Tests

Tests

A Comprehensive Reference for Assessments in Psychology, Education, and Business

FOURTH EDITION

Edited by
Taddy Maddox

pro·ed
An International Publisher

8700 Shoal Creek Boulevard
Austin, Texas 78757-6897

©1997, 1991, 1986, 1984, 1983 by PRO-ED, Inc.
8700 Shoal Creek Boulevard
Austin, Texas 78757-6897

Library of Congress Cataloging-in-Publication Data

Tests : a comprehensive reference for assessments in psychology,
    education, and business. — 4th ed. / edited by Taddy Maddox.
        p.   cm.
    Includes bibliographical references and indexes.
    ISBN 0-89079-707-2 (hard cover : alk. paper). — ISBN
0-89079-709-9 (soft cover : alk. paper)
    1. Psychological tests.   2. Educational tests and measurements.
    3. Occupational aptitude tests.   I. Maddox, Taddy.
BF176.T43   1997   96-38299
150'.28'7—dc20   CIP

This book is designed in Garamond and Frutiger.

Production Manager: Alan Grimes
Production Coordinator: Karen Swain
Managing Editor: Tracy Sergo
Art Director: Thomas Barkley
Reprints Buyer: Alicia Woods
Editor: Teri Sperry
Production Assistant: Claudette Landry
Editorial Assistant: Suzi Hunn

Printed in the United States of America

3   4   5   6   7   8   9   10   01   00   99   98

Contents

. . . .

Preface

As this fourth edition of *Tests* is published, it is appropriate to comment on the project's development and background and recognize the contributions of people who made the task possible. Richard C. Sweetland and Daniel J. Keyser prepared *Tests: First Edition* in response to the need for a resource containing consistent codified information describing and cataloging tests available for use by psychologists, educators, and human resources personnel. The professional community received *Tests,* published in 1983, enthusiastically. Within one year of publication, the first edition was in its third printing, indicating to the editors that thousands of professionals had come to rely on its quick-scanning, easy-to-read format. Committed to providing readers with the most current information possible on assessment instruments, Sweetland and Keyser launched a "search and find" effort that resulted in the 1984 publication of *Tests: Supplement,* a complement to the first edition that contained information on more than 500 new tests. The supplement was followed by *Tests: Second Edition* in 1986.

Sweetland and Keyser's ongoing "search and find" efforts, which uncovered information on hundreds of new tests; rapid developments in areas such as substance abuse, eating disorders, and chronic illness; the increasing role of technology in assessment; and Sweetland and Keyser's continued firm commitment to providing users with quick access to current test information resulted in the third edition, published in 1991. PRO-ED continues this commitment to provide a reference that can be used by professionals in the fields of psychology, education, and business to obtain information about testing instruments in the fourth edition.

As the editor of the fourth edition, I have attempted to maintain the consistency of the previous editions. The fourth edition does have a few changes to aid the reader in finding information. Cross-referencing has been moved from the text to an index, and new indexes have been added for tests and publishers that were in the third edition and are not included in the fourth.

I thank the readers for the numerous suggestions they have offered, particularly for providing the names of assessment instruments not referenced in the previous edition. A special thank-you is extended to the many test publishers and authors who generously and graciously contributed their staff time, information, and support for this book. Particular recognition must be given to Ally Macredie and Gwenn Long for their tireless entering of the data necessary to prepare this text.

Special acknowledgment is given to Richard C. Sweetland and Daniel J. Keyser, previous editors of this text. The foundation that they established made my job far easier.

How To Use This Book

T*ests,* a reference guide containing information on thousands of assessment instruments, is designed especially for psychologists, educators, and human resources personnel who search for tests to satisfy their assessment needs. In addition, students, librarians, and other nonspecialists who need to familiarize themselves with the broad range of available tests will find the contents and format helpful. *Tests* does not attempt to review or evaluate tests; its purpose is to present concise descriptions in a quick-scanning, easy-to-read format. This fourth edition, which presents the tests of 221 publishers, updates the information contained in the third edition and presents descriptions of new and revised tests.

How *Tests* Is Organized

The assessments described herein are organized according to a system of primary classification and cross-referencing intended to make information as accessible to the reader as possible. Each of the book's three main sections—Psychology, Education, and Business—is divided into subsections. For example, Psychology contains 19 subsections; Education, 50 subsections; and Business, 20 subsections. Each test has been given a primary classification in one of the Psychology, Education, or Business subsections and is described in detail in that subsection. Each test is also cross-referenced in the Index of Cross-References. Some tests are cross-referenced in several places. The tests within each subsection are listed alphabetically by title.

In order to establish subsections that would be practical and functional for the reader, the editor sought considerable consultation from professionals who use tests on a daily basis. Based on feedback from these sources, the editor reorganized the subsections in this fourth edition both to facilitate the reader's search for assessments and to reflect contemporary terminology.

Format and Content of Descriptions

The format and content of each test entry are designed to provide the basic information necessary to decide whether a particular test is appropriate to consider for a given assessment need. Each test entry is structured as follows: test title and author(s), copyright date, population for which the test is intended, a purpose statement, a brief description highlighting the test's major features, format information, scoring method, relevant cost and availability information, and primary publisher. Each of these components will be explained in greater detail.

The **title** of each test is presented exactly as it appears in the test publisher's materials, but without any articles (e.g., *the, a, an*). For example, one would find the description of *The Wonderlic Personnel Test* listed as *Wonderlic Personnel Test*. Readers who are familiar with a test's common or popular name rather than its published title may find the Index of Authors useful if they encounter difficulty in finding the test.

The test **author** names appear below the test title. Corporate authors are not listed; only specific individuals are.

The **copyright date** is the next entry. This date reflects the date the instrument or its revision was published.

A description of the intended consumers of the test is listed in the **population** entry. For children, the target age or grade of the examinee may be provided.

The **purpose** statement offers a succinct overview of the test's intended application and what it purports to measure, assess, diagnose, evaluate, or identify.

The **description** presents the number of test items, test format (paper–pencil, true–false, projective, oral, observational, etc.), factors or variables measured, materials used, manner in which the test is administered, foreign language availability, and special features.

The **format** section describes how the test is administered (individual and/or group), estimated time of administration, and whether the instrument is timed (when the information has been provided by the publisher).

The **scoring** description provides information about the method used to score the test: hand key, examiner evaluated, machine scored, or computer scored. Hand key indicates that the test is scored using an answer key or template provided by the test publisher. An examiner-evaluated test is scored using an examiner's opinion, skills, and knowledge. A computer- or machine-scored test uses answer sheets that are scored by machine or computer. When a combination of these terms appears in the scoring section, the first listed is the primary method employed.

The **cost** section contains price information that is as accurate at the editor could establish at the time of the book's publication. Because the pricing structure for some tests (covering the various forms, kits, options, etc.) is so extensive, only representative costs are included here. The editor encourages readers to contact the publisher for complete cost information.

The **publisher** lines identify the test's primary publisher. The Index of Publishers contains complete address and telephone information. The editor attempted to confirm the accuracy of every test entry through direct correspondence with the test publisher. But despite repeated contact attempts, some publishers did not respond to queries. Those publishers who did not respond are listed in the Index of Publishers Not in the Fourth Edition.

Indexes

Tests: Fourth Edition contains eight indexes. The indexes were compiled to make this reference book user-friendly. Information provided by the publishers in response to specific questions regarding foreign language and computer availability enabled the editor to compile these indexes.

The **Index of Test Titles** lists each of the tests described in this book. The title of each test is presented exactly as it appears in the test publisher's materials, but without any articles (e.g., *the, a, an*) to allow for true alphabetical listing. British spelling has been retained in proper titles.

The **Index of Tests Not in the Fourth Edition** lists those instruments that were in the third edition but are not found in this fourth edition. There are a variety of reasons for the exclusion of an instrument, including lack of response from the publisher, a publisher no longer in business, or tests that are out of print.

The **Index of Publishers Not in the Fourth Edition** lists those publishers who had tests listed in the third edition but not in this edition. For example, this listing includes those publishers who did not reply to the initial request for information or those publishers for whom current address and phone information is available but who did not return information on their instruments.

The **Index of Tests Available in Foreign Language** contains tests that are available in language versions other than English. Tests are arranged by language and listed alphabetically.

The **Index of Computer-Scored Tests** lists tests that may be scored by computer, either on-site or via mail-in or teleprocessing services. Publishers are currently introducing computer scoring for more instruments, so if an instrument does not list computer scoring as an option, contact the publisher to see if computer scoring is now available.

The **Index of Authors** lists all test authors except for corporate and institutional staffs. This listing is in alphabetical order and includes all authors of each instrument, not just the first author.

The **Index of Publishers** provides addresses, telephone numbers, and fax numbers for each publisher. This listing includes page numbers for each instrument that each publisher has listed in the book.

The **Index of Cross-References** groups the test instruments into areas of focus (e.g., Psychology: Personality; Business: Personality). Some instruments are listed in several areas.

The purpose of *Tests* from the outset has been to provide a quick reference for tests available in the English language. When the first edition of this volume was published, the editors decided to omit reliability, validity, and normative data—aspects considered too complex to reduce to the quick-scanning desk-reference format. The editors were aware, however, that a fuller treatment of each test was needed, and they were encouraged by librarians, educators, psychologists, and forensic specialists to create the *Test Critiques* series, which serves as a complement to *Tests* and is a vital component within the array of test review resources currently available.

Use of the Book

The system of classification used in *Tests* and the inclusion of the indexes just described are designed to accommodate readers who need information about a particular test as well as those conducting a general search for appropriate assessment instruments. The following suggestions for using *Tests* are intended to minimize the reader's efforts to locate information.

- The editor encourages readers to scan the Index of Cross-References sections relevant to their particular assessment needs. The "scanning-by-section" approach may be most helpful to readers who know how the particular test for which they are searching is likely to be classified or for readers whose search is focused on an assessment area rather than on a particular test.

- Readers who are unable to locate a test using the Index of Test Titles or the Index of Cross-References should consult the Index of Authors and/or the Index of Publishers if these elements are known.

- Tests that cannot be located in the previously mentioned sections may be found in the Index of Tests Not in the Fourth Edition. The reader should be aware that these instruments may not be out of print, but the editor was unable to determine current information about availability, price, and/or revisions.

PRO-ED fully supports the ethical and professional standards established by national and state professional organizations. The inclusion of specific restrictions on test accessibility noted in some descriptions in this book usually has been requested by the publisher or author; the fact that a test description does not list restrictions does not imply that such restrictions do not exist. When ordering tests, the reader should ask each publisher for the standards or requirements for purchasing.

Order forms, catalogs, and further information regarding tests may be obtained from each publisher. Anyone interested in ordering a specific test should contact the publisher, which can be facilitated by using the Index of Publishers, which provides mailing addresses and telephone/fax numbers.

Although the information in this book was obtained from primary sources, the editor is aware of possibilities for error. Each test entry has been researched, screened, written, edited, and read by professional test administrators; however, the editor asks that the reader understand that the job of checking and ensuring the accuracy of a book such as this is a process that will continue throughout the publication of subsequent editions. The editor welcomes on an ongoing basis the submission of information about new tests and encourages test publishers and authors to apprise the PRO-ED staff of errors in the test descriptions or of test revisions made available since publication of this edition.

Psychology Instruments

The tests presented and described in the Psychology section have been selected on the basis of their appropriate usage in a clinical or counseling setting. In general, tests found in this section are those that might be used by a mental health professional, rather than by an educator or human resources specialist The classification of tests on the basis of typical usage or function is, of course, arbitrary, and the reader is encouraged to review the Education and Business sections for additional assessment instruments.

Attention Deficit

Adult Attention Deficit Disorder Behavior Rating Scale
Ned Owens, Betty R. Owens

Copyright: 1983

Population: Adults; ages 17 and above

Purpose: Identifies children and adolescents with attention deficit disorder; used for referral to medical doctors and as a follow-up to measure academic and behavioral improvement

Description: Fifty-item paper–pencil rating scale identifying attention deficit disorder. Teachers or parents rate items on a 5-point scale ranging from "You have not noticed this behavior before" to "You have noticed this behavior to a very large degree." The test contains three primary, or organic, scales (Inattention, Impulsivity, Hyperactivity) and seven secondary, or emotional, scales (Anger Control, Academics, Anxiety, Confidence, Aggressiveness, Resistance, Social). Results distinguish between individuals with attention deficit disorder without hyperactivity and attention deficit disorder with hyperactivity.

Format: Self-administered; untimed: 15 minutes

Scoring: Self-scored

Cost: $40.00

Publisher: Ned Owens, M.Ed., Inc.

Attention Deficit Disorder Behavior Rating Scales (ADDBRS)
Ned Owens, Betty R. Owens

Copyright: 1982

Population: Children, adolescents; ages 6 to 16

Purpose: Screens for attention deficit disorder; used for behavior counseling

Description: Fifty-question paper–pencil rating scale identifying attention deficit disorder. Teachers or parents rate items on a 5-point scale ranging from "You have not noticed this behavior before" to "You have noticed this behavior to a very large degree." The test contains three primary, or organic, scales (Inattention, Impulsivity, Hyperactivity) and seven secondary, or emotional, scales (Anger Control, Academics, Anxiety, Confidence, Aggressiveness, Resistance, Social). Results distinguish between individuals with attention deficit disorder with and without hyperactivity.

Format: Self-administered; untimed: 15–30 minutes

Scoring: Examiner evaluated

Cost: Kit (25 rating sheets, 25 profile sheets, manual) $15.00

Publisher: Ned Owens, M.Ed., Inc.

Attention Deficit Disorders Evaluation Scale (ADDES)– Revised

Stephen B. McCarney

Copyright: 1995

Population: Children, adolescents; Grades K to 12

Purpose: Used to diagnose attention deficit, hyperactivity, and impulsivity

Description: The scale includes the most currently recognized subscales of inattention and hyperactivity/impulsivity. The results provided by the scale are commensurate with criteria used by educational, psychiatric, and pediatric personnel to identify attention deficit/hyperactivity disorder in children and youth. The scale comes in both a School Version and a Home Version. Available in Spanish. A computer version using IBM-compatible or Macintosh computers is available.

Format: Individual administration

Scoring: Self-scored; computer scored

Cost: Complete kit $206.00

Publisher: Hawthorne Educational Services, Inc.

Attention-Deficit Hyperactivity Disorder

Sue Larson, Teresa Frields

Copyright: 1995

Population: Children

Purpose: Used for identification of ADHD

Description: Resource Book provides an in-depth summary of the disorder; two separate checklists are included, one for school personnel and one for the child's parent to complete to identify the ADHD individual. These checklists follow the APA guidelines for identification of ADHD and provide an overview of the core elements of ADHD and classroom suggestions used in programming for the ADHD student. This ADHD package is appropriate for Chapter 1 and Head Start programs, all educators, and therapists and responsible adults working in special interest and volunteer programs.

Format: Examiner required; not suitable for group use; untimed: 1 hour

Scoring: Hand key; may be computer scored

Cost: Complete kit $52.00; Resource Book $32.00; Checklist for School/Educational and Parent/Home Settings $24.00

Publisher: Slosson Educational Publications, Inc.

Attention-Deficit/Hyperactivity Disorder Test (ADHDT)

James E. Gilliam

Copyright: 1995

Population: Ages 3 through 23

Purpose: Identifies and evaluates attention deficit disorders

Description: Multiple-item checklist that is completed by teachers, parents, or others who are knowledgeable about a referred individual. Based on the diagnostic criteria for attention-deficit/hyperactivity disorder of the DSM–IV, the instrument contains 36 items that describe characteristic behaviors of persons with ADHD. These items comprise three subtests representing the core symptoms necessary for the diagnosis of ADHD: hyperactivity, impulsivity, and inattention. Results are reported in standard scores and percentiles that are interpreted related to degree of severity and probability for males and females.

Format: Questionnaire, 10 minutes

Scoring: Examiner scoring and interpretation

Cost: Complete kit (manual, protocols, and storage box) $69.00

Publisher: PRO-ED, Inc.

Brown Attention-Deficit Disorder Scales

Thomas A. Brown

Copyright: 1996

Population: Adolescents, adults; ages 12 through adult

Purpose: Evaluates cognitive and affective indications of ADD in adolescents and adults

Description: Self-report instrument that allows

for screening of ADD by examining a wide variety of factors believed to be associated with ADD. Adolescent (ages 12–18) and adult forms are available. Ready Score form gives an immediate summary score indicating overall impairment. Diagnostic Form includes guidelines and worksheets for conducting a clinical interview, scoring summary, multirater evaluation form, analysis of IQ subtest data relevant to ADD, screener for comorbid disorders, and an overall diagnostic summary form.

Format: Examiner required; not suitable for group use; untimed: 20–40 minutes

Scoring: Examiner evaluated

Cost: Starter Kit (manual, treatment monitoring worksheet, answer documents) $70.00

Publisher: The Psychological Corporation

Children's Attention and Adjustment Survey (CAAS)
Nadine Lambert, Carolyn Hartsough, Jonathan Sandoval

Copyright: 1990

Population: Ages 5 to 13

Purpose: Evaluates behaviors related to hyperactivity and attention deficit in children

Description: A survey that identifies behavior problems associated with ADD and ADHD. Four scales are provided to provide more precise intervention planning: Inattentiveness, Impulsivity, Hyperactivity, and Conduct Problems/Aggressiveness. Since children's behavior often varies with their environment, CAAS uses an interactive systems model. The survey assesses behaviors observed both at home and at school through two forms: the Home Form (completed by the parent or primary caregiver) and the School Form (completed by the teacher or other school professional). Each form contains 31 items. Behaviors are classified according to criteria determined by DSM.

Format: Survey format, individual, 5–10 minutes

Scoring: Examiner interpretation

Cost: Starter Set (manual, home and school protocols, and scoring profile) $104.95

Publisher: American Guidance Service

Conners' Continuous Performance Test (CPT)– Version 3.1
C. Keith Conners

Copyright: 1994

Population: Ages 4 to 50

Purpose: Helps assess attention problems

Description: Computer-administered test requiring subject responses to 360 stimuli that appear on a computer screen. The test measures error rates, reaction time, and variability of reaction time. Statistics measure aspects of attention.

Format: Individual administration; examiner required; timed: 14.5 minutes

Scoring: Computer scored

Cost: Manual and disk $495.00

Publisher: Multi-Health Systems, Inc.

Conners' Parent and Teacher Rating Scales
C. Keith Conners

Copyright: 1989

Population: Children, adolescents; ages 3 to 17

Purpose: Measures hyperactivity and other patterns of child behavior

Description: Paper–pencil or computer-administered instrument used to evaluate problem behaviors of children as reported by the child's teacher, parents, or alternate caregiver. The Teacher Version is available in a 28-item (CTRS-28) or 39-item (CTRS-39) form and includes the following scales: Hyperactivity, Conduct Problem, Emotional Overindulgent, Anxious–Passive, Asocial, and Daydream Attendance Problem. The Parent Version is available in a 48-item (CPRS-48) or 93-item (CPRS-93) form and includes the following scales: Conduct Disorder, Psychosomatic, Learning Problem–Immature, Restless–Disorganized, Fearful–Anxious, Obsessional, Hyperactive–Immature, Impulsive–Hyperactive, and Antisocial. Derived *T*-scores can be obtained for the teacher and parent versions.

Format: Self-administered; not suitable for group use; untimed: time varies

Scoring: Carbonized QuikScore forms: may be computer scored

Cost: Complete Kit (test manual, 25 Quik-Score forms for each of 4 versions) $80.00; IBM PC–compatible version (50 administrations and scorings for each of 4 versions) $145.00

Publisher: Multi-Health Systems, Inc.

Disruptive Behavior Rating Scale (DBRS)
Bradley T. Erford

Copyright: 1993

Population: Ages 5 to 10

Purpose: Identifies attention deficit disorder, attention deficit disorder with hyperactivity, oppositional disorders, and antisocial conduct problems; identifies "at-risk" children; facilitates decisions for student placement

Description: Fifty-item inventory. Administration can be performed by both professionals and paraprofessionals. The DBRS is ideal for individual and mass screenings. The wording of the teacher and parent versions is nearly identical, allowing legitimate comparisons between their responses. Scale items were specifically written to allow direct teacher transfer to behavior-modification plans, IEPs, or 504 plans. The DBRS provides separate norms for teacher, mother, and father responses. Normative data were obtained from 1,766 children, mothers of 1,399 children, and fathers of 1,252 children for boys and girls 5 to 10 years of age. Normative data are also provided to convert raw scores into T-scores and percentile ranks, as well as standard error of measurement and critical item determination. The computer-generated report calculates a summary statistics table, T-scores, percentile ranks, and interpretation ranges and will also identify critical items of importance.

Format: Individual or group administration; examiner required; untimed: 7 minutes.

Scoring: Hand key; computer scored

Cost: Complete kit $120.00

Publisher: Slosson Educational Publications, Inc.

Early Childhood Attention Deficit Disorders Evaluation Scale (ECADDES)
Stephen B. McCarney

Copyright: 1995

Population: Children; ages 24 to 72 months

Purpose: Diagnoses attention deficit/hyperactivity disorder

Description: The School Version of the scale includes 56 items easily observed and documented by educational personnel. The Home Version includes 50 items representing behavior exhibited in and around the home environment and is completed by the parent or guardian.

Format: Individual administration; untimed; time varies

Scoring: Self/computer scored

Cost: Complete kit $147.00

Publisher: Hawthorne Educational Services, Inc.

Visual Search and Attention Test (VSAT)
Max R. Trenerry, Bruce Crosson, James DeBoe, William R. Leber

Copyright: 1990

Population: Adults

Purpose: Measures attentional processes

Description: Paper–pencil. Four visual cancellation tasks yielding the following scores: overall attention and left- and right-side performance. Materials used include a manual and stimulus and scoring forms. Examiner must be C-level qualified.

Format: Individual administration; examiner required; timed: 6 minutes

Scoring: No key necessary

Cost: Kit $54.00

Publisher: Psychological Assessment Resources, Inc.

Drug Knowledge

Information Test on Drugs and Drug Abuse
Glenn C. Leach, Frederick H. Kilander

Copyright: 1974

Population: Adolescents, adults; Grades 10 and above

Purpose: Measures high school and college students' knowledge of drugs and drug abuse; used for drug abuse counseling

Description: Thirty-item paper–pencil, multiple-choice test covering legal and illegal drug use

Format: Self-administered; suitable for group use; timed: 30 minutes

Scoring: Hand key

Cost: Free

Publisher: Glenn C. Leach, Ed.D.

Smoking and Health
H. Frederick Kilander, Glenn C. Leach

Copyright: 1974

Population: Adolescents, adults; Grades 10 to 13

Purpose: Assesses an individual's commitment to and knowledge of smoking; used for analysis of smoking behavior and research

Description: Paper–pencil 33-item multiple-choice and objective test on smoking

Format: Self-administered; suitable for group use; timed: 25 minutes

Scoring: Hand key

Cost: Free

Publisher: Glenn C. Leach, Ed.D.

Family

Ackerman-Schoendorf Scales for Parent Evaluation of Custody (ASPECT)
Marc J. Ackerman, Kathleen Schoendorf

Copyright: Not provided

Population: Adults

Purpose: Used to evaluate parent effectiveness in child custody evaluations

Description: ASPECT offers a practical, standardized, and defensible approach to child custody evaluations. It draws information from a variety of sources, reducing the likelihood of examiner bias. It yields three scale scores: Observational (a measure of the parent's appearance and presentation), Social (a measure of the parent's interaction with others, including the child), and Cognitive–Emotional (a measure of the parent's psychological and mental functioning). Research has shown 90% agreement between ASPECT recommendations and custody decisions made by judges. It has also proved effective in identifying those parents who will need supervision during child visitations. The clinician must answer 56 yes-or-no questions, based on information drawn from the parent questionnaire, interviews with and observations of each parent with and without the child, and test data.

Format: Individually administered; examiner required

Scoring: Examiner evaluated/hand key or computer scoring service

Cost: Kit (includes 20 parent questionnaires, 10 AutoScore™ answer forms, 1 manual, 2 test report prepaid mail-in answer sheets for computer scoring and interpretation) $110.00

Publisher: Western Psychological Services

American Home Scale
W. A. Kerr, H. H. Remmers

Copyright: 1982

Population: Adolescents, adults; Grades 8 and above

Purpose: Evaluates the cultural, aesthetic, and economic factors of an individual's home environment; used for counseling students and other individuals who may be experiencing problems due to their home environment

Description: Multiple-item paper–pencil inventory assessing an individual's home environment. Construction of the test is based on profile and factor analyses. The test discriminates between sociological areas. The norms are based on over 16,000 eighth-grade students in more than 40 American cities.

Format: Examiner required; suitable for group use; timed: 40 minutes

Scoring: Examiner evaluated

Cost: Specimen Set $4.00; 25 surveys $5.00

Publisher: Psychometric Affiliates

Borromean Family Index: For Married Persons
Panos D. Bardis

Copyright: 1988

Population: Adolescents, adults

Purpose: Measures a married person's attitudes and feelings toward his or her immediate family; used for clinical assessment, family and marriage counseling, family attitude research, and discussions in family education

Description: Eighteen-item paper–pencil test in which the subject rates nine statements about "forces that attract you to your family" on a scale from 0 (absent) to 4 (very strong) and nine statements about "forces that pull you away from your family" on a scale from 0 (does not pull you away at all) to 4 (very strong). Suitable for individuals with physical and hearing disabilities.

Format: Examiner/self-administered; suitable for group use; untimed: 10 minutes

Scoring: Examiner evaluated

Cost: Free

Publisher: Panos D. Bardis, Ph.D.

Borromean Family Index: For Single Persons
Panos D. Bardis

Copyright: 1988

Population: Adolescents, adults

Purpose: Measures an individual's attitudes and feelings toward his or her family; used for clinical assessment, family counseling, family attitude research, and discussion in family education

Description: Eighteen-item paper–pencil test in which the subject rates nine statements about "forces that attract you to your family" from 0 (absent) to 4 (very strong) and nine statements about "forces that pull you away from your family" from 0 (does not pull you away at all) to 4 (very strong). Suitable for use with individuals with physical and hearing disabilities.

Format: Examiner/self-administered; suitable for group use; untimed: 10 minutes

Scoring: Examiner evaluated

Cost: Free

Publisher: Panos D. Bardis, Ph.D.

Children's Version of the Family Environment Scale
C. J. Pino, Nancy Simons, Mary Jane Slawinowski

Copyright: Not provided

Population: Ages 5 to 12

Purpose: Assesses characteristics of the family environment as seen from the child's perspective; used for family therapy

Description: Thirty-item paper–pencil forced-choice test consisting of 90 illustrations measuring 10 dimensions of the family environment: cohesion, expressiveness, conflict, independence, achievement orientation, intellectual–cultural orientation, active–recreational orientation, moral–religious emphasis, organization, and control.

Format: Examiner required; suitable for group use; untimed: 15–20 minutes

Scoring: Examiner evaluated

Cost: Complete kit (manual, 10 test booklets, 50 each of profiles, examiner's worksheets, student answer sheets) $84.80

Publisher: Consulting Psychologists Press, Inc.

Dyadic Parent–Child Coding System–DPICS II
Sheila M. Eyberg, Elizabeth Robinson, K. Bessmer, Newcomb, D. Edwards

Copyright: 1994

Population: Children to adults; ages 2 to adult.

Purpose: Measures quality of social interactions of families; used in family counseling and social services

Description: Multiple-item paper–pencil test

Format: Examiner required

Scoring: Examiner evaluated

Cost: $72.00

Publisher: Select Press

Faces II
D. H. Olson, R. Bell, J. Portner

Copyright: 1992

Population: Ages 10 and above

Purpose: Used in research and family counseling to assess family adaptability and cohesion

Description: Thirty-item paper–pencil Likert scale with 16 cohesion items and 14 flexibility items. Couple and family forms are used. Available in foreign language.

Format: Individual/self-administered; untimed

Scoring: Hand key

Cost: Contact publisher

Publisher: Family Social Science

Familism Scale
Panos D. Bardis

Copyright: 1988

Population: Adolescents, adults

Purpose: Assesses individual attitudes toward both nuclear and extended families; used for clinical evaluation, marriage and family counseling, research on the family, and discussion in family life education

Description: Sixteen-item paper–pencil test in which the subject reads 10 statements about nuclear family relationships and 6 statements about extended family relationships and rates them according to his or her personal beliefs on a scale from 0 (strongly disagree) to 4 (strongly agree). The "famlism" score equals the sum of the 16 numerical responses. The theoretical range of scores extends from 0 (least familistic) to 64 (most familistic). Separate scores may be obtained for "nuclear family integration" and "extended family integration." Suitable for use with individuals with physical and hearing disabilities.

Format: Examiner/self-administered; suitable for group use; untimed: 10 minutes

Scoring: Examiner evaluated

Cost: Free

Publisher: Panos D. Bardis, Ph.D.

Familism Scale: Extended Family Integration
Panos D. Bardis

Copyright: 1988

Population: Adolescents, adults

Purpose: Measures attitudes toward the extended family (beyond the nuclear family, but within the kinship group); used for clinical assessment, marriage and family counseling, family attitude research, and discussions in family education

Description: Six-item paper–pencil test in which the subject reads a list of statements concerning extended family relationships and rates them according to personal beliefs on a scale from 0 (strongly disagree) to 4 (strongly agree). The "famlism" score is the sum of the six numerical responses. The theoretical range of scores extends from 0 (least familistic) to 24 (most familistic). Suitable for use with individuals with physical and hearing disabilities.

Format: Examiner/self-administered. Suitable for group use; untimed: 5 minutes

Scoring: Examiner evaluated

Cost: Free

Publisher: Panos D. Bardis, Ph.D.

Familism Scale: Nuclear Family Integration
Panos D. Bardis

Copyright: 1988

Population: Adolescents, adults

Purpose: Measures attitudes toward the solidarity of the nuclear family; used for clinical assessment, marriage and family counseling, family attitude research, and discussion in family education

Description: Ten-item paper–pencil test in which the subject rates 10 statements about family relationships from 0 (strongly disagree) to 4 (strongly agree). The "familism" score equals the sum of the 10 numerical responses. The theoretical range of scores extends from 0 (least familistic) to 40 (most familistic). Suitable for use with individuals with physical and hearing disabilities.

Format: Self-administered; suitable for group use; untimed: 5 minutes

Scoring: Hand key

Cost: Free

Publisher: Panos D. Bardis, Ph.D.

Family Adjustment Test (Elias Family Opinion Survey)
Gabriel Elias, H. H. Remmers

Copyright: 1972

Population: Adolescents, adults

Purpose: Measures intrafamily homeyness–homelessness (acceptance–rejection) while appearing to be concerned only with attitudes toward general community life; used for clinical evaluations and research

Description: Paper–pencil or oral-response projective test measuring adult and adolescent feelings of family acceptance. The test yields 10 subscores: attitudes toward mother, attitudes toward father, relatives preferences, oedipal,

independence struggle, parent–child friction, interparental friction, family status feeling, child rejection, and parental quality. Subtest scores and clinical indicators of a number of adjustment trends, as well as an overall index of feelings of intrafamily homeyness–homelessness, are provided. Percentile norms are provided by sex for the following age groups: ages 12 to 13, 14 to 15, 16 to 18, and 19 and older. Interpretation is provided in terms of subtest profiles. Norms for specific parent–child relationships are provided also. No third party should be present if the test is administered orally.

Format: Examiner required; the paper–pencil format is suitable for group use; timed: 45 minutes

Scoring: Hand key; scoring service available

Cost: Specimen Set (test, manual, key) $5.00; 25 tests $8.50

Publisher: Psychometric Affiliates

Family Apperception Test
Alexander Julian III, Wayne M. Sotile, Susan E. Henry, Mary O. Sotile

Copyright: Not provided

Population: All ages

Purpose: Used by therapists to generate family systems hypotheses from the assessment of a single family member

Description: The instrument includes 21 Stimulus Cards, which depict common family activities, constellations, and situations. These are shown to the client, one at a time, and responses are recorded. Following instructions provided in the Manual, the test can be scored for: obvious conflict, conflict resolution, limit setting, quality of relationships, boundaries, dysfunctional circularity, abuse, unusual responses, refusals, and emotional tone. A Total Dysfunction Index can also be computed. The manual presents interpretive guidelines and evidence of the scoring system's reliability and validity.

Format: Individually administered; examiner required; 30 minutes

Scoring: Hand scored

Cost: Kit (includes 1 set of stimulus cards, 100 scoring sheets, 1 manual) $125.00

Publisher: Western Psychological Services

Family Assessment Measure (FAM III)

Harvey A. Skinner, Paul D. Steinhauer, Jack Santa-Barbara

Copyright: 1992

Population: Children to adults

Purpose: Assesses family functioning; used in family counseling

Description: Paper–pencil test with a general, dyadic, and self scale. Categories include task accomplishment, communication, involvement, values and norms, role performance, affective expression, control, social desirability, and defensiveness. Scores are yielded for each subscale and a total score. These scores can be converted to standard scores and plotted on a color-coded profile sheet. A fifth-grade reading level is required.

Format: Self-administered; untimed: 10–15 minutes

Scoring: Hand key

Cost: Kit $125.00

Publisher: Multi-Health Systems, Inc.

Family Environment Scale

Rudolf H. Moos, Bernice S. Moos

Copyright: Not provided

Population: Adolescents, adults

Purpose: Assesses characteristics of family environments; used for family therapy

Description: Ninety-item paper–pencil test measuring 10 dimensions of family environments: cohesion, expressiveness, conflict, independence, achievement orientation, intellectual–cultural orientation, active–recreational orientation, moral–religious emphasis, organization, and control. These dimensions are further grouped into three categories: relationship, personal growth, and system maintenance. Materials include the Real Form (Form R), which measures perceptions of current family environments; the Ideal Form (Form I), which measures conceptions of ideal family environments; and the Expectancies Form (Form E), which measures expectations about family settings. The revised manual has been extensively updated and expanded with new normative data.

Format: Examiner required; suitable for group use; untimed; typical time not available

Scoring: Examiner evaluated

Cost: Preview Kit (Form R booklet, answer sheet, report form, manual) $39.00

Publisher: Consulting Psychologists Press, Inc.

Family Relationship Inventory (FRI)

Ruth B. Michaelson, Harry L. Bascom

Copyright: 1982

Population: Ages 5 to adult

Purpose: Evaluates family relationships along positive and negative lines. Used as an aid in individual child–adult counseling, family therapy, youth groups, high school instruction, and marriage and family enrichment programs

Description: Fifty-item paper–pencil test measuring self-esteem, positive or negative perception of self and significant others, most- and least-esteemed family members, and closest and most distant relationships within the family. One numbered item is printed on each of 50 cards. Items 1 to 25 have positive valence, and items 26 to 50 have negative valence. The subject lists "self" and "family members" across the top of a tabulating form and assigns each item to self, significant other, or the wastebasket column and tallies the data on scoring forms with the help of a counselor. Materials include item cards, tabulating forms, scoring forms, a relationship wheel to graphically portray the responses, a Familygram to show family interrelationships, and a test manual.

Format: Examiner required; suitable for group use; untimed: 30–45 minutes

Scoring: Examiner evaluated

Cost: Complete FRI Kit (manual, 50 reusable item cards, 50 tabulating forms, 25 scoring forms, 50 individual relationship sheets, 25 Familygrams) $70.00

Publisher: Psychological Publications, Inc.

Family Story Pictures
Morten Nissen

Copyright: 1984

Population: Children; ages 4 to 12

Purpose: Assesses a child's perception of and reaction to parents' divorce

Description: Thirteen-picture verbal test used in divorce counseling to assess the child's cognitive understanding, perception of the future, expectations of the future, and perception of the possibilities of influencing his or her own situation. Examiner must be a qualified psychologist. Also available in Danish.

Format: Individually administered; examiner required; untimed

Scoring: Examiner evaluated

Cost: $53.00 (DKK 302)

Publisher: Dansk psykologisk Forlog

Family Violence Scale
Panos D. Bardis

Copyright: 1988

Population: Adolescents, adults

Purpose: Measures the degree of verbal and physical violence in an individual's family during childhood; used for clinical assessment, marriage and family counseling, research on attitudes toward family and violence, and classroom discussion

Description: Paper–pencil test in which the subject rates 25 statements about family violence on a scale from 0 (never) to 4 (very often). The "family violence" score equals the sum of the 25 numerical responses. The theoretical range of scores extends from 0 (least violent) to 100 (most violent). Suitable for use with physically and hearing impaired.

Format: Self-administered; suitable for group use; untimed: 10 minutes

Scoring: Examiner evaluated

Cost: Free

Publisher: Panos D. Bardis, Ph.D.

Grandparent Strengths and Needs Inventory (GSNI)
Robert D. Strom, Shirley K. Strom

Copyright: 1993

Population: Adults

Purpose: Identifies favorable qualities of grandparents.

Description: Sixty-item multiple-choice test with six subscales: satisfaction, success, teaching, difficulty, frustration, and information needs. Scores yielded are always (4), often (3), seldom (2), and never (1). Three versions—grandparent, parent, and grandchild—are available. Booklets, profiles, and a pencil are used. Examiner must be certified for assessment.

Format: Individual/self-administered; suitable for group use; examiner required; untimed

Scoring: Hand key

Cost: Specimen Set $22.05

Publisher: Scholastic Testing Service, Inc.

Home Screening Questionnaire (HSQ)
C. Cooms, E. Gay, A. Vandal, C. Ker, William F. Frankenberg

Copyright: 1981

Population: Children; ages 0 to 6

Purpose: Evaluates the quality of a child's home environment; used to indicate need for further evaluation

Description: Paper–pencil 64-item questionnaire filled out by the parents and scored by an examiner. Suspect results must be followed by an evaluation of the home by a trained professional to see if intervention is needed. A 30-item blue form is available for children up to age 3, and a 34-item white form is available for ages 3 to 6. Both forms have toy checklists. The questionnaires are written at third- and fourth-grade reading levels.

Format: Self-administered; not suitable for group use; untimed: 15–20 minutes

Scoring: Hand key

Cost: 25 test forms $7.75; manual $7.75

Publisher: Denver Developmental Materials, Inc.

Interview Questionnaire on Attitudes Toward Family Planning in Black Community
Ian D. McMahon

Copyright: 1976

Population: Adults

Purpose: Measures resistance to family planning in the black community

Description: Paper–pencil 193-item test

Format: Group administered; examiner required; untimed

Scoring: Examiner evaluated

Cost: $15.00

Publisher: Select Press

Inventory of Anger Communication
Millard J. Bienvenu

Copyright: 1974

Population: Adolescents, adults; ages 13 and older

Purpose: Assesses subjective and interactional aspects of anger communication; used in individual, marriage, and group counseling and human relations training

Description: Thirty-item yes–no–sometimes test. A seventh-grade reading level is required. Examiner must have experience in anger management.

Format: Self-administered; suitable for group use; untimed: 15 minutes

Scoring: Hand key

Cost: $.75 per copy; guide $2.00; minimum order $10.00

Publisher: Northwest Publications

Life Interpersonal History Enquiry (LIPHE)
Will Schutz

Copyright: 1989

Population: Adults

Purpose: Evaluates an individual's retrospective account of relationship to parents before age 6; used for counseling and therapy

Description: Paper–pencil report of an individual's early relationship with parents in areas of inclusion, control, and affection at both the behavioral and the feeling levels. Separate scores are obtained for the father, the mother, and the respondent's perception of the relationship between the parents.

Format: Examiner/self-administered; suitable for group use; untimed: typical time not available

Scoring: Hand key

Cost: Sampler Set $25.00, permission for 200 uses $90.00

Publisher: Mind Garden, Inc.

Marital Communication Inventory
Millard J. Bienvenu

Copyright: 1969

Population: Adults; ages 17 and above

Purpose: Assesses the level of communication of couples; used in marriage counseling, enrichment, research, and teaching

Description: Forty-six items. A seventh-grade reading level is required. Examiner must have experience in couple counseling.

Format: Self-administered; suitable for group use; untimed

Scoring: Hand key

Cost: Forms F and M $1.50; guide $2.00; minimum order of $10.00

Publisher: Northwest Publications

Maryland Parent Attitude Survey (MPAS)
Donald K. Pumroy

Copyright: Not provided

Population: Adults

Purpose: Assesses parents' attitudes toward the way they rear their children; particularly useful as a research instrument

Description: Paper–pencil 95-item test in which the subject chooses one of each pair of A or B forced-choice statements that best represents the parents' attitudes toward childrearing: indulgent, disciplinarian, protective, and rejecting. The survey indicates childrearing "type" or approach. Materials consist of a cover letter, a copy of the research articles, and scoring keys.

Format: Self-administered; suitable for group use; untimed: 45 minutes

Scoring: Hand key

Cost: Complete set $5.00

Publisher: Donald K. Pumroy, Ph.D.

Michigan Screening Profile of Parenting (MSSP)
Ray E. Helfer, James K. Hoffmeister, Carol J. Schneider

Copyright: 1978

Population: Adults

Purpose: Evaluates an individual's perceptions in areas that are critically important for positive parent–child interactions; profiles segments of the individual's early childhood experiences and current relationships

Description: Multiple-item paper–pencil self-report questionnaire for parents and prospective parents. The questionnaire consists of four sections. Section A provides information about family characteristics, the respondent's health history, and relationships with employers, social agencies, and spouse. Section B provides information regarding respondent perceptions of childhood experiences and current interactions with family and friends. Section C (answered only by individuals having one or more children) provides information about the respondent's child (or children) and current parent–child interactions. Section D (answered only by individuals who do not have children) provides information with regard to the respondent's expectations for future interactions with pro-spective children. Section A requires various types of answers depending on the type of biographical information being requested. Sections B, C, and D use 7-point Likert scales to rate responses to individual test items.

Format: Self-administered; suitable for group use; untimed: time varies

Scoring: Computer scored

Cost: 25 questionnaires (including scoring service) $50.00

Publisher: Test Analysis and Development Corporation

Parent As a Teacher Inventory (PAAT)
Robert D. Strom

Copyright: 1995

Population: Adults

Purpose: Assesses parents' attitudes toward their parent–child relationship; used with parents of children ages 3 to 9

Description: Multiple-choice inventory measuring parental attitudes in the following areas: feelings toward the parent–child interactive system, standards for assessing the importance of certain aspects of child behavior, and value preferences and frustrations concerning child behavior. Available in Spanish.

Format: Individual/self-administered; suitable for group use; untimed: 30 minutes

Scoring: Hand key

Cost: Starter Set (inventory manual, 20 inventory booklets/identification questionnaires, 20 profiles) $30.00; Specimen Set $20.90

Publisher: Scholastic Testing Service, Inc.

Parent Behavior Form
Leonard Worell, Judith Worell

Copyright: Not provided

Population: Parents

Purpose: Assesses dimensions of perceived parent behavior

Description: Rates parent behavior by their school-aged or adult children; form for self-rating is available. Fifteen scores are yielded: acceptance, active involvement, egalitarianism, cognitive independence, cognitive understanding, cognitive competence, lax control, conformity, achievement, strict control, punitive control, hostile control, rejection, inconsistent responding, and social desirability. Five forms are used: PBF, PBF-S, PBF Elementary, Form A, Form C-B.

Format: Individual/group administration

Scoring: Hand key

Cost: Contact publisher

Publisher: Judith Worell

Parent–Adolescent Communication Inventory
Millard J. Bienvenu

Copyright: 1969

Population: Adolescent, adult; ages 13 and older

Purpose: Assesses communication in parent–adolescent relationships; used in family counseling, family life education, teaching, and research

Description: Forty-item yes–no–sometimes test. A seventh-grade reading level is required. Examiner must have family counseling experience.

Format: Self-administered; suitable for group use; untimed: 15 minutes

Scoring: Hand key

Cost: $.50 per copy; Guide $1.00; minimum order $10.00

Publisher: Northwest Publications

Parent–Child Relationship Inventory (PCRI)
Anthony B. Gerard

Copyright: Not provided

Population: Parents of 3- to 15-year-old children

Purpose: Used to evaluate parenting skills and attitudes, child custody arrangements, family interaction, and physical or sexual abuse of children

Description: Self-report inventory with 78 items covering seven scales: parental support, involvement, limit setting, role orientation, satisfaction with parenting, communication, and autonomy. Includes two validity scales and separate norms for mothers and fathers.

Format: Examiner not required; suitable for group use; 15 minutes

Scoring: Hand key or computer scored

Cost: Kit (includes 25 AutoScore™ answer sheets, 1 manual, 2 test report prepaid mail-in answer sheets for computer scoring and interpretation) $95.00

Publisher: Western Psychological Services

Parental Acceptance–Rejection Questionnaire (PAPQ)
Ronald P. Rohner, Jose M. Saavedra, Emeline O. Granum

Copyright: 1978

Population: Children 7 to 11 and parents or primary caregivers

Purpose: Measures parental acceptance and rejection

Description: Sixty-item four-point scale questionnaire that measures warmth/affection, aggression/hostility, neglect/indifference, and rejection. Three versions available: Adult I, Adult II, and Child.

Format: Individually administered; requires examiner; untimed

Scoring: Examiner evaluated

Cost: $15.00

Publisher: Select Press

Parental Acceptance–Rejection Questionnaire (PARQ)
Ronald P. Rohner

Copyright: Child and Adult 1976, Parent 1978

Population: Ages 7 to adult

Purpose: Assesses perceived parental acceptance and rejection; used for screening with clinical populations, in research studies with student and community populations and as a tool for parental education programs

Description: Sixty-item paper–pencil questionnaire measuring perceived parental acceptance and rejection in four scales: Warmth/Affection (20 items), Hostility/Aggression (15 items), Indifference/Neglect (15 items), and Undifferentiated Rejection (10 items). The test, designed to cut across social classes and available in 15 languages, can be combined with the formal interview (Parental-Acceptance Rejection Interview Schedule) and behavior observations. It is scored on a four-point scale (almost always to almost never), with some items with reversed scoring to reduce response bias. Scores range from 60 (maximum acceptance, minimum rejection) to 240 (maximum rejection, minimum acceptance). Three versions are available: Mother (includes father; reflects on what they do to child), Adult (adult reflects back on own childhood), and Child (reflects on present actions in family). Available in Arabic, Bengali, Czech, French, Hindi, Korean, Spanish, Swedish, Tamil, Telugu, Tiv, Urdu, Japanese.

Format: Examiner/self-administered; suitable for group use

Scoring: Hand key; may be computer scored

Cost: Handbook $15.00

Publisher: Center for the Study of Parental Acceptance and Rejection

Parenthood Motivation Questionnaire
Burleigh Seaver, Elizabeth P. Kirchuer, Margaret K. Straw, Maria E. Vegega

Copyright: 1977

Population: Adults

Purpose: Assesses motivations of future parents for/against parenthood

Description: Paper–pencil/oral response questionnaire containing 22 subscales for females, 21 subscales for males.

Format: Group or individual administration; examiner required; untimed

Scoring: Examiner evaluated

Cost: $15.00

Publisher: Select Press

Parenting Stress Index (PSI)
Richard R. Abidin

Copyright: 1995

Population: Adults

Purpose: Used in family counseling, stress management, and forensic evaluation to identify parent–child problem areas

Description: Paper–pencil yes–no Likert scale index with four short form scales: Total Stress, Parental Distress, Parent–Child Dysfunctional Interaction, Difficult Child. Long-form Domains and Subscales include Total Stress, Child Domain (distractibility/hyperactivity, adaptability, reinforces parent, demandingness, mood, acceptability), Parent Domain (competence, isolation, attachment, health, role restriction, depression, spouse), Life Stress. A computer version using an IBM PC or compatible is available.

Format: Individual administration; examiner required; untimed

Scoring: Computer scored; hand scorable answer sheet

Cost: Short Form Kit $50.00; Long Form Kit $69.00

Publisher: Psychological Assessment Resources, Inc.

Perceptions of Parental Role Scales
Lucia A. Gilbert, Gary R. Hansen

Copyright: 1982

Population: Adults

Purpose: Measures perceived parental role responsibilities; used with male and female adults for education, counseling, and research

Description: Paper–pencil 78-item instrument assessing parental perceptions in three domains yielding 13 scales: teaching a child (cognitive development, social skills, handling of emotions, physical health, norms and social values, personal hygiene, and survival skills), meeting a child's basic needs (health care, child care, emotional needs, and food, clothing, and shelter), and serving as the interface between the child and the family and other social institutions (social institutions and family unit). The test takes into account current societal views about men's and women's roles. An eighth-grade reading level is required.

Format: Self-administered; suitable for group use; untimed: 15 minutes

Scoring: Hand key

Cost: Kit (manual, 25 questionnaires) $32.00; 50 Questionnaires $26.00

Publisher: Marathon Consulting and Press

Religion Scale
Panos D. Bardis

Copyright: 1961

Population: Adolescents, adults

Purpose: Measures attitudes toward religion; used for clinical assessment, family and marriage counseling, research on attitudes toward religion, and discussion in religion and social science classes

Description: Paper–pencil 25-item test in which the subject reads 25 statements about religious issues and rates them according to his or her beliefs on a scale from 0 (strongly disagree) to 4 (strongly agree). The score is the sum of the 25 numerical responses. The theoretical range of scores extends from 0 (least religious) to 100 (most religious). Suitable for individuals with physical and hearing disabilities.

Format: Examiner/self-administered; suitable for group use; 10 minutes

Scoring: Examiner evaluated

Cost: Free

Publisher: Panos D. Bardis, Ph.D.

Rossetti Pediatric Case History and Family Needs Profile
Louis Rossetti, Jack E. Kile,
Charles A. Osborne, Mary Jeanne
Schaffmeyer, Stephanie Thomas,
Paula L. Wilkening

Copyright: 1995

Population: Children; birth to 3

Purpose: Assesses infants and toddlers who are at risk or have disabilities and their families; used in marital counseling

Description: Oral response criterion-referenced short answer with nine areas of assessment, plus a Family Needs Profile. The areas of assessment are family background, statement of the problem, prenatal and birth history, hearing history, speech and language development, motor development, play behaviors, social/emotional development, educational history, and a family needs profile. No scores are generated. Examiners must be SLPs or early interventionists. Suitable for individuals with visual, physical, hearing, and mental disabilities.

Format: Individual administration; examiner required; untimed

Scoring: Examiner evaluated; no scoring service available

Cost: 15 profiles $19.95

Publisher: LinguiSystems, Inc.

Staffan Roijeus Family Game (SRF)
Staffan Roijen

Copyright: 1993

Population: Children to Adults

Purpose: Assesses family interaction

Description: Four-item show-tell test measuring the family now, the effect on the family of a two-week vacation, the effect of one member of the family moving away, new learning about the family during the game. Examiner must be a qualified psychologist or psychiatrist. Available also in Danish.

Format: Individually administered; suitable for group use; examiner required; untimed

Scoring: Examiner evaluated

Cost: $132.00 (DKK 750)

Publisher: Dansk psykologisk Forlag

Tasks and Rating Scales for Lab Assessment of Infant Temperament

A. Methany, R. Wilson

Copyright: 1981

Population: Children; ages 3 to 30 months

Purpose: Assesses age-appropriate sequence of interactions between child and mother/caregiver

Description: Multiple-item criterion-referenced paper–pencil/oral response assessment

Format: Individual or group administration; examiner required; untimed

Scoring: Hand key; examiner evaluated

Cost: $18.00

Publisher: Select Press

Uniform Child Custody Evaluation System (UCCES)

Harry L. Munsinger, Kevin N. Karlson

Copyright: 1994

Population: Individuals involved in child custody litigation

Purpose: Provides a uniform custody evaluation procedure

Description: Paper–pencil short answer test; 25 forms are organized into three categories: general data and administration forms, parent forms, and child forms. Materials used include a manual and 25 different forms used to document and evaluate.

Format: Individual administration; examiner required; untimed

Scoring: Examiner evaluated

Cost: Kit $85.00

Publisher: Psychological Assessment Resources, Inc.

Workbook–Coder Training Manual for DPICS II

Sheila M. Eyberg, D. Edwards, K. Bessmer, V. Litwin

Copyright: 1994

Population: Children to adults; ages 2 to adult

Purpose: Measures quality of social interactions of families; used in family counseling and social services

Description: Paper–pencil instrument

Format: Individually administered; examiner required; timed: time not available

Scoring: Examiner evaluated

Cost: $27.50

Publisher: Select Press

Geropsychology

· ·

Assessment of Living Skills and Resources (ALSAR)

Theresa J. K. Drinka, Jane H. Williams, Martha Schram, Jean Farrell-Holtan, Rennie Euhardy

Copyright: 1991

Population: Community-dwelling elders

Purpose: Assesses ability to function in the community

Description: Eleven task scores (telephoning, reading, leisure, medication management, transportation, shopping, meal preparation, laundering, housekeeping, home maintenance) measured on an instrument that looks at daily tasks that require a high level of cognitive function, or Instrumental Activities of Daily Living (IADLs).

Format: Individual administration, 15–20 minutes

Scoring: Examiner evaluation and interpretation

Cost: $5.00 per master, $55.00 for each of 2 videotapes

Publisher: Madison VA Geriatric Research, Education, and Clinical Center

Clock Test
H. Tuokko, T. Hadjistavropoulos,
J. A. Miller, A. Horton, B. L. Beattie

Copyright: 1995

Population: Adults; ages 50 and older

Purpose: Screens for dementia; used for neurology and geriatric counseling

Description: Paper–pencil drawn response test comprised of three subtests: Clock drawing (1 clock must be drawn), clock setting (5 clocks must be set), and clock reading (5 times must be read). A score is obtained for each of the subtests, the scores are plotted on a profile sheet, and the pattern is used to screen for dementia.

Format: Individual administration; examiner required; untimed

Scoring: Hand key

Cost: Kit $160.00

Publisher: Multi-Health Systems, Inc.

Dementia Rating Scale (DRS)
Steven Mattis

Copyright: 1988

Population: Adults; ages 65 to 81

Purpose: Provides a brief, comprehensive measure of cognitive status in individuals with cortical impairment, particularly of the degenerative type

Description: Oral-response 36-task short-answer verbal and copying test comprised of 5 subscales that measure attention, initiation/perseveration, construction, conceptualization, and memory. It provides a measure of cognitive function at lower levels of ability. Test–retest reliability for the DRS Total Score is .97; subscale correlations range from .61 to .94. The split-half reliability coefficient for the DRS is .90. Validity is supported by DRS Total Score correlations with the Wechsler Memory Scale Memory Quotient, WAIS Full Scale IQ, and cortical metabolism of .70, .67, and .59, repectively. The manual includes further studies describing the development and validation of the DRS. Materials include manual, scoring/recording forms, and stimulus cards. Examiner must meet APA guidelines, C level.

Format: Examiner required; not suitable for group use; untimed: 15–45 minutes

Scoring: Examiner evaluated

Cost: DRS Kit (manual, 25 scoring/recording forms, and set of stimulus cards) $61.00

Publisher: Psychological Assessment Resources, Inc.

Fuld Object-Memory Evaluation
Paula Altman Fuld

Copyright: 1977

Population: Adults; ages 70 to 90

Purpose: Measures memory and learning in adults regardless of vision, hearing, or language handicaps; cultural differences; or inattention problems

Description: Ten common objects in a bag are presented to the patient to determine whether he or she can identify them by touch. The patient names the item and then pulls it out of the bag to see if he or she was right. After being distracted, the patient is asked to recall the items from the bag. The patient is given four additional chances to learn and recall the objects. The test provides separate scores for long-term storage, retrieval, consistency of retrieval, and failure to recall items even after being reminded. The test also provides a chance to observe naming ability, left–right orientation, stereognosis, and verbal fluency. Separate norms are provided for total recall, storage, consistency of retrieval, ability to benefit from reminding, and ability to say words in categories.

Format: Examiner required; not suitable for group use; timed: 60 seconds for each first trial, 30 seconds for each second trial

Scoring: Examiner evaluated

Cost: Complete kit (testing materials, manual, record forms) $65.00; 30 record forms $25.00

Publisher: Stoelting Company

Geriatric Depression Scale
T. L. Brink, Jerome Yesavage, P. Heersema,
O. Lum, M. Adey, T. L. Rose, V. O. Leirer,
V. Huang

Copyright: Not provided

Population: Adolescents, adults, elders

Purpose: Screens for depression

Description: This 30-item scale may be administered orally, in writing, over the telephone, or by computer. The yes–no response format is especially appropriate for oral administration. The lack of somatic items makes the test appropriate for general medical patients, elders, and those with chronic physical conditions. Spanish, Hebrew, Yiddish, Portuguese, Japanese, and Chinese translations are available.

Format: Untimed: 2–7 minutes

Scoring: Hand key

Cost: Free, along with annotated bibliography

Publisher: T. L. Brink, Ph.D.

Human Figure Drawing Test (HFDT): An Illustrated Handbook for Clinical Interpretation and Standardized Assessment of Cognitive Impairment
Jerry Mitchell, Richard Trent,
Roland McArthur

Copyright: Not provided

Population: Ages 15 to adult

Purpose: Used to evaluate cognitive deterioration in adults

Description: A complete scoring and interpretation system for human figure drawings that provides adult norms for cognitive impairment. Using the handbook and the AutoScore™ form, a complete qualitative evaluation can be made. The HFDT provides four measures of cognitive status: Impairment Score, Distortion Score, Simplification Score, and Organic Factors Index. These scores are helpful in discriminating cognitive impairment caused by thought disorders from that caused by organic conditions. Norms are based on a sample of 800 individuals (over age 15), including the following groups: nonclinical, depressed, antisocial, manic, paranoid, schizophrenic, organic, and mentally retarded.

Format: Individually administered; examiner required

Scoring: Examiner evaluated/hand key

Cost: Kit (includes handbook, 25 AutoScore™ forms, 25 drawing forms) $87.50

Publisher: Western Psychological Services

Hypochondriasis Scale: Institutional Geriatric
T. L. Brink, James Bryant, Judy Belanger,
Diane Capri, Suzanne Jascula,
Connie Janakes, Charmaine Oliveira

Copyright: Not provided

Population: Adolescents, adults, elders

Purpose: Assesses hypochondriacal attitudes

Description: This 6-item scale may be administered orally, in writing, over the telephone, or by computer. The yes–no format is especially appropriate for oral administration. The scale has false positives but not false negatives. Spanish, Hebrew, and Yiddish translations are available.

Format: Untimed: 1–2 minutes

Scoring: Hand key

Cost: Free, along with annotated bibliography

Publisher: T. L. Brink, Ph.D.

Older Persons Counseling Needs Survey (OPCNS)
Jane E. Myers

Copyright: 1993

Population: Adults; ages 60 and above

Purpose: Assesses an elderly person's needs and desires for counseling

Description: Likert-type scale with 56 items measuring personal, social, activity, and environment concerns. A fifth-grade reading level is required.

Format: Individual administration; suitable for group use; examiner required; untimed: 10–15 minutes

Scoring: Examiner evaluated

Cost: Sampler Set $25.00; Permission Set for 200 users $90.00

Publisher: Mind Garden, Inc.

Ross Information Processing Assessment–Geriatric (RIPA–G)
Deborah G. Ross-Swain, Paul Fogle

Copyright: 1996

Population: Adults; ages 55 and over

Purpose: Assesses cognitive–linguistic deficits in geriatric patients who are residents in skilled nursing facilities, hospitals, and clinics

Description: Multiple-item paper–pencil instrument that incorporates questions from the Minimum Data Set used by nursing staffs to provide correlational data with nursing staff's assessments of patients' cognitive–linguistic abilities. Enables examiner to quantify deficits, determine severity levels for the skills areas (Immediate Memory, Recent Memory, Temporal Orientation, Spatial Orientation, Orientation to Environment, Recall of General Information, Problem Solving and Abstract Reasoning, Organization of Information, Auditory Processing and Comprehension, and Problem Solving and Concrete Reasoning), and develop rehabilitation goals and objectives.

Format: Individual administration; untimed: 45–60 minutes

Scoring: Hand key

Cost: Complete kit (manual protocols, picture book) $134.00

Publisher: PRO-ED, Inc.

Scale for Paranoia/Observer Rated Geriatric (SPORG)
T. L. Brink, J. Sheikh

Copyright: Not provided

Population: Elders

Purpose: Assesses paranoia in institutionalized elders

Description: This 20-item scale is designed for nursing home staff to assess the level of paranoia in institutionalized geriatric patients.

Format: Untimed: 2–3 minutes per examiner per patient

Scoring: Hand key

Cost: Free

Publisher: T. L. Brink, Ph.D.

Illness

Chronic and Terminal

Battery for Health Improvement™ (BHI™)
J. Mark Disorbio, Daniel Bruns

Copyright: Not provided

Population: Adults

Purpose: Measures factors that would interfere with a patient's normal course of recovery from an injury; used for evaluation of patients in treatment or recovery from an injury

Description: Multiple-choice/oral-response 202-item computer or paper–pencil test. Scales measure depression, anxiety, hostility, borderline dependency, failure to succeed, substance abuse, family dysfunction, job dissatisfaction, doctor dissatisfaction, somatic and pain complaints. Validity index. Sixth-grade reading level required.

Format: Self-administered; suitable for group use; untimed: 25–40 minutes

Scoring: Hand key; computer scored

Cost: Hand score $1.50; profile reports $7.00–$10.00

Publisher: NCS Assessments

Health Attribution Test (HAT)
Jeanne Achterberg, G. Frank Lawlis

Copyright: 1990

Population: Adults

Purpose: Measures attitudes toward health responsibility of patients regarding their own health maintenance or treatment program; used in rehabilitation therapy and for chronic illness treatments

Description: Paper–pencil 22-item test with three dimensions: Internal scale, Powerful Others scale, and Chance Dimension. A sixth-grade reading level is required.

Format: Self-administered; untimed

Scoring: Hand key; no scoring service available

Cost: Package of 25 tests $23.00; test user's guide $14.00

Publisher: Institute for Personality and Ability Testing

Psychosocial Adjustment to Illness Scale (PAIS–SR)
Leonard R. Derogatis

Copyright: 1983

Population: Adults

Purpose: Assesses the psychological and social adjustment of medical patients or their immediate families to a clinically significant medical illness

Description: Paper–pencil 46-item self-report instrument or structured interview guide assessing the psychosocial adjustment of medical patients and their immediate families in terms of seven principal domains: health care orientation, vocational environment, domestic environment, sexual relationships, extended family relationships, social environment, and psychological distress. A total score summarizes overall adjustment to illness. The self-report form (PAIS–SR) and the interview guide (PAIS) measure equivalent items. Norms and profile/score sheets are available for lung cancer, essential hypertension, burn patients, gynecology, cancer, and renal dialysis patients for the self-report form. SCORPAIS Version 2.1 is a microcomputer scoring program. It generates 7 primary domain scores and an adjustment to illness score, which may be converted to standardized score formats for any of the available norm groups (renal dialysis, cardiac bypass, lung cancer, acute burn, and essential hypertension).

Format: Examiner required; self-report form suitable for group use; interview guide individually administered; untimed: 20–30 minutes

Scoring: Examiner evaluated; may be computer scored

Cost: Interview booklet $3.00; self-report form $.75; score/profile sheets $.40 and $.70; manual $26.00; SCORPAISPC Version 2.1 available on a per use basis

Publisher: Clinical Psychometric Research, Inc.

Questionnaire on Resources and Stress (QRS)
Jean Holroyd

Copyright: 1987

Population: Adults

Purpose: Measures stress in families of ill or disabled persons; used with families of individuals with developmental disabilities, psychiatric problems, renal disease, cystic fibrosis, neuromuscular disease, and cerebral palsy

Description: True–false 285-item paper–pencil test with 15 subtests assessing the impact of an individual's illness or disability on other family members. The subtests are Poor Health/Mood, Excess Time Demands, Negative Attitude, Overprotection/Dependency, Lack of Social Support, Overcommitment/Martyrdom, Pessimism, Lack of Family Integration, Limits on Family Opportunity, Financial Problems, Physical Incapacitation, Lack of Activities, Occupational Limitations, Social Obtrusiveness, and Difficult Personality Characteristics. The test yields information about the examinee, the family, and the disabled individual. Raw scores are converted to standard scores. A long form and a short form are available. A sixth-grade reading level is required.

Format: Self-administered; not suitable for group use; untimed: 1 hour or less

Scoring: Hand key; may be examiner evaluated

Cost: Complete kit (manual, protocols, and scoring templates) $79.00

Publisher: PRO-ED, Inc.

Depression

Children's Depression Rating Scale, Revised (CDRS–R)
Elva O. Poznanski, Hartmut B. Mokros

Copyright: Not provided

Population: Ages 6 to 12 years

Purpose: Used to diagnose depression and determine its severity

Description: In clinical contexts, the CDRS–R can be used to diagnose depression and to monitor treatment response. In nonclinical contexts, such as schools and pediatric clinics, it serves as a screening tool, identifying children who need professional intervention. This is a brief rating scale based on a semistructured interview with the child. The scale requires the interviewer to rate 17 symptom areas (including those that serve as DSM–IV criteria for a diagnosis of depression): school work, capacity to have fun, social withdrawal, eating patterns, sleep patterns, excessive fatigue, physical complaints, irritability, guilt, self-esteem, depressed feelings, morbid ideation, suicidal ideation, weeping, facial expressions of affect, tempo of speech, and hyperactivity. The majority of these symptom areas are rated on an expanded 7-point scale. The CDRS–R gives a single Summary Score along with a clear interpretation of, and recommendations for, six different score ranges.

Format: Individual administration; examiner required; 15–20 minutes

Scoring: Hand key

Cost: Kit (includes 25 answer booklets, 1 manual) $55.00

Publisher: Western Psychological Services

Children's Depression Scale– Second Research Edition
Moshe Lange, Miriam Tisher

Copyright: 1983

Population: Children, adolescents; ages 9 to 16

Purpose: Measures depression in children; identifies depressed children in need of further evaluation

Description: Scale with 66 items (48 "depressive" and 10 "positive") measuring six aspects of childhood depression: affective response, social problems, self-esteem, preoccupation with own sickness or death, guilt, and pleasure. Items are presented on cards which the child sorts into five boxes ranging from "very right" to "very wrong" according to how he or she feels the item applies to herself or himself. A paper–pencil questionnaire identical in content to the cards but appropriately reworded, is available for use with parents, teachers, or other adults familiar with the child. The complete set of materials includes 66 cards, five boxes, 25 record forms, and a manual.

Format: Examiner required; not suitable for group use; untimed: time varies

Scoring: Examiner evaluated

Cost: Contact publisher

Publisher: The Australian Council for Educational Research Limited

Depressive Life Experience Scale (DLES)
W. E. Snell, Jr., R. C. Hawekins, S. S. Belk

Copyright: 1986

Population: Adults

Purpose: Measures stressful and distressful aspects of depression; used in depression therapy

Description: Multiple-item paper–pencil questionnaire

Format: Individual administration; examiner required; untimed

Scoring: Examiner evaluated

Cost: $21.00

Publisher: Select Press

Draw a Story: Screening for Depression (DAS)
Rawley A. Silver

Copyright: 1993

Population: Ages 5 through 21

Purpose: Screens for depression; assesses concepts of self and others

Description: The examinee views two sets of stimulus drawings of 14 people, animals, places, or things and is asked to choose two subjects to imagine something happening between them. A picture is then drawn of what is imagined, followed by a written story. The information is rated on a 1- to 5-point scale.

Format: Individual administration; suitable for group use; untimed: 10 minutes

Scoring: Examiner administration and interpretation

Cost: $25.00

Publisher: Ablin Press Distributors

Hamilton Depression Inventory (HDI)
William H. Reynolds, Kenneth A. Kobak

Copyright: 1995

Population: Adults

Purpose: Used as a comprehensive screening for symptoms of depression; used in private practice, hospitals, and correctional institutions

Description: Paper–pencil 23-item 3- to 5-point scale with the following categories: Depressed Mood, Loss of Interest/Pleasure, Weight Loss, Insomnia/Hypersomnia, Psychomotor Retardation/Agitation, Fatigue, Worthlessness, Indecisiveness, Suicide Ideation. Materials used include a manual, item booklet, summary sheet, answer sheet, and short-form test booklet. A fifth-grade reading level is required. Examiner must be B-level qualified.

Format: Self-administered; examiner required; untimed

Scoring: Hand-scorable answer sheet

Cost: Intro kit $59.00

Publisher: Psychological Assessment Resources, Inc.

IPAT Depression Scale
Samuel E. Krug, James E. Laughlin

Copyright: 1976

Population: Adults

Purpose: Diagnoses depression in adults of most educational levels; used for both clinical diagnosis and psychological research on depression

Description: Forty-item paper–pencil questionnaire diagnosing and measuring depression in adults. Norms are provided for adult, college, prison, and certain clinical populations. A fifth-grade reading level is required.

Format: Self-administered; suitable for group use; untimed: 10 minutes

Scoring: Hand key

Cost: Complete kit $16.00; manual $11.75; 25 nonreusable test booklets $10.50; scoring key $4.00

Publisher: Institute for Personality and Ability Testing, Inc.

Martin S–D Inventory
William T. Martin

Copyright: 1970

Population: Adolescents, adults

Purpose: Identifies persons with depressive and suicidal tendencies; serves as a screening instrument for suicide prevention centers and mental health facilities; also used for research on suicide and depression

Description: Fifty-item paper–pencil inventory measuring behavioral and cognitive aspects related to depression and suicide. Subjects rate statements (both negative and positive) on a scale from 1 to 4 as they apply to their own beliefs and behavior. A total Adjusted Score is derived, with norms provided for normals, depressed persons, and psychiatric patients. Suggested cutoff scores are provided for persons considered depressed, moderately depressed, and significantly depressed. The inventory may be used in conjunction with the S–D Proneness Checklist. A pamphlet on suicide/depression also is available.

Format: Examiner required; suitable for group use; untimed: 15 minutes

Scoring: Hand key; examiner evaluated

Cost: Specimen Set $9.00; 25 tests $8.25; scoring templates $2.75; manual $6.75

Publisher: Psychologists and Educators, Inc.

Multiscore Depression Inventory for Children (MDI-C)
David J. Berndt, Charles F. Kaiser

Copyright: Not provided

Population: Ages 8 to 17

Purpose: Used to assess depression in children and adolescents

Description: Paper–pencil or computer-administered 79-item inventory, written or revised by children, used to assess depression in 8- to 17-year-olds. The inventory contains eight scales: anxiety, self-esteem, social introversion, instrumental helplessness, sad mood, pessimism, low energy, and defiance. The inventory yields scores for each of these scales, plus a total score, and several validity indicators. This inventory is a downward extension of the Multiscore Depression Inventory.

Format: Examiner required; not suitable for group use; 10–20 minutes

Scoring: Hand key or computer scored

Cost: Kit (includes 25 AutoScore™ test forms, 1 manual, 2 test report prepaid mail-in answer sheets for computer scoring and interpretation) $105.00; MDI-C Microcomputer Disk (IBM 3.5" or 5.25") (good for 25 uses) $295.00

Publisher: Western Psychological Services

North American Depression Inventories (NADI)
James Battle

Copyright: 1988

Population: Ages 5 to adulthood

Purpose: Assesses depression, is applicable for psychotherapy/depression counseling, and is suitable for most populations

Description: Total number of items: Form A—for adults, 40 items; Form C—for children, 25 items. Scores yielded and reports available: classifications, percentile ranks, *T*-scores. Paper–pencil, criterion-referenced response format, Available in large print, on audiocassette, and in French and Spanish; may be used for persons with visual, physical, hearing, or mental disabilities.

Format: Individual or group administration; untimed: 0–15 minutes

Scoring: hand key and computer scored; test scoring service available from publisher

Cost: $120.00 U.S.; $150.00 Canadian

Publisher: James Battle and Associates, Ltd.

Revised Hamilton Rating Scale for Depression (RHRSD)
W. L. Warren

Copyright: Not provided

Population: Adults

Purpose: Used to evaluate depression in adult clinical populations and in medical or mental health settings

Description: The RHRSD was developed in a medical setting and used concurrently with antidepressant medication to evaluate treatment response. The RHRSD covers both psychoaffective and somatic symptoms. It gives three levels of interpretation: Overall Symptom Severity, Groups of Symptoms, Specific Symptom Areas. Can be used to quickly evaluate symptom severity, to confirm a diagnosis of depression, to explore depressive symptoms, and to measure treatment outcome. Several new features: a self-report version (can be completed in the waiting room by the client), a WPS AutoScore™ Form, and eight new critical items which help confirm diagnoses of depression.

Format: Self-administered; untimed: 5–10 minutes

Scoring: Hand or computer scored

Cost: Kit (includes 10 WPS AutoScore™ RHRSD Clinician Forms; 10 WPS AutoScore™ Self-Report Problem Inventories; 1 manual) $70.00; RHRSD (IBM) Microcomputer Disk (each disk good for 25 uses) $215.00

Publisher: Western Psychological Services

Reynolds Adolescent Depression Scale (RADS)
William M. Reynolds

Copyright: 1987

Population: Adolescents; ages 13 to 18

Purpose: Measures depression in adolescents; used for identification of depression in school and clinical groups, research on depression, clinical assessment, evaluation of treatment programs, screening of behavior/conduct disorder referrals, and academic problems

Description: Thirty-item paper–pencil test to which students respond on a 4-point Likert-type scale. The test is available in three forms: HS, I, and G. Form HS is the hand-scorable version. Form I, for use with individuals and small groups, includes a four- to five-page report that includes a validity check, score comparisons against cutoff and normative data, critical item responses, and total item responses. Form G, designed for large groups and mail-in scoring, is used in research and for program evaluation. The survey report includes group summary data, a list of protocols above the cutoff, protocols above the 95th percentile, invalid protocols, scores for all protocols, and means and ranges for all scores. A scoring service is available from the publisher.

Format: Self-administered; suitable for group use; untimed: 5–10 minutes

Scoring: Form HS hand key; Forms I and G computer scored

Cost: Professional Kit (manual, 25 Form HS answer sheets, scoring key) $55.00; 50 Form G prepaid mail-in answer sheets (scoring and report) $105.00; 10 Form I prepaid mail-in answer sheets (scoring and report) $49.00

Publisher: Psychological Assessment Resources, Inc.

Reynolds Child Depression Scale (RCDS)
William M. Reynolds

Copyright: 1989

Population: Children; Grades 3 to 6

Purpose: Assesses and screens depressive symptomatology

Description: Thirty-item multiple-choice paper–pencil test. Percentiles by grade and sex are provided for the total score. Second-grade reading level required. One test in the Reynolds Depression Scale series. May be used with individuals with visual, hearing, physical, and mental disabilities. Examiner must meet APA B-Level guidelines.

Format: Examiner required; suitable for group use; untimed: 10 minutes

Scoring: Hand key; test scoring service available from publisher

Cost: Kit (manual, 25 handscorable answer sheets, and scoring key) $55.00

Publisher: Psychological Assessment Resources, Inc.

State–Trait Depression Adjective Checklists (ST–DACL)
Bernard Lubin

Copyright: 1994

Population: Ages 14 to 89

Purpose: Used in counseling to measure both state and trait feelings of depression

Description: Paper–pencil checklists ranging from 32 to 34 adjectives. Materials used include a manual, Forms 1 and 2, Form A-B, Form C-D, and Profile Form.

Format: Self-administered; suitable for group

use; examiner required; untimed: 2–3 minutes

Scoring: Hand scored

Cost: Kit $65.00

Publisher: Psychological Assessment Resources, Inc.

Trait Anxiety and Depression Scales
Albert Mehrabian

Copyright: 1994

Population: Adolescents, adults; ages 14 and older

Purpose: Assesses trait anxiety and depression; used for research and in counseling

Description: Paper–pencil 36-item test with two subtests: Trait anxiety—16 items; Depression—20 items; A 10th-grade reading level is required.

Format: Self-administered; suitable for group use; untimed: 10 minutes

Scoring: Hand key; test scoring service available from publisher

Cost: Test kit $31.00

Publisher: Albert Mehrabian, Ph.D.

Eating Disorders

Eating Disorder Inventory–2 (EDI–2)
David M. Garner

Copyright: 1991

Population: Adolescents, adults

Purpose: Assesses the psychological and behavioral traits common in eating disorders; distinguishes individuals with serious psychopathology from normal dieters; used in the treatment of individuals with eating disorders

Description: Paper–pencil or computer-administered 64-item self-report inventory consisting of eight subscales (Drive for Thinness, Bulimia, Body Dissatisfaction, Ineffective-ness, Perfectionism, Interpersonal Distrust, Interoceptive Awareness, and Maturity Fears) measuring specific cognitive and behavioral dimensions related to eating disorders. The inventory identifies individuals with serious eating disorders and differentiates between subgroups of eating disorders. The computer version operates on IBM PC systems and compatibles. Available in Swedish and Italian.

Format: Suitable for group use; untimed: 20 minutes

Scoring: Hand key; computer scored.

Cost: Kit (manual, manual supplement, scoring keys, 25 test booklets, 25 profile forms) $75.00; computer version $345.00

Publisher: Psychological Assessment Resources, Inc.

Eating Inventory
Albert J. Stunkard, Samuel Messick

Copyright: 1988

Population: Adults; ages 17 and older

Purpose: Measures behavior important to the understanding and treatment of eating-related disorders such as anorexia and bulimia; also used to predict response to weight-loss programs, weight gain after quitting smoking, and weight change during depression

Description: Paper–pencil 51-item questionnaire measuring three dimensions of eating behavior: cognitive restraint of eating, disinhibition, and hunger. This test is for use only by persons with at least a master's degree in psychology or a related discipline. Registration is required.

Format: Self-administered; suitable for group use; untimed: 15 minutes

Scoring: Hand key

Cost: Examination Kit (manual, 25 questionnaires, and 25 Ready Score answer sheets) $95.00; manual $39.50

Publisher: The Psychological Corporation

Substance Abuse

Adolescent Chemical Dependency Inventory (ACDI)

Copyright: 1989

Population: Ages 12 to 18

Purpose: Screens for and evaluates adolescent substance abuse; used in intake/referral settings, adolescent chemical dependency treatment programs, and juvenile court/probation systems

Description: Paper–pencil or computer-administered 104-item multiple-choice and true–false inventory containing five scales: Truthfulness, Alcohol, Drugs, Adjustment, and Distress. The Truthfulness scale measures how truthfully the examinee responded to ACDI items. The Alcohol scale measures alcohol-related problems. The Drugs scale measures drug use or abuse-related problems. The Adjustment scale measures overall level of adjustment (personal, home, school, authority, relationship). The Distress scale measures anxiety and depression levels. Results are reported as percentiles, corrected raw scores, and risk-level classifications (low, low–medium, high–medium, high). Narrative explanations and recommendations are presented in automated reports. The computer version operates on IBM PC–compatible systems. Floppy diskettes containing 50, 100, 150 ACDS test applications provided; computer scoring on-site. A sixth-grade reading level is required. Available in Spanish.

Format: Self-administered; suitable for group use; untimed: 20 minutes

Scoring: Computer scored

Cost: Contact publisher; volume discounts available

Publisher: Behavior Data Systems, Ltd.

Adolescent Diagnostic Interview (ADI)

Ken C. Winters, George H. Henly

Copyright: Not provided

Population: 12- to 18-year-olds

Purpose: Systematically assesses psychoactive substance use disorders and evaluates psychosocial stressors, school and interpersonal functioning, and cognitive impairment

Description: Used by chemical dependency practitioners, clinical psychologists, and social workers, the ADI consists of a series of questions about behaviors, events, and attitudes related to DSM–III–R and DSM–IV diagnostic criteria for psychoactive substance use disorders. The interviewer reads the questions from the Administration Booklet and enters the client's responses. When the ADI is scored, it yields the following information: presence or absence of a DSM–III–R or DSM–IV diagnosis, level of functioning, severity of psychosocial stressors, and rating of memory and orientation.

Format: Individually administered; examiner required; 45 minutes or more

Scoring: Examiner evaluated

Cost: Kit (includes 5 administration booklets, 1 manual) $75.00

Publisher: Western Psychological Services

Adolescent Drinking Index (ADI)

Adele V. Harrell, Philip W. Wirtz

Copyright: 1989

Population: Adolescents; ages 12 to 17

Purpose: Assesses alcohol abuse in adolescents with emotional or behavioral problems; used for screening and treatment planning

Description: Multiple-choice 24-item index. A manual and test booklet are used. A fifth-grade reading level is required. Examiner must be level B qualified.

Format: Individual administration; suitable for group use; untimed: 5 minutes

Scoring: Hand key

Cost: Kit $48.00

Publisher: Psychological Assessment Resources, Inc.

Alcadd Test–Revised

Morse P. Manson, Lisa A. Melchior

Copyright: 1988

Population: Adults; ages 18 and older

Purpose: Assesses the extent of alcohol addiction; used for diagnosis, treatment, and alcoholism research

Description: Multiple-choice 65-item paper–pencil test consisting of five subscales measuring regularity of drinking, preference for drinking over other activities, lack of controlled drinking, rationalization of drinking, and excessive emotionality. Materials include WPS Autoscore Form or ALCADD Microcomputer Disk. Computer versions available for IBM PC, XT, or AT (or compatible). Fourth-grade reading level required. This test is suitable for individuals with visual, hearing, and physical disabilities. Can be read to individuals with visual impairments. This is a revision of the 1978 ALCADD Test.

Format: Self-administered; suitable for group use; untimed: 5–15 minutes

Scoring: Hand key; computer scored

Cost: Kit $55.00; disk (25 uses) $125.00

Publisher: Western Psychological Services

Alcohol and Drug Use Scales

Albert Mehrabian

Copyright: 1994

Population: Adolescents, adults; ages 14 and older

Purpose: Measures alcohol/drug abuse; used for research and counseling

Description: Paper–pencil 18-item test with two subscales: extent of alcohol use/abuse (11 items), extent of drug use/abuse (7 items). A 10th-grade reading level is required.

Format: Self-administered; suitable for group use; untimed: 10 minutes

Scoring: Hand key

Cost: Test kit $31.00

Publisher: Albert Mehrabian, Ph.D.

Alcohol Dependence Scale (ADS)

Harvey A. Skinner, John L. Horn

Copyright: 1984

Population: Adults

Purpose: Measures severity of alcohol dependence; used for addiction counseling

Description: 25-item paper–pencil test

Format: Individual administration; untimed

Scoring: Self-scored

Cost: 25 forms $6.50

Publisher: Addiction Research Foundation

Alcohol Use Inventory (AUI)

J. L. Horn, K. W. Wanberg, F. M. Foster

Copyright: 1987

Population: Adults

Purpose: Identifies patterns of behavior, attitudes, and symptoms associated with the use and abuse of alcohol; used for planning treatments

Description: Self-report inventory with 228 items measuring the alcohol-related problems of addicted, dependent, binge, and violent drinkers along four domains: benefits, styles, consequences, and concerns associated with alcohol use. The test contains 24 scales (17 primary, 6 second-order, and 1 general) covering drinking for social or mental improvement, drinking to manage moods, gregarious vs. solo drinking, compulsive obsession about drinking, sustained vs. periodic drinking, social role maladaption, loss of control over behavior when drinking, perceptual and somatic withdrawal symptoms, relationship of marital problems and drinking, quantity of alcohol consumed when drinking, guilt and worry associated with drinking, prior attempts to deal with drinking, and awareness of drinking problems and readiness for help. A profile report is included. Items are written at a sixth-grade reading level.

Format: Self-administered; suitable for group use; untimed: 35–60 minutes

Scoring: Computer scored; hand scoring materials available

Cost: Specimen Set (manual, test booklet, profile report answer sheet) $14.95

Publisher: NCS Assessments

American Drug and Alcohol Survey™

Copyright: 1996

Population: Children, adolescents; Grades 4 to 12

Purpose: Assesses substance abuse experience and attitudes; used for prevention program planning and evaluation

Description: Multiple-choice paper–pencil test. Adolescent's form has 58 questions; Children's form has 51 questions. The ADAS is not an instrument for clinical use with individuals. It is an anonymous survey to be administered to a group. Reports present percentages of respondents who answer in certain ways. RMBSI scans surveys, runs analyses, and produces comprehensive reports on the student population surveyed. Forms are optical-scan forms processed by the publisher. Adolescent form is available in Spanish.

Format: Self-administered; suitable for group use; untimed: approximately 30 minutes

Scoring: Test scoring service available from publisher

Cost: Varies based on number of forms and reports ordered

Publisher: Rocky Mountain Behavioral Science Institute, Inc.

Brief Drinker Profile (BDP)
William R. Miller, G. Allan Marlatt

Copyright: 1987

Population: Adults

Purpose: Evaluates problem drinking; used as a component of a screening battery in mental health facilities, forensic centers, medical and hospital settings, and alcohol treatment centers

Description: Multiple-item paper–pencil intake interview covering an individual's family and employment status, demographic, history of problem development, current drinking pattern, alcohol-related problems, severity of dependence, other drug use, additional life problems, and motivation for treatment. The instrument, which is a shortened version of the Comprehensive Drinker Profile (CDP), incorporates the Michigan Alcoholism Screening Test (MAST). The BDP is used in situations not requiring the degree of information elicited by the CDP. Cards from the CDP card deck are required, and the CDP manual is used for scoring and interpretation. A new CDP manual supplement provides administration instructions.

Format: Examiner required; not suitable for group use; untimed: 50 minutes

Scoring: Examiner evaluated

Cost: 25 BDP forms $39.00; CDP manual supplement $12.00; CDP manual $15.00; CDP card sets $15.00

Publisher: Psychological Assessment Resources, Inc.

Children of Alcoholics Screening Test (CAST)
John W. Jones

Copyright: 1983

Population: Children and adults

Purpose: Identifies children of alcoholics, adult children of alcoholics, and their chemically dependent parents; applicable for school or marital counseling

Description: Thirty-item paper–pencil true–false test yielding an overall score which assists diagnosis of parental alcoholism. Standard form (alcohol abuse) and Researchers form (drug and alcohol abuse) used. Available also in Spanish and French. Suitable for individuals with visual, physical, and hearing disabilities.

Format: Individual/group administration; self-administered; untimed

Scoring: Hand key

Cost: Manual with 50 forms $30.00 + shipping; discounts for researchers or large-scale testing

Publisher: Camelot Unlimited

Collateral Interview Form (CIF)
William R. Miller, G. Allan Marlatt

Copyright: 1987

Population: Adults

Purpose: Assesses the problem drinker from the perspective of the significant other

Description: Multiple-item paper–pencil structured interview designed to verify the accuracy of the information supplied by the drinker, obtain information and perspectives not available from the drinker, increase the accuracy of information offered by the drinker through awareness that his or her information will be checked, and involve persons close to the drinker in the change process. The test is adapted from the Comprehensive Drinker Profile (CDP). The CDP manual is used for scoring and interpretation. A CDP manual supplement provides administration instructions.

Format: Examiner required; not suitable for group use; untimed: typical time not available

Scoring: Examiner evaluated

Cost: 15 CIF forms $23.00; CDP manual supplement $12.00; CDP manual $15.00

Publisher: Psychological Assessment Resources, Inc.

Comprehensive Drinker Profile (CDP)
G. Alan Marlatt, William R. Miller

Copyright: 1987

Population: Adults

Purpose: Assesses alcoholism in men and women; used for intake-screening in alcohol abuse treatment programs; provides a basis for selecting, planning, and implementing individualized treatment programs

Description: Multiple-item paper–pencil structured interview guide assessing an individual's history and current status regarding the use and abuse of alcohol. The profile measures items in the following areas: basic demographics, family and employment status, history of problem development, current drinking pattern and problem status, severity of dependence, social aspects of alcohol use, associated behaviors, relevant medical history, motivations for drinking and seeking treatment, and problem areas other than drinking. The profile yields scores on problem duration, family history of alcoholism, alcohol consumption, alcohol dependence, range of drinking situations, quantity and frequency of other drug use, emotional factors related to drinking, and life problems other than drinking. The profile is used by professionals, including physicians, psychologists, psychiatrists, social workers, nurses, and alcohol abuse counselors.

Format: Examiner required; not suitable for group use; untimed: 1–2 hours

Scoring: Examiner evaluated

Cost: Interview kit (manual, 25 interview forms, 8 reusable card sets) $66.00

Publisher: Psychological Assessment Resources, Inc.

Driver Risk Inventory (DRI)

Copyright: 1987

Population: Ages 16 and older

Purpose: Measures the driving risk of DWI (driving while intoxicated) or DUI (driving under the influence) offenders; used to identify problem drinkers, substance abusers, and high-risk drivers

Description: Paper–pencil or computer-administered 130-item multiple-choice and true–false screening inventory containing five scales. The Validity, or Truthfulness, scale measures how truthfully the examinee responded to DRI items. The Alcohol Scale measures the examinee's alcohol proneness and related problems. The Drugs Scale measures the examinee's drug use or abuse proneness and related problems and distinguishes between alcohol and drug abuse. The Driver Risk Scale measures driver risk potential, identifying the problem-prone driver independent of respondent's substance abuse history. The Stress Coping Abilities Scale is a measure of the examinee's ability to cope with stress. Results are presented in the DRI Profile and as percentiles. Risk ranges (low, low–medium, high–medium, high) for each scale as well as scores for all five scales are reported. Available in Spanish. An IBM PC or compatible is required for operation of the computer version.

Format: Self-administered; untimed: 25 minutes

Scoring: Computer scored

Cost: Contact publisher

Publisher: Behavior Data Systems, Ltd.

Drug Abuse Screening Test (DAST–20)

Copyright: 1982

Population: Adults

Purpose: Gauges severity of addiction to drugs other than alcohol; used for application and addiction counseling

Description: 20-item paper–pencil test

Format: Individual administration; 5 minutes

Scoring: Examiner/self-scored; hand key

Cost: 100 forms $5.50

Publisher: Addiction Research Foundation

Follow-up Drinker Profile (FDP)
William K. Miller, G. Allan Marlatt

Copyright: 1987

Population: Adults

Purpose: Evaluates the progress of diagnosed alcoholics

Description: Multiple-item paper–pencil structured interview designed for evaluating, at regular intervals, the progress of alcoholics after treatment. The content of the FDP parallels that of the Comprehensive Drinker Profile and the Brief Drinker Profile (see individual descriptions). The CDP manual is used for scoring and interpretation, and cards from the CDP card deck are required for administration. A new CDP manual supplement provides administration instructions.

Format: Examiner required; not suitable for group use; untimed: 30–50 minutes

Scoring: Examiner evaluated

Cost: 15 FDP forms $23.00; CDP manual

supplement $12.00; CDP manual $15.00; CDP card sets $15.00

Publisher: Psychological Assessment Resources, Inc.

Inventory of Drinking Situations (IDS–100)
Helen M. Annis, J. Martin Graham, Christine S. Davis

Copyright: 1987

Population: Adults

Purpose: Provides profile of situations where person drank heavily during the past year; used for addiction counseling

Description: Multiple-choice 100-item paper–pencil test. A computer version using IBM compatibles is available. Also available in French.

Format: Self-administered

Scoring: Hand key

Cost: 25 paper tests $14.95; computer test $450.00 for 200 uses

Publisher: Addiction Research Foundation

Inventory: Drug Abuse Research Instruments
Ernest W. Ferneau, Jr.

Copyright: 1972

Population: Adults

Purpose: Assesses drug abuse

Description: Seventy items; includes bibliographies of all research instruments on drug abuse.

Format: Group administered; examiner required; untimed

Scoring: Examiner evaluated

Cost: $15.00

Publisher: Select Press

Manson Evaluation–Revised
Morse P. Manson, George J. Huba

Copyright: 1987

Population: Adults

Purpose: Assesses alcohol abuse proneness and

eight related personality characteristics

Description: Paper–pencil 72-item true–false computer-administered test with seven sub-scales measuring anxiety, depressive fluctuations, emotional sensitivity, resentfulness, incompleteness, aloneness, and interpersonal relations. Raw scores, *T*-scores, and percentiles are yielded. This revised version provides 1985 norms as well as a new, easy-to-use test form featuring the WPS AutoScore system. This makes it possible for the administrator to score, profile, and interpret the test in just a minute or two. It can be used for personnel screening, diagnosis, therapy, research, and alcohol abuse programs. A computer version for IBM PC, XT, or AT (or compatible) with 128K is available. Materials include the paper-and-pencil version or the microcomputer version.

Format: Examiner required; suitable for group use; untimed: 5–10 minutes

Scoring: Hand key; computer scored; test scoring service available from the publisher

Cost: Kit (25 WPS AutoScore™ Test/Profile forms, 1 manual) $55.00

Publisher: Western Psychological Services

Personal Experience Inventory (PEI)

Ken C. Winters, George H. Henly

Copyright: 1989

Population: Adolescents; ages 12 to 18

Purpose: Assesses chemical dependency of adolescents

Description: Paper–pencil 300-item multiple-choice computer administered two-part test. Part I contains 129 items relating to personal involvement with chemicals, effects of drug use, social benefits of drug use, consequences of drug use, polydrug use, social-recreational use, psychological benefits of drug use, transitional use, preoccupation with drugs, and loss of control. In addition to documenting the degree, duration, and onset of drug use, this section provides several clinical scales, validity indexes, and a problem severity section. Part II consists of 147 items that measure aspects of psychosocial functioning related to patterns of drug use

and treatment responsiveness. Eight personal risk factor scales and four environmental risk factor scales are included in this section. Scores are used to generate a PEI computer report and PEI chromagraph. A sixth-grade reading level is required.

Format: Self-administered; suitable for group use; untimed: 40–50 minutes

Scoring: Computer scored; test scoring service available from publisher

Cost: Kit (10 WPS test reports, PEI answer booklets, manual) $170.00; computer disk (25 uses) $270.00

Publisher: Western Psychological Services

Personal Experience Inventory for Adults (PEI-A)

Ken C. Winters

Copyright: Not provided

Population: Adults; age 19 or older

Purpose: Used to identify alcohol and drug problems, make referrals, and plan treatment; also assesses psychosocial difficulties

Description: Self-report inventory provides comprehensive information about substance abuse patterns in adults. It is designed to address the broad scope of problems associated with substance abuse. The PEI-A has two parts—the Problem Severity Section (120 items) and the Psychosocial Section (150 items). The interpretive report for the PEI-A presents results for each validity indicator; a graphic profile of all scale scores; the raw score, drug clinic *T*-score, and nonclinical *T*-score for each scale; results of the drug use frequency and duration items; and a narrative interpretation, including analysis of the Treatment Receptiveness scale score.

Format: Examiner required; suitable for group use; 45–60 minutes

Scoring: Computer scored (scoring service)

Cost: Kit (includes 5 test report prepaid mail-in answer booklets, manual) $135.00; microcomputer disk (IBM) (good for 25 uses) $275.00

Publisher: Western Psychological Services

Personal Experience Screening Questionnaire (PESQ)
Ken C. Winters

Copyright: Not provided

Population: Ages 12 to 18

Purpose: Used to identify and refer teenagers who may be chemically dependent

Description: This self-report questionnaire identifies teenagers who should be referred for a complete chemical dependency evaluation. The questionnaire includes 40 items divided into three sections: problem severity, psychosocial items, drug use history. Two validity scales measure response distortion.

Format: Examiner required; suitable for group use; 10 minutes

Scoring: Hand key

Cost: Kit (25 AutoScore™ test forms, 1 manual) $70.00

Publisher: Western Psychological Services

Recovery Attitude and Treatment Evaluation, Clinical Evaluation (RAATE–CE)
David Mee-Lee, Norman G. Hoffman

Copyright: 1987

Population: Adults

Purpose: Measures factors related to substance abuse treatment; used in treatment, planning, and placement

Description: 35-item clinician rating form

Format: Individual administration; examiner required

Scoring: Hand key; examiner evaluated

Cost: 25 packets $59.75

Publisher: New Standards, Inc.

Situational Confidence Questionnaire (SCQ–39)
Helen M. Annis, J. Martin Graham

Copyright: 1988

Population: Adults

Purpose: Measures an alcoholic client's self-confidence in dealing with a variety of high-risk situations that may lead to relapse

Description: 39-item multiple-choice and computer-administered response format

Format: Individual or self-administered

Scoring: Hand key or computer scored

Cost: 25 paper tests $14.75; computer tests $225.00 for 200 uses

Publisher: Addiction Research Foundation

Smoker Complaint Scale (SCS)
Nina G. Schneider

Copyright: 1984

Population: Adults

Purpose: Assesses withdrawal symptoms of individuals during smoking cessation

Description: Twenty-item 7-point Likert Scale test designed to measure changes in physiological/emotional/craving states as a function of smoking cessation

Format: Self-administered; suitable for group use; untimed: 1–5 minutes

Scoring: Examiner evaluated

Cost: Free

Publisher: Nina G. Schneider, Ph.D.

Structured Addictions Assessment Interview for Selecting Treatment (ASIST)

Copyright: 1984

Population: Adults

Purpose: Assesses alcohol and psychoactive drug use, physical and mental health, family, employment, and legal problems

Description: Twelve sections consisting of multiple-choice, paper–pencil, oral response, short answer, verbal. Also available in French.

Format: Individual administration

Scoring: Examiner/self scored; hand key

Cost: 10 forms $25.00

Publisher: Addiction Research Foundation

Substance Abuse Questionnaire (SAQ)

Copyright: 1985

Population: Ages 18 and older

Purpose: Screens and evaluates adult chemical dependency; used as an intake/referral device, in chemical dependency treatment settings, and in the criminal justice system

Description: Paper–pencil or computer-administered 151-item multiple-choice and true–false test designed to screen for and evaluate chemical dependency. The Truthfulness Scale measures how truthfully the examinee responded to the SAQ items. The Alcohol Scale measures the examinee's alcohol-related problems and proneness. The Drugs Scale measures drug use or abuse-related problems and proneness. The Aggressivity Scale measures the examinee's risk-taking behavior and aggressiveness. The Resistance Scale measures uncooperativeness and resistance to assistance. The Stress Coping Abilities Scale measures the examinee's ability to cope with stress, tension, and anxiety. The SAQ Profile reports scores, percentiles, and risk levels (low, low–medium, medium, high–medium, high) for all six scales. The computer version operates on IBM PC and compatible systems. Floppy diskettes containing 50, 100, or 150 test applications are provided. A sixth-grade reading level is required. Available in Spanish.

Format: Self-administered; suitable for group use; untimed: 25 minutes

Scoring: Computer scored

Cost: Contact publisher; volume discounts available

Publisher: Behavior Data Systems, Ltd.

Substance Abuse Relapse Assessment (SARA)

Lawrence Schonfeld, Roger Peters, Addis Dolente

Copyright: 1993

Population: Adolescents; adults

Purpose: Used in substance abuse counseling and treatment to assess and monitor relapse causes and coping skills

Description: Oral-response 39-item interview with the following categories: Substance Abuse Behavior, Antecedents of Substance Abuse, Consequences of Substance Abuse, and Responses to Slips. Materials used include a manual, stimulus card, interview record form, and relapse prevention planning forms 1, 2, and 3. Examiner must be B-Level qualified.

Format: Individual administration; examiner required; untimed: 1 hour

Scoring: Examiner evaluated

Cost: Kit $59.00

Publisher: Psychological Assessment Resources, Inc.

Substance Abuse Screening Test (SAST)

Terry L. Hibpshman, Sue Larson

Copyright: 1993

Population: Ages 13 to adult

Purpose: Facilitates early identification and reliable referral of individuals who are abusing substances or are "at risk"

Description: The SAST elicits simple "yes" or "no" responses to questions which target critical areas of an individual's daily functioning. Responses may be written or verbal. The SAST may be administered by teachers, nurses, counselors, social workers, psychologists, and by well-informed adults who are under the supervision of a professional. The respondent's score can be interpreted by the use of a simple "pass–fail" table or by the use of a traditional standard score table. A comprehensive and user-friendly manual addresses critical subjects such as administration, scoring and interpretation, and statistics.

Format: Individual or group administration; approximately 5 minutes

Scoring: Hand key

Cost: Complete $55.00

Publisher: Slosson Educational Publications, Inc.

Substance Abuse Subtle Screening Inventory (SASSI)

Copyright: 1988

Population: Ages 12 to 20—Adolescent form; Ages 18 and up—Adult form

Purpose: Screens for substance-related disorders; used in alcohol/drug treatment, mental health, and corrections

Description: Computer-administered or paper–pencil test with 62 true–false items, 12 alcohol items, and 14 drug items. The substance abuse classification is based on eight subscale scores. A fourth- to sixth-grade reading level is required. Examiner must be degreed, alcohol/drug certified, and SASSI trained. Suitable for individuals with visual, physical, hearing, and mental disabilities.

Format: Individual administration; suitable for group use; examiner required; untimed: 10–12 minutes

Scoring: Hand key; computer scored; machine scored

Cost: Contact publisher

Publisher: The SASSI Institute

Substance Use Disorder Diagnostic Schedule–IV (SUDDS–IV)

Norman G. Hoffmann, Patricia A. Harrison

Copyright: 1995

Population: Adults

Purpose: Assesses diagnoses of substance use disorders; used for substance abuse/dependency diagnosis and treatment planning

Description: Oral response test with 64 items. Software available for in-office administration and scoring.

Format: Examiner required; untimed

Scoring: Hand key; examiner evaluated

Cost: 25 packets $59.75

Publisher: New Standards, Inc.

Triage Assessment for Addiction Disorders

Norman G. Hoffmann

Copyright: 1995

Population: Adults

Purpose: Screens for substance use disorders; part of CARES three-part battery

Description: 31-item structured interview

Format: Individual administration; examiner required; untimed

Scoring: Hand key; examiner evaluated

Cost: 25 packets $59.75

Publisher: New Standards, Inc.

Western Personality Inventory (WPI)

Morse P. Manson

Copyright: 1963

Population: Adults

Purpose: Diagnoses the presence and degree of alcoholism; useful in alcohol rehabilitation programs

Description: Paper–pencil or computer-administered test that combines the "Manson Evaluation," which identifies the potential alcoholic personality, and the "Alcadd Test," which measures the extent of alcohol addiction, into one booklet. The computer version is available on IBM PC or compatible systems. Computer scoring is available via mail-in services or on-site.

Format: Examiner required; suitable for group use; untimed: 15–20 minutes

Scoring: Hand key; may be computer scored

Cost: Kit (5 WPS AutoScore™ test forms, 1 Manson Evaluation Manual, 1 Alcadd Manual, 2 WPS Test Report answer sheets) $90.00

Publisher: Western Psychological Services

Workers Wide Range Assessment of Problems (WWRAP)

Norman G. Hoffmann

Copyright: 1995

Population: Adults

Purpose: For treatment and placement planning; part of the CARES three-part battery

Description: Fifty-item paper–pencil test. Scores are on 12 scales.

Format: Self-administered; untimed

Scoring: Hand key; examiner evaluated

Cost: 25 packets $59.75

Publisher: New Standards, Inc.

Intelligence

Alternate Uses (AU)
Paul R. Christensen, J. P. Guilford,
Philip R. Merrifield, Robert C. Wilson

Copyright: 1978

Population: Adolescents, adults; Grades 7 and above

Purpose: Measures ability to spontaneously produce ideas in response to objects or other ideas

Description: Multiple-item paper–pencil test measuring an aspect of creativity that translates into spontaneous flexibility of thinking or the ability to produce or adapt ideas relating to the use of an object. Scales include flexibility of thinking, spontaneous flexibility, adaptive flexibility, and divergent production.

Format: Group; 12 minutes

Scoring: Examiner administration and interpretation

Cost: Sampler Set $25.00; Permission Set $90.00

Publisher: Mind Garden, Inc.

Arlin Test of Formal Reasoning (ATFR)
Patricia Kennedy Arlin

Copyright: 1984

Population: Children, adolescents; Grades 6 to 12

Purpose: Assesses student's cognitive abilities; used by teachers to plan curriculum, modify teaching techniques, and identify gifted students

Description: Paper–pencil 32-item multiple-choice test assessing students' cognitive abilities at one of five levels: concrete, high concrete, transitional, low formal, and high formal reasoning in the application of Piaget's developmental theory. The interpretation of both the total test score and the subtest scores is based on Inhelder and Piaget's description of formal operational thought and the eight schemata associated with that thought (multiplicative compensation, probability, correlations, combinational reasoning, proportional reasoning, forms of conservation beyond direct verification, mechanical equilibrium, and coordination of two or more systems or frames of reference). Two computer scoring packages are available. Package 1 provides an alphabetical pupil list indicating subtest scores, total test scores, and cognitive level designation. A sixth-grade reading level is required.

Format: Examiner required; suitable for group use; untimed: 1 hour

Scoring: Hand key; may be computer scored

Cost: Test kit (manual, 35 test booklets, 35 answer sheets, template, Teaching for Thinking) $69.00

Publisher: Slosson Educational Publications, Inc.

Arthur Point Scale of Performance, Form I
Grace Arthur

Copyright: 1943

Population: Ages 4 to adult

Purpose: Measures intelligence of children and adults; used as a nonverbal supplement to the highly verbalized Binet tests, especially with people with language, speech, emotional, or cultural problems

Description: Ten nonverbal task-assessment subtests measuring intelligence: Mare-Foal Formboard, Sequin-Goddard Formboard, Pintner-Paterson 2-Figure Formboard, Casuist Formboard, Pintner-Manikin Test, Knox-Kempf Feature Profile Test, Knox Cube Imitation Test, Healy Pictorial Completion Test 1, Kohs Block Design Test, and Porteus Mazes. The test is particularly useful as a supplement to the Binet scale in cases in which a child's environmental conditions vary widely from those of the average child. The comparison is of value whether it confirms the Binet ratings or reveals a disparity in verbal and nonverbal development.

Format: Examiner required; not suitable for group use; untimed: typical time not available

Scoring: Examiner evaluated

Cost: Complete kit (tests, 50 record cards, manual) $625.00; 50 record cards $30.00

Publisher: Stoelting Company

Canadian Cognitive Abilities Test: Multilevel Edition (CCAT), Levels A-H, Form 7
E. Wright, Robert L. Thorndike, Elizabeth P. Hagen

Copyright: 1989

Population: Children, adolescents; Grades 3 to 12

Purpose: Assesses students' abilities in three parallel batteries: verbal, nonverbal, and quantitative

Description: Series of multiple-choice paper–pencil subtests for three parallel batteries: Verbal, Nonverbal, and Quantitative. Materials include test booklets, examiner's manual, and answer sheets. A consumable booklet for Level A for younger children is also available. It is accompanied by a supplementary manual with a key insert. This test is a Canadian adaptation of the Cognitive Abilities test published by Riverside Publishing Company. Examiner must have a teaching certificate.

Format: Examiner required; suitable for group use; timed: 90 minutes

Scoring: Test scoring service available from publisher; hand key

Cost: Test booklets $10.40; 35 answer sheets $23.05; scoring mask $14.50; teacher's guide $19.20

Publisher: Nelson Canada

Canadian Cognitive Abilities Test: Primary Battery (CCAT), Levels 1 and 2, Form 7
E. Wright, Robert L. Thorndike, Elizabeth P. Hagen

Copyright: 1989

Population: Children; Grades K.5 to 3

Purpose: Assesses students' verbal, nonverbal, and quantitative abilities

Description: Series of multiple-choice paper–pencil subtests in three areas; Verbal, Nonverbal, and Quantitative. Materials include test booklets, examiner's manual, and a score key for each level tested. Examiner must have a teaching certificate.

Format: Examiner required; suitable for group use; untimed: time varies

Scoring: Hand key

Cost: 35 test booklets $48.35; examiner's manual $18.10; scoring key $6.60

Publisher: Nelson Canada

Children's Auditory Verbal Learning Test–2 (CAVLT–2)
Jack L. Talley

Copyright: 1993

Population: Children, adolescents; ages 6 years 6 months to 17 years 11 months

Purpose: Measures auditory verbal learning and memory abilities; used for psychoeducational or neuropsychological assessment

Description: Oral response verbal test with the following seven scales: Immediate Memory Span, Level of Learning, Interference Trial, Immediate Recall, Delayed Recall, Recognition Accuracy, Total Intrusions

Format: Individual administration; examiner required; untimed

Scoring: Hand scored

Cost: Introduction Kit $66.00

Publisher: Psychological Assessment Resources, Inc.

CHIPS—Children's Problem Solving
Mogens Hansen, Svend Kreiner,
Carsten Rosenberg Hanson

Copyright: 1995

Population: Children; ages 5 to 13

Purpose: Assesses the child's actual problem-solving strategies when faced with tasks of different cognitive complexity; used in the teacher's planning of classroom learning (global cognition, analytic/synthetic cognition, comprehensive cognition)

Description: Forty-item multiple-choice test requiring global cognition (11 items), analytic/synthetic cognition (14 items), comprehensive cognition (15 items). Profiles depict the child's development through the stages of cognitive development. One group version and one individual version is used along with a test booklet with four items for the group version and a special test book with one item a page for individual use. Examiner must be a teacher or psychologist. Available in Danish and Slovakian but not in English.

Format: Individual administration; suitable for group use; examiner required; untimed

Scoring: Hand key

Cost: Specimen Set $27.00 (DKK 152)

Publisher: Dansk psykologisk Forlag

Cognitive Diagnostic Battery (CDB)
Stanley R. Kay

Copyright: 1982

Population: Ages 2 to 65

Purpose: Distinguishes between mental subnormality and abnormality; used for mental health assessment for mentally retarded and psychotic populations

Description: Contains five subtests: Color-Form Preference Test, Color-Form Representation Test, Egocentricity of Thought Test, Progressive Figure Drawing Test, and Span of Attention Test.

Format: Untimed

Scoring: Score computed on records form

Cost: Intro Kit $63.00

Publisher: Psychological Assessment Resources, Inc.

Cognitive Symptom Checklist (CSC)
Christine O'Hara, Minnie Harrell,
Eileen Bellingrath, Katherine Lisicia

Copyright: 1993

Population: Adults; ages 16 and older

Purpose: Evaluates areas of impaired cognitive functioning; used in rehabilitation counseling and occupational therapy

Description: Paper–pencil short-answer checklist with five cognitive areas: Visual Processes, Attention/Concentration, Memory, Language, and Executive Functions. A clinician guide for each of the five checklists is used. A seventh-grade reading level is required. Examiner must be B-Level qualified and trained in therapeutic approaches to rehabilitation of cognition.

Format: Rater required; untimed: 10 to 20 minutes per checklist

Scoring: Examiner evaluated

Cost: Introductory Kit $47.00

Publisher: Psychological Assessment Resources, Inc.

Columbia Mental Maturity Scale (CMMS)
Bessie B. Burgemeister, Lucille Hollander
Blum, Irving Lorge

Copyright: 1972

Population: Children; ages 3 years 6 months to 10 years

Purpose: Assesses mental ability; used with preschoolers, kindergartners, or children with physical or verbal disabilities

Description: Test of general reasoning abilities, with 92 items arranged in a series of eight overlapping levels. The level administered is determined by the child's chronological age. Items are printed on 95 (6″ x 9″) cards. The child responds by selecting from each series of drawings the one that does not belong. Materials include item cards and a Guide for Administration and Interpretation, which includes directions in Spanish.

Format: Examiner required; not suitable for group use; untimed: 15–20 minutes

Scoring: Examiner evaluated

Cost: CMMS Kit (95 item cards, guide for administering and interpreting, 35 record forms) $451.00; 35 Individual Record Forms $47.00

Publisher: The Psychological Corporation

Comprehensive Test of Nonverbal Intelligence (CTONI)
Donald D. Hammill, Nils A. Pearson,
J. Lee Wiederholt

Copyright: 1996

Population: Ages 7 through 89

Purpose: Measures nonverbal reasoning abilities of individuals for whom most other mental ability tests are either inappropriate or biased

Description: Six subtests (Pictorial Analogies, Geometric Analogies, Pictorial Categories, Geometric Categories, Pictorial Sequences, and Geometric Sequences) require students to look at a group of pictures or designs to solve problems. Individuals indicate their answer by pointing to alternative choices. Three composite scores are computed: Nonverbal Intelligence Quotient, Pictorial Nonverbal Intelligence Quotient, and Geometric Nonverbal Intelligence Quotient. No oral responses, reading, writing, or object manipulation are required to take the test. Instructions for administration include pantomime and oral delivery.

Format: Individual administration; computer administration on IBM compatible; 60 minutes

Scoring: Examiner administered and interpreted

Cost: Complete kit (manual, picture books,

protocols, and storage box) $239.00; computer assisted $298.00

Publisher: PRO-ED, Inc.

Culture Fair Intelligence Tests
Raymond B. Cattell, A. K. S. Cattell

Copyright: 1960

Population: Ages 4 and older

Purpose: Measures individual intelligence for a wide range of ages without, as much as possible, the influence of verbal fluency, cultural climate, and educational level. Identifies learning and emotional problems. Used in employee selection and placement.

Description: Nonverbal paper–pencil tests arranged in three scales to cover the age range of 4 years to adult. Test items require only that the subject be able to perceive relationships in shapes and figures. Scale I differs from Scales 2 and 3 in that it is not wholly nonverbal or wholly group administered. It consists of eight subtests, four of which must be individually administered. A set of cards and some common objects are required for two of the subtests. Scales 2 and 3 contain four paper–pencil subtests of perceptual tasks: Completing Series, Classifying, Solving Matrices, and Evaluating Conditions. Scale 2 can be used with children and adults. Scale 3 is more difficult than Scale 2. The choice of scales administered is based on the examiner's evaluation of the potential ability level to be tested. Available in Spanish.

Format: Examiner required; suitable for group use; timed: Scale 1, 22 minutes; Scales 2 and 3, 12½ minutes per form

Scoring: Hand key

Cost: Scale 1: reusable classification test cards $21.00; 25 test booklets $19.00; scoring key $3.50; handbook $4.75. Scales 2 and 3: 25 reusable test booklets $20.25; 50 answer sheets $10.75; scoring keys $3.50; audiocassette tape $33.00

Publisher: Institute for Personality and Ability Testing, Inc.

Full-Range Picture Vocabulary Test (FRPV)

R. B. Ammons, H. S. Ammons

Copyright: 1950

Population: Ages 2 to adult

Purpose: Assesses individual intelligence; may be used for testing special populations, such as individuals who are physically disabled, uncooperative, or aphasic, or very young subjects

Description: Test of verbal comprehension. Each of the 16 items is matched to one of four drawings on 16 cards. The subject points to one of the four drawings that best represents a particular word. The subject also may respond by indicating "yes" or "no" as the examiner points to each drawing. No reading or writing is required of the subject. Two parallel forms, A and B, which use the same set of stimulus plates, are available.

Format: Examiner required; not suitable for group use; untimed: 5–10 minutes

Scoring: Hand key; examiner evaluated

Cost: Set of plates, with instructions, norms, and sample answer sheets $15.00

Publisher: Psychological Test Specialists

Goodenough-Harris Drawing Test

Florence L. Goodenough, Dale B. Harris

Copyright: Not provided

Population: Children, adolescents; ages 3 to 15

Purpose: Assesses mental ability without requiring verbal skills

Description: Measures intelligence through three drawing tasks in three tests: Goodenough Draw-a-Man Test, Draw-a-Woman Test, and the experimental Self-Drawing Scale. The man and woman drawings may be scored for the presence of up to 73 characteristics. Materials include Quality Scale Cards, which are required for the short-scoring method. Separate norms are available for males and females.

Format: Examiner required; suitable for group use; untimed: 10–15 minutes

Scoring: Hand key

Cost: Complete kit (test booklet, manual, quality scale cards) $84.00; 35 test booklets $45.50; manual $40.00; Quality Scale Cards $43.50

Publisher: The Psychological Corporation

Graded Anagram Task (GAT)

Lawrence Scrima

Copyright: 1979

Population: Adolescents, adults; ages 13 to 100; Grades 8 and above

Purpose: Assesses memory following exposure to a complex associative information task; used in research for investigating various aspects of information processing, including relationship to developmental cognition, problem solving, and creative thinking

Description: Oral-response test consisting of 10 lists of 10 five-letter anagrams each. The letters in each anagram can be unscrambled to form two words. Two of the lists are used for practice, and one of the remaining eight lists then is administered. As the examinee solves each anagram, he or she first must say and spell aloud the word that it forms and then associate the word with something. The examinee then searches for the second possible word that can be formed from the anagram, one minute per anagram. This process is repeated for all 10 anagrams. After completing the task, the examinee is instructed to do whatever the examiner deems appropriate (e.g., card game to prevent rehearsal, simply allow time to elapse, etc.). Following a controlled interval, the examinee is asked to recall and spell the words that he or she formed earlier (free recall test). Finally, the examinee is given another trial using the same list of anagrams (cued recall test).

Format: Examiner required; not suitable for group use; timed: 10 minutes (1 minute per anagram)

Scoring: Examiner evaluated

Cost: 10 card lists, instructions $30.00

Publisher: Preventive Measures, Inc.

Haptic Intelligence Scale

Harriet C. Shurrager, Phil S. Shurrager

Copyright: 1925

Population: Adults with blindness

Purpose: Measures the intelligence of blind and partially sighted adults; used as a substitute for or supplement to the Wechsler Adult Intelligence Scale

Description: Seven nonverbal (except for instructions) task assessments measuring the intelligence of blind and partially sighted adults. The subtests are Digit Symbol, Object Assembly, Block Design, Plan-of-Search, Object Completion, Pattern Board, and Bead Arithmetic. Wechsler's procedures were followed in establishing age categories and statistical treatment of the data.

Format: Examiner required; not suitable for group use; timed: 1 hour 30 minutes

Scoring: Examiner evaluated

Cost: Complete kit (25 record blanks, testing materials, manual) $850.00

Publisher: Stoelting Company

Hiskey–Nebraska Test of Learning Aptitude (H–NTLA)

Marshall S. Hiskey

Copyright: 1966

Population: Ages 2 years 6 months to 18 years 6 months

Purpose: Evaluates learning potential of deaf children and those with hearing, speech, or language disabilities.

Description: Battery of 12 subtests measuring visual–motor coordination, sequential memory, visual retention or stimuli in a series, visual discrimination and matching, and awareness of environment. The subtests are Bead Patterns, Memory for Color, Picture Association, Paper Folding Patterns, Visual Attention Span, Block Patterns, Completion of Drawings, Memory for Digits, Puzzle Blocks, Picture Analogies, and Spatial Reasoning. The scales are nonverbal and have norms for evaluating either hearing or deaf children.

Format: Individual administration; examiner required; 50 to 60 minutes

Scoring: Examiner evaluated

Cost: Complete kit (25 record forms, pad of 25 picture sheets) $24.00

Publisher: PRO-ED, Inc.

Intermediate Booklet Category Test (IBCT)

Paul A. Byrd

Copyright: 1987

Population: Children, adolescents; ages 9 to 14

Purpose: Assesses concept formation and abstract reasoning; used by clinicians to detect brain dysfunction

Description: Test with 168 items replicating in booklet format the slides used in the Halstead Category Test. Figures are presented one at a time to the subject, who responds with a number between one and four. The test consists of six subtests. A cutoff score is derived.

Format: Examiner required; not suitable for group use; untimed: 30–60 minutes

Scoring: Examiner evaluated

Cost: Complete kit (IBCT in 2 volumes, manual, 50 scoring forms) $225.00

Publisher: Psychological Assessment Resources, Inc.

Junior South African Individual Scales (JSAIS)

Copyright: 1979

Population: Children; ages 3 to 7

Purpose: Assesses cognitive functioning of children; used for psychological-educational diagnosis

Description: Measure of various aspects of a child's cognitive abilities. Twelve empirically selected scales yield the following IQ measures: General Intellectual Ability (GIQ), Verbal Ability (VIQ), and Perceptual-Performance Ability (PIQ), as well as estimates of memory and quantitative ability. Any scale or group of scales may be administered.

Format: Examiner required; not suitable for group use; untimed: typical time not available

Scoring: Hand key; examiner evaluated

Cost: Contact publisher

Publisher: Human Sciences Research Council

Kahn Intelligence Test (KIT:EXP) A Culture-Minimized Experience
T. C. Kahn

Copyright: 1960

Population: All ages

Purpose: Assesses individual intelligence; may be used for special groups, such as the blind and deaf or individuals from different educational and cultural backgrounds

Description: Performance measure of several aspects of intelligence, including concept formation, recall, and motor coordination. A special scale for assessment of blind subjects' intelligence is included. The test requires no reading, writing, or verbal knowledge. It uses the same materials as the Kahn Test of Symbol Arrangement (KTSA): 16 plastic objects and a cloth strip containing 15 equal segments. The manual contains instructions for obtaining mental age, IQ, or developmental level. The test may be used only by psychologists, psychiatrists, counselors, and others with comparable training.

Format: Examiner required; not suitable for group use; untimed: 15 minutes

Scoring: Hand key; examiner evaluated

Cost: Complete set $52.00

Publisher: Psychological Test Specialists

Kasanin-Hanfmann Concept Formation Test (Vygotsky Test) and Modified Vygotsky Concept Formation Test
Paul L. Wang

Copyright: 1983

Population: All ages

Purpose: Measures an individual's ability to think in abstract concepts; used with uneducated adults, children, and special groups such as psychotic patients

Description: Task-assessment test consisting of 22 blocks that the subject analyzes and sorts. The blocks are of different colors, shapes, and sizes but are alike in some way. The subject must determine the common factor and sort the blocks according to that factor. The Modified Vygotsky Concept Formation Test provides a new method of administering and scoring. The modification standardizes and simplifies the observation of the subject and adds a divergent thinking test. The modification is particularly useful in the study of mental retardation, schizophrenia, and cerebral organicity (e.g., frontal lobe pathology).

Format: Examiner required; not suitable for group use; untimed: typical time not available

Scoring: Examiner evaluated

Cost: Test materials $195.00; Modified Vygotsky Concept Formation Manual $25.00; 30 record forms $25.00

Publisher: Stoelting Company

Knox's Cube Test (KCT)
Mark Stone, Benjamin Wright

Copyright: 1983

Population: Children, adolescents

Purpose: Measures children's and adults' short-term memory and attention span, which together constitute the most elementary stage of mental activity; used to evaluate deaf, language-impaired, and foreign-speaking persons.

Description: Multiple-task assessment of attention span and short-term memory measuring how accurately an individual can repeat simple rhythmic figures tapped out for him or her by the examiner. Test materials include four cubes attached to a wooden base and a separate tapping block. Directions can be delivered in pantomime. The manual provides procedures and rationale for administering, scoring, and interpreting a comprehensive version of KCT, which incorporates all previous versions. This revision utilizes Rasch measurement procedures to develop an objective psychometric variable, along which both items and persons can be positioned. Two versions are available: KCT JR (ages 2 to 8) and KCT SR (ages 8 and above).

Format: Examiner required; not suitable for group use; timed: time not available

Scoring: Examiner evaluated

Cost: Both versions complete (testing materials, manual, record forms) $95.00 each

Publisher: Stoelting Company

Kohs Block Design Test
S. C. Kohs

Copyright: 1919

Population: Mental ages 3 to 19

Purpose: Measures intelligence of persons with a mental age of 3 to 19 years. Used for testing individuals with language and hearing disabilities, the disadvantaged, and non-English-speaking individuals.

Description: Multiple-item task-assessment test consisting of 17 cards containing colored designs and 16 colored blocks that the subject uses to duplicate the designs on the cards. Performance is evaluated for attention, adaptation, and autocriticism. This test also is included in the Merrill-Palmer and Arthur Performance scales. The complete set includes cubes, cards, a manual, and 50 record blanks.

Format: Examiner required; suitable for group use; timed: 40 minutes or less

Scoring: Examiner evaluated

Cost: Complete kit $135.00

Publisher: Stoelting Company

Leiter Adult Intelligence Scale (LAIS)

Copyright: 1972

Population: Adults

Purpose: Measures general intelligence in adults; used with individuals from the upper and lower levels of the socioeconomic hierarchy and with the psychologically disabled

Description: Six oral-response and task-performance tests assessing verbal and nonverbal intelligence. The verbal tests are Similarities–Differences, Digits Forward and Backward, and Free Recall–Controlled Recall. The nonverbal tests are Pathways (following a prescribed sequence), Stencil Designs (reproduction of designs), and Painted Cube Test (duplication of designs). Test results identify deficits in cogni-

tive, psychophysical, or social areas and provide a measure of functional efficiency for psychologically disabled and superior individuals.

Format: Examiner required; not suitable for group use; untimed: 40 minutes

Scoring: Examiner evaluated

Cost: Test kit (all test materials, manual, 100 record blanks) $225.00

Publisher: Stoelting Company

Leiter International Performance Scale (Arthur Adaptation)

Copyright: 1979

Population: Children; ages 2 to 12

Purpose: Assesses general intelligence of nonverbal or non-English-speaking individuals

Description: Multiple-item nonverbal intelligence test consisting of 54 subtests contained in two trays for measuring intelligence of individuals ages 2 to 7 (Tray 1) and 8 to 12 (Tray 2). The test requires no verbal instructions or responses. Individuals match blocks with corresponding characters in a wooden frame. Categories of matching are concretistics (matching of specific relationships), symbolic transformation (judging relationships between two events), quantitative discriminations, spatial imagery, genus matching, progression discriminations, and immediate recall. There are significant positive correlations between this test and the Stanford-Binet, Wechsler, Peabody Picture Vocabulary, and others. The test can be used with individuals who are deaf, cerebral palsied, non-English speaking, culturally disadvantaged, mentally retarded, and mentally superior.

Format: Examiner required; not suitable for group use; untimed: time varies

Scoring: Examiner evaluated

Cost: Complete set (test materials, manual, carrying case, 100 record forms) $625.00

Publisher: Stoelting Company

Leiter International Performance Scale (LIPS)
Russell G. Leiter

Copyright: 1979

Population: Children, adolescents; ages 2 to 18

Purpose: Measures intelligence and mental age for all individuals ages 2 to 18, including individuals who are deaf, cerebral palsied, non-English-speaking, and culturally disadvantaged

Description: Multiple-item nonverbal task assessment of intelligence in which the subject matches blocks with corresponding characteristic strips positioned in a sturdy wooden frame. The difficulty of the task increases at each level. The categories measured are concretistics (matching of specific relationships), symbolic transformation (judging relationships between to events), quantitative discriminations, spatial imagery, genus matching, progression discriminations, and immediate recall. Test materials include three trays of blocks and strips that make up the 54 subtests. Tray 1 covers ages 2 to 7, Tray 2 covers ages 8 to 12, and Tray 3 covers ages 13 to 17. Instructions for all levels are delivered by easily learned pantomime. The LIPS yields Mental Age and IQ. The Binet-type year scale has four tests at each year level from Year 2 through Year 16 and six tests at year 17. The test kit includes all materials, wooden frame, carrying case, 100 record cards, and manual.

Format: Examiner required; not suitable for group use; untimed: 45 minutes

Scoring: Examiner evaluated

Cost: Complete kit $795.00; 25 record forms $27.00

Publisher: Stoelting Company

Leiter–R
Gale H. Roid, Lucy Miller

Copyright: 1996

Population: Ages 2 to 20

Purpose: Assesses intelligence, visualization, and reasoning; used for diagnosis and placement in educational settings

Description: A revision of the original Leiter Scale. Twenty subtests, two segment tests.

Format: Individual administration; examiner required; untimed: 60 minutes

Scoring: Examiner evaluated

Cost: Contact publisher

Publisher: Stoelting Company

Matrix Analogies Test–Expanded Form (MAT–EF)
Jack A. Naglieri

Copyright: 1985

Population: Children, adolescents; ages 5 to 17

Purpose: Measures the nonverbal reasoning ability of students

Description: Paper–pencil 64-item multiple-choice test consisting of abstract designs or matrices from which an element in progression is missing. The child chooses the missing element from six alternatives. Items are organized in four groups: pattern completion, reasoning by analogy, serial reasoning, and spatial visualization. The test yields standard scores, percentile ranks, age equivalents for the total score, and item group scores. Since minimal verbal comprehension and response are required, the test can be used for assessment of bilingual and gifted and those with learning disabilities, mental retardation, hearing and/or language disabilities, physical disabilities, or limited response capabilities. The test can be administered by psychologists, counselors, school psychologists and diagnosticians, rehabilitation psychologists, and other professionals with proper training and experience in testing.

Format: Examiner required; not suitable for group use; untimed: 20–25 minutes

Scoring: Hand key

Cost: Complete kit (examiner's manual, stimulus manual, 50 answer sheets, and case) $132.00

Publisher: The Psychological Corporation

Matrix Analogies Test–Short Form (MAT–SF)
Jack A. Naglieri

Copyright: 1985

Population: Children, adolescents; ages 5 years to 17 years 11 months

Purpose: Measures nonverbal reasoning abilities of students; designed to screen large numbers of children with learning difficulties or potentially gifted bilingual or educationally disadvantaged students

Description: Paper–pencil 35-item test consisting of abstract designs with missing elements and matrices containing progressive elements that predict the next element in progression. Test items are part of the larger MAT–Expanded Form. The test features norms on a large nationally representative U.S. sample and a six-option, multiple-choice format. When used with the Multi-Level Academic Survey Test, this test also may be used to screen for children with learning disabilities identified on the basis of an ability–achievement discrepancy. The test yields percentile ranks, stanines by half-year age intervals, and age equivalents from 5-0 to 17-11.

Format: Examiner required; suitable for group use; may be administered individually to a child with a physically handicapping condition; untimed: 20 minutes

Scoring: Hand key

Cost: Examination kit (examiner's manual, reusable test booklet, self-scoring answer sheet) $28.50

Publisher: The Psychological Corporation

McCarthy Scales of Children's Abilities
Dorothea McCarthy

Copyright: 1972

Population: Children; ages 2 years 6 months to 8 years 6 months

Purpose: Assesses intellectual and motor development of children

Description: Measure of five aspects of children's thinking, motor, and mental abilities. The subtests are Verbal Ability, Short-Term Memory, Numerical Ability, Perceptual Performance, and Motor Coordination. The verbal, numerical, and perceptual performance scales are combined to yield the General Cognitive Index. Items involve puzzles, toylike materials, and gamelike tasks. Six of the 18 task components that predict the child's ability to cope with schoolwork in the early grades form the McCarthy Screening Test.

Format: Examiner required; not suitable for group use; untimed: 45–60 minutes

Scoring: Examiner evaluated

Cost: Complete set (stimulus and manipulable materials, manual, 25 record forms, 25 drawing booklets, and case) $455.50; Screening Test complete set (manual, 25 record forms, 25 drawing booklets, and case) $178.00

Publisher: The Psychological Corporation

Merrill-Palmer Scale
Rachel Stutsman Ball

Copyright: 1948

Population: Children; ages 18 months to 4 years

Purpose: Measures intelligence in children; used as a substitute for or a supplement to the Binet Scale.

Description: Task-assessment and oral-response tests measuring language skills, motor skills, dexterity, and matching. The 19 subtests are Stutsman Color Matching Test; Wallin Pegboards A and B; Stutsman Buttoning Test; Stutsman Stick and String; Scissors; Stutsman Language Test; Stutsman Picture Formboards 1, 2, and 3; Mare-Foal Formboard; Seguin-Goddard Formboard; Pintner-Manikin Test; Decroly Matching Game; Stutsman Nested Cubes; Woodworth-Wells Association Test; Stutsman Copying Test; Stutsman Pyramid Test; Stutsman Little Pink Tower Test; and Kohs Blocks. The test deals directly with the problem of resistance in the testing situation and provides a comprehensive listing of the many factors influencing a child's willingness to cooperate. Refused and omitted items are considered when arriving at a total score, which may then be converted into mental age, sigma value, or percentile rank. The test is significant in its complete independence from The Stanford-Binet Scale.

Format: Examiner required; not suitable for

group use; untimed: time varies

Scoring: Examiner evaluated

Cost: Complete kit (tests, 50 record blanks, carrying case) $750.00

Publisher: Stoelting Company

Multidimensional Aptitude Battery–Form L
Douglas N. Jackson

Copyright: 1984

Population: Ages 16 to adult

Purpose: Assesses aptitudes and intelligence for adolescents and adults; used for clinical and research purposes with normal and deviant populations, including prison inmates, neurotic, psychotic, and neurologically impaired psychiatric patients

Description: Multiple-item paper–pencil multiple-choice test consisting of two batteries of five subtests each. The Verbal Battery includes the following subtests: Information, Comprehension, Arithmetic, Similarities, and Vocabulary. The Performance Battery subtests include Digit Symbol, Picture Completion, Spatial, Picture Arrangement, and Object Assembly. Verbal, Performance, and Full Scale IQs and standard scores for the 10 subtests have been calibrated to those of another popular IQ test and permit appraisal of intellectual functioning at nine different age levels, ranging from ages 16 to 74. Separate test booklets and answer sheets are provided for the two batteries. One battery of five subtests (7 minutes per test) can be administered in one sitting. An optional tape recording of instruction and timing may be used to administer all subtests. Scoring templates are available for hand scoring. On-line software is available.

Format: Examiner required; suitable for group use; timed: 7 minutes per subtest

Scoring: Hand key; computer scored; scoring service available from publisher

Cost: Machine Scoring Examination Kit $21.00; Hand Scoring Examination Kit $33.00

Publisher: Sigma Assessment Systems, Inc.

Ohio Classification Test
DeWitt E. Sell, Robert W. Scollay

Copyright: 1977

Population: Adults

Purpose: Assesses general mental ability; used for evaluation of penal populations, factory workers, general populations, management, and student populations

Description: Four-subtest performance measure of general intellectual ability. The subtests include Block-Counting, Digit-Symbol, Number Series, and Memory Span for Objects. The directions are given by the examiner. Some number reading is required. The test may be used in any situation where a culture-fair measure of intelligence is needed.

Format: Examiner required; not suitable for group use; timed: 20 minutes

Scoring: Hand key

Cost: Specimen Set $5.00; 25 tests $8.75; 25 answer sheets $7.00

Publisher: Psychometric Affiliates

Porteus Mazes
S. D. Porteus

Copyright: 1965

Population: All ages

Purpose: Assesses mental ability of subjects with verbal handicaps; used in anthropological studies and in research on the effects of drugs and neurosurgery

Description: Nonlanguage test of mental ability in which the items are mazes. Materials include the Vineland Revision, Porteus Maze Extension, and Porteus Maze Supplement. The Vineland Revision, consisting of 12 mazes, is the basic test. The Porteus Maze Extension is a series of eight mazes designed for retesting and is not intended for use as an initial test. The Porteus Maze Supplement is designed for a third testing in clinical and research settings.

Format: Examiner required; not suitable for group use; untimed: 25 minutes per scale

Scoring: Examiner evaluated

Cost: Basic Set (mazes and 100 score sheets) $155.50; Porteus Maze Extension (mazes and 100 score sheets) $115.00; Porteus Maze Supplement (100 each of eight Mazes); manual $39.00

Publisher: The Psychological Corporation

Proverbs Test
Donald R. Gorham

Copyright: 1956

Population: All ages

Purpose: Assesses abstract verbal functioning; used for individual clinical evaluation, screening, and clinical research

Description: Two formats (12 and 40 items) measure verbal comprehension. The subject is required to explain the meanings of proverbs. The 12-item free-answer format allows the subject to respond in his or her own words. The 40-item form is in a multiple-choice format. The free-response forms are scored for abstractness and pertinence on a 3-point scale. The multiple-choice form is scored with a hand stencil. Forms I, II, and III are available for free-answer administration.

Format: Examiner required; multiple-choice suitable for group use; 20–40 minutes

Scoring: Hand key; examiner evaluated

Cost: Complete kit $13.00

Publisher: Psychological Test Specialists

Quick-Test (QT)
R. B. Ammons, C. H. Ammons

Copyright: 1962

Population: Ages 2 to adult

Purpose: Assesses individual intelligence; may be used for evaluation of individuals with severe physical disability, individuals with short attention spans, or uncooperative subjects

Description: Fifty-item test of general intelligence. The subject looks at plates with four line drawings and indicates which picture best illustrates the meaning of a given word. The subject usually responds by pointing. The test requires no reading, writing, or speaking. Usual admin-istration involves the presentation of 15 to 20 of the items. Materials include plates with stimulus pictures and three alternate forms.

Format: Examiner required; suitable for group use; 3–10 minutes

Scoring: Hand key; examiner evaluated

Cost: Complete kit $16.00

Publisher: Psychological Test Specialists

Ross Test of Higher Cognitive Processes
John D. Ross, Catherine M. Ross

Copyright: 1976

Population: Ages 9 to 11

Purpose: Assesses abstract and critical thinking skills among gifted and nongifted intermediate-grade students; used to screen students for special programs and to evaluate program effectiveness

Description: Paper–pencil 105-item multiple-choice test in eight sections, each dealing with a specific level of higher cognitive processes within the areas of analysis, synthesis, and evaluation. Test is taken in two sittings. Responses may be recorded directly in the student test booklet or on an optional answer sheet. Materials include overlays for the scoring of answer sheets and an audiotape of the test.

Format: Individual or group administration; first sitting 63 minutes, second sitting 58 minutes

Scoring: Examiner administered; hand key

Cost: Test kit (manual, 10 student test booklets, 25 answer/profile forms, 2 overlays for quick scoring, in vinyl folder) $60.00

Publisher: Academic Therapy Publications

Schaie–Thurstone Adult Mental Abilities Test (STAMAT)
K. Warner Schaie

Copyright: Not provided

Population: Adults; ages 22 to 84

Purpose: Measures five separate factors of intelligence

Description: Multiple-item paper–pencil test in two forms measuring verbal, spatial, reasoning, number, and word fluency abilities of adults. Form A (adult) is the original Thurstone Primary Mental Abilities Test, Form 11–17, with new adult norms. Form OA (older adult) is a large-type version of the original test plus two additional scales relevant for adults ages 55 and older. The test was used by Schaie for assessing the development of adult intelligence longitudinally and cross-sectionally. New normative data are based on 4,500 people from ages 22 to 84. Instructions have been written to enhance performance by older adults.

Format: Examiner required; suitable for group use; timed: Form A, 26 minutes; Form B, 37 minutes

Scoring: Hand key

Cost: Preview Kit (booklet, scoring key, manual) $39.00

Publisher: Consulting Psychologists Press, Inc.

Schubert General Ability Battery
Herman J. P. Schubert

Copyright: 1979

Population: Adolescents, adults

Purpose: Measures general mental abilities; used for scholastic and industrial placement and guidance in high school, college, and industry

Description: Multiple-item paper–pencil battery of tests assessing general mental abilities in order to predict educational and employment success. The battery yields scores for verbal skills, precise thinking, arithmetic reasoning, and logical analysis.

Format: Examiner required; suitable for group use; timed: time varies

Scoring: Hand key

Cost: Kit (25 test booklets, answer key, manual) $55.00

Publisher: Slosson Educational Publications, Inc.

Shipley Institute of Living Scale
Walter C. Shipley

Copyright: Not provided

Population: Ages 14 to adult

Purpose: Used as a measure of intellectual ability and impairment

Description: The Shipley measures cognitive impairment and is composed of two brief subtests: a 40-item vocabulary test, and a 20-item abstract thinking test. The scale produces six summary scores: vocabulary, abstraction, total, conceptual quotient (an index of impairment), abstraction quotient (the conceptual quotient adjusted for age), and estimated full-scale WAIS or WAIS–R IQ scores.

Format: Self-administered; suitable for group use; timed: 20 minutes

Scoring: Hand or computer scored

Cost: Kit (100 test forms, 1 manual, 1 hand scoring key, 2 AutoScore™ test forms) $96.00; microcomputer disk (IBM; good for 25 uses) $210.00

Publisher: Western Psychological Services

Silver Drawing Test of Cognition and Emotion
Rawley A. Silver

Copyright: 1996

Population: Ages 5 to adult; Grades 1 to 12

Purpose: Assesses cognitive skills, screens for depression, provides access to fantasies and attitudes toward self and others

Description: Three multiple-item paper–pencil subtests with cognitive and emotional components. Predictive Drawing measures concepts of horizontal, verticality, and sequential order. Examinees are asked to add lines to outline drawings. Responses are scored for ability to show how objects would appear if filled, tilted, or moved. Drawing from Observation measures concept of space. Examinees are asked to draw an arrangement of cylinders. Responses are scored for ability to represent left–right, above–below, and front–back relationships. Drawing from Imagination measures cognitive skills, creative skills, and attitudes toward self and others. Examinees are asked to choose subjects from an array of 15 stimulus drawings and create narrative drawings with titles. Responses are scored for ability to select (content), ability to combine (form), ability to represent (creativity), and emotional content. Skill in drawing is not evaluated. Instruction may be pantomimed.

Format: Individual or group administration; 12–20 minutes

Scoring: Examiner administration and interpretation

Cost: $32.00

Publisher: Ablin Press Distributors

Slosson Full-Range Intelligence Test (S-FRIT)
Bob Algozzine, Ronald C. Eaves, Lester Mann, H. Robert Vance

Copyright: 1993

Population: Ages 5 to 21

Purpose: Provides a balanced measure of verbal/performance/memory cognitive assessments; screens nonverbal from verbal abilities even when language skills are limited; used for screening new school entrants and planning educational programming

Description: The S-FRIT is intended to supplement the use of more extensive cognitive assessment instruments to facilitate screening in charting cognitive progress. The test can be given by regular or special education teachers, psychologists, counselors or other personnel who have taken basic courses in statistics and/or tests and measurements. Items are arranged according to levels of difficulty, and the examiner presents items at suggested starting points by chronological age. When the examinee fails 8 items in a row, testing is completed and the examiner very quickly gets a picture of the individual's mental abilities in the following areas: Verbal Skills/Quantitative/Recall Memory/Abstract Performance Reasoning.

Format: Individual administration; 15–30 minutes

Scoring: Examiner evaluated

Cost: Complete $115.00; Examiner's Manual $26.00; Normative/Technical Manual $24.00;

Picture Book $22.00; 50 Motor Response Forms $20.00; 50 Brief Score Forms $20.00; 50 Item Profile/Score Summaries $20.00

Publisher: Slosson Educational Publications, Inc.

Slosson Intelligence Test–Revised (SIT–R)
Richard L. Slosson, Charles L. Nicholson, Terry L. Hibpshman

Copyright: 1990

Population: Ages 4 to 65

Purpose: Measures the mental age and IQ level of children and adults; used by psychologists, guidance counselors, special educators, and learning disability and remedial reading teachers to provide a quick assessment of a person's mental abilities

Description: Oral screening instrument consisting of 187 questions arranged on a scale of chronological age. The administrator finds the basal, then adds the questions passed after the basal to find the raw score. Test scores range from 36 (moderate M/H) to 164 (very superior IQ). The national restandardization creates a Total Standard Score (TSS), establishes a 95% or 99% confidence interval, Mean Age Equivalent, T-score, stanine, Normal Curve Equivalent, and percentiles, based on the TSS. Norms include regular and special populations, as well as the visual disabled and the blind. Quantitative reasoning questions were designed to be administered to populations who use metric or standard references, using language common to both. Six cognitive areas of measurement include vocabulary, general information, similarities and differences, comprehension, quantitative, and auditory memory.

Format: Examiner required; not suitable for group use; untimed: 10–20 minutes

Scoring: Examiner evaluated

Cost: Complete kit (manual, directions, 50 SIT–R score sheets, norms tables/technical manual) $78.00

Publisher: Slosson Educational Publications, Inc.

Snyders-Oomen Non-Verbal Intelligence Test Revised (SON–R 2½–7)

J. Th. Snijders, P. J. Tellegen, J. A. Laros

Copyright: 1988

Population: Ages 2 years 6 months to 7 years

Purpose: Measures nonverbal intelligence

Description: Paper–pencil test consisting of multiple-choice, oral response, short answer, and true–false items. Seven subtests. Test may be administered to students with or without hearing impairments and language difficulties. Instructions may be given orally or with gestures. Responses may be verbal, point-to, or show-tell. Manual available in Dutch, German, and English.

Format: Individual administration; examiner required; untimed: 90 minutes

Scoring: Examiner evaluated

Cost: Contact publisher

Publisher: SWETS and Zeitlinger B V

Stanford–Binet Intelligence Scale, Form L–M

Lewis M. Terman, Maud A. Merrill, Robert L. Thorndike

Copyright: 1972

Population: Ages 2 to adult

Purpose: Measures an individual's mental abilities

Description: Verbal and nonverbal IQ test with 142 items assessing language, memory, conceptual thinking, reasoning, numerical reasoning, visual motor, and social reasoning. In most cases, only 18 to 24 test items need to be administered to a subject. First, the basal age is established. Testing continues until the ceiling age is reached. Responses then are scored according to established procedures to yield mental age and IQ. The results identify children and adults who would benefit from specialized learning. Form L–M materials will be available until current stock is exhausted.

Format: Individual administration by professionally trained, certified examiners; 45–90 minutes

Scoring: Examiner evaluated

Cost: Examiner's Kit (Manual, 1 set of protocols, materials) $622.00

Publisher: Riverside Publishing Company

Stanford–Binet Intelligence Scale–Fourth Edition

Robert L. Thorndike, Elizabeth P. Hagen, Jerome M. Sattler

Copyright: 1986

Population: Ages 2 to adult

Purpose: Assesses intelligence and cognitive abilities

Description: Verbal and nonverbal performance test assessing mental abilities in four areas: verbal reasoning (vocabulary, comprehension, verbal relations, absurdities), abstract/visual reasoning (pattern analysis, matrices, paper folding and cutting, copying), quantitative reasoning (quantitative, number series, equation building), and short-term memory (memory for sentences, memory for digits, memory for objects, and bead memory). Items are arranged according to item type and order of difficulty. The following scores can be obtained: raw percentages and scaled scores for each of the 15 subtests, four content area scores, a composite of the four area scores, a composite of any combination of the four area scores, and a profile on all 15 subtests. Results identify children and adults who would benefit from specialized learning environments.

Format: Individual administration by professionally trained, certified examiners; 45–90 minutes

Scoring: Examiner evaluated; scoring service available from publisher

Cost: Examiner's Kit (Item Books, Guide for Administration, Technical Manual, 1 record booklet, scissors, paper, and all materials in briefcase) $595.00

Publisher: Riverside Publishing Company

Swanson Cognitive Processing Test (S–CPT)

H. Lee Swanson

Copyright: 1996

Population: Children, adults; ages 4 years 5 months to 78 years 6 months

Purpose: Measures different aspects of intellectual abilities and information processing potential

Description: Battery of 11 subtests that can be administered in abbreviated form (five subtests) or in a complete form under traditional, or interactive, testing conditions. Information is drawn from the work on information processing theory and dynamic assessment. Normative data for the S–CPT were gathered between 1987 and 1994. The test was individually administered to 1,611 children and adults (ages 4 years 5 months to 78 years 6 months) in 10 U.S. states and two Canadian provinces. The sample closely matches the 1990 U.S. census figures for ethnicity, gender, region, and community size. The S–CPT includes test–teach–test conditions that required measures of internal reliability. The total coefficient alpha score for the S–CPT is highly reliable. The results of composite and component scores indicate that the majority of scores range from .82 to .95, with 64% (16 of 25) of the reliabilities at .90 or greater. High construct and criterion-related validity coefficients are reported.

Format: Individual administration; timed: time varies

Scoring: Examiner evaluated

Cost: Complete kit (examiner's manual, 25 profile/examiner record booklets, picture book, card decks, strategy cards, storage box) $169.00

Publisher: PRO-ED, Inc.

System of Multicultural Pluralistic Assessment (SOMPA)

Jane R. Mercer, June F. Lewis

Copyright: 1978

Population: Children; ages 5 to 11

Purpose: Assesses cognitive abilities, sensorimotor abilities, and adaptive behavior of children; used for assessing children of diverse cultural backgrounds

Description: Multiple-instrument measure covering various aspects of functioning of children from diverse cultural backgrounds. The test has two major components: The Parent Interview and Student Assessment Materials. The Parent Interview is conducted in the home and requires the administration of the Adaptive Behavior Inventory for Children (ABIC), Sociocultural Scales, and Health History Inventories. Student Assessment Materials data are collected in the school and include administration or completion of the following tests and tasks: Physical Dexterity, Weight by Height, Visual Acuity, Auditory Acuity, Bender Visual Motor Gestalt Test, and the WISC–R or WPPSI. The test should be interpreted by a psychologist or a qualified team. Normative data are provided for black, Hispanic, and white children. The Parent Interview is available in Spanish.

Format: Examiner required; not suitable for group use; untimed: Parent Interview, 20 minutes; Student Assessment Materials, 60 minutes in addition to time required for the Wechsler and Bender-Gestalt tests.

Scoring: Examiner evaluated

Cost: Basic kit (parent interview manual, 25 parent interview record forms, set of 6 ABIC scoring keys, student assessment manual, 25 student assessment record forms, 25 profile folders, and technical manual) $206.00

Publisher: The Psychological Corporation

Test of Nonverbal Intelligence– Third Edition (TONI–3)

Linda Brown, Rita J. Sherbenou, Susan K. Johnsen

Copyright: 1997

Population: Ages 6 years 0 months through 89 years 11 months

Purpose: Provides a language-free measure of intelligence, aptitude, and reasoning; used with subjects suspected of having difficulty in reading, writing, listening, or speaking

Description: The administration of the test requires no reading, writing, speaking, or listening on the part of the test subject. There are two equivalent forms of the TONI–3. The items include problem-solving tasks that increase in difficulty.

Format: Individual or small group (5) administration; 10–15 minutes

Scoring: Examiner evaluated and interpreted

Cost: Complete kit (manual, picture book, protocols, and storage box) $219.00

Publisher: PRO-ED, Inc.

Visual Gestalt Test
Ruth Andersen

Copyright: 1989

Population: Adults

Purpose: Assesses cognitive dysfunction related to cerebral deficits applicable for research with patients with right-hemisphere dysfunction

Description: Four-item paper–pencil test measuring quantitative and qualitative assessment of visual gestalts using figures in: circle, triangle, rectangle, semi-circle. Materials include four stimulus cards, four pads with figure outlines, a scoring key, and a scoring sheet. Examiner must be a qualified neuropsychologist. Available also in Danish.

Format: Individual administration; examiner required; untimed

Scoring: Hand key

Cost: Specimen Set $38.00 (DKK 215)

Publisher: Dansk psykologisk Forlag

Vulpe Assessment Battery
Shirley German Vulpe

Copyright: 1994

Population: Ages 0 to 6

Purpose: Evaluates the developmental status of atypically developing children

Description: Performance analysis/developmental assessment of functioning in eight developmental skill areas (basic senses and functions, gross-motor behaviors, fine-motor behaviors, language behaviors, cognitive processes, specific concepts, the organization of behavior, activities of daily living) and one environmental domain (environment). Information about an individual child is obtained through direct observation or from a knowledgeable informant. Includes 1,127 items.

Format: Examiner required; not suitable for group use; untimed: typical time not available

Scoring: Examiner evaluated

Cost: Complete battery $99.00; 50 record sheets $15.00

Publisher: Slosson Educational Publications, Inc.

Wechsler Preschool and Primary Scale of Intelligence–Revised (WPPSI–R)
David Wechsler

Copyright: 1989

Population: Children; ages 3 years to 7 years 3 months

Purpose: Measures intellectual abilities in young children

Description: A revision of the original 1967 WPPSI. It retains the conceptual and technical foundations while incorporating new features and extending the age range. Contains the original 11 subtests, plus an additional performance subtest, Object Assembly. Pegs (formerly Animal House) and Sentences are now optional subtests. Provides norms for 17 age groups divided by 3-month intervals. Verbal, Performance, and Full Scale IQ scores are provided. Numerous validity studies were conducted. Optional scoring and reporting software available.

Format: Examiner required; not suitable for group use; requires about 75 minutes

Scoring: Examiner evaluated; may be computer scored

Cost: Complete set (in case) $553.00; (in box) $517.00

Publisher: The Psychological Corporation

Wechsler Adult Intelligence Scale–Revised (WAIS–R)
David Wechsler

Copyright: 1981

Population: Adolescents, adults; ages 16 to 74

Purpose: Assesses intelligence in adolescents and adults

Description: Eleven subtests divided into two major divisions yielding a Verbal IQ, a Performance IQ, and a Full Scale IQ for individuals ages 16 and older. Some units of the test require verbal responses from the subject, and others require the subject to manipulate test materials to demonstrate performance ability. The verbal section of the test consists of the following subtests: Information, Comprehension, Arithmetic, Similarities, Digit Span, and Vocabulary. The performance or nonverbal section of the test consists of the following subtests: Digit Symbol, Picture Completion, Block Design, Picture Arrangement, and Object Assembly. Raw scores are converted into scale scores after the examiner records and scores the subject's performance. The WAIS–R is a revision of the 1955 edition of the WAIS. Available in Spanish.

Format: Examiner required; not suitable for group use; untimed: 75 minutes

Scoring: Examiner evaluated

Cost: Complete set (all necessary stimulus and manipulative materials, manual, 25 record forms, 25 mazes booklets, 50 geometric design sheets, and attaché case) $595.00; Complete set without attaché case $550.00

Publisher: The Psychological Corporation

Wechsler Intelligence Scale for Children–Third Edition (WISC–III)
David Wechsler

Copyright: 1991

Population: Children, adolescents; ages 6 to 16

Purpose: Assesses intellectual ability in children

Description: A revision of the 1974 edition of the WISC–R. While retaining the basic structure and content of that instrument, this test offers updated normative data and improved items and design. Ten core subtests plus three supplementary subtests provide three composite scores; Verbal IQ, Performance IQ, and Full Scale IQ. Verbal subtests include Information, Similarities, Arithmetic, Vocabulary, and Comprehension, plus Digit Span. Performance subtests include Picture Completion, Coding, Picture Arrangement, Block Design, Object Design, plus Symbol Search and Mazes. Both verbal responses and manipulation of test materials are required of individual. Optional scoring and report writing software available.

Format: Examiner required; not suitable for group use; core subtests, 50–70 minutes; Supplemental subtests, 10–15 minutes

Scoring: Examiner evaluated; may be computer scored

Cost: Complete kit (in case) $595.00; (in box) $550.00

Publisher: The Psychological Corporation

Wide Range Intelligence Personality Test (WRIPT)
Joseph F. Jastak

Copyright: 1978

Population: Ages 9½ to adult

Purpose: Measures general mental ability and personality structure. Used for clinical diagnosis and research relating personality to intelligence, academic achievement, and vocational aptitudes and performances

Description: Ten paper–pencil subtests measuring verbal, numeric, pictorial, spatial, social competency, and other abilities. The test provides a *g* (global) or intelligence score and identifies the extent to which this general factor influences behavior. The test also provides cluster (lobal) scores for language, reality set, motivation, and psychomotor skills. In addition, the test offers several areas of special effectiveness: measuring mental abilities through a wide range of abilities; studying personality makeup; measuring changes in specific personality traits due to age, health, education, or other factors; demonstrating the role of group (lobal) factors in schooling, job selection, and social adjustment; studying variances contributing to the diagnosis of mental retardation, mental illness, learning disabilities, and antisocial and asocial behavior; showing how cultural neglect or environmental limits influence a person's applications.

Format: Examiner required; suitable for group use; timed: 50 minutes

Scoring: Hand key

Cost: Starter Set $85.00

Publisher: Wide Range, Inc.

Woodcock-Johnson®–Revised Tests of Cognitive Ability (WJ–R®)
Richard W. Woodcock, M. Bonner Johnson

Copyright: 1989

Population: Ages 2 to 90+

Purpose: Assesses cognitive abilities, aptitudes, and oral language

Description: Seven cognitive factors are measured: long-term retrieval, short-term memory, processing speed, auditory processing, visual processing, comprehension–knowledge, and fluid reasoning. There are two to four tests for each cognitive factor, a measure of oral language, and five differential aptitude clusters. There are 21 tests in the complete cognitive battery. The first seven tests are the Standard Battery. The remaining 14 tests are supplemental and can be used selectively to obtain information on cognitive factors, intracognitive discrepancies, oral language, or differential aptitudes.

Format: Individual administration; examiner required; 5 minutes per subtest

Scoring: Examiner interpretation; computer software available for PC, Mac, and Apple formats

Cost: Complete battery with case (Standard and Supplemental Test Books, examiner's manual, norm tables, audiocassettes, 25 test records) $498.00

Publisher: Riverside Publishing Company

Marital

Premarital

Dating Scale
Panos D. Bardis

Copyright: 1988

Population: Adolescents, adults

Purpose: Measures attitudes toward various aspects of dating; used for clinical assessment, marriage and family counseling, research on attitudes toward dating, and discussion in family education

Description: Two-item paper–pencil test in which the subject notes 25 statements about dating from 0 (strongly disagree) to 4 (strongly agree). The score equals the sum of the 25 numerical responses. Theoretical range of scores extends from 0 (least liberal) to 100 (most liberal). Suitable for use with individuals with physical and hearing disabilities.

Format: Examiner/self-administered; suitable for group use; untimed: 10 minutes

Scoring: Examiner evaluated

Cost: Free

Publisher: Panos D. Bardis, Ph.D.

Marriage and Family Attitude Survey
Donald V. Martin, Maggie Martin

Copyright: 1982

Population: Adolescents, adults

Purpose: Assesses attitudes toward a variety of marital issues; used as an aid in premarriage and marriage counseling

Description: Sixty-item paper–pencil multiple-choice test assessing attitudes toward finances, health, children, and in-laws. A fifth-grade reading level is required.

Format: Examiner/self-administered; suitable for group use; untimed: 10 minutes

Scoring: Hand key

Cost: Specimen Set (includes manual) $5.00; replacement manual $4.50; 25 test forms $15.00

Publisher: Psychologists and Educators, Inc.

Premarital Communication Inventory
Millard J. Bienvenu

Copyright: 1968

Population: Adults; ages 17 and older

Purpose: Assesses marriageability of a couple; used in premarital counseling, marriage preparation, and teaching

Description: Forty item yes–no–sometimes test. A seventh-grade reading level is required. Examiner must have counseling experience.

Format: Self-administered; suitable for group use; untimed: 15 minutes

Scoring: Hand key

Cost: $.75 per copy; guide $2.00; minimum order $10.00

Publisher: Northwest Publications

Role-Played Dating Interactions (RPDI)
Linda D. Rhyne, Marion L. MacDonald, Robert A. McGrath, Carol Ummel Lindquist, Judith A. Kramer

Copyright: 1974

Population: Adults

Purpose: Assesses male social dating skills

Description: Oral response test consisting of three 4-minute encounters.

Format: Individual administration; examiner required; timed: 12 minutes

Scoring: Examiner evaluated

Cost: $15.00

Publisher: Select Press

Relations

Abortion Scale
Panos D. Bardis

Copyright: 1988

Population: Adolescents, adults

Purpose: Measures attitudes toward many aspects of abortion; used in clinical assessment, marriage and family counseling, research on attitudes toward abortion, and discussion in family education

Description: Paper–pencil 25-item test in which the subject reads statements about issues concerning abortion and rates them according to his or her personal beliefs on a scale from 0 (strongly disagree) to 4 (strongly agree). The score equals the sum of the 25 numerical responses. Theoretical range of scores extends from 0 (lowest approval of abortion) to 100 (highest approval). Suitable for use with individuals with physical or hearing disabilities.

Format: Examiner/self-administered; suitable for group use; untimed: 10 minutes

Scoring: Examiner evaluated

Cost: Free

Publisher: Panos D. Bardis, Ph.D.

Abuse Risk Inventory (ARI)
Bonnie L. Yegidis

Copyright: 1987

Population: Adult women

Purpose: Identifies abused or at-risk-for-abuse women; used for marital or relationship counseling and by social service agencies, physicians, and health care providers

Description: Four-point Likert Scale with 25 items. Scores provide sociodemographic information. Examiner must be trained in proper use and interpretation.

Format: Self-administered; suitable for group use; untimed: 10–15 minutes

Scoring: Hand key, examiner evaluated

Cost: Sampler Set $25.00; Permission Set for 200 users $90.00

Publisher: Mind Garden, Inc.

Caring Relationship Inventory (CRI)
Everett L. Shostrom

Copyright: 1966

Population: Adults

Purpose: Measures the essential elements of caring (or love) in the relationship between a man and a woman; used for evaluation and discussion in marriage and family counseling

Description: Paper–pencil 83-item true–false test consisting of a series of statements that the subject applies first to the other member of the couple (spouse, fiancée, etc.) and second to his or her "ideal" mate. Responses are scored on seven scales: affection, friendship, eros, empathy, self-love, being love, and deficiency love. Separate forms are available for adult males and females. Items were developed based on the responses of criterion groups of successfully married couples, troubled couples in counseling, and divorced individuals. Percentile norms for successfully married couples are presented separately for men and women. Means and standard deviations are presented for troubled couples and divorced individuals. The CRI is a component of the Actualizing Assessment Battery (AAB).

Format: Examiner required; suitable for group use; untimed: 40 minutes

Scoring: Hand key

Cost: Specimen Set (manual, all forms) $7.00

Publisher: EdITS/Educational and Industrial Testing Service

Coitometer
Panos D. Bardis

Copyright: 1988

Population: Adolescents, adults

Purpose: Measures knowledge of the anatomical and physiological aspects of coitus; used for clinical assessment, marriage and family counseling, research on human sexuality, and discussion in family and human sexuality classes

Description: Fifty-item paper–pencil true–false four-page instrument consisting of the questionnaire and a measure key; suitable for use with individuals with physical or hearing disabilities.

Format: Examiner/self-administered; suitable for group use; untimed: 12 minutes

Scoring: Hand key

Cost: Free

Publisher: Panos D. Bardis, Ph.D.

Derogatis Interview for Sexual Functioning (DISF/DISF–SR)
Leonard R. Derogatis

Copyright: 1987

Population: Adolescents, adults

Purpose: Assesses quality of sexual functioning for clinical trials, outcomes, and effectiveness studies

Description: Test with 26 items, five domains, and a Total Score. Categories include Sex–Cognition/Fantasy, Arousal, Sex Experience, Orgasm, Drive/Relationship. Male and female forms of the DISF interview and the DISF-SR self report are available. High school reading level is required. Available in French, German, Spanish, Dutch, and Italian.

Format: Examiner required; self-administered for SR Form; suitable for group use; untimed: 15-20 minutes

Scoring: Examiner evaluated; test scoring service available from publisher

Cost: 50 profile forms $25.00; $37.50 for package of 50

Publisher: Clinical Psychometric Research, Inc.

Derogatis Sexual Functioning Inventory (DSFI)
Leonard R. Derogatis

Copyright: 1978

Population: Adults

Purpose: Measures and describes the quality of an individual's sexual functioning

Description: Paper–pencil or computer-administered 255-item inventory consisting of 10 subtests assessing the following factors related to an individual's sexual functioning: information, experience, drive, attitude, psychological symptoms, affects, gender role definition, fantasy, body image, and sexual satisfaction. Available in over 20 languages. Norms are available separately for men and women. Provides scaled scores for each subtest and a combined sexual functioning score.

Format: Suitable for group use; 30–40 minutes; PC format administration

Scoring: Examiner interpretation

Cost: 25 test booklets $50.00 or $33.00; 25 profile forms $10.00; manual $10.00; computer version sold on a per-use basis

Publisher: Clinical Psychometric Research, Inc.

Developing a Comparative Measure of Family Interaction
George Levinger

Copyright: 1972

Population: Adults

Purpose: Assesses marital interaction

Description: Paper–pencil questionnaire

Format: Individually administered; requires examiner; untimed

Scoring: Examiner evaluated

Cost: $21.00

Publisher: Select Press

Dimensional Structure of SPAT (Spouse Adjective Test)
Robert G. Ryder

Copyright: 1971

Population: Adults

Purpose: Assesses attitudes of spouses toward each other

Description: Short answer/true–false adjective test

Format: Individually administered; examiner required; untimed

Scoring: Hand key; examiner evaluated

Cost: $15.00

Publisher: Select Press

Dyadic Adjustment Scale (DAS)
Graham Spanier

Copyright: 1989

Population: Adults

Purpose: Measures relationship dissatisfaction for use in marital counseling

Description: Paper–pencil or computer-administered 32-item self-report measure consisting of four factored subscales: Dyadic Satisfaction, Dyadic Cohesion, Dyadic Consensus, and Affectional Expression. A total score below 100 points indicates relationship distress. Computer version generates interpretive statements.

Format: Self-administered; suitable for group use; untimed: time varies

Scoring: Carbonized QuikScore forms; may be computer scored

Cost: Kit (manual, 20 QuikScore Forms) $40.00; IBM PC compatible (50 administrations and scorings) $125.00

Publisher: Multi-Health Systems, Inc.

Eidetic Parents Test
Akhter Ahsen

Copyright: 1972

Population: Adults

Purpose: Assists clinical patients and marriage and family counsultees to aid in exploring emotional attachments that affect current functioning

Description: Stimuli are provided that are meant to arouse eidetic images of parents.

Verbal reporting by individuals of subjective visual images of increasingly surrealistic situations.

Format: Individual administration; minimum 60 minutes

Scoring: Examiner administration and interpretation

Cost: $20.00 per manual; includes test

Publisher: Brandon House, Inc.

Erotometer: A Technique for the Measurement of Heterosexual Love
Panos D. Bardis

Copyright: 1988

Population: Adolescents, adults

Purpose: Measures the intensity of an individual's love for a member of the opposite sex; used for clinical assessment, marriage and family counseling, research on love, and discussions in family and sex education

Description: Fifty-item paper–pencil test in which the subject reads statements concerning actual feelings, attitudes, desires, and wishes regarding one specific member of the opposite sex and rates them on the following scale: 0 (absent), 1 (weak), 2 (strong). The score equals the sum of the 50 numerical responses. The theoretical range of scores extends from 0 (no love) to 100 (strongest love). Suitable for use with individuals with physical or hearing disabilities.

Format: Self-administered; suitable for group use; untimed: 12 minutes

Scoring: Examiner evaluated

Cost: Free

Publisher: Panos D. Bardis, Ph.D.

Golombok Rust Inventory of Sexual Satisfaction (GRISS)
John Rust, Susan Golombok

Copyright: 1986

Population: Adults

Purpose: Used in marital counseling to assess the quality of sexual relationships

Description: Paper–pencil 28-item 5-point scale with the following categories: Male: Impotence, Premature Ejaculation, Male Non-Sensuality, Male Avoidance, Male Dissatisfaction Infrequency; Female: Non-Communication, Female Dissatisfaction, Female Avoidance, Female Non-Sensuality, Vaginismus, Anorasmia. Materials used include a manual, male questionnaire/profile, female questionnaire/profile. Examiner must be B-Level qualified.

Format: Self-administered; untimed

Scoring: Hand scored

Cost: Introductory kit (manual and protocols) $53.00

Publisher: Psychological Assessment Resources, Inc.

Gravidometer
Panos D. Bardis

Copyright: 1988

Population: Adolescents, adults

Purpose: Measures knowledge of the anatomical and physiological aspects of pregnancy; used in clinical assessments, marriage and family counseling, and research on human sexuality and family classes

Description: Fifty-item paper–pencil true–false test measuring knowledge of human pregnancy; suitable for use with individuals with physical and hearing disabilities.

Format: Self-administered; suitable for group use; untimed: 12 minutes

Scoring: Hand key

Cost: Free

Publisher: Panos D. Bardis, Ph.D.

Grow
Thomas J. Henry, Virginia M. Henry, Samuel E. Krug

Copyright: 1984

Population: Adults

Purpose: Assessment and development program for use in professional relationship counseling and enrichment

Description: Program of assessment, learning activities, and personal development. The 189-item paper–pencil multiple-choice inventory is divided into four sections assessing various areas of personality. Results of the inventory are used to develop four individualized lessons covering bonding, communication, decision making, and definition of roles. Each lesson contains a self-evaluation exercise to increase individual awareness of the topic area. Combined, the assessment and lessons are designed to provide a program of marital growth and communication. The assessment is based on the Adult Personality Inventory.

Format: Self-administered; suitable for group use; untimed: inventory 45 minutes, lessons vary

Scoring: Computer scored through publisher

Cost: $18.40 to $48.00 per couple, depending on quantities and options

Publisher: MetriTech

Male–Female Relations Questionnaire
Janet T. Spence, Robert L. Helmreich, Linda Leavitt Sarvin

Copyright: 1970
Population: Adults
Purpose: Assesses sex role behaviors and preferences in males and females

Description: Thirty-item paper–pencil test with the following categories: social interactions, marital roles, and two sex-unique scales.

Format: Group or individual administration; examiner required; untimed

Scoring: Examiner evaluated
Cost: $18.00
Publisher: Select Press

Marital Attitudes Evaluation (MATE)
Will Schutz

Copyright: 1989
Population: Adults
Purpose: Explores the relationship between

spouses or other closely related persons; measures the amount of satisfaction respondents feel toward someone close to them; used in marital, relationship, and family counseling

Description: Six-point Likert scale test. An eighth-grade reading level is required.

Format: Individual administration; suitable for group use; examiner required; untimed: 10–15 minutes

Scoring: Hand key; examiner evaluated

Cost: Sampler Set $25.00, permission for up to 200 uses $90.00

Publisher: Mind Garden, Inc.

Marital Evaluation Checklist
Leslie Navran

Copyright: 1984
Population: Adults
Purpose: Assesses common characteristics and problem areas in a marital relationship. Used as a survey instrument in clinical and counseling settings to initiate the consultation process and introduce the client to formal diagnostic testing

Description: Paper–pencil 140-item test organized in three sections: reasons for marrying, current problems, and motivation for counseling. Areas surveyed include interpersonal/emotional, material/economic, social, personal, money and work, sex, personal characteristics, and marital relationships.

Format: Self-administered; suitable for group use; untimed: 10–20 minutes

Scoring: Examiner evaluated
Cost: 50 checklists $34.00
Publisher: Psychological Assessment Resources, Inc.

Marital Satisfaction Inventory (MSI)
Douglas K. Snyder

Copyright: 1981
Population: Adults
Purpose: Identifies the nature and extent of marital distress; used in marital and family counseling

Description: Multiple-item paper–pencil or computer-administered true–false test providing information concerning nine basic measured dimensions of marriage: affective communication, problem-solving communication, time together, disagreement about finances, sexual dissatisfaction, role orientation, family history of distress, dissatisfaction with children, and conflict over childrearing. In addition, a validity scale and a global distress scale measure each spouse's overall dissatisfaction with the marriage. The test is available in two forms: a 280-item version for couples with children and a 239-item version for childless couples. The results for both spouses are recorded on the same profile form, graphically identifying the areas of marital distress. Each spouse's scores can be individually evaluated as well as directly compared, thereby facilitating diagnostic and intervention procedures. Group mean profiles for each sex are provided for couples seeking general marital therapy.

Format: Examiner required; not suitable for group use; untimed: 30–40 minutes

Scoring: Hand key; may be computer scored

Cost: Kit (2 reusable administration booklets, 50 hand-scored answer sheets, 50 profile forms, 1 set of hand scoring keys, 1 manual, 2 WPS Test Report answer sheets) $145.00

Publisher: Western Psychological Services

Marriage Scale
J. Gustav White

Copyright: 1971

Population: Adults; ages 16 and older

Purpose: Assesses various aspects of marital relationships

Description: Paper–pencil 21-item inventory measuring factors related to marital life and compatibility. Each partner is asked to rate on a 10-point scale statements pertaining to the following topics: mutual understanding, outlook on life, religion, love, intercommunication, objectionable habits, pleasures, relatives, children, sex, occupation, interests, aesthetic tastes, finances, major plans, and so forth. Each partner's profile is copied onto the profile of the other partner for a direct comparison of their responses. A four-page folder serves as a permanent file record. Not suitable for persons with below-average reading ability.

Format: Self-administered; suitable for group use; untimed: 10–15 minutes

Scoring: Hand key; examiner evaluated

Cost: Specimen Set $5.00; 25 Rating Folders $15.00

Publisher: Psychologists and Educators, Inc.

Menometer
Panos D. Bardis

Copyright: 1988

Population: Adolescents, adults

Purpose: Measures knowledge of the anatomical and physiological aspects of menstruation; used for clinical assessment, marriage and family counseling, research on human sexuality, and discussion in family and human sexuality classes

Description: Fifty-item paper–pencil true–false test in which the subject marks the appropriate answers. Suitable for use with individuals with physical or hearing disabilities.

Format: Examiner/self-administered; suitable for group use; 12 minutes

Scoring: Hand key

Cost: Free

Publisher: Panos D. Bardis, Ph.D.

Pair Attraction Inventory (PAI)
Everret L. Shostrom

Copyright: 1970

Population: Adults

Purpose: Measures aspects contributing to adults' selection of a mate or friend; used for premarital, marital, and family counseling

Description: Paper–pencil 224-item test assessing the feelings and attitudes of one member of a male–female pair about the nature of the relationship. Percentile norms are provided based on adult samples. The inventory may be used as a component of the Actualizing Assessment Battery (AAB).

Format: Examiner required; suitable for group use; untimed: 30 minutes

Scoring: Hand key

Cost: Kit (3 male, 3 female booklets; 50 answer sheets, 50 profiles, manual) $18.75

Publisher: EdITS/Educational and Industrial Testing Service

Partner Relationship Inventory (PRI)
Carol Noll Hoskins

Copyright: Not provided

Population: Adults

Purpose: Identifies the perceived act within a relationship; assesses interactional, emotional, and sexual needs and points to conflict areas

Description: Available in two forms. The Long Form contains 80 items within two scales. Form I consists of two alternate forms: IA and IB. This is the "short form" of the inventory, and each contains 40 items. The manual provides theoretical background and research information, as well as administration, scoring, and interpretive information.

Format: Examiner required; suitable for use with groups of couples; untimed: 10–30 minutes

Scoring: Hand key; examiner evaluated

Cost: Preview Kit (booklet, scoring form, manual) $27.00

Publisher: Consulting Psychologists Press, Inc.

Pill Scale
Panos D. Bardis

Copyright: 1988

Population: Adolescents, adults

Purpose: Measures attitudes toward oral contraceptives; used for clinical assessment, marriage and family counseling, family attitude research, and discussions in family and sex education

Description: Paper–pencil 25-item test in which the subject reads statements concerning moral, sexual, psychological, and physical aspects of "the pill" and rates them on a scale

from 0 (strongly disagree) to 4 (strongly agree). The score equals the sum of the 25 numerical responses. The theoretical range of scores extends from 0 (least liberal) to 100 (most liberal). Suitable for use with individuals with physical and hearing disabilities.

Format: Examiner/self-administered; suitable for group use; 10 minutes

Scoring: Examiner evaluated

Cost: Free

Publisher: Panos D. Bardis, Ph.D.

Sex-Role Egalitarianism Scale (SRES)
Lynda A. King, Daniel W. King

Copyright: 1993

Population: Adolescents, adults; ages 12 and above

Purpose: Measures attitudes toward equality; used in marital counseling and prevention of sexual harassment

Description: Five-point Likert scale with 95 items and five subscales of educational roles, marital roles, employment roles, social–interpersonal–heterosexual roles, and parental roles. Alternate forms include 25 items. Requires a sixth-grade reading level for the examinee.

Format: Individual and group administration; 25 minutes

Scoring: Examiner interpretation

Cost: Kit $28.00

Publisher: Sigma Assessment Systems, Inc.

Sexometer
Panos D. Bardis

Copyright: 1988

Population: Adolescents, adults

Purpose: Assesses knowledge of human reproductive anatomy and physiology; used for clinical assessment, marriage and family counseling, research on sex knowledge, and discussion in family and sex education

Description: Fifty-item paper–pencil test consisting of short-answer and identification questions concerning human reproduction, anatomy, function, physiology, disease, birth control, and sexual behavior. Materials include the test form and answer key. Suitable for use with individuals with physical and hearing disabilities.

Format: Examiner/self-administered; suitable for group use; 15 minutes

Scoring: Hand key

Cost: Free

Publisher: Panos D. Bardis, Ph.D.

Sexual Communication Inventory
Millard J. Bienvenu

Copyright: 1980

Population: Adults; ages 17 and older

Purpose: Assesses sexual communication in couples; used in marital counseling and in communication skills training for couples 17 years and older

Description: Thirty-item yes–no–sometimes test. A seventh-grade reading level is required. Examiner must have couples counseling experience.

Format: Self-administered; suitable for group use; untimed: 12 minutes

Scoring: Hand key

Cost: $.50 per copy; guide $2.00; minimum order $10.00

Publisher: Northwest Publications

Sexuality Experience Scales
J. Frenken, P. Vennix

Copyright: Not provided

Population: Adults; ages 18 to 55

Purpose: Assesses characteristics of heterosexual behavior; used in counseling, therapy, and social and medical research

Description: Paper–pencil 83-item instruments measuring four dimensions of sexual experience. SES-1 (21 items) measures restrictive sexual morality (rejection versus acceptance); SES-2 (15 items) measures psychosexual stimulation (seeking, allowing versus avoiding of symbolic sexual stimuli); SES-3 (29 items)

measures sexual motivation (approach tendency versus avoidance tendency in sexual interaction with partner); and SES-4 (18 items) measures attraction to own marriage (low versus high). SES-1 and SES-2 are administered to persons who have no sexual partners. The latter two are administered to persons who have durable heterosexual relationships. The tests, derived from item analysis and factor analysis, have 14 relatively independent subscales. Norms are available for married men and women ages 18 to 55 and for women complaining of sexual dysfunction and their male partners.

Format: Examiner/self-administered; not suitable for group use; untimed: typical time not available

Scoring: Computer scored

Cost: Contact publisher

Publisher: SWETS and Zeitlinger B V

Socio-Sexual Knowledge and Attitudes Test (SSKAT)
Joel Wish, Katherine F. McCombs, Barbara Edmonson

Copyright: 1948

Population: Individuals with developmental disabilities; ages 18 to 42

Purpose: Measures sexual knowledge and attitudes of individuals with developmental disabilities of all ages; used for educational and clinical counseling, planning, and placement

Description: Stimulus picture book (227 pages) presents realistic pictures illustrating "yes or no" and point-to response questions relevant to 14 sociosexual topic areas: anatomy terminology, menstruation, dating, marriage, intimacy, intercourse, pregnancy and childbirth, birth control, masturbation, homosexuality, venereal disease, alcohol and drugs, community risks and hazards, and a terminology check. Subjects to be tested must have visual and verbal comprehension; expressive language requirements are minimal. This is a criterion test to determine what the subject knows, believes, and does not know about human sexuality. It does not establish standards. Normative data are based on individuals with developmental disabilities ages 14 to 42, although the test also is used in determining the sexual knowledge and attitudes of persons without retardation of all ages. The manual presents data on reliability and item-total correlations for each subtest.

Format: Examiner required; not suitable for group use; untimed: open ended

Scoring: Examiner evaluated

Cost: Complete kit (record forms, stimulus picture book, manual) $150.00

Publisher: Stoelting Company

Vasectomy Scale: Attitudes
Panos D. Bardis

Copyright: 1988

Population: Adolescents, adults

Purpose: Measures attitudes toward the social and psychological aspects of vasectomy; used for clinical assessment, marriage and family counseling, research on human sexuality, and discussions in family and sex education

Description: Paper–pencil 25-item test in which the subject rates 25 statements concerning vasectomy on a scale from 0 (strongly disagree) to 4 (strongly agree). The score equals the sum of the 25 numerical responses. The theoretical range of scores extends from 0 (lowest approval of vasectomy) to 100 (highest approval). Suitable for use with individuals with physical or hearing disabilities.

Format: Examiner/self-administered; suitable for group use; 10 minutes

Scoring: Examiner evaluated

Cost: Free

Publisher: Panos D. Bardis, Ph.D.

Neuropsychology

300 Series Valpar Dexterity Modules

Copyright: 1995

Population: All ages

Purpose: Used in cognitive assessment and psychomotor functioning to assess motor, manual, and finger coordination; intended for individuals with brain injuries and industrial rehabilitation

Description: Criterion-referenced performance test. The 300 Series Dexterity Modules include five 6-inch square plates (numbered 301–305) that fasten, one at a time, onto a lightweight plastic box (the Basic Unit). Each plate has several unique exercises of short duration which assess various aspects of hand function and upper extremity range of motion. The exercises may be administered to the client either horizontally or at a 45-degree angle of presentation. The exercises focus primarily on tasks which require fine finger and manual dex-

terity and eye-hand coordination. The exercises assess upper-body range of motion, strength, flexibility, ability to follow instructions, memory, and many secondary work-related characteristics. All of the exercises have Methods–Time Measurement (MTM) industrial work rate standards to aid in the interpretation of scores.

Format: Individual administration; examiner required; untimed

Scoring: Examiner evaluated

Cost: Contact publisher

Publisher: Valpar International Corporation

Adult Neuropsychological Questionnaire
Fernando Melendez

Copyright: 1978

Population: Adolescents, adults; ages 16 and older

Purpose: Evaluates conditions that may suggest underlying brain dysfunction or other organic conditions; used as a symptom checklist for making appropriate referrals to other doctors and for further neuropsychological testing

Description: Paper–pencil 59-item questionnaire evaluating complaints, symptoms, and signs that may suggest brain dysfunction. The questionnaire also monitors the course of a person's recovery or decline over a period of time. The examiner asks questions and instructs the subject to elaborate when appropriate.

Format: Examiner required; not suitable for group use; available in Spanish; untimed: 10–15 minutes

Scoring: Examiner evaluated

Cost: Complete kit (50 forms, manual) $32.00

Publisher: Psychological Assessment Resources, Inc.

Barry Rehabilitation Inpatient Screening of Cognition (BRISC)
Phillip Barry

Copyright: 1995

Population: All ages

Purpose: Assesses eight categories of cognitive function for patients with severe brain injuries; provides information on the patient's status and weekly changes, suggests methods of treatment, and predicts what kinds of cognitive problems the patient may experience

Description: Paper–pencil oral-response short-answer verbal test. Scores on the individual subtests may be compared to norms provided for adults and for children in separately normed Grades 2 through 12. The total score provides a reliable index of the relative severity of dysfunction and progress in the early stages of recovery. The subtests are Reading, Design Copy, Verbal Concepts, Orientation, Mental Imagery, Mental Control, Initiation, and Memory. A total score of under 120 points is indicative of impaired function in persons between the ages of 12 and 39. Scores between 110 and 120 should be interpreted cautiously in older adults.

Format: Individual administration; examiner required; untimed

Scoring: Examiner evaluated

Cost: Set (1 manual, pad of 5 BRISCs) $74.95

Publisher: Valpar International Corporation

Bender Visual Motor Gestalt Test
Lauretta Bender

Copyright: Not provided

Population: Ages 3 to adult

Purpose: Assesses visual–motor functions; also used to evaluate perceptual maturity, possible neurological impairment, and emotional adjustment

Description: Test consists of nine figures that are presented, one at a time, to the person being tested, who copies them on a blank piece of paper. Responses are scored according to the development of the concepts of form, shape, pattern, and orientation in space.

Format: Individual or group administration; examiner required; 15–20 minutes.

Scoring: Examiner evaluated

Cost: Comprehensive Bender Gestalt Test Materials (set includes all materials for Adults and Children tests) $400.00; Bender Gestalt Test–Adults $160.00; Bender Gestalt Test–Children $250.00

Publisher: Western Psychological Services

Booklet Category Test (BCT)
Nick A. DeFilippis, Elizabeth McCampbell

Copyright: 1991

Population: Adolescents, adults; ages 15 and older

Purpose: Diagnoses brain dysfunction; used for clinical assessment of brain damage

Description: Test of concept formation and abstract reasoning with 208 items. Figures are presented one at a time to the subject, who responds with a number between 1 and 4. This is the booklet version of the Halstead Category Test. The first four subtests may be used to predict total error scores if time limitations do not allow administration of the entire BCT. Cutoff scores are used.

Format: Examiner required; not suitable for group use; untimed: 30–60 minutes

Scoring: Examiner evaluated

Cost: Complete set (BCT in 2 volumes, manual, 50 scoring forms) $225.00

Publisher: Psychological Assessment Resources, Inc.

California Verbal Learning Test–Adult Version (CVLT®)
Dean C. Delis, Joel H. Kramer,
Edith Kaplan, Beth A. Ober

Copyright: 1987

Population: Adolescents, adults; ages 17 and older

Purpose: Assesses verbal learning and memory deficits and aids in designing and monitoring rehabilitation; used with the elderly and the neurologically impaired

Description: Multitrial verbal-learning task consisting of 16 categorized words used in immediate and delayed free-recall, cued-recall, and recognition trials. A second word list also is presented to obtain interference measures. Indices of learning strategies, error types, primacy/recency effects, and other process data are provided. Optional software provides a scoring and administration system that produces graphic representations of test data and automatically calculates over 25 critical parameters of learning and memory.

Format: Examiner required; not suitable for group use; untimed: 30 minutes, plus a 20-minute delay period

Scoring: Examiner evaluated; may be computer scored

Cost: Set (manual and 25 record forms) $113.00; CVLT Administration and Scoring System $253.00

Publisher: The Psychological Corporation

California Verbal Learning Test–Children's Version (CVLT®–C)
Dean C. Delis, Joel H. Kramer,
Edith Kaplan, Beth A. Ober

Copyright: 1994

Population: Ages 5 through 16 years

Purpose: Measures verbal learning and memory within the context of an everyday memory task

Description: Multitrial verbal-learning task consisting of a 15-word shopping list used in immediate and delayed free-recall, cued-recall, and recognition trials. Aged-based norms available on 27 key indices. Optional software provides a scoring and administration system available in Windows and Macintosh versions.

Format: Examiner required; not suitable for group use; untimed: 15–20 minutes, plus a 20-minute delay period

Scoring: Examiner evaluated; may be computer scored

Cost: Complete kit (manual, 25 record forms, CVLT–C Scoring Assistant disks and user's guide) $295.00

Publisher: The Psychological Corporation

Canter Background Interference Procedure (BIP) for the Bender Gestalt Test
Arthur Canter

Copyright: 1975

Population: Adolescents, adults; ages 15 and older

Purpose: Assesses the probability of organic brain damage among individuals ages 15 and older; used for diagnosis and to plan rehabilitation programs

Description: Ten-item paper–pencil test comparing the subject's results on the standard Bender Gestalt Test (in which the subject is presented with stimulus cards and asked to copy the designs on a blank sheet of paper) with the results of a Bender Gestalt Test in which the subject reproduces the designs on a special sheet with intersecting sinusoidal lines that provide a background "noise" or interference during the copying task. The difference between the standard and the BIP results provides the basis for defining the subject's level of impairment. Specific ranges of adequacy and inadequacy of performance are defined to permit a measure of impairment having a high probability of association with organic brain damage or disease. Scoring is a modification of the standard Pascal-Suttell system.

Format: Examiner required; not suitable for group use; untimed: 20–30 minutes

Scoring: Examiner evaluated

Cost: Kit (25 tests, manual) $70.00

Publisher: Western Psychological Services

Category Test–Computer Version
Nick A. DeFilippis

Copyright: 1993

Population: Adults; ages 15 and above

Purpose: Measures concept formation and abstract thinking; distinguishes between individuals with and without brain damage

Description: Computer-administered version of the Halstead Category test. Examiner must be a qualified neuropsychologist.

Format: Self-administered; untimed

Scoring: Computer scored

Cost: $395.00

Publisher: Psychological Assessment Resources, Inc.

Child Neuropsychological Questionnaire
Fernando Melendez

Copyright: 1978

Population: Children, adolescents; ages 6 to 16

Purpose: Evaluates children suspected of having brain dysfunction; used as part of a comprehensive evaluation that should include a neuropsychological and pediatric neurological examination

Description: Paper–pencil 41-item questionnaire reviewing possible complaints, symptoms, and signs that suggest underlying brain dysfunction. The test encourages the examiner to consider alternative problems and make appropriate referrals for further studies. The questionnaire can be used as a basis for discussion with the child's parents. Available in Spanish.

Format: Examiner required; not suitable for group use; untimed: 10–15 minutes

Scoring: Examiner evaluated

Cost: Complete kit (50 forms, manual) $32.00

Publisher: Psychological Assessment Resources, Inc.

Closed Head Injury Screener (CHIS)
Michael Ivan Friedman

Copyright: 1994

Population: Patients with head injury

Purpose: A systematic interview procedure based on neurobehavioral symptoms; determines a basis for evaluation and rehabilitation; used for clinicians evaluating postconcussion syndrome

Description: Oral-response yes–no test reporting the day-to-day manifestations of cortical functions

Format: Individual administration; examiner required; untimed: 30 minutes

Scoring: Examiner evaluated

Cost: Sampler Set $25.00; permission for up to 200 uses $90.00

Publisher: Mind Garden, Inc.

Cognitive Participation Rating Scale (CPRS)
Rosamond Gianutsos

Copyright: 1987

Population: Adolescents, adults

Purpose: Assesses progress following head injury or CVA

Description: Computer-administered 23-item index of the cognitive status of individuals undergoing rehabilitation for brain injury. The behavioral domains covered are Awareness of Therapy, Planning, Memory (Recent), Orientation, Quality of Participation, and Social/Metacognition. The scale focuses on how well the individual meets the challenges presented in therapy situations. The computer program, which operates on Apple II series 80-column display and IBM PC systems (and compatibles, CGA display), displays items, individual scale points, and normal ranges. For each item and scale, the program also provides definitions, illustrations, and suggestions for unusual situations. Full and subscale scores are compiled, results are displayed and printed, and scores may be saved to disk for analysis.

Format: Examiner required; not suitable for group use; untimed: time varies

Scoring: Computer scored

Cost: $75.00

Publisher: Life Science Associates

CogScreen Aeromedical Edition
Gary G. Kay

Copyright: 1995

Population: Adults; ages 25 to 73

Purpose: Assesses neuropsychological functioning of aviators and pilots seeking medical recertification

Description: Computer-administered point-to test with the following subtests: Overview of Backward Digit Span (BDS), Overview of Math, Overview of Visual Sequence Comparison (VSC), Overview of Symbol Digit Coding (SDC), Overview of Auditory Sequence Comparison (ASC), Overview of Manikan (MAN), Overview of Matching-to-Sample (MTS), Overview of Shifting Attention Test (SAT), Overview of Pathfinder, Overview of Dual Task Test (DTT), and Overview of Dividend Attention Test (DAT). Examiner must be C-level qualified with professional training in neuropsychology.

Format: Self-administered; examiner required; timed and untimed

Scoring: Computer scored

Cost: Software kit (with light pen) $849.00

Publisher: Psychological Assessment Resources, Inc.

Comprehensive Norms for an Expanded Halstead-Reitan Battery
Robert K. Heaton, Igor Grant, Charles G. Matthews

Copyright: 1992

Population: Adults; ages 20 to 80

Purpose: Provides normative data for 54 measures based on age, education, and sex

Description: A comprehensive norms book is used. Computer version available. The authors analyze the influence of demographic variables on raw and corrected scores for all test measures. The distributional properties of the corrected scores are examined, and the performance of the correction system is checked at different age and education levels. Issues related to using corrected scores in clinical interpretation and research applications are addressed. Case studies illustrate using scaled and standard scores in interpretation.

Format: Individual administration

Scoring: Hand key

Cost: $59.00; book with WAIS-R Supplement $69.00

Publisher: Psychological Assessment Resources, Inc.

Continuous Visual Memory Test (CVMT)
Donald E. Trahan, Glenn J. Larrabee

Copyright: 1988

Population: Adults; ages 18 and above

Purpose: Assesses the visual memory of individuals with neurological impairment.

Description: Multiple-item verbally administered oral-response visual memory test in three parts. The Acquisition Task (recognition memory) requires the individual to discriminate between new and old repeated stimuli from among 112 designs presented at 2-second intervals. The Delayed Recognition Task measures retrieval from long-term storage and is administered after a 30-minute delay. The Visual Discrimination Task assesses the individual's ability to perceive and discriminate stimuli, thus distinguishing visual discrimination deficits from visual memory problems.

Format: Examiner required; not suitable for group use; untimed: 45–50 minutes (includes 30–minute delay)

Scoring: Examiner evaluated

Cost: Kit (manual, stimulus cards, 50 scoring forms) $87.00

Publisher: Psychological Assessment Resources, Inc.

Driving Advisement System (DAS)
Rosamond Gianutsos

Copyright: 1988

Population: Adults

Purpose: Assesses an individual's readiness to drive after experiencing head injury or stroke

Description: Five-task computer-administered program assessing the cognitive abilities required to operate a motor vehicle, including choice and execution of components of reaction time, response to complex processing demands, impulse control, ability to sustain performance, flexibility (ability to adjust readily to changed circumstances), eye-hand coordination (tracking), and judgment (based on self-appraisal). Also included is a Report Generation program that displays the individual's scores in comparison to the scores of over 70 safe drivers representing a variety of age groups. The system, which operates on an Apple II series or IBM PC (or compatible, CGA display) computer system, is sold as a package that includes the software, steering and foot pedal modules, a computer interface, and a 1-day application seminar. User qualifications and a description of the professional setting in which the program is to be used must accompany all orders.

Format: Examiner required; not suitable for group use; untimed: 1 hour

Scoring: Computer scored

Cost: Complete system $1,200.00

Publisher: Life Science Associates

Error Detection in Texts (DETECT)
Rosamond Gianutsos, Georgine Vroman, Pauline Matheson

Copyright: 1986

Population: Ages 10 to adult

Purpose: Measures foveal imperception in patients with reading deficiencies and those with head injury or stroke

Description: Paper–pencil test of ability to locate errors in a text. The patient reads 10 typewritten paragraphs and locates errors systematically placed in the left or right half of the page. Some errors are at the beginning of the word, others at the end. The test is available in two forms: A and B. The subject must be able to read simple English words.

Format: Examiner required; not suitable for group use; untimed: 20 to 30 minutes

Scoring: Hand key

Cost: $10.00

Publisher: Life Science Associates

Free Recall (FREEREC)
Rosamond Gianutsos, Carol Klitzner

Copyright: 1981

Population: Ages 10 to adult

Purpose: Measures short- and long-term memory; used to assess head injury or stroke as it affects verbal memory

Description: Computer-administered test measuring short- and long-term retention. Subjects are required to memorize word lists and recall them after either a short delay or an intervening task. Words are commonly used, monosyllabic nouns from the 1944 Thorndike-Lorge list.

Format: Examiner required; not suitable for group use; untimed: 10–12 minutes

Scoring: Computer scored

Cost: $35.00

Publisher: Life Science Associates

Halstead Russell Neuropsychological Evaluation System (HRNES)
Elbert W. Russell, Regina I. Starkey

Copyright: Not provided

Population: All ages

Purpose: Provides a complete neuropsychological evaluation, generating age- and education-corrected scores for a full range of cognitive functions

Description: Uses a scaling system based on 10 index tests. The program takes raw scores from the tests you choose to administer, corrects them for age and education, and converts them to scaled scores. HRNES generates three overall indexes of brain function: Percent Score, Average Index Score, and Lateralization Key.

Format: Computer Scoring System

Scoring: Hand key

Cost: Kit (includes manual, 10 recording booklets, 3.5" or 5.25" unlimited-use HRNES microcomputer disk) $450.00

Publisher: Western Psychological Services

Hooper Visual Organization Test (HVOT)
H. Elston Hooper

Copyright: 1985

Population: Adolescents, adults

Purpose: Assesses organic brain pathology of both hemispheres; used for clinical diagnosis

Description: Thirty-item pictorial test differentiating between functional and motivational disorders. The subject is presented with drawings of simple objects cut into several parts and rearranged and is asked to name the objects.

Format: Examiner required; suitable for group use; untimed: 15 minutes

Scoring: Hand key

Cost: Kit (4 test booklets, 1 manual, 25 test booklets, 100 answer sheets, 1 scoring key) $180.00

Publisher: Western Psychological Services

Human Information Processing Survey (HIP Survey)
E. Paul Torrance, William Taggart, Barbara Taggart-Hausladen

Copyright: 1984

Population: Adults

Purpose: Used in human resource development to assess learning styles and brain hemisphere dominance

Description: Forty-item paper–pencil survey with left-brain, right-brain, or integrated categories. Raw scores, standard scores, and percentiles are yielded. Research and Professional Forms are available. Booklets, profiles, and pencils are used. Examiner must be certified for assessment.

Format: Individual/self-administered; suitable for group use; untimed: 20–30 minutes

Scoring: Self-scored; no scoring service available

Cost: Specimen Set $23.10

Publisher: Scholastic Testing Service, Inc.

International Version of Mental Status Questionnaire
T. L. Brink

Copyright: Not provided

Population: Adults, elders

Purpose: Assesses confusion

Description: This 10-item test is best administered orally. It assesses the confusional state associated with the inability to process new information. Patients suffering from clinically significant delirium and dementia will score poorly, but this test has various types of false positives and is not a measure of organicity. One version is for elders residing in the community and another version is for institutionalized elders. Spanish, Hebrew, and Yiddish translations are available.

Format: Untimed: 1–2 minutes

Scoring: Hand key

Cost: Free, along with annotated bibliography

Publisher: T. L. Brink, Ph.D.

Jump: Eye Movement Exercise
Rosamond Gianutsos, Georgine Vroman, Pauline Matheson

Copyright: 1986

Population: Ages 8 to adult

Purpose: Assesses rapidity of eye movements; used to assess head injury, stroke, or visual system damage

Description: Computer-administered test of visual and oculomotor systems. Symbols flash at the left or right edge of the screen, and the subject judges whether they are the same or different. Rapid lateral saccadic movements are required, both left-to-right and right-to-left. The program finds and adjusts to the patient's ability level.

Format: Self-administered; not suitable for group use; untimed: 8 to 12 minutes

Scoring: Computer scored

Cost: $35.00

Publisher: Life Science Associates

Kahn Test of Symbol Arrangement (KTSA)
Theodore C. Kahn

Copyright: 1957

Population: All ages

Purpose: Assesses personality dynamics and the extent of cerebral competence; used for individual diagnosis and therapy as well as vocational counseling

Description: Multiple-task performance test of a subject's cultural/symbolic thinking. The subject is required to sort plastic objects of varying size, color, thickness, and translucence in several ways. The examiner evaluates the subject's symbol pattern and compares it to patterns of normal and clinical groups. For use only by clinical psychologists, psychiatrists, counseling psychologists, school psychologists, and others with professional competence in clinical assessment.

Format: Examiner required; not suitable for group use; untimed: 15 minutes

Scoring: Hand key; examiner evaluated

Cost: Complete kit (plastic objects, felt strip, 10 individual record sheets, manual, clinical manual) $50.00

Publisher: Psychological Test Specialists

Kaufman Short Neuropsychological Assessment Procedure (K-SNAP)
Alan S. Kaufman, Nadeen L. Kaufman

Copyright: 1994

Population: Ages 11 to 85 and over

Purpose: Can be used as a short cognitive evaluation or as part of a comprehensive neuropsychological or intellectual assessment in such places as clinics, hospitals, schools, private practices, and nursing facilities

Description: Individual assessment of an adolescent's or adult's cognitive functioning at three levels of complexity. Each kit includes a manual, an easel, and 25 record booklets.

Format: Individual administration; 20–30 minutes; must be interpreted by a professional with knowledge of psychometrics and individual assessment

Scoring: Examiner administration and interpretation, standard scores

Cost: Kit $145.00; with nylon carrying case $170.00

Publisher: American Guidance Service

Learning and Memory Battery (LAMB)
James P. Schmidt, Tom N. Tombaugh

Copyright: 1995

Population: Adults

Purpose: Assesses learning and memory abilities; used for neurological assessment

Description: Paper–pencil oral response test with seven subtests. The subtests are Paragraph Learning, Word List, Word Pairs, Digit Span, Supraspan, Simple Figure, and Complex Figure. All subtests contribute to an overall assessment of learning and memory abilities. All components of memory are considered, including storage and retrieval. Scores are yielded for each of the subtests. These scores are plotted on a profile sheet for easy comparison to norms. A computer version using IBM PC and Windows is available.

Format: Individual administration; examiner required; untimed: 1 hour

Scoring: Hand key; computer scored

Cost: Paper–pencil kit $295.00, computer scoring program $295.00

Publisher: Multi-Health Systems

Line Bisection (BISECT)
Rosamond Gianutsos, Georgine Vroman, Pauline Matheson

Copyright: 1986

Population: Ages 8 to adult

Purpose: Measures visual hemi-imperception; used to assess head injury, stroke, or visual system damage

Description: Computer-administered test measuring the presence of an intact visual system. The computer presents horizontal or vertical lines that have a visible gap somewhere near the center. The subject attempts to center the gap using the arrow keys.

Format: Examiner required; not suitable for group use; untimed: 6–8 minutes

Scoring: Computer scored

Cost: $35.00

Publisher: Life Science Associates

Luria-Nebraska Neuropsychological Battery (LNNB)
Charles J. Golden, Arnold D. Purisch, Thomas A Hammeke

Copyright: 1984

Population: Adolescents, adults; ages 15 and older

Purpose: Assesses a broad range of neuropsychological functions for individuals ages 15 and older; used to diagnose specific cerebral dysfunction and to select and assess rehabilitation programs

Description: Multiple-item verbal, observational test available in two forms: Form I (269 items) and Form II (279 items). The discrete, scored items produce a profile for the following scales: Motor, Rhythm, Tactile, Visual, Receptive Speech, Expressive Speech, Writing, Reading, Arithmetic, Memory, Intellectual, Pathognomonic, Left Hemisphere, Right Hemisphere, Impairment, and Profile Evaluation. Form II also assesses intermediate memory. The battery diagnoses the presence of cerebral dysfunction and determines lateralization and localization. Test materials include six stimulus cards, an audiotape, comb, quarter, and stopwatch. A manual provides instructions for administering the test, evidence of reliability and validity, interpretive guides, and copies of the Administration and Scoring Booklet and the Patient Response Booklet. The Administration and Scoring Booklet includes the Profile Form and Computation of Critical Level Tables. It is used to record all scores during administration.

Format: Examiner required; not suitable for group use; untimed: 1½ to 2½ hours

Scoring: Hand key; may be computer scored

Cost: Complete kit Form I (1 set of test materials, 10 administration and scoring booklets, 10 patient response booklets, 1 manual, 2 WPS Test Report answer sheets); $450.00; Complete kit Form II $425.00

Publisher: Western Psychological Services

Luria-Nebraska Neuropsychological Battery–Children's Revision (LNNB–C)
Charles J. Golden

Copyright: 1987

Population: Children; ages 8 to 12

Purpose: Measures cognitive strengths and weaknesses; used to diagnose cerebral dysfunction and to select and assess rehabilitation programs

Description: Verbal, observational 149-item adaptation of the Luria-Nebraska Neuropsychological Battery assessing cognitive functioning. The clinical scales are Motor Functions, Tactile Functions, Receptive Speech, Writing, Arithmetic, Intellectual Processes, Rhythm, Visual Functions, Expressive Speech, Reading, and Memory. The summary scales are Pathognomonic, Left Sensorimotor, and Right Sensorimotor. Two optional scales, Spelling and Motor Writing, are available. Microcomputer software for use with IBM PC or Apple II computers is available for computer scoring and interpretation.

Format: Examiner required; not suitable for group use; untimed: 2 hours 30 minutes

Scoring: Hand key

Cost: Kit (1 set of test materials, 10 administration and scoring booklets, children's revision, 10 patient response booklets, children's revision, 1 manual, children's revision, 2 WPS Test Report answer sheets, carrying case) $400.00

Publisher: Western Psychological Services

Memory Assessment Scales (MAS)
J. Michael Williams

Copyright: 1991

Population: Ages 18 to 90

Purpose: Used in clinical rehabilitation and neuropsychology to assess memory functioning

Description: Contains the following subtests: List Learning, Prose Memory, List Recall, Verbal Span, Visual Span, Visual Recognition, Visual Reproduction, Names–Faces, Delayed List Recall, Delayed Prose Memory, Delayed Visual Recognition, Delayed Names–Faces Recall. Materials used include a manual, stimulus card set, 25 record forms, and attaché case. Examiner must be Level C qualified.

Format: Individual administration; examiner required; untimed: 40–45 minutes

Scoring: Record form scored without a key

Cost: Intro Kit $171.00

Publisher: Psychological Assessment Resources, Inc.

Memory Span (SPAN)
Rosamond Gianutsos, Carol Klitzner

Copyright: 1981

Population: Ages 10 to adult

Purpose: Measures concentration and short-term memory; may also be used as a retraining exercise with patients with head injury or stroke

Description: Computer-administered test providing assessment and remediation of memory deficits. A list of words appears on the screen one at a time. After the entire list has appeared, the patient tries to recall a certain number of words from the end of the list. On the first five trials, the patient is asked to recall the last two words; the number to be recalled increases by

one for each set of five lists up to a maximum of seven. The patient must be able to read simple English words.

Format: Examiner required; not suitable for group use; untimed: 8–12 minutes

Scoring: Computer scored

Cost: $35.00

Publisher: Life Science Associates

Memory-for-Designs Test (MFD)
Frances K. Graham, Barbara S. Kendall

Copyright: 1960

Population: Ages 8 years 6 months to 60 years

Purpose: Assesses perceptual-motor coordination; used to differentiate between functional behavior disorders and those associated with brain injury

Description: Fifteen-item performance measure of perceptual-motor coordination. Items consist of designs on cardboard cards. The subject is shown a design for 5 seconds and then attempts to draw it from memory. This procedure is repeated for the 15 items. Diagnostic testing and evaluation should be closely supervised by a clinical or school psychologist, psychiatrist, neurologist, or pediatrician.

Format: Examiner required; not suitable for group use; 10 minutes

Scoring: Hand key; examiner evaluated

Cost: Complete kit $17.00

Publisher: Psychological Test Specialists

Mini Inventory of Right Brain Injury (MIRBI)
Patricia A. Pimental, Nancy A. Kingsbury

Copyright: 1989

Population: Adults; ages 18 and older

Purpose: Identifies severity of right brain injury; used by psychologists, speech pathologists, neurologists, psychiatrists, occupational therapists, physical therapists, nurses, and other health care professionals

Description: Multiple-item screening test of right brain injury. Items require visual scanning, finger gnosis, stereognosis, 2-point discrimination, unilateral neglect, reading, writing, attention, visuosymbolic processing and calculating, praxis, visuomotor skills, affective language, understanding of humor, explanations of figurative language, explanations of similarities, general expressive language ability, emotion and affect processing, general behavior, and psychic integrity. The test provides a severity index and a deficit profile based on underlying process disorders. Cutoff scores are provided for individuals with and without brain injury. Results are printed as percentiles in the various deficit areas. A narrative triplicate report form that can be used to answer consultations is generated.

Format: Examiner required; not suitable for group use; untimed: typical time not available

Scoring: Examiner evaluated

Cost: Complete kit (examiner's manual, test booklets, report forms, storage box) $94.00

Publisher: PRO-ED, Inc.

Neuropsychological Status Examination (NSE)

Copyright: 1983

Population: Adults

Purpose: Evaluates and collects data pertaining to an individual's neuropsychological functioning; used for a variety of neuropsychological assessments ranging from screening procedures to extensive workups and preparation for expert-witness testimony

Description: Ten-page multiple-item paper–pencil assessment evaluating neuropsychological information, such as patient data, observational findings, test administration parameters, neuroanatomical correlates, reports of test findings, clinical impressions, and recommendations for treatment. The instrument consists of 13 sections, including patient and referral data; neuropsychological symptom checklist (NSC); premorbid status; physical, emotional, and cognitive status; results of neuropsychological testing; and diagnostic comments and follow-up and treatment recommendations. The NSC is a two-page screening instrument used to assess the status of potential neurological/neuropsy-

chological signs and symptoms. Each section was designed with consideration of base rate data for common findings in neuropsychological evaluations. The manual includes a discussion of the rationale of the logic underlying the structure of the instrument and provides suggestions for its most efficient use.

Format: Examiner required; not suitable for group use; untimed: time varies

Scoring: Examiner evaluated

Cost: Examination kit (manual, 25 NSE and NSC forms) $32.00

Publisher: Psychological Assessment Resources, Inc.

NeuroPsychology Behavior and Affect Profile (NBAP)
Linda Nelson, Paul Satz, Louis F. D'Elia

Copyright: 1994

Population: Adults, individuals with brain impairment

Purpose: Assesses affective change used for clinical evaluation; intended for stroke patients, outpatients with dementia, and survivors of closed head injury

Description: Agree/disagree 106-item test measuring reliability and validity data for indifference, inappropriateness, pragnosia, depression, and mania

Format: Self-administered; untimed

Scoring: Examiner evaluated

Cost: Sampler set $25.00; permission for 200 uses $90.00

Publisher: Mind Garden, Inc.

Number Series Problems (NSERIES)
Linda Laatsch

Copyright: 1986

Population: Ages 10 to adult

Purpose: Measures simple problem-solving ability; used to assess head injury, stroke, or visual system damage

Description: Computer-administered test of problem-solving ability in which the subject solves addition (10, 12, 14, ?), subtraction (75, 70, 65, ?), and pattern (9, 8, 8, 9, ?) series. Two levels of difficulty are provided. The user receives feedback and can choose to receive a prompt. Scoring is separate for each type of series.

Format: Examiner required; not suitable for group use; untimed: 5–12 minutes

Scoring: Computer scored

Cost: $35.00

Publisher: Life Science Associates

Oars Multidimensional Functional Assessment Questionnaire

Copyright: 1988

Population: Adults

Purpose: Assesses the functional status of adults, particularly the elderly; suitable for use with individuals with visual, physical, mental, and hearing disabilities

Description: Criterion-referenced 101-item paper–pencil and oral-response test assessing five areas of functioning: social (13 items), economic (20 items), mental health (15 items), physical health (22 items), and ADL (14 items). The test also contains a 24-item services section, demographic information, and interviewer sections. The test yields both subscore ratings and summary ratings on 6-point scales for social, economic, mental health, physical health, and ADL. A videocassette is available for training purposes. Norms for the elderly (age 60+) are provided. Available also in Spanish, Portuguese, French, and Italian. Suitable for individuals with physical, hearing, and visual disabilities.

Format: Examiner/self-administered; not suitable for group use

Scoring: Examiner evaluated; may be computer scored

Cost: $29.95

Publisher: Lawrence Erlbaum Associates, Inc.

Paired Word Memory Task (PAIRMEM)
Rosamond Gianutsos

Copyright: 1984

Population: Ages 8 to adult

Purpose: Assesses immediate memory in patients with head injury and stroke

Description: Computer-administered test of verbal memory. The computer displays a random list of words one by one. The subject then types the list in order. Both number of words in the list and duration of exposure are adjustable. The subject must have some visual function, the ability to read simple English words, rudimentary keyboarding skills, and the ability to follow simple instructions.

Format: Self-administered/extensive user data recording capability; not suitable for group use; untimed: 8–12 minutes

Scoring: Computer scored

Cost: $50.00

Publisher: Life Science Associates

Pediatric Early Elementary Examination (PEEX2)
Melvin D. Levine

Copyright: 1995

Population: Children; ages 6 to 9

Purpose: Assesses neurological development, behaviors, and health of children; used by clinicians in health care and other settings for educational planning, counseling, use of medication, and general programming

Description: Multiple-item response test providing standardized observation procedures for characterizing children's functional health and its relationship to neurodevelopmental and physical status. The test enables clinicians to integrate medical, developmental, and neurological findings while making observations of behavioral adjustment and style.

Format: Examiner required; not suitable for group use; untimed: 45–60 minutes

Scoring: Examiner evaluated

Cost: Record Forms and Response Booklets $40.90; Stimulus Booklet $12.00; Examiner's Manual $10.25; Complete Set $62.00; Specimen Set (record form, manual) $9.70; Training Video $30.00

Publisher: Educators Publishing Service, Inc.

Pediatric Examination of Educational Readiness at Middle Childhood (PEERAMID2)
Melvin D. Levine

Copyright: 1995

Population: Children, adolescents; ages 9 to 15

Purpose: Assesses children's and adolescents' neurological development, behaviors, and health; used by clinicians in health care and other settings

Description: Multiple-item response test providing standardized observation procedures for characterizing children's and adolescents' functional health and its relationship to neurodevelopmental and physical status. The test assesses wide range of functions, including neuromaturation, attention, many aspects of memory, motor efficiency, language, and other areas critical to the academic and social adjustment of older children. It is particularly sensitive to the often subtle developmental dysfunction of junior high school students.

Format: Examiner required; not suitable for group use; untimed: 45–60 minutes

Scoring: Examiner evaluated

Cost: Record Forms and Response Booklets $47.75; Stimulus Booklet $12.00; Examiner's Manual $10.25; Complete Set $72.90; Specimen Set (manual, form) $10.85; Training Video $30.00

Publisher: Educators Publishing Service, Inc.

Pediatric Extended Examination at Three (PEET)
Melvin D. Levine

Copyright: 1986

Population: Children; ages 3 to 4

Purpose: Enables clinicians to integrate medical, developmental, and neurological findings and make observations of behavioral adjustment and style and assists them in identifying specific interventions; used for diagnosis, screening, research, and training

Description: Verbal paper–pencil, show–tell performance measure of five developmental areas: gross motor, language, visual–fine motor, memory, and intersensory integration. The child is asked to perform gross motor tasks (jumping, throwing and kicking a small ball), identify pictures, name objects and directions, and copy figures with a pencil; tasks are presented using numerous miscellaneous items (sticks, crayon, doll) contained in kit; words and sentences are provided for language assessment. The examination produces an empirically derived profile of the child in the developmental areas, based on her or his performance of age-appropriate tasks, which can be used to clarify concerns, determine need for further evaluation in specific areas, and initiate services or continued surveillance.

Format: Examiner administered; not suitable for group use; untimed: about 1 hour

Scoring: Examiner evaluated

Cost: Record Forms $18.20; Examiner's Manual $9.15; Stimulus Book $12.00; Kit $31.85; Complete Set $71.00; Specimen Set (manual, record form) $9.70

Publisher: Educators Publishing Service, Inc.

Philadelphia Head Injury Questionnaire
Lucille M. Curry, Richard G. Ivins, Thomas L. Gowen

Copyright: Not provided

Population: All ages

Purpose: Used as a history-gathering instrument specifically for individuals who have sustained head injuries

Description: The questionnaire is composed of six sections: identifying information, accident description, persistent symptoms, cognitive aspects, personality changes, pertinent personal/medical history. Each section includes 8

to 16 questions; virtually all questions can be answered with a yes or no response. Questionnaire provides organized information about head trauma.

Format: Examiner not required, but recommended; not suitable for group use; 20 minutes

Scoring: Hand key

Cost: Pad of 100, with a brief manual $22.50

Publisher: Western Psychological Services

Pin Test
Paul Satz, Lou D'Elia

Copyright: 1989

Population: Adolescents, adults; ages 16 to 69

Purpose: Assesses manual dexterity; used in neuropsychological evaluation

Description: A four-trial (30 seconds each) test measuring manual dexterity. The examinee is required to push a pin through a pattern of circles. Scores yield percentiles and standard scores for total hits for each hand. Advantage Index provided. Materials include Pin Test Manual, record forms, trial sheets, and test components. Examiner must meet APA B-level guidelines.

Format: Examiner required; not suitable for group use; timed: 2 minutes

Scoring: Hand scored without key

Cost: Kit (test, manual, 50 recording forms, 200 trial sheets, 5 resistance cardboard pieces, 10 pins) $88.00

Publisher: Psychological Assessment Resources, Inc.

Portable Tactual Performance Test (P-TPT)

Copyright: 1984

Population: Children, adolescents; ages 5 to adult

Purpose: Measures spatial perception in children and adults

Description: Multiple-task examination measuring spatial perception, discrimination of forms, manual or construction ability, motor coordination, and the ability to meet new situations. This portable version features a wooden

carrying case, which can be set up for standardized administration.

Format: Examiner required; not suitable for group use; untimed: not available

Scoring: Examiner evaluated

Cost: Kit (manual, 50 record forms) $315.00

Publisher: Psychological Assessment Resources, Inc.

Quick Neurological Screening Test (QNST)
Harold M. Sterling, Margaret Mutti, Norma V. Spalding

Copyright: 1978

Population: Ages 5 to 18

Purpose: Assesses neurological integration as it relates to the learning abilities of children and teenagers

Description: Multiple-task nonverbal test of 15 functions, each involving a motor task similar to those observed in neurological pediatric examinations. The areas measured include maturity of motor development, skill in controlling large and small muscles, motor planning and sequencing, sense of rate and rhythm, spatial organization, visual and auditory perceptual skills, balance and cerebellarvestibular function, and disorders of attention. Materials include geometric form reproduction sheets and flipcards printed with directions for administration and scoring. Scoring occurs simultaneously, and neurodevelopmental difficulties result in an increasingly larger numerical score.

Format: Individual administration; 20 minutes

Scoring: Examiner evaluated

Cost: Test kit (manual, 25 scoring forms, 25 geometric form reproduction sheets, 25 remedial guideline forms, flipcards, in vinyl folder) $70.00

Publisher: Academic Therapy Publications

Randt Memory Test
C. T. Randt, E. R. Brown

Copyright: 1983

Population: Adults; ages 20 to 80

Purpose: Measures memory processes in individuals with neurological impairment, including the elderly.

Description: Computer-administered test of memory changes in areas including process of association, primary memory deficits, recall vs. recognition memory, and transfer to and retrieval from secondary store memory. Test materials include picture recognition cards documentation; a program for test administration control; response recording; and computation of scaled scores, standard scores, and summary of test scores. Norms are included for age decades from 20 to 80.

Format: Examiner/self-administered; not suitable for group use; untimed: time varies

Scoring: Hand key; may be computer scored

Cost: Test, manual scoring $85.00; Apple computer scoring pogram $40.00

Publisher: Life Science Associates

Reaction Time Measure of Visual Field (REACT)
Rosamond Gianutsos, Carol Klitzner

Copyright: 1981

Population: Ages 8 to adult

Purpose: Diagnoses and trains visual field deficits and blind spots; used to assess head injury, stroke, or visual system damage

Description: Computer-administered test detecting slowed response to visual stimuli. The patient presses any key on the keyboard to stop the "runaway numbers" on the screen. The numbers are presented in different locations in the visual field while the subject fixates on a point. Possible modifications include a hand-held or other specially arranged switch for responding.

Format: Examiner required; not suitable for group use; timed: 8 minutes

Scoring: Computer scored

Cost: $35.00

Publisher: Life Science Associates

Ross Information Processing Assessment—Second Edition (RIPA–2)
Deborah G. Ross-Swain

Copyright: 1996

Population: Ages 15 to 90

Purpose: Enables the examiner to quantify cognitive–linguistic deficits, determine severity levels for each skill area, and develop rehabilitation goals and objectives

Description: The RIPA–2 provides quantifiable data for profiling 10 key areas basic to communicative and cognitive functioning: Intermediate Memory, Recent Memory, Temporal Orientation (Recent Memory), Temporal Orientation (Remote Memory), Spatial Orientation, Orientation to Environment, Recall of General Information, Problem Solving and Abstract Reasoning, Organization, and Auditory Processing and Retention. The study sample included 126 individuals with traumatic brain injury in 17 states. The sample was representative of TBI demographics for gender, ethnicity, and socioeconomic status. Internal consistency reliability was investigated, and the mean reliability coefficient for RIPA–2 subtests was .85, with a range of .67 to .91. This indicates that test error was minimal and that the RIPA–2 can be used with confidence. Content, construct, and criterion-related validity also were thoroughly studied.

Format: Individual administration; untimed: 45–60 minutes

Scoring: Hand key

Cost: Complete kit (examiner's manual, record forms, profile/summary forms, storage box) $96.00

Publisher: PRO-ED, Inc.

Screening Test for the Luria-Nebraska Neuropsychological Battery: Adult and Children's Forms
Charles J. Golden

Copyright: 1987

Population: Ages 8 to adult

Purpose: Assesses cognitive functioning; used to identify individuals who will show a significant degree of impairment when administered the complete battery; also used for neuropsychological screening in schools and alcohol abuse programs

Description: Fifteen-item screening test predicting overall performance on the Luria-Nebraska Neuropsychological Battery. Testing is discontinued when the client reaches the critical score. Materials include an administration and scoring booklet, spiral-bound stimulus cards, and easel. Forms are available for children ages 8 to 12 and adults ages 13 and older.

Format: Examiner required; suitable for schools and drug abuse programs; untimed: 20 minutes or less

Scoring: Examiner evaluated

Cost: Kit (1 set of stimulus cards, 25 administration and scoring booklets, 1 manual) $130.00

Publisher: Western Psychological Services

Search for the Odd Shape (SOSH)
Rosamond Gianutsos, Georgine Vroman

Copyright: 1986

Population: Ages 6 to adult

Purpose: Assesses foveal imperception and differentiates scanning skill from shape examination and matching hemi-imperception; used to assess head injury, stroke, or visual system damage

Description: Computer-administered nonverbal shape comparison task. The subject scans an array of identical patterns for the "odd" one.

Format: Examiner required; not suitable for group use; untimed: 8 to 10 minutes

Scoring: Computer scored

Cost: $35.00

Publisher: Life Science Associates

Search-a-Word (SAW)
Rosamond Gianutsos, Carol Klitzner

Copyright: 1981

Population: Ages 6 to adult

Purpose: Diagnoses hemi-imperception and visual attentional deficits; used to assess head injury, stroke, or visual system damage

Description: Thirty-task paper–pencil test of intact visual systems and central visual process-ing. The subject scans a 13″×13″ character array and stops when a target three-character word is found. Materials include the SAW test booklet, stopwatch, and a pencil. The subject must be able to read simple English words.

Format: Examiner required; not suitable for group use; untimed: 8–20 seconds per task

Scoring: Hand key

Cost: $10.00

Publisher: Life Science Associates

Searching for Shapes (SEARCH)
Rosamond Gianutsos, Carol Klitzner

Copyright: 1981

Population: Ages 8 to adult

Purpose: Detects and treats differences in attention and responsiveness on the two sides of the visual field; used to assess head injury, stroke, or visual system damage

Description: Computer-administered test of visual systems and central visual processing. The subject looks at a shape in the center of the screen and searches for a match elsewhere on the screen as quickly as possible. Examiner then indicates whether or not the response is correct. The computer stores the search times for correct responses and the number of incorrect responses for later display.

Format: Examiner required; not suitable for group use; untimed: 10 minutes

Scoring: Computer scored

Cost: $35.00

Publisher: Life Science Associates

Seguin-Goddard Formboards (Tactual Performance Test)

Copyright: Not provided

Population: Children, adolescents; ages 5 to 14

Purpose: Measures spatial perception in children; used in a variety of neuropsychological applications

Description: Multiple-task examination of spatial perception, discrimination of forms, manual or construction ability, motor coordination, and the ability to meet new situations.

The test materials consist of 10 sturdy blocks cut in the geometric forms of semicircle, triangle, cross, elongated hexagon, oblong, circle, square, flatted oval, star, and lozenge, and a base with corresponding shapes cut into it. The child must place the blocks in the appropriate spaces on the formboard base. Two types of bases are available: one with raised geometric figures and one with flush geometric figures.

Format: Examiner required; not suitable for group use; untimed: typical time not available

Scoring: Examiner evaluated

Cost: Raised formboard (used in Halstead-Reitan Battery) $340.00; flush formboard (used in Merrill-Palmer Scale) $185.00

Publisher: Stoelting Company

Self-Administered Free Recall (FRSELF)
Rosamond Gianutsos

Copyright: 1989

Population: Ages 10 to adult

Purpose: Measures short- and long-term verbal memory in individuals with head injury and stroke

Description: Computer-administered test of verbal memory in which the subject memorizes word lists and recalls them after either a short delay or an intervening task. This test is similar to FREEREC but is designed to be self-administered. The subject must be able to read simple English words.

Format: Self-administered; extensive user data recording capability; not suitable for group use; untimed: 8–12 minutes

Scoring: Computer scored

Cost: $50.00

Publisher: Life Science Associates

Sequence Recall (SEQREC)
Rosamond Gianutsos, Carol Klitzner

Copyright: 1981

Population: Ages 10 to adult

Purpose: Assesses wide-range, nonverbal memory; used to diagnose severe memory deficits

Description: Computer-administered test of nonverbal memory. Shapes, short words, or pictures are presented one at a time and are followed by a "menu" of items that may or may not have appeared. The subject is asked to indicate which ones appeared. Because it does not require reading aloud, this program can be used for diagnosis and treatment with patients unable to process verbal material, including non-English speakers, aphasics, and others. It can be set to a wide range of difficulty.

Format: Examiner required; not suitable for group use; untimed: 10–15 minutes

Scoring: Computer scored

Cost: $35.00

Publisher: Life Science Associates

Shape Matching (MATCH)
Rosamond Gianutsos, Georgine Vroman, Pauline Matheson

Copyright: 1986

Population: Ages 6 to adult

Purpose: Assesses foveal imperception associated with head injury, stroke, or visual system damage

Description: Computer-administered nonverbal shape comparison task. Two detailed shapes are displayed one above the other. The subject has to decide whether they are the same or different in some small but distinct way.

Format: Examiner required; not suitable for group use; untimed: 8–10 minutes

Scoring: Computer scored

Cost: $35.00

Publisher: Life Science Associates

Short Category Test, Booklet Format
Linda C. Wetzel, Thomas J. Boll

Copyright: 1987

Population: Adolescents, adults; ages 15 and older

Purpose: Assesses brain dysfunction; used for clinical diagnosis of brain damage

Description: Multiple-item paper–pencil test

assessing adaptability, abstract concept formation, capacity to learn from experience, and cognitive flexibility. This booklet format reduces the length and complexity of the Category Test of the Halstead-Reitan Neuropsychological Battery by using only half the items of the original and eliminating the equipment necessary for administering it. The test may be administered at bedside.

Format: Examiner required; not suitable for group use; untimed: 15–30 minutes

Scoring: Examiner evaluated

Cost: Kit (1 set of stimulus cards, 100 answer sheets, 1 manual) $175.00

Publisher: Western Psychological Services

Single and Double Simultaneous Stimulation (SDSS)
Rosamond Gianutsos, Georgine Vroman, Pauline Matheson

Copyright: 1986

Population: Ages 6 to adult

Purpose: Assesses imperception due to unilateral visual field loss; used to assess head injury, stroke, or visual system damage

Description: Computer-administered test for intact visual systems and central visual processing. The subject indicates whether symbols appear on the left, right, both, or neither side of the screen.

Format: Examiner required; not suitable for group use; untimed: 8–10 minutes

Scoring: Computer scored

Cost: $35.00

Publisher: Life Science Associates

Software for the Individual Emerging from Coma into Consciousness
Rosamond Gianutsos

Copyright: 1988

Population: All ages

Purpose: Assists in evaluating and treating the cognitive aspects of response capability in patients emerging from comas

Description: Ten computer-administered programs assessing the responsivity of the emerging coma patient. The therapist is guided by a hierarchy of "milestones" that begin with a single discrete response to multiswitch response differentiation. Using an input interface, responses can be recorded from any switches (microswitches, pedals, finger-extension, etc.). The programs, which operate on Apple II series and IBM PC computers (or compatible CGA display), use sound and bold displays when possible and can be customized by user. Scores are automatically stored on computer for analysis of performance across sessions.

Format: Examiner required (special training with programs required); not suitable for group use; untimed: time varies

Scoring: Computer scored

Cost: Program (specify computer model) $200.00; input interface $109.00; pedal switch $19.95; finger extension switch $29.95

Publisher: Life Science Associates

Speeded Reading of Word Lists (SRWL)
Rosamond Gianutsos, Carol Klitzner

Copyright: 1981

Population: Ages 8 to adult

Purpose: Diagnoses and trains visual scanning; used to assess head injury, stroke, or visual system damage

Description: Computer-administered test of four basic functions of visual information processing: anchoring at the margin, scanning horizontally, identification of words within the perceptual span, and monitoring the periphery. Words are presented by the computer in different positions on the screen. The user can vary word displacement from the center and display time. Once an individual's problems have been diagnosed, SRWL can be used for rehabilitation.

Format: Examiner required; not suitable for group use; untimed: 10–15 minutes

Scoring: Computer scored

Cost: $35.00

Publisher: Life Science Associates

Stimulus Recognition Test

T. L. Brink, James Bryant,
Mary Lou Catalono, Connie Janaker,
Charmaine Oliveira

Copyright: Not provided

Population: Adults, elders

Purpose: Assesses confusion

Description: This 10-item test is administered orally. It assesses the confusional state associated with the inability to process new information. Patients suffering from clinically significant delirium and dementia will score poorly, but this test has various types of false positives and is not a measure of organicity. The test uses seven audio and visual trials (on large cards) and three audio-only trials for assessing very short-term memory in a recognition format.

Format: Untimed: 2–5 minutes

Scoring: Hand key

Cost: Free, along with annotated bibliography

Publisher: T. L. Brink, Ph.D.

Stroop Neuropsychological Screening Test (SNST)

Max. R. Trenerry

Copyright: 1989

Population: Adults; ages 18 to 79

Purpose: Screens neuropsychological functioning

Description: A two-part (Color Task, Color Word Task) oral-response short-answer test measuring neuropsychological functioning. Scores yield percentile and probability values for Color Score and Color-Word Score. Materials include Form C Stimulus Sheets, Form C-W Stimulus Sheets, record form, and manual. Examiner must meet APA C-Level guidelines.

Format: Examiner required; not suitable for group use; timed: 4 minutes

Scoring: Hand scored

Cost: Kit (manual, 25 Form C stimulus sheets, 25 Form C-W stimulus sheets, 25 record forms) $55.00

Publisher: Psychological Assessment Resources, Inc.

Symbol Digit Modalities Test (SDMT)

Aaron Smith

Copyright: 1982

Population: Ages 8 to 75

Purpose: Measures brain damage; used to screen and predict learning disorders and to identify children with potential reading problems

Description: Multiple-item test in which the subject is given 90 seconds to convert as many meaningless geometric designs as possible into their appropriate numbers according to the key provided. When group administered, the test may be used as a screening device. The test may be administered orally to individuals who cannot take written tests. Since numbers are nearly universal, the test is virtually culture-free.

Format: Examiner required; suitable for group use; timed: 90 seconds

Scoring: Hand key

Cost: Complete kit (25 WPS AutoScore™ test forms, 1 manual) $60.00

Publisher: Western Psychological Services

Tachistoscopic Reading (FASTREAD)

Rosamond Gianutsos

Copyright: 1989

Population: Ages 10 to adult

Purpose: Assesses areas of attention deficits, foveal imperception, and difficulty in planning and articulating words; used with head injury and stroke victims

Description: Computer-administered reading test in which the computer flashes a word and the subject types what he or she saw. The task speed adjusts to the subject's performance. The program may be used for retraining and has diagnostic capabilities.

Format: Self-administered; extensive user data recording capability; not suitable for group use; untimed: 8–12 minutes

Scoring: Computer scored

Cost: $50.00

Publisher: Life Science Associates

Test of Memory and Learning (TOMAL)
Cecil R. Reynolds, Erin D. Bigler

Copyright: 1994

Population: Children, adolescents; ages 5 through 19

Purpose: Evaluates children and adolescents referred for learning disabilities, traumatic brain injury, neurological diseases, serious emotional disturbance, and attention-deficit/hyperactivity disorder.

Description: The TOMAL includes 10 regular subtests and 4 supplementary subtests that evaluate general and specific memory functions; features composite memory scores for Verbal Memory, Nonverbal Memory, Delayed Recall, and a Composite Memory Index; has supplementary composite scores that include a Learning Index, Attention and Concentration Index, Sequential Memory Index, Free Recall Index, and an Associate Recall Index; and includes highly interpretable and relevant scores, scaled to a familiar metric. TOMAL scores include standardized or scaled scores and percentiles. Subtest scaled scores appear in a familiar metric with a mean of 10 and a standard deviation of 3. Composite scores and indexes are also scaled to a familiar metric for ease of use and comparability with other tests.

Format: Individual administration; timed: less than 45 minutes

Scoring: Examiner evaluated

Cost: Complete kit (examiner's manual, picture book, record forms and administration booklets, supplementary analysis forms, facial memory picture book, facial memory chips, visual selective reminding test board, delayed recall cue cards) $189.00

Publisher: PRO-ED, Inc.

Test of Perceptual Organization (TPO)
William T. Martin

Copyright: 1970

Population: Adults

Purpose: Measures abstract reasoning abilities, psychomotor functioning, and the ability to follow specific, exacting instructions in an accurate manner; identifies persons with emotional disturbance or perceptual–motor disabilities

Description: Ten-item paper–pencil test consisting of abstract reasoning and visual–motor tasks. Test items consist of written statements (instructions for plotting points on a map) presented in order of increasing difficulty. The subjects read the instructions and mark an X at each of the 10 coordinate points on a street map containing 54 1″ square blocks confined within a 6″×9″ area. Objective scoring discriminates between persons with emotional disturbance and/or perceptual motor disabilities and those with one or few of these problems. Subjective analysis of the test protocol identifies persons with emotional disturbances or intellect–abstraction problems. Clinical analysis must be done in terms of personality dynamics and visual–motor theory. A fourth-grade reading level is required.

Format: Examiner required; suitable for group use; timed: 10 minutes

Scoring: Hand key; examiner evaluated

Cost: Examiner's Set $40.00; 25 test forms $15.00; keys $2.75; 25 profile sheets $8.25; manual $6.75

Publisher: Psychologists and Educators, Inc.

Triplet Recall (TRIPREC)
Rosamond Gianutsos, Carol Klitzner

Copyright: 1981

Population: Ages 10 to adult

Purpose: Measures short- and long-term memory; used to assess head injury or stroke as it affects verbal memory

Description: Computer-administered test measuring short- and long-term retention. The task is easier than that in Free Recall and can be used for practice and remediation with patients for whom Free Recall is too difficult. Three words are presented one at a time and followed by 0, 3, or 9 words to be read, but not recalled, after a constant time interval.

Format: Examiner required; not suitable for group use; untimed: 10–15 minutes

Scoring: Computer scored

Cost: $35.00

Publisher: Life Science Associates

Visual Attention Tasks (ATTEND)
Linda Laatsch

Copyright: 1986

Population: Ages 10 to adult

Purpose: Diagnoses attention and vigilance deficits; used to assess head injury, stroke, or visual system damage

Description: Computer-administered test of attentional skills in which the examiner selects targets to which the subject responds and non-targets to which the subject inhibits response. The stimuli appear at selectable intervals, randomly or nonrandomly. The task can be constructed to suit the level of the deficit.

Format: Examiner required; not suitable for group use; untimed: 2–15 minutes

Scoring: Computer scored

Cost: $35.00

Publisher: Life Science Associates

Visual Memory Task (VISMEM)
Rosamond Gianutsos

Copyright: 1989

Population: Ages 8 to adult

Purpose: Measures visual, nonverbal memory in individuals with head injury and stroke

Description: Computer-administered test of visual memory. Irregular shapes are presented for study. The subject then "paints" the shape as recalled.

Format: Self-administered; extensive user data recording capability; not suitable for group use; untimed: 8–12 minutes

Scoring: Computer scored

Cost: $25.00

Publisher: Life Science Associates

Visual Scanning (SCAN)
Linda Laatsch

Copyright: 1986

Population: Ages 10 to adult

Purpose: Diagnoses visual scanning deficits; used to assess head injury, stroke, or visual system damage

Description: Computer-administered test of visual scanning deficits. Two formats are provided: TEXTSCAN and LINESCAN. In TEXTSCAN, letters move across the screen. The subject must respond when the target letter is briefly bracketed. In LINESCAN, a letter or number appears briefly at the right or left edge of the screen, and the same or a different letter or number appears at the opposite edge. The subject must indicate whether they are the same. The required scanning speed is adjustable over a wide range in both formats. May be used in retraining and for diagnosis.

Format: Examiner required; not suitable for group use; untimed: 5–12 minutes

Scoring: Computer scored

Cost: $35.00

Publisher: Life Science Associates

Wechsler Memory Scale–Revised (WMS–R)
David Wechsler, C. P. Stone

Copyright: 1987

Population: Adolescents and adults; ages 16 to 74

Purpose: Assesses memory functioning; used with individuals with aphasia or organic brain injury and with the elderly

Description: Ten-subtest verbal and nonverbal scale assessing memory functioning. Three new subtests have been added: Figural Memory, Visual Paired Associates, and Visual Memory Span. The Logical Memory, Verbal Paired Associates, Visual Paired Associates, and Visual Reproduction subtests are administered twice to provide separate estimates of immediate and delayed recall. The revised edition also features more explicit scoring guidelines for the Logical Memory and Visual Reproduction subtests.

This test is for use only by persons with at least a master's degree in psychology or a related discipline. The WMS–R is a revision of the 1974 edition of the WMS.

Format: Examiner required; not suitable for group use; untimed: 50 minutes, including 30-minute delayed recall procedure

Scoring: Examiner evaluated

Cost: Complete set (all necessary materials for proper administration, manual, 25 record forms, and carrying case) $294.00; manual $67.50; 25 record forms $30.50

Publisher: The Psychological Corporation

Wide Range Assessment of Memory and Learning (WRAML)
Wayne Adams, David Sheslow

Copyright: 1990

Population: Ages 5 to 17

Purpose: Measures an individual's verbal and visual memory ability; will be helpful in measuring memory-related learning ability and problems within the psychological, educational, and medical communities

Description: Nine subtests, some with repetitive trials and recall administrations. Subtests include Picture Memory, Design Memory, Verbal Learning, Story Memory, Finger Windows, Sound Symbol Learning, Sentence Memory, Visual Learning, and Number/Letter Memory. National stratified norms including over 2,300 individuals controlled for age, sex, race, region, and residence.

Format: Individual administration; examiner required; untimed: approximately 45 minutes

Scoring: Hand key

Cost: Kit $305.00

Publisher: Wide Range, Inc.

Wisconsin Card Sorting Test (WCST)
David A. Grant, Esta A. Berg

Copyright: 1993

Population: Children, adults; ages 6 years 6 months to 89 years

Purpose: Assesses perseveration and abstract thinking; used for neuropsychological assess-ment of individuals suspected of having brain lesions involving the frontal lobes; the test can help discriminate frontal from nonfrontal lobes

Description: Multiple-task nonverbal test in which the subject matches cards in two response decks to one of four stimulus cards for color, form, or number. Responses are recorded on a form for later scoring. The test provides measures of overall success and particular sources of difficulty. A computerized version operates on Apple II systems with a color monitor, two floppy disk drives, and a paddle. The scoring program operates on IBM PC systems with 256K and two disk drives. Available in Dutch.

Format: Examiner required; not suitable for group use; untimed: typical time not available

Scoring: Examiner evaluated; may be computer scored

Cost: Complete kit $169.00

Publisher: Psychological Assessment Resources, Inc.

Wisconsin Card Sorting Test: Computer Version–2, Research Edition
Robert K. Heaton

Copyright: 1993

Population: Ages 6 years 6 months to 89 years

Purpose: Assesses perseveration and abstract thinking; used for neuropsychological assessment of individuals suspected of having brain lesions involving the frontal lobes; this edition is designed for research purposes only

Description: Nonverbal computer-administered test in which the subject, using a paddle, matches color reproductions of the print version's two decks of response cards to one of four reproduced stimulus cards for color, form, or number. The test produces a scored protocol. Results may be saved on disk. The program is designed for use on PC format.

Format: Examiner required; not suitable for group use; untimed

Scoring: Computer scored

Cost: $495.00

Publisher: Psychological Assessment Resources, Inc.

Word Memory Task (WORDMEM)
Rosamond Gianutsos

Copyright: Not provided

Population: Ages 8 to adult

Purpose: Assesses immediate memory in individuals with head injury and stroke

Description: Computer-administered test of verbal memory. The computer displays a random list of words one by one. The subject then types the list in order. Both number of words in the list and duration of exposure are adjustable. The subject must have some visual function, the ability to read simple English words, rudimentary keyboarding skills, and the ability to follow simple instructions.

Format: Individual administration; 8–12 minutes

Scoring: Computer scored

Cost: Contact publisher

Publisher: Life Science Associates

Pain

. . . .

Chronic Pain Battery™ (CPB)
Stephen R. Levitt

Copyright: 1983

Population: Adolescents, adults; ages 13 and above

Purpose: Collects medical, psychological, behavioral, and social data and assesses correlates of chronic pain; used by health professionals to suggest treatment and management approaches of individuals suffering from chronic malignant or nonmalignant pain

Description: Paper–pencil or computer-administered 215-item multiple-choice true–false test including SCL-90-R with a 10-page narrative. The results are used to coordinate therapeutic strategies in multidisciplinary health care settings and to aid the private practitioner's specific evaluation. The report topics include demographic and social history, past and current pain history, pain intensity ratings, medication and treatment history, medical history, personality and pain coping style, psychosocial factors (stress, psychological dysfunction, and support system), behavioral-learning factors (prior models, illness-behavior reinforcement, litigation-compensation, activity assessment), patient expectations and goals, and patient problem ratings. Two scoring options are available: mail-in and computer-scoring. The examiner must meet APA guidelines. An eighth-grade reading level is required. Also available in Spanish.

Format: Self-administered; suitable for group use; untimed

Scoring: Computer scored; test scoring service available from publisher

Cost: $14.00 to $28.00

Publisher: Pain Resource Center

Pain Apperception Test
Donald V. Petrovich

Copyright: 1973

Population: Adults

Purpose: Examines the emotional aspects of pain; used in settings in which pain might be experienced or anticipated

Description: Oral-response 25-item projective test assessing pain's emotional aspects within a psychological context by measuring an individual's perception of intensity and duration of pain and by focusing on total reactions and not just thresholds. Items consist of 25 picture cards dealing with three major groups of pain situations: felt pain sensations, anticipation versus felt-sensation of pain, and self-inflicted versus other-inflicted pain. Responses are recorded on the protocol sheet. Adult normative data are provided.

Format: Examiner required; suitable for group

use; untimed: 15–20 minutes

Scoring: Examiner evaluated

Cost: Kit (100 protocol sheets, 1 set of picture cards, manual) $87.50

Publisher: Western Psychological Services

Pain Patient Profile™ (P-3™)
C. David Tollison, Jerry C. Langley

Copyright: 1996

Population: Adults; ages 17 to 76

Purpose: Assesses psychological factors that can influence the severity and persistence of pain

Description: Multiple-choice 44-item computer or paper–pencil test measuring psychological factors that influence patient pain. Scales include depression, anxiety, and somatization. Includes a validity index. Eighth-grade reading level required.

Format: Self-administered; suitable for group use; untimed: 15 minutes

Scoring: Hand key; computer scored; test scoring service available from publisher

Cost: Narrative report $7.50–$10.00; hand score answer sheet (includes profile form) $1.50; quantity discounts available

Publisher: NCS Assessments

Psychosocial Pain Inventory (PSPI)
Robert K. Heaton, Ralph A. W. Lehman, Carl J. Getto

Copyright: 1985

Population: Adults

Purpose: Evaluates psychosocial factors related to chronic pain problems; used in the treatment of individuals with chronic pain

Description: Eight-page multiple-item paper–pencil inventory assessing the following psychosocial factors considered important in maintaining and exacerbating chronic pain problems: several forms of secondary gain, the effects of pain behavior on interpersonal relationships, the existence of stressful life events that may contribute to subjective distress or promote avoidance learning, and components of past history that familiarize the patient with

the chronic invalid role and with its personal and social consequences. Ratings take into account that patients differ in the degree to which they are likely to be influenced by potential sources of secondary gain. The inventory yields a total score. High scores predict poor response to medical treatment for pain.

Format: Examiner required; not suitable for group use; untimed: time varies

Scoring: Examiner evaluated

Cost: Test kit (25 PSPI forms, manual) $32.00

Publisher: Psychological Assessment Resources, Inc.

TMJ Scale™
Stephen R. Levitt, Tom F. Lundeen, Michael W. McKinney

Copyright: 1985

Population: Ages 11 and above

Purpose: Screens for TMJ disorders, craniofacial pain, and dysfunction; used by dental practitioners; physicians; ear, eyes, nose, and throat specialists; and psychologists

Description: Multiple-item paper–pencil self-report tool measuring physical and psychosocial factors contributing to craniomuscular dysfunction. The TMJ Scale Report™ yields 10 scored scales in three domains: Physical (Pain Report, Palpation Pain, Perceived Malocclusion, Joint Dysfunction, Range of Motion Limitation, and Non-TM Disorder), Psychosocial (Psychological Factors, Stress, Chronicity), and Global. Patients may complete the report at home or in the office. A narrative report and a printout of the patient's scores and responses is generated. The TMJ Scale Profile™ presents patient's scale scores graphically. Tests may be scored using TMJ/Score™ IBM compatible. Disk sizes 3½″ and 5¼″ available. Available in Spanish.

Format: Self-administered; suitable for group use; untimed: 15 minutes

Scoring: Computer scored

Cost: Contact publisher

Publisher: Pain Resource Center

Personality

· ·

Child

Burks' Behavior Rating Scales–Preschool and Kindergarten Edition

Harold F. Burks

Copyright: 1977

Population: Children; Grades PreK through K

Purpose: Identifies patterns of behavior problems in children ages 3 to 6; used to aid differential diagnosis

Description: Paper–pencil 105-item inventory used by parents and teachers to rate a child on the basis of descriptive statements of observed behavior. The inventory contains 18 subscales: excessive self-blame, anxiety, withdrawal, dependency, suffering, sense of persecution, aggressiveness, resistance, poor ego strength, physical strength, coordination, intellectuality, attention, impulse control, reality contact, sense of identity, anger control, and social conformity. This inventory is a downward extension of Burk's Behavior Rating Scale.

Format: Examiner required; not suitable for group use; untimed: 15–20 minutes

Scoring: Hand key

Cost: Kit (25 Profile sheets and booklets, manual) $60.00

Publisher: Western Psychological Services

California Preschool Social Competency Scale

Samuel Levine, Freeman F. Elzey, Mary Lewis

Copyright: Not provided

Population: Children; ages 2 years 6 months to 5 years 6 months

Purpose: Assesses the social competency of preschool children; used by teachers for diagnosis, placement, or measurement of the development of young children

Description: Thirty-item paper–pencil rating scale providing objective, numerical evaluations of the social competency of preschool children. The items call for specific behaviors (preschool children's interpersonal behavior and the degree to which they assume social responsibility). The manual provides percentile norms for children from high and low occupational levels for four age groups (by sex).

Format: Examiner required; not suitable for group use; untimed: typical time not available

Scoring: Hand key

Cost: Preview kit (scales, manual) $10.00

Publisher: Consulting Psychologists Press, Inc.

California Q-Sort (Child)

Jeanne Block, Jack Block

Copyright: 1980

Population: Children

Purpose: Describes individual behavior and personality in contemporary psychodynamic terms; used for research in child development

Description: Formulation of personality descriptions using 100 descriptive personality statements sorted from most to least applicable to the subject. Materials include individual 2¼"×3½" cards.

Format: Examiner required; not suitable for group use; untimed: typical time not available

Scoring: Examiner evaluated

Cost: Sampler Set $25.00

Publisher: Mind Garden, Inc.

Child Anxiety Scale (CAS)

John S. Gillis

Copyright: 1978

Population: Children; ages 5 to 12

Purpose: Diagnoses adjustment problems in children; helps to prevent emotional and behavioral disorders in later life by identifying children who would benefit from therapeutic intervention at an early age; used for clinical evaluations and counseling

Description: Paper–pencil test measuring anxiety-based disturbances in young children. Test items are based on extensive research of the form anxiety takes in the self-report of 5- to 12-year-olds. An audiocassette tape is used to present the questionnaire items, and brightly colored, easy-to-read answer sheets are specially designed for use with children of this age group. The CAS manual contains reliability and validity information, scoring instructions, and percentiles and standard scores for both sexes separately and combined.

Format: Examiner required; suitable for group use; untimed: 15 minutes

Scoring: Hand key

Cost: CAS introductory kit $43.25; CAS manual $11.50; 50 handscoring answer sheets $10.75; scoring key $6.00; cassette tape $15.00

Publisher: Institute for Personality and Ability Testing, Inc.

Children's Apperceptive Story-Telling Test (CAST)
Mary F. Schneider

Copyright: 1989

Population: Children; ages 6 to 13

Purpose: Evaluates the emotional functioning of school-age children

Description: Multiple-item apperceptive test employing colored picture stimuli to evoke stories from students. The test yields a *T*-score profile for four major factors (adaptive, nonadaptive, immature, and uninvested) and 15 adaptive, nonadaptive, and problem-solving scales. Profiles are available for children with attention deficit, conduct disorder, anxiety disorder, oppositional disorder, and childhood depression.

Format: Examiner required; not suitable for group use; untimed: time varies

Scoring: Examiner evaluated

Cost: Complete kit (examiner's manual, 31 colorful picture cards, record-scoring forms, storage box) $129.00

Publisher: PRO-ED, Inc.

Children's Apperception Test (CAT–A)
Leopold Bellak, Sonya Sorel Bellak

Copyright: 1949, revised 1991

Population: Ages 3 to 10

Purpose: Assesses children's personality; used in clinical evaluation and diagnosis

Description: Ten-item oral-response projective personality test measuring the traits, attitudes, and psychodynamics involved in the personalities of children ages 3 to 10. Each test item consists of a picture of animals in a human social context through which the child becomes involved in conflicts, identities, roles, and family structures. Examinees are required to tell a story about each picture. The test also includes informational material on the history, nature, and purpose of CAT, Ego Function Graph, test interpretation, use of the Short Form, research possibilities, and bibliography. Available also in Spanish, Indian, French, German, Japanese, Flemish, Portuguese, and Italian.

Format: Examiner required; not suitable for group use; untimed: 20–30 minutes

Scoring: Examiner evaluated

Cost: Complete kit (pictures, manual) $25.00

Publisher: C.P.S., Inc.

Children's Apperception Test–Human Figures (CAT–H)
Leopold Bellak, Sonya Sorel Bellak

Copyright: 1965

Population: Ages 3 to 10

Purpose: Assesses children's personality; used for clinical evaluation and diagnosis

Description: Ten-item oral-response projective personality test measuring the traits, attitudes, and psychodynamics involved in the personalities of children. The test consists of 10 pictures of human figures in situations of concern to children: conflicts, identified roles, and family structure. The test also includes a review of the literature concerning the use of animal versus human figures in projective techniques, a discussion of the process of transposing animal figures to human forms, a copy of Haworth's Schedule of Adaptive Mechanisms in CAT Responses, and a bibliography. Available also in Spanish, Portuguese, Flemish, and Japanese.

Format: Examiner required; not suitable for group use

Scoring: Examiner evaluated

Cost: Complete kit (10 pictures and manual) $25.00

Publisher: C.P.S., Inc.

Children's Apperception Test–Supplement (CAT–S)
Leopold Bellak, Sonya Sorel Bellak

Copyright: 1951, revised 1991

Population: Ages 3 to 10

Purpose: Assesses children's personality; used for clinical evaluation and diagnosis

Description: Ten-item oral-response projective personality test measuring the traits, attitudes, and psychodynamics at work in the personalities of children ages 3 to 10. The test items consist of 10 pictures of animal figures in family situations that are common but not as universal as those of the Children's Apperception Test. Among the situations depicted are prolonged illness, physical disability, mother's pregnancy, and separation of parents. The picture plates are constructed like pieces of a large jigsaw puzzle, with irregularly shaped outlines. Children who do not relate stories readily can manipulate these forms in play techniques. The test also includes informational material on test techniques and a bibliography. Available also in Spanish, French, Flemish, and Italian.

Format: Examiner required; not suitable for group use; untimed: 20–30 minutes

Scoring: Examiner evaluated

Cost: Complete kit (10 pictures, manual) $29.00

Publisher: C.P.S., Inc.

Children's Personality Questionnaire (CPQ)
Rutherford B. Porter, Raymond B. Cattell

Copyright: 1973

Population: Children, adolescents; ages 8 to 12

Purpose: Assesses personality development in children; used for clinical evaluations and educational and personal counseling

Description: Paper–pencil 140-item test measuring 14 primary personality traits useful in predicting and evaluating the course of personal, social, and academic development. The traits measured include emotional stability, self-concept level, excitability, and self-assurance. Scores for extraversion, anxiety, and other broad trait patterns are obtained as combinations of the primary scales. Percentiles and standard scores are presented for both sexes together and separately. The test is available in four forms: A, B, C, and D. Each form is divided into two parts for scheduling convenience in school settings. A third-grade reading level is required. Available in Spanish and German.

Format: Examiner required; suitable for group use; untimed: 30–60 minutes per form

Scoring: Computer scored; scoring service available from publisher; teletest

Cost: CPQ Introductory Kit $29.95; handbook with norms $14.75; 25 reusable test booklets $18.00; 50 answer sheets $10.75; 50 profile sheets $10.75; 50 answer-profile sheets $15.00; scoring key $13.50

Publisher: Institute for Personality and Ability Testing, Inc.

Children's Problems Checklist
John A. Schinka

Copyright: 1985

Population: Parents of children ages 5 to 12

Purpose: Assesses children's problems as reported by parent or guardian; used as a survey instrument in clinical and counseling settings to initiate the consultation process and introduce the client to formal diagnostic testing

Description: Paper–pencil 190-item test completed by a parent or guardian and identifying problems in 11 areas: emotions, self-concept, peers/play, school, language/thinking, concentration/organization, activity level/motor control, behavior, values, habits, and health. The test is a component of the Clinical Checklist Series.

Format: Self-administered; suitable for group use; untimed: 10–20 minutes

Scoring: Examiner evaluated

Cost: 50 checklists $34.00

Publisher: Psychological Assessment Resources, Inc.

Differential Test of Conduct and Emotional Problems (DT/CEP)
Edward J. Kelly

Copyright: Not provided

Population: Grades K through 12

Purpose: Identifies children and adults without disabilities who have conduct problems

Description: Screening test reliably differentiates between three critical populations: conduct disorder (socially maladjusted), emotionally disturbed, and noninvolved. The DT/CEP facilitates educational decisions (special education/ regular education). Emphasizes simple but effective screening identification, verification, and diagnostic steps to facilitate more accountable placement and programming for students with conduct problems and emotional disorders. Includes nine case studies. Standardized.

Format: Examiner required; suitable for group use; untimed: 15–20 minutes

Scoring: Hand key

Cost: Complete $67.00

Publisher: Slosson Educational Publications, Inc.

Early Childhood Behavior Scale (ECBS)
Stephen B. McCarney

Copyright: 1992

Population: Children; ages 36 months to 72 months; Grades PreK to 1

Purpose: Provides the standardized profile information and specific indicators necessary to determine which students are in need of intervention, behavioral support, and the opportunity to learn more appropriate behavior

Description: The subscales of Social Relationships, Personal Adjustment, and Academic Progress were carefully developed with the use of behaviors appropriate for children ages 36 to 72 months in preschool and kindergarten situations. Results provided by primary observers such as teachers, mental health workers, or parents are used to document the behaviors which indicate areas of most concern. Children in the standardization sample represented all geographic regions of the United States, with attention given to racial and ethnic minorities in the creation of the national norms. Internal consistency, test retest, and interrater reliability; item and factor analysis; and content, criterion-related, diagnostic, and construct validity are well documented and reported for the scale. A computer version using IBM/Macintosh PCs is available.

Format: Individual administration; untimed: 15–20 minutes

Scoring: Self/computer scored

Cost: Complete kit $89.50

Publisher: Hawthorne Educational Services, Inc.

Early School Personality Questionnaire (ESPQ)
Raymond B. Cattell, Richard W. Coan

Copyright: 1976

Population: Children; ages 6 to 8

Purpose: Measures personality in children in the early school years; used for clinical evaluation and educational and personal counseling

Description: Paper–pencil 160-item test measuring personality in children. Questions are read aloud by the administrator (an optional tape recording may be used instead), and the students mark their answers on the answer sheet. To use the answer sheet, children need only be able to discriminate the letter and other common objects. Percentiles and standard scores are provided for both sexes separately and together. The test is divided into two equal parts of 80 items each for scheduling convenience. Also available in Spanish.

Format: Examiner required; suitable for group use; untimed: 1 hour

Scoring: Hand key

Cost: ESPQ Introductory Kit $23.00; manual $10.00; 25 answer booklets $10.00; 50 profile sheets $15.00; 2 scoring keys $12.00; tape recording $13.65

Publisher: Institute for Personality and Ability Testing, Inc.

Hirsch Opinions About Psychological and Emotional Disorders in Children (HOPE)
Joseph A. Hirsch

Copyright: 1995

Population: Children

Purpose: Designed for teachers, psychologists, social workers, and day care workers to provide opinions about psychological and emotional disorders

Description: Paper/pencil 42-item survey on a Likert scale that measures two factors (Biases and Dynamic/Clinical). The Biases factor has 24 items while the Dynamic/Clinical assesses treatment efficacy and psychodymanic etiology. Scaled scores are provided for each factor with separate norms for special populations. Requires a sixth-grade reading level.

Format: Individual or group administration; untimed

Scoring: Examiner scoring and interpretation

Cost: $25.00 per 50

Publisher: Joseph A. Hirsch, Ph.D., Psy.D.

House Tree Person and Draw a Person
Valerie Van Hutton

Copyright: 1994

Population: Children; ages 7 to 11

Purpose: Used in outpatient counseling and school psychology to screen for sexual abuse

Description: Paper–pencil projective four-drawing test with the following categories: Preoccupation with Sexually Relevant Con-

cepts, Aggression and Hostility, Withdrawal and Guarded Accessibility, Alertness for Danger, Suspiciousness, and Lack of Trust. Materials used include HIP/DAP book and HIP/DAP scoring booklets. Examiner must be C-level qualified.

Format: Individual administration; examiner required; untimed

Scoring: Examiner evaluated; scoring criteria

Cost: Kit (book and 10 scoring books) $47.00

Publisher: Psychological Assessment Resources, Inc.

Joseph Preschool and Primary Self-Concept Screening Test (JPPSST)
Jack Joseph

Copyright: 1979

Population: Children; ages 3 years 5 months to 9 years

Purpose: Measures social–emotional development of children; used to identify children who may have learning difficulties due to negative self-appraisals and to monitor progress in early childhood programs and special education classes

Description: Paper–pencil and oral-response 16-item test in two parts. First, the child draws his or her own face on a blank figure of the corresponding sex. Next, the child answers two simple oral-response questions and 13 questions asking the child to select from pairs of pictures the one with which he or she identifies more closely. The face drawing is evaluated qualitatively, and the 15 questions are scored objectively. The test generates a Global Self-Concept Score based on five dimensions and provides objective high-risk cutoff points. The effects of socially desirable responses are corrected for at upper ranges (ages 5 to 9). Both quantitative and qualitative indices regarding possible cognitive deficits and experiential or receptive language lags are developed. The manual provides normative data, measures of validity and reliability, item analysis, specific case illustrations, and research considerations.

Format: Examiner required; not suitable for group use; untimed: 5–7 minutes

Scoring: Examiner evaluated

Cost: Complete kit $150.00

Publisher: Stoelting Company

Junior Eysenck Personality Inventory (JEPI)
Sybil B. G. Eysenck

Copyright: 1965

Population: Children, adolescents; ages 7 to 16

Purpose: Measures the major personality dimensions of children; used as a research instrument

Description: Sixty-item paper–pencil yes–no inventory measuring extraversion–introversion (24 items) and neuroticism–stability (24 items). A falsification scale (12 items) detects response distortion. Scores are provided for E—Extraversion, N—Neuroticism, and L—Lie. American norms are available for selected samples of majority and minority children. Available in Spanish.

Format: Examiner required; suitable for group use; untimed: 10 minutes

Scoring: Hand key

Cost: Specimen Set (manual, one copy of all forms) $6.50

Publisher: EdITS/Educational and Industrial Testing Service

Katz-Zalk Projective Prejudice Test
Sue Rosenberg Zalk, Phyllis A. Katz

Copyright: 1976

Population: Children; Grades 1 through 5

Purpose: Measures racial attitudes in children

Description: Paper–pencil true–false test with slides; available in two forms: urban or suburban

Format: Group administration; examiner required; untimed

Scoring: Examiner evaluated

Cost: $18.00

Publisher: Select Press

Measure of Child Stimulus Screening (Converse of Arousability)
Albert Mehrabian, Carol Falender

Copyright: 1978

Population: Children; ages 3 months to 7 years

Purpose: Measures major components of a child's arousability and stimulus screening; used for research, counseling, and education program selection purposes

Description: Multiple-item paper–pencil observational inventory measuring parents' descriptions of their children's arousability (responses of one parent are sufficient). Test results indicate the child's characteristic arousal response to complex, unexpected, or unfamiliar situations. Stimulus screening/arousability has been shown to be a major component of many important personality dimensions, such as anxiety, neuroticism, extroversion, or hostility. This test is based on the same conceptual framework used to develop the corresponding adult measure.

Format: Examiner required; suitable for group use; untimed: 10 minutes

Scoring: Hand key

Cost: Test kit (scale, scoring directions, norms, descriptive material) $31.00

Publisher: Albert Mehrabian, Ph.D.

Measure of Stimulus Screening (Converse of Arousability)
Albert Mehrabian

Copyright: 1994

Population: Adults

Purpose: Measures major components of arousability and stimulus screening; used for research, counseling, and job placement purposes

Description: Multiple-item verbal questionnaire assessing the extent of an individual's arousal response to complex, unexpected, or unfamiliar situations. The test items are based on extensive factor-analytic and experimental investigations of all major components of arousability and stimulus screening. Stimulus screening/arousability has been shown to be a major component of many important emotional characteristics, such as anxiety, neuroticism, extroversion, or hostility.

Format: Self-administered; suitable for group use; untimed: 10 minutes

Scoring: Examiner evaluated

Cost: Test kit (scales, scoring directions, norms, descriptive material) $31.00

Publisher: Albert Mehrabian, Ph.D.

Mental Status Checklist™– Children
Edward H. Dougherty, John A. Schinka

Copyright: 1988

Population: Ages 5 to 12

Purpose: Surveys the mental status of children; used to identify problems and establish rapport in order to prepare individuals for further diagnostic testing; also provides written documentation of presenting problems

Description: Paper–pencil or computer-administered 153-item checklist covering presenting problems, referral data, demographics, mental status, personality function and symptoms, diagnosis, and disposition. The computer version operates on IBM PC.

Format: Self-administered; suitable for group use; untimed: 10–20 minutes

Scoring: Examiner evaluated

Cost: 25 checklists $34.00; computer version $295.00

Publisher: Psychological Assessment Resources, Inc.

Murphy-Meisgeier Type Indicator for Children (MMTIC)
Charles Meisgeier, Elizabeth Murphy

Copyright: Not provided

Population: Children; Grades 2 through 8

Purpose: Determines the Jungian types of children in order to identify individual learning styles

Description: Seventy-item test measuring four preference scales: Extraversion–Introversion

(16 items), Sensing–Intuition (18 items), Thinking–Feeling (18 items), and Judgment–Perception (18 items). The inventory is designed to affirm the child's strengths to increase self-esteem; contribute to the rearing, teaching, counseling, and overall understanding of children; and provide a means through which children can understand individual differences. The manual contains statistical information as well as descriptions of learning styles associated with each type. Three booklets introducing type to children, parents, and teachers are available. The computer report identifies the individual preferences and reports information on learning styles. The reading level of the items is most appropriate for students in Grades 3 through 6; however, teachers may read the items aloud to second graders or any examinee with reading difficulties.

Format: Examiner required; suitable for group use; untimed: typical time not available

Scoring: Hand key; may be computer scored

Cost: Preview kit (booklet, answer sheet, teacher's guide, manual) $37.00

Publisher: Consulting Psychologists Press, Inc.

Personality Inventory for Children (PIC)–Revised Format
Robert D. Wirt, David Lachar, James E. Klinedinst, Philip D. Seat, William E. Broen, Jr.

Copyright: 1984

Population: Children, adolescents; ages 3 to 16

Purpose: Evaluates the personality attributes of children and adolescents; used by professionals for counseling and identification of psychopathology, developmental problems, and social disabilities

Description: Paper–pencil 280-item true–false inventory completed by one of the child's parents producing a profile of 16 scales: Intellectual Screening, Family Relations, Hyperactivity, Somatic Concern, Social Skills, Achievement, Development, Depression, Delinquency, Withdrawal, Psychosis, Anxiety, Lie Frequency, Defensiveness, and Adjustment. A 420-item version is available for higher scale reliabilities, and a 131-item version is available for screening.

Format: Examiner required; not suitable for group use; untimed: 25–30 minutes

Scoring: Hand key; may be computer scored

Cost: Kit (1 reusable administration booklet, 100 profile forms, 25 hand-scored answer sheets, 1 set of scoring keys, 1 manual, 1 manual supplement for the revised PIC, 2 WPS Test Report answer sheets) $225.00

Publisher: Western Psychological Services

Pictorial Scale of Perceived Competence and Social Acceptance for Young Children
Susan Harter, Robin Pike

Copyright: 1983

Population: Ages 4 to 7

Purpose: Assesses cognitive competence, physical competence, maternal acceptance, and peer acceptance

Description: There are two versions of this instrument, one for preschool/kindergarten children and one for first/second graders. Includes 24 items.

Format: Examiner required; not suitable for group use

Scoring: Examiner evaluated

Cost: Manual $20.00, plates $30.00

Publisher: Susan Harter

Piers-Harris Children's Self-Concept Scale (PHCSCS)
Ellen V. Piers, Dale B. Harris

Copyright: 1984

Population: Children, adolescents; Grades 4 through 12

Purpose: Measures a child's self-concept; identifies problem areas in a child's self-concept; used for research

Description: Eighty-item paper–pencil test assessing six aspects of a child's self-esteem: behavior, intellectual and school status, physical appearance and attributes, anxiety, popularity, and happiness and satisfaction. Items are writ-

ten at a third-grade reading level and require a simple "yes–no" answer. Percentile and standard scores are provided for the total score and for each of the six subscales. Scores can be used for research purposes or to identify extreme problem areas. The manual provides the information necessary for administering and interpreting the scale, as well as the information included in Research Monograph #1 concerning use of the scale with minority and special education groups.

Format: Examiner/self-administered; suitable for group use; untimed: 15–20 minutes

Scoring: Hand key; may be computer scored

Cost: Kit (25 test booklets, 25 profile forms, 1 scoring key, 2 WPS Test Report answer sheets, 1 manual) $115.00

Publisher: Western Psychological Services

Questionnaire for Process Analysis of Social Skills/Oriented Group Therapy of Children
Daniel S. Kirschenbaum, Joanne L. Pedro, Joyce B. DeVage

Copyright: 1977

Population: Children

Purpose: Measures results of group therapy

Description: Multiple-item questionnaire

Format: Individual administration; examiner required; untimed

Scoring: Hand key; examiner evaluated

Cost: $15.00

Publisher: Select Press

Roberts Apperception Test for Children
Glen E. Roberts, Dorothea S. McArthur

Copyright: 1982

Population: Children, adolescents; ages 6 to 15

Purpose: Identifies emotionally disturbed children; used for clinical diagnosis, particularly with children just entering counseling or therapy

Description: Sixteen-item oral-response test in which the child is shown cards containing realistic line illustrations and is asked to make up stories about each. The illustrations depict adults and children in up-to-date clothing and emphasize the everyday, interpersonal events of contemporary life, including (in addition to the standard situations of the TAT and CAT) such situations as parental disagreement, parental affection, observation of nudity, and school and peer interpersonal events. Stimuli are chosen to elicit psychologically meaningful responses. The clinical areas measured and reported on the Interpersonal Chart are conflict, anxiety, aggression, depression, rejection, punishment, dependency, support, closure, resolution, unresolved indicator, maladaptive outcome, and deviation response. Other measures include the Ego Functioning Index, the Aggression Index, and the Levels of Projection Scale. The manual includes a number of case studies and examples.

Format: Examiner required; not suitable for group use; untimed: 20–30 minutes

Scoring: Examiner evaluated

Cost: Kit (set of test pictures, 25 record booklets, manual) $115.00; test pictures for black children $59.50

Publisher: Western Psychological Services

Self-Concept Adjective Checklist
Alan J. Politte

Copyright: 1974

Population: Children; Grades K through 8

Purpose: Measures personality and self-concept; used for diagnosis, screening, and measuring changes due to therapy

Description: Paper–pencil 114-item test of self-concept in which the items are categorized as physical traits, social values, intellectual abilities, and miscellaneous. Children in Grades K through 3 check "I am" or "I Am Not" for each item. Children in Grades 4 through 8 have the additional choice of an "I Would Like To Be" column. The items may be rated by the student or an observer.

Format: Examiner required; suitable for group use; untimed: 10 minutes

Scoring: Hand key; examiner evaluated

Cost: Specimen Set $5.00; 25 rating checklists $15.00

Publisher: Psychologists and Educators, Inc.

Tasks and Rating Scales for LAB Assessment of Social Interaction
Adam P. Metheny, Jr., Ronald S. Wilson, Sharon M. Nuss

Copyright: 1984

Population: Children; ages 3 to 4 years

Purpose: Measures social behavior of twins

Description: Multiple-item show–tell test

Format: Individual administration; examiner required; untimed

Scoring: Examiner evaluated

Cost: $15.00

Publisher: Select Press

Temperament Assessment Battery for Children (TABC)
Roy P. Martin

Copyright: 1988

Population: Ages 3–7

Purpose: Measures the basic personality behavioral dimensions or temperaments of children

Description: Multiple-item paper–pencil test assessing six temperamental variables: Activity, Adaptability, Approach/Withdrawal, Intensity, Distractibility, and Persistence. Items are rated on a 7-point scale ranging from "hardly ever" to "almost always." Three forms are used. The 48-item Parent Form describes the child's behavior at home. The 48-item Teacher Form reflects the child's classroom behavior. The Clinician Form is a questionnaire used by professionals involved in the child's psychoeducational evaluation. The test produces a description of the child and a comparison of other children in the same age range. Three factor scores are yielded: Emotionality, Persistence, and Sociability. Raw scores are converted to percentile equivalents for each temperament and factor scale.

Format: Examiner required; not suitable for group use; untimed: 12 minutes

Scoring: Hand key; examiner evaluated

Cost: Complete Kit (manual test forms) $69.00

Publisher: PRO-ED, Inc.

Adolescent and Adult

16PF Fifth Edition Questionnaire
Raymond B. Cattell, A. Karen S. Cattell,
Heather E. P. Cattell

Copyright: 1993

Population: Adolescents, adults; ages 16 and over

Purpose: Measures 16 personality factors and 5 global factors; used for personnel selection, career development, couples counseling, guidance counseling, and vocational and rehabilitation counseling

Description: Multiple-choice 185-item computer-administered or paper–pencil test yielding 16 Personality Factors: Warmth (A), Reasoning (B), Emotional Stability (C), Dominance (E), Liveliness (F), Rule-Consciousness (G), Social Boldness (H), Sensitivity (I), Vigilance (L), Abstractedness (M), Privateness (N), Apprehension (O), Openness to Change (Q1), Self-Reliance (Q2), Perfectionism (Q3), Tension (Q4). Global Factors yielded: Extraversion, Anxiety, Tough-Mindedness, Independence, Self-Control. Response Style Indices yielded: Impression Management, Infrequency, and Acquiescence. A fifth-grade reading level is required. Examiner qualifications: Level 2 requires a master's degree in psychology, counseling, social work, or a related field, plus relevant coursework in tests and measurement.

Format: Self-administered; suitable for group use; untimed: 35–50 minutes (paper–pencil), 25 minutes (computer)

Scoring: Hand key; examiner evaluated; machine scored; computer scored; test scoring service available from publisher

Cost: Package of 10 reusable questionnaires $12.50; package of 25 answer sheets $12.50

Publisher: Institute for Personality and Ability Testing

16PF Questionnaire Fourth Edition
Raymond B. Cattell

Copyright: 1978

Population: Adolescents, adults; ages 16 and older

Purpose: Multiple-item paper–pencil test measuring 16 primary personality traits, including levels of assertiveness, emotional maturity, shrewdness, self-sufficiency, tension, anxiety, neuroticism, and rigidity

Description: For business, the 16PF predicts job-related criteria, such as sales effectiveness, work efficiency, and tolerance for routine. In diagnostic settings, measures are provided for anxiety, neuroticism, and rigidity. Educators can use the 16PF to counsel college-bound students and to identify potential dropouts, drug users, and low achievers. There are five forms of the test. Six types of computer-analyzed reports are available: Personal Career Development Profile, Karson Clinical Report, Marriage Counseling Report, 16PF Narrative Scoring Report, Human Resources Department Report, and a Law Enforcement and Development Report. The manual is a nontechnical guide for administration, scoring, and basic interpretation of Forms A, B, C, and D. A videotape recording of the Form A test booklet in American Sign Language is available. Also available in Spanish.

Format: Examiner/self-administered; suitable for group use; untimed: 45–60 minutes

Scoring: Hand key; may be computer scored

Cost: 25 reusable test booklets $24.00–$28.25; 25 machine-scorable answer sheets $10.75; 50 hand-scorable answer sheets $10.75; 50 profile sheets $10.75; scoring keys $14.75–$16.50

Publisher: Institute for Personality and Ability Testing, Inc.

16PF Report
Giles D. Rainwater

Copyright: 1984

Population: Adults

Purpose: Provides an automated interpretation of the 16 Personality Factor Test; assesses and evaluates personality

Description: Eighteen-item report

Format: Individual administration; examiner required; untimed

Scoring: Scoring service for test available from another company

Cost: $49.95

Publisher: Psychometric Software, Inc.

A-B Therapy Scale Norms
Dale T. Johnson, Charles W. Neville, Jr., Larry E. Bentler

Copyright: 1973

Population: Adults

Purpose: Initial effort to standardize criterion group selection

Description: Questionnaire with 31 items used for group selection

Format: Self-administered; suitable for group use; untimed

Scoring: Examiner evaluated

Cost: $15.00

Publisher: Select Press

Aberrant Behavior Checklist (ABC)
Michael G. Aman, Nirbhay N. Singh

Copyright: Residential 1986, Community 1994

Population: Children to adults

Purpose: Assesses problem behaviors of children and adults with mental retardation at home, in residential facilities, ICFs/MR, and work training centers

Description: Checklist with 58 items resolved into five subscales: Irritability, Agitation; Lethargy, Social Withdrawal; Stereotypic Behavior; Hyperactivity, Noncompliance; and Inappropriate Speech. The ABC asks for degree of retardation, the person's medical status, and current medication condition. Then 58 specific symptoms are rated, and an extensive manual gives comprehensive descriptions for each assessed behavior. The checklist can be completed by parents, special educators, psychologists, direct caregivers, nurses and others with knowledge of the person being assessed. Average subscale scores are available for both U.S. and overseas residential facilities and for children and adults living in the community.

Format: Individual and group administration; 25 minutes

Scoring: Examiner interpretation

Cost: Residential complete $52.00; Community complete $52.00

Publisher: Slosson Educational Publications, Inc.

ACDI Corrections Version II

Copyright: 1989

Population: Ages 12 to 17

Purpose: Measures six areas of concern for troubled juveniles

Description: Designed for troubled youth assessment for juvenile courts and probation, the test contains six scales: Truthfulness, Alcohol, Drugs, Violence, Distress, and Adjustment. Each scale provides specific recommendations for intervention, supervision, and treatment. There are 143 multiple-choice/true–false items. Measures juveniles' truthfulness, evaluates their overall adjustment, and assesses their anxiety and depression level, as well as violence proneness. Truth-corrected scores. Computer-generated report summarizes risk range and recommendations. Standardized and normed on the juvenile population. Available in English or Spanish.

Format: Self-administered; suitable for group use; 20–25 minutes

Scoring: Computer scored

Cost: Contact publisher

Publisher: Risk and Needs Assessment, Inc.

Achievement Experience Questionnaire
William P. Gaeddert, Dale C. Noelting

Copyright: 1986

Population: Adults

Purpose: Assesses goals and performance evaluation standards; used in research

Description: Multiple-item criterion-referenced 5-point "does not describe"/"describes" paper–pencil questionnaire with four categories: social goals, competitive goals, extrinsic standards, and intrinsic standards.

Format: Self-administration; suitable for group use; untimed

Scoring: Examiner evaluated

Cost: $15.00

Publisher: Select Press

Achievement Orientation Attitude Scale (AOAS)
Joan Daniels Pedro

Copyright: 1980

Population: Adolescent females; ages 12 to 15

Purpose: Assesses individual attitudes toward vicarious or direct achievement

Description: Paper–pencil 25-item questionnaire administered to junior high school females

Format: Individual or group administration; requires examiner; untimed

Scoring: Examiner evaluated

Cost: $15.00

Publisher: Select Press

Activity Performance Scales Based on SYS Derived
T. W. Cunningham, David F. Slavaker, N. Blythe Riegel

Copyright: 1975

Population: Adults

Purpose: Ergometric approach to interest measurement; used in career counseling for undergraduate students

Description: Adaptation of OAI—Occupational Analysis Inventory, OVIS—Ohio Vocational Inventory Survey, and VAPP—Vocational Activity Preference Profile. Includes 22 scales.

Format: Individual administration

Scoring: Hand key

Cost: $34.68

Publisher: Select Press

Actualizing Assessment Battery (AAB)
Everett L. Shostrom

Copyright: 1976

Population: Adults

Purpose: Measures an individual's sense of actualization with self and within relationships with others; used by therapists, marriage and family counselors, personnel administrators, and school psychologists for a wide variety of counseling situations

Description: Four paper–pencil tests measuring 13 dimensions of a person's sense of actualization: being, weakness, synergistic integration, time orientation, core centeredness, love, trust in humanity, creative living, mission, strength, manipulation awareness, anger, and potentiation. The Personal Orientations Dimensions (POD) and the Personal Orientation Inventory (POI) primarily measure intrapersonal actualizing, and the Caring Relationship Inventory (CRI) and the Pair Attraction Inventory (PAI) primarily measure interpersonal actualizing. The AAB may be scored locally by using the POI, CRI, and PAI or may be sent to EdITS for scoring. Results are reported through the AAB Interpretation Brochure, a six-page booklet containing descriptions and profiles for each of the four tests.

Format: Examiner required; suitable for group use; untimed: approximately 3 hours

Scoring: Computer scored

Cost: Contact publisher

Publisher: EdITS/Educational and Industrial Testing Service

Adolescent Coping Scale
Erica Frydenberg, Ramon Lewis

Copyright: 1993

Population: Adolescents; Grades 7 to 12

Purpose: Assesses a broad range of coping strategies, focusing on what an individual does

Description: Paper–pencil instrument in a general and specific Long Form (80 items, 18 scales) and Short Form (1 item from each scale). The main focus in on psychological well-being and adaptive strategies for coping. It can be used for initiating self-directed and behavioral change and stimulating group discussion. The Long Form can be computer or hand scored. Data can then be transferred to a Profile Chart. A Practitioner's Kit has been specially produced.

Format: Examiner required; individual or group administration; Long form—10 minutes, Short Form—2 minutes

Scoring: Hand key or computer scoring

Cost: Contact publisher

Publisher: The Australian Council for Educational Research Limited

Adult Personality Inventory
Samuel E. Krug

Copyright: 1984

Population: Adolescents, adults; ages 16 and older

Purpose: Evaluates individual personality characteristics, interpersonal relations, and lifestyle; used by professionals in industry, public service, health care, and education

Description: Multiple-item paper–pencil inventory assessing personality characteristics. While it maintains continuity with Cattell's theory of behavior first introduced more than 40 years ago, the Adult Personality Inventory offers several significant contemporary features. Items have been shortened in order to increase the number of items on the inventory (for increased reliability), and the required reading level has been lowered to the fourth-grade level. The computer scoring service provides a nine-page verbal and graphic report examining significant individual characteristics, interpersonal relations, and lifestyle.

Format: Examiner required; suitable for group use; untimed: 1 hour

Scoring: Scoring service available from publisher

Cost: Test booklets (package of 10) $15.50; 25 answer sheets $10.75; decision-making worksheets (package of 10) $12.00

Publisher: Institute for Personality and Ability Testing, Inc.

Age Projection Test
Akhter Ahsen

Copyright: 1988

Population: Adults

Purpose: Designed to reveal self-images

Description: An imagery test aimed at revealing self-images at various age (and self) levels and their associated structures of imagery functioning that is useful toward the understanding of a presented problem or a symptom

Format: Individual administration; 1–2 hours

Scoring: Examiner evaluated and interpreted

Cost: $20.00 per manual; includes test

Publisher: Brandon House, Inc.

Anxiety Scales for Children and Adults (ASCA)
James Battle

Copyright: 1993

Population: Ages 5 to Adulthood

Purpose: Measures anxiety, is applicable for Psychotherapy–Anxiety Therapy, and is suitable for most populations

Description: Total number of items: for children, Form Q, 25 items; for adults, Form M, 40 items; Scores yielded: Classifications, percentile ranks, T-Scores. Forms available: for children, Form Q; for Adults, Form M. Materials used: Test protocols, Paper–pencil, criterion-referenced response format. Available in large print, on audiocassette, in French and Spanish. May be used for those with visual, physical, hearing, or mental disabilities.

Format: Examiner/self-administration; untimed: 0–15 minutes

Scoring: Hand key/computer scored; test scoring service available from publisher

Cost: $120.00 U.S., $150.00 Canadian

Publisher: James Battle and Associates, Ltd.

Asch-Type Conformity Scale with Control for Acquiescence Response Set
A. P. McDonald, Jr.

Copyright: 1973

Population: Adults

Purpose: Measures control for acquiescence response; used for therapy

Description: Paper–pencil questionnaire. Includes six studies and eight scales and tables.

Format: Individually administered; untimed

Scoring: Examiner evaluated

Cost: $15.00

Publisher: Select Press

Assessment of Interpersonal Relations (AIR)
Bruce A. Bracken

Copyright: 1993

Population: Adolescents

Purpose: Assesses the quality of interpersonal relationships in a hierarchical fashion, including global relationship quality and relationship quality

Description: Three domains—Family (mother and father), Social (male and female peer relations), and Academic (teacher relations)—measure primary relationships that can be assessed independently by administering any of the respective 35-item subscales. All five subscales administered in combination reflect global interpersonal relations.

Format: Individual or group administration; 20 minutes

Scoring: Examiner administration and interpretation

Cost: Complete kit (manual and protocols) $79.00

Publisher: PRO-ED, Inc.

Assessment of Maternal Attitudes Toward Employment
A. M. Farel

Copyright: 1981

Population: Adult women

Purpose: Measures women's motivation to work

Description: Multiple-item paper–pencil questionnaire consisting of the following categories:

motivation to work, attitudes toward needs of young children, sex role stereotyping

Format: Individual or group administration; requires examiner; untimed

Scoring: Examiner evaluated

Cost: $15.00

Publisher: Select Press

Association Adjustment Inventory (AAI)
Martin M. Bruce

Copyright: 1959

Population: Adults

Purpose: Evaluates the extent to which the subject is maladjusted, immature, and deviant in ideation; used as an aid in predicting potential deviant behavior and job tenure

Description: Inventory with 100 items in which the subject matches one of four words with a stimulus word, allowing the examiner to score for ideational deviation, general psychosis, depression, hysteria, withdrawal, paranoia, rigidity, schizophrenia, impulsiveness, psychosomapathia, and anxiety. The scores are compared to "norms" to measure deviation. Available also in Spanish and German. Suitable for individuals with physical, hearing, or visual impairment.

Format: Examiner/self-administered; suitable for group use; untimed: 10 minutes

Scoring: Hand key

Cost: Reusable tests for use with IBM answer sheets $54.50; manual supplement (1984) $15.50; fan key $54.50; manual $14.75; profile sheets $25.50; scoring stencil test $43.00; fan key set $20.00

Publisher: Martin M. Bruce, Ph.D.

Attitudes Toward Aging
A. Sheppard

Copyright: 1981

Population: Adults; ages 17 to 49 years

Purpose: Measures attitudes toward aging in younger adults

Description: Paper–pencil 20-item questionnaire with the following categories: physical, psychological, and social

Format: Individual or group administration; requires examiner; untimed

Scoring: Examiner evaluated

Cost: $15.00

Publisher: Select Press

Attitudes Toward Physical Attractiveness Scale (ATPAS)
A. C. Downs, M. A. Reagan, C. Garrett, P. Kolodzy

Copyright: 1982

Population: Adolescents, adults

Purpose: Assesses stereotypes based on physical appearance

Description: Agree/disagree scale with 34 items and 7 points

Format: Self or group administration; untimed

Scoring: Examiner evaluated

Cost: $15.00

Publisher: Select Press

Attitudes Toward Women Scale (AWS)
Janet T. Spence, Robert Helmreich

Copyright: 1972

Population: Adults

Purpose: Measures attitudes toward the rights and roles of women in contemporary society

Description: Multiple-choice/short-answer 55-item paper–pencil questionnaire with six categories: Vocation, Education, Intelligence; Freedom and Independence; Dating; Drinking/Dirty Jokes; Sexual Behavior; and Marriage.

Format: Self-administered; suitable for group use; untimed

Scoring: Hand key

Cost: $21.00

Publisher: Select Press

Balanced Emotional Empathy Scale (BEES)
Albert Mehrabian

Copyright: 1996

Population: Adolescents, adults; ages 14 and above

Purpose: Assesses emotional empathy (sensitivity) to others; used for research, job placement, and counseling

Description: Thirty-item paper–pencil test yielding a single total score. A 10th grade reading level is required.

Format: Self-administered; suitable for group use; untimed: 10 minutes

Scoring: Hand key; test scoring service available from publisher

Cost: Test Kit $31.00

Publisher: Albert Mehrabian, Ph.D.

Basic Personality Inventory (BPI)
Douglas N. Jackson

Copyright: 1988, 1995

Population: Adolescents, adults

Purpose: Identifies personality dimensions indicating personal strengths as well as psychopathological dimensions; used in psychological, psychiatric, and counseling practices as well as psychiatric hospitals and community mental health centers

Description: Paper–pencil or computer-administered 240-item true–false multiphasic personality inventory used with both normal and clinical populations to identify personal strengths or sources of maladjustment. The test contains 11 substantive clinical scales and 1 critical item scale: Hypochondriasis, Anxiety, Depression, Thinking Disorder, Denial, Impulse Expression, Interpersonal Problems, Social Introversion, Alienation, Self-Depreciation, Persecutory Ideas, and Deviation (critical item scale). The computer version, which operates on IBM PC/ AT/XT and compatible systems, yields scores, profiles, and reports.

Format: Examiner required; suitable for group use; untimed: 20–45 minutes

Scoring: Hand key; scoring service available from publisher; computer scored

Cost: Examination kit (test manual, 10 test booklets, 25 answer sheets, 25 profile sheets, scoring template, and one basic report) $56.00;

software (licensed for 25 scorings, includes manual and key overlays) $175.00

Publisher: Sigma Assessment Systems, Inc.

BASIS–A Inventory (Basic Adlerian Scales for Interpersonal Success–Adult Form)
Mary S. Wheeler, Roy M. Kern, William L. Curlette

Copyright: 1993

Population: Adults

Purpose: Helps one understand how an individual's beliefs developed in early childhood relate to present functioning; used for individual/marital counseling, vocational counseling, organizational settings, and educational settings

Description: Paper–pencil 65-item Likert scale test with five BASIS–A Scales and five HELPS Scales. The BASIS–A scales are Belonging–Social Interest (9 items), Going Along (8 items), Taking Charge (8 items), Wanting Recognition (11 items), and Being Cautious (8 items). The HELPS scales are Harshness (H), Entitlement (E), Liked by All (L), Striving for Perfection (P), and Softness (S). Individuals receive *T*-scores on the five BASIS–A Scales and cutoff scores on the five HELPS scales. Profiles are part of the self-scoring test booklet. Materials used include test items, responses, scoring directions, and brief interpretations of scales, all contained in a self-scoring test booklet.

Format: Individual/group administered; self/examiner administered; untimed: approximately 20–30 minutes

Scoring: Self-scored; examiner evaluated

Cost: Introductory Kit (2 manuals, 15 self-scoring test booklets, and 15 interpretive guides) $95.00; Sampler Kit (one self-scoring test booklet, one interpretive guide) $7.00 plus shipping and handling

Publisher: TRT Associates, Inc.

Bass Orientation Inventory (ORI)
Bernard M. Bass

Copyright: 1977

Population: Adolescents, adults

Purpose: Measures attitudes toward achieve-

ment and rewards; used for personnel assessment, high-school and college vocational counseling, and group research

Description: Paper–pencil 27-item forced-choice test of three types of orientation toward satisfaction and rewards: self-orientation, interaction orientation, and task orientation. Results help to predict an individual's success and performance in various types of work. The inventory is based on Bass' theory of interpersonal behavior in organizations.

Format: Examiner required; suitable for group use; untimed: 10–15 minutes

Scoring: Hand key

Cost: Sampler Set $25.00; Permission Set $90.00

Publisher: Mind Garden, Inc.

Behavior Status Inventory
William T. Martin

Copyright: 1971

Population: Adolescents, adults

Purpose: Measures behavioral traits of adults and adolescents in mental health settings; used to evaluate patients with emotional disturbance, brain damage, and mental retardation; used to monitor patient progress in response to therapy

Description: Observational inventory with 91 items assessing seven behavioral areas: personal appearance, manifest (obvious) behavior, attitude, verbal behavior, social behavior, work behavior, and cognitive behavior. An aide or staff member familiar with the individual can complete the questionnaire, rating each of the behavioral statements from 1 to 4 based on observed patient behavior during the past week. Scores for each of the seven subscales and a Total Patient Asset Score are derived. Item analysis and subscale scores can be machine scored for one time or for ongoing patient or program analysis.

Format: Examiner required; suitable for group use; untimed: no time limit

Scoring: Examiner evaluated

Cost: Specimen Set $5.00; 25 forms $15.00; 25 profile sheets $6.75

Publisher: Psychologists and Educators, Inc.

Beliefs About Women Scale (BAWS)

Sharyn S. Belk, William E. Snell

Copyright: 1986

Population: Adults

Purpose: Assesses stereotypic beliefs about women; used in research

Description: Agree/disagree 75-item, 5-point scale questionnaire with 15 subscales

Format: Self-administration; suitable for group use; untimed

Scoring: Examiner evaluated

Cost: $21.00

Publisher: Select Press

Bell Object Relations and Reality Testing Inventory (BORRTI)

Morris D. Bell

Copyright: Not provided

Population: Adults

Purpose: Used by clinicians to evaluate adults with character disorders and psychoses

Description: Composed of 90 items, the inventory measures object relations and reality testing on seven scales: Object Relations–Alienation, Egocentricity, Insecure Attachment, Social Incompetence; Reality Testing Reality Distortion, Uncertainty of Perception. The test report profiles scores, describes client characteristics, makes diagnostic suggestions, and provides individualized treatment recommendations. Lists specific clinical themes that apply to client in question.

Format: Individually administered by examiner; 15–20 minutes

Scoring: WPS Scoring Service; fax or mail-in

Cost: Kit (includes 5 WPS Test Reports, prepaid BORRTI mail-in answer sheets, 1 manual) $125.00; BORRTI microcomputer disk (IBM) $250.00; microcomputer answer sheet (pads of 100) $15.00

Publisher: Western Psychological Services

Bem Sex-Role Inventory (BSRI)

Sandra L. Bem

Copyright: 1978, 1981

Population: Adults

Purpose: Measures masculinity and femininity; used for research on psychological androgyny

Description: Sixty-item paper–pencil measure of integration of masculinity and femininity. Items are three sets of 20 personality characteristics: masculine, feminine, and neutral. The subject indicates on a 7-point scale how well each characteristic describes him- or herself. Materials include a 30-item short form.

Format: Self-administered; suitable for group use; untimed: 10 minutes

Scoring: Hand key

Cost: Sampler Set $25.00; Permission Set $90.00; test booklets $25.00

Publisher: Mind Garden, Inc.

Bi/Polar® Inventories of Core Strengths

J. W. Thomas, T. J. Thomas

Copyright: 1977, 1995

Population: Ages 14 to adult

Purpose: Determines personality strengths; used in marital counseling, communication, and self-awareness

Description: Paper–pencil 45-item test in which the examinee uses a Likert-type scale to rate personality statements on three scales (Basic Strengths, Thinking Strengths, and Risking Strengths). A scoring service is available from the publisher. Training required for certification to administer. Available in Spanish and Finnish.

Format: Self-administered; suitable for group use; untimed

Scoring: Computer scored; test scoring service available from publisher

Cost: $40.00

Publisher: Institute of Foundational Training and Development

Bloom Sentence Completion Attitude Survey
Wallace Bloom

Copyright: Not provided

Population: Adolescents, adults

Purpose: Assesses adult and student attitudes toward self and important factors in everyday living; used to identify change in an individual over time and to compare individuals and groups

Description: Forty-item paper–pencil free-response test consisting of sentence stems which the subject completes in his or her own words. The responses measure attitudes toward age mates or people, physical self, family, psychological self, self-directedness, education or work (depending on which version is used), accomplishments, and irritants. Two versions are available: one for adults and one for unmarried students. The scoring system facilitates use of the test as both an objective and a projective instrument.

Format: Examiner required; suitable for group use; untimed: 25 minutes

Scoring: Examiner evaluated

Cost: Complete kit (specify version; 30 test forms, 30 analysis record forms, manual) $44.00

Publisher: Stoelting Company

Brief Symptom Inventory (BSI)
Leonard R. Derogatis

Copyright: 1975

Population: Adolescents, adults; ages 13 years and up

Purpose: Used to screen for psychological problems and measures progress

Description: Multiple-choice 53-item computer-administered or paper–pencil test with a 5-point rating scale of 0 to 4. The nine primary dimensions are somatization, obsessive–compulsive, interpersonal sensitivity, depression, anxiety, hostility, phobic anxiety, paranoid ideation, and psychoticism. A sixth-grade reading level is required. Examiner must be M-level qualified. A computer version using an IBM compatible 486 PC or higher is available. The test is available on audiocassette and in 23 foreign languages; 13 additional languages are available for research purposes only.

Format: Self-administered; suitable for group use; untimed: 8–10 minutes

Scoring: Hand key; computer scored; test scoring service not available

Cost: Contact publisher

Publisher: NCS Assessments

California Life Goals Evaluation Schedules
Milton E. Hahn

Copyright: 1974

Population: Adults; ages 15 and older

Purpose: Differentiates "life goals" from "interests" by identifying significant motivational forces in normal individuals; used for career planning, adjusting to aging or retirement, evoking insights in areas of psychological normality, and college counseling

Description: Paper–pencil 150-item test measuring 10 life goals: esteem, profit, fame, leadership, power, security, social service, interesting experiences, self-expression, and independence. Using a 5-point acceptance or rejection scale, the subject responds to "debatable" statements. Norms are presented based on age, sex, occupation, familial relationships, and projected academic studies.

Format: Self-administered; suitable for group use; untimed: 20–30 minutes

Scoring: Hand key

Cost: Kit (50 profile forms, manual, 10 reusable test booklets, key, 50 answer sheets) $89.50

Publisher: Western Psychological Services

California Psychological Inventory™, Third Edition (CPI™)
Harrison G. Gough

Copyright: 1987

Population: Adolescents, adults; ages 14 and up

Purpose: Assesses personality characteristics important for daily living; used in business, in schools and colleges, in clinics and counseling agencies, and for cross-cultural and other research

Description: True–false 434-item paper–pencil test measuring behavioral tendencies along 20 scales: Dominance, Capacity for Status, Sociability, Social Presence, Self-Acceptance, Independence, Empathy, Responsibility, Socialization, Self-Control, Good Impression, Communality, Well-Being, Tolerance, Achievement via Independence, Achievement via Conformance, Intellectual Efficiency, Psychological-Mindedness, Flexibility, and Femininity/Masculinity. There are three vector scales that define a theoretical model of personality structure and 13 special purpose scales such as Managerial Potential, Work Orientation, Creative Temperament, and Anxiety. Four personality types (Alphas, Betas, Gammas, and Deltas) are described across seven levels. Windows-based scoring and mail-in computer scoring are available. Reports available are the CPI Profile, CPI Narrative Report, CPI Configural Analysis Supplement, and Police and Public Safety Selection Report.

Format: Self-administered; suitable for group use; untimed: 45–60 minutes

Scoring: Hand key; may be computer scored

Cost: Profile Preview Kit $12.00; Narrative Preview Kit $25.00; Configural Analysis Supplement Preview Kit $30.00; Police and Public Safety Preview Kit $22.00

Publisher: Consulting Psychologists Press, Inc.

California Q-Sort Revised (Adult)
Jack Block, Daryl Bem

Copyright: 1990
Population: Adults
Purpose: Describes individual personality in contemporary psychodynamic terms; used for research
Description: Test with 100 items used to formulate personality descriptions. Items are descriptive personality statements on cards sorted from most to least applicable to the subject's ex-

perience. Materials include individual $2\frac{1}{4}''\times3\frac{1}{2}''$ cards and a sorting guide. May be sorted by professionals or laypersons.

Format: Examiner required; not suitable for group use; untimed: typical time not available

Scoring: Examiner evaluated

Cost: Sampler Set $25.00

Publisher: Mind Garden, Inc.

Career Area Rotation Model
Richard B. Williams, Larry T. Looper, Rodney Morton

Copyright: 1974
Population: Adults
Purpose: Used as managerial tool for evaluation of diverse policy interactions
Description: Multiple-item paper–pencil test
Format: Individual or group administration; requires examiner; untimed
Scoring: Examiner evaluated
Cost: $41.28
Publisher: Select Press

Carlson Psychological Survey (CPS)
Kenneth A. Carlson

Copyright: 1982
Population: Adolescents, adults
Purpose: Assesses and classifies criminal offenders; used to evaluate persons presenting behavioral or substance-abuse problems and analyze the effects of intervention programs
Description: Fifty-item paper–pencil questionnaire in a five-category response format with space for the respondent's comments. The scales measured are Chemical Abuse, Thought Disturbance, Antisocial Tendencies, Self-Depreciation, and Validity. The test is designed for offenders, those charged with crimes, and others who have come to the attention of the criminal justice or social welfare systems. The results are classified into 18 offender types. A companion edition, the Psicológico Texto (PT), is designed for use with Spanish-literate offenders. A fourth-grade reading level is required.

Available in French.

Format: Examiner required; suitable for group use; untimed: 15 minutes

Scoring: Hand key; computer scored; scoring service available from publisher

Cost: Examination kit $28.00; software $175.00

Publisher: Sigma Assessment Systems, Inc.

Clinical Analysis Questionnaire
Raymond B. Cattell, Samuel Krug

Copyright: 1970

Population: Adolescents, adults; ages 16 and older

Purpose: Evaluates personality and psychiatric/psychological difficulties; used as a measure of primary behavioral dimensions in adults and adolescents; and for clinical diagnosis, evaluation of therapeutic progress, and vocational and rehabilitation guidance

Description: Paper–pencil 331-item multiple-choice test measuring 16 personality factors (the 16PF factors) as well as hypochondriasis, agitated depression, suicidal depression, anxious depression, guilt, energy level, boredom, and five other dimensions in the pathology domain. Norms are provided for adults and college men and women. Special adolescent norms are provided for Part II. The manual contains profiles for a number of special groups, including alcoholics, narcotic addicts, people with various types of neurotic and psychotic disorders, criminals, and others. The test has been organized in two parts so that the entire test need not be given in a single sitting. A sixth-grade reading level is required.

Format: Self-administered; suitable for group use; untimed: 2 hours

Scoring: Hand key; may be computer scored

Cost: 25 hand-scorable answer sheets $10.75; manual $16.00; scoring keys $23.00; computer profile and interpretation $18.00–$25.00; 25 reusable test booklets $34.25; for teleprocessing and computer software contact publisher

Publisher: Institute for Personality and Ability Testing, Inc.

Clinical Checklist Series

Copyright: 1984–1989

Population: Adolescents, adults

Purpose: Assesses personal, marital, and health problems; used for initiating the consultation process and introducing the client to formal diagnostic testing

Description: Multiple-item paper–pencil or computer-administered series of five checklists used, as appropriate, with adolescents and adults to identify relevant problems, establish rapport, and provide written documentation of presenting problems consistent with community standards of care. Checklists include Personal Problems Checklist–Adult, Personal Problems Checklist–Adolescent, Children's Problems Checklist, Marital Evaluation Checklist, and Health Problems Checklist. Items are presented in terms understood by adolescents and adults from most educational and occupational levels.

Format: Self-administered; suitable for group use; untimed: 10–20 minutes

Scoring: Examiner evaluated

Cost: 50 Checklists $34.00

Publisher: Psychological Assessment Resources, Inc.

Close Air Support Mission: CAS
Gary S. Thomas

Copyright: 1985

Population: Adults; military

Purpose: Measures pilot performance and combat readiness

Description: Multiple-choice, projective paper–pencil/oral test

Format: Individual administration; examiner required; untimed

Scoring: Hand key; examiner evaluated

Cost: $15.00

Publisher: Select Press

College Adjustment Scales (CAS)
William D. Anton, James R. Reed

Copyright: 1991

Population: Adults; ages 17 to 30

Purpose: Used by college counselors to identify psychological adjustment problems experienced by college students

Description: Paper–pencil 108-item 4-point Likert scale measuring anxiety, depression, suicidal ideation, substance abuse, self-esteem problems, interpersonal problems, family problems, academic problems, and career problems. A manual, item booklet, and answer sheet are used. A fifth-grade reading level is required. Examiner must be B–Level qualified with graduate training in psychology.

Format: Individual administration; suitable for group use; examiner required; untimed

Scoring: Hand scored

Cost: manual, 25 reusable item books, 25 answer sheets $59.00

Publisher: Psychological Assessment Resources, Inc.

Community Integration Scale
Janet Taylor

Copyright: 1979

Population: Adults

Purpose: Assesses treatment outcome in the community

Description: Seven-item paper–pencil scale measuring success of therapy

Format: Individual administration; requires examiner; untimed

Scoring: Examiner evaluated

Cost: $15.00

Publisher: Select Press

Comprehensive Emotional-State Scales
Albert Mehrabian

Copyright: 1995

Population: Adolescents, adults; ages 14 and older

Purpose: Measures three basic dimensions of affect: pleasure, arousal, and dominance; used

for research and counseling

Description: Paper–pencil 34-item test with three subscales: pleasure–displeasure, 16 items; arousal–nonarousal, 9 items; dominance–submissiveness, 9 items. A 10th-grade reading level is required.

Format: Self-administered; suitable for group use; untimed: 10 minutes

Scoring: Hand key; test scoring service available from publisher

Cost: Test Kit $31.00

Publisher: Albert Mehrabian, Ph.D.

Comrey Personality Scales (CPS)
Andrew L. Comrey

Copyright: 1970

Population: Adolescents, adults

Purpose: Measures major personality characteristics of adults and high school and college students; used in educational, clinical, and business settings where personality structure and stability are important

Description: Paper–pencil 180-item test consisting of eight personality dimensions scales (20 items each), a validity scale (8 items), and a response bias scale (12 items). The eight personality scales are Trust vs. Defensiveness, Orderliness vs. Lack of Orderliness, Social Conformity vs. Rebelliousness, Activity vs. Lack of Energy, Emotional Stability vs. Neuroticism, Extraversion vs. Introversion, Masculinity vs. Femininity, and Empathy vs. Egocentrism. Subjects respond to items according to 7-point scales ranging from "never" or "definitely not" to "always" or "definitely." The profile presents a description of the personality structure of "normal" socially functioning individuals. Extreme scores on any of the scales may provide a clue to the source of current difficulties, predict future problems, aid in selection of therapy programs, and screen job applicants. Norms are presented as T-scores for male and female college students.

Format: Examiner required; suitable for group use; untimed: 30–50 minutes

Scoring: Hand key; may be computer scored

Cost: Specimen Set (manual, all forms) $29.25

Publisher: EdITS/Educational and Industrial Testing Service

Consequences (CQ)
Paul R. Christensen, Philip R. Merrifield, J. P. Guilford

Copyright: 1980

Population: Adults

Purpose: Measures ability to produce spontaneously original ideas in response to associated ideas

Description: Clients are asked to write consequences for five new and unusual situations; it is used to predict academic achievement and job performance and in researching personality and creativity

Format: Examiner required; untimed: 10 minutes

Scoring: Hand key

Cost: Sampler Set $25.00, permission for up to 200 uses $90.00

Publisher: Mind Garden, Inc.

Construction of a Personal Autonomy Inventory
D. J. W. Strumpfer

Copyright: 1976

Population: Males ages 19 to 60

Purpose: Assesses need for autonomy or independence

Description: Paper–pencil 415-item questionnaire

Format: Examiner required; not suitable for group use; untimed

Scoring: Examiner evaluated

Cost: $15.00

Publisher: Select Press

Coping Operations Preference Enquiry (COPE)
Will Schutz

Copyright: 1962

Population: Adults

Purpose: Measures individual preference for certain types of coping or defense mechanisms; used for counseling and therapy

Description: Six-item paper–pencil test measuring the characteristic use of five defense mechanisms: denial, isolation, projection, regression–dependency, and turning-against-the-self. Each item describes a person and his or her behavior in a particular situation. The respondent ranks five alternative ways he or she might feel; the alternatives represent the inventory's five coping mechanisms. Materials include separate forms for men and women.

Format: May be self-administered; an examiner is recommended; suitable for group use; untimed

Scoring: Examiner evaluated

Cost: Sampler Set $25.00, permission for up to 200 uses $90.00

Publisher: Mind Garden, Inc.

Coping Resources Inventory (CRI)
Allen L. Hammer, M. Susan Marting

Copyright: Not provided

Population: Adults

Purpose: Measures an individual's resources for coping with stress; used in individual counseling, workshops, and health settings

Description: Sixty-item paper–pencil inventory consisting of five scales measuring an individual's cognitive, social, physical, emotional, and values resources. The results identify the resources a person has developed for coping with stress and those that still must be developed. The manual includes scale descriptions, reliability and validity information, separate norms for males and females, and case illustrations for interpreting the profiles.

Format: Examiner required; suitable for group use; untimed: 10 minutes

Scoring: Hand key; may be computer scored

Cost: Sampler (booklet, answer sheet, manual) $22.00

Publisher: Consulting Psychologists Press, Inc.

Cornell Index
Arthur Weider

Copyright: 1958

Population: Adults

Purpose: Evaluates an individual's psychiatric history; identifies individuals with serious personal and psychosomatic disturbances; used for clinical evaluations and research purposes

Description: Paper–pencil 101-item questionnaire measuring neuropsychiatric and psychosomatic symptoms. Administered in the form of a structures interview. Analysis of responses provides a standardized evaluation of an individual's psychiatric history and statistically differentiates individuals with serious personal and psychiatric disturbances.

Format: Self-administered; suitable for group use; untimed: 5 minutes

Scoring: Template and examiner evaluated

Cost: 25 questionnaires $9.00; 100 copies $35.00; Specimen Set $20.00

Publisher: Arthur Weider, Ph.D.

Cornell Word Form
Arthur Weider

Copyright: 1958

Population: Adults

Purpose: Assesses an individual's adaptive mechanisms; used in a variety of clinical and research settings

Description: Multiple-item paper–pencil test employing a modification of the word association technique. For each test item, the subject selects one word of a pair of printed responses that he or she associates with a given stimulus word. Analysis of the responses contributes to a descriptive sketch of the subject's adaptive mechanisms in a manner not easily apparent.

Format: Self-administered; suitable for group use; untimed: 5 minutes

Scoring: Template and examiner evaluated

Cost: Specimen Set $20.00; 25 copies $9.00; 100 copies $35.00

Publisher: Arthur Weider, Ph.D.

Curtis Completion Form
James W. Curtis

Copyright: 1971

Population: Adolescents, adults

Purpose: Evaluates the emotional adjustment of older adolescent and adults; used in employment situations to screen individuals whose emotional adjustment makes them poor employment risks; also used in educational and industrial counseling

Description: Multiple-item paper–pencil free-response sentence-completion test measuring emotional adjustment. It is similar to a projective test, but is scored using relatively objective, standardized criteria.

Format: Examiner required; suitable for group use; untimed: 30 minutes

Scoring: Examiner evaluated

Cost: Kit (25 forms, 1 manual) $37.50

Publisher: Western Psychological Services

Defense Mechanisms Inventory
Goldine C. Gleser, David Ihilevich

Copyright: 1993

Population: Adolescents, adults; ages 10 and above

Purpose: Assesses an individual's use of such defense mechanisms as projection and reversal

Description: Ten vignettes (male and female forms) with five defensive responses to a variety of situations are presented to the subject. Each vignette is followed by four questions: "What would you do?", "What would you like to do?", "What do you think?", and "How do you feel?" There are five possible responses to each question corresponding to the following five defense mechanisms: turning against an object, projection, principalization, turning against self, and reversal. Materials include adolescent, adult, and elderly male and female forms, answer sheets, a manual, and male and female profiles. The adult version may be used in clinical settings; the adolescent and elderly versions are restricted to research applications. Available in German, French, and Portuguese.

Format: Self-administered; suitable for group use; untimed: 40 minutes

Scoring: Hand key

Cost: Comprehensive Kit $115.00

Publisher: Psychological Assessment Resources, Inc.

Defining Issues Test of Moral Judgment (DIT)
James R. Rest

Copyright: 1979

Population: Adolescents, adults; ages 12+; English-speaking populations

Purpose: Assesses moral judgment development; used for education evaluations and psychological assessment

Description: Paper–pencil 72-item test consisting of six short stories, each followed by 12 related statements. The stories present social problems or moral dilemmas, and the statements present a range of considerations to be taken into account as one tries to determine what a proper course of action would be in a given situation. Individuals indicate each consideration's importance by rating each statement on a 5-point scale ranging from "none" to "great." Individuals then rank in order of importance the 4 statements they consider the most important of the 12 statements provided for each story. A proficiency in English and an eighth-grade reading level are required. Suitable for individuals with visual, physical, hearing, and mental disabilities.

Format: Self-administered; suitable for group use; untimed: 40 minutes

Scoring: Examiner evaluated; computer scored

Cost: $.70 each to $1.95 each, depending on quantity ordered

Publisher: Center for the Study of Ethical Development

Derogatis Affects Balance Scale (DABS)
Leonard R. Derogatis

Copyright: 1975

Population: Adolescents, adults

Purpose: Evaluates psychological adjustment and well-being in terms of mood and affect balance

Description: Forty-item paper–pencil self-report adjective mood scale assessing four positive affect dimensions (joy, contentment, vigor, and affection) and four negative affect dimensions (anxiety, depression, guilt, and hostility). Scoring and interpretation procedures are structured on the concept that healthy psychological adjustment is based on the presence of active positive emotions and the relative absence of negative emotions. The overall score of the test is expressed as the affect balance index, reflecting the balance between positive and negative affects in terms of standardized scores. SCORABS Version 2.1 is a computer scoring program designed for IBM DOS systems. It generates eight positive and negative primary affect dimension scores, positive and negative affect total scores, an Affects Balance Index, and two additional global scores.

Format: Examiner required; suitable for group use; untimed: 3–5 minutes

Scoring: Examiner evaluated; may be computer scored

Cost: 100 test forms $50.00; 100 profile sheets $40.00

Publisher: Clinical Psychometric Research, Inc.

Derogatis Psychiatric Rating Scale™ (DPRS®)
Leonard R. Derogatis

Copyright: 1978

Population: Adolescents, adults

Purpose: Screens for psychological problems and measures progress; used in adolescent and adult personality assessment

Description: Computer or paper–pencil test using a clinician rating scale. The DPRS enables the clinician to rate his or her observations of a patient's psychological symptomatic distress on the same nine primary dimensional scales as measured by the SCL-90-R or BSI. The nine primary scales are: somatization, obsessive–compulsive, interpersonal sensitivity, depression, anxiety, hostility, phobic anxiety, paranoid ideation, and psychoticism. The eight additional scales are: sleep disturbance, psychomotor retardation, hysterical behavior, abjection–disinterest, conceptual dysfunction, disorientation, excitement, and euphoria. The examiner must have A-level qualifications. A computer version is available using an IBM-compatible 486 PC or higher.

Format: Individual administration; examiner required; untimed: 2–5 minutes

Scoring: Examiner evaluated; computer or hand scored; no scoring service available

Cost: Contact publisher

Publisher: NCS Assessments

Description of Body Scale (DOBS)
R. E. Carney

Copyright: 1980

Population: Adolescents, adults; ages 12 and older; Grades 7 and above

Purpose: Measures perceived masculinity/femininity of body

Description: Fourteen-item paper–pencil test utilizing a 6-point scale ranging from male to female. Items are divided evenly between the Present Body scale and the Ideal Body scale. The test yields a Total Masculinity (S) score, Ideal Masculinity (I) score, Inconsistency (K) score, and a Present-Ideal Incongruence (C) score. The test form integrates items, scoring, and a profile. A scoring service is available from the publisher. Examinees must have a seventh-grade reading level. Test forms must be ordered in quantities of 50 or more.

Format: Examiner/self-administered; suitable for group use; untimed: time varies

Scoring: Hand key; may be computer scored

Cost: 50 forms $25.00; Specimen Set (manual, form) $12.00

Publisher: TIMAO Foundation for Research and Development

Domestic Violence Inventory

Copyright: 1991

Population: Adult domestic violence offenders

Purpose: Used for evaluating domestic violence offenders

Description: Designed for domestic violence risk and needs assessment, the test contains six scales: Truthfulness, Violence, Alcohol, Drugs, Agressivity, and Stress Coping Ability. Each scale provides specific recommendations for intervention, supervision, and treatment. There are 157 multiple-choice/true–false items. Truth-corrected scores. Computer-generated report summarizes risk range and recommendations; on-site reports within 4 minutes of test completion. Designed specifically for assessing domestic violence. Available in English or Spanish.

Format: Self-administered; suitable for group use; 30 minutes

Scoring: Computer scored

Cost: Contact publisher

Publisher: Risk and Needs Assessment, Inc.

Dynamic Personality Inventory (DPI)
Charles Saltzman, James Creaser, Jo-Ann Ashbaugh

Copyright: 1976

Population: Adults

Purpose: Measures normative results of U.S. college population

Description: Paper–pencil 39-item instrument

Format: Group or individual administration; examiner required; untimed

Scoring: Hand key; examiner evaluated

Cost: $15.00

Publisher: Select Press

Educational Values (VAL-ED)
Will Schutz

Copyright: 1962, 1977

Population: Adults

Purpose: Assesses an individual's attitudes toward education; used to evaluate the working relationships of students, teachers, administrators, and community members

Description: Multiple-item paper–pencil survey of values regarding interpersonal relationships in school settings. The factors included relate to inclusion, control, and affection at both the feeling and the behavioral levels and to the purpose and importance of education.

Format: Examiner/self-administered; suitable for group use; untimed: typical time not available

Scoring: hand key

Cost: Sampler Set $25.00; Permission Set $90.00

Publisher: Mind Garden, Inc.

Edwards Personal Preference Schedule (EPPS)
A. L. Edwards

Copyright: 1959

Population: Adults; ages 18 and older

Purpose: Assesses an individual's personality; used for both personal counseling and personality research

Description: Paper–pencil forced-choice test designed to show the relative importance of 15 needs and motives: achievement, deference, order, exhibition, autonomy, affiliation, intraception, succorance, dominance, abasement, nurturance, change, endurance, heterosexuality, and aggression.

Format: Self-administered; suitable for group use; untimed: 45 minutes

Scoring: Hand key

Cost: Examination Kit (manual, schedule booklet, hand-scorable answer sheet, and IBM 805 and NCS Answer Sheets) $35.00

Publisher: The Psychological Corporation

Ego Function Assessment (EFA)
Leopold Bellak

Copyright: 1989

Population: Adolescents, adults; ages 13 and older

Purpose: Assesses ego functions; used for a variety of purposes including personnel assessment, drug effects, and evaluation

Description: Oral-response criterion-referenced test measuring 12 ego functions

Format: Examiner administered; not suitable for group use; untimed: time varies

Scoring: Examiner evaluated

Cost: $12.00

Publisher: C.P.S., Inc.

Eight State Questionnaire: Forms A and B (8SQ)
James P. Curran, Raymond B. Cattell

Copyright: 1974

Population: Adolescents, adults; ages 17 and older

Purpose: Assesses the state of mind of adults and adolescents; measures experimental manipulations of a person's moods and progress of related therapeutic intervention; used for clinical evaluation and personal counseling

Description: Multiple-item paper–pencil questionnaire measuring eight important mood states: anxiety, stress, depression, regression, fatigue, guilt, extraversion, and arousal. The questionnaire is available in two equivalent forms to allow for accurate retesting. Standard scores and percentiles are presented for men and women together, men alone, women alone, and male prisoners. A sixth-grade reading level is required.

Format: Self-administered; suitable for group use; untimed: 30 minutes

Scoring: Hand key

Cost: Specimen Set $10.75; manual $7.75; 10 reusable test booklets (for both Forms A and B) $13.25; 25 answer sheets $10.75; 25 profile sheets $10.75; and scoring key $11.00

Publisher: Institute for Personality and Ability Testing, Inc.

Embedded Figures Test (EFT)
Herman A. Witkin

Copyright: Not provided

Population: Ages 10 to adult

Purpose: Assesses cognitive style in perceptual tasks; used in counseling

Description: Twelve-item verbal-manual test of perceptual processes including field dependence–independence. The task requires the subject to locate and trace a previously seen simple figure within a larger complex figure. Performance is related to analytic ability, social behavior, body concept, and preferred defense mechanisms. Materials include cards with complex figures, cards with simple figures, and a stylus for tracing. A stopwatch with a second hand is needed also. Two alternate forms are available.

Format: Examiner required; not suitable for group use; untimed: 10–45 minutes

Scoring: Examiner evaluated

Cost: Test kit (card sets, stylus, 25 recording sheets) $63.60; manual $22.25

Publisher: Consulting Psychologists Press, Inc.

Emotional Problem Scale (EPS)
H. Thompson Prout, Douglas C. Strohmer

Copyright: 1991

Population: Ages 14 and above

Purpose: Used in behavioral counseling to assess emotional and behavioral problems in individuals with mild mental retardation and borderline intelligence

Description: Multiple-choice paper–pencil yes–no scale with two categories: a Behavior Rating Scale (BRS) and a Self Report Inventory (SRI). The BRS measures thought/behavior disorder, verbal aggression, physical aggression, sexual maladjustment, distractability, somatic concerns, depression, withdrawal, low self-esteem, and externalizing/internalizing problems. The SRI measures positive impression, thought/ behavior disorder, impulse control, anxiety, depression, low self-esteem, and total pathology. Materials used include a manual, BRS test BK, SRF test BK, SRI scoring key, and EPS profile form. A fourth-grade reading level is required. Examiner must be B-Level qualified.

Format: Self-administered; examiner required; untimed

Scoring: Hand key

Cost: Introductory Kit (manual, protocols, and scoring keys) $77.00

Publisher: Psychological Assessment Resources, Inc.

Emotions Profile Index
Robert Plutcik, Henry Kellerman

Copyright: 1974

Population: Adolescents, adults

Purpose: Measures personality traits and conflicts in adults and adolescents; used for counseling and guidance, therapy, and diagnostic evaluations

Description: Paper–pencil 62-item forced-choice test in which the subject chooses which of the two words presented in each item best describes her- or himself. Four bipolar scales measure eight dimensions of emotions: Timed vs. Aggressive, Trustful vs. Distrustful, Controlled vs. Dyscontrolled, and Gregarious vs. Depressed. A unique circular profile displays percentile scores and compares the basic personality dimensions. Norms are provided on 1,000 normal adult men and women. Data also are given for certain special groups.

Format: Examiner required; suitable for group use; untimed: 10–15 minutes

Scoring: Hand key

Cost: Kit (25 tests and profile sheets, 1 manual) $40.00

Publisher: Western Psychological Services

Employee Assistance Program Inventory (EAPI)
William D. Anton, James R. Reed

Copyright: 1994

Population: Adults

Purpose: Used in employee assistance programs and counseling to screen for identification of common psychiatric problems in 10 areas

Description: Inventory with 120 items using the following 4-point scales: Anxiety, Depression, Self-Esteem, Marital Problems, Family Problems, External Stressors, Interpersonal Conflict, Work Adjustment, Problem Minimization, Effects of Substance Abuse. Items used include a manual, item booklet, and an answer profile sheet. A third-grade reading level is required. Examiner must be B-Level qualified.

Format: Self-administered; suitable for group use; untimed

Scoring: Hand-scorable answer sheet

Cost: Intro Kit $55.00

Publisher: Psychological Assessment Resources, Inc.

Endler Multidimensional Anxiety Scales (EMAS)

Norman S. Endler, Jean M. Edwards, Romeo Vitelli

Copyright: Not provided

Population: Adolescents, adults

Purpose: Used to evaluate phobias, panic attacks, generalized anxiety disorder, test anxiety, posttraumatic stress disorder, and treatment outcome

Description: Three related self-report measures that assess and predict anxiety across situations and measure treatment response. The first scale measures state anxiety—the individual's actual transitory anxiety response. It assesses both physiological and cognitive responses. The second scale measures the individual's predisposition to experience anxiety in four different types of situations. The third scale evaluates the individual's perception of the type and intensity of threat in the immediate situation. The scales can be given separately or as a set.

Format: Suitable for group use; examiner required; 25 minutes

Scoring: Hand or computer scored

Cost: Kit (includes 10 AutoScore™ test forms for each scale, 1 manual, 2 test report prepaid mail-in answer sheets for computer scoring and interpretation) $80.00

Publisher: Western Psychological Services

EPS Problems Checklist (PC)

H. Thomas Prout, Douglas C. Strohmer

Copyright: 1993

Population: Adolescents, adults

Purpose: Used in behavioral/educational counseling to survey common client problems across 13 areas; intended for individuals with mild mental retardation or borderline intelligence

Description: Checklist with 200 items and the following categories: Interpersonal Relationships/Getting Along with Others, Psychological Functioning/About Myself, Sexuality and Relationships/Sex, Dating and the Opposite Sex, Family/My Family, Residential Living and Adjustment/Where I Live, Behavior/What I Do and How I Act, Financial Concerns/Money, Attitudes Toward Disability/Being Different, Independence/Doing Things on My Own, Adjustment to Change and Adaptability/Changes in My Life, Health/My Health, Responsibility/Being Responsible, School or Work/School or Work and Jobs. Materials used include a professional user's guide, problems checklist, and school or nonschool forms. A fourth-grade reading level is required. Examiner must be B-Level qualified.

Format: Self-administered; examiner required; untimed

Scoring: Examiner evaluated

Cost: Kit (guide and booklets) $30.00

Publisher: Psychological Assessment Resources, Inc.

EPS Sentence Completion Technique (SCT)

Douglas C. Strohmer, H. Thomas Prout

Copyright: 1991

Population: Adolescents, adults

Purpose: Used in behavioral counseling to assess problem areas in mild mental retardation and borderline intelligence subjects

Description: Forty-item paper–pencil projective test with the following categories: Interpersonal Relations, Psychological Functioning, Work or School, Independence, Sexuality, Family, Residential Living, Behavior, and Health. Materials used include a professional user's guide, SCT school version test booklets, and SCT nonschool version test booklets. A fourth-grade reading level is required. Examiner must be B-Level qualified.

Format: Self-administered; examiner required; untimed

Scoring: Examiner evaluated

Cost: Kit (Guide and booklets) $21.00

Publisher: Psychological Assessment Resources, Inc.

Eysenck Personality Inventory (EPI)

H. J. Eysenck, Sybil B. G. Eysenck

Copyright: 1963

Population: Adolescents, adults

Purpose: Measures extraversion and neuroticism, the two dimensions of personality which account for most personality variance; used for counseling, clinical evaluation, and research

Description: Paper–pencil 57-item yes–no inventory measuring two independent dimensions of personality: extraversion–introversion and neuroticism–stability. A falsification scale detects response distortion. Scores are provided for three scales: E—Extraversion, N—Neuroticism, and L—Lie. The inventory is available in two equivalent forms, A and B, for pre- and posttesting. The instrument also is available in Industrial Form A-I for industrial workers. College norms are presented in percentile form for Forms A and B both separately and combined. Adult norms are presented for Form A-I. Available in Spanish.

Format: Self-administered; suitable for group use; untimed: 10–15 minutes

Scoring: Hand key; may be computer scored

Cost: Specimen Set (manual, one copy of all forms) $7.75

Publisher: EdITS/Educational and Industrial Testing Service

Facial Interpersonal Perception Inventory (FIPI)

J. Luciani, R. E. Carney

Copyright: 1980

Population: Ages 3 to adults

Purpose: Assess an individual's self-perception

Description: Paper–pencil 26-item nonverbal projective point-to instrument using cartoon faces to assess present and ideal self-perception or perception of others, as well as incongruence between present and ideal perception. The items are divided into two categories, Present Perception (13 items) and Ideal Perception (13 items). The test yields 15 scores: Total Positive Perception, Pleasant–Unpleasant, Attention–Rejection, Sleep–Tension, Total Inconsistency, Systematic, Inconsistency, Unsystematic Inconsistency, Inconsistency F Ratio, Total Incongruence, Pleasant–Unpleasant Incongruence, Attention–Rejection Incongruence, Sleep–Tension Incongruence, Systematic Incongruence, Unsystematic Incongruence, and Incongurence F Ratio. The test form integrates items, scoring, and a profile. A scoring service is available from the publisher. The test requires no reading skills; however, if the subject is illiterate, the examiner must speak the subject's native language. Available in Spanish.

Format: Examiner or self-administered; not suitable for group use

Scoring: Hand key; may be computer scored; scoring service available from publisher

Cost: 50 forms $25.00; Specimen Set (manual, form) $12.00; forms must be ordered in quantities of 50 or more

Publisher: TIMAO Foundation for Research and Development

Feminist Attitude Toward Rape Scale

Marsha B. Jacobson, Paula M. Papovich, David W. Biers

Copyright: 1980

Population: Adults

Purpose: Measures male/female attitudes toward rape

Description: Paper–pencil 46-item agree/disagree-extent statements

Format: Individual/self-administered; examiner required; untimed

Scoring: Hand key; examiner evaluated

Cost: $18.00

Publisher: Select Press

Fundamental Interpersonal Relations Orientation–Feelings (FIRO–F)

Will Schutz

Copyright: Not provided

Population: Adults

Purpose: Evaluates an individual's characteristic feelings toward others; used to assess both individual and interactional traits as an aid to counseling and therapy

Description: Paper–pencil 54-item test measuring six dimensions of an individual's feelings toward others: expressed significance, expressed competence, expressed lovability, wanted significance, wanted competence, and wanted lovability. Dimensions parallel the three dimensions of the FIRO–B. The FIRO–F is identical to the FIRO–B except the questions are phrased to assess feelings rather than behaviors.

Format: Examiner/self-administered; suitable for group use; untimed: 15–20 minutes

Scoring: hand key

Cost: 25 test booklets $29.75; scoring key $42.50

Publisher: Consulting Psychologists Press, Inc.

Giannetti On-Line Psychosocial History (GOLPH)
Ronald A. Giannetti

Copyright: 1988

Population: Adults

Purpose: Gathers information on an individual's background and current life circumstances; used to obtain psychosocial history for general or psychiatric patients, and to evaluate job applicants' work history and criminal offenders' history of legal difficulties

Description: Multiple-item multiple-choice and completion-item questionnaire presented on microcomputer. Questions and their order of appearance are determined by answers to the preceding items. The examiner selects from the following areas to gather appropriate information: current living situation, family of origin, client development, educational history, marital history/present family, occupational history/current finances, legal history, symptom screening (physical), symptom screening (psychological), and military history. Questions are presented at a sixth-grade reading level. The length of the examination depends on the areas chosen for exploration and the extent of the individual's problems. A 3- to 12-page report presents the individual's responses in narrative fashion.

Format: Computer/self-administered; not suitable for group use; untimed: 30 minutes–2 hours

Scoring: PC-based MICROTEST™ system required for GOLPH use

Cost: MICROTEST™ system (10 administrations) $80.00; 50 administrations $337.50; 100 administrations $600.00

Publisher: NCS Assessments

Gordon Personal Profile and Inventory (GPP-I)
Leonard V. Gordon

Copyright: 1993

Population: Adolescents, adults

Purpose: Assesses aspects of an individual's personality that are significant in the functioning of the normal person

Description: Paper–pencil measure of eight aspects of personality. The Personal Profile measures ascendancy, responsibility, emotional stability, and sociability. Four traits combine to yield the Self-Esteem score. The Personal Inventory measures cautiousness, original thinking, personal relations, and vigor. Respondents mark one item in each group of three as being most like them and one item as being least like them.

Format: Self-administered; suitable for group use; untimed: 10–15 minutes per instrument

Scoring: Hand key; may be machine scored locally

Cost: Examination Kit (profile/inventory booklet, one profile booklet, one inventory booklet, and manual) $48.00; 25 booklets: profile/inventory $73.75, profile $33.00, inventory $33.00

Publisher: The Psychological Corporation

Guilford-Zimmerman Temperament Survey (GZTS)
J. P. Guilford, Wayne S. Zimmerman

Copyright: Not provided

Population: Adults

Purpose: Identifies nonclinical personality and temperament; can be used for crisis intervention, assertiveness training, and desensitization

Description: Records orientation on 10 scales (general activity, restraint, ascendancy, sociability, emotional stability, objectivity, friendliness, thoughtfulness, personal relations, and masculinity/femininity) to identify positive and negative temperament.

Format: Individual administration; 45 minutes

Scoring: Examiner interpretation; can be computer scored

Cost: Preview Kit (booklet, answer sheet, manual) $20.00

Publisher: Consulting Psychologists Press, Inc.

Hassles and Uplifts Scale (HSUP)
Richard S. Lazarus, Susan lolkman

Copyright: 1989

Population: Adults

Purpose: Measures respondents' attitudes about daily situations; used in counseling and in clinical settings

Description: Likert scale measuring the frequency and severity of hassles and the frequency and intensity of uplifts. An eighth-grade reading level is required.

Format: Self-administered; suitable for group use; untimed

Scoring: Examiner evaluated

Cost: Sampler Set $25.00; permission for 200 uses $90.00

Publisher: Mind Garden, Inc.

Health and Daily Living Form (HDL)
Rudolph H. Moos, Ruth C. Cronkite, John W. Finney

Copyright: 1990

Population: Adolescents, adults

Purpose: Assesses both patient and community groups' health-related factors, life stressors, social functioning, and resources; used by health psychologists and clinicians

Description: Yes–no test. An eighth-grade reading level is required.

Format: Individual administration; examiner required; untimed

Scoring: Examiner evaluated

Cost: Sampler Set $25.00; permission for 200 uses $90.00

Publisher: Mind Garden, Inc.

Heterosocial Adequacy Test (HAT)
Michael G. Perric, Steven Richards, Jerry D. Goodrich

Copyright: 1978

Population: Adults

Purpose: Role-playing to assess heterosexual skills in male college students

Description: Paper–pencil 484-item instrument measuring 60 salient situations

Format: Group or individual administration; examiner required; untimed

Scoring: Hand key; examiner evaluated

Cost: $18.00

Publisher: Select Press

High School Personality Questionnaire (HSPQ)
Raymond B. Cattell, Mary D. Cattell, Edgar Johns, Mark McConville

Copyright: 1968

Population: Adolescents; ages 12 to 18

Purpose: Identifies adolescents with high potentials for dropping out of school, drug abuse, and low achievement; used in correctional situations to facilitate parent–teacher, parent–officer, and parent–clinic cooperation

Description: Paper–pencil 142-item questionnaire measuring 14 primary personality dimensions, such as stability, tensions, warmth, and enthusiasm. Scores for anxiety, extraversion, creativity, leadership, and other broad trait patterns are also obtained. The test is available in four equivalent forms, A, B, C, and D. Percentiles and standard scores for separate and combined sex tables are provided. A sixth-grade reading level is required. Also available in Spanish.

Format: Examiner required; suitable for group use; untimed: 45–60 minutes per form

Scoring: Hand key; scoring and interpretation services available

Cost: Computer Interpretation Intro Kit $22.95; manual $13.00; 25 reusable test booklets $18.00–$29.50; 25 machine-scorable answer sheets $10.75; 50 hand-scorable answer sheets $10.75; 50 hand-scorable answer-profile sheets $10.75; and 2 scoring keys $13.50

Publisher: Institute for Personality and Ability Testing, Inc.

Hilson Adolescent Profile (HAP)
Robin E. Inwald

Copyright: 1984

Population: Adolescents; ages 10 to 18

Purpose: Identifies and predicts troubled and/or delinquent behavior in adolescents

Description: Behaviorally oriented 310-item paper–pencil true–false test consisting of a validity measure and 15 scales assessing specific external behaviors, attitudes and temperament, interpersonal adjustment measures, and internalized conflict measures: Guardedness, Alcohol, Drugs, Educational Adjustment Difficulties, Law/Society Violations, Frustration Tolerance, Antisocial/Risk-Taking Attitudes, Rigidity/Obsessiveness, Interpersonal/Assertiveness Difficulties, Homelife Conflicts, Social/Sexual Adjustment, Health Concerns, Anxiety/Phobic Avoidance, Depression/Suicide Potential, Suspicious Temperament, and Unusual Responses. Raw scores and three sets of T-scores are provided for each scale. T-scores are based on juvenile offender norms, clinical inpatient norms, and student norms. A fifth- to sixth-grade reading level is required. A computer scoring service available from the publisher provides mail-in and teleprocessing services.

Format: Self-administered; suitable for group use; untimed: 30–45 minutes

Scoring: Computer scored

Cost: Starter Kit (technical manual, test booklet, answer sheets for 3 computer-scored reports) $45.00; reusable test booklets $2.00; processing fees range from $7.50–$21.50

Publisher: Hilson Research, Inc.

Hogan Personality Inventory
Robert Hogan

Copyright: 1990

Population: Adults

Purpose: Measures normal personality for personnel selection and assessment

Description: True–false 206-item test with seven primary scales: Adjustment concerns confidence, self-esteem, and composure under pressure; Ambition concerns initiative, competitiveness, and leadership potential; Sociability concerns extraversion, gregariousness, and a need for social interaction; Likeability concerns warmth, charm, and the ability to maintain relationships; Prudence concerns responsibility, self-control, and conscientiousness; Intellectance concerns imagination, curiosity, and creative potential; School Success concerns interest in education and the degree to which a person stays up-to-date on business and technical matters. Booklets, answer sheets, and computer software are used. A fourth-grade reading level is required. Also available in Spanish.

Format: Suitable for group use; examiner required; untimed: 20 minutes

Scoring: Computer scored; test scoring service available from publisher

Cost: Contact publisher

Publisher: Hogan Assessment Systems, Inc.

Home–Career Conflict Measure
Helen S. Farmer, Gail Rooney, Kathryn Lyssy

Copyright: 1982

Population: Adults

Purpose: Measures whether women are experiencing conflict or not; used in research and clinical applications

Description: Four-item paper–pencil test

Format: Group or individual administration; examiner required; timed: 20 minutes

Scoring: Examiner evaluated

Cost: $18.00

Publisher: Select Press

How Well Do You Know Yourself
Thomas N. Jenkins

Copyright: 1976

Population: Adolescents, adults; Grades 10 and above

Purpose: Assesses normal personality; used for educational guidance

Description: Multiple-item paper–pencil test measuring 17 personality traits: irritability, practicality, punctuality, novelty-loving, vocational assurance, cooperativeness, ambitiousness, hypercriticalness, dejection, general morale, persistence, nervousness, seriousness, submissiveness, impulsiveness, dynamism, and emotional control. Two additional measures of response style consistency and test objectivity are included.

Format: Examiner required; suitable for group use; untimed: 20 minutes

Scoring: Hand key

Cost: Complete kit (3 test booklets of each edition and manual) $10.00; 25 tests (specify secondary, college, or personnel) $20.00; keys $6.75; manual $6.75

Publisher: Psychologists and Educators, Inc.

Human Relations Inventory
Raymond S. Bemberg

Copyright: 1981

Population: Adolescents, adults; Grades 10 and above

Purpose: Measures a person's tendency toward social or lawful conformity; differentiates between conformist and nonconformist individuals

Description: Multiple-item paper–pencil test measuring an individual's sense of social conformity. Social conformity is defined and tested in terms of moral values, positive goals, reality testing, ability to give affection, tension level, and impulsivity. The test is constructed using the "direction of perception" technique, and the purpose of the test is disguised from subjects to produce more valid results. The test discriminates between samples of law violators and ordinary conformists. Norms are provided for senior high school boys, college students, regular churchgoers, Los Angeles police officers, male inmates of a California youth prison, adult male inmates of the Los Angeles County Jail, and adult female inmates of the Los Angeles County Jail.

Format: Examiner required; suitable for group use; untimed: typical time not available

Scoring: Examiner evaluated

Cost: Specimen Set $5.00; 25 inventories $5.00

Publisher: Psychometric Affiliates

Impact Message Inventory
Donald J. Kiesler, Jack C. Anchin, Michael J. Perkins, Bernie M. Chirico, Edgar M. Kyle, Edward J. Federman

Copyright: 1991

Population: Adolescents, adults

Purpose: Measures the affective, behavioral, and cognitive reactions of one individual to another; helpful in clarifying interpersonal transactions in any dyad, including teacher–student, friends, employer–employee, and therapist–client

Description: Paper–pencil 90-item inventory assessing one individual's reactions to the interpersonal or personality style of another person. Items describe ways in which people are emotionally engaged or affected when interacting with another person. Individuals respond on a 4-point scale ranging form "not at all" to "very much so" to indicate the extent to which each item describes the feeling aroused by the other person, behaviors they want to direct toward the other person, or descriptions of the other person that come to mind when in the other person's presence. Each test item describes a reaction elicited by a person high on one of 15 interpersonal dimensions. Scores are derived for each of the 15 subscales as well as for 4 cluster scores. Kiesler has completed a revised manual, Research Manual for the Impact Message Inventory. The manual includes descriptions of the subscales and tables for converting raw scores to T-scores.

Format: Examiner required; suitable for group use; untimed: 15 minutes

Scoring: Examiner evaluated

Cost: Sampler Set $25.00, permission for 200 uses $90.00; test booklets $25.00

Publisher: Mind Garden, Inc.

Indexing Elementary School-Aged Children's Views of Attractive and Unattractive People
A. Chris Downs, Marie V. Currie

Copyright: 1983

Population: Children; ages 5 to 11

Purpose: Measures attitudes toward physical attractiveness

Description: Paper–pencil/oral response 16-item instrument

Format: Group or individual administration; examiner required; untimed

Scoring: Hand key; examiner evaluated

Cost: $15.00

Publisher: Select Press

Interpersonal Adjective Scales (IAS)
Jerry S. Wiggins

Copyright: 1995

Population: Adults

Purpose: Used in personality assessment to measure the two most important dimensions of interpersonal behavior: dominance and nurturance

Description: Paper–pencil 64-item 8-point scale with the following categories: Cold Hearted, Aloof–Introverted, Unassured–Submissive, Unassuming–Ingenious, Warm–Agreeable, Gregarious–Extroverted. Materials used include a manual, test booklet, scoring booklet, and glossaries. A 10th-grade reading level is required. Examiner must be B–Level qualified. A computer version using IBM-compatible computers is available. Available in Spanish.

Format: Self-administered; suitable for group use; examiner required; untimed: 15 minutes

Scoring: Hand-scored answer sheet

Cost: Intro Kit $60.00

Publisher: Psychological Assessment Resources, Inc.

Interpersonal Communication Inventory
Millard J. Bienvenu

Copyright: 1969

Population: Adolescents, adults; ages 13 and older

Purpose: Assesses the level and characteristics of an individual's communication with others; used in counseling, management training, teaching, research, and communication skills training

Description: Forty-item yes–no–sometimes test. A seventh-grade reading level is required. Examiner must have communication skills experience.

Format: Self-administered; suitable for group use; untimed: 15 minutes

Scoring: Hand key

Cost: $.75 per copy; guide $3.00; minimum order of $10.00

Publisher: Northwest Publications

Interpersonal Relations Questionnaire (IRQ)

Copyright: 1981

Population: Adolescents; ages 12 to 15

Purpose: Assesses personal adjustment in adolescence; used for counseling and guidance

Description: Test with 260 or 100 items measuring 12 components of adjustment: self-confidence, self-esteem, self-control, nervousness, health, family influences, personal freedom, general sociability, sociability with the opposite sex, sociability with the same sex, moral sense, and formal relations. Items are answered on a 4-point scale. A 100-item abridged questionnaire provides a more general indication of adjustment involving five components.

Format: Examiner required; suitable for group use; untimed: 2 hours; abridged questionnaire 1 hour

Scoring: Hand key; examiner evaluated

Cost: Contact publisher

Publisher: Human Sciences Research Council

Interpersonal Style Inventory (ISI)
Maurice Lorr, Richard P. Youniss

Copyright: 1985

Population: Adolescents, adults; ages 14 and older

Purpose: Assesses an individual's manner of interacting with other people and style of impulse control; used for self-understanding, counseling and therapy, personnel guidance, and research

Description: Paper–pencil 300-item true–false inventory assessing an individual's style of interpersonal interactions along 15 primary scales: Directive, Sociable, Help-Seeking, Nurturant, Conscientious, Trusting, Tolerant, Sensitive, Deliberate, Independent, Rule Free, Orderly, Persistent, Stable, and Approval Seeking. Each item is a statement describing ways in which people relate and respond to each other. The individual reads each statement and decides whether it is mostly true or not true for herself or himself. High school and college norms are provided by sex. The computer report includes a full-color WPS ChromaGraph profile of major scores.

Format: Self-administered; suitable for group use; untimed: 30 minutes

Scoring: Computer scored

Cost: Test Kit (2 reusable administration booklets; 5 WPS Test Report prepaid ISI mail-in answer sheets for computer scoring and interpretation; 1 manual) $100.00

Publisher: Western Psychological Services

Intra and Interpersonal Relations (IIRS)

Copyright: 1973

Population: Children, adolescents

Purpose: Measures the relationship with self and parental figures; used for counseling and assessment

Description: Paper–pencil test of relationships with self and others. The scale also measures the relationship between the real and ideal selves and indicates self-acceptance.

Format: Examiner required; suitable for group use; untimed: 30 minutes

Scoring: Hand key; examiner evaluated

Cost: Contact publisher

Publisher: Human Sciences Research Council

Inventory of Positive Thinking Traits
Millard J. Bienvenu

Copyright: 1992

Population: Adolescents, adults; ages 13 and older

Purpose: Assesses negativity and positivity in individuals; used in counseling, human relations, training, and teaching

Description: Yes–no–sometimes test with 34 items. A seventh-grade reading level is required. Examiner must be trained in human relations.

Format: Self-administered; suitable for group use; untimed: 10 minutes

Scoring: Hand key

Cost: $.50 each; guide $1.00; minimum order of $10.00

Publisher: Northwest Publications

IPAT Anxiety Scale (or Self-Analysis Form)
Raymond B. Cattell, Ivan H. Scheier

Copyright: 1976

Population: Adolescents, adults; Grades 10 and above

Purpose: Measures anxiety in senior high-school students and adults of most educational levels; used for both clinical diagnosis and psychological research on anxiety

Description: Forty-item paper–pencil questionnaire measuring the five principal 16 PF factors of anxiety: emotional instability (C–), suspiciousness (L+), guilt-proneness (0+), low integration (Q3–), and tension (Q4+). Norms are provided for adult, college, and high school populations, with both separate and combined sex tables. A sixth-grade reading level is required.

Format: Examiner required; suitable for group use; untimed: 10 minutes

Scoring: Hand key

Cost: Anxiety Scale Testing Kit $15.00; Anxiety Scale Handbook $10.75; scoring key $4.00; 25 nonreusable test booklets $10.50

Publisher: Institute for Personality and Ability Testing, Inc.

Jackson Personality Inventory Revised (JPI–R)
Douglas N. Jackson

Copyright: 1994

Population: Adolescents, adults

Purpose: Assesses personality characteristics of normal people who have average and above-average intelligence; used to evaluate behavior in a wide range of settings, including those involving work, education, organizations, interpersonal relations, and performance.

Description: Paper–pencil 300-item true–false test covering 15 substantive scales and one validity scale. The scales measured are Complexity, Breadth of Interest, Innovation, Tolerance, Empathy, Anxiety, Cooperativeness, Sociability, Social Confidence, Energy Level, Social Astuteness, Risk Taking, Organization, Traditional Values, and Responsibility. To hand score the test, materials needed include a manual, a reusable test booklet, a quickscore answer sheet, and a profile sheet; no template is required. Norms include updated college norms, and new norms for blue- and white-collar workers. This test differs from the Personality Research Form (PRF) in terms of the nature of the variables measured and is a further refinement of substantive psychometric and computer-based strategies for scale development. Machine readable answer sheets may be mailed to the publisher for a computer-generated report. Test booklets are available in French.

Format: Examiner required; suitable for group use; untimed: 45 minutes

Scoring: Hand key; computer scored; scoring service available from publisher

Cost: Examination kit $59.00; software $175.00

Publisher: Sigma Assessment Systems, Inc.

Jung Personality Questionnaire (JPQ)

Copyright: 1983

Population: All ages

Purpose: Assesses personality; assists in vocational guidance

Description: Multiple-item paper–pencil test of personality based on the theory of Carl Gustav Jung; the personality factors measured are extraversion, introversion, thought, feeling, sensation, intuition, judgment, and perception

Format: Examiner required; suitable for group use; untimed: 25 minutes

Scoring: Hand key; examiner evaluated; may be machine scored

Cost: Contact publisher

Publisher: Human Sciences Research Council

Kirton Adaption–Innovation Inventory (KAI)
Michael J. Kirton

Copyright: 1985

Population: Adolescents, adults

Purpose: Evaluates an individual's cognitive style preference in creativity, problem solving, and decision making; used in personality and occupational psychology and in business management for training and team building

Description: Paper–pencil 33-item test containing three subtests: Sufficiency, Efficiency Preference, and Rule/Group Conformity Preference. Scores are yielded for each subtest. The preferred cognitive style measured is unrelated to an individual's capacity; however, it is strongly related to a critical cluster of personality traits. Available in Italian, Dutch, Slavic, German, French, Spanish, Russian, and Czech.

Format: Suitable for group use; 10–15 minutes

Scoring: Examiner evaluated and interpreted, hand key

Cost: 25 response sheets $32.00; manual $40.00

Publisher: Occupational Research Centre

Least Preferred Coworker Scale
Willam M. Fox

Copyright: 1976

Population: Adults

Purpose: Used in research and development

Description: Instrument measures on 32 scales

Format: Untimed

Scoring: Examiner evaluated

Cost: $21.00

Publisher: Select Press

Level of Service Inventory– Revised (LSI–R)
Don A. Andrews, James L. Bonta

Copyright: 1995

Population: Adults; ages 18 and older

Purpose: Assesses risk and needs in criminal offenders; used for criminal corrections and probation decisions

Description: Test with 54 items and 9 categories: criminal history (10 items), education/employment (12 items), family/marital (4 items), accumulation (3 items), leisure/recreation (2 items), companions (5 items), alcohol/drug problem (9 items), emotional/personal (5 items), attitudes/orientation (4 items). The total score indicates the level of risk/needs. Examiner must be familiar with APA standards and understand test interpretations and limitations.

Format: Individual administration; examiner required; untimed

Scoring: Hand key; examiner evaluated

Cost: Kit $145.00

Publisher: Multi-Health Systems, Inc.

Life History Questionnaire (LHQ)
Roger Bakeman, Robert Helmreich, John Wilhelm

Copyright: 1974

Population: Children through adults; ages 1 through 19

Purpose: Used in research and development

Description: Multiple-item paper–pencil test

Format: Individual administration; examiner required; untimed

Scoring: Examiner evaluated

Cost: $18.00

Publisher: Select Press

Life History Questionnaire (Short Form)
Robert Helmreich, John Wilhelm

Copyright: 1975

Population: Children through adults; ages 1 through 19

Purpose: Assesses correlation with IQ, self-esteem, grades, etc.

Description: Paper–pencil/oral-response test with five questions answered five times

Format: Individual administration; examiner required; untimed

Scoring: Examiner evaluated

Cost: $21.00

Publisher: Select Press

Make a Picture Story (MAPS)
Edwin S. Shneidman

Copyright: 1947

Population: Adolescents, adults

Purpose: Measures fantasies, defenses, and impulses

Description: Projective oral-response test consisting of 22 stimulus cards and a set of 67 "cut-out" figures. Stimulus cards range from structured situations (bedroom, bathroom, schoolroom, baby's room) to more ambiguous presentations (a blank doorway, a cave, and a totally blank card). Figures include men, women, boys, girls, policemen, mythical characters, animals, cripples, nudes, and a variety of frequently encountered individuals. The examiner asks the patient to select a stimulus card, place figures on the background stimulus card, and tell a story explaining those choices. He or she may also be asked to act out a story about the figures and their environment. The Location Sheet is used to record the placement of the figures on the stimulus card.

Format: Examiner required; not suitable for group use; untimed: time varies

Scoring: Examiner evaluated

Cost: Kit (set of test materials, manual, 25 Location Sheets) $90.00

Publisher: Western Psychological Services

Manual for the Activity Feeling Scale (AFS)
Johnmarshall Reeve

Copyright: 1986

Population: Adults

Purpose: Assesses five affect experiences

Description: Paper–pencil 11-point Likert-scale 15-adjective questionnaire

Format: Group or individual administration; examiner required; untimed

Scoring: Hand key; examiner evaluated

Cost: $21.00

Publisher: Select Press

Manual for the Sac Participation Rating Scale
Stanley R. Kay

Copyright: 1984

Population: Children through adults

Purpose: Assesses physical/emotional commitment to social activities; used in behavioral treatment of individuals with schizophrenia and mental retardation

Description: Multiple-item examiner-observation questionnaire using a 6-point scale

Format: Individual administration; examiner required; untimed

Scoring: Examiner evaluated

Cost: $18.00

Publisher: Select Press

Math Attribute Scale
Elizabeth Fennema, Patricia Wolleat, Joan Daniels Pedro

Copyright: 1979

Population: Adolescents

Purpose: Measures high school students' attributions of the causes of their successes and failures in math

Description: Paper–pencil test with eight subscales measuring success versus failure

Format: Group or individually administered; examiner required; untimed

Scoring: Hand key; examiner evaluated

Cost: $15.00

Publisher: Select Press

Measure of Achieving Tendency
Albert Mehrabian

Copyright: 1994

Population: Adults

Purpose: Assesses an individual's motivation to achieve; used for research, counseling, and employee selection and placement purposes

Description: Multiple-item verbal questionnaire assessing all major components of achievement. Test items are based on extensive factor-analytic investigation of most experimentally identified components of achievement.

Format: Self-administered; suitable for group use; untimed: 10 minutes

Scoring: Hand key

Cost: Test Kit (scales, scoring directions, norms, test manual) $31.00

Publisher: Albert Mehrabian, Ph.D.

Measure of Arousal Seeking Tendency
Albert Mehrabian

Copyright: 1978

Population: Adults

Purpose: Assesses an individual's desire for change, stimulation, and arousal; used for research, job placement, and counseling purposes

Description: Multiple-item verbal questionnaire measuring an individual's arousal-seeking tendencies. Test items are based on extensive factor-analytic and experimental studies of all aspects of change seeking, sensation seeking, variety seeking, and, generally, desire to master high-uncertainty situations.

Format: Self-administered; suitable for group use; untimed: 10 minutes

Scoring: Hand key

Cost: Test Kit (scale, scoring directions, norms, descriptive material) $31.00

Publisher: Albert Mehrabian, Ph.D.

Measurement of Attitudes Toward Sex Role Differences
Joseph W. Critell

Copyright: 1979

Population: Adults

Purpose: Measures extent of separate/distinct behavior life roles of males and females; test of Fromm/Reik theories

Description: Multiple-item paper–pencil/oral response questionnaire

Format: Group or individually administered; examiner required; untimed

Scoring: Examiner evaluated

Cost: $15.00

Publisher: Select Press

Measures of Affiliative Tendency and Sensitivity to Rejection
Albert Mehrabian

Copyright: 1994

Population: Adults

Purpose: Assesses an individual's friendliness, sociability, and general interpersonal and social approach–avoidance characteristics; used for research and counseling purposes

Description: Multiple-item verbal questionnaire consisting of two subscales: affiliative tendency and sensitivity to rejection. The standardized sum of the scores on both subscales also provides a reliable and valid measure of dependency.

Format: Self-administered; suitable for group use; untimed: 10 minutes per scale

Scoring: Hand key

Cost: Test Kit (scales, scoring directions, norms, descriptive material) $31.00

Publisher: Albert Mehrabian, Ph.D.

Measures of Psychosocial Development (MPD)
Gwen A. Hawley

Copyright: 1988

Population: Adolescents, adults; ages 13 and older

Purpose: Provides an index of overall psychosocial health and personality development through the eight stages of the life span based on Erik Erikson's criteria

Description: Multiple-choice 112-item paper–pencil test that provides a measure of the positive and negative attitudes or attributes of personality associated with each developmental stage, the status of conflict resolution at each stage, and overall psychosocial health. The items are rated on a 5-point scale ranging from "very much like me" to "not at all like me." Results are reported as T-scores or percentiles and can be plotted on profile forms which are available separately for males and females by age groups from 13 to 50+. Interpretation of the MPD is consistent with Erikson's focus on healthy personality development and growth, rather than a pathology-oriented focus. A sixth-grade reading level is required. Materials include manual, reusable item booklets, answer sheets, and male and female profile forms. Examiner must meet APA guidelines.

Format: Examiner required; suitable for group use; untimed: 15–20 minutes

Scoring: Hand key

Cost: MPD Kit (manual, 25 reusable item booklets, 50 answer sheets, 25 male and 25 female profile forms) $72.00

Publisher: Psychological Assessment Resources, Inc.

Mental Status Checklist™– Adolescent
Edward H. Dougherty, John A. Schinka

Copyright: 1988

Population: Ages 13 to 17

Purpose: Surveys the mental status of adolescents; used to identify problems and establish rapport in order to prepare individuals for further diagnostic testing; also provides written documentation of presenting problems

Description: Paper–pencil or computer-administered 174-item checklist covering presenting problems, referral data, demographics, mental status, personality function and symptoms, diagnosis, and disposition. The computer version operates on IBM PC.

Format: Self-administered; suitable for group use; untimed: 10–20 minutes

Scoring: Examiner evaluated

Cost: 25 checklists $34.00; computer version $295.00

Publisher: Psychological Assessment Resources, Inc.

Mental Status Checklist™–Adult
John A. Schinka

Copyright: 1988

Population: Adults

Purpose: Surveys the mental status of adults; used to identify problems and establish rapport in order to prepare individuals for further diagnostic testing; also provides written documentation of presenting problems

Description: Paper–pencil or computer-administered 120-item checklist covering presenting problems, referral data, demographics, mental status, personality function and symptoms, diagnosis, and disposition. The computer version operates on IBM PC systems with 256K and two floppy disk drives.

Format: Self-administered; suitable for group use; untimed: 10–20 minutes

Scoring: Examiner evaluated

Cost: 25 checklists $34.00; computer version $295.00

Publisher: Psychological Assessment Resources, Inc.

Millon Adolescent Personality Inventory (MAPI)
Theodore Millon, Catherine J. Green, Robert B. Meagher, Jr.

Copyright: 1982

Population: Adolescents; ages 13 to 18

Purpose: Evaluates adolescent personality; used as an aid to clinical assessment and academic and vocational guidance; identifies student behavioral and emotional problems

Description: True–false 150-item test covering eight personality style scales, eight expressed concern scales (such as peer security), and four behavioral correlates scales (such as impulse control). The clinical version is coordinated with DSM–III–R and is available to those with experience in the use of self-administered clinical tests. The test may be computer scored in three ways: via mail-in services, Arion II teleprocessing, or PC-based MICROTEST™ Assessment system.

Format: Suitable for group use; untimed: 20–30 minutes

Scoring: Computer scored

Cost: Manual $17.50; Clinical Interpretive Report $14.55 to $19.90 depending on quantity and scoring method; Guidance Interpretive Report $6.10 to $9.95 depending on quantity and scoring method

Publisher: NCS Assessments

Millon Behavioral Health Inventory (MBHI)
Theodore Millon, Chaterine J. Green, Robert B. Meagher, Jr.

Copyright: 1982

Population: Adults; ages 18 and older

Purpose: Assesses attitudes of physically ill adults toward daily stress factors and health care personnel; used for clinical evaluation of possible psychosomatic complications

Description: True–false 150-item inventory covering eight basic coping styles (e.g., cooperation), six psychogenic attitudes (e.g., chronic tension), three psychosomatic correlatives (e.g., allergic inclinations), and three prognostic indexes (e.g., pain treatment responsivity). The test is designed for use with medical patients by examiners experienced in the use of clinical instruments.

Format: Self-administered; suitable for group use; untimed: 20 minutes

Scoring: Computer scored by NCS

Cost: Manual $16.50; Interpretive Report $12.95 to $18.15 depending on quantity and scoring method

Publisher: NCS Assessments

Millon Clinical Multiaxial Inventory (MCMI)
Theodore Millon

Copyright: 1976

Population: Adults; ages 18 and older

Purpose: Diagnoses emotionally disturbed adults; used to screen individuals who may require more intensive clinical evaluation and treatment

Description: True–false 175-item test evaluating adults who have psychological or psychiatric difficulties. The test covers three categories that include eight basic personality patterns (DSM–III, Axis II) reflecting a patient's lifelong traits existing prior to the behavioral dysfunctions; three pathological personality disorders (DSM–III, Axis II) reflecting chronic or severe abnormalities, and nine clinical symptom syndromes (DSM–IIII, Axis I) describing episodes or states in which active pathological processes are clearly evidenced. This instrument is intended for use only with psychiatric–emotionally disturbed populations. The examiner must be experienced in the use of clinical tests. Interpretation is available exclusively from NCS, and test results are available immediately via Arion II teleprocessing or PC-based MICROTEST™ Assessment system. Mail-in computer scoring services also are provided.

Format: Self-administered; suitable for group use; untimed: 25 minutes

Scoring: Computer scored; may be hand scored

Cost: Manual $21.00; Interpretive Report $21.25 to $28.35 depending on quantity and scoring method; Profile Report $5.75 to $8.00 depending on quantity and scoring method

Publisher: NCS Assessments

Millon Clinical Multiaxial Inventory–II (MCMI–II)
Theodore Millon

Copyright: 1987

Population: Adults; ages 18 and older

Purpose: Diagnoses adults with personality disorders; used in private or group practice, mental health centers, out-patient clinics, and general and psychiatric hospitals and clinics with individuals in assessment or treatment programs

Description: True–false 175-item test evaluating adults with emotional or interpersonal problems. The revised version of the MCMI contains 25 scales measuring both the state and the trait features of personality. The Clinical Personality Pattern scales are Schizoid, Avoidant, Dependent, Histrionic, Narcissistic, Antisocial, Aggressive/Sadistic, Compulsive, Passive/Aggressive, and Self-Defeating. There are three Modifier Indices—Disclosure, Desirability, and Debasement—and three Severe Pathology scales—Schizotypal, Borderline, and Paranoid. The Clinical Syndrome scales are Anxiety Disorder, Somatoform Disorder, Hypomanic Disorder, Dysthymic Disorder, Alcohol Dependence, and Drug Dependence. There are three Severe Syndrome Scales: Thought Disorder, Major Depression, and Delusional Disorder. A validity index is included also. The new edition is intended to reflect proposed DSM–III–R diagnoses changes. Of the 175 items in the revised edition, 45 are new or reworded.

Format: Self-administered; suitable for group use; untimed: 20–30 minutes

Scoring: Computer scored

Cost: Manual $21.00; Interpretive Report $21.25 to $28.35 depending on quantity and scoring method; Profile Report $5.75 to $8.00 depending on quantity and scoring method

Publisher: NCS Assessments

Minnesota Multiphasic Personality Inventory (MMPI) Scoring and Interpretation Report
David Lachar

Copyright: Not provided

Population: Adolescents/Adults

Purpose: Interpretive report based on extensive research used for scoring and interpretation of MMPI

Description: The MMPI Scoring and Interpretation Service provides well-documented, highly professional reports of the Minnesota Multiphasic Personality Inventory. It is available using either WPS Test Report prepaid mail-in answer sheets or Fax service, which provides immediate scoring and interpretation via fax. Features of the report include Client Anonymity, Complete Age Norms, Profile Code, Statement Reference, Critical Items, Response Frequencies, Validated Decision Rules, and Prompt Service.

Format: Individual administration

Scoring: Service scored

Cost: Kit (includes 2 test report MMPI answer sheets, 1 MMPI test booklet, 1 test report MMPI user's manual) $80.00; mail-in answer sheet (prices include all processing and reports) 1–9 $34.50 each

Publisher: Western Psychological Services

MMPI–Report
Giles D. Rainwater

Copyright: 1989

Population: Adults

Purpose: Generates interpretations of the MMPI profiles

Description: Report with 27 items

Format: Individual administration; examiner required; untimed

Scoring: Scoring service available from publisher

Cost: $195.95

Publisher: Psychometric Software, Inc.

Mooney Problem Check Lists
R. L. Mooney, L. V. Gordon

Copyright: 1950

Population: Adolescents, adults; Grades 7 and above

Purpose: Identifies individuals who want or need help with personal problems; used for individual counseling, increasing teacher understanding of students, and preparing students for counseling interviews

Description: Multiple-item paper–pencil self-assessment of personal problems. The subjects read examples of problems, underline those of "some concern," circle those of "most concern," and write a summary in their own words. The areas covered vary from form to form but include health and physical development, home and family, boy and girl relations, morals and religion, courtship and marriage, economic security, school or occupation, and social and recreational. Materials include separate checklists for junior high students, high school students, college students, and adults.

Format: Self-administered; suitable for group use; untimed: 30 minutes

Scoring: Hand key; may be machine scored

Cost: Examination Kit (checklist and manual): Junior High School $8.00, High School $8.00, College $8.00, Adult $8.00, All levels combined $25.50

Publisher: The Psychological Corporation

Multidimensional Self-Esteem Inventory (MSEI)
Edward J. O'Brien, Seymour Epstein

Copyright: 1987

Population: College-age students

Purpose: Assesses global self-esteem and its components; used to evaluate job dissatisfaction, eating disorders, anxiety/depression, and treatment intake/outcome

Description: Multiple-choice 116-item paper–pencil test that measures global self-esteem and eight components of self-esteem: Competence, Lovability, Likability, Personal Power, Self-Control, Moral Self-Approval, Body Appearance, and Body Functioning. The MSEI uses a 5-point response format, reporting results as *T*-scores and percentiles. A 10th-grade reading level is required. Materials include manual, reusable test booklets, rating forms, and profile forms. Examiner must meet APA B-Level guidelines.

Format: Examiner required; suitable for group use; untimed: 15–30 minutes

Scoring: Hand key

Cost: MSEI Kit (manual, 25 test booklets, 25 rating forms, and 25 profile forms) $49.00

Publisher: Psychological Assessment Resources, Inc.

Multiphasic Sex Inventory
H. R. Nichols, Ilene Molinder

Copyright: 1984

Population: Adolescents, adults

Purpose: Measures the sexual characteristics of adolescent and adult male sexual offenders; used to evaluate sexual deviance and assess progress in the treatment of sexual deviance

Description: Paper–pencil 300-item true–false test of psychosexual characteristics from which 20 scales and a 50-item sexual history are derived. Six of the 20 scales are validity scales. The inventory also contains a Treatment Attitudes Scale. The sex deviance scales include the Child Molest Scale, Rape Scale, and Exhibitionism Scale. There are five atypical sexual outlet scales: Fetish, Voyeurism, Obscene Call, Bondage and Discipline, and Sado-Masochism. The four sexual dysfunction scales include Sexual Inadequacy, Premature Ejaculation, Impotence, and Physical Disabilities. There is also a Sexual Knowledge and Beliefs Scale. The 50-item Sexual History includes a sex deviance development section, marriage development section, gender identity section, gender orientation development section, and a sexual assault behav-

ior section. Scores are yielded for all 20 scales and are recorded on the profile form. Two forms are available: Adult and Juvenile Male.

Format: Examiner/self-administered; suitable for group use; untimed: 45 minutes

Scoring: Hand key

Cost: Complete Kit (manual, 5 test booklets, 25 answer sheets, 25 profile forms, set of 13 scoring templates, audiocassette of test items) $80.00; shipping and handling $5.00

Publisher: Nichols and Molinder

Multiple Affect Adjective Checklist–Revised (MAACL–R)
Marvin Zuckerman, Bernard Lubin

Copyright: 1965

Population: Adolescents, adults; Grades 10 and above

Purpose: Measures positive and negative affects as both traits and states; used in studies of stress and stress reduction, diagnosis and treatment of psychological disorders, and basic research on personality and emotions

Description: Multiple-item paper–pencil inventory measuring the affects of Anxiety (A), Depression (D), Hostility (H), Positive Affect (PA), and Sensation Seeking (SS). This revised edition contains trait and state forms that have been shown to differentiate patients with affective disorders from other types of patients and normals. The test yields two summary scores: Dysphoria (A+D+H) and Positive Affect and Sensation Seeking (PA+SS).

Format: Examiner/self-administered; suitable for group use; untimed: 5 minutes per form

Scoring: Hand key; may be computer scored

Cost: Specimen Set $7.25

Publisher: EdITS/Educational and Industrial Testing Service

Multiscore Depression Inventory for Adolescents and Adults (MDI)
David J. Berndt

Copyright: 1983

Population: Adolescents, adults; ages 13 and older

Purpose: Measures the severity and specific aspects of depression and detects subtle variations in mild forms of depression; used with normal individuals

Description: Paper–pencil or computer-administered 118-item true–false questionnaire containing 10 subscales: Low Energy Level, Cognitive Difficulty, Guilt, Low Self-Esteem, Social Introversion, Pessimism, Irritability, Sad Mood, Instrumental Helplessness, and Learned Helplessness. An interpretive report that provides a general score as well as scores for each subscale is available. In addition, one section of the report indicates the probability that the examinee is a depressed, conduct disordered, psychotic, suicidal, bulimic, anorexic, or nondepressed individual; an individual with a mixed diagnoses; an individual with endogenous depression; or a chronic pain sufferer. The computer version, which is designed for use on IBM PC, XT, or AT systems with 128K, offers on-line scoring that generates the interpretive report; a mail-in scoring service that yields the report is available for the paper–pencil version. A short form consisting of the first 47 items of the full-length inventory is also available.

Format: Self-administered; suitable for group use; untimed: 20 minutes

Scoring: Paper–pencil version, hand key or scoring service; computer version, computer scored

Cost: Kit (50 hand-scored test/answer sheets, 50 profile forms, 1 set of hand scoring keys, 1 manual, 2 WPS Test Report answer sheets) $110.00

Publisher: Western Psychological Services

Myers-Briggs Type Indicator (MBTI)

Isabel Briggs Myers, Katharine C. Briggs

Copyright: Not provided

Population: Adolescents, adults; ages 14 through adult

Purpose: Measures personality dispositions and interests based on Jung's theory of types; used in personal, vocational, and marital counseling, executive development programs, educational settings, and personality research

Description: Six different forms—166-item Form F for research, 126-item Form G, 94-item Form G self-scorable, 126-item Form G in Spanish, 131-item Form K for understanding differences, or 290-item Form J for clinical settings test of four bipolar aspects of personality: Introversion–Extraversion, Sensing–Intuition, Thinking–Feeling, and Judging–Perceiving. The various combinations of these preferences result in 16 personality types. The inventory is at the eighth-grade reading level. The available reports are: Profile, Narrative Report, Team Report, Organizational Report, Career Report, Expanded Analysis Report, Type Differentiation Indicator Report, and Relationship Report. Many interpretive guides are available to aid the examiner. A software package is available for use with the IBM-compatible PC.

Format: Self-administered; suitable for group use; untimed: 20–30 minutes

Scoring: Hand key; scoring service available; may be computer scored

Cost: Self-Scorable Preview Kit $10.00; Profile Preview Kit $10.00; Narrative Preview Kit $15.00; Narrative Report/Organizations Preview Kit $17.00; Team Report Preview Kit $75.00; Career Report Preview Kit $14.00; Relationship Report Preview Kit $24.00

Publisher: Consulting Psychologists Press, Inc.

Neo–Five Factor Inventory (NEO–FFI)

Paul T. Costa, Jr., Robert R. McCrae

Copyright: 1989

Population: Adults; ages 19 to 93

Purpose: Assesses the five major personality domains; used in clinical psychology, psychiatry, behavioral medicine, vocational counseling, and industrial psychology

Description: Multiple-choice 60-item paper–pencil test providing a general description of an adult's personality. The NEO–FFI is a shortened version of the NEO Personality Inventory. Domains assessed are Neuroticism (N), Extraversion (E), Openness to Experience (O), Agreeableness (A), and Conscientiousness (C). The NEO–FFI is based on NEO–PI–R normative data and is interpreted in the same manner. Correlations with NEO–PI–R validimax factors range from .75 to .89. Materials include manual, summary sheet, and test booklets. Examiner must meet APA Level-B guidelines.

Format: Examiner required; suitable for group use; untimed: time varies

Scoring: Hand-scorable answer sheet

Cost: Kit (manual, manual supplement, 25 test booklets, 25 summary feedback sheets) $75.00

Publisher: Psychological Assessment Resources, Inc.

Neuroticism Scale Questionnaire (NSQ)
Raymond B. Cattell, Ivan H. Scheier

Copyright: 1961

Population: Adolescents, adults; Grades 10 and above

Purpose: Measures neuroticism in senior high school students and adults of most educational levels; used for clinical evaluation, personal counseling, and research on neuroticism

Description: Paper–pencil 40-item questionnaire measuring degree of "neurotic trend" in adults and adolescents. Standard scores are provided for men, women, and men and women together. A sixth-grade reading level is required.

Format: Self-administered; suitable for group use; untimed: 10 minutes

Scoring: Hand key

Cost: Testing kit $14.00; handbook $9.50; 25 test booklets $11.50; scoring key $4.00

Publisher: Institute for Personality and Ability Testing, Inc.

Objective Analytic Batteries (O–A)
Raymond B. Cattell, James M. Schueiger

Copyright: 1971

Population: Adolescents, adults; ages 14 and older

Purpose: Evaluates personality in adults and adolescents; used for clinical evaluations, research on personality source traits, and personal counseling

Description: Ten paper–pencil tests providing an objective measure of 10 personality source traits: ego strength, anxiety, independence, extraversion, regression, control, cortertia, depression, and others. The batteries are arranged in a kit, from which tests for ½ hour, 1 hour, 2 hours, etc., may be scheduled, according to purpose and testing time. The handbook for the O–A Kit combines practical tests with broad developments in psychometry and in personality theory concerning the source-trait structures and their mode of interaction. The handbook is designed explicitly as supportive reading and realistic illustration for courses on personality theory. Norms are calculated directly for each of the 10 factors; the norm base covers ages 14 to 30 years of age; age trends are included for other situations.

Format: Examiner required; suitable for group use; untimed: 30 minutes

Scoring: Hand key

Cost: Professional Testing Kit $139.25; handbook $53.50; test kit $40.50; 10 expendable booklets (OA359) $10.40; (OA360) $8.25; (OA361) $10.40; 25 answer sheets (OA362) $8.25

Publisher: Institute for Personality and Ability Testing, Inc.

Occupational Sex-Typing Using 2 Unipolar Scales
R. Barry Ruback, D. Emily Simerly

Copyright: 1983

Population: Adults

Purpose: Assesses sex type of different occupations; used for career counseling of college students

Description: Paper–pencil questionnaire containing 100 occupations

Format: Group or individual administration; examiner required; untimed

Scoring: Hand key; examiner evaluated

Cost: $15.00

Publisher: Select Press

Offer Self-Image Questionnaire for Adolescents–Revised (OSIQ–R)
D. Offer, E. Ostrov, K. I. Howard, S. Dolan

Copyright: Not provided

Population: Ages 13 to 19

Purpose: Used to measure adjustment and self-image in adolescents

Description: Composed of 129 simple statements, the questionnaire measures adjustment in 12 areas: impulse control, emotional tone, body image, social functioning, self-reliance, sexuality, family functioning, self-confidence, vocational attitudes, ethical values, mental health, and idealism. It uses a 6-point response scale. The OSIQ–R yields conventional *T*-scores and validity checks.

Format: Examiner required; not suitable for group use; 30 minutes

Scoring: Computer scored; scoring service

Cost: Kit (1 manual, 2 reusable administration booklets, 5 test report prepaid mail-in answer sheets for computer scoring and interpretation) $115.00; OSIQ–R microcomputer disk (IBM) $225.00

Publisher: Western Psychological Services

Panic and Somatization Scales
Albert Mehrabian

Copyright: 1994

Population: Adolescents, adults; ages 14 and older

Purpose: Assesses panic disorder and somatization or hypochondria; used for research and counseling

Description: Paper–pencil 18-item test with two subtests: Panic (8 items) and Somatization (10 items). A 10th-grade reading level is required.

Format: Self-administered; suitable for group use; untimed: 10 minutes

Scoring: Hand key; test scoring service available from publisher

Cost: Test Kit $31.00

Publisher: Albert Mehrabian, Ph.D.

Patterns of Selfhood
Fred McKinney, Thomas L. Sexton

Copyright: 1977

Population: Adults

Purpose: Assesses validation of Bakan's Agency and role behavior

Description: Paper–pencil 130-item questionnaire

Format: Group or individual administration; examiner required; untimed

Scoring: Examiner evaluated

Cost: $15.00

Publisher: Select Press

Perception of Control
Carmen Barroso-Fundacao, Carlos Chagas

Copyright: 1977

Population: Adults

Purpose: Measures construction of a multi-dimensional scale

Description: Multiple-item paper–pencil questionnaire with 24 situations

Format: Group or individual administration; examiner required; untimed

Scoring: Hand key; examiner evaluated

Cost: $15.00

Publisher: Select Press

Personal Attributions Questionnaire
Janet I. Spence, Robert Helmreich, Joy Stapp

Copyright: 1974

Population: Adults

Purpose: Measures college students' sex role stereotypes/masculinity/femininity

Description: Paper–pencil 138-item questionnaire containing six polar items

Format: Group or individual administration; examiner required; untimed

Scoring: Hand key; examiner evaluated

Cost: $18.00

Publisher: Select Press

Personal Feelings Booklet
Janet Taylor

Copyright: 1978

Population: Adults

Purpose: Assesses treatment outcomes of mental health patients

Description: Paper–pencil 25-item questionnaire

Format: Group or individual administration; examiner required; untimed

Scoring: Examiner evaluated

Cost: $15.00

Publisher: Select Press

Personal Orientation Dimensions (POD)
Everett L. Shostrom

Copyright: 1975

Population: Adults

Purpose: Measures attitudes and values in terms of concepts of the actualizing person; used to introduce humanistic value concepts, indicate a person's level of positive mental health, and measure the effects of various treatment and training techniques

Description: Paper–pencil 260-item two-choice test consisting of bipolar pairs of statements of comparative values and behavior judgments. The subject must choose from each pair the statement that is closest to his or her beliefs. Items are stated both negatively and positively; opposites are dictated not by word choice but by context. Test items are nonthreatening in order to facilitate communication of the results and provide a positive approach for measuring the following personality dimensions: orientation (time orientation and core centeredness), polarities (strength/weakness and love/anger), integration (synergistic integration and potenti-

ation), and awareness (being, trust in humanity, creative living, mission and manipulation awareness). Test results indicate whether (and to what degree) an individual is actualizing or nonactualizing. The inventory may be used as a component of the Actualizing Assessment Battery (AAB).

Format: Examiner required; suitable for group use; untimed: 30–40 minutes

Scoring: Computer scored

Cost: Specimen Set (manual, all forms) $7.25

Publisher: EdITS/Educational and Industrial Testing Service

Personal Orientation Inventory (POI)
Everett L. Shostrom

Copyright: 1963

Population: Adolescents, adults

Purpose: Measures values and behaviors important in the development of the actualizing person; used in counseling and group training sessions and as a pre- and posttherapy measure to indicate a person's level of positive mental health.

Description: Paper–pencil 150-item two-choice test containing bipolar pairs of statements of comparative values and behavioral judgments. The subject must choose from each pair the statement that is closest to his or her beliefs. The inventory is scored for two major scales and 10 subscales: Time Ratio, Support Ratio, Self-Actualizing Value, Existentially, Feeling, Reactivity, Spontaneity, Self-Regard, Self-Acceptance, Nature of Man, Synergy, Acceptance of Aggression, and Capacity for Intimate Contact. College norms are presented in percentile scores. Adult mean scores and profiles are provided. Means, standard deviations, and plotted profiles are provided for clinically nominated self-actualized and non–self-actualized groups, as well as for many other clinical and industrial samples. The inventory may be used as a component for group use.

Format: Examiner required; suitable for group use; untimed: 30 minutes

Scoring: Hand key; may be computer scored

Cost: Specimen Set (manual, all forms) $7.50

Publisher: EdITS/Educational and Industrial Testing Service

Personal Problems Checklist–Adolescent
John A. Schinka

Copyright: 1985

Population: Adolescents; ages 13 to 17

Purpose: Assesses personal problems of adolescents; used as a survey instrument in clinical and counseling settings to initiate the consultation process and introduce the client to formal diagnostic testing

Description: Paper–pencil or computer-administered 240-item test identifying common problems cited by adolescents in 13 areas: social, appearance, job, family, home, school, money, religion, emotions, dating, health, attitude, and crises.

Format: Self-administered; suitable for group use; untimed: 10–20 minutes

Scoring: Evaluated by teacher, parent, or guardian

Cost: 50 checklists $34.00

Publisher: Psychological Assessment Resources, Inc.

Personal Problems Checklist–Adult
John A. Schinka

Copyright: 1985

Population: Adults

Purpose: Assesses the personal problems of adults; used as a survey instrument in clinical and counseling settings to initiate the consultation process and introduce the client to formal diagnostic testing

Description: Paper–pencil 211-item test identifying problems in 13 areas: social, appearance, vocational, family and home, school, finances, religion, emotions, sex, legal, health and habits, attitude, and crises.

Format: Self-administered; suitable for group use; untimed: 10–20 minutes

Scoring: Examiner evaluated

Cost: 50 checklists $34.00

Publisher: Psychological Assessment Resources, Inc.

Personal Styles Inventory PSI–120
Joseph T. Kunce, Corrine S. Cope, Russel M. Newton

Copyright: 1990

Population: Adolescents, adults; ages 14 and above

Purpose: Assesses basic personality characteristics for vocational, marital, and personal counseling

Description: Multiple-choice 120-item paper–pencil test broken down into emotional styles (8 scales), physical styles (8 scales), and cognitive styles (8 scales). Available also in Spanish.

Format: Self-administered; suitable for group use; untimed: 25 minutes

Scoring: Computer scored; test scoring service available from publisher

Cost: $47.50

Publisher: Educational and Psychological Consultants, Inc.

Personality Adjective Check List (PACL)
Stephen Strack

Copyright: 1991

Population: Adolescents, adults; ages 16 and above

Purpose: Used in counseling, personnel selection, and research to assess personality

Description: Paper–pencil or computer-administered 153-item test. Personality scores yielded are: introversive (IN), inhibited (IH), cooperative (CO), sociable (SO), confident (CN), forceful (FO), respectful (RE), sensitive (SE), problem indicator (PI). Response style scales are random (R), favorable (F), and unfavorable (F). Profile and narrative interpretation reports are available. A single 8½″×11″ test sheet is used. An eighth-grade reading level is required. Examiner must have an M.A., M.S., M.F.C.C., M.S.W., or Ph.D. in the mental health field.

Format: Individual/self-administered; suitable for group use; untimed: 10–15 minutes

Scoring: Hand key; computer scored

Cost: Start-Up Kit (manual, scoring keys, 50 test sheets, 50 profile sheets) $79.00

Publisher: Twenty-first Century Assessment

Personality Assessment Inventory (PAI)
Leslie C. Morey

Copyright: 1991

Population: Adults; ages 18 and older

Purpose: Used in forensic psychology and personality assessment to assess adult psychopathology

Description: Paper–pencil 4-point Likert scale with the following categories: 4 Validity Scales: inconsistency (ICN), infrequency (INF), negative impression (NIM), positive impression (PIM); 11 Clinical Scales and Subscales: somantic complaints (SOM), anxiety (ANX), anxiety-related disorders (ARD), depression (DEP), mania (MAN), paranoia (PAR), schizophrenia (SCZ), borderline features (BOR), antisocial features (ANT), alcohol problems (ALC), drug problems (DRG); 5 Treatment Scales: aggression (AGG), suicidal ideation (SUI), stress (STR), nonsupport (NON), treatment rejection (RXR); Interpersonal Scales: dominance (DOM), warmth (WRM). Materials used include a manual, reusable item book, hand-scorable answer sheet, profile form, critical item form. A fourth-grade reading level is required. Examiner must be C-level qualified. A computer version using IBM PC and compatibles is available. Spanish version available.

Format: Individual administration; examiner required; untimed: 50–60 minutes

Scoring: Computer scored; hand-scored answer sheet

Cost: Comprehensive Kit $135.00

Publisher: Psychological Assessment Resources, Inc.

Personality Disorder Interview–IV (PDI–IV)
Thomas A. Widiger, Steve Mangine, Elizabeth M. Corbitt, Cynthia G. Ellis, Glenn V. Thomas

Copyright: 1994

Population: Adults; ages 18 and older

Purpose: Assists in the diagnosis of DSM–IV personality disorders

Description: Oral-response structured interview with the following booklets: Thematic Content Interview Booklet (attitudes toward self, attitudes toward others, security of comfort of others, friendships and relationships, conflicts and disagreements, work and leisure, social norms, mood, appearance and perception) and Personality Disorders Interview Booklet (antisocial personality disorder, avoidant personality disorder, borderline personality disorder, dependent personality disorder, histrionic personality disorder, narcissistic personality disorder, obsessive–compulsive personality disorder, paranoid personality disorder, schizoid personality disorder, schizotypal personality disorder, depressive personality disorder, passive–aggressive personality disorder, administration and scoring of the PDI–IV). Examiner must be C-level qualified.

Format: Individual administration; examiner required; untimed: 2 hours

Scoring: Hand key

Cost: Intro Kit (PDI–IV book, 2 of each interview booklet and personality disorders booklet, 10 profile forms) $69.00

Publisher: Psychological Assessment Resources, Inc.

Personality Research Form (PRF)
Douglas N. Jackson

Copyright: 1984

Population: Adolescents, adults; Grades 6 and above

Purpose: Assesses personality traits relevant to the functioning of an individual in a variety of situations; used in self-improvement courses and guidance centers and for personnel selection

Description: True–false paper–pencil or computer-administered test in five forms. Forms AA and BB contain 440 items covering 22 areas of normal functioning. Form E has 352 items in 22 scales. Forms A and B have 300 items in 15 scales. The 22 scales measured are Abasement, Achievement, Affiliation, Aggression, Autonomy, Change, Cognitive Structure, Defendance, Dominance, Endurance, Exhibition, Harm-Avoidance, Impulsivity, Nurturance, Order, Play, Sentience, Social Recognition, Succorance, Understanding, Infrequency, and Desirability. A 90-minute cassette tape with simplified wording is available for use with those who have limited verbal skills or sight or reading problems. Materials include a manual, reusable test booklet, answer sheets, profiles, and a scoring template. The computer version operates on IBM PC and compatible systems. Form E available in French and Spanish.

Format: Suitable for group use; Form E 1 hour, Forms A and B 45 minutes, Forms AA and BB 1 hour 15 minutes, audiotape 90 minutes

Scoring: Hand key; computer scored; scoring service available from publisher

Cost: Examination Kit $53.00; computer version (licensing agreement and 25 uses) $175.00

Publisher: Sigma Assessment Systems, Inc.

Personality Scales of Bender-Gestalt Test
Martin F. Rosenman, Gail J. Albergottie

Copyright: 1973

Population: Adults

Purpose: Measures relationship of personality process in rehabilitation clients

Description: Paper–pencil test containing 16 questionnaire scales

Format: Group or individual administration; examiner required; untimed

Scoring: Hand key; examiner evaluated

Cost: $15.00

Publisher: Select Press

Pictorial Study of Values
Charles Shooster

Copyright: 1986

Population: Adults

Purpose: Examines personal values; used for self-awareness programs, discussion groups, and research on values and mores

Description: Multiple-item paper–pencil test measuring reactions to six basic value areas: social, political, economic, religious, aesthetic, and theoretical. Test items are composed of photographs. College norms are provided. Suitable for illiterate and non-English-speaking persons.

Format: Examiner required; suitable for group use; untimed: 20 minutes

Scoring: Examiner evaluated

Cost: Specimen Set $5.00; 25 tests $5.00

Publisher: Psychometric Affiliates

Picture Personality Test for Indian South Africans (PPT–ISA)

Copyright: 1982

Population: Adults; ages 16 and older

Purpose: Measures attitudes of Indian South Africans

Description: Multiple-item paper–pencil projective test predicting job success in industry and business and indicating relations with significant others for clinical purposes. A picture album (one for males and one for females) is used for determining attitude toward demands, family relationships, father–son or mother–daughter relationships, mother–son or father–daughter relationships, attitude toward Indian authority, self-concept, sexual relationship, attitude toward white authority, social adjustment and aggression. The test has 11 picture cards (constructs) that can be selected according to the purpose of the evaluation. Distinction can be made for Hindus, Mohammedans, and Christians. The test can be analyzed for positive (favorable), negative (hostile), and ambivalent (unsure) reactions. An item analysis also can be performed. Individual testing is recommended for individuals who have only a primary school qualification.

Format: Examiner required; suitable for group use; untimed: 2 hours

Scoring: Hand key

Cost: Contact publisher

Publisher: Human Sciences Research Council

Polyfactorial Study of Personality
Martin M. Bruce

Copyright: 1959

Population: Adults

Purpose: Aids in the clinical evaluation of an individual's personality

Description: Pencil-paper 300-item true–false test measuring 11 aspects of psychopathology: hypochondriasis, sexual identification, anxiety, social distance, sociopathy, depression, compulsivity, repression, paranoia, schizophrenia, and hyperaffectivity. Suitable for individuals with physical, hearing, or visual impairment.

Format: Self-administered; suitable for group use; untimed: 45 minutes

Scoring: Hand key

Cost: Manual and manual supplement $38.50; IBM scoring stencil $34.00; profile sheets $24.50; IBM answer sheets $24.50; Specimen Set $53.50

Publisher: Martin M. Bruce, Ph.D.

Positive and Negative Syndrome Scale (PANSS)
Stanley R. Kay, Lewis A. Opler

Copyright: 1992

Population: Adults; ages 18 and older

Purpose: Assesses positive and negative symptomology in schizophrenics; used in psychotherapy

Description: Test with 33 items rated by a therapist. The test is broken up into eight scales and one composite score. The scales are positive symptoms (7 items), negative symptoms (7 items), general (16 items), aneria (4 symptoms), thought disturbance (4 items), activation (3

items), paranoid (3 items), depression (4 items). Scores for all subscales plus a composite and General Psychopathology score are obtained. A profile form is used to convert raw scores into standard scores.

Format: Individually administered; examiner required; untimed

Scoring: Hand key

Cost: Kit $95.00

Publisher: Multi-Health Systems

Preliminary Manual for State-Trait Personality Inventory (STPI)
D. Spielberger, G. Jacobs, R. Crone, R. Russell, L. Westberry, L. Barker, E. Johnson, J. Knight

Copyright: 1986

Population: Adults

Purpose: Assesses college students' personal well-being

Description: Paper–pencil/oral-response 60-item questionnaire containing six subscales measuring state/trait, anxiety, curiosity, anger.

Format: Group or individual administration; examiner required; untimed

Scoring: Hand key; examiner evaluated

Cost: $15.00

Publisher: Select Press

Prison Inmate Inventory

Copyright: 1991

Population: Adult prison inmates

Purpose: Designed for inmate risk assessment and needs identification; reports help determine risk and establish supervision levels and readiness for classification or status changes

Description: Designed for prison inmate risk and needs assessment, the test contains 10 scales: Validity, Violence, Antisocial, Risk, Self Esteem, Alcohol, Drugs, Judgment, Distress, and Stress Coping Abilities. There are 157 multiple-choice/true–false items. Truth-corrected scores. Computer-generated report summarizes risk range and recommendations for each scale;

on-site reports within four minutes of test completion. Available in English or Spanish.

Format: Self-administered; suitable for group use; 45 minutes

Scoring: Computer scored

Cost: Contact publisher

Publisher: Risk and Needs Assessment, Inc.

Problem Behavior Inventory–Adolescent Symptom Screening Form
Leigh Silverton

Copyright: Not provided

Population: Adolescents

Purpose: Used to help clinicians structure and focus diagnostic interview

Description: This inventory lists more than 100 DSM–IV–R-related symptoms in clear, simple language. The adolescent checks those symptoms that he or she has experienced. This inventory identifies areas where personality testing might be helpful.

Format: Self-administered; suitable for group use; 10–15 minutes

Scoring: Hand key

Cost: Package of 25 carbonized AutoScore™ forms $32.00

Publisher: Western Psychological Services

Problem Behavior Inventory–Adult Symptom Screening Form
Leigh Silverton

Copyright: Not provided

Population: Adults

Purpose: Used to help clinicians structure and focus diagnostic interview

Description: This inventory lists more than 100 DSM–III–R-related symptoms in clear, simple language. The client checks those symptoms that he or she has experienced. This inventory guides the initial interview, provides material for the intake report, and identifies areas where personality testing might be helpful.

Format: Self-administered; suitable for group use; 10–15 minutes

Scoring: Hand key

Cost: Package of 25 carbonized AutoScore™ forms $32.50

Publisher: Western Psychological Services

Problem Experiences Checklist–Adolescent Version
Leigh Silverton

Copyright: Not provided

Population: Adolescents

Purpose: Checklist used to pinpoint problems and identify areas for discussion prior to the initial clinician interview

Description: This checklist gives the clinician a quick picture of the adolescent's life situation, indicating what kind of difficulties he or she is experiencing. More than 250 problems and troubling life events are listed under the following headings: school, opposite sex concerns, peers, family, goals, crises, emotions, recreation, habits, neighborhood, life phase transition, beliefs and attitudes, and occupational and financial circumstances. The adolescent checks the problems that he or she is experiencing.

Format: Self-administered; 10–15 minutes

Scoring: Hand key

Cost: Package of 25 $32.00

Publisher: Western Psychological Services

Problem Experiences Checklist–Adult Version
Leigh Silverton

Copyright: Not provided

Population: Adults

Purpose: Used to help clinicians structure and focus diagnostic interview

Description: This checklist gives the clinician a quick picture of the client's life situation, indicating what kind of difficulties he or she is experiencing. More than 20 problems and troubling life events are listed under the following headings: marital relationship, children–parents, financial–legal, bereavement, personal habits, work adjustment, life transition, beliefs and goals, painful memories, and emotions. The client checks the problems that he or she is experiencing.

Format: Self-administered; suitable for group use; 10–15 minutes

Scoring: Hand key

Cost: Package of 25 $32.50

Publisher: Western Psychological Services

Profile of Mood States (POMS)
Douglas M. McNair, Maurice Lorr, Leo Droppleman

Copyright: 1971

Population: Adolescents, adults; ages 18 and older

Purpose: Assesses dimensions of affect or mood in individuals ages 18 and older; used to measure outpatients' response to various therapeutic approaches, including drug evaluation studies

Description: Paper–pencil 65-item test measuring six dimensions of affect or mood: tension–anxiety, depression–dejection, anger–hostility, vigor–activity, fatigue–inertia, and confusion–bewilderment. An alternative POMS–Bipolar Form measures the following mood dimensions in terms of six bipolar affective states identified in recent research: composed–anxious, elated–depressed, agreeable–hostile, energetic–tired, clearheaded–confused, and confident–unsure. Norms are provided for POMS Bipolar for high school, college, and outpatient populations. POMS is available in a shortened form and large print. Also available in French and Japanese.

Format: Examiner required; suitable for group use; untimed: 3–5 minutes

Scoring: Hand key, may be computer scored

Cost: Specimen Set (manual, all forms) $8.25

Publisher: EdITS/Educational and Industrial Testing Service

Psychiatric Diagnostic Interview–Revised (PDI–R)
Ekkehard Othmer, Elizabeth C. Penick, Barbara J. Powell, Marsha Read, Sigliende Othmer

Copyright: Not provided

Population: Adults

Purpose: Identifies frequently encountered psychiatric disorders; used in all phases of diagnostic screening, intake, and follow-up

Description: Multiple-item verbally administered oral-response or computer-administered test consisting of questions usually requiring a "yes" or "no" answer. The test offers diagnostic summaries evaluating the following basic syndromes: organic brain syndrome, alcoholism, drug abuse, mania, depression, schizophrenia, antisocial personality, somatization disorder, anorexia nervosa, obsessive–compulsive neurosis, phobic neurosis, anxiety neurosis, mental retardation, bulimia, posttraumatic stress disorder, generalized anxiety, and adjustment disorder. In addition, four derived syndromes are evaluated: polydrug abuse, schizoaffective disorder, manic–depressive disorder, and bulimarexia. The questions for each of the basic syndromes are divided into four sections. If simple response criteria are not met, the interviewer omits the remainder of the questions for that syndrome and proceeds to the next syndrome. All positive syndromes are recorded on the Time Profile.

Format: Examiner required; not suitable for group use; untimed: 15–60 minutes

Scoring: Examiner evaluated; may be computer scored

Cost: Kit (1 administration booklet, 25 recording booklets, 1 manual) $97.50

Publisher: Western Psychological Services

Psychological Dimensions of Work
Regis H. Walther

Copyright: 1972

Population: Adults

Purpose: Uses a self-report inventory in evaluating performance

Description: Multiple-item paper–pencil/oral-response test with 50 occupational groups

Format: Group or individual administration; examiner required; untimed

Scoring: Examiner evaluated

Cost: $15.00

Publisher: Select Press

Psychological Screening Inventory (PSI)
Richard I. Lanyon

Copyright: 1978

Population: Adolescents, adults

Purpose: Identifies adults and adolescents who may need a more extensive mental health examination or professional attention; used in clinics, hospitals, schools, courts, and reformatories

Description: True–false 130-item test covering five scales: Alienation, Social Nonconformity, Discomfort, Expression, and Defensiveness. Materials include a manual, question and answer sheet, scoring templates, and profile sheet. Available in Spanish.

Format: Examiner required; suitable for group use; untimed: 15 minutes

Scoring: Hand key

Cost: Examination Kit $48.00

Publisher: Sigma Assessment Systems, Inc.

Psychological/Social History Report

Copyright: 1988

Population: Adults

Purpose: Gathers basic information relevant to a psychological intake interview; used for initiating discussion between the clinician and patient

Description: Multiple-item paper–pencil or computer-administered psychological intake interview covering presenting problem, family/developmental history, education, financial history/status, employment history, military service, alcohol/drug history, medical history, marital/family life, diet/exercise, and psychological/social stressors. The program generates an Important Responses section of patient responses that may be clinically significant. This section allows the clinician to see areas requiring further evaluation. The program operates on IBM PC.

Format: Examiner required; not suitable for group use; untimed: 30–45 minutes

Scoring: Examiner evaluated; may be computer scored

Cost: Computer version $295.95; Package of paper–pencil questionnaires $10.95

Publisher: Psychometric Software, Inc.

Psychosexual Life History (PSLH)
H. R. Nichols, Ilene Molinder

Copyright: 1995

Population: Adult sex offenders

Purpose: Used for clinical interview and assessment of behavior patterns, emotional states, attitudes, and personal history of sex offenders

Description: Short-answer 16-page questionnaire detailing experiences, thoughts, and feelings from childhood through adult life. Categories are Sexual History, Health, Parental and Family, Childhood and Adolescent Development and Behaviors, Education, Work, Substance Abuse, Marital, Adult Behaviors, and Treatment. A sixth-grade reading level is required.

Format: Individual administration; untimed

Scoring: Examiner evaluated

Cost: 10 Inventories $20.00

Publisher: Nichols and Molinder Assessments

Psychotic Inpatient Profile
Maurice Lorr, Norris D. Vestre

Copyright: 1968

Population: Adults

Purpose: Measures the behavior patterns of adult psychiatric patients; used with difficult patients and to evaluate treatment progress

Description: Paper–pencil 96-item inventory consisting of questions about the subject's behavior, which a nurse or psychiatric aide answers by indicating frequency of observation. Analysis of the responses provides objective and quantitative measures of 12 syndromes of observable psychotic behavior: excitement, hostile belligerence, paranoid projection, anxious depression, retardation, seclusiveness, care needed, psychotic disorganization, grandiosity, perceptual distortion, depressive mood, and disorientation. The six-page test booklet is a revised and expanded version of the Psychotic Reaction Profile. Norms are provided for men and women, both drug free and drug treated.

Format: Examiner required; not suitable for group use; untimed: 20–30 minutes

Scoring: Hand key

Cost: Kit (25 forms, 1 manual) $45.00

Publisher: Western Psychological Services

Purpose in Life (PIL)
James C. Crumbaugh, Leonard T. Maholick

Copyright: 1981

Population: Adults

Purpose: Measures degree to which an individual has found meaning in life; used with addicted, retired, disabled, and philosophically confused individuals for purposes of clinical assessment, student counseling, vocational guidance, and rehabilitation

Description: Paper–pencil 34-item test assessing an individual's major motivations in life. Subjects must rate 20 statements according to their own beliefs, complete 13 sentence stems, and write an original paragraph describing their aims, ambitions, and goals in life. Based on Victor Frankl's "Will to Meaning," the test embraces his logo therapeutic orientation in recognition of threat of the existential vacuum. Norms are provided for mental patients and non-mental patients. A fourth-grade reading level is required. Available in Spanish and Portuguese.

Format: Self-administered; suitable for group use; untimed: 10–15 minutes

Scoring: Scoring service available

Cost: Specimen Set (test, manual, bibliography) $4.00; 25 tests $5.00

Publisher: Psychometric Affiliates

Quality of Life Inventory (QOLI)
Michael B. Frisch

Copyright: 1994

Population: Adults; ages 18 and above

Purpose: Measures satisfaction/dissatisfaction with life; used for personal counseling, marriage counseling, and outcomes assessment

Description: Multiple-choice 32-item computer-administered or paper–pencil test with a 3-point rating scale for importance and a 6-point scale for satisfaction. A sixth-grade reading level is required. Examiner must have B-level qualification. A computer version is available using an IBM-compatible 486 PC or higher.

Format: Self-administered; suitable for group use; untimed: 5 minutes

Scoring: Hand key; computer scored; test scoring service not available

Cost: Contact publisher

Publisher: NCS Assessments

Racial Attitude Survey
Thomas J. Rundquist

Copyright: 1995

Population: Adolescents, adults

Purpose: Evaluates and assesses racial attitude; used by sociologists, public relations professionals, and educators studying prejudice and racial (and ethnic) views of any selected grouping

Description: Computer-administered survey comprised of questions on Physical, Ego Strength (Dominance, Control, Anxiety, Ethnic, General Social, and on the Job). Also rates attitudes from Boss to Marriage Partner in terms of social/sexual contact. Also data on an anonymous basis compiles traits as to age, sex, marital status, race, education, and other traits.

The program operates on PC systems and Novell networks. Previous version on paper also available, but examiner would need to compile own statistics.

Format: Examiner required; suitable for group or individual use; untimed: usually takes only a few minutes

Scoring: Computer scored

Cost: Windows Version $39.95

Publisher: Nova Media Inc.

Rating of Behavior Scales (ROBS)
Robert C. Newman II, Richard E. Carney

Copyright: 1980

Population: Adolescents, adults; ages 12 and older

Purpose: Assesses an individual's adoption of stereotypic sex-role behaviors, androgyny, and degree and type of motivation to change role behaviors. May be used with individuals with visual, physical, or hearing disabilities.

Description: Paper–pencil 40-item multiple-choice test measuring sex-role adoption and androgyny. The items are presented in two sections: present behavior (20 items) and ideal behavior (20 items). The test yields several scores, including Total Behavior (S), Male Behavior (M), Female Behavior (F), Total Inconsistency (K), Inconsistency Between Sex Roles (K1), Inconsistency Within Sex Roles (K2), F Ratio for Androgeny (K3), Total Incongruence (C; present vs. ideal), Difference Between Female Items (F1), Difference Between Male and Female Difference (C1), Inconsistency Within Male and Female Items (C2), and F Ratio Between C1 and C2 (C3). A computer scoring service is available from the publisher. A sixth-grade reading level is required. The test may be read to those with visual disabilities.

Format: Self-administered; suitable for group use; untimed: time varies

Scoring: Hand key; may be computer scored

Cost: 50 forms $25.00; Specimen Set (manual, form) $12.00

Publisher: TIMAO Foundation for Research and Development

REHAB: Rehabilitation Evaluation Hall and Baker
Roger Baker, John N. Hall

Copyright: 1983

Population: Adults; ages 17 to 95

Purpose: A multipurpose rating scale designed to assess the behavior of people with a major psychiatric handicap; assesses behavioral change, selects inpatients with potential for discharge to the community, selects groups, and helps in planning treatment

Description: Paper–pencil 23-item test yielding the Total Deviant Behavior Score (7 items) and Total General Behavior Score (16 items), which also yields five factor scores: Social Ability (6 items), Speech Skills (2 items), Disturbed Speech (2 items), Self Care (5 items), and Community Skills (2 items). An integrated package of materials comprising assessment forms, rater's guides, user's manual, score sheets, scoring template, and individual and group presentation sheets. Purchaser must be a qualified mental health professional, or an institution.

Format: Individual administration; examiner required; untimed

Scoring: Hand key

Cost: Complete set of materials with carrying case $385.00; Specimen Set $11.50

Publisher: Vine Publishing Ltd.

Relationship Inventory: Developments and Adaptations
G. T. Barrett-Lannard

Copyright: 1978

Population: Adults

Purpose: Assesses five theoretically critical variables of therapist/counselor–client relationships

Description: Multiple-item paper–pencil questionnaire containing four scales

Format: Individual or group administration; examiner required; untimed

Scoring: Examiner evaluated

Cost: $21.00

Publisher: Select Press

Revised NEO Personality Inventory (NEO–PI–R™)
Paul T. Costa, Jr., Robert R. McCrae

Copyright: 1992

Population: Adults

Purpose: Measures five major personality domains of adults; used in clinical psychology, psychiatry, behavioral medicine, vocational counseling, and industrial psychology

Description: Paper–pencil 240-item test providing a general description of an adult's personality. Domains assessed are Neuroticism (N), Extraversion (E), Openness to Experience (O), Agreeableness (A), and Conscientiousness (C). Facet scales for all domains yield a more detailed analysis of personality structure. Domain N scales are Anxiety, Hostility, Depression, Self-Consciousness, Impulsiveness, and Vulnerability. Domain E scales are Warmth, Gregariousness, Assertiveness, Activity, Excitement-Seeking, and Positive Emotions. Domain O scales are Fantasy, Aesthetics, Feelings, Actions, Ideas, and Values. Domain K facets are Trust, Straightforwardness, Altruism, Compliance, Modesty, Tender-Mindedness. Domain C facets are Competence, Order, Dutifulness, Achievement, Striving, Self discipline, Deliberation. Two versions of the inventory are available. Form S, appropriate for men and women, is self-administered. Answers are provided on a 5-point scale.

Format: Examiner/self-administered; suitable for group use; untimed: 30 minutes

Scoring: Hand key; may be computer scored

Cost: Comprehensive Kit (manual, scoring keys, reusable test booklets, profile forms, answer sheets, and feedback sheets) $115.00; Computer PGM (contact publisher)

Publisher: Psychological Assessment Resources, Inc.

Risk of Eruptive Violence Scale
Albert Mehrabian

Copyright: 1996

Population: Adults

Purpose: Identifies adolescents and adults who, although generally quiet and nonaggressive, have a tendency to become extremely violent and destructive

Description: Paper–pencil 35-item measure that deals with a wide range of fantasy, cognitive, emotional, and frustrated violent impulses. It has been shown to be a moderately strong negative correlate of Emotional Empathy, to be a positive correlate of other measures of Aggressiveness and Violence, and to clearly differentiate between violent incarcerated adolescents and adults versus controls.

Format: Self-administered; suitable for group use; untimed: 10 minutes

Scoring: Hand key

Cost: Test Kit (scale, scoring directions, norms, descriptive material) $31.00

Publisher: Albert Mehrabian, Ph.D.

Rogers Criminal Responsibility Assessment Scales (r-CRAS)
Richard Rogers

Copyright: 1984

Population: Adults

Purpose: Evaluates the criminal responsibility of individuals who may or may not, depending on their sanity or insanity at the time they committed a crime, be held legally accountable for their actions

Description: Multiple-item paper–pencil inventory evaluating criminal responsibility. The instrument quantifies essential psychological and situational variables at the time of the crime that are to be used in a criterion-based decision model. This allows the clinician to quantify the impairment at the time of the crime, conceptualize the impairment with respect to the appropriate legal standards, and render an expert opinion with respect to those standards. Descriptive criteria are provided on scales measuring the individual's reliability, organicity, psychopathology, cognitive control, and behavioral control at the time of the alleged crime. Part I establishes the degree of impairment on psychological variables significant to the determination of insanity. Part II articulates the decision process toward rendering an accurate opinion on criminal responsibility with the ALI standard and includes experimental criteria and decision models for guilty-but-mentally-ill (GBMI) and M'Naughten standards.

Format: Examiner required; not suitable for group use; untimed: time varies

Scoring: Examiner evaluated

Cost: Test Kit (manual and 15 examination booklets) $39.00

Publisher: Psychological Assessment Resources, Inc.

Rotter Incomplete Sentences Blank–Second Edition (RISB™)
Julian B. Rotter, Michael I. Lah, Janet E. Rafferty

Copyright: 1992

Population: Adolescents, adults

Purpose: Studies personality by using sentence completion

Description: Paper–pencil 40-item test of personality. Items are stems of sentences to be completed by the subject. Responses may be classified into three categories: conflict or unhealthy responses, neutral responses, and positive or healthy responses. The test is available in high school, college, and adult forms.

Format: Self-administered; suitable for group use; untimed: 20–40 minutes

Scoring: Hand key; examiner evaluated

Cost: Incomplete Sentences Blanks 25-count $23.00, 100-count $84.50 (high school, college, or adult); manual $54.50

Publisher: The Psychological Corporation

S-14 Personal Value Inventory/Theory and Preliminary Findings
Dale D. Simmons

Copyright: 1978

Population: Adults

Purpose: Measures value choices of individuals

Description: Multiple-item paper–pencil questionnaire

Format: Individual or group administration; examiner required; untimed

Scoring: Examiner evaluated

Cost: $15.00

Publisher: Select Press

S-D Proneness Checklist
William T. Martin

Copyright: 1971

Population: Adolescents, adults

Purpose: Identifies persons with depressive and suicidal tendencies; used by persons and agencies involved in suicide prevention; may be administered via telephone

Description: Paper–pencil 30-item inventory assessing a person's level of depression and suicide tendencies. Any trained counselor can complete the questionnaire, based on information gained through interviews and observation. The evaluator rates each of the statements on a 5-point scale ranging from "does not apply" to "most significant." Three scores are derived: Suicidal Score, Depression Score, and Total Suicide-Depression Proneness Score. Interpretive guidelines are provided with each form, including suicide correction factors. A pamphlet on suicide/depression also is available.

Format: Examiner required; not suitable for group use; untimed: open ended

Scoring: Examiner evaluated

Cost: Specimen Set $5.00; 25 rating forms $8.25

Publisher: Psychologists and Educators, Inc.

SAQ-Adult Probation II

Copyright: 1994

Population: Adults on probation

Purpose: Measures eight areas of concern with adults on probation

Description: Version II contains eight scales: Truthfulness, Alcohol, Drugs, Resistance, Aggressivity, Violence, Antisocial, and Stress Coping Abilities. Multiple-choice and true–false, 181

items, computer or paper–pencil administered. Computer-generated results are available within 4 minutes of test completion. Truth-corrected scores. Computer-generated report includes summary reports on each scale. Standardized and normed on probationers and parolees. Available in English or Spanish.

Format: Self-administered; suitable for group use; untimed: 35 minutes

Scoring: Computer scored

Cost: Contact publisher

Publisher: Risk and Needs Assessment, Inc.

Scale for Measuring Attitudes About Masculinity
Robert Brannon

Copyright: 1983

Population: Adults

Purpose: Measures attitudes of male undergraduates about male sex role and masculinity

Description: Multiple-item paper–pencil questionnaire containing seven homogeneous subscales

Format: Individual or group administration; examiner required; untimed

Scoring: Examiner evaluated

Cost: $15.00

Publisher: Select Press

Scale of Intrinsic Versus Extrinsic Orientation in the Classroom
Susan Harter

Copyright: 1980

Population: Ages 8 to 18

Purpose: Assesses preference for challenge versus preference for easy assignments, curiosity/interest versus doing what the teacher requires, independent mastery versus dependence on teacher, independent judgment versus reliance on teacher's judgment

Description: Test with 30 items.

Format: Examiner required; not suitable for group use

Scoring: Examiner evaluated

Cost: $20.00

Publisher: Susan Harter

Scale To Measure Benevolent Versus Malevolent Perceptions of the Environment
W. Larry Gregory, George T. Brennan, Ivan D. Steiner, Ann Detrick

Copyright: 1978

Population: Adults

Purpose: Measures perceptions of whether RG, association, and nature have been advantageous or not

Description: Paper–pencil 22-item questionnaire

Format: Individual or group administration; examiner required; untimed

Scoring: Examiner evaluated

Cost: $18.00

Publisher: Select Press

School Motivation Analysis Test (SMAT)
Samuel E. Krug, Raymond B. Cattell, Arthur B. Sweney

Copyright: 1970

Population: Adolescents; ages 12 to 18

Purpose: Assesses the psychological motivations of adolescents; used for clinical evaluation, educational and personal counseling, and psychological research on adolescent motivations

Description: Paper–pencil 190-item multiple-choice test measuring 10 important achievement, social, and comfort needs of 12- to 18-year-olds. Six of the needs are basic drives: protectiveness, caution, self-assertion, sexual identity, aggressiveness, and self-indulgence. Four are interests that develop and mature through learning experiences: interest in school, dependency, responsibility, and self-fulfillment. Test items consist of objective devices, which are less susceptible to deliberate faking or distortion than standard questionnaires or checklists. For each of the 10 interest areas, scores measure drive or need level, satisfaction level, degree of conflict, and total motivational strength. Norms are provided for males and females separately. A fourth-grade reading level is required.

Format: Examiner required; suitable for group use; untimed: 45–60 minutes

Scoring: Hand key

Cost: Specimen Set $17.25; handbook $15.00; 10 reusable test booklets $20.50; 25 answer sheets $12.75; 3 scoring keys $18.00

Publisher: Institute for Personality and Ability Testing, Inc.

SCL-90® Analogue
Leonard R. Derogatis

Copyright: 1976

Population: Adolescents, adults

Purpose: Screens for psychological problems; used for adolescent and adult personality assessment

Description: Paper–pencil test with an observer rating scale. The nine primary dimensions are: somatization, obsessive–compulsive, interpersonal sensitivity, depression, anxiety, hostility, phobic anxiety, paranoid ideation, and psychoticism. Can be used with SCL–90–R or BSI self-report tests. Examiner must be B-Level qualified.

Format: Individual administration; examiner required; untimed: 1–3 minutes

Scoring: Examiner evaluated; no scoring service available

Cost: Contact publisher

Publisher: NCS Assessments

Seeking of Noetic Goals Test (SONG)
James C. Crumbaugh

Copyright: 1977

Population: Adolescents, adults

Purpose: Measures the strength of a person's motivation to find meaning in life; used for

pre- and posttesting of logotherapy programs with addicted, retired, disabled, and philosophically confused individuals

Description: Paper–pencil 20-item test consisting of statements that the subject rates on a 7-point scale according to his or her own beliefs. The test is used in conjunction with the Purpose in Life Test to predict therapeutic success. The manual includes a discussion of the test's rationale, validity, reliability, administration, scoring, norms, and other technical data. A fourth-grade reading level is required. Available in Portuguese.

Format: Self-administered; suitable for group use; untimed: 10 minutes

Scoring: Scoring service available

Cost: Specimen Set (test, manual) $4.00; 25 tests $5.00

Publisher: Psychometric Affiliates

Self-Esteem Inventory
Millard J. Bienvenu

Copyright: 1995

Population: Adolescents, adults; ages 13 and older

Purpose: Assesses how individuals perceive themselves in positives, negatives, strengths, and weaknesses

Description: Forty-item yes–no–sometimes test. A seventh-grade reading level is required. Examiner must be trained in counseling/human relations.

Format: Self-administered; suitable for group use; untimed: 15 minutes

Scoring: Hand key

Cost: $1.00 each; guide $1.50; minimum order of $10.00

Publisher: Northwest Publications

Self-Interview Inventory
H. Birnet Hovey

Copyright: 1983

Population: Adults

Purpose: Measures an individual's level of emotional adjustment and identifies individuals with neurotic tendencies; used for self-awareness and counseling programs with both psychiatric and nonpsychiatric patients

Description: Paper–pencil 185-item inventory containing a high loading level of unique content. A Composite Neurotic score is derived from subscores on current complaints, emotional insecurity, and guilt feelings. A Composite Maladjustment score is derived from subscores on prepsychotic and psychotic behavior and childhood illness. Two validating scores are also provided: one on carefulness and one on truthfulness of response. Norms are provided for control groups.

Format: Examiner/self-administered; suitable for group use; untimed: 30 minutes

Scoring: Hand key

Cost: Specimen Set $4.00; 25 inventories $5.00; 25 answer sheets $5.00; 25 profiles $5.00

Publisher: Psychometric Affiliates

Self-Perception Inventory
William T. Martin

Copyright: 1972

Population: Adolescents, adults; ages 12 and older

Purpose: Evaluates an individual's personality and general level of adjustment; used for screening procedures, clinical research on personality, and evaluation of therapeutic progress

Description: Paper–pencil 200-item true–false test of personality. Test items consist of symptomatic and descriptive statements grouped according to the following syndromes: consistency, self-actualization, supervision, rigidity–dogmatism, authoritarianism, anxiety, depression, and paranoia. Subscale scores are provided for each syndrome. General Adjustment and General Maladjustment scores are derived from these subscales to provide an index of personality patterning. A fifth-grade reading level is required.

Format: Examiner required; suitable for group use; untimed: 20–35 minutes

Scoring: Hand key

Cost: Examiner's manual (10 tests, 25 answer sheets, 25 profile sheets, keys, manual) $40.00; 25 tests $27.50; 25 answer and 25 profile sheets $6.75 each; keys $9.00; manual $6.75

Publisher: Psychologists and Educators, Inc.

Self-Perception Profile for Adolescents
Susan Harter

Copyright: 1988

Population: Ages 14 to 18

Purpose: Assesses scholastic competence, athletic competence, social acceptance, physical appearance, behavioral conduct, close friendship, romantic appeal, job competence, and global self-worth

Description: Test with 45 items

Format: Examiner required; not suitable for group use

Scoring: Examiner evaluated

Cost: $20.00

Publisher: Susan Harter

Self-Perception Profile for Adults
Bonnie Messer, Susan Harter

Copyright: 1986

Population: Ages 20 to 55

Purpose: Assesses intelligence, job competence, athletic competence, physical appearance, sociability, close friendship, intimate relationships, morality, sense of humor, nurturance, household management, adequacy as a provider, and global self-worth

Description: This 50–item test is designed for adults in the world of work and family.

Format: Examiner required; not suitable for group use

Scoring: Examiner evaluated

Cost: $20.00

Publisher: Susan Harter

Self-Perception Profile for College Students
Susan Harter

Copyright: 1986

Population: Ages 18 to 23

Purpose: Assesses scholastic competence, intellectual ability, creativity, job competence, athletic competence, physical appearance, peer acceptance, close friendship, romantic relationships, relationships with parents, morality, and sense of humor

Description: Test with 54 items

Format: Examiner required; not suitable for group use

Scoring: Examiner evaluated

Cost: $20.00

Publisher: Susan Harter

Self-Perception Profile for Learning Disabled Students
Mari Jo Renick, Susan Harter

Copyright: 1988

Population: Ages 8 to 18

Purpose: Assesses general intellectual ability, reading competence, math competence, writing competence, spelling competence, social acceptance, athletic competence, physical appearance, behavioral conduct, and global self-worth

Description: Test with 46 items

Format: Examiner required; not suitable for group use

Scoring: Examiner evaluated

Cost: $20.00

Publisher: Susan Harter

Self-Rating Scale for Somatotyping
Joseph C. Lagey, Ashton Munroe

Copyright: 1972

Population: Adults

Purpose: Measures college students' responses in association with various components of body type

Description: Multiple-item paper–pencil test

Format: Self-administration; untimed

Scoring: Examiner evaluated

Cost: $15.00

Publisher: Select Press

Senior Apperception Technique (SAT)
Leopold Bellak, Sonya Sorel Bellak

Copyright: 1973

Population: Adults

Purpose: Assesses personality in individuals age 60 and older; used by psychiatrists, psychologists, physicians, nurses, and social workers for clinical evaluation and diagnosis

Description: Oral-response 16-item projective personality test measuring the traits, attitudes, and psychodynamics involved in the personalities of individuals age 60 and older. Each test item consists of a picture of human figures in situations of concern to the elderly. The examinee is asked to tell a story about each picture. The test also includes informational material on technique, administration, research possibilities, and a bibliography. Available also in Spanish and Japanese.

Format: Examiner required; not suitable for group use; untimed: 20–30 minutes

Scoring: Examiner evaluated

Cost: Complete kit (pictures, manual) $19.75

Publisher: C.P.S., Inc.

Sentence Completion Series (SCS)
Larry H. Brown, Michael A. Unger

Copyright: 1992

Population: Adolescents, adults

Purpose: Used in counseling to identify themes, underlying concerns, and specifications of distress

Description: Paper–pencil projective, sentence-completion series with 50 items per form. The categories are as follows: Adult, Adolescent, Family, Marriage, Parenting, Work, Illness, and Aging. Materials used include a professional user's guide and forms for each of the categories. Examiner must be B-level qualified.

Format: Self-administered; examiner required; untimed: 15–45 minutes

Scoring: Examiner evaluated

Cost: Kit $75.00

Publisher: Psychological Assessment Resources, Inc.

Sentence Completion Test
Floyd S. Irvin

Copyright: 1972

Population: Adolescents, adults; Grades 10 and above

Purpose: Assesses personality functioning; used for clinical counseling and academic guidance

Description: Paper–pencil 90-item test measuring six aspects of personality, including self-need for achievement, learning attitude, and body image. Items are sentence stems, which the subject completes. They are scored on a 5-point scale ranging from outright positive to outright negative.

Format: Examiner required; not suitable for group use; untimed: 15 minutes

Scoring: Hand key; examiner evaluated

Cost: Specimen Set $6.75; 25 forms $8.25

Publisher: Psychologists and Educators, Inc.

Sex Adjustment Inventory

Copyright: 1991

Population: Sex offenders

Purpose: Designed to identify sexually deviate and paraphiliac behavior in people accused or convicted of sexual offenses

Description: Screens sexual offenders and measures degree of severity of sexually deviate and paraphiliac behavior. The test contains 13 scales: Test Item Truthfulness, Sex Item Truthfulness, Sexual Adjustment, Child Molest, Sexual Assault, Exhibitionism, Incest, Alcohol, Drugs, Violence, Antisocial, Distress, and Judgment. There are 214 multiple-choice/true–false

items. Computer-generated report summarizes risk range and recommendations for each scale; on-site reports within 4 minutes of test completion. Two separate truthfulness scales permit comparison of client's test-taking attitude to sex-related and non–sex-related questions, which provides insight into client's attitude, motivation, and assessment-related behavior. Truth-corrected scores.

Format: Self-administered; suitable for group use; 45 minutes

Scoring: Computer scored

Cost: Contact publisher

Publisher: Risk and Needs Assessment, Inc.

Shoplifting Inventory

Copyright: 1995

Population: Adolescent/adult shoplifters

Purpose: Designed for shoplifter evaluation

Description: This assessment inventory contains nine scales: Truthfulness, Entitlement, Shoplifting, Antisocial, Peer Pressure, Self-Esteem, Impulsiveness, Alcohol, and Drugs and evaluates people charged or convicted of shoplifting. There are 185 multiple-choice/true–false items. Computer-generated report summarizes risk range and recommendations for each scale. Truth-corrected scores, on-site reports within 4 minutes of test completion. Available in English or Spanish.

Format: Self-administered; suitable for group use; 45 minutes

Scoring: Computer scored

Cost: Contact publisher

Publisher: Risk and Needs Assessment, Inc.

Situational Preference Inventory (SPI)
Carl N. Edwards

Copyright: 1973

Population: Adults; ages 17 and above

Purpose: Assesses an individual's preferred styles of social interaction; used for counseling and research purposes

Description: Paper–pencil 28-item rating scale assessing preferred styles of social interaction. Each test item consists of a set of three statements, each representing a different style of interaction: cooperational, instrumental, or analytic. Individuals are asked to indicate which of the three statements they agree with most and which they agree with least, leaving the third statement unmarked (neutral). Independent scores are derived for each of the three interactional styles. Norms are available by sex for 14 populations.

Format: Self-administered; suitable for group use; untimed: time varies

Scoring: Examiner evaluated

Cost: Contact publisher

Publisher: Four Oaks Institute

Social Reticence Scale (SRS)
Warren H. Jones

Copyright: 1986

Population: Adolescents, adults

Purpose: Assesses shyness and interpersonal problems in high school and college students and adults; used to provide client feedback and to assess the effectiveness of therapeutic interventions; also used in research of interpersonal relationships

Description: Paper–pencil 20-item measure of shyness. Items are answered using a 5-point Likert-type scale.

Format: Examiner required; suitable for group use; untimed: 5–10 minutes

Scoring: Not available

Cost: Sampler Set $25.00; Permission Set for 200 users $90.00

Publisher: Mind Garden, Inc.

Social Support Scale for Children and Adolescents
Susan Harter

Copyright: 1985

Population: Ages 8 to 18

Purpose: Taps support/regard from four sources: parents, teachers, close friends, and classmates

Description: Test with 24 items

Format: Examiner required; not suitable for group use

Scoring: Examiner evaluated

Cost: $20.00

Publisher: Susan Harter

Somatic Inkblot Series II
Wilfred A Cassell

Copyright: 1988

Population: All ages

Purpose: Used for somatic issues and conversion reactions for diagnostic purposes

Description: Paper–pencil 62-item short-answer, projective test containing inkblot cards for assessing perceptions. An examiner is required. Suitable for those with hearing, physical, and mental disabilities. Test available on videocassette (video purchase requires certification).

Format: Individual administration; examiner required; untimed: 90 minutes

Scoring: Examiner evaluated; test scoring service available from publisher

Cost: SIS-II Booklets: $4.50 to $3.00 (for 20) SIS-V video: $39.95 including certification and training

Publisher: Behaviordyne, Inc.

SRD/PE Attitude Inventory
Agnes Chrietzberg

Copyright: 1979

Population: Adults; secondary physical education teachers

Purpose: Assesses attitudes toward sex role differences in physical education; used in career counseling

Description: Multiple-item paper–pencil questionnaire

Format: Individual or group administration; examiner required; untimed

Scoring: Hand key

Cost: $15.00

Publisher: Select Press

State Trait Anger Expression Inventory (STAXI)
Charles D. Spielberger

Copyright: 1996

Population: Adolescents, adults; ages 13 to 65

Purpose: Measures type and expression of anger; used as a screening and outcome measure in psychotherapy and stress management programs, with particular application in behavioral medicine

Description: Paper–pencil 44-item Likert-type test assessing anger along six scales: State Anger, Trait Anger, Anger Expression, Anger Control, and Subtypes of Trait Anger (Angry Temperament and Angry Reaction). A scoring service is available from PAR. Available in German, Swedish, and Italian.

Format: Self-administered; suitable for group use; untimed: 10 minutes

Scoring: Hand key; may be machine scored

Cost: Kit (manual, 50 item booklets, 50 rating sheets) $69.00

Publisher: Psychological Assessment Resources, Inc.

State-Trait Anxiety Inventory for Adults (STAI)
Charles D. Spielberger

Copyright: 1983

Population: Adolescents, adults

Purpose: Differentiates between longstanding (trait) and temporary (state) anxiety; used for research and clinical practice

Description: Paper–pencil 40-item Likert scale. State anxiety and Trait anxiety scores are yielded. An eighth-grade reading level is required.

Format: Self-administered; suitable for group use; untimed: 5–20 minutes

Scoring: Hand key; test scoring service available from publisher

Cost: Sample Set $25.00, permission for up to 200 uses $90.00

Publisher: Mind Garden, Inc.

State-Trait Anxiety Inventory for Children
Charles D. Spielberger, C. D. Edwards, J. Montuori, R. Lushene

Copyright: 1973

Population: Children, adolescents; Grades 4 through 8

Purpose: Assesses anxiety in children; used for research screening and treatment evaluation

Description: Two 20-item scales measuring two types of anxiety: state anxiety (current level of anxiety, or S-Anxiety) and trait anxiety (anxiety-proneness, or T-Anxiety). The S-Anxiety scales ask how the child feels at a particular moment in time, and the T-Anxiety scales ask how he or she generally feels. The inventory is based on the same concept as the State-Trait Anxiety Inventory and is used in conjunction with the adult form manual.

Format: Self-administered; suitable for group use; untimed: 10–20 minutes

Scoring: Hand key: examiner evaluated

Cost: Sample Set $25.00; Permission Set $90.00; Scoring Key $10.00

Publisher: Mind Garden, Inc.

Stereotypes About Male Sexuality Scale
William E. Snell, Jr., Sharyn S. Belk, Raymond C. Hawkins, II

Copyright: 1986

Population: Adults

Purpose: Measures an individual's beliefs and influences in personal life

Description: Paper–pencil 10-item questionnaire

Format: Individual or group administration; examiner required; untimed

Scoring: Examiner evaluated

Cost: $21.00

Publisher: Select Press

Structured Interview of Reported Symptoms
Richard Rogers, R. Michael Bagby, Susan E. Dickens

Copyright: 1992

Population: Adults

Purpose: Used for forensic assessment to detect malingering and feigning of psychiatric symptoms

Description: Oral-response 172-item short-answer interview with the following scales: Rare Symptoms, Symptom Combinations, Improbable or Absurd Symptoms, Blatant Symptoms, Subtle Symptoms, Severity of Symptoms, Selectivity of Symptoms, Reported vs. Observed Symptoms. Supplemental Scales include Direct Appraisal of Honesty, Defensive Symptoms, Symptom Onset, Overly Specified Symptoms, and Inconsistency of Symptoms. Materials used are a manual and interview booklets. Examiner must be C-Level qualified.

Format: Individual administration; examiner required; untimed: under 1 hour

Scoring: Examiner evaluated

Cost: Kit $91.00

Publisher: Psychological Assessment Resources, Inc.

Structured-Objective Rorschach Test (SORT)

Copyright: 1975

Population: Ages 11 to 54

Purpose: Evaluates personality tendencies of white South Africans; used in guidance, selection, and placement

Description: Multiple-item paper–pencil test of mental functioning (8 components), interests (2 components), responsiveness (2 components), and temperament (13 components). The test was adapted from J. B. Stone's SORT and standardized for white South Africans of both sexes and both official languages (Afrikaans and English). There is a training course for interpreting the test.

Format: Examiner required; suitable for group use; untimed: 30 minutes

Scoring: Hand key

Cost: Contact publisher

Publisher: Human Sciences Research Council

Suicidal Ideation Questionnaire (SIQ)
William M. Reynolds

Copyright: 1988

Population: Adolescents; ages 13 to 18

Purpose: Assesses suicidal ideation in adolescents

Description: Paper–pencil 30-item test utilizing a 7-point Likert-type response format designed as a companion instrument to the Reynolds Adolescent Depression Scale. The 15-item SIQ–JR version is available for students in Grades 7 through 9. Both the full version and the JR version are available in Form G, which is designed for use with large groups and with mail-in answer sheets.

Format: Self-administered; suitable for group use; untimed: typical time not available

Scoring: Hand key; Form G computer scored

Cost: Professional Kit (manual, 25 each of SIQ and SIQ–JR Form HS answer sheets, scoring keys) $73.00; manual $25.00; 25 SIQ answer sheets (specify SIQ or SIQ–JR) $25.00; scoring key (specify version) $11.00; 50 Form G pre-paid mail-in answer sheets $105.00

Publisher: Psychological Assessment Resources, Inc.

Suicide Behavior History Form (SBHF)
William M. Reynolds, James J. Mazza

Copyright: 1992

Population: Adolescents, adults

Purpose: Documents a history of suicide behavior

Description: Oral-response 29-item interview with the following categories: Client Information, History of Suicide Attempts, Description of Most Recent Attempt, Prior Attempt History, Current Status, Additional Test and Clinical Information, and Recommendations. Materials used include a clinician's guide and an interview book.

Format: Individual administration; examiner required; untimed: 10–15 minutes

Scoring: Examiner evaluated

Cost: Kit $55.00

Publisher: Psychological Assessment Resources, Inc.

Suicide Probability Scale (SPS)
John G. Cull, Wayne S. Gill

Copyright: 1982

Population: Ages 14 to 65

Purpose: Predicts the probability of suicidal behavior; used by clinicians to assess the probability that an individual may harm herself or himself; may be used for screening, monitoring changes in suicide potential over time, clinical exploration, and research

Description: Paper–pencil or computer-administered 36-item test in which the subject uses a 4-point scale ranging from "none or little of the time" to "most or all of the time" to indicate how often the behavior described in the statements would be descriptive of his or her behavior or feelings. The test itself does not mention suicide. Items are broken down into four subscales: Hopelessness, Suicide Ideation, Negative Self-Evaluation, and Hostility. Scoring yields a total weighted score, a normalized *T*-score, and a Suicide Probability Score. The manual presents cutoff scores indicating the level of probable suicide behavior, interpretive guidelines, and clinical strategies for each level. The computer version is available for IBM PC or compatible systems.

Format: Examiner required; suitable for group use; untimed: 5–10 minutes

Scoring: Hand key; may be computer scored

Cost: Kit (25 tests, 1 manual, 25 profile sheets) $80.00

Publisher: Western Psychological Services

Survey of Interpersonal Values
Leonard V. Gordon

Copyright: 1960

Population: Adolescents, adults; Grades 10 and above

Purpose: Measures individuals' values by assessing what they consider important in relationships with others; used to measure values associated with adjustment and performance for selection, placement, employment counseling, and research purposes

Description: Paper–pencil 30-item inventory assessing interpersonal values. Each item consists of a triad of value statements. For each triad, examinees must indicate most and least important values. Six values are measured: support, conformity, recognition, independence, benevolence, and leadership.

Format: Self-administered; suitable for group use; untimed: 15 minutes

Scoring: Hand key

Cost: 25 test booklets $44.00; scoring stencil $10.00; examiner's manual $15.00

Publisher: McGraw-Hill/London House

Symptom Checklist–90–Revised (SCL–90–R)
Leonard R. Derogatis

Copyright: 1975

Population: Adolescents, adults; ages 13 years and above

Purpose: Screens for psychological problems and measures progress

Description: Multiple-choice 90-item computer-administered or paper–pencil test with a 5-point rating scale of 0 to 4. The nine primary dimensions are somatization, obsessive–compulsive, interpersonal sensitivity, depression, anxiety, hostility, phobic anxiety, paranoid ideation, and psychoticism. A sixth-grade reading level is required. Examiner must be M-level qualified. A computer version using an IBM-compatible 486 PC or higher is available. The test is available on audiocassette and in 23 foreign languages. 24 additional languages are available for research purposes only.

Format: Self-administered; suitable for group use; untimed: 12–15 minutes

Scoring: Hand key; computer scored; test scoring service not available

Cost: Contact publisher

Publisher: NCS Assessments

Tasks of Emotional Development Test (TED)
Geraldine Weil, Haskel Cohen

Copyright: Not provided

Population: Ages 6 to 18

Purpose: Used to identify specific areas of emotional difficulty, potential maladaptive behavior, and reasons why a student is having difficulty with academic learning

Description: Projective test uses photographs of children in situations structured to represent the specific emotional developmental tasks that children must meet in the process of growing up. The instrument is grounded in the theoretical framework of psychoanalytic ego psychology, but the photos are less ambiguous than in similar tests. It helps identify core problems of the child and their severity, as well as suggests intervention strategies.

Format: Individual administration; untimed: 30 minutes

Scoring: Examiner administered and interpreted

Cost: Complete set $60.00; textbook $50.00

Publisher: Massachusetts School of Professional Psychology

Taxonomy of Human Performance (THS)
George C. Thologus, Edwin A. Fleishman

Copyright: 1973

Population: Adults

Purpose: Validates ability scales for classifying human tasks; used in career counseling

Description: Paper–pencil 38-task test

Format: Individual or group administration; examiner required; untimed

Scoring: Hand key; examiner evaluated

Cost: $24.00

Publisher: Select Press

Taylor-Johnson Temperament Analysis
Robert M. Taylor, Lucille P. Morrison

Copyright: 1996

Population: Adolescents, adults; ages 13 to adult

Purpose: Provides a clinical assessment of personality; used for individual premarital, marital, and family counseling, educational and vocational guidance, and substance abuse counseling

Description: Paper–pencil 180-item test measuring common personality traits to assist in assessing individual adjustment and formulation of an overall counseling plan. The regular edition, for ages 17 to adult, has a special feature allowing "criss-cross" testing in which questions are answered as applied to self and again as applied to significant other, thereby adding the dimension of interpersonal perception to counseling perspective. An eighth-grade reading level is required. The secondary edition, for ages 13 to 17 and adults who are poor readers, is presented in direct-question format with simplified vocabulary for lower-level readers. A fifth-grade reading level is required. Evaluation is presented as bipolar graphs of trait pairs: nervous/composed, depressive/lighthearted, active–social/quiet, expressive–responsive/inhibited, sympathetic/indifferent, subjective/objective, dominant/submissive, hostile/tolerant, and self-disciplined/impulsive.

Format: Suitable for group use; untimed: 20–30 minutes

Scoring: Hand key; may be computer scored

Cost: Basic package $140.00; practice scoring

training packet $25.00; manual $75.00; 10 test booklets $15.00; 100 handscorable answer sheets $20.00; 100 computer-scorable answer sheets $20.00; 20 report booklets $25.00

Publisher: Psychological Publications, Inc.

Temperament Inventory Tests
Peter Blitchington, Robert J. Cruise

Copyright: 1979

Population: Adolescents, adults

Purpose: Assesses an individual's basic temperament traits according to the four-temperament theory; used by professionals and laypersons in marital, vocational, social, moral, and spiritual counseling settings

Description: Paper–pencil 80-item test determining an individual's basic temperamental traits. The test is available in a self-report form and a group form. The self-report form consists of a 42-page booklet, Understanding Your Temperament, containing the test and instructions for self-administration, self-scoring, and interpreting the scores from a Christian viewpoint. The group form, called the Temperament Inventory, is administered and scored with temperament templates by the examiner or group leader. Interpretive material is not included with the group form. Also available in French, German, and Spanish.

Format: Self-administered; untimed: time varies

Scoring: Self-scored; examiner evaluated

Cost: $1.25

Publisher: Andrews University Press

Tennessee Self Concept Scale (TSCS)
William H. Fitts

Copyright: 1988

Population: Adolescents, adults; ages 12 to adult

Purpose: Measures an individual's self-concept in terms of identity, feelings, and behavior; used for a wide range of clinical applications

Description: Paper–pencil 100-item test consisting of self-descriptive statements which sub-jects rate on a scale ranging from 1 (completely false) to 5 (completely true). The test is available in two forms: Counseling (Form C) and Clinical and Research (Form C and R). Form C is appropriate if the results are to be used directly with the subject. It provides a number of measures, including response defensiveness, a total score, and self-concept scales that reflect "What I Am," "How I Feel," and "What I Do." The scales include Identity, Self Satisfaction, Behavior, Physical Self, Moral–Ethical Self, Personal Self, Family Self, and Social Self. It does not require scoring keys. Form C and R yields the same scores as Form C as well as the following six empirical scales, which require special scoring keys: Defensive Positive, General Maladjustment, Psychosis, Personality Disorder, Neurosis, and Personality Integration. Both forms use the same test booklet but require different answer-profile sheets.

Format: Self-administered; suitable for group use; untimed: 10–20 minutes

Scoring: Computer scored; hand key (only Form C and R)

Cost: Kit (5 reusable test booklets, 10 hand-scored answer-profile forms, 1 set of hand-scoring keys, 1 manual, 2 WPS Test Report answer sheets) $125.00

Publisher: Western Psychological Services

Test Anxiety Inventory (TAI)
Charles D. Spielberger

Copyright: 1980

Population: Adolescents, adults; Grades 10 and above

Purpose: Measures individual differences in test-taking anxiety; used for research

Description: Paper–pencil 20-item test of two major components of test anxiety: worry and emotionality. Respondents report how frequently they experience specific anxiety symptoms in examination situations. Similar in structure and concept to the T-Anxiety scale of the State-Trait Anxiety Inventory.

Format: May be self-administered; suitable for group use; untimed: 5–10 minutes

Scoring: Hand key

Cost: Sample Set $25.00; permission for up to 200 uses $90.00

Publisher: Mind Garden, Inc.

Texas Social Behavior Inventory (TSBI)
Robert Helmreich, Joy Stapp, Charles Ervin

Copyright: 1974

Population: Adults

Purpose: Measures self-esteem or social competence

Description: Questionnaire with 32 items

Format: Individual or group administration; examiner required; untimed

Scoring: Examiner evaluated

Cost: $15.00

Publisher: Select Press

Trait Arousability Scale (Converse of Stimulus Screening)
Albert Mehrabian

Copyright: 1994

Population: Adolescents, adults; ages 14 and older

Purpose: Assesses general emotionality or emotional reactivity; used for clinical research and counseling

Description: Paper–pencil 34-item test yielding a single total score. A 10th-grade reading level is required.

Format: Self-administered; suitable for group use; untimed: 10 minutes

Scoring: Hand key; test scoring service available from publisher

Cost: Test Kit $31.00

Publisher: Albert Mehrabian, Ph.D.

Trait Dominance–Submissiveness Scale
Albert Mehrabian

Copyright: 1994

Population: Adults

Purpose: Measures aspects of dominance and submissiveness in an individual's personality; used for research, counseling, job placement purposes, and matching of co-workers

Description: Multiple-item verbal questionnaire assessing personality characteristics related to dominance and submissiveness. Test items are based on extensive factor-analytic and experimental studies on aspects of dominance (controlling, taking charge) versus submissiveness characteristics. This measure has been shown to be a basic component of many important personality attributes such as extroversion, dependency, anxiety, and depression.

Format: Self-administered; suitable for group use; untimed: 10 minutes

Scoring: Hand key

Cost: Test Kit (scale, scoring directions, norms, descriptive material) $31.00

Publisher: Albert Mehrabian, Ph.D.

Trait Pleasure–Displeasure Scale
Albert Mehrabian

Copyright: 1994

Population: Adolescents, adults; ages 14 and older

Purpose: Measures general psychological adjustment/maladjustment; used with clinical work, counseling, and research

Description: Paper–pencil 22-item test with a single total score

Format: Self-administered; suitable for group use; untimed: 10 minutes

Scoring: Hand key; test scoring service available from publisher

Cost: Test Kit $31.00

Publisher: Albert Mehrabian, Ph.D.

Trauma Symptom Inventory (TSI)
John Briere

Copyright: 1995

Population: Adults

Purpose: Evaluates acute and chronic post-traumatic symptomology

Description: Paper–pencil 100-item 4-point scale (anxious arousal, dissociation, depression, sexual concerns, anger, dysfunctional sexual behavior, intrusive experiences, impaired self-reference, defensive avoidance, and tension reduction behavior). Materials used include a manual, item booklet, hand-scorable answer sheet, and male/female profile forms. A fifth- to seventh-grade reading level is required. Examiner must be B-Level qualified.

Format: Individual administration; suitable for group use; examiner required; untimed: 20 minutes

Scoring: Computer scored; hand-scored answer sheet

Cost: Kit $89.00

Publisher: Psychological Assessment Resources, Inc.

Triadal Equated Personality Inventory

Copyright: 1961

Population: Adults

Purpose: Assesses personality; used to predict job success and to measure personal adjustment

Description: Paper–pencil 633-item test of personality. Items are simple adjectives equated for response popularity. The test yields 21 self-image scores: dominance, self-confidence, decisiveness, independence, toughness, suspicion, introversion, activity, depression, foresight, industriousness, warmth, enthusiasm, conformity, inventiveness, persistence, sex drive, recognition, drive, cooperativeness, humility tolerance, and self-control.

Format: Examiner required; suitable for group use; untimed: 50–120 minutes

Scoring: Examiner evaluated

Cost: Professional Examination Kit (for 24) $50.00

Publisher: Psychometric Affiliates

Violence Scale
Panos D. Bardis

Copyright: 1973

Population: Adolescents, adults

Purpose: Measures attitudes toward violence (words and actions aimed at property damage and personal injury); used for clinical assessment, marriage and family counseling, research on violence, and discussions in social science classes

Description: Paper–pencil 25-item test in which the subjects rate 25 statements concerning various aspects of violence on a scale from 0 (strongly disagree) to 4 (strongly agree). The "violence" score equals the sum of the 25 numerical responses. The theoretical range of scores extends from 0 (lowest approval of violence) to 100 (highest approval). Suitable for use with individuals with physical and hearing disabilities.

Format: Examiner/self-administered; suitable for group use; 10 minutes

Scoring: Examiner evaluated

Cost: Free

Publisher: Panos D. Bardis, Ph.D.

Wahler Physical Symptoms Inventory
H. J. Wahler

Copyright: 1973

Population: Adults

Purpose: Discriminates between patients with medical ailments and those with psychogenic complaints; used to screen new patients

Description: Paper–pencil 42-item test consisting of physical problems on which the subjects must rate themselves using a 6-point frequency scale ranging from "almost never" to "nearly every day." The test helps identify conversion hysteria, hypochondriases, and psychophysiological reactions, as well as physically determined disorders.

Format: Self-administered; suitable for group use; untimed: 15–20 minutes

Scoring: Hand key

Cost: Kit (100 inventory sheets, 1 manual) $45.00

Publisher: Western Psychological Services

Walstadt and Altruistic Other Orientation Scale (AOO)
Joyce Jennings Walstadt

Copyright: 1977

Population: Adults

Purpose: Measures personalities of married/unmarried middle-class women age 34 or older

Description: Multiple-item paper–pencil questionnaire consisting of 54 statements, and six filler items

Format: Individual or group administration; examiner required; untimed

Scoring: Examiner evaluated

Cost: $15.00

Publisher: Select Press

Whitaker Index of Schizophrenic Thinking (WIST)
Leighton C. Whitaker

Copyright: 1980

Population: Adolescents, adults; Grades 8 and above

Purpose: Provides an index of schizophrenic thinking; used for intake screening

Description: Paper–pencil 25-item multiple-choice test discriminating between schizophrenic and nonschizophrenic thinking. The test can be completed by anyone with an eighth-grade education. The test is available in two equivalent forms. A revised (1980) manual provides a discussion of relevant diagnostic issues and the development of the test, directions for administration and scoring, standardization and validity data, a discussion of diagnostic and clinical uses, case illustrations, references, and specimen copies of the test forms.

Format: Self-administered; suitable for group use; untimed: 15 minutes

Scoring: Hand key

Cost: Kit (50 tests, 1 key, 1 manual) $75.00

Publisher: Western Psychological Services

Women's Liberation Scale
Carlos Goldberg

Copyright: 1976

Population: Adults

Purpose: Measures attitudes toward positions advocated by women's groups

Description: Paper–pencil 14-item questionnaire

Format: Group or individual administration; examiner required; untimed

Scoring: Examiner evaluated

Cost: $15.00

Publisher: Select Press

Work and Family Questionnaire (WFO)
Robert Helmreich, Janet T. Spence

Copyright: 1978

Population: Adults

Purpose: Used by college students, scientists with Ph.D.s, and athletes

Description: Paper–pencil 32-item questionnaire

Format: Group or individual administration; examiner required; untimed

Scoring: Examiner evaluated

Cost: $18.00

Publisher: Select Press

Multiage

Adjustment Scales for Children and Adolescents (ASCA)
Paul A. McDermott

Copyright: 1994

Population: Children, adolescents; ages 5 through 17; Grades K through 12

Purpose: Assesses social and behavioral adjustment for use in educational and psychological diagnosis and intervention

Description: Paper–pencil teacher behavioral rating test for special education. Materials include a user's manual and male/female self-scoring forms. An adult reading level is required. Examiners must be qualified educational and psychological specialists.

Format: Self-administered; suitable for group use; untimed: 10–20 minutes

Scoring: Self scored

Cost: Contact publisher

Publisher: Ed and Psych Associates, Inc.

Automated Child/Adolescent Social History (ACASH)
Mark Rhode

Copyright: Not provided

Population: Children, adolescents; ages 5 to 19

Purpose: Assists in obtaining child/adolescent psychosocial history information

Description: Series of computer-administered questions yielding a narrative summary of a child or adolescent seeking counseling treatment. Questions address the following areas: reason for referral-identifying information; developmental history, childhood to present; educational history; current family members and background; and problem identification. Ninth-grade reading level required of examiner.

Format: Examiner/parent or guardian administered; not suitable for group use; untimed: 45–90 minutes

Scoring: Computer administered and scored via MICROTEST Assessment Software only

Cost: Contact publisher

Publisher: NCS Assessments

Bar-Ilan Picture Test for Children
Rivkah Itskowitz, Helen Strauss

Copyright: 1985

Population: Children; ages 4 to 16

Purpose: Assesses the child's perception of daily life situations

Description: Nine-item projective verbal test used in child guidance. Measures the child's perception of his or her place at home, in the learning situation, and in the peer group. The material contains specific sex-related items for both sexes. Examiner must be a qualified psychologist. Available also in Danish.

Format: Individual administration; suitable for group use; examiner required; untimed

Scoring: Examiner evaluated

Cost: $60.00 (DKK 343)

Publisher: Dansk psykologisk Forlag

Behavior Dimensions Rating Scale (BDRS)
Lyndal M. Bullock, Michael J. Wilson

Copyright: 1989

Population: Ages 5 to adult

Purpose: Measures behavior patterns in individuals

Description: Rating scale (with 43 items) used by psychologists, teachers, counselors, or parents to rate subjects' behavior on a 7-point scale. Scores provide a profile of four behavior subscales: Aggressive/Acting Out, Irresponsible/Inattentive, Socially Withdrawn, and Fearful/Anxious. Record forms are on carbonless NCR paper. Results are automatically transferred to the scoring sheet.

Format: Self-administered; suitable for group use; 5–10 minutes

Scoring: Self scored; examiner interpretation

Cost: Complete kit (Manual and record forms) $85.50

Publisher: Riverside Publishing Company

Behavioral Academic Self-Esteem (BASE)
Stanley Coopersmith, Ragnar Gilberts

Copyright: Not provided

Population: Children, adolescents; Grades PreK through 8

Purpose: Measures academic self-esteem; used for counseling and research

Description: Paper–pencil 16-item test consisting of a behavioral rating scale assessing five factors related to self-esteem: student initiative, social attention, success/failure, social attraction, and self-confidence. The test may be used with children as young as 4 years of age and by teachers, parents, and other professionals who can observe the child directly. May be used in conjunction with the Coopersmith Self-Esteem Inventory to improve the accuracy and stability of self-esteem measurements.

Format: Self-administered; suitable for group use; untimed: 5 minutes

Scoring: Hand key; examiner evaluated

Cost: 25 rating scales $10.55; manual $23.25

Publisher: Consulting Psychologists Press, Inc.

Bender Report
Giles D. Rainwater

Copyright: 1984

Population: Children, adolescents, adults

Purpose: Scores and interprets the Bender Gestalt Test; assesses and evaluates personality

Description: Multiple-choice reporting program that helps to systematically score and interpret child and adult protocols. The report includes relevant normative comparisons, associated behavioral/personality characteristics, level of severity, diagnostic indications, treatment recommendations, and important clinical hypotheses. The scoring system and the interpretive format for adults is largely based on the work done by Max Hutt and has 27 items that report personality and organic indicators. The child version is largely based on the work of Elizabeth Koppitz and has 12 items that report developmental and behavioral indicators. These computer versions are available for IBM PC. Examiners must be professionals trained in personality assessment evaluation.

Format: Examiner required; not suitable for group use; timed/untimed

Scoring: Computer scored

Cost: $199.95

Publisher: Psychometric Software, Inc.

Blue Pearl
Lotte Bggild, Sonja Overby

Copyright: 1992

Population: Children; ages 7 to 14

Purpose: Evaluates the well-being of immigrant children

Description: Seven-picture projective verbal test measuring seven everyday life situations from classroom, school yard, shower room, and at home. Used in child guidance for children with a background in the Muslim farming culture. Only one form is used, but the material contains specific sex-related items for both sexes. Must be supervised by a psychologist. Also available in Danish.

Format: Individual administration; examiner required; untimed

Scoring: Examiner evaluated

Cost: $57.00 (DKK 325)

Publisher: Dansk psykologisk Forlag

Bristol Social Adjustment Guides, American Edition (BSAG)
D. H. Stott

Copyright: 1970

Population: Children, adolescents; ages 5 to 16

Purpose: Diagnoses the nature and extent of behavioral disturbances and social adjustment in children; used by teachers and school psychologists

Description: Multiple-item paper–pencil observational instrument consisting of short phrases describing a child's behavior. The phrases that apply to the child being evaluated are underlined by an adult familiar with the child. The guides are concerned with observable behavior rather than with inferences based on projective techniques or the child's self-assessment. An overall assessment of maladjustment, subscores for five core syndromes (unforthcomingness, withdrawal, depression, inconsequence, hostility), and four additional associated groupings (peer maladaptiveness, nonsyndromic overreaction, nonsyndromic underreaction, and neurological symptoms) are provided. The test is available in separate forms for boys and girls. Separate norms based on students from city, county, and church schools are provided for boys and girls.

Format: Examiner required; suitable for group use; untimed: 10–15 minutes

Scoring: Hand key

Cost: Specimen Set (includes manual, all forms) $7.25

Publisher: EdITS/Educational and Industrial Testing Service

Burks' Behavior Rating Scales
Harold F. Burks

Copyright: 1977

Population: Children, adolescents; Grades 1 through 9

Purpose: Identifies patterns of behavior problems in children; used as an aid in differential diagnosis

Description: Paper–pencil 110-item inventory used by parents and teachers to rate a child on the basis of descriptive statements of observed behavior. Nineteen subscales measure excessive self-blame, anxiety, withdrawal, dependency, suffering, sense of persecution, aggressiveness, resistance, poor ego strength, physical strength, coordination, intellectuality, academics, attention, impulse control, reality contact, sense of identity, anger control, and social conformity. The Parents' Guide and the Teacher's Guide define each of the scales, present possible causes for the problem behavior, and offer suggestions on how to deal with the undesirable behavior from the point of view of the parent or teacher. The manual discusses causes and manifestations and possible intervention approaches for each of the subscales as well as use with special groups, such as educable individuals with mental retardation and individuals with educational, orthopedic, speech, and hearing disabilities.

Format: Examiner required; not suitable for group use; untimed: 15–20 minutes

Scoring: Hand key

Cost: Kit (25 booklets and profile sheets, manual, 2 parents' guides, 2 teacher's guides) $110.00

Publisher: Western Psychological Services

Checklist for Child Abuse Evaluation (CCAE)
Joseph Petty

Copyright: 1990

Population: Children, adolescents

Purpose: Used for investigating and evaluating subjects who may have been abused or neglected

Description: Multiple-choice 264-item evaluation with the following categories: Sexual Abuse, Physical Abuse, Neglect, Child's Psychological Status, Credibility/Competence of Child, Conclusions of Six Categories. Treatment recommendations are yielded. A manual and checklist are used. Examiner must be trained in the evaluation of child abuse.

Format: Individual administration; examiner required; untimed

Scoring: Computer evaluated

Cost: Introductory Kit $44.00

Publisher: Psychological Assessment Resources, Inc.

Coopersmith Self-Esteem Inventories (CSEI)
Stanley Coopersmith

Copyright: Not provided

Population: Ages 8 to adult

Purpose: Measures attitudes toward the self in social, academic, and personal contexts; used for individual diagnosis, classroom screening, pre/postevaluations, and clinical and research studies

Description: Paper–pencil 58- or 25-item test of self-attitudes in four areas: social–self–peers, home–parents, school–academic, and general–self. Materials include the 58-item School Form and 25-item Adult Form. The School Form is suitable for use with individuals ages 8 to 15; the Adult Form is administered to individuals ages 16 and older. The School Form may be used with Behavioral Academic Self-

Esteem (BASE) for individual diagnosis, classroom screening, and pre- and postevaluations, as well as in clinical and research studies.

Format: Self-administered; suitable for group use; untimed: 15 minutes

Scoring: Hand key

Cost: School Preview Kit (form, key, manual) $23.00; Adult Preview Kit (form, key, manual) $23.00

Publisher: Consulting Psychologists Press, Inc.

Culture-Free Self-Esteem Inventories–Second Edition (CFSEI–2)
James Battle

Copyright: 1992

Population: Grades 3 and above

Purpose: Assesses the self-esteem of children and adults; identifies individuals needing psychological assistance

Description: Multiple-item paper–pencil test assessing five areas of self-esteem: general, school-related, peer-related, parent-related, and defensiveness. Raw scores for each subscale and a total score are obtained with acetate scoring templates. Percentile ranks and standard scores are provided for children in Grades 3 through 9 and adults. Separate forms are available for children and adults; parallel forms are available for children for pre- and posttesting. The test may be administered orally or with an audiotape to low-level readers.

Format: Suitable for group use; untimed: 10–15 minutes

Scoring: Hand key; may be computer scored

Cost: Complete Kit (examiner's manual, forms A, forms B, forms AD, scoring acetate, and administrative audiocassette) $119.00

Publisher: PRO-ED, Inc.

d2 Test: Test of Concentration and Endurance Under Pressure
R. Brickenkamp

Copyright: 1996

Population: Children, adolescents, adults; ages 9 to 59 years

Purpose: Psychodiagnostic instrument used for measuring concentration, particularly visual attention; used for personnel selection and clinical, educational, and developmental psychology assessment

Description: Detail discrimination paper-pencil test used to assess individuals' visual attention and concentration. Giving the test is virtually language dependent since the test taker is intensively engaged in simply crossing out certain items on a sheet of many possibilities. Available in German.

Format: Self-administered; suitable for group use; timed: 8 minutes

Scoring: Hand key

Cost: Complete test $64.50 U.S., $84.50 Canadian; Manual $39.50 U.S., $52.00 Canadian

Publisher: Hogrefe and Huber Publishers

Dimensions of Depression Profile for Children and Adolescents
Susan Harter, Mary Nowakowski

Copyright: 1987

Population: Ages 8 to 18

Purpose: Assesses affect, energy level, self-worth, self-blame, and suicidal ideation

Description: Thirty-item test

Format: Examiner required; not suitable for group use

Scoring: Examiner evaluated

Cost: $20.00

Publisher: Susan Harter

Dysphorimeter
Leopold Bellak

Copyright: 1989

Population: All ages

Purpose: Assesses degree of dysphoria; used in therapy

Description: Criterion-referenced instrumental analog to subjective dysphoria states, such as depression, anxiety, depersonalization, and pain. The subject matches his or her subjective way of feeling to the sound on some point of the scale from 1 to 10.

Format: Examiner administered; not suitable for group use; untimed: time varies

Scoring: No scoring service available

Cost: $130.00

Publisher: C.P.S., Inc.

Early Memories Procedure
Arnold R. Bruhn

Copyright: 1989

Population: Ages 10+; individuals with fourth-grade reading and writing skills; counseling

Purpose: Assesses current major unresolved issues for the individual, group, family, or married couples

Description: Twenty-one specific, one-time memories are recalled in this paper–pencil short-answer, projective, essay, verbal-response format. Fourth-grade reading level required. Suitable for individuals with visual, physical, or hearing impairment.

Format: Individual/group administration; examiner or scribe required; untimed: 1.5–2.25 hours

Scoring: Examiner evaluated; no scoring service available

Cost: 25 tests: $112.50/contact publisher

Publisher: Arnold R. Bruhn, Ph.D.

Emotional and Behavior Problem Scale (EBPS)
Stephen B. McCarney

Copyright: 1989

Population: Children, adolescents; ages 4 years 5 months to 21 years

Purpose: Provides results for both a Theoretical and Empirical construct of Emotionally Disturbed/Behaviorally Disordered, providing both an educational and more clinical perspective of Emotional Disturbance/Behavior Disorders

Description: The Empirical Interpretation provides five "conditions" of behavior while the Theoretical Interpretation is composed of five subscales representing the five characteristics of Emotional Disturbance/Behavior Disorders contained in IDEA. Students in the standardization sample represented all geographic regions of the United States, with particular attention given to the inclusion of racial and ethnic minorities in the creation of the national norms. Internal consistency, test–retest, and interrater reliability; item and factor analysis; and content, criterion-related, diagnostic, and construct validity are all well documented and reported for the scale.

Format: Individual administration; untimed: 15 minutes

Scoring: Self/computer scored

Cost: Complete Kit $66.50

Publisher: Hawthorne Educational Services, Inc.

Eysenck Personality Questionnaire (EPQ)
H. J. Eysenck, Sybil B. G. Eysenck

Copyright: 1975

Population: Adolescents, adults; ages 7 to adult

Purpose: Measures the personality dimensions of extraversion, emotionality, and toughmindedness (psychoticism in extreme cases) in individuals ages 7 to adult; used for clinical diagnosis, educational guidance, occupational counseling, and personnel selection

Description: Paper–pencil 90-item yes–no inventory measuring three important dimensions of personality: extraversion–introversion (21 items), neuroticism–stability (23 items), and psychoticism (25 items). The falsification scale consists of 21 items. The questionnaire deals with normal behaviors which become pathological only in extreme cases; hence, use of the term "toughmindedness" is suggested for nonpathological cases. Scores are provided for E-Extraversion, N-Neuroticism or emotionality, P-Psychoticism or toughmindedness, and L-Lie. College norms are presented in percentile form for Forms A and B both separately and combined. Adult norms are provided for an industrially employed sample. An 81-item junior form is available for testing young children.

Format: Self-administered; suitable for group use; untimed: 10–15 minutes

Scoring: Hand key

Cost: Specimen Set (manual, one copy of each form) $7.75

Publisher: EdITS/Educational and Industrial Testing Service

Four Picture Test
D. J. VanLennep, R. Houwink

Copyright: Not provided

Population: Ages 10 and older

Purpose: Assesses personality; used for diagnosis and individual counseling

Description: Four-item projective test of personality in which the subject looks at four pictures for 1 minute. The pictures are removed, and the subject is asked to write a single story based on memory in which all four pictures are used. Materials include four picture cards and manual.

Format: Examiner required; suitable for group use; untimed: 30–45 minutes

Scoring: Examiner evaluated

Cost: Contact publisher

Publisher: SWETS and Zeitlinger B V

Fundamental Interpersonal Relations Orientation–Behavior Characteristics (FIRO–BC)
Will Schutz, Marilyn Wood

Copyright: Not provided

Population: Child, adolescent

Purpose: Measures characteristic behavior of children toward other people; used for counseling and therapy

Description: Paper–pencil 54-item test containing six Guttman-type scales measuring the characteristic behavior of children in the areas of inclusion, control, and affection—the three dimensions of interpersonal behavior described by the author in his book, *The Interpersonal Underworld.* The test measures the relative strength of the needs within the individual. Because it does not compare a person with a population, norms are not provided.

Format: Examiner/self-administered; suitable for group use; untimed: typical time not available

Scoring: Hand key

Cost: 25 test booklets $27.50; scoring key $27.50

Publisher: Consulting Psychologists Press, Inc.

Group Embedded Figures Test (GEFT)
Philip K. Oltman, Evelyn Raskin, Herman A. Witkin

Copyright: Not provided

Population: Ages 10 to adult

Purpose: Assesses cognitive style in perceptual tasks; used in counseling

Description: Pencil–paper 25-item test of perceptual processes, including field dependence–independence. Performance is related to analytic ability, social behavior, body concept, and preferred defense mechanisms. Subjects find one of eight simple figures in the 18 complex designs.

Format: Examiner required; suitable for group use; untimed: 20 minutes

Scoring: Hand key

Cost: Sample Set (test booklet, scoring key) $2.00; manual $3.75; tests $18.50; scoring key $1.25

Publisher: Consulting Psychologists Press, Inc.

Group Personality Projective Test (GPPT)
Russell N. Cassel, T. C. Kahn

Copyright: 1961

Population: Ages 11 and older

Purpose: Measures major personality characteristics; used to screen potentially pathological personalities

Description: Paper–pencil 90-item test measuring seven aspects of personality, including tension, nurturance, withdrawal, neuroticism, affiliation, succorance, and total. Items are stick drawings accompanied by five descriptive or interpretative statements. The subject chooses the statement he or she believes is most accurate.

Format: Self-administered; suitable for group use; untimed: 40 minutes

Scoring: Hand key; examiner evaluated

Cost: Examiner's Set (manual, 7 scoring keys, 12 test booklets, 100 answer and profile sheets) $27.00

Publisher: Psychological Test Specialists

Hand Test
Edwin E. Wagner

Copyright: Not provided

Population: Ages 5 to adult

Purpose: Used to measure action tendencies such as acting out and aggressive behavior

Description: Using pictures of hands as the projective medium, the Hand Test elicits responses that reflect behavioral tendencies. The client is shown 10 picture cards containing simple line drawings of a hand in various positions. The client's task is to explain what each hand is doing. It is scored by classifying responses according to clear-cut quantitative and qualitative scoring categories. The quantitative scores reflect the individual's overt behavior. The qualitative scores generally reflect feelings and motivations underlying the impaired action tendencies. The test also provides six summary scores, including an index of overall pathology and an acting-out ratio, which is used to predict aggressive behavior. Manual supplement: Interpreting Child and Adolescent Responses.

Format: Individually administered; examiner required; 10 minutes

Scoring: Hand key

Cost: Kit (includes 25 scoring booklets, 1 set of picture cards, 1 manual, 1 Hand Test manual supplement) $130.00

Publisher: Western Psychological Services

Holtzman Inkblot Technique (HIT)
W. H. Holtzman

Copyright: 1972

Population: Ages 5 to adult

Purpose: Assesses an individual's personality characteristics; used for diagnosis and therapy planning

Description: Projective 45-item measure of personality in which the examinee responds to 45 inkblots. Some inkblots are asymmetric, and some are in a color other than black. An objective scoring system has been developed. Materials include two alternate and equivalent forms, A and B, for a total of 90 stimulus cards.

Format: Examiner required; not suitable for group use; untimed: typical time not available

Scoring: Examiner evaluated

Cost: Complete Set, Form A or B $255.00; Forms A and B combined $475.00

Publisher: The Psychological Corporation

House-Tree-Person (H-T-P) Projective Technique
John N. Buck

Copyright: 1970

Population: Ages 3 and older

Purpose: Assesses personality disturbances in individuals ages 3 and older in psychotherapy, school, and research setting; may be used with individuals who are culturally disadvantaged, educationally deprived, mentally retarded, and aged

Description: Multiple-item paper–pencil and oral-response test providing a projective study of personality. The test consists of two steps. The first, which is nonverbal, creative, and almost completely unstructured, requires the subject to make a freehand drawing of a house, a tree, and a person. The second step, which is verbal, apperceptive, and more formally structured, gives the subject an opportunity to describe, define, and interpret the drawings and their respective environments.

Format: Examiner required; not suitable for group use; untimed: 15–20 minutes

Scoring: Hand key; examiner evaluated

Cost: Complete Set (manual and interpretive guide; 1 copy of *H-T-P Drawings: An Illustrated Handbook;* 1 copy of *Catalog of the Qualitative Interpretation of the H-T-P;* 25 H-T-P Interpretation Booklets; 25 H-T-P Drawing Forms $165.00

Publisher: Western Psychological Services

IES Test
Lawrence A. Dombrose, Morton S. Slobin

Copyright: 1958

Population: Ages 10 and older

Purpose: Assesses the relative strengths of various personality forces; used for individual diagnosis, clinical evaluation, and research

Description: Four-subtest 57-item projective measure of personality. Picture Title is a 12-item test in which the subject creates titles for pictures. Picture Story Completion requires the subject to select a cartoon to end each of 13 incomplete cartoon stories. Photo-Analysis consists of nine men's photographs with two objectively scored questions about each. Arrow-Dot is a set of 23 graphic problems requiring the subject to draw a line from an arrow to a dot goal without creating or crossing barriers. All responses are scored Impulse (I), Ego (E), or Superego (S). Use is limited to psychologists, psychiatrists, and other professionals in the areas of clinical and research psychology.

Format: Examiner required; not suitable for group use; untimed: 30 minutes

Scoring: Examiner evaluated

Cost: Complete Kit (Picture Title cards, Picture Story Completion cards, Photo-Analysis cards, 25 Arrow-Dot test forms, 25 record forms, separate instruction cards, general manual, heavy storage boxes) $43.50

Publisher: Psychological Test Specialists

Intermediate Personality Questionnaire for Indian Pupils (IPQI)

Copyright: 1974

Population: Children, adolescents

Purpose: Assesses personality; used for guidance of children with social and emotional problems; used in vocational guidance

Description: Multiple-item paper–pencil measure of 10 aspects of personality: social extraversion, verbal intelligence, emotional stability, adventuresomeness, creativity, dominance, perseverance, relaxedness, spirit of enterprise, and environment relatedness.

Format: Examiner required; suitable for group use; untimed: 30–45 minutes

Scoring: Hand key

Cost: Contact publisher

Publisher: Human Sciences Research Council

Interpersonal Behavior Survey (IBS)
Paul A. Mauger, David R. Adkinson, Suzanne K. Zoss, Gregory Firestone, J. David Hook

Copyright: 1980

Population: Adolescents, adults; Grades 9 and above

Purpose: Measures and distinguishes assertive and aggressive behaviors among adolescents and adults; used for assertiveness training, marriage counseling, and in a variety of clinical settings

Description: Paper–pencil 272-item test in which the subject responds to statements written in the present tense to provide sensitivity to ongoing changes. The test yields eight aggressiveness scales (including one that measures general aggressiveness over a broad range of item content, including aggressive behaviors, feelings, and attitudes), nine assertiveness scales (including one that measures general assertiveness over a broad range of behaviors), three validity scales, and three relationship scales (Conflict Avoidance, Dependency, and Shyness). Two shorter forms are available: a 38-item form providing a general sampling of behaviors and a 133-item form providing information on all scales. The Profile Form provides a display of raw scores, *T*-scores, and percentiles. Norms are provided for adult males, adult females, high-school students, college students, and blacks. The manual presents validity and reliability data, interpretive guidelines, and a number of illustrated cases.

Format: Self-administered; suitable for group use; untimed: 10–45 minutes depending on form

Scoring: Hand key

Cost: Kit (5 booklets, 50 profile forms, 50 answer sheets, key, manual) $65.00

Publisher: Western Psychological Services

Interpersonal Dependency Inventory
Robert Hirschfeld

Copyright: 1977

Population: Adolescents, adults; ages 15 and above; Grades 10 and above

Purpose: Measures feelings of insufficiency and lack of self-confidence resulting in dependency; used for identifying vulnerability to depression, problems of self-esteem, and dependency

Description: This 48-item weighted-response test is scored for three subscales, from which a total score indicative of interpersonal dependency is obtained. The first two subscales (Emotional Reliance on Others, and Lack of Social Self-Confidence) are indicative of dependency, and the third (Assertion of Autonomy) is contraindicative. Qualified users, according to the standards of the American Psychological Association, may obtain a copy of the test form, a sheet giving scoring instructions and norms, and a list of current references from the custodian of the inventory. Only one form is available. A test blank is used.

Format: Suitable for group use; self-administered; untimed: 10 minutes

Scoring: Hand key, computer scored; no scoring service available

Cost: Free

Publisher: Harrison G. Gough, Ph.D.

Kinetic Drawing System for Family and School
Howard M. Knoff, H. Thompson Prout

Copyright: Not provided

Population: Children, adolescents; ages 5 to 20

Purpose: Provides personalized themes within school and family contexts; used for school psychology referrals

Description: Paper–pencil oral-response projective system integrating Kinetic Family Drawing and Kinetic School Drawing covering a broad range of the most frequent areas of child and adolescent distress—family and school. It consists of two drawings with a series of suggested projective questions in relation to the action between figures; figure characteristics; position, distance, and barriers style; and symbols. Each has a projective interpretation for family and school forms and a variable number of items subject to examiner discretion.

Format: Examiner required; not suitable for group use; untimed: time varies

Scoring: Examiner evaluated

Cost: Kit (1 manual, 25 scoring booklets) $57.50

Publisher: Western Psychological Services

Louisville Behavior Checklist
Lovick C. Miller

Copyright: 1984

Population: Children, adolescents; ages 4 to 17

Purpose: Measures the entire range of social and emotional behaviors indicative of psychopathological disorders in children and adolescents; used as an intake screening device

Description: Paper–pencil or computer-administered 164-item true–false inventory in which parents record their child's behavior by answering questions that provide relevant information on a number of interpretive scales. The inventory is available in three forms for three different age groups: Forms E1 (ages 4 to 6), Form E2 (ages 7 to 12), and Form E3 (ages 13 to 17).

Format: Examiner required; not suitable for group use; untimed: 20–30 minutes

Scoring: Hand key; may be computer scored

Cost: Kit (30 reusable questionnaires, 1 manual, 100 answer-profile sheets, 3 scoring keys, 2 WPS Test Report prepaid LBC mail-in answer sheets for computer scoring and interpretation) $195.00

Publisher: Western Psychological Services

M-Scale: Inventory of Attitudes Toward Black/White Relations
James H. Morrison

Copyright: 1969

Population: Adolescents, adults

Purpose: Initiates discussions of black–white relations in training sessions; used as a self-examination to sensitize a person to his or her attitudes toward race relations and for research

Description: Paper–pencil 28-item inventory measuring attitudes toward black–white relations in the United States on an integrationist–separationist continuum. Instructions are read to the subjects, who are allowed as much time as necessary to complete the test. Requires a 10th-grade reading level.

Format: Self-administration; 25 minutes

Scoring: Examiner interpretation

Cost: $4.00 for 20 inventories with manual

Publisher: James H. Morrison

Non-Verbal Scale of Suffering (N-V SOS)
Theodore C. Kent

Copyright: 1981

Population: Ages 5 and above

Purpose: Assesses the level of sadness and low self-esteem; used as a pictorial screening instrument to identify suicide proneness and suffering and to provide clues of its origin

Description: Paper–pencil 24-item oral-response and point-to test of experienced suffering. Each item presents five nonverbal figures reflecting different degrees of distress, and subjects are asked to circle the drawing that best reflects their current feelings. The test measures degree of subjective suffering, self-image, denial of feelings, and inconsistency of feelings. Six scoring categories are used: No Suffering, No Significant Suffering, Mild Suffering, Significant Suffering, Severe Suffering, and Profound Suffering. Instructions may be given in any language; English and Spanish instructions are provided on the test blank. The test may be used with individuals with mental, physical, and hearing disabilities.

Format: Examiner/self-administered; suitable for group use; untimed: 10 minutes

Scoring: Examiner evaluated; objective scoring

Cost: Free guide ($25.00 deposit); copies must be made of test and manual and returned

Publisher: Human Sciences Center

Personality Assessment Questionnaire (PAQ)
Ronald P. Rohner

Copyright: Child 1977; Adult 1977; Parent 1979

Population: Ages 7 to adult

Purpose: Predicts personality and mental health outcome of variations in perceived parental acceptance–rejection

Description: Multiple-item paper–pencil instrument measuring seven personality dimensions: Hostility/Aggression, Dependence/Independence, Self-Esteem, Self-Adequacy, Emotional (Un)Responsiveness, Emotional (In)Stability, and World View. Theoretically, these dispositions are linked to the acceptance–rejection process. The test is available in a child version, an adult version, and a mother version. The questionnaire yields seven scale scores in addition to the Total Test score, which is often used as a measure of overall mental health. A computer scoring program is available for IBM PC systems. The examiner may read the items to visually impaired individuals and explain the meanings of words to very young individuals or those with mental disabilities. The Handbook for the Study of Parental Acceptance and Rejection contains all versions of the PAQ and provides scoring instructions, descriptions of validity and reliability, and other information needed for administration, scoring, and interpretation.

Format: Examiner/self-administered; suitable for group use; untimed: 10 minutes

Scoring: Self-scored; may be computer scored

Cost: Handbook $15.00; software (PARScore) $25.00

Publisher: Center for the Study of Parental Acceptance and Rejection

Personality Rating Scale
Mary Amatora

Copyright: 1985

Population: Children, adolescents; Grades K through 12

Purpose: Assesses personality strengths and weaknesses of children; identifies children needing further psychological evaluation

Description: Paper–pencil 22-item test of personality functioning. The items are characteristics of good and poor habits of interaction acquired in childhood and strengthened in early adolescence that affect personality development and the process of maturation. The rating scale may be completed by the child, teacher, or peers. The test may be used with students in Grades K through 3 with the special instructions provided in manual.

Format: Self-administered; suitable for group use; untimed: 30–40 minutes

Scoring: Hand key; examiner and student evaluated

Cost: Specimen Set $5.00; complete kit (35 scales, 35 pupil rating sheets, 3 class record sheets, key, manual) $15.50; additional manuals $2.00 each

Publisher: Educators'/Employers' Tests and Services Associates

Politte Sentence Completion Test (PSCT)
Alan J. Politte

Copyright: 1971

Population: Children, adolescents; Grades 1 through 12

Purpose: Evaluates personality traits and adjustment of children; used to assess personality in educational, counseling, and clinical areas

Description: Paper–pencil 35-item free-response projective test measuring personality. Students are told that the test is a "questionnaire" or an "exercise" in which they are to read the stems and then complete the sentences. The test serves as a screening device through which the examiner can gain further insight into the thinking processes of the student. It is not an instrument that provides a "score" or normative reference for the student. Persons without training in clinical psychology should use the test as an aid in interview or counseling settings. Clinically trained psychologists can base their

interpretations from a psychoanalytic, social, behavioral, or similar approach. The test is available in two forms: Elementary for Grades 1 through 6 and Secondary for Grades 7 through 12.

Format: Examiner/self-administered; suitable for group use; untimed: 15 minutes

Scoring: Examiner evaluated

Cost: Specimen Set $4.50; 25 tests (manual included; specify form) $8.25

Publisher: Psychologists and Educators, Inc.

Q-Tags Test of Personality
Arthur G. Storey, Louis I. Masson

Copyright: Not provided

Population: Ages 6 and older

Purpose: Measures individual personality traits; used for counseling, self-examination, and research

Description: Using 54 cards, this test measures five factors of personality: assertive, effective, hostile, reverie, and social. By sorting cards, subjects are able to describe themselves both as they are and as they wish to be. The test was developed with norms for age, grade, occupation, and sex based on a wide range of subjects.

Format: Self-administered; suitable for group use; untimed: 30 minutes

Scoring: Examiner evaluated

Cost: Contact publisher

Publisher: Institute of Psychological Research, Inc.

Revised Children's Manifest Anxiety Scale (RCMAS)
Cecil R. Reynolds, Bert O. Richmond

Copyright: Not provided

Population: 6- to 19-year-olds

Purpose: Measures the level and nature of anxiety in children

Description: The RCMAS helps pinpoint the problems in a child's life. A brief self-report inventory provides scores for Total Anxiety and four subscales: Worry/Oversensitivity, Social Concerns/Concentration, Physiological Anxiety, and Lie Scale. It is composed of 37 yes-or-no items. The scale is useful to clinicians who are treating children for academic stress, test anxiety, peer and family conflicts, or drug problems. It provides objective data on anxiety that can inform and guide treatment.

Format: Suitable for group use; examiner required; 15 minutes

Scoring: Hand key

Cost: Kit (includes 100 test forms, 1 scoring key, 1 manual) $80.00

Publisher: Western Psychological Services

Risk-Taking Attitude-Values Inventory (RTAVI)
R. E. Carney

Copyright: 1979

Population: All ages; ages 3 and older

Purpose: Measures basic values and needs, behavior potentials for risks, credibility of sources of help (ways of changing behavior)

Description: Paper–pencil, 71- to 101-item (depending on form) multiple-choice test based on the subjective utility model of risk–taking. It measures values and needs (16 items), utilities and expectations of behavior (30–50 items), frequencies of behavior (15–25 items), and ways of changing behavior (10 items). The test yields several scores, including Total Need, Need for Affection, Respect, Skill, Knowledge, Power, Wealth, Need for Well-Being, 15–25 behavior potential scores (depending on form used), Socially Disapproved Behavior Style (SDB), Masculine-Aggressive Behavior Style (MAB), Socially Approved Behavior Style (SAB), Institutional Ways of Change (IST), and Interpersonal Ways of Change (INT). The test form integrates items, scoring, and a profile. Several forms are available: Preschool–Primary, Elementary, Secondary, Post-Secondary, and Adult. Materials must be ordered in quantities of 50 or more.

Format: Examiner/self-administered; suitable for group use; untimed: typical time not available

Scoring: Hand key; may be computer scored; scoring service available from publisher

Cost: 50 forms (specify form) $30.00; Specimen Set (includes all forms) $15.00

Publisher: TIMAO Foundation for Research and Development

Rorschach Inkblot Test
Hermann Rorschach

Copyright: Not provided

Population: All ages

Purpose: Evaluates personality tendencies

Description: 10 Rorschach color inkblot plates used for psychodiagnostic purposes. Examiner shows one at a time to client and records responses.

Format: Individually administered; examiner required

Scoring: Examiner evaluated

Cost: Set (includes 1 set plates, 1 pad of 100 miniature inkblots in color/summary forms, 25 record booklets and summary forms) $145.00

Publisher: Western Psychological Services

Rorschach Psychodiagnostic Test—Rorschach Ink Blot Test
Hermann Rorschach

Copyright: Not provided

Population: Ages 3 and older

Purpose: Evaluates personality through projective technique; used in clinical evaluation

Description: Ten-plate oral-response projective personality test in which the subject is asked to interpret what he or she sees in 10 inkblots, based on the assumption that the individual's perceptions and associations are selected and organized in terms of his motivations, impulses, and other underlying aspects of personality. Extensive scoring systems have been developed. Although many variations are in use, this entry refers only to the Psychodiagnostic Plates first published in 1921. Materials include inquiry charts, tabulation sheets, and a set of 10 inkblots. A set of 10 Kodaslides of the inkblots may be imported on request. Trained examiner required.

Format: Individually administered; examiner required; untimed

Scoring: Examiner evaluated

Cost: $75.00

Publisher: Hogrefe and Huber Publishers

Rosenzweig Picture-Frustration Study (P-F)
Saul Rosenzweig

Copyright: 1978

Population: Ages 4 through adult

Purpose: Measures aggression in personality; used in clinical counseling

Description: Paper–pencil semiprojective technique assessing an individual's patterns of response to everyday frustration or stress. It consists of 24 cartoon pictures, each depicting two persons in a frustrating situation. One person is acting as the frustrator. The subject provides a reply for the anonymous frustrated person in the second picture. The instrument measures three types of aggression (obstacles-dominance, ego-defense, and need-persistence) and three directions of aggression (extraggression, imaggression, and intraggression). Nine factors, derived by combining the types and directions of aggression, constitute the score. The scoring guide is provided in the manual. Three versions are available: adult, adolescent, and child.

Format: Examiner required; suitable for group use; timed: 15–20 minutes

Scoring: Hand key

Cost: Study Kit (manual, manual supplement, 25 test booklets and scoring sheets) $50.00; specify version

Publisher: Psychological Assessment Resources, Inc.

Scenotest
G. von Staabs

Copyright: 1991

Population: Children; adolescents

Purpose: To quickly assess emotional problems in children

Description: Specifically developed to evaluate children's and adolescents' unconscious problems, the test is suited for working with adults and families. It permits accessing consciously denied or personally unknown relationships in the attitudes of the subjects to themselves and their social environment. Flexible dolls and a supply of additional material (selected according to psychological and dynamic considerations) such as animals, trees, symbolic figures, and important objects from everyday life, are used as standard stimuli to prompt the subject easily to form and play out scenes which reveal real-life experiences, relations, fears, wishes, and coping strategies. Initial sessions reveal considerable matter which could not be tapped by direct questioning. In particular, neurotic disturbances can be revealed, and differential diagnosis is strongly supported. Used as part of an explicit therapy, it helps the patient see his or her problems at a distance and cope with them.

Format: Individually administered; untimed

Scoring: Examiner evaluated

Cost: Complete test kit $775.00 (DM 1,362.00); manual $35.00 (DM 69.00); German version is also available from publisher

Publisher: Hogrefe and Huber Publishers

Self-Concept Evaluation of Location Form (SELF)
R. E. Carney, C. W. Weedman, G. Spielberger

Copyright: 1980

Population: Ages 12 and older

Purpose: Assesses self-concept

Description: Multiple-choice 32-item paper–pencil self-rating instrument assessing present self (16 items) and ideal self (16 items). The test yields 15 scores: Total Positive Self-Concept Evaluation (E), Potency Self-Concept (P), Activity Self-Concept (A), Total Inconsistency (K), Systematic Inconsistency (K1), Unsystematic Inconsistency (K2), Inconsistency F ratio (K3), Total Incongruence (C), Evaluation Incongruence (E1), Potency Incongruence (P1), Activity Incongruence (A1), Systematic Incongruence (C1), Systematic Incongruence (C1), Unsystematic Incongruence (C2), and Incongruence F ratio (C3). The test form integrates items, scoring, and a profile. A scoring service is available from the publisher. When used as a self-rating instrument, examinees must be at least 12 years old. Examinees must have a sixth-grade reading level. The test is suitable for use with individuals with hearing and visual disabilities. Test booklets must be purchased in quantities of 50 or more.

Format: Examiner/self-administered; suitable for group use; untimed: time varies

Scoring: Hand key; may be computer scored; test scoring service available from publisher

Cost: 50 test forms $25.00; Specimen Set $12.00

Publisher: TIMAO Foundation for Research and Development

Self-Esteem Index (SEI)
Linda Brown, Jacquelyn Alexander

Copyright: 1991

Population: Ages 7 to 18

Purpose: Measures the way individuals perceive and value themselves

Description: Paper–pencil 120-item survey assessing self-esteem. Items are divided into four scales: Perception of Familial Acceptance, Perception of Academic Competence, Perception of Peer Popularity, and Perception of Personal Security. Results are reported as standard scores and percentiles.

Format: Self-administered; suitable for group use; untimed: 30 minutes

Scoring: Computer scored

Cost: Complete Kit (examiner's manual, student response booklets, profile and record forms, storage box) $104.00

Publisher: PRO-ED, Inc.

Self-Esteem Questionnaire (SEQ–3)
James K. Hoffmeister

Copyright: 1971

Population: Grades 4 to adult

Purpose: Evaluates how individuals feel about various aspects of themselves, including their capabilities, worth, and acceptance by others

Description: Paper–pencil 21-item self-report rating scale consisting of two subscales: Self-Esteem (12 items) and Self–Other Satisfaction (9 items). Items on the Self-Esteem subscale consist of statements such as "Most of my friends accept me as much as they accept other people" that the individual rates on a 5-point scale from one ("not at all") to five ("yes, very much"). Items on the Self–Other Satisfaction subscale immediately follow items on the Self-Esteem subscale and take the form "Does the situation described in [the previous question] upset you?" These items are rated on a 5-point scale also. Scores are provided for both subscales according to the computerized convergence analysis process (a score is computed only if the individual has responded in a reasonably consistent fashion to the items used to measure that factor). The manual includes a description of the test's variables and content and directions for administering and scoring the questionnaire.

Format: Examiner required; suitable for group use; untimed: time varies

Scoring: Computer scored

Cost: 50 questionnaires (includes computer scoring service) $50.00

Publisher: Test Analysis and Development Corporation

Self–Other Location Chart
Theodore C. Kent

Copyright: 1988

Population: All ages

Purpose: Measures self-esteem; used in counseling settings to identify feelings of superiority and inferiority

Description: A projective test in which examinees respond to an illustration of a group of figures walking. They indicate where they think they are in the illustration, where they would like to be, who they think the leader is, and who they think the loser is. May be used with individuals with hearing, physical, or mental disabilities.

Format: Group; untimed

Scoring: Examiner administration and interpretation

Cost: Sample furnished for a $25.00 deposit (returned)

Publisher: Human Sciences Center

Self-Perception Profile for Children
Susan Harter

Copyright: 1985

Population: Ages 8 to 13

Purpose: Assesses scholastic competence, athletic competence, social acceptance, physical appearance, behavioral conduct, and global self-worth

Description: Test with 36 items. The manual includes a teacher rating scale, as well as a rating scale to tap children's perceptions of the importance of each domain.

Format: Examiner required; not suitable for group use

Scoring: Examiner evaluated

Cost: $20.00

Publisher: Susan Harter

Semistructured Clinical Interview for Children and Adolescents (SCICA)
Stephanie H. McConaughy,
Thomas M. Achenbach

Copyright: 1994

Population: Children, adolescents; ages 6 to 18

Purpose: Used in mental health and special education applications to assess behavioral and emotional problems

Description: Paper–pencil short-answer rating scales with 247 problem items. The following profiles are yielded: anxious; anxious/depressed; aggressive; attention problems; family problems; resistant; strange; and withdrawn. Practical and rating forms are used by an interviewer. Examiner must be an experienced interviewer. A computer version using all IBM compatibles is available.

Format: Individual administration; examiner required; untimed: 60–90 minutes

Scoring: Hand key; computer scored

Cost: Package of 25 forms $10.00

Publisher: University of Vermont Department of Psychiatry

Social–Emotional Dimension Scale (SEDS)
Jerry B. Hutton, Timothy G. Roberts

Copyright: 1986

Population: Ages 5 years 6 months to 18 years 6 months

Purpose: Assesses student performance in physical/fear reaction, depressive reaction, avoidance of peer interaction, avoidance of teacher interaction, aggressive interaction, and inappropriate behaviors

Description: Well-standardized, norm-referenced 32-item rating scale that can be used by teachers, counselors, and psychologists to screen students who are at risk for conduct disorders, behavior problems, or emotional disturbance. It assesses student performance in six areas: physical/fear reaction, depressive reaction, avoidance of peer interaction, avoidance of teacher interaction, aggressive interaction, and inappropriate behaviors. Statements on the rating scale were written to represent observable student behavior in each of the six areas. To complete the rating scale, teachers or other school personnel familiar with the student rate each item by determining whether the behavior is observed never or rarely, occasionally, or frequently. The rating scale can be completed after an observation period of approximately 3 weeks. Ample reliability and validity data are provided for nondisabled students. Coefficient alphas and test–retest reliability coefficients exceed .80.

Format: Examiner required; timed: time varies

Scoring: Examiner evaluated

Cost: Complete Kit (examiner's manual, 50 profile/examiner record forms, storage box) $69.00

Publisher: PRO-ED, Inc.

Stroop Color and Word Test
Charles J. Golden

Copyright: 1978

Population: Grades 2 and above

Purpose: Evaluates personality, cognition, stress response, psychiatric disorders, and other psychological phenomena; used to differentiate non–brain-damaged psychiatric from brain-damaged subjects

Description: Multiple-item response test of an

individual's ability to separate word and color stimuli and react to them independently. The test consists of three pages: a Word Page containing color words printed in black ink; a Color Page with a series of X's printed in colored inks; and a Word-Color page on which the words on the first page are printed in the colors of the second page except that the word and color do not match. The subject is given all three pages and asked to read the Word Page. He or she then names the colors of the X's on the Color Page. Next he must name the color of the ink in which the words on the Word-Color Page are printed, ignoring the semantic meaning of the words. The test requires a second-grade reading level.

Format: Examiner required; not suitable for group use; timed: 5 minutes

Scoring: Examiner evaluated

Cost: Complete Kit (manual, 25 sets of 3 sheets) $60.00

Publisher: Stoelting Company

TEMAS (Tell-Me-a-Story)

Giuseppe Costantino, Robert G. Malgady, Lloyd Rogler

Copyright: 1986

Population: Children, adolescents; ages 5 to 18

Purpose: Measures strengths and deficits in cognitive, affective, interpersonal, and intrapersonal functioning in children and adolescents

Description: Multicultural thematic apperception test designed for use with minority and nonminority children and adolescents ages 5 to 18. The test, which features 35 scales, uses 23 full-color stimulus cards to elicit stories from the examinee. Two parallel forms, minority and nonminority, are available. Separate norms are available for blacks, Hispanics, and whites.

Format: Examiner required; not suitable for group use; untimed: short form 1 hour; long form 3 hours

Scoring: Examiner evaluated

Cost: Kit (set of stimulus cards, set of minority stimulus cards, 25 record booklets, administration instruction card, 1 manual) $260.00

Publisher: Western Psychological Services

Test of Social Insight: Youth and Adult Editions

Russell N. Cassel

Copyright: 1959

Population: 10 to adult

Purpose: Measures the subject's understanding of and adaptation to acceptable patterns of culture in the United States

Description: Paper–pencil 60-item multiple-choice test involving five ways of responding to interpersonal problems: withdrawal, passivity, cooperation, competition, and aggression. The potential conflict areas covered include home and family, authority figures, avocational contacts, and work situations. The Youth Edition is appropriate for individuals ages 10 to 18; the Adult Edition is designed for individuals ages 18 and older. A fifth-grade reading level is required. Suitable for individuals with physical, hearing, or visual disabilities.

Format: Self-administered; suitable for group use; untimed: 30–40 minutes

Scoring: Hand key

Cost: Manual and manual supplement $42.50; reusable tests $64.00; profile sheets $25.50; IBM scoring stencils $31.00; IBM answer sheets $25.50; Specimen Set $52.50

Publisher: Martin M. Bruce, Ph.D.

Thematic Apperception Test (TAT–Z)

Copyright: 1976

Population: Ages 10 and older

Purpose: Measures personality characteristics; used for assessment and diagnosis of personality

Description: Ten-card projective measure of personality using the method of choosing cards which reveal the level of Westernization and adjustment to Western demands. The subject chooses pictures that relate to the following 10 areas: degree and direction of acculturation, family relationships, father–son relationship, mother–son relationship, attitude toward black authority, attitude toward white authority, self-concept, heterosexual relationships, social relationships, and handling of aggression.

Format: Examiner required; not suitable for group use; untimed: 2 hours

Scoring: Hand key; examiner evaluated

Cost: Contact publisher

Publisher: Human Sciences Research Council

Welsh Figure Preference Test (WFPT)
George S. Welsh

Copyright: 1987

Population: Ages 6 to adult

Purpose: Evaluates individual personality traits through figure identification; used for counseling and research

Description: Paper–pencil 400-item nonverbal test measuring an individual's personality traits by evaluating his or her preference for types of black-and-white figures. The subject responds by indicating "likes" or "dislikes" for each figure. Scales include Conformity, Male–Female, Neuropsychiatric, Consensus, Origence, Intellectence, Barron-Welsh Original Art Scale, Revised Art Scale, Repression, Anxiety, Children, Movement, Figure–Ground Reversal, Sex Symbol, and several measuring preferences for specific kinds of geometric figures. All scales need not be scored. The Barron-Welsh Art Scale (86 items) is available separately.

Format: Examiner required; suitable for group use; untimed: 50 minutes

Scoring: Hand key

Cost: Sample Set $25.00; permission for up to 200 uses $90.00

Publisher: Mind Garden, Inc.

Youth Self-Report (YSR)
Thomas M. Achenbach

Copyright: 1995

Population: Adolescents; ages 11 to 18; Grades 4 through 12

Purpose: Used in mental health and special education applications to assess behavioral and emotional problems

Description: Paper–pencil short-answer rating scales with 102 problem items and 17 competence items. The following profiles are yielded: aggressive, anxious/depressed, attention problems, delinquent, social problems, somatic, thought problems, and withdrawn. A form completed by the youth is used. A fifth-grade reading level is required. A computer version using all IBM compatibles and Apple II computers is available. A client-entry program is available.

Format: Individual administration; suitable for group use; untimed: 15–20 minutes

Scoring: Hand key; machine scored; computer scored

Cost: Package of 25 forms $10.00

Publisher: University of Vermont Department of Psychiatry

Research

Cognitive Behavior Rating Scales (CBRS)–Research Edition
J. Michael Williams

Copyright: 1987

Population: Adults

Purpose: Determines the presence and assesses

the severity of cognitive impairment, behavioral deficits, and observable neurological signs in individuals with possible brain impairment; also used to assess dementia

Description: Paper–pencil 116-item instrument consisting of nine scales intended to elicit information about the examinee's daily behaviors: Language Deficit, Agitation, Need for Routine, Depression, Higher Cognitive Deficits, Memory Disorder, Dementia, Apraxia, and Disorientation. The items on the scales are rated by the examinee's significant other. *T*-scores and percentiles are reported for each of the nine scale scores.

Format: Examiner required; not suitable for group use; untimed: 15–20 minutes

Scoring: Examiner evaluated

Cost: Kit (manual, 25 reusable item booklets, 50 rating booklets) $47.00

Publisher: Psychological Assessment Resources, Inc.

Fundamental Interpersonal Relations Orientation–Behavior (FIRO–B)
Will Schutz

Copyright: Not provided

Population: All ages

Purpose: Measures an individual's characteristic behavior toward others; used in individual and group psychotherapy, in executive development programs, and as a measure of compatibility in relationships

Description: Paper–pencil or computer-administered 54-item test measuring six dimensions of an individual's behavior toward others: expressed inclusion, expressed control, expressed affection, wanted inclusion, wanted control, and wanted affection. Software for administration and scoring is available for IBM PC or compatible systems with 386 processor with 4 MB RAM.

Format: Examiner/self-administered; suitable for group use; untimed: paper–pencil version 20 minutes; computer version 10 minutes

Scoring: Hand key; may be computer scored

Cost: Self-Scorable Preview Kit (booklet, client's guide, results guide) $14.00

Publisher: Consulting Psychologists Press, Inc.

Kohn Problem Checklist (KPC)–Research Edition
Martin Kohn

Copyright: 1988

Population: Children; PreK through K

Purpose: Assesses the presence or absence of behavior problems in children

Description: Paper–pencil 49-item unipolar behavior rating scale measuring the presence or absence of pathological behavior. The ratings of two teachers are combined to yield angry–defiant and apathetic–withdrawn behavior dimension scores. These scores can be merged with scores obtained on the Kohn Social Competence (KSC) Scale to yield pooled-instrument scores across the two scales. The test is available only to institutions with a staff member who has completed an advanced-level course in testing from an accredited college or university.

Format: Examiner required; not suitable for group use; untimed: 10 minutes or less

Scoring: Hand key

Cost: Complete KPC/KSC Combined Kit (25 answer sheets for KPC, 25 answer sheets for KSC, and manual) $86.00

Publisher: The Psychological Corporation

Kohn Social Competence Scale (KSC)–Research Edition
Martin Kohn

Copyright: 1988

Population: Children; PreK through K

Purpose: Assesses the social–emotional functioning of young children

Description: Paper–pencil 64- or 73-item bipolar behavior rating scale measuring social competency along the following dimensions: cooperative–compliant versus angry–defiant and interest–participation versus apathetic–withdrawn. One or two teachers evaluate the child. Their scores are combined to produce scores along the bipolar behavior dimensions. Scores can be merged with scores from the Kohn Problem Checklist to yield pooled-instrument scores across the two scales. The 64-item version is designed for children enrolled in half-day programs, and the 73-item version for children in full-day programs. The test is available only to institutions with a staff member who has completed an advanced level-course in testing from an accredited college or university. Registration is required.

Format: Examiner required; not suitable for group use; untimed: 5–10 minutes

Scoring: Hand key

Cost: Complete KPC/KSC Combined Kit (includes 25 Ready Score answer sheets for the KPC, 25 Ready Score answer sheets for the KSC, and manual) $86.00

Publisher: The Psychological Corporation

Physical Punishment Questionnaire (PPQ)
Ronald P. Rohner

Copyright: 1995

Population: Children, adults; Grades 3 and above

Purpose: Assesses experiences of children and adults with physical punishment received; parents report use of physical punishment; used for research on antecedents and consequences of physical punishment

Description: Paper–pencil oral-response verbal test consisting of 59 items on child and adult forms; 29 items on the parent form. Measures major variables: frequency, severity, consistency, predictability, incidence, deservedness, timing, and explanation of punishment; 13 specific forms of punishment; four write-in forms of punishment experienced; sum of different forms of punishment experienced from major caretaker; sum of different forms of punish-

ment experienced from major disciplinarian; harshness of punishment received; justness of punishment received. Third-grade reading level required. Soon available in Spanish, Arabic, and other languages.

Format: Examiner/self-administered; suitable for group use; untimed: 10–15 minutes

Scoring: Hand key

Cost: Test and manual $15.00

Publisher: Center for the Study of Parental Acceptance and Rejection

Test of Basic Assumptions
James H. Morrison
Martin Levit

Copyright: 1959

Population: Adolescents, adults

Purpose: Diagnoses philosophical preferences; used to examine assumptions about reality or philosophy and for research and group discussion

Description: Paper–pencil 20-item measure of realism, idealism, and pragmatism. Instructions are read to the subjects, who are allowed as much time as they need to complete the test. A minimum 12th-grade reading level is necessary. The test should not be used for prediction purposes.

Format: Self-administration; 40 minutes

Scoring: Examiner interpretation

Cost: $4.00 for 20 inventories with manual

Publisher: James H. Morrison

Stress

At Ease!
Giles D. Rainwater

Copyright: 1985

Population: Adolescents, adults

Purpose: Assists in coping with stress and frustration, making more effective use of rest

breaks, improving concentration and attention, and dealing with cognitive rehabilitation

Description: Computer-administered program consisting of eight categories—progressive muscle relaxation, deep breathing, meditation, relaxation, pleasant scene, paced breathing, quick relaxation, visual relaxation—and print instructions. Computer program available for IBM PC. Examiners must be professionals trained in providing psychotherapy.

Format: Examiner required; suitable for group use; timed and untimed

Scoring: Computer scored

Cost: $69.95

Publisher: Psychometric Software, Inc.

Brief Computerized Stress Inventory (Brief CSI)
Allan N. Press, Lynn Osterkamp

Copyright: 1996

Population: Adults; ages 18 and above

Purpose: Assesses levels of stress in over 30 lifestyle areas; used in health, mental health, educational, business, and military settings

Description: Assessment (with 15 items) of over 16 lifestyle areas, such as work or primary activity, time, family relationships, self-esteem, and physical symptoms of stress. Can be computer administered or responses from the six-page written questionnaire can be operator entered in 90 seconds. The program generates an eight-page individualized profile plus graph of the respondent's levels of stress and satisfaction. Introduced in 1987 and normed on a national sample of over 3,500 respondents, the Brief CSI is available for IBM PC and Macintosh systems. The purchase price includes unlimited use of the software and master questionnaire. Data files are written to disk and can be aggregated into a group or corporate report or used to generate research scores. The questionnaire and report can be customized for a specific population or setting.

Format: Individual/self-administered; untimed: 20 minutes

Scoring: Computer scored

Cost: $300.00 for unlimited use of both computer-administered and paper–pencil versions

Publisher: Preventive Measures, Inc.

Comprehensive Computerized Stress Inventory (Comprehensive CSI)
Allan N. Press, Lynn Osterkamp

Copyright: 1996

Population: Adults; ages 18 and above

Purpose: Assesses levels of stress in over 30 lifestyle areas; used in health, mental health, educational, business, and military settings

Description: Branching inventory consisting of more than 400 items that assesses over 30 lifestyle areas, such as work or primary activity, family relationships, life changes, eating habits, time management, worrying, and self-esteem. Can be computer administered or responses from the 19-page written questionnaire can be operator entered in 4 minutes. The CSI generates a 16-page individualized narrative profile plus graph of the respondent's levels of stress and satisfaction. The report makes suggestions for reducing stress and encourages respondents to make positive lifestyle changes. Introduced in 1984 and normed on a national sample of over 1,500 respondents, the Comprehensive CSI is available for IBM PC and Macintosh systems. The purchase price includes unlimited use of the software and master questionnaire. Data files are written to disk and can be aggregated into a group or corporate report or used to generate research scores. The questionnaire and report can be customized for a specific population.

Format: Individual/self-administered; untimed: 60 minutes

Scoring: Computer scored

Cost: $325.00 for unlimited use of both computer-administered and paper-and-pencil versions

Publisher: Preventive Measures, Inc.

Coping Inventory for Stressful Situations (CISS)
Norman Endler, James Parker

Copyright: 1989

Population: Adolescents, adults

Purpose: Measures coping styles in individuals

Description: Paper–pencil or computer-administered 48-item instrument measuring three major types of coping styles: Task Oriented, Emotion Oriented, and Avoidance Coping. The CISS also identifies two types of Avoidance Coping patterns: Distraction and Social Support. Scores provide a profile of an individual's coping strategy. Adult and adolescent forms available.

Format: Self-administered; suitable for group use; untimed: 10 minutes

Scoring: Carbonized scoring forms; may be computer scored

Cost: Kit (test manual, 25 QuikScore forms) $40.00; IBM PC–compatible version (50 administrations and scorings) $160.00

Publisher: Multi-Health Systems, Inc.

Coping Responses Inventory (CRI)
Rudolf H. Moos

Copyright: 1993

Population: Adolescents, adults; ages 12 and above

Purpose: Used in counseling and stress management education to identify and monitor coping strategies

Description: Paper–pencil short-answer 4-point scale with the following categories: Logical Analysis, Positive Reappraisal, Seeking Guidance and Support, Problem Solving, Cognitive Avoidance, Acceptance or Resignation, Seeking Alternative Rewards, and Emotional Discharge. Two forms are available: youth and adult. Materials used include an adult manual, youth manual, adult actual and ideal test booklets, youth ideal and actual test booklets, and answer sheets. A sixth-grade reading level is required. Examiner must be B-Level qualified with training in clinical and counseling psychology.

Format: Self-administered; examiner required; untimed

Scoring: Hand-scored answer sheet; test scoring service available from publisher

Cost: Youth or adult kit $55.00

Publisher: Psychological Assessment Resources, Inc.

Daily Stress Inventory (DSI)
Philip J. Brantley, Glenn N. Jones

Copyright: 1989

Population: Adults; ages 17 and above

Purpose: Used in behavioral counseling and stress management to monitor changes in daily stress

Description: Paper–pencil 58-item 7-point scale with the following categories: Impact (perceived stressfulness), Event (frequency), and I/E Ratio (sensitivity to events). Materials used include a manual, rating booklet, and stress tracking chart. A seventh-grade reading level is required. Examiner must be B-Level qualified and trained in educational assessment.

Format: Self-administered; untimed

Scoring: Hand-scorable answer sheet

Cost: Intro Kit $47.00

Publisher: Psychological Assessment Resources, Inc.

Derogatis Stress Profile (DSP)
Leonard R. Derogatis

Copyright: 1980

Population: Adults

Purpose: Measures the levels of stress an individual experiences in terms of interactional stress theory

Description: Paper–pencil 77-item test assessing 11 dimensions of stress grouped in the following three domains: environmental stress, personality mediators, and emotional response. In addition to 11 dimension scores and three domain scores, two global stress indices are also derived. An optical scanning version, SCANTRON, is available for use with computer scoring and interpretation services.

Format: Examiner required; suitable for group use; untimed: 12–15 minutes.

Scoring: Examiner evaluated; may be computer scored

Cost: 50 self-scoring forms $50.00; 100 self-scoring forms $85.00; 50 score/profile forms $25.00; 100 score/profile forms $40.00; SCORDSP Version 2.1 available on a per use basis

Publisher: Clinical Psychometric Research, Inc.

Fear Survey Schedule (FSS)
Joseph Wolpe, Peter J. Land

Copyright: 1969

Population: Adults

Purpose: Evaluates the manner in which an individual deals with fear-related situations; particularly useful in behavior therapy

Description: Multiple-item paper–pencil survey of a patient's reactions to a variety of possible sources of maladaptive emotional reactions. The reactions are unpleasant and often fearful, fear tinged, or fear related. The schedule reveals reactions to many stimulus classes in a short time.

Format: Examiner required; suitable for group use; untimed: 3 minutes

Scoring: Examiner evaluated

Cost: Response forms and manual $11.50

Publisher: EdITS/Educational and Industrial Testing Service

Hilson Career Satisfaction Index (HCSI)
Robin E. Inwald

Copyright: 1988

Population: Adults

Purpose: Identifies and predicts stress-related behavior patterns and career satisfaction

Description: Paper–pencil 161-item true–false instrument consisting of 4 scales: Stress Pattern Content Areas, Anger/Hostility Content Areas, Dissatisfaction Content Areas, and Defensiveness Validity Scale. Total score measures overall level of stress and dissatisfaction related to current work-oriented activities. This score should be used only as a general indicator and individual scale elevations should be reviewed whenever conclusions are drawn about test results. The teleprocessing software allows input of test responses.

Format: Self-administered; suitable for group use; untimed: 25–35 minutes

Scoring: Computer scored

Cost: $6.00 per test; reusable test booklets $1.50

Publisher: Hilson Research, Inc.

Life Stressors and Social Resources Inventory (LISRES)
Rudolf H. Moos

Copyright: 1994

Population: Adolescents, adults

Purpose: Measures ongoing life stressors and social resources and their changes over time

Description: Multiple-choice paper–pencil yes–no inventory with the following scales: LISRES-Y Life Stressors Scales (physical health, home and money, parents, siblings, extended family, school, friends, boyfriend/girlfriend, negative life events); LISRES-Y Social Resources Scales (parents, siblings, extended family, school, friends, boyfriend/girlfriend, positive life events); LISRES-A Life Stressors Scales (physical health, home and neighborhood, financial, work, spouse or parent, children, extended family, friends, negative life events); LISRES-A Social Resources Scales (financial, work, spouse or partner, children, extended family, friends, positive life events). A sixth-grade reading level is required. Examiner must be B-Level qualified.

Format: Self-administered; suitable for group use; untimed: 30 minutes

Scoring: Hand-scored answer sheet

Cost: Professional Kit $59.00

Publisher: Psychological Assessment Resources, Inc.

Life/Time Manager
Giles D. Rainwater

Copyright: 1985

Population: Adults

Purpose: Used to evaluate time management

Description: Computer-administered short-answer program with four categories: develop goals, develop activities, develop schedules, and develop to-do items. Computer version available for IBM PC.

Format: Self-administered; not suitable for group use

Scoring: Computer scored

Cost: $49.95

Publisher: Psychometric Software, Inc.

Maslach Burnout Inventory–Second Edition
Christina Maslach, Susan E. Jackson

Copyright: Not provided

Population: Adults

Purpose: Measures burnout among social and human service personnel; used in job counseling to reduce burnout symptoms and by school districts to detect potential problems among school staffs

Description: Paper–pencil 22-item inventory consisting of three subscales measuring various aspects of burnout: Emotional Exhaustion, Personal Accomplishment, and Depersonalization. Examinees answer each item on the basis of how frequently they experience the feeling described in the item. The Demographic Data Sheet may be used to obtain biographical information. The revised manual contains more research data and more extensive norms than the previous manual, future research suggestions, and a supplement on burnout in education. In addition, a new MBI Educators Survey and an Educators Demographic Data Sheet are available.

Format: Examiner/self-administered; suitable for group use; untimed: 20–30 minutes

Scoring: Hand key

Cost: Preview Kit (Human Services booklet, Educators Survey booklet, scoring keys, manual) $27.00

Publisher: Consulting Psychologists Press, Inc.

Quick Computerized Stress Inventory (Quick CSI)
Allan N. Press, Lynn Osterkamp

Copyright: 1996

Population: Adults; age 18 and above

Purpose: Screens and assesses levels of stress and life satisfaction in 11 lifestyle areas; used in health, mental health, educational, business, and military settings

Description: Thirty-item screening assessment of 11 major sources of stress and life satisfaction, such as work or primary activity, relationships, feelings about self, managing time, and physical health. Can be computer administered, or responses from the two-page written questionnaire can be operator entered in 25 seconds. The program generates a two-page individualized profile plus graph of the respondent's levels of stress and satisfaction. Introduced in 1990 and normed on several national samples, the Quick CSI is available for IBM PC and Macintosh systems. The purchase price includes unlimited use of the software and master questionnaire. Data files are written to disk and can be aggregated into a group or corporate report or used to generate research scores. The questionnaire and report can be customized for a specific population or setting.

Format: Individual/self-administered; untimed: 5 minutes

Scoring: Computer scored

Cost: $275.00 for unlimited use of both computer-administered and paper-and-pencil versions

Publisher: Preventive Measures, Inc.

Schedule of Recent Experience (RE)
Thomas H. Holmes

Copyright: 1988

Population: Adolescents, adults

Purpose: Measures how often various stress-producing events have occurred in an individual's life during the recent past; used for counseling and discussion purposes and as an aid in general health maintenance programs

Description: Paper–pencil 42-item inventory assessing the amount of psychological change (adaptive behavior) an individual has undergone in the recent past. Each test item is an event that causes change in a person's life that has been observed in a large number of patients preceding the onset of their medical illness or clinical symptoms. Test items include stress-related socially undesirable events and socially desirable events (birth of a baby or a promotion at work). The individual indicates for each item how often the event has occurred during a specific time period (ranging from less than 1 year up to 10 years). The inventory also may be used as a framework for a structured interview. The manual includes instructions for administering the test to individuals of all ages, sample test forms (both 1-year and 3-year versions), templates for scoring both versions, a report of the studies on which the test is based, and a list of suggested preventive measures.

Format: Examiner/self-administered; suitable for group use; untimed: time varies

Scoring: Hand key

Cost: Complete package (manual, 50 1-year test forms or 50 3-year test forms, templates, vinyl folder) $35.00, $50.00

Publisher: University of Washington Press

Wellness

Health Problems Checklist
John A. Schinka

Copyright: 1984

Population: Adults

Purpose: Assesses the health problems of adults; used as a survey instrument in clinical and counseling settings to initiate the consultation process and introduce the client to formal diagnostic testing

Description: Paper–pencil 200-item test identifying health problems that may affect overall psychological well-being. The test, which can be used as a screening tool for medical referrals, covers 13 areas: general health, cardiovascular/pulmonary, endocrine/hematology, gastrointestinal, dermatological, visual, auditory/olfactory, mouth/throat/nose, orthopedic, neurological, genitourinary, habits, and history. The test is a component of the Clinical Checklist Series.

Format: Self-administered; suitable for group use; untimed: 10–20 minutes

Scoring: Examiner evaluated

Cost: 50 checklists $34.00

Publisher: Psychological Assessment Resources, Inc.

Menstrual Distress Questionnaire (MDQ)
Rudolf H. Moos

Copyright: Not provided

Population: Adolescents, adults; ages 13 and older

Purpose: Assesses the characteristics of a woman's menstrual cycle in order to diagnose and treat premenstrual symptoms

Description: Multiple-item paper–pencil or computer-administered questionnaire assessing the examinee on eight characteristics (pain, concentration, behavior change, autonomic reactions, water retention, negative affect, arousal, and control) during each of three phases of the menstrual cycle: premenstrual, menstrual, and intermenstrual. A diskette for administration, scoring, and interpretation on IBM PC and compatible systems is available. The paper–pencil version provides mail-in answer sheets.

Format: Self-administered; suitable for group use; untimed: typical time not available

Scoring: Computer scored

Cost: Kit (10 questionnaires, form C, 1 manual, 2 WPS Test Report answer sheets) $79.00

Publisher: Western Psychological Services

Quality of Life Questionnaire (QLQ)
David Evans, Wendy Cope

Copyright: 1989

Population: Adults

Purpose: Measures an individual's quality of life

Description: Paper–pencil or computer-administered 192-item self-report measure consisting of 15 content scales and a social desirability scale. The five major domains are General Well-Being, Interpersonal Relations, Organizational Activity, Occupational Activity, and Leisure and Recreational Activity. An overall Quality of Life score is obtained from the questionnaire. A computer version generates a narrative report summarizing the findings.

Format: Self-administered; suitable for group use; untimed: 30 minutes

Scoring: Carbonized scoring forms; may be computer scored

Cost: Kit (manual, 10 question booklets, 25 forms) $45.00; IBM PC–compatible computer version (50 administrations and scorings) $125.00

Publisher: Multi-Health Systems, Inc.

Recovery Attitude and Treatment Evaluation–Questionnaire I (RAATE–QI)
David Mee-Lee, Norman G. Hoffman

Copyright: 1987

Population: Adults

Purpose: Used for treatment planning and placement

Description: Paper–pencil 94-item test. Software available for in-office administration and scoring.

Format: Self-administered; untimed

Scoring: Hand key; examiner evaluated

Cost: 25 packets $59.75

Publisher: New Standards, Inc.

Spiritual Well-Being Scale
Craig W. Eilison, Raymond F. Paloutzian

Copyright: 1982

Population: Adolescents, adults; ages 16 and above

Purpose: Measures spiritual wellness; used in medical fields, social science, pastoral counseling, church congregational analysis, and individual counseling

Description: Multiple-choice 20-item paper–pencil test measuring overall spiritual well-being with religious and existential well-being subscales. A high school reading level is required. Also available in French and Spanish.

Format: Self-administered; examiner required; suitable for group use; untimed: 10–15 minutes

Scoring: Hand key; examiner evaluated; self scored

Cost: Contact publisher

Publisher: Life Advance, Inc.

Education Instruments

Tests classified in the Education section generally are used in an educational or school setting to assess the cognitive and emotional growth and development of persons of all ages. Typically, professionals who use the tests listed in this section are school psychologists, school counselors, and classroom teachers. As the classification of tests by function or usage is somewhat arbitrary, the reader is encouraged to check the Psychology and Business sections for additional tests that may be helpful in meeting assessment needs.

Academic Achievement

ACER Advanced Test B40 (Revised)

Copyright: 1989

Population: Adolescents, adults; ages 15 and older

Purpose: Measures intelligence of students ages 15 years and older

Description: Paper–pencil 77-item test measuring general mental abilities, including both verbal and numerical reasoning. The revised manual includes norms for adults and supplementary data for 15-year-olds and first-year college students. Materials include an expendable booklet, score key, manual, and specimen set.

Format: Examiner required; suitable for group use; untimed: 1 hour

Scoring: Hand key

Cost: Contact publisher

Publisher: The Australian Council for Educational Research Limited

ACER Higher Tests: WL-WQ, ML-MQ (Second Edition) and PL-PQ

Copyright: 1989

Population: Adolescents, adults; ages 13 and older

Purpose: Measures the intelligence of students

Description: Paper–pencil 72-item tests of general mental abilities available in three forms: WL-WQ for students ages 13 and older and parallel forms ML-MQ and PL-PQ for students ages 15 and older. The L section (36 items) of each form has a linguistic bias; the Q section (36 items) is quantitative. Australian norms are provided for both sections separately and for a combined score.

Format: Examiner required; suitable for group use; timed: L section 15 minutes, Q section 20 minutes

Scoring: Hand key; examiner evaluated

Cost: Contact publisher

Publisher: The Australian Council for Educational Research Limited

ACER Intermediate Test F

Copyright: 1982

Population: Children, adolescents; ages 10–14

Purpose: Measures the intelligence of students

Description: Paper–pencil 80-item test measuring general mental abilities in the following areas: classification, jumbled sentences, number series, synonyms and antonyms, arithmetical and verbal problems, and proverbs. Materials include a four-page booklet, scoring key, manual, and specimen set. Australian norms are provided.

Format: Examiner required; suitable for group use; timed: 30 minutes

Scoring: Hand key

Cost: Contact publisher

Publisher: The Australian Council for Educational Research Limited

ACER Intermediate Test G

Copyright: 1982

Population: Children, adolescents; ages 10 to 15

Purpose: Measures intelligence of students

Description: Paper–pencil 75-item test measuring general mental abilities: verbal comprehension, verbal reasoning, and quantitative reasoning. Australian age and grade norms are provided. Not available to Australian government schools.

Format: Examiner required; suitable for group use; timed: 30 minutes

Scoring: Hand key

Cost: Contact publisher

Publisher: The Australian Council for Educational Research Limited

ACT Assessment (ACT)

Copyright: Yearly

Population: Adolescents, adults; Grades 11 and above

Purpose: Used for college admissions, course placement, and academic advising

Description: Multiple-choice 215-item paper–pencil test with the following categories: English Test—75 items, 45 minutes; Math Test—60 items, 60 minutes; Reading Test—40 items, 35 minutes; Science Reasoning Test—40 items, 35 minutes. An English Test total score and two subscores: Usage/Mechanics and Rhetorical Skills; Math Test total score and three subscores: Pre-Algebra/Elementary Algebra, Intermediate Algebra/Coordinate Geometry, Plane Geometry/Trigonometry; Reading Test total score and two subscores: Arts/Literature and Social Studies/Sciences; Science Reasoning Test total score. Raw scores are converted to scale scores; scale scores for the four tests and the composite range from a low of 1 to a high of 36. Subscores are reported on a scale score ranging from a low of 1 to a high of 18. Multiple forms are in use. Test booklets, answer folders, registration forms, and supplemental publications are used. May be used with individuals with visual, physical, hearing, and mental disabilities.

Format: Suitable for group use; examiner required; timed: 175 minutes

Scoring: Machine scored; test scoring service available from publisher

Cost: $18.00 to $21.00

Publisher: American College Testing

ACT Proficiency Examination Program: Regents College Examinations (ACT PEP RCE)

Copyright: Varies for each test

Population: Adults; college level

Purpose: Assesses college-level academic achievement; used to grant college credit and advanced placement in academic courses to students at over 800 colleges and universities, including the New York Regents College

Description: Thirty-eight paper–pencil tests measuring achievement in a wide range of fields: Arts and Sciences (13 tests), Business (8 tests), Education (1 test), Nursing (17 tests). Most of the tests are objective (110–150 items) and some are essay. College-level achievement is measured from introductory to advanced levels of study. There are no restrictions on who may take the tests. Individuals seeking credit should contact their local college for information. These tests are known as Regents College Examinations in New York State.

Format: Examiner required; suitable for group use; timed: 3 hours per test

Scoring: Machine scored and examiner evaluated

Cost: Varies from $50.00 to $90.00 each for multiple-choice and $160 for each essay test

Publisher: American College Testing

Adult Basic Learning Examination–Second Edition (ABLE)

Bjorn Karlsen, Eric F. Gardner

Copyright: 1986

Population: Adults; ages 17 and older

Purpose: Measures adult achievement in basic learning

Description: Multiple-item paper–pencil measure of vocabulary knowledge, reading comprehension, spelling and arithmetic computation, and problem-solving skills. The test is divided into three levels. Level 1 is for adults with from 1 to 4 years of formal education. Level 2 is for adults with from 5 to 8 years of schooling. Level 3 is for those with at least 8 years of schooling and who may or may not have graduated from high school. Because the vocabulary test is dictated, no reading is required. The Arithmetic Problem-Solving test is dictated at Level 1. A short test, SelectABLE, is available for use in determining the appropriate level of ABLE for each applicant. The test is available in two alternate forms, E and F, at each level. SelectABLE is available in only one form. Available in Spanish. Screening Battery can be used for Level 2 when testing time is limited.

Format: Examiner required; suitable for group use; untimed: SelectABLE, 15 minutes; Level 1, 2 hours 10 minutes; Levels 2 and 3, 2 hours 55 minutes

Scoring: Hand key; may be computer scored; Levels 2 and 3 self-scored

Publisher: Harcourt® Brace Educational Measurement

Analytic Learning Disability Assessment (ALDA-EZ)

Robert G. Criss

Copyright: 1986

Population: Children

Purpose: Measures neurological efficiency

Description: The ALDA-EZ provides the psychologist with a detailed report, including all the information available from the ALDA. The user-friendly program will provide indications of neurological efficiency, learning impairment, and learning-channel functioning. The report describes the most efficient method for a child to learn the basic subjects of Reading, Spelling, Math, and Handwriting. It may be used to design remedial approaches and improve academic functioning. Hardware: Apple II with 64K, IBM PC and compatibles.

Format: Individual administration; time varies

Scoring: Computer administered and scored

Cost: ALDA-EZ (Apple) $195.00; ALDA-EZ (IBM) 3½" $195.00

Publisher: Slosson Educational Publications, Inc.

AP Examination: Advanced Placement Program

Copyright: 1989

Population: Adolescents; Grades 10 through 12

Purpose: Measures academic achievement in a wide range of fields; used by participating colleges to grant credit and placement in these fields to gifted/advanced students and to measure the effectiveness of a school's Advanced Placement AP Program

Description: The AP exams are a part of the AP Program, which provides course descriptions, exams, and curricular materials to high schools to allow those students who wish to pursue college-level studies while still in secondary school to receive advanced placement and/or credit upon entering college. The AP Program provides descriptions and exams on 29 introductory college courses in the following 15 fields: art, biology, chemistry, computer science, economics, English, French, German, government and politics, history, Latin, math, music, physics, and Spanish. No test is longer than 3 hours. All exams are paper–pencil tests (except for the art portfolios) with an essay or problem-solving section and a multiple-choice section. Using the operational services provided by the Educational Testing Service, the AP Exams are administered in May by schools throughout the world. Any school may participate. Fee reductions are available for students with financial need. Available in Braille and large print. Grades are sent to students, their schools, and colleges in July.

Format: Examiner required; suitable for group use; timed: 3 hours maximum

Scoring: Computer scored; examiner evaluated

Cost: Per student/per test $72.00; Contact publisher

Publisher: The College Board

ASSET

Copyright: 1993

Population: Adults; ages 18 and above

Purpose: Assesses writing, reading, numerical, and advanced math skills for course placement

Description: Multiple-choice 192-item paper–pencil test with the following categories: Writing—36 items; Reading—24 items; Numerical—32 items; Elementary Algebra—25 items; Intermediate Algebra—25 items; College Algebra—25 items; and Geometry—25 items. Scores yielded are Entering Student Descriptive Report, Returning Student Retention Report, Course Placement Service, Underprepared Student Follow-up. Forms B, B2, C1, and C2 are used. A test booklet, answer sheet, and a #2 pencil are used. May be modified for students with disabilities.

Format: Individual administration; suitable for group use; examiner required; timed: 25 minutes each subtest

Scoring: Hand key; machine scored; computer scored; scoring service available from publisher

Cost: 25 test booklets $30.00

Publisher: American College Testing

Basic Achievement Skills Individual Screener (BASIS)

Copyright: 1983

Population: Grades 1 and above

Purpose: Measures achievement in reading, mathematics, and spelling; assesses individual students' academic strengths and weaknesses with both norm-referenced and criterion-referenced information

Description: Three subtests assessing academic achievement in reading, mathematics, and spelling. Test items are grouped in grade-referenced clusters, which constitute the basic unit of administration. Testing begins at a grade cluster with which the student is expected to have little difficulty and continues until the student fails to reach the criteria for a particular cluster. The clusters range from Readiness through Grade 8 for reading and mathematics and from Grades 1–8 for spelling. The reading test assesses comprehension of graded passages. The student is required to read the passages aloud and supply the missing words. Comprehension at the lower levels is assessed by word reading and sentence reading, and readiness is measured by letter identification and visual discrimination. The mathematics test consists of a readiness subtest and assesses computation and problem solving above that level. The student works on the computation items directly in the record form. Word problems are dictated by the teacher and require no reading on the part of the student. The spelling test for Grades 1–8 consists of clusters of words that are dictated in sentence contexts. The student writes the words on the record form.

Format: Examiner required; not suitable for group use; untimed: 1 hour

Scoring: Hand key

Cost: Examiner's Kit (manual, content booklet, 2 record forms) $111.50

Publisher: Harcourt® Brace Educational Measurement

BRIGANCE® Diagnostic Comprehensive Inventory of Basic Skills (CIBS)

Albert H. Brigance

Copyright: 1983

Population: Children, adolescents; Grades PreK through 9

Purpose: Measures attainment of basic academic skills; used to meet minimal competency requirements, develop IEPs, and determine academic placement

Description: Test includes 203 skill sequences

in the following 22 sections: readiness, speech, word recognition, grade placement, oral reading, reading comprehension, listening, functional word recognition, word analysis, reference skills, graphs and maps, spelling, writing, math grade placement, numbers, number facts, computation of whole numbers, fractions and mixed numbers, decimals, percents, word problems, metrics, and math vocabulary. Assessment is initiated at the skill level at which the student will be successful and continues until the student's level of achievement for that skill is attained. The following assessment methods may be used to accommodate different situations: parent interview, teacher observation, group or individual, and informal appraisal of student performance in daily work. Two alternate forms, A and B, are available for pre- and posttesting for 51 skill sequences. All skill sequences are referenced to specific instructional objectives and grade-level expectations. The comprehensive book graphically indicates at each testing the level of competency the student has achieved. A videotape for in-service training of examiners is available.

Format: Examiner required; many sections are suitable for group use

Scoring: Examiner evaluated

Cost: Assessment Book $139.00; Class Record Book $12.95; 30 IEP Objective Forms $16.95; CIBS excerpts available at no charge; 10 Comprehensive Record Books $32.95

Publisher: Curriculum Associates®, Inc.

BRIGANCE® Diagnostic Inventory of Basic Skills

Albert H. Brigance

Copyright: 1977

Population: Children, adolescents; Grades K to 6

Purpose: Assesses basic strengths and weaknesses in 14 major skill areas; provides a systematic performance record, in grade level terms, for diagnosis and evaluation, defines instructional objectives, and determines a child's level of achievement

Description: Comprises the original BRIG-ANCE® Inventory with 141 subtests in the following areas: readiness, word recognition, reading, word analysis, vocabulary, handwriting, grammar and mechanics, spelling, reference skills, math placement, numbers, operations, measurement, and geometry. The tester selects assessments for evaluation based on individual student needs. An introductory section outlines how to administer the tests, assess skill levels, record results, identify instructional objectives, and develop IEPs. Individual Student Record Books indicate competency levels and progress and serve to communicate ongoing instructional goals to teachers, specialists, and parents. An optional Class Record Book forms a convenient matrix for skills mastered and objectives set for 35 students.

Format: Examiner required; many assessments may be made by observation, adapting the tests for group administration

Scoring: Examiner evaluated

Cost: Assessment Book $129.00; Record Books (10-pack) $26.95; Class Record Book $12.95

Publisher: Curriculum Associates®, Inc.

BRIGANCE® Diagnostic Inventory of Essential Skills

Albert H. Brigance

Copyright: 1981

Population: Children, adolescents; Grades 4 to 12

Purpose: Measures a student's mastery of academic skills and skills essential to success as a citizen, consumer, worker, and family member; used in secondary programs serving students with special needs; used to develop IEPs

Description: Test includes 186 paper–pencil or oral-response skill assessments measuring minimal academic and vocational competencies in reading, language arts, and math. The inventory includes rating scales to measure applied skills that cannot be assessed objectively, such as health and attitude, job interview preparation, and communication. Test results identify basic skills that have and have not been mastered, areas of strengths and weaknesses in academic and practical skills, and instructional objectives for a specified skill level. Individual record books graphically indicate at each testing the level of competency the student has achieved and the student's current instructional goals. An optional class record book monitors the progress of 15 students and forms a matrix of specific student competencies. IEP objective forms are available for reading, writing and spelling, math, and individual use (blank form). Tests may be administered by teachers, aides, or parent volunteers. A videotape program for inservice training of examiners is available.

Format: Examiner required; some sections are suitable for group use; untimed: time varies

Scoring: Examiner evaluated

Cost: Assessment Book $149.95; Class Record Book $12.95; Pre Test Excerpt available; 10-pack Essential Skills Record Books $36.95

Publisher: Curriculum Associates®, Inc.

Calibration of an Item Pool for Adaptive Measurement of Achievement
I. Bejar, D. J. Weiss, G. G. Kingsbury

Copyright: 1978

Population: Adults

Purpose: Measures achievement of naval personnel; used in career counseling

Description: Multiple-item multiple-choice paper–pencil questionnaire

Format: Individual or group administration; requires examiner; untimed

Scoring: Examiner evaluated

Cost: $18.00

Publisher: Select Press

California Achievement Tests, Fifth Edition (CAT/5)

Copyright: 1992

Population: Grades K through 12

Purpose: Assesses academic achievement

Description: A paper–pencil assessment sys-

tem that evaluates students' academic achievement from Kindergarten through Grade 12. The number of criterion-referenced/multiple-choice items varies from 126 to 408, depending on the format/form. Tests assess performance in reading, language, spelling, mathematics, study skills, science, and social studies. Normative, objectives-based, and other reports available. Test is available in large print or Braille. May be used for persons with visual, hearing, physical, or mental disabilities.

Format: Group administered; examiner required; timed: 1½–5¼ hours

Scoring: Computer scored (by publisher) or hand key

Cost: Varies by format/form

Publisher: CTB/McGraw-Hill

California Diagnostic Tests (CDMT/CDRT)

Copyright: 1990

Population: Grades 1 through 12

Purpose: Assesses basic reading and math skills

Description: The California Diagnostic Mathematics Test (CDMT) and the California Diagnostic Reading Test (CDRT) are two diagnostic assessments that help educators identify strengths and areas of need for students in Grades 1 through 12. Norm-referenced scores produced can be used to evaluate progress.

Format: Examiner required; suitable for group use; including sample items and breaks, approximately 100–150 minutes

Scoring: Hand key or computer scored

Cost: CDRT and CDMT Test Books—35 count, machine scorable $99.40, hand scorable $61.20, reusable (answer sheets ordered separately) $45.50

Publisher: CTB/McGraw-Hill

Canadian Tests of Basic Skills: High School Battery (CTBS), Levels 15–18, Form 7
E. King-Shaw, D. Scannell

Copyright: 1989

Population: Adolescents; Grades 9 through 12

Purpose: Assesses students' abilities in reading comprehension, mathematics, written expression, using sources of information, and applied proficiency skills

Description: Four test levels (15–18) consisting of a series of multiple-choice paper–pencil subtests which include Reading Comprehension, Mathematics, Written Expression, Using Sources of Information, and Applied Proficiency Skills. This is an adaptation of the Tests of Achievement and Proficiency published by the Riverside Publishing Company.

Format: Examiner required; suitable for group use; timed: 160 minutes

Scoring: Hand key; machine scored; test scoring service available from publisher

Cost: Examination Kit $31.90

Publisher: Nelson Canada

Canadian Tests of Basic Skills: Multilevel (CTBS), Levels 5–18, Form 7/8
E. King-Shaw, A. Hieronymus, D. Scannell

Copyright: 1989

Population: Children, adolescents; Grades K.2 to 12

Purpose: Assesses students' abilities in vocabulary, reading comprehension, spelling, capitalization, punctuation, usage, visual materials, reference materials, mathematics concepts, mathematics problem solving, and mathematics computation

Description: Three test levels (Primary, Multilevel, and High School), each consisting of a series of multiple-choice paper–pencil subtests which include Vocabulary, Reading Comprehension, Spelling, Capitalization, Punctuation, Usage, Visual Materials, Reference Materials, Mathematics Concepts, Mathematics Problem Solving, and Mathematics Computation. Materials include test booklets, answer sheets, scoring masks, teacher's guide, and supplementary materials as required. This is an adaptation of the Iowa Tests of Basic Skills published by the Riverside Publishing Company.

Mathematics available in French. Examiner must have a teaching certificate.

Format: Examiner required; suitable for group use; timed: Primary 235 minutes, Multilevel 256 minutes, High School 160 minutes

Scoring: Hand key; machine scored; test scoring service available from publisher

Cost: Test booklets $10.45; 35 answer sheets $14.95; scoring masks $14.95; teachers' guide $19.95

Publisher: Nelson Canada

Canadian Tests of Basic Skills: Primary Battery (CTBS), Levels 5–8, Form 7
E. King-Shaw, A. Hieronymus

Copyright: 1989

Population: Children; Grades K.2 to 3.5

Purpose: Assesses students' abilities in listening, vocabulary, word analysis, language, reading, mathematics, and work study

Description: Four test levels (5–8) consisting of a series of multiple-choice paper–pencil subtests which include Listening, Vocabulary, Word Analysis, Language, Reading, Mathematics, and Work Study. Materials should include test booklets, scoring masks, a teacher's guide, and supplementary materials as required. Examiner must have a teaching certificate. This test is a Canadian adaptation of the Iowa Tests of Basic Skills published by the Riverside Publishing Company.

Format: Examiner required; suitable for group use; untimed: 115–235 minutes (varies according to level)

Scoring: Hand key; machine scored; test scoring service available from publisher

Cost: 25 test booklets $43.95; scoring mask $29.95; teacher's guide $18.95

Publisher: Nelson Canada

Career Programs Assessment (CPAt)

Copyright: 1988

Population: Adults; ages 18 and above

Purpose: Used for course placement to assess basic language, reading, and numerical skills

Description: Multiple-choice 115-item paper–pencil test with the following categories: Language Usage (60 items), Reading Skills (30 items), and Numerical Skills (25 items). Scores for each content area; standard CPAt Summary Report; Customized CPAt Summary Report; CPAt Retention Report. A test booklet, answer sheet, and #2 pencil are used. Forms A, B, and C are available.

Format: Individual administration; suitable for group use; examiner required; timed: 60 minutes

Scoring: Hand key

Cost: $150.00 per campus; $1.00 per test booklet; 50 answer sheets $107.50

Publisher: American College Testing

CASAS Secondary Diploma Program Assessment

Copyright: 1991

Population: Adults, adolescents; native and nonnative speakers of English

Purpose: Measures a learner's reading comprehension, critical thinking, and problem solving capabilities in eight core academic subjects; programs use the tests to award high school credit and for placement, monitoring progress, and targeting instruction

Description: Multiple-choice test. Tests include: Mathematics, Economics, American Government, United States History, English/Language Arts, World History, Biological Science, Physical Science. CASAS scaled scores identify general skill level and enable comparison of performance across CASAS tests. Training required.

Format: Group administered

Scoring: Hand key

Cost: Each subject area: set of 5 pretests, 5 posttests $42.00; Program Implementation Guide $50.00

Publisher: Comprehensive Adult Student Assessment System

College BASE
Steven J. Osterlind

Copyright: 1994

Population: College students

Purpose: Measures mastery of the college core curriculum

Description: Multiple-item multiple-choice and essay achievement test measuring proficiency in English, mathematics, science, and social studies. In addition to these subject skills, the test assesses three cross-disciplinary competencies: Interpretive Reasoning, Strategic Reasoning, and Adaptive Reasoning. These skills and competencies represent a core curriculum for most colleges and universities. Each of the four academic subjects is organized into levels of increasing specificity: subjects, clusters, skills, and enabling subskills. The Regular Edition contains the Complete Test Battery. It consists of 180 items and a writing exercise. The Institutional Matrix Edition includes items from all subject areas in the Complete Battery, plus Writing. This edition yields summary data only, not individual student information.

Format: Examiner required; suitable for group use; Regular 45 minutes per test, Institutional 60 minutes

Scoring: Hand key; may be machine scored

Cost: Contact publisher for current prices

Publisher: Riverside Publishing Company

College Basic Academic Skills Examination (C-BASE)
S. J. Osterlind

Copyright: 1995 (current form LJ)

Population: Adults; college students

Purpose: Assesses knowledge of basic academic skills

Description: Applicable for campus assessment; teaches education placement, 4 categories: English, mathematics, science, social studies. The instrument has 180 total items. Institutional and individual student report with composite score available. Multiple-choice and essay response format. Test available in large print.

Format: Group administration; requires examiner; untimed

Scoring: Examiner evaluated; machine-scored; test scoring service available from publisher

Cost: Contact publisher

Publisher: Assessment Resource Center

College Outcome Measures Program (COMP) COMP Activity Inventory

Copyright: 1996

Population: Adults; ages 17 and above

Purpose: Assesses participation in activities outside of course requirements

Description: Multiple-choice 54-item paper–pencil test with the following categories: Social Sciences, Natural Sciences, Arts/Humanities, Communicating, Solving Problems, and Clarifying Values. Six subscores are yielded. Form 8 is available.

Format: Individual/self-administered; suitable for group use; examiner required; untimed: 60–90 minutes

Scoring: Machine scored; test scoring service available from publisher

Cost: $5.25 per person

Publisher: American College Testing

College-Level Examination Program (CLEP)

Copyright: 1995

Population: Adolescents, adults; Grades 12 and above

Purpose: Enables any student to earn college credit by recognizing college-level achievement acquired outside the conventional college classroom; anyone may take the tests; used by businesses to allow employees to earn required continuing education credits

Description: Five general exams and 30 subject exams assessing college-level proficiency in a wide range of fields. The general exams measure achievement in 5 areas of the liberal arts: English composition, humanities, math, natural sciences, and social sciences and history. The material tested is referred to as the general/liberal education requirement. The subject exams measure achievement in specific college courses and are used to grant exemption from and credit in specific college courses. The exams stress concepts, principles, relationships, and applications of course material. They contain questions of varying difficulty. Exams are administered each month at more that 1,000 test centers located on college campuses throughout the country. Approximately 48 hours after, test scores and a booklet explaining them are sent to the candidates and their specified recipients. Institutions honoring CLEP test scores for credit are listed in "CLEP Colleges," available free from the publisher.

Format: Examiner required; suitable for group use; timed: 1 hour 30 minutes per test

Scoring: Computer scored; free-response sections examiner evaluated locally

Cost: Contact publisher

Publisher: The College Board

Combining Achievement Test Data Through Normal Curve Equivalent Scaled Scores
Richard M. Jaeger

Copyright: 1978

Population: Children, adolescents

Purpose: Evaluates Title 1 programs in elementary and secondary education

Description: Paper–pencil checklist; contains eight norm tables

Format: Group administration; requires examiner; untimed

Scoring: Examiner evaluated

Cost: $5.00

Publisher: Select Press

COMP Composite Examination

Copyright: 1996

Population: Adults

Purpose: Assesses applied skills and general education

Description: Multiple-choice 99-item paper–pencil oral response criterion-referenced short-answer, essay/verbal test. The categories are Speaking, Writing, Communication, Solving Problems, Clarifying Values, Using the Arts, Using Science, and Functioning in Social Situations. Total Speaking and Total Writing have three subscores each. Forms 10–12 are available.

Format: Suitable for group use; examiner required; timed: 240 minutes

Scoring: Examiner evaluated; machine scored; scoring service available from publisher

Cost: $15.75 per student; $27.00 to rate per student

Publisher: American College Testing

COMP Objective Test

Copyright: 1996

Population: Adults; ages 17 and above

Purpose: Assesses general education skills

Description: Multiple-choice 120-item paper–pencil test with the following categories: Communicating, Solving Problems, Clarifying Values, Using the Arts, Using Science, and Functioning in Social Situations.

Format: Suitable for group use; examiner required; timed: 120 minutes

Scoring: Machine scored; test scoring service available from publisher

Cost: $15.75 per student

Publisher: American College Testing

Comprehensive Scales of Student Abilities (CSSA)
Donald D. Hammill, Wayne P. Hresko

Copyright: 1994

Population: Ages 6 through 16 years 11 months

Purpose: Assesses developmental abilities seen in school settings for identification of need for referral

Description: Multiple-item rating scale to quantify a teacher's knowledge of students' abilities to include in the referral. Nine areas are measured: Verbal Thinking, Speech, Reading, Writing, Handwriting, Mathematics, General Facts in Science and Social Studies, Basic Motor Generalizations, and Social Behavior. The instrument contains a 9-point rating scale for 68 items. Descriptions contain clarifying information to aid the educator in the completion of the checklist. Scores obtained include standard scores and percentiles for the nine areas. Computer administration available on Mac and Windows format.

Format: Teacher checklist

Scoring: Examiner scored and interpreted; 10 minutes

Cost: Complete Kit (manual, protocols, and storage box) $69.00; computer version $134.00

Publisher: PRO-ED, Inc.

Comprehensive Testing Program (CTP III)

Copyright: 1992

Population: Children, adolescents; Grades 1 through 12

Purpose: Measures the verbal and mathematical skills of students; used for evaluation of student progress, assessing the effectiveness of instructional programs, and guidance counseling

Description: Multiple-item paper–pencil tests arranged in six levels, A through F, that span Grades 1 through 12. Lower levels of the test measure Auditory Comprehension, Reading Comprehension, Word Analysis, Writing Mechanics, and Mathematics. Upper levels measure Verbal Ability, Quantitative Ability, Reading Comprehension, Writing Mechanics, Writing Process, and Mathematics. Algebra I, Algebra II, and Geometry are offered as end-of-course tests. Consumable test booklets for Levels A, B, and C. Separate answer sheets for Levels D, E, and F. Norms: National, Suburban (public) Schools, and Independent Schools. Use of the test is restricted to ERB member schools.

Format: Examiner required; suitable for group use; untimed: Levels A and B (varies with level), approximately 200 minutes; timed: Levels C, D, E, and F (varies with level), 255 to 290 minutes

Scoring: Machine-scored; test scoring service available from the publisher; hand keys also available

Cost: Refer to ERB Test Catalog for prices of CTP III test materials and scoring services

Publisher: Educational Records Bureau

Comprehensive Tests of Basic Skills–Fourth Edition (CTBS®–4)

Copyright: 1989

Population: Grades K through 12

Purpose: Assesses basic skills in reading, language, mathematics, science, and social studies

Description: Multiple-item multiple-choice paper–pencil test measuring basic academic skills. Eleven levels assess the following: visual and sound recognition, word analysis, vocabulary, comprehension, spelling, language mechanics and expression, mathematics computation, mathematics concepts and applications, study skills, science, and social studies. The test is available in 11 levels (K–21/22); Level K is a "readiness" rather than "achievement" measure and is not scaled.

Format: Examiner required; suitable for group use; timed: complete battery 2–4 hours

Scoring: Hand key; scoring service available from publisher

Cost: Complete battery (35 booklets) $94.75

Publisher: CTB/McGraw-Hill

Computerized Adaptive Placement Assessment and Support System (COMPASS)

Copyright: 1997

Population: Adults; ages 18 and above

Purpose: Used for placement and diagnosis to assess writing, reading, and math skills

Description: Multiple-choice computer-administered test with placement tests (7 separate scores) and diagnostic tests (28 separate scores). The categories are Writing Skills Placement (465 items); Reading Placement (205 items); Math Placement: Pre algebra (234 items), Algebra (235 items), College Algebra (165 items), Geometry (187 items), Trigonometry (200 items); Math Diagnostic Tests: 20 items per category: Operations with Integers, Operations with Fractions, Operations with Decimals, Exponents, Ratios and Proportions, Percentages, Averages; Reading Diagnostic Tests: Main Idea (30 items), Implicit Information (90 items), Explicit Information (60 items), Vocabulary (100 items); Writing Skills Diagnostic Tests: Punctuation (40 items), Verbs (40 items), Usage (40 items), Relationships of Clause (40 items), Shifts in Construction (40 items), Organization (40 items), Spelling (40 items), Capitalization (40 items). Requires a PC 286, 15MB disk space, 640K RAM, EGA monitor, and a disk drive.

Format: Individual administration; examiner required; untimed.

Scoring: Computer scored

Cost: Site License $500.00; Administration Unit $1.00 each

Publisher: American College Testing

Criterion Test of Basic Skills

Kerth Lundell, William Brown, James Evans

Copyright: 1976

Population: Ages 6 through 11

Purpose: Assesses reading and arithmetic skills

Description: Multiple-item paper–pencil criterion-referenced test. The Reading subtest measures letter recognition, letter sounding, blending, sequencing, special sounds, and sight words. The Arithmetic subtest measures number and numerical recognition, addition, subtraction, multiplication, and division. Each part of the test offers optional objective for evaluation. The manual contains over 200 teacher-directed, independent, and peer-tutoring activities correlated to the skill areas assessed, and arranged according to increasing difficulty.

Format: Individual administration; suitable for group use; 10–15 minutes

Scoring: Examiner administered and interpreted

Cost: Test Kit (manual, protocols, and stimulus cards in vinyl folder) $55.00

Publisher: Academic Therapy Publications

CTB Portfolio Assessment

Copyright: 1992

Population: Grades 1 through 8

Purpose: Assesses classroom performance

Description: Test includes 8–20 real-life performance tasks that allow students and teachers to work together to monitor development of skills and concepts, emphasizing development and encouraging students to rethink and improve their work. Subcategories include language arts and mathematics. Five levels are available.

Format: Examiner required; suitable for group use; untimed

Scoring: Examiner evaluated

Cost: Classroom Module (Language Arts or Mathematics)—all materials required for instruction and assessment of 35 students $89.60/level

Publisher: CTB/McGraw-Hill

CTB Task Bank

Copyright: 1994

Population: Grades 3 through 12

Purpose: Assesses performance on tasks and task-related activities to gain important information on student progress in particular areas of math or language arts

Description: Each task in the bank comprises one or more theme-based activities. Item banks are shipped either in electronic form, as a CurriculumBuilder bank, or in printed form, as a notebook.

Format: Individual administration

Scoring: Computer scored

Cost: IBM 3.5″ or 5.25″ disk—Reading or Math—electronic or printed $645.00; electronic and printed $845.00

Publisher: CTB/McGraw-Hill

Curriculum Frameworks Assessment

Copyright: 1990

Population: Grades 1 through 12

Purpose: Assesses mastery of state and local curriculum in four categories: English–Language Arts, History–Social Science, Science, and Mathematics

Description: Multiple-item paper–pencil multiple-choice test that measures how well students meet the educational goals of state and local curriculum. Available in 10 grades/levels containing four categories: English–language arts, history–social science, science, and mathematics. Individual and group scores, national norms, minimum proficiency scores, and district-set criteria are available.

Format: Examiner required; suitable for group use; timed: time varies by level

Scoring: Hand key; scoring service available

Cost: 35 test books and examiner's manual $101.80 (machine-scorable), $64.00 (hand-scorable)

Publisher: CTB/McGraw-Hill

Developing Skills Checklist (DSC)

Copyright: 1990

Population: Grades PreK through K̇

Purpose: Evaluates the full range of skills children develop from pre-kindergarten through the end of kindergarten

Description: Multiple-item point-to, oral-response checklist that measures the following skills and concepts: language, visual, auditory, mathematical concepts and operations, memory, social and emotional, fine and gross motor, and print and writing. The Spanish version is Lista de Destreza en Desarollo.

Format: Examiner required; individually administered; untimed: 30–45 minutes

Scoring: Examiner evaluated; machine scored

Cost: Test Kit (materials for 25 students) $259.30

Publisher: CTB/McGraw-Hill

Diagnostic Achievement Battery–Second Edition (DAB–2)
Phyllis L. Newcomer

Copyright: 1990

Population: Ages 6 to 14 years 11 months

Purpose: Assesses a child's ability to listen, speak, read, write, and perform simple mathematics operations; diagnoses learning disabilities

Description: Multiple-item paper–pencil and oral-response subtests assessing the following five components of a child's verbal and mathematical skills: Listening (Story Comprehension and Characteristics), Speaking (Synonyms and Grammatic Completion), Reading (Alphabet/Word Knowledge and Reading Comprehension), Writing (Capitalization, Punctuation, Spelling, and Writing Composition), and Math (Math Reasoning and Math Calculation). Results, converted to standard scores, provide a profile of the child's strengths and weaknesses. The components of the test may be administered independently, depending on the needs of the child being tested.

Format: Individual administration; suitable for group use; examiner required; 1 to 2 hours

Scoring: Examiner scored and interpreted; computer (IBM and Apple II) interpretation available

Cost: Complete Kit (examiner's manual, picture book, protocols, and storage box) $169.00

Publisher: PRO-ED, Inc.

Diagnostic Achievement Test for Adolescents–Second Edition (DATA–2)
Phyllis L. Newcomer, Brian R. Bryant

Copyright: 1993

Population: Ages 12 to 18 years 11 months

Purpose: Measures the spoken language ability and academic achievement levels

Description: Multiple-item paper–pencil and oral-response test consisting of 10 core subtests and 3 supplemental subtests. The core subtests are Receptive Vocabulary, Receptive Grammar, Expressive Grammar, Expressive Vocabulary, Word Identification, Reading Comprehension, Math Calculations, Math Problem Solving, Spelling, and Writing Composition. The supplemental subtests are Science, Social Studies, and Reference Skills. Nine composite standard scores are generated.

Format: Individual or group administration; examiner required; 1 to 2 hours

Scoring: Examiner scored and interpreted; computer (IBM and Apple II) interpretation available

Cost: Complete Kit (examiner's manual, picture book, protocols, and storage box) $124.00

Publisher: PRO-ED, Inc.

Diagnostic Screening Test: Achievement (DSTA)
Thomas D. Gnagey, Patricia A. Gnagey

Copyright: 1977

Population: Children, adolescents; Grades K through 14

Purpose: Measures basic knowledge of science, social studies, and literature and the arts to help determine a course of study for special education students

Description: Multiple-choice 108-item paper–pencil test measuring a student's conceptual level in science, social studies, and literature and the arts. Scores are obtained for practical knowledge and estimated mental age. The manual discusses subtest pattern analysis of student motivation, cultural versus organic retardation, cultural deprivation, reading and study skill problems, and possession of practical versus formal knowledge. The examiner explains the procedure to individuals or groups and reads the test if the students have poor reading skills.

Format: Examiner required; suitable for group use; untimed: 5–10 minutes

Scoring: Hand key

Cost: Manual and 50 test forms $50.00

Publisher: Slosson Educational Publications, Inc.

EXPLORE

Copyright: 1993

Population: Adolescents

Purpose: Measures educational achievement for counseling and evaluation

Description: Multiple-choice 128-item paper–pencil test with the following categories: English Test (40 items, 30 minutes), Math Test (30 items, 30 minutes), Reading Test (30 items, 30 minutes), and Science Reasoning (28 items, 30 minutes). A pencil, paper, and test booklet are used. Suitable for individuals with visual, physical, hearing, and mental impairments.

Format: Suitable for group use; examiner required; timed: 120 minutes

Scoring: Hand key; machine scored; test scoring service available from publisher

Cost: Contact publisher

Publisher: American College Testing

First Grade Reading and Mathematics Test (FGRMT)

Copyright: 1992

Population: Grade 1, Title I eligible students

Purpose: Measures academic achievement

Description: Five R/LA objectives, 5 math objectives, precursor to Grade 2 of statewide achievement test for collection of scores for Title I. Form X available, multiple-choice response format.

Format: Group administration; requires examiner; untimed

Scoring: Machine-scored; test scoring service available from publisher

Cost: $3.75/booklet

Publisher: Assessment Resource Center

Graduate Record Examinations (GRE)

Copyright: Updated yearly

Population: Adults, college graduates

Purpose: Measures academic abilities and knowledge of graduate school applicants; used by graduate schools for screening the qualifications of applicants and by organizations for selecting fellowship recipients

Description: Multiple-item paper–pencil multiple-choice battery of advanced achievement and aptitude tests. The General Test measures verbal, quantitative, and analytical abilities. The Subject Tests are available for the following 17 subjects: biology, chemistry, computer science, economics, education, engineering, French, geology, history, literature in English, mathematics, music, physics, political science, psychology, sociology, and Spanish. The tests are administered on specified dates at centers established by the publisher. The General Test is also offered on computer, taken at the examinee's convenience at Sylvan Learning Centers.

Format: Examiner required; suitable for group use; timed: General test 3½ hours, subject tests 2 hours 50 minutes each

Scoring: Computer scored

Cost: Contact publisher

Publisher: Educational Testing Service

Guidance Test Battery for Secondary Pupils (GBS)

Copyright: 1981

Population: Adolescents

Purpose: Measures scholastic achievement; used for educational guidance

Description: Paper–pencil test of pupils' proficiency in English, Afrikaans, Mathematics, Nonverbal Reasoning, and Verbal Reasoning. Two forms, A and B, are available. The test publisher notes that this test is "normed on Blacks only."

Format: Examiner required; suitable for group use; timed: 3½ hours

Scoring: Hand key; examiner evaluated; may be machine scored

Cost: Contact publisher

Publisher: Human Sciences Research Council

High Level Battery B/75

Copyright: Not provided

Population: Adults

Purpose: Assesses educational abilities of older students; used with individuals entering college or higher

Description: Multiple-item paper–pencil multiple-choice tests of academic abilities. The six tests are Mental Alertness, Language Ability in English and Afrikaans, Reading Comprehension, Vocabulary, Spelling, and Arithmetic.

Format: Examiner required; suitable for group use; timed: 1 hour 53 minutes

Scoring: Hand key

Cost: Contact publisher

Publisher: Human Sciences Research Council

Hudson Education Skills Inventory (HESI)

Floyd G. Hudson, Steven E. Colson, Doris L. Hudson Welch, Alison K. Banikowski, Teresa A. Mehring

Copyright: 1989

Population: Children, adolescents; Grades K through 12

Purpose: Assesses basic education skills, including mathematics, reading, and writing; used to plan instruction for students with dysfunctional learning patterns

Description: Multiple-item curriculum-based series of three separate tests for assessing mathematics, reading, and writing skills. Each of the three curriculum skills tests is divided into specific subskills. A Student Book containing problems and items that require a visual stimulus is used to evoke the student's responses. The series is based on the Test-Down/Teach-Up model, in which the examiner ends the test at the student's actual level of performance. Once the student's level of performance has been established, the teacher "teaches up" the Curriculum Skills Sequence. The series, which complies with assessment guidelines in the Education of All Handicapped Children Act of 1975, is designed so that all or only one of the tests may be administered as needed for planning instruction.

Format: Examiner required; suitable for group use; untimed

Scoring: Computer scored

Cost: Complete Battery (1 each of complete HESI Math, Reading, and Writing Kits) $249.00; Math Complete Kit $89.00; Reading Complete Kit $89.00; Writing Complete Kit $89.00

Publisher: PRO-ED, Inc.

Independent School Entrance Examination (ISEE)

Copyright: 1989

Population: Children, adolescents; Grades 6 through 12

Purpose: Measures academic achievement and ability for admission to independent schools

Description: Multiple-choice paper–pencil test. Two levels: Middle (applicants to Grades 6, 7, 8) and Upper (applicants to Grades 9, 10, 11, 12). Each level consists of four subtests: Verbal Ability, Quantitative Ability, Reading Comprehension, and Mathematics Achievement. The test also includes a 30-minute essay that is not scored. Available in large print and Braille. Use of the test is restricted to ERB member schools for selecting IEP goals and objectives or measuring progress in a particular skill area. The Examiner's Manual includes sample items and the Curriculum Skills Sequence. The Instructional Planning Form provides a detailed format for recording and monitoring assessment and instructional planning decisions.

Format: Individual or group administration; examiner required; timed: 160 minutes

Scoring: Machine scored; test scoring service available from publisher; norms: applicants to independent schools

Cost: Refer to ISEE Student Guide for prices and information on test sites

Publisher: Educational Records Bureau

Initial Evaluation Tests in English and Mathematics

Copyright: Not provided

Population: Children, adolescents

Purpose: Measures achievement in English and math; used for educational evaluation at the beginning of a new standard

Description: Nine tests measuring achievement in English and mathematics. Initial Evaluation Tests in English are available at Standards 5 and 8. Seven Initial Evaluation Tests in Mathematics are available for Standards 1 to 7. Two alternate forms, A and B, are available for each of the nine tests. Tests should be administered as soon as possible after the beginning of the school year.

Format: Examiner required; suitable for group use; untimed: typical time not available

Scoring: Hand key; examiner evaluated

Cost: Contact publisher

Publisher: Human Sciences Research Council

Intermediate Battery B/77

Copyright: Not provided

Population: Adults

Purpose: Assesses academic achievement and clerical aptitudes of individuals who have 10–12 years of schooling

Description: Multiple-item paper–pencil set of seven subtests, six of which are similar to those in the High Level Battery (mental alertness, English, reading comprehension, vocabulary, spelling, and arithmetic). This battery does not include the Afrikaans reading comprehension, vocabulary, and spelling tests. However, it does include a clerical perception test.

Format: Examiner required; suitable for group use; timed: 2 hours 45 minutes

Scoring: Hand key

Cost: Contact publisher

Publisher: Human Sciences Research Council

Iowa Tests of Basic Skills®, Form M (ITBS®)

H. D. Hoover, A. N. Hieronymus,
D. A. Frisbie, S. B. Dunbar

Copyright: 1996

Population: Grades K through 9 (Levels 5 through 14)

Purpose: Assesses the development of basic academic skills; identifies individual students' strengths and weaknesses and evaluates the effectiveness of instructional programs

Description: Paper–pencil multiple-choice tests assessing proficiency in the basic skills required for academic success. The Iowa Tests consist of 10 levels: K and Grade 1 Levels 5 and 6; Grades 1–3 Levels 7 and 8; and Grades 3–9 Levels 9–14 used according to time of year. The tests are Vocabulary, Reading, Language, Mathematics, Social Studies, Science, Sources of Information, Student Questionnaire (optional), Performance Assessments (optional), Iowa Writing Assessment (optional), and Listening Assessment (optional). Scores are reported for each of the tests in the Complete and Survey Batteries at each level. Total scores are reported for Reading, Language, Mathematics, and either the Core Battery tests or the Survey Battery.

Format: Examiner required; suitable for group use; Complete Battery 310 minutes; Survey Battery 100 minutes

Scoring: Hand key; may be machine scored

Cost: Contact publisher for current prices

Publisher: Riverside Publishing Company

Iowa Tests of Basic Skills®, Forms G, H, and J (ITBS®)

A. N. Hieronymus, H. D. Hoover,
E. F. Lindquist

Copyright: 1988

Population: Grades K through 9 (Levels 5 through 14)

Purpose: Assesses the development of basic academic skills; identifies individual students' strengths and weaknesses and evaluates the effectiveness of instructional programs

Description: Paper–pencil multiple-choice tests assessing proficiency in the basic skills required for academic success. The Multilevel/Separate Level Editions (Grades 3–9) measure the following skill areas at each level: vocabulary, reading, language, work study, and mathematics. Schools can track listening skills through junior high school and offer paper–

pencil generative writing assessments for Grades 3–8. The Early Primary (Levels 5–6) and Primary (Levels 7–8) batteries (Grades K–3.5) include tests in listening, vocabulary, reading (except for Level 5), word analysis, language, and mathematics. The Primary Battery (Grades 1.7–3.5) also contains a work-study test. The Complete Battery Plus Social Studies and Science for Levels 7 and 8 for the Complete Battery, a Source of Information Total, and Composite Score are also reported. For Title I reporting, Advanced Skills scores are available for Reading, Language, and Mathematics. If the optional Questionnaire is used, results are tabulated for teachers and guidance counselors as part of central scoring services.

Format: Examiner required; suitable for group use; Complete Battery 4 hours 16 minutes, Basic Battery 2 hours 15 minutes

Scoring: Hand key; may be machine scored

Cost: Contact publisher for current prices

Publisher: Riverside Publishing Company

Iowa Tests of Basic Skills®, Forms K and L (iTBS®)
A. N. Hieronymus, H. D. Hoover,
S. B. Dunbar, D. A. Frisbie

Copyright: 1993

Population: Grades K through 9 (Levels 5 through 14)

Purpose: Assesses the development of basic academic skills; identifies individual students' strengths and weaknesses and evaluates the effectiveness of instructional programs

Description: Assessment program for students in Kindergarten through Grade 9. Available in three different editions: Complete Battery, Core Battery, and Survey Battery. The Complete Battery is a comprehensive battery covering important objectives of the instructional program of a given grade. An optional Questionnaire for Grades 3–9 is designed to collect information about students which is useful to counselors and teachers as they work with individual students. The Core Battery contains wholly intact tests from the Complete Battery that provides reading, language, and mathe-

matics scores for Levels 7–9. The Survey Battery is limited to 30 minutes per test in reading, language, and mathematics, plus the Questionnaire. Contains all of the Complete Battery tests as well as tests in social studies and science.

Format: Examiner required; suitable for group use; Complete Battery 310 minutes, Survey Battery 90 minutes

Scoring: Hand key; may be machine scored

Cost: Contact publisher for current prices

Publisher: Riverside Publishing Company

Junior Aptitude Tests (JAT)

Copyright: 1974

Population: Children, adolescents

Purpose: Measures scholastic aptitude; used for educational counseling

Description: Multiple-item paper–pencil test measuring specific scholastic aptitudes: classification, reasoning, number ability, synonyms, comparison, spatial (2D), spatial (3D), memory (paragraph), memory (words and symbols), and mechanical insight.

Format: Examiner required; suitable for group use; untimed: 2 hours 45 minutes

Scoring: Hand key; examiner evaluated; may be machine scored

Cost: Contact publisher

Publisher: Human Sciences Research Council

Kaufman Functional Academic Skill Test (K-FAST)
Alan S. Kaufman, Nadeen L. Kaufman

Copyright: 1994

Population: Ages 15 to 85

Purpose: Designed to be used as a supplement to intelligence, achievement, or adaptive behavior inventories

Description: Two-subtest measure of ability to demonstrate competence in reading and math as applied to daily life situations. Materials included in kit: manual, easel, and 25 record booklets.

Format: Individual administration; 15–25 minutes

Scoring: Examiner administration and interpretation; standard scores

Cost: Complete Kit $89.95; with nylon carrying case $114.95

Publisher: American Guidance Service

Kaufman Test of Educational Achievement (K-TEA)
Alan S. Kaufman, Nadeen L. Kaufman

Copyright: 1985

Population: Grades 1 through 12

Purpose: Evaluates students referred for learning problems

Description: Individually administered measure of academic achievement. Materials included in kit: Comprehensive Form—Manual, Test Easel, 25 Individual Test Records, Sample Report to Parents; Brief Form—Manual, Test Easel, 25 Individual Test Records, and a Sample Report to Parents.

Format: Individual administration; Comprehensive Form 60–75 minutes, Brief Form 30 minutes

Scoring: Examiner administration and interpretation; standard scores; ASSIST available for PC, Apple II

Cost: Complete kit for Comprehensive and Brief (test easels, manuals, protocols, reports to parents, carrying bag) $225.95

Publisher: American Guidance Service

Mini-Battery of Achievement
Richard W. Woodcock, Kevin McGrew, Judy Werder

Copyright: 1994

Population: Ages 4 to adult

Purpose: Provides a brief screening of achievement

Description: Designed to give broader coverage of the skills included in each achievement area, the MBA has four subtests: reading, mathematics, writing, and factual knowledge. Reading test tests a variety of aspects of reading, including sight recognition, comprehension, and vocabulary. Mathematics test includes cal-culation, reasoning, and concepts. Writing skills test includes spelling dictation, punctuation, usage, and proofing. The Factual Knowledge test helps assess general information in science, social studies, and the humanities. Each of the four subtests can be administered and scored independently of the others. Reading, writing, and mathematics scores can be combined to obtain a Basic Skills Cluster score. The MBA includes a computer program that will print a one-page narrative report summarizing all test results in a matter of seconds.

Format: Individually administered; examiner required; 20 minutes

Scoring: Computer program (IBM, MAC, or Apple)

Cost: Complete test (test book with manual, 25 test records with subject worksheets, and 5.25" and 3.5" computer disks) $149.00

Publisher: Riverside Publishing Company

Monitoring Basic Skills Progress (MBSP)
Lynn S. Fuchs, Carol Hamlett, Douglass Fuchs

Copyright: 1990, 1996

Population: Children

Purpose: Monitors progress in three academic areas: basic reading, basic math, and basic spelling

Description: Computer-assisted measurement series of three separate disks that test and monitor progress in basic reading, basic math, and basic spelling. With Basic Reading, students are routinely tested at the computer on instructional-level reading material using a multiple-choice cloze procedure. With Basic Math, students are periodically tested at the computer on a different alternate test that includes each problem type to be taught during the school year. With Basic Spelling, students' spelling proficiency is assessed by having them type words in the computer from a year-long curriculum. The computer generates and administers the tests and automatically scores the students' performance during administration. The computer shows students results of the testing and provides a graph of scores over time. The complete MBSP program includes one each of Basic Reading, Basic Math, and Basic Spelling. Available for use with an Apple II family computer with 64K.

Format: Self-administered; not suitable for group use; untimed: time varies

Scoring: Computer scored; Reading available on Mac only, Math and Spelling available on Apple II

Cost: Complete Program (one each of Basic Reading, Basic Math, and Basic Spelling) $298.00; Basic Reading $109.00; Basic Math $109.00; Basic Spelling $98.00

Publisher: PRO-ED, Inc.

National Educational Development Test (NEDT)

Copyright: 1984

Population: Grades 9 through 10

Purpose: Assesses students' strengths and weaknesses in English, math, social studies, reading, natural sciences, and educational ability

Description: Paper–pencil 209-item test measuring the ability to apply rules and principles of grammar and general English usage, understand mathematical concepts, and apply principles in solving quantitative problems, comprehend reading selections, and apply critical reading skills. The test is semisecure (forms and keys are not released). The test is used only in schools that choose to serve as designated test centers.

Format: Examiner required; suitable for group use; timed: 2 hours 30 minutes

Scoring: Computer scored

Cost: Test materials and scoring service $5.75 per student for Fall 1996 (prices change annually)

Publisher: CTB/McGraw-Hill

Norris Educational Achievement Test (NEAT)

Janet Switzer, Christian P. Gruber

Copyright: Not provided

Population: Ages 4 to 17

Purpose: Used as a standard assessment of basic educational abilities

Description: A diagnostic achievement battery featuring alternate forms, optional measures of written language and oral reading and comprehension, separate grade and age norms, tables identifying discrepancies between IQ and achievement, and a standardization sample. Readiness Tests are used to assess children between 4 and 6 years of age, and Achievement Tests are used to evaluate examinees age 6 and older.

Format: Individually administered; examiner required; 30 minutes

Scoring: Hand key

Cost: Kit (10 test booklets, 1 administration and scoring manual, 1 technical manual) $120.00

Publisher: Western Psychological Services

Objectives-Referenced Bank of Items and Tests (ORBIT)

Copyright: 1982

Population: Grades K through 12

Purpose: Allows the development of customized criterion-referenced tests; offers objectives designed to meet educational needs

Description: Criterion-referenced bank of multiple-choice questions covering objectives in reading, language arts, mathematics, and social studies. Four test items are provided for each objective.

Format: Examiner required; suitable for group use; untimed: time varies

Scoring: Machine scored; hand key; computer scored

Cost: Contact publisher

Publisher: CTB/McGraw-Hill

Peabody Individual Achievement Test–Revised (PIAT–R)

Frederick C. Markwardt, Jr.

Copyright: 1989

Population: Grades K through 12

Purpose: Used to screen academic achievement

Description: PIAT–R is an individually administered achievement test providing wide-range screening in six content areas. Materials included in kit: test easel in four volumes (Volume I, General Information and Reading Recognition; Volume II, Reading Comprehension; Volume III, Mathematics; Volume IV, Spelling and Written Expression), 50 combined Test Records and Written Expression Response Booklets, manual.

Format: Individual administration; 60 minutes

Scoring: Examiner interpreted, standard scores, ASSIST available for DOS, Macintosh, and Windows

Cost: Complete Kit (Volumes I–IV subtests, 50 Combined Test Record and Written Expression Response Booklets, manual) $269.95

Publisher: American Guidance Service

Performance Assessments for California (PAC)

Copyright: 1993

Population: Grades 3 through 10

Purpose: Assesses students in reading/language arts and mathematics; supports the instructional methods and learning goals of California and other schools where whole language concepts and problem solving in mathematics are emphasized

Description: Multiple-item paper–pencil short-answer/essay test used to measure academic achievement in reading/language arts and mathematics. Components include: English/language arts, literary tasks; English/language arts, informative tasks; mathematics assessments. Levels include Elementary (Grades 3–4), Middle School (Grades 7–8), and High School (Grades 9–10). Test yields rubric-based performance scores.

Format: Examiner required; suitable for group use; untimed

Scoring: Examiner evaluated

Cost: Package of 35 test books, examiner's manual and scoring guide: price varies by module

Publisher: CTB/McGraw-Hill

PLAN

Copyright: Revised yearly

Population: Adolescents; Grade 10

Purpose: Used in student guidance and program evaluation to assess educational achievement

Description: Multiple-choice 145-item paper–pencil test with the following categories: English Test—50 items, 30 minutes; Math Test—40 items, 40 minutes; Reading Test—25 items, 20 minutes; Science Reasoning Test—30 items, 25 minutes. An English Test total score and two subscores: Usage/Mechanics and Rhetorical Skills; Math Test total score and two subscores: Pre-Algebra/Algebra and Geometry; Reading Test total score; Science Reasoning Test total score. Raw scores are converted to scale scores; scale scores for the four tests and the composite range from a low of 1 to a high of 32. Subscores are reported on a scale score ranging from a low of 1 to a high of 16. A pencil, test booklet, answer sheet, and supplemental publications are used.

Format: Suitable for group use; examiner required; timed: 115 minutes

Scoring: Hand key; machine scored; test scoring service available from publisher

Cost: $7.00 per individual; reduced price for quantity orders

Publisher: American College Testing

Pre-Professional Skills Test (PPST)

Copyright: Not provided

Population: College students

Purpose: Measures the basic academic skills and achievement of individuals preparing for careers as elementary or high school teachers

Description: Multiple-item paper–pencil multiple-choice and essay test assessing proficiency in reading, writing, and mathematics. The 50-minute Reading test (40 questions) assesses the ability to understand, analyze, and evaluate short passages (100 words), long passages (200 words), and short statements. The 50-minute Mathematics test (40 questions) evaluates the ability to judge mathematical relations. The two-part Writing test consists of a 45-item multiple-choice test of functional written English (30 minutes) and an essay (30 minutes). Each part is graded separately and combined for a single Writing score.

Format: Examiner required; suitable for group use; timed: 3 hours

Scoring: Computer scored; examiner evaluated

Cost: Contact publisher

Publisher: Educational Testing Service

Proficiency Batteries—JSPB, SPB, APP, and SPT-HT

Copyright: Varies

Population: All ages

Purpose: Assesses achievement in scholastic fields; used for selection and placement of students and applicants

Description: Four paper–pencil measures of proficiency in a range of scholastic fields. The JSPB (Standards 5 to 7) measures proficiency in first language (English or Afrikaans), mathematics, natural sciences, geography, history, and second language. The SPB (Standards 8 to 10) measures social sciences, commercial sciences, natural sciences, arithmetic, and home language (English or Afrikaans). APP (first-year university students) tests proficiency in social sciences, commercial sciences, natural sciences, mathematical sciences, and home language. The SPT-HT (adults whose proficiency is at the higher primary level) measures performance in mathematics, English, and Afrikaans.

Format: Examiner required; suitable for group use; timed: JSPB 2½ hours, SPB 1¾ hours; APB 1¾ hours

Scoring: Hand key; examiner evaluated

Cost: Contact publisher

Publisher: Human Sciences Research Council

Proficiency Battery in English and Mathematics for Indian South Africans (PEMISA)

Copyright: 1982

Population: Adolescents; Standards 6 to 7

Purpose: Evaluates the English and mathematics proficiency of Indian South African students; may be used to select and place students in courses

Description: Paper–pencil 120-item multiple-choice battery assessing students' skills in English and mathematics. The English Language Test is composed of two subtests. Language Usage (45 items) covers spelling, word usage, and the knowledge of the meaning of words, phrases, and sentences. Reading Comprehension (30 items) contains questions based on passages the student reads. The 45-item Mathematics Test measures factual knowledge, terminology and general principles, and general skills. The tests are available on two levels, Standard 6 and Standard 7, and in English only.

Format: Examiner required; suitable for group use; untimed: 2 hours 30 minutes

Scoring: Hand key; machine scored

Cost: Contact publisher

Publisher: Human Sciences Research Council

Project SAIL

Copyright: 1994

Population: Grades 2 through 6

Purpose: Used as an integrated assessment–instructional system for use in Grades 2 through 6

Description: An electronic item bank integrating Reading/Language Arts, Mathematics, and Social Studies using a thematic model incorporating dynamic real-world situations. Materials include assessment items, lesson plans, and student activities. Used with CurriculumBuilder.

Format: Suitable for group assessment

Scoring: Hand key

Cost: Bank and notebook $2,095.00

Publisher: CTB/McGraw-Hill

Quic Tests
Oliver Anderhalter

Copyright: 1989

Population: Children, adolescents; Grades 2 through 12

Purpose: Used as an estimation of grade placement to assess achievement in communications and math

Description: Multiple-choice test with five to eight items per grade. Grade equivalent scores and competency-based grade equivalent scores are yielded. Forms A and B for both Communicative Arts and Mathematics are available. A booklet, answer sheet, and pencil are used. Examiner must be certified for assessment.

Format: Individual/self-administered; suitable for group use; examiner required; timed: 30 minutes

Scoring: Hand key; examiner evaluated

Cost: Starter Set $50.70

Publisher: Scholastic Testing Service, Inc.

Quick-Score Achievement Test (Q-SAT)
Donald D. Hammill, Jerome J. Ammer, Mary E. Cronin, Linda H. Mandlebaum, Sally S. Quinby

Copyright: 1987

Population: Children, adolescents; Grades 1 through 12

Purpose: Identifies students with subject matter content difficulties; used by teachers, psychologists, and diagnosticians

Description: Multiple-item paper–pencil test measuring student proficiency in reading, writing, arithmetic, and facts about science, social studies, health, and language arts. Results are reported as standard scores and percentiles. The test is available in two equivalent forms, A and B, and is suited for English-speaking children regardless of nationality.

Format: Examiner required; not suitable for group use; untimed: 40 minutes

Scoring: Hand key

Cost: Complete Kit (examiner's manual, 50 summary/profile sheets, 25 student record forms for Form A, and 25 student record forms for Form B) $98.00

Publisher: PRO-ED, Inc.

SAT II: Subject Tests

Copyright: 1989

Population: Adolescents; Grades 10 through 12

Purpose: Used to predict college performance and by some schools for admissions selection and course placement in specific subject areas

Description: Paper–pencil multiple-choice tests in Writing, Literature, American History and Social Studies, World History, Math (Levels I, IC, and IIC), Biology, Chemistry, Physics, French, German, Modern Hebrew, Italian, Latin, and Spanish. An individual may take up to three SATII: Subject Tests on a single test date. The use of a calculator is allowed on Math Level IC and Math Level IIC. They require a scientific calculator.

Format: Examiner required; suitable for group use; timed: 1 hour

Scoring: Computer scored

Cost: Contact publisher

Publisher: The College Board

Scholastic Abilities Test for Adults (SATA)
Brian R. Bryant, James R. Patton, Caroline Dunn

Copyright: 1991

Population: Adolescents, adults; ages 16 and older

Purpose: Measures an individual's scholastic aptitude and achievement; used to identify an individual's strengths and weaknesses and identify persons who may need special assistance in secondary and postsecondary training and educational settings

Description: Multiple-item paper–pencil assessment battery consisting of nine subtests: Verbal Reasoning—understanding verbal analogies; Nonverbal Reasoning—using geometric forms to assess nonverbal problem solving; Quantitative Reasoning—determining problem-solving abilities using numbers; Reading Vocabulary—recognizing synonyms and antonyms in print; Reading Comprehension—reading passages silently and responding to multiple-choice items; Math Calculation—computing arithmetic, geometry, and algebra problems; Math Application—reading and computing story problems; Writing Mechanics—writing sentences that require spelling, capitalization, and punctuation skills; and Writing Composition—writing a story that is checked for content maturity and vocabulary.

Format: Examiner required; suitable for group use; timed: time varies by subtest

Scoring: Hand key; may be computer scored

Cost: Complete Kit (manual, test books, response booklets, profile/examiner record forms) $139.00

Publisher: PRO-ED, Inc.

Scholastic Aptitude Test Batteries for Standards 2, 3 and 5 (SATB and JSATB)

Copyright: 1980

Population: Children

Purpose: Assesses academic and scholastic aptitudes; used for psychoeducational counseling

Description: Multiple-item test batteries measuring a broad range of scholastic aptitudes. SATB (Standards 2 and 3) measures mathematics, nonverbal reasoning ability, and proficiency in English, Afrikaans, and one of seven mother tongues: Northern Sotho, Southern Sotho, Tswanga, Tsonga, Venda, Xhosa, and Zulu. JSATB (Standard 5) assesses abilities in language, mathematics, and verbal and nonverbal reasoning ability. Individual subtest raw scores are converted to estimated grade equivalents, standard scores ($M = 10$, $SD = 3$), and percentiles. Several composite scores are also generated: General Aptitude, Total Achievement, Reading, Mathematics, and Writing. Composite scores are reported as estimated grade equivalents, standard scores ($M = 100$,

$SD = 15$), and percentiles.

Format: Examiner required; suitable for group use; SATB 3 hours, JSATB 2½ hours

Scoring: Hand key; examiner evaluated

Cost: Contact publisher

Publisher: Human Sciences Research Council

Scholastic Proficiency Test–Higher Primary Level (SPT–HP)

Copyright: 1976

Population: Adults

Purpose: Assesses proficiency in mathematics, English, and Afrikaans; used in South Africa with adult blacks with an educational level of Standards 2–5 for selection and placement in training programs or occupations

Description: Multiple-item paper–pencil test of scholastic proficiency in mathematics, English, and Afrikaans. Norms indicate the typical performance of people passing Standards 2–5. The test can be used for selecting and placing adults in training courses or occupations requiring a higher primary scholastic level.

Format: Examiner required; suitable for group use; untimed: 3 hours 15 minutes

Scoring: Hand key

Cost: Contact publisher

Publisher: Human Sciences Research Council

School Archival Records Search (SARS)
Hill M. Walker, Alice Block-Pedego, Bonnie Todis, Herbert H. Severson

Copyright: 1991

Population: Children; Grades K through 6

Purpose: Provides the school professional with a profile of a student's status on 11 archival variables usually contained in school records

Description: The SARS profile can be used for determining at-risk status for dropout, meeting the requirement that a referred student's school history be systematically examined in eligibility decision-making processes, validating school assessments, and an optional fourth stage of screening in conjunction with the SSBD program. Included is a User's Guide and Technical Manual and an Instrument Packet with quantities sufficient to conduct a record search on 50 students.

Format: Individual administration; untimed

Scoring: Examiner evaluated

Cost: $35.00

Publisher: Sopris West, Inc.

School Improvement Follow-Up Survey

Copyright: 1994

Population: Adults; postsecondary students and graduates

Purpose: Measures success of academic programs and the extracurricular climate for learning

Description: Multiple-choice response format with comments section. For students in their first and fifth years following graduation.

Format: Individual administration; untimed

Scoring: Machine-scored; test scoring service available from publisher

Cost: $35.00/pkg. of 50; scoring .50/survey

Publisher: Assessment Resource Center

Secondary School Admission Test (SSAT)

Copyright: Not provided

Population: Children, adolescents; Grades 5 through 10

Purpose: Measures the abilities of students applying for admission to Grades 6–11 of selective schools; used by independent schools for student selection

Description: Multiple-item paper–pencil multiple-choice test measuring verbal and quantitative abilities and reading comprehension. The test consists of four sections: one measuring verbal ability, two measuring mathematical ability, and one measuring reading comprehension. An upper-level form is administered to students in Grades 8–10; a lower form is administered to students in Grades 5–7. Scores are normed on the student's grade level at the time of testing. Norms for each grade level are developed annually on the basis of the most recent three-year sample of candidates tested. The test is administered on specific dates (six Saturdays during the school year and biweekly during the summer) at designated test centers. Students may designate six score recipients. Accommodations are available for individuals with disabilities.

Format: Examiner required; suitable for group use; timed: time varies

Scoring: Computer scored; hand key

Cost: Domestic Test Fee (administration, parents' score report, six designated school reports) $25.00; Foreign Test Fee (including Canada, Puerto Rico, U.S. territories) $45.00

Publisher: Educational Testing Service

Stanford Achievement Test™ Series–9th Edition

Copyright: 1996

Population: Children, adolescents; Grades K through 13

Purpose: Assesses school achievement status of children in reading, mathematics, language, spelling, study skills, science, social studies, and listening

Description: Multiple-item paper–pencil test with a combination of multiple-choice and open-ended subtests. Three forms, S, SA, and T. Form T is secure and available by special arrangement only. Form SA features an alternate integrated language subtest. Provides norms-, criterion-, content-, and objective-referenced scores.

Format: Examiner required; suitable for group use; timed: time varies

Scoring: Hand key; computer scoring service available

Cost: Examination Kit (for preview only) $24.00 per level

Publisher: Harcourt® Brace Educational Measurement

STS: High School Placement Test (HSPT)–Closed Form

Copyright: 1995

Population: Adolescents; Grades 8.3 through 9.3

Purpose: Assesses academic achievement and aptitude

Description: Multiple-choice 298-item test with five subtests: verbal cognitive skills, quantitative skills, reading, mathematics, and language. Alphabetical lists, rank-order lists, group summary reports, performance profiles, and item analysis reports are provided. Optional tests on Catholic religion, mechanical aptitude, and science are available. A booklet, answer sheet, and pencil are used. Examiner must be certified for assessment. Available in large print. A special program permits individuals with physical or visual disabilities to take the test with up to double the amount of testing time per section.

Format: Suitable for group use; examiner required; timed: 2½ hours

Scoring: Machine scored; test scoring service available from publisher

Cost: Specimen Set $19.48

Publisher: Scholastic Testing Service, Inc.

STS: High School Placement Test (HSPT)–Open Form

Copyright: 1982

Population: Adolescents; Grades 8.3 through 9.3

Purpose: Assesses academic achievement and aptitude

Description: Multiple-choice 298-item test with five subtests: verbal cognitive skills, quantitative skills, reading, mathematics, and language. Cognitive Skills Quotients, basic skills scores, and a composite score are yielded. Optional tests available are Catholic Religion, mechanical aptitude, and science. A pencil, booklet, and answer sheet are used. Examiner must be certified for assessment. Available in large print.

Format: Suitable for group use; examiner required; timed: 2½ hours

Scoring: Hand key

Cost: Specimen Set $19.48

Publisher: Scholastic Testing Service, Inc.

TerraNova (CTB5–5)

Copyright: 1996

Population: Grades K through 12

Purpose: Assesses academic achievement in multiple measures format

Description: Multiple-item paper–pencil norm- and criterion-referenced multiple-choice/short-answer/essay assessment system with multiple components. Consists of reading/language arts, mathematics, science, and social studies subtests. Available in Forms A or B. Spanish version available.

Format: Examiner required; suitable for group use; timed: time varies by subtest

Scoring: Hand key; image scored; hand-score of constructed response

Cost: Contact publisher

Publisher: CTB/McGraw-Hill

Tests of Achievement and Proficiency™: Form M (TAP®)

Dale P. Scannell, Oscar H. Haugh, Brenda H. Loyd, C. Frederick Risinger

Copyright: 1996

Population: Grades 9 through 12

Purpose: Provides a comprehensive and objective measure of students' progress in a high school curriculum

Description: Paper–pencil multiple-choice battery assessing student achievement in the basic skills of reading, writing, mathematics, social studies, science, and information processing. The tests are organized into four levels that correspond to the four high school grades. Each level is available in a Survey Battery and a Complete Battery. The Survey Battery covers Reading with Vocabulary and Comprehension, Written Expression, Math Concepts and Problem Solving, and optional Math

Computation. The Complete Battery consists of Vocabulary, Reading Comprehension, Written Expression, Math Concepts and Problem Solving, optional Math Computation, Social Studies, Science, and Information Processing. For the Complete Battery, scores are reported for each of the seven individual tests, a Reading Total, a Core Total, and a Battery Composite. For the Survey Battery, scores are reported for Reading, Math, and Battery Total. Predicted ACT and SAT scores are available to help with educational guidance.

Format: Examiner required; suitable for group use; Complete Battery 255 minutes, Survey Battery 90 minutes

Scoring: Hand key; may be machine scored

Cost: Contact publisher for current prices

Publisher: Riverside Publishing Company

Tests of Achievement and Proficiency™: Forms G, H, and J (TAP®)

Dale P. Scannell, Oscar M. Haugh, Alvin H. Schild, Gilbert Ulmer

Copyright: 1990, 1986

Population: Grades 9 through 12

Purpose: Provides a comprehensive and objective measure of students' progress in a high school curriculum

Description: Paper–pencil multiple-choice battery assessing student achievement in the basic skills of reading, writing, listening, mathematics, using sources of information, social studies, and science. The tests are organized into four levels that correspond to the four high school grades. Each level is available in a Basic Battery and a Complete Battery. The Basic Battery covers Reading with Comprehension, Mathematics, Written Expression, and Using Sources of Information. The Complete Battery consists of Reading Comprehension, Written Expression, Mathematics, Using Sources of Information, Social Studies, and Science. Optional Listening and Writing Tests are also available. For the Complete Battery, scores are reported for each of the six individual tests, a Reading Total, a Core Total, and a Battery

Composite. For the Survey Battery, scores are reported for Reading, Math, and Battery Total. Predicted ACT and SAT scores are available to help with educational guidance.

Format: Examiner required; suitable for group use; Complete Battery 240 minutes, Basic Battery 160 minutes

Scoring: Hand key; may be machine scored

Cost: Contact publisher for current prices

Publisher: Riverside Publishing Company

Tests of Achievement and Proficiency™: Forms K and L (TAP®)

Copyright: 1993

Population: Grades 10 and 11

Purpose: Provides a comprehensive and objective measure of students' progress in a high school curriculum

Description: Paper–pencil multiple-choice battery assessing student achievement in the basic skills of reading, writing, listening, mathematics, using sources of information, social studies, and science. Available in a Complete Battery, Core Battery, and Survey Battery.

Format: Examiner required; group administered

Scoring: Hand key; may be machine scored

Cost: Contact publisher for current prices

Publisher: Riverside Publishing Company

Tests of Achievement in Basic Skills (TABS)

Copyright: 1985

Population: Children, adolescents; Grades 2 through 13

Purpose: Evaluates individual student progress in reading, mathematics, and geometry; used to measure overall class and school achievement growth related to specific academic objectives

Description: Paper–pencil 66-item criterion-referenced tests measuring student achievement in mathematics and reading comprehension. Two parallel forms, 1 and 2, are available at four ability levels. Test items are arranged in three parts. Part I, Arithmetic Skills, consists of 30 items measuring basic arithmetic skills. Part II, Geometry–Measurement–Application, consists of 25 items measuring basic geometric concepts, arithmetic measurements, and application to practical problems. Part III, Modern Concepts, consists of 11 items measuring modern mathematics concepts.

Format: Examiner required; suitable for group use; untimed: 1 class period

Scoring: Scoring service available

Cost: Contact publisher

Publisher: EdITS/Educational and Industrial Testing Service

Tests of Adult Basic Education (TABE), Forms 7 and 8

Copyright: 1994

Population: Adults

Purpose: Measures adult proficiency in reading, mathematics, and language; used to identify individual strengths and needs, establish appropriate level of instruction, and measure growth after instruction

Description: Multiple-item paper–pencil multiple-choice test measuring an adult's grasp of the reading, mathematics, language skills, and spelling required to function in society. The test is available in four levels ranging from easy to advanced. A large-print edition is available. Scores may be used to estimate performance on the GED tests. Spanish version available. Computerized version available.

Format: Examiner required; suitable for group use; complete battery 2 hours 45 minutes, survey form 1 hour 30 minutes

Scoring: Hand key; may be computer scored

Cost: Multi-Level Review Kit $19.10

Publisher: CTB/McGraw-Hill

Tests of Adult Basic Education (TABE–PC™)

Copyright: 1994

Population: Adults

Purpose: Provides automatic scoring of the TABE™ basic skills assessments

Description: Computerized version of the TABE™ basic skills assessments. Available for TABE Forms 5 and 6, TABE Forms 7 and 8, TABE Work-Related Foundation Skills (TABE–WF), and TABE Español.

Format: Examiner required; administered on computer; complete battery 2 hours 45 minutes, survey form 1 hour 30 minutes

Scoring: Computer scored

Cost: IBM 3.5″ or 5.25″ disk Starter Module $60.00; Additional Administrations $220.00 for 50, $420.00 for 100

Publisher: CTB/McGraw-Hill

3-R's® Test
Nancy S. Cole, E. Roger Trent,
Dena C. Wadell, Robert L. Thorndike,
Elizabeth P. Hagen

Copyright: 1982

Population: Grades K through 12

Purpose: To assess student progress in the fundamental skills

Description: Three paper–pencil multiple-choice batteries assessing academic achievement and ability: the Achievement Edition, the Class Period Edition, and a Spanish Edition. The Achievement Edition measures students' achievement in the readiness skills and the mathematics, reading, and language skills most essential to student development. The Class Period Edition measures achievement in the most basic skills in just 40 minutes and yields a single overall achievement score. La Prueba is the Spanish language edition. It is designed to determine the degree to which students are literate in Spanish and to assess the achievement of students whose primary language is Spanish. La Prueba de Realización also measures achievement in science and social studies.

Format: Examiner required; suitable for group use; 40–190 minutes depending on the edition and grade level

Scoring: Hand key; may be machine scored

Cost: Contact publisher for current prices

Publisher: Riverside Publishing Company

Wechsler Individual Achievement Test® (WIAT®)

Copyright: 1992

Population: Ages 5 through 19

Purpose: Measures academic abilities to evaluate discrepancies between aptitude and achievement

Description: Eight subtests (Basic Reading, Mathematics Reasoning, Spelling, Reading Comprehension, Numerical Operations, Listening Comprehension, Oral Expression, and Written Expression) that are linked with the WISC–III and WPPSI–R for meaningful comparisons between achievement scores and ability test performance. A screening test offers measurement of basic reading, mathematics reasoning, and spelling skills.

Format: Examiner required; individual administration; Battery 30–75 minutes, Screener 10–18 minutes

Scoring: Hand key

Cost: Complete Kit (manual, stimulus booklets, protocols, and Screener in box) $227.00

Publisher: Harcourt® Brace Educational Measurement

Wide Range Achievement Test–Third Edition (WRAT–3)
Gary S. Wilkinson

Copyright: 1993

Population: Ages 5 to 75

Purpose: Used in the measurement of basic academic codes and diagnosing learning disabilities to assess reading, spelling, and arithmetic; intended for school populations, special education, and clinical use

Description: Paper–pencil test with three subtests: Reading, spelling, and arithmetic. Standard scores, percentiles, absolute scores, and grade ratings are yielded. A test form, #2 pencil, profile form, and a manual for interpretation are used. Available in large print.

Format: Individual/group administered; examiner required; timed and untimed

Scoring: Hand key; examiner evaluated

Cost: Starter Set $105.00

Publisher: Wide Range, Inc.

Woodcock-Johnson®–Revised Tests of Achievement (WJ–R®)
Richard W. Woodcock, M. Bonner Johnson

Copyright: 1989

Population: Ages 2 to 90+

Purpose: Provides a comprehensive assessment of achievement

Description: The tests are divided into two batteries: standard and supplemental. The Standard Battery contains nine tests covering the areas of reading, mathematics, written language, and knowledge. These tests yield six cluster scores: Broad Reading, Broad Mathematics, Mathematics Reasoning, Broad Written Language, Broad Knowledge, and Skills. The Supplemental Battery contains tests that can be used in conjunction with the tests in the Standard Battery to obtain the following cluster scores: Basic Reading, Reading Comprehension, Basic Mathematics, Basic Writing Skills, and Written Expression. Alternate forms are available for pretest and posttest administration.

Format: Individual administration; examiner required; 5 minutes per subtest

Scoring: Examiner interpretation; computer software available for PC, Mac, and Apple formats

Cost: Form A or B (standard and supplemental test books, examiner's manual, norm tables, 25 test records, 25 Subject Response Booklets, with case) $308.00

Publisher: Riverside Publishing Company

Academic Aptitude

Academic Aptitude Test, Standard 10 (AAT)

Copyright: 1974

Population: Adolescents

Purpose: Assesses academic abilities; used for vocational guidance

Description: Battery of 10 tests measuring specific academic aptitudes: Nonverbal Reasoning, Verbal Reasoning, English Vocabulary, English Reading Comprehension, Numerical Comprehension, Afrikaans Vocabulary, Afrikaans Proficiency.

Format: Examiner required; suitable for group use; timed: 7 hours

Scoring: Hand key; examiner evaluated

Cost: Contact publisher

Publisher: Human Sciences Research Council

Academic Aptitude Test, University (AAT)

Copyright: 1976

Population: Adolescents, adults

Purpose: Assesses academic abilities at the university level; used for vocational guidance

Description: Multiple-item battery of tests measuring 10 specific academic aptitudes: Nonverbal Reasoning, Verbal Reasoning, English Vocabulary, English Reading Comprehension, Numerical Comprehension, Afrikaans Vocabulary, Afrikaans Reading Comprehension, Squares, Spatial Perception (3D), and Mathematical Proficiency.

Format: Examiner required; suitable for group use; timed: 7 hours

Scoring: Hand key; examiner evaluated

Cost: Contact publisher

Publisher: Human Sciences Research Council

Academic-Technical Aptitude Tests for Coloured Pupils in Standards 6, 7, and 8 (ATA)

Copyright: 1969

Population: Adolescents

Purpose: Measures the differential aptitudes of pupils in Standards 6–8; used for vocational and educational guidance

Description: Multiple-item battery of 10 paper–pencil tests, including verbal reasoning, nonverbal reasoning, computations, spatial perception (2D), mechanical reasoning, language comprehension, spatial perception (3D), comparison, coordination, and writing speed. Stanines and percentile ranks are available for each standard.

Format: Examiner required; suitable for group use; untimed: 4 hours

Scoring: Hand key

Cost: Contact publisher

Publisher: Human Sciences Research Council

ACER Tests of Learning Ability (TOLA)

Copyright: 1976

Population: Children, adolescents; ages 8 years 6 months to 13 years 2 months

Purpose: Measures the language and reasoning aspects of general intellectual ability important for academic success for students ages 8 years 6 months to 13 years 2 months

Description: Multiple-item paper–pencil test of general academic aptitude is available at two levels: TOLA 4 (Year 4 of schooling or ages 8-6 to 11-5) and TOLA 6 (Year 6 of schooling or ages 10-3 to 13-2). Each level contains three separately timed subtests: Verbal Comprehension (vocabulary), General Reasoning (problem solving in a mathematical framework), and Syllogistic Reasoning (verbal analogies).

Australian norms are provided in the form of stanines and percentile ranks.

Format: Examiner required; suitable for group use; timed: 33 minutes

Scoring: Hand key; may be machine scored

Cost: Contact publisher

Publisher: The Australian Council for Educational Research Limited

Ann Arbor Learning Inventory
Barbara Meister Vitale, Waneta Bullock

Copyright: 1996

Population: Grades K through 8

Purpose: Evaluates the central processing and perceptual skills necessary for reading, writing, and spelling to identify learning difficulties and deficits and suggest appropriate remedial strategies

Description: Multiple-item task-performance oral-response and paper–pencil test measuring the following central processing skills: Visual Discrimination, Visual Memory, Auditory Discrimination, and Auditory Memory. Test items are presented in order of natural cognitive development, beginning with pictures, proceeding to objects and geometric forms, and finally to letters, words, and phrases. Tasks involve listening, manipulating, showing, matching, visualizing, telling, and writing. Results also provide objective data on developmental levels for prereading readiness, precomputational skills, kinesthetic and motor skills, and comprehension and critical thinking. Instrument is criterion referenced.

Format: Individual or group administration; untimed

Scoring: Examiner administered and interpreted

Cost: Manuals (Levels A, B, or C) $10.00; test booklets (Levels A, B, or C) $12.00; stimulus cards (Level C) $8.00

Publisher: Academic Therapy Publications

Aptitude Test Battery for Pupils in Standards 6 and 7 (ATB)

Copyright: 1970

Population: Adolescents

Purpose: Measures aptitudes of students in Standards 6 and 7; used in South Africa for educational placement and for identifying underachievement in black pupils

Description: Multiple-item paper–pencil battery of multiple-choice tests for determining academic aptitude and achievement. The core battery of six tests includes English (reading comprehension and vocabulary), spatial perception, nonverbal reasoning, mathematics, Afrikaans (reading comprehension and vocabulary), and verbal reasoning. The supplementary tests are comparison, numerical, and mechanical insight. Stanines are calculated for the third term.

Format: Examiner required; suitable for group use; untimed: 5 hours

Scoring: Hand key; may be machine scored

Cost: Contact publisher

Publisher: Human Sciences Research Council

Aptitude Test for Adults (AA)

Copyright: 1979

Population: Adults

Purpose: Assesses scholastic aptitudes; used for psychoeducational evaluation

Description: Paper–pencil 225-item test measuring nine scholastic aptitudes, including comparison, figural series, calculations, reasoning, mechanical insight, spatial visualization (2-D), classification, spatial visualization (3-D), and spare parts.

Format: Examiner required; suitable for group use; timed: 3½ hours

Scoring: Hand key; examiner evaluated

Cost: Contact publisher

Publisher: Human Sciences Research Council

Aptitude Tests for Indian South Africans (JATISA and SATISA)

Copyright: JATISA 1974; SATISA 1977

Population: Children, adolescents

Purpose: Assesses aptitudes of Indian children; used for vocational guidance

Description: Multiple-item paper–pencil test batteries measuring scholastic and vocational aptitudes. JATISA (Standards 6 to 8) consists of 10 subtests: Verbal Reasoning, Series Completion, Social Insight, Language Usage, Numerical Reasoning, Spatial Perception (2-D), Spatial Perception (3-D), Visual Arts, Clerical Speed and Accuracy, and Mechanical Insight. SATISA (Standards 9 and 10) consists of 11 subtests: Verbal Reasoning, Numerical Reasoning, Spatial Perception (3-D), Series Completion, Mechanical Insight, Classification, Spatial Perception (2-D), Comparison, Language Usage, Memory, and Filing.

Format: Examiner required; suitable for group use; timed: Junior 3½ hours, Senior 4½ hours

Scoring: Hand key; examiner evaluated

Cost: Contact publisher

Publisher: Human Sciences Research Council

Ball Aptitude Battery™ (BAB)

Copyright: 1995

Population: Grades 8 to 12 and above

Purpose: Measures aptitudes for career exploration and self-knowledge

Description: Multiple-choice and short-answer, paper–pencil format. Instrument has 12 subtests: 1. Clerical (Perceptual Speed)— ability to see and differentiate pairs of numbers quickly and accurately. 2. Word Association— personality characteristics of objective vs. subjective orientation. 3. Writing Speed—ability to write fast. 4. Ideaphoria—ability to generate a rapid and abundant flow of ideas. 5. Associative Memory—short-term memorization of letter–number combinations. 6. Auditory Memory Span—short-term auditory memory. 7. Inductive Reasoning—ability to find common elements in a series of pictures. 8. Paper Folding (Spatial Visualization)—ability to visualize a 3-dimensional figure in 2-dimensional space. 9. Vocabulary—ability to understand relationships between concepts and organize them in a systematic manner. Different forms for differ-

ent grade levels. Accommodations for individuals with disabilities.

Format: Group administration; examiner required; timed

Scoring: Hand and computer scored; test scoring service available from publisher; scores provided include subtests, overall aptitude profile, and 5-page personalized narrative report

Cost: Technical, Counselor, and Administration Manuals $0.25 each; contact publisher for test prices

Publisher: Ball Foundation

Beery Picture Vocabulary Test (PVT)
Keith E. Beery, Colleen M. Taheri

Copyright: 1992

Population: Children to adults; ages 30 months to 40 years

Purpose: Used in educational/developmental counseling to measure expressive nominal vocabulary

Description: Oral-response 165-item verbal test. Materials used include a manual, stimulus card set, and Berry PVT record forms. Examiner must be B-Level qualified.

Format: Individual administration; examiner required; untimed: 10–15 minutes

Scoring: Hand key

Cost: Introductory Kit (manual, card set, protocols) $99.00

Publisher: Psychological Assessment Resources, Inc.

Beery Picture Vocabulary Screening Series (BEERY PVS)
Keith E. Beery, Colleen M. Taheri

Copyright: 1992

Population: Children, adolescents; Grades 2 to 12

Purpose: Used in emotional counseling to screen for problems in intellectual development or achievement; intended for students in grades 2 to 12 having adequate visual motor abilities

Description: Paper–pencil series with 11 subtests (1 for each grade), 16 pictures per test. Materials used include professional manual and booklets for each of Grades 2 through 12. Examiners must be teachers or education specialists.

Format: Individual administration; suitable for group use; examiner required; timed: 10 minutes

Scoring: Hand key

Cost: Complete Kit (manual and 5 of each booklet) $65.00

Publisher: Psychological Assessment Resources, Inc.

California Program for Learning Assessment

Copyright: Not provided

Population: Grades 3 through 10

Purpose: Assesses students' ability to think critically, respond effectively in writing, and apply problem-solving strategies

Description: Provides performance assessments in English-language arts and mathematics in both English and Spanish. One authentic literary selection and a series of open-ended questions begin each assessment. All passages are drawn from published materials, and literary passages in Spanish are authentic works, not translations. Assessment content reflects the California English-Language Arts Framework. A group activity serves as a bridge between the reading and writing portions of the assessment, which culminates with a related extended writing activity.

Format: Group administered; examiner required; time varies

Scoring: Examiner evaluated

Cost: English-Language Arts Assessments (includes blackline masters for 3 assessments plus Directions for Administration and Scoring)—Elementary or Intermediate $108.50, Secondary $72.50; Mathematics—Elementary or Intermediate $72.50, Secondary $47.00

Publisher: Riverside Publishing Company

Cognitive Abilities Test™: Form 4 (CogAT®)

Robert L. Thorndike, Elizabeth P. Hagen

Copyright: 1986

Population: Grades K to 12

Purpose: Assesses students' abilities in reasoning and problem solving using verbal, quantitative, and spatial (nonverbal) symbols

Description: Multiple-item paper–pencil multiple-choice test measuring the development of students' cognitive skills. The Primary Battery, organized into two levels (Level 1 for Grades K–1, Level 2 for Grades 2–3), measures the factors of oral vocabulary, verbal classification, figure matrices, and quantitative concepts. The Multilevel/Separate Level Editions are available for Levels A–H for Grades 3 to 12. Each level contains a verbal battery assessing sentence completion, verbal classification, and verbal analogies; a quantitative battery assessing quantitative relations, number series, and equation building; and a nonverbal battery measuring figure classification, figure analogies, and figure analysis.

Format: Examiner required; suitable for group use; approximately 90 minutes

Scoring: Hand key; may be machine scored

Cost: Contact publisher for current prices

Publisher: Riverside Publishing Company

Cognitive Abilities Test™: Form 5 (CogAT®)

Robert L. Thorndike, Elizabeth P. Hagen

Copyright: 1993

Population: Grades K to 12

Purpose: Assesses students' abilities in reasoning and problem solving using verbal, quantitative, and spatial (nonverbal) symbols

Description: Multiple-item paper–pencil multiple-choice test measuring the development of students' cognitive skills. The Primary Battery, organized into two levels (Level 1 for Grades K–1, Level 2 for Grades 2–3), measures the factors of oral vocabulary, verbal classification, figure matrices, and quantitative concepts. The

Multilevel/Separate Level Editions are available for Levels A–H for Grades 3 to 12. Each level contains a verbal battery assessing sentence completion, verbal classification, and verbal analogies; a quantitative battery assessing quantitative relations, number series, and equation building; and a nonverbal battery measuring figure classification, figure analogies, and figure analysis. All levels of the test contain three batteries which provide separate scores for verbal, quantitative, and nonverbal reasoning abilities. A Composite score is also available. Each item on the verbal tests has been reviewed for appropriateness of vocabulary level and sentence structure. All items have been reviewed to eliminate content that could be biased toward any group of individuals.

Format: Examiner required; suitable for group use; approximately 90 minutes

Scoring: Hand key; may be machine scored

Cost: Contact publisher for current prices

Publisher: Riverside Publishing Company

COMP Assessment of Reasoning and Communication (ARC)

Copyright: 1996

Population: Adults; ages 17 and above

Purpose: Assesses speaking, writing, and reasoning

Description: Paper–pencil 33-item oral-response criterion-referenced essay/verbal test with the following categories: Speaking, Writing, and Reasoning. Total Speaking, Total Writing, and Total Reasoning each have three subtests. Forms 10–12 are available.

Format: Individual administration; suitable for group use; examiner required; timed: 69 minutes

Scoring: Examiner evaluated; machine scored

Cost: $15.75 per student; $23.00+ to rate per student

Publisher: American College Testing

Cornell Critical Thinking Test, Level X

Robert H. Ennis, Jason Millman

Copyright: 1985

Population: Children, adolescents; Grades 4 to 14

Purpose: Assesses an individual's ability to think critically; used for research, teaching of critical thinking, or as one of several criteria for admission to positions/areas requiring ability to think critically

Description: Paper–pencil 71-item multiple-choice measure of critical thinking divided into four sections. In the first section, the examinee reads a conclusion and decides which of several premises supports the conclusion. The second section measures the examinee's ability to judge the reliability of information. The third section tests the examinee's ability to judge whether a statement follows from premises. The fourth section involves the identification of assumptions. Level X is somewhat easier than Level Z.

Format: Examiner required for Grades 4–6; suitable for group use; timed: 50–62 minutes

Scoring: Computer/hand scored; answers and norms in TM

Cost: Specimen Set (tests, manual) $14.95; 10 tests $16.95; 10 machine-scorable answer sheets $7.95

Publisher: Critical Thinking Books and Software

Cornell Critical Thinking Test, Level Z

Robert H. Ennis, Jason Millman

Copyright: 1985

Population: Adolescents, adults

Purpose: Assesses an individual's ability to think critically; used for research, teaching of critical thinking, or as one of several criteria for admission to positions or areas requiring ability for critical thinking

Description: Paper–pencil 52-item multiple-choice measure of critical thinking divided into seven sections directed at assessing the examinee's ability to decide whether a statement follows from a given premise, detect equivocal arguments, judge reliability of observation and authenticity of sources, judge direction of support for a hypothesis, judge possible predictions for their value in guiding experiments, and find assumptions of various types. Level Z is somewhat more difficult than Level X.

Format: Self-administered; suitable for group use; timed: 50 minutes

Scoring: Computer/hand scored; answers and norms in TM

Cost: Specimen Set (manual, tests) $14.95; 10 tests $16.95; 10 machine-scorable answer sheets $7.95

Publisher: Critical Thinking Books and Software

CTB Performance Assessment

Copyright: 1994

Population: Grades K through 11

Purpose: Assesses students' complex thinking and learning skills

Description: Short answer/essay paper–pencil test consisting of 12–25 open-ended tasks in four subtest areas: Reading/Language Arts, Mathematics, Science, and Social Studies. Twelve levels. Integrated outcomes report available when used with CAT/5 or CTBS/4.

Format: Examiner required; group or individual administration; timed: 30 minutes to 1 hour each subtest

Scoring: Examiner evaluated; scoring service available from publisher

Cost: Test books (pkg. of 30, examiner's manual) $45.90

Publisher: CTB/McGraw-Hill

Detroit Tests of Learning Aptitude–Adult (DTLA–A)
Donald D. Hammill, Brian R. Bryant

Copyright: 1991

Population: Ages 16 to 79

Purpose: Measures general and specific aptitudes to identify deficiencies and provide an index of optimal-level performance; permits interpretation in terms of current theories of intellect and behavior domains

Description: The battery's 12 subtests and 16 composites measure both general intelligence and discrete ability areas. The instrument was normed on more than 1,000 adults from more than 20 states. The overall composite is formed by combining the scores of all 12 subtests in the battery. Because of this, the overall composite is probably the best estimate of g in that it reflects status on the widest array of different developed abilities. The DTLA–A includes a Verbal and Nonverbal Composite, an Attention-Enhanced and an Attention-Reduced Composite, and a Motor-Enhanced and a Motor-Reduced Composite.

Format: Individual administration, examiner required, requires 1½ –2½ hours

Scoring: Examiner scored and interpreted; computer (IBM and Apple II) interpretation available

Cost: Complete kit (examiner's manual, picture books, protocols, and storage box) $249.00

Publisher: PRO-ED, Inc.

Detroit Tests of Learning Aptitude–Primary: Second Edition (DTLA–P:2)
Donald D. Hammill, Brian R. Bryant

Copyright: 1991

Population: Ages 3 to 9 years

Purpose: Measures general and specific aptitudes of children and identifies deficiencies; serves as a standardized instrument in research

Description: Oral-response and paper–pencil 100-item battery yielding six subtest scores (Verbal, Nonverbal, Attention-Enhanced, Attention-Reduced, Motor-Enhanced, and Motor-Reduced) and a General Mental Ability score. These scores provide a detailed profile of a student's abilities and deficiencies. The test is useful with low-functioning school-aged children.

Format: Individual administration; examiner required; 15–45 minutes

Scoring: Examiner scored and interpreted; computer (IBM and Apple II) interpretation available

Cost: Complete Kit (examiner's manual, picture book, protocols, and storage box) $139.00

Publisher: PRO-ED, Inc.

Detroit Tests of Learning Aptitude–Third Edition (DTLA–3)
Donald D. Hammill, Brian R. Bryant

Copyright: 1991

Population: Ages 6 to 17 years

Purpose: Measures general and specific aptitudes of children and identifies deficiencies; serves as a standardized instrument in research

Description: Includes 11 subtests and 16 composites that measure both general intelligence and discrete ability areas to permit interpretation in terms of current theories of intellect and behavior domains. Provides an index of optimal level performance. Subtests are Word Opposites, Design Sequences, Sentence Imitation, Reversed Letters, Story Construction, Design Reproduction, Basic Information, Symbolic Relations, Word Sequences, Story Sequences, and Picture Fragments. Composite scores that can be obtained are Verbal, Nonverbal, Attention-Enhanced, Attention-Reduced, Motor-Enhanced, and Motor-Reduced.

Format: Individual administration; examiner required; 50 minutes to 2 hours

Scoring: Examiner scored and interpreted; computer (IBM and Apple II) interpretation available

Cost: Complete kit (examiner's manual, picture book, protocols, and storage box) $239.00

Publisher: PRO-ED, Inc.

Differential Aptitude Tests™, Fifth Edition (DAT™)
G. K. Bennett, H. G. Seashore,
A. G. Wesman

Copyright: 1990

Population: Adolescents; Grades 8 through 12

Purpose: Assesses aptitude and interest; used for educational and vocational guidance in junior and senior high schools

Description: Multiple-item paper–pencil test

of eight abilities: verbal reasoning, numerical ability, abstract reasoning, clerical speed and accuracy, mechanical reasoning, space relations, spelling, and language usage. A ninth score is obtained by summing the verbal reasoning and numerical ability scores. The Career Planning Questionnaire is optional. Two levels: Level 1 for Grades 8 and 9, and Level 2 for Grades 10 through 12.

Format: Examiner required; suitable for group use; timed: complete battery 2½ hours

Scoring: Hand key; may be machine or computer scored; scoring service available

Cost: Examination Kit $22.50

Publisher: Harcourt® Brace Educational Measurement

Ennis-Weir Critical Thinking Essay Test
Robert H. Ennis, Eric Weir

Copyright: 1985

Population: Adolescents, adults; Grades 7 and above

Purpose: Measures the ability to think critically; used for teaching and in research

Description: Paper–pencil essay test incorporating the following aspects of critical thinking: getting the point, seeing the reasons and assumptions, stating one's point, offering good reasons, seeing other possibilities, responding appropriately to/avoiding equivocation, irrelevance, circularity, reversal of an if–then relationship, overgeneralization, credibility questions, and the use of emotive language to persuade.

Format: Self-administered; suitable for group use; untimed: 40 minutes

Scoring: Examiner evaluated

Cost: Manual (includes scoring directions, 1 test, 1 scoring sheet) $9.95

Publisher: Critical Thinking Books and Software

Graduate Management Admissions Test (GMAT)

Copyright: Updated yearly

Population: College graduates

Purpose: Measures verbal and quantitative abilities related to success in graduate management schools; used for admission to graduate management school

Description: Paper/pencil multiple-choice test used by many graduate schools of business and management as one criterion for admission. In 1994, an analytical writing assessment was added to GMAT. The test is administered four times annually at centers established by the publisher, and registration materials are available at no charge. The test is not available for institutional use.

Format: Group; 4 hours

Scoring: Examiner required; computer scored by publisher

Cost: Contact publisher

Publisher: Educational Testing Service

Group Test for Indian Pupils

Copyright: 1968

Population: Children, adolescents

Purpose: Measures general mental ability; used for psychoeducational evaluation

Description: Six-subtest paper–pencil measure of general mental ability. Three subtests are verbal and three are nonverbal. Tests provide three scores: verbal, nonverbal, and total. The test is divided into three series: Junior, Intermediate, and Senior. Two alternative forms are available for the Junior and Intermediate Series.

Format: Examiner required; suitable for group use; timed: 2 hours

Scoring: Hand key; examiner evaluated

Cost: Contact publisher

Publisher: Human Sciences Research Council

Group Tests for 5/6 and 7/8 Year Olds

Copyright: 1960

Population: Children; ages 5 to 8

Purpose: Assesses intellectual ability; used for measurement of school readiness

Description: Six-subtest measure of general intellectual ability. Materials include bilingual (English, Afrikaans) test booklets. The child should be able to handle a pencil and follow instructions without emotional distress.

Format: Examiner required; suitable for group use; untimed: no time limit

Scoring: Hand key; examiner evaluated

Cost: Contact publisher

Publisher: Human Sciences Research Council

Group Tests–1974

Copyright: 1974

Population: Children

Purpose: Assesses developmental intelligence; used for psychological educational evaluation

Description: Six-subtest measure of general intelligence. Three subtests are verbal, three are nonverbal. The test provides three scores: verbal, nonverbal, and total. Materials include three series: Junior Series for Standards 4 to 6, Intermediate Series for Standards 6 to 8, and Senior Series for Standards 8 to 10.

Format: Examiner required; suitable for group use; timed: 2½ hours

Scoring: Hand key; examiner evaluated

Cost: Contact publisher

Publisher: Human Research Council

Henmon-Nelson Test of Mental Ability (Canadian Edition)

M. J. Nelson, Tom Lamke, Joseph French

Copyright: 1989

Population: Children, adolescents; Grades 3 to 12

Purpose: Assesses students' academic aptitude

Description: Series of multiple-choice paper–pencil subtests that test students' academic aptitude. This is a revision of the Henmon-Nelson Form 1 by Riverside (1973). Materials include test booklets, answer sheets, and record sheets. Examiner must have a teaching certificate.

Format: Examiner required; suitable for group use; timed: 30 minutes

Scoring: Self-scored; hand key; scoring service available from publisher

Cost: Contact publisher

Publisher: Nelson Canada

Henmon-Nelson Tests of Mental Ability
Joseph L. French, Tom A. Lamke, Martin J. Nelson

Copyright: 1973

Population: Grades K through 12

Purpose: Provides a quick and reliable measure of cognitive ability

Description: Battery of paper–pencil multiple-choice tests available on four levels for Grades K–2, 3–6, 6–9, and 9–12. Types of items related to academic success—vocabulary, sentence completion, opposites, general information, verbal analogies, verbal classification, verbal inference, number series, arithmetic reasoning and figure analogies—are arranged in omnibus-cycle form in the tests for Grades 3–12. The Grade K–2 battery consists of three subtests—Listening, Picture Vocabulary, and Size and Number—measuring nine abilities. No reading is required for the Primary Battery.

Format: Examiner required; suitable for group use; Grades K–2 25 to 30 minutes, Grades 3–12 30 minutes

Scoring: Hand key; may be machine scored

Cost: Contact publisher for current prices

Publisher: Riverside Publishing Company

Individual Scale for Indian South Africans (ISISA)

Copyright: 1971

Population: Children, adolescents; ages 8 to 17

Purpose: Assesses intelligence in Indian pupils; used for psychological–educational evaluation

Description: Ten-subtest measure of general intellectual ability. Five subtests are verbal; five are nonverbal. Scores obtained include Vocabulary, Comprehension, Similarities, Problems, Memory, Pattern Completion, Blocks, Absurdities, Formboard, and Mazes. The test may be administered in an abbreviated form. The test was adapted for Indians from the New South African Individual Scale.

Format: Examiner required; not suitable for group use; untimed: 1 hour 20 minutes

Scoring: Hand key; examiner evaluated

Cost: Contact publisher

Publisher: Human Sciences Research Council

Iowa Tests of Educational Development® (ITED®), Form M
Leonard S. Feldt, Robert A. Forsyth, Timothy N. Ansley, Stephanie D. Alnot

Copyright: 1996

Population: Grades 9 through 12

Purpose: Assesses intellectual skills that represent the long-term goals of secondary education, particularly the critical thinking skills of analysis and evaluation

Description: Available in a Complete Battery and Survey Battery. The Complete Battery contains seven tests that require students to apply knowledge and skills in new settings and give students an opportunity to demonstrate different competencies in a variety of contexts: Vocabulary, Ability To Interpret Literary Materials, Correctness and Appropriateness of Expression, Ability To Do Quantitative Thinking, Analysis of Social Studies Materials, Analysis of Science Materials, and Use of Sources of Information. The Survey Battery consists of three tests: Reading, Correctness and Appropriateness of Expression, and Ability To Do Quantitative Thinking. For the Complete Battery, scores are reported for each of the seven tests and a composite. For the Survey Battery, scores are reported for each test and an Advanced Skills score. Predicted ACT and SAT scores are available to help with educational guidance. If the optional Questionnaire is used, results may be tabulated for teachers and guidance counselors as part of central scoring services.

Format: Examiner required; suitable for group use; Complete Battery 235 minutes, Survey Battery 90 minutes

Scoring: Hand key; may be machine scored

Cost: Contact publisher for current prices

Publisher: Riverside Publishing Company

Iowa Tests of Educational Development® (ITED®), Forms K and L
Leonard S. Feldt, Robert A. Forsyth, Timothy N. Ansley, Stephanie D. Alnot

Copyright: 1993

Population: Grades 9 through 12

Purpose: Assesses intellectual skills that represent the long-term goals of secondary education, particularly the critical thinking skills of analysis and evaluation

Description: Available in a Complete Battery and Survey Battery. The Complete Battery contains seven tests that require students to apply knowledge and skills in new settings and give students an opportunity to demonstrate different competencies in a variety of contexts: Vocabulary, Ability To Interpret Literary Materials, Correctness and Appropriateness of Expression, Ability To Do Quantitative Thinking, Analysis of Social Studies Materials, Analysis of Science Materials, and Use of Sources of Information. The Survey Battery consists of three tests: Reading, Correctness and Appropriateness of Expression, and Ability To Do Quantitative Thinking. For the Complete Battery, scores are reported for each of the seven tests and an Advanced Skills score. For the Survey Battery, scores are reported for each test and a composite. Predicted ACT and SAT scores are available to help with educational guidance. If the optional Questionnaire is used, results may be tabulated for teachers and guidance counselors as part of central scoring services.

Format: Examiner required; suitable for group use; Complete Battery 235 minutes, Survey Battery 90 minutes

Scoring: Hand key; may be machine scored

Cost: Contact publisher for current prices

Publisher: Riverside Publishing Company

Junior South African Individual Scales (JSAIS)

Copyright: 1979

Population: Children; ages 3 to 7

Purpose: Assesses cognitive functioning of children; used for psychological–educational diagnosis

Description: Measure of various aspects of a child's cognitive abilities using 22 scales. Twelve empirically selected scales yield the following IQ measures: General Intellectual Ability (GIQ), Verbal Ability (VIQ), and Perceptual-Performance Ability (PIQ), as well as estimates of memory and quantitative ability. Any scale or group of scales may be administered.

Format: Examiner required; not suitable for group use; untimed: typical time not available

Scoring: Hand key; examiner evaluated

Cost: Contact publisher

Publisher: Human Sciences Research Council

Kaufman Adolescent and Adult Intelligence Test (KAIT)
Alan S. Kaufman, Nadeen L. Kaufman

Copyright: 1993

Population: Ages 11 to 85 years and above

Purpose: Intended as a comprehensive measure of intelligence in test batteries used in clinical, neuropsychological, psychoeducational, and vocational evaluations within school systems, clinics, residential treatment centers, and hospitals

Description: The KAIT is a comprehensive measure of general intelligence. It includes separate Crystallized and Fluid Scales. Materials included in the kit: manual, 2 easels, 6 blocks in a box, audiocassette tape, Mystery Code Item Booklets, individual test records, briefcase. Special features: includes a well-standardized measure of Mental Status, provides age-based norms through age 85, and a measure of Fluid Intelligence.

Format: Individual administration; Core Battery 1 hour, Expanded Battery 1½ hours

Scoring: Examiner administration and interpretation; standard scores; ASSIST available for PC

Cost: Complete Kit (2 test easels, manual, 25 individual test records, 25 Mystery Code Item Booklets, auditory comprehension audiocassette, set of 6 Memory-for-Design blocks with holder) $495.00

Publisher: American Guidance Service

Kaufman Assessment Battery for Children (K-ABC)
Alan S. Kaufman, Nadeen L. Kaufman

Copyright: 1983

Population: Ages 2 years 6 months to 12 years 5 months

Purpose: Measures individual cognitive assessment

Description: Individually administered intelligence battery based on Luria-Das model of Sequential vs. Simultaneous information processing. Materials included in kit: administration and scoring manual, interpretive manual, three easel kits, Magic Window disk, triangles, photo series cards, Matrix Analogies Chips, and individual test records.

Format: Individual administration, 35 minutes at age 2½, 50 to 60 minutes at age 5, 75 to 85 minutes at ages 7 and above

Scoring: Examiner scored; scoring ASSIST program available for Apple II

Cost: Complete Kit (administration and scoring manual, interpretive manual, 25 individual test records) $329.95; with Deluxe Briefcase $399.95

Publisher: American Guidance Service

Kaufman Brief Intelligence Test (K-BIT)
Alan S. Kaufman, Nadeen L. Kaufman

Copyright: 1990

Population: Ages 4 to 90

Purpose: Used to obtain an estimate of intelligence; could be used for screening for giftedness, as part of a personality assessment, for reevaluations, or as part of routine intake for prisoners, patients, or recruits

Description: A brief, two-subtest measure of verbal and nonverbal intelligence. Special features: wide age range, excellent normative sample for such a brief test, and can be administered by nonpsychologists.

Format: Individual administration; 15 to 30 minutes

Scoring: Examiner administration and interpretation; standard scores

Cost: Complete Kit (easel, manual, individual test records) $105.95, with nylon carrying case $130.95

Publisher: American Guidance Service

Kuhlmann-Anderson Tests (KA), 8th Edition
Frederick Kuhlmann, Rose G. Anderson

Copyright: 1982

Population: Children, adolescents: Grades K through 12

Purpose: Evaluates students' academic ability and potential; used for placement and diagnosing individual learning abilities

Description: Multiple-item multiple-choice test with eight subtests, four of which are nonverbal in nature. The test is available in seven levels: Kindergarten, Grade 1, Grades 2–3, Grades 3–4, Grades 5–6, Grades 7–9, and Grades 9–12. The test yields standard scores for verbal, nonverbal, and full battery; national and local percentiles; and stanines. A booklet, answer sheet, and pencil are used. Available in large print. May be machine scored.

Format: Examiner required; suitable for group use; timed: 50–75 minutes

Scoring: Hand key; machine scored; scoring service available from publisher

Cost: Specimen Set (specify level) $18.40

Publisher: Scholastic Testing Service, Inc.

Measure of Questioning Skills
Garnet W. Miller

Copyright: 1993

Population: Children, adolescents; Grades 3–10

Purpose: Assesses critical thinking skills development; used to improve thinking skills

Description: Short-answer test shows four pictures. Time limit of 4 minutes on each item. Forms A and B are available. A booklet and pencil are used. Examiner must be certified for assessment.

Format: Individual administration; suitable for group use; examiner required; timed: 20 minutes

Scoring: Examiner evaluated

Cost: Starter Set $40.75

Publisher: Scholastic Testing Service, Inc.

Miller Analogies Test™ (MAT™)

Copyright: Updated yearly

Population: Adults

Purpose: Assists with the selection of candidates for graduate school

Description: A high-level mental ability test requiring the solution of problems stated as analogies. It consists of 100 partial analogies. One term in each analogy has been replaced with four options, only one of which is correct. The examinee is expected to select the option that creates a valid analogy.

Format: Examiner required; suitable for group use; timed: 50 minutes.

Scoring: Scored by The Psychological Corporation

Cost: Contact publisher

Publisher: The Psychological Corporation

National Academic Aptitude Tests: Non-Verbal Intelligence
Andrew Kobal, J. Wayne Wreightstone, Karl R. Kuntze

Copyright: 1964

Population: Adolescents, adults; Grades 10 and above

Purpose: Assesses mental abilities; used to indicate aptitude for academic training in such areas as engineering, chemistry, and other sciences

Description: Three nonverbal paper–pencil tests measuring mental aptitudes. The tests are Nonverbal Test of Spatial Relations, Comprehension of Physical Relations, and Graphic Relations. The test detects the ability to handle nonverbal materials at a high mental level. Items include pictorial and graphic work.

Format: Examiner required; suitable for group use; timed: 26 minutes

Scoring: Hand key

Cost: Specimen Set $4.00; 25 tests $13.75

Publisher: Psychometric Affiliates

National Academic Aptitude Tests: Verbal Intelligence
Andrew Kobal, J. Wayne Wreightstone, Karl R. Kuntze

Copyright: 1984

Population: Adolescents, adults; Grades 12 and above

Purpose: Assesses mental aptitudes important in academic and professional work; used for evaluation of applicants for employment and school programs

Description: Three verbal paper–pencil tests measuring mental aptitudes. The tests cover general information, academic and general science, mental alertness, comprehension, judgment, arithmetic reasoning, comprehension of relations, logical selection, analogies, and classification. Norms are provided for Grades 7–12, college students, administrative and executive employees, physicians, lawyers, and other professionals.

Format: Examiner required; suitable for group use; timed: 40 minutes

Scoring: Hand key

Cost: Specimen Set $4.00; 25 tests $13.75

Publisher: Psychometric Affiliates

New Jersey Test of Reasoning Skills
Virginia Shipman

Copyright: 1985

Population: Children, adolescents; ages 10 to 17; Grades 4 through 12

Purpose: Measures thinking and language-related reasoning skills

Description: Fifty-item paper–pencil multiple-choice test of reasoning ability in 22 skill areas, including converting statements, analogical reasoning, detecting underlying assumptions, detecting ambiguities, distinguishing differences of kind and degree, recognizing dubious authority, contradicting statements, and discerning causal relationships.

Format: Examiner required; suitable for group use; untimed: 40 minutes

Scoring: Hand key

Cost: $2.40

Publisher: Institute for the Advancement of Philosophy for Children

New South African Group Test (NSAGT)

Copyright: 1965

Population: Children, adolescents; ages 8 to 17

Purpose: Assesses intellectual ability; used for psychological and educational evaluation

Description: Six-subtest measure of general intellectual ability. Three subtests are verbal, and three are nonverbal. The test is available at three levels: Junior, Intermediate, and Senior. Two equivalent forms are available for the Junior and Senior Series. The test is available only to departments of education and private schools or to schools training teachers for the purpose of training and research.

Format: Examiner required; not suitable for group use; timed: 2 hours

Scoring: Hand key; examiner evaluated; may be machine scored

Cost: Contact publisher

Publisher: Human Sciences Research Council

Normal Battery A/76

Copyright: Not provided

Population: Adults

Purpose: Assesses academic ability; used for educational evaluation

Description: Multiple-item paper–pencil battery of six multiple-choice tests: Mental Alertness, Language Ability in English and Afrikaans, Reading Comprehension, Vocabulary, Spelling, and Arithmetic. Norms are available.

Format: Examiner required; suitable for group use; timed: 2 hours

Scoring: Hand key

Cost: Contact publisher

Publisher: Human Sciences Research Council

Otis-Lennon School Ability Test–Seventh Edition (OLSAT–7)
Arthur S. Otis, Roger T. Lennon

Copyright: 1995

Population: Children, adolescents; Grades K through 12

Purpose: Assesses general mental ability or scholastic aptitude

Description: Multiple-item test covering a broad range of cognitive abilities. Processes are measured on five item types: verbal comprehension, verbal reasoning, pictorial reasoning, figural reasoning, and quantitative reasoning. There are seven levels of the test for different grade levels.

Format: Examiner required; suitable for group use; timed: time varies by level, 75 minutes maximum

Scoring: Hand key; may be machine scored; computer scoring service available

Cost: Examination Kit (test booklet and directions for administering, practice test and directions for administering, machine-scorable answer document, practice test answer document) $16.00

Publisher: Harcourt® Brace Educational Measurement

Performance Assessments for ITBS® and TAP®/ITED®

Copyright: 1993/1994

Population: Grades 1 through 12

Purpose: Assesses students' strategic thinking and problem-solving capabilities

Description: Norm-referenced, free-response assessments in Integrated Language Arts, Mathematics, Social Studies, and Science. These assessments give students in Grades 1–12 an opportunity to apply content-area concepts and high-order thinking processes in real-life situations. The assessments are designed to evaluate the application of problem-solving processes; they provide a complement to multiple-choice achievement test batteries. They were developed to minimize the need to apply prior knowledge of specific content information. Performance assessments provide in-depth evaluation of the processes students use to mobilize prior knowledge and/or solve problems. Tasks in each assessment are weighted toward the higher levels of cognitive complexity. Each assessment uses a scenario to engage students in a real-world situation that requires them to use their strategic thinking and problem-solving capabilities. Assessments include Integrated Language Arts, Mathematics, Social Studies, and Science.

Format: Group administered; examiner required; about 1 hour

Scoring: Examiner evaluated

Cost: Each Assessment (pkg. of 25, includes Teacher's Directions) $25.50 each grade level; Manual for Scoring and Interpretation (each assessment and grade level) $14.50

Publisher: Riverside Publishing Company

Preliminary SAT/National Merit Scholarship Qualifying Test
Admissions Testing Program

Copyright: 1989

Population: Adolescents; Grade 11

Purpose: Assesses high school students' verbal and math reasoning abilities and evaluates readiness for college-level study; used as a preview of the SAT and serves as the qualifying test for student competitions conducted by the National Merit Scholarship Corp.

Description: Paper–pencil 115-item multiple-choice test measuring verbal and mathematical achievement and aptitude. The verbal section consists of 65 questions of four types: antonyms, sentence completion, analogies, and reading comprehension. The mathematical section consists of 50 questions applying graphic, spatial, numerical, symbolic, and logical techniques at a knowledge level no higher than elementary algebra and geometry. Special testing arrangements can be made for away-from-school testing, for students abroad, and for students with visual and other disabilities.

Format: Examiner required; suitable for group use; timed: 1 hour 40 minutes

Scoring: Computer scored

Cost: Contact publisher

Publisher: The College Board

Prescriptive Teaching Series
Sue Martin

Copyright: 1971

Population: Grades 1 through 8

Purpose: Measures individual child development; used for assessment of a child's strengths and weaknesses and for planning educational experiences

Description: Six-scale test of development in the following areas: visual, visual–motor, motor, auditory, reading and language, and math. The Visual Skills Test is composed of 22 skills with 104 subitems. The Visual–Motor Skills Booklet is composed of 28 items in four areas: body imagery, spatial orientation, visual–motor discrimination, and writing skills. The Motor Skills booklet consists of 166 items. The Auditory Skills Booklet consists of 31 items in several areas: auditory stimuli, speech response to auditory stimuli, oral reading, and phonetic analysis. The Reading and Language Skills booklet is composed of 152 skills, and Math Skills is composed of 315 skills. Each assessment uses a scenario to engage students in a real-world situation that requires them to use their strategic-thinking and problem-solving capabilities. Assessments include Integrated Language Arts, Mathematics, Social Studies, and Science.

Format: Examiner required; not suitable for group use; untimed: each rating period 15 minutes

Scoring: Hand key; examiner evaluated

Cost: Examiner's Set (10 copies all booklets, manual) $5.00; 25 Visual Skills, 25 Visual–Motor Skills each $15.00; 25 Motor Skills, 25 Auditory Skills, 25 Reading and Language Skills each $20.00; 25 Math Skills $35.00

Publisher: Psychologists and Educators, Inc.

Proverbs Test
Donald R. Gorham

Copyright: Not provided

Population: All ages

Purpose: Assesses abstract verbal functioning; used for individual clinical evaluation, screening, and clinical research

Description: Power test with 12 or 40 items measuring verbal comprehension. The subject is required to explain the meanings of proverbs. The 12-item free-answer format allows the subject to respond in his or her own words. A 40-item multiple-choice format is also available. The free-response forms are scored for abstractness and pertinence on a 3-point scale. The multiple-choice form is scored with a hand stencil. Forms I, II, and III are available for free-answer administration.

Format: Examiner required; individual test 10–30 minutes, group multiple-choice test 20–40 minutes

Scoring: Hand key; examiner evaluated

Cost: Complete kit (general manual, clinical manual, 10 each Forms I, II, III, scoring cards, 10 free-response form booklets, scoring stencils) $13.00

Publisher: Psychological Test Specialists

Quick Screening Scale of Mental Development
Katherine M. Banham

Copyright: 1963

Population: Children; ages 6 months to 10 years

Purpose: Assesses a child's mental development; identifies children in need of clinical evaluation; used in clinics, hospitals, and special schools

Description: Task-assessment and observational instrument arranged in five behavioral categories to measure a child's mental development. The test booklet consists of brief descriptions of behavior occurring in certain situations. The situations are to be checked and scored directly on the booklet. Instructions for administering are provided in the manual. Professional persons skilled in clinical psychology should interpret the results. The test provides a profile of scores in the five behavior categories for diagnostic purposes and educational guidance. Tentative norms for 50 children, along with the children's scores on the Cattell Infant Scale and the Stanford-Binet Scale, are provided.

Format: Examiner required; not suitable for group use; untimed: 30 minutes

Scoring: Hand key

Cost: Specimen Set $5.00; 25 tests $5.00

Publisher: Psychometric Affiliates

Riverside Performance Assessment Series (R-PAS)

Copyright: 1993

Population: Grades 1 through 12 (Levels A–F)

Purpose: Assesses students' thinking and process skills and problem-solving strategies

Description: Consists of constructed-response assessments in Reading, Mathematics, and Writing. These assessments provide students with an opportunity to engage in authentic activities involving strategic thinking and problem-solving skills and strategies. Reading assessments provide students with opportunities to construct and extend meaning by composing both brief and extended responses to questions, or by completing charts and diagrams. Writing assessments provide students with opportunities to engage in prewriting activities and to demonstrate drafting, composing, and revising skills. Mathematics assessments establish a context in which students exercise their problem-solving skills and reasoning capabilities.

Format: Group administered; examiner required; 50 minutes to 2 hours

Scoring: Examiner evaluated

Cost: Reading, Writing, or Mathematics Student Booklets (includes 25 booklets, 1 Teacher's Directions and Scoring Guide) $24.00 each level

Publisher: Riverside Publishing Company

SAT I: Scholastic Assessment Test—Reasoning Test

Copyright: 1989

Population: Adolescents; Grades 11 through 12

Purpose: Measures verbal and mathematics reasoning abilities that are related to successful performance in college; used to supplement secondary school records and other information in assessing readiness for college-level work

Description: Paper–pencil 135-item multiple-choice test measuring reading comprehension, vocabulary, and mathematical problem-solving ability involving arithmetic reasoning, algebra, and geometry. The test consists of two verbal sections of 85 questions, including 25 antonyms, 20 analogies, 15 sentence completion, and 25 reading questions and two mathematical sections of 50 questions, including approximately ⅔ multiple-choice and ⅓ quantitative comparison questions.

Format: Examiner required; suitable for group use; timed: 2½ hours

Scoring: Computer scored

Cost: Contact publisher

Publisher: The College Board

Senior Academic–Technical Aptitude Tests for Coloureds in Standards 8, 9, and 10 (SATA)

Copyright: 1977

Population: Adolescents, adults

Purpose: Measures the differential aptitudes of students and young adults with an educational

level of Standards 8–10; used for educational and occupational guidance

Description: Multiple-item paper–pencil battery of tests in two forms assessing aptitudes. Forms A and B include 10 tests: Verbal Reasoning, Nonverbal Reasoning I (figure series), Nonverbal Reasoning II (dominoes), computations, reading comprehension, spelling and vocabulary, mechanical reasoning, spatial perception (3D), comparison, and price controlling. Form B has an additional filing test. Stanines and percentile ranks are available.

Format: Examiner required; suitable for group use; untimed: 4 hours 30 minutes

Scoring: Hand key

Cost: Contact publisher

Publisher: Human Sciences Research Center

Senior Aptitude Tests (SAT)

Copyright: 1978

Population: Adolescents, adults

Purpose: Measures scholastic aptitude; used for educational counseling

Description: Multiple-item paper–pencil test of 12 specific aptitudes: verbal comprehension, calculations, disguised words, comparison, pattern completion, figural series, spatial (2D), spatial (3D), memory (paragraph), memory (symbols), coordination, and writing speed.

Format: Examiner required; suitable for group use; timed: 2 hours

Scoring: Hand key; examiner evaluated; may be machine scored

Cost: Contact publisher

Publisher: Human Sciences Research Council

Senior South African Individual Scale (SSAIS)

Copyright: 1964

Population: Children, adolescents; ages 6 to 17

Purpose: Assesses general intelligence in children; used for psychological–educational evaluation

Description: Nine-subtest measure of general

intellectual ability consisting of five verbal subtests and four nonverbal subtests. Verbal, Nonverbal, and Total IQ scores may be obtained.

Format: Examiner required; not suitable for group use; untimed: 50 minutes

Scoring: Hand key; examiner evaluated

Cost: Contact publisher

Publisher: Human Sciences Research Council

Structure of Intellect Learning Abilities Test (SOI)
Mary Meeker, Robert Meeker

Copyright: 1975

Population: Grades K to adult

Purpose: Measures an individual's learning abilities; used for cognitive clinical assessment, diagnosis, screening for giftedness, and identification of specific learning deficiencies

Description: Paper–pencil 430-item multiple-choice free-response test. The test measures 26 factors identified by Guilford's Structure-of-Intellect model. The operations of cognition, memory, evaluation, convergent production, and divergent production are applied to figural, symbolic, and semantic content. The test is available in two equivalent forms, A and B, and five shorter forms (gifted-screening, math, reading, primary screening, and reading readiness). The shorter forms use 10–12 subtest factors, printed test forms, and a manual with visual aids for group presentations. Training in administration and usage is required.

Format: Examiner required; suitable for group use in some situations; untimed: 2½ hours

Scoring: Hand key

Cost: Kit (10 test booklets, 5 each of Form A and Form B, manual, set of scoring keys, set of stimulus cards, 10 worksheets and profile forms) $210.00

Publisher: Western Psychological Services

Test of Cognitive Skills, Second Edition (TCS®/2)

Copyright: 1992

Population: Children, adolescents; Grades 2 through 12

Purpose: Assesses skills important for success in school settings; used for predicting school achievement and screening students for further evaluation

Description: Multiple-item paper–pencil multiple-choice test consisting of four subtests (Sequences, Analogies, Memory, Verbal Reasoning) assessing cognitive skills. The test is divided into six levels spanning grades 2–12. The test yields the following scores: number of correct responses, age or grade percentile rank, scale score, and cognitive skills index.

Format: Examiner required; suitable for group use; timed: 1 hour

Scoring: Hand key; may be computer scored

Cost: Multi-Level Examination Kit $52.00

Publisher: CTB/McGraw-Hill

Watson-Glaser Critical Thinking Appraisal™ (WGCTA™)
Goodwin Watson, Edward M. Glaser

Copyright: 1980

Population: Adults

Purpose: Measures the ability to think critically

Description: Eighty-item measure of the individual's ability to draw inferences based on sufficient data, recognize assumptions taken for granted in statements, reason by deduction to a conclusion that necessarily follows a statement, decide whether certain interpretations can be logically made, and determine whether arguments concerning a series of questions are strong or weak. Requires a ninth-grade reading level. Available in alternate forms.

Format: Examiner required; suitable for group use; timed: 40 minutes; untimed: 60 minutes

Scoring: Hand key

Cost: Examination Kit (Form A and B test booklets, answer document, and manual) $41.25

Publisher: The Psychological Corporation

Word and Number Assessment Inventory (WNAI)
Charles B. Johansson, Jean C. Johansson

Copyright: 1977

Population: Adolescents, adults

Purpose: Measures individual verbal and numerical aptitude; used for career and school counseling and employment screening

Description: Eighty-item paper–pencil multiple-choice test consisting of 50 vocabulary and 30 mathematics items on combined question-answer forms. The scores are compared to those of individuals at several educational levels and in a number of occupations. The test may be computer scored via mail-in service or using Arion II Teleprocessing.

Format: Self-administered; suitable for group use; untimed: 1 hour

Scoring: Computer scored

Cost: Manual $12.50; Interpretive Report $7.50 to $9.50 depending on quantity; Profile Report $4.75 to $5.50 depending on quantity

Publisher: NCS Assessments

Auditory

. . . .

Auditory Memory Span Test
Joseph M. Wepman, Anne Morency

Copyright: 1975

Population: Children; ages 5 to 8

Purpose: Measures the ability of children ages 5 to 8 to retain and recall words as auditory units, an essential capacity for learning how to speak and read accurately; used to identify specific auditory learning disabilities

Description: Oral-response test assessing the development of a child's ability to retain and recall familiar, isolated words received aurally. The test items are based on the most frequently used words in the spoken vocabulary of 5-year-old children. Norms are provided for children ages 5, 6, 7, and 8. Available in two equivalent forms, 1 and 2.

Format: Examiner required; not suitable for group use; untimed: 5–10 minutes

Scoring: Hand key

Cost: Complete Kit (includes 100 each of Forms 1 and 2, 1 manual) $55.00

Publisher: Western Psychological Services

Auditory Sequential Memory Test
Joseph M. Wepman, Anne Morency

Copyright: 1975

Population: Children; ages 5 to 8

Purpose: Measures the ability of children ages 5 to 8 to remember and repeat what they have just heard; used to diagnose specific auditory learning disabilities

Description: Oral-response test assessing a child's ability to repeat from immediate memory an increasing series of digits in the exact order of their verbal presentation. The test is useful for determining a child's readiness for learning to read and speak with accuracy and is also a determinant of spelling and arithmetic achievement. Norms are provided for children ages 5, 6, 7, and 8. Available in two equivalent forms, 1 and 2.

Format: Examiner required; not suitable for group use; untimed: 5 minutes

Scoring: Hand key

Cost: Complete Kit (100 each of Forms 1 and 2, manual) $55.00

Publisher: Western Psychological Services

Carrow Auditory–Visual Abilities Test (CAVAT)
Elizabeth Carrow-Woolfolk

Copyright: 1981

Population: Children; ages 4 to 10

Purpose: Measures auditory and visual perceptual, motor, and memory skills in children; used to identify language/learning problems, to analyze sources of auditory and/or visual difficulties, and for instructional programming

Description: Multiple-item set of two norm-referenced paper–pencil verbal–visual batteries containing 14 subtests. They allow comparison of individual performances in auditory and visual abilities by providing data on interrelationships among discrimination, memory, and motor skills. In the Visual Abilities battery, the categories are visual discrimination matching, visual discrimination memory, visual–motor copying, visual–motor memory, and motor speed. In the Auditory Abilities battery, the categories are picture memory, picture sequence selection, digits forward, digits backward, sentence repetition, word repetition, auditory blending, auditory discrimination in quiet, and auditory discrimination in noise. The Visual battery is not appropriate for blind subjects; the Auditory is not appropriate for the deaf.

Format: Examiner required; not suitable for group use; timed: 90 minutes for entire test, 2–13 minutes per test

Scoring: Examiner evaluated

Cost: Complete Kit (manual, response/score booklets, entry test book, auditory abilities battery book, visual abilities battery book, cassette, carrying case) $219.00

Publisher: PRO-ED, Inc.

Denver Audiometric Screening Test (DAST)
William K. Frankenburg, Marion Dreris, Elinor Kuzuk

Copyright: Not provided

Population: Ages 3 and above

Purpose: Detects children with hearing deficiencies; used to screen for 25dB loss; those who fail the test are referred for additional examination

Description: Function test in which a trained examiner creates a tone with an audiometer and checks the child's response; the child indicates whether the tone can be heard at different decibel levels.

Format: Examiner and audiometer required; not suitable for group use; untimed: 5–10 minutes

Scoring: Examiner evaluated

Cost: 25 tests $5.00; manual/workbook $10.25

Publisher: Denver Developmental Materials, Inc.

Goldman-Fristoe-Woodcock Test of Auditory Discrimination
Ronald Goldman, Macalyne Fristoe, Richard W. Woodcock

Copyright: 1974

Population: Ages 3 years 8 months to 70 years

Purpose: Measures the ability to discriminate speech sounds against two different backgrounds, quiet and noise

Description: Specifically designed to assess young children. Geared to children's vocabulary levels and limited attention spans. The individual responds by pointing to pictures of familiar objects. Writing and speaking are not required. In addition, the test can be used successfully with adults—particularly those with disabilities. Three parts, Training Procedure, Quiet Subtest, and Noise Subtest, provide practice in word–picture associations and provide two measures of speech–sound discrimination for maximum precision.

Format: Individual; 20–30 minutes

Scoring: Examiner administration and interpretation; standard scores; error analysis

Cost: Test kit (Easel-Kit containing test plates, manual, 50 response forms, audiocassette) $78.95

Publisher: American Guidance Service

Lindamood Auditory Conceptualization Test (LAC)
Charles H. Lindamood, Patricia C. Lindamood

Copyright: 1971

Population: All ages

Purpose: Measures an individual's ability to discriminate one speech sound from another and to perceive the number, order, and sameness or difference of speech sounds in sentences; used to diagnose auditory–conceptual dysfunctions and the need for remedial training

Description: Forty-item criterion-referenced test in which the subject arranges colored blocks (each symbolizing one speech sound) in a row to represent a sound pattern spoken by the examiner. The color of the blocks indicates sameness or difference, with a repeated sound symbolized by the same color block and a different sound by a different color. Materials include the manual, cassette, 24 wooden blocks in six colors, test forms, and examiner's cue sheets. A separate product, *Auditory Discrimination in Depth,* provides a training program. Available in Spanish.

Format: LAC (not appropriate for deaf subjects) administered by an examiner; not suitable for group use; untimed: 10 minutes

Scoring: Examiner evaluated

Cost: Complete Set $46.00

Publisher: PRO-ED, Inc.

Listening Assessment for ITBS®
H. D. Hoover, A. N. Hieronymus, Kathleen Oberley, Nancy Cantor

Copyright: 1994, 1987

Population: Grades 3 through 9 (Levels 9–14)

Purpose: Assesses strengths and weaknesses in the listening development of individuals and groups so that effective instruction can be planned; provides a model to help teachers and students become more aware of the importance of good listening strategies

Description: Emphasizes learning through reading, listening, and the use of visual materials. Consists of questions that measure Literal Meaning, Inferential Meaning, Following Directions, Visual Relationships, Numerical/Spatial/Temporal Relationships, and Speaker's Purpose, Point of View, or Style. There are a total of 95 questions on the test. Each test level is different, although questions that are included at the end of one test level also appear at the middle of the next level and toward the beginning of the next higher level. This is be-

cause tasks that would be relatively difficult for a third-grade student would be somewhat easier for a fourth-grade student, and much easier for a fifth-grader.

Format: Group administered; examiner required; approximately 35 minutes

Scoring: Scored by Riverside

Cost: Mark Reflex® Listening Answer Folder (pkg. of 50, includes 1 Directions for Administration and Score Interpretation and materials needed for machine scoring) $51.50

Publisher: Riverside Publishing Company

Listening Assessment for TAP®/ITED®
Oscar M. Haugh, Dale P. Scannell

Copyright: 1994, 1987

Population: Grades 9 through 12 (Levels 15–18)

Purpose: Assesses the developed listening skills of high school students; identifies and supports the most effective methods and procedures for enhancing students' listening skills

Description: The Listening Assessment for TAP/ITED is provided as a supplement to the Complete and Survey Batteries of Tests of Achievement and Proficiency (TAP) and the Iowa Tests of Educational Development (ITED). This assessment provides teachers and students with valuable insights into students' strengths and weaknesses in the important art of listening. The assessment consists of questions that measure the following content objectives: Literal Meaning, Inferential Meaning, and Speaker's Purpose or Point of View. In addition, questions are cross-classified according to four levels of cognition: knowledge/information, comprehension, application/analysis, and synthesis/evaluation. The test consists of 100 questions in four overlapping levels.

Format: Group administered; examiner required; approximately 40 minutes

Scoring: Scored by Riverside

Cost: Mark Reflex® Listening Answer Folder (pkg. of 50, includes 1 Directions for Administration and Score Interpretation and materials needed for machine scoring) $44.00

Publisher: Riverside Publishing Company

Listening Comprehension Tests in English for Standards 5 and 8

Copyright: 1979

Population: Children, adolescents

Purpose: Measures ability to understand spoken English; used for educational evaluation

Description: Multiple-item paper–pencil tests of listening comprehension for students in Standards 5 and 8. Pupils listen to recorded questions and mark answers on answer sheets. Materials include an audiocassette tape with questions for two alternate forms, A and B.

Format: Examiner required; suitable for group use; untimed: 50 minutes

Scoring: Hand key; examiner evaluated

Cost: Contact publisher

Publisher: Human Sciences Research Council

Listening Test

Mark Barrett, Rosemary Huisingh, Linda Bowers, Carolyn LoGiudice, Jane Orman

Copyright: 1992

Population: Children; ages 6 to 11; Grades 1 through 6

Purpose: Evaluates the effect of listening on children's ability to learn in the classroom; helps them transfer what they learn to daily life; used with communicative disorders, low academic performance, and classroom behavior difficulties

Description: Oral-response 75-item verbal, point-to test with five subtests and a classroom listening scale: Main Idea, Details, Concepts, Reasoning, and Story Comprehension. Suitable for individuals with physical, hearing, or mental impairment.

Format: Individual administration; examiner required; untimed: approximately 35 minutes

Scoring: Examiner evaluated; no scoring service available

Cost: Manual and 20 test forms $59.95

Publisher: LinguiSystems, Inc.

Oliphant Auditory Discrimination Memory Test

Genevieve Oliphant

Copyright: 1971

Population: Grades 1 through 8

Purpose: Evaluates the ability of grade-school students to hear and discriminate sounds and words; used to identify students needing further testing and to diagnose the relationship between perceptual problems and learning disabilities

Description: Paper–pencil 20-item test measuring how well students discriminate sounds and remember what they hear. Each item presents the student with two words, which are either alike or minimally different. The examiner then presents a third word, and the student is asked to decide whether that word is the same as the first or second word or whether all three words are the same. The words are all single syllable in a consonant–vowel–consonant format.

Format: Group; 30–45 minutes

Scoring: Examiner administration and interpretation

Cost: Kit $4.00 each; Specimen Set $1.60

Publisher: Educators Publishing Service, Inc.

Oliphant Auditory Synthesizing Test

Genevieve Oliphant

Copyright: 1971

Population: Grades 1 through 8

Purpose: Evaluates the ability of grade-school students to hear and discriminate sounds and words; used to identify students needing further testing and to diagnose the relationship between perceptual problems and learning disabilities

Description: Paper–pencil 20-item test measuring how well students discriminate sounds and remember what they hear. Each item presents the student with two words, which are either alike or minimally different. The examiner then presents a third word, and the student is asked to decide whether that word is the same as the first or second word or whether all three words are the same. The words are all single syllable in a consonant–vowel–consonant format.

Format: Group; 30–45 minutes

Scoring: Examiner administration and interpretation

Cost: Kit $4.00 each; Specimen Set $1.60

Publisher: Educators Publishing Service, Inc.

SCAN: Screening Test for Auditory Processing Disorders
Robert W. Keith

Copyright: 1986

Population: Children; ages 3 to 11

Purpose: Identifies central auditory disorders in children

Description: Multiple-item standardized response test consisting of four subtests of auditory abilities. In the Filtered Words subtest, the child hears words in which high-frequency sounds have been filtered. In the Auditory Figure Ground subtest, the child hears words with background noise. In the Auditory Fusion subtest, the child hears words that consist of low- and high-pass filtered bands presented to both ears separately, then split and presented to different ears simultaneously. In the Competing Words subtest, the child hears a different word in each ear simultaneously.

Format: Examiner required; not suitable for group use; untimed: 15 minutes

Scoring: Hand scored

Cost: Complete Program (manual, audiocassette, and protocol) $100.50

Publisher: The Psychological Corporation

Test for Auditory Figure–Ground Discrimination (TAFD)

Copyright: 1981

Population: Children; ages 5 to 10

Purpose: Measures ability to attend to one sound and to perceive it in relation to, but separate from, competing sounds; used for educational evaluation

Description: Seven-subtest measure of auditory perception of specific sounds against a variety of background sounds (e.g., a bicycle bell against traffic noise or speech against background music). The child responds verbally to tape-recorded stimuli. Materials include a cassette recording of the TAFD. Available to professional personnel affiliated with education departments and others who can document their expertise.

Format: Examiner required; not suitable for group use; timed: 1 hour

Scoring: Examiner evaluated

Cost: Contact publisher

Publisher: Human Sciences Research Council

Wepman's Auditory Discrimination Test, 2nd Edition
Joseph M. Wepman

Copyright: 1987

Population: Children; ages 4 to 8

Purpose: Measures the auditory discrimination ability of children ages 4 to 8; used to identify specific auditory learning disabilities for possible remediation

Description: Oral-response test in which children are verbally presented pairs of words and asked to discriminate between them. The test predicts articulatory speech defects and certain remedial reading problems. The second edition is identical to the original edition except for scoring. In the second edition, scoring is based on a correct score rather than on the "error" basis of the original edition. The 1987 manual contains standardization tables for children ages 4 to 8, a 5-point qualitative rating scale, an interpretation section discussing how the test results may be used, reports on research using the test, and selected references.

Format: Examiner required; not suitable for group use; untimed: 10–15 minutes

Scoring: Hand key

Cost: Complete Kit (100 each of Forms 1A and 2A; 1 manual) $80.00

Publisher: Western Psychological Services

Wepman's Auditory Memory Battery
Joseph M. Wepman
Anne Morency

Copyright: Not provided

Population: Ages 5 to 8

Purpose: Assesses auditory memory in young children

Description: These two tests help determine whether children have the basic memory skills required for reading, spelling, and arithmetic.

Auditory Memory Span Test assesses ability to retain and recall familiar, isolated words received aurally, one of the basic abilities needed in order to learn to read phonetically and to speak accurately. Auditory Sequential Memory Test assesses ability to repeat from immediate memory an increasing series of digits.

Format: Individually administered; examiner required; 5 minutes each test

Scoring: Examiner evaluated

Cost: Set (1 kit for each test; kits include 100 each of Forms 1 and 2, 1 manual) $100.00

Publisher: Western Psychological Services

Behavior and Counseling

Attitudes

Achievement Identification Measure (AIM)
Sylvia B. Rimm

Copyright: 1985

Population: Children, adolescents; Grades K through 12

Purpose: Identifies characteristics contributing to underachievement in students; used by teachers and parents for communication and intervention

Description: Paper–pencil 77-item inventory in which parents assess their child's characteristics in five areas (Competition, Responsibility, Independence/Dependence Achievement, Achievement Communication, Respect/Dominance) by responding "no," "to a small extent," "average," "more than average," or "definitely" to each item. The test distinguishes between achievers and underachievers. Parents receive a computer-scored report with a manual that explains the meaning of the scores.

Format: Self-administered; suitable for group use; untimed: 20 minutes

Scoring: Computer scored

Cost: Class set of 30 tests and computer scoring $100.00; Specimen Set $12.00

Publisher: Educational Assessment Service, Inc.

Achievement Identification– Teacher Observation (AIM–TO)
Sylvia B. Rimm

Copyright: 1988

Population: Children, adolescents; Grades K through 12

Purpose: Identifies characteristics contributing to achievement in students; used by teachers

Description: Paper/pencil 70-item inventory in which teachers assess students' achievement characteristics in five areas (Competition, Responsibility, Achievement Communication, Independence/Dependence, Respect, Dominance). A computer scoring service is available.

Format: Examiner required; not suitable for group use; timed: 20 minutes

Scoring: Computer scored

Cost: 30 tests $100.00; Specimen Set $12.00

Publisher: Educational Assessment Service, Inc.

Achievement Motivation Profile (AMP)

Jotham Friedland, Harvey Mandel, Sander Marcus

Copyright: Not provided

Population: Adolescents, adults

Purpose: Used to evaluate underachieving or unmotivated students age 14 and older

Description: This self-report inventory is composed of 140 brief, self-descriptive statements which produce scale scores in four areas: motivation for achievement, interpersonal strengths, inner resources, and work habits. Students respond to items using a 5-point scale. The AMP is designed specifically to measure motivation and is validated against objective measures of achievement.

Format: Self-administered; suitable for group use; 20–30 minutes

Scoring: Hand key or computer scored

Cost: Kit (25 AutoScore™ forms, 1 manual, 2 test report prepaid mail-in answer sheets for computer scoring and interpretation) $98.00; microcomputer disk (IBM; good for 25 uses) $185.00

Publisher: Western Psychological Services

Achieving Behavioral Competencies

Lawrence T. McCarron, Kathleen M. Ford, Melody B. McCarron

Copyright: 1992

Population: Adolescents, adults; ages 13 and above

Purpose: Assesses coping skills, work habits, and peer relationships; used for the development of social and emotional skills

Description: Eighty-item teacher rating scale comprised of 20 competencies within four skill areas.

Format: Rating scale; Untimed

Scoring: Computer scored; test scoring service included

Cost: $137.50

Publisher: McCarron-Dial Systems, Inc.

ACTeRS: Parent Form

Rina K. Ullmann, Esther K. Sleator, Robert L. Sprague

Copyright: 1996

Population: Grades Pre-K through 12

Purpose: Aids in diagnosis of attention-deficit disorder with or without hyperactivity; used as a screening device to differentiate children with ADD and those who may have other learning disabilities; useful for monitoring medication levels

Description: Paper–pencil or computer-administered 25-item multiple-choice test assessing behavior relevant to Attention-Deficit Disorder. Provides separate scores for five factors: Attention, Hyperactivity, Social Skills, Opposition Behavior, and Early Childhood. The computer version for IBM PC and compatible systems supports both the ACTeRS: Parent Form and the ADD-H: Comprehensive Teacher's Rating Scale (ACTeRS).

Format: Examiner required; not suitable for group use; untimed: 10 minutes

Scoring: Computer scored; hand key

Cost: Kit (100 rating/profile forms, manual) $64.00; 50-administration software $100.00; 100-administration software $175.00

Publisher: MetriTech, Inc.

ADD-H Comprehensive Teacher's Rating Scale (ACTeRS)

Rina K. Ullmann, Ester K. Sleator, Robert L. Sprague

Copyright: 1987

Population: Children; Grades K through 8

Purpose: Aids in diagnosis of attention-deficit disorder with or without hyperactivity; used as a screening device to differentiate between children with ADD and those who may have other learning disabilities; useful in monitoring children's medication levels

Description: Paper–pencil or computer-administered 24-item multiple-choice test assessing behavior relevant to the diagnosis of attention-deficit disorder. Provides separate scores for four factors: Attention, Hyperactivity,

Social Skills, and Oppositional. The classroom teacher rates items on a 5-point scale ranging from "almost never" to "almost always." An ACTeRS Profile (Boys' and Girls'; forms) is generated. The computer version for IBM PC and compatible systems supports both the teacher's form and the ACTeRS: Parent Form. APA purchase restrictions apply.

Format: Examiner required; not suitable for group use; untimed: 10 minutes

Scoring: Hand scored; computer scored

Cost: Kit (100 rating/profile forms/profiles, manual) $64.00; Computer software—50 administrations $100.00, 100 administrations $175.00

Publisher: MetriTech, Inc.

American Drug and Alcohol Survey (ADAS)

Copyright: 1996

Population: Children, adolescents; Grades 4 through 12

Purpose: Assesses substance abuse experience and attitudes; used for prevention program planning and evaluation

Description: Multiple-choice paper–pencil test. Adolescent Form has 58 questions; Children's Form has 51 questions. The ADAS is not an instrument for clinical use with individuals. It is an anonymous survey to be administered to a group. Reports present percentage of respondents who answer in certain ways. RMBSI scans surveys, runs analyses, and produces comprehensive reports on the student population surveyed. Forms are optical-scan forms processed by the publisher. Adolescent Form is available in Spanish.

Format: Self-administered; suitable for group use; untimed: approximately 30 minutes

Scoring: Test scoring service available from publisher

Cost: Varies based on number of forms and reports ordered

Publisher: Rocky Mountain Behavioral Science Institute, Inc.

Arlin-Hills Attitude Surveys
Marshall Arlin, David Hills

Copyright: 1976

Population: Children, adolescents; Grades K through 12

Purpose: Assesses student attitudes; used for research on student attitudes

Description: Four 15-item paper–pencil questionnaires measuring student attitudes in the following areas: attitude toward teachers, attitude toward learning, attitude toward language, and attitude toward arithmetic. Items are presented in a cartoon format. Because group results are used, the four instruments may be distributed at random to students within a classroom. Each instrument is divided into three levels: Primary for Grades K–3, Elementary for Grades 4–6, and High School for Grades 7–12. Computer scoring is recommended for groups.

Format: Examiner required; suitable for group use; untimed: 5–10 minutes

Scoring: Hand key; may be computer scored

Cost: Contact publisher

Publisher: Psychologists and Educators, Inc.

Children's Academic Intrinsic Motivation Inventory (CAIMI)
Adele E. Gottfried

Copyright: 1986

Population: Children; Grades 4 through 8

Purpose: Assesses academic motivation in children; used to identify students with academic difficulties and to differentiate motivation from achievement and ability factors; also used in course selection and individual and district-level program planning

Description: Paper–pencil 122-item instrument measuring motivation for learning in both general and specific areas. The 44 questions comprise five scales: Reading, Math, Social Studies, Science, and General. A profile form is provided. Results are reported as *T*-scores or percentiles.

Format: Examiner/self-administered; suitable for group use; untimed: 20–30 minutes

Scoring: Hand key

Cost: Kit (manual, 25 test booklets, 25 profile forms) $49.95

Publisher: Psychological Assessment Resources, Inc.

Fennema/Sherman Math Attitudes Scales
Elizabeth Fennema, Julia A. Sherman

Copyright: 1976

Population: Adolescents

Purpose: Measures high school adolescents' attitudes toward learning mathematics by males/females

Description: Paper–pencil 173-item Likert-type scales

Format: Group or individual administration; examiner required; untimed

Scoring: Hand key; examiner evaluated

Cost: $18.00

Publisher: Select Press

Group Achievement Identification Measure (GAIM)
Sylvia B. Rimm

Copyright: 1986

Population: Children, adolescents; ages 10 to 18; Grades 5 through 12

Purpose: Identifies students with characteristics that may contribute to underachievement; used by classroom teachers to help underachieving students

Description: Paper–pencil 90-item inventory assessing achievement characteristics. The inventory directs both teachers and parents to the areas in which the child must change in order to achieve in school. The test yields a Total Score as well as five dimension scores: Competition, Responsibility, Achievement Communication, Independence/Dependence, and Respect Dominance. The test is used for both male and female. A computer scoring service is available from the publisher.

Format: Examiner required; suitable for group use; untimed; time varies

Scoring: Computer scored

Cost: Specimen set $12.00; class set of 30 tests $100.00

Publisher: Educational Assessment Service, Inc.

Interest-a-Lyzer
Joseph S. Renzulli

Copyright: 1977

Population: Children, adolescents

Purpose: Examines the present and potential interests of upper-elementary and junior high school students; used as a basis for group discussions and in-depth counseling

Description: Multiple-item paper–pencil instrument consisting of a series of open-ended questions structured to highlight general patterns of interest. Items cover mathematical, historical, political, scientific, artistic, and technical interest areas.

Format: Examiner required; suitable for group use; untimed: time varies

Scoring: Examiner evaluated

Cost: 100 questionnaires $28.95

Publisher: Creative Learning Press, Inc.

Inventory for Counseling and Development
Norman S. Giddan, F. Reid Creech, Victor R. Lovell

Copyright: 1987

Population: College students

Purpose: Identifies the strengths, assets, and coping skills of college students; used in on-campus counseling centers, private and community mental health centers, college health centers, and hospitals as a predictor of personal, social, and academic functioning

Description: True–false 449-item test consisting of 23 scales. The 15 substantive scales measure personality dimensions affecting an individual's personal, social, and academic functioning. Four criterion scales measure academic characteristics. One criterion scale measures stereotypes related to sex role, and three validity scales assess response-style characteristics. A profile report is available.

Format: Untimed: 1 hour

Scoring: Computer scored; hand scoring materials available

Cost: Manual $12.95; interpretive reports $7.50 to $9.50; profile reports $4.50 to $5.95

Publisher: NCS Assessments

Learning Process Questionnaire (LPQ)
J. Biggs

Copyright: 1989

Population: Adolescents; Grades 8 through 12

Purpose: Assesses a student's general orientation toward learning by identifying the motives and strategies that comprise an approach to learning; used by teachers and counselors

Description: Paper–pencil 36-item test identifying the motives and strategies that comprise a student's approach to learning. Items are rated in a Likert-scale format. Stanine and percentile rank scores are yielded for total raw score conversion. Separate profiles are provided for motive and strategy subscales. One of two tests in a series (see entry for Study Process Questionnaire).

Format: Examiner required; suitable for group use; timed: 20 minutes

Scoring: Hand key; may be machine scored

Cost: Contact publisher

Publisher: The Australian Council for Educational Research Limited

MSI Mentoring Style Indicator
William A. Gray, Terry D. Anderson

Copyright: 1987

Population: Adults

Purpose: Selects, matches, and trains mentors and protégés for schools

Description: Six-situation multiple-choice paper–pencil test. A 10th-grade reading level is required. Forms are available for college stu-

dents and new teachers. Computer version is available for PC format.

Format: Self-administered; suitable for group use; untimed

Scoring: Self-scored

Cost: $8.00/test

Publisher: Mentoring Institute, Inc.

My Book of Things and Stuff: An Interest Questionnaire for Young Children
Ann McGeevy

Copyright: 1982

Population: Children; ages 6 to 11

Purpose: Assesses the interests of young children

Description: Multiple-item paper–pencil questionnaire including over 40 illustrated items focusing on the special interests and learning styles of students. The book also includes a teacher's section, an interest profile sheet, sample pages from a journal, and bibliographies of interest-centered books and magazines for children. All questionnaire pages are perforated and prepared on blackline masters so that copies can be made for an entire class.

Format: Examiner required; suitable for group use; untimed: time varies

Scoring: Examiner evaluated

Cost: Questionnaire booklet $14.95

Publisher: Creative Learning Press, Inc.

Parent's Observation of Study Behaviors Survey
Mary Elizabeth Paterra

Copyright: 1991

Population: Adults

Purpose: Measures a parent's changes in study behaviors and attitudes

Description: Paper–pencil 28-item test with the following subtests: Positive Attitudes, Useful Work Habits, Efficient Learning Tools, and Effective Test Taking. Pre/posttest comparable numerical totals are yielded. A pencil and three-page survey questionnaire are used. A seventh-grade reading level is required.

Format: Individual/self-administered; untimed

Scoring: Self-scored

Cost: Pre/Posttest $3.00

Publisher: Cambridge Stratford, Ltd.

PHSF Relations Questionnaire

Copyright: 1970

Population: Children, adolescents

Purpose: Assesses adjustment level of high school students; used for counseling and guidance

Description: Paper–pencil questionnaire of 12 aspects of personal adjustment, including self-confidence, self-esteem, self-control, nervousness, health, family influences, personal freedom, sociability-G, sociability-S, moral sense, formal relations, and a desirability scale.

Format: Examiner required; suitable for group use; untimed: 30 minutes

Scoring: Hand key; examiner evaluated; may be machine scored

Cost: Contact publisher

Publisher: Human Sciences Research Council

Responsibility and Independence Scale for Adolescents (RISA)
John Salvia, John T. Neisworth, Mary W. Schmidt

Copyright: 1990

Population: 12 years to 19 years 11 months

Purpose: Measures adolescents' adaptive behavior

Description: Nationally standardized instrument specifically designed to measure adolescents' behavior in terms of responsibility and independence. Whereas most measures of adaptive behavior target low-level skills, RISA assesses higher-level behaviors. Subscales include domestic skills, money management, citizenship, personal planning, transportation skills, career development, self-management,

social maturity, and social communication.

Format: Individually administered; examiner required; 30–45 minutes

Scoring: Examiner evaluated

Cost: Complete program (test book, examiner's manual, 25 response forms) $135.00

Publisher: Riverside Publishing Company

School Attitude Measure (SAM)
Marci M. Enos, Larry Dolan, John Wick

Copyright: 1989

Population: Children, adolescents; ages 5 to 18

Purpose: Used to identify students at risk; assesses student attitude as it relates to school achievement

Description: Five-level multiple-choice paper–pencil test divided into five scales: Motivation for Schooling, Academic Self-Concept: Performance Based, Academic Self-Concept: Reference Based, Student's Sense of Control over Performance, and Student's Instructional Mastery. Each scale consists of a set of statements followed by four response choices: never agree, sometimes agree, usually agree, and always agree. Level C/D is used with Grades 1–2; Level E/F is used with Grades 3–4; Level G/H is used with Grades 5–6; Level I/J is used with Grades 7–8; and Level K/L is used with Grades 9–12. Raw scores are transformed by statistical analysis using the Rasch model. The user, then, will have available both the raw scores and logit scores derived through the Rasch analysis. This facilitates comparison between student scores and between the scores on the five scales. This is one test in the Comprehensive Assessment Program series and is a revision of the 1980 SAM.

Format: Examiner required; suitable for group use; timed: time varies by level

Scoring: Machine-scored; hand key; test scoring available through publisher

Cost: Machine-scorable test booklets (packages of 25) Levels C/D and E $37.10; Reusable Test Booklets (package of 25) Levels E–L $28.75; answer sheets (package of 35) $12.40; directions $3.90

Publisher: American College Testing

School Environment Preference Survey
Leonard V. Gordon

Copyright: 1978

Population: Children, adolescents; Grades 1 through 12

Purpose: Measures work role socialization as it occurs in the traditional school setting; used for academic and disciplinary student counseling, vocational counseling, and instructional planning

Description: Paper–pencil 24-item test measuring a student's levels of commitment to the set of attitudes, values, and behaviors necessary for employment and that are fostered and rewarded in most school settings. The scales measured are structured role orientation, self-subordination, traditionalism, rule conformity, and uncriticalness.

Format: Examiner required; suitable for group use; untimed: 10–15 minutes

Scoring: Hand key; may be computer scored

Cost: Specimen Set $6.75; 25 forms $9; keys $13.50; manual $3.75

Publisher: EdITS/Educational and Industrial Testing Service

Search Institute Profiles of Student Life: Alcohol and Other Drugs

Copyright: 1988, 1990

Population: Adolescents; ages 11 to 18

Purpose: Assesses student attitudes, behaviors, and perceptions concerning alcohol and other drugs; used as baseline information for programming in public and private schools and youth-serving agencies

Description: Paper–pencil 119-item survey that provides a portrait of alcohol and drug use patterns for establishing program needs and priorities. May be used to evaluate the impact of prevention programs. The information is

analyzed and presented in a 35-page school report containing graphics and explanatory text.

Format: Examiner required; suitable for group use; untimed: 30 minutes

Scoring: Machine scored; test scoring service provided by publisher

Cost: Charge per student $2.00; report $500.00

Publisher: Search Institute

Search Institute Profiles of Student Life: Attitudes and Behavior

Copyright: 1989

Population: Adolescents; ages 11 to 18

Purpose: Assesses the behaviors and attitudes that affect student motivation and achievement; used as baseline information for programming in public and private schools and youth-serving agencies

Description: Paper–pencil 152-item survey that includes topics such as student attitudes and efforts in school, prosocial and antisocial behavior, sexuality, peer and parent relationships, self-esteem, alienation, alcohol and other drug use and nonuse, stress, abuse, eating disorders, general well-being, and program interests. Yields a comprehensive report of students' attitudes, understandings, and responses to student life.

Format: Examiner required; suitable for group use; untimed: 45 minutes

Scoring: Machine scored; test scoring service provided by publisher

Cost: Charge per student $2.00; report $500.00

Publisher: Search Institute

Student Adjustment Inventory
James R. Barclay

Copyright: 1989

Population: Children, adolescents; Grades 5 through 14

Purpose: Assesses common affective-social problem areas; results help students understand their own attitudes and feelings that may interfere with learning and school adjustment

Description: Computer-administrated or paper–pencil 78-item inventory yielding scores in self-esteem, group interaction and social processes, self-discipline, communication, energy/effort, learning/studying, and attitude toward the learning environment. IBM PC–compatible computer software administers and scores the test and generates reports.

Format: Self administered; suitable for small group use; untimed: 30 minutes

Scoring: Computer scored; mail-in service

Cost: 50-administration software $225.00; mail-in report kit (test materials, manual, and processing fee for 5 reports) $34.00

Publisher: MetriTech, Inc.

Student Assessment of Study Behaviors
Mary Elizabeth Paterra

Copyright: 1991

Population: Adolescents; Grades 7 through 12

Purpose: Used in conjunction with study skills instruction to measure changes in study behaviors and attitudes

Description: Paper–pencil 42-item test with the following subtests: positive attitudes, useful work habits, efficient learning tools, good comprehension, high-performance writing, and effective test taking. Pre- and posttest comparable numerical totals are yielded. A pencil and a four-page survey questionnaire are used. A seventh-grade reading level is required.

Format: Self-administered; suitable for group use; untimed: 20 minutes

Scoring: Self scored

Cost: Pre Post Set $3.00

Publisher: Cambridge Stratford, Ltd.

Student Evaluation Scale (SES)
William T. Martin, Sue Martin

Copyright: 1974

Population: Ages 6 to 21

Purpose: Assesses attitudes and behaviors of elementary and secondary school children; used to evaluate educational and social–emotional responses to school

Description: Paper–pencil 52-item test of two areas of student attitudes: educational response and social–emotional response. Items are rated by teachers or guidance personnel after observing students for a 2- to 3-week period. The rating scale ranges from 0 (never) to 3 (always).

Format: Self-administered; suitable for group use; untimed: 5 minutes

Scoring: Examiner evaluated

Cost: Specimen Set (includes manual) $5.00; 25 rating and profile forms $6.75

Publisher: Psychologists and Educators, Inc.

Student Motivation Diagnostic Questionnaire
Kevin M. Matthews, Carvin L. Brown

Copyright: 1989

Population: Children, adolescents; ages 5 to 18; Grades K through 12

Purpose: Assesses student motivation

Description: Paper–pencil 64-item multiple-choice test assessing student motivation. Each of the student's subject areas are assessed by four subtests: Teacher Expectation, Student Self-Concept of Ability, Future Utility of Subject, and Student Attitude Toward Teacher. The test is used by schools to determine teacher motivation, which also affects student motivation.

Format: Examiner required; suitable for group use; untimed: time varies

Scoring: Machine scored; may be computer scored

Cost: 25 forms $55.00

Publisher: Humanics Psychological Test Corporation

Student Motivation Diagnostic Questionnaire (Short Form Second Revision)
Kenneth M. Matthews

Copyright: 1994

Population: Grades 4 through 12

Purpose: Identifies aspects of student motivation in need of improvement

Description: Paper–pencil 16-item questionnaire assessing teachers' expectations, students' beliefs about relevance, attitudes toward teachers, and calculative self-concepts in Language Arts, Mathematics, Science, and Social Studies.

Format: Untimed: less than 20 minutes

Scoring: Hand scored; computer scoring available

Cost: 25 forms $55.00

Publisher: Kenneth M. Matthews, Ed.D.

Study Attitudes and Methods Survey (SAMS)
William B. Michael, Joan J. Michael, Wayne S. Zimmerman

Copyright: 1985

Population: Adolescents, adults; Grades 7 and above

Purpose: Diagnoses habits and attitudes which may be preventing junior high school, high school, and college students from achieving full academic potential; used in the classroom and for schoolwide screening to identify students likely to benefit from counseling

Description: Multiple-item paper–pencil inventory assessing dimensions of a motivational, noncognitive nature that relate to school achievement and contribute to a student's performance beyond those measured by traditional ability tests. The student's profile can provide the requisite insights and guidelines for study habit improvement. Scales measured by the SAMS are Academic Interest/Love of Learning, Academic Drive, Study Methods, Lack of Anxiety, Lack of Manipulation, and Lack of Alienation toward Authority. Norms are provided for high school and college level.

Format: Examiner required; suitable for group use; untimed: 20–30 minutes

Scoring: Hand key; may be computer scored

Cost: Specimen Set (manual, all forms) $6.75, 25 booklets and answer sheets $12.75; keys

$13.50; manual $3.00

Publisher: EdITS/Educational and Industrial Testing Service

Study Process Questionnaire (SPQ)
J. Biggs

Copyright: 1989

Population: Tertiary students

Purpose: Assesses a student's general orientation toward learning by identifying the motives and strategies that comprise an approach to learning; used by teachers or counselors

Description: Paper–pencil 42-item test identifying the motives and strategies that comprise the student's approach to learning. Items are rated on a Likert-scale format. Stanine and percentile rank scores are presented for total raw score conversion. Separate profiles are presented for motive and strategy subscales. The test is one of two in a series (see entry for Learning Process Questionnaire).

Format: Examiner required; suitable for group use; timed: 20 minutes

Scoring: Hand key; may be machine scored

Cost: Contact publisher

Publisher: The Australian Council for Educational Research Limited

Subsumed Abilities Test—A Measure of Learning Efficiency (SAT)
Martin M. Bruce

Copyright: 1957

Population: Adolescents, adults; Grades 6 and above

Purpose: Measures, nonverbally, the subject's ability and willingness to learn; used for student placement, vocational counseling, and job selection

Description: Paper–pencil 60-item test consisting of 30 pairs of items, each of which is composed of four line drawings. The student analyzes one with three others, resulting in a Potential Abilities Score and a Demonstrated Abilities Score based on the student's ability to conceptualize, form abstractions, and recognize identicals. Designed for individuals with at least a sixth-grade education. Suitable for individuals with physical, hearing, or visual disabilities.

Format: Examiner required; may be self-administered; suitable for group use; timed: 30 minutes

Scoring: Hand key

Cost: Package of tests $55.00; manual and manual supplement (1984) $38.50; key-tabulation sheets $25.50; Specimen Set $42.50

Publisher: Martin M. Bruce, Ph.D.

Test of Attitude Toward School (TAS)

Guy Thibaudeau

Copyright: 1984

Population: Children, adolescents; Grades 1 through 12

Purpose: Assesses an individual's attitude toward school

Description: Oral-response test assessing two principal components of scholastic attitude: emotional disposition toward school and tendencies to action. The administrator presents to the child drawings showing situations that arise at school and notes how the examinee interprets the situations depicted. The number of situations liked and hated are calculated. Also available in French.

Format: Examiner required; not suitable for group use; untimed: time varies

Scoring: Examiner evaluated

Cost: Manual $15.00; set of drawings $12.00; 25 questionnaires $18.00

Publisher: Institute of Psychological Research, Inc.

Learning Style

Cornell Learning and Study Skills Inventory (Classic)

Walter Pauk, Russell N. Cassel

Copyright: Not provided

Population: Adolescents, adults; Grades 7 through 12, college

Purpose: Assesses skills important to effective

learning in high school and college; used for educational counseling

Description: Paper–pencil 120-item test of study skills yielding scores in goal orientation, activity structure, scholarly skills, lecture mastery, textbook mastery, examination mastery, and self-mastery and a study efficiency total score. Twenty-two of the items are included in a Reading Validity Index, which determines whether the student has responded thoughtfully. Two forms, the College Form and the Secondary School Form, are available. College Form items are answered on a 5-point ordinal scale ranging from seldom to always. The Secondary School Form items are written in a true–false format.

Format: Self-administered; suitable for group use; untimed: 30–45 minutes

Scoring: Hand key

Cost: Specimen Set $9.00; 25 tests $20.00; 25 answer sheets, 25 profile sheets $6.75 each; keys $6.75; manual $6.75 (specify Secondary or College form)

Publisher: Psychologists and Educators, Inc.

Culture-Free Performance Test of Learning Aptitude

James K. Arima

Copyright: 1978

Population: Adults

Purpose: Measures native ability of individuals who do not score well on traditional tests; used for placement and career counseling of naval recruits

Description: Multiple-item paper–pencil test using six pairs of random polygons as stimuli in a two-choice multiple discrimination

Format: Individual administration; requires examiner; timed: 6 minutes

Scoring: Examiner evaluated

Cost: $18.00

Publisher: Select Press

Learning and Study Strategies Inventory (LASSI)

Claire E. Weinstein, David Palmer, Ann Schulte

Copyright: 1987

Population: Adults; college freshmen

Purpose: Assesses learning, study practices, and attitudes; used as a counseling tool and a diagnostic measure

Description: Ten-scale 77-item multiple-choice computer-administered or paper–pencil test measuring attitude, motivation, time management, information processing, test strategies, anxiety, concentration, selecting main ideas, study aid, and self-testing. A chart yielding statistically valid and reliable percentile rankings are available. Computer version using IBM 3.5" and 5.25"/MAC is available.

Format: Self-administered; suitable for group use; untimed: 30 minutes

Scoring: Self or computer scored

Cost: 1–49 $3.00 each, 50–499 $2.50 each, 500–2,000 $2.00 each

Publisher: H and H Publishing Co., Inc.

Learning and Study Strategies Inventory–High School (LASSI–HS)
Claire E. Weinstein, David R. Palmer, Ann Schulte

Copyright: 1990

Population: Adolescents; Grades 9 through 12

Purpose: Measures learning, study practices, and attitudes; used as a counseling tool for diagnostic measure

Description: Ten-scale multiple-choice, paper–pencil test measuring attitude, motivation, time management, information processing, test strategies, anxiety, concentration, selecting main ideas, study aid, and self-testing. A chart yielding statistically valid and reliable percentile rankings is used as is a self-scored form or a scanable NCS form. A seven-page booklet and a pen or pencil is needed.

Format: Suitable for group use; self-administered; untimed: 30 minutes

Scoring: Machine/self-scored

Cost: 1–100 tests $2.25, 200+ $2.10

Publisher: H and H Publishing Company, Inc.

Learning and Working Styles Inventory
Helena Hendrix-Frye

Copyright: 1991–1994

Population: Adolescents, adults; ages 12 and older

Purpose: Assesses individual learning styles

Description: Multiple-choice paper–pencil or computer-administered test measuring cognitive learning style, social learning style, expressive learning style, and working (environmental) learning style. Suitable for individuals with visual, hearing, physical, or mental impairments. Computer versions available for Apple II, Mac, and PC (MS DOS). Computer printouts for individual and group profiles are provided, graphically indicating major and minor learning styles. Specific teaching and learning strategies are also outlined based on each individual's scores. All results are saved to disk and may be edited or printed at any time. Based on the Hendrix-Frye Working Learning Styles and the C.I.T.E. Academic Learning Styles.

Format: Suitable for group use; timed (14 minutes); untimed (10 to 30 minutes)

Scoring: Examiner administration and interpretation; computer scored, hand key, or optical machine

Cost: C.I.T.E. version $395.00; Working Styles version $495.00

Publisher: Piney Mountain Press, Inc.

Learning Style Inventory (LSI)
Rita Dunn, Kenneth Dunn, Gary E. Price

Copyright: 1995

Population: Children, adolescents; Grades 3 through 12

Purpose: Identifies students' preferred learning environments; used for designing instructional environments and counseling

Description: Paper–pencil or computer-administered 104-item Likert scale test assessing the conditions under which students prefer to learn. Individual preferences are measured in the following areas: immediate environment (sound, heat, light, and design), emotionality (motivation, responsibility, persistence, and structure), sociological needs (self-oriented, peer-oriented, adult-oriented, or combined ways), and physical needs (perceptual preferences, time of day, food intake, and mobility). Test items consist of statements about how people like to learn. Students indicate whether they agree or disagree with each item. Results identify student preferences and indicate the degree to which a student's responses are consistent. Suggested strategies for instructional and environmental alternatives are provided to complement the student's revealed learning style. Computerized results are available in three forms: individual profile (raw scores for each of 22 areas, standard score in each area), group summary (identifies students with significantly high or low scores and groups individuals with similar preferences), and a subscale summary. Available in two levels: Grades 3–4 and 5–12.

Format: Self-administered; suitable for group use; untimed: 30 minutes

Scoring: Computer scored

Cost: Specimen Set (manual, research report, inventory booklet, answer sheet) $12.00; diskette (100 administrations per licensing agreement) $295.00; each additional 100 administrations $60.00; NCS Scanner Program $395.00; 100 answer sheets for NCS $60.00

Publisher: Price Systems, Inc.

Learning Style Inventory (LSI)
David A. Kolb

Copyright: 1985

Population: Adolescents, adults; ages 14 and above

Purpose: Describes the way one learns and how one deals with ideas and day-to-day situations; used to enhance teaching and training programs, further team development, understand problem solving, manage others and set goals, and understand learning styles

Description: Multiple-choice 12-item paper–pencil test. Results are plotted onto two graphs: Cycle of Learning and Learning Type grid. There is a scrambled scoring format, LSI IIA,

and the LSI is also available in French and Spanish.

Format: Self-administered; untimed: 20–30 minutes

Scoring: Self-scored

Cost: 10 forms $65.00

Publisher: McBer and Company, Inc.

Learning Styles Inventory
Richard M. Cooper, Jerry F. Brown

Copyright: 1978

Population: Adolescents

Purpose: Assesses learning styles

Description: Paper–pencil or computer-administered 45-item multiple-choice and Likert-scale test assessing learning styles through the following subtests: Visual Language, Visual Numeric, Auditory Language, Auditory Numeric, Tactile Concrete, Social Individual, Social Group, Oral Expressiveness, and Written Expressiveness. The test yields several scores, including Class Composite, Individual vs. Class, Teacher vs. Class, Class Prescriptive Information, and Individual Prescriptive Information. The computer program operates on Apple, DOS, and Macintosh computer systems.

Format: Self-administered; suitable for group use; untimed: time varies

Scoring: Computer scored

Cost: Diskettes and documentation $98.00

Publisher: Educational Activities, Inc.

Learning Styles Inventory (LSI)
Joseph S. Renzulli, Linda H. Smith

Copyright: 1978

Population: Grades 4 through 12

Purpose: Assesses the methods through which students prefer to learn; used to assist teachers in individualizing the instructional process

Description: Paper–pencil 65-item inventory assessing student attitudes toward nine modes of instruction: projects, drill and recitation, peer teaching, discussion, teaching games, independent study, programmed instruction, lecture, and stimulation. Various classroom learning experiences associated with these nine teaching/learning style approaches are described, and students use a 5-point scale ranging from "very unpleasant" to "very pleasant" to indicate their reaction to each activity. A teacher form is included so that teachers respond to items that parallel those on the student form. The resulting profile of instructional styles can be compared to individual student preferences and serve to facilitate a closer match between how teachers instruct and the styles to which students respond most favorably.

Format: Suitable for group use; time varies

Scoring: Examiner administration and interpretation, computer scored

Cost: Test Kit (30 student forms, two teacher forms, manual, and computer analysis) $24.95; Specimen Set $8.95

Publisher: Creative Learning Press, Inc.

Learning Styles Inventory (LSI)
Albert A. Canfield

Copyright: Not provided

Population: Adolescents, adults

Purpose: Identifies an individual's preferred learning methods; identifies individuals with little or no interest in independent or unstructured learning situations; used to maximize teaching and learning efficiency

Description: Paper–pencil 30-item forced-rank inventory measuring individual learning needs (interacting with others, goal setting, competition, friendly relations with instructor, independence in study, classroom authority); preferred mediums (listening, reading, viewing pictures, graphs, slides, or direct experience); and areas of interest (numeric concepts, qualitative concepts, working with inanimate things and people). The inventory also indicates student perceptions as to how they will perform in the learning situation and identifies learning problems associated with either traditional or innovative teaching methods. The test is available in two forms: Form S-A for use with most adults and Form E for use with persons whose reading level is as low as the fifth grade. The test booklets are reusable. Separate norms are available for males and females.

Format: Self-administered; suitable for group use; untimed: 30 minutes

Scoring: Self-scored

Cost: Kit (8 inventory booklets, 2 each of forms A, B, C, and E, 1 manual, 2 WPS Test Report inventory booklets, 1 form ABC, and 1 form E) $99.50

Publisher: Western Psychological Services

Perceptual Memory Task (PMT)
Lawrence T. McCarron

Copyright: 1985

Population: Ages 4 and older; Grades Pre-K and above

Purpose: Assesses individual learning style; used with special education and rehabilitation populations at any level of intellectual functioning and with individuals with physical, mental, emotional, or functional behavior disabilities

Description: Oral-response and show–tell 62-item test utilizing stimulus materials to assess fundamental information processing skills essential for learning and performance, including perception and memory for spatial relationships; visual and auditory sequential memory, intermediate-term memory, and discrimination of detail. To test hearing and visually impaired examinees (those with visual acuity of 20/400 or worse in either eye), supplementary procedures involving two alternate subtasks are provided. The instrument also assesses information processing skills dependent on right and left cerebral functioning. Age-corrected norm tables are used to convert each subtest score to a standard score that can be profiled on the PMT Score Form to portray graphically the individual's relative strengths and/or weaknesses. Factor scores also may be determined and compared to indicate relative strengths and weaknesses in specific memory processes.

Format: Examiner required; not suitable for group use; untimed: time varies

Scoring: Hand key

Cost: Complete Set $390.00; PMT Computer Report $350.00

Publisher: McCarron-Dial Systems

Reading Style Inventory (RSI)
Marie L. Carbo

Copyright: Not provided

Population: Ages 6 to adult

Purpose: Assesses learning style for reading or reading style; used to implement reading instruction

Description: Multiple-choice 68-item computer-administered/paper–pencil point-to test yielding an individual profile and a group profile. A computer version is available for PC, Apple II, and Mac formats. A Spanish version is available. The adult version is available on audiocassette.

Format: Individual or group administration; suitable for group use; untimed

Scoring: Examiner required; computer scored

Cost: Approximately $1.00 per student

Publisher: National Reading Styles Institute

Student Styles Questionnaire
Thomas Oakland, Joseph Glutting, Connie Horton

Copyright: 1996

Population: Children, adolescents; ages 8 through 17

Purpose: Measures styles of learning, relating, and working in students

Description: Patterned after the original Jungian constructs in four scales: Extroverted/Introverted, Thinking/Feeling, Practical/Imaginative, and Organized/Flexible. Students respond to 69 forced-choice questions related to real-life situations to express their individual styles; each item is a brief description of an everyday event. Includes classroom applications booklet for activity ideas in specific subject areas appropriate for each student style (personal, educational, and occupational). Optional scoring software generates a report for the child or adolescent and the professional.

Format: Examiner required; suitable for group use; untimed: can be completed in less than 30 minutes

Scoring: Examiner evaluated; may be computer scored

Cost: Starter Kit (manual, classroom applications booklet, answer documents, booklet) $65.00

Publisher: The Psychological Corporation

Surveys of Problem-Solving and Educational Skills (SEDS and SPRS)
Lynn J. Meltzer

Copyright: 1987

Population: Children, adolescents; ages 9 to 15

Purpose: Assesses the problem-solving and learning strategies of students in middle childhood

Description: Paper–pencil short-answer test comprised of nonlinguistic subtests, linguistic–verbal subtests, reading inventory, writing inventory, spelling inventory, and mathematics inventory. The score provides accurate information to determine the appropriate educational plan. A fourth-grade reading level is required.

Format: Individual administration; examiner required; untimed: 1–1½ hours

Scoring: Examiner evaluated

Cost: SEDS Workbook $20.55; Examiner's Manual $10.00; video $37.90; SPRS Record Forms $18.75; SPRS Stimulus Book $9.45; SEDS Stimulus Book $7.10; SEDS Record Form $21.75

Publisher: Educators Publishing Service, Inc.

Your Style of Learning and Thinking (SOLAT)
E. Paul Torrance, Bernice McCarthy, Mary Kolesinski, Jamie Smith

Copyright: 1988

Population: Children, adolescents; Grades K through 12

Purpose: Assesses learning styles

Description: Paper–pencil test with 25 to 28 items per questionnaire. Categories are left-brained, right-brained, or whole-brained. Raw scores, standard scores, and percentiles are yielded. A Youth Form and an Elementary Form are available. A questionnaire and pencil are used. Examiner must be certified for assessment.

Format: Individual/self-administered; suitable for group use; untimed

Scoring: Self-scored

Cost: Specimen Set $18.90

Publisher: Scholastic Testing Service, Inc.

Personality Factors

Children's Inventory of Self-Esteem (CISE)
Richard A. Campbell

Copyright: 1990

Population: Children; ages 5 to 12; Grades K through 6

Purpose: Used by parent workshops, parent conferences, and teacher consultations to compare relative strengths and weaknesses among four components of self-esteem as observed by parents and/or teachers

Description: True–false 64-item test with the following subtests: Belonging (16 items), exceptionality (16 items), control (16 items), and ideals (16 items). A "Component Scores" report reveals the weakest of the four components. A "Coping Strategies" profile shows passive and aggressive tendencies. Male and female forms are available. Examiner must have an advanced degree in a mental health or testing field.

Format: Individual/self-administered; suitable for group use; untimed: 10 minutes

Scoring: Hand key; examiner evaluated

Cost: Contact publisher

Publisher: Brougham Press

Computerized Personal Skills Map System (CPSMS)

Copyright: 1994

Population: Adolescents; Grades 7 through 12

Purpose: Provides a computerized research-based positive assessment of intrapersonal, interpersonal, and life management skills directly related to achievement, performance, adjustment, and healthy living

Description: Multiple-choice 200-question computer-administered (other NCS and Scantron) survey of Grades 7–12. Categories are self-esteem, growth motivation, change orientation, interpersonal assertion, interpersonal aggression, interpersonal deference, interpersonal awareness, empathy, drive strength, decision making, time management, sales orientation, commitment ethic, and stress management. Materials necessary for assessment: CPSMS Software Package. Necessary for intervention: Becoming a Champion Personal Success System and Student Workbook (6–12), Becoming a Champion Teacher's Guide (3–12), Support Materials: Becoming a Champion Mentor Guide, Becoming a Champion Parent Guide, Becoming a Champion Research Manual. Computer version available for MS-DOS, Macintosh, and Network. Suitable for individuals with hearing impairment.

Format: Self-administered; suitable for group use; untimed: 25–30 minutes

Scoring: Machine scored (NCS, Scantron)

Cost: 1–5 diskettes, each $300.00; 6–10 diskettes, each $287.50; 11–15 diskettes, each $275.00; 16–20 diskettes, each $262.50; 20+ diskettes, each $250.00 (50 administrations per diskette)

Publisher: Chronicle Guidance Publications, Inc.

Coping Inventory (Observation Form)
Shirley Zeitlin

Copyright: 1985

Population: Children, adolescents; ages 3 to 16

Purpose: Assesses personality

Description: Paper–pencil criterion-referenced test assesses two categories: coping with self (productive, active, flexible) and coping with environment (productive, active, and flexible). Scores yielded are: not effective (1), minimally effective (2), effective in some but not others (3), effective more often than not (4), effective most of the time (5). A booklet and manual are used. Examiner must be certified for assessment. Available in large print.

Format: Individual administration; examiner required; suitable for group use; untimed

Scoring: Hand key; examiner evaluated

Cost: Starter Set (manual and 20 forms) $47.40

Publisher: Scholastic Testing Service, Inc.

Coping Inventory (Self-Rated Form)
Shirley Zeitlin

Copyright: 1985

Population: Adolescents; ages 15 and above

Purpose: Assesses personality

Description: Paper–pencil criterion-referenced test assesses two categories: coping with self (productive, active, flexible) and coping with environment (productive, active, and flexible). Scores yielded are: not effective (1), minimally effective (2), effective in some but not others (3), effective more often than not (4), effective most of the time (5). A booklet and manual are used. Examiner must be certified for assessment. Available in large print.

Format: Individual/self-administered; suitable for group use; examiner required; untimed: 45 minutes

Scoring: Examiner evaluated; hand key; self-scored

Cost: Starter Set (manual and 10 forms) $30.85

Publisher: Scholastic Testing Service, Inc.

Dimensions of Self-Concept (DOSC)
William B. Michael, Robert A. Smith

Copyright: 1977

Population: Children, adolescents; Grades 4 and above

Purpose: Identifies students who might have difficulty with schoolwork due to low self-esteem and diagnoses factors contributing to low self-esteem

Description: Multiple-item paper–pencil questionnaire assessing level of aspiration, anxiety, academic interest and satisfaction, leadership and initiative, and identification vs. alienation. Form E is available for Grades 4–6; Form S for Grades 7–12; Form H for college. Percentile ranks are presented for Grades 4–6, 7–9, and 10–12.

Format: Examiner required; suitable for group use; untimed: Form E 20–40 minutes, Form S 15–35 minutes, Form H 15–35 minutes

Scoring: Machine scored by publisher

Cost: 25 test forms $10.00; manual $4.00; Specimen Set $7.00

Publisher: EdITS/Educational and Industrial Testing Service

Inferred Self-Concept Scale
E. L. McDaniel

Copyright: 1973

Population: Children; Grades 1 to 6

Purpose: Evaluates the self-concept of children based on their behavior in school

Description: Paper–pencil 30-item inventory evaluating a child's self-concept. Based on observation of the child, a teacher or counselor familiar with the child rates him or her on a 5-point scale ranging from "never" to "always." With the aid of standardized scoring and interpretation, the child's self-concept is assessed based on this behavior profile. Administered by a teacher or counselor familiar with the child.

Format: Examiner required; not suitable for group use; untimed: 15–20 minutes

Scoring: Hand key

Cost: Kit (100 scales, manual) $45.00

Publisher: Western Psychological Services

Martinek-Zaichkowsky Self-Concept Scale for Children (MZSCS)
Thomas J. Martinek,
Leonard D. Zaichkowsky

Copyright: 1971

Population: Children, adolescents; Grades 1 through 8

Purpose: Measures the global self-concept of children, identifies children with low self-esteem, and evaluates the impact of the educational process on a child's self-perception; may be used with non–English-speaking children; used for research and referral

Description: Paper–pencil 25-item forced-choice test measuring physical, behavioral, and emotional aspects of a child's self-confidence. Five factors are covered: satisfaction and happiness; home and family relationships and circumstances; ability in games, recreation, and sports; personality traits and emotional tendencies; and behavioral and social characteristics in school. Each test item consists of a page in the test booklet that presents the child with a pair of pictures representing positive and negative roles. The child circles the picture he or she considers to be most like herself or himself. The test requires little or no reading ability and is culture-free.

Format: Examiner required; suitable for group use; untimed: 10–15 minutes

Scoring: Hand key; examiner evaluated

Cost: Specimen Set $10.00; 25 tests $35.00; manual $6.75

Publisher: Psychologists and Educators, Inc.

Perception of Ability Scale for Students (PASS)
Frederic J. Boersma, James W. Chapman

Copyright: Not provided

Population: Grades 3 through 6

Purpose: Used to measure school-related self-concept

Description: The scale includes 70 items with a yes–no response format. Scores are provided for the full scale and for six subscales: general ability, math, reading/spelling, penmanship and neatness, school satisfaction, and confidence in academic ability. Raw scores convertible to stanines, percentiles, and T-scores for comparison to the norm group.

Format: Examiner required; suitable for group use; 15 minutes

Scoring: Hand key or computer service scored

Cost: Kit (10 AutoScore™ answer forms, 1 manual, 2 test report prepaid mail-in answer sheets for computer scoring and interpretation) $72.50; microcomputer disks available

Publisher: Western Psychological Services

Personal Skills Map (PSM)

Copyright: 1992

Population: Adolescents, adults

Purpose: Provides a research-based positive assessment of intrapersonal, interpersonal, and life management skills directly related to achievement, performance, adjustment and healthy living

Description: Survey with 200 questions for grades 7–12, 300 questions for adults; multiple-choice, paper–pencil test consisting of the following categories: self-esteem, growth motivation, change orientation, interpersonal assertion, interpersonal aggression, interpersonal deference, interpersonal awareness, empathy, drive strength, decision making, time management, sales orientation, commitment ethic, and stress management. Materials used for assessment: Personal Skills Map and Interpretation Guide. For intervention: Becoming a Champion, Becoming a Champion Personal Success System and Student Workbook (6–12), Becoming a Champion Teacher's Guide (3–12). Support materials: Becoming a Champion Mentor Guide, Becoming a Champion Parent Guide, Becoming a Champion Research Manual. Suitable for those with hearing impairment.

Format: Self-administered; suitable for group use; untimed: 30–50 minutes

Scoring: Hand key

Cost: 1–4 packages, each $125.00; 5–10 packages, each $118.75; 11+ packages $112.50 (25 administrations per package)

Publisher: Chronicle Guidance Publications, Inc.

Self Concept As a Learner (SCAL)
Walter B. Waetjen

Copyright: 1967

Population: Children, adolescents; ages 10 to 20; Grades 4 through 14

Purpose: Assesses self-concept in the school setting

Description: Paper–pencil 50-item test with five subtests. A fourth-grade reading level is required. Available in Spanish. Yields a total score and four subtest scores.

Format: Examiner required; untimed: 20 minutes

Scoring: Hand key

Cost: $.25 per copy

Publisher: Walter B. Waetjen

Self-Perception Profile for Adolescents
Susan Harter

Copyright: 1988

Population: Ages 14 to 18

Purpose: Assesses scholastic competence, athletic competence, social acceptance, physical appearance, behavioral conduct, close friendship, romantic appeal, job competence, and global self-worth

Description: Paper–pencil measurement

Format: Examiner required; individual administration; time varies

Scoring: Hand key

Cost: $15.00

Publisher: Susan Harter

Self-Perception Profile for Children
Susan Harter

Copyright: 1985

Population: Children, adolescents; ages 8 to 13

Purpose: Assesses scholastic competence, athletic competence, social acceptance, physical appearance, behavioral conduct, and global self-worth

Description: The manual includes a teacher rating scale, as well as a rating scale to tap children's perceptions of the importance of each domain.

Format: Examiner required; individual administration; time varies

Scoring: Hand key

Cost: $18.00

Publisher: Susan Harter

Self-Profile Q-Sort (SPQS)
Alan F. Politte

Copyright: 1974

Population: Children, adolescents; Grades 2 and above

Purpose: Assesses student's feelings toward self; used for elementary school counseling

Description: Test of self-perception in which the child indicates whether or not each of 63 items describes his or her feelings. The test is administered orally to younger children; older children may read the items themselves.

Format: Examiner required; suitable for group use; untimed: 10 minutes

Scoring: Examiner evaluated

Cost: Specimen Set $4.50; 25 forms $6.75

Publisher: Psychologists and Educators, Inc.

Student Self-Concept Scale (SSCS)
Frank M. Gresham, Stephen N. Elliott, Sally E. Evans-Fernandez

Copyright: 1993

Population: Level 1 (Grades 3 through 6), Level 2 (Grades 7 through 12)

Purpose: Used to assist in screening, classifying, and planning interventions for children and adolescents; can be used as a screener or as part of a comprehensive evaluation

Description: Multidimensional self-report measure of self–concept; materials include a manual, Level 1 and Level 2 Questionnaire. Response format: person reads item and responds by circling the selected option.

Format: Individual or group administration; 15–25 minutes

Scoring: Examiner interpretation; standard scores for scales and composites

Cost: Manual $39.95, Level I and Level 2 Student Questionnaires (25) $31.95

Publisher: American Guidance Service

Problem Behaviors

Behavior Assessment System for Children (BASC)
Cecil R. Reynolds, Randy W. Kamphaus

Copyright: 1992

Population: Ages 4 to 18

Purpose: Facilitates differential diagnosis and educational classification of a variety of children's emotional and behavioral disorders and aids in the design of treatment plans

Description: The BASC is a multimethod, multidimensional approach to evaluating the behavior and self-perceptions of children. It has five components that can be used individually or in any combination. The three core components are Teacher Rating Scales (TRS), Parent Rating Scales (PRS), and Self-Report of Personality (SRP). Additional components include Structured Developmental History (SDH) and Student Observation System (SOS). The BASC measures positive (adaptive) as well as negative (clinical) dimensions of behavior and personality.

Format: Individual administration; TRS/PRS 10–20 minutes, SRP 30 minutes, SDH varies from family to family, SOS 15 minutes

Scoring: Computerized scoring available in the BASC Enhanced ASSIST and the BASC Plus software for IBM and compatibles with 640K memory

Cost: BASC Enhanced ASSIST (set for IBM PC, XT, AT, PS/2 and compatibles with 640 K includes 5.25″ program diskette and 3.5″ program diskette, manual) $225.95

Publisher: American Guidance Service

Behavior Dimensions Scale (BDS)
Stephen B. McCarney

Copyright: 1995

Population: Children, adolescents; ages 5 to 19; Grades K through 12

Purpose: Assesses dimensions of behavior of attention-deficit/hyperactivity disorder, oppositional defiant, conduct disorder, avoidant personality, anxiety, and depression

Description: Each dimension of behavior is clarified by behavioral items which are observable overt descriptors of the behavior problems which are documented by primary observers of the child or adolescent's behavior (i.e., teachers and parents). Frequency-based quantifiers provide precise measures of the rate of problematic behavior. Available in both a School Version, a reporting form for educators, and a Home Version, a reporting form for parent output. A computer version using IBM/Macintosh PCs is available. Also available in Spanish.

Format: Individual administration

Scoring: Self/computer scored

Cost: Complete Kit $148.00

Publisher: Hawthorne Educational Services, Inc.

Behavior Disorders Identification Scale (BDIS)
Stephen B. McCarney

Copyright: 1988

Population: Children, adolescents; Grades K through 12

Purpose: Identifies behaviorally disordered/emotionally disturbed students

Description: Includes School and Home Versions to provide a comprehensive profile of student behavior problems. The scale relies on direct behavioral observations by educators and parents or guardians. The BDIS focuses on both the overt indicators of behavior disorders, as well as the more subtle indicators of withdrawal, depression, and suicidal tendencies. The standardized sample represented all geographic regions of the United States, with particular attention given to the inclusion of racial and ethnic minorities in the creation of the national norms. Internal consistency, test–retest, interrater reliability, item analysis, factor analysis, content validity, criterion-related validity, diagnostic validity, and construct validity are all reported. A computer version using IBM/ Macintosh PCs is available. Available also in Spanish.

Format: Individual administration; untimed: 15–20 minutes

Scoring: Self/computer scored

Cost: Complete Kit $167.00

Publisher: Hawthorne Educational Services, Inc.

Behavior Evaluation Scale–2 (BES–2)
Stephen B. McCarney

Copyright: 1990

Population: Children, adolescents; ages 5 to 19; Grades K through 12

Purpose: Provides results that assist school personnel in making decisions about eligibility, placement, and programming for students with behavior problems who have been referred for evaluation

Description: The scale yields relevant behavioral information about students regardless of disabilities and may be used with students who have learning disabilities, mental retardation, physical impairments, and other conditions. The scale is based on the IDEA definition of behavior disorders/emotional disturbance. Standard scores and percentile ranks are provided for total scale performance across 76 items as well as for each of the five subscales.

Format: Individual administration

Scoring: Self/computer scored

Cost: Complete Kit $191.00

Publisher: Hawthorne Educational Services, Inc.

Behavior Rating Profile–Second Edition (BRP–2)
Linda L. Brown, Donald D. Hammill

Copyright: 1990

Population: Ages 6 years 6 months to 18 years 6 months

Purpose: Identifies elementary and secondary students thought to have behavior problems and the settings in which those problems seem prominent; also identifies individuals who have differing perceptions about the behavior of a student

Description: Multiple-item paper–pencil battery consisting of six independent, individually normed measures: Student Rating Scales (Home, School, and Peer), Parent Rating Scale, Teacher Rating Scale, and the Sociogram. May be used with emotionally disturbed students.

Format: Individual administration, checklist format

Scoring: Examiner administration and interpretation

Cost: Complete kit (manual; student, parent, and teacher rating forms; profile sheets; and storage box) $169.00

Publisher: PRO-ED, Inc.

Child Behavior Checklist for Ages 2–3 (CBCL/2–3)
Thomas M. Achenbach

Copyright: 1988

Population: Children; ages 2 to 3

Purpose: Used in mental health and special education applications to assess behavioral and emotional problems

Description: Paper–pencil 100-item short-answer rating scales with the following profiles: aggressive, anxious/depressed, destructive, sleep problems, somatic problems, and withdrawn. A fifth-grade reading level is required. A computer version using IBM PCs and compatibles and Apple II computers is available.

Format: Individual administration; examiner required; untimed: 10 minutes

Scoring: Hand key; computer scored

Cost: Package of 25 forms $10.00

Publisher: University of Vermont Department of Psychiatry

Child Behavior Checklist for Ages 4–18 (CBCL/4–18)
Thomas M. Achenbach

Copyright: 1995

Population: Children, adolescents; ages 4 to 18

Purpose: Used in mental health and special education applications to assess behavioral and emotional problems

Description: Paper–pencil short-answer rating scales with 120 problem items and 20 competence items. The following profiles are yielded: aggressive, anxious/depressed, attention problems, delinquent, social problems, somatic, thought problems, and withdrawn. Separate scoring profiles for males and females ages 4–11 and 12–18 are available. A form completed by the parent is used. A fifth-grade reading level is required. A computer version using IBM PCs and compatibles and Apple II computers is available. A client-entry program is available.

Format: Individual administration; examiner required; untimed: 15–20 minutes

Scoring: Hand key; machine scored; computer scored

Cost: Package of 25 forms $10.00

Publisher: University of Vermont Department of Psychiatry

Demos D (Dropout) Scale
George D. Demos

Copyright: Not provided

Population: Adolescents

Purpose: Measures student attitudes

Description: Brief, objective, 29-question scale measures student attitudes in four areas: toward teachers, influences by peers or parents, toward

education, and school behavior. A fifth-grade reading level is required. A Total Score and basic Area Scores are converted to probabilities of dropping out of school. Widely used at junior and senior high levels, this scale is easy to administer, score, and interpret.

Format: Self-administered; timed: time varies

Scoring: Examiner evaluated

Cost: Kit (25 forms, 1 manual) $30.00

Publisher: Western Psychological Services

Devereux Elementary School Behavior Rating Scale (DESB–II)
Marshall Swift

Copyright: 1982

Population: Children; ages 6 to 12

Purpose: Assesses overt classroom behaviors at the elementary school level; diagnoses problem behaviors that interfere with classroom performance; used for screening procedures and group placement decisions in response to specific programs

Description: Paper–pencil 52-item inventory assessing the symptomatic classroom behavior patterns of children. The classroom teacher rates each item according to how he or she feels the subjects' behavior compares to the behavior of normal children their age. The test yields 10 behavior factors (Work Organization, Creative Initiative/Involvement, Positive Toward Teacher, Need for Direction in Work, Socially Withdrawn, Failure Anxiety, Impatience, Irrelevant Thinking/TALK, Blaming, Negative/Aggressive) and 4 behavior clusters (Perseverance, Peer Cooperation, Confusion, and Inattention).

Format: Self-administered by teacher; not suitable for group use; untimed: 10–15 minutes

Scoring: Examiner evaluated

Cost: Package of 25 $9.00; manual $5.00

Publisher: The Devereux Foundation

Direct Observation Form (DOF)
Thomas M. Achenbach

Copyright: 1986

Population: Children, adolescents; ages 5 to 14; Grades K through 9

Purpose: Used in mental health and special education to assess behavioral and emotional problems for individuals with BED, LD, and EH

Description: Paper–pencil short-answer rating scales with 97 problem items; on-task behavior at 1-minute intervals. The following profiles are yielded: withdrawn–inattentive; nervous–obsessive; depressed; hyperactive; attention demanding; aggressive. An observation form is used and scored by an observer. Examiner must be an experienced observer. A computer version using all IBM compatibles and Apple II computers is available.

Format: Individual administration; examiner required; timed: 10 minutes

Scoring: Hand key; computer scored

Cost: Package of 25 forms $10.00

Publisher: University of Vermont Department of Psychiatry

Draw a Person: Screening Procedure for Emotional Disturbance (DAP: SPED)
Jack A. Naglieri, Timothy J. McNeish, Achilles N. Bardos

Copyright: 1991

Population: Children, adolescents; ages 6 to 17

Purpose: Helps identify children and adolescents who have emotional problems and require further evaluation

Description: The DAP: SPED has items that are used to rate the drawings of a man, a woman, and the self. The items were based on an exhaustive review of the literature on human figure drawings, and the test was written to be objective and fast to score. The test blends the clinical skills and knowledge reported in the literature over the past 75 years with a modern psychometric approach to test construction. The DAP: SPED was normed on a nationwide sample of 2,260 students representative of the nation as a whole with regard to gender, race, ethnicity, geographic region, and socioeco-

nomic status. Evidence of various types of reliability and validity is well documented in the test manual. The DAP: SPED yields a standard score (T score) that is used to determine if further assessment is (a) not indicated, (b) indicated, or (c) strongly indicated.

Format: Individual administration; suitable for group use; timed: time varies

Scoring: Examiner evaluated

Cost: Complete Kit (examiner's manual, 10 scoring templates, 25 record forms, storage box) $79.00

Publisher: PRO-ED, Inc.

Emotional or Behavior Disorder Scale (EBDS)
Stephen B. McCarney

Copyright: 1991

Population: Children, adolescents; ages 4 years 5 months to 21 years; Grades K through 12

Purpose: Provides the perspective of emotional or behavioral disorders and the criteria by which identification is now being made

Description: Multiple-item rating scale in the areas of academic performance, social relationships, and personal adjustment. Both a School and Home Version are available. A computer version using IBM PCs is available.

Format: Individual administration

Scoring: Self/computer scored

Cost: Complete Kit $109.00

Publisher: Hawthorne Educational Services, Inc.

Emotional/Behavioral Screening Program (ESP)
Jack G. Dial, Garry Amann

Copyright: 1988

Population: Children, adolescents; ages 9 and older

Purpose: Analyzes emotional and behavioral functioning; used with special needs students

Description: Paper–pencil 35-item checklist for rating an individual on the basis of observed behavior, reliable case history reports, or information provided by a reliable informant. The checklist, called the Behavioral Checklist for Students (BCS), contains seven categories of items: Impulsivity–Frustration, Anxiety, Depression–Withdrawal, Socialization, Self-Concept, Aggression, and Reality Discrimination. Raw subtest scores are entered into the computer. Users may choose from three types of reports. The Analysis Report is an analysis of emotional/behavioral functions with possible diagnostic categories. The Classroom Report describes emotional/behavioral characteristics the teacher may anticipate and lists specific recommendations for educational management. The Comprehensive Report integrates features of both the Analysis Report and the Classroom Report. The software operates on Macintosh and IBM PC and compatible systems.

Format: Examiner/self-administered; not suitable for group use; untimed: time varies

Scoring: Examiner evaluated; may be computer scored

Cost: Complete Kit (comprehensive manual, 25 copies of BCS, computer program with operating manual) $250.00

Publisher: McCarron-Dial Systems

Eyberg Child Behavior Inventory
Shelia M. Eyberg, J. Sutter

Copyright: 1996

Population: Children, adolescents; ages 2 to 16

Purpose: Used by health professionals to assess disruptive behavior in school

Description: Multiple-choice 36-item paper–pencil test with an Intensity scale and a Problem scale. The Intensity scale indicates how often behavior currently occurs; the Problem scale identifies behaviors that are currently problems. Each item has an intensity part and a problem part; therefore there are 36 items for each scale. Forms A and B, male and female, are used. A manual and questionnaire are used. Examiner must be B-Level qualified.

Format: Individual administration; examiner required; untimed: 10–15 minutes

Scoring: Hand scorable

Cost: Contact publisher

Publisher: Psychological Assessment Resources, Inc.

Humanics National After-School Assessment Form: Ages 6 to 9
Jackson Rabbit, Sylvia B. Booth, Marilyn L. Perling

Copyright: 1995

Population: Children; ages 6 to 9; Grades 1 through 4

Purpose: Assesses child behavior; used for after-school assessment and developmental activities

Description: Paper–pencil oral-response criterion-referenced verbal, show-tell, point-to test. The test has five categories: Social Emotional, Language, Cognitive, Motor Skills, Hygiene/Self-Help. All categories have 18 questions each. A developmental profile is yielded. Adaptation of the Humanics National Assessments 0–3 and 3–6.

Format: Individual administration; examiner required; untimed

Scoring: Examiner evaluated; no scoring service available

Cost: Package of 25 forms $29.95

Publisher: Humanics Psychological Test Corporation

Life Adjustment Inventory
Ronald C. Doll, F. Wayne Wrightstone

Copyright: 1962

Population: Adolescents; Grades 9 through 12

Purpose: Measures general adjustment to high school curriculum; used for curriculum surveys and diagnosis of maladjusted pupils for individual guidance

Description: Multiple-item paper–pencil test of general adjustment to the high school curriculum. The test measures the feeling of needing additional experiences in 13 specific areas, such as consumer education; religion, morals, and ethics; family living; vocational orientation and preparation; reading and study skills; and citizenship education. The test conforms with the U.S. Office of Education's Life Adjustment Program.

Format: Examiner required; suitable for group use; untimed: 25 minutes

Scoring: Hand key

Cost: Specimen Set $5.00; 25 inventories $8.75

Publisher: Psychometric Affiliates

Preschool and Kindergarten Behavior Scales (PKBS)
Kenneth W. Merrell

Copyright: 1994

Population: Ages 3 to 6

Purpose: Assesses social skills and problem behaviors

Description: Multiple-choice 76-item paper–pencil test consisting of eight subtests and two categories: Problem Behavior scale—42 items, Social Skills—34 items. This instrument is designed to be used as a screening tool for early detection of developing social–emotional problems, as part of a multimethod assessment battery for classifications and eligibility purposes, to develop intervention programs, and to gauge subsequent behavioral change.

Format: Individual administration; untimed: 8–12 minutes

Scoring: Hand scored with scoring key provided adjacent to the rating scale

Cost: Complete Kit (manual and forms) $39.00

Publisher: PRO-ED, Inc.

Revised Behavior Problem Checklist (RBPC)
Herbert C. Quay,
Donald R. Peterson

Copyright: 1987

Population: Children, adolescents; Grades K through 12

Purpose: Measures behavior problems in children and adolescents

Description: Paper–pencil 89-item 3-point rating scale with the following categories: Conduct Disorder, Socialized Aggression, Attention Problems/Immaturity, Anxiety/Withdrawal, Psychotic Behavior, and Motor Excess. Materials used include a manual, checklist, and scoring key. Examiner must be B-Level qualified.

Format: Individual administration; examiner required; untimed: 10 minutes

Scoring: Hand key

Cost: Kit $50.00

Publisher: Psychological Assessment Resources, Inc.

School Behavior Checklist
Lovick C. Miller

Copyright: Not provided

Population: Ages 4 to 13

Purpose: Used as assessment of children's behavior in classroom

Description: Teacher-completed checklist of true–false statements and 11 global judgments describing the child's classroom behavior. This gives professional mental health workers a standardized evaluation of the child's classroom behavior in the following areas: need achievement, cognitive or academic deficit, aggression, hostile isolation, anxiety, extroversion. There are two forms: Form A1, for children 4 to 6 years; and Form A2, for children aged 7 to 13 years.

Format: Examiner completed; 8–10 minutes

Scoring: Hand key

Cost: Set (50 reusable checklists, 50 answer sheets, 2 sets of scoring templates, 1 manual) $90.00

Publisher: Western Psychological Services

School Social Behavior Scales (SSBS)
Kenneth W. Merrell

Copyright: 1993

Population: Children, adolescents; Grades K through 12

Purpose: Provides an integrated rating of both social skills and antisocial problem behaviors

Description: Multiple-choice 65-item paper–pencil two-scale test measuring social competence and antisocial behavior. The Social Competence Scale includes 32 items that measure adaptive, prosocial skills and includes three subscales (Interpersonal Skills, Self Management Skills, and Academic Skills). The Antisocial Behavior scale includes 33 items that measure socially linked problem behaviors and also includes three subscales (Hostile–Irritable, Antisocial–Aggressive, and Disruptive–Demanding). This instrument is designed to be used as a screening instrument for early detection of developing social–behavioral problems and as part of a multimethod assessment battery for conducting comprehensive assessments, determining program eligibility, and developing intervention plans.

Format: Examiner required; not suitable for groups; untimed: 5–10 minutes

Scoring: Hand scored with an easy-to-use scoring key; examiner evaluated

Cost: complete kit $39.00

Publisher: PRO-ED, Inc.

School Social Skills Rating Scale (S3 Rating Scale)
Laura Brown, Donald Black, John Downs

Copyright: 1984

Population: Elementary to high school students

Purpose: Assists school personnel in identifying student deficits in school-related social behaviors; provides an inventory of a student's ability to apply the skills necessary to achieve success in school settings and for eventual success in employment

Description: The 40-item scale of observable prosocial skills has been socially validated and determined to be important for student school success in the areas of Adult Relations (12 items), Peer Relations (16 items), School Rules (6 items), Classroom Behaviors (6 items). The S3 Rating Scale is quick and easy to administer,

taking approximately 10 minutes per student. Ratings are done on a 6-point Likert Scale and are based on observation of student behavior over the previous month. The S3 Manual accompanies the S3 Rating Scale and provides complete behavioral descriptions of each of the 40 skills and the conditions under which they should be used. The S3 Rating Scale is a criterion-referenced instrument that yields knowledge of a student's strengths and deficiencies. Both the test–retest and the interrater reliability data indicate the S3 Rating Scale has comparable reliability with residential, special education, and regular education students.

Format: 10 minutes per individual

Scoring: Examiner evaluated

Cost: S3 Complete $55.00; S3 Manual $24.00; 50 S3 Rating Scales $36.00

Publisher: Slosson Educational Publications, Inc.

Social Behavior Assessment Inventory (SBAI)
Thomas H. Stephens, Kevin D. Arnold

Copyright: 1992

Population: Children, adolescents; Grades K through 9

Purpose: Used by teachers, counselors, and parents to measure children's social behaviors

Description: Paper–pencil 136-item rating scale with the following content areas and subscales: Environmental Behaviors (care for the environment, dealing with emergency, lunchroom behavior, movement around environment), Interpersonal Behaviors (accepting authority, coping with conflict, gaining attention, greeting others, helping others, making conversation, organized play, positive attitude toward others, playing informally, property: own and others), Self-Related Behaviors (accepting consequences, ethical behavior, expressing feelings, positive attitude toward self, responsible behavior, self-care), Task-Related Behaviors (asking and answering questions, attending behavior, classroom discussion, completing tasks, following directions, group activities, independent work, on-task behavior, performing before others, quality of work). Materials used include Social Skills in the Classroom, SBAI Manual Rating Book. Examiner must be B-Level qualified.

Format: Individual administration; examiner required; untimed: 30–45 minutes

Scoring: Rating booklet scored without key

Cost: Intro Kit $88.00

Publisher: Psychological Assessment Resources, Inc.

Social Skills Rating System (SSRS)
Frank M. Gresham, Stephen N. Elliott

Copyright: 1990

Population: Preschool (age 3), Elementary (Grades K–6), Secondary (Grades 7–12)

Purpose: Assists professionals in screening and classifying children suspected of having significant social behavior problems and aids in the development of appropriate interventions for identified children

Description: Multirater assessment of the perceived frequency and importance of a student's social behaviors.

Format: Individual or group administration; 15–25 minutes

Scoring: Examiner interpretation; standard scores for scales and subscales

Cost: Starter Set: Preschool/Elementary Level (10 copies each of teacher, parent, and student questionnaires; 10 assessment-intervention records, manual) $109.95. Secondary Level $99.95

Publisher: American Guidance Service

Social–Emotional Dimension Scale (SEDS)
Jerry B. Hutton, Timothy G. Roberts

Copyright: 1986

Population: Children, adolescents; ages 5 years 6 months to 18 years 6 months

Purpose: Identifies students who may have conduct disorders or emotional disturbance behavior problems; used by teachers, counselors, and psychologists

Description: Test with 32 items assessing inappropriate behaviors of students, including physical/fear reaction, depressive reaction, avoidance of peer interaction, avoidance of teacher interaction, inappropriate behaviors, and aggressive interaction. The test provides percentiles and standard scores.

Format: Examiner required; not suitable for group use; untimed: 15–20 minutes

Scoring: Examiner evaluated

Cost: Complete Kit (examiner's manual and 50 profile/examiner record forms) $69.00

Publisher: PRO-ED, Inc.

Stress Response Scale
Louis A. Chandler

Copyright: 1993

Population: Children, adolescents; ages 5 to 14

Purpose: Assesses the emotional status of children ages 5 to 14 with nonorganic and mild to moderate emotional problems; used in schools and clinics for screening and diagnosis

Description: Paper–pencil 40-item inventory indicating the maladaptive coping efforts of children. Adults rate children on a 6-point scale. The test is based on a model that predicts five behavior styles: acting out, overactive, passive–aggressive, repressed, and dependent. Test results may be profiled to suggest the child's preferred response pattern. The test should not be used with individuals with mental retardation, psychoneurological learning disabilities, or severe emotional disabilities. A computer scoring program is available for IBM PC or Apple II systems.

Format: Examiner required; not suitable for group use; untimed: time varies

Scoring: Hand key; may be computer scored

Cost: Kit (manual, set of forms) $54.00

Publisher: Psychological Assessment Resources, Inc.

Student Referral Checklist
John A. Schinka

Copyright: 1988

Population: Children; adolescents

Purpose: Used by teachers or school personnel to provide a comprehensive review of student problems in a school

Description: Paper–pencil 180-item checklist with the following categories: Emotions, Self-Concept/Self-Esteem, Peer Relations, School Attitude, Motor Skill/Activity Level, Language and Cognition, Behavioral Style, Moral Development, Health and Habits, and Additional Problems. Materials used include a student referral checklist K–6 and Jr./Sr. High.

Format: Individual administration; examiner required; untimed

Scoring: Examiner evaluated

Cost: 50 checklists $34.00

Publisher: Psychological Assessment Resources, Inc.

Sutter-Eyberg Student Behavior Inventory (SESBI)
J. Sutter, S. Eyberg

Copyright: Currently in development

Population: Ages 2 to 16

Purpose: Used in education/school settings to assess disruptive behavior in school

Description: Multiple-choice 36-item paper–pencil yes/no test with two scales: Intensity and Problem. The Intensity scale indicates how often behavior currently occurs; the Problem scale identifies behaviors that are currently problems. Each item has an intensity and a problem part; therefore there are 36 items for each scale. Forms A and B are available. A manual and questionnaire are used. Examiner must be B-Level qualified.

Format: Individual administration; examiner required; untimed: 10–15 minutes

Scoring: Hand scorable

Cost: Contact publisher

Publisher: Psychological Assessment Resources, Inc.

Systematic Screening for Behavior Disorders (SSBD)
Hill M. Walker, Herbert H. Severson

Copyright: 1990

Population: Children; Grades K through 6

Purpose: Used in public schools to screen for behavior disorders

Description: The SSBD screening process is proactive and incorporates a three-stage, multi-gated process. SSBD relies on teacher judgments and direct observation. Extensively field-tested, the SSBD Kit contains three manuals (User's Guide and Administration Manual, Technical Manual, and Observer Training Manual), a videotape, and forms for screening in 30 classrooms. In Stage I, the teacher identifies two groups of ten students each that most closely resemble behavioral profiles of externalizing and internalizing behavior problems. The teacher then ranks the students, and the three highest-ranked students on each list move to Stage II. In Stage II, the teacher completes three brief rating instruments for each of the six students. Only those students who exceed the SSBD Stage II screening criteria move to Stage III student in two separate 15-minute classroom and 15-minute playground observations.

Format: Individual and group administration; examiner required; timed and untimed sections

Scoring: Examiner evaluated

Cost: $195.00

Publisher: Sopris West, Inc.

Teacher's Report Form (TRF)
Thomas M. Achenbach

Copyright: 1995

Population: Children, adolescents; ages 5 to 18

Purpose: Used in mental health and special education applications to assess behavioral and emotional problems for individuals with BED, LD, and EH

Description: Paper–pencil short answer rating scales with 120 problem items and 5 adaptive items. The following profiles are yielded: aggressive, anxious/depressed, attention problems, delinquent, social problems, somatic, thought problems, and withdrawn. Separate scoring profiles for males and females ages 5 to 11 and 12 to 18 are available. A form completed by the teacher is used. A fifth-grade reading level is required. A computer version using all IBM compatibles and Apple II computers is available. A client-entry program is available.

Format: Individual administration; untimed: 15–20 minutes

Scoring: Hand key; machine scored; computer scored

Cost: Package of 25 forms $10.00

Publisher: University of Vermont Department of Psychiatry

Walker Problem Behavior Identification Checklist
Hill M. Walker

Copyright: 1983

Population: Children; Grades Pre-K through 6

Purpose: Identifies children with behavior problems; used to evaluate children for counseling and possible referral

Description: Paper–pencil 50-item true–false inventory consisting of behavior statements that are applied to the child being rated. The checklist can be completed by anyone familiar with the child, although it is used primarily by teachers. The test provides a Total Score, a cutoff score for classifying children as disturbed, and scores for the following five scales: Acting-Out, Withdrawal, Distractibility, Disturbed Peer Relations, and Immaturity.

Format: Examiner required; suitable for group use; untimed: 5 minutes

Scoring: Hand key

Cost: Kit (200 checklists and profiles, 100 each of male and female forms, 1 manual) $72.00

Publisher: Western Psychological Services

Study Skills

Inventory of Learning Processes (ILP)
Ronald Schmeck

Copyright: 1991

Population: Ages 16 and above

Purpose: Assesses study strategies and personality correlates; used for counseling students regarding study strategies

Description: Contains 90 items, 18 scales, 5 Likert items per scale. Paper–pencil test comprised of Self Efficacy–Organization, Self Efficacy–Critical Thinking, Self Efficacy–Fact Retention, Motivation–Academic Interest, Motivation–Personal Responsibility, Motivation–Effort, Academic Self-Esteem, Academic Assertion, Conventional Attitudes, Methodical Approach, Deep-Semantic, Deep-Thinking, Elaborative–Episodic, Elaborative–Self Actualization, Agentic–Serial, Agentic–Analytic, Literal Memorization, and Lie.

Format: Individual administration; suitable for group use; untimed

Scoring: Examiner evaluated; machine scored; computer scored

Cost: Contact publisher

Publisher: Ronald Schmeck

Survey of Study Habits and Attitudes (SSHA)
W. F. Brown, W. H. Holtzman

Copyright: 1967

Population: Adolescents, adults; Grades 7 through college

Purpose: Measures study methods, motivation for studying, and certain attitudes toward scholastic activities that are important in the classroom

Description: Paper–pencil 100-item test measuring four basic aspects of study habits and attitudes: delay avoidance, work methods, teacher approval, and education acceptance. Students rate themselves according to their own habits and attitudes. The test yields a Study Habits subtotal, a Study Attitude subtotal, and total Study Orientation scores. Two forms, Form H (Grades 7–12) and Form C (college students) are available. Available in Spanish.

Format: Self-administered; suitable for group use; untimed: 20–25 minutes

Scoring: Hand key; may be machine scored

Cost: Examination Kit (survey, IBM 805 answer document, key, manual) $30.50; 25 surveys $43.00; 50 IBM 805 answer documents $38.00; manual and keys $25.50

Publisher: Harcourt® Brace Educational Measurement

Teacher Rating of Academic Achievement Motivation (TRAAM)

Terry A. Stinnett, Judy Oehler-Stinnett

Copyright: 1996

Population: Grades 2 through 6

Purpose: Assessment for helping determine whether poor school performance is caused by academic skills deficit or motivation deficits; used by psychologists, counselors, and educators

Description: Multiple-choice 50-item test assessing four factors: Mastery/Effort, Curiosity/Persistence, Academic/Cognitive Skills, and Academic Work Completion.

Format: Examiner required; not suitable for group use; untimed: 30 minutes

Scoring: Computer scored

Cost: Contact publisher

Publisher: MetriTech, Inc.

Test Alert®

Copyright: 1993, 1991

Population: Grades 1 through 8

Purpose: Develops fundamental test-taking skills to prepare students for standardized achievement tests

Description: The goal of this program is to produce test scores that accurately reflect student achievement. Level A, Grades 1 and 2, attempts to familiarize students with the standardized test format before they have ever been tested. The only prerequisite skill for this program is knowledge of letters and numbers, not reading. It can also be used with kindergarten children toward the end of the school year. It is organized into five lessons, one for each day of the school week, each progressing from simple to more complex skills: Good Listening, Good Guessing, A Closer Look at Numbers, A Closer Look at Words, and Using Clues. At Levels B and C, Grades 3–6, the listening skills that are so important at Level A are replaced with an emphasis on reading and language. The 10 lessons of Levels B and C are organized into four units: Mechanics of Test Taking, Reading Strategies, Mathematics Strategies, and Language Strategies. At Level D, Grades 7 and 8, there is more emphasis on interpretive reasoning and less call for practice with separate answer sheets. Level D reflects this change of emphasis in its four units: Mechanics of Test Taking, Reading Strategies, Mathematics Strategies, and Language Strategies.

Format: Group administered; examiner required; Level A, 30–45 minutes/lesson; Levels B and C, 45 minutes/lesson

Scoring: Examiner evaluated

Cost: Level A Classroom Package (25 activity books, Teacher's Guide, and merit badges) $81.00; Levels B, C, and D Classroom Packages (25 activity books, Teacher's Guide) $111.00 each level

Publisher: Riverside Publishing Company

Business Education

ACT PEP RCE: Business: Business Policy and Strategy

Copyright: 1994

Population: Adults; college level

Purpose: Measures upper-level knowledge and understanding of business policy and strategy;

used to grant college credit and advanced placement in academic courses

Description: Nine-item essay test. Two forms are available. A test booklet, answer sheet, and pen are used. Examiner must have experience with test administration at the college level. May be used for persons with visual, hearing, physical, and mental disabilities.

Format: Examiner required; suitable for group use; timed: 4 hours

Scoring: Machine scored

Cost: $140.00

Publisher: American College Testing

ACT PEP RCE: Business: Corporation Finance

Copyright: 1990

Population: Adults; college level

Purpose: Measures lower-level knowledge and understanding of material taught in introductory corporation finance courses; used to grant college credit and advanced placement in academic courses

Description: Paper–pencil 131-item multiple-choice test. Scale scores range from 20 to 80. Two forms are available. A test booklet, answer sheet, and pen are used. Examiner must have experience with test administration at the college level. May be used for persons with visual, hearing, physical, and mental disabilities.

Format: Examiner required; suitable for group use; timed: 3 hours

Scoring: Machine scored

Cost: $55.00

Publisher: American College Testing

ACT PEP RCE: Business: Human Resources Management

Copyright: 1994

Population: Adults; college level

Purpose: Used by adults wanting to earn college credit by examination; assesses upper-level knowledge of human resource management

Description: Extended-response essay test with 10 to 14 items. Two forms are available. A test booklet, answer document, and a pen are used. A college reading level is required. Examiner must have experience with college test administration. May be used for persons with visual, physical, hearing, and mental disabilities.

Format: Suitable for group use; examiner required; timed: 3 hours

Scoring: Examiner evaluated

Cost: $140.00

Publisher: American College Testing

ACT PEP RCE: Business: Labor Relations

Copyright: 1994

Population: Adults; college level

Purpose: Used by adults wanting to earn college credit by examination; assesses upper-level knowledge in labor relations

Description: Extended-response essay test with 10 to 14 items. Two forms are available. A test booklet, answer document, and pen are used. A college reading level is required. Examiner must have experience with college test administration. May be used for individuals with visual, physical, hearing, and mental disabilities.

Format: Suitable for group use; examiner required; timed: 3 hours

Scoring: Examiner evaluated

Cost: $140.00

Publisher: American College Testing

ACT PEP RCE: Business: Organizational Behavior

Copyright: 1994

Population: Adults; college level

Purpose: Used by adults wanting to earn college credit by examination; assesses upper-level knowledge of organizational behavior

Description: Extended-response essay test with 10 to 14 items. Two forms are available. A test booklet, answer document, and a pen are used. A college reading level is required. Examiner must have experience with college test administration. May be used for individuals with visual, physical, hearing, and mental disabilities.

Format: Suitable for group use; examiner required; timed: 3 hours

Scoring: Examiner evaluated

Cost: $140.00

Publisher: American College Testing

ACT PEP RCE: Business: Principles of Management

Copyright: 1992

Population: Adults; college level

Purpose: Used by adults wanting to earn college credit by examination; assesses intro-level management knowledge

Description: Multiple-choice 141-item test. Scale scores range from 20 to 80. Two forms are available. A test booklet, answer sheet, and pencil are used. A college reading level is required. Examiner must have experience with test administration at the college level. Available in large print. May be used for individuals with visual, physical, hearing, and mental disabilities.

Format: Suitable for group use; examiner required; timed: 3 hours

Scoring: Machine scored

Cost: $55.00

Publisher: American College Testing

ACT PEP RCE: Business: Production/Operations Management

Copyright: 1991

Population: Adults; college level

Purpose: Used by adults wanting to earn credit by examination; assesses intro-level knowledge in production/operations management

Description: Paper–pencil 125-item multiple-choice test. Scale scores range from 20 to 80. Two forms are available. A test booklet, answer sheet, and pencil are used. Examiner must have experience with test administration at the college level. May be used for persons with visual, physical, hearing, and mental disabilities.

Format: Examiner required; suitable for group use; timed: 3 hours

Scoring: Machine scored

Cost: $140.00

Publisher: American College Testing

Development and Readiness

AGS Early Screening Profiles (ESP)

Patti Harrison, Alan Kaufman,
Nadeen Kaufman, Robert Bruininks,
John Rynders, Steven Ilmer, Sara Sparrow,
Domenic Cicchetti

Copyright: 1990

Population: Ages 2 years to 6 years 11 months

Purpose: Used for screening

Description: The ESP is an ecological assessment battery that uses multiple domains, settings, and sources to measure the cognitive, motor, self-help/social, articulation, health development, and home environment of young children. ESP screens the five major developmental areas specified by the Education of the Handicapped Amendments of 1986: cognitive, language, motor, self-help, and social development. Materials included in each kit: administration manual, easel, Motor Profile booklet, bag of manipulatives, packet of record forms, packet of Self-Help/Social Profiles, packet of Home/Health questionnaires, and a packet of Score Summaries.

Format: Individually administered, either as a mass screening or one-on-one by a single examiner; 15–30 minutes

Scoring: ESP uses a two-level scoring system: Level I scores available for two subscales of

Cognitive/Language Profile; subscales and subtests of the Cognitive/Language Profile can be scored using Level II scores.

Cost: Test kit (manuals, easel, 25 test records, 25 self-help/Social Profile Questionnaires, 25 score summaries, sample Home/Health History Survey, tape measure, beads) $278.95

Publisher: American Guidance Service

AGS Edition of the Developmental Indicators for the Assessment of Learning–Revised (DIAL–R)
Carol Mardell-Czudnowski
Dorothea S. Goldenberg

Copyright: 1990

Population: Ages 2 years to 5 years 11 months

Purpose: Used for screening

Description: DIAL–R is an individually administered screening test designed to identify young children in need of further diagnostic assessment of curricular modification. Subtests assess behaviors in the motor, concepts, and language areas. Test includes a checklist of social/emotional behavior.

Format: Individually administered in a station format by a team of professionals/paraprofessionals; 20–30 minutes for entire test, 5–8 minutes per subtest

Scoring: Task scores summed to obtain an item raw score, then converted into an item scaled score, then they are summed to obtain the DIAL–R Total score.

Cost: Test kit (manual, 50 record booklets, 100 cutting cards, 50 parent information forms, training packet, area subtests for motor, concepts, and language areas with manipulatives and dials) $278.95

Publisher: American Guidance Service

Aptitude Tests for School Beginners (ASB)

Copyright: 1974

Population: Children; ages 5 to 8

Purpose: Assesses aptitudes of children begin-

ning school; used for placement, program planning, and prediction of future achievement

Description: Multiple-item paper–pencil test measuring eight areas important in the early school years: perception, spatial, reasoning, numerical, gestalt, coordination, memory, and verbal comprehension. The test yields a differential aptitude profile rather than IQ-type score. Administration during the first two months of the school year is recommended.

Format: Examiner required; suitable for group use; timed: 7 hours

Scoring: Hand key; examiner evaluated

Cost: Contact publisher

Publisher: Human Sciences Research Council

Assessing Prelinguistic and Early Linguistic Behaviors
Lesley Olswang, Carol Stoel-Gammon, Truman Coggins, R. Carpenter

Copyright: 1987

Population: Children; ages 9 months to 24 months

Purpose: Identifies early emerging speech and language behaviors for children ages 9 to 24 months and older children whose functional age is below 24 months; used for developing assessment procedures and generating normative data documenting language development

Description: Program containing five scales assessing prelinguistic and early linguistic development: Cognitive Antecedents to Word Meaning, Play, Communicative Intention, Language Comprehension, and Language Production. This assessment protocol is described in a 165-page manual, *Assessing Prelinguistic and Early Linguistic Behaviors in Developmentally Young Children.* For each scale, the manual discusses the scale's theoretical foundation; describes the administration procedures, behaviors, and normative data; and provides a training supplement. The manual is accompanied by a videotape (optional) that demonstrates the methods used in assessing the behaviors outlined in the manual.

Format: Examiner required; not suitable for

group use; timed: time not available

Scoring: Examiner evaluated

Cost: Manual (binder format) $40.00; ½" VHS video $225.00

Publisher: University of Washington Press

Basic School Skills Inventory–Diagnostic (BSSI–D)
Donald D. Hammill, James E. Leigh

Copyright: 1983

Population: Ages 4 years to 6 years 11 months

Purpose: Determines the special learning needs of children by pinpointing both the general areas and the specific readiness skills that need remedial attention

Description: Paper–pencil 110-item test enabling the examiner to view a child's performance individually or compared with peers. Measures six areas of school performance: daily living skills, spoken language, reading readiness, writing readiness, math readiness, and classroom behavior.

Format: Individual administration; checklist format

Scoring: Examiner administration and interpretation

Cost: Complete kit (manual, answer sheets, picture book, and storage box) $84.00

Publisher: PRO-ED, Inc.

Basic School Skills Inventory–Screen (BSSI-S)
Donald D. Hammill, James E. Leigh

Copyright: 1983

Population: Ages 4 years to 6 years 11 months

Purpose: Diagnoses children who are "high risk" for school failure, need more in-depth assessment, and should be referred for further evaluation; assesses a child's overall readiness for school

Description: Paper–pencil 20-item observational screening device that examines daily living skills, spoken language, reading readiness, writing readiness, math readiness, and classroom behavior. The examiner checks off the answers he or she knows about the child; further investigation may be needed for some items.

Format: Individual administration; checklist format; 5–8 minutes

Scoring: Examiner administration and interpretation

Cost: Complete kit (manual, answer sheets, picture book, and storage box) $29.00

Publisher: PRO-ED, Inc.

Battelle Developmental Inventory (BDI)
Jean Newborg, John R. Stock, Linda Wnek, John Guidubaldi, John Svinicki

Copyright: 1984

Population: Ages birth through 8

Purpose: Evaluates the development of children from infant to primary levels; screens and diagnoses developmental strengths and weaknesses

Description: Multiple-item test assessing key developmental skills in five domains: personal–social, adaptive, motor, communication, and cognition. Information is obtained through structured interactions with the child in a controlled setting, observation of the child, and interviews with the child's parents, caregivers, and teachers. Test items contain content and sequence directly compatible with infant and preschool curricula. The test may be administered by a team of professionals or by an individual service provider. Directions for modifications are included for children with various disabilities. A Screening test containing 96 items is included in the complete BDI kit.

Format: Individual administration; examiner required; 1–2 hours for Complete, 10–30 minutes for Screening

Scoring: Examiner interpretation; scoring service available from publisher

Cost: Complete Program (test books, examiner's manual, scoring booklets, visuals, and case) $249.00

Publisher: Riverside Publishing Company

Bayley Scales of Infant Development®–Second Edition (BSID®–II)

Nancy Bayley

Copyright: 1993

Population: Children; ages 1 month to 42 months

Purpose: Assesses mental, motor, and behavioral development; used for assessing developmental progress, comparison with peers, and providing an objective basis for determining eligibility for special services

Description: Two-scale test of infant mental and motor development. The Mental Development assesses sensory–perceptual behavior, learning ability, and early communication attempts. The Index-Psychomotor measures general body control, coordination of large muscles, and skills in fine-muscle control of hands. The materials include a kit containing stimulus items and the Behavior Rating Scale for noting qualitative aspects of behavior.

Format: Examiner required; not suitable for group use; untimed: 25–60 minutes

Scoring: Examiner evaluated; hand scorable

Cost: Complete Kit (manual, stimulus booklet, 25 each of the mental scale record forms, motor scale record forms, and behavior rating scale record forms; visual stimulus cards, map) $760.00

Publisher: Harcourt® Brace Educational Measurement

Birth to Three Assessment and Intervention System (BTAIS)

Tina E. Bangs, Susan Dodson

Copyright: 1986

Population: Ages 0 to 3

Purpose: Comprehensive program that allows examiners to identify, measure, and address developmental delays

Description: Includes a norm-referenced screening test, a criterion-referenced checklist, and an intervention manual. The screening test has standard scores, percentiles, and stanines. It measures language (receptive and expressive), avenues for learning, social–emotional development, and motor ability. Checklist results can be used to prepare a development plan, while the Intervention Manual details how to set up a program for parents to assist their children who are at risk.

Format: Individual administration; untimed

Scoring: Examiner administration and interpretation

Cost: Complete Kit (manuals, test forms, checklist forms) $198.00; Screening Test Kit (screening manual and test forms) $79.00

Publisher: PRO-ED, Inc.

Boehm Test of Basic Concepts–Preschool Version

Ann E. Boehm

Copyright: 1986

Population: Children; ages 3 to 5

Purpose: Measures a young child's knowledge of 26 basic relational concepts; used to identify weaknesses in basic concept comprehension for development of appropriate remediation

Description: Test with 52 items utilizing a pictorial booklet to display the concepts to be tested. The child responds to oral instructions by pointing to one of several pictures. The examiner records the child's responses on the record form. Each concept is tested twice.

Format: Examiner required; not suitable for group use; untimed: 10–15 minutes

Scoring: Hand key

Cost: Complete Kit (picture book, manual, 35 individual record forms, class record) $102.00

Publisher: Harcourt® Brace Educational Measurement

Boehm Test of Basic Concepts–Revised (BOEHM–R)

Ann E. Boehm

Copyright: 1986

Population: Children; Grades K through 2

Purpose: Measures children's mastery of basic concepts used in classroom instruction; identifies individual children with low level of concept development; targets specific areas for basic concept remediation

Description: Paper–pencil 50-item multiple-choice picture test of concepts in such contexts as quantity, space, and time. The child responds to oral instructions by marking one of several pictures. Two alternate forms, C and D, measure the same concepts. A new 26-item Applications level for Grades 1 and 2 requires the child to respond to combinations of basic concepts. Available in Spanish.

Format: Examiner required; suitable for group use; untimed: 30 minutes

Scoring: Hand key

Cost: Examination Kit (1 copy each booklet Form C, D, and Applications, Directions, Manual, Class Record, Parent–Teacher Conference Report, Hand Key) $42.00

Publisher: Harcourt® Brace Educational Measurement

Bracken Basic Concept Scale (BBCS)
Bruce A. Bracken

Copyright: 1984

Population: Children; ages 2 years 6 months to 8 years

Purpose: Measures a child's acquisition of basic concepts; used with both regular and special education populations

Description: Verbal 258-item "point-to" test using picture stimuli to evaluate 11 categories of basic concept acquisition, including color, shape, size, quantity, counting, letter identification, direction/position, time/sequence, texture, comparisons, and social/emotional responses. The four-option multiple-choice items are intended to reduce the probability of guessing. The instrument is available as a complete diagnostic scale that measures 258 basic concepts and as a screening test. Results of the diagnostic scale can be applied in planning therapy or lessons. The screening test identifies kindergarten and first-grade students whose concept development is below age-level expectations. Two alternate forms facilitate pre- and posttest assessment.

Format: Examiner required; not suitable for group use; untimed: 20–40 minutes

Scoring: Hand key

Cost: Complete Program (examiner's manual, diagnostic scale stimulus manual, 25 diagnostic scale record forms, one screening test Form A, one screening test Form B) $153.50

Publisher: Harcourt® Brace Educational Measurement

Bracken Basic Concept Scale–Screening Test (BBCS–Screening)
Bruce A. Bracken

Copyright: 1984

Population: Children; ages 2 years 6 months to 8 years

Purpose: Helps identify kindergartners and first graders whose ability to distinguish concepts is below age-level expectations; used as a guide for further testing

Description: Paper–pencil 30-item multiple-choice test in which books of picture stimuli assess different concepts of approximately equal difficulty in eight categories of basic concept acquisition. The test yields a single norm-referenced standard score. Two alternate forms are available for pre- and posttesting.

Format: Examiner required; suitable for group use; timed: 5–10 minutes

Scoring: Hand key

Cost: Contact publisher

Publisher: Harcourt® Brace Educational Measurement

BRIGANCE® Diagnostic Inventory of Early Development–Revised
Albert H. Brigance

Copyright: 1991

Population: Children; developmental ages 0 to 7

Purpose: Measures the development of children functioning below the developmental age of 7 years; diagnoses developmental delays and monitors progress over a period of time; used to develop IEPs

Description: Two hundred paper–pencil oral-response and direct-observation skill assessments measuring psychomotor, self-help, communication, general knowledge and comprehension, and academic skill levels. Test items are arranged in developmental sequential order in the following major skill areas: preambulatory, gross motor, fine motor, prespeech, speech and language, general knowledge and comprehension, readiness, basic reading, manuscript writing, and basic math skills. An introductory section outlines how to administer the tests, assess skill levels, record the results, identify specific instructional objectives, and develop IEPs. Results, expressed in terms of developmental ages, are entered into the individual record book, which indicates graphically that five optional advanced assessments are included for students scoring 95% or above on the basic first-grade assessment. Optional forms for teacher/parent rating and examiner observations are reproducible. Separate pupil data sheets are required, each testing the level of competency the individual has achieved. An optional group record book monitors the progress of 15 individuals.

Format: Examiner required; not suitable for group use; untimed: time varies

Scoring: Examiner evaluated

Cost: Assessment Book $124.00; Group Record Book $12.95; Free Test Excerpts available; 10-pack Developmental Record Books $26.90

Publisher: Curriculum Associates®, Inc.

BRIGANCE® K and 1 Screen–Revised
Albert H. Brigance

Copyright: 1992

Population: Children; Grades K through 1

Purpose: Screens the basic skills necessary for success in Grades K–1; identifies students needing special service referral, determines appropriate pupil placement, and assists in planning instructional programs and developing IEPs

Description: Multiple-item paper–pencil oral-response and direct-observation assessments

measuring the following basic skills: personal data response, color recognition, picture vocabulary, visual discrimination, visual–motor skills, standing gross-motor skills, draw-a-person, rote counting, identification of body parts, reciting the alphabet, following verbal directions, numeral comprehension, recognizing lowercase letters, auditory discrimination, printing personal data, syntax and fluency, and numerals in sequence. Class summary record folders are available. Criterion-referenced results are translated directly into curriculum or program objectives to meet the needs of individual pupils. Test items are cross-referenced to the BRIGANCE Inventory of Basic Skills and the Inventory of Early Development–Revised to facilitate further evaluation of skill deficiencies. Validation study completed in 1995.

Format: Examiner required; not suitable for group use; untimed: 12 minutes

Scoring: Examiner evaluated

Cost: Assessment Manual $64.90; 30 Pupil Data Sheets $19.85, 10-pack Summary Record Folder for Grade K $23.85; 30 Pupil Data Sheets $20.15; 10-pack Summary Record Folder for Grade 1 $23.80; free validation study summary available

Publisher: Curriculum Associates®, Inc.

BRIGANCE® Preschool Screen
Albert H. Brigance

Copyright: 1985

Population: Children; ages 3 to 4

Purpose: Evaluates basic developmental and readiness skills of children; used for program planning, placement, and special service referrals

Description: Multiple-item oral-response and task-performance test evaluating basic developmental and readiness skills. Children identify body parts, objects, and colors; demonstrate gross and visual motor skills; match colors; explain the use of objects; repeat sentences; build with blocks; and provide personal data. Number concepts, picture vocabulary, use of plurals, -ing endings, prepositions, and irregular plural nouns are tested also. Rating forms and supplementary skill assessments allow for additional observations and extended screening options. Validation study completed in 1995.

Format: Examiner required; suitable for group use; untimed: 12 minutes

Scoring: Examiner evaluated

Cost: SCREEN (with building blocks for tests) $64.00; 30 3-year-old child data sheets $20.90; 30 4-year-old child data forms $20.50; free validation study summary available

Publisher: Curriculum Associates®, Inc.

Caregiver's School Readiness Inventory (CSRI)
Marvin L. Simmer

Copyright: 1989

Population: Children; ages 4 to 5 years

Purpose: Assesses school readiness; predicts early school problems

Description: Three-item paper–pencil checklist. Scores yield at-risk odds.

Format: Individual administration; examiner required; untimed: 2–3 minutes

Scoring: Hand key

Cost: $11.50

Publisher: Phylmar Associates

Cattell Infant Intelligence Scale
Psyche Cattell

Copyright: Not provided

Population: Children; ages 3 months to 30 months

Purpose: Assesses the mental development of infants

Description: Test of early development rating infant verbalizations and motor control, such as the manipulation of cubes, pencils, pegboards, and other stimulus items. The test has been modified with items from the Gesell, Minnesota Preschool, and Merrill-Palmer scales and is applicable to a younger age range than the Stanford-Binet Intelligence Scale. Materials include a kit containing stimulus items.

Format: Examiner required; not suitable for group use; untimed: 20–30 minutes

Scoring: Examiner evaluated

Cost: Contact publisher

Publisher: The Psychological Corporation

Cognitive Abilities Scale (CAS)
Sharon Bradley-Johnson

Copyright: 1987

Population: Ages 2 to 3

Purpose: Identifies children with cognitive developmental deficiencies; used for planning instructional programs and as an overall performance measure for children who will not talk or whose speech is unintelligible

Description: Test with 88 items in which toys are used as stimuli to assess language, imitation, reading, memory, mathematics, handwriting, and other skills important for school success. A total score, five subtest scores, and percentile and standard scores are obtained.

Format: Individual administration; 30–45 minutes

Scoring: Examiner scoring and interpretation

Cost: Complete Kit (manual, child's book, protocols, picture cards, toys, and storage box) $134.00

Publisher: PRO-ED, Inc.

Communicative Evaluation Chart
Ruth M. Anderson, Madeline Miles, Particia A. Matheny

Copyright: 1963

Population: Children; infancy to 5 years

Purpose: Assesses children's development of overall abilities in language and visual–motor–perceptual skills; identifies children needing referral for clinical evaluation

Description: Items listed on chart are evaluated: physical well-being, normal growth and development, motor coordination, beginning visual–motor–perception skills.

Format: Examiner required

Scoring: Examiner interpretation

Cost: $1.25 each; pkg. of 50 $44.00

Publisher: Educators Publishing Service, Inc.

Comprehensive Identification Process (CIP)–Second Edition
R. Reid Zehrbach

Copyright: 1996

Population: Children; ages 2 years 5 months to 5 years 5 months

Purpose: Evaluates the mental and physical development of young children; used to identify those in need of special medical, psychological, or educational help before entering kindergarten or first grade

Description: Criterion-referenced and perceptual multiple-item verbal response and task-assessment test of eight areas of child development: cognitive–verbal, fine motor, gross motor, speech and expressive language, hearing, vision, social/affective behavior, and medical history. The screening kit contains administrator's and interviewer's manuals, screening booklet, 35 parent interview forms, 35 observation of behavior forms, 35 speech and expressive language forms, symbol booklet, 35 record folders, and the materials required for the tasks (blocks, balls, beads, buttons, crayons, etc.). The test can be administered by trained paraprofessionals supervised by professionals in the preschool area. The test helps meet the Child-Find requirements of P.L. 101-476 (IDEA).

Format: Examiner required; not suitable for group use; untimed: time varies

Scoring: Examiner evaluated

Cost: Screening Kit $168.00

Publisher: Scholastic Testing Service, Inc.

Concept Assessment Kit–Conservation (CAK)
Marcel L. Goldschmid, Peter M. Bentler

Copyright: 1968

Population: Children; ages 4 to 7

Purpose: Assesses the cognitive development of preschool and early school-age children; used to assess the effect of training based on Piaget's theories

Description: Multiple-item task-assessment and oral-response test measuring the develop-

ment of the concept of conservation. Two parallel forms, A and B, measure conservation in terms of two-dimensional space, number, substance, continuous quantity, discontinuous quantity, and weight. Form C measures conservation in terms of area and length. Test items are constructed to assess the child's conservation behavior and comprehension of the principle involved. The items require the child to indicate the presence or absence of conservation and specify the reason for his or her judgment. CAK is relatively independent of IQ but correlates significantly with school performance. The two parallel forms assess the effect of training, and Form C tests the transfer effects of the training. Norms are provided separately for boys and girls ages 4 to 7.

Format: Examiner required; not suitable for group use; untimed: 15 minutes per form

Scoring: Hand key

Cost: Complete Kit (Forms A, B, C; manual) $52.25

Publisher: EdITS/Educational and Industrial Testing Service

DABERON Screening for School Readiness–Second Edition (DABERON–2)
Virginia A. Danzer, Mary Frances Gerber, Theresa M. Lyons, Judith K. Voress

Copyright: 1991

Population: Ages 4 to 6

Purpose: Provides a standardized assessment of school readiness in children including those with learning or behavior problems who are functioning at the early elementary level

Description: Measurement of development, categorization, and other developmental abilities that relate to early academic success. The Learning Readiness Equivalency Age score may be used to identify children at risk for school failure. The test can help identify instructional objectives and develop IEPs. It includes the Classroom Summary Form and the Report on Readiness, a summary of performance, and practical suggestions for parents. The test samples knowledge of body parts, color and number concepts and gross motor and fine motor skills.

Format: Individual administration; 20–40 minutes

Scoring: Examiner evaluated

Cost: Complete Kit (administration manual, 25 screen forms, 25 reports on readiness, 5 classroom summary forms, 24 presentation cards, object kit of manipulatives, storage box) $114.00

Publisher: PRO-ED, Inc.

Denver Child Health Passport
William K. Frankenburg,
Benjamin Gitterman

Copyright: 1994

Population: Children; ages 0 to 6

Purpose: Monitors health care given

Description: A monitor of health care comprised of screenings, examinations, tests, lab work, and health education. Materials include a passport/record book. A sixth-grade reading level is required. Must be administered by a physician or nurse.

Format: Individual administration; examiner required

Scoring: Computer scored

Cost: $30.00

Publisher: Denver Developmental Materials, Inc.

Denver Developmental Activities
William K. Frankenburg

Copyright: Not provided

Population: Children; ages 0 to 6

Purpose: Used as suggestions to parents for activities promoting development

Description: No-response examination with more than 100 items suitable for all populations. Forms are available according to age groups: birth to age 6. Categories include personal–social, fine motor, language, gross motor. A sixth-grade reading level is required.

Format: Not applicable

Scoring: Not applicable

Cost: $11.25 and $16.50

Publisher: Denver Developmental Materials, Inc.

Denver II
William K. Frankenburg, Josiah Dodds,
Philip Archer, Howard Shapiro,
Beverly Bresnick

Copyright: 1989

Population: Children; ages 0 to 6

Purpose: Assesses personal, social, fine- and gross-motor, language, and adaptive abilities as a means of identifying possible problems and screening for further evaluation

Description: Verbal 125-item test in which personal–social, fine-motor, adaptive language is measured. Available also in Spanish.

Format: Individual administration; examiner required; timed: 10–20 minutes

Scoring: Examiner evaluated

Cost: 100 test forms $19.00; kit $40.00; manual $21.00; technical manual $22.00

Publisher: Denver Developmental Materials, Inc.

Developmental Activities Screening Inventory–Second Edition (DASI–II)
Rebecca R. Fewell, Mary Beth Langley

Copyright: 1984

Population: Ages 0 to 5 years

Purpose: Detects early developmental disabilities in children

Description: Total-response and task-performance 67-item test assessing 15 developmental skill categories ranging from sensory intactness, means–end relationships, and causality to memory, seriation, and reasoning. Test items may be administered in different sequences in one or two sittings. Instructions are given either verbally or visually. Each test item includes adaptations for use with visually impaired children.

Format: Individual administration, can be given by teacher; 20–40 minutes

Scoring: Examiner scored and interpreted

Cost: Complete kit (manual, protocols, picture cards, configuration cards, numeral cards, word cards, shape cards, and storage box) $74.00

Publisher: PRO-ED, Inc.

Developmental History Checklist
Edward H. Dougherty
John A. Schinka

Copyright: 1989

Population: Children; ages 5 to 12

Purpose: Assesses development of children

Description: Designed to be completed by a parent, guardian, or clinician. Includes 136 items covering family history, developmental history, educational history, family background, medical history, and current behavior. Computer version using IBM PCs and compatibles available.

Format: Checklist

Scoring: Examiner evaluated

Cost: Package of 25 $34.00; computer version $295.00

Publisher: Psychological Assessment Resources, Inc.

Developmental Observation Checklist System (DOCS)
Wayne P. Hresko, Shirley A. Miguel,
Rita J. Sherbenou, Steve D. Burton

Copyright: 1994

Population: Ages birth through 6 years

Purpose: Measures the areas of language, motor, social, and cognitive development to identify possible developmental delay

Description: Multiple-item screening questionnaire that meets the mandates of the Education of the Handicapped Amendments of 1986 and is based on current theory. The test can be completed by parents or caregivers. It has a sufficient number of items, interactive play items at the earlier developmental levels, and environmental input on family stress and support as well as problematic child behaviors. Responses are based on careful observation of the child's daily behaviors. The three-part system provides standard scores, percentiles, and NCE equivalents in Overall Development, Developmental Cognition, Developmental Language, Developmental Social Skills, and Developmental Motor Skills.

Format: Questionnaire; 30 minutes

Scoring: Examiner scoring and interpretation

Cost: Complete Kit (manual, protocols, and storage box) $104.00

Publisher: PRO-ED, Inc.

Developmental Profile II (DP–II)
Gerald D. Alpern, Thomas Boll,
Marsha Shearer

Copyright: 1986

Population: Children; ages 0 to 9

Purpose: Evaluates the age-equivalent physical, social, and mental development of children with or without disabilities; used for counseling, school planning, and research

Description: Paper–pencil or computer-administered 186-item interview test covering five areas: physical, self-help, social, academic, and communication. Developmental age scores are derived by interviewing a parent or through teacher observation. From birth to age 4, the scales are graded by half-year increments. From ages 5 to 9, they are graded in yearly increments. The test also provides an IQ equivalency score. Materials include test books, profile and scoring forms, a manual, and step-by-step procedures for test administration and interpretation. The computer version is suitable for use with IBM PC or compatible systems. The manual must be purchased separately for the computer version. A computer report is available through mail-in service or on-site (if the computer version is used).

Format: Examiner required; suitable for group use; untimed: 20–40 minutes

Scoring: Examiner evaluated; may be computer scored

Cost: Paper–pencil Version Complete Kit (25 scoring/profile forms, manual, 2 WPS Test Report Answer Sheets) $120.00

Publisher: Western Psychological Services

Developmental Tasks for Kindergarten Readiness–II

Walter J. Lesiak, Judi Lucas Lesiak

Copyright: 1994

Population: Children; ages 4 years 6 months to 6 years 2 months

Purpose: Assesses successful performance in kindergarten; intended for preschool and kindergarten students

Description: Fifteen subtests: Social Interaction, Name Printing, Body Concepts–Awareness, Body Concepts–Use, Auditory Sequencing, Auditory Association, Visual Discrimination, Visual Memory, Visual Motor, Color Naming, Relational Concepts, Number Counting, Number Use, Number Naming, Alphabet Knowledge.

Format: Examiner required; not suitable for groups; untimed: 20–30 minutes

Scoring: Hand key

Cost: Complete kit $74.00

Publisher: PRO-ED, Inc.

Early Coping Inventory

Shirley Zeitlin, G. Gordon Williamson, Margery Szczepanski

Copyright: 1988

Population: Children; ages 4 months to 36 months

Purpose: Assesses the coping-related behaviors of infants and toddlers

Description: Behavioral observation 48-item inventory designed to assess the coping-related behaviors of infants and toddlers who function in the 4- to 36-month age range. Items are divided into three subtests: sensorimotor organization, reactive behavior, and self-initiated behaviors. The manual contains instructions for rating, scoring, and implementing results. Available in large print.

Format: Examiner required; suitable for group use; untimed: time varies

Scoring: Hand key

Cost: Starter Set $47.40

Publisher: Scholastic Testing Service, Inc.

Early School Assessment (ESA)

Copyright: 1990

Population: Grades Pre-K through 1

Purpose: Assesses skills that are characteristic of kindergarten children and prerequisite to formal instruction in reading and mathematics

Description: Multiple-item two-level paper–pencil multiple-choice test used to assess skills in the following scales: language, visual, auditory, math concepts and operations (number concepts), math concepts and operations (logical operations), and memory. Six testing sessions.

Format: Examiner required; suitable for group use; untimed: 15–30 minutes per scale

Scoring: Hand key; scoring service available from publisher

Cost: Review Kit $18.20

Publisher: CTB/McGraw-Hill

Early Screening Project (ESP)

Hill H. Walker, Herbert H. Severson, Edward G. Feil

Copyright: 1995

Population: Children; ages 3 to 5

Purpose: Diagnoses behavior disorders

Description: Enables educators to proactively screen and identify children in the 3- to 5-year age range who are experiencing preschool adjustment problems—whether internalizing or externalizing. Using standardized criteria to evaluate both the frequency and intensity of adjustment problems, ESP screens for children whose social behavior may indicate at-risk status for emotional problems, speech and language difficulties, impaired cognitive ability, attention deficits, hyperactivity, and other barriers to learning. Each ESP Kit contains a User's Manual, ESP Instrument Packet, a Social Observation Training Video, and a stopwatch.

Format: Individual administration; suitable for group use; examiner required; untimed

Scoring: Examiner evaluated

Cost: $95.00

Publisher: Sopris West, Inc.

Einstein Measurement of Children's Cognitions (E=MC²)
Ruth L. Gottesman, Jo Ann Doino-Ingersoll, Frances M. Cerullo

Copyright: Not provided

Population: Grades K through 5

Purpose: Used to identify children who are "at risk" for or experiencing school learning difficulties

Description: The test has six levels, one for each grade. Major skill areas underlying school achievement are measured: Language/Cognition, Letter Recognition, Word Recognition, Oral Reading, Reading Comprehension, Auditory Memory, Arithmetic, and Visual–Motor Integration. The total score reflects the child's overall performance on a variety of tasks that assess school-related skills.

Format: Individual administration; examiner required; untimed: 7–10 minutes

Scoring: Hand key

Cost: Complete (specify level) $60.00

Publisher: Slosson Educational Publications, Inc.

Eliot-Price Test
John Eliot, Lewis Price

Copyright: 1976

Population: Ages 5 and up

Purpose: Measures perspective taking for Piagetian research

Description: The test consists of 30 items in a multiple-choice paper–pencil format. Results are to be forwarded to John Eliot.

Format: Group or individual; 15 minutes

Scoring: Examiner administration and interpretation

Cost: Free

Publisher: University of Maryland

Essential Skills Screener (ESS)
Bradley T. Erford, Gary J. Vitali, RoseMary Haas, Rita R. Boykin

Copyright: 1995

Population: Ages 3 to 11

Purpose: Identifies children "at-risk" for school readiness or learning problems

Description: Reading, writing, and math skills are assessed for children in three age ranges: 3 to 5, 6 to 8 and 9 to 11. The ESS provides both grade and age norms. Interpretation is simplified through the use of percentile ranks, performance ranges, and standard scores. Age scores and grade scores are provided.

Format: Individual administration; suitable for group use; 10 minutes

Scoring: Hand key

Cost: Complete $169.00

Publisher: Slosson Educational Publications, Inc.

Extended Merrill-Palmer Scale
Rachel Stutsman Ball, Philip R. Merrifield, Leland H. Stott

Copyright: 1978

Population: Children; ages 3 to 5

Purpose: Measures intelligence in children

Description: Task-assessment 16-item and oral-response test measuring the mental processes of evaluation and production with both semantic and figural units. The 16 tasks include tower building, ambiguous forms, food naming, dot joining, word meaning, pie completion, action agents, copying, round things, block sorting, following directions, 3-cube pyramid, 6-cube pyramid, action agents, stick manipulation, and design productions. Scores and percentile ranges are provided in six intervals from ages 3 to 5 for four specific abilities, each of which is tested by four of the tasks. The abilities are semantic production, figural production, semantic evaluation, and semantic production.

Format: Examiner required; suitable for group use; timed: 4–5 minutes

Scoring: Examiner evaluated

Cost: Complete Kit (test materials, record forms, scoring forms, manual, carrying case) $500.00

Publisher: Stoelting Co.

Fisher-Landau Early Childhood Screening (FLECS)

Francee R. Sugar, Amy Stone Belkin

Copyright: 1995

Population: Grades through K through 1

Purpose: Assesses a young student's abilities on a range of language, perceptual–motor, and readiness skills

Description: Identifies strengths and weaknesses so that teachers may tailor curriculum to an individual student or whole class.

Format: Examiner required; individual administration; untimed

Scoring: Examiner evaluated

Cost: Examiner's Manual $9.15; Stimulus Book $14.00; test booklets $24.00; Specimen Set $25.15

Publisher: Educators Publishing Service, Inc.

Five P's: Parent/Professional Preschool Performance Profile

Judith Simon Bloch

Copyright: 1987

Population: Children; ages 2 to 6 years functioning between 6 and 60 months

Purpose: Assesses the development of young children with disabilities in the home and at school; used for the IFSP

Description: Observational 458-item assessment instrument consisting of 13 scales grouped in six developmental areas: Classroom Adjustment, Self-Help Skills, Language Development, Social Development, Motor Development, and Cognitive Development. Scale items describe developmental skills and interfering behaviors. Items are observed by teacher and parent on a 3-point Likert scale. The assessment is completed periodically to monitor change and to provide a means of ongoing assessment linked to remediation. Also available in Spanish.

Format: Individual administration; time varies

Scoring: Examiner evaluated

Cost: Sample Packet $75.00; Educational Assessment for class of 10 children $125.00;

Computerized Preschool Short-Term Instructional Objectives (IBM) $350.00; video $45.00; manual $25.00

Publisher: Variety Pre-Schooler's Workshop

Goodman Lock Box

Joan Goodman

Copyright: 1981

Population: Children; Pre-K

Purpose: Screens preschool children for mental retardation, fine-motor problems, and distractibility/hyperactivity; used as a nonthreatening warm-up instrument for more extensive preschool screening

Description: Multiple-task assessment of a preschooler's ability to organize a free-choice situation. The child is presented with a box with 10 locked doors to open and investigate. A toy is behind each door. The manner in which the child removes the toys is observed to determine whether the child is systematic and organized or poorly focused and distractible. The test relies entirely on spontaneous behavior (no questions asked). It supplements, without duplicating, other intelligence tests. Norms are provided at 6-month intervals for normally developing children and at yearly intervals for mentally retarded children.

Format: Examiner required; not suitable for group use; timed: 6 1/2 minutes

Scoring: Examiner evaluated

Cost: Complete Kit (testing materials, manual, record forms) $895.00

Publisher: Stoelting Company

Humanics National Child Assessment Form: Ages 0 to 3

Copyright: 1992

Population: Children; ages 0 to 3

Purpose: Records children's skills and behaviors; used by parents and teachers for planning educational and developmental experiences

Description: Paper–pencil 90-item checklist for assessing the development of a child's skills and behaviors in five areas: social–emotional, language, cognitive, gross motor, and fine motor. Items are arranged in developmental sequence. Space is provided for recording observations 3 times during 1 year.

Format: Examiner required; not suitable for group use; untimed: time varies

Scoring: Examiner evaluated

Cost: 25 forms $29.95; handbook $15.95; Specimen Set (handbook and 5 forms) $22.95

Publisher: Humanics Psychological Test Corporation

Humanics National Child Assessment Form: Ages 3 to 6

Copyright: 1993

Population: Children; ages 3 to 6

Purpose: Records children's skills and behaviors; used by parents and teachers for planning educational activities

Description: Multiple-item paper–pencil checklist for measuring skills and behaviors of children. Teachers or teacher aides record observations for educational planning. The checklist is useful in helping parents understand their child's growth and development.

Format: Examiner required; not suitable for group use; untimed: time varies

Scoring: Examiner evaluated

Cost: 25 forms $29.95; handbook $17.95; Specimen Set (handbook and 5 forms) $24.95

Publisher: Humanics Psychological Test Corporation

Infant Reading Tests
M. A. Brimer, B. Raban

Copyright: 1979

Population: Children; ages 4 to 6

Purpose: Assesses the reading-related skills of children

Description: Multiple-item task-performance diagnostic tests measuring reading-related abilities. The three prereading tests, used with children who have not begun formal reading instruction, examine linguistic competence, the

ability to use printed symbols, recognition of speech sounds, and discrimination of printed shapes. The three reading tests examine word recognition, sentence completion, and reading comprehension skills. Together, the tests yield a profile of maturation and learning. Rather than standardized scores and reading ages, the tests provide a scale ranging from 1 to 7, derived in the same manner as the new British Ability Scales. A score of 2 or lower indicates that a child lacks the skill tested. A score of 5 or higher indicates that the child has mastered the skill.

Format: Examiner required; suitable for group use; untimed: 20 minutes

Scoring: Hand key

Cost: Contact publisher

Publisher: Educational Evaluation Enterprises

K1 Assessment Activities

Copyright: Not provided

Population: Grades K through 1

Purpose: Assesses performance in areas of reading/language arts and mathematics of young children

Description: Various group, partner, and individual activities used to assess outcomes and encourage independent and cooperative work. Scores are entered on Summary Profiles in back of book and are based on classroom observation and specific guidelines for evaluating student work.

Format: Examiner required; suitable for group use; untimed

Scoring: Examiner evaluated

Cost: K-1 Assessment Activities (includes product overview and all activities, activity sheets, and scoring sections) $40.25

Publisher: CTB/McGraw-Hill

Kaufman Developmental Scale (KDS)
Harvey Kaufman

Copyright: 1974

Population: Children

Purpose: Evaluates school readiness, developmental deficits, and all levels of retardation for normal children through age 9 and persons with MR of all ages; used in programming accountability

Description: Task-assessment 270-item test consisting of behavioral evaluation items that are actually expandable teaching objectives. The KDS yields a Developmental Age and Developmental Quotient, as well as individual age scores and quotients for the following areas of behavioral development: gross motor, fine motor, receptive, expressive, personal behavior, and interpersonal behavior.

Format: Examiner required; not suitable for group use; untimed: typical time not available

Scoring: Examiner evaluated

Cost: Complete Kit (testing materials, manual, 25 record forms, carrying case) $400.00

Publisher: Stoelting Company

Kaufman Infant and Preschool Scale (KIPS)
Harvey Kaufman

Copyright: 1981

Population: Children

Purpose: Measures early high-level cognitive process and indicates possible need for intervention in nonretarded children ages 1 month to 4 years and in retarded children and adults with mental ages of 4 years or less

Description: Multiple-item task-assessment and observation measure of high-level cognitive thinking. The child is observed and asked to perform a number of tasks indicative of his or her level. All test items are "maturational prototypes" that can be taught to enhance maturation. The test covers general reasoning, storage, and verbal communication. The test yields the following scores: Overall Functioning Age (Mental Age) and Overall Functioning Quotient. Based on a child's performance on the scale, the manual suggests types of activities and general experience the child needs for effective general adaptive behavior.

Format: Examiner required; not suitable for group use; untimed: 30 minutes

Scoring: Examiner evaluated

Cost: Complete Kit (manipulatives, stimulus cards, 10 evaluation booklets) $300.00

Publisher: Stoelting Company

Kaufman Survey of Early Academic and Language Skills (K-SEALS)
Alan S. Kaufman, Nadeen L. Kaufman

Copyright: 1993

Population: Ages 3 years to 6 years 11 months

Purpose: Measures language skills, pre-academic skills, and articulation

Description: Three subtests (Vocabulary; Numbers, Letters, and Words; and Articulation) provide an expanded and enhanced version of the Cognitive/Language Profile in the AGS Early Screening Profiles. The scores reflect many aspects of the child's language and early academic development.

Format: Individual administration; 15–25 minutes

Scoring: Examiner interpreted

Cost: Complete Kit (manual, easel, test protocols, carrying bag) $149.95

Publisher: American Guidance Service

Kent Infant Development Scale (KID Scale)
Jeanette M. Reuter, Lewis Katoff

Copyright: 1978 to 1995

Population: Infants or children; developmental ages 0 to 14 months

Purpose: Uses caregiver reports to screen and assess the developmental strengths and needs of infants and young children with disabilities who are chronologically or developmentally under 14 months of age

Description: Paper–pencil or computer-administered 252-item inventory that has caregivers describe behaviors characteristic of infants in the first year of life. Test items cover five behavioral domains: cognitive, motor, language, self-help, and social. Developmental ages for each domain and for the full-scale are based on a normative sample of healthy infants. Specifically, the test can be used to assess the developmental status of healthy infants (0 to 14 mos.), infants at risk (0 to 20 mos.), and severely handicapped young children (2 to 8 years). The scale has been used for evaluating early intervention projects, monitoring the developmental progress of NICU graduates, teaching teenage mothers about their child's development, and evaluating at-risk infants. Also available in Spanish, Dutch, German, Russian, and Hungarian.

Format: Individual administration; untimed: 30–40 minutes

Scoring: Hand key or computer scored

Cost: Template Kit (hand score) $72.50; Computer Kit (MS-DOS program) $172.50

Publisher: Kent Developmental Metrics, Inc.

Kindergarten Readiness Test (KRT)

Sue Larson, Gary J. Vitali

Copyright: 1988

Population: Ages 4 to 6

Purpose: Identifies school readiness

Description: Consolidates critical areas of various developmental tests into one single form, making identification of school readiness more efficient and valid. The KRT targets and screens key developmental traits across a broad range of skills necessary to begin school: Reasoning, Language, Auditory and Visual Attention, Numbers, Fine Motor Skills, and several other cognitive and sensory-perception areas. Test booklet and additional forms are designed for use in parent conferences or interprofessional presentations. The KRT may be used to identify possible disabilities at an early age and facilitate writing developmental plans.

Format: Examiner required; individual administration; 15 minutes

Scoring: Hand key

Cost: Complete $92.00

Publisher: Slosson Educational Publications, Inc.

Koontz Child Developmental Program: Training Activities for the First 48 Months

Charles W. Koontz

Copyright: 1974

Population: Children; developmental ages 1 month to 48 months

Purpose: Evaluates the development of children with and without retardation who are functioning at developmental levels of 1 to 48 months; used for evaluating and developing skills; may be modified for use with children with hearing and visual disabilities

Description: Paper–pencil 550-item inventory of observable performance items arranged to parallel development in a normal child. A parent, teacher, or therapist checks off the specific behaviors that have been observed in the child's routine activities in order to establish the level of functioning in each of four areas of evaluation (gross motor, fine motor, social, and language). Progress is recorded in relation to performance items, and the training activities are designed to reinforce and develop each skill. The test pages, which are made of cardboard, are organized so that different developmental age levels of each of the four areas appear at the same time. Consequently, an examiner working with a child functioning at different levels in any of the four areas has all the appropriate activities visible simultaneously.

Format: Examiner required; not suitable for group use; untimed: typical time not available

Scoring: Hand key

Cost: Complete Kit (50 record cards, 1 copy of *Koontz Child Developmental Programs: Training Activities for the First 48 Months*) $65.00

Publisher: Western Psychological Services

Lollipop Test: A Diagnostic Screening Test of School Readiness

Alex L. Chew

Copyright: 1992

Population: Children; Pre-K through Grade 1

Purpose: Evaluates the school readiness of preschoolers, kindergartners, and first graders; used to plan individualized programs in Grades K–1

Description: Multiple-item oral-response and task-assessment measuring a preschooler's attainment of the developmental skills necessary for success in Grades K–1. Test items are culture-free. Results identify both deficiencies and strengths for each child tested. The test may be administered before and after preschool programs to assess progress in readiness skills booklets. Available in Spanish. The four areas have all the appropriate activities visible simultaneously.

Format: Examiner required; suitable for group use

Scoring: Examiner evaluated

Cost: Test Kit (manual, 7 cards, 25 booklets) $49.95; manual $14.95; stimulus cards $10.95; 25 booklets $29.95

Publisher: Humanics Psychological Test Corporation

McCarthy Screening Test (MST)
Dorothea McCarthy

Copyright: 1978

Population: Children; ages 4 through 6 years

Purpose: Screens for potential learning problems

Description: Includes six component scales, all drawn from the McCarthy Scales of Children's Abilities, that are predictive of a child's ability to cope with schoolwork in the early grades. The MST helps educators identify children who may be "at risk" for learning problems. The subtests measure cognitive and sensorimotor functions central to the successful performance of school tasks, including Verbal Memory, Right–Left Orientation, Leg Coordination, Draw-A-Design, Numeric Memory, and Conceptual Grouping. Although interpretation of the MST requires training in psychology, it can be easily administered and scored by the classroom teacher or trained paraprofessional.

Format: Individual administration; approximately 20 minutes

Scoring: Hand scored

Cost: Complete Set (manual, 25 record forms, 25 drawing booklets) $178.00

Publisher: The Psychological Corporation

Metropolitan Readiness Tests: Sixth Edition (MRT6)
Joanne R. Nurss

Copyright: 1995

Population: Children; ages 4 to 7; Pre-K to Grade 1

Purpose: Assesses underlying skills important for early school learning; for use in identifying each individual child's needs

Description: Multiple-item paper–pencil test of skills important for learning reading and mathematics and for developing language. The test is divided into two levels. Level 1 assesses literacy development in Pre-K and beginning kindergarten children. Level 2 assesses beginning reading and mathematics development in the middle and end of kindergarten and at the beginning of Grade 1.

Format: Examiner required; Level 1—individual administration, Level 2—suitable for group use; timed: Level 1, 85 minutes, Level 2, 100 minutes

Scoring: Hand scorable

Cost: Level 1 Complete Kit $75.00; Level 2 Examination Kit $10.00

Publisher: Harcourt® Brace Educational Measurement

Mullen Scales of Early Learning: AGS Edition
Eileen M. Mullen

Copyright: 1995

Population: Birth to 68 months

Purpose: A comprehensive scale of cognitive functioning in multiple developmental domains; used to assess learning styles, strengths, and weaknesses

Description: Consists of a Gross Motor Scale (birth to 33 months) together with four cognitive scales—Visual Reception, Fine Motor,

Receptive Language, and Expressive Language (birth to 68 months each). An Early Learning Composite score is derived from the scores on the cognitive scales. Results provide a profile of cognitive strengths and weaknesses that can be used to develop individualized program plans. Items are performance based, involving the child in a variety of activities. The kit includes a manual, item administration book, stimulus book, record forms (pkg. of 25), and many attractive, colorful manipulatives.

Format: Individual administration; 15–30 minutes (birth to 2 years), 40–60 minutes (3 to 5 years)

Scoring: Examiner administration and interpretation, *T*-scores on each scale, test age scores; composite standard score; ASSIST is available for PC, Macintosh, and Windows formats

Cost: Complete Kit $599.00

Publisher: American Guidance Service

Newborn Behavior Inventory
Barbara J. Anderson, Kay Stanley

Copyright: 1979

Population: Newborns

Purpose: Assesses parents' perception of infant neonatal behavior

Description: True–false 24-item test. Materials include 24 cards.

Format: Individual administration; examiner required; untimed

Scoring: Examiner evaluated

Cost: $15.00

Publisher: Select Press

PACE
Lisa K. Barclay, James R. Barclay

Copyright: 1986

Population: Preschoolers; ages 4 to 6 years

Purpose: Assesses academic and social readiness and identifies learning skill deficits in preschool children; used by school psychologists, special educators, teachers, and other professionals involved in preschool screening, educational placement, and remediation

Description: Task-performance 68-item instrument in which the examiner observes the child's behavior in 12 areas: motor coordination, eye–hand coordination, small muscle coordination, visual perception, rhythm recognition, listening, visual matching, tactile skills, motor behavior memory, verbal memory, attending, and social interaction. Parents' observations may be integrated and compared with classroom results. A short form (FAST PACE) that includes 18 of the original items can be used as a brief, preliminary screening device. The computer software operates on IBM PC systems.

Format: Examiner required; suitable for small group use; untimed: 30 to 45 minutes

Scoring: Examiner evaluated; computer scored

Cost: PACE 50 administration software $87.50; Fast PACE 100 administration software $100.00

Publisher: MetriTech, Inc.

Parent Behavior Checklist
Robert A. Fox

Copyright: 1994

Population: Parents of children aged 1 year to 4 years 11 months

Purpose: Assesses how parents raise their young children; professionals can use the instrument to assess parenting strengths and weaknesses to plan intervention

Description: Test with 100 items and three scales: Expectations Scale—50 items; Discipline Scale—30 items; and Nurturing Scale—20 items. A manual and test form is used. A 3.0 reading level is required.

Format: Self/examiner administered; not suitable for groups; untimed: 10–20 minutes

Scoring: Hand key

Cost: Complete kit (Manual and forms) $44.00

Publisher: PRO-ED, Inc.

Phelps Kindergarten Readiness Scale
Leadelle Phelps

Copyright: 1991

Population: Children; Pre-K, early K

Purpose: Assesses kindergarten readiness

Description: Paper–pencil oral-response short-answer point-to test with eight subtests: Vocabulary, Verbal Reasoning, Analogies, Visual Discrimination, Perceptual Motor, Auditory Discrimination, Auditory Digit Memory, and Memory of Sentences and Stories. Available in Spanish.

Format: Individual administration; examiner required; untimed: 15–20 minutes

Scoring: Examiner evaluated

Cost: Evaluation Set $25.00; materials prices are on a sliding scale

Publisher: Psychology Press, Inc.

Preschool Evaluation Scale (PES)
Stephen B. McCarney

Copyright: 1992

Population: Children; ages birth to 72 months

Purpose: Used in child development to screen for developmental delays and behavior problems

Description: Subscales are large muscle skills, small muscle skills, cognitive thinking, expressive language, social/emotional behavior, and self-help skills. Irregularities in normal development are determined in order to provide an appropriate intervention plan to remediate. A computer version using IBM/Macintosh PCs is available.

Format: Individual administration

Scoring: Self/computer scored

Cost: Complete Kit $74.50

Publisher: Hawthorne Educational Services, Inc.

Preschool Screening Instrument (PSI)
Stephen Paul Cohen

Copyright: 1994

Population: Children; ages 4 years to 5 years 3 months

Purpose: Identifies prekindergarten children with learning disabilities; used to meet IDEA screening requirements

Description: Multiple-item task-assessment test in which the child is told he or she will be "playing some games" with the examiner, who administers the following subtests: Figure Drawing, Circle Drawing, Tower Building, Cross Drawing, Block Design, Square Drawing, Broad Jumping, Balancing, Ball Throwing, Hopping, Whole Name, Picture Responses, Comprehension, and Oral Vocabulary. The child's responses are evaluated in seven developmental areas: visual–motor perception, fine-motor development, gross-motor skills, language development, verbal fluency, conceptual skills, and speech and behavioral problems.

Format: Examiner required; not suitable for group use; untimed: 5–8 minutes

Scoring: Examiner evaluated

Cost: Complete Kit (25 student record books, manual, 16 wooden blocks, picture story card, 6 kindergarten-size pencils) $75.00

Publisher: Stoelting Company

Prescreening Developmental Questionnaire (PDQ)
William F. Frankenburg, W. VanDoorninck, T. Liddell, N. Dick

Copyright: 1975

Population: Children; ages 3 months to 6 years

Purpose: Determines whether children can perform certain skills performed by most children their age; used as an indicator for further testing

Description: Paper–pencil 97-item test administered by the parents, who are given response forms color-coded by age with 10 questions appropriate for each age group. Forms are available for the following age groups: 3 to 8 months, 9 to 15 months, 16 to 24 months, 2 years 1 month to 4 years 9 months, and 5 to 6 years. Examiners must have at least a high school education. Also available in Spanish and French.

Format: Examiner required; suitable for group use; untimed: 2–5 minutes

Scoring: Hand key

Cost: 100 forms (specify age group) English $15.00–$17.00; Spanish $18.00–$20.00; French $19.00–$21.00; directions and interpretive instructions included

Publisher: Denver Developmental Materials, Inc.

Preverbal Assessment-Intervention Profile (PAIP)
Patricia Connrad

Copyright: 1984

Population: All ages

Purpose: Assesses communication and motor performance of students and adults whose communication performance is between the developmental range of 0 to 9 months; diagnoses communication needs and evaluates prelinguistic behavior of preverbal individuals

Description: Multiple-item three-stage observational procedure for observing and reporting performance in a natural environment. The test assesses the sensorimotor domains of auditory, visual, vocal/oral, and motor in a manner that yields an individualized preverbal/motor assessment profile. The examiner records information supplied by parents, caregivers, and teachers; observes behaviors during eating, bathing, dressing, and playing; and presents structured tasks using spoons, mirrors, lights, spinning and pull toys, and so forth. The test, used primarily with severely retarded, profoundly retarded, or multidisabled individuals, can be adapted for stroke patients.

Format: Examiner required; not suitable for group use; untimed: typical time not available

Scoring: Examiner evaluated

Cost: Complete Kit (assessment manual and 5 assessment record booklets) $59.00

Publisher: PRO-ED, Inc.

Primary Test of Cognitive Skills (PTCS)

Copyright: 1990

Population: Grades K through 1

Purpose: Assesses intellectual functioning of young children, including verbal, spatial, memory, and concepts; used by teachers to identify students who may be gifted or have learning disabilities or "unique" developmental delays

Description: Multiple-item paper–pencil multiple-choice test divided into four subtests: verbal, spatial, memory, and concepts. It yields four subscales that combine with the child's age to produce a single Cognitive Skills Index (CSI). May be used with the CAT/5 or CTBS/4 to produce an Anticipated Achievement score to screen children for potential learning disabilities.

Format: Examiner required; suitable for group use; untimed: 30 minutes per subtest

Scoring: Machine scored; examiner evaluated

Cost: Review Kit $18.20

Publisher: CTB/McGraw-Hill

Printing Performance School Readiness Test (PPSRT)
Marvin L. Simmer

Copyright: 1990

Population: Children; ages 4 to 5 years

Purpose: Predicts early school problems

Description: Paper–pencil criterion-referenced test. Scores yield at-risk odds.

Format: Individual administration; examiner required; untimed: 10–15 minutes

Scoring: Hand key

Cost: $25.00

Publisher: Phylmar Associates

Reading Readiness Test: Reversal Tests (Bilingual)
Ake W. Edfeldt

Copyright: Not provided

Population: Children; Grade 1

Purpose: Measures degree of speech reversal tendencies in young children before they learn to read; used by educators and speech therapists to predict reading problems in first grade

Description: Oral-response test based on

research into the cause and effect of word transposition tendencies of children. The test was developed to diagnose and prevent these difficulties. A child who is scored either as "control case" or as "not yet ready to read" is not considered ready to master reading and therefore should postpone instruction.

Format: Examiner required; not suitable for group use; untimed: typical time not available

Scoring: Hand key; examiner evaluated

Cost: Contact publisher

Publisher: Institute of Psychological Research, Inc.

Revised Pre-Reading Screening Procedures to Identify First Grade Academic Needs
Beth H. Slingerland

Copyright: 1977

Population: Children; Grades K through 1

Purpose: Tests evaluate auditory, visual, and kinesthetic strengths in order to identify children who may have some form of dyslexia or specific language disability; should be used with students who have had no introduction to reading

Description: Series of 12 verbal–visual subtests measuring visual perception; visual discrimination; visual recall; visual-motor skills; auditory recall; auditory discrimination; auditory perception; letter knowledge; and language skills, such as vocabulary, enunciation, comprehension of oral directions, oral expression, and recall of new words. The test also evaluates motor coordination, hobbies and interests, attention span, and mental growth. The test identifies children who are ready for formal instruction in reading, writing, and spelling and are able to learn through conventional methods; children who, while appearing to be ready, reveal indications of a language disability and need immediate multisensory instruction; children who show language confusion but whose maturity indicates a need to begin strengthening their language background; children of any age who are unready to begin reading instruction and who would benefit from more readi-

ness and social development training. The examiner first explains the directions to the students, and then they proceed with the task.

Format: Examiner required; suitable for group use; untimed: 2–3 hours

Scoring: Hand key; examiner evaluated

Cost: 12 test booklets $15.95; teacher's manual $5.75; teachers cards and chart $7.45; Specimen Set (teacher's manual, test booklet) $6.00

Publisher: Educators Publishing Service, Inc.

Revised Prescreening Developmental Questionnaire (R–PDQ)

Copyright: 1986

Population: Children; ages 0 to 6

Purpose: Determines whether a child possesses developmental skills acquired by most other children of his or her age; used to indicate further testing

Description: Paper–pencil 105-item prescreening test administered by the child's parents. This updated version is designed to include more age-appropriate items, simplified parent scoring, and easier norm comparisons. Forms are available for the following age ranges: 0 to 9 months, 9 to 24 months, 2 to 4 years, and 4 to 6 years. Examiners must have at least a high school education.

Format: Examiner required; suitable for group use; untimed: office assistant 2 minutes; parents 10 minutes

Scoring: Hand key

Cost: 100 forms $15.00–$17.00

Publisher: Denver Developmental Materials, Inc.

Riley Preschool Developmental Screening Inventory
Clara M. D. Riley

Copyright: 1969

Population: Children; Grades Pre-K through 1

Purpose: Measures readiness to attend school and identifies children most likely to need assistance in adjusting to normal school situations; used for counseling and to meet the requirements of IDEA

Description: Multiple-item observational test providing a child's developmental age and self-concept and determining serious developmental and maturational problems. The instrument can be administered at the beginning of preschool, kindergarten, or first grade. It was developed and has been used widely in Head Start programs. Suggested cutoff scores are provided. Test instructions are in both Spanish and English.

Format: Examiner required; suitable for group use; untimed: 15–20 minutes

Scoring: Examiner evaluated

Cost: Kit (25 tests, 1 manual) $35.00

Publisher: Western Psychological Services

Ring and Peg Tests of Behavior Development for Infants and Preschool Children
Katherine M. Banham

Copyright: 1963

Population: Children; ages 0 to 6

Purpose: Measures the development of infants and preschool children and helps identify the social and motivational factors influential in a child's development; used for clinical assessment of infant and child development

Description: Task-assessment test measuring five categories of behavioral performance and ability: ambulative, manipulative, communicative, social–adaptive, and emotive. The test covers a wider range of items than standard intelligence tests in order to provide the clinical psychologist with diagnosis information. The scale yields a point score and a behavior age for the whole test, as well as for each of the five categories. A developmental quotient (D 1) may be derived from the full-scale behavior age. The test kit includes minimally culture-bound manipulation objects, manual, test booklet, and scoring sheet.

Format: Examiner required; not suitable for group use; untimed: 45 minutes

Scoring: Hand key

Cost: Professional Examination Kit (25 tests, handbook) $20.00; 25 score sheets $5.00

Publisher: Psychometric Affiliates

Rockford Infant Developmental Evaluation Scales (RIDES)

Copyright: Not provided

Population: Children; ages birth to 4

Purpose: Evaluates the level of a child's skill and behavioral development; used for initial assessment by special education teachers to guide and objectify their observations of a child

Description: Multiple-item criterion-referenced evaluation of 308 developmental behaviors in five skill areas: personal-social/self-help, fine motor/adaptive, receptive language, expressive language, and gross motor. Children respond verbally or by pointing. Each behavioral item is determined to be present, emerging, or absent in the child. Test results relate these single items to major developmental patterns and competencies and provide an informal indication of a child's development. The format calls for one eight-page booklet per child. An Individual Child Progress Graph on the back page shows progress and allows comparison of levels across developmental areas. The manual contains a section detailing development, use, and interpretation of the test. The entries for all 308 behaviors provide scoring criteria, developmental significance, equipment specifications, and references to further information. An appendix containing master equipment list, skill group listing, notes, and bibliography is included. Examiner must be certified for assessment.

Format: Individually administered; examiner required; not suitable for group use; untimed: time varies

Scoring: Examiner evaluated

Cost: Starter Set $75.95

Publisher: Scholastic Testing Service, Inc.

Rossetti Infant-Toddler Language Scale
Louis Rossetti

Copyright: 1990

Population: Children; ages birth to 3

Purpose: Assesses language skills of children from birth through 36 months of age; used for communicative disorders, early childhood intervention, developmental delays, and behavior disorders for use with premature and at-risk infants/toddlers

Description: Oral response 291-item criterion-referenced projective, verbal, point-to, gesture, vocalization test comprised of six domains: interaction attachment, pragmatics, gesture, play, language comprehension, and language expression. An examiner's manual with scoring standards and interpretation is available. A Parent Questionnaire is also included.

Format: Individual administration; examiner required; untimed

Scoring: Examiner evaluated; no scoring service available

Cost: Manual, 10 test forms, and 10 parent questionnaires $54.95

Publisher: LinguiSystems, Inc.

School Readiness Evaluation by Trained Testers (SETT)

Copyright: 1984

Population: Children; preschool

Purpose: Evaluates the developmental level of children about to begin school; used by teachers for classifying entering students and by psychologists for diagnostic purposes

Description: Test with 36 items evaluating the language and general, physical and motor, and emotional and social development of children entering school. Items are constructed to create learning situations similar to those that occur in the classroom and to promote interaction between the teacher and the student. Scores yield five groups of beginners distinguished according to the types of problems that may interfere with academic development.

Format: Examiner required; not suitable for group use; untimed: 30 minutes

Scoring: Examiner evaluated

Cost: Contact publisher

Publisher: Human Sciences Research Council

School Readiness Survey
F. L. Jordan, James Massey

Copyright: Not provided

Population: Children; ages 4 to 6

Purpose: Assesses a child's understanding of numbers, colors, words, and forms; used to determine readiness for kindergarten

Description: Paper–pencil 95-item verbal test consisting of eight school readiness subtests: Number Concept, Discrimination of Form, Color Naming, Symbol Matching, Speaking Vocabulary, Listening Vocabulary, General Information, and General Readiness. The test may be administered by parents or an examiner. Parent-administered scores are correlated with teacher-administered scores. Materials include suggestions to parents for developing the child's skill areas.

Format: Examiner required; not suitable for group use; untimed: typical time not available

Scoring: Examiner evaluated

Cost: Preview Kit (booklet, manual) $10.00

Publisher: Consulting Psychologists Press, Inc.

School Readiness Test (SRT)
O. F. Anderhalter, Jan Perney

Copyright: 1990

Population: Children; Grades K through 1

Purpose: Determines individual and group readiness for first grade; used to identify and diagnose students with skill deficiencies

Description: Multiple-choice criterion-referenced test designed for children entering first grade. The test reveals readiness for formal instruction by assessing eight skill areas: number knowledge, handwriting ability, vocabulary, identifying letters, visual discrimination, auditory discrimination, comprehension and interpretation, and spelling ability. Raw scores, national percentiles, stanines, and norm curve equivalents are yielded. The test results, which can be used as the basis for placement, show a child at one of six readiness levels. A booklet and pencil are used. Examiner must be certified for assessment.

Format: Examiner required; suitable for group use; both timed and untimed sections

Scoring: Hand key

Cost: Starter Set $48.50

Publisher: Scholastic Testing Service, Inc.

Screening Children for Related Early Educational Needs (SCREEN)
Wayne P. Hresko, D. Kim Reid, Donald D. Hammill, Herbert P. Ginsburg, Arthur J. Baroody

Copyright: 1988

Population: Children; ages 3 to 7

Purpose: Identifies intraindividual abilities in educationally relevant areas; used to identify mildly disabled students and to document student growth and program effectiveness

Description: Multiple-item picture-response test. The five standard scores obtained with SCREEN can be used to document student growth and program effectiveness. SCREEN was standardized on 1,355 children from 20 states. Characteristics of the normative sample are provided and approximate those reported in the 1986 *Statistical Abstract of the United States.* Internal consistency reliability of global and component scores exceeds .80 across all age groups. Test–retest reliability exceeds .85. Criterion-related validity is evidenced by significant correlations with other achievement tests. Construct validity is evidenced by correlations with the DTLA–2, WISC–R, and Human Figures Drawing Test, among others.

Format: Examiner required; timed: time varies

Scoring: Examiner evaluated

Cost: Complete Kit (examiner's manual, profile/record forms, student workbooks and picture book, storage box) $119.00

Publisher: PRO-ED, Inc.

Screening Test for Educational Prerequisite Skills (STEPS)
Frances Smith

Copyright: Not provided

Population: Ages 4 to 5

Purpose: Used by schools/teachers to provide a clear picture of needs and skills of beginning kindergartners

Description: STEPS screens five areas: intellectual skills, verbal information skills, cognitive strategies, motor skills, and attitudes in learning styles. The child performs several tasks: copying shapes and words, identifying colors, classifying objects, following directions, and remembering digits. The test is scored as it is given.

Format: Individual administration; examiner required; 8–10 minutes

Scoring: Hand key or computer scored

Cost: Kit (1 set of test materials, 25 Auto-Score™ forms, 25 AutoScore™ home questionnaires, 1 manual) $135.00; microcomputer disk (IBM) (good for 50 uses) $89.50

Publisher: Western Psychological Services

Slosson Test of Reading Readiness (STRR)
Leslie Anne Perry, Gary J. Vitale

Copyright: Not provided

Population: Later kindergarten through Grade 1

Purpose: Assesses reading readiness in young children

Description: The test was designed to identify children who are "at-risk" of failure in programs of formal reading instruction. STRR subtests include recognition of capital letters, recognition of lowercase letters, matching capital and lowercase letters, visual discrimination, auditory discrimination, sequencing, and opposites. Test items focus on cognitive, auditory, and visual abilities.

Format: Individual administration; examiner required; untimed: 15 minutes

Scoring: Hand key; examiner evaluated

Cost: STRR Complete $62.00

Publisher: Slosson Educational Publications, Inc.

Smith-Johnson Nonverbal Performance Scale

Alathena J. Smith, Ruth E. Johnson

Copyright: 1977

Population: Children; ages 2 to 4

Purpose: Provides a nonverbal assessment of the developmental level of children; used to evaluate hearing-impaired, language-delayed, culturally deprived, and disabled children

Description: Fourteen-category examination using nonverbal tasks to measure the developmental level of a broad range of skills in young children. Each category consists of a series of subtasks presented in order of increasing difficulty. With the exception of two tasks, the examiner proceeds to the first task in the next category as soon as the child has failed two consecutive tasks. All but one of the tasks are untimed. The test measures strengths and weaknesses across a broad range of skills without constricting the evaluation by labeling the child with a single quantitative score. Norms are provided for children with and without hearing disabilities.

Format: Examiner required; not suitable for group use; untimed: 30–45 minutes

Scoring: Hand key

Cost: Kit (1 set of test materials, 100 record sheets, 1 manual) $198.00

Publisher: Western Psychological Services

Sugar Scoring System for the Bender Gestalt Visual Motor Test

Francee R. Sugar

Copyright: 1995

Population: Grades K through 1

Purpose: Assesses visual–motor functions and developmental problems in young children

Description: The system is designed for teachers and psychologists to assess a young child's production of six of the Bender designs from both a qualitative and a quantitative point of view.

Format: Examiner required; individual administration; untimed

Scoring: Examiner evaluated

Cost: $3.15

Publisher: Educators Publishing Service, Inc.

System to Plan Early Childhood Services (SPECS)

Stephen J. Bagnato, John T. Neisworth, Jean Gordon, George McCloskey

Copyright: 1990

Population: Ages 2 to 6

Purpose: A decision-making system that links team assessment, intervention, and evaluation for children who are disabled or at risk

Description: Decision-making system for use by early childhood service teams. SPECS Starter Set consists of 50 Developmental Specs forms, 25 Team Specs forms, 25 Program Specs forms, and a manual. SPECS is used during team meetings and is expected to reduce the amount of time needed for the process.

Format: Examiner required; time varies

Scoring: Developmental Specs results are profiled, discussed during the team meeting, and used to determine service needs

Cost: Starter Set (50 Developmental Specs, 25 Team Specs, 25 Program Specs, manual $95.95

Publisher: American Guidance Service

Teacher's School Readiness Inventory (TSRI)

Marvin L. Simmer

Copyright: 1986

Population: Children; ages 4 to 5 years

Purpose: Assesses school readiness; predicts early problems

Description: Five-item paper–pencil checklist yielding at-risk odds.

Format: Individual administration; examiner required; untimed: 2–3 minutes per child

Scoring: Examiner evaluated

Cost: $12.50

Publisher: Phylmar Associates

Test of Sensory Functions in Infants (TSFI)

Georgia A. DeGangi, Stanley I. Greenspan

Copyright: Not provided

Population: Infants; ages 4 months to 18 months

Purpose: Used to identify infants with sensory integrative dysfunction

Description: Composed of 24 items, the test provides objective criteria for determining presence and extent of deficits in sensory functioning in infants. TSFI provides an overall measure of sensory processing and reactivity and also assesses these subdomains: reactivity to tactile deep pressure, visual–tactile integration, adaptive motor function, ocular motor control, and reactivity to vestibular stimulation.

Format: Individually administered; examiner required; 20 minutes

Scoring: Examiner evaluated

Cost: Kit (set of test materials, 100 administration and scoring forms, manual, plastic carrying case) $165.00

Publisher: Western Psychological Services

Tests of Basic Experiences–Second Edition (TOBE–2)

Margaret H. Moss

Copyright: 1978

Population: Children; Grades K through 1

Purpose: Measures the degree to which young children have acquired concepts and experiences related to effective school participation; used for evaluation of school readiness

Description: Multiple-item battery of paper–pencil tests measuring quantity and quality of children's early learning experiences. The test is divided into two overlapping levels, covering programs from preschool through first grade. Each level contains a language, mathematics, science, and social studies test. Each test item consists of a verbal stimulus and four pictured responses. An instructional activities kit contains materials for teaching concepts and skills.

Format: Examiner required; suitable for group use; untimed: 45 minutes per test

Scoring: Hand key

Cost: Test books (package of 30) $58.90

Publisher: CTB/McGraw-Hill

Driver's Education

. . . .

Theory Tests for Licenses

Copyright: Not provided

Population: Adults

Purpose: Assesses knowledge of driving skills; used for issuance of driver's and learner's licenses

Description: Multiple-item paper–pencil measures of vehicle driver's knowledge of the rules of the road, road traffic signs, and vehicle controls. The test also covers relevant portions of the Road Traffic Ordinances of the Provinces. Three equivalent forms are available. These tests are available only to licensing authorities with the power to issue learners' and drivers' licenses and who have examiners with certificates of competency issued by the publisher.

Format: Examiner required; suitable for group use; untimed: driver's 45 minutes, learner's 1 hour

Scoring: Hand key; examiner evaluated

Cost: Contact publisher

Publisher: Human Sciences Research Council

Wilson Driver Selection Test

Clark L. Wilson

Copyright: 1961

Population: Adults

Purpose: Evaluates visual attention, depth visualization, eye–hand coordination, steadiness, and recognition of details; used by driver selection and evaluation companies and schools to screen personnel in order to reduce the risk of operator-caused accidents

Description: Six-part paper–pencil nonverbal test measuring visual attention, depth perception, recognition of simple and complex details, eye–hand coordination, and steadiness. The booklet includes norms for males and females, as well as items on the subject's accident record and personal history. Suitable for individuals with physical, hearing, and visual disabilities.

Format: Examiner required; suitable for group use; timed: 26 minutes

Scoring: Hand key

Cost: Manual and manual supplement $39.50; key $2.95; package of tests $62.50; Specimen Set $42.00

Publisher: Martin M. Bruce, Ph.D.

English As a Second Language and Bilingual Education

. . . .

Basic Inventory of Natural Language (BINL)
Charles H. Herbert

Copyright: 1996

Population: Ages 4 years to adult; Grades Pre-K to college

Purpose: Measures students' language proficiency; used in bilingual, language development, and speech and language remediation programs

Description: Oral-response test in which each test item consists of a color photograph that is used to elicit language samples from the students. The language samples are transcribed and analyzed at three levels: word class (determiner, noun, verb, adjective, adverb, preposition, gerund, etc.); type of phrase employed (noun phrase, verb phrase, etc.); and sentence type (simple, compound, compound/complex, etc). Four BINL kits are available. Forms A and B are elementary kits for use with Grades K–6. Forms C and D are secondary kits for use with Grades 7–12. The kits include an instruction manual, 20 full-color photographs on heavy posterboard, 400 individual oral scoring sheets, class profile cards, sorting envelopes to prepare the tests for machine scoring, and materials for teaching the prescription activities included in the instructions manual. Three BINL computer-scoring programs are available. BINL I scoring is available from the publisher. The reports from this program include individual scores, class and grade level, graphs of student placement, and classification of students into four categories: Non, Limited, Functional, and Proficient. The program is available in English, Spanish, and 24 other languages.

Format: Examiner required; not suitable for group use; untimed: time varies

Scoring: Computer scored; scoring service available

Cost: Kit $59.00

Publisher: CHECpoint Systems, Inc.

....

Ber-Sil Spanish Tests: Elementary Test 1987 Revision
Marjorie L. Beringer

Copyright: 1987

Population: Ages 5 to 12

Purpose: Assesses the functioning level of children ages 5 to 12 in Spanish; used to assist in placing Spanish-speaking and speech-impaired students for efficient instruction

Description: Multiple-item paper–pencil criterion-referenced test consisting of five sections: Vocabulary (Spanish; 100 words), Action Responses to directions (13 items), Visual–Motor Activity (3 parts), Mathematics (70 items), and Vocabulary (English; 100 words) Writing samples, geometric figures, and figure drawings are included in the test. Spanish Vocabulary,

Comprehension of Spanish, Visual–Motor Abilities, Math Skills, and English Vocabulary scores are yielded. The revision includes the math and English vocabulary tests. Directions are on audiotape. Available in Spanish, Mandarin, Cantonese, Tagalog, Ilocano, Korean, and Persian translations.

Format: Examiner required; not suitable for group use; untimed: 30–60 minutes

Scoring: Hand key; examiner evaluated

Cost: Complete Kit $50.00; Combination Kit (elementary and secondary) $85.00; translation tapes $15.00

Publisher: The Ber-Sil Company

Ber-Sil Spanish Tests: Secondary Test
Marjorie L. Beringer

Copyright: 1984

Population: Ages 13 to 17

Purpose: Assesses Spanish-language and mathematics abilities of junior and senior high school students; used to assist in placing secondary Spanish-speaking or speech-impaired students for efficient instruction

Description: Multiple-item multiple-choice paper–pencil and point-to criterion-referenced test in four sections: Spanish Vocabulary (100 words), Dictation in Spanish (4 sentences), Draw a Boy or Girl (maturity level), and Mathematics (70 items). Scores indicating the level of the examinee's ability in Spanish vocabulary, Spanish grammar and spelling, maturity level, and mathematical processes are generated. The test is administered with audiotape instructions by psychologists, psychometricians, counselors, and speech specialists. It is useful for curriculum planning and academic counseling. Available in Ilocano and Tagalog translations.

Format: Examiner required; not suitable for group use; untimed: 20–30 minutes

Scoring: Hand key; examiner evaluated

Cost: Complete Kit $50.00; Combination Kit (elementary and secondary) $85.00; translation tapes $15.00

Publisher: The Ber-Sil Company

Bilingual Syntax Measure I and II (BSM)
Marina K. Burt, Heidi C. Dulay, Eduardo Hernandez

Copyright: 1978

Population: Children, adolescents; Grades K through 12

Purpose: Measures children's mastery of basic oral syntactic structures in both English and Spanish; used for diagnosis and placement in bilingual and other special language programs

Description: Multiple-item measure testing strengths and weaknesses in basic language construction by using cartoon-type pictures and simple questions to elicit natural speech patterns. The test also places pupils in a proficiency level category (in English and in Spanish). Scores may be used for determining English readiness or program exit in bilingual and other special programs. The test is available on two levels: BSMI for Grades K–2 and BSMII for Grades 3–12. The manual provides proficiency rating and equivalent LAU categories established by federal guidelines. Available in English and Spanish.

Format: Examiner required; not suitable for group use; untimed: 10–15 minutes

Scoring: Hand key

Cost: Contact publisher

Publisher: The Psychological Corporation

Brigance® Diagnostic Assessment of Basic Skills–Spanish Edition
Albert H. Brigance

Copyright: 1984

Population: Children, adolescents; Grades Pre-K through 9

Purpose: Measures the academic skills of Spanish-speaking students; distinguishes language barriers from learning disabilities; used by bilingual, ESL, migrant, and bilingual special educators to identify, develop, and implement academic programs

Description: Test composed of 102 skill sequences assessing Spanish-speaking students'

abilities in readiness, speech, functional word recognition, oral reading, reading comprehension, word analysis, listening, writing and alphabetizing, numbers and computation, and measurement. Directions to the examiner are written in English; directions to the student are written in Spanish. Assessments used for dominant language screening present directions to the student in English and Spanish. The diagnostic tests identify skills the student has and has not mastered and students who might have learning disabilities. The diagnostic tests help to determine individual instructional objectives. The dominant language screening form provides a means of comparing a student's performance in English and Spanish on all of the oral language and literacy diagnostic assessments. Results of the screening are used to place students in appropriate ESL and bilingual programs. The seven grade-level screens assess skills that indicate grade-level competency in Grades K–6. The results are used to place students at their appropriate instructional levels and to identify students who need further evaluation. Individual student record books record the level of competency the student has achieved.

Format: Examiner required; many sections are suitable for group use; untimed: time varies

Scoring: Examiner evaluated

Cost: Assessment Book $129.00; Class Record Book $12.95; 10 Student Record Books $27.95

Publisher: Curriculum Associates®, Inc.

English Placement Test (EPT)
Mary Spann, Laura Strowe, A. Corrigan, B. Dobson, E. Kellman, S. Tyma

Copyright: 1993

Population: Adults

Purpose: Assesses facility with the English language; used to group low to advanced intermediate proficiency adult nonnative speakers of English into homogenous ability levels as they enter an intensive English course

Description: Paper–pencil 100-item multiple-choice test of listening comprehension, grammar in conversational contexts, vocabulary

recognition, and reading comprehension of sentences. A tape is available for use with the listening comprehension items. Three forms (A, B, C) are available.

Format: Examiner required; suitable for group use; timed: 1 hour 5 minutes

Scoring: Hand key

Cost: Testing Package (examiner's manual, scoring stencil, 20 test booklets, 100 answer sheets, cassette) $38.00

Publisher: English Language Institute

Institutional Testing Program (ITP)

Copyright: Not provided

Population: Adolescents, adults

Purpose: Measures English proficiency of nonnative speakers of English

Description: Multiple-choice 150-item test composed of Listening Comprehension (50 items), Structure and Written Expression (40 items), Vocabulary and Reading Comprehension (60 items). This test uses retired forms of the Test of English as a Foreign Language (TOEFL). The test yields three section scores and one total score. Suitable for individuals with visual, physical, and hearing disabilities.

Format: Examiner required; suitable for group use; timed: 150 minutes

Scoring: Hand key; test scoring service available from publisher

Cost: Minimum order of 10 tests: 200 or fewer tests $14.00 each, more than 200 tests $12.00 each

Publisher: Educational Testing Service— TOEFL

IRCA Pre-Enrollment Appraisal

Copyright: 1988

Population: Adult ESL students

Purpose: Measures learners' English ability in the context of basic life skills as well as the history and government of the United States

Description: Includes a multiple-choice reading test, a short oral interview, and a two-sentence listening dictation to assess basic writing ability. The appraisal is a screening and placement test battery for beginning and intermediate limited-English–speaking adults. May be used in private postsecondary ESL programs that receive Pell Grants and are required to administer a test to show students' "ability to benefit" from instruction. The test is approved by the U.S. Dept. of Education only for students enrolling in ESL programs.

Format: Group administered

Scoring: Self-scored

Cost: Set of 25 reusable tests $44.00; Set of 25 answer sheets $25.00; administration manual $33.00

Publisher: Comprehensive Adult Student Assessment System

Language Assessment Scales–Oral (LAS–O)
Sharon E. Duncan, Edward A. DeAvila

Copyright: 1990

Population: Grades 1 through 12

Purpose: Assesses oral language abilities of students whose primary language is not English

Description: Multiple-item paper–pencil multiple-choice/oral-response test available in two levels and two forms in English, two levels and one form in Spanish. The test is based on an analysis of four primary language subsystems: phonemic, lexical, syntactical, and pragmatic. Its five sections are divided into two components: the Oral Language Component and the Pronunciation Component. Can be used with LAS Reading and Writing.

Format: Examiner required; individually administered; untimed 10–20 minutes

Scoring: Examiner evaluated

Cost: Examiner's Kit $108.50

Publisher: CTB/McGraw-Hill

Language Proficiency Test (LPT)
Joan E. Gerald, Gloria Weinstock

Copyright: 1981

Population: Ages 15 to adult

Purpose: Evaluates ability to use English language; identifies competency levels and detects specific deficiencies of ESL students

Description: Multiple-item paper–pencil criterion-referenced test in three major sections: aural/oral, reading, and writing. An optional translation section is included for ESL students. Materials were designed to be appropriate for older students. The majority of the nine subtests can be group administered. Raw scores are converted to a percentage and plotted on a profile chart that indicates level of English language competency.

Format: Individual and group administration; 1 hour 30 minutes

Scoring: Examiner administered and interpreted

Cost: Test kit (manual and protocols in vinyl folder) $45.00

Publisher: Academic Therapy Publications

LAS® Reading/Writing (LAS R/W)
Sharon E. Duncan, Edward A. DeAvila

Copyright: 1994

Population: Grades 2 through 12

Purpose: Assesses nonnative English-speaking students' reading and writing proficiency

Description: Multiple-item paper–pencil multiple-choice/essay test available in two forms and three levels in English, and one form and three levels in Spanish. Vocabulary, fluency, reading comprehension, and mechanics are assessed objectively with multiple-choice items, while writing is evaluated directly using performance assessment.

Format: Examiner required; suitable for group use; timed: 90 minutes

Scoring: Examiner evaluated; hand key

Cost: Review Kit $20.85 (English or Spanish version)

Publisher: CTB/McGraw-Hill

Listening Comprehension Test (LCT)
John Upshur, H. Koba, Mary Spaan, Laura Strowe

Copyright: 1986

Population: Adults

Purpose: Measures an individual's understanding of spoken English; used to predict the academic success of nonnative speakers of English

Description: Paper–pencil 45-item multiple-choice test of aural comprehension of English. The student is read a short question or statement and responds by marking the appropriate written answer. A tape recording of the verbal questions and statements is available. The test is available in three forms: 4, 5, and 6. This test is a retired, nonsecure component of the Michigan Test Battery. It is sold only to educational institutions for internal use (e.g., to measure the learning progress of ESL/EFL students who have already been admitted to a program or to confirm the level of proficiency of matriculated students). The tests are not to be used for initial university admission purposes or to report scores to other institutions.

Format: Examiner required; suitable for group use; timed: 15 minutes

Scoring: Hand key

Cost: Testing Package (manual, 20 test booklets, 100 answer sheets, 3 scoring stencils) $46.00

Publisher: English Language Institute

Macualitis Assessment of Competencies (MAC)
Jean D'Arcy Maculaitis

Copyright: 1994

Population: All ages

Purpose: Assesses English language proficiency for ESL and LEP individuals in reading, writing, speaking, and listening

Description: Multiple-choice paper–pencil oral-response criterion-referenced short-answer essay, verbal, point-to test with subtests: Oral Expression, Vocabulary Knowledge, Listening Comprehension, Word Recognition, and Reading Comprehension. Materials used include an administration book, record form, student booklet, and answer sheet.

Format: Examiner required; individual/group administration; timed and untimed

Scoring: Hand key; examiner evaluated

Cost: $55.00

Publisher: Steck-Vaughn/Berrent Publications

Michigan Test of English Language Proficiency (MTELP)
John Upshur

Copyright: 1977

Population: Adults

Purpose: Assesses an individual's facility with the English language; used to predict the academic success of advanced-proficiency adult nonnative speakers of English

Description: Paper–pencil 100-item multiple-choice test of grammar, reading comprehension, and vocabulary. Available in nine alternate forms (F, G, H, J, K, L, P, Q, R). These materials are retired, nonsecure components of the Michigan Test Battery and should not be used as an admission test; however, it is suitable for placement of students who already have been admitted.

Format: Examiner required; suitable for group use; timed: 1 hour 15 minutes

Scoring: Hand key

Cost: Testing Package (includes manual, scoring stencil, 20 test booklets, 100 answer sheets) $32.00

Publisher: English Language Institute

Oral Communication Applied Performance Appraisal (OCAPA)

Copyright: 1991

Population: Adults, adolescents; Native and nonnative speakers of English

Purpose: Assesses speaking, listening, reading, writing, and thinking skills in functional contexts; used as an appraisal of a client's communication skills upon entry into a job training program or to determine readiness for program exit

Description: Eight competency tasks set in an employment (primarily office) context, presented in a modified role-play format. Training is recommended. Checklist for scoring of performance on competency tasks is provided.

Format: Individual administration; oral and written responses

Scoring: Test administrator uses standardized scoring rubric

Cost: Reusable test and 30 scoring materials $50.00

Publisher: Comprehensive Adult Student Assessment System

Oral English or Spanish Proficiency Placement Test

Copyright: 1995

Population: Grades 1 through 6 and Grades 7 through 12 (adult)

Purpose: Designed to measure oral English-speaking ability of limited-English–speaking students

Description: Oral test administered in English that measures language-speaking ability. Initial directions given in the student's native language. Spanish placement test measures the oral Spanish-speaking ability of the student.

Format: Examiner required; individual administration

Scoring: Examiner evaluated

Cost: $20.00

Publisher: Moreno Education Company

Pre-LAS
Sharon E. Duncan, Edward A. DeAvila

Copyright: 1985

Population: Ages 4 to 6

Purpose: Assesses children's oral language abilities

Description: Multiple-item paper–pencil verbal/oral-response test available in two forms in English, and one form in Spanish. The test assesses expressive and receptive abilities in three linguistic components of oral language: morphology, syntax, and semantics.

Format: Examiner required; individually administered; untimed: 15–20 minutes

Scoring: Examiner evaluated

Cost: Examiner's Kit $110.75

Publisher: CTB/McGraw-Hill

Secondary Level English Proficiency Test (SLEP)

Copyright: Not provided

Population: Adolescents; ages 12 to 17

Purpose: Assesses English language proficiency of nonnative speakers; used as an admissions test by private secondary schools and as a placement test by both public and private secondary schools

Description: Paper–pencil 150-item multiple-choice test measuring two components (75 items each) of English proficiency: listening comprehension and reading comprehension (structure and vocabulary). The test does not measure productive language skills. A tape recorder is required to administer the listening comprehension sections. An audiotape is included. Raw and converted scores are provided for both the listening comprehension and reading comprehension sections. The test is available in three equivalent forms.

Format: Examiner required; suitable for group use; timed: 1 hour 20 minutes

Scoring: Hand key

Cost: Complete Kit (reusable materials, 25 test booklets, 100 answer sheets, cassette, 2 keys, manual) $100.00

Publisher: Educational Testing Service— TOEFL

Spanish and English Reading Comprehension Test

Copyright: 1993

Population: Grades 1 through 6 and Grades 7 through 12 (adult)

Purpose: Measures Spanish reading achievement based on Mexican norms to determine learning ability and learning potential; used as a tool to evaluate bilingual education programs and for research

Description: Compares Spanish reading ability with that of Mexican readers. Based on Mexican curriculum materials, standardized and normed in Mexico. Measures both Spanish and English reading comprehension. Developed and designed for use in the United States. Can be used by psychologists and evaluators for the identification of individuals who are mentally gifted and those who have learning disorders.

Format: Individual administration; suitable for group use; 25 minutes

Scoring: Examiner administration and interpretation

Cost: Elementary $20.00; Secondary $20.00 (answer sheets may be duplicated as needed)

Publisher: Moreno Education Company

Spanish Reading Comprehension Test (Evaluación de Comprensión de la Lectura)

Copyright: 1994

Population: Spanish-speaking adults and adolescents

Purpose: Used for people learning Spanish as a second language; assesses basic reading comprehension in Spanish

Description: Multiple-choice competency-based test of reading comprehension in Spanish. Contains reading selections drawn from authentic Spanish language material in functional life skill contexts. Difficulty level from 3 to 9 years of schooling. May be used as entrance appraisal, progress test, or exit measure in Spanish language instructional programs. Forms A and B are available.

Format: Group administered

Scoring: Self-scoring answer sheets

Cost: Set of 25 reusable answer sheets $44.00; Set of 25 answer sheets $25.00

Publisher: Comprehensive Adult Student Assessment System

Speaking Proficiency English Assessment Kit (SPEAK)

Copyright: 1982 to present

Population: Adults; international teaching assistants

Purpose: Assesses spoken English for international teaching assistants

Description: Twelve-item oral-response test available for purchase by institutions. Under this program, test forms are administered and scored by institutions, at their convenience, using their own facilities and staff. Scores are reported on a scale from 20 to 60 in 5-point increments. Materials used include a test book, audio test cassette, and an audio answer cassette/response tape. Revised version available for Spring 1996.

Format: Examiner required; suitable for group use; timed: 30 minutes total

Scoring: Examiner evaluated; no scoring service available

Cost: To be announced

Publisher: Educational Testing Service—TOEFL

Test of English as a Foreign Language (TOEFL)

Copyright: Not provided

Population: Adults

Purpose: Assesses proficiency in English for nonnative speakers; used as a college admission and placement test

Description: Paper–pencil 150-item multiple-choice test measuring three aspects of English ability: listening comprehension, structure and written expression, and reading comprehension. Items involve comprehension of spoken and written language. The test is administered monthly on either Friday or Saturday.

Format: Examiner required; suitable for group use; timed: 3 hours

Scoring: Computer scored

Cost: Contact publisher

Publisher: Educational Testing Service—TOEFL

Test of Spoken English (TSE)

Copyright: Not provided

Population: Adults

Purpose: Assesses nonnative speakers' proficiency in spoken English; used to evaluate applicants for graduate-level teaching assistant-ships and for certification in health-related professions whose native language is not English.

Description: Twelve-item oral-response test assessing nonnative speakers' proficiency in spoken English. A test tape leads the examinee through questions requiring controlled responses to less structured free answers that demand more active use of English. The subject's answers are taped and evaluated by two raters at ETS. The test yields scores in three areas: grammar, fluency, and pronunciation. TSE is part of the Test of English as a Foreign Language (TOEFL) program and is designed to complement the TOEFL, which does not measure oral English proficiency. The institutional version, the Speaking Proficiency English Assessment Kit (SPEAK), is available for local testing. Two additional test forms, SPEAK II and SPEAK III, are available (refer to separate listing for a full description).

Format: Examiner required; suitable for group use; untimed: 20 minutes

Scoring: Computer scored; examiner evaluated

Cost: Contact publisher

Publisher: Educational Testing Service—TOEFL

Test of Written English (TWE)
Velma R. Andersen, Sheryl K. Thompson

Copyright: 1992

Population: Adolescents, adults; students entering college

Purpose: Measures written English ability of nonnative speakers of English who wish to study at the college level; used for admissions and placement

Description: Paper–pencil criterion-referenced essay, verbal test using answer sheets, paper, pencil, and a test booklet. TWE uses a 6-point holistic score scale. This is a secure test; publisher arranges all administrations, scoring, etc. Suitable for individuals with visual, physical, or hearing disabilities.

Format: Group administration; timed: 30 minutes

Scoring: Examiner evaluated; test scoring service required from publisher

Cost: TWE is given with the TOEFL test; no additional fee

Publisher: Educational Testing Service—TOEFL

Woodcock Language Proficiency Battery–Revised (WLPB–R) English Form
Richard W. Woodcock

Copyright: 1991

Population: Ages 2 to 90+

Purpose: Assesses language skills in English; used for purposes of eligibility and determination of level of language proficiency

Description: Provides an overall measure of language proficiency in measures of oral language, reading, and written language. The subtests are Memory for Sentences, Picture Vocabulary, Oral Vocabulary, Listening Comprehension, Verbal Analogies (Oral Language); Letter–Word Identification, Passage Comprehension, Word Attack, Reading Vocabulary (Reading); Dictation, Writing Samples, Proofing, Writing Fluency; Punctuation and Capitalization, Spelling and Usage, and Handwriting (Written Language). The tests are primarily measures of language skills predictive of success in situations characterized by Cognitive Academic Language Proficiency (CALP) requirements.

Format: Individual administration; examiner required; 20–60 minutes depending on the number of subtests administered

Scoring: Examiner interpretation; computer software available for PC and Apple formats

Cost: Complete Program (Test book, audio cassette, test records, response booklets, examiner's manual, norm tables) $246.00

Publisher: Riverside Publishing Company

Woodcock Language Proficiency Battery–Revised (WLPB–R) Spanish Form
Richard W. Woodcock,
Ana F. Muñoz-Sandoval

Copyright: 1995

Population: Ages 2 to 90+

Purpose: Assesses language skills in Spanish; used for purposes of eligibility and determination of level of language proficiency

Description: Provides an overall measure of language proficiency in measures of oral language, reading, and written language. The subtests are Memory for Sentences, Picture Vocabulary, Oral Vocabulary, Listening Comprehension, Verbal Analogies (Oral Language); Letter–Word Identification, Passage Comprehension, Word Attack, Reading Vocabulary (Reading); Dictation, Writing Samples, Proofing, Writing Fluency; Punctuation and Capitalization, Spelling and Usage, and Handwriting (Written Language). The tests are primarily measures of language skills predictive of success in situations characterized by Cognitive Academic Language Proficiency (CALP)

requirements. When both versions of the WLPB–R have been administered, a Comparative Language Index that allows direct comparison between English and Spanish scores will be obtained. CALP levels are provided from Advanced to Negligible.

Format: Individual administration; examiner required; 20–60 minutes depending on the number of subtests administered

Scoring: Examiner interpretation; computer software available for PC formats

Cost: Complete Program (test book, audio cassette, test records, response booklets, English examiner's manual, English norm tables, supplemental manual) $246.00

Publisher: Riverside Publishing Company

Fine Arts

Aptitude for and Sensitivity to Music–Junior Form (ASM J)

Copyright: 1982

Population: Children; Standards 3–5

Purpose: Measures aptitude and sensitivity to music

Description: Multiple-item paper–pencil test in which students listen to taped music and answer questions designed to assess their musical aptitude and sensitivity. The five subtests are Fantasy, Various Ending, Interval, Rhythm, and Mood. A record player is required for playing the three albums on which the test is recorded.

Format: Examiner required; suitable for group use; untimed: 1 hour 30 minutes

Scoring: Hand key

Cost: Contact publisher

Publisher: Human Sciences Research Council

Aptitude for and Sensitivity to Music–Senior Form (ASM S)

Copyright: 1982

Population: Adolescents, adults; Standards 6–10 and college

Purpose: Measures aptitude and sensitivity to music

Description: Multiple-item paper–pencil test in which students listen to taped music and answer questions designed to assess their musical aptitude and sensitivity. The test consists of eight subtests: Selective Listening, Performance, Accompaniment, Interval, Harmony, Rhythm, Mood, and Degrees of Musical Enjoyment. A record player is required for playing the three albums of music.

Format: Examiner required; suitable for group use; untimed: 2 hours 15 minutes

Scoring: Hand key

Cost: Contact publisher

Publisher: Human Sciences Research Council

Instrument Timbre Preference Test
Edwin E. Gordon

Copyright: 1984

Population: Ages 9 and older

Purpose: Assesses the timbre preference of students ages 9 and older. Used to help students select appropriate brass or woodwind instruments.

Description: Multiple-item paper–pencil test identifying the timbre preferences of students. Students listen to different melodic synthesized sounds on a cassette recording and indicate their preferences on an answer sheet. Results help students choose instruments that match their timbre preferences, which improves the performance of beginning band students and reduces dropout rates.

Format: Examiner required; suitable for group use; untimed: 30 minutes

Scoring: Hand key; may be machine scored

Cost: Complete Kit (cassette, 100 test sheets, scoring masks, manual) $44.00

Publisher: GIA Publications, Inc.

Intermediate Measures of Music Audiation
Edwin E. Gordon

Copyright: 1986

Population: Children; Grades 1 through 6

Purpose: Measures the music aptitude of children

Description: Multiple-item paper–pencil test measuring and discriminating among the music aptitudes of children who obtained exceptionally high scores on the Primary Measures of Music Audiation or who are slightly older than the students targeted for the primary test. The test requires no language or music skills. Children listen to tonal and rhythm tape recordings, decide if pairs of patterns are the same or different, and circle an appropriate picture on the answer sheet. The manual contains information on converting raw scores to percentile ranks, interpreting results, and formal and informal music instruction suggestions.

Format: Examiner required; suitable for group use; untimed: 24 minutes

Scoring: Hand key

Cost: Complete Kit $85.00

Publisher: GIA Publications, Inc.

Iowa Tests of Music Literacy (ITML)
Edwin E. Gordon

Copyright: 1991

Population: Grades 4 through 12

Purpose: Assesses strengths and weaknesses in music achievement

Description: Six-level multiple-choice paper–pencil test with two categories: Tonal Concepts (45 minutes) and Rhythm Concepts (45 minutes). Listening, reading, and writing reports are available. A rhythm sheet, tonal sheet, cassette, and scoring mask are used.

Format: Suitable for group use; examiner required; timed: 90 minutes

Scoring: Hand key; no scoring service available

Cost: Entire kit $295.00

Publisher: GIA Publications, Inc.

Modern Photography Comprehension
Martin M. Bruce

Copyright: 1969

Population: Adolescents, adults

Purpose: Assesses knowledge of photography; used for vocational guidance and as a measure of classroom progress

Description: Paper–pencil 40-item multiple-choice test measuring photographic understanding. Individuals are rated on a scale of superior, high average, average, and low average. Materials include a manual and grading keys. Suitable for individuals with physical, hearing, or visual impairment.

Format: Self-administered; suitable for group use; untimed: 20–25 minutes

Scoring: Hand key

Cost: 20 tests $49.50; manual $2.00; keys $2.25; Specimen Set $8.50

Publisher: Martin M. Bruce, Ph.D.

Musical Aptitude Tests—Musat J and Musat S

Copyright: 1977

Population: Children, adolescents

Purpose: Assesses musical aptitude; used for educational evaluation

Description: Two tests of musical ability. MUSAT J (Standards 1 to 5) measures ability to perceive seven aspects of music: interval, harmony, timbre, rhythm, duration, speed, and counting units. MUSAT S (Standards 6 to 10) measures 10 aptitudes: interval, harmony, rhythm, duration, speed, counting, loudness of tone, intonation, and selective listening. Materials include records containing music especially composed for this test. A record player is required for test administration. Groups should not contain more than 20 students.

Format: Examiner required; suitable for group use; untimed: Junior 1 hour 30 minutes, Senior 2 hours 30 minutes

Scoring: Hand key; examiner evaluated

Cost: Contact publisher

Publisher: Human Sciences Research Council

Primary Measures of Music Audiation (K–3)
Edwin E. Gordon

Copyright: 1986

Population: Children; Grades K–3

Purpose: Measures the music aptitude of students

Description: Multiple-item paper–pencil test diagnosing the musical potential of students with average to low musical aptitudes. The test requires no language or music skills. Children listen to tonal and rhythm patterns sound the same or different and circle an appropriate picture on the answer sheet. The manual contains information on converting raw scores to percentile ranks, interpreting results, and formal and informal music instruction.

Format: Examiner required; suitable for group use; untimed: 24 minutes

Scoring: Hand key

Cost: Complete Kit $62.00

Publisher: GIA Publications, Inc.

Foreign Language

AATG First Level Test

Copyright: 1996

Population: High school and college students

Purpose: Measures knowledge of basic German used with secondary and college-level students

Description: Paper–pencil 70-item test assessing understanding of the German language by secondary school students completing one year of study and by college or university students completing one semester of study.

Format: Examiner required; suitable for group use

Scoring: Hand key

Cost: $3.00

Publisher: American Association of Teachers of German

AATG National German Examination for High School Students

Copyright: 1996

Population: Adolescents; Grades 9 through 12

Purpose: Measures German language achievement of high school students in their second, third, and fourth year of study; used to place transfer students, assess the progress of students and entire classes, and compare the results of various teaching methods

Description: Multiple-item paper–pencil test assessing the German language competency of high school students. Test sections include listening comprehension, grammar, situational questions, and comprehension of connected passages. Questions are of graded difficulty. Tests are administered annually in school or in an AATG chapter test center. In-school testing is accomplished under the supervision of the school's testing personnel. Students may be tested in school or at a chapter test center. AATG will send Regional Chairpersons a copy of test orders submitted from their chapter area. Regional Chairpersons will establish chapter test centers and inform teachers who have requested this service when and where testing is to occur. Students are eligible to take the test designed for the level on which they are studying at the time of test administration. Students who take a test below their current level of work, or take more than one test, will be excluded from any awards program. The test company returns scores to test administrators and regional chairpersons in February. A total score, as well as scores for each section of the test, is provided. Practice tests are available.

Format: Examiner required; suitable for group use

Scoring: All tests scored by Software Design, Inc.

Cost: $4.00 per student

Publisher: American Association of Teachers of German

Advanced Russian Listening Comprehension/Reading Proficiency Test (ARPT)

Copyright: Not provided

Population: Adults, college students

Purpose: Measures the listening comprehension and reading proficiency of native English-speaking students' Russian; appropriate for use with students who have completed the equivalent of 3 to 5 years or more of college-level study

Description: Multiple-item orally administered and paper–pencil test in two major sections: Listening Comprehension and Reading Proficiency. The Listening Comprehension section is administered via a tape recording that presents the student with a variety of material spoken in Russian. Questions about this material are printed in a test booklet, and students respond on machine-scorable answer sheets. In the Reading Proficiency section, the student reads passages printed in Russian and selects responses that complete or answer the questions.

Format: Examiner required; suitable for group use; timed: 2 hours

Scoring: Computer scored

Cost: Test booklet $15.00 each

Publisher: Educational Testing Service

Arabic Proficiency Test (APT)
Raji M. Rammuny

Copyright: 1992

Population: Adolescents, adults; college and above

Purpose: Measures reading and listening proficiency for placement, selection, and evaluation

Description: Multiple-choice 100-question paper–pencil test comprised of Listening and Reading Comprehension. Forms A and B available. Materials used include an audiocassette player, test booklet, and test answer sheet. Suitable for individuals with physical impairment.

Format: Individual/group administered; examiner required; timed: 110 minutes

Scoring: Hand key, machine scored; test scoring service available from publisher

Cost: $14.00–$25.00 per examinee depending on the number of examinees

Publisher: Center for Applied Linguistics

Arabic Speaking Test (AST)
Raji M. Rammuny

Copyright: 1992

Population: Adolescents, adults; college and above

Purpose: Measures oral proficiency in Arabic

Description: Oral-response 15-item test measuring oral language proficiency in Arabic.

Ratings are based on the speaking proficiency scale of the American Council on the Teaching of Foreign Languages (ACTFL). Available in forms A and B. Playback and tape-recording equipment used. Test available on audiocassette. May be used with individuals with physical disabilities.

Format: Examiner required; timed: 55 minutes

Scoring: Examiner evaluated; test scoring service available from publisher

Cost: $115.00 per examinee for operational costs and certified rating service

Publisher: Center for Applied Linguistics

CASAS Basic Citizenship Skills Examination

Copyright: 1996

Population: Adults who are eligible to become citizens of the United States

Purpose: Approved by the U.S. Immigration and Naturalization Service to satisfy the history and government requirement for individuals applying to become U.S. citizens

Description: Multiple-choice 20-question test in simple language test knowledge of basic U.S. history and government. The English version also has a writing section with two dictated sentences. The exam is offered through CASA-approved citizenship testing centers. Tests are available in Spanish, Korean, Vietnamese, Cambodian, Lao, and Hmong.

Format: Group administered

Scoring: Official scoring and certification of results is provided by CASAS

Cost: $26.00–$30.00 per examinee

Publisher: Comprehensive Adult Student Assessment System

Chinese Proficiency Test (CPT)

Copyright: 1983

Population: Adolescents, adults; high school and above

Purpose: Measures listening and reading proficiency used for placement, evaluation, and selection

Description: Multiple-choice 150-question paper–pencil test comprised of Listening Comprehension, Reading Comprehension, and Structure. Form A available. Materials used include an audio cassette player, test booklet, and test answer sheet. Suitable for those with physical disabilities.

Format: Individual/group administered; examiner required; timed: 120 minutes

Scoring: Machine scored

Cost: $14.00–$25.00 per examinee depending on the number of examinees

Publisher: Center for Applied Linguistics

Chinese Speaking Test (CST)

Copyright: 1994

Population: Adolescents, adults; college and above

Purpose: Assesses the ability to speak Chinese in contemporary, real-life language-use contexts

Description: Oral-response 15-item test measuring oral language proficiency in Chinese. Via a question tape and test booklet, the examinees are asked six types of questions: Personal Conversation, Giving Directions, Detailed Descriptions, Picture Sequences, Topic of Discourse, and Situations. The examinee's oral responses to the six item types are recorded and then sent to the publisher for scoring. Ratings are based on the speaking proficiency scale of the American Council on the Teaching of Foreign Language (ACTFL). Three forms (A, B, and C) are available. May be used with individuals with physical impairments.

Format: Examiner required; suitable for group use; timed: 45 minutes

Scoring: Publisher scored

Cost: $115.00 per examinee for operational costs and certified rating service

Publisher: Center for Applied Linguistics

CLEP Subject Examination: Foreign Languages: College French Levels 1 and 2

Copyright: 1990

Population: Adolescents, adults; Grades 12 and above

Purpose: Measures knowledge and ability equivalent to that of students who have completed from two to four semesters of college-level French; also used by some businesses to allow employees to earn required continuing education credits

Description: Multiple-item paper–pencil test in two separately timed sections assessing proficiency in the skills typically achieved from the end of the first year through the second year of college-level French. In the 90-item Reading section (1 hour), examinees are assessed on vocabulary mastery, grammatical control, and reading comprehension. In the 55-item Listening section (30 minutes), items are presented orally via a tape and test phonemic discrimination, listening comprehension, and ability to understand native speakers in dialogues and narratives. Levels 1 and 2 are incorporated into a single examination.

Format: Examiner required; suitable for group use; timed: 1 hour 30 minutes

Scoring: Computer scored

Cost: Contact publisher

Publisher: College Level Examinations

French Computerized Adaptive Placement Exam (F-CAPE)

Jerry W. Larson, Kim L. Smith,
Don C. Jensen

Copyright: 1995

Population: Adults

Purpose: Measures the achievement level in French; used for placement into 1st, 2nd, and 3rd semester classes; intended for university/college students

Description: Total number of items varies according to the ability of the examinee. Categories include grammar, vocabulary, and reading. Full performance or simplified compiled reports are available. A Macintosh or PC computer and test disks are used.

Format: Individually/self-administered; untimed

Scoring: Computer scored

Cost: $995.00 for site license

Publisher: Brigham Young University

French Speaking Test (FST)

Copyright: 1995

Population: Adolescents, adults; high school and above

Purpose: Measures oral proficiency in French

Description: Oral-response 16-item test measuring oral language proficiency in French. Via playback and tape-recording equipment, the oral response is recorded. Forms A, B, and C are available. Ratings are based on the speaking proficiency scale of the American Council on the Teaching of Foreign Languages (ACTFL). Available on audiocassette. Suitable for individuals with physical impairment.

Format: Individual/group administered; examiner required; timed: 45 minutes

Scoring: Examiner evaluated; test scoring service available from publisher

Cost: $115.00 per examinee for operational costs and certified rating service

Publisher: Center for Applied Linguistics

German Computerized Adaptive Placement Exam (G-CAPE)

Jerry W. Larson, Kim L. Smith,
Randall L. Jones

Copyright: 1995

Population: Adults

Purpose: Measures the achievement level in German; used for placement into 1st, 2nd, and 3rd semester classes; intended for university/college students

Description: Total number of items varies according to the ability of the examinee. Categories include grammar, vocabulary, and reading. A full performance or simplified compiled reports are available. A Macintosh or PC computer and test disks are used.

Format: Individually/self-administered; untimed

Scoring: Computer scored

Cost: $995.00 for site license

Publisher: Brigham Young University

German Speaking Test (GST)

Copyright: 1995

Population: Adolescents, adults; high school and above

Purpose: Measures oral proficiency in German

Description: Oral-response 16-item test measuring oral language proficiency in German. Via playback and tape-recording equipment, the examinee's oral response is recorded. The test is available on audiocassette. Forms A, B, and C are available. Suitable for individuals with physical impairment.

Format: Individual/group administration; examiner required; timed: 45 minutes

Scoring: Examiner evaluated; test scoring service available from publisher

Cost: $115.00 per examinee for operational costs and certified rating service

Publisher: Center for Applied Linguistics

Hausa Speaking Test (HAST)

Copyright: 1989

Population: Adolescents, adults; college and above

Purpose: Assesses the ability to speak Hausa in contemporary, real-life language-use contexts

Description: Oral-response 16-item test measuring oral language proficiency in Hausa. Via a question tape and test booklet, the examinee's oral responses of five item types are recorded and then sent to the publisher for scoring. Ratings are based on the speaking proficiency scale of the American Council on the Teaching of Foreign Languages (ACTFL). A, B, Male, and Female forms are available. May be used with individuals with physical impairments.

Format: Examiner required; suitable for group use; timed: 45 minutes

Scoring: Publisher scored

Cost: $115.00 per examinee for operational costs and certified rating service

Publisher: Center for Applied Linguistics

Hebrew Speaking Test (HEST)

Copyright: 1989

Population: Adolescents, adults; college and above

Purpose: Assesses the ability to speak Hebrew in contemporary, real-life language-use contexts

Description: Oral-response 16-item test measuring oral language proficiency in Hebrew. Via a question tape and test booklet, the examinees are asked six types of questions: Personal Conversation, Giving Directions, Detailed Descriptions, Picture Sequences, Topical Discourse, and Situations. The examinee's oral responses to the six item types are recorded and then sent to the publisher for scoring. Ratings are based on the speaking proficiency scale of the American Council on the Teaching of Foreign Language (ACTFL). U.S. and Israeli versions are available in male, female, A, and B forms. May be used with individuals with physical impairments.

Format: Examiner required; suitable for group use; timed: 45 minutes

Scoring: Publisher scored

Cost: $115.00 per examinee for operational costs and certified rating service

Publisher: Center for Applied Linguistics

Indonesian Speaking Test (IST)

Copyright: 1989

Population: Adolescents, adults; college and above

Purpose: Assesses the ability to speak Indonesian in contemporary, real-life language-use contexts

Description: Oral-response 27-item test measuring oral language proficiency in Indonesian. Via a question tape and test booklet, the examinees are asked five types of questions: Personal Conversation, Giving Directions, Picture Sequences, Topical Discourse, and Situations. The examinee's oral responses to the five item types are recorded and then sent to the publisher for scoring. Ratings are based on the proficiency scale of the American Council on the Teaching of Foreign Language (ACTFL). Two forms (A, B) are available. May be used with individuals with physical impairments.

Format: Examiner required; suitable for group use; timed: 45 minutes

Scoring: Publisher scored

Cost: $60.00

Publisher: Center for Applied Linguistics

Japanese Speaking Test (JST)

Copyright: 1992

Population: Adolescents, adults; college and above

Purpose: Measures oral proficiency in Japanese for evaluation, placement, and selection

Description: Oral-response 15-item test using playback and tape-recording equipment to record examinee's oral response. Ratings are based on the speaking proficiency scale of the American Council on the Teaching of Foreign Languages (ACTFL). Suitable for individuals with physical impairment.

Format: Individual/group administered; examiner required; timed: 45 minutes

Scoring: Examiner evaluated; test scoring service available from publisher

Cost: $115.00 per examinee for operational costs and certified rating service

Publisher: Center for Applied Linguistics

Lista de Destrezas en Desarrollo (La Lista)

Copyright: 1993

Population: Grades Pre-K through K

Purpose: Evaluates a wide range of skills in Spanish-speaking children that develop from prekindergarten through the end of kindergarten

Description: Multiple-item point-to, oral-response checklist that measures the following skills and concepts: language, visual, auditory, mathematical concepts and operations, mem-

ory, fine and gross motor, and print and writing. La Lista is a supplement to CTB's Developing Skills Checklist (DSC), the English language assessment of early childhood development. (Note: one must have the English DSC kit in order to administer La Lista.)

Format: Examiner required; individually administered; untimed

Scoring: Hand key; machine scored

Cost: Test Kit (materials for 25 students) $134.55

Publisher: CTB/McGraw-Hill

National Spanish Examinations

Copyright: 1996

Population: Grades 6 to 12

Purpose: Assesses reading and listening comprehension skills; used for secondary school with Spanish students

Description: Spanish exams covering four levels developed each year by teachers who are members of AATSP. A multiple-choice test that has both aural and written sections that measure the knowledge of Spanish after each year of study at the secondary school level. There are 30 listening comprehension questions, 50 reading comprehension questions, and an additional 20 reading comprehension questions for bilingual native students. The 1997 NSE will be proficiency based.

Format: Suitable for group use; timed: 1 hour

Scoring: Examiner required; computer scored

Cost: Contact publisher

Publisher: National Spanish Examinations

Performance Assessment in Spanish (PAIS)

Copyright: Not provided

Population: Children; Grades 3 through 4

Purpose: Assesses Spanish-speaking students' reading/language arts skills

Description: Multiple-item paper–pencil short-answer/essay test covering reading/language arts that measures informative and literary tasks. Three assessment sections (reading, group work, and writing) are administered in three separate sessions. Activities are based on the following: marginal notes, initial response, text-focused questions, graphic response, beyond-the-text-questions, final response, working with your group, and extended writing.

Format: Examiner required; suitable for group use; untimed: minimum time 45 minutes per section

Scoring: Examiner evaluated

Cost: Literary or Informative Tasks Package (includes 35 test booklets and teacher's guide and scoring guidelines) $56.95

Publisher: CTB/McGraw-Hill

Polish Proficiency Test (PPT)

Copyright: 1992

Population: Adolescents, adults; college and above

Purpose: Measures listening and reading proficiency; used for placement, evaluation, and selection

Description: Multiple-choice 135-question paper–pencil test comprised of listening comprehension, reading comprehension, structure, and total. Form A available. Test available on audiocassette. Suitable for individuals with physical impairment.

Format: Individual/group administration; examiner required; timed: 150 minutes

Scoring: Machine scored; test scoring service available from publisher

Cost: $14.00–$25.00 per examinee depending on the number of examinees

Publisher: Center for Applied Linguistics

Portuguese Speaking Test (PST)

Copyright: 1988

Population: Adolescents, adults; college and above

Purpose: Assesses the ability to speak Portuguese in contemporary, real-life language-use contexts

Description: Oral-response 16-item test measuring oral language proficiency in Portuguese. Via a question tape and test booklet, the examinees are asked six types of questions: Personal Conversation, Giving Directions, Detailed Descriptions, Picture Sequences, Topical Discourse, and Situations. Their oral responses are recorded and then sent to the publisher for scoring. Ratings are based on the speaking proficiency scale of the American Council on the Teaching of Foreign Languages (ACTFL). A, B, and C forms are available. Available also in Brazilian and Lusitanian.

Format: Examiner required; suitable for group use; timed: 45 minutes

Scoring: Scored by publisher

Cost: $115.00 per examinee for operational costs and certified rating service

Publisher: Center for Applied Linguistics

Preliminary Chinese Proficiency Test (Pre-CPT)

Copyright: 1991

Population: Adolescents, adults; high school and above

Purpose: Measures reading and listening proficiency for placement, evaluation, and selection

Description: Multiple-choice 125-question paper–pencil test comprised of Listening Comprehension, Reading Comprehension, and Structure. Materials used include audiocassette player, test booklet, and test answer sheet. Form A available. Suitable for individuals with physical disabilities.

Format: Individual/group administered; examiner required; timed: 90 minutes

Scoring: Machine scored; test scoring service available from publisher

Cost: $14.00–$25.00 per examinee depending on the number of examinees

Publisher: Center for Applied Linguistics

Preliminary Japanese Speaking Test (Pre-JST)

Copyright: 1991

Population: Adolescents, adults; high school and above

Purpose: Measures oral proficiency in Japanese for placement, evaluation, and selection

Description: Eight-item oral-response test using playback tape and recording equipment to record oral responses. Forms A and B available. Ratings are based on the speaking proficiency scale of the American Council on the Teaching of Foreign Languages (ACTFL). Suitable for individuals with physical disabilities.

Format: Individual/group administration; examiner required; timed: 25 minutes

Scoring: Examiner evaluated; test scoring service available from publisher

Cost: $90.00 per examinee for operational costs and certified rating service

Publisher: Center for Applied Linguistics

Russian Computerized Adaptive Placement Exam (R-CAPE)

Jerry W. Larson, Kim L. Smith, Marshall R. Murray

Copyright: 1995

Population: Adults

Purpose: Measures the achievement level in Russian; used for placement into first, second, and third semester classes; intended for university/college students

Description: Total number of items varies according to ability of examinee. Categories include grammar, vocabulary, and reading. A full performance or simplified compiled reports are available. A Macintosh or PC computer and test disks are used.

Format: Individually/self-administered; untimed

Scoring: Computer scored

Cost: $995.00 for site license

Publisher: Brigham Young University

Spanish Assessment of Basic Education–Second Edition (SABE®–2)

Copyright: 1991

Population: Children, adolescents; Grades 1 through 8

Purpose: Assesses the basic reading and mathematics skills of Spanish-speaking LEP students

Description: Multiple-item paper–pencil multiple-choice test covering word attack, vocabulary, reading comprehension, mathematics computation, mathematics concepts and applications, spelling, language mechanics, language expression, and study skills. The examiner must speak fluent Spanish.

Format: Examiner required; suitable for group use; timed: 180–255 minutes

Scoring: Hand key; machine scored; test scoring service

Cost: Package of 35 tests $87.00

Publisher: CTB/McGraw-Hill

Spanish Computerized Adaptive Placement Exam (S-CAPE)

Jerry W. Larson, Kim L. Smith

Copyright: 1995

Population: Adults

Purpose: Measures the achievement level in Spanish; used for placement into first, second, and third semester classes; intended for university/college students

Description: Total number of items varies according to ability of examinee. Categories include grammar, vocabulary, and reading. Full performance or simplified compiled reports are available. A Macintosh or PC computer and test disks are used.

Format: Individually/self-administered; untimed

Scoring: Computer scored

Cost: $995.00 for site license

Publisher: Brigham Young University

Spanish Proficiency Test (SPT)

Copyright: 1994

Population: Adolescents, adults; high school/college students

Purpose: Assesses Spanish language proficiency of nonnative speakers of Spanish; used for assessment, placement, evaluation of programs, and selection of students for immersion programs

Description: Multiple-choice paper–pencil oral response, essay, verbal test composed of four categories: Listening—25 multiple choice questions, Reading—40 multiple choice questions, Writing—three essay or constructed response prompts, Speaking—simulated dialogue with 15 inquiries. Raw scores and ACTFL proficiency ratings for Listening and Reading (scored by ETS); ACTFL proficiency ratings for Writing and Speaking (scored at institutions).

Format: Examiner required; suitable for group use; timed: 90 minutes total

Scoring: Test scoring service available from publisher

Cost: 4 Skills $25.00, Listening and Reading $17.00, Writing and Speaking $15.00

Publisher: Educational Testing Service

Spanish Speaking Test (SST)

Copyright: 1995

Population: Adolescents, adults; high school and above

Purpose: Measures oral proficiency in Spanish for placement, evaluation, and selection

Description: Oral-response 16-item test. Oral response of examinee is recorded using playback and tape-recording equipment. Forms A, B, and C available. Ratings are based on the speaking proficiency scale of the American Council on the Teaching of Foreign Languages (ACTFL).

Format: Individual/group administered; examiner required; timed: 45 minutes

Scoring: Examiner evaluated; test scoring service available from publisher

Cost: $115.00 per examinee for operational costs and certified rating service

Publisher: Center for Applied Linguistics

Guidance

General

Ability Explorer
Thomas F. Harrington, Joan C. Harrington

Copyright: 1996

Population: Level 1: Grades 6 through 8; Level 2: Grades 9 through 12 and adults

Purpose: To help students, and adults in transition, explore their abilities as they relate to the world of work and career and educational planning

Description: The Ability Explorer is a measure of self-reported abilities which provides information on 14 work-related abilities relevant to the workplace of today and the future. The work-related ability areas include Artistic, Clerical, Interpersonal, Language, Leadership, Manual, Musical/Dramatic, Numerical/Mathematical, Organizational, Persuasive, Scientific, Social, Spatial, and Technical/Mechanical. Level 1 helps middle school and junior high school students explore abilities and careers, begin career planning, and select courses for high school. Level 2 helps high school students and adults learn about their abilities, do advanced career and/or educational exploration, develop career plans and portfolios, and begin the transition from school to work and/or postsecondary education or training.

Format: Group or individually administered; examiner required for machine-scorable, recommended for hand-scorable; less than one class period

Scoring: Examiner/student evaluated, machine evaluated

Cost: Hand Scorable Assessment Booklet $35.00 (includes 25 assessment documents and

Directions for Administration); Spanish Version (hand-scorable only) Machine-Scorable Assessment Document $45.00 (includes 25 booklets, and Directions for Administration)

Publisher: Riverside Publishing Company

Adult Career Concerns Inventory (ACCI)
Donald E. Super, Albert S. Thompson, Richard H. Lindeman

Copyright: Not provided

Population: Adults

Purpose: Measures career and life stages of adults; used in counseling and research

Description: Paper-pencil 51-item measurement of Donald Super's theory of Life Stages (Exploration, Establishment, Maintenance, Disengagement) and a special Career Change Status Scale. Each of the 51 concerns is rated on a 5-point scale. Counselors can use the inventory for assessing a client's career stage and growth. Researchers may use it for assessing how life stage affects productivity, creativity, turnover, etc. The computer scoring service profile plots 5 career stages, 12 subscales, and group summary data for answer sheets scored simultaneously.

Format: Self-administered; suitable for group use; untimed: 30 minutes

Scoring: Hand key; may be computer scored

Cost: Preview Kit (booklet, answer sheet, and manual) $40.00

Publisher: Consulting Psychologists Press, Inc.

Air Force Occupational Attitude Inventory Development (OAI)
R. Bruce Gould

Copyright: 1979

Population: Adults

Purpose: Validates 35 hypothesized job dimensions; used in job placement with the military

Description: Multiple-item short-answer paper–pencil questionnaire

Format: Individual or group administration; requires examiner; untimed

Scoring: Hand key

Cost: $24.00

Publisher: Select Press

Applied Knowledge Test (AKT)
M. A. Brimer

Copyright: 1979

Population: Adolescents; ages 14 to 18

Purpose: Measures the ability to use knowledge of mathematics, English, science, and spatial relationships; used for vocational guidance

Description: Multiple-item paper–pencil measures of a student's competence in the four employment-related subject areas of mathematics, English, science, and spatial relationships. Results can be used to validate interest scores from the Occupational Interest Rating Scale (OIRS).

Format: Examiner/self-administered; suitable for group use; timed subtests: total time 55 minutes

Scoring: Hand key

Cost: £14.00 Sterling

Publisher: Educational Evaluation Enterprises

APTICOM
Jeffrey A. Harris, Howard C. Dansky

Copyright: 1985

Population: Adults; high school students

Purpose: Assesses aptitudes, interests, and work-related math and language skills; used for vocational guidance and counseling

Description: Multiple-item aptitude battery measuring general learning ability, verbal aptitude, numerical aptitude, spatial aptitude, form perception, clerical perception, motor coordination, finger dexterity, manual dexterity, and eye–hand–foot coordination. The Interest Inventory assesses preference for U.S. Department of Labor interest areas. The Educational Skills Development Battery assesses math and language achievement levels defined by the U.S. Department of Labor as General Educational Development. Tests are presented via panels mounted on APTICOM, a portable computerized desktop console. APTICOM times and scores tests and generates score and recommendation reports when interfaced with a printer. The aptitude battery has separate norm bases for three levels: Adult/Grades 11–12, Grade 10, Grade 9. The Interest Inventory has vocational (i.e., adult) and prevocational (roughly 17 years and younger) norm bases. Available in Spanish.

Format: Examiner required; suitable for use with groups of four using optional master control; timed: Aptitude 29 minutes, Educational Skills Development Battery 25 minutes; Untimed: Interest Inventory 10 minutes

Scoring: Computer scored

Cost: Contact publisher

Publisher: Vocational Research Institute

Aptitude Based Career Decision (ABCD)

Copyright: 1986

Population: Adolescents, adults

Purpose: Assesses battery of seven aptitude tests; used in vocational/educational guidance for employees, students, and unemployed workers

Description: Multiple-choice computer-administered or paper–pencil test measuring: clerical perception, 240 items; vocabulary, 80 items; numerical computation, 20 items; numerical reasoning, 20 items; spatial visual, 24 items; inductive reasoning, 30 items; analytical reasoning, 18 items. IBM/compatible required. Also available in Spanish.

Format: Individual administration or suitable for group use; examiner required; timed: 104 minutes

Scoring: Computer scored; no scoring service available

Cost: Contact publisher

Publisher: Centec Learning

Armed Services Vocational Aptitude Battery (ASVAB)

Copyright: Updated yearly

Population: Adolescents, adults; Grades 10 and over

Purpose: Evaluates high school students' vocational interests and aptitudes; used for counseling and by the military services to identify eligible graduates for possible recruitment

Description: Paper–pencil 334-item test of aptitudes in various vocational and technical fields. Factors measured include electronics, mechanical comprehension, general science, automotive and shop information, numerical operations, coding speed, word knowledge, arithmetic, reasoning, paragraph comprehension, and mathematics knowledge. Indicates ability in the following areas: verbal; math; academic; mechanical and crafts; business and clerical; electronics and electrical; and health, social, and technologies. A military service recruiter will assist each school in administering the test, and the Defense Manpower Data Center provides the examiner. Individual test results are delivered to school counselors, and copies of the scores are given to the recruiting services.

Format: Examiner required; suitable for group use; timed: 3 hours

Scoring: Computer scored

Cost: No charge to schools for administration, materials, and scoring

Publisher: Defense Manpower Data Center

Assessing Specific Competencies Pre-Test/Post-Test

George Cunningham, Shelley M. Mauer

Copyright: 1995

Population: Adolescents, adults; ages 15 and above; Grades 9 and above

Purpose: Assesses the participant's knowledge of the employability and work maturity skills

Description: Multiple-choice 110-item computer-administered paper–pencil test with 11 categories: Making Career Decisions, 10 items; Using Labor Market Information, 10 items; Developing a Resume, 10 items; Completing a Job Application, 10 items; Interviewing for a Job, 10 items; Maintaining Regular

Attendance, 10 items; Completing Tasks Effectively, 10 items; Being Consistently Punctual, 10 items; Positive Attitudes/Behavior, 10 items; Good Interpersonal Relations, 10 items; and Presenting Appropriate Appearance, 10 items. These sections correspond to the U.S. Dept. of Labor's 11 core competencies for pre-employability and work maturity skills. Scoring ranges from 0 to 100%. Based on test score, self-prescribed plan of the scores is given to the recruiting services.

Format: Self-administered; suitable for group use; examiner required; untimed: 30–45 minutes

Scoring: Hand key, computer scored; test scoring service available from publisher

Cost: 25 Pre-Tests $52.00, 25 Post-Tests $52.00

Publisher: Education Associates, Inc.

Assessment of Career Decision Making (ACDM)
Vincent A. Harren, Jacqueline N. Buck

Copyright: Not provided

Population: High school and college students

Purpose: Used to help students select careers

Description: Comprised of 96 true–false items covering six scales: decision-making styles (rational, intuitive, and dependent), and decision-making tasks (school adjustment, occupation, and major). Inventory is designed to help students select a career that is compatible with their particular interests and abilities; it can also identify students who need career counseling.

Format: Self-administered; suitable for group use

Scoring: Computer/service scored

Cost: Kit (4 test report prepaid mail-in answer sheets for computer scoring and interpretation, 1 manual) $79.50

Publisher: Western Psychological Services

Barriers to Employment Success Inventory (BESI)
John J. Liptak

Copyright: 1996

Population: Adolescents, adults

Purpose: Identifies key barriers that keep people from conducting successful job searches; used for work with the unemployed

Description: Fifty-statement multiple-choice short-answer true–false test with the following categories: Personal/Financial, Emotional/Physical, Career Decision-Making/Planning, Job Seeking Knowledge, and Education and Training. Reports a person's barrier to a successful job search. An eighth-grade reading level is required.

Format: Individual/self-administered; untimed: 20 minutes

Scoring: Self-scored

Cost: 25 forms $37.50

Publisher: JIST Works, Inc.

California Critical Thinking Disposition Inventory (CCTDI)
Peter A. Facione, Noreen C. Facione

Copyright: 1992

Population: Grades 7 through 12; college-level students and graduates

Purpose: Measures disposition toward critical thinking; used for evaluation of groups and programs, personnel development and management training

Description: Paper–pencil 75-item test. Five-page test booklet includes specialized answer sheet. Categories include truth-seeking, inquisitiveness, analyticity, systematicity, open-mindedness, cognitive maturity, and reasoning confidence. Available also in Spanish, French, Hebrew, and Chinese.

Format: Individual/group administration; examiner required; untimed: 20 minutes

Scoring: Hand key/machine scored

Cost: Kits $75.00; tests by quantity $1.75 to $1.05

Publisher: California Academic Press

California Critical Thinking Skills Test (CCTST)
Peter A. Facione

Copyright: Form A 1990, Form B 1992

Population: Adults; college and graduate students

Purpose: Assesses core cognitive skills in critical thinking

Description: Multiple-choice 34-item paper–pencil test with five subtests. Categories include analysis, inference, evaluation, inductive reasoning, deductive reasoning. Forms A and B available. CCTST test booklet (10 pages) used; answer form is optional. Available also in Spanish. Suitable for individuals with hearing impairment.

Format: Individual administration; suitable for group use; timed: 45 minutes, untimed: up to 60 minutes

Scoring: Machine scored; no scoring service available

Cost: Kit $60.00, tests by quantity: $1.13 to $1.60

Publisher: California Academic Press

CAM 2001 Computerized One-Stop

Copyright: 1989

Population: Adolescents, adults; ages 14 and above

Purpose: Assesses interests, aptitudes, attitudes, temperament, and learning styles

Description: A comprehensive software module determines skills that are transferred from an individual's past work history to other skilled or semiskilled jobs utilizing those same occupationally significant skills. Provided in an on-line testing format for a one-stop objective assessment to match skills to job skills; links with a new case management system.

Format: Group

Scoring: Computerized on-site

Cost: Contact publisher

Publisher: PESCO, International

Campbell Interest and Skill Survey (CISS)
David Campbell

Copyright: 1992

Population: Adolescents, adults; ages 15 and above

Purpose: Assesses self-reported interests and skills; used for career exploration and development and educational planning

Description: Multiple-choice 320-item computer-administered paper–pencil test divided into 200 interest categories and 120 skill categories. A sixth-grade reading level is required. Examiner must have a B.A. with a test measurement course, or attendance at a CISS workshop. A computer version is available using a Windows-based computer.

Format: Self-administered; suitable for group use; untimed: 35 minutes

Scoring: Computer scored; test scoring service available from publisher

Cost: $4.25 to $5.95 depending on quantity; manual $21

Publisher: NCS Assessments

Career Assessment Inventory– The Enhanced Version
Charles B. Johansson

Copyright: 1986

Population: Adolescents, adults; Grades 9 and above

Purpose: Assesses the career interests of students and individuals reentering the job market or considering a career change; used for making decisions about career interests, screening job applicants, and providing career and vocational assistance

Description: Paper–pencil 370-item test in which items are answered on a 5-point Likert-type scale ranging from "like very much" to "dislike very much." Items are divided into three major categories: activities, school subjects, and occupations. The test, which focuses on careers requiring up to and including 4 years of college, covers 111 occupations. Six General Occupational Theme scores (Holland's RIASEC) and 25 Basic Interest scale scores that divide the 6 general scores into specific areas are provided. A narrative report, profile report, and optional group reports are available. Items are written at an eighth-grade reading level. This is a revision of the Career Assessment Inventory–The Vocational Version, which focuses on skilled trade.

Format: Self-administered; suitable for group use; untimed: 40 minutes

Scoring: Computer scored by publisher

Cost: Manual $18.00; Narrative Report $6.00–$8.50 depending on quantity; Profile Report $3.75–$5.50 depending on quantity

Publisher: NCS Assessments

Career Beliefs Inventory (CBI)
John D. Krumboltz

Copyright: 1991

Population: Adolescents, adults; ages 14 and above

Purpose: Assesses individuals' beliefs and assumptions about themselves and the world of work

Description: Multiple-choice 96-item paper–pencil test intended for career counseling for use in high school, college, or during mid-life career transitions. The profile yields 25 scales organized into five categories: My Current Career Situation, What Seems Necessary for My Happiness, Factors That Influence My Decisions, Changes I Am Willing to Make, Effort I Am Willing to Initiate. Response choices range from strongly agree to strongly disagree. An eighth-grade reading level is required. Also available in French Canadian. Materials used include an item booklet, prepaid answer sheet or a nonprepaid answer sheet, a report booklet, and a scoring key. A client workbook is also available.

Format: Self-administered; suitable for group use; examiner required; untimed: 10–20 minutes

Scoring: Hand key; test scoring service available from publisher

Cost: Preview Kit (item booklet, answer sheet, test, manual) $39.00

Publisher: Consulting Psychologists Press, Inc.

Career Development Inventory (College and University Form)
Donald E. Super, Albert S. Thompson, Richard H. Lindeman, Jean P. Jordaan, Roger A. Myers

Copyright: Not provided

Population: College students

Purpose: Assesses knowledge and attitudes about career choices; used with college and university students for guidance and for designing and evaluating career counseling programs

Description: Multiple-item paper–pencil inventory for determining knowledge and attitudes of college and university students regarding careers; students respond on computer-scored answer sheets. The computer scoring service provides individual student profiles, a group roster, response analysis by occupational group, and response analysis of the Career Planning and Career Exploration items. The User's Manual contains information on development, use, and interpretation of the test, as well as case studies and norms. The Technical Manual contains statistical and research information. Test booklets are reusable.

Format: Examiner required; suitable for group use; untimed: 55–65 minutes

Scoring: Computer scored

Cost: Preview Kit (item booklet, answer sheet, manual, tech guide) $42.00

Publisher: Consulting Psychologists Press, Inc.

Career Development Inventory (School Form)
Donald E. Super, Albert S. Thompson, Richard H. Lindeman, Jean P. Jordaan, Roger A. Myers

Copyright: Not provided

Population: Adolescents; Grades 10 through 12

Purpose: Assesses individual attitudes, knowledge, and skills related to vocational decisions; used in career counseling courses

Description: Paper–pencil 120-item test covering eight dimensions of vocational decision making: career planning, career exploration, decision making, world-of-work information, knowledge of preferred occupational group, career development attitudes, career development knowledge and skills, and career orientation total. The scoring service offered by the publisher consists of individual student profiles, a group roster, a response analysis by occupation, and a response analysis of the Career Planning and Career Direction items. May be administered in one 65-minute session or one 40-minute and one 25-minute session.

Format: Examiner required; suitable for group use; untimed: 55–65 minutes

Scoring: Computer scored

Cost: Preview Kit (item booklet, answer sheet, manual, tech guide) $42.00

Publisher: Consulting Psychologists Press, Inc.

Career Directions Inventory
Douglas N. Jackson

Copyright: 1986

Population: Adolescents, adults

Purpose: Helps evaluate career interests of high school and college students and adults; used for educational and vocational planning and counseling

Description: Paper–pencil or computer-administered 100-item inventory consisting of a triad of statements for each item, describing job-related activities. Computer scoring yields a sex-fair profile of 15 basic interest scales. The pattern of these interests is compared to the interest patterns shown by individuals in a wide variety of occupations. This new test evolved from the Jackson Vocational Interest Survey; the content and vocabulary are easier, and more emphasis is placed on activities involved in sales, service, and technical occupations. Reports are available through the mail-in batch scoring service. The computer version operates on IBM PC and compatible systems.

Format: Examiner required; suitable for group use; untimed: 30–45 minutes

Scoring: Computer scored; scoring service available from publisher

Cost: Examination Kit (manual, question-and-answer document, computerized scoring for one individual) $19.00; Computer Version (licensing agreement with 25 scorings) $175.00

Publisher: Sigma Assessment Systems, Inc.

Career Guidance Inventory
James E. Oliver

Copyright: Continuously updated

Population: Adolescents, adults

Purpose: Measures comparative strength of interests in 25 trades, services, and technologies; used to counsel non–college-bound students

Description: Paper–pencil 240-item test covering 14 engineering-related trades and 11 others: carpentry, masonry, mechanical repair, painting and decorating, plumbing–pipe fitting, printing, tool and die making, sheet metal and welding, drafting and design technology, and industrial production. Students rate their interest in each area on a scale from 1 (very low) to 20 (very high).

Format: Examiner required; suitable for group use; untimed: 1 hour 30 minutes

Scoring: Hand key

Cost: Booklet $3.00; manual $6.00; 25 self-scoring answer sheets and profiles $35.00

Publisher: Wintergreen/Orchard House, Inc.

Career Planning Program (CPP)

Copyright: 1993

Population: Adolescents, adults; Grades 8 and above

Purpose: Evaluates an individual's career-related abilities, interests, and experiences; used for vocational counseling and placement

Description: Items on two levels designed to help the examinee identify and explore personally relevant occupations and educational programs. Six factors are measured in each of four areas: background and plans, work-related experiences, self-rating of abilities, and interest inventory). The ability tests measure Reading Skills, Language Usage, Clerical Speed/Accuracy,

Space Relations, Numerical Skills, and Mechanical Reasoning. Level I is used with eighth and ninth graders and Level II is used with Grades 11 and 12 and adults.

Format: Examiner required; suitable for group use; timed: 2½ hours

Scoring: Computer scored by ACT

Cost: $4.80 per test

Publisher: American College Testing

CASAS Employability Competency System

Copyright: 1994

Population: Adults, adolescents; native and nonnative speakers of English

Purpose: Helps programs identify the skills needed by adults and youth in today's workforce and to place them into appropriate education and employment training programs and jobs; agencies can place learners into appropriate instructional levels

Description: Multiple-choice survey achievement tests that assess reading comprehension and basic math skills at four levels, A–D and, for assessment in English as a second language (ESL), listening comprehension tests at levels A–C. Each test has two forms for pre-/posttesting. Includes an appraisal for placement purposes, certification tests, preemployment and work maturity checklists, critical thinking assessment, and occupation-specific tests. Tests are competency based; content covers a range of employment-related contexts. CASAS scaled scores identify general skill level and enable comparison of performance across CASAS tests. Scannable answer sheets are available.

Format: Group administered

Scoring: Self/computer scored

Cost: 25 reusable tests $44.00; 25 listening tests with audiotape $51.00

Publisher: Comprehensive Adult Student Assessment System

Computerized Assessment (COMPASS)

Copyright: 1994

Population: Children to adults; ages 9 and above

Purpose: Used in occupational exploration and career counseling to screen for Dept. of Labor *Dictionary of Occupational Titles (DOT)* work-related factors; designed to quickly establish that evaluees have various degrees of work-related and academic skills

Description: Multiple-choice computer-administered test with 13 computer-based subtests plus three short work samples and a paper–pencil survey. The three work samples are Alignment and Driving, Machine Tending, and Writing. The 13 subtests are Placing, Color Discrimination, Reading, Size Discrimination, Shape Discrimination, Short-Term Visual Memory, Spelling, Vocabulary, Mathematics, Language Development (Editing), Problem Solving, and Eye–Hand–Foot Coordination. The paper–pencil survey is: Guide to Occupational Exploration (GOE). Subtest level scores and DOT-type factors are yielded. A computer, control panel, foot pedal, and three out-of-computer work samples are used. A fourth-grade reading level is required.

Format: Individual administration; examiner required; timed and untimed

Scoring: Computer scored

Cost: Contact publisher

Publisher: Valpar International Corporation

Development of the Occupation Analysis Inventory

J. W. Cunningham, Thomas C. Tuttle, John R. Floyd, Joe A. Bates

Copyright: 1974

Population: Adults

Purpose: Inventories work activities, conditions, and requirements; used in curriculum development, occupational testing, and placement

Description: Criterion-referenced 622-item paper–pencil inventory with five categories: information received, mental activities, physical work behavior, representational work behavior, and interpersonal work.

Format: Individually/self-administered; untimed

Scoring: Examiner evaluated; hand key

Cost: Contact publisher for current prices

Publisher: Select Press

Educational Development Series
O. F. Anderhalter, Jan Perney

Copyright: 1992

Population: Children, adolescents; Grades K through 12

Purpose: Assesses academic achievement, aptitude, and career interests; used by guidance counselors, teachers, and others for counseling and diagnosis

Description: Multiple-choice battery in four formats: Complete Battery, Core Achievement Battery, Basic Skills Battery, and Cognitive and Basic Skills Battery. The Complete Battery (Grades 4–12) contains ten subtests: Career Interests, School Plans, Non-Verbal Cognitive Skills, Verbal Cognitive Skills, Reference Skills, Reading, Language Arts, Mathematics, Science, and Social Studies. The Core Achievement Battery (Grades 2–12) contains eight subtests: Career Interests and School Plans, School Interests, Reference Skills, Reading, Language Arts, Mathematics, Science, and Social Studies. Five subtests are included in the Basic Skills Battery (Grades K–12): Career Interests and School Plans, School Interests, Reading, Language Arts, and Mathematics. The Cognitive and Basic Skills Battery (Grades K–12) contains seven subtests: Career Interests and School Plans, School Interests, Non-Verbal Cognitive Skills, Verbal Cognitive Skills, Reading, Language Arts, and Mathematics. Reports provided are Alphabetical Lists, Group Summary Reports, Performance Problems, Narrative Reports, and Item Analysis Reports. A booklet, answer sheets, and manual are used. Examiner must be certified for assessment.

Format: Examiner required; suitable for group use; timed: 2–5 hours

Scoring: Machine scored; hand key; computer scored

Cost: Specimen Set (specify level and form) $18.40

Publisher: Scholastic Testing Service, Inc.

Educational Interest Inventory (EII)
James E. Oliver

Copyright: Continuously updated

Population: Adolescents, adults

Purpose: Measures relative interest in instructional programs for students planning to attend college or university; used in career/educational counseling

Description: Test consists of 235 paired activity descriptions. Measures relative interest in 47 postsecondary academic majors in baccalaureate degrees. Scores yield an individual profile.

Format: Examiner required; individual/group administered; untimed: approximately 60 minutes

Scoring: Self-scored

Cost: Booklet $3.00; manual $6.00; 25 self-scoring answer sheets and profiles $35.00

Publisher: Wintergreen/Orchard House

Enlistment Screening Test Forms
John J. Mathews Malcolm James Ree

Copyright: 1982

Population: Adults

Purpose: Measures development and calibration of Air Force enlistees; used in career counseling

Description: Paper–pencil instrument

Format: Group or individual administration; examiner required; untimed

Scoring: Hand key; examiner evaluated

Cost: $15.00

Publisher: Select Press

Forer Vocational Survey: Men–Women
Bertram R. Forer

Copyright: 1957

Population: Adolescents, adults

Purpose: Evaluates attitudes and goals related to work situations among adolescents and adults; useful for career planning, vocational guidance, and employee selection and placement

Description: Paper–pencil 80-item multiple-choice test in which the subject completes structured sentence stems measuring three areas of occupational activity: reactions to specified situations, causes of feelings and actions, and vocational goals. Results reveal interpersonal behavior, attitudes toward work, supervision, authority, people, and work dynamics.

Format: Self-administered; suitable for group use; untimed: 20–30 minutes

Scoring: Examiner evaluated

Cost: Kit (25 men and 25 women forms, 1 manual) $50.00

Publisher: Western Psychological Services

Gordon Occupational Check List II
Leonard V. Gordon

Copyright: 1981

Population: Adolescents, adults; Grades 8 and above

Purpose: Identifies areas of job interest; used for counseling of non–college-bound high school students

Description: Multiple-item paper–pencil test consisting of 240 activities, each related to a different occupation within six broad vocational interest categories: business, arts, outdoors, technical–mechanical, technical–industrial, and service. The categories are further divided into the area and work group classifications used in the Department of Labor's *Guide for Occupational Exploration.*

Format: Examiner required; suitable for group use; untimed: 20–25 minutes

Scoring: Examiner evaluated

Cost: Examination Kit (checklist, manual, and job title supplement) $23.50

Publisher: Harcourt® Brace Educational Measurement

Guide for Occupational Exploration (GOE) Inventory

Copyright: 1996

Population: Adolescents, adults

Purpose: Explores career, education, and lifestyle options; used in career counseling

Description: Multiple-choice 84-item true–false test yielding a graphic interest profile on seven factors leading to career options: Leisure Activities, Home Activities, Education and School Subjects, Training, Work Settings, Work Experience, and Overall Interest. An eighth-grade reading level is required.

Format: Individual/self-administered; untimed

Scoring: Self-scored

Cost: 25 forms $36.95

Publisher: JIST Works, Inc.

Guilford-Zimmerman Aptitude Survey (GZAS)
J. P. Guilford, Wayne S. Zimmerman

Copyright: Not provided

Population: Adults

Purpose: Measures verbal and abstract intelligence, numerical facility, and perception for career counseling, industrial and organizational psychology research, and intelligence and aptitude research

Description: Instrument tests verbal comprehension, general reasoning, numerical operation, perceptual speed, spatial orientation, and spatial visualization. The measures can be used independently or in combination.

Format: Individual administration

Scoring: Examiner administration and interpretation

Cost: Assessment Kit (manual, scoring keys, materials for 25 examinees) $265.00

Publisher: Consulting Psychologists Press, Inc.

Harrington-O'Shea Career Decision-Making System (CDM–Revised)
Thomas F. Harrington, Arthur J. O'Shea

Copyright: Manual, 1993

Population: Level 1: 7th–10th grade, Level 2: 11th and 12th grade, adults reentering

Purpose: Involves the client with self-understanding of values and abilities needed for successful career choices and development; focuses the client on those school subjects pertinent to career choices and provides direction for career exploration

Description: The CDM–R is an interest inventory with a sound theoretical basis that provides valid and reliable assessment of career interests. It also surveys values, training plans, and abilities. It incorporates career information and presents a model for career decision making. The CDM–R is based on the Holland theory of vocational development—that is, that most people can be categorized by a single type or a combination of personality types. The CDM–R uses these six types—Crafts, Scientific, the Arts, Social, Business, and Office Operations. These six areas provide raw scores which are used to define the client's preferred work environment.

Format: Level 1: 20 minutes; Level 2: 30–40 minutes; individual or group administration

Scoring: Level 1 is hand scored; Level 2 hand or machine scored

Cost: Hand-Scored Edition (Levels 1 and 2: 25 booklets, directions $49.95 each, 5–19 packages $44.95 each, 20+ packages $41.95 each); Machine-Scored Edition (survey booklets Level 2 $33.95, answer sheets Level 2 $24.95); Group Identification Sheet free

Publisher: American Guidance Service

Key Educational Vocational Assessment System (KEVAS)

Copyright: 1994

Population: Adolescents, adults

Purpose: Measures vocational interests and aptitudes and matches individual interests and functional capabilities with locally available jobs and training programs; used with individuals with and without special needs.

Description: Multiple-choice computer-administered or paper–pencil criterion-referenced test measuring Auditory Acuity, Auditory Localization, Auditory Memory, Visual Acuity, Color Vision, Visual Memory, Hand Strength, Manual Persistence, Fine Motor Skills, Reaction Times, Spatial Reasoning, Problem Solving, Word Knowledge, Reading Comprehension, Reading Level, Arithmetic Skills, Vocational Interest, Social Functioning, and Work-Related Temperament Factors. The KEVAS software also enables scoring and on-site report production. Group data are aggregated, and statistical reports and research services are available.

Format: Examiner/self-administered; suitable for group use; untimed: 2 to 3 hours

Scoring: Computer scored; examiner evaluated

Cost: KEVAS IBM-compatible testing station $2,000.00. License Fees include one year's test usage for $2,500.00 and up. Additional usage varies from $6.00 to $11.00 each, depending on volume.

Publisher: Key Education, Inc.

Knowledge of Occupations Test
Leroy G. Baruth

Copyright: 1974

Population: Adolescents; Grades 10 through 12

Purpose: Assesses high school students' knowledge of occupations; used for vocational guidance

Description: Paper–pencil 96-item multiple-choice measure of what students know about occupations. Item content was drawn from sources including the *Occupational Outlook Handbook* and the *Encyclopedia of Career and Vocational Guidance.*

Format: Examiner required; suitable for group use; timed: 40 minutes

Scoring: Hand key; may be machine scored

Cost: Specimen Set $9.00; 25 tests $20.00; 25 profile sheets, 25 answer sheets $8.25 each; key $2.75; manual $6.75

Publisher: Psychologists and Educators, Inc.

My Vocational Situation
John L. Holland

Copyright: Not provided

Population: Adults

Purpose: Assesses the problems that may be troubling an individual seeking help with career decisions; used in career counseling and guidance

Description: Two-page multiple-item paper–pencil questionnaire determining which of three difficulties may be troubling an individual in need of career counseling: lack of vocational identity, lack of information or training, and environmental or personal barriers. The questionnaire is completed by the individual just prior to the counseling interview and may be tabulated by the counselor at a glance. Responses may offer clues for the interview itself and treatments relevant to each individual's need. The manual discusses development of the diagnostic scheme and reports statistical properties of the three variables.

Format: Self-administered; suitable for group use; untimed: 5–10 minutes

Scoring: Examiner evaluated

Cost: Booklets $9.40 manual $3.50

Publisher: Consulting Psychologists Press, Inc.

Non-Verbal Reasoning

Copyright: 1994

Population: Adolescents, adults; ages 12 and above

Purpose: Used in career counseling and vocational exploration; assesses nonverbal reasoning of DOL GED R levels 4, 5, and 6

Description: The evaluee is presented with a series of 333 grids. Eight of the cells contain geometric pictures that bear some relationship to one another. The evaluee must choose from a list the item that best completes the grid. A test booklet, answer sheet, and a manual are used.

Format: Individual/group administration; examiner required; timed: 20 minutes

Scoring: Machine/computer scored

Cost: Contact publisher

Publisher: Valpar International Corporation

Occupational Clues
J. Michael Farr

Copyright: 1993

Population: Adults

Purpose: Explores career alternatives; used in career counseling with adults with above-average reading skills

Description: Multiple-choice true–false test with six groups of checklists: Occupational Interests, Work-Related Values, Leisure Activities, Home Activities, School, Training, and Work Experience. Short and long versions are available.

Format: Individual/self-administered; untimed: 60 minutes

Scoring: Self-scored

Cost: Long Version—25 Forms $48.95; Short Version—25 Forms $36.95

Publisher: JIST Works, Inc.

Occupational Scale Based on Job Competency
Herman J. P. Schubert

Copyright: 1977

Population: Adults

Purpose: Assesses establishment of social class; used in career counseling

Description: Multiple-item paper–pencil questionnaire

Format: Group or individual administration; examiner required; untimed

Scoring: Hand key; examiner evaluated

Cost: $15.00

Publisher: Select Press

Perceptions Expectations, Emotions, and Knowledge About College (PEEK)
Claire E. Weinstein, David R. Palmer

Copyright: 1995

Population: Adolescents; 12th graders, college freshmen

Purpose: Assesses thoughts, beliefs, and expectations about personal, social, and academic changes that may occur in a college setting; used for counseling, course development, and college success courses

Description: Three-scale 30-item multiple-choice computer-administered test measuring academic experiences (10 items), personal experiences (10 items), and social experiences (10 items). A Distribution Report showing responses, percents, median, mode, mean, and standard deviation; a Student Profile; and a Summary Report are yielded. A #2 pencil is used along with a 1-page scannable form.

Format: Suitable for group use; self-administered; untimed: 20–30 minutes

Scoring: Machine scored; test scoring service available from publisher

Cost: 1–499 $1.25 each; 500+ $1.00 each

Publisher: H and H Publishing Co., Inc.

Pictorial Interest Inventory Development
James M. Wilbourn, William E. Alley

Copyright: 1980

Population: Adults

Purpose: Measures job qualifications of Air Force personnel; used in career counseling

Description: Paper–pencil/oral-response 180-item test. Materials include 180 35mm color slides.

Format: Group or individual administration; examiner required; untimed

Scoring: Hand key; examiner evaluated

Cost: $15.00

Publisher: Select Press

Program for Assessing Youth Employment Skills (PAYES)

Copyright: Not provided

Population: Adolescents

Purpose: Measures the attitudes, knowledge, and interests of students preparing for entry-level employment; used by program directors, counselors, and teachers working with dropouts and disadvantaged youth in government training programs and skill centers

Description: Three orally administered paper–pencil tests assessing attitudes, knowledge, and interests related to entry-level employment. Test Booklet I measures attitudes toward job-holding skills (supervisor's requests, appropriate dress, punctuality), attitudes toward supervision by authority figures, and self-confidence in social and employment situations. Measurements are made by assessing responses to multiple-choice questions based on statements, real-life situations, and scenes. Test Booklet II provides cognitive measures, including job knowledge, job seeking skills, and practical job-related reasoning in situations that require following directions. Test Booklet III measures seven vocational interest clusters. Respondents indicate their degree of interest in specific job tasks that are described verbally and pictured. Students mark answers directly in test booklets.

Format: Examiner required; suitable for group use; untimed: time varies

Scoring: Examiner evaluated

Cost: Complete Set (20 each of Test Booklets I, II, and III, score sheets) $90.00; User's Guide $4.50; Administrators' Manual $5.50

Publisher: Educational Testing Service

PSB Health Occupations Aptitude Examination

Copyright: 1992

Population: Adults; health occupations students

Purpose: Measures abilities, skills, knowledge, and attitudes important to successful performance in various health care occupations; used as an admission test for schools and programs in health occupations

Description: Multiple-item paper–pencil battery of five tests assessing areas important to performance in health care occupations: academic aptitude, spelling, reading comprehension, the natural sciences, and vocational adjustment. The test predicts an individual's readiness for specialized instruction in numerous health care positions, including medical record technician, dental assistant, psychiatric aide, histologic technician, nursing assistant, respiratory therapy technician, and radiologic technologist.

Format: Examiner required; suitable for group use; timed: 2 hours 15 minutes

Scoring: Machine scored

Cost: Reusable test booklets $7.00; answer sheets (scoring and reporting service) $7.00

Publisher: Psychological Services Bureau

Self-Directed Search® Career Explorer (SDS® CE)
John L. Holland, Amy B. Powell

Copyright: 1994

Population: Adolescents

Purpose: Used to help students assess and explore interests for future education and career planning; intended for middle and junior high school students

Description: Paper–pencil yes–no test. Materials used include a technical information book, teacher's guide, self-assessment booklet, career booklet, and exploring your future with the SDS booklet. A sixth-grade reading level is required. A computer version using IBM PCs and compatibles is available.

Format: Self-administered; suitable for group use; untimed: 30 minutes

Scoring: Self/computer scored

Cost: Intro Kit $85.00

Publisher: Psychological Assessment Resources, Inc.

Self-Directed Search® Form E (SDS® Form E)
John L. Holland

Copyright: 1990

Population: Adolescents, adults

Purpose: Used in career counseling to assess career interests among individuals with lower educational levels

Description: Paper–pencil yes–no form. Materials used include a user's guide, technical manual, Form E assessment booklet, jobs finder, and You and Your Job booklet. Available in Spanish and English Canadian. An SDS summary code is yielded.

Format: Self-administered; suitable for group use; untimed: 20–30 minutes

Scoring: Self scored

Cost: Intro Kit $90.00

Publisher: Psychological Assessment Resources, Inc.

Self-Directed Search® Form R (SDS® Form R)

Copyright: 1994

Population: Adolescents, adults

Purpose: Used to explore career interests

Description: Paper–pencil yes–no test. Materials used include professional user's guide, technical manual, Form R assessment booklet, occupations finder, You and Your Career booklet, leisure activity finder, educational opportunity finder. Computer version using IBM PCs and compatibles is available. Versions available in South African, Japanese, Australian, Dutch, Danish, Hebrew, and New Zealand editions. An eighth-grade reading level is required.

Format: Self-administered; suitable for group use

Scoring: Machine, self, and computer scored

Cost: Kit $156.00

Publisher: Psychological Assessment Resources, Inc.

Self-Directed Search® Career Planner (SDS® CP)
John L. Holland

Copyright: 1990

Population: Adults

Purpose: Used in career counseling as an assessment for long-term career planning; intended for individuals on the career development path

Description: Paper–pencil yes–no test. Materials used include a professional user's guide, technical manual, Form CP assessment booklets, career option finders, and Exploring Career Options booklet. An eighth-grade reading level is required. A computer version using IBM PCs and compatibles is available.

Format: Self-administered; suitable for group use; untimed: 15–25 minutes

Scoring: Machine, self, and computer scored; test scoring service available from publisher

Cost: Intro Kit $112.00

Publisher: Psychological Assessment Resources, Inc.

Spatial Aptitude

Copyright: 1994

Population: Adolescents, adults; ages 12 and above

Purpose: Used in career counseling and vocational exploration to assess the top three levels of APT–S

Description: The evaluee is presented with a series of two-dimensional drawings that could fold into a three-dimensional object. The evaluee must select the proper object from a group of three-dimensional projections. DOL spatial aptitude levels 1 and 2 scores are yielded. A test booklet, answer sheet, and manual are used.

Format: Individual/group administration; examiner required; timed: 10 minutes

Scoring: Machine/computer scored

Cost: Contact publisher

Publisher: Valpar International Corporation

Student Adaptation to College Questionnaire (SACQ)
Robert W. Baker, Bohad Siryk

Copyright: Not provided

Population: Adults

Purpose: Measures overall student adjustment to college; used for college counseling

Description: Multiple-choice 67-item questionnaire with four subscales that measure academic adjustment, social adjustment, personal–emotional adjustment, and attachment to the college. Yields T-Scores. A computer version for IBM and compatible personal computers is available.

Format: Self-administered; suitable for group use; untimed: 30 minutes

Scoring: Machine scored; computer scored; self-scored; test scoring service available from publisher

Cost: Kit (25 hand-scored questionnaires, 1 manual, 2 WPS Test Report answer sheets) $87.50

Publisher: Western Psychological Services

Student Developmental Task and Lifestyle Inventory (SDTLI)
Roger B. Winston, Jr., Theodore K. Miller, Judith S. Prince

Copyright: 1987

Population: Adults; ages 17 to 24; college students

Purpose: Measures the psychosocial development of traditional-aged college students

Description: Paper–pencil 140-item true–false test covering the following psychosocial areas: Establishing and Clarifying Purpose Task (Educational Involvement, Career Planning, Lifestyle Planning, Cultural Participation, Life Management), Developing Mature Interpersonal Relationships (Tolerance, Peer Relationships, Emotional Autonomy), Academic Autonomy Task, Salubrious Lifestyle Scale, Intimacy Scale, and Response Bias Scale. A 12th-grade reading level is required. This inventory is an adaptation of the Student Developmental Task Inventory (SDTI2). Suitable for individuals with visual, hearing, and physical disabilities.

Format: Self-administered; suitable for group use; untimed: 20–30 minutes

Scoring: Self-scored

Cost: 50 booklets $50.00; 50 answer sheets $25.00; 50 interpretive guides $15.00

Publisher: Student Developmental Associates, Inc.

Student Profile and Assessment Record (SPAR)

Theodore K. Miller, Roger B. Winston, Jr.

Copyright: 1985

Population: College students; ages 17 to 23

Purpose: Assesses perceptions of entering college students; used by academic advisers, counselors, residence hall staff, and others

Description: Multiple-item paper–pencil comprehensive self-assessment tool providing information in six categories: general (home address, marital status, disabilities, need for financial assistance, emergency contact person), academic (perceptions of subjects, decisions about major, noncredit academic interests and long-range plans, instructional approach preference, academic strengths and weaknesses), career, health and wellness, activities and organizations, and special concerns and other considerations. The SPAR folder has space for recording the student's test profile, high school academic record, and other pertinent information, including educational goals and objectives. The instrument is useful in the initial phases of orientation. It is recommended for use in conjunction with the Student Developmental Task and Lifestyle Inventory.

Format: Self-administered; not suitable for group use; untimed: time varies

Scoring: Self-scored

Cost: 50 folders $25.00

Publisher: Student Development Associates, Inc.

Study Skills Counseling Evaluation

George D. Demos

Copyright: Not provided

Population: Adolescents, adults; Grades 10 through college

Purpose: Evaluates the study habits and attitudes of high school and college students

Description: Paper–pencil 50-item questionnaire in which students use a scale ranging from "very often" to "very seldom" to rate themselves on time distribution, study conditions, taking notes, examinations, and habits and attitudes. The questionnaire contains "critical items" that differentiate between B and C students.

Format: Self-administered; suitable for group use; untimed: 10–20 minutes

Scoring: Hand key

Cost: Kit (25 forms, 1 manual) $35.00

Publisher: Western Psychological Services

System for Assessment and Group Evaluation (SAGE)

Copyright: 1980

Population: Adolescents, adults; ages 14 and above

Purpose: Measures educational development, vocational aptitudes, vocational interests, temperaments, and work attitudes

Description: Paper–pencil, multiple-choice, hands-on assessment battery measuring four categories. A fourth-grade reading level is required. Used for vocational planning and guidance with populations who have physical/mental disabilities, are disadvantaged, or have been dislocated or injured as workers. Computer scoring is available.

Format: Individual administration; suitable for group use; examiner required; timed and untimed

Scoring: Machine/computer scored

Cost: Contact publisher

Publisher: PESCO, International

Technical and Scientific Information Test (A/9) and Technical Reading Comprehension Test A/10

Copyright: Not provided

Population: Adults

Purpose: Assesses scientific and technical understanding of people with little or no schooling in scientific or technical areas; used for predicting job success in these fields after training

Description: Multiple-item paper–pencil tests of general scientific knowledge and the ability to comprehend technical information. The two tests should be given together and sequentially. The first is a list of questions on general scientific information likely to be known by individuals who have had little or no formal scientific training. The second test consists of five paragraphs assessing whether a person with little or no formal schooling in technical subjects can comprehend articles of a technical nature. The tests predict job success after technical and scientific training. Norms are available.

Format: Examiner required; suitable for group use; timed: 30 minutes

Scoring: Hand key

Cost: Contact publisher

Publisher: Human Sciences Research Council

Test on Appraising Observations (Constructed Response Version)
Stephen P. Norris

Copyright: 1986

Population: Adolescents, adults

Purpose: Measures an individual's ability to appraise observations reported by others; used in teaching and diagnosis

Description: Paper–pencil 25-item short-answer test assessing an individual's ability to evaluate observation. The test is based on a set of principles for appraising observations related to characteristics of the observer, the observation conditions, and the observation statement. A sixth-grade reading level is required. Suitable for use with individuals with hearing and physical disabilities.

Format: Examiner/self administered; suitable for group use; untimed: 45 minutes

Scoring: Examiner evaluated

Cost: Contact publisher

Publisher: Faculty of Education, Memorial University of Newfoundland

Test on Appraising Observations (Multiple-Choice Version)
Stephen P. Norris, Ruth King

Copyright: 1986

Population: Adults

Purpose: Measures the ability of senior high school and college students to appraise observations reported by others; used in critical thinking research and evaluation, classroom instruction and evaluation, and selection and placement of students

Description: Paper–pencil 50-item test consisting of two stories and related items. Each item consists of two observation statements. Examinees decide which statement, if either, is more believable. The test is based on a set of principles for appraising observations related to characteristics of the observer, the observation conditions, and the observation statement. The publisher offers a scoring service that generates a statistical report. A sixth-grade reading level is required.

Format: Examiner/self-administered; suitable for group use; untimed: 50–60 minutes

Scoring: Hand key; may be computer scored

Cost: 35 test forms $35.00; 100 answer sheets (NCS General Purpose) $10.00; scoring key $1.00; manual $5.00; technical report of test design $10.00; scoring service $0.75 per answer sheet; standard statistical report $10.00; data diskette $10.00

Publisher: Faculty of Education, Memorial University of Newfoundland

Transition Behavior Scale (TBS)
Stephen B. McCarney

Copyright: 1989

Population: Adolescents; ages 16 to 20; Grades 10 and above

Purpose: Provides a measure of behaviors necessary for success in employment and independent living

Description: The subscales measure a student's behavior in the areas of Work Related Behavior, Interpersonal Relations, and Social/Community Expectations. The TBS provides teachers a convenient mechanism for measuring the student's skills and readiness for transition activities. Students in the standardization sample represented all geographic regions of the United States, with particular attention given to the inclusion of racial and ethnic minorities in the creation of the national norms. Internal consistency, test–retest, and interrater reliability; item and factor analysis; and content, criterion-related, diagnostic, and construct validity are well documented and reported for the scale.

Format: Individual administration

Scoring: Machine/self/computer scored

Cost: Complete Kit $63.50

Publisher: Hawthorne Educational Services, Inc.

VCWS 19—Dynamic Physical Capacities

Copyright: 1986

Population: Adults

Purpose: Measures the Physical Demands factor of the Worker Qualifications Profile of the DOT (*Dictionary of Occupational Titles*). Evaluates an individual's endurance and strength; may be used in postinjury cases

Description: Objective measure of functional capacity in terms of strength. The exercise measures each of the strength levels represented in the Physical Demands factor of the Worker Qualifications Profile of the DOT: sedentary, light, medium, heavy, and very heavy. The examinee, who assumes the role of a shipping and receiving clerk, handles materials varying in weight from 5 pounds to 115 pounds. The examinee begins with exercises on the sedentary level and gradually moves through the range of strengths until his or her capacity is reached. The test may be discontinued at any time. The test should be administered only to individuals who are able to walk, are free of visual handicaps, and have use of their upper extremities.

Format: Examiner required; not suitable for group use; timed: time not available

Scoring: Examiner evaluated

Cost: $4,295.00

Publisher: Valpar International Corporation

VCWS 201—Physical Capacities/Mobility Screening

Copyright: 1989

Population: Adolescents, adults; ages 13 and older

Purpose: Screens physical demands required in work/training settings; used for placement and career planning

Description: Criterion-referenced test consisting of demonstrated performance of lifting, continuous lifting, two-handed grip, palm press, horizontal press, vertical press, balancing, walk forward, walk backward, walk heel–toe, and climbing. Examiner qualifications as required by testing site. Materials include weight scale, standing platform, lifting apparatus, hinged climbing board, and tape measure. This test is suitable for individuals with hearing, physical, and mental impairments. Signing for hearing impairment necessary.

Format: Examiner required; not suitable for group use; untimed: 10–15 minutes

Scoring: Examiner evaluated

Cost: $695.00

Publisher: Valpar International Corporation

Vocational Information and Evaluation Work Samples (VIEWS)

Copyright: 1980

Population: Adults; high school students

Purpose: Assesses vocational interests and abilities of persons with MR; used for vocational guidance

Description: Work simulating tests of abilities consisting of 16 work samples. The tasks performed include sorting, cutting, collating, assembling, weighing, tying, measuring, using hand tools, tending a drill press, and electric machine feeding. The assessment process includes client orientation, demonstration by the examiner, training, and timed assessment. A separate training phase and observation of the client help distinguish between learning and performance and provide information about learning, quality of work, and productivity. The test requires no reading ability. VIEWS is normed on a national sample of mentally retarded individuals with a mean IQ of 52. MODAPTS, or industrial performance comparisons, are computed for each sample to indicate the ability to perform at a competitive level of work.

Format: Examiner required; suitable for small group use; untimed: 4–5 days

Scoring: Examiner evaluated

Cost: Contact publisher

Publisher: Vocational Research Institute

Vocational Integration Index (VII)
Wendy S. Parent, John Kregel, Paul Wehman

Copyright: 1992

Population: Adults

Purpose: For special and rehabilitation professionals, employment specialists, and consumers; designed to identify employment opportunities for individuals with disabilities

Description: The index is an easy-to-use instrument that consists of two scales and a manual. Each scale contains 32 items that describe the characteristics of the company, the work area, the employees, and the benefits that relate to overall employee integration. The Job Scale is used to evaluate a job site to determine available opportunities for vocational integration. The Consumer Scale is used to assess the degree to which a worker with a disability takes advantage of such opportunities and to identify how job satisfaction could be enhanced. The Examiner's Manual contains detailed instructions for administering, scoring, and interpreting the instruments, illustrated through the use of case study examples. Complete validity and reliability analysis is included.

Format: Examiner required; timed: time varies

Scoring: Examiner evaluated

Cost: Complete Kit (examiner's manual, 20 job scale forms, and 20 consumer scale forms) $59.00

Publisher: PRO-ED, Inc.

Vocational Preference Inventory
John L. Holland

Copyright: 1985

Population: Adolescents, adults; Grades 10 and above

Purpose: Assesses personality using occupational item content; developed for high school students and adults for vocational exploration

Description: Multiple-item paper–pencil or computer-administered test yielding a profile based on 11 dimensions of personality: realistic, investigative, scientific, conventional, enterprising, artistic, self-control, masculinity/femininity, status, infrequency, and acquiescence. Items are all occupational titles, and the subjects indicate which they like or dislike. This revision contains new items as well as answer sheet and stencil revisions. The computer version operates on Apple systems with 64K, an 80-column card, and two disk drives and on IBM PC systems and compatibles. Available in French.

Format: Examiner/self-administered; suitable for group use; untimed: 15–30 minutes

Scoring: Hand-scorable answer sheet; may be computer scored

Cost: Professional Kit $32.00

Publisher: Psychological Assessment Resources, Inc.

Vocational Research Interest Inventory (VRII)

Copyright: 1988

Population: Adolescents, adults

Purpose: Identifies the interests of high school juniors and seniors and adults; used for vocational counseling and job exploration

Description: Paper–pencil or computer-administered 162-item inventory assessing an individual's interests in 12 areas tied to the jobs listed in the *Dictionary of Occupational Titles* and the *Guide for Occupational Exploration:* artistic, scientific, plants/animals, protective, mechanical, industrial, business detail, selling, accommodating, humanitarian, lead/influence, and physical performing. Each form includes score profiles and explanations for the U.S. Department of Labor's Occupational Exploration Systems. Separate norms are provided for prevocational and vocational students. The computer version runs on Apple IIe, Apple II+, Apple IIGS, IBM, and IBM-compatible systems with one disk drive. The examinee uses the arrow and return keys to respond. Responses can be scored either automatically or on disk for later scoring and evaluation. The program allows reports to be generated based on data manually entered from the paper–pencil version. The Spanish translation, Inventario Investigativo de Interés Vocacional (IIIV), is designed to be accessible to native speakers of Spanish in all regions of the United States. Both tests provide an Individual Profile Analysis and ideographic interpretation.

Format: Self-administered; suitable for group use; untimed: 15–20 minutes

Scoring: Hand key; computer scored on site

Cost: Specimen Kit, paper–pencil version (manual, 5 test forms) $12.50; software package $295.00

Publisher: Vocational Research Institute

Work Adjustment Inventory (WAI)
James E. Gilliam

Copyright: 1994

Population: Ages 12 to 22

Purpose: Assesses work-related temperament

Description: A multidimensional, norm-referenced instrument designed for use in schools and clinics. The WAI provides vital information to counselors, psychologists, personnel directors, and others. The WAI can be used in the development of individual transition plans for students with disabilities (required under IDEA) and has application for at-risk students. Six scales measure six work-related temperament traits: Activity, Empathy, Sociability, Assertiveness, Adaptability, and Emotionality. Each scale provides a standard score for age and gender, and combination of the standard scores generates an overall quotient of work temperament and adjustment. These scores can be dis-

played graphically. The WAI standardization (on more than 7,000 students, 10% with disabilities) is the largest and most representative of the 1990 U.S. population of any test of temperament. The WAI norms constitute the most current and representative temperament norms available. Studies of both internal consistency and test–retest reliability produced appropriately high coefficients. Evidence of reliability of the WAI is provided in the form of coefficients alpha.

Format: Individual administration; suitable for group use; timed: 20 minutes

Scoring: Examiner evaluated

Cost: Complete Kit (examiner's manual, 50 response record forms, storage box) $69.00

Publisher: PRO-ED, Inc.

Work Adjustment Scale (WAS)
Stephen B. McCarney

Copyright: 1991

Population: Adolescents; ages 16 and above; Grades 10 and above

Purpose: Provides the profile necessary to determine a student's readiness for success in the workplace

Description: Includes 54 items easily observed and documented by educational personnel. Separate norms are provided for male and female students.

Format: Individual administration; untimed: 12–15 minutes

Scoring: Self/computer scored

Cost: Complete Kit $59.50

Publisher: Hawthorne Educational Services, Inc.

World of Work and You
U.S. Department of Labor

Copyright: 1990

Population: Adolescents

Purpose: Used in career exploration; teaches the importance of values and education in career planning

Description: Career exploration booklet (32

pages) identifies such factors as work satisfiers, values, and training in educational options. Job matching chart included. Eighth-grade reading level is required.

Format: Individual/self-administered; untimed

Scoring: Self-scored

Cost: 25 forms $48.95

Publisher: JIST Works, Inc.

Aptitude

Academic–Technical Aptitude Tests—ATA and SATA

Copyright: ATA 1969; SATA 1977

Population: Children, adolescents

Purpose: Assesses differential job aptitudes; used for vocational and educational guidance

Description: Multiple-item paper–pencil batteries measuring occupational aptitudes. The ATA battery (for pupils in Standards 6, 7, and 8) consists of 10 tests: Verbal Reasoning, Nonverbal Reasoning, Computations, Spatial Perceptions (2-D), Mechanical Reasoning, Language Comprehension, Spatial Perception (3-D), Comparison, Coordination, and Writing Speed. SATA (for pupils in Standards 8, 9, and 10) is available in two forms, A and B. Form A consists of the following 10 tests: Verbal Reasoning, Nonverbal Reasoning I: Figure Series, Nonverbal Reasoning II: Dominoes, Computations, Reading Comprehension, Spelling and Vocabulary, Mechanical Reasoning, Spatial Perception (3-D), Comparison, and Price Controlling. Form B has one additional subtest, Filing.

Format: Examiner required; suitable for group use; timed: ATA 4 hours; SATA 4½ hours

Scoring: Hand key; examiner evaluated

Cost: Contact publisher

Publisher: Human Sciences Research Council

Career Ability Placement Survey (CAPS)

Lila F. Knapp, Robert R. Knapp

Copyright: 1994

Population: Adolescents, adults

Purpose: Measures abilities keyed to entry requirements for the majority of jobs in each of the 14 COPSystem Career Clusters; used with students for career and vocational guidance and academic counseling

Description: Eight paper–pencil subtests measuring career-related abilities. The tests are Mechanical Reasoning, Spatial Relations, Verbal Reasoning, Numerical Ability, Language Usage, Word Knowledge, Perceptual Speed and Accuracy, and Manual Speed and Dexterity. The eight tests are keyed to the COPSystem Career Clusters. An audiotape of recorded instructions is available.

Format: Examiner/self-administered; suitable for group use; timed: 51 minutes

Scoring: Self scored; may be computer scored

Cost: Specimen Set (one copy of each test, manual) $7.00

Publisher: EdITS/Educational and Industrial Testing Service

McCarron-Dial System (MDS)

Lawrence T. McCarron, Jack G. Dial

Copyright: 1986

Population: Adolescents, adults; ages 16 and older

Purpose: Assesses verbal–spatial–cognitive, sensory, motor, emotional, and integration–coping factors; used primarily in educational and vocational programming, development, and placement of special education and rehabilitation populations

Description: Multiple-item paper–pencil oral-response point-to task-performance battery consisting of six separate instruments: *Peabody Picture Vocabulary Test–Revised* (PPVT–R), *Bender Visual Motor Gestalt Test* (BVMGT), *Behavior Rating Scale* (BRS), *Observational Emotional Inventory* (OEI), *Haptic Visual Discrimination Test* (HVDT), and *McCarron Assessment of Neuromuscular Development* (MAND). The standard format for comprehensive reporting includes specific scores, vocational and residential placement scores, behavioral observations, case history information, lists of strengths and weaknesses, programming priorities, and programming recommendations. The system is designed to predict the level of vocational and residential functioning the individual may achieve after training. This level can be used to establish vocational goals and /or appropriate vocational program placement. The system is targeted toward individuals with learning disabilities, emotional disturbance, mental retardation, cerebral palsy, closed head injury, social disabilities, and cultural disadvantages. It also can be used with persons with blindness or deafness. The examiner must be trained.

Format: Examiner required; not suitable for group use; timed: time not available; untimed: time varies

Scoring: Hand key; examiner evaluated

Cost: Complete MDS $2,575.00; HVDT $965.00; MAND $1,125.00

Publisher: McCarron-Dial Systems

Occupational Aptitude Survey and Interest Schedule–Second Edition: Aptitude Survey (OASIS–2:AS)
Randall M. Parker

Copyright: 1991

Population: Adolescents; Grades 8–12

Purpose: Evaluates a high school student's aptitude for various occupations; used for occupational guidance and counseling

Description: Paper–pencil 245-item survey measuring general, verbal, numerical, spatial, perceptual, and manual abilities through five subtests: Vocabulary (40 items, 9 minutes), Computation (30 items, 12 minutes), Spatial Relations (20 items, 8 minutes), Word Comparison (95 items, 5 minutes), Making Marks (60 items, 1 minute). Subtest raw scores, percentiles, stanines, and 5-point scores are yielded. A companion test to the Interest Schedule, scores for both surveys are keyed directly to the *Dictionary of Occupational Titles,*

Guide for Occupational Exploration, and the *Worker Trait Group Guide.*

Format: Examiner required; suitable for group use; timed: 35 minutes

Scoring: Examiner evaluated

Cost: Complete Kit (examiner's manual, 10 student test booklets, 50 hand-scorable answer sheets, 50 profile sheets, storage box) $124.00

Publisher: PRO-ED, Inc.

Self-Directed Learning Readiness Scale (SDLRS)
Lucy M. Guglielmino

Copyright: Not provided

Population: Assesses an individual's learning preferences and attitudes toward learning; used to measure readiness for self-directed learning

Description: Paper–pencil/computer-administered 58-item self-report multiple-choice test assessing readiness for self-directed learning. The test is available on two levels, Elementary and Adult. A Business form and a Self-Scoring form are available at the adult level. A sixth-grade reading level is required. Form ABE, suitable for adults with lower reading levels and nonnative speakers of English, is also available. The software program operates on Apple IIc systems. Raw scores may be converted to percentile rankings. Adult form available in Spanish, French, German, Chinese, Japanese, and Finnish. Form ABE available in Spanish.

Format: Self-administered; suitable for group use; 20 minutes

Scoring: Computer scored (except self-scoring form)

Cost: $3.00 per copy including scoring; $3.95 for self-scoring form; quantity discounts available

Publisher: Guglielmino and Associates, Inc.

Skills Assessment Module (S.A.M.)
Michelle Rosinek

Copyright: 1985–1992

Population: Adolescents, adults; ages 14 years and older

Purpose: Assesses basic skill level in 13 career skill areas; used for career training placement

Description: Paper–pencil show-tell format with 12 hands-on modules: Digital Discrimination, Clerical/Verbal, Motor Coordination, Clerical/Numerical, Written Instructions, Finger Dexterity, Measurement Skill, Manual Dexterity, Form Perception, Spatial Perception, Color Perception, Following Diagrammed Instructions. A Career Training Performance matrix is generated. Computer version for Apple, Macintosh, and IBM personal computers is available. Available in Spanish.

Format: Suitable for group/individual use; examiner required; timed: 1 hour 45 minutes

Scoring: Examiner evaluated; computer scored

Cost: $2,495.00

Publisher: Piney Mountain Press, Inc.

Trade Aptitude Test (TRAT)

Copyright: 1983

Population: Adolescents, adults

Purpose: Assesses aptitudes of adult blacks for training in trades; used for screening prospective trade school students

Description: Paper–pencil 16-subtest measure of skills important to trade training, including skill, coordination, patterns, spare parts, classification, assembling, calculations, inspection, graphs, mechanical insight, mathematics, spatial perception (2-D), vocabulary, figure series, and spatial perception (3-D).

Format: Examiner required; suitable for group use; untimed: 4 hours 45 minutes

Scoring: Hand key; examiner evaluated; may be machine scored

Cost: Contact publisher

Publisher: Human Sciences Research Council

Vocational Transit

Copyright: 1989

Population: Adolescents, adults; ages 14 and older

Purpose: Assesses vocational potential: aptitudes, learning style, and work rate stability; used for vocational counseling and placement of individuals who have mental retardation, brain injury, or severe learning disabilities

Description: Computer-driven vocational assessment system for measurement of Motor Coordination (60 seconds), Manual Dexterity (90 seconds), Finger Dexterity (without assembly—60 seconds; with assembly—90 seconds), and Form Perception. Each motor test has a demonstration, practice, and testing phase. Form Perception test incorporates multiple-choice format and is preceded by three pretest phases; form-board, flip-chart, and attribute orientation. Formal testing involves three phases during which interventions are progressively introduced to provide cognitive structure. Yields raw scores, aptitude levels (1–5), percentiles using MR and/or nonimpaired norm bases, and work rate stability scores. This test is suitable for individuals with hearing and mental impairments. Computer versions for IBM and compatibles, Mac, and Apple II are available.

Format: Examiner required; not suitable for group use; untimed: 1 to 3 hours

Scoring: Computer scored

Cost: $5,850.00

Publisher: Vocational Research Institute

Interest

19 Field Interest Inventory (19FII)

Copyright: 1970

Population: Adolescents, adults

Purpose: Assesses vocational interests of high school students; used for vocational guidance

Description: Paper–pencil measure of 19 broad areas of vocational interest: fine arts, performing arts, language, historical, service, social work, sociability, public speaking, law, creative thought, science, practical—male, practical—female, numerical, business, clerical, travel, nature, and sports. Scores on two aspects of interests, work-hobby and active-passive, also are obtained.

Format: Examiner required; suitable for group use; untimed: 45 minutes

Scoring: Hand key; examiner evaluated; may be machine scored

Cost: Contact publisher

Publisher: Human Sciences Research Council

Awareness of Occupational Experience Scale II (AOES)
Philip C. Kendall, A. J. Finch, Jr., J. Mikulka, William Coleson

Copyright: 1980

Population: Adolescents; high school females

Purpose: Measures knowledge of facts about the female occupational experience; used in career counseling

Description: True–false 25-item paper–pencil questionnaire

Format: Individual or group administration; requires examiner; untimed

Scoring: Hand key; examiner evaluated

Cost: $15.00

Publisher: Select Press

Career Assessment Battery (CAB)

Copyright: 1991–1994

Population: Ages 13 to adult

Purpose: Measures career interests for career counseling

Description: A live-action video provides participants access to 12 occupational situations to make informed choices. Each category takes 3 minutes and provides aptitude, career cluster, and job title matches. Computer scoring on MAC/IBM/Apple is included in the package. Machine and scoring service are available.

Format: Individual or group administration; 40 minutes

Scoring: Examiner administration and interpretation

Cost: $595.00

Publisher: Piney Mountain Press, Inc.

Career Assessment Inventory–Vocational Version
Charles B. Johansson

Copyright: 1982

Population: Adolescents, adults

Purpose: Measures occupational interests of high school students who want immediate, non–college-graduate business or technical training; used for employment decisions, vocational rehabilitation, and self-employment

Description: Paper–pencil 305-item test in a five-response Likert format. The inventory covers six general occupational themes (Holland's RIASEC), 22 basic interest scales, and 91 occupational scales. The test may be computer scored by NCS in one of three ways: via mail-service, Arion II Teleprocessing, or MICROTEST™ assessment system. Available in French, Spanish, and English.

Format: Self-administered; suitable for group use; untimed: 25 to 30 minutes

Scoring: Computer scored by publisher

Cost: Manual $18.00; Narrative Report $6.00–$8.50 depending on quantity; Profile Report $3.75–$5.50 depending on quantity

Publisher: NCS Assessments

Career Exploration Inventory (CEI)
John J. Liptak

Copyright: 1994

Population: Adolescents, adults

Purpose: Career test that integrates work, leisure, and learning interests; used for career guidance

Description: Multiple-choice 120-item true–false yes–no test identifying interests with *Guide for Occupational Exploration* occupational clusters. Also available in Spanish. A seventh-grade reading level is required. Yields graphic interest profile.

Format: Self-administered; designed for group use; untimed

Scoring: Self-scored

Cost: 25 forms $29.95

Publisher: JIST Works, Inc.

Career Orientation Placement and Evaluation Survey (COPES)

Copyright: 1995

Population: Adolescents, adults; Grades 8 and above

Purpose: Measures personal values related to the type of work an individual chooses and the satisfactions derived from the occupation; used for career evaluation and guidance and to supplement other types of information used to improve self-awareness

Description: Multiple-item paper–pencil inventory measuring the following 16 value dimensions related to career evaluation and selection: investigative vs. accepting, practical vs. carefree, independent vs. conformity, leadership vs. supportive, orderliness vs. flexibility, recognition vs. privacy, aesthetic vs. realistic, and social vs. reserved. The COPES value dimensions are based on theoretical and factor analytic research and are keyed to the COPSystem Career Clusters. Norms are provided for high school and college levels. Measures both ends of each scale.

Format: Self-administered; suitable for group use; untimed: 30 minutes

Scoring: Self-scored; may be computer scored

Cost: Specimen Set (manual, all forms) $6.25

Publisher: EdITS/Educational and Industrial Testing Service

Career Survey

Copyright: 1983

Population: Adolescents, adults; Grades 7 and above

Purpose: Measures and profiles students' interests and abilities; used in guidance and vocational counseling

Description: Paper–pencil 132-item multiple-choice test covering 12 areas of career interest: accommodating/entertaining, humanitarian/caretaking, plant/animal/caretaking, mechanical, business detail, sales, numerical, communications/promotion, science/technology, artistic expression, educational/social, and medical.

The interest scales were built around a two-dimensional model: people–things and data–ideas. Also included is a 40-item ability survey measuring verbal and nonverbal reasoning ability.

Format: Examiner/self-administered; suitable for group use; timed: ability scales 24 minutes total

Scoring: Machine scored; hand key; scoring service available from publisher

Cost: 35 test booklets, 35 orientation booklets, directions for administration $45.00; scoring and reporting services extra

Publisher: American College Testing

Chronicle Career Quest® (CCQ)

Copyright: 1992

Population: Adolescents; Grades 7 through 12

Purpose: A comprehensive interest inventory used for career counseling

Description: Multiple-choice paper–pencil test. Form S (Grades 7–10) and Form L (Grades 9–12) are available. Materials used include an interest inventory (SandL), interpretation guide (SandL), career crosswalk, occupational profiles/summary sheets, report to parents, and career paths. Suitable for individuals with hearing disabilities.

Format: Self-administered; suitable for group use; untimed: 30–35 minutes

Scoring: Hand key

Cost: CCO Form S: package of 25 II, 25 IG, 1 AG, $40.50; CCO Form L: package of 25 II, 25 IG, 1 AG, $49.50

Publisher: Chronicle Guidance Publications, Inc.

Copsystem Interest Inventory (COPS)

Robert. R. Knapp, Lila F. Knapp

Copyright: 1995

Population: Adolescents, adults; Grades 7 and above

Purpose: Measures job activity interests related to occupational clusters appropriate for college-

and vocationally oriented individuals; used for academic counseling, career planning, and vocational guidance

Description: Multiple-item paper–pencil inventory measuring interests related to both professional and skilled positions in science, technology, business, arts, and service and to occupations in communication, consumer economics, clerical, and outdoor fields. Each cluster is keyed to curriculum choice and major sources of detailed job information, including the *Dictionary of Occupational Titles* and the *Occupational Outlook Handbook.* On-site scoring provides immediate feedback of results. The instrument may be used with the CAPS and COPES as part of the COPSystem. Percentile norms are presented separately for high school and college levels. Also available in Spanish and Canadian.

Format: Self-administered; suitable for group use; untimed: 20 minutes

Scoring: Self-scoring; may be computer scored

Cost: Specimen set (all forms, technical manual) $8.25; 25 self-scoring test booklets $11.75; 25 self-interpretation guides and profile guides $11.50; 25 machine-scoring booklets and answer sheets $12.25; handscoring keys $17.75; examiner's manual $2.50

Publisher: EdITS/Educational and Industrial Testing Service

Copsystem Interest Inventory–Form R (COPS–R)
Robert. R. Knapp, Lila F. Knapp

Copyright: 1994

Population: Adolescents; Grades 6 through 12

Purpose: Measures job activity interests related to occupational clusters; used for academic counseling, career planning, and vocational guidance

Description: Multiple-item paper–pencil inventory measuring interests related to both professional and skilled positions in science, technology, business, arts, and service and to occupations in communication, consumer economics, clerical, and outdoor fields. COPS–R is parallel to the COPS Interest Inventory but uses simpler language and a single norms profile. Items are written at a sixth-grade reading level, and the whole unit is presented in a single booklet. The instrument may be used with CAPS and COPES as a part of the Copsystem. A self-scoring form and a machine-scoring form for processing and scoring by EdITS are available. Percentile norms are provided at the high school level.

Format: Self-administered; suitable for group use; untimed: 20 minutes

Scoring: Self-scored; may be computer scored

Cost: Specimen Set (manual, all forms) $6.50; 25 self-scoring forms (includes self-scoring booklet and self-interpretation guide) $23.00; 25 machine-scoring booklets and answer sheets $12.25; examiner's manual $2.50

Publisher: EdITS/Educational and Industrial Testing Service

Copsystem Intermediate Inventory (COPS II)
Robert. R. Knapp, Lila F. Knapp

Copyright: 1994

Population: Adolescents; Grades 4 through 7

Purpose: Measures the career-related interests of students in Grades 4–7 and older students for whom language or reading might present more difficulty; used for academic counseling and guidance

Description: Multiple-item paper–pencil inventory providing a rating of student's job-related interests based to a large extent on knowledge of school activities. COPS II extends interest measurement to younger students and to older students with reading or language difficulties for whom motivational considerations are of special concern. Items are written at a fourth-grade reading level.

Format: Self-administered; suitable for group use; untimed: response 20–30 minutes; scoring 15–20 minutes

Scoring: Self-scored

Cost: Specimen Set (includes manual) $5.00; 25 self-scoring forms $24.25 (combined self-scoring booklet and self-interpretation guide);

Set of 14 COPSystem Occupational Cluster Charts with COPSystem II Cartoons $44.00; 25 pocket-size cluster charts $6.50

Publisher: EdITS/Educational and Industrial Testing Service

Copsystem Professional Level Interest Inventory (COPS–P)
Lisa Knapp-Lee, Lila F. Knapp, Robert R. Knapp

Copyright: 1993

Population: Adolescents, adults; Grades 7 and above

Purpose: Measures the career-related interests of professionally minded high school and college students; used for college major and occupational selection and orientation

Description: Multiple-item paper–pencil inventory measuring interests related to professional-level occupations in the following career clusters: Science (medical, life, physical), Technology (civil, electrical, mechanical), Outdoor (agribusiness, nature), Business (management, finance), Computation, Communication (written, oral), Arts (design, performing), and Service (social, instructional). Separate percentile norms are provided for high school and college levels.

Format: Self-administered; suitable for group use; untimed: 30–40 minutes

Scoring: Self-scored; may be computer scored

Cost: Specimen Set $8.75; 25 expendable self-scoring test booklets $11.75; 25 self-interpretation guides and profile guides $11.50; 25 machine-scoring booklets and answer guides $12.25

Publisher: EdITS/Educational and Industrial Testing Service

Educational Opportunities Finder
Donald Rosen, Kay Holmberg, John L. Holland

Copyright: 1995

Population: Adolescents

Purpose: Used in college counseling to aid in identifying fields of study that match one's interests; intended for college or college-bound individuals

Description: Materials used include SDS assessment booklet and educational opportunities finder. A computer version using IBM PCs and compatibles is available.

Format: Examiner/self-administered; suitable for group use; untimed: 20–30 minutes

Scoring: Hand key; computer scored

Cost: Package of 25 $42.00

Publisher: Psychological Assessment Resources, Inc.

Geist Picture Interest Inventory
Harold Geist

Copyright: 1975

Population: Adolescents, adults; Grades 8 and above

Purpose: Identifies an individual's vocational and avocational interests; used for vocational guidance and placement, especially with culture-limited and educationally deprived individuals

Description: Multiple-item paper–pencil multiple-choice test requiring minimal language skills. The subject circles one of three pictures depicting the vocational and avocational scenes he or she prefers. Occupational norms are provided for Grades 8–12, college, and adult. A Motivation Questionnaire can be administered separately to explore motivation behind occupational choices.

Format: Examiner/self-administered; suitable for group use; untimed: 20–30 minutes

Scoring: Hand key

Cost: Kit (10 male and 10 female tests, manual) $78.50

Publisher: Western Psychological Services

Hall Occupational Orientation Inventory (HALL)–Adult Basic Form
Lacy G. Hall

Copyright: 1976

Population: Adults with reading deficiencies

Purpose: Used in career counseling/guidance to assess vocational interests for adults in basic education programs

Description: Paper–pencil criterion-referenced test with 220 items focusing on 22 occupational and personality characteristics. A booklet, response sheet, and interpretive folder are used. Examiner must be certified for assessment. Reading level can be modified for the test. Available in large print.

Format: Individual/self-administered; suitable for group use; examiner required; untimed: 45 minutes

Scoring: Self-scored; examiner evaluated

Cost: Specimen Set $27.60

Publisher: Scholastic Testing Service, Inc.

Hall Occupational Orientation Inventory (HALL)–Form II
Lacy G. Hall

Copyright: 1989

Population: Adolescents, adults; junior high and above

Purpose: Used in career guidance/counseling to assess vocational interests

Description: Paper–pencil criterion-referenced test with 150 items focusing on career opportunities and development. Items are referenced to six interest scales, eight worker trait scales, and nine value/needs scales. A booklet, response sheet, and interpretive folder are used. Examiner must be certified for assessment. Available in large print.

Format: Individual/self-administered; suitable for group use; examiner required; untimed: 45 minutes

Scoring: Self-scored; examiner evaluated

Cost: Specimen Set $35.30

Publisher: Scholastic Testing Service, Inc.

Hall Occupational Orientation Inventory (HALL)–Intermediate Form
Lacy G. Hall

Copyright: 1976

Population: Children, adolescents; Grades 3 through 7

Purpose: Used in elementary career guidance to assess vocational interests

Description: Paper–pencil criterion-referenced test with 110 school-focused items and 22 work and personality characteristics. A booklet, response sheet, and interpretive folder are used. Examiner must be certified for assessment. Available in large print.

Format: Individual/self-administered; suitable for group use; examiner required; untimed: 45 minutes

Scoring: Self-scored; examiner evaluated

Cost: Specimen Set $27.60

Publisher: Scholastic Testing Service, Inc.

Hall Occupational Orientation Inventory (HALL)–Young Adult/College Form
Lacy G. Hall

Copyright: 1992

Population: Adolescents, adults; high school and above

Purpose: Used in career guidance/counseling to assess vocational interests

Description: Paper–pencil criterion-referenced test with 220 items focusing on 22 occupational and personality characteristics. A booklet, response sheet, and interpretive folder are used. Examiner must be certified for assessment. Available in large print.

Format: Individual/self-administered; suitable for group use; untimed: 45 minutes

Scoring: Self-scored

Cost: Specimen Set $27.60

Publisher: Scholastic Testing Service, Inc.

High School Interest Questionnaire (HSIQ)

Copyright: 1973

Population: Adolescents; Grades 10 through 12

Purpose: Measures vocational interests of non-white students; used for vocational guidance

Description: Paper–pencil 200-item test of eight interest areas: language, performing arts, fine arts, social, science, technical, business, and office work. The pupil responds "like," "indifferent," or "dislike" to each item.

Format: Examiner required; suitable for group use; untimed: 45–60 minutes

Scoring: Hand key; examiner evaluated

Cost: Contact publisher

Publisher: Human Sciences Research Council

How Well Do You Know Your Interests
Thomas N. Jenkins

Copyright: Not provided

Population: Adolescents, adults; Grades 10 and above

Purpose: Assesses attitudes toward work activities; used for vocational guidance

Description: Multiple-item paper–pencil test measuring interests in 10 vocational areas: business, mechanical, outdoor, service, research, visual art, amusement, literacy, music, and general work attitudes. Items are rated on a 6-point scale ranging from "like tremendously" to "dislike tremendously."

Format: Examiner required; suitable for group use; untimed: 10 minutes

Scoring: Hand key

Cost: Complete Kit (3 test booklets of each edition and manual) $10.00; 25 tests (specify secondary, college, or personnel) $20.00; keys $6.75; interpretations handbook $6.75; manual $6.75

Publisher: Psychologists and Educators, Inc.

Interest Based Career Decision (IBCD)

Copyright: Not provided

Population: Adolescents, adults

Purpose: Assesses interests to identify the likes and dislikes of individuals and matches them to what is done and not done on jobs; helps individuals select an occupation they will find rewarding; used for career exploration, vocational/educational guidance

Description: Multiple-choice 200-item computer-administered or paper–pencil test assessing an individual's preferences. The individual responds to a 200-picture inventory containing activity statements. Responses are recorded in the test booklet for computer scoring or on cards for on-site scoring. A generated profile across the 20 dimensions of work describes the individual's approach/avoid pattern as numerical indicators related to activity preferences. The data bank consists of profiles of the 66 Occupational Families of the GOE, which were compiled by using the same survey instrument administered to the individuals tested. The program compares the individual's interest profile to job requirement profiles in the Occupational Families. Available also in Spanish. IBM/compatible required for computer version.

Format: Individual administration or suitable for group use; examiner required; untimed: 30–45 minutes

Scoring: Computer scored; no scoring service available

Cost: Contact publisher

Publisher: Centec Learning

Interest Determination, Exploration, and Assessment System (IDEAS)
Charles B. Johansson

Copyright: 1990

Population: Adolescents; Grades 6 through 12

Purpose: Measures career-related interests of junior high and high school students; used in career planning and occupational exploration

Description: Paper–pencil 128-item inventory assessing a range of career interests. Test items present five response choices. The areas covered are mechanical/fixing, nature/outdoors, science, writing, child care, protective services, mathematics, medical, creative arts, community service, educating, public speaking, business, sales, office practices, and food service. The test is scored on a 5-point Likert-type scale and is sold in a self-contained package that can be scored and interpreted by the student. A sixth-grade reading level is required.

Format: Self-administered; suitable for group use; untimed: 30 to 40 minutes

Scoring: Hand key

Cost: Manual $5.50; 50 booklets $48.95–$53.95 depending on quantity

Publisher: NCS Assessments

Inventory of Vocational Interests
Andrew Kobal, J. Wayne Wrightstone, Karl R. Kunze, Andrew J. MacElroy

Copyright: 1966

Population: Adolescents, adults; Grades 10 and above

Purpose: Assesses vocational interests; used for vocational guidance

Description: Paper–pencil 25-subject test of occupational interests. Each of the 25 topics contains 10 responses. The test, which provides insight into both major and minor interests, measures academic, artistic, mechanical, business and economic, and farm–agricultural areas. Materials include an inventory and occupation index arranged by vocational categories in the manual.

Format: Examiner required; suitable for group use; timed: 35 minutes

Scoring: Examiner evaluated

Cost: Specimen Set $4.00; 25 tests $5.00; 25 answer sheets $5.00

Publisher: Psychometric Affiliates

Jackson Vocational Interest Survey (JVIS)
Douglas N. Jackson

Copyright: 1977, 1985, 1991, 1995

Population: Adolescents, adults; Grades 9 and above

Purpose: Helps evaluate career interests of high school and college students and adults in career transition; used for educational and vocational planning and counseling and for personnel placement

Description: Paper–pencil or computer-administered 289-item inventory consisting of paired statements covering 34 basic interest scales and 10 occupational themes: expressive, logical, inquiring, practical, assertive, socialized, helping, conventional, enterprising, and communicative. The subject marks one of two responses. Scoring yields a sex-fair profile of 34 basic interest scales. A seventh-grade reading level is required. The computer version operates on IBM PC and compatible systems. Also available in French and Spanish.

Format: Examiner required; suitable for group use; untimed: 45–60 minutes

Scoring: Hand key; computer scored; scoring service available from publisher

Cost: Examination Kit $41.95; computer software (licensed package with 25 scorings) $175.00

Publisher: Sigma Assessment Systems, Inc.

Kuder General Interest Survey, Form E, Revised 1991
Frederic Kuder

Copyright: 1991

Population: Adolescents; Grades 6 through 12

Purpose: Assesses students' preferences for various activities related to general interest areas. Used to guide educational planning toward future employment

Description: Paper–pencil 168-item inventory measuring preferences in 10 general interest areas: outdoor, mechanical, scientific, computational, persuasive, artistic, literary, musical, social science, and clerical. The general manual contains general, technical, and interpretive information, including a script from a sample counseling session. Optional Job and College Majors Charts are available. A sixth-grade reading level is required.

Format: Examiner required; suitable for group use; untimed: 45–60 minutes

Scoring: Hand key; may be machine scored or computer scored locally

Cost: Complete set (materials and scoring for 25 students, machine-scored version) $44.85; software for computer- scored version $340.20;

Job and College Majors charts $14.35; general manual included in order

Publisher: CTB/McGraw-Hill

Kuder Occupational Interest Survey, Form DD (KOIS), Revised 1991

Frederic Kuder

Copyright: 1991

Population: Adolescents, adults; Grades 11 and above

Purpose: Measures how an individual's interest compares with those of satisfied workers in a number of occupational fields or students in various college majors; used with students and adults for career planning, vocational guidance, and academic counseling

Description: Paper–pencil 100-item inventory assessing the subject's interests in a number of areas related to occupational fields and college majors. Survey items consist of a list of three activities. The subject indicates for each item which activity he or she likes the most and which the least. The survey reports comparison to the subject's norm group by sex in 10 vocational areas and those of satisfied workers in approximately 100 specific occupational groups. A sixth-grade reading level is required.

Format: Self-administered; suitable for group use; timed; 30–40 minutes

Scoring: Computer scored

Cost: Materials and Scoring—complete package for 20 survey takers $106.80

Publisher: CTB/McGraw-Hill

Kuder Vocational Preference Record, Form C

Copyright: 1991

Population: Adolescents/adults; Grades 9 and above

Purpose: Evaluates occupational interests of students and adults; used for vocational counseling and employee screening and placement

Description: Paper–pencil 168-item survey measuring interests in 10 occupational areas:

outdoor, mechanical, scientific, computational, persuasive, artistic, literary, musical, social science, and clerical. A high school reading level is required.

Format: Self-administered; suitable for group use; untimed: 30–40 minutes

Scoring: Hand key

Cost: Test booklets (package of 25) $58.70; manual $6.50

Publisher: CTB/McGraw-Hill

Leisure/Work Search Inventory

John J. Liptak

Copyright: 1994

Population: Adolescents, adults

Purpose: Connects leisure interests with employment opportunities; used for employment counseling

Description: Multiple-choice 96-item test containing a career planning guide to help organize career actions. A seventh-grade reading level is required. Yields a graphic interest profile.

Format: Self-administered; untimed: 25 minutes

Scoring: Self-scored

Cost: 25 forms $29.95

Publisher: JIST Works, Inc.

Occupational Aptitude Survey and Interest Schedule–Second Edition: Interest Survey (OASIS–2:IS)

Randall M. Parker

Copyright: 1991

Population: Adolescents; Grades 8 through 12

Purpose: Evaluates a high school student's areas of interest, as related to various occupations; used for occupational guidance and counseling

Description: Paper–pencil or computer-administered 240-item self-rating scale measuring the following interest areas: artistic, scientific, nature, protective, mechanical, industrial, business detail, selling, accommodating, humanitarian, leading/influencing, and physical performing. The test yields scale raw scores, percentiles, and stanines. A companion test is the Aptitude Survey. Scores for both surveys are keyed directly to the *Dictionary of Occupational Titles, Guide for Occupational Exploration,* and the *Worker Trait Group Guide.* The computer version operates on Apple II+, IIe, IIc, or compatible systems. Questions may be read aloud to those with visual disabilities.

Format: Examiner required; suitable for group use; untimed: 30 minutes

Scoring: Examiner evaluated; may be computer scored

Cost: Complete Kit (examiner's manual, 25 student test booklets, 50 hand-scorable answer sheets, 50 profile sheets, 50 scoring forms, storage box) $124.00

Publisher: PRO-ED, Inc.

Occupational Interest Rating Scale (OIRS)
M. A. Brimer

Copyright: 1977

Population: Adolescents; ages 14 through 18

Purpose: Identifies the vocational interests of adolescents; used for vocational counseling

Description: Multiple-item paper–pencil instrument using a two-way classification system for determining vocational interests. Seven occupational areas (business, technical, care, aesthetic, scientific, numerical, and field) and five directions of involvement (persuasive, operational, empathic, making, and intellectual) are covered in the inventory. The test provides two forms in the same booklet for examining the stability of interest. Used with the Applied Knowledge Tests (AKT), expressed interests can be matched with performance in the cognitive domain. This test minimizes the need to know specific terminology and uses a sample-free ability scale scoring system. Each area and direction of involvement is measured on a scale of 0–10 based on techniques adopted for the new British Intelligence Scale. Strengths of interests between areas and between persons can be compared.

Format: Self-administered; suitable for group use; untimed: time varies

Scoring: Hand key; computer scored

Cost: £14.35 Sterling

Publisher: Educational Evaluation Enterprises

Ohio Vocational Interest Survey–Second Edition (OVIS–II)

Copyright: 1981

Population: Adults; Grades 7 through college

Purpose: Assesses occupational and vocational interests; used for educational and vocational counseling

Description: Paper–pencil 253-item test of job-related interests. Items are job activities to which the student responds on a 5-point scale ranging from "like very much" to "dislike very much." Used in conjunction with the *Dictionary of Occupational Titles,* OVIS–II classifies occupations according to three elements: data, people, and things. Materials include a Career Planner Workbook, Handbook for Exploring Careers, and filmstrips to aid counselors in administering and interpreting the test. The interest inventory is combined with an optional Career Planning Questionnaire and Local Survey and includes 23 Interest Scales.

Format: Examiner required; suitable for group use; untimed: 45 minutes

Scoring: Hand key; may be machine scored; MRC scoring service available

Cost: Examination Kit (student booklet, directions for administering MRC answer document, MRC scoring certificate, hand-scorable answer document, and norms and scale clarity tables) $18.50

Publisher: Harcourt® Brace Educational Measurement

Picture Vocational Interest Questionnaire for Adults (PVI)

Copyright: 1981

Population: Adolescents, adults

Purpose: Assesses vocational interests; used for vocational guidance

Description: Measure of interest with 110 items in 11 areas: clerical work, advanced engineering trades, lower engineering trades, woodwork, painting trades, building, domestic work, food preparation, agriculture, tailoring, and leather work. The subject indicates preference, dislike, or neutral for each item.

Format: Examiner required; suitable for group use; untimed: 30–45 minutes

Scoring: Hand key; examiner evaluated

Cost: Contact publisher

Publisher: Human Sciences Research Council

Reading Free Vocational Interest Inventory–Revised (R-FVII–Revised)
Ralph Leonard Becker

Copyright: 1988

Population: Adolescents, adults; ages 13 and older

Purpose: Measures vocational preferences of individuals with mental retardation, learning disabilities, and other disadvantages in job areas that are within the individuals' capabilities; used for vocational guidance counseling, selection of prospective job trainees, and placement

Description: Paper–pencil 165-item forced-choice test measuring the vocational preferences of educable mentally retarded (EMR), learning disabled (LD), trainable mentally retarded (TMR), and adult disadvantaged persons. The test items consist of 55 sets of three drawings each, depicting job tasks from the unskilled, semiskilled, and skilled levels, Each artist-drawn picture is typical of the kind and type of job in which EMR, LD, and TMR individuals are known to be proficient and productive. From the three alternatives in each set, individuals select the one picture or job task they most prefer. The examiner may describe the pictorial items for examinees requiring assistance. Scores are obtained for 11 vocational interest clusters: automotive, building, trades, clerical, animal care, food service, patient care, horticulture, housekeeping, personal service, laundry service, and materials handling. The test yields standard scores, percentiles, stanines,

and individual vocational profiles using percentiles. Test booklets include a detachable scoring sheet and individual profile sheet. The Occupational Title Lists (OTL) provides an expanded description of the occupational categories as well as a list of up to 50 job titles within each category.

Format: Examiner required; suitable for group use; untimed: 20 minutes or less

Scoring: Hand key; self-scored

Cost: Sample Set (10 test booklets, 1 manual) $28.00

Publisher: Elbern Publications

Safran Students Interest Inventory (Third Edition)
C. Safran

Copyright: 1985

Population: Adolescents; Grades 5 through 12

Purpose: Assesses occupational interests of students

Description: Multiple-item three-part paper–pencil inventory determining the relationship of students' interests and occupational characteristics. Section 1 requires students to choose one alternative from 168 pairs of occupational alternatives categorized in the areas of economic, technical, outdoor, service, humane, artistic, and scientific preferences. Section II measures school subject interests, and Section III contains a self-rated Levels of Ability Chart (academic, mechanical, social, and clerical). Student interests are referenced to the *Canadian Classification and Dictionary of Occupations* (CCDO) and the Student Guidance Information System (SGIS). The inventory is available on two levels: Level 1 (Grades 5–9) and Level 2 (Grades 8–12).

Format: Examiner/self-administered; suitable for group use; untimed: 40 minutes

Scoring: Hand key

Cost: Specimen Set (test booklets Levels 1 and 2, student manual, counselor's manual) $19.95; 35 student booklets $44.95

Publisher: Nelson Canada

Seventh Revision VPI Vocational Preference Inventory
Gary D. Gottfredson, John L. Holland, Jean E. Holland

Copyright: 1978

Population: Adults; high school/college students

Purpose: Assesses core options of occupational groups; used in career counseling

Description: Multiple-item paper–pencil questionnaire.

Format: Individual or group administration; examiner required; untimed

Scoring: Hand key

Cost: $15.00

Publisher: Select Press

Strong Interest Inventory
E. K. Strong, Jr., Jo-Ida C. Hansen, David P. Campbell

Copyright: 1994

Population: Adolescents, adults; Grades 8 and above

Purpose: Measures occupational interests in a wide range of career areas; used to make long-range curricular and occupational choices and for employee placement, career guidance, development, and vocational rehab placement

Description: Paper–pencil 317-item multiple-choice test requiring the examinee to respond in various ways to items covering a broad range of familiar occupational tasks and daily activities. Topics include occupations, school subjects, activities, leisure activities, types of people, preference between two activities, "your characteristics," and preference in the world of work. The response is scored on six general occupational themes, 25 basic interest scales, occupational scales, and four personal style scales. The scoring services provide 11 additional nonoccupational and administrative indexes as a further guide to interpreting the results.

Format: Self-administered; suitable for group use; untimed: 35–40 minutes

Scoring: Computer scored

Cost: Profile Preview Kit $12.00; Interpretive Preview Kit $15.00; Professional Preview Kit $15.00; Career Preview Kit $10.00

Publisher: Consulting Psychologists Press, Inc.

Technical Training Inventory and Exploration Survey (TECH-TIES)
Nancy Scott

Copyright: 1991–1994

Population: Ages 13 to adult

Purpose: Identifies technical training interests of junior high and high school students

Description: Paper–pencil multiple-choice test examining technical training interests. A descriptive report of the examinee's technical training interests is generated. Computer scoring in Mac/IBM/Apple format is included. This instrument does not require reading ability.

Format: Group presented in video format

Scoring: Examiner administration and interpretation

Cost: $495.00

Publisher: Piney Mountain Press, Inc.

Vocational Interest Exploration (VIE) System
Lawrence T. McCarron, Harriette P. Spires

Copyright: 1991

Population: Adolescents, adults; ages 14 and above

Purpose: Assesses preferences for work conditions and orientation to work; used for vocational guidance, work adjustment, and occupational planning

Description: Multiple-choice work preference questionnaire. A fourth-grade reading level is required. A computer version is available for Apple, Macintosh, and IBM/compatibles. Available in Spanish, French-Canadian, and Hebrew.

Format: Individual administration; suitable for group use; untimed

Scoring: Test scoring service included

Cost: $350.00

Publisher: McCarron-Dial Systems, Inc.

Vocational Interest Inventory–Revised (VII–R)
Patricia W. Lunneborg

Copyright: 1981

Population: Adolescents, adults; Grades 11 and above

Purpose: Measures high school students' interests in a number of vocational areas; used for vocational and educational guidance

Description: Paper–pencil or computer-administered 112-item inventory measuring the relative strengths of students' interests in eight occupational areas: service, business contact, organization, technical, outdoor, science, general culture, and arts and entertainment. Each item is a forced-choice statement which pulls interests apart. Two copies of a narrative report are provided for each student. The report includes a profile of scores by percentile; a summary of percentiles and *T*-scores for each scale; an analysis and discussion of all scores at or above the 75th percentile; a college majors profile, which compares a student's scores with the mean scores of college majors who took the VII when they were in high school; and a discussion of nontraditional areas for exploration for students who scored between the 50th and 75th percentiles in an area that has been considered nontraditional for his or her sex (test items are controlled for sex bias). An eight-page Guide to Interpretation describes the types of people typical of each of the eight interests groups and gives examples of jobs typical of each group for five levels of education and training. The microcomputer version is available for PC systems.

Format: Self-administered; suitable for group use; untimed: 20 minutes

Scoring: Computer scored

Cost: Kit (4 WPS Test Report answer sheets, 1 manual) $79.50

Publisher: Western Psychological Services

Vocational Interest Profile (VIP)
Giles D. Rainwater

Copyright: 1984

Population: Adults

Purpose: Administers, scores, and interprets the Interest Check List developed by the U.S. Department of Labor

Description: Multiple-choice 210-item computer-administered paper–pencil inventory relating to work activities. All items were selected to reflect a sampling of jobs found in 12 work categories: artistic, scientific, plants and animals, protective, mechanical, industrial, business detail, selling, accommodative, humanitarian, leading–influencing, and physical performing. The 5–7 page report examines the top three interest categories in depth. This inventory can be administered by the computer or by using a pencil and paper format. The VIP Report can be used with the USES Guide for Occupational Exploration. Computer version available for IBM PC. Examiners must be professionals trained in providing counseling.

Format: Examiner required; not suitable for group use; untimed

Scoring: Computer scored

Cost: $99.95

Publisher: Psychometric Software, Inc.

Vocational Interest Questionnaire for Pupils in Standards 6–10 (VIQ)

Copyright: 1974

Population: Adolescents

Purpose: Assesses vocational interests; used for vocational and study guidance

Description: Paper–pencil test of 10 fields of vocational interest, including technical, outdoor, social service, natural sciences, office work (clerical), office work (numerical), music, art, commerce, and language.

Format: Examiner required; suitable for group use; untimed: 1 hour–1 hour 30 minutes

Scoring: Hand key; examiner evaluated; may be machine scored

Cost: Contact publisher

Publisher: Human Sciences Research Council

Vocational Interest, Experience and Skill Assessment (VIESA)– Second Canadian Edition

Copyright: 1995

Population: Grades 8 and above

Purpose: Measures vocational interests, experiences, and skills of individuals; used by educators and professional in career counseling with individuals and for group programs.

Description: Multiple-item two-part paper–pencil assessment providing career counseling information. Individuals link personal characteristics determined using the Career Guidebook to more than 500 occupations on a World of Work Map that shows how occupations relate to each other. The Job Family Charts list occupations according to typical preparation level, including high school courses, post–high school preparation, and college majors. Occupations are referenced to National Occupational Classification (NOC) and the *Canadian Classification and Dictionary of Occupation* (CCDO). The test is available on two levels: Level 1 (Grades 8–10) and Level 2 (Grades 11–adult). A seventh-grade reading level is required.

Format: Examiner/self-administered; suitable for group use; untimed: 40–45 minutes

Scoring: Hand key

Cost: Examination Kit Levels 1 and 2 $19.95; 25 student booklets $47.95

Publisher: Nelson Canada

Wide Range Interest-Opinion Test (WRIOT)

Joseph F. Jastak, Sarah Jastak

Copyright: 1979

Population: Ages 5 to adult

Purpose: Provides information about vocational interests (without language requirements); assesses levels of self-projected ability, aspiration level, and social conformity; used in vocational and career planning and counseling and employee selection and placement

Description: Paper–pencil 150-item test measuring individuals' occupational motivation according to their likes and dislikes. The test booklet contains 150 pages with three pictures on each page. Each picture shows an individual or group performing a specific job. Subjects must select the picture they like the most and the least for each page. The results are presented on a report form that graphically shows an individual's strength of interest in 18 interest and 8 attitude clusters (normed on seven age groups from ages 5 to adult, separately for males and females). The occupational range is from unskilled labor to the highest levels of training. The test may be used with individuals with educational and cultural disadvantages, learning disabilities, mental retardation, and deafness. The picture titles can be read to those with visual disabilities. Individual administration is necessary for those unable to complete a separate answer sheet.

Format: Examiner required; suitable for group use (except where noted); untimed: 40 minutes

Scoring: Hand key; may be computer scored

Cost: Manual $27.00; 50 test forms $15.00; 50 report forms $45.00; stencils $15.00; filmstrip $85.00

Publisher: Wide Range, Inc.

Health Education

ACT PEP RCE: Nursing: Adult Nursing

Copyright: 1993

Population: Adults; college level

Purpose: Assesses knowledge of adult nursing

care; used to grant college credit and advanced placement in academic courses

Description: Paper–pencil 122-item multiple-choice test. Scale scores range from 20 to 80. Two forms are available. A test booklet, answer sheet, and pencil are used. Examiner must have experience with test administration at the college level. May be used for persons with visual, physical, hearing, and mental disabilities.

Format: Examiner required; suitable for group use; timed: 3 hours

Scoring: Machine scored

Cost: $45.00

Publisher: American College Testing

ACT PEP RCE: Nursing: Commonalities in Nursing Care: Area A

Copyright: 1995

Population: Adults; college level

Purpose: Used by adults wanting to earn credit by examination; assesses knowledge in common concepts of nursing care

Description: Paper–pencil 138-item multiple-choice test. Scale scores range from 20 to 80. Two forms are available. A test booklet, answer sheet, and pencil are used. Examiner must have experience with test administration at the college level. May be used for persons with visual, physical, hearing, and mental disabilities.

Format: Examiner required; suitable for group use; timed: 3 hours

Scoring: Machine scored

Cost: $80.00

Publisher: American College Testing

ACT PEP RCE: Nursing: Commonalities in Nursing Care: Area B

Copyright: 1995

Population: Adults; college level

Purpose: Used by adults wanting to earn credit by examination; assesses knowledge in common concepts of nursing care

Description: Paper–pencil 140- to 146-item multiple-choice test. Scale scores range from 20 to 80. Two forms are available. A test booklet, answer sheet, and pencil are used. Examiner must have experience with test administration at the college level. May be used for persons

with visual, physical, hearing, and mental disabilities.

Format: Examiner required; suitable for group use; timed: 3 hours

Scoring: Machine scored

Cost: $80.00

Publisher: American College Testing

ACT PEP RCE: Nursing: Differences in Nursing Care: Area A

Copyright: 1992

Population: Adults; college level

Purpose: Used by adults wanting to earn credit by examination; assesses knowledge in health care problems

Description: Paper–pencil 144- to 145 item multiple-choice test. Scale scores range from 20 to 80. Two forms are available. A test booklet, answer sheet, and pencil are used. Examiner must have experience with test administration at the college level. May be used for persons with visual, physical, hearing, and mental disabilities. Knowledge of differences in nursing care related to oxygenation and cell growth and resulting from specific health problems and the individual's response to clinical situations and of anatomy, physiology, pharmacology, and nutrition is assumed. Designed for and standardized at the A.S. degree level. Individuals seeking credit should contact their local colleges for information.

Format: Examiner required; suitable for group use; timed: 3 hours

Scoring: Machine scored

Cost: $80.00

Publisher: American College Testing

ACT PEP RCE: Nursing: Differences In Nursing Care: Area B

Copyright: 1993

Population: Adults; college level

Purpose: Used by adults wanting to earn credit

by examination; assesses knowledge in health care problems

Description: Paper–pencil 120-item multiple-choice test. Scale scores range from 20 to 80. Two forms are available. A test booklet, answer sheet, and pencil are used. Examiner must have experience with test administration at the college level. May be used for persons with visual, physical, hearing, and mental disabilities.

Format: Examiner required; suitable for group use; timed: 3 hours

Scoring: Machine scored

Cost: $80.00

Publisher: American College Testing

ACT PEP RCE: Nursing: Differences in Nursing Care: Area C

Copyright: 1992

Population: Adults; college level

Purpose: Used by adults wanting to earn credit by examination; assesses knowledge in health care problems

Description: Paper–pencil 145- to 147-item multiple-choice test. Scale scores range from 20 to 80. Two forms are available. A test booklet, answer sheet, and pencil are used. Examiner must have experience with test administration at the college level. May be used for persons with visual, physical, hearing, and mental disabilities.

Format: Examiner required; suitable for group use; timed: 3 hours

Scoring: Machine scored

Cost: $80.00

Publisher: American College Testing

ACT PEP RCE: Nursing: Fundamentals of Nursing

Copyright: 1994

Population: Adults; college level

Purpose: Assesses proficiency in nursing skills and procedures; used to grant college credit and/or advanced placement in academic courses

Description: Paper–pencil 120-item multiple-choice test measuring terms, facts, and trends and the ability to apply principles and theories to nursing situations. Examination is based on conventional nursing content. Designed for and standardized for the associate degree level. Examiner must have experience with test administration at the college level. May be used for persons with visual, physical, hearing, and mental disabilities.

Format: Examiner required; suitable for group use; timed: 3 hours

Scoring: Machine scored

Cost: $45.00

Publisher: American College Testing

ACT PEP RCE: Nursing: Health Restoration: Area I

Copyright: 1995

Population: Adults; college level

Purpose: Used by adults wanting to earn credit by examination; assesses upper-level nursing knowledge of client wellness

Description: Paper–pencil 141-item multiple-choice test. Scale scores range from 20 to 80. Two forms are available. A test booklet, answer sheet, and pencil are used. Examiner must have experience with test administration at the college level. May be used for persons with visual, physical, hearing, and mental disabilities.

Format: Examiner required; suitable for group use; timed: 3 hours

Scoring: Machine scored

Cost: $80.00

Publisher: American College Testing

ACT PEP RCE: Nursing: Health Restoration: Area II

Copyright: 1995

Population: Adults; college level

Purpose: Used by adults wanting to earn credit by examination; assesses upper-level nursing knowledge of client wellness

Description: Paper–pencil 136- to 137-item multiple-choice test. Scale scores range from 20 to 80. Two forms are available. A test booklet, answer sheet, and pencil are used. Examiner must have experience with test administration at the college level. May be used for persons with visual, physical, hearing, and mental disabilities.

Format: Suitable for group use; examiner required; timed: 3 hours

Scoring: Machine scored

Cost: $80.00

Publisher: American College Testing

ACT PEP RCE: Nursing: Health Support: Area I

Copyright: 1994

Population: Adults

Purpose: Used by adults wanting to earn college credit by examination; assesses basic-level nursing knowledge of client wellness

Description: Multiple-choice 141-item test. Two forms are available. A test booklet, answer sheet, and pencil are used. A college reading level is required. Examiner must have experience with college test administration. Available in large print. May be used for individuals with visual, physical, hearing, and mental disabilities.

Format: Suitable for group use; examiner required; timed: 180 minutes

Scoring: Machine scored

Cost: Contact publisher

Publisher: American College Testing

ACT PEP RCE: Nursing: Health Support: Area II

Copyright: 1995

Population: Adults; college level

Purpose: Used by adults wanting to earn college credit by examination; assesses basic-level nursing knowledge of clients' wellness

Description: Multiple-choice 136- to 137-item test. Scale scores range from 20 to 80.

Two forms are available. A test booklet, answer sheet, and a pen are used. A college reading level is required. Examiner must have experience with test administration at the college level. Available in large print. May be used for individuals with visual, physical, hearing, and mental disabilities.

Format: Suitable for group use; examiner required; timed: 180 minutes

Scoring: Machine scored

Cost: $80.00

Publisher: American College Testing

ACT PEP RCE: Nursing: Maternal and Child Nursing (Associate)

Copyright: 1993

Population: Adults; college level

Purpose: Used by adults wanting to earn college credit by examination; assesses maternity and child nursing knowledge

Description: Multiple-choice 120-item paper–pencil test. Scale scores range from 20 to 80. Two forms are available. A test booklet, answer sheet, and a pen are used. A college reading level is required. Examiner must have experience with test administration at the college level. May be used for individuals with visual, physical, hearing, and mental disabilities. Designed for and standardized at the associate degree level.

Format: Examiner required; suitable for group use; timed: 3 hours

Scoring: Machine scored

Cost: $45.00

Publisher: American College Testing

ACT PEP RCE: Nursing: Maternal and Child Nursing (Baccalaureate)

Copyright: 1993

Population: Adults; college level

Purpose: Used by adults wanting to earn college credit by examination; assesses maternity and child nursing knowledge

Description: Multiple-choice 120-item paper–pencil test. Scale scores range from 20 to 80. Two forms are available. A test booklet, answer sheet, and pen are used. A college reading level is required. Examiner must have experience with test administration at the college level. May be used for individuals with visual, physical, hearing, and mental disabilities.

Format: Examiner required; suitable for group use; timed: 3 hours

Scoring: Machine scored

Cost: $45.00

Publisher: American College Testing

ACT PEP RCE: Nursing: Maternity Nursing

Copyright: 1994

Population: Adults; college level

Purpose: Used by adults wanting to earn college credit by examination; assesses maternity nursing and normal health care maintenance for the well and ill child at birth

Description: Paper–pencil 70-item multiple-choice test. Items are based on terminology, facts, principles, theories, and trends. Designed and standardized at the Associate of Science degree level. A test booklet, answer sheet, and pencil are used. Examiner must have experience with test administration at the college level. May be used for individuals with visual, physical, hearing, and mental disabilities.

Format: Examiner required; suitable for group use; timed: 3 hours

Scoring: Machine scored

Cost: $45.00

Publisher: American College Testing

ACT PEP RCE: Nursing: Professional Strategies in Nursing

Copyright: 1992

Population: Adults; college level

Purpose: Used by adults wanting to earn college credit by examination; assesses upper-level knowledge of the professional roles within nursing

Description: Paper–pencil 137- to 141-item multiple-choice test. Scale scores range from 20 to 80. Two forms are available. A test booklet, answer sheet, and pen are used. A college reading level is required. Examiner must have experience with test administration at the college level. May be used for individuals with visual, physical, hearing, and mental disabilities.

Format: Examiner required; suitable for group use; timed: 3 hours

Scoring: Machine scored

Cost: $80.00

Publisher: American College Testing

ACT PEP RCE: Nursing: Psychiatric/Mental Health Nursing

Copyright: 1992

Population: Adults; college level

Purpose: Used by adults wanting to earn college credit by examination; assesses psychiatric/mental health nursing knowledge

Description: Paper–pencil 137- to 141-item multiple-choice test. Scale scores range from 20 to 80. Two forms are available. A test booklet, answer sheet, and pen are used. A college reading level is required. Examiner must have experience with test administration at the college level. May be used for individuals with visual, physical, hearing, and mental disabilities.

Format: Examiner required; suitable for group use; timed: 3 hours

Scoring: Machine scored

Cost: $45.00

Publisher: American College Testing

Allied Health Aptitude Test® (AHAT)

Copyright: Updated yearly

Population: Adults

Purpose: Assists in selection and placement of applicants to 1- and 2-year allied health programs

Description: Approximately 300 multiple-choice questions focusing on four major areas: verbal ability, numerical ability, science, and reading comprehension. Administered at the convenience of participating programs.

Format: Examiner required; timed: 2.5 hours

Scoring: Scored by the publisher

Cost: Contact publisher

Publisher: The Psychological Corporation

Allied Health Professions Admission Test® (AHPAT)

Copyright: Updated yearly

Population: Adults

Purpose: Assists in selection and placement of students to four-year allied health programs

Description: Approximately 300 multiple-choice questions focusing on five major areas: verbal ability, quantitative ability, biology, chemistry, and reading comprehension. Given four times per academic year at designated test centers.

Format: Examiner required; timed: 4 hours

Scoring: Scored by the publisher

Cost: Contact publisher

Publisher: The Psychological Corporation

Entrance Examination for Schools of Nursing™ (RNEE)

Copyright: Updated yearly

Population: Adults

Purpose: Measures academic achievement to assist in selection and placement of students

Description: Approximately 215 multiple-choice questions focusing on five major content areas: verbal ability, numerical ability, life sciences, physical sciences, and reading comprehension. Administered at the convenience of participating programs.

Format: Examiner required; timed: 3 hours

Scoring: Scored by the publisher

Cost: Contact publisher

Publisher: The Psychological Corporation

Entrance Examination for Schools of Practical/Vocational Nursing™ (PBEE)

Copyright: Updated yearly

Population: Adults

Purpose: Provides measure of academic achievement to assist with the selection and placement of students

Description: Approximately 300 multiple-choice questions focusing on four major areas: verbal ability, numerical ability, science, and reading comprehension. Administered at the convenience of participating programs.

Format: Examiner required; timed: 3 hours

Scoring: Scored by the publisher

Cost: Contact publisher

Publisher: The Psychological Corporation

Kilander-Leach Health Knowledge
H. Frederick Kilander, Glenn C. Leach

Copyright: 1972

Population: Adolescents, adults; Grades 10 and above

Purpose: Measures high school and college students' general knowledge of health; used as a pre- or end-of-course exam in high school health education classes and as a pre- or posttest for colleges and schools of nursing

Description: Paper–pencil 100-item multiple-choice test measuring health knowledge, including personal health, nutrition, community health, sanitation, communicable diseases, safety, first aid, family living, and mental health

Format: Self-administered; proctor desirable; suitable for group use; untimed: 45–50 minutes

Scoring: Hand key

Cost: 100 booklets $35.00; 35 copies $20.00 (prices include answer sheet and breakdown of questions by health areas)

Publisher: Glenn C. Leach, Ed. D.

National Achievement Tests: Health and Science Tests—Health Education

John S. Shaw, Maurice E. Troyer, Clifford L. Brownell

Copyright: 1964

Population: Adolescents; Grades 7 and above

Purpose: Assesses health knowledge; used for educational evaluation

Description: Paper–pencil test of newer phases of health information. The test contains problems with which students in high school and college should be familiar. Two equivalent forms, A and B, are available.

Format: Examiner required; suitable for group use; timed: 40 minutes

Scoring: Hand key

Cost: Specimen Set (test, manual, key) $4.00; 25 tests $8.75; 25 answer sheets $4.00

Publisher: Psychometric Affiliates

NLN Achievement Tests for Practical Nursing: Comprehensive Nursing Achievement Test for Practical Nursing Students (Form 54-3514)

Copyright: 1989

Population: Practical nursing students

Purpose: Measures the full range of knowledge needed by graduating students in practical/vocational nursing programs for beginning practice; assesses readiness for the nurse licensure examination

Description: Approximately 170-item paper–pencil multiple-choice test measuring the full range of material presented in programs preparing students for practical nursing. Questions pertain to case situations representative of conditions commonly encountered by the beginning practitioner in health care settings, including care of the adult, care of the elderly, nursing during childbearing, and nursing of children. The questions call for the application of knowledge in the assessment of client status, planning, intervention in basic nursing situations,

evaluating, recording, and reporting. Questions related to growth and development, mental health concepts, basic communication techniques, medication administration and effects, as well as nutrition are integrated. A total score, along with subscores in broad clinical areas, are reported in the form of individual diagnostic profiles. Two copies are provided: one for distribution to students and one for faculty analysis. Norms are provided for practical nursing students. The test should be administered at the end of the program to assess readiness for the nurse licensure examination and to provide practice in taking a nationally standardized test of nursing knowledge.

Format: Examiner required; suitable for group use; untimed: 3 hours

Scoring: Computer scored

Cost: Test service (test booklets, answer sheets, directions for administration, scoring service) $10.00 per student

Publisher: National League for Nursing

NLN Achievement Tests for Practical Nursing: Fundamentals for Practical Nursing Students (Form 25-4615)

Copyright: 1986

Population: Practical nursing students

Purpose: Measures individual achievement of practical/vocational nursing students in body structure and function, nursing procedures, and normal nutrition

Description: Approximately 100-item paper–pencil multiple-choice test measuring the ability to identify basic bodily structures and functions, select appropriate measures for giving care to patients, and identify nutritional requirements and the nutritional elements of food. Items on nursing practice include principles of therapeutic communication, the nursing process, vital signs, body mechanics, and aseptic technique. A total score and three subscores (Anatomy and Physiology, Normal Nutrition, Nursing Practice) are provided. Norms are reported for practical nursing students. The test should be administered early in the program, after completion of the areas covered by the test. The test is available for faculty review.

Format: Examiner required; suitable for group use; untimed: 2 hours

Scoring: Computer scored

Cost: Test service (test booklets, answer sheets, directions for administration, scoring service) $5.00

Publisher: National League for Nursing

NLN Achievement Tests for Practical Nursing: Maternity Nursing for Practical Nursing Students (Form 4019)

Copyright: 1989

Population: Practical nursing students

Purpose: Measures the individual achievement of practical/vocational nursing students in objectives related to maternity nursing

Description: Approximately 110-item paper–pencil multiple-choice test measuring student knowledge of the objectives of maternity nursing related to nursing measures, including medications, nutrition, and communication. A total score and three subscores (antepartum, intra- and postpartum, neonate) are reported. Norms are reported for practical nursing students. The test should be administered after completion of the course in maternity nursing. The test is available for faculty review.

Format: Examiner required; suitable for group use; untimed: 2 hours

Scoring: Computer scored

Cost: Test service (test booklets, answer sheets, directions for administration, scoring service) $5.00 per student

Publisher: National League for Nursing

NLN Achievement Tests for Practical Nursing: Medical–Surgical Nursing for Practical Nursing Students (Form 4218)

Copyright: 1988

Population: Practical nursing students

Purpose: Measures individual achievement of practical/vocational nursing students in medical–surgical nursing

Description: Approximately 120-item paper–pencil multiple-choice test measuring knowledge and application of the facts and principles related to the care of patients with medical and surgical conditions. Questions refer to patient situations and represent a variety of ages and common conditions. Items relating to the practical nurse's role in drug and diet therapy, communications, and patient teaching are integrated. A total score and two subscores (medical nursing and surgical nursing) are reported for practical nursing students. The test should be administered when the student's program is near completion. The test is available for faculty review.

Format: Examiner required; suitable for group use; untimed: 2 hours

Scoring: Computer scored

Cost: Test service (test booklets, answer sheets, directions for administration, scoring service) $5.00 per student

Publisher: National League for Nursing

NLN Achievement Tests for Practical Nursing: Mental Health Concepts for Practical Nursing Students (Form 4415)

Copyright: Not provided

Population: Practical nursing students

Purpose: Measures practical nursing students' understanding of the principles of mental health and their application to the general practice of practical/vocational nursing

Description: Paper–pencil 102-item test focusing on the mental health concepts applicable to the basic care of persons with physical impairment and mental illness. The test also includes questions on the psychological aspects of children. A total score and two subscores (behaviors/concepts and nursing interventions) are reported. Scores are based on the number of questions answered correctly. Norms for practical nursing students are provided. The test is available for faculty review.

Format: Examiner required; suitable for group use; untimed: 2 hours

Scoring: Computer scored

Cost: Test service (test booklets, answer sheets, directions for administration, scoring service) $4.00 per student

Publisher: National League for Nursing

NLN Achievement Tests for Practical Nursing: Nursing of Children for Practical Nursing Students (Form 4119)

Copyright: 1989

Population: Practical nursing students

Purpose: Measures individual achievement of practical/vocational nursing students in pediatric nursing

Description: Paper–pencil 107-item multiple-choice test measuring achievement of major objectives related to the nursing of children. Questions assess knowledge of normal growth and development in children and nursing measures based on age-related needs, including preventive measures; knowledge and recognition of various pathophysiological processes and treatments, including nutrition and expected outcomes; knowledge of nursing measures commonly used in the care of children who are ill, including drug administration and communication skills. Questions about teaching and providing emotional support to family members are included also. A total score is reported in addition to three subscores (Normal Growth and Development, Pathophysiology and Treatment, and Nursing Measures). Scores are based on the number of questions answered correctly. Norms are reported for practical nursing students. The test should be administered to students who have completed their major learning experience in the content area of the test. The test is available for faculty review.

Format: Examiner required; suitable for group use; untimed: 2 hours

Scoring: Computer scored

Cost: Test service (test booklets, answer sheets, directions for administration, scoring service)

$5.00

Publisher: National League for Nursing

NLN Achievement Tests for Practical Nursing: Pharmacology for Practical Nursing Students (Form 83-4514)

Copyright: Not provided

Population: Practical nursing students

Purpose: Measures individual achievement of practical/vocational nursing student's knowledge of facts and principles related to drugs and drug administration

Description: Approximately 100-item paper–pencil multiple-choice test measuring general knowledge of pharmacology, chiefly through the interpretation of orders and observations necessary for detecting the effects of common drugs and assessing the basic principles of drug administration. A total score is reported together with two subscores (Principles of Drug Administrations, Calculations, and other Implications for Nursing; and Effects, Therapeutic and Other). Norms are reported for practical nursing students. The test should be administered when the program is completed. The test is available for faculty review.

Format: Examiner required; suitable for group use; untimed: 1½ hours

Scoring: Computer scored

Cost: Test service (test booklets, answer sheets, directions for administration, scoring service) $5.00 per student

Publisher: National League for Nursing

NLN Achievement Tests for Registered Nursing: Anatomy and Physiology (Form 76-1212)

Copyright: Not provided

Population: Registered nursing students

Purpose: Measures individual achievement of registered nursing students in anatomy and physiology

Description: Approximately 115-item paper–pencil multiple-choice test measuring knowledge of anatomy and physiology in the following subject-matter areas: cellular metabolism and integumentary system, musculoskeletal system, circulatory system (including lymphatics and fetal circulation), respiratory system, gastrointestinal system, endocrine system, reproductive system, nervous system, special senses, urinary system, and water, electrolyte, and acid-base regulation. For the items scored, total score and two subscores (anatomy and physiology) are reported. Separate norms are reported for students in associate degree, baccalaureate, and diploma programs. The test is available for faculty review.

Format: Examiner required; suitable for group use; untimed: 2 hours

Scoring: Computer scored

Cost: Test service (test booklets, answer sheets, directions for administration, scoring service) $5.00 per student

Publisher: National League for Nursing

NLN Achievement Tests for Registered Nursing: Basic Nursing Care I and II (Forms 34-0414 and 35-0424)

Copyright: Not provided

Population: Registered nursing students

Purpose: Measures individual achievement of registered nursing students in the basics of nursing care and attainment of nationally accepted objectives in nursing

Description: Series of two 100-item paper–pencil multiple-choice tests that may be administered separately or in combination. Basic Nursing Care I emphasizes nursing process, nursing diagnosis, and the nursing care plan. Items are included that test basic nursing measures for the care of dependent clients with stable conditions, including hygiene, positioning, nutrition, hydration, vital signs, skin care, application of heat or cold, catheter care, and other basic nursing skills. Basic Nursing Care II consists of questions that pertain to the calculation of dosages and principles of administration of common medications (oral, parenteral, opthalmic, and rectal); such nursing measures

as peroperative care, aseptic technique, assessment and management of pain, oxygen therapy, blood transfusions, and common laboratory tests.

Format: Examiner required; suitable for group use; untimed: 2 hours

Scoring: Computer scored

Cost: Test service (test booklets, answer sheets, directions for administration, scoring service) $5.00 per student

Publisher: National League for Nursing

NLN Achievement Tests for Registered Nursing: Comprehensive Nursing Achievement Test (Form 90-3615)

Copyright: Not provided

Population: Registered nursing students

Purpose: Measures achievement of graduating students in registered nursing programs in a range of knowledge needed by the beginning practitioner; assesses readiness for the nurse licensure examination

Description: Approximately 210-item multiple-choice paper–pencil test of a graduating student's knowledge of human functioning, the nursing process, and clinical content. This test assesses readiness for the registered nurse licensure examination, NCLEX–RN. Questions are presented as case situations drawn from a variety of clinical areas and are written within the nursing process framework. A total raw score is reported with an indication of the likelihood of passing NCLEX–RN for students performing at same level. A variety of subscores are reported as well to complete the individual diagnostic profiles. A copy is provided for the student and another for faculty analysis.

Format: Examiner required; suitable for group use; untimed: 3½ hours

Scoring: Computer scored

Cost: Test service (test booklets, answer sheets, directions for administration, scoring service) $17.00 per student

Publisher: National League for Nursing

NLN Achievement Tests for Registered Nursing: Diagnostic Test for RN Licensure (Form 96-3514)

Copyright: Not provided

Population: Registered nursing students

Purpose: Assesses knowledge and skills needed for entry-level practice as measured by the RN licensing examination

Description: Paper–pencil 172-item multiple-choice test identifying areas of strength and weakness for students preparing for RN licensure. An individualized performance profile provides an estimate of the student's probability of success on the licensing examination NCLEX–RN. In addition, the profile indicates in 31 separate graphs the student's relative strengths and weaknesses in several categories, including nursing process (5 areas), client needs (4 areas), human functioning (8 areas), health alterations (10 areas), and clinical nursing (4 areas). A customized study guide is included. Content frameworks are described on the report. Class summary reports are provided for educators returning groups of answer sheets.

Format: Examiner/self administered; untimed: 3 hours

Scoring: Computer scored

Cost: $23.00 per answer sheet returned for scoring

Publisher: National League for Nursing

NLN Achievement Tests for Registered Nursing: Diet Therapy and Applied Nutrition (Form 3313)

Copyright: Not provided

Population: Registered nursing students

Purpose: Measures individual achievement of registered nursing students in diet therapy and applied nutrition

Description: Approximately 120-item paper–pencil multiple-choice test measuring knowledge of the facts and principles of nutrition and the ability to apply that knowledge to situations involving patients who have specific nutritional problems. A total score, a facts and principles subscore, and an application of knowledge subscore are provided. Separate norms are reported for students in associate degree, baccalaureate, and diploma programs. The test should be administered at the end of the student's program and is not a substitute for the NLN achievement test in normal nutrition. The test is available for faculty review.

Format: Examiner required; suitable for group use; untimed: 2 hours

Scoring: Computer scored

Cost: Test service (test booklets, answer sheets, directions for administration, scoring service) $5.00 per student

Publisher: National League for Nursing

NLN Achievement Tests for Registered Nursing: Fundamentals of Drug Therapy (Form 1414)

Copyright: Not provided

Population: Registered nursing students

Purpose: Measures individual achievement of registered nursing students in drug therapy

Description: Approximately 110-item paper–pencil multiple-choice test measuring knowledge of the general principles of drug administration, calculations, and drug effects. A total score and three subscores (calculations, principles of drug administration, and drug effects) are reported based on the number of questions answered correctly. Separate norms are reported for associate degree, baccalaureate, and diploma programs. The test is intended for use relatively early in the program (knowledge of clinical nursing is not required) and is not a substitute for the NLN achievement test in pharmacology in clinical nursing. The test is available for faculty review.

Format: Examiner required; suitable for group use; untimed: 2 hours

Scoring: Computer scored

Cost: Test service (test booklets, answer sheets, directions for administration, scoring service) $5.00 per student

Publisher: National League for Nursing

NLN Achievement Tests for Registered Nursing: Microbiology (Form 77-1713)

Copyright: Not provided

Population: Registered nursing students

Purpose: Measures individual achievement of registered nursing students in microbiology as it applies to nursing

Description: Approximately 115-item paper–pencil multiple-choice test measuring the nursing student's understanding of facts and principles related to the causative microorganisms of infectious diseases. For the 89 items scored, a total score and subscores for three areas are provided: the basic processes occurring during the cellular activity of microorganisms, the structural and functional differences of the microorganisms, and techniques and measures for studying and culturing microorganisms that cause infectious disease; substances developed for immunization, the body's immunological response to foreign substances, and the antimicrobials used in controlling diseases; and the transmission of organisms, the incidence, manifestation, and progression of communicable diseases, as well as methods used to destoy microorganisms. Each score is based on the number of questions answered correctly. Separate norms are provided for students in associate degree, baccalaureate, and diploma programs. The test is available for faculty review.

Format: Examiner required; suitable for group use; untimed: 2 hours

Scoring: Computer scored

Cost: Test service (test booklets, answer booklets, directions for administration, scoring service) $5.00

Publisher: National League for Nursing

NLN Achievement Tests for Registered Nursing: Nursing Care of Adults, Parts I and II (Forms 0217 and 0227)

Copyright: Not provided

Population: Registered nursing students

Purpose: Measures individual achievement of registered nursing students in nursing care of adults with pathophysiological disturbances and attainment of nationally accepted objectives in nursing

Description: Two approximately 130-item paper–pencil multiple-choice tests measuring knowledge of the nursing care of adults with pathophysiological disturbances. Part I measures knowledge of problems related to deficiencies in providing oxygen or nutrients to cells, alterations in patterns of elimination, and failures in regulation of metabolism. Part II measures alterations in urinary functions, impaired mobility, impaired skin integrity, and alterations in sensory and perceptual functions. Most of the questions are presented as case situations and relate to hospitalized patients. The health problems selected reflect those occurring most frequently in the adult population of the United States. The questions emphasize the knowledge of communicable diseases, as well as methods used to destroy microorganisms. Each score is based on the number of questions answered correctly. Separate norms are provided for students in associate degree, baccalaureate, and diploma programs. The test is available for faculty review.

Format: Examiner required; suitable for group use; untimed: Part I, 2 hours; Part II, 2 hours

Scoring: Computer scored

Cost: Test service, specify Part I or Part II (test booklets, answer sheets, directions for administration, scoring service) $5.00 per student

Publisher: National League for Nursing

NLN Achievement Tests for Registered Nursing: Nursing of Children (Form 0118)

Copyright: Not provided

Population: Registered nursing students

Purpose: Measures individual achievement of registered nursing students in nursing care for children

Description: Approximately 120-item paper–pencil multiple-choice test measuring understanding of facts and principles related to the nursing care of children and the ability to apply those principles. Questions relating to growth and development, teaching, interpersonal relations, nutrition, pharmacology, and the basic sciences are integrated. A total score and three subscores (care of infants, care of toddlers and preschoolers, and care of school-age children and adolescents) are reported based on the number of questions answered correctly. Separate norms are reported for students in associate degree, baccalaureate, and diploma programs. The test is available for faculty review.

Format: Examiner required; suitable for group use; untimed: 2 hours

Scoring: Computer scored

Cost: Test service (test booklets, answer sheets, directions for administration, scoring service) $5.00 per student

Publisher: National League for Nursing

NLN Achievement Tests for Registered Nursing: Nursing the Childbearing Family (Form 19-0013)

Copyright: Not provided

Population: Registered nursing students

Purpose: Assesses knowledge related to nursing the childbearing family; used with registered nursing students completing the maternity nursing sequence

Description: Paper–pencil 123-item multiple-choice test measuring understanding of the facts and principles related to nursing the childbearing family and the ability to apply them. Questions on nutrition, pharmacology, the basic sciences, and interpersonal relations are integrated. While emphasis is on the normal, questions dealing with common health problems of the mother and newborn are included. Questions are written in the framework of the nursing process. A total score and three subscores (antepartal care, intrapartal and post-

partal care, and fetal and newborn development and care) are provided. Scores are based on the number of questions answered correctly. Separate norms are reported for students in associate degree and baccalaureate degree programs. For each test, a total score and two sets of subscores are reported based on the number of questions answered correctly. One set of subscores reflects the objectives of the test: pathophysiology, nursing measures, and therapeutic management (including drugs and diet). The second set of subscores reflects the nursing process.

Format: Examiner required; suitable for group use; untimed: 2 hours

Scoring: Computer scored

Cost: Test service (test booklet, answer sheets, directions for administration, scoring service) $5.00 per student

Publisher: National League for Nursing

NLN Achievement Tests for Registered Nursing: Pharmacology in Clinical Nursing (Form 3418)

Copyright: Not provided

Population: Registered nursing students

Purpose: Measures individual achievement of registered nursing students in applied pharmacology

Description: Approximately 110-item paper–pencil multiple-choice test measuring understanding of facts and principles related to drugs and drug administration, including the actions of pharmacologic agents, undesirable effects of drugs and their control, drug administration, and the calculation of dosages. Case situations are drawn from maternity nursing, nursing care of children, nursing care of adults with mental illness, nursing care of adults with pathophysiological disturbances, and geriatric nursing. A total test score is reported. Norms are reported for students in all registered nursing programs, in addition to separate norms for associate and baccalaureate degree students. The test is available for faculty review.

Format: Examiner required; suitable for group use; untimed: 2 hours

Scoring: Computer scored

Cost: Test service (test booklets, answer sheets, directions for administration, scoring service) $5.00 per student

Publisher: National League for Nursing

NLN Achievement Tests for Registered Nursing: Psychiatric Nursing (Form 88-0312)

Copyright: Not provided

Population: Registered nursing students

Purpose: Measures individual achievement of registered nursing students in psychiatric nursing

Description: Approximately 110-item paper–pencil multiple-choice test measuring knowledge of theory and practice in psychiatric nursing, including patient situations. The therapeutic role of the nurse in the care of patients with mental disorders is emphasized. For the 100 items scored, a total score and two subscores (concept/process and planning/intervention) are reported. Separate norms are reported for students in associate degree, baccalaureate, and diploma programs. The test should be administered after students have completed their major learning experiences in psychiatric nursing. The test is available for faculty review.

Format: Examiner required; suitable for group use; untimed: 2 hours

Scoring: Computer scored

Cost: Test service (test booklets, answer sheets, directions for administration, scoring service) $5.00 per student

Publisher: National League for Nursing

NLN Achievement Tests for Registered Nursing: Normal Nutrition (Form 45-1312)

Copyright: Not provided

Population: Registered nursing students

Purpose: Measures individual achievement of registered nursing students in normal nutrition

Description: Approximately 110-item paper–pencil multiple-choice test measuring knowledge of the facts and principles of normal nutrition and the ability to apply those principles. Test items cover nutrients in food and the role of nutrition in health. A total score, a knowledge and interpretation of information basic to normal nutrition subscore, and an application of knowledge of normal/nutrition subscore are provided based on a correction-for-guessing formula. Separate norms are reported for students in associate degree, baccalaureate, and diploma programs. This test should be administered after the student completes initial major learning experience in normal nutrition. (Knowledge of clinical nursing is not required.) The test is available for faculty review.

Format: Examiner required; suitable for group use; untimed: 2 hours

Scoring: Computer scored

Cost: Test service (test booklets, answer sheets, directions for administration, scoring service) $5.00

Publisher: National League for Nursing

NLN Baccalaureate-Level Achievement Tests for Registered Nursing: Community Health Nursing (Form 38-2315)

Copyright: Not provided

Population: Baccalaureate-level registered nursing students

Purpose: Measures individual student achievement in community health nursing in baccalaureate-level registered nursing programs

Description: Approximately 100-item paper–pencil multiple-choice test measuring students' ability to apply the principles of community health planning and organization of health care services in contemporary society and knowledge of the nursing process as it is applied to the community and to family groups and individuals in community settings. The test is based on an approach to community health nursing that stresses promotion of maximum health with respect for cultural differences and individual values and with recognition of the ethical–legal constraints within which the community health nurse functions. Knowledge basic to nursing practice in any setting, such as communication, nutrition, and pharmacology, is tested within the context of the community setting where nurses practice. A total score and three subscores (human ecology, individual in systems, community health planning/health care system) are provided. Norms are reported for baccalaureate-level students only. The test should be administered to students in baccalaureate programs who have completed a major learning experience in community health nursing. The test is available for faculty review.

Format: Examiner required; suitable for group use; untimed: 1½ hours

Scoring: Computer scored

Cost: Test service (test booklets, answer sheets, directions for administration, scoring service) $5.00 per student

Publisher: National League for Nursing

NLN Baccalaureate-Level Achievement Tests for Registered Nursing: Comprehensive Nursing Achievement Test for Baccalaureate Nursing Students (Form 60-3110)

Copyright: Not provided

Population: Baccalaureate-level registered nursing students

Purpose: Measures individual achievement of students ready to graduate from baccalaureate-level registered nursing programs

Description: Approximately 210-item paper–pencil multiple-choice test measuring students' ability to apply knowledge derived from nursing science, as well as from the natural, behavioral, and social sciences. The test focuses on the cumulative results of the educational program rather than on the content of individual clinical components. To accommodate the heterogeneity of baccalaureate nursing curricula, an attempt has been made to construct a test that reflects a number of representative conceptual frameworks. Performance reports are based

on 200 items scored. Subscores are reported for each of the following content areas: clients being assessed for health status, including risk factors; clients experiencing a knowledge deficit; clients experiencing alteration of physiological functioning; clients with dysfunctional patterns of behavior; and leadership and research process. The six subscores reflect the percentage of questions answered correctly within the diagnostic cluster. The total score is a standard score. The score report includes information about individual student performance as well as group performance. Norms are reported for baccalaureate students.

Format: Examiner required; suitable for group use; untimed: 4 hours

Scoring: Computer scored

Cost: Test service (test booklets, answer sheets, directions for administration, scoring services) $8.00 per student

Publisher: National League for Nursing

NLN Baccalaureate-Level Achievement Tests for Registered Nursing: Health and Illness: Adult Care (Form 2117)

Copyright: Not provided

Population: Baccalaureate-level registered nursing students

Purpose: Measures individual achievement in medical–surgical nursing for students in baccalaureate-level registered nursing programs

Description: Approximately 120-item paper–pencil test measuring students' knowledge of facts and principles related to medical–surgical nursing and the ability to apply them to patient care situations. The questions relate to adult patients in a variety of age groups. The client situations represent the health–illness continuum. The questions emphasize the assessment, decision-making, and teaching skills of the nurse. A total score and two subscores are provided: care of healthy patients and patients with early changes in health status, and care of acutely ill patients and patients in need of rehabilitation. Norms are reported for baccalaureate students. The test should be administered after students in baccalaureate programs complete their major learning experience in the care of adults in health and illness. The test is available for faculty review.

Format: Examiner required; suitable for group use; untimed: 2 hours

Scoring: Computer scored

Cost: Test service (test booklets, answer sheets, directions for administration, scoring service) $5.00 per student

Publisher: National League for Nursing

NLN Baccalaureate-Level Achievement Tests for Registered Nursing: Nursing Care in Mental Health and Mental Illness (Form 64-2213)

Copyright: Not provided

Population: Baccalaureate-level registered nursing students

Purpose: Measures individual achievement in psychiatric nursing in baccalaureate-level registered nursing programs

Description: Approximately 12-item paper–pencil multiple-choice test measuring knowledge of the concepts and principles essential in the care of clients with a variety of mental disorders. The case situations cover a number of different settings, and questions covering primary and tertiary prevention are included. Although the test focuses on the knowledge required for caring for clients with mental disorders, questions covering new approaches to treatment and concepts of a broader nature are integrated. A total score and three subscores (knowledge/concepts, assessing/analyzing/evaluating, planning/implementing) are reported based on the number of questions answered correctly. Norms are reported for baccalaureate students. The test should be administered to students who have completed their major learning experience in psychiatric nursing. The test is available for faculty review.

Format: Examiner required; suitable for group use; untimed: 2 hours

Scoring: Computer scored

Cost: Test service (test booklets, answer sheets, directions for administration, scoring service) $5.00

Publisher: National League for Nursing

NLN Baccalaureate-Level Achievement Tests for Registered Nursing: Parent–Child Care (Form 2019)

Copyright: Not provided

Population: Baccalaureate-level registered nursing students

Purpose: Measures individual achievement in parent–child nursing care in baccalaureate-level registered nursing programs

Description: Approximately 110-item paper–pencil multiple-choice test measuring knowledge of nursing interventions for individuals during infancy, childhood, and adolescence and for families during the childbearing and child-rearing years. In addition to measuring the achievement of learning objectives pertinent to all areas of nursing practice, such as principles of communication, the test measures learning objectives specific to the nursing of parents and children, including psychosocial and physical development of children and parents and normal and unexpected physical changes related to childhood and childbearing. The test presents nursing situations in a variety of inpatient and outpatient settings where parents and children requiring health care are encountered. A total score and two subscores (childbearing, including fetal development and the neonate to 1 month of age; and care of the child from 1 month to young adulthood, including family health concepts) are provided. Norms are reported for baccalaureate students. The test assesses students' knowledge of all steps of the nursing process and should be administered to students who have completed the major learning experiences.

Format: Examiner required; suitable for group use; untimed: 2 hours

Scoring: Computer scored

Cost: Test service (test booklets, answer sheets, directions for administration, scoring service) $5.00 per student

Publisher: National League for Nursing

NLN Nursing Mobility Profile I

Copyright: Not provided

Population: Registered nursing students

Purpose: Evaluates previous learning and experience in order to establish credit and placement in programs preparing individuals for registered nursing practice; administered to licensed practical nurses

Description: Approximately 400-item paper–pencil multiple-choice battery assessing three content areas: foundations of nursing (200 items), nursing care during childbearing (100 items), and nursing care of the child (100 items). Book One (foundations of nursing) includes questions related to nursing care to meet basic physiological and psychosocial needs of clients with stable conditions. The first section of Book Two (nursing care during childbearing) includes questions related to nursing care during antepartal, intrapartal, and neonatal periods. The second section of Book Two (nursing care of the child) includes questions related to nursing care of the hospitalized infant, toddler, preschooler, school-age child, and adolescent. The two test books may be administered separately or together as determined by individual needs. Questions are based on the nursing care of clients in health care settings and are presented in case situations representative of those commonly encountered in nursing practice. A total score is reported for each of the three content areas. Diagnostic scores are provided as a supplement to faculty evaluations of students. Suggested methods for institutional setting are available upon request.

Format: Examiner required; suitable for group use; timed: Book One 3½ hours; Book Two 3½ hours

Scoring: Computer scored

Cost: Test service, specify book (test booklets, answer sheets, directions for administration, scoring service) $34.50 per book administered

Publisher: National League for Nursing

NLN Nursing Mobility Profile II

Copyright: Not provided

Population: Registered nursing students

Purpose: Evaluates previous learning and experience in order to establish credit and placement in baccalaureate nursing programs; administered to registered nurses seeking placement in a baccalaureate nursing program

Description: Approximately 560-item paper–pencil multiple-choice battery assessing four content areas: care of the adult client (220 items), care of the client during childbearing (110 items), care of the child (110 items), and care of the client with mental disorder (120 items). Test books may be administered in any order or combination as determined by individual needs. Book One (care of the adult client) includes content related to the nursing care of individual clients whose delivery of oxygen to the cells is deficient; clients with digestive and metabolic problems and difficulty providing nutrients to the cells; clients with sensorimotor function impairment; and clients with genitourinary or reproductive system dysfunctions. The first section of Book Two (care of the client during childbearing) includes content related to nursing care during the antepartal, intrapartal, postpartal, and neonatal periods. The second section of Book Two (care of the child) includes content related to nursing care of the infant, the toddler and preschooler, and the school-age child and adolescent. Book Three (care of the client with mental disorder) contains content related to nursing care of adults with psychological, adjustmental, and organic mental disorders.

Format: Examiner required; suitable for group use; timed: Book One 4 hours; Book Two 4 hours; Book Three 2 hours

Scoring: Computer scored

Cost: Test service, specify book (test booklets, answer sheets, directions for administration, scoring service) $34.50 per book administered

Publisher: National League for Nursing

NLN Pre-Admission Examination–RN (PAX–RN)

Copyright: Not provided

Population: Nursing program applicants

Purpose: Measures ability and academic achievement in specific content areas that predict academic success in programs preparing students for beginning registered nursing practice; assists schools in making admissions and placement decisions

Description: Battery of three multiple-item paper–pencil multiple-choice tests measuring ability in the following areas: verbal ability, mathematics achievement, and science achievement. The verbal ability test consists of word knowledge and reading comprehension sections. The word knowledge section measures the ability to recognize the meaning of a word as it is used in a sentence. Applicants choose the answer that best completes a statement. The reading section is composed of passages of a scientific or general nature with associated questions suitable for measuring reading comprehension skills. The mathematics test measures skills in basic arithmetic calculations, as well as elementary algebraic and geometric concepts. Straight computational, as well as reading problems, are included. The science test evaluates knowledge of high-school-level general science, chemistry, physics, and biology, with particular emphasis on areas most applicable to the nursing curriculum. Experimental questions are included for test development purposes only and are not included in scoring. The test is administered at scheduled sessions throughout the country at test sites established by NLN Test Service.

Format: Examiner required; suitable for group use; timed: 3½ hours

Scoring: Computer scored

Cost: One administration with two score reports (one for the applicant and one for a designated school of nursing) $20.00; additional reports $8.00

Publisher: National League for Nursing

Nutrition Information Test
H. Frederick Kilander, Glenn C. Leach

Copyright: 1968

Population: Adolescents, adults; Grades 10 and above

Purpose: Determines nutrition knowledge and attitudes of high school and college students

Description: Paper–pencil 33-item multiple-choice test covering various aspects of nutrition, including calories, diseases, physical health, and weight control

Format: Self-administered; suitable for group use; untimed: 15 minutes

Scoring: Hand key

Cost: Free

Publisher: Glenn C. Leach, Ed. D.

Optometry Admission Test (OAT)

Copyright: 1987–1996

Population: Adults; applicants to optometry schools

Purpose: Assesses achievement in various sciences; used for admissions purposes

Description: Multiple-choice test comprised of Reading Comprehension (50 items), Quantitative Reasoning (50 items), Biology (40 items), General Chemistry (30 items), Organic Chemistry (30 items), and Physics (40 items).

Format: Suitable for group use; examiner required; timed: approximately 4 hours

Scoring: Computer scored; test scoring service available from publisher only

Cost: $80.00

Publisher: Optometry Admission Testing Program

Pharmacy College Admission Test™ (PCAT™)

Copyright: Updated yearly

Population: Adults

Purpose: Measures academic achievement to assist with the selection and placement of students

Description: Approximately 300 multiple-choice questions focusing on five major areas: verbal ability, quantitative ability, biology, chemistry, and reading comprehension. Given three times per academic year at designated test centers.

Format: Examiner required; timed: 4 hours

Scoring: Scored by the publisher

Cost: Contact publisher

Publisher: The Psychological Corporation

Student Health Survey

Copyright: 1993

Population: Grades 6 through 12

Purpose: Assesses use of alcohol, tobacco and drugs and AIDS awareness

Description: Multiple-choice response format

Format: Group administration; requires examiner; 50 minutes

Scoring: Machine scored; test scoring service available from publisher

Cost: $.90/survey; $.50/survey for scoring

Publisher: Assessment Resource Center

Veterinary College Admission Test™ (VCAT™)

Copyright: Updated yearly

Population: Adults

Purpose: Measures academic achievement to assist with the selection and placement of students

Description: Approximately 300 multiple-choice questions focusing on five major areas: verbal ability, quantitative ability, biology, chemistry, and reading comprehension. Given four times per academic year at designated test centers.

Format: Examiner required; timed: 4 hours

Scoring: Scored by the publisher

Cost: Contact publisher

Publisher: The Psychological Corporation

Industrial Arts

. . . .

Mechanical Comprehension Test A3/1

Copyright: Not provided

Population: Adolescents

Purpose: Measures mechanical abilities

Description: Multiple-item paper–pencil test assessing the ability to apply the laws and principles of physics and mechanics; the test is based on the secondary school syllabus

Format: Examiner required; suitable for group use; untimed: 30–35 minutes

Scoring: Hand key

Cost: Contact publisher

Publisher: Human Sciences Research Council

VCWS 15—Electrical Circuitry and Print Reading

Copyright: 1977

Population: Adults

Purpose: Measures the ability to understand, comprehend, and apply the principles and functions of electrical circuitry through the modality of electronic components; provides insight into potential without basing performance exclusively on prior knowledge

Description: Measures the ability to understand and apply principles and functions of electrical circuits. The examinee performs various exercises in three areas: testing for circuit continuity using probes; testing and repairing circuits using probes, wires, and pliers; and reading an electrical schematic print and inserting wires, diodes, and two types of resistors as specified by the print. The examinee is given trays containing various electrical components and appropriate tools. The various electrical circuits to be tested range from very simple to complex. The examinee tests each circuit, records malfunctions, and, if necessary, repairs nonfunctioning circuits. No previous experience with electrical or electronic principles is required. The results indicate potential for success in an entry-level position in fields that require electrical circuitry and print reading skills. The test relates to work activities such as repairing materials, dexterous use of the hands, inspecting products, and selecting appropriate tools and materials. The test should not be used with individuals with severe impairment of the upper extremities, severe visual impairment, or severe coordination problems.

Format: Examiner required; not suitable for group use; timed: time not available

Scoring: Examiner evaluated

Cost: $1,695.00

Publisher: Valpar International Corporation

VCWS 202—Mechanical Assembly/Alignment and Hammering

Copyright: 1989

Population: Adolescents, adults; ages 13 and older

Purpose: Assesses worker qualification profile factors for job/curricula placement and career planning

Description: Criterion-referenced test consisting of demonstrated performance of block assembly, alignment driving, block disassembly, and hammering. Spatial aptitude, motor coordination, finger dexterity, and manual dexterity are measured. The test yields MTM standard and percentile scores. Materials include assembly block, assorted small tools and parts, and hammering cards. This test is suitable for individuals with hearing, physical, and mental impairments. Signing for individuals with hearing impairment necessary.

Format: Examiner required; not suitable for group use; timed: 10–15 minutes

Scoring: Examiner evaluated

Cost: $995.00

Publisher: Valpar International Corporation

VCWS 203—Mechanical Reasoning and Machine Tending

Copyright: 1989

Population: Adolescents, adults; ages 13 and older

Purpose: Assesses worker qualification profile factors for job/curricula placement and career planning

Description: Criterion-referenced test consisting of demonstrated performance of platform assembly, disassembly using fingers, and small tools. Measures vocational reasoning, motor coordination, manual dexterity, finger dexterity, and general learning ability. The test yields MTM standard and percentile scores. Materials include four-legged platform, machine tending board, nut driver, and felt marker. This test is suitable for individuals with hearing, physical, and mental disabilities. Signing for hearing impairment is necessary.

Format: Examiner required; not suitable for group use; timed: 10–15 minutes

Scoring: Examiner evaluated

Cost: $995.00

Publisher: Valpar International Corporation

Library Skills

Diagnostic Test of Library Skills
Barbara Feldstein, J. Rawdon

Copyright: 1992

Population: Children, adolescents; Grades 5 to 8

Purpose: Evaluates student's working knowledge of essential library skills

Description: Paper–pencil 50-item multiple-choice test measuring library skills in the following areas: definitions of library terms, use of the title page, use of the table of contents, use of an index, use of the card catalog, library arrangement, and use of reference materials. The results are recorded on an analytic sheet that indicates areas that require general class or small-group attention. Further examination of individual answer sheets indicates specific needs. The test is available in equivalent forms A and B with interchangeable answer key. A bibliography of sources providing instruction and learning experiences for concepts included in this test is provided in the teacher's guide. A computer version is available for Apple II, Macintosh, and IBM PC and compatibles.

Format: Examiner required; suitable for group use; untimed: time varies

Scoring: Hand key; computer scoring available

Cost: Test kit, specify form (50 test booklets, 100 answer sheets, scoring key, teacher's guide) $26.95; computer version (disk, teacher's guide, student record sheet) $39.95

Publisher: Learnco, Inc.

Diagnostic Test of Library Skills–Advanced

Susan Bailey

Copyright: Not provided

Population: High school students

Purpose: Evaluates student's working knowledge of essential library skills

Description: Multiple-item paper–pencil multiple-choice test measuring library skills in the following areas: definitions of library terms, use of the title page, use of the table of contents, use of an index, use of the card catalog, library arrangement, and reference materials. The results are recorded on an analytic sheet that indicates areas that require general class or small-group attention. Further examination of individual answer sheets indicates specific needs. A computer version is available for Apple II, Macintosh, and IBM compatibles.

Format: Examiner required; suitable for group use; untimed: time varies

Scoring: Hand key; computer scoring available

Cost: Test kit, specify form (50 test booklets, 100 answer sheets, scoring key, teacher's guide) $29.95; computer version (disk, teacher's guide, student record sheet) $39.95

Publisher: Learnco, Inc.

Math

Basic

ACER Mathematics Tests

Copyright: 1989

Population: Children, adolescents; Grades K through 11

Purpose: Measures achievement in mathematics; used for diagnosing individual student strengths and weaknesses

Description: Multiple-choice paper–pencil tests of basic mathematics skills: addition, subtraction, multiplication, and division. Tests are ACER Class Achievement Test in Mathematics (CATIM), a criterion-referenced test for years 4 to 5 and ACER Class Achievement Test in Mathematics (CATIM), years 6 to 7.

Format: Examiner required; suitable for group use; timed: time varies

Scoring: Hand key

Cost: Contact publisher

Publisher: The Australian Council for Educational Research Limited

Arithmetic Test A/8

Copyright: Not provided

Population: Adolescents, adults

Purpose: Measures general arithmetic ability

Description: Multiple-item paper–pencil test assessing arithmetic skills. Norms are available on request.

Format: Examiner required; suitable for group use; timed: 30–40 minutes

Scoring: Hand key

Cost: Contact publisher

Publisher: Human Sciences Research Council

Canadian Test of Basic Skills: Mathematics French Edition (CTBS), Levels 9–14, Form 7

E. King-Shaw, A. Hieronymus

Copyright: 1989

Population: Children; Grades 3 through 8

Purpose: Assesses students' abilities in mathematics concepts, mathematics problem solving, and mathematics computation

Description: Series of multiple-choice paper–pencil subtests which include Mathematics Concepts, Mathematics Problem Solving, and Mathematics Computation. Materials include CTBS Mathematics French Edition Test Booklets, CTBS Multilevel Teacher's Guide, the supplementary guide and key, and answer sheets. The CTBS Mathematics French Edition is an adaptation of the Iowa Tests of Basic Skills published by the Riverside Publishing Company. Examiner must have a teaching certificate.

Format: Examiner required; suitable for group use; timed: 66 minutes

Scoring: Hand key; machine scored; test scoring service available from publisher

Cost: Test booklets $4.35; CTBS Multilevel Teacher's Guide $12.00; supplementary guide and key $4.95; 35 answer sheets $13.45

Publisher: Nelson Canada

College Assessment of Academic Progress (CAAP) Mathematics Test

Copyright: 1996

Population: Adults; ages 17 and above

Purpose: Assesses mathematics skills

Description: Multiple-choice 35-item paper–pencil test. A test booklet, answer sheet, and pencil are used. May be used for persons with visual, physical, hearing, and mental disabilities.

Format: Suitable for group use; examiner required; timed: 40 minutes

Scoring: Machine scored; test scoring service available from publisher

Cost: $8.50

Publisher: American College Testing

Math Tests Grade I/Sub A–Standard 10

Copyright: 1981

Population: Children

Purpose: Measures understanding of mathematics; used for educational evaluation and placement

Description: Nineteen separate paper–pencil tests of mathematics achievement and understanding. Particular subtests vary, but generally they include Mechanical, Insight, and Problem Solving. Two alternate forms, A and B, are available for all standards except Grade I/Sub A.

Format: Examiner required; suitable for group use; untimed: typical time not available

Scoring: Hand key; examiner evaluated

Cost: Contact publisher

Publisher: Human Sciences Research Council

Mathematics Competency Test

John F. Izard, Ken M. Miller

Copyright: 1996

Population: Adoléscents, adults; ages 11 to 18; Grades 7 through 12

Purpose: Used as a general screening and identification of strengths and weaknesses to provide a profile of math competency

Description: Multiple-choice 46-item paper–pencil short-answer true–false test. Scores yielded are Full Test, Using and Applying Mathematics, Number and Algebra, Shape and Space, and Data.

Format: Individual administration; suitable for group use; examiner required; timed

Scoring: Hand key; examiner evaluated

Cost: Contact publisher

Publisher: The Australian Council for Educational Research Limited

Metropolitan Achievement Tests™, Sixth Edition Mathematics Diagnostic Tests
Thomas P. Hogan, Roger C. Farr, George A. Prescott, Irving H. Balow

Copyright: 1986

Population: Children, adolescents; Grades 1 through 9

Purpose: Assesses mathematics skills and competence; used for providing prescriptive information on educational performance of individual pupils

Description: Multiple-item series of paper–pencil tests measuring major components of mathematics skills, including numeration, geometry, measurement, problem solving, operations, whole numbers, laws, properties, fractions, decimals, graphs, and statistics. The test is divided into five levels: Primary 1 and 2, Elementary, Intermediate, and Advanced. Suitable for Title 1 use. Clusters of related objectives help teachers determine the level of instruction for optimal growth.

Format: Examiner required; suitable for group use; timed: time varies

Scoring: Hand key; may be machine scored; scoring service available

Cost: Examination Kit $14.50

Publisher: Harcourt® Brace Educational Measurement

National Achievement Tests for Arithmetic and Mathematics— American Numerical Test
John J. McCarty

Copyright: 1962

Population: Adolescents, adults

Purpose: Assesses arithmetic and numerical ability; used for educational evaluation and vocational guidance

Description: Paper–pencil 60-item test arranged in sequences of the four basic arithmetical operations. Items require numerical alertness and adaptation. Validity studies include specific fields of secretarial training, automotive, machine tools, construction technology, accounting, and machine drafting and design.

Format: Group; 4 minutes

Scoring: Hand key

Cost: Specimen set (test, key, manual) $4.00; 25 tests $5.00

Publisher: Psychometric Affiliates

National Achievement Tests for Elementary Schools: Arithmetic and Mathematics—Fundamentals and Reasoning (Grades 3–6)
Robert K. Speer, Samuel Smith

Copyright: 1962

Population: Children, Grades 3 through 6

Purpose: Assesses students' achievement in arithmetic; used to identify strengths and weaknesses as part of an educational evaluation

Description: Five-part paper–pencil test of arithmetic reasoning and fundamentals, including computation, arithmetical judgments, problem reading, and problem solving. Special norms for students with high and low IQs are provided. Two equivalent forms, A and B, are available.

Format: Examiner required; suitable for group use; timed: 30 minutes per part

Scoring: Hand key

Cost: Specimen Set (test, key, manual) $4.00; 25 tests $5.00

Publisher: Psychometric Affiliates

National Achievement Tests for Elementary Schools: Arithmetic and Mathematics—Fundamentals and Reasoning (Grades 6–8)
Robert K. Speer, Samuel Smith

Copyright: 1962

Population: Adolescents; Grades 6 through 8

Purpose: Assesses students' achievement in

arithmetic; used to identify strengths and weaknesses as part of an educational evaluation

Description: Five-part paper–pencil test of arithmetic reasoning and fundamentals, including fundamentals, number comparisons, mathematical judgments, problem reading, and problem solving. Special norms for students with high and low IQs are provided. Two equivalent forms, A and B, are available.

Format: Examiner required; suitable for group use; timed: 30 minutes per part

Scoring: Hand key

Cost: Specimen Set (test, key, manual) $4.00; 25 tests $5.00

Publisher: Psychometric Affiliates

National Achievement Tests for Elementary Schools: Arithmetic and Mathematics—General Mathematics
Stanley J. Lejeune

Copyright: 1969

Population: Children; Grades 4 through 6

Purpose: Assesses students' achievement in general mathematics; used to identify strengths and weaknesses as part of an educational evaluation

Description: Multiple-item paper–pencil power test of student comprehension of 11 major topics in general mathematics: the numeration system; addition, subtraction, multiplication, and division; common fractions; decimal fractions and percentages; measurements; geometry; solving written problems; graphs and scale drawings; set terminology; mathematical structure; and money. Two equivalent forms, A and B, are available.

Format: Examiner required; suitable for group use; untimed: approximately 2–3 class periods

Scoring: Hand key

Cost: Specimen Set (test, key, manual) $5.00; 25 tests $9.00; 25 answer sheets $3.50

Publisher: Psychometric Affiliates

National Achievement Tests for Elementary Schools: Arithmetic and Mathematics—General Mathematics
Robert K. Speer, Samuel Smith

Copyright: 1962

Population: Children, adolescents; Grades 3–8

Purpose: Assesses students' achievement in basic arithmetic skills; used to identify strengths and weaknesses as part of an educational evaluation

Description: Multiple-item paper–pencil test covering three basic areas of arithmetic skills: speed and accuracy in computation; judgment, speed, and accuracy in comparing computations; and skill and understanding, without special reference to speed. Two equivalent forms, A and B, are available.

Format: Examiner required; suitable for group use; timed: 45 minutes

Scoring: Hand key

Cost: Specimen Set (test, key, manual) $4.00; 25 tests $5.00

Publisher: Psychometric Affiliates

National Achievement Tests for Elementary Schools: Arithmetic and Mathematics—General Mathematics
Harry Eisner

Copyright: 1962

Population: Adolescents; Grades 7 through 9

Purpose: Assesses students' achievement in general mathematics; used to identify strengths and weaknesses as part of an educational evaluation

Description: Multiple-item paper–pencil test of student's knowledge of essential concepts, skills, and insights that should be developed in junior high school mathematics. The abilities measured are arithmetic, algebraic, and geometric concepts; applications; problem analysis; and reasoning. Two equivalent forms, A and B, are available.

Format: Examiner required; suitable for group use; timed: Section 1, 10 minutes; Section 2, 15 minutes; Section 3, 27 minutes

Scoring: Hand key

Cost: Specimen Set (test, key, manual) $4.00; 25 tests $9.00

Publisher: Psychometric Affiliates

Sequential Assessment of Mathematics Inventory—Standardized Inventory (SAMI)

Fredricka K. Reisman

Copyright: 1985

Population: Children, adolescents; Grades K through 8

Purpose: Provides a comprehensive profile of a student's overall standing in the mathematics curriculum, including the specific strengths and weaknesses that affect the student's performance

Description: Paper–pencil 243-item test measuring math performance in eight content areas: math language, ordinality, number/notation, measurement, geometry, computation, word problems, and math applications. Norms reported include standard scores, percentile ranks, stanines, and grade equivalents.

Format: Examiner required; not suitable for group use; untimed: 30–60 minutes

Scoring: Hand key

Cost: Complete Program (easel, examiner's manual, 12 student response booklets, 12 record forms) $109.50

Publisher: Harcourt® Brace Educational Measurement

Slosson-Diagnostic Math Screener (S-DMS)

Bradley T. Erford, Rita R. Boykin

Copyright: Not provided

Population: Ages 6 to 13

Purpose: Assesses children's mathematical skills

Description: Test assesses conceptual develop-

ment, problem solving, and computation skills in five grade ranges (Grades 1–8). Provides an overall view for entire class when group scored. Used for screening "at risk" students or checking new school entrants and eligibility assessments. Criterion- or norm-referenced curriculum evaluation. S-DMS tasks include math concepts, math problem solving, and math computation.

Format: Examiner required; suitable for group use; 30–50 minutes

Scoring: Hand key

Cost: Complete $160.00

Publisher: Slosson Educational Publications, Inc.

Comprehensive

Arithmetic Skills Assessment Test

Copyright: 1995

Population: Children, adults

Purpose: Provides profile of students' strengths and weaknesses in 119 math skills

Description: Computer-generated test measuring students' math skills, including addition, subtraction, multiplication, and division of whole numbers, fractions, and decimals. Students work out problems on worksheets and enter answers in the computer. Results may be printed or viewed on-screen. Macintosh/Windows versions also give approximate grade level.

Format: Self-administered

Scoring: Computer scored

Cost: Diskette and worksheets $89.00

Publisher: Educational Activities, Inc.

Diagnostic Math Tests

Copyright: 1976

Population: Children, adolescents

Purpose: Assesses skills in arithmetic; used for determining nature of specific pupil problems

Description: Three paper–pencil tests of math ability: Diagnostic Arithmetic Tests (Standards 2 to 8); Diagnostic Tests in Basic Algebra (Standards 7 and 8); and Mathematics Tests,

Diagnostic, Primary Level (Standards 1 to 5). Each test is divided into subtests. Aspects tested by the Diagnostic Tests in Basic Algebra are basic operations; simple algebraic expressions and linear equations; sets; exponents; number systems; ratio, rate, and proportion; substitution; and factors.

Format: Examiner required; suitable for group use; untimed: typical time not available

Scoring: Hand key; examiner evaluated

Cost: Contact publisher

Publisher: Human Sciences Research Council

Diagnostic Screening Test: Math, Third Edition (DTSM)
Thomas D. Gnagey

Copyright: 1980

Population: Children, adolescents; Grades 1 through 10

Purpose: Determines a student's conceptual and computational mathematical skills

Description: Multiple-item paper–pencil test in two sections: Basic Processes Section and Specialized Section. The Basic Processes Section consists of 36 items arranged developmentally within four major areas: addition skills, subtraction skills, multiplication, and division. Each area yields a separate Grade Equivalent Score and Consolidation Index Score and scores in nine supplemental categories: process, sequencing, simple computation, complex computation, special manipulations, use of zero, decimals, simple fractions, and manipulation in fractions. The Specialized Section consists of 37–45 items evaluating conceptual and computational skills in five areas: money, time, percent, U.S. measurement, and metric measurement. The examiner explains the procedure and the student completes the problems. The test is available in alternate forms, A and B.

Format: Examiner required; suitable for group use; untimed: 5–20 minutes

Scoring: Hand key

Cost: Complete Kit (manual, 25 Form A tests, 25 Form B tests) $48.00

Publisher: Slosson Educational Publications, Inc.

KeyMath–Revised: A Diagnostic Inventory of Essential Mathematics
Austin J. Connolly

Copyright: 1988

Population: Grades K through 9

Purpose: Assesses mathematics comprehension and application

Description: KeyMath–R is an individually administered instrument designed to prove comprehensive assessment of a student's understanding and application of important mathematics concepts and skills. Materials included in the kit: manual, Form A and B test easels, 25 of each forms A and B test records, sample report to parents.

Format: Individual administration; 35–50 minutes depending on grade level

Scoring: Examiner interpreted; standard scores, ASSIST available for PC, Apple II

Cost: Contact publisher

Publisher: American Guidance Service

Michigan Prescriptive Program in Math
William E. Lockhart

Copyright: 1996

Population: Grades 6 to adult

Purpose: Measures mathematics skills to identify skill deficits

Description: Multiple-item paper–pencil test assessing the following high school–level mathematics skills: addition; subtraction; multiplication; division; fractions; averaging; decimals; chancing decimals to percents; simple and compound interest; denominate numbers; reading line, bar, and circle graphs; finding perimeter, area, and volume; square roots; proportions; set theory; laws of operation; Roman numerals; exponents; signs; simple equations; inequalities; sum of angles; coordinate geometry; theorems; graphical solutions; and slope.

This pretest accompanies a program that provides remediation that is used to help students obtain a 10th-grade equivalency to pass the GED test in mathematics.

Format: Individual and group administration

Scoring: Examiner administered and interpreted

Cost: Math Study Guide $14.00; Pre-Test Booklets $15.00; Response and Prescriptive Sheets $8.00; scoring template $3.00

Publisher: Academic Therapy Publications

Multilevel Academic Survey Tests (MAST)
Kenneth W. Howell, Stanley H. Zucker, Mada K. Morehead

Copyright: 1985

Population: Children, adolescents; Grades K through 12

Purpose: Assesses academic performance to ensure meaningful placement and curriculum decisions

Description: Multiple-item paper–pencil test using two methods, Grade Level and Curriculum Level. In the Grade Level tests, three levels are available: Primary, Short (reading and mathematics), and Extended (includes reading comprehension and problem solving). The Curriculum Level tests include comprehensive reading and mathematics.

Format: Examiner required; suitable for group use; untimed: varies from 10 minutes to 30 minutes

Scoring: Examiner evaluated

Cost: Examination Kit $55.00

Publisher: Harcourt® Brace Educational Measurement

National Proficiency Survey Series (NPSS): Mathematics
Dale P. Scannell

Copyright: 1989

Population: Grades 8 through 12

Purpose: Assesses student proficiency in high school courses

Description: Multiple-item multiple-choice

paper–pencil tests used for evaluating student proficiency in mathematics courses. The General Mathematics test measures computation skill with integers and the knowledge of basic geometric concepts. The Algebra 1 test measures understanding of real numbers and variables and their operations in equations and inequalities. The Algebra 2 test measures an understanding of real numbers and polynomials; solving of linear, quadratic, and trigonometric equations; and the graphing of functions. The Geometry test measures an understanding of the nature and relationships of points, lines, angles, planes, circles, polygons, and solids.

Format: Examiner required; suitable for group use; 40 minutes

Scoring: Self-scored; hand key

Cost: Scanning and Scoring System Kit available; contact publisher for current prices

Publisher: Riverside Publishing Company

Stanford Diagnostic Mathematics Test, Third Edition (SDMT)
Leslie S. Beatty, Richard Madden, Eric F. Gardner, Bjorn Karlsen

Copyright: 1984

Population: Grades 1 through 12

Purpose: Measures progress in basic mathematics concepts and skills

Description: Multiple-item paper–pencil test with two alternate and equivalent forms on four levels

Format: Examiner required; suitable for group use; timed: varies

Scoring: Hand key; computer scoring service available

Cost: Examination Kit $27.50

Publisher: Harcourt® Brace Educational Measurement

Steenburgen Diagnostic Prescriptive Math Program and Quick Math Screening Test
Fran Steenburgen Gelb

Copyright: 1978

Population: Ages 6 to 11

Purpose: Determines an elementary school student's exact level of functioning in mathematics; used to plan programs for children and older remedial students whose math skills are still at the elementary level

Description: Multiple-item paper–pencil screening test measuring ability in simple addition, subtraction, one-digit carrying, addition of mixed numbers, and long division. The items are arranged in a sequential hierarchy according to the grade level at which each skill is introduced. Level I includes problems appropriate for Grades 1–3, and Level II contains problems for Grades 4–6. Scores can be plotted on a profile sheet that graphically shows a student's progress from pre- to posttest. After the student's strengths and weaknesses are identified, the diagnostic–prescriptive program consisting of 55 reproducible worksheets can be used by the student until skills are mastered.

Format: Individual or group administration

Scoring: Examiner administered; hand key

Cost: Manual (includes the Reproducible Quick Math Screening Test and Answer Key, Diagnostic–Prescriptive Guide, Prescriptive Worksheets, and answer key) Levels I and II $17.00

Publisher: Academic Therapy Publications

Test of Early Mathematics Ability–Second Edition (TEMA–2)
Herbert P. Ginsburg, Arthur J. Baroody

Copyright: 1990

Population: Children; ages 3 to 8

Purpose: Measures the mathematics performance of children; diagnoses individual strengths and weaknesses; used with children with mental retardation and learning disabilities to measure progress, evaluate programs, screen for readiness and to identify giftedness and problems

Description: Oral-response or paper–pencil 50-item test assessing mathematical abilities in two domains: informal mathematics (concepts of relative magnitude, counting, and calculation) and formal mathematics (knowledge of conventional number facts, calculation, and base-10 concepts). A picture card is used to present test items. Raw scores may be converted to standard scores, percentiles, and age equivalencies. Criterion-referenced interpretation leads directly to instructional objectives. The examiner should be competent in the administration of educational, psychological, and language tests.

Format: Examiner required; not suitable for group use; untimed: time varies

Scoring: Examiner evaluated

Cost: Complete Kit (examiner's manual, picture book, 50 profile/examiner record forms, assessment probes, instructional activities, and storage box) $149.00

Publisher: PRO-ED, Inc.

Test of Mathematical Abilities–Second Edition (TOMA–2)
Virginia L. Brown, Mary E. Cronin, Elizabeth McEntire

Copyright: 1994

Population: Children, adolescents; Grades 3 through 12

Purpose: Assesses the mathematical attitudes and aptitudes of students. Used to plan and assess instructional programs in mathematics, identify gifted students and those with learning disabilities, determine strengths and weaknesses, document progress, and conduct research

Description: Five paper–pencil subtests assessing knowledge, mastery, and attitudes in two major skill areas: story problems (17 items) and computation (25 items). In addition to measuring the student's abilities, the following broad diagnostic areas are assessed: expressed attitudes toward mathematics (15 items), understanding of vocabulary as applied to mathematics (20 items), the functional use of mathematics as applied to our general culture, and the relationship between a student's attitudes and abilities and those of her or his peers.

Normative information related to age and IQ, as well as graded mastery expectations for the "400" basic number facts, is provided for students ages 8 to 17. Scores differentiate diagnostically between students who have problems in mathematics and those who do not. Examiners should be competent in the administration of educational, psychological, and language tests.

Format: Examiner required; suitable for group use; untimed: time varies

Scoring: Examiner evaluated

Cost: Complete Kit (examiner's manual, 25 profile/record forms, storage box) $74.00

Publisher: PRO-ED, Inc.

Specific

Achievement Test for Accounting Graduates (ATAG)

Copyright: Updated yearly

Population: Adults

Purpose: Measures academic achievement in elementary accounting

Description: Available in two forms, each consisting of 75 multiple-choice questions, 60% in financial accounting and 40% in managerial accounting

Format: Examiner required; suitable for group use; timed: 3 hours

Scoring: Hand key

Cost: Examination Kit (booklet, Ready Score Answer Document, and handbook) $50.00

Publisher: The Psychological Corporation

Iowa Algebra Aptitude Test™
Harold L. Schoen, Timothy N. Ansley, H. D. Hoover, Beverly S. Rich, Sheila I. Barron, Robert A. Bye

Copyright: 1993

Population: Grades 7 through 8; suitable for high school or junior college testing

Purpose: Assesses student readiness for Algebra 1

Description: Mathematics educators have long recognized that Algebra 1 classes tend to have high student failure rates. That failure creates frustration and lost time for both teacher and students. The IAAT can promote student success in algebra classes by helping educators more accurately determine which students should be placed into Algebra 1 and into pre-algebra courses. The content of the IAAT has been aligned with current NCTM recommendations, both for pre-algebra and algebra curricula and for testing.

Format: Group administered; examiner required; 50 minutes

Scoring: Examiner evaluated or by Trans-Optic scanning equipment

Cost: Test Booklets (pkg. of 25, includes 1 Directions for Administration) Form 1 and Form 2 $69.50; Answer Documents (pkg. of 25, includes 1 class record sheet) $31.00; Class Record Sheets (pkg. of 25) $19.50; Scanning and Scoring System (IBM) $990.00

Publisher: Riverside Publishing Company

National Achievement Tests for Arithmetic and Mathematics— Algebra Test for Engineering and Science
A. B. Lonski

Copyright: 1973

Population: Adolescents, adults

Purpose: Assesses achievement in intermediate algebra; used for screening students planning to register in an engineering college or technical school

Description: Paper–pencil test of algebra knowledge. Items represent mistakes made in algebra by college freshmen who failed the subject in engineering and science courses. The test represents minimum essentials for entry into regular freshmen mathematics.

Format: Examiner required; suitable for group use; untimed: typical time not available

Scoring: Hand key

Cost: Specimen Set (test, key, manual) $4.00; 25 tests $17.50; 25 answer sheets $3.00

Publisher: Psychometric Affiliates

National Achievement Tests for Arithmetic and Mathematics— First Year Algebra Test
Ray Webb, Julius H. Hlavaty

Copyright: 1962

Population: Adolescents

Purpose: Assesses achievement in first-year algebra; used to identify strengths and weaknesses as part of an educational evaluation

Description: Paper–pencil test measuring pupils' knowledge of first-year algebra. Two equivalent forms, A and B, are available.

Format: Examiner required; suitable for group use; timed: 40 minutes

Scoring: Hand key

Cost: Specimen Set (test, key, manual) $4.40; 25 tests $6.00; 25 answer sheets $4.50

Publisher: Psychometric Affiliates

National Achievement Tests for Arithmetic and Mathematics— Plane Geometry, Solid Geometry, and Plane Trigonometry Tests
Ray Webb, Julius H. Hlavaty

Copyright: 1970

Population: Adolescents

Purpose: Assesses achievement in geometry and trigonometry; used to identify strengths and weaknesses as part of an educational evaluation

Description: Three paper–pencil tests measuring essential concepts, skills, and insight in three content areas: plane geometry, solid geometry, and plane trigonometry. Two equivalent forms, A and B, are available.

Format: Examiner required; suitable for group use; timed: 40 minutes

Scoring: Hand key

Cost: Specimen Set (test, key, manual) $4.00; 25 tests $8.75; 25 answer sheets $3.50

Publisher: Psychometric Affiliates

Orleans-Hanna Algebra Prognosis Test (Revised)
Gerald S. Hanna, Joseph B. Orleans

Copyright: 1982

Population: Adolescents; Grades 7 through 12

Purpose: Identifies students likely to experience difficulties in an algebra course; used in counseling, selecting, and grouping algebra students

Description: Multiple-item test of three variables related to the prognosis of success in an algebra course: aptitude, achievement, and interest and motivation. Items include a questionnaire and work samples. Students complete the questionnaire by indicating recent grades and estimating their algebra grade. Then they complete the 60-item work sample.

Format: Examiner required; suitable for group use; timed: 40 minutes

Scoring: Hand key; may be machine scored; computer scoring service available

Cost: Examination Kit $14.00

Publisher: Harcourt® Brace Educational Measurement

Motor Skills

Bruininks-Oseretsky Test of Motor Proficiency
Robert H. Bruininks

Copyright: 1978

Population: Ages 4 years 6 months to 14 years 6 months

Purpose: Assists in assessing motor skill for individual students, in developing and evaluating motor training programs, and in assessing serious motor dysfunctions and developmental disabilities in children

Description: The test provides a comprehensive index of motor proficiency as well as differentiated measures of gross and fine motor skills. The Complete Battery contains eight subtests comprised of 46 separate items. The Short Form consists of 14 items from the Complete Battery and provides a quick, brief survey. One score provides an index of general motor proficiency. The Short Form may be used when large numbers of children must be tested in a limited amount of time.

Format: Individually administered; Complete Battery: 45–60 minutes, Short Form 15–20 minutes

Scoring: Hand scored; raw scores recorded as each subtest is administered; raw scores are converted to point scores and then to derived scores

Cost: Test Kit Manual, 25 Student Booklets, 25 Individual Record Forms for Complete Battery/Short Form (plus sample of alternate Short Form), testing equipment $399.95

Publisher: American Guidance Service

Children's Handwriting Evaluation Scale (CHES)
Joanne M. Phelps, Lynn Stempel

Copyright: 1984

Population: Ages 6 to adult; Grades 1 through college

Purpose: Intended for all levels of students to assess handwriting and legibility

Description: Paper–pencil scale with a paragraph to copy and a manual to score. A raw score, standard score, percentile for rate, and description quality are yielded.

Format: Examiner required; individual administration; suitable for group use; timed and untimed: 8 minutes

Scoring: Examiner evaluated

Cost: $35.00

Publisher: CHES

Children's Handwriting Evaluation Scale–Manuscript (CHES–M)
Joanne M. Phelps, Lynn Stempel

Copyright: 1987

Population: Grades 1 and 2

Purpose: Intended for all levels of students to assess handwriting and legibility

Description: Paper–pencil scale with a paragraph to copy and a manual to score. A raw score, standard score, percentile for rate, and description quality are yielded.

Format: Examiner required; individual administration; suitable for group use; timed and untimed: 8 minutes

Scoring: Examiner evaluated

Cost: $20.00

Publisher: CHES

College Handwriting Evaluation Scale–College (CHES–C)
Joanne M. Phelps, Lynn Stempel

Copyright: 1985

Population: College students

Purpose: Intended for all levels of students to assess handwriting and legibility

Description: Paper–pencil scale with a paragraph to copy and a manual to score. A raw score, standard score, percentile for rate, and description quality are yielded.

Format: Examiner required; suitable for group use; timed and untimed: 8 minutes

Scoring: Examiner evaluated

Cost: $10.00

Publisher: CHES

Denver Handwriting Analysis (DHA)
Peggy L. Anderson

Copyright: 1983

Population: Ages 8 through 13

Purpose: Assesses the general ability of a student's cursive handwriting to provide detailed information related to handwriting instruction

Description: Multiple-item paper–pencil test consisting of five areas: near-point copying, writing the alphabet from memory, far-point copying, manuscript-cursive transition, and dictation. Detailed information that relates directly to handwriting instruction is provided. The instrument can also be used for continuing assessment.

Format: Individual administration; suitable for group use; 20 to 60 minutes

Scoring: Examiner administered and interpreted

Cost: Test Kit (manual, wall chart, protocols, and remedial checklists in vinyl folder) $40.00

Publisher: Academic Therapy Publications

Functional Writing Assessment

Copyright: 1995

Population: Adults, adolescents; native and nonnative speakers of English

Purpose: Assesses learners' general writing levels and provides diagnostic information about which writing skills the learners need to target; appropriate for low literacy levels

Description: Three writing tasks: Process Task, Picture Task, Form Task. Students describe the process or picture or fill out the form. Training is required.

Format: Students choose writing prompt and write in test booklet

Scoring: Writing samples are scored analytically or holistically using standardized detailed rubrics and annotated scoring anchors.

Cost: Various

Publisher: Comprehensive Adult Student Assessment System

Infant/Toddler Symptom Checklist

Georgia De Gangi, Susan Poisson,
Ruth Sickel, Andrea Santman

Copyright: 1995

Population: 7 months to 30 months

Purpose: Screens for sensory and regulatory diseases

Description: Paper–pencil point-to test screening sensory and regulatory diseases used for occupational and physical therapy

Format: Untimed

Scoring: Hand key; no scoring service available

Cost: Test kit (manual and score sheet sets) $52.00

Publisher: Communication Skill Builders, Inc.

Jordan Left–Right Reversal Test–Revised (JLRRT)

Brian T. Jordan

Copyright: 1990

Population: Ages 5 through 12

Purpose: Assesses the extent to which a child reverses letters, numbers, and words

Description: Multiple-item paper–pencil examination on two levels. Level I measures reversals of letters, numerals, and words. Level II reveals reversed lowercase letters within words and whole-word reversals within sentences. The manual includes detailed remediation exercises for reversal problems. The Laterality Checklist is an informal survey that determines whether a student prefers use of one side of his or her body, and the Remedial Checklist provides a list of activities that can be used to develop laterality. Norm-referenced instrument provides developmental age.

Format: Individual and group administration; 20 minutes

Scoring: Examiner administered and interpreted

Cost: Test kit (manual, protocols, and checklists in vinyl folder) $63.00

Publisher: Academic Therapy Publications

Lincoln-Oseretsky Motor Development Scale

William Sloan

Copyright: 1954

Population: Children, adolescents

Purpose: Measures motor development of children; used to supplement information obtained from other techniques concerning intellectual, social, emotional, and physical development

Description: Task assessment of a child's motor development. The areas covered in the 36 items are static coordination, dynamic coordination, speed of movement and asynkinesia (finger dexterity), eye–hand coordination, and gross activity of the hands, arms, legs, and trunk. Both unilateral and bilateral tasks are involved. The test items, arranged in order of difficulty, include walking backwards, crouching on tip-toe, standing on one foot, touching nose, touching fingertips, tapping rhythmically with feet and fingers, jumping over a rope, finger movement, standing heel to toe, closing and opening hands alternately, making dots, catching a ball, making a ball, winding thread, balancing a rod crosswise, describing circles in the air, tapping, placing coins and matchsticks, jumping and turning about, putting matchsticks in a box, winding thread while walking, throwing a ball, sorting matchsticks, drawing lines, cutting circle, putting coins in a box, tracing mazes, balancing on tiptoe, tapping with feet and fingers, jumping and touching heels, tapping feet and describing circles, standing on one foot, jumping and clapping, balancing on tiptoe and opening and closing hands, and balancing a rod vertically.

Format: Examiner required; not suitable for group use; untimed: typical time not available

Scoring: Examiner evaluated

Cost: Complete Kit (test materials, 50 record blanks, manual) $235.00

Publisher: Stoelting Company

Peabody Developmental Motor Scales and Activity Cards

M. Rhonda Folio, Rebecca R. Fewell

Copyright: 1983

Population: Birth to 83 months

Purpose: Assesses students' thinking and process skills and problem-solving strategies

Description: Multiple-item task-performance test consisting of a comprehensive sequence of gross- and fine-motor skills from which the child's relative developmental skill level can be determined. The test may be used to analyze a wide range of skills identified as questionable by prior screening or to diagnose specific characteristics of a motor problem. Norms are provided for each skill category at each level and for the total test. The instructional program components include a tab-indexed card file of 170 gross motor and 112 fine-motor activities referenced to the items on the test. These activity cards provide an instructional curriculum to fill developmental gaps, strengthen emerging skills, and set objectives for skills not yet attained.

Format: Individually or group administered; examiner required; 20–30 minutes per scale

Scoring: Examiner evaluated

Cost: Test kit (manual, 15 scoring booklets, 282 activity cards, cubes, pegboard, pegs, form board and shapes, bottle, beads and laces, box, dowel and string, etc.) $180.00

Publisher: PRO-ED, Inc.

Test of Gross Motor Development (TGMD)

Dale A. Ulrich

Copyright: 1985

Population: Ages 3 to 10

Purpose: Assess common motor skills of children; use for educational planning and research and to evaluate existing special education programs

Description: Multiple-item task-performance test consisting of two subtests. The Locomotor Skills subtest measures the run, gallop, hop, skip, horizontal jump, leap, and slide. The Object Control Skills subtest measures the two-hand strike, stationary bounce, catch, kick, and overhand throw. Test findings are reported in terms of subtest standard scores, percentiles, and a composite quotient that represents total gross motor development performance.

Format: Individual administration; 15 minutes

Scoring: Examiner administration and interpretation

Cost: Complete kit (manual, protocols, and storage box) $64.00

Publisher: PRO-ED, Inc.

Reading, Language Arts, and English

Elementary

Computer Crossroads
Stuart Paltrowitz, Donna Paltrowitz

Copyright: 1985

Population: Children

Purpose: Diagnoses weaknesses and strengths in reading comprehension skills of children with interest levels of Grades 2–5 and reading levels of Grades 1.8–2.8; used in school settings

Description: Computer-administered test of reading comprehension skills, including finding the main idea, sequencing, noting details, predicting outcomes, and inferring. The program allows students to create a story through which they journey with "computer pets," which the students also create. The program, which operates on Apple IIe computer systems, provides practice toward remediation and diagnostic information.

Format: Examiner required; not suitable for group use; untimed: time varies

Scoring: Computer scored

Cost: Complete Kit (3 diskettes, 3 backups, management, documentation, and reproducible activity masters) $99.95

Publisher: Educational Activities, Inc.

Diagnostic Reading Scales–Revised Edition (DRS)
George D. Spache

Copyright: 1982

Population: Children

Purpose: Identifies a student's reading strengths and weaknesses; used by educators to determine placement and to prescribe instruction

Description: Multiple-item reading skills test consisting of a series of graduated scales containing 3 word-recognition lists, 22 reading sections, and 12 phonics and word analysis tests.

Format: Examiner required; not suitable for group use; timed: 1 hour

Scoring: Examiner evaluated

Cost: Specimen Set, 1981 Edition (test book, record book, manual, test reviewer's guide) $34.65

Publisher: CTB/McGraw-Hill

Durrell Analysis of Reading Difficulty–Third Edition
Donald D. Durrell, Jane H. Catterson

Copyright: 1980

Population: Children; Grades 1 through 6

Purpose: Assesses reading behavior; used for diagnosis, measurement of prereading skills, and planning remedial programs

Description: Multiple-item series of tests and situations measuring 10 reading abilities: oral reading, silent reading, listening comprehension, listening vocabulary, word recognition/word analysis, spelling, auditory analysis of words and word elements, pronunciation of word elements, visual memory of words, and prereading phonics abilities. Supplementary paragraphs for oral and silent reading are provided for supplementary testing or retesting. Materials include a spiral-bound booklet containing items to be read and a tachistoscope with accompanying test card.

Format: Examiner required; not suitable for group use; untimed: 30–45 minutes

Scoring: Examiner evaluated

Cost: Examiner's Kit (five record booklets, tachistoscope, reading booklet, and manual) $89.00

Publisher: Harcourt® Brace Educational Measurement

Gillingham-Childs Phonics Proficiency Scales: Series I, Basic Reading and Spelling and Series II, Advanced Reading

Sally B. Childs, Ralph de S. Childs

Copyright: 1970 (Series I); 1971 (Series II)

Population: Grades 1 through 8

Purpose: Evaluates student progress in the mastery of phonic and beginning reading skills to provide teachers with an index of remedial progress

Description: Multiple-item primarily verbal examination in two series: Series I contains 12 scales dealing with basic reading and spelling skills; letter–sound relationships; three-letter words; consonant digraphs and blends; one-syllable words ending with *f, l,* or *s;* silent *e* words; syllabication rules; sight words; and suffix rules. Series II contains 16 scales measuring advanced reading skills. There is no spelling test in Series II. The original version of the scales was developed by Anna Gillingham.

Format: Individual administration; 30 minutes–1 hour

Scoring: Examiner administration and interpretation

Cost: Series I $17.10; Series II $11.40

Publisher: Educators Publishing Service, Inc.

Informal Reading Comprehension Placement Test

Eunice Insel, Ann Edson

Copyright: 1994

Population: Children to adults; reading levels 1–12

Purpose: Measures reading comprehension; determines students' instructional placement level; correlates to TABE (Mac and Windows versions)

Description: Computer-administered 68-item test assessing word and passage comprehension. The 60-item word comprehension test uses a word analogy format to measure students' knowledge of word meanings and thinking skills. The passage comprehension test consists of a series of eight graded selections and questions ranging in difficulty from the primary level through eighth grade. Students are placed in an instructional reading range of first through eighth grade in word comprehension and passage comprehension. The test is totally administered, scored, and managed by the microcomputer. A diskette is available for the AppleII+ and IIe, MS-DOS, Windows, and Macintosh microcomputers.

Format: Examiner required; not suitable for group use; untimed: time varies

Scoring: Computer scored

Cost: Diskette (specify model) $59.95

Publisher: Educational Activities, Inc.

Language Arts Assessment Portfolio (LAAP)

Bjorn Karlsen

Copyright: 1992

Population: Level I—Grade 1, Level II—Grades 2–3, Level III—Grades 4–6

Purpose: Provides an alternative assessment of language arts (reading, writing, listening, speaking)

Description: Alternative classroom assessment system for the language arts that makes use of both portfolio and performance-based assessment techniques. The Evaluation Booklet is used by the teacher to observe and rate students' performance in language arts. The Self-Evaluation Booklet is used by the student to help develop self-awareness of language arts skills. Portfolio folders and blackline masters are used together to assemble and evaluate samples of the student's work.

Format: Individual administration; untimed

Scoring: For each language arts area, both the Self-Evaluation Booklet and the Evaluation Booklet list specific skills, which the student and teacher use as the basis of their ratings.

Cost: Complete Kit (Level I) $104.95, (Level II) $104.95, (Level III) $104.95

Publisher: American Guidance Service

O'Brien Vocabulary Placement Test

Janet O'Brien

Copyright: 1989

Population: Children; Grades 1 through 6

Purpose: Measures the reading ability of elementary-school students; used to identify children who have reading deficiencies

Description: Paper–pencil 10-item test in six sections, one for each grade through the sixth. Each test contains a list of words for which the student selects the antonym from four possible choices. The test enables a teacher to find the independent reading level of an entire class in 15 minutes. The test also can be used individually for new students and those in special education classes.

Format: Examiner required; suitable for group use; untimed: 15 minutes

Scoring: Hand key

Cost: Apple IIe diskette $29.95

Publisher: Educational Activities, Inc.

Observation Survey of Early Literacy

Marie M. Clay

Copyright: 1985

Population: Grades K, 1, and 2

Purpose: Assesses reading skills; used for diagnosing individual reading deficiencies

Description: Multiple-item test for observing and screening the emergent reading skills of children in Grades 1 and 2. Materials include a set of two test booklets (*Sand* and *Stones)*, a guide, and a textbook, *The Patterning of Complex Behavior. The Early Detection of Reading Difficulties* guide presents the theoretical background, administration details, and scoring interpretation of the tests.

Format: Examiner required; suitable for group use; untimed: typical time not available

Scoring: Hand score

Cost: *Early Detection of Reading Difficulties* $15.00; *Sand* $3.00; *Stones* $3.00

Publisher: Heinemann Educational Books, Inc.

Prereading Expectancy Screening Scale (PRESS)

Lawrence C. Hartlage, David G. Lucas

Copyright: 1973

Population: Children; ages 6 to 9

Purpose: Assesses skills important in reading; used for predicting reading problems for beginning readers

Description: Multiple-item paper–pencil test measuring a child's recognition of the numbers 1–9 and the following shapes: cross, circle, star, square, and diamond. The scale consists of four subtests: Sequencing, Spatial, Memory, and Letter Identification. Items are read by the teacher.

Format: Examiner required; suitable for group use; untimed: 35 minutes

Scoring: Hand key; examiner evaluated

Cost: Specimen Set $9.00; 25 tests $15.00; 25 profile sheets (specify boys or girls) $6.75; manual $6.75

Publisher: Psychologists and Educators, Inc.

Test of Children's Language (TOCL)

Edna Barenbaum, Phyllis Newcomer

Copyright: 1996

Population: Ages 5 years to 8 years 11 months

Purpose: Identifies students' specific strengths and weaknesses in language components and in recognizing students who are at risk for failure in reading and writing; also helps with documentation of students' progress as a consequence of early intervention

Description: Unit 1 uses a storybook format featuring the antics of animal characters to assess children's ability in spoken language and reading. In Unit 2, students undertake a series of writing tasks that range from basic writing skills to creative writing. Materials in the TOCL are familiar to primary-level classrooms. Test results provide the teacher with authentic information about specific students' performances in all aspects of language, permit comparisons with national norms, and yield useful guidelines for further assessment and instruction. The skills included in Unit 1 of the TOCL include aspects of spoken language known to be correlates of reading and writing, including semantics, syntax, and listening comprehension, as well as three other skills related to reading: knowledge about print, phonological awareness, and letter knowledge. Additional items in this section assess the two major components of reading: word recognition and reading comprehension. Unit 2 is divided into three parts: Part A measures various types of writing ability, Part B requires the children to write the story they have read previously, and in Part C children write an original story about the animal characters in the storybook.

Format: Individual administration; untimed: 30–40 minutes

Scoring: Hand key

Cost: Complete Kit (examiner's manual, "A Visit with Mr. Turtle" Storybook, Story Picture Sheet, 25 student workbooks, 25 profile/examiner record forms, storage box) $119.00

Publisher: PRO-ED, Inc.

Test of Early Reading Ability–Second Edition (TERA–2)
D. Kim Reid, Wayne P. Hresko, Donald D. Hammill

Copyright: 1989

Population: Children; ages 3 years to 9 years 11 months

Purpose: Determines the actual reading ability (not "readiness") of preschool, kindergarten, and primary level students; used to identify problems, document progress, conduct research, and suggest instructional practices

Description: Multiple-item paper–pencil test examining three areas related to early learning: contextual meaning, alphabet, and the conventions of reading (e.g., book orientation and format). Scaled scores, percentiles, age equivalents, and reading quotients are yielded. Results can be used to document early reading ability. Two equivalent forms (A and B) are available. Examiners must be competent in the adminis-

tration of educational, psychological, and language tests.

Format: Examiner required; not suitable for group use; untimed: time varies

Scoring: Examiner evaluated

Cost: Complete Kit (examiner's manual, picture book, 25 Form A and 25 Form B profile/examiner record forms, storage box) $149.00

Publisher: PRO-ED, Inc.

Test of Early Written Language–Second Edition (TEWL–2)
Wayne P. Hresko, Shelley R. Herron, Pamela K. Peak

Copyright: 1996

Population: Ages 3 years to 10 years 11 months

Purpose: Measures the emerging written language skills of young children; used to identify mildly handicapped students and to document student growth and program effectiveness

Description: Multiple-item paper–pencil test covering areas with a direct relationship to a young child's school-related activities, including transcription, conventions of print, communication, creative expression, and record keeping. Picture cards are used to prompt writing samples. The test yields standard scores and percentiles, which can be used with other cognitive and academic measures to identify intraindividual abilities. The scores obtained are Global Writing Quotient, Basic Writing Quotient, and Contextual Writing Quotient.

Format: Examiner required; not suitable for group use; untimed: 10–30 minutes

Scoring: Examiner evaluated

Cost: Complete Kit (examiner's manual, 25 profile/record forms, 25 student workbooks, 7 picture cards, storage box) $98.00

Publisher: PRO-ED, Inc.

Test of Phonological Awareness (TOPA)
Joseph K. Torgesen, Brian R. Bryant

Copyright: 1994

Population: Children; Grades K through 2

Purpose: Measures young children's awareness of the individual sounds in words

Description: The TOPA can be used to identify children in kindergarten who may profit from instructional activities to enhance their phonological awareness in preparation for reading instruction. Additionally, since kindergarten scores on the TOPA are strongly related to reading growth in first grade, the TOPA also will be useful as part of kindergarten screening activities to identify children who are at risk for learning difficulties in school. The Early Elementary version of the TOPA can be used to determine if first- and second-grade students' difficulties in early reading are associated with delays in development of phonological awareness. The test has been standardized on a large sample of children representative of the population characteristics reported in the U.S. census. The manual provides information about general percentiles and a variety of standard scores. Internal consistency reliability estimates range from .89 to .91 at different ages. Evidence of content, predictive, and construct validity also is provided in the manual.

Format: Examiner administered; timed: time varies

Scoring: Examiner evaluated

Cost: Complete Kit (examiner's manual, 25 student booklets—kindergarten, 25 student booklets—early elementary, 25 profile/examiner record forms—kindergarten, 25 profile/examiner record forms—early elementary, storage box) $124.00

Publisher: PRO-ED, Inc.

High School and College

ACER Reading Tests

Copyright: 1989

Population: Adolescents, adults; ages 15 and older

Purpose: Measures intelligence of students ages 15 and older at secondary and tertiary levels

Description: Multiple-item paper–pencil intelligence test available in two parallel forms: AL-AQ (Second Edition) and BL-BQ. The L section of both forms contains linguistic items, and the Q section contains quantitative items. Norms are presented for upper-secondary level and first-year samples from TAFE colleges and Colleges of Advanced Education. Materials include expendable booklets for each section (AL, BL, AQ, or BQ), scoring keys for each section, manual, and specimen set.

Format: Examiner required; suitable for group use; timed: AL, BL 15 minutes; AQ, BQ 20 minutes

Scoring: Hand key; examiner evaluated

Cost: Contact publisher

Publisher: The Australian Council for Educational Research Limited

ACT PEP RCE: Education: Reading Instruction in the Elementary School

Copyright: 1993

Population: Adults; college level

Purpose: Assesses knowledge of a two-semester course in elementary reading instruction; used to grant college credit and advanced placement in academic courses

Description: Paper–pencil 120-item multiple-choice test. Scale scores range from 20 to 80. Two forms are available. A test booklet, answer sheet, and pencil are used. Examiner must have experience with test administration at the college level. May be used for persons with visual, physical, hearing, and mental disabilities.

Format: Examiner required; suitable for group use; timed: 3 hours

Scoring: Machine scored

Cost: $45.00

Publisher: American College Testing

Adult Language Assessment Scales (Adult LAS®)

Sharon E. Duncan, Edward A. DeAvila

Copyright: 1991

Population: Adults

Purpose: Assesses English language proficiency in adults whose primary language is not English

Description: Multiple-item paper–pencil multiple-choice/oral-response/short-answer test available in two levels. The test consists of oral language, writing, reading, and mathematics components. There are four subtests, divided into subsections that allow for identification of problem areas. Results of all test components are combined to give one measure of language proficiency.

Format: Examiner required; suitable for group use; untimed: 5–30 minutes per subsection

Scoring: Examiner evaluated; hand key

Cost: Oral Examiner's Kit (Form A) $134.55; test books (Reading/Math) $73.25/25; (Writing) $50.00/50; Answer sheets (R/M) $29.00/50

Publisher: CTB/McGraw-Hill

College Assessment of Academic Progress (CAAP) Reading Test

Copyright: 1996

Population: Adults; ages 17 and above

Purpose: Assesses reading skills

Description: Multiple-choice 36-item paper–pencil test with two categories: Referring and Reasoning. A test booklet, answer sheet, and pencil are used. May be used for persons with visual, physical, hearing, and mental disabilities.

Format: Suitable for group use; examiner required; timed: 40 minutes

Scoring: Machine scored; test scoring service available from publisher

Cost: $8.50

Publisher: American College Testing

College Assessment of Academic Progress (CAAP) Writing Essay Test

Copyright: 1996

Population: Adults; ages 17 and above

Purpose: Assesses writing skills

Description: Paper–pencil essay test. A test booklet, answer sheet, and pencil are used. May be used for persons with visual, physical, hearing, and mental disabilities.

Format: Suitable for group use; examiner required; timed: 40 minutes

Scoring: Examiner evaluated; test scoring service available from publisher

Cost: $8.50

Publisher: American College Testing

College Assessment of Academic Progress (CAAP) Writing Skills Test

Copyright: 1996

Population: Adults; ages 17 and above

Purpose: Assesses English usage/mechanics and rhetorical skills

Description: Multiple-choice 72-item paper–pencil test with the following categories: Usage/Mechanical and Rhetorical Skills. Two subscores are yielded. A test booklet, answer sheet, and pencil are used. May be used for persons with visual, physical, hearing, and mental disabilities.

Format: Suitable for group use; examiner required; timed: 40 minutes

Scoring: Machine scored; test scoring service available from publisher

Cost: $8.50

Publisher: American College Testing

COMP Speaking Assessment

Copyright: 1996

Population: Adults; ages 17 and above

Purpose: Assesses speaking proficiency

Description: Six-item oral-response criterion-referenced verbal test with the following categories: Audience, Discourse, and Delivery. Six subscores are yielded. Forms 10–12 are available.

Format: Individual administration; suitable for

group use; examiner required; timed: 9 minutes

Scoring: Examiner evaluated; machine scored

Cost: $5.25 per person; $7.25 to rate per person

Publisher: American College Testing

COMP Writing Assessment

Copyright: 1996

Population: Adults; ages 17 and above

Purpose: Assesses writing proficiency

Description: Nine-item paper–pencil criterion-referenced essay test with the following categories: Audience, Organization, and Language. Three subscores are yielded. Forms 10–12 are available.

Format: Suitable for group use; examiner required; timed: 60 minutes

Scoring: Examiner evaluated; machine scored; test scoring service available from publisher

Cost: $5.25 per person; $7.25 to rate per person

Publisher: American College Testing

National Achievement Tests: English, Reading, Literature, and Vocabulary Tests—American Literacy Test
Andrew Kobal

Copyright: 1962

Population: Adults

Purpose: Assesses literacy in adults; used for detecting functional illiteracy

Description: Paper–pencil 50-item test measuring vocabulary or depth of literacy. Items require knowledge of approximate synonyms. The test discriminates degrees of literacy, from illiterate to the highly sophisticated.

Format: Examiner required; suitable for group use; timed: 4 minutes

Scoring: Hand key

Cost: Specimen Set (test, manual, key) $4.00; 25 scales $5.00

Publisher: Psychometric Affiliates

National Achievement Tests: English, Reading, Literature, and Vocabulary Tests—College English for High School and College
A. C. Jordon

Copyright: 1961

Population: Adolescents, adults; Grades 10 and above

Purpose: Assesses English achievement of high school and college students; used for evaluating prospective college students

Description: Multiple-item paper–pencil test measuring a range of English skills, including the ability to use correct capitalization, punctuate correctly, use proper syntax, determine subject/verb agreement, vary sentence structure, use modifiers correctly, and apply language principles. Two equivalent forms, A and B, are available.

Format: Examiner required; suitable for group use; timed: 45 minutes

Scoring: Hand key

Cost: Specimen Set (test, manual, key) $4.00; 25 tests $8.75

Publisher: Psychometric Affiliates

National Proficiency Survey Series (NPSS): Language Arts
Dale P. Scannel

Copyright: 1989

Population: Grades 8 through 12

Purpose: Assesses student proficiency in high school courses

Description: Multiple-item multiple-choice paper–pencil tests used for evaluating student proficiency in Language Arts courses. The Writing Fundamentals test covers spelling and vocabulary in addition to grammar, usage, and mechanics. The Literature test evaluates literal and inferential comprehension, drawing from the works of a wide variety of authors and from different types of literature. The English IV test evaluates a student's ability to use language effectively to organize and support ideas.

Format: Examiner required; suitable for group use; 40 minutes

Scoring: Self-scored; hand key

Cost: Scanning and Scoring System Kit available; contact publisher

Publisher: Riverside Publishing Company

Nelson-Denny Reading Test: Forms E and F

James I. Brown, J. Michael Bennett, Gerald S. Hanna

Copyright: 1981

Population: Grade 9 to adult

Purpose: Assesses student achievement and progress in vocabulary, comprehension, and reading rate

Description: Paper–pencil 136-item reading survey test in two parts. Part I, the Vocabulary Test, measures vocabulary development. Part II, the Comprehension Test, assesses comprehension and reading rate. The test is available in two parallel forms.

Format: Examiner required; suitable for group use; 35 minutes

Scoring: Hand key; may be machine scored

Cost: Contact publisher

Publisher: Riverside Publishing Company

Nelson-Denny Reading Test: Forms G and H

James I. Brown, Vivian Vick Fishco, Gerald S. Hanna

Copyright: 1993

Population: Grades 9 and above

Purpose: Assesses student achievement and progress in vocabulary, comprehension, and reading rate

Description: A two-part test that measures vocabulary development, comprehension, and reading rate. Part I (Vocabulary) is a 15-minute timed test; Part II (Comprehension and Rate) is a 20-minute test. The first minute of the

Comprehension Test is used to determine reading rate. A unique feature of this edition is the extended-time administration of the test to meet the needs of special populations. Other changes from previous editions include a reduction in the number of vocabulary items from 100 to 80 and inclusion of 7 rather than 8 reading comprehension passages. Special norms are available for the extended-time administration and for law-enforcement academies.

Format: Examiner required; suitable for group use; 35 minutes standard or 56 minutes extended

Scoring: Hand key; may be machine scored

Cost: Contact publisher

Publisher: Riverside Publishing Company

PSB Reading Comprehension Examination

Copyright: 1993

Population: Health occupations students

Purpose: Measures an individual's ability to understand material read; used to identify students in the health professions who need counseling or remedial assistance

Description: Multiple-item paper–pencil test sampling essential functional elements of reading comprehension. It is specifically designed for secondary, postsecondary, and professional programs and may be used as an adjunct to PSB tests in practical nursing, health occupations, and nursing.

Format: Examiner required; suitable for group use; timed: 60 minutes

Scoring: Machine scored

Cost: Reusable test booklets $7.00; answer sheets (scoring and reporting service) $5.00

Publisher: Psychological Services Bureau, Inc.

Test of Basic Literacy in the Sotho Languages

Copyright: 1982

Population: Adults

Purpose: Assesses the literacy skills of adults in the South Sotho, North Sotho, and Tswana languages; also used to assess higher primary level students

Description: Series of three multiple-item paper–pencil tests assessing proficiency in the South Sotho, North Sotho, and Tswana languages. Each language is covered in a separate test, and each test is available in two forms, I and II. All forms contain three subtests: Reading Comprehension (items relate to practical knowledge or coping skills), Reading Comprehension (items cover a continuous prose passage and a letter written in cursive script), and Writing Skill (dictation items and form completion). Subtests may be administered separately. Questions are answered directly in the test booklets.

Format: Examiner required; suitable for group use; untimed: 1 hour 30 minutes

Scoring: Examiner evaluated

Cost: Contact publisher

Publisher: Human Sciences Research Council

Multiple Level

American Literacy Profile Scales
Patrick Griffin, Patricia Smith, Lois Burrill

Copyright: 1995

Population: Primary to middle school students

Purpose: Describes students' accumulation of literacy related to behaviors and attributes; serves as a framework for authentic assessment

Description: The scales provide a manageable way of observing, interpreting, and recording children's progress. They merge assessment and teaching to map indicators of progress in nine levels, from primary to middle school. The instruments were developed with educators in Australia and the United States.

Format: Individual

Scoring: Examiner interpretation

Cost: Contact publisher

Publisher: Heinemann Educational Books, Inc.

Bench Mark Measures
Aylett Cox

Copyright: 1986

Population: Children, adolescents

Purpose: Assesses a student's general phonic knowledge, including reading, alphabet and dictionary skills, handwriting, and spelling, as a means of diagnosing particular deficiencies and to gauge progress during remediation

Description: Three paper–pencil verbal tests arranged in sequence to cover four areas of remedial language: alphabet and dictionary skills, reading, handwriting, and spelling. The alphabet and reading sections must be administered individually, but the handwriting and spelling schedules may be administered to groups. A Guide to Bench Mark Measures contains testing, scoring, and interpretation information. Designed for use with the Alphabetic Phonics Curriculum, but can be used independently.

Format: Individual and group (last 2 sections); 30 minutes to 1 hour for each of the 4 levels

Scoring: Examiner administration and interpretation

Cost: $64.40

Publisher: Educators Publishing Service, Inc.

Composition Profile
Holly Jacobs, Jane B. Hughey,
V. Faye Hartfiel, Deanna R. Wormuth

Copyright: 1995

Population: All ages

Purpose: Assesses proficiency, mastery, and diagnostic growth or progress in written composition

Description: One-item computer-administered paper–pencil criterion-referenced essay verbal-production test. Content, organization, vocabulary, language use, and mechanics are the profiles available. Forms available are English: Levels I, II, III; English as a second language: Forms A, B, C, Spanish, French. Available in Spanish and French.

Format: Examiner required; individual/group administered; timed/untimed

Scoring: Examiner evaluated; scoring service available from publisher

Cost: $4.00–$25.00

Publisher: Writing Evaluation Systems, Inc.

CTB Writing Assessment System®

Copyright: 1993

Population: Grades 2 through 12

Purpose: Assesses reading-related and independent writing skills in Grades 2–12

Description: Multiple-item paper–pencil essay test used independently or combined with CAT/5 results. The test offers two kinds of writing assignments or prompts: independent and reading-related. Independent prompts test writing ability independent of the ability to comprehend a reading passage. Reading-related prompts combine reading comprehension with writing tasks to reflect the whole-language instructional approach. Writing tasks elicit one of the following types of writing: personal expression (narrative or descriptive), informative, or persuasive. The assessment has four levels between the Grades 2 and 12.

Format: Examiner required; suitable for group use; timed: time varies by level/type

Scoring: Examiner evaluated; scoring service available

Cost: 30 tests and scoring service $33.80/writing type

Publisher: CTB/McGraw-Hill

Degrees of Reading Power® (DRP)

Copyright: 1995

Population: Children, adolescents, adults; Grades 1 through 12, college

Purpose: Assesses reading comprehension of students; used to identify and place students in reading programs, assess reading goals and standards, relate reading ability to functional reading situations, and make admission decisions

Description: Multiple-item multiple-choice text-referenced paper–pencil test in which students read a series of nonfiction prose passages, each with seven deleted words. Students supply the missing words from among five choices provided for each deletion. The passages progress from easy to difficult. The test yields six scores: raw score, independent level score (indicates the difficulty of textbooks the student can read with a 90% chance of understanding the material), three instructional level scores (70%, 75%, and 80% chance of student comprehending materials), and frustration level score (indicates probability of comprehension of 50% or less). Percentile ranks and NCEs are available for Grades 1–12. The test is available in two alternate series, G and H, for Grades 1–12.

Format: Examiner required; suitable for group use; untimed: about 1 class period

Scoring: Hand key; scoring service available from publisher

Cost: DRP Examination Set $35.00; 30 Primary (machine-scorable) Booklets $80.00; 30 Standard DRP Test Booklets $60.00; handbook $25.50; norms $21.50; scoring key $13.00; basic scoring: Primary (machine-scorable booklet) $2.60 and Standard $1.70

Publisher: Touchstone Applied Science Associates, Inc.

Degrees of Word Meaning (DWM)

Copyright: 1993

Population: Children, adolescents; Grades 3 through 9

Purpose: Used in literary assessment to measure the size of students' reading vocabularies

Description: Multiple-choice 40-item paper–pencil criterion-referenced test. M-2 through M-7 are available.

Format: Examiner required; suitable for group use; untimed: 45–50 minutes

Scoring: Hand key, machine scored; test scoring service available from publisher

Cost: DWM Examination Set $35.00; 30 test booklets $46.00; answer sheets $14.50; user's manual $32.00; scoring key $13.00; basic scoring $1.70

Publisher: Touchstone Applied Science Associates

Diagnostic Assessments of Reading with Trial Teaching Strategies (DARTTS)

Copyright: 1992

Population: Pre-reading through high school

Purpose: Assesses reading skills and provides instructional materials

Description: The DARTTS Program Kit is packaged in a file box. The program box contains one each of the DAR and TTS Teacher's Manuals, DAR Student Book, TTS envelopes A–J, and StoryBooks 1–6. Also included are one package of 15 each of the consumable materials: the DAR response record with Directions for Administration, the DAR student record booklet, and the TTS record booklet. Teacher's manuals provide general information about the tests plus complete directions for scoring the tests and recording results; TTS Manual suggests ways to interpret the DAR results with students, provides model case studies, and describes common patterns of strengths and weaknesses in reading. StoryBooks are filled with interesting, high-quality stories, poems, riddles, and sayings at reading Levels 1–6 that are of proven interest even to reluctant readers. The companion book *Creating Successful Readers: A Practical Guide to Testing and Teaching at All Levels* provides the theoretical and research bases for the program and also includes 20 annotated case studies. The book outlines the stages of normal reading development and describes remedies for less-than-average progress.

Format: Individually administered; examiner required

Scoring: Examiner evaluated

Cost: Program Kit $178.00; *Creating Successful Readers: A Practical Guide to Testing and Teaching at All Levels* $27.00

Publisher: Riverside Publishing Company

Diagnostic Screening Test: Language, Second Edition (DSTL)
Thomas D. Gnagey, Patricia A. Gnagey

Copyright: 1980

Population: Children, adolescents; Grades K through 13

Purpose: Determines a student's ability to write English and diagnoses common problems in the use of the language

Description: Multiple-choice 110-item paper–pencil test yielding six scores: total, sentence structure, grammar, punctuation, capitalization, and formal spelling rules. All subtests yield applied versus formal knowledge for a total of 12 scores in all. The examiner explains the procedure to individuals or groups and reads the test if the students have poor reading skills.

Format: Examiner required; suitable for group use; untimed: 5–10 minutes

Scoring: Hand key

Cost: Manual, 50 test forms $50.00

Publisher: Slosson Educational Publications, Inc.

Diagnostic Screening Test: Reading, Third Edition (DSTR)
Thomas D. Gnagey, Particia A. Gnagey

Copyright: 1982

Population: Children, adolescents; Grades 1 through 13

Purpose: Determines reading achievement levels and diagnoses common reading problems by testing word recognition and reading and listening comprehension

Description: Paper–pencil 84-word test yielding two major scores (Word Recognition and Reading Comprehension Grade Equivalents) and eight diagnostic scores that reflect skills in using seven basic word attack skills, as well as sight vocabulary. The student reads a word list and comprehension passages aloud and answers prescribed questions. The examiner then reads a passage aloud and the student answers questions. The test yields a consolidation index which reflects how solid or spotty each skill is.

The test is available in two equivalent forms, A and B.

Format: Examiner required; not suitable for group use; untimed: 5–10 minutes

Scoring: Hand key

Cost: Manual, 25 Form A, 25 Form B $48.00

Publisher: Slosson Educational Publications, Inc.

Diagnostic Screening Test: Spelling, Third Edition (DSTS)
Thomas D. Gnagey

Copyright: 1982

Population: Children, adolescents; Grades 1 through 12

Purpose: Measures a student's ability to spell words and diagnoses common spelling problems

Description: Pencil–paper 78-item test measuring sight or phonics orientation for spelling instruction; relative efficiency of verbal and written testing procedures; analysis of sequential and gross auditory memory; and spelling potential. A pretest is available to determine the appropriate level of entry. The examiner, using the test form, pronounces 78 developmentally arranged words and the student spells them orally; the examiner then repronounces difficult words and the student writes them. When administered to groups, the test yields a grade equivalent score. The test is available in Forms A and B.

Format: Examiner required; suitable for group use; untimed: 5–10 minutes

Scoring: Hand key

Cost: Manual, 25 Form A, 25 Form B $48.00

Publisher: Slosson Educational Publications, Inc.

Diagnostic Spelling Potential Test (DSPT)
John Arena

Copyright: 1982

Population: Ages 7 to adult

Purpose: Provides comprehensive information about spelling skills

Description: Multiple-item paper–pencil test with four subtests: Spelling, Word Recognition, Visual Recognition, and Auditory–Visual Recognition. Standard scores, percentile, and grade equivalents are provided. Results provide a detailed profile that compares spelling efficiency with requisite skills, such as decoding and visual recall. Two parallel forms are available. Three of the four subtests may be given in group format.

Format: Individual or group administration; 25 to 40 minutes

Scoring: Examiner administered and interpreted

Cost: Test Kit (manual, protocols, and analysis charts in vinyl folder) $50.00

Publisher: Academic Therapy Publications

Diagnostic Word Patterns: Tests 1, 2, and 3
Evelyn Buckley

Copyright: 1978

Population: Grades 3 and above

Purpose: Assesses basic phonic knowledge; used to help classroom teachers determine general word attack concepts to review with an entire class and to identify individual students' strengths and weaknesses to develop suitable reading programs

Description: Three verbal paper–pencil 100-word tests, each of which can be used to test spelling and/or word recognition. Can be used as a spelling or word-recognition test. Test 1 deals with short vowels, nonphonetic words, and consonant digraphs. Test 2 covers vowel digraph and diphthong patterns and nonphonetic words. Test 3 contains suffixes, two-syllable words, and more material from Tests 1 and 2.

Format: Spelling—group; Word Recognition—individual; 20 to 45 minutes

Scoring: Examiner administration and evaluation

Cost: Manual $4.60; individual student charts $4.50; cards for word recognition tests $5.15

Publisher: Educators Publishing Service, Inc.

English First and Second Language Tests

Copyright: 1981

Population: All ages

Purpose: Measures understanding of English as a first or second language; used for educational placement and guidance

Description: Nineteen separate paper–pencil tests of English comprehension for each standard or level of pupil. Particular subtests vary but generally include Language Usage, Vocabulary, Reading Comprehension, and Spelling. Two alternate forms, A and B, are available for each standard.

Format: Examiner required; suitable for group use; untimed: typical time not available

Scoring: Hand key; examiner evaluated

Cost: Contact publisher

Publisher: Human Sciences Research Council

ERB Writing Assessment Program (WAP)

Copyright: 1989

Population: Children, adolescents; Grades 3 through 12

Purpose: Assesses writing skills in six areas: Topic Development, Organization, Support, Sentence Structure, Word Choice, Mechanics

Description: Essay test. Use of the test is restricted to ERB member schools.

Format: Individual/group administration; examiner required; untimed: given in two class periods, usually on successive days

Scoring: Analytically scored by ERB readers; norms: Suburban (public) Schools and Independent Schools

Cost: Refer to ERB Test Catalog for prices of WAP test materials and scoring services

Publisher: Educational Records Bureau

Formal Reading Inventory (FRI)
J. Lee Wiederholt

Copyright: 1985

Population: Ages 6 years 6 months to 17 years 11 months

Purpose: Assesses silent reading comprehension and diagnoses the oral reading miscues of students to develop teaching strategies

Description: Multiple-item paper–pencil and oral-response test in four forms assessing reading comprehension and miscues. Each form contains 13 developmentally sequenced passages with five literal, inferential, critical, and affective multiple-choice questions following each story. Form A is used to derive a silent reading quotient. Form B, read orally by the student and marked by the examiner on a separate worksheet, is used to note reading behaviors, including comprehension strategies, appropriate grammar forms, word attack strategies, self-correction strategies, omissions, additions, dialect, and reversals. Form C (silent) and Form D (oral) are used as posttests.

Format: Individual administration

Scoring: Examiner evaluated

Cost: Complete Kit (manual, student book, record forms, and storage box) $89.00

Publisher: PRO-ED, Inc.

Gates MacGinitie Reading Test, Second Canadian Edition (GMRT)
Walter MacGinitie

Copyright: 1992

Population: Children, adolescents; Grades K through 12

Purpose: Measures student's reading and vocabulary achievement levels; used for placement and class planning

Description: Multiple-item paper–pencil test of vocabulary and reading comprehension. The basic Level R contains 54 items. Levels A–F contain 85–89 items.

Format: Examiner required; suitable for group use; timed: 55 minutes; untimed: (Level R) 65 minutes

Scoring: Hand key; may be computer scored

Cost: 35 booklets $36.95; manual $22.50; key $4.95

Publisher: Nelson Canada

Gates-MacGinitie Reading Tests, Third Edition

Walter H. MacGinitie, Ruth K. MacGinitie

Copyright: 1989

Population: Grades K through 12

Purpose: Measures reading achievement; used to identify students who would benefit from remedial or accelerated programs, to evaluate instructional programs, and to counsel students and report progress to parents

Description: Multiple-item paper–pencil test assessing reading comprehension and vocabulary development. The test is available on nine levels: PRE (Grade K), R (Grade 1), 1 (Grade 1.3–1.9), 2 (Grade 2), 3 (Grade 3), 4 (Grade 4), 5/6 (Grades 5–6), 7/9 (Grades 7–9), and 10/12 (Grades 10–12). Level PRE is a readiness test that assesses the student's knowledge of important background concepts on which beginning reading skills are built. Level R measures beginning reading achievement in four skill areas: Initial Consonants and Consonant Clusters, Final Consonant and Consonant Clusters, Vowels, and Use of Context. Test levels 1 through 10/12 each include two tests—a vocabulary test and a comprehension test.

Format: Examiner required; suitable for group use; timed: time varies per level

Scoring: Hand key; may be machine scored

Cost: Contact publisher for current prices

Publisher: Riverside Publishing Company

Gray Oral Reading Tests–Diagnostic (GORT–D)

Brian R. Bryant, J. Lee Wiederholt

Copyright: 1991

Population: Ages 5 years 6 months through 12 years 11 months

Purpose: Evaluates specific abilities and weaknesses in reading

Description: Multiple-item test that uses two alternate equivalent forms to assess students' specific abilities and weaknesses. There are seven subtests that are organized under the three major cue systems believed to affect reading proficiency: meaning cues, function cues, and graphic/phonemic cues. Paragraph Reading requires the student to orally read passages and respond to comprehension questions. If the student performs poorly on the first subtest, the remaining subtests are administered: Decoding (Consonant/Cluster Recognition, Phonogram Recognition, Blending), Word Identification Attack, Morphemic Analysis, Contextual Analysis, and Word Ordering. Standardized scores are provided for the three components and a composite.

Format: Individual administration; 15–30 minutes

Scoring: Examiner evaluated

Cost: Complete kit (manual, student book, Forms A and B, and storage box) $139.00

Publisher: PRO-ED, Inc.

Gray Oral Reading Tests–Third Edition (GORT–3)

J. Lee Wiederholt, Brian R. Bryant

Copyright: 1992

Population: Ages 7 years through 18 years 11 months

Purpose: Measures growth in oral reading and diagnoses reading difficulties in students

Description: Multiple-item oral-response test in two alternate, equivalent forms. The student reads 13 developmentally sequenced passages and responds to five comprehension questions. The Passage Score, derived from reading rate and errors, and the Oral Reading Comprehension score are reported as standard scores, percentiles, and grade equivalents. A system of miscue analysis provides criterion information in Meaning Similarity, Function Similarity, Graphic/Phonemic Similarity, and Self-Correction. A total score for Oral Reading is also provided.

Format: Individual administration; 15–30 minutes

Scoring: Examiner evaluation

Cost: Complete kit (manual, student book, Form A and B protocols, and storage box) $139.00

Publisher: PRO-ED, Inc.

Integrated Literature and Language Arts Portfolio Program
Nambury Raju

Copyright: 1991

Population: Grades 2 through 8

Purpose: Assesses students' reading and language arts proficiency

Description: The Integrated Literature and Language Arts Portfolio Program offers a performance assessment that uses intact selections of authentic literature and an open-ended testing format. It focuses on listening and speaking as well as reading and writing. Each assessment includes an Individual Student's Interest and Experience Survey and performance exercises. Performance exercises provide three selections from literature, one to be read aloud by the teacher and two—one fiction and the other nonfiction—to be read by the student. Selection-related test items follow an interactive model of listening/reading. Items are designed to focus on prior knowledge/predicting content, reading strategies, passage-relevant vocabulary, and constructing meaning. Emphasis is placed on higher-order thinking skills. The performance-based format provides special opportunities for the evaluation of student writing. All items have been reviewed to eliminate bias or stereotyping.

Format: Group administered; examiner required; three 45-minute sessions

Scoring: Examiner evaluated

Cost: Student Activity Booklets (two forms each for Levels 2–8 allow for pre- and posttesting; pkg. of 25, includes teacher's Directions and Class Record Form) $46.00 each level. Student Activity Booklet Scoring Guide $9.00 each level

Publisher: Riverside Publishing Company

Iowa Writing Assessment
H. D. Hoover, A. N. Hieronymus,
D. A. Frisbie, S. B. Dunbar, L. S. Feldt,
R. A. Forsyth, T. N. Ansley, S. D. Alnot

Copyright: 1994

Population: Grades 3 through 12 (Levels 9–18)

Purpose: Assesses students' ability to generate, organize, and express ideas in a variety of written forms

Description: Measures students' ability to generate, organize, and express ideas in four different modes of discourse: narrative, descriptive, persuasive, and expository. Used in conjunction with the ITBS, TAP, and ITED, the Iowa Writing Assessment provides a measure of students' productive writing skills in response to specific writing tasks.

Format: Group administration; examiner required; 50 minutes

Scoring: Examiner evaluated

Cost: Classroom Test Packages (directions and testing materials for 25 students) $31.50 each level/writing mode; Manual for Scoring and Interpretation $17.00 each level/writing mode

Publisher: Riverside Publishing Company

McCarthy Individualized Diagnostic Reading Inventory
William G. McCarthy

Copyright: 1976

Population: Grades 2 and above

Purpose: Diagnoses the development of specific areas of reading skills for placement and the selection of appropriate instructional materials

Description: Eleven brief reading selections ranked from primer to Grade 12, read by the student to the examiner. The factors measured are oral reading, reading comprehension, critical thinking skills, vocabulary, phonics, word recognition, sight vocabulary, and study skills. The last part of the test moves into prescription by providing structure to develop a preliminary plan for reading instruction based on the information gained in the inventory.

Format: Individual; 1 to 1½ hours

Scoring: Examiner administration and interpretation

Cost: Information Booklet $2.90; Teacher Administration Booklet $7.70; Pupil Booklet $2.00; record forms $8.85

Publisher: Educators Publishing Service, Inc.

Metropolitan Achievement Tests™, Sixth Edition Language Diagnostic Tests

Irving H. Balow, Thomas P. Hogan, Roger C. Farr, George A. Prescott

Copyright: 1986

Population: Children, adolescents; Grades 1 through 9

Purpose: Assesses basic skill areas in language arts; used for providing prescriptive information on educational performance of individual pupils

Description: Multiple-item series of paper–pencil tests measuring major components of language arts skills, including listening comprehension, punctuation and capitalization, usage, grammar and syntax, spelling, and study skills. The test is divided into five levels: Primary 1 and 2, Elementary, Intermediate, and Advanced 1. Suitable for Title 1 use. Clusters of related objectives help teachers determine the level of instruction for optimal growth.

Format: Examiner required; suitable for group use; timed: time varies

Scoring: Scoring service available

Cost: Examination Kit $14.50

Publisher: Harcourt® Brace Educational Measurement

Metropolitan Achievement Tests™, Sixth Edition Reading Diagnostic Tests

Roger C. Farr, George A. Prescott, Irving H. Balow, Thomas P. Hogan

Copyright: 1986

Population: Children; Grades K through 9

Purpose: Measures reading skills; used for providing prescriptive information on the educational performance of individual pupils

Description: Multiple-item series of paper–pencil tests measuring major components of reading skills, including visual discrimination, letter recognition, auditory discrimination, letter recognition, auditory discrimination, sight vocabulary, phoneme/grapheme: consonants, phoneme/grapheme: vowels, vocabulary in context, word-part clues, rate of comprehension, skimming and scanning, and reading comprehension. The test is divided into six levels: Primer, Primary 1 and 2, Elementary, Intermediate, and Advanced 1. Suitable for Title 1 use. Clusters of related objectives help teachers determine the level of instruction for optimal growth.

Format: Examiner required; suitable for group use; timed: time varies

Scoring: Hand key; may be machine scored; scoring service available

Cost: Examination Kit $14.50

Publisher: Harcourt® Brace Educational Measurement

Metropolitan Achievement Test™, Seventh Edition (MAT™7)

Copyright: 1992

Population: Children, adolescents; Grades K through 12

Purpose: Assesses school achievement; used for measuring performance of large groups of students

Description: Multiple-choice paper–pencil tests of school achievement divided into 14 levels: Preprimer, Primer, Primary 1 and 2, Elementary 1 and 2, Intermediate 1, 2, 3, and 4, and Secondary 1, 2, 3, and 4. The Basic Battery for all levels consists of tests in reading vocabulary, reading comprehension, mathematics, and language. The Complete Battery for the Primary 1 through the Advanced 1 levels also includes social studies and science tests. Materials include two alternate and equivalent forms. MAT™7 Short Form is an abridged version, but it takes only 30 minutes to administer each of 3 tests (Reading Comprehension, Mathematics Concepts and Problem Solving, and Language.)

Format: Examiner required; suitable for group use; timed: varies from 1 hour 35 minutes for kindergarten to 4 hours 10 minutes for Grades 6 through 9

Scoring: Hand key; may be machine/computer scored; scoring service available

Cost: Examination Kit $16.50 for each level

Publisher: Harcourt® Brace Educational Measurement

Michigan Prescriptive Program in English (Grammar)
William E. Lockhart

Copyright: 1996

Population: Grade 6 to adults

Purpose: Measures English grammar, punctuation, spelling, and word usage (synonyms, homonyms, antonyms) abilities to identify skill deficits

Description: Multiple-item paper–pencil test measuring the following high school–level English grammar skills: capitalization, subjects, verbs, verb tense, moods, prepositions, case, possessive and indefinite pronouns, adjectives, adverbs, punctuation, synonyms, homonyms, plurals, and spelling. This pretest accompanies a program that provides remediation that is used to help students obtain a 10th-grade equivalency to pass the GED test in English grammar.

Format: Individual and group administration

Scoring: Examiner administered and interpreted

Cost: English Study Guide $10.00; 10 Pre-test Booklets $15.00; 10 Response and Prescriptive Sheets $8.00; Scoring Template $3.00

Publisher: Academic Therapy Publications

National Achievement Tests: English, Reading, Literature, and Vocabulary Tests—Reading
Robert K. Speer, Samuel Smith

Copyright: 1961

Population: Adolescents, adults; Grades 7 and above

Purpose: Assesses students' reading achievement; used to identify student strengths and weaknesses as part of an educational evaluation

Description: Multiple-item paper–pencil test of reading skills important for achievement, including vocabulary, word discrimination, sentence meaning, noting details, and interpreting paragraphs. Two equivalent forms, A and B, are available.

Format: Examiner required; suitable for group use; timed: 40 minutes

Scoring: Hand key

Cost: Specimen Set (test, manual, key) $5.00; 25 tests $13.75

Publisher: Psychometric Affiliates

National Achievement Tests: English, Reading, Literature, and Vocabulary Tests—Vocabulary (Grades 3–8)
Robert K. Speer, Samuel Smith

Copyright: 1961

Population: Children, adolescents; Grades 3 through 8

Purpose: Assesses the vocabulary knowledge of children; used as part of an educational evaluation

Description: Multiple-item paper–pencil test of vocabulary knowledge. For each item, the base word is printed in capital letters in a meaningful sentence. The pupil selects a synonym for the base word from a group of words. The base words are more difficult than synonyms. Two equivalent forms, A and B, are available.

Format: Examiner required; suitable for group use; timed: 15 minutes

Scoring: Hand key

Cost: Specimen Set (test, manual, key) $4.00; 25 tests $3.50

Publisher: Psychometric Affiliates

National Achievement Tests: English, Reading, Literature, and Vocabulary Tests—Vocabulary (Grade 7–College)
Robert K. Speer, Samuel Smith

Copyright: 1971

Population: Adolescents; Grades 7 and above

Purpose: Assesses students' vocabulary knowledge; used as part of an educational evaluation

Description: Multiple-item paper–pencil test measuring knowledge and judgment related to word meaning and word discrimination. Two equivalent forms, A and B, are available.

Format: Examiner required; suitable for group use; timed: 15 minutes

Scoring: Hand key

Cost: Specimen Set (test, manual, key) $4.00; 25 tests $3.50

Publisher: Psychometric Affiliates

Neale Analysis of Reading Ability–Revised
M. D. Neale

Copyright: 1989

Population: Children, adolescents; ages 5 years 6 months to 11 years 11 months

Purpose: Assesses the reading ability of children and adolescents; used by teachers for diagnostic purposes; suitable for use with students with learning disabilities

Description: Series of reading passages that the student reads aloud. The test is available in two parallel forms, Form 1 and Form 2, and a Diagnostic Tutor Form that extends test options. The test yields stanine and percentile rank and range scores, Neale (Rasch) scale scores, and reading ages. This test is a revised version of the Neale Analysis of Reading Ability published by Macmillan Education.

Format: Examiner required; not suitable for group use; untimed: 30 minutes

Scoring: Hand key; examiner evaluated

Cost: Contact publisher

Publisher: The Australian Council for Educational Research Limited

Nelson Reading Skills Tests: Forms 3 and 4
Gerald S. Hanna, Leo M. Schell, Robert L. Schreiner

Copyright: 1977

Population: Grades 3 through 9

Purpose: Assesses student achievement and progress in word attack skills, vocabulary, reading comprehension, and reading rate

Description: Paper–pencil multiple-choice survey test. Two parallel forms, each with three test levels, are available. All three test levels have a Word Meaning (Vocabulary) test and a Reading Comprehension test. An optional Word Parts test for Grades 3–4 (Level A) permits diagnosis of students' decoding skills, including sound/symbol correspondence, root words, and syllabication. An optional Reading Rate test is available for Grades 5–6 and 7–9 (Levels B and C). A short Comprehension subtest is provided with the Reading Rate test to check comprehension of the reading rate passage.

Format: Examiner required; suitable for group use; 35–56 minutes

Scoring: Hand key; may be machine scored

Cost: Contact publisher for current prices

Publisher: Riverside Publishing Company

New Assessments for Teaching and Learning (NAT'L or "National")

Copyright: 1995

Population: Children, adolescents; Grades 3 through 11

Purpose: Assesses students in a standards-based, performance-based manner; provides classroom-based assessment of reading and writing; prepares students for state, performance-based assessments

Description: Multiple-item paper–pencil short-answer/essay test covering Reading/ Language Arts that measures informative and literary tasks. Three assessment sections (reading, group work, and writing) are administered in three separate sessions. Activities are based on the following: initial understanding, developing understanding, personal response, critical evaluation, learning together, and extended writing.

Format: Examiner required; suitable for group use; untimed: minimum time 45 minutes per section

Scoring: Examiner evaluated

Cost: Literary or Informative Tasks Package (includes 35 test booklets and a teacher's guide and scoring guidelines) $56.95; available in Elementary (Grades 3–5), Middle Grade (Grades 6–8), and High School (Grades 9–11)

Publisher: CTB/McGraw-Hill

Reading Efficiency Tests
Lyle L. Miller

Copyright: 1982

Population: Adolescents, adults; Grades 7 and above

Purpose: Measures pre- and posttesting of reading rate, comprehension, and efficiency

Description: Five tests that include content on history, geography, government, culture, and the people of Brazil, Japan, India, New Zealand, and Switzerland. Each reading test contains 5,000 words, and each line of the test is numbered. Each answer sheet contains 50 items about the content of the reading selection. When the timed test is stopped, each student marks the line on which he or she was reading and is tested only on the material read.

Format: Examiner required; suitable for group use; timed: 10 minutes per test

Scoring: Hand key

Cost: 20 booklets $15.00; 20 answer sheets $5.00; Specimen Set $5.00

Publisher: Developmental Reading Distributors

Slosson Oral Reading Test–Revised (SORT–R)
Richard L. Slosson, Charles L. Nicholson

Copyright: 1990

Population: Children, adolescents; Grades 1 through 12

Purpose: Measures reading ability and identifies reading handicaps

Description: Oral screening test providing an estimate of a person's word-recognition level. The SORT–R is based on the ability to pronounce words at different levels of difficulty, primer through high school.

Format: Examiner required; not suitable for group use; untimed: 3–5 minutes

Scoring: Examiner evaluated

Cost: Complete $48.00

Publisher: Slosson Educational Publications, Inc.

Sort-A-Sentence Test (SAST)
Alan M. Brimer

Copyright: 1994

Population: Children, adolescents; ages 7 to 18

Purpose: Assesses reading comprehension for reading skills

Description: Multiple-choice 64-item paper–pencil test yielding standardized scores and percentiles. Examiner must be a teacher or psychologist. Two forms, A and B, are used.

Format: Group administration; timed: 25 minutes

Scoring: Hand key, computer scored; test scoring service available from publisher

Cost: £28 Sterling

Publisher: Educational Evaluation Enterprises/ Irish Educational Research Centre

South African Written Language Test (SAWLT)

Copyright: 1981

Population: Grades II–Standard 5

Purpose: Measures written language ability of

English-speaking primary school students; used for educational guidance

Description: Test of written language requiring the subject to write a passage in response to a stimulus photo. Materials include the stimulus photo, which should be provided to each subject in group administrations.

Format: Examiner required; suitable for group use; untimed: 30 minutes

Scoring: Hand key; examiner evaluated

Cost: Contact publisher

Publisher: Human Sciences Research Council

Spadafore Diagnostic Reading Test (SDRT)
Gerald J. Spadafore

Copyright: 1983

Population: Age 6 to adult

Purpose: Assesses reading skills of students in Grades 1–12 and adults; used as a screening and diagnostic instrument for academic placement and career guidance counseling

Description: Four subtests assess word recognition, oral reading and comprehension, silent reading comprehension, and listening comprehension. Criterion-referenced test items are graded for difficulty. Independent, Instructional, and Frustration reading and comprehension levels are designated for performance at each grade level. Test results may be used for screening to determine whether reading problems exist at a student's current grade placement. Administration for diagnostic purposes requires 30 minutes for all four subtests and yields a comparison of decoding reading skills. Guidelines are provided for interpreting performance in terms of vocational literacy. Provisions for conducting a detailed error analysis of oral reading are included.

Format: Individual administration; screening 30 minutes, diagnosis 1 hour

Scoring: Examiner administered and evaluated

Cost: Test kit (manual, test plates, 10 test booklets) $55.00

Publisher: Academic Therapy Publications

Spellmaster Assessment and Teaching System
Claire R. Greenbaum

Copyright: 1987

Population: All ages

Purpose: Measures spelling abilities and diagnoses individual and group spelling difficulties; used to plan instructional and remedial spelling programs and provide direct teaching for classroom teachers and qualified professionals

Description: Multiple-item paper–pencil tests measuring eight levels of spelling abilities corresponding to grade levels 1–8. Regular word tests, irregular word tests, and homophone tests are provided for all levels. Entry-level tests are provided to determine the appropriate level of regular word, irregular word, and homophone tests to administer to each student. The Regular Word tests (Levels 1–2, 20 words each; Levels 3–8, 40 words each) are criterion-referenced diagnostic tests, each featuring a unique scoring form that identifies specific erroneous elements within words. The Irregular Words tests (Level 1, 20 words; Levels 2–8, 40 words) measure mastery of frequently used words that violate phonic rules. The Homophone Tests (Level 1, 20 words; Levels 2–8, 40 words) measure mastery of words whose spelling must be learned in conjunction with meaning. The examiner's manual provides instructions for the administration and instructions for the administration and scoring of all tests and contains detailed teaching aids and techniques, analysis of errors, and specific teaching suggestions for each regular phonic and structural element as well as for irregular words and homophones. This test is a revision of the Spellmaster Diagnostic Spelling System.

Format: Examiner required; suitable for group use; untimed: time varies

Scoring: Hand key; examiner evaluated; self-scored

Cost: Complete Kit (examiner's manual, 50 student answer sheets, 8 pads of 25 scoring forms for each diagnostic level [1–8], storage box) $98.00

Publisher: PRO-ED, Inc.

Standardized Reading Inventory (SRI)

Phyllis L. Newcomer

Copyright: 1986

Population: Children, adolescents; Grades 1 through 8

Purpose: Evaluates a student's idiosyncratic reading skills

Description: Criterion-referenced reading test consisting of 10 graded passages containing key words designed to assess oral and silent reading from the preprimer to eighth-grade levels. After reading the passages, the student answers a series of comprehension questions. Each passage yields scores in word recognition and comprehension, revealing the student's independent, instructional, and frustration reading levels. The test is available in two forms, A and B.

Format: Examiner required; not suitable for group use; untimed: typical time not available

Scoring: Hand key; examiner evaluated

Cost: Complete Kit (examiner's manual, student booklet, 50 summary/record sheets, storage box) $89.00

Publisher: PRO-ED, Inc.

Stanford Diagnostic Reading Test, Third Edition (SDRT)

Bjorn Karlsen, Eric F. Gardner

Copyright: 1984

Population: Children, adolescents; Grades 1 through 12

Purpose: Measures major components of the reading process; used for diagnosing specific student needs

Description: Multiple-item paper–pencil test measuring four aspects of reading: comprehension, vocabulary, decoding, and rate. The test is divided into four levels.

Format: Examiner required; suitable for group use; timed: time varies by level

Scoring: Hand key; computer scoring service available

Cost: Examination Kit $27.50

Publisher: Harcourt® Brace Educational Measurement

Test of Inference Ability in Reading Comprehension (TIA)

Linda M. Phillips

Copyright: 1987–1989

Population: Adolescents; ages 11 to 15

Purpose: Measures inference ability in reading comprehension

Description: Paper–pencil 36-item multiple-choice and short-answer test designed to measure a student's inference ability on the basis of full-length passages representative of the three kinds of discourse commonly found at the middle grade levels. Requires fifth-grade reading level.

Format: Group; 30 minutes

Scoring: Evaluator administration and interpretation; machine scoring available from publisher

Cost: Test (set of 35) $35.00; manual $10.00; technical report $12.00

Publisher: Faculty of Education, Memorial University of Newfoundland

Test of Reading Comprehension–Third Edition (TORC–3)

Virginia L. Brown, Donald D. Hammill, J. Lee Wiederholt

Copyright: 1995

Population: Children, adolescents; Grades 2 through 12

Purpose: Assesses students' reading comprehension; used to diagnose reading problems in terms of current psycholinguistic theories of reading comprehension as a constructive process involving both language and cognition

Description: Eight multiple-item paper–pencil subtests measuring aspects of reading comprehension. Three of the subtests (General Vocabulary, Syntactic Similarities, and Paragraph Reading) are combined to determine a basic Comprehension Core, which is expressed as a Reading Comprehension Quotient (RCQ). Three subtests measure students' abilities to read the vocabularies of math, science, and social studies. Subtest 7, Reading the Directions of Schoolwork, is a diagnostic tool for younger or remedial students. The eighth subtest is Sentence Sequences. Scaled scores are provided for each subtest.

Format: Examiner required; not suitable for group use; untimed: 1 hour 45 minutes

Scoring: Hand key

Cost: Complete Kit (examiner's manual, 50 answer sheet and Subtest 8 forms, 50 profile/examiner record forms, 10 student booklets, storage box) $134.00

Publisher: PRO-ED, Inc.

Test of Written Expression (TOWE)
Ron McGhee, Brian R. Bryant, Stephen C. Larsen, Diane M. Rivera

Copyright: 1995

Population: Ages 6 years 6 months through 14 years 11 months

Purpose: Provides a comprehensive assessment of writing achievement

Description: The TOWE uses two assessment methods to evaluate a student's writing skills. The first method involves administering a series of 76 items that tap different skills associated with writing. The second method requires students to read or hear a prepared story starter and use it as a stimulus for writing an essay (i.e., the beginning of the story is provided, and the writer continues the story to its conclusion). The TOWE provides an excellent source of writing samples that can be used independently in a norm-referenced assessment of writing or as a component of a student's portfolio of written products. The 76 items assess a broad array of writing skills (i.e., ideation, vocabulary, grammar, capitalization, punctuation, and spelling) to determine the students' general writing proficiency. The overall writing score derived can be converted to normative data. Examiners also can conduct an item analysis to examine strengths and weaknesses across the content assessed by the items. In the second method of assessment, a storyteller is provided to the student, who writes a completion of the tale.

Format: Individual administration; suitable for group use; timed: time varies

Scoring: Examiner evaluated

Cost: Complete Kit (examiner's manual, 25 profile/examiner record forms, 25 student booklets, storage box) $109.00

Publisher: PRO-ED, Inc.

Test of Written Language–Third Edition (TOWL–3)
Donald D. Hammill, Stephen C. Larsen

Copyright: 1988

Population: Children, adolescents; ages 7 to 17; Grades 2 through 12

Purpose: Identifies students who have problems in written expression and pinpoints specific areas of deficit; also useful for documenting progress and conducting research; may be used with language and communication disabilities and students in special education.

Description: Paper–pencil free-response test in which students write a story about a given theme. The test yields information in eight areas of writing competence, in contrived and spontaneous formats: Vocabulary, Spelling, Style, Logical Sentences, Sentence Combining, Contextual Conventions, Contextual Language, and Story Construction. The information is derived from an analysis of a sample of continuous writing, as well as from an analysis of subtest performance. Subtest raw scores, standard scores, percentiles, a Contrived Writing Quotient, Spontaneous Writing Quotient, and Overall Written Language Quotient are generated. The test is available in Forms A and B.

Format: Examiner required; suitable for group use; untimed: 90 minutes

Scoring: Examiner evaluated; computer scored

Cost: Complete Kit (examiner's manual, 25 student response booklets A, 25 student response booklets B, and 50 profile/story scoring forms, storage box) $159.00

Publisher: PRO-ED, Inc.

Test of Written Spelling–Third Edition (TWS–3)
Stephen C. Larsen, Donald D. Hammill

Copyright: 1994

Population: Children, adolescents; ages 6 years 7 months to 18 years 6 months

Purpose: Measures students' spelling abilities by using both words that are easily predictable by their sound and words that are more irregular; identifies the spelling strengths and weaknesses of students, identifies words to be studied, and measures progress

Description: Paper–pencil 100-item test assessing student spelling performance with three groups of words: words readily predictable in sound-spelling pattern, words less predictable, and both types of words presented together. Standard scores and percentiles are provided for each of the three groups. In addition, a Written Spelling Quotient, a Predictable Words Quotient, and an Unpredictable Words Quotient are calculated. Test items were developed after review of 2,000 spelling rules, with words drawn from 10 basal spelling programs. Braille typing is available for individuals with visual disabilities.

Format: Examiner required; suitable for group use; untimed: 20 minutes

Scoring: Examiner evaluated

Cost: Complete Kit (examiner's manual, 50 summary/response forms, storage box) $69.00

Publisher: PRO-ED, Inc.

Tests of Reading Comprehension (TORCH)
L. Mossenson, P. Hill, G. Masters

Copyright: 1989

Population: Children, adolescents; Grades 3 through 10

Purpose: Assesses the extent to which a student is able to obtain meaning from text

Description: Multiple-item paper–pencil modified–cloze-response reading comprehension test yielding both diagnostic and achievement information. The test consists of 14 passages of graded difficulty. Each passage contains approximately 24 items. The test yields both stanine and percentile rank scores and TORCH (Rasch) scale scores.

Format: Examiner required; suitable for group use; untimed: 30 minutes

Scoring: Hand key; examiner evaluated

Cost: Contact publisher; complete kit must be initial purchase

Publisher: The Australian Council for Educational Research Limited

Woodcock Reading Mastery Tests–Revised (WRMT–R)
Richard W. Woodcock

Copyright: 1987

Population: Ages 5 to 75

Purpose: Used for screening and to provide an in-depth diagnosis of reading skills

Description: WRMT–R is a comprehensive individual assessment of reading ability. WRMT–R is available in two parallel forms: Forms G and H. Test/subtest names: Test 1, Visual–Auditory Learning (Form G), measures ability to form associations between visual stimuli and oral responses. Test 2, Letter Identification (Form G), measures ability to identify letters presented in uppercase or lowercase forms. Supplementary Letter Checklist (Form G) is used to determine which letters the subject can name or identify by sound. Test 3, Word Identification, requires the subject to identify isolated words that appear in large type on the subject pages in the test easel. Test 4, Word Attack, requires the subject to read either nonsense words or words with a very low frequency of occurrence in English. It measures ability to apply phonic and structural analysis skills to pronounce unfamiliar words. Test 5, Word Comprehension, measures reading vocabulary at several different levels of cognitive processing and consists of three subtests: Antonyms, Synonyms, and Analogies. Test 6, Passage Comprehension, measures ability to identify a key word.

Format: Individual administration; 10–30 minutes for each cluster of tests

Scoring: Examiner interpreted, standard scores (age and grade based), age and grade equivalents; ASSIST computer scoring available for DOS, Macintosh, and Windows

Cost: Combined Kit (Form G and H test books, 25 each Form G and H test records, sample Form G and H summary record form, pronunciation guide cassette, sample report to parents, examiner's manual) $299.95

Publisher: American Guidance Service

Woodcock-Muñoz Language Survey, English Form, Spanish Form

Richard W. Woodcock,
Ana F. Muñoz-Sandoval

Copyright: 1993

Population: Age 4 to adult

Purpose: To provide a broad sampling of proficiency in oral language, reading, and writing

Description: Use of the English Form in conjunction with the Spanish Form enables examiners to obtain information on which of the two languages is dominant and information regarding the subject's proficiency in each language compared to others at the same age or grade level. The Language Surveys provide a means for classifying a subject's language proficiency into five levels based on proficiency with language tasks. This gives examiners a sound procedure for classification of a subject's English or Spanish language proficiency, for determining eligibility for bilingual services, and for assessing a subject's progress or readiness for English-only instruction. Age and grade equivalents can be obtained directly from the test record. Percentile ranks, standard scores, and relative mastery indexes can be obtained through use of the Scoring and Reporting Program which comes with the test.

Format: Individually administered; examiner required; 20 minutes

Scoring: Examiner evaluated; computer Scoring and Reporting Program

Cost: Complete Program, English or Spanish

Form (comprehensive manual, 25 test records, and test book with Scoring and Reporting Program disk[s]) $159.00

Publisher: Riverside Publishing Company

Word Meaning Through Reading—WM(R)

Copyright: 1995

Population: Children, adolescents; ages 7 to 16

Purpose: Measures reading vocabulary to be used in conjunction with WM(L)

Description: 60 items, two forms: A and B

Format: Examiner required; group administration; untimed: 20 minutes

Scoring: Scoring service available from publisher

Cost: £8.60 Sterling

Publisher: Educational Evaluation Enterprises

Written Language Assessment (WLA)

J. Jeffrey Grill, M. M. Kirwin

Copyright: 1989

Population: Ages 8 to 18 and older

Purpose: Assesses written language

Description: Essay test offering direct assessment of written language through an evaluation of writing samples that reflect three modes of discourse: expressive, instructive, and creative writing. Analytic scoring techniques are used to yield scores in General Writing Ability, Productivity, Word Complexity, and Readability. A Written Language Quotient that is a composite of the four subscores is also reported. Raw scores for the four subskill areas and the Written Language Quotient can be converted to scaled scores and percentile ranks and plotted on the scoring/profile form.

Format: Individual or group administration; 1 hour

Scoring: Examiner administered and interpreted

Cost: Test kit (manual, 25 each of three Writing Record Forms, 25 Scoring/Profile Forms, and Hand Counter, in vinyl folder) $60.00

Publisher: Academic Therapy Publications

Religious

ACT PEP RCE: Arts and Sciences: Religions of the World

Copyright: 1994

Population: Adults; college level

Purpose: Used by adults wanting to earn college credit by examination; assesses knowledge of major world religions in social and historical content

Description: Essay test with three extended-response questions. Two forms are available. A test booklet, answer sheet, and pen are used. A college reading level is required. Examiner must have experience as a college test administrator. Available in large print. May be used for individuals with visual, physical, hearing, and mental disabilities.

Format: Suitable for group use; examiner required; timed: 3 hours

Scoring: Examiner evaluated

Cost: $140.00

Publisher: American College Testing

New Testament Diagnostic
Fred R. Johnson

Copyright: 1985

Population: Adults; ages 17 and older

Purpose: Measures and assesses New Testament knowledge

Description: Paper–pencil 150-item multiple-choice test with five subtests: Introduction to New Testament World and Records, Gospels, Acts, Epistles, and Revelation. Raw scores are converted to 100% scale and percentile ranks.

Format: Individual or group administration; 45 minutes

Scoring: Examiner administered; hand key

Cost: Test $1.00; 100 tests $75.00

Publisher: Accrediting Association of Bible Colleges

Partial Index of Modernization: Measurement of Attitudes Toward Morality
Panos D. Bardis

Copyright: 1972

Population: Adolescents, adults

Purpose: Measures attitudes toward traditional concepts of sin; used for clinical assessment, counseling, research on religion and morals, and discussions in religion and social science classes

Description: Paper–pencil 10-item test in which the subject rates 10 statements about sin and morality from 0 (least amount of agreement) to 10 (highest amount of agreement). The score equals the sum of the 10 numerical responses. The theoretical range of scores extends from 0 (least modern) to 100 (most modern).

Format: Group and individual administration; 5 minutes

Scoring: Examiner evaluated and interpreted

Cost: Free

Publisher: Panos D. Bardis, Ph.D.

Standardized Bible Content Tests

Copyright: 1959

Population: Adults

Purpose: Evaluates knowledge of the Bible; used for college entrance examinations, class assignment, assessment (pretest, posttest), and comparing national and institutional norms

Description: Paper–pencil 150-item multiple-choice test measuring biblical knowledge: people, history, doctrine, geography, and quotations. The test is recommended for institutions of higher education. Forms D and E are available in Spanish.

Format: Individual or group administration; 45 minutes

Scoring: Examiner evaluated; hand key

Cost: 100 tests (specify form) $75.00; 100 answer sheets $7.50; scoring key $2.00; manual $5.00

Publisher: Accrediting Association of Bible Colleges

Standardized Bible Content Tests–E, F

Copyright: 1976

Population: Adult

Purpose: Measures and assesses biblical knowledge; used for college admissions, class assignments, assessment (pretest, posttest), and comparing national and institutional norms

Description: Paper–pencil 150-item multiple-choice test measuring biblical knowledge: people, history, doctrine, geography, and quotations. The test is recommended for institutions of higher education. Forms D and E are available in Spanish.

Format: Individual or group administration

Scoring: Examiner evaluated; hand key

Cost: Test $1.00 each; 100 tests $75.00; answer sheets $0.10 or 100 for $75.00

Publisher: Accrediting Association of Bible Colleges

Standardized Bible Content Tests–G, H, GS, HS

Copyright: 1993

Population: Adults

Purpose: Assesses Bible knowledge

Description: GS and HS: 50-item multiple-choice paper/pencil test. Scores are reported as percentiles relative to AABC member colleges. G and H: 150-item multiple-choice paper–pencil test

Format: Individual or group administration; 45 minutes

Scoring: Examiner administered; hand key

Cost: 100 GS and HS $100.00; all others $75.00

Publisher: Accrediting Association of Bible Colleges

Standardized Bible Content Tests–Form SP

Copyright: 1976

Population: Ages 15 and older

Purpose: Measures and assesses Bible knowledge for counseling, Bible college readiness, and missionary candidacy

Description: Paper–pencil 150-item multiple-choice test. Scores are reported as percentiles relative to AABC member colleges.

Format: Individual or group administration; 45 minutes

Scoring: Examiner administered; hand key

Cost: Test $1.00; 100 tests $75.00

Publisher: Accrediting Association of Bible Colleges

Thanatometer
Panos D. Bardis

Copyright: 1986

Population: Adolescents, adults

Purpose: Measures awareness and acceptance of death

Description: Paper–pencil 20-item Likert-scale assessing attitudes toward death and dying. Examinee responds by indicating degree of agreement with each item. Suitable for use with individuals with physical and hearing disabilities.

Format: Self-administered; suitable for group use; 12 minutes

Scoring: Hand key

Cost: Free

Publisher: Panos D. Bardis, Ph.D.

Speech and Language

Comprehensive

ACTFL Oral Proficiency Interview

Copyright: Not provided

Population: All ages

Purpose: Measures language production holistically by determining patterns of strengths and weaknesses and establishing a speaker's level of consistent functional ability as well as the clear upper limitations of competence

Description: A 10- to 30-minute tape-recorded interview conducted either face-to-face or via telephone by an ACTFL certified tester. It resembles a natural conversation. The interview does not measure discrete aspects of language use or knowledge about the language. There are four categories of assessment criteria: the global tasks or functions performed with the language; the social contexts and the content areas in which the language can be used; the accuracy features which define how well the speaker performs the tasks pertinent to those contexts and content areas; and the oral text types produced, from individual words to extended discourse. ACTFL OPIs are used for assessing the speaking skills of college-level adults and business people. Available in 28 languages.

Format: Tape-recorded interview via telephone or by an examiner; untimed: 10–30 minutes

Scoring: Scored by LTI

Cost: $115.00

Publisher: Language Testing International

Adapted Sequenced Inventory of Communication Development for Adolescents and Adults with Severe Handicaps
Sandra E. McClennen

Copyright: 1989

Population: Adolescents, adults

Purpose: Evaluates the communication abilities of severely handicapped adolescents and adults whose language skills are in the range of birth to 4 years; used for remedial programming by speech–language pathologists, audiologists, psychologists, and teachers

Description: Inventory with 76 items assessing and diagnosing language disorders in adolescents and adults. The receptive communication section (27 items) includes a processing profile for auditory perception and pragmatic, semantic, and syntactic language and a concepts profile for awareness, words, directions, questions, and attributes. The expressive communication section (31 items) includes a processing profile for pragmatic and semantic/syntactic language and imitation and a behavioral profile for imitating motor behavior, motor and/or vocal/verbal initiating behavior, and motor and/or vocal/verbal responding behavior. An observation/interview section (18 items) is also included. Approach is based on order of difficulty concept, and mode of expression is defined to recognize alternatives to vocal communication. The resulting Communication Profile provides guidelines for developing remedial programs for adolescents and adults who have little or no speech or who are understood only by those closest to them. Handicapping conditions represented in the norm group include severe hearing loss, legal blindness, epilepsy, spastic quadriplegia, and nonambulation. Adaptations are described for clients with cerebral palsy and other motor handicaps.

Format: Examiner required; not suitable for group use; untimed: time varies

Scoring: Examiner evaluated

Cost: Complete Kit (manuals, 50 receptive skills checklists and profiles, 50 expressive skills checklists and profiles, 50 assessment booklets, stimulus objects, plastic carrying case) $250.00

Publisher: Western Psychological Services

Adolescent Language Screening Test (ALST)
Denise L. Morgan, Arthur M. Guilford

Copyright: 1984

Population: Ages 11 through 17

Purpose: Screens the dimensions of oral language use, content, and form

Description: Multiple-item, thorough method of screening through seven subtests: Pragmatics, Receptive Vocabulary, Concepts, Expressive Vocabulary, Sentence Formulation, Morphology, and Phonology. The results provide the clinician with a solid foundation for recommending a total communication evaluation and outline the language dimensions on which extension testing should focus.

Format: Individual administration; 15 minutes

Scoring: Examiner administered and interpreted

Cost: Complete kit (manual, picture book, protocols, and storage box) $104.00

Publisher: PRO-ED, Inc.

Analyzing Storytelling Skills
Natalie L. Hedberg, Carol E. Westby

Copyright: 1993

Population: Children to adults

Purpose: Assesses the ability to produce and comprehend stories

Description: Oral-response test used to assess ability to produce and comprehend stories. Used for speech–language pathology applications. Suitable for individuals with hearing and mental impairment.

Format: Individual administration; examiner required

Scoring: Examiner analysis of story/narrative produced

Cost: Test kit (manual) $49.00

Publisher: Communication Skill Builders, Inc.

Bankson Language Test–Second Edition (BLT–2)
Nicholas W. Bankson

Copyright: 1990

Population: Children; ages 3–0 to 6–11

Purpose: Provides examiners with a measure of children's psycholinguistic skills

Description: The device is organized into three general categories that assess a variety of areas: Semantic Knowledge—body parts, nouns, verbs, categories, functions, prepositions, opposites; Morphological/Syntactical Rules—pronouns, verb usage/verb tense, verb usage (auxiliary, modal, copula), plurals, comparatives/superlatives, negation, questions; Pragmatics—ritualizing, informing, controlling, imagining. The selection of subtests to be included in the BLT–2 was predicated on a review of those areas that language interventions frequently test and remediate in younger children. Test results may be reported in terms of standard scores and percentile ranks, which are provided for children age 3-0 through 6-11. The normative sample consisted of more than 1,200 children living in 19 states. The demographic features of the sample are representative of the U.S. population as a whole on a variety of variables as provided by the Statistical Abstract of the United States (1985). Evidence of internal consistency reliability is provided in the test manual, and reliability coefficients exceed .90. Support for content, concurrent, and construct validity also is provided.

Format: Examiner required; not suitable for group use; untimed

Scoring: Hand key

Cost: Complete Kit (examiner's manual, 25 profile/examiner's record booklets, 25 screen record forms, picture book, storage box) $114.00

Publisher: PRO-ED, Inc.

CAT/5 Listening and Speaking Checklist

Copyright: 1993

Population: Grades K through 12

Purpose: Assesses oral language proficiency in children and adolescents

Description: Oral-response checklist that is teacher scored and individually administered to evaluate students' listening behavior, listening comprehension, critical listening, speaking behavior, and participation. The teacher uses one checklist per student to rate each student's ability based on classroom observation and experience. Students receive an overall rating which classifies them as basic, proficient, or advanced.

Format: Examiner required; individually administered; untimed: time varies

Scoring: Examiner evaluated

Cost: Classroom package (30 checklists, teacher's guide, and class summary folder) $22.80 each level

Publisher: CTB/McGraw-Hill

Child Language Ability Measures (CLAM)
Albert Mehrabian, Christy Moynihan

Copyright: 1979

Population: Children; ages 2 to 7

Purpose: Measures the language production and language comprehension abilities of children; identifies linguistic abilities and difficulties; used by educators, speech–language pathologists, testers, and child psychologists to plan language development programs

Description: Six multiple-item oral-response and nonverbal task-performance tests measuring a child's expressive and receptive language abilities, including vocabulary comprehension, grammar comprehension, inflection production, grammar imitation, "grammar formedness" judgment, and grammar equivalence judgment. The tests assess a child's knowledge of syntactic, semantic, and phonological rules and do not confound measurement of language development with intellectual skills such as memory span, knowledge of real-world facts, or ability to form abstract relationships. Administration procedures contain built-in safeguards against tester bias (such as encouraging one child more than another). The six tests may be administered separately or together. Norms are provided to calculate standardized scores for each test and for combinations of

tests. The manual includes details regarding the construction of the tests, statistics on item selection and test reliabilities, appropriate age ranges for each test, and scoring procedures and norms. Two administration books are available. Sample answer sheets are provided at the end of each test administration booklet and can be copied by the examiner for use in recording children's answers.

Format: Examiner required; not suitable for group use; untimed: 15 minutes per test

Scoring: Examiner evaluated

Cost: Manual $12.00; Test Administration Booklets $20.00 each

Publisher: Albert Mehrabian, Ph.D.

Clinical Evaluation of Language Fundamentals®–Third Edition (CELF®–3)
Eleanor Semel, Elisabeth H. Wiig, Wayne A. Secord

Copyright: 1995

Population: Children, adolescents; Grades K through 12

Purpose: Yields detailed diagnostic information on language processing and production skills to identify children with language disabilities

Description: Multiple-item oral-response assessment consisting of two screening tests (Elementary for Grades K–5 and Advanced for Grades 5–12) and a diagnostic battery. The Elementary screening test is administered using a "Simon Says" format. The Advanced screening test utilizes playing cards to elicit language processing skills. The Diagnostic Battery employs 13 criterion- and norm-referenced subtests to probe language processing, language production, and receptive and expressive phonological factors. These 13 subtests can be administered in their entirety, in part, or in any sequence.

Format: Examiner required; not suitable for group use; untimed: 1–2 hours

Scoring: Examiner evaluated

Cost: Contact publisher

Publisher: The Psychological Corporation

Communication Profile
Joan C. Payne

Copyright: 1994

Population: Adults

Purpose: Assesses communication skills in adult and geriatric clients

Description: Oral-response survey/checklists measuring communication skills for speech–language pathology applications. Suitable for individuals with hearing and mental disabilities.

Format: Individual administration; not suitable for group use

Scoring: Hand key; examiner evaluated (uses examiner's knowledge), no scoring service available

Cost: Test kit (manual, scoring forms) $42.00

Publisher: Communication Skill Builders, Inc.

CommunicationLab Profile
Ellen Pritchard Dodge

Copyright: 1994

Population: Children, adolescents; ages 6 to 14; Grades 1 through 8

Purpose: Assesses a child's communication skills in real-life situations; used in individual assessment, small groups, and the classroom

Description: Criterion-referenced 28-item test with seven areas of communication. The subtests are as follows: Nonverbal, Listening, Speech/Voice, Turn-Taking, Cooperation, Discussions, Confidence, and Communication Think Sheet. No standardized score is determined. Each item is ranked rarely (1), sometimes (2), or usually (3). The score is totaled. Student performance is categorized into three levels based on overall score: 1—Shows competence, 2—Acceptable, 3—Needs instruction. Suitable for individuals with visual, physical, hearing, and mental disabilities.

Format: Individual administration; examiner required; suitable for group use; untimed

Scoring: Examiner evaluated; no scoring service available

Cost: $29.95

Publisher: LinguiSystems, Inc.

Communicative Abilities in Daily Living (CADL)
Audrey L. Holland

Copyright: 1980

Population: Aphasic adults

Purpose: Assesses functional communication skills; used for planning treatment programs

Description: Multiple-item oral-response test. Descriptive data are provided in 10 categories: reading/writing/calculating; speech acts; content utilization; role-playing; sequential relationships; social conventions; divergences; nonverbal symbols; deixis (movement-related communicative behavior); and humor, metaphor, and absurdity. The test employs both traditional and role-playing methods. Provides cutoff scores for determining functional communication disorders.

Format: Individual administration

Scoring: Examiner scored and interpreted

Cost: Complete Kit (manual, scoring kit, picture book, audiotape, and storage box) $144.00

Publisher: PRO-ED, Inc.

Comprehensive Receptive and Expressive Vocabulary Test (CREVT)
Gerald Wallace, Donald D. Hammill

Copyright: 1994

Population: Ages 4 years through 17 years 11 months

Purpose: Measures receptive and expressive oral vocabulary

Description: Receptive vocabulary is measured with the use of a picture book that has 10 color pictures for 61 items for the "point-to-the-picture-of-the-word-I-say" technique. Five to eight words are associated with each picture plate, spread evenly across grade levels 1 through 13. On the Expressive subtest, the words pertain to the same 10 common themes used in the Receptive Vocabulary subtest. The individual defines the word given. A combined score is provided on two equivalent forms.

Format: Individual administration; untimed: 20–30 minutes

Scoring: Hand key

Cost: Complete Kit (manual, photo album, protocols in storage box) $149.00

Publisher: PRO-ED, Inc.

Early Language Milestone Scale–Second Edition (ELM–2)
James Coplan

Copyright: 1993

Population: Ages birth to 36 months

Purpose: Assesses speech and language development

Description: The ELM–2 is ideally suited to help clinicians implement the mandate to serve the developmental needs of children. It also can be used with older children with developmental delays whose functional level falls within this range. The ELM–2 consists of 43 items arranged in three divisions: Auditory Expressive (which is further subdivided into Content and Intelligibility), Auditory Receptive, and Visual. May be used by examiners with varying levels of prior knowledge of early language development. The ELM–2 may be administered using either a pass/fail or a point scoring method. The pass/fail method yields a global "pass" or "fail" rating for the test as a whole, whereas the point scoring method yields percentile values, standard score equivalents, and age equivalents for each area of language function (Auditory Expressive, Auditory Receptive, and Visual), as well as Global Language score. The pass/fail method is preferred whenever large numbers of low-risk subjects must be evaluated. The point scoring method is preferred whenever more detailed information than a global "pass" or "fail" is desired, including high-risk setting (e.g., neonatal intensive care unit follow-up clinics).

Format: Pass/fail or point scoring method; 1–10 minutes

Scoring: Hand key

Cost: Complete Kit (examiner's manual, object kit, 100 record forms, storage box) $109.00

Publisher: PRO-ED, Inc.

English Picture Vocabulary Test (EPVT) Full Range
Alan M. Brimer, Lloyd M. Dunn

Copyright: 1973

Population: Children to adults; ages 3 to 18 and over

Purpose: Assesses listening vocabulary; used by teachers and speech therapists for identifying reading difficulty and other verbal learning handicaps

Description: Multiple-item response test measuring verbal comprehension. The examinee matches a picture with a spoken word. The test is available on five levels: Test 1 (40 items) for ages 5 years to 8 years 11 months; Test 2 (40 items) for ages 7 years to 11 years 11 months (group and individual versions); Test 3 (48 items) for ages 11 years to 18 years; and a full-range version (125 items arranged in order of increasing difficulty) for ages 3 years to 18 years. No reading is required.

Format: Examiner required; suitable for group use depending on level; untimed: time varies

Scoring: Hand key

Cost: £27.60 Sterling

Publisher: Educational Evaluation Enterprises

English Picture Vocabulary Test 2; EPVT–2, EPVT–2(G)
Alan M. Brimer, Lloyd M. Dunn

Copyright: Individual 1963, Group 1970

Population: Children; ages 7 years to 11 years 11 months

Purpose: Used for screening

Description: Multiple-choice 48-item paper–pencil show-tell point-to test yielding standardized scores and percentiles. Individual and group forms are available. Suitable for individuals with physical and mental disabilities.

Format: Individual/group administration; examiner required; untimed: 20 minutes

Scoring: Hand key; test scoring service available from publisher

Cost: Individual £14.55 Sterling; Group £8.60 Sterling

Publisher: Educational Evaluations Enterprises

English Picture Vocabulary Test 3 (EPVT) G

Copyright: Not provided

Population: Children

Purpose: Used for screening

Description: Multiple-choice 48-item paper–pencil show-tell, point-to test. Adapted from the Peabody Picture Vocabulary Test. Examiner must be a qualified teacher, psychologist, or speech therapist. Suitable for those with physical and mental disabilities.

Format: Individual/group administration; examiner required; untimed

Scoring: Hand key; test scoring service available from publisher

Cost: £8.60 Sterling

Publisher: Educational Evaluation Enterprises

Evaluating Acquired Skills in Communication (EASIC)–Revised
Anita Marcott Riley

Copyright: 1991

Population: Ages 3 months to 8 years

Purpose: Assesses the language abilities of individuals with a language age of 3 months to 8 years and an interest level age of 4 years to 20 years; used for planning therapy programs for clients with severe language impairment.

Description: Multiple-item oral-response test consisting of five inventories assessing a child's abilities in semantics, syntax, morphology, and pragmatics. The examiner uses picture stimuli to elicit spontaneous, cued, imitated, manipulated, noncompliant, or incorrect responses. The test helps determine emerging communication skills, including before meaningful speech; understanding of simple noun labels, action verbs, and basic concepts; emerging modes of communication; understanding of more complex language functions; and use of more complex communication. The test includes goals for individual education prescriptions. It is used with autistic, mentally impaired, developmentally delayed, and preschool language-delayed children and adolescents.

Format: Examiner required; not suitable for group use; untimed: typical time not available

Scoring: Hand key

Cost: Test Kit (manual, picture book, cards, test booklets, skill profiles, storage box) $82.00

Publisher: Communication Skill Builders, Inc.

Fluharty Preschool Speech and Language Screening Test (FPSLST)
Nancy Buono Fluharty

Copyright: 1968

Population: Ages 2 to 6

Purpose: Evaluate the language performance of preschoolers to identify children with delayed or abnormal language development

Description: Multiple-item oral-response test assessing syntax, articulation, and auditory comprehension. Picture stimuli (10 cards) are used to elicit language samples. Cutoff scores are provided for each age level of each area screened.

Format: Individual administration; 5–10 minutes

Scoring: Examiner administration and interpretation

Cost: Complete kit (manual, picture cards, and response forms in plastic case) $59.00

Publisher: PRO-ED, Inc.

Fullerton Language Test of Adolescents–Second Edition (FLTA–2)
Arden R. Thorum

Copyright: 1986

Population: Age 11 through adulthood

Purpose: Measures receptive and expressive

language skills to identify language impairment

Description: Standardized instrument that contains eight subtests: Auditory Synthesis, Morphology Competency, Oral Commands, Convergent Production, Divergent Production, Syllabication, Grammatic Competency, and Idioms. The test diagnoses strengths and weaknesses and gives remediation suggestions.

Format: Individual administration; 1 hour

Scoring: Examiner evaluated

Cost: Complete kit (manual, stimulus items, and protocols) $69.00

Publisher: PRO-ED, Inc.

Functional Communication Profile
Larry I. Kleiman

Copyright: 1994

Population: Ages 3 to adult

Purpose: Measures communicative effectiveness in clients with developmental delays; used in speech and language therapy and family counseling with individuals with developmental delay, autism, cerebral palsy, Down Syndrome, and other chromosomal abnormalities.

Description: Oral-response criterion-referenced verbal show-tell, point-to test comprised of nine categories: sensory/motor functioning, attentiveness, receptive language, expressive language, pragmatic/social skills, speech, voice, oral functioning, and fluency. Interpretation of results is in the manual. Examiner must be a qualified speech pathologist or intern, special education teacher, or grad student in communicative disorders.

Format: Individual administration; examiner required; untimed

Scoring: Examiner evaluated; no scoring service available

Cost: Manual and 15 forms $31.95

Publisher: LinguiSystems, Inc.

Interaction Checklist for Augmentative Communication (INCH)
Susan Oakander Bolton, Sallie E. Dashiell

Copyright: 1991

Population: Children and adults

Purpose: Evaluates and remediates the interaction skills of nonspeaking individuals

Description: The INCH checklist evaluates responding to greetings from others, introducing self when appropriate, using AAC system without prompting, seeking help when needed, using pauses or spaces for greater clarity, and restating a message. Can be used as an initial and follow-up measure of communicative effectiveness with either an electronic or manual device. Authors include suggestions for remediating interaction skills and for writing goals and objectives.

Format: Individual; untimed

Scoring: Examiner administration and interpretation

Cost: Manual and 15 checklists $32.95

Publisher: Imaginart International, Inc.

Kindergarten Language Screening Test (KLST)
Sharon V. Gauthier, Charles L. Madison

Copyright: 1983

Population: Children; ages 4 to 7

Purpose: Tests receptive and expressive language competency and assesses language deficits that may cause kindergartners to fail academically

Description: Eight-item oral-response test identifying children for further diagnostic testing for language deficits that may accelerate academic failure. The child identifies name, age, colors, body parts, and number concepts, follows commands, repeats sentences, and engages in spontaneous speech. The test is based on the verbal language abilities considered average for children of kindergarten age.

Format: Examiner required; individual administration; untimed 4–5 minutes

Scoring: Examiner evaluated

Cost: Complete kit (manual, picture cards, protocols in storage box) $49.00

Publisher: PRO-ED, Inc.

Language Processing Test–Revised (LPT–R)

Gail J. Richard, Mary Anne Hanner

Copyright: 1995

Population: Children; ages 5 to 11; Grades K through 6

Purpose: Evaluates the ability to attach increasingly more meaning to information received auditorily and to determine a child's ability to handle increasing language demands of the classroom; used for communicative disorders and low academic performance

Description: Oral-response 84-item verbal test with two pretests and six subtests. Pretests: Labeling and Stating Functions. Subtests: Associations, Categorization, Similarities, Differences, Multiple Meanings, and Attributes. Numbers of subjects, means, medians, and standard deviations for each subtest and total test by six-month age groups. Age equivalents of raw scores for each subtest and total test. Percentile ranks and standard score values for each subtest and total test raw scores by age. Test–retest reliability coefficients and standard errors of measurement for each subtest and total test by age. Reliability based on item homogeneity. Print biserial correlations between subjects with and without language disorder by age level for raw score means by subtest and total test. Tests for differences between male and female mean scores for each subtest and total test by age. Suitable for individuals with physical, hearing, and mental disabilities.

Format: Individual administration; examiner required; untimed: approximately 35 minutes

Scoring: Examiner evaluated; no scoring service available

Cost: Manual and 20 test forms $64.95

Publisher: LinguiSystems, Inc.

Oral Speech Mechanism Screening Examination–Revised (OSMSE–R)

Kenneth O. St. Louis, Dennis M. Ruscello

Copyright: 1987

Population: All ages

Purpose: Evaluates speech, language, and other related skills; used for examining oral speech mechanisms in language and speech clients of all ages

Description: Oral-response instrument examining the lips, tongue, jaw, teeth, hard palate, soft palate, pharynx, velopharyngeal function, breathing, and diadochokinetic rates. The revised edition yields separate numerical scores for Structure and Function in addition to the total score.

Format: Examiner required; not suitable for group use; untimed: 5–10 minutes

Scoring: Examiner evaluated

Cost: Hand key

Publisher: PRO-ED, Inc.

OWLS: Oral and Written Language Scales Listening Comprehension and Oral Expression: Written Expression

Elizabeth Carrow-Woolfolk

Copyright: 1995

Population: Ages 3 to 21 (LC and OE); ages 5 to 21 (WE)

Purpose: Provides speech–language pathologists, school psychologists, and other professionals a way of measuring language knowledge and processing skills in preschoolers through young adults

Description: OWLS is a theoretically based, individually administered assessment of receptive and expressive (oral and written) language for children and young adults aged 3 through 21 years. OWLS consists of three scales: Listening Comprehension (LC), Oral Expression (OE), and Written Expression (WE). The scales were developed and normed as part of the same assessment. The oral language components (LC and OE) are packaged together with one manual. The WE scale is packaged separately with its own manual. The LC scale is designed to measure the understanding of spoken language. The OE scale is designed to measure the understanding and use of spoken language. The WE scale is designed to measure the ability to communicate meaningfully using written linguistic forms. Tasks in LC address the lexical (vocabulary), syntactic (grammar), and supralinguistic (higher-order thinking) skills. Tasks in OE address lexical, syntactic, supralinguistic, and pragmatic, or functional language skills. Tasks address conventions (rules of spelling, capitalization, punctuation, etc.), linguistics (modifiers, phrases, verb forms, etc.), and content (ability to communicate meaningfully). Items are administered by age-appropriate item sets.

Format: Individual administration; LC approximately 5–15 minutes, OE approximately 10–25 minutes, WE approximately 10–40 minutes

Scoring: Examiner interpreted, standard scores; ASSIST computer scoring available

Cost: LC and OE Scales Kit (manual, listening comprehension easel, oral expression easel, 25 record forms) $150.00; WE Expression Scale Kit $79.95

Publisher: American Guidance Service

Porch Index of Communicative Ability (PICA)
Bruce E. Porch

Copyright: 1981

Population: Adults

Purpose: Quantifies a patient's ability to communicate

Description: A standardized test for adults with aphasia, the PICA makes possible sensitive measurement and comparison, even when tests are administered by different clinicians. Because of this, it has been used extensively by clinicians for decades. A basic battery of 18 subtests and a multidimensional scoring system were constructed and evaluated over a 6-year period. The 18 subtests sample gestural, verbal, and graphic abilities at various levels of difficulty.

Format: Examiner administered; timed: time varies

Scoring: Examiner evaluated

Cost: Complete kit $229.00

Publisher: PRO-ED, Inc.

Preschool Language Scale–3 (PLS–3)
Irla Lee Zimmerman, Violette G. Steiner, Robert Evatt Pond

Copyright: 1992

Population: Ages birth through 6

Purpose: Provides a diagnostic measure of receptive and expressive language

Description: Multiple-item test assessing both auditory comprehension and verbal ability. Items measure sensory discrimination, logical thinking, grammar and vocabulary, memory and attention span, temporal/spatial relations, and self-image at most age levels in each of the two domains. Available in Spanish.

Format: Examiner required; not suitable for group use; untimed: 20–30 minutes

Scoring: Examiner evaluated

Cost: Complete kit (picture book, manual, and record forms) $103.00

Publisher: Harcourt® Brace Educational Measurement

Rating Scale to Measure Attitudes of Children
Lee T. Magid, Ernest M. Weiler, Maryc Schalk

Copyright: 1975

Population: Children; Grades 3 through 6

Purpose: Measures attitudes toward speech pathology

Description: Twenty-item questionnaire

Format: Individual administration; examiner required; untimed

Scoring: Hand key; examiner evaluated

Cost: $15.00

Publisher: Select Press

Receptive–Expressive Emergent Language Scale–Second Edition (REEL–2)
Kenneth R. Bzoch, Richard League

Copyright: 1991

Population: Children; birth to 3 years

Purpose: Used for the multidimensional analysis of emergent language

Description: Designed for use with a broad range of infants and toddlers who are at risk in the new multidisciplinary programs developing under the Education of the Handicapped Act Amendments of 1986. The REEL–2 is a system of measurement and intervention planning based on neurolinguistic development and is designed to help public health nurses, pediatricians, and educators identify young children who have specific language problems based on specific language behaviors. These behaviors have been systematically selected based on extensive research, and all are age related. Results of the evaluation are given in terms of an Expressive Language Age, a Receptive Language Age, and a Combined Language Age.

Format: Examiner required

Scoring: Hand key

Cost: Complete kit (examiner's manual, 25 profile/test forms, storage box) $69.00

Publisher: PRO-ED, Inc.

Revised Token Test (RTT)

Malcolm M. McNeil, Thomas E. Prescott

Copyright: 1978

Population: Adults; ages 20 through 80

Purpose: Used for designing effective rehabilitation programs and in quantifying small amounts of patient change for both clinical and research purposes

Description: The Revised Token Test (RTT), a clinical and research tool, is a revision of the Token Test by DeRenzi and Vignolo. The RTT is a sensitive quantitative and descriptive test battery for auditory processing inefficiencies and disorders associated with brain damage, aphasia, and certain language and learning disabilities. Percentile ranks are available for normal, right, and left hemisphere brain damaged adults for each of the 10 RTT subtests and for overall performance. Experimental evidence is reported for concurrent and construct validity, as well as for test–retest, intrascorer, and interscorer reliability.

Format: Examiner required; timed: time varies

Scoring: Examiner evaluated

Cost: Complete kit (examiner's manual, administration manual, scoring forms, profile forms, tokens, storage box) $119.00

Publisher: PRO-ED, Inc.

Reynell Developmental Language Scales

Joan K. Reynell, Christian P. Gruber

Copyright: Not provided

Population: Used for measuring language skills in young or developmentally delayed children

Purpose: These scales assess two processes essential to language development: verbal comprehension and expressive language

Description: Battery of 134 items includes colorful test materials. Useful in evaluating language processes in young children, the test identifies the nature and extent of each child's language difficulty.

Format: Individually administered; examiner required; 30 minutes

Scoring: Examiner evaluated

Cost: Kit (set of stimulus materials, 10 test booklets, 1 manual, carrying case) $495.00

Publisher: Western Psychological Services

Rhode Island Test of Language Structure (RITLS)

Elizabeth Engen, Trygg Engen

Copyright: 1983

Population: Ages 3 to 20

Purpose: Measures English language development in hearing children ages 3 to 6 or children and adults (ages 3 to 20) with hearing impairment; used for educational planning

Description: Multiple-choice 100-item verification test assessing understanding of language structure (syntax). The test presents 20 sentence types, both simple and complex. The test is used for educational planning, such as determination of school readiness, bilingual programming, and language introduction procedures. It can also be used where language development is a concern, including mental retardation, learning disability, and bilingual programs.

Format: Examiner required; not suitable for group use; timed: 30 minutes

Scoring: Hand key

Cost: Complete kit (test booklet, 10 response sheets/10 analysis sheets, manual, storage box) $114.00

Publisher: PRO-ED, Inc.

Screening Kit of Language Development (SKOLD)
Lynn S. Bliss, Doris V. Allen

Copyright: 1983

Population: Children; ages 2 to 5

Purpose: Assesses language disorders and delays in young children; used by speech–language pathologist paraprofessionals in day care and by health care/nursing and preschool specialists

Description: Oral-response 135-item test measuring language development in children speaking either Black English or Standard English. Picture stimuli are used to assess vocabulary, comprehension, story completion, individual and paired sentence repetition with pictures, individual sentence repetition without pictures, and comprehension of commands. The test consists of six subtests, three for Black English and three for Standard English, in each of the following age ranges: 30–36 months, 37–42 months, and 43–48 months. Norms are provided for speakers of Black and Standard English. The manual includes guidelines for administration and scoring and the linguistic characteristics of Black English.

Format: Examiner required; not suitable for group use; untimed: 15 minutes

Scoring: Examiner evaluated

Cost: Test kit (manual, stimulus book, set of either Black or Standard English scoring forms) $80.00

Publisher: Slosson Educational Publications, Inc.

Sequenced Inventory of Communication Development (SICD)
Dona Lea Hendrick, Elizabeth M. Prather, Annette R. Tobin

Copyright: 1984

Population: Children functioning between 4 months and 4 years

Purpose: Evaluates the communication abilities of children with and without retardation

Description: The inventory can be used in remedial programming of the young child with language disorders, mental retardation, and specific language problems. It has been used successfully with children with sensory impairments and with children with varying degrees of retardation. In assessing the communication development of very young children, examiners face the challenge of maintaining the children's cooperation. The objects in this kit are effective aids in obtaining information with the most effective use of time.

Format: Examiner required; timed: time varies

Scoring: Examiner evaluated

Cost: Complete kit (instruction manual and test manual, receptive scales, expressive scales, profiles and objects for administration, carrying case) $349.00

Publisher: PRO-ED, Inc.

Sequenced Inventory of Communication Development–Revised Edition
Dona Lea Hedrick, Elizabeth M. Prather, Annett R. Tobin

Copyright: 1984

Population: Children; ages 4 months to 4 years

Purpose: Evaluates the communication abilities of children with and without retardation functioning between the ages of 4 months and 4 years; used for remedial programming by speech–language pathologists, audiologists, psychologists, and teachers

Description: Inventory with 210 items assessing and diagnosing language disorders in young children. The receptive language section (92 items) includes behavioral items that test sound and speech discrimination and awareness and understanding. The expressive language section (118 items) includes three types of expressive behaviors (imitating, initiating, and responding) and measures verbal output for length, grammatic and syntactic structure, and articulation. The resulting Communication Profile provides guidelines for developing remedial programs for young children with language disorders, mental retardation, specific language problems, and hearing or visual impairments. Some items have been adapted from the REP Scale, the Denver Development Scale, and the Illinois Test of Adaptive Abilities. The test kit includes over 100 objects used as stimuli for test items. The test has been used with autistic and other difficult-to-test children, those with hearing impairment, and Yupik-speaking Eskimo children. A Cuban Spanish edition is available.

Format: Examiner required; not suitable for group use; untimed: time varies

Scoring: Examiner evaluated

Cost: Complete kit (manual, 50 receptive test booklets, 50 expressive test booklets, stimulus objects, plastic carrying case) $275.00

Publisher: Western Psychological Press

Speech and Language Evaluation Scale (SLES)

Stephen B. McCarney

Copyright: 1989

Population: Children, adolescents; ages 4 years 5 months to 18 years

Purpose: Diagnoses speech and language disorders

Description: The SLES is designed for in-school screening and referral of students with speech and language problems. The scale is designed to provide the clinician with input from classroom teachers, without requiring anecdotal reporting. The scale includes the most commonly recognized subscales of speech (articulation, voice, fluency) and language (form, content, and pragmatics). A computer

version using IBM/Macintosh PCs is available.

Format: Individual administration; untimed: 15–20 minutes

Scoring: Self/computer scored

Cost: Complete kit $117.50

Publisher: Hawthorne Educational Services, Inc.

Studies in Convergent Communication

Thelma Brown, Catherine Garvey

Copyright: 1972

Population: Children

Purpose: Assesses communication accuracy of children

Description: Three-task observation test

Format: Individual administration; examiner required; untimed

Scoring: Examiner evaluated

Cost: $21.00

Publisher: Select Press

Test for Auditory Comprehension of Language–Revised (TACL–R)

Elizabeth Carrow-Woolfolk

Copyright: 1985

Population: Ages 3 years 9 months to 11 years

Purpose: Measures auditory comprehension of children; also used with adults

Description: Multiple-item response test assessing auditory understanding of word classes and relations, grammatical morphemes, and elaborated sentence constructions. The test requires no oral response. This revised edition provides high reliability and validity, a more efficient scoring system, and a variety of normative comparisons. The test yields percentile ranks, standard scores, and age equivalents. Guidelines for administering the test to adults also are provided.

Format: Examiner required; not suitable for group use; untimed: 10–20 minutes

Scoring: Examiner evaluated; may be computer scored

Cost: Complete kit (examiner's manual, test book, and 25 record forms) $159.00

Publisher: PRO-ED, Inc.

Test for Examining Expressive Morphology (TEEM)
Kenneth G. Shipley, Terry A. Stone, Marlene B. Sue

Copyright: 1983

Population: Children, adolescents

Purpose: Assesses the expressive morpheme development of children (language age 3 to 8 years; interest level 3 to 16 years), measures general language level, and monitors student progress; used in language remediation, hearing impairment, early childhood, and special education

Description: Oral-response 54-item sentence-completion test assessing the allomorphic variations of six major morphemes: present progressives, plurals, possessives, past tenses, third-person singulars, and derived adjectives. The examiner presents each stimulus picture while reading the stimulus phrase, and the child completes the phrase while viewing the picture. Results identify specific morphemes and allomorphic variations requiring stimulation or instruction. The manual includes administration and instructions and technical data.

Format: Examiner required; not suitable for group use; untimed: 7 minutes

Scoring: Examiner evaluated

Cost: Test kit (manual, 25 scoring forms, test book) $32.00

Publisher: Communication Skill Builders, Inc.

Test of Adolescent Language–Third Edition (TOAL–3)
Donald D. Hammill, Virginia L. Brown, Stephen C. Larsen, J. Lee Wiederholt

Copyright: 1994

Population: Ages 12 years to 24 years 11 months

Purpose: Assesses the linguistic aspects of listening, speaking, reading, and writing

Description: Internal consistency, test–retest, and scores reliability were investigated. All reliability coefficients exceed .80. Content, criterion-related, and construct validity have been thoroughly studied. TOAL–3 is also related to IQ and age. The TOAL–3 scores distinguished dramatically between groups known to have language problems and those known to have normal language. The 10 composites are Listening—the ability to understand the spoken language of other people; Speaking—the ability two express one's ideas orally; Reading—the ability to comprehend written messages; Writing—the ability to express thoughts in graphic form; Spoken Language—the ability to listen and speak; Written Language—the ability to read and write; Vocabulary—the ability to understand and use words in communication; Grammar—the ability to understand and generate syntactic structures; Receptive Language—the ability to comprehend both written and spoken language; and Expressive Language—the ability to produce written and spoken language.

Format: Individual administered; suitable for group use; timed: 1–3 hours

Scoring: Examiner evaluated

Cost: Complete kit (examiner's manual, 50 answer booklets, 10 test booklets, 50 profile/examiner record forms, storage box) $149.00

Publisher: PRO-ED, Inc.

Test of Early Language Development–Second Edition (TELD–2)
Wayne P. Hresko, D. Kim Reid, Donald D. Hammill

Copyright: 1991

Population: Children; ages 3 years to 7 years 11 months

Purpose: Measures content and form in the receptive and expressive language abilities of children; used to identify problems, document progress, conduct research, and guide instructional practices

Description: Oral-response and point-to 38-item test using a variety of semantic and syntactic tasks to assess different aspects of receptive/expressive language. Standard scores, percentiles, age equivalents, and language quotients are calculated. Examiners must be competent in the administration of educational, psychological, and language tests.

Format: Examiner required; not suitable for group use; untimed: 15 minutes

Scoring: Examiner evaluated

Cost: Complete kit (examiner's manual, 25 Form A profile/examiner record forms, 25 Form B profile/examiner record forms, picture book, storage box) $129.00

Publisher: PRO-ED, Inc.

Test of Language Competence–Expanded (TLC–Expanded)
Elisabeth H. Wiig, Wayne Secord

Copyright: 1989

Population: Children, adolescents; ages 5 through 18

Purpose: Measures metalinguistic, higher-level language functions

Description: Multiple-item response test for diagnosing language disabilities by assessing language strategies rather than language skill. The Recreating Sentences subtest examines the ability to perceive the nature of a communication and recreate a semantically, syntactically, and pragmatically appropriate sentence. The Understanding Metaphoric Expressions subtest has students interpret an expression and select another one with the same meaning. The Understanding Ambiguous Sentences subtest evaluates the ability to recognize and interpret alternative meanings of lexical and structural ambiguities. The Making Inferences subtest has students identify permissible inferences based on causal relationships or chains. The test's features include norm-referenced scores, extension teaching and testing formats for each subtest, and individual education program guidelines. Two levels for different age groups.

Format: Examiner required; not suitable for group use; untimed: less than 1 hour

Scoring: Hand key

Cost: Complete kit (manuals, materials, and protocols for both levels with briefcase) $279.50

Publisher: The Psychological Corporation

Test of Language Development–Intermediate: Third Edition (TOLD–I:3)
Donald D. Hammill, Phyllis L. Newcomer

Copyright: 1997

Population: Children; ages 8 years 6 months to 12 years 11 months

Purpose: Assesses the expressive and receptive language abilities of children; identifies children with language problems

Description: Multiple-item oral-response test consisting of six subtests measuring different aspects of spoken language. The Generals (25 items), Vocabulary (35 items), and Malapropisms (30 items) subtests assess the understanding and meaningful use of spoken words. The Sentence Combining (20 items) and Grammatic Comprehension (40 items) subtests assess different aspects of grammar. Test results are reported in terms of raw scores, standard scores, percentiles, and age equivalents. By combining various subtest scores, it is possible to diagnose a child's abilities in relation to specific language skills, including overall spoken language, listening (receptive language), speaking (expressive language), semantics (the meaning of words), and syntax (grammar).

Format: Examiner required; suitable for group use; untimed: 40 minutes

Scoring: Hand key; may be computer scored

Cost: Complete kit (examiner's manual, 50 profile/examiner record forms, storage box) $149.00

Publisher: PRO-ED, Inc.

Test of Language Development–Primary: Third Edition (TOLD–P:3)
Phyllis L. Newcomer, Donald D. Hammill

Copyright: 1997

Population: Children; ages 4 years to 8 years 11 months; Grades K through 3

Purpose: Assesses the expressive and receptive abilities of children; used as a language achievement test and to identify children with language problems, including mental retardation, learning and reading disabilities, speech delays, and articulation problems

Description: Oral-response and point-to 190-item test consisting of seven subtests measuring different components of spoken language. The Picture Vocabulary (35 items) and Oral Vocabulary (30 items) subtests assess the understanding and meaningful use of spoken words. The Grammatic Understanding (25 items), Sentence Imitation (30 items), and Grammatic Completion (30 items) subtests assess different aspects of grammar. The Word Articulation (20 items) and Word Discrimination (20 items) subtests are supplemental tests measuring the ability to pronounce words correctly and distinguish between words that sound familiar. Test results are reported in terms of standard scores, percentiles, age equivalents, Spoken Language Quotient, Semantics Quotient, and Phonology Quotient. By combining various subtest scores, it is possible to diagnose a child's abilities in relation to specific language skills, including overall spoken language, listening (receptive language), speaking (expressive language), semantics (the meaning of words), and syntax (grammar). The examiner must have formal training in assessment.

Format: Examiner required; not suitable for group use; untimed: 40 minutes

Scoring: Examiner evaluated; computer scored

Cost: Complete kit (examiner's manual, picture book, 50 profile/examiner record forms, storage box) $213.00

Publisher: PRO-ED, Inc.

Token Test for Children (TTFC)
Frank DiSimoni

Copyright: 1978

Population: Children; ages 3 years to 12 years 6 months

Purpose: Measures functional listening ability in children and identifies receptive language dysfunction; used in language therapy

Description: Test with 61 items in which the child arranges wooden tokens in response to the examiner's oral directions. The results can be used to indicate a need for further testing of lexicon and syntax or to rule out language impairment in a child with reading difficulties. Materials include the tokens, manual, and scoring forms. Age and grade scores available. The test is not appropriate for individuals with deafness.

Format: Examiner required; not suitable for group use; untimed: 10 minutes

Scoring: Examiner evaluated

Cost: Complete kit (examiner's manual, 20 tokens, and 50 scoring forms) $79.00

Publisher: PRO-ED, Inc.

TOPS–R Elementary (Test of Problem Solving)
Linda Bowers, Rosemary Huisingh, Mark Barrett, Jane Orman, Carolyn LoGiudice

Copyright: 1994

Population: Children; ages 6 to 11; Grades 1 through 6

Purpose: Assesses how children use language to think; used with communicative disorders, social or psychological difficulties, behavior disorders, and cognitive disorders

Description: Oral-response 72-item verbal test. Profiles and reports yielded are as follows: numbers of subjects, means, medians, and standard deviations by age in 6-month age groupings; age equivalents of raw scores; percentile ranks and standard score values for raw scores by age; test–retest reliability coefficients and standard errors of measurement by age; reliability based on item homogeneity: Kuder Richardson coefficients by age; point biserial correlations between item scores and total test by age; T values for differences between normal and language disordered subjects by age level for raw score means; T tests for differences between male and female mean scores by age; numbers, means, and standard deviations for raw scores for normal subjects for the Classroom Problem Solving Scale; T values for differences between normal and language disordered subjects by age level for raw score means for the Classroom Problem Solving Scale. Suitable for individuals with physical, hearing, and mental disabilities. This is a revised version of TOPS: Test of Problem Solving (1984).

Format: Individual administration; examiner required; untimed: approximately 35 minutes

Scoring: Examiner evaluated; no scoring service available

Cost: Manual and 20 test forms $79.95

Publisher: LinguiSystems, Inc.

Utah Test of Language Development–Third Edition (UTLD–3)
Merlin J. Mecham

Copyright: 1989

Population: Children, adolescents; ages 1 to 14

Purpose: Identifies children with language-learning disabilities who may need further assistance

Description: Task-assessment oral-response 51-item test measuring the following factors: receptive semantic language, expressive semantic language, receptive sequential language, and expressive sequential language. Test items are arranged in developmental order. The examiner begins testing at or just below a child's expected level of ability and works down until eight consecutive correct answers are obtained, whereupon he or she works upward from the starting point. When eight consecutive incorrect answers are obtained, the test is discontinued. Items are scored as correct (plus) or incorrrect (minus). The total score is the total number of pluses. Results are presented as percentiles, stanines, language-age equivalents, and raw scores. Restricted to persons trained in psychological or educational testing.

Format: Examiner required; not suitable for group use; untimed: 20–30 minutes

Scoring: Examiner evaluated

Cost: Complete kit (examiner's manual, administration/picture book, 50 profile/examiner record forms, storage box) $104.00

Publisher: PRO-ED, Inc.

Word Meaning Through Listening—WM (L)
Alan M. Brimer

Copyright: 1995

Population: Children, adolescents; ages 6 to 16

Purpose: Measures the understanding of spoken English words used for screening verbal ability

Description: Multiple-choice 60-item paper–pencil test yielding standardized scores and percentiles. Test is related to the *Listening for Meaning Test.*

Format: Group administration; examiner required; untimed: 20 minutes

Scoring: Test scoring service available from publisher

Cost: £8.60 Sterling

Publisher: Educational Evaluation Enterprises

Articulation and Phonology

Arizona Articulation Proficiency Scale–Second Edition
Janet Barker Fudala, William M. Reynolds

Copyright: 1986

Population: Children; ages 1 year 6 months to 13 years

Purpose: Measures the speaking abilities of children; used to identify children requiring speech therapy

Description: Oral-response 48-item measure of articulation performance in which the child responds to pictures and sentences presented on 48 stimulus cards. The examiner records all errors in the protocol booklet. A sentence test is provided as an alternative for use with older children. Scores provided include total articulatory proficiency and percentage of improvement. Norms are provided. A survey form is available for compiling an abbreviated articulation record of 10 children on a single sheet.

Format: Examiner required; suitable for group use; untimed: 10–15 minutes

Scoring: Hand key

Cost: Kit (1 set of picture test cards, 25 protocol booklets, 10 survey forms, 1 manual) $100.00

Publisher: Western Psychological Services

Assessment of Phonological Processes–Revised (APP–R)
Barbara Williams Hodson

Copyright: 1986

Population: Ages 3 to 12

Purpose: Evaluates the ability of children with severe speech disorders to use phonetics

Description: Fifty-item test measuring spontaneous utterances naming three-dimensional stimuli. The examiner records speech deviations using narrow phonetic transcription. Materials include recording, analysis, summary, and preschool and multisyllabic screening forms, as well as 12 pictures for multisyllabic screening and 12 picture cards for hard-to-find objects. Explicit descriptions for more than 30 phonological processes along with examples and clear instructions for scoring are found in the manual.

Format: Individual administration; requires speech pathologist; 15–20 minutes

Scoring: Examiner administration and interpretation

Cost: Complete kit (manual, protocols, and storage box) $89.00; Object Kit $32.00

Publisher: PRO-ED, Inc.

Children's Articulation Test (CAT)
George S. Haspiel

Copyright: 1989

Population: Ages 4 to 11; Grades K through 6

Purpose: Assesses articulation adequacy

Description: Oral-response 77-item short-answer point-to test with four categories: B, Vowel-Diphthong Errors; C, Final Consonant Errors; D, Initiating Consonant Errors; E,

Error Grid I; F, Error Grid II.

Format: Individual administration; examiner required; untimed: 12 minutes

Scoring: Hand key; no scoring service available

Cost: $36.25/$6.50 separately

Publisher: Dragon Press

Compton Phonological Assessment of Children
Arthur J. Compton

Copyright: Not provided

Population: Children

Purpose: Evaluates and analyzes patterns of speech errors in children

Description: Evaluation tool that uses a step-by-step approach that provides a visual display of error patterns, provides phonological rule analysis, and does a phonological process analysis. The first 15 items can function as a screening evaluation. Pictures are used as prompts. Response booklet provides results in a color-coded, easy-to-read format.

Format: Individual administration; 45–60 minutes

Scoring: Examiner administration and interpretation

Cost: Set (manual, pictures, protocols) $45.00

Publisher: Carousel House

Compton Phonological Assessment of Foreign Accent
Arthur J. Compton

Copyright: Not provided

Population: All ages

Purpose: Identifies the accent patterns of foreign-born clients

Description: Evaluation kit gives a quick, detailed analysis of client's problem sounds and accent patterns. Assessment is based on research on over 1,500 people and 95 different languages. A tape-recorded speech analysis gives a phonetically balanced sampling of speech sounds in single words, sentences and phrases, oral reading, and conversational speech. The results are organized in a clear, color-coded display of problem sounds and accent patterns.

Format: Individual administration; 90 minutes

Scoring: Examiner administration and interpretation

Cost: Set (manual, stimulus words, reading passage, protocols) $45.00

Publisher: Carousel House

Compton Speech and Language Screening Evaluation
Arthur J. Compton

Copyright: Not provided

Population: Ages 3 to 6

Purpose: Estimates articulation and language development of young children

Description: Multiple-item oral-response test utilizing common objects to elicit verbal responses from the child. The test, which measures both production and comprehension, covers the following areas: articulation, vocabulary, colors, shapes, memory span, language (plurals, opposites, progressive and past tenses, prepositions, multiple commands, possessive pronouns), spontaneous language, fluency, voice, and oral mechanism. The materials include revised response forms with age profiles, pass/fail guidelines, and an audiogram. Available in English and Spanish versions.

Format: Examiner required; not suitable for group use; untimed: 6–10 minutes

Scoring: Examiner evaluated; Spanish version requires bilingual pathologist or aide

Cost: Complete kit (manual, carrying case, stimulus objects, pictures, 25 response forms) $50.00

Publisher: Carousel House

Denver Articulation Screening Exam (DASE)
Amelia F. Drumwright

Copyright: 1971

Population: Children; ages 2 years 6 months to 7 years

Purpose: Detects speech articulation problems in children; screens for more sophisticated testing

Description: Test measuring a child's intelligibility (does not assess language ability, vocabulary, school readiness, or intelligence). The examiner shows 22 pictures displayed on 11 cards to the child, says a word, and the child repeats it. The test is not recommended for shy or younger children.

Format: Examiner required; not suitable for group use; untimed: 5 minutes

Scoring: Examiner evaluated

Cost: 25 tests $5.00; manual/workbook $14.00; picture cards $5.50

Publisher: Denver Developmental Materials, Inc.

Fisher-Logemann Test of Articulation Competence
Hilda B. Fisher, Jerilyn A. Logemann

Copyright: 1971

Population: Preschool through adults

Purpose: Implements the examination of the phonological system, provides ease in recording and analyzing phonetic notations of articulation, and facilitates accurate analysis of articulation errors

Description: Two test forms (pictures and sentences) provide a method for eliciting spontaneous responses that are prestructured for required phonemic occurrence and analyzed and summarized according to distinctive features which are violated. The test consists of a Test Portfolio of 35 cards with 109 large, full-color illustrations and a Sentence Test with 15 sentences to be repeated.

Format: Individual administration; examiner required; untimed

Scoring: Examiner scored and interpreted

Cost: Complete kit (manual, portfolio, and record forms) $149.00

Publisher: PRO-ED, Inc.

Goldman-Fristoe Test of Articulation (GFTA)

Ronald Goldman, Macalyne Fristoe

Copyright: 1986

Population: Ages 2 to 16 and over

Purpose: Provides descriptive information about an individual's articulation skills

Description: A systematic method for identifying and recording articulatory errors of consonant sounds. Materials included in the kit: response forms for recoding and evaluating responses, manual, and easel of stimulus pictures.

Format: Individual administration; 10–15 minutes

Scoring: Level 1: each sound production judged for presence of error; Level 2: each sound production judged for type of error; both levels used

Cost: Complete G-F Test of Articulation Kit: 1986 Edition (test easel, manual, 25 response forms) $134.95

Publisher: American Guidance Service

Khan-Lewis Phonological Analysis (KLPA)

Linda M. L. Khan, Nancy P. Lewis

Copyright: 1986

Population: Ages 2 years 5 months to adult

Purpose: Provides link between disordered speech and therapy plans

Description: The KLPA is used after giving a complete GFTA. It breaks speech production into 15 phonological processes.

Format: Individual administration; scoring takes 15–40 minutes

Scoring: KLPA measures usage of 15 phonological processes; 12 are characteristic of normal speech development, 3 are not

Cost: Complete Kit (manual, 25 analysis forms) $69.95

Publisher: American Guidance Service

Phonological Awareness Profile

Carolyn Robertson, Wanda Salter

Copyright: 1995

Population: Children; ages 5 to 8; Grades K through 3

Purpose: Used to diagnose deficits in phonological processing and phoneme/grapheme correspondence

Description: Oral-response criterion-referenced test. Nine total tasks are assessed, divided into two areas. Suitable for individuals with visual, physical, hearing, or mental disabilities.

Format: Individual administration; examiner required; untimed: 10–20 minutes

Scoring: Examiner evaluated; no scoring service available

Cost: Manual and 20 test forms $34.95

Publisher: LinguiSystems, Inc.

Photo Articulation Test–Second Edition (PAT)

K. Pendergast, S. Dickey, J. Selmar, A. Soder

Copyright: 1997

Population: Children; ages 3 to 11

Purpose: Measures articulation skills; used for screening and analysis in schools and clinics and for therapy

Description: Test composed of 72 color photographs arranged with nine pictures on each of eight sheets to measure articulation of consonants, consonant blends, vowels, and diphthongs. The test categorizes defective sounds as tongue, lip, or vowel sounds. The subject names the items in the color photographs as the examiner points to the pictures and records responses on the recording sheet. Materials include a supplementary test words list.

Format: Examiner required; not suitable for group use; untimed: 5 minutes

Scoring: Examiner evaluated

Cost: Complete kit (manual, picture cards, 100 recording sheets, storage container) $98.00

Publisher: PRO-ED, Inc.

Riley Articulation and Language Test–Revised

Glyndon D. Riley

Copyright: 1971

Population: Children; Grades K through 2

Purpose: Measures the language proficiency of young children; used to identify children most in need of speech therapy

Description: Oral-response screening test consisting of three subtests (Language Proficiency and Intelligibility, Articulation Function, and Language Function) measuring phonemic similarity, stimulability, number of defective sounds, error consistency, frequency of occurrence, and developmental expectancy. The test yields an objective articulation loss score and standardized language loss and language function scores.

Format: Examiner required; not suitable for group use; untimed: 2–3 minutes

Scoring: Hand key

Cost: Kit (25 tests, 1 manual) $35.00

Publisher: Western Psychological Services

Slosson Articulation, Language Test with Phonology (SALT-P)

Wilma Jean Tade

Copyright: Not provided

Population: Ages: 3 to 5

Purpose: Assesses articulation, phonology, and language in young children

Description: Indicates the communicative competency of a young child. Screening format utilizes structured conversation centering around stimulus pictures. The articulation section assesses 22 initial and 18 final consonants, 10 clusters/blends, plus 8 vowels and diphthongs. Phonological processes probed are initial and final consonant deletion, fronting, stopping, and cluster reduction. The language subscore reflects errors on 31 language behaviors normally acquired between ages 2½ to 6. Statistical section included in the manual.

Format: Individual administration; examiner required; untimed: 7–10 minutes

Scoring: Hand key; examiner evaluated

Cost: Complete $65.00

Publisher: Slosson Educational Publications, Inc.

Speech-Ease Screening Inventory (K–1)

Teryl Pigott, Jane Barry, Barbara Hughes, Debra Eastin, Patricia Titus, Harriett Stensel, Kathleen Metcalf, Belinda Porter

Copyright: 1985

Population: Children; Kindergarten through Grade 1

Purpose: Assesses the articulation and language development of children; used to identify students needing speech–language services

Description: Multiple-item response test evaluating the speech and language development of children. The basic section assesses articulation, language association, auditory recall, expressive vocabulary, and concept development. An optional section includes additional auditory items, a section on similarities and differences, a language sample, and a section on linguistic relationships.

Format: Examiner required; not suitable for group use; untimed: 7–10 minutes

Scoring: Examiner evaluated

Cost: Complete kit (examiner's manual, 100 screening forms, 50 kindergarten summary sheets, 50 first-grade summary sheets, 3 picture plates, storage box) $84.00

Publisher: PRO-ED, Inc.

Structured Photographic Articulation Test Featuring Dudsberry (SPAT-D)

Janet I. Dawson, Patricia Tattersall

Copyright: 1993

Population: Children; ages 3 to 9 years

Purpose: Designed to assess phonological repertoire in a natural manner and provide a systematic means of assessing the child's articulation

Description: Uses 48 actual photographs to spontaneously elicit the child's production of 59 consonant singletons according to syllabic function and manner of articulation. Identifies articulation errors on 21 consonant blends containing the phonemes /s/, /r/, and /l/. Allows for analysis of production of /s/, /r/, and /l/ in more complex phonetic contexts. Examines the phonological processes which are commonly used by preschool and school-age children. Examiner must be a speech–language pathologist.

Format: Individual administration; examiner required

Scoring: Examiner evaluated

Cost: Complete kit (manual, 48 photographs, and 25 response forms) $79.00

Publisher: Janelle Publications, Inc.

Templin-Darley Tests of Articulation
Margaret Templin, Frederick Darley

Copyright: 1969

Population: Children, adolescents

Purpose: Assesses adequacy of oral pressure for speech-sound production

Description: Test with 141 items divided into nine overlapping subjects; the 50-item Screening Test indicates general articulation adequacy; the 43 items constituting the Iowa Pressure Articulation Test assess the adequacy of oral pressure for speech-sound production and the adequacy of velopharyngeal closure. Other subtests which help identify areas of needed speech correction are a 42-item grouping of initial and final consonant singles, 31 two- and three-phoneme /r/ clusters, 18 two- and three- phoneme /l/ clusters, 17 two- and three-phoneme /s/ clusters, 9 miscellaneous two-phoneme clusters, 11 vowels, and 6 diphthong and combination items. The manual contains complete instructions for administration and scoring, 57 stimulus cards, and norms for the Diagnostic Test as a whole and for each of the nine subtests. Cards are used with young children. For older subjects 141 test sentences elicit the same sounds. The four-page Articulation Test Form includes the numbered test items, an outline for analysis of test results, and space for additional comments on speech performance. Reusable overlays for the nine subtests facilitate scoring.

Format: Individual administration; suitable for group use

Scoring: Hand key

Cost: Specimen Set $10.00; manual $7.00; test forms $.15; scoring overlay $3.00

Publisher: University of Iowa

Test of Minimal Articulation Competence (T-MAC)
Wayne Secord

Copyright: 1981

Population: Ages 3 to adult

Purpose: Assesses the severity of articulation disorders; used to identify children needing therapy, monitor speech development in terms of research-based minimal expectations for age level, and target the most trainable phonemes for remediation

Description: Multiple-item verbal-response test using one of the following procedures: picture identification, sentence reading, or sentence repetition. The test provides a flexible format for obtaining a diagnostic measure of articulation performance on 24 consonant phonemes; frequently occurring *s, r,* and *l* blends; 12 vowels; 4 diphthongs; and variations of vocalic *r.* The test kit includes a manual and 25 record forms.

Format: Examiner required; not suitable for group use; untimed: 10–20 minutes

Scoring: Examiner evaluated

Cost: Complete Program (manual and protocols) $80.50

Publisher: The Psychological Corporation

Weiss Comprehensive Articulation Test (WCAT)
Curtis E. Weiss

Copyright: 1980

Population: Ages 3 to adult

Purpose: Determines articulation disorders or delays and identifies misarticulation patterns and other problems; used in articulation therapy

Description: Multiple-item criterion-referenced test in two forms: an easel-stand flip book of 85 pictures for subjects who cannot read and a card with 38 sentences for those who can. With the pictures, the child supplies the missing word in a sentence spoken by the examiner; with the sentences, the child does the reading. Materials include the picture cards and forms.

Format: Individual administration; examiner required; not appropriate for nonverbal subjects; untimed: 20 minutes

Scoring: Examiner evaluated

Cost: Complete kit (examiner's manual, picture cards, sentence card, 100 picture response forms, and 100 sentence response forms) $84.00

Publisher: PRO-ED, Inc.

Aphasia, Apraxia, Dysarthria, and Dysphagia

Apraxia Battery for Adults (ABA)
Barbara L. Dabul

Copyright: 1979

Population: Adults

Purpose: Used in supporting or refuting a prior impression of apraxia to gain an estimate of severity

Description: A systematic set of tasks with an objective scoring system that provides the clinician with an initial step toward assessing recovery in relation to severity of apraxia. The instrument has six subtests: Diadochokinetic Rate, Increasing Word Length, Limb Apraxia and Oral Apraxia, Latency and Utterance Time for Polysyllabic Words, Repeated Trials Test, and Inventory of Articulation Characteristics of Apraxia.

Format: Individual administration; 20 minutes

Scoring: Examiner administered and interpreted

Cost: Complete kit (manual [including picture plates], protocols, and storage box) $84.00

Publisher: PRO-ED, Inc.

Assessment of Intelligibility of Dysarthric Speech (AIDS)
Kathryn Yorkston, David Beukelman, Charles Traynor

Copyright: 1984

Population: Adolescents, adults

Purpose: Quantifies the single-word intelligibility, sentence intelligibility, and speaking rates of dysarthric individuals

Description

Multiple-item verbal and listening test containing speaker tasks, recording techniques, and listener response formats to obtain a variety of intelligibility and communication efficiency measures. The clinical software version provides for quick and efficient quantifying without tedious stimuli selection or computation. Both versions can be readministered repeatedly with reliable results.

Format: Individual administration; requires speech pathologist

Scoring: Examiner administration and interpretation

Cost: Print version (manual, picture book, and storage box) $98.00; computer version (Apple II) $169.00

Publisher: PRO-ED, Inc.

Bedside Evaluation and Screening Test of Aphasia
Joyce Fitch-West, Elaine S. Sands

Copyright: 1986

Population: Adults

Purpose: Assesses language deficits for patients to provide a profile of severity

Description: Uses seven subtests to measure competence across three modalities: Speaking, Comprehension, and Reading. The subtests include Conversational Expression, Naming Objects, Describing Objects, Repeating Sentences, Point-to Objects, Pointing to Parts of a Picture, and Reading. After administration and scoring, a summary form is completed that is suitable for placement in medical charts or patient folders. An overall score reflective of the impairment's severity is produced; descriptors relative to the patient's degree of impairment can also be used to match the objective numerical score.

Format: Individual administration; untimed: time varies

Scoring: Hand key

Cost: Complete kit (manual, protocols, and manipulatives in storage box) $154.00

Publisher: PRO-ED, Inc.

Bedside Evaluation of Dysphagia (BED)
Edward Hardy

Copyright: 1995

Population: Adults with neurological impairment

Purpose: Assesses adult patients with dysphagia at bedside

Description: Comprised of a screening of behavior, cognition, and communication abilities; oral–motor assessment of structure and function of the lips, cheeks, tongue, soft palate, mandible, and larynx. An Oral–Pharyngeal Dysphagia Symptoms Assessment is designed to assess oral, and to some degree, pharyngeal abilities. The Summary Report is detachable.

Format: Individual; untimed

Scoring: Examiner administration and interpretation

Cost: Manual and 10 evaluation forms $35.95; 20 evaluation forms $27.00

Publisher: Imaginart International, Inc.

Boston Assessment of Severe Aphasia (BASA)
Nancy Helm-Estabrooks, Gail Ramsberger, Alisa R. Morgan, Marjorie Nicholas

Copyright: 1989

Population: Stroke patients

Purpose: Provides diagnostic information needed for immediate treatment

Description: This aphasia test is designed to be given to poststroke cases soon after the onset of symptoms, preferably at bedside. It can be given long before most other assessments are appropriate. The BASA probes the spared language abilities of persons with severe aphasia and provides diagnostic information needed for immediate treatment. The 61 items measure a wide variety of tasks and modalities, including auditory comprehension, buccofacial or limb praxis, gesture recognition, oral and gestural expression, reading comprehension, writing, and visual–spatial tasks. Both gestural and verbal responses to the items are scored, and refusals, affective responses, and perseverative responses are recorded. Gestural and verbal responses may be scored in combination or separately, and both scores may be expressed as fully or partially communicative.

Format: Individual administration

Scoring: Hand key

Cost: Complete kit (examiner's manual, custom clipboard, manipulatives, stimulus cards, 24 record forms, briefcase) $249.00

Publisher: PRO-ED, Inc.

Boston Diagnostic Aphasia Test
Harold Goodglass, Edith Kaplan

Copyright: 1983

Population: Adults

Purpose: Measures the presence and type of aphasic syndrome, leading to inferences concerning cerebral localization for both initial determination and detection of change over time, and comprehensive assessment of the assets and liabilities of the patient

Description: Multiple-item instrument that provides severity rating in fluency, auditory comprehension, naming, oral reading, repetition, paraphasia, automatic speech, reading comprehension, writing, music, and spatial and computational areas. The patient responds to oral, pictorial, and written prompts.

Format: Examiner required; not suitable for group use; untimed: time varies

Scoring: Examiner evaluated

Cost: Complete package $47.00

Publisher: Williams & Wilkins

Boston Naming Test

Edith Kaplan, Harold Goodglass,
Sandra Weintraub, Osa Segal

Copyright: 1983

Population: Children; adults

Purpose: Measures object naming ability in individuals with aphasia

Description: Sixty-item test of line-drawn objects of graded difficulty from "bed" to "abacus." The pictures have been selected so as to eliminate items that have alternative acceptable names. In the administration of this test, the individual is provided with the initial sound (phonemic cue) if unable to name correctly without help. Rate of success with phonemic cues is counted separately but not included in the count of items correct. Norms are provided for children ages 5 years 5 months to 10 years 5 months and adults.

Format: Examiner required; not suitable for group use; untimed: time varies

Scoring: Examiner evaluated

Cost: Picture booklet $10.95; Scoring booklet $9.00 per 25

Publisher: Williams & Wilkins

Contextual Memory Test

Joan P. Toglia

Copyright: 1993

Population: Adults

Purpose: Measures client's use of memory strategies and awareness of memory limitations

Description: Oral-response test suitable for individuals with physical and mental disabilities.

Format: Examiner required; not suitable for group use

Scoring: Hand scorable by examiner

Cost: Test kit (manual, cards, picture cards, score sheets, carrying case) $89.00

Publisher: Communication Skill Builders, Inc.

Dysarthria Examination Battery

Sakina S. Drummond

Copyright: 1993

Population: Children to adults

Purpose: Assesses motor speech disorders for speech pathology applications

Description: Suitable for individuals with hearing and mental disabilities

Format: Examiner required; not suitable for group use; untimed

Scoring: Examiner evaluated

Cost: Test kit (manual, test, stimulus cards, scoring forms) $59.00

Publisher: Communication Skill Builders, Inc.

Examining for Aphasia–Third Edition (EFA–3)

Jon Eisenson

Copyright: 1994

Population: Adolescents and adults

Purpose: Helps determine areas of strength and weakness for receptive and expressive functions

Description: A revised version of a "classic" assessment of aphasia and aphasic impairments relative to receptive and evaluative (decoding) and expressive and productive (encoding) impairments. EFA–3 acknowledges cognitive, personality, and linguistic modifications that are associated with acquired aphasia. The test reflects current positions and interpretations of aphasic impairments on subsymbolic and symbolic levels. The EFA–3's 33 subtests help determine areas of strength and weakness for receptive and expressive functions. EFA–3 tests for agnosia (visual, auditory, and tactile); linguistic reception (oral and written) of words, sentences, and paragraphs; and expressive impairments, including simple skills, automatic language, arithmetic computations, and language items that parallel those for receptive tasks. An optional "Tell a Story" test in response to a picture assesses self-organized language content. The examiner's manual has been completely rewritten and redesigned for ease of administration and interpretation. It includes the author's position on the nature and purposes of assessment for diagnosis prognosis, and on therapy.

Format: Examiner required; individual administration; time varies

Scoring: Hand key

Cost: Complete kit (examiner's manual, picture book, 25 profile/response forms, 25 examiner record booklets, object kit, storage box) $139.00

Publisher: PRO-ED, Inc.

Frenchay Dysarthria Assessment
P. Enderby

Copyright: 1983

Population: Age 12 to adult

Purpose: Assesses and provides differential description and diagnosis of dysarthria

Description: Task-performance and behavioral-observation 29-item test measuring speech impairment due to neuromuscular disorders. The test items cover reflex, respiration, lips, jaw, palate, larynx, tongue, intelligibility, influencing factors (sight, teeth, language, mood, posture), rate, and sensation. The results are recorded graphically on multicopy forms using a 9-point rating scale.

Format: Individual administration

Scoring: Examiner administration and interpretation

Cost: Complete kit (manual and protocols) $39.00

Publisher: PRO-ED, Inc.

Reading Comprehension Battery for Aphasia (RCBA)
Leonard L. LaPointe, Jennifer Horner

Copyright: 1979

Population: Adults

Purpose: Evaluates the nature and degree of reading impairment in aphasic adults and provides a focus for therapy

Description: Multiple-item stimulus-response test utilizing pictures to assess the reading comprehension of adults with aphasia. The 10 subtests included are Single Word Comprehension (Visual Confusions, Auditory Confusions, and Semantic Confusions), Functional Reading, Synonyms, Sentence Comprehension (Picture), Short Paragraph Comprehension (Picture), Paragraphs (Factual and Inferential Comprehension—2 subtests), and Morpho-Syntactic Reading with Lexical Controls.

Format: Examiner required; not suitable for group use; untimed: typical time not available

Scoring: Examiner evaluated

Cost: Complete kit (examiner's manual, stimulus items, picture plates, 50 response record forms, storage box) $89.00

Publisher: PRO-ED, Inc.

Screening Test for Developmental Apraxia of Speech (STDAS)
Robert W. Blakeley

Copyright: 1980

Population: Children; ages 4 to 12

Purpose: Assists in the differential diagnosis of developmental apraxia of speech

Description: Multiple-item test diagnosing the developmental apraxia of speech through eight subtests. The subtests are Expressive Language Discrepancy, Vowels and Diphthongs, Oral Motor Movement, Verbal Sequencing, Motorically Complex Words, Articulation, Transpositions, and Prosody. The testing results of 169 children of normal intelligence with multiple articulation errors are reported.

Format: Examiner required; not suitable for group use; untimed: 10 minutes

Scoring: Examiner evaluated

Cost: Complete kit (examiner's manual, 50 response record forms, storage box) $69.00

Publisher: PRO-ED, Inc.

Sklar Aphasia Scale–Revised
Maurice Sklar

Copyright: 1983

Population: Adults

Purpose: Assesses auditory decoding, visual decoding, oral encoding, and graphic encoding; used for adults with suspected speech–language disturbances

Description: Oral-response 100-item criterion-referenced short-answer verbal point-to true–false test providing objective measurement and evaluations of speech and language disorders resulting from brain damage. Provides a reliable determination of the kind and extent of disturbance and potential for benefitting from therapy. Yields raw scores and impairment profile for five scales, plus total.

Format: Examiner required; not suitable for group use; untimed: time varies

Scoring: Examiner evaluated

Cost: Kit (25 protocol booklets; 1 manual; stimulus cards) $75.00

Publisher: Western Psychological Services

Western Aphasia Battery (WAB)
Andrew Kertesz

Copyright: 1982

Population: Adolescents, adults

Purpose: Evaluates an individual's ability to read, write, and calculate; measures the language functions of content, fluency, auditory comprehension, repetition, and naming; used to evaluate the severity of language impairment (aphasia)

Description: Three-part test covering oral language; reading, writing, calculation, and praxis; and nonverbal skills (apraxia, drawing, block design, calculation, Raven's matrices). The nonverbal part is optional. The oral part requires a stopwatch, four Kohs blocks, and a *Raven's Colored Progressive Matrices* test to measure spontaneous speech, comprehension, naming, repetition, and aphasia. The subtests require conversational speech in response to questions and a picture interview. The reading and writing tests measure functional communication, spontaneous speech and fluency, and comprehension.

Format: Examiner required; not suitable for group use; timed: 1 hour

Scoring: Examiner evaluated

Cost: Complete kit (manual, test booklet, and stimulus cards) $100.50

Publisher: The Psychological Corporation

Fluency and Voice

Assessment of Fluency in School-Age Children (AFSC)
Julia Thompson

Copyright: 1983

Population: Ages 5 to 18

Purpose: Evaluates speech deficiencies; used to assess individuals who stutter to provide therapy; also used in school programs

Description: A diagnostic, criterion-referenced instrument that uses sequenced tasks to determine speech, expressive language, and physiological (oral motor and breath control) functioning. Paper–pencil 37-item test. Materials needed (but not included) are a tape recorder, picture stimuli, and stopwatch. The accompanying resource guide provides reference information describing management placement in public school settings as well as complete directions for administration.

Format: Individual administration; parent and teacher interview; requires speech pathologist

Scoring: Examiner administration and interpretation

Cost: Complete kit (resource guide, protocols, and storage box) $89.00

Publisher: PRO-ED, Inc.

Fluency Development System for Young Children (TFDS)
Susan Meyers Fosnot, Lee L. Woodford

Copyright: 1992

Population: Children

Purpose: Assesses and treats young children with fluency disorders; involves each child's parent, child care provider, or teacher in the child's counseling

Description: Three sections provide valuable information to help in multidimensional assessment. Differential Assessment of Fluency Disorders describes procedures for a differential diagnosis of fluency disorders, including intake techniques, discussion of a standard battery of tests to be given, and techniques and tips on how to most effectively administer these tests. The Child Treatment Program section adapts principles from well-known fluency and cognitive intervention programs for young children, including providing group therapy instructions, incorporating individual child-centered intervention, and implementing parent counseling activities. Basic Principles of Group Counseling incorporates basic principles of counseling to increase your knowledge base pertaining to theories and applications of counseling, update information about parent counseling and fluency disorders, and implement a model parent counseling program using a team approach. An appendix contains valuable reproducible forms and references. Various manipulatives and an audiotape help you embellish the stories and games, enhancing fluency techniques.

Format: Examiner required; timed: time varies

Scoring: Examiner evaluated

Cost: Complete program $297.00

Publisher: PRO-ED, Inc.

Source Profile: Oral–Facial and Neck

Debra C. Gangale

Copyright: 1995

Population: All ages

Purpose: Measures a client's oral–motor functioning, care plan goals, progress, and current status; used for communicative disorders for patients with stroke, head trauma, craniofacial abnormalities, cleft palate, or reconstructive surgery

Description: Criterion-referenced test with the following categories: orientation, observation and palpitation, musculature rating, current nutritional inventory, swallowing function, care plan, and objectives. A clinician interprets overall findings and observations. Examiner must be a qualified speech–language pathologist, occupational therapist, nurse, physical therapist, physician, physician's assistant, dentist, or oral hygienist.

Format: Individually administered; examiner required; untimed

Scoring: Examiner evaluated; no scoring service available

Cost: Manual and 10 test forms $29.95

Publisher: LinguiSystems, Inc.

Stuttering Prediction Instrument for Young Children (SPI)

Glyndon D. Riley

Copyright: 1981

Population: Children; ages 3 to 8

Purpose: Determines whether a child should be scheduled for therapy to treat stuttering

Description: Diagnostic test utilizing pictures, parent interview, observation, and taped recordings of the child's speech to assess the child's history, reactions, part-word repetitions, prolongations, and frequency of stuttered words

Format: Examiner required; timed: time varies

Scoring: Examiner evaluated

Cost: Complete kit (examiner's manual with picture plates and test forms, storage box) $74.00

Publisher: PRO-ED, Inc.

Stuttering Severity Instrument for Children and Adults (SSI)

Glyndon D. Riley

Copyright: 1994

Population: All ages

Purpose: Measures the severity of stuttering and evaluates the effects of treatment; used by clinicians and researchers

Description: Oral-response test utilizing pictures to measure the frequency of repetition and prolongation of sounds and syllables, estimated duration of the longest stuttering events, and observable concomitants.

Format: Examiner required; not suitable for group use; untimed: typical time not available

Scoring: Examiner evaluated

Cost: Complete kit (examiner's manual, picture plates, 50 test record and frequency computation forms, storage box) $79.00

Publisher: PRO-ED, Inc.

Test of Oral Structures and Functions (TOSF)
Gary J. Vitali

Copyright: 1986

Population: Ages 7 to adult

Purpose: Assesses oral structures, nonverbal oral functioning, and verbal oral functioning; used by speech pathologists for screening, differential diagnosis, caseload management decisions, and pre- and posttreatment assessment

Description: Multiple-item paper–pencil and oral-response test assessing oral structures and motor integrity during verbal and nonverbal oral functioning and establishing the nature of structural, neurological, or functional disorders. The test is composed of five subtests: Speech Survey, Verbal Oral Functioning, Nonverbal Motor Functioning, Orofacial Structures, and History/ Behavioral Survey. The Speech Survey targets articulation, rate/prosody, fluency, and voice during spontaneous or elicited speech. The Verbal Oral Functioning subtest assesses the integrity of oral–nasal resonance balance during imitated and spontaneous speech and articulatory precision and rate/prosody during tests which control for performance loading effects, syllable position effects, voicing, manner of articulation, and placement of articulation. The Nonverbal Motor Functioning subtest assesses volitional and automatic oral functioning during essentially static and sequenced activities controlled for general anatomic site of functioning. The Orofacial Structures subtest is an observational survey of intraoral and orofacial structures at rest.

Format: Examiner required; not suitable for group use; timed: 20 minutes

Scoring: Examiner evaluated

Cost: Complete kit (manual, 25 test booklets, finger cots, tongue blades, balloons, oroscope penlight) $75.00

Publisher: Slosson Educational Publications, Inc.

Voice Assessment Protocol for Children and Adults (VAP)
Rebekah H. Pindzola

Copyright: 1987

Population: Children, adults

Purpose: Evaluates voice pitch, loudness, quality, breath features, and rate/rhythm

Description: Clinical tasks are guided step by step, and immediate interpretations of normalcy are facilitated by a grid-marking system. The VAP is equally applicable to functional and neurogenic voice disorders. The VAP includes a pitch level sample audiocassette for clinical use. By using these taped samples, musical instruments and sophisticated pitch determination equipment are not necessary for a voice assessment. The cassette contains whole notes of the musical scale between E2 and C6. The tape is arranged for clinical practicality. Each whole note and octave is identified, played on a piano, then followed by a vocal demonstration.

Format: Examiner required; timed: time varies

Scoring: Examiner evaluated

Cost: Complete kit (examiner's manual, audiocassette, 25 protocols, storage box) $49.00

Publisher: PRO-ED, Inc.

Pragmatics

Test of Pragmatic Language (TOPL)
Diana Phelps-Terasaki

Copyright: 1992

Population: Kindergarten through junior high; adult remedial

Purpose: Assesses the student's ability to effectively use pragmatic language

Description: TOPL test items provide information within six core subcomponents of pragmatic language: physical setting, audience, topic, purpose (speech acts), visual–gestural cues, and abstraction. The test includes 44 items, each of which establishes a social context. After a verbal stimulus prompt from the examiner, who also displays a picture, the student responds to the dilemma presented. The TOPL is designed for use by speech–language pathologists, teachers, counselors, psychologists, mental health professionals, and administrators. It is also appropriate for use as part of a comprehensive psychological battery of tests to aid in the evaluation of social skills and social language use. Norms are provided for individuals from 5 years to 13 years 11 months; however, test items can be used as a criterion-referenced assessment for older individuals. The TOPL was standardized on a sample of 1,016 children residing in 21 states. Characteristics of the normative sample match those from the 1990 U.S. census data with regard to gender, residence, race, geographic region, and ethnicity. Internal consistency of the TOPL was determined using the coefficient alpha technique at each age level.

Format: Individual administration; timed: time varies

Scoring: Examiner evaluated

Cost: Complete kit (examiner's manual, picture book, 25 profile/examiner record forms, storage box) $109.00

Publisher: PRO-ED, Inc.

Semantics

Assessing Semantic Skills Through Everyday Themes (ASSET)
Mark Barrett, Linda Bowers, Rosemary Huisingh

Copyright: 1988

Population: Children; ages 3 to 9; preschool through Grade 4

Purpose: Assesses the receptive and expressive vocabulary and semantic skills of preschool and early elementary children

Description: Test with 150 items examining semantics through a theme approach that utilizes 20 pictures depicting the day-to-day life experiences of preschool and early elementary children. The themes include learning and playing, shopping, around the house, working, eating, and health and fitness. The types of tasks that are evaluated receptively and expressively are labeling, categorizing, attributes, functions, and definitions. The test provides standardized analyses of a child's strengths and weaknesses as well as an overall estimate of the individual child's semantic and vocabulary abilities in relation to other children the child's age. Standard scores, percentile ranks, age equivalents, and standard deviations are available. In addition, the normative data from a sample of children with language disorders who were administered the test is available.

Format: Examiner required; not suitable for group use; untimed: time varies

Scoring: Examiner evaluated

Cost: Test kit (manual, picture stimuli book, 20 test forms) $79.95

Publisher: LinguiSystems, Inc.

Expressive One-Word Picture Vocabulary Test–Revised (EOWPVT–R)
Morrison F. Gardner

Copyright: 1990

Population: Ages 2 through 11 years 11 months

Purpose: Provides in-depth assessment of speaking vocabulary

Description: Verbal test of definitional and interpretational skills. The instrument consists of 100 pictures presented one at a time to the examinee, who names each picture. Standard scores, scaled scores, percentiles, stanines, and age equivalents are provided. Spanish record forms are available.

Format: Individual administration; under 20 minutes

Scoring: Examiner administered and interpreted

Cost: Test kit (manual, test plates, and English protocols in vinyl folder) $75.00

Publisher: Academic Therapy Publications

Expressive One-Word Picture Vocabulary Test: Upper Extension (EOWPVT: UE)
Morrison F. Gardner

Copyright: 1983

Population: Ages 12 through 15 years 11 months

Purpose: Provides in-depth assessment of speaking vocabulary

Description: Multiple-item oral-response test in which the student demonstrates ability to understand and use words by naming pictures that range from simple objects to representations of abstract concepts. The instrument is a diagnostic tool for evaluating a bilingual student's English/Spanish fluency. Standard scores, stanines, percentiles, and language ages are provided. Spanish forms are available.

Format: Individual administration; 5–10 minutes

Scoring: Examiner administered and interpreted

Cost: Test kit (manual, test plates, English record forms in vinyl folder) $70.00

Publisher: Academic Therapy Publications

Joliet 3-Minute Speech and Language Screen (JMSLS)–Revised

Mary C. Kinzler,
Constance Cowing Johnson

Copyright: 1992

Population: Kindergarten, Grades 2 and 5

Purpose: Identifies students' potential problems in grammar, semantics, and phonology

Description: Multiple-item individually administered oral-response test assessing receptive vocabulary, expressive syntax, voice, fluency, and phonological competence. Line drawings are used to elicit receptive vocabulary. Sentences are used to identify expressive syntax, morphology, and phonological competence.

Format: Individually administered, but suitable for group use; 3 minutes

Scoring: Examiner evaluated

Cost: Test kit (manuals, Apple II disk, vocabulary plates, scoring sheets, ring binder) $59.00

Publisher: Communication Skill Builders, Inc.

Listening for Meaning Test

M. A. Brimer

Copyright: 1981

Population: Children; ages 3 to 18

Purpose: Measures the level of intelligent verbal functions of which an individual is capable; used by teachers, psychologists, or speech therapists

Description: Multiple-item picture-response test using an individual's understanding of spoken English words as a means of measuring the individual's level of verbal functioning. The individual indicates which picture represents the meaning of a word spoken by the examiner. A focusing scale is used to determine at which point testing should begin within 10 hierarchically ordered scales of 12 items each.

Format: Examiner required; not suitable for group use; untimed: time varies

Scoring: Examiner evaluated

Cost: £19.95 Sterling

Publisher: Educational Evaluation Enterprises

Peabody Picture Vocabulary Test–Revised (PPVT–R)

Lloyd M. Dunn, Leota M. Dunn

Copyright: 1981

Population: Ages 2 years 6 months to adult

Purpose: Used as a quick estimate of verbal ability; evaluates individuals referred for remedial education or speech therapy

Description: A measure of receptive vocabulary. One may buy kit of combined forms or each form individually. Form L or Form M test kit includes an easel of 175 test plates, manual, and package of 25 test records. Combined kit includes both easels, one manual, and two packages of test records (one L and one M). Special editions of Form L or M with wipeable test plates are also available.

Format: Individual administration, 10–20 minutes

Scoring: Examiner interpreted, standard scores

Cost: Complete kit (both test easels, protocols, manual) $154.95

Publisher: American Guidance Service

Receptive One-Word Picture Vocabulary Test (ROWPVT)
Morrison F. Gardner

Copyright: 1985

Population: Ages 2 years through 11 years 11 months

Purpose: Assesses receptive vocabulary of bilingual, speech-impaired, immature, withdrawn, and emotionally and physically impaired children

Description: Response test using 100 picture plates, each with four illustrations presented horizontally across the page. The child identifies the illustration that matches the word presented by the examiner. When used with the Expressive One-Word Picture Vocabulary Test, comparisons can be made between a student's receptive and expressive vocabulary skills.

Format: Examiner required; not suitable for group use; 20 minutes

Scoring: Examiner administered and interpreted

Cost: Test kit (manual, test plates, 50 English record forms) $70.00

Publisher: Academic Therapy Publications

Receptive One-Word Picture Vocabulary Test–Upper Extension (ROWPVT–UE)
Rich Brownell

Copyright: 1987

Population: Children, adolescents; ages 12 to 15

Purpose: Assesses receptive vocabulary; used with bilingual, speech-impaired, immature/withdrawn, and emotionally/physically impaired children

Description: Multiple-item nonverbal assessment of receptive vocabulary. The examinee points to an illustration that matches the word presented by the examiner. The test is an upward extension of the ROWPVT. When the ROWPVT is used with the Expressive One-Word Picture Vocabulary Test–Upper Extension, the two measures evaluate differences in speaking and hearing vocabularies. Tables for converting raw scores to language standard scores, percentile ranks, stanines, and language ages are provided.

Format: Examiner required; individual administration; untimed: 20 minutes

Scoring: Examiner evaluated

Cost: kit (manual, test plates, 50 English record forms, vinyl folder) $70.00

Publisher: Academic Therapy Publications

Test de Vocabulario en Imágenes Peabody (TVIP)
Lloyd M. Dunn, Delia E. Lugo, Eligio R. Padilla, Leota M. Dunn

Copyright: 1986

Population: Ages 2 years 6 months to 18

Purpose: For use with Spanish-speaking and bilingual students to measure Spanish vocabulary

Description: A measure of receptive vocabulary. One may buy kit of combined forms or each form individually. Form L or Form M test kit includes an easel of 175 test plates, manual, and package of 25 test records. User must be B-Level qualified.

Format: Individual administration, 10–15 minutes

Scoring: Examiner interpreted, standard scores

Cost: Test kit (test easel, Spanish manual, 25 record forms) $84.95

Publisher: American Guidance Service

Test of Adolescent/Adult Word Finding (TAWF)
Diane J. German

Copyright: 1990

Population: Ages 12 to 80; Grades 7 through 12

Purpose: Assesses word-finding disorders

Description: Test with 107 items (or 40 in the brief version) with five naming sections: Picture Naming: Nouns; Picture Naming: Verbs; Sentence Completion Naming; Description

Naming; and Category Naming. The TAWF includes a special sixth comprehension section that allows the examiner to determine if errors are a result of word-finding problems or are due to poor comprehension. The test provides formal and informal analyses of two dimensions of word finding: speed and accuracy. The formal analysis yields standard scores, percentile ranks, and grade standards for item response time. The informal analysis yields secondary characteristics (gestures and extra verbalization) and substitution types. Speed can be measured in actual or estimated item response time. The estimated response time can be done during testing and eliminates the need for a stopwatch or tape recorder.

Format: Examiner required; timed: 20–30 minutes

Scoring: Examiner evaluated

Cost: Complete kit (examiner's manual, technical manual, test book, and 25 response forms) $179.00

Publisher: PRO-ED, Inc.

Test of Awareness of Language Segments (TALS)
Diane J. Sawyer

Copyright: 1987

Population: Children; ages 4 years 6 months through 7 years

Purpose: Provides information that will help teachers plan reading instruction

Description: Forty-six items are distributed across three subtests to quickly and accurately assess which units of language children can explicitly manipulate. TALS indicates whether or not a child's language has developed to meet the instructional demands of a beginning program, helps teachers decide which reading approach to use with a student, and provides clues for selecting materials and activities appropriate to the language awareness level of the student. Cutoff scores are available based on inferences drawn from research studies involving more than 1,000 children at each grade level—kindergarten and first grade.

Format: Examiner required; timed: time varies

Scoring: Examiner evaluated

Cost: Complete kit (examiner's manual, 50 record forms, set of blocks, storage box) $98.00

Publisher: PRO-ED, Inc.

Test of Word Finding (TWF)
Diane J. German

Copyright: 1989

Population: Children, adolescents; ages 6 years 6 months to 12 years 11 months

Purpose: Diagnoses expressive language problems resulting from word retrieval difficulties; used in educational and clinical settings with children with language disorders, learning disabilities, and mental retardation, as well as children with no disabilities, for planning, evaluating, and conducting research

Description: Multiple-item test in which a child responding to naming tasks is scored for accuracy and item response time, resulting in one of four profiles of word-finding patterns: fast and accurate, slow and accurate, fast and inaccurate, slow and inaccurate. Percentile ranks, standard scores, and means and standard deviations for response and completion times are obtained. An easel-binder test book is used for administration.

Format: Examiner required; not suitable for group use; untimed: 20–30 minutes

Scoring: Examiner evaluated

Cost: Complete kit (examiner's manual, technical manual, test book, and 25 response forms) $149.00

Publisher: PRO-ED, Inc.

Test of Word Finding in Discourse (TWFD)
Diane J. German

Copyright: 1991

Population: Children

Purpose: Helps answer questions related to word-finding difficulties

Description: In the TWFD the child views three stimulus pictures contained in the manual and responds to standard auditory prompts.

The elicited language sample is tape-recorded and then scored through a process of transcribing and segmenting the child's narrative. Scores obtained include the Productivity Index, a quantitative measure of how much language is produced in a child's discourse, and the Word Finding Behaviors Index, a frequency measure of specific word-finding behaviors present in a child's discourse, such as repetitions, reformulations, substitutions, insertions, empty words, time fillers, and delays. Percentile ranks and standard scores can be obtained for both indexes.

Format: Examiner required; timed: time varies

Scoring: Examiner evaluated

Cost: Complete kit (administration, scoring, interpretation, technical manual, and 25 record forms) $98.00

Publisher: PRO-ED, Inc.

Troubled Talk Test
James Kubeck

Copyright: 1973

Population: Adults

Purpose: Assesses understanding of the book *Troubled Talk*

Description: Can be used to present basic principles involved in human communication and human relations.

Format: Group or individual; untimed

Scoring: Examiner interpretation; self-scored

Cost: $.50 each (minimum of 10)

Publisher: International Society for General Semantics

Uncritical Inference Test
William V. Haney

Copyright: 1982

Population: Adolescents and adults

Purpose: Measures uncritical inferencing

Description: Instrument helps students learn to distinguish between observations and inferences. Multiple-choice paper–pencil test.

Format: Group or individual; untimed

Scoring: Examiner interpretation; self-scored

Cost: $.50 each (minimum of 10)

Publisher: International Society for General Semantics

WORD Test–Adolescent
Linda Bowers, Rosemary Huisingh, Mark Barrett, Jane Orman, Carolyn LoGuidice

Copyright: 1989

Population: Ages 12 to 18; Grades 7 through 12

Purpose: Assesses students' expressive vocabulary and semantic skills using common as well as unique contexts; tasks reflect language usage typical of school assignments and life experiences

Description: A 60-item oral response test assessing a student's facility with language and word meaning. The four subtests assess the following expressive vocabulary and semantic tasks: Brand Names, Synonyms, Sign of the Times, and Definitions. Tasks are presented both auditorily and in printed or graphic form. Test results yield age equivalencies, standard scores, standard deviations, and percentile ranks for students aged 12 to 18. Demonstration items are provided. A discussion of performance and suggestions for remediation are included in the test manual.

Format: Examiner required; not suitable for group use; untimed: approximately 25 minutes

Scoring: Examiner evaluated

Cost: Test kit (manual and 20 test forms) $59.95

Publisher: LinguiSystems, Inc.

WORD Test–Revised (Elementary)
Rosemary Huisingh, Mark Barrett, Linda Bowers, Carolyn LoGiudice, Jane Orman

Copyright: 1990

Population: Children; ages 7 to 11; Grades 2 through 6

Purpose: Assesses expressive vocabulary and

semantics; evaluates how a child understands and uses critical semantic features to attach meaning to words; used for communicative disorders and low academic performance especially in vocabulary and language arts

Description: Oral-response 90-item verbal test with six subtests: Associations, Synonyms, Semantic Absurdities, Antonyms, Definitions, and Multiple Definitions. Profiles and reports yielded are as follows: number of subjects, means, medians, and standard deviations of each task and total test by age in 6-month intervals; age equivalents of raw scores for each task and total test; percentile ranks and standard score values for each task and total test raw scores by age in 6-month intervals; test–retest reliability coefficients and standard errors of measurement of each task and total test by age; reliability based on item homogeneity; Kuder Richardson (KR20) coefficients of each task by age; point biserial correlations between item scores and task scores by age; average task intercorrelations and average correlations between tasks and total test across all ages; task intercorrelations and correlations between tasks and total test across all ages; correlations between the *WORD Test* and the *WORD Test–R* (Elementary) for each task and total test by age; *t* values for differences between subjects with and without language disorder by age level for raw score means by task and total test; subject distribution for item selection study.

Format: Individual administration; examiner required; untimed: 25–35 minutes

Scoring: Examiner evaluated; no scoring service available

Cost: Manual and 20 forms $59.95

Publisher: LinguiSystems, Inc.

Syntax

Carrow Elicited Languages Inventory (CELI)
Elizabeth Carrow Woolfolk

Copyright: 1974

Population: Ages 3 years to 7 years 11 months

Purpose: Assesses a child's knowledge of grammatical structures and syntax through the use of elicited imitation

Description: Instrument is norm referenced, resulting in means, percentile ranks, and standard scores. The child is asked to repeat verbatim sentences of increasing word length and syntactic complexity. Children with good grasp of grammar and syntactic rules are found to be able to repeat longer sentences than those who do not have such an ability.

Format: Individual administration; 25 minutes

Scoring: Examiner scoring and interpretation

Cost: Complete kit (manual, training guide, protocols, audiotape, and binder) $98.00

Publisher: PRO-ED, Inc.

Language Sampling, Analysis, and Training (LSAT)
Dorothy Tyack, Robert Gottsleben

Copyright: 1974

Population: Ages 2 to adult

Purpose: Describes the procedures for analyzing the morphological and syntactical elements of sentences; also used as a resource for training children whose language delays are serious enough to warrant intervention

Description: Based on established linguistic and behavioral principles, this method is appropriate for both group and individual teaching. The authors suggest that the assessment of children's use of sentences provides a sample of what they typically produce in connected speech. This speech sample demonstrates the rules that each child has acquired to form sentences. Analyzing these data enables teachers and clinicians to write Individualized Education Programs that are precisely tailored to specific linguistic needs. The book contains four main chapters: Eliciting and Transcribing Language, Analyzing the Sample, Training Programs, and Measuring Change. Included with the handbook are the following worksheets: Transcription, Word/Morpheme Tally and Summary; Sequence of Language Acquisition Sheet; Baseline Analysis Sheet; Training Worksheet; and a Score Sheet. Scored or unscored samples are provided for practice.

Format: Examiner required; individual administration; time varies

Scoring: Hand key

Cost: Complete kit (handbook, transcription sheets, word/morpheme tally and summary sheets, sequence of language acquisition sheets, baseline analysis sheets, training worksheets, score sheets) $29.00

Publisher: PRO-ED, Inc.

Patterned Elicitation Syntax Test (PEST) (Revised)
Edna Carter Young, Joseph J. Perachio

Copyright: 1993

Population: Children; language age 3 years to 7 years 6 months

Purpose: Determines whether a child's expressive grammatical skills are age appropriate; identifies children needing further evaluation

Description: Multiple-item oral-response test using the delayed imitation technique to assess a child's use of 44 syntactic structures. The child listens to three consecutive modeled sentences with a common syntactic pattern but varying vocabulary while looking simultaneously at corresponding illustrations. The child then repeats the sentences with the aid of the drawings. The first two sentences serve as models. The third sentence, which is most distant from the examiner's model, is scored. In addition to determining the child's language age, criterion-referenced interpretation of the child's responses provides an in-depth analysis of the child's use of grammatical structures. The manual includes stimulus pictures, a demonstration page, normative data, and instructions for administration and scoring. The response form is used to record the child's utterances, the assessment form includes grammatical analysis, and the individual data form is used for record keeping.

Format: Examiner required; not suitable for group use; untimed: 20 minutes

Scoring: Examiner evaluated

Cost: Test kit (stimulus pictures, demonstration page, normative data, instructions, response sheets, assessment sheets, individual data form) $55.00

Publisher: Communication Skill Builders, Inc.

Structured Photographic Expressive Language Test–II (SPELT–II)
Janet I. Dawson

Copyright: 1974, revised 1983; updated 1995

Population: Children; ages 4 years to 9 years 5 months

Purpose: Measures expressive use of morphology and syntax

Description: Oral-response verbal test with 50 photographs. Standard scores, percentile ranks, and age equivalent scores are yielded. Photographic pictures are used.

Format: Individual administration; examiner required; untimed: 15–20 minutes

Scoring: Examiner evaluated

Cost: $79.00

Publisher: Janelle Publications, Inc.

Structured Photographic Expressive Language Test–Preschool (SPELT–P)
Ellen O'Hara Werner, Janet I. Dawson

Copyright: 1983

Population: Ages 3 years to 5 years 11 months

Purpose: Measures difficulty in expression of early developing morphological and syntactic features

Description: Oral-response verbal test with 25 photographs. Raw scores, means, standard deviations, and cutoff scores are yielded. Spanish version available.

Format: Individual administration; examiner required; untimed: 10–15 minutes

Scoring: Examiner evaluated

Cost: $69.00

Publisher: Janelle Publications, Inc.

Test for Oral Language Production (TOLP)

Copyright: 1980

Population: Children; ages 4 years 6 months to 10 years 6 months

Purpose: Measures oral language ability; used for educational evaluation

Description: Multiple-item verbal test of 16 aspects of language production covering productivity, syntactic complexity, correctness, fluency, and content. Materials include stimulus materials that the subject responds to orally. The TOLP is available only to professional personnel attached to education departments and others with sufficient knowledge of sentence analysis to score the test.

Format: Examiner required; not suitable for group use; untimed: 30 minutes–1 hour 30 minutes

Scoring: Hand key; examiner evaluated

Cost: Contact publisher

Publisher: Human Sciences Research Council

School and Institutional Environments

Classroom Environment Scale (CES)
Rudolf H. Moos, Edison J. Trickett

Copyright: Not provided

Population: Adolescents; Grades 7 through 12

Purpose: Assesses the teaching atmosphere of junior and senior high school classrooms in order to evaluate the effects of course content, teaching methods, teacher personality, and class composition

Description: Paper–pencil 90-item test measuring nine dimensions of classroom atmosphere: involvement, affiliation, teacher support, task orientation, competition, order and organization, rule clarity, teacher control, and innovation. These dimensions are grouped into four sets: relationship, personal development, system maintenance, and system change. Materials include four forms: The Real Form (Form R), which measures current perceptions of classroom atmosphere; the Ideal Form (Form I), which measures conceptions of the ideal classroom atmosphere; the Expectations Form (Form E), which measures expectations about a new classroom; and a 36-item Short Form (Form S). Forms I and E are not published, although reworded instructions and items are listed in the manual.

Format: Examiner required; suitable for group use; untimed: typical time not available

Scoring: Examiner evaluated; scoring service available

Cost: Preview kit (booklet, profile, answer sheet, scoring keys, manual) $26.00

Publisher: Consulting Psychologists Press, Inc.

Community Oriented Programs Environment Scale (COPES)
Rudolf H. Moos

Copyright: 1988

Population: Adults

Purpose: Assesses the social environments of community-based psychiatric treatment programs

Description: Paper–pencil 100-item true–false test of 10 aspects of social environment: involvement, support, spontaneity, autonomy, practical orientation, personal problem orientation, anger and aggression, order and organization, program clarity, and staff control. Materials include the Real Form (Form R), which measures perceptions of a current program; the 40-item Short Form (Form S); and the Ideal Form (Form I), which measures conceptions of a new program. Forms I and E are not published, but items and instructions are printed in the appendix of the COPES manual. Items are modified from the *Ward Atmosphere Scale*. One in a series of nine *Social Climate Scales*.

Format: Examiner required; untimed: 20 minutes

Scoring: Hand key

Cost: Sampler Set $25.00; permission for up to 200 uses $90.00

Publisher: Mind Garden, Inc.

Correctional Institutions Environment Scale (CIES)
Rudolf H. Moos

Copyright: 1974, 1987

Population: Adults

Purpose: Assesses the social environment of juvenile and adult correctional programs

Description: Paper–pencil 90-item true–false test of nine aspects of social environment: involvement, support, expressiveness, autonomy, practical orientation, personal problem orientation, order and organization, clarity, and staff control. Materials include four forms: the Real Form (Form R), which measures perceptions of the current correctional program; the 36-item Short Form (Form S); the Ideal Form (Form I), which measures conceptions of an ideal program; and the Expectations Form (Form E), which measures expectations of a new program. Forms I and E are not published, but items and instructions appear in the appendix of the CIES manual. Items and subscales are similar to those used in the *Ward Atmosphere Scale*. One of a series of nine *Social Climate Scales*.

Format: Examiner administered; suitable for group use; untimed: typical time not available

Scoring: Hand key

Cost: Sampler Set $25.00; permission for up to 200 uses $90.00

Publisher: Mind Garden, Inc.

Effective School Battery (ESB)
Gary D. Gottfredson

Copyright: 1984

Population: Adolescents; Grades 7 through 12

Purpose: Assesses the school environment of middle, junior, and senior high schools; used by administrators, board members, and teachers to identify excellence, diagnose problems, plan and develop programs, monitor progress, and research aspects of the school

Description: Multiple-item paper–pencil survey used with students and teachers for determining perceptions about school climate and characteristics of students and teachers in the school. Results describe 34 specific aspects of school climate and student and teacher characteristics. Four profiles that describe the school and can be used to compare any school with other schools are produced.

Format: Examiner required; suitable for group use; untimed: 50 minutes

Scoring: Computer scored

Cost: Introductory kit (user's manual, coordinator's manual, survey administrator's instructions, one each of student and teacher survey booklets, answer sheets) $25.00; user's manual $20.00

Publisher: Psychological Assessment Resources, Inc.

Institutional Functioning Inventory
Earl J. McGrath

Copyright: Not provided

Population: Adults

Purpose: Evaluates functioning of educational institutions; used in self-studies for accreditation, planning, and research

Description: Paper–pencil 132-item test assessing 11 dimensions of institutional functioning: intellectual–aesthetic, extracurricular, freedom, human diversity, concern for undergraduate learning, democratic governance, meeting local needs, self-study and planning, concern for advanced knowledge, concern for innovation, and institutional esprit. The inventory is distributed to a random sample of college community members, including the faculty, administration, and students. Available in French for Canadian institutions.

Format: Self-administered; suitable for group use; untimed: 45 minutes

Scoring: Computer scored

Cost: Reusable faculty booklet $0.50; reusable student booklet $0.35; answer sheet $0.10 each

Publisher: Educational Testing Service

Instructional Climate Inventory–Students

Larry A. Braskamp, Martin L. Maehr

Copyright: 1988

Population: Grades 3 to 12

Purpose: Assesses school culture from the student perspective; used by elementary and secondary school administrators to assess student and teacher attitudes toward the school and its instructional learning climate

Description: Twenty-item paper–pencil multiple-choice test measuring school loyalty and the strength of the school's climate. Additional scales describe the climate on four dimensions: accomplishment, recognition, power, and affiliation.

Format: Examiner/self-administered; suitable for group use; untimed: 5 to 10 minutes

Scoring: Computer scored by publisher

Cost: Contact publisher

Publisher: MetriTech, Inc.

Instructional Environment System–II (TIES–II)

James Ysseldyke, Sandra Christenson

Copyright: 1993

Population: Children, adolescents; Grades K through 12

Purpose: Used by special educators and school psychiatrists to assess the instructional needs of individual students

Description: Based on the belief that student performance in school is a function of an interaction between the student and the learning (instructional) environment, TIES–II provides a set of observational and interview forms, administration procedures, and an organizational structure that allows educators to both identify and address the instructional needs of individual students. While TIES–II can be used to assess the learning needs of all students, it is especially potent when applied to the needs of the tough to teach. TIES–II enables education professionals to identify ways to change instruction—or the learning environment—so that the student will respond to instruction more positively and thus more successfully. TIES–II provides education professionals with essential information for: prereferral intervention; instructional consultation; student/staff support teams (SSTs, TATs, etc.); intervention assistance; and collaborative intervention planning.

Format: Individual administration; examiner required; untimed

Scoring: Examiner evaluated

Cost: $55.00

Publisher: Sopris West, Inc.

Military Environment Inventory (MEI)

Rudolph H. Moos

Copyright: 1986

Population: Adults

Purpose: Assesses the social environment of various military contexts; used to detect individuals and units at risk for morale and performance problems

Description: Multiple-item paper–pencil inventory assessing individuals' and units' perceptions of the military environment. The test yields seven scores: Involvement, Peer Cohesion, Officer Support, Personal Status, Order and Organization, Clarity, and Officer Control. Additional subscales are related to military performance and sick-call rates.

Format: Self-administered; suitable for group use; untimed: typical time not available

Scoring: Hand key

Cost: Sampler Set $25.00; Permission Set $90.00; test booklets $25.00

Publisher: Mind Garden, Inc.

Small College Goals Inventory (SCGI)

Copyright: Not provided

Population: Adolescents, adults; college students

Purpose: Assesses the educational goals of small colleges; used to establish priorities and to provide direction for present and future planning

Description: Paper–pencil 90-item test assessing the educational goals of small colleges. The 20 goal areas are divided into two types, outcome goals and process goals. The outcome goals are academic development, intellectual orientation, individual personal development, humanism/altruism, cultural/aesthetic awareness, traditional religiousness, vocational preparation, advanced training, research, meeting local needs, public service, social egalitarianism, and social criticism/activism. The process goals are freedom, democratic governance, community, intellectual/aesthetic environment, innovation, off-campus learning, and accountability/efficiency. The inventory is distributed to a random sample of students, faculty, and administrators. Materials include space for 20 additional locally written goals.

Format: Self-administered; suitable for group use; untimed: 45 minutes

Scoring: Computer scored

Cost: Booklets $0.65; processing $1.75

Publisher: Educational Testing Service

Student Outcomes Information Service (SOIS)—Student Outcomes Questionnaires

Copyright: 1981

Population: College students

Purpose: Collects, analyzes, and evaluates the experiences, goals, accomplishments, and attitudes of college students; used by university administrators to study retention, review program utilization, and assess trends in needs for student services

Description: Series of six paper–pencil multiple-item instruments, administered to college students at six intervals before and after college, covering experiences, goals, accomplishments, and attitudes. Each questionnaire is available in a 2-year and 4-year version. A manual, data procession, and questionnaire analysis are included.

Format: Self-administered; suitable for group use; untimed: typical time not available

Scoring: Computer scored

Cost: Contact publisher

Publisher: The College Board

Student Reactions to College: Four Year College Edition (SRC/4)

Copyright: Not provided

Population: Adolescents, adults; college students

Purpose: Assesses the needs and concerns of students enrolled in four-year colleges; used in institutional self-assessment for developing programs and services for students

Description: Paper–pencil 150-item test assessing four dimensions of student concerns: processes of instruction, program planning, administrative affairs, and out-of-class activities. These four dimensions are divided further into such areas as content of courses, appropriateness of coursework to occupational goals, satisfaction with teaching procedures, student–faculty relations, educational and occupational decisions, effectiveness of advisers and counselors, registration, regulations, availability of classes, housing, employment, financial aid, and satisfaction with campus environment. The test is distributed to random samples of students.

Format: Self-administered; suitable for group use; untimed: 50 minutes

Scoring: Computer scored

Cost: Booklet $0.65; processing $1.75

Publisher: Educational Testing Service

Student Reactions to College: Two Year College Edition (SRC/2)

Copyright: Not provided

Population: Adolescents, adults; college students

Purpose: Assesses the needs and concerns of students enrolled in two-year colleges; used in institutional self-assessment for developing programs and services for students

Description: Paper–pencil 150-item test assessing four dimensions of student concerns: processes of instruction, program planning, administrative affairs, and out-of-class activities. These four dimensions are divided further into such areas as content of courses, appropriateness of coursework to occupational goals, satisfaction with teaching procedures, student–faculty relations, educational and occupational decisions, effectiveness of advisers and counselors, registration, regulations, availability of classes, housing, employment, financial aid, and satisfaction with campus environment. The test is distributed to a random sample of students.

Format: Self-administered; suitable for group use; untimed: 50 minutes

Scoring: Computer scored

Cost: Booklet $0.65; processing $1.75

Publisher: Educational Testing Service

University Residence Environment Scale (URES)
Rudolf H. Moos, Marvin S. Gerst

Copyright: 1988

Population: College students, adults

Purpose: Assesses the social environment of university residence halls and dormitories

Description: Paper–pencil 100-item true–false test of 10 dimensions of the social climate of college dormitories: involvement, emotional support, independence, traditional social orientation, competition, academic achievement, intellectuality, order and organization, student influence, and innovation. Materials include the Real Form (Form R), which measures current perceptions of a residence; the 40-item Short Form (Form S); the Expectations Form (Form E), which measures expectations of a new residence; and the Ideal Form (Form I), which measures conceptions of an ideal residence hall environment. Forms I an E are not in published form, but items and instructions appear in the Appendix of the URES manual. One in a series of nine *Social Climate Scales*.

Format: Examiner required; suitable for group use; untimed: typical time not available

Scoring: Hand key; examiner evaluated

Cost: Sample Set $25.00; permission for up to 200 uses $90.00

Publisher: Mind Garden, Inc.

Ward Atmosphere Scale (WAS)
Rudolf H. Moos

Copyright: 1974

Population: Adolescents, adults

Purpose: Assesses the social environments of hospital-based psychiatric treatment programs; used to evaluate organizational effectiveness

Description: Paper–pencil 100-item true–false test covering 10 aspects of social environment and yielding 10 scores: involvement, support, spontaneity, autonomy, practical orientation, personal problem orientation, anger and aggression, order and organization, program clarity, and staff control. Three "treatment outcome" scales may be used: Dropout, Release Rate, and Community Tenure. Materials include the Real Form (Form R), which measures perceptions of a current program; the 40-item Short Form (Form S); the Ideal Form (Form I), which measures conceptions of an ideal program; and the Expectations Form (Form E), which measures expectations of a new program. Forms I and E are not published, but items and instructions appear in the appendix of the *WAS Climate Scales*.

Format: Examiner required; suitable for group use; untimed: 20 minutes

Scoring: Hand key; examiner evaluated

Cost: Sample Set $25.00, permission for up to 200 uses $90.00

Publisher: Mind Garden, Inc.

School Leadership Aptitude

Instructional Climate Inventory–Teachers

Larry A. Braskamp, Martin L. Maehr

Copyright: 1988

Population: Adults

Purpose: Assesses instructional leadership behavior, satisfaction, and school culture from the teacher's perspective; used by elementary and secondary school administrators to assess teacher attitudes toward the school and the effectiveness of school leadership

Description: Paper-pencil 108-item multiple-choice test measuring instructional leadership and school climate. Climate is described on four dimensions: accomplishment, recognition, power, and affiliation. Additional scales measure strength of culture, degree of commitment or loyalty to the school, and job satisfaction, plus the research-based dimensions of instructional leadership: Defines Mission, Manages Curriculum, Supervises Teaching, Monitors Student Progress, and Promotes Instructional Climate. Items were adapted from the Organizational Assessment Survey.

Format: Examiner/self-administered; suitable for group use; untimed: 25 minutes

Scoring: Computer scored through publisher

Cost: Contact publisher

Publisher: MetriTech, Inc.

Instructional Leadership Inventory

Martin L. Maehr, Russell Ames

Copyright: 1985

Population: Adults

Purpose: Evaluates the leadership goals and behaviors of school administrators

Description: Paper-pencil 100-item multiple-choice inventory evaluating the leadership goals and behaviors of school administrators on five broad categories of instructional leadership: Defines Mission, Manages Curriculum, Supervises Teaching, Monitors Student Progress, and Promotes Instructional Climate. An additional set of items assess the individual's perception of contextual factors relating to staff, students, and community. A mail-in scoring service is available from the publisher. APA purchase guidelines apply.

Format: Self-administered; suitable for group use; untimed: 30 to 60 minutes

Scoring: Computer scored

Cost: $20.00 per report

Publisher: MetriTech, Inc.

Leadership Skills Inventory (LSI)

Frances A. Karnes, Jane C. Chauvin

Copyright: 1985

Population: Children, adolescents; Grades 4 through 12

Purpose: Assesses leadership abilities of students; used by students, teachers, consultants, curriculum planners, and teacher trainers

Description: Multiple-item paper-pencil or computer-administered inventory assessing fundamentals of leadership, written and oral communication, group dynamics, problem-solving, personal development, decision making, and planning abilities. The results help students understand and develop leadership abilities. The inventory may be used for pre- and postevaluation. An activities manual is included.

Format: Self-administered; suitable for group use; untimed: time varies

Scoring: Self-scored

Cost: Complete kit (administration manual, activities manual, and 25 evaluation forms) $69.00

Publisher: PRO-ED, Inc.

School Administrator Assessment Survey

Larry A. Braskamp, Martin L. Maehr

Copyright: 1988

Population: Adults

Purpose: Assesses organizational culture and employee commitment, assesses worker motivation by determining personal values and incentive, and evaluates the opportunities for fulfillment that individuals perceive in their present jobs

Description: Likert scale with 200 items measuring four aspects of the person, the job, and the culture of the school. Each element is assessed in terms of the same four characteristics: accomplishment, recognition, power, and affiliation. Reports help administrators identify specific objectives for individual improvement and personal development. This instrument is an adaptation of the Organizational Assessment Survey.

Format: Examiner/self-administered; suitable for group use; untimed: 1 hour

Scoring: Computer scored through publisher

Cost: $20.00 per report

Publisher: MetriTech, Inc.

School Principal Job Functions Inventory (SP-JFI)
Melany E. Baehr, Frances M. Burns,
R. Bruce McPherson, Columbus Salley

Copyright: 1976

Population: Adults

Purpose: Assesses the relative importance of functions performed in a particular type of principalship and the principal's ability to perform the functions; used to clarify a school principal's job responsibilities and to diagnose training needs

Description: Multiple-item paper-pencil inventory assessing the relative importance of 17 basic functions for overall successful performance in a given principalship: personal handling of student adjustment problems, organizations and extracurricular activities, individual student development, utilization of specialized staff, evaluation of teacher performance, collegial contacts, racial and ethnic group problems, troubleshooting and problem solving, community involvement and support, dealing with gangs, curriculum development, instructional materials, staffing, working with unions, working with central office, safety regulations, and fiscal control. Items are rated by the incumbent principal. The inventory also may be used to have incumbents rate their relative ability to perform these functions. Separate forms are available for rating the importance of various functions and for self-rating of the incumbent's abilities.

Format: Examiner required; suitable for group use; untimed: 45–60 minutes

Scoring: Hand key

Cost: 25 test booklets $30.00; 25 score sheets $10.00; examiner's manual $15.00

Publisher: McGraw-Hill/London House

Science

General

College Assessment of Academic Progress (CAAP) Science Reasoning Test

Copyright: 1996

Population: Adults; ages 17 and above

Purpose: Assesses science reasoning

Description: Multiple-choice 36-item paper–pencil test with two categories: Referring and Reasoning. A test booklet, answer sheet, and pencil are used. May be used for persons with visual, physical, hearing, and mental disabilities.

Format: Suitable for group use; examiner required; timed: 40 minutes

Scoring: Machine scored; test scoring service available from publisher

Cost: $8.50

Publisher: American College Testing

General Science Test

Copyright: Not provided

Population: College students

Purpose: Assesses scientific understanding of college entrants and students in higher education

Description: Multiple-item paper–pencil test in two parts assessing general scientific knowledge and understanding of technical materials. The first part contains questions on general science, and the second part consists of several paragraphs that determine the extent to which the examinee understands technical articles. Norms are available.

Format: Examiner required; suitable for group use; timed: 55 minutes

Scoring: Hand key

Cost: Contact publisher

Publisher: Human Sciences Research Council

National Proficiency Survey Series (NPSS): Science
Dale P. Scannell

Copyright: 1989

Population: Grades 8 to 12

Purpose: Assesses student proficiency in high school courses

Description: Multiple-item multiple-choice paper–pencil tests used for evaluation of student proficiency in science courses. The biology test measures information about the living world, ranging from single-celled organisms to the human body. The chemistry test measures understanding of atomic theory and the nature of matter and its states. The physics test examines the nature of energy and the relationship between energy and matter from mechanics through nuclear reactions.

Format: Examiner required; suitable for group use; 40 minutes

Scoring: Self-scored; hand key

Cost: Scanning and Scoring System Kit available; contact publisher for current prices

Publisher: Riverside Publishing Company

Science Tests—Standard 5 Through Standard 8 Higher Grade

Copyright: 1981

Population: Children, adolescents

Purpose: Assesses achievement in science courses; used for educational evaluation and placement

Description: Six paper–pencil tests of science knowledge in Standards 5 through 8 Higher Grade. General Science–Standard 5 consists of the following subtests: Measurement of Matter, Heat, Magnetism, and Biology. Physical Science–Standard 6 has three subtests: Matter, Classification of Matter, Oxygen, Hydrogen, and Carbon Dioxide; Water; and Force, Work, Energy, and Electricity. Physical Science–Standard 7 is very similar to Standard 6. Standard 8 and above measures eight aspects of physical science: light; sound: heat, light, and energy; electricity; atomic structure; chemical reactions, acids, bases, and salts; chemical reactions; and electricity. Biology tests for Standards 6 and 7 measure some of the following areas: reproduction, growth and development, nutrition, and gaseous exchange during respiration.

Format: Examiner required; suitable for group use; untimed: typical time not available

Scoring: Hand key; examiner evaluated

Cost: Contact publisher

Publisher: Human Sciences Research Council

Specific

ACT PEP RCE: Arts and Sciences: Abnormal Psychology

Copyright: 1994

Population: Adults

Purpose: Measures upper-level knowledge and understanding of abnormal psychology; used to grant college credit and/or advanced placement in academic courses

Description: Multiple-choice 119-item paper–pencil test assessing knowledge of material normally taught in one semester. Uses test booklet, answer sheet, and pencil. Examiner must have experience with test administration at the college level. May be used for persons with visual, hearing, physical, and mental disabilities.

Format: Examiner required; suitable for group use; timed: 3 hours

Scoring: Machine scored

Cost: $45.00

Publisher: American College Testing

ACT PEP RCE: Arts and Sciences: Anatomy and Physiology

Copyright: 1994

Population: Adults

Purpose: Measures lower-level knowledge and understanding of anatomy and physiology; used to grant college credit and advanced placement in academic courses

Description: Paper–pencil 120-item multiple-choice test assessing knowledge of anatomical terminology and facts and physiological concepts and principles. Uses test booklet, answer sheet, and pencil. Examiner must have experience with test administration at the college level. May be used for persons with visual, physical, hearing, and mental disabilities.

Format: Examiner required; suitable for group use; timed: 3 hours

Scoring: Computer scored by ACT

Cost: $45.00

Publisher: American College Testing

ACT PEP RCE: Arts and Sciences: Foundations of Gerontology

Copyright: 1994

Population: Adults

Purpose: Measures upper-level knowledge and understanding of the biological, psychological, and social aspects of aging; used to grant college credit and advanced placement in academic courses

Description: Paper–pencil 110-item multiple-choice test assessing knowledge of material normally taught in a one-semester introductory course in gerontology at the undergraduate level. Uses test booklet, answer sheet, and pencil. Examiner must have experience with test administration at the college level. May be used for persons with visual, physical, hearing, and mental disabilities.

Format: Examination required; suitable for group use; timed: 3 hours

Scoring: Machine scored

Cost: $45.00

Publisher: American College Testing

ACT PEP RCE: Arts and Sciences: Microbiology

Copyright: 1993

Population: Adults

Purpose: Measures lower-level knowledge and understanding of microbiology; used to grant college credit and advanced placement in academic courses

Description: Paper–pencil 120-item multiple-choice test assessing knowledge of material normally taught in a one-semester, introductory course in microbiology at the undergraduate level. Examiner must have experience with test administration at the college level. May be used with individuals with visual, physical, hearing, and mental disabilities.

Format: Examiner required; suitable for group use; timed: 3 hours

Scoring: Machine scored

Cost: $45.00

Publisher: American College Testing

ACT PEP RCE: Arts and Sciences: Statistics

Copyright: 1996

Population: Adults; college level

Purpose: Measures knowledge and understanding of statistics; used to grant college credit and advanced placement in academic courses

Description: Paper–pencil 120-item multiple-choice test of material normally taught in one semester of descriptive and inferential statistics. Test booklet, answer sheet, and pencil are used. Examiner must have experience with test administration at the college level. May be used for persons with visual, physical, hearing, and mental disabilities.

Format: Examiner required; suitable for group use; timed: 3 hours

Scoring: Examiner evaluated

Cost: $45.00

Publisher: American College Testing

ACT PEP RCE: Psychology: Life Span Developmental Psychology

Copyright: 1996

Population: Adults; college level

Purpose: Used by adults wanting to earn college credit by examination; assess the development of psychology over a life span

Description: Paper–pencil 120-item multiple-choice test. Scale scores range from 20 to 80. Two forms are available. A test booklet, answer sheet, and pen are used. A college reading level is required. Examiner must have experience with test administration at the college level. May be used for individuals with visual, physical, hearing, and mental disabilities.

Format: Suitable for group use; examiner required; timed: 180 minutes

Scoring: Machine scored

Cost: Contact publisher

Publisher: American College Testing

CLEP Subject Examination: History and Social Sciences: Educational Psychology

Copyright: 1990

Population: Adolescents, adults; Grades 12 and above

Purpose: Measures competency in educational psychology at the introductory college-course level; also used by some businesses to allow employees to earn required continuing education credits

Description: Paper–pencil 100-item objective test in two separately timed sections assessing knowledge and comprehension of basic information, concepts, and principles to the psychology of education, including one's ability to integrate various aspects of this content as it applies to teaching situations and problems. The categories covered are theories and theorists, evaluation, teaching, education, development, motivation, and learning. The optional four-item essay section assesses factors such as accuracy of information, comprehensiveness and relevance of treatment, organization of materials, approach to problems from a psychological frame of reference, and logic and imaginativeness.

Format: Examiner required; suitable for group use; timed: 45 minutes each section: essay 90 minutes

Scoring: Computer scored; essay section examiner evaluated locally

Cost: Contact publisher

Publisher: The College Board

Dental Admission Test (DAT)

Copyright: Updated yearly

Population: Ages 21 to 22; college students applying to dental schools; 63% have completed 60–120 semester hours

Purpose: Measures knowledge of mathematics, biology, and chemistry, as well as reading comprehension and spatial/perceptual abilities; provides national, standardized admission criteria for dental schools in the United States

Description: Quantitative Reasoning—40 items, 45 minutes; Reading Comprehension—50 items, 50 minutes; Survey of Natural Sciences—100 items, 90 minutes; Biology—40 items; General Chemistry—30 items; Organic Chemistry—30 items; Perceptual Ability—90 items, 60 minutes. The test is administered only to individuals who have completed at least one year of college, including courses in natural sciences. No books, rulers, slide rules, paper, calculators, or other resource materials are permitted in the exam room. Administered biannually in specific cities only.

Format: Examiner required (provided by the testing center); suitable for group use; ½ day

Scoring: Computer scored

Cost: Candidate Fee $75.00

Publisher: American Dental Association

Human Reproduction

Copyright: 1967

Population: Adolescents, adults; Grades 10 and above

Purpose: Measures high school and college students' knowledge of the human reproductive system; used for health and human sexuality courses

Description: Paper–pencil 33-item multiple-choice test assessing knowledge of human reproduction

Format: Self-administered; suitable for group use; timed: 30 minutes

Scoring: Hand key

Cost: Free

Publisher: Glenn C. Leach, Ed. D.

PSB Aptitude for Practical Nursing Examination

Copyright: 1993

Population: Adults; practical nursing students

Purpose: Measures abilities, skills, knowledge, and attitudes important to successful performance as a practical nurse; used as an admission test for schools and programs of practical nursing

Description: Multiple-item paper–pencil battery of five tests assessing areas important for performance as a practical nurse: General Mental Ability, Spelling, the Natural Sciences, Judgment in Practical Nursing, and Readiness for Specialized Instruction in Practical Nursing.

Format: Examiner required; suitable for group use; timed: 2 hours 15 minutes

Scoring: Machine scored

Cost: Reusable test booklets $7.00; answer sheets (scoring and reporting service) $7.00

Publisher: Psychological Services Bureau, Inc.

PSB Nursing School Aptitude Examination (RN), 1991 Revision

Copyright: 1991

Population: Adults; nursing school candidates

Purpose: Measures abilities, skills, knowledge, and attitudes important to successful performance as a nurse; used as an admission test for schools and departments of nursing

Description: Multiple-item paper–pencil battery of five tests assessing areas important for performance as a nurse: academic aptitude, spelling, reading comprehension, information in the natural sciences, and vocational adjustment. The battery predicts readiness for instruction in nursing at the diploma or associate degree levels. Both the original version and the revised versions are available.

Format: Examiner required; suitable for group use; timed: 1 hour 45 minutes

Scoring: Machine scored

Cost: Reusable test booklets $7.00; answer sheets (scoring and reporting service) $7.00

Publisher: Psychological Services Bureau, Inc.

Special Education

General

Adaptive Behavior Evaluation Scale (ABES)–Revised

Stephen B. McCarney

Copyright: 1995

Population: Children, adolescents; ages 5 to 19; Grades K through 12

Purpose: Used as a measure of adaptive behavior in the identification of students with mental retardation, behavioral disorders, learning disabilities, vision or hearing impairment, and physical disabilities

Description: The revised ABES represents the 10 adaptive behavior skill areas of Communication Skills, Self-Care, Home Living, Social Skills, Community Use, Self-Direction, Health and Safety, Functional Academics, Leisure, and Work Skills. A computer version using IBM/Macintosh PCs is available. Also available in Spanish.

Format: Individual administration

Scoring: Self/computer scored

Cost: Complete kit $146.00

Publisher: Hawthorne Educational Services, Inc.

Adaptive Behavior Inventory for Children (ABIC)

Jane R. Mercer, June F. Lewis

Copyright: 1982

Population: Children; ages 5 through 11

Purpose: Measures a child's social role performance in his or her family, peer group, and community

Description: Inventory in a 242-item interview format measuring six aspects of adaptive behavior, including family, community, peer relations, nonacademic school rules, earner/consumer, and self-maintenance. Items are divided into two sections. The first section is applicable to all children, and the second section consists of age-graded questions. The ABIC is one component of the System of Multicultural Pluralistic Assessment (SOMPA). The manual includes the ABIC questions in both Spanish and English.

Format: Examiner required; not suitable for group use; untimed: 45 minutes

Scoring: Hand key; examiner evaluated

Cost: Basic kit (manual, 25 record forms, six scoring keys) $93.50

Publisher: Harcourt® Brace Educational Measurement

Anser System—Aggregate Neurobehavioral Student Health and Educational Review

Melvin D. Levine

Copyright: 1989

Population: Children, adolescents; ages 3 to 18

Purpose: Gathers information from parents and teachers for the educator/clinician who has questions about a child with learning and/or behavioral problems; used in schools, health care, and counseling centers to evaluate children with disabilities

Description: Three separate short-answer paper–pencil questionnaires for parents and school personnel to evaluate three age groups: Form 1 (ages 3 to 5), Form 2 (ages 6 to 11), and Form 3 (ages 12 and over). Form 4 is a self-administered student profile to be completed by students ages 9 and older. The parent questionnaire surveys family history, possible pregnancy problems, health problems, functional problems, early development, early educational experience, skills and interests, activity–attention problems, associated behaviors, and associated strengths. The school questionnaire covers the educational program and setting, special facilities available, and the results of previous testing. The self-administered Student Profile asks the student to rate herself or himself on a series of statements in the following categories: fine motor, gross motor, memory, attention, language, general efficiency, visual–spatial processing, sequencing, general academic performance, and social interaction. Follow-up questionnaires document frequency and changes of behaviors and environment, assisting in monitoring and evaluation of progress and deficiency of intervention programs.

Format: Examiner required; not suitable for group use; untimed: 30–60 minutes

Scoring: Examiner evaluated

Cost: Interpreter's Guide for (Forms 1–6 $10.25; Specimen Set (guide, sample of each form 1–6) $10.25; all questionnaires available for purchase in one- or two-dozen lots

Publisher: Educators Publishing Service, Inc.

Becker Work Adjustment Profile (BWAP)

Ralph L. Becker

Copyright: 1989

Population: Adolescents, adults; ages 15 to adult

Purpose: Assesses the vocational adjustment and competency of individuals with mental retardation, cerebral palsy, cultural disadvantage, learning disabilities, emotional disturbance, and physical disabilities

Description: Likert-type 63-item questionnaire completed by someone familiar with the individual's work. Two editions of the questionnaire are available: a Short Scale and a Full Scale. Vocational adjustment and competency are evaluated in four domains: Work Habits/Attitudes (10 items), Interpersonal Relations (12 items), Cognitive Skills (19 items), and Work Performance Skills (22 items). In addition to scores in each domain, a global score is obtained. The raw scores are converted to percentiles, *T*-scores, and stanines using an appropriate norm for those with mental retardation, physical disabilities, emotional disturbances, or learning disabilities. Two profiles are available: a Peer Profile to interpret an individual's work adjustment compared with other people who have the same disability, and an Employability Status Profile which provides a graphic picture of the person's vocational competency for placement in one of five program tracks: Day Care, Work Activity, Sheltered Workshop, Transitional, and Community–Competitive. A complete report/analysis is given on different individuals with disabilities.

Format: Examiner required; not suitable for group use; untimed: 10–20 minutes

Scoring: Examiner required

Cost: Starter Set (2 short scales, 2 full scales, 2 profiles and 1 manual) $16.50

Publisher: Elbern Publications

CASAS Life Skills Assessment System

Copyright: 1994

Population: Adults, adolescents; native and nonnative speakers of English

Purpose: Used by programs to identify basic skills in reading, math, and listening needed by individuals to function successfully in today's workplace, community, and society; learners can be placed into educational programs to assess learning gains

Description: Multiple-choice survey achievement series includes reading comprehension and math tests at four levels, A–D, and, for assessment in English as a second language (ESL), listening comprehension tests at levels A–C. Each test has two forms, pre- and posttesting. Includes a life skills appraisal and an ESL appraisal for placement purposes, a reading certification test, and a beginning literacy reading assessment. Tests are competency based; content covers general life skills in a variety of content areas. CASAS scaled scores identify general skill level and enable comparison of performance across CASAS tests. Scannable answer sheets are available.

Format: Group administered

Scoring: Self/computer scored

Cost: 25 reusable tests $44.00; 25 listening tests and audiotape $51.00

Publisher: Comprehensive Adult Student Assessment System

Checklist of Adaptive Living Skills
Lanny E. Morreau, Robert H. Bruininks

Copyright: 1991

Population: All ages

Purpose: Comprehensive, criterion-referenced checklist that targets specific behaviors each individual needs to develop

Description: Organized into four broad domains: Personal Living Skills, Home Living Skills, Community Living Skills, and Employment Skills, CALS presents 24 specific skill modules spanning a wide range of behaviors. Evaluates 794 important life skills. It determines instructional needs, develops individual training objectives, and provides continuous record of progress. Linked to two norm-referenced tests—*Scales of Independent Behavior and Inventory for Client and Agency Planning.*

Format: Individual administration; examiner required

Scoring: Examiner evaluated

Cost: Complete program (manual, 25 checklists) $79.00

Publisher: Riverside Publishing Company

Children's Adaptive Behavior Report (CABR)
Bert O. Richmond, Richard H. Kicklighter

Copyright: 1982

Population: Children; ages 5 to 11

Purpose: Assesses the adaptive behavior of children; used to plan remediation programs

Description: Multiple-item paper–pencil observational inventory covering five areas of adaptive behavior: language development, independent functioning, family role performance, economic vocational activity, and socialization. A teacher or school psychologist completes the inventory based on direct observation of the child and evaluates the results according to guidelines presented in the manual.

Format: Self-administered; suitable for group use; untimed: time varies

Scoring: Examiner evaluated

Cost: Test kit (manual, picture book, 5 record forms) $29.95

Publisher: Humanics Psychological Test Corporation

Scales of Independent Behavior–Revised (SIB–R)
Robert H. Bruininks, Richard W. Woodcock, Richard F. Weatherman, Bradley K. Hill

Copyright: 1996

Population: Infants to adults

Purpose: Measures adaptive and problem behavior; used to determine independence of individuals with varying degrees of mental, emotional, behavioral, or physical disability

Description: Multiple-item structured interview or checklist procedure with 14 subtests

assessing motor skills, social interaction and communication skills, personal living skills, community living skills, and problem behaviors. In addition, four maladaptive behavior indexes measure the frequency and severity of problem behaviors: General Maladaptive Index, Internalized Maladaptive Index, Externalized Maladaptive Index, and Asocial Maladaptive Index. Age scores, percentile ranks, standard scores, relative mastery indexes, expected range of independence, and training implication range are obtained. The SIB–R offers five administration options: full battery, short form, early development scale, individual clusters, and a problem behavior scale. This test is related structurally and statistically to the Woodcock-Johnson Psycho-Educational Battery–Revised (1989). Because common norms are provided for the two tests, an individual's adaptive behavior may be interpreted in relation to cognitive ability.

Format: Individual administration; examiner required; complete battery 45–60 minutes, other forms 10–15 minutes

Scoring: Examiner evaluated; may be computer scored

Cost: Complete program (Interview Book, Interviewer's Comprehensive Manual, 15 Full-scale response booklets, 5 Short-Form response booklets, 5 Early Development Form response booklets) $150.00

Publisher: Riverside Publishing Company

Autism

Adolescent and Adult Psychoeducational Profile (AAPEP)
Gary B. Mesibov, Eric Schopler, Bruce Schaffer, Rhoda Landrus

Copyright: 1988

Population: Adolescents and adults with developmental disability

Purpose: Measures the learning abilities and characteristics of individuals with severe developmental disabilities; used by service providers, teachers, and parents for preparing and maintaining individuals in community-based programs

Description: Multiple-item task-performance test assessing the learning abilities of individuals who have autism and developmental disability. The test results comprise a profile reflecting the individual characteristics of the person. Emphasis is on evaluating functional skills from three areas: direct observation, home, and school work. The profile is translated into an appropriately individualized set of goals and objectives for each individual.

Format: Individual administration

Scoring: Examiner scored and interpreted

Cost: Manual $59.00

Publisher: PRO-ED, Inc.

Autism Screening Instrument for Educational Planning–Second Edition (ASIEP–2)
David A. Krug, Joel R. Arick, Patricia J. Almond

Copyright: 1993

Population: Ages 18 months to adult

Purpose: Assesses the behavioral, social, and educational development of students with autism, mental retardation, deafness, blindness, and emotional disturbance; used to establish IEPs, evaluate program effectiveness, and monitor student progress

Description: Multiple-item paper–pencil observational inventory consisting of five subtests: Autism Behavior Checklist (ABC), Sample of Vocal Behavior, Interaction Assessment, Educational Assessment, and Prognosis of Learning Rate. The observational methods involved in all five subtests allow all students to be "testable."

Format: Examiner required; not suitable for group use; untimed: time varies

Scoring: Examiner evaluated

Cost: Complete kit (manual, summary booklets, autism behavior checklist record forms, sample of vocal behavior record forms, interac-

tion assessment record forms, educational assessment record forms, prognosis of learning rate record forms) $174.00

Publisher: PRO-ED, Inc.

Behavior Rating Instrument for Autistic and Other Atypical Children–Second Edition (BRIAAC)
Bertram Ruttenberg, Beth Kalish, Charles Wenar, Enid Wolf

Copyright: 1991

Population: Children

Purpose: Evaluates the status of low functioning, atypical, and autistic children of all ages; used to evaluate children who will not or cannot cooperate with formal testing procedures

Description: Paper–pencil inventory of observations taken over a two-day period assessing a child's present level of functioning and measuring behavioral change in eight areas: relationship to an adult, communication, drive for mastery, vocalization and expressive speech, sound and speech reception, social responsiveness, body movement (passive and active), and psychobiological development. Each of the eight scales begins with the most severe autistic behavior and progresses to behavior roughly comparable to that of a normally developing 3½ to 4½-year-old. The complete BRIAAC includes a manual, report forms, individual scale score sheet, total score sheet, intrascale and interscale profile forms, descriptive guides, and suggested individual plans.

Format: Examiner required; not suitable for group use; untimed: 2 days

Scoring: Examiner evaluated

Cost: Complete kit (manual, all required forms) $124.50

Publisher: Stoelting Company

Childhood Autism Rating Scale (CARS)
Eric Schopler, Robert J. Reichler, Barbara Rochen Renner

Copyright: 1988

Population: Children, adolescents

Purpose: Diagnoses children with autism syndrome and distinguishes them from children with developmental disabilities who are not autistic; used for psychological, medical, or educational evaluations

Description: Fifteen-item behavior rating scale. Items include relating to people; imitation; emotional response; body use; object use; adaptation to change; visual response; listening response; taste, smell, and touch response and use; fear or nervousness; verbal communication; nonverbal communication; activity level; level and consistency of intellectual response; and general impression. The child is rated on each of the 15 items using a 7-point scale that indicates the degree to which the child's behavior deviates from that of a normal child of the same age. A total score is then computed by summing the individual ratings. Children who score above a given point are categorized as autistic. Scores within the autistic range can then be divided into two categories: mild-to-moderate autism and severe autism.

Format: Examiner required; not suitable for group use; untimed: time varies

Scoring: Examiner evaluated

Cost: Kit (25 rating scales, 1 manual) $55.00

Publisher: Western Psychological Services

Gilliam Autism Rating Scale (GARS)

James E. Gilliam

Copyright: 1995

Population: Ages 3 through 22

Purpose: Helps identify and diagnose autism and to estimate the severity of the problem

Description: Items on the GARS are based on the definitions of autism adopted by the Autism Society of America and the *Diagnostic and Statistical Manual of Mental Disorders–Fourth Edition* (DSM–IV). The items are grouped into four subtests: Stereotyped Behaviors, Communication, Social Interaction, and Developmental Disturbances. The GARS has the following characteristics: (1) Three core

subtests describe specific and measurable behaviors. (2) An optional subtest (Developmental Disturbances) allows parents to contribute data about their child's development during the first 3 years of life. (3) The test was normed on 1,092 representative subjects with autism from 45 states, Puerto Rico, and Canada. Both validity and reliability of the instrument are high. (4) Behaviors are assessed using objective, frequency-based ratings. (5) The entire scale can be completed in approximately 5 to 10 minutes. (6) The scale is easily completed by those who have knowledge of the subject's behavior.

Format: Examiner required; timed: time varies

Scoring: Examiner evaluated

Cost: Complete kit (examiner's manual, 25 summary/response forms, storage box) $69.00

Publisher: PRO-ED, Inc.

Psychoeducational Profile–Revised (PEP–R)

Eric Schopler, Robert F. Reichler, Ann Bashford, Margaret D. Lansing, Lee M. Marcus

Copyright: 1990

Population: Developmentally disabled children

Purpose: Measures the learning abilities and characteristics of autistic and related developmentally disordered children; used to establish individualized special education curricula or home programs for developmentally disabled children

Description: Multiple-item task-performance test assessing the learning abilities of autistic and developmentally disabled children. The test results comprise a learning profile reflecting the individual characteristics of the child. This profile is translated into an appropriately individualized special education curriculum or home program according to the teaching strategies described in Volume II of the manual. The manual, Individualized Assessment for Autistic and Developmentally Disabled Children, is published in two volumes by PRO-ED. Volume I describes the psychoeducational profile, and Volume II discusses teaching strategies for parents and professionals.

Format: Examiner required; not suitable for group use; untimed: time varies

Scoring: Examiner evaluated

Cost: Complete program $59.00

Publisher: PRO-ED, Inc.

Deafness and Hearing Disabilities

Carolina Picture Vocabulary Test (CPVT)
Thomas L. Layton, David W. Holmes

Copyright: 1985

Population: Children; ages 4 years to 11 years 6 months

Purpose: Measures the receptive sign vocabulary in individuals where manual signing is the primary mode of communication

Description: Norm-referenced, validated, receptive sign vocabulary test for children who have deafness or hearing impairment. The population (N = 767) used in the standardization research was based on a nationwide sample of children who use manual signs as their primary means of communication. Stratification of the sample was based on geographic region, educational facility, parental occupation, sex, race, age, grade, etiology, age of onset of hearing impairment, number of years of signing, IQ, and threshold of hearing loss in the better ear. The CPVT consists of 130 items with suggested basal and ceiling levels. Scale scores, percentile ranks, and age equivalency scores are provided.

Format: Individual administration; untimed: 10–15 minutes

Scoring: Hand key

Cost: Complete kit (examiner's manual, picture book, record forms, storage box) $109.00

Publisher: PRO-ED, Inc.

Central Institute for the Deaf Preschool Performance Scale (CID-PPS)
Ann E. Geers, Helen S. Lane

Copyright: 1984

Population: Preschoolers with hearing and language disabilities

Purpose: Measures intellectual potential using completely nonverbal testing procedures; predicts school achievement in preschoolers with hearing and language disabilities

Description: Multiple-item task-performance test assessing the intellectual abilities of preschoolers without requiring a single spoken word from either the examiner or the child (optional verbal clues are provided for hearing children). Six subtests assess intellectual abilities in the following areas: manual planning (block building, Montessori cylinders, and two-figure form board); manual dexterity (buttons and Wallin pegs); form perception (Decroly pictures, Seguin form board); perceptual/motor skills (Knox cube, drawing, and paper folding); preschool skills (color sorting and counting sticks); and part/whole relations (Manikin and Stutsman puzzles). Test materials were selected from existing mental tests for children ages 2 to 5 to obtain a broad, clinical picture of the child's ability and a numerical rating (Deviation IQ) that would correlate with a Stanford-Binet IQ. The test is an adaptation of the early Randall's Island Performance Series.

Format: Examiner required; not suitable for group use; untimed: time varies

Scoring: Examiner evaluated

Cost: Complete kit (manual, record forms, manipulatives for subtests) $850.00

Publisher: Stoelting Company

Test of Early Reading Ability–Deaf or Hard of Hearing (TERA–D/HH)
D. Kim Reid, Wayne P. Hresko, Donald D. Hammill, Susan Wiltshire

Copyright: 1991

Population: Children

Purpose: Assesses hearing loss

Description: This is the only individually administered test of reading designed for children with moderate to profound hearing loss (ranging from 41 to beyond 91 decibels, corrected). TERA–D/HH is also the only individually administered reading test designed for children younger than age 8 who are deaf or hard of hearing. It has equivalent forms and taps the child's ability to construct meaning, knowledge of the alphabet and its functions, and awareness of print conventions. Results are reported as standard scores, percentile rankings, and normal curve equivalents. TERA–D/HH was standardized on a national sample of more than 1,000 students who were deaf or hard of hearing from 20 states. Normative data are given for every 6-month interval from 3-0 through 13-11. Internal consistency and test–retest reliability are reported in the manual. In all instances, coefficients approach or exceed .90. Validity coefficients for TERA–D/HH with other reading, language, intelligence, and achievement tests frequently used with students who are deaf or hard of hearing also are reported in the manual.

Format: Individual administration; timed: time varies

Scoring: Examiner evaluated

Cost: Complete kit (examiner's manual, picture book, 25 Form A and 25 Form B profile/examiner record forms, storage box) $149.00

Publisher: PRO-ED, Inc.

Gifted and Talented

Center for Talented Youth Spatial Tests
John Eliot, Heirrich Stumpl

Copyright: 1992

Population: Grades 7 and up; gifted individuals

Purpose: Measure spatial intelligence

Description: Fourteen subtests in Forms AA, BB, EE, and FF have a multiple-choice paper–pencil format.

Format: Group administration; 3 hours

Scoring: Examiner administration and interpretation

Cost: Free

Publisher: Center for Talented Youth

Collegiate Assessment of Academic Progress (CAAP) Critical Thinking Test

Copyright: 1996

Population: Adults; ages 17 and above

Purpose: Assesses critical thinking

Description: Multiple-choice 32-item paper–pencil test. A test booklet, answer sheet, and pencil are used. Examiner must have experience with test administration at the college level. May be used for persons with visual, physical, hearing, and mental disabilities.

Format: Suitable for group use; examiner required; timed: 40 minutes

Scoring: Machine scored; test scoring service available from publisher

Cost: $8.50

Publisher: American College Testing

Creativity Assessment Packet (CAP)
Frank E. Williams

Copyright: 1980

Population: Ages 6 to 18

Purpose: Measures cognitive thought factors of fluency, flexibility, elaboration, originality, vocabulary, and comprehension that are related to the creative process; identifies gifted students

Description: Instrument consists of two group-administered instruments for children: the Test of Divergent Thinking (Forms A and B) and the Test of Divergent Feeling. A third instrument, The Williams Scale, is a rating instrument for teachers and parents of the same tested factors among children. All three instruments can be used to evaluate, screen, and identify the most important factors of creativity found in some degree among all children.

Format: Group administration

Scoring: Self-scoring; examiner interpreted

Cost: Complete kit (manual, forms, storage box) $94.00

Publisher: PRO-ED, Inc.

Creativity Attitude Survey (CAS)
Charles E. Schaefer

Copyright: 1971

Population: Children; Grades 4 through 6

Purpose: Assesses attitudes important for creative thinking; used in the evaluation of training programs in creativity

Description: Paper–pencil 32-item test measuring five dimensions associated with creative thinking: confidence in own ideas; appreciation of fantasy; theoretical and aesthetic orientation; openness to impulse expression; and desire for novelty. The items are statements to which the child indicates agreement or disagreement.

Format: Examiner required; suitable for group use; untimed: 10 minutes

Scoring: Hand key

Cost: Specimen Set $5.00; manual $4.50; 25 tests $15.00

Publisher: Psychologists and Educators, Inc.

Gifted Evaluation Scale (GES)
Stephen B. McCarney

Copyright: 1987

Population: Children, adolescents; ages 5 to 19; Grades K through 12

Purpose: Identifies gifted and talented students based on the current federal definition of giftedness adopted by the U.S. Office of Education in 1978

Description: The scale provides a measure of Intellectual Ability, Creativity, Specific Academic Ability, Leadership Ability, and Performing and Visual Arts Skills. The completed rating form and student profile provides standard scores for the five subscales, a quotient score, and a percentile score based on the national standardization sample.

Format: Individual administration

Scoring: Self/computer scored

Cost: Complete kit $63.50

Publisher: Hawthorne Educational Services, Inc.

Group Inventory for Finding Creative Talent (GIFT)
Sylvia B. Rimm

Copyright: 1980

Population: Children, Grades K through 6

Purpose: Assesses creativity; used to identify gifted students

Description: Multiple-item paper–pencil test of interests and attitudes related to creativity. The test yields the following dimension scores: Imagination, Independence, and Many Interests. Validation groups include minorities, urban and suburban students, students with learning disabilities, and gifted students. Available also in Spanish.

Format: Examiner required; suitable for group use

Scoring: Machine scored

Cost: Specimen Set $10.00; Class Set of 30 $65.00 (indicate grade level); scoring included in price

Publisher: Educational Assessment Service, Inc.

Group Inventory for Finding Interests (GIFFI)
Sylvia B. Rimm, Gary A. Davis

Copyright: 1979

Population: Children, adolescents; Grades 6 through 12

Purpose: Assesses creativity in children; used to identify gifted children

Description: Multiple-item paper–pencil test of interests and attitudes related to creativity. The test yields the following dimension scores: Creative Art and Writing, Confidence, Imagination, Challenge-Inventiveness, and Many Interests. Validation groups include minorities, urban and suburban students, students learning disabilities, and gifted children. Also available in Spanish.

Format: Self-administered; suitable for group use; untimed: 20–40 minutes

Scoring: Machine scored

Cost: Specimen Set $12.00; Class Set of 30 tests and scoring $80.00 (indicate grade level)

Publisher: Educational Assessment Service, Inc.

Khatena Torrance Creative Perception Inventory (KTCPI)
Joe Khatena, E. Paul Torrance

Copyright: 1976

Population: Adolescents, adults; ages 12 and above

Purpose: Identifies candidates for gifted programs

Description: Paper–pencil criterion-referenced test with two subtests: Something About Myself (SAM) and What Kind of Person are You (WKOPAY). Both subtests have 50 items each. Raw scores and standard scores are yielded. A manual and test sheet are used. Examiner must be certified for assessment. Available in large print.

Format: Individual/self-administered; suitable for group use; examiner required; untimed: 20–40 minutes

Scoring: Examiner evaluated; self-scored

Cost: Starter Set $56.20

Publisher: Scholastic Testing Service, Inc.

Khatena-Morse Multitalent Perception Inventory (KMMPI)
Joe Khatena, David T. Morse

Copyright: 1985

Population: Children to adults; Grades 5 and above

Purpose: Assesses giftedness in art, music, and leadership

Description: Paper–pencil criterion-referenced test that measures five factors: art, music, creative imagination, initiative, and leadership. Form A has 19 items; Form B has 20 items. Raw scores, national percentile ranks, standard scores, and stanines are yielded. A manual, test

sheet, and pencil are used. Examiner must be certified for assessment. Available in large print.

Format: Individual/self-administered; suitable for group use; examiner required; untimed: 30–45 minutes

Scoring: Examiner evaluated; self-scored

Cost: Starter Set (manual and 35 questionnaires) $55.15

Publisher: Scholastic Testing Service, Inc.

Preschool and Kindergarten Interest Descriptor (PRIDE)
Sylvia B. Rimm

Copyright: 1983

Population: Children; ages 3 to 6

Purpose: Identifies creatively gifted preschool and kindergarten children; used for academic placement in gifted programs

Description: Paper–pencil 50-item inventory in which parents assess their child's attitudes and interests by responding "no," "to a small extent," "average," "more than average," or "definitely" to each item. Scores are provided on four dimensions: Many Interests, Independence–Perseverance, Imagination–Playfulness, and Originality. All scoring is completed by publisher.

Format: Self-administered; suitable for group use; untimed: 20–35 minutes

Scoring: Computer scored

Cost: Specimen set $12.00; class set of 30 tests and computer scoring $80.00

Publisher: Educational Assessment Service, Inc.

Scales for Rating the Behavioral Characteristics of Superior Students (SRBCSS)
Joseph S. Renzulli, Linda H. Smith, Alan J. White, Carolyn M. Callahan, Robert K. Hartman

Copyright: 1977

Population: Children, adolescents

Purpose: Assesses the behavioral characteristics related to the objectives of gifted and talented elementary and junior high school programs; used to supplement measures of intelligence, achievement, and creativity in selecting students for gifted programs

Description: Paper–pencil 95-item inventory consisting of 10 subscales, each of which assesses a different dimension of behavioral characteristics related to gifted and talented educational objectives. The following 10 dimensions are evaluated: learning, motivation, creativity, leadership, art, music, dramatics, planning, precise communication, and expressive communication. Each scale consists of 4–15 statements describing behaviors attributed to gifted and talented students. The teacher rates each item on a 4-point scale from "seldom" to "almost always," reflecting the degree to which the presence or absence of each characteristic has been observed. The 10 subscales represent 10 distinct sets of behavioral characteristics; therefore, no total score is derived. Only scales relevant to program objectives should be selected for use in a given program.

Format: Self-administered by teacher; suitable for group use; untimed: time varies

Scoring: Examiner evaluated

Cost: Test kit $8.95; additional sets of 100 tests $49.95

Publisher: Creative Learning Press, Inc.

Screening Assessment for Gifted Elementary Students (SAGES)

Susan K. Johnsen, Anne L. Corn

Copyright: 1987

Population: Children; ages 7 years to 12 years 11 months

Purpose: Assesses aptitude, achievement, and creativity; used to identify gifted children

Description: Multiple-item paper–pencil test consisting of three subtests. The Reasoning subtest, which measures aptitude, requires the child to solve problems by identifying relationships among pictures and figures. In the School Acquired Information subtest, the child answers multiple-choice questions assessing social studies, science, and math achievement.

The Divergent Production subtest measures ideational fluency, an aspect of creativity. Standard scores and percentile ranks are provided for each subtest.

Format: Examiner required; Divergent Production subtest—individual administration; Reasoning and School Acquired Information subtests—suitable for group use; untimed: 30–50 minutes

Scoring: Hand key

Cost: Complete kit (examiner's manual, picture book, 50 profile and response sheets, storage box) $104.00

Publisher: PRO-ED, Inc.

Screening Assessment for Gifted Elementary Students–Primary (SAGES–P)

Susan K. Johnsen, Anne L. Corn

Copyright: 1992

Population: Children; ages 5 years to 8 years 11 months

Purpose: Helpful in identifying gifted students in kindergarten through third grade; samples aspects of two of the most commonly used areas for identifying young gifted students: aptitude and achievement

Description: Aptitude is measured by the Reasoning subtest. The child is asked to solve analogical problems by identifying relationships among pictures and figures. The General Information subtest assesses achievement. The child answers questions about everyday concepts and those introduced in the primary school years by selecting from a series of pictures, symbols, or words. The subtests may be used to examine the relationships among aptitude, achievement, and total performance. Standard scores and percentile ranks are provided for subtests, and full-scale scores are given for both gifted and normal samples. The SAGES–P was standardized on a large, nationally representative sample of more than 2,500 normal students and 1,000 gifted students residing in 24 states. The demographic characteristics of the normal sample approximate those of the nation as a whole with regard to sex, race, ethnicity, geographic region, and urban/rural residence. Data are provided supporting test–retest and internal consistency reliability and content, construct, and criterion-related validity. Validity studies indicate that the SAGES–P scores differentiate among groups within the gifted sample and between normal and gifted children.

Format: Examiner required; suitable for group; timed: approximately 30 minutes

Scoring: Examiner evaluated

Cost: Complete kit (examiner's manual, student response booklets, profile and response forms, storage box) $89.00

Publisher: PRO-ED, Inc.

Thinking Creatively in Action and Movement (TCAM)
E. Paul Torrance

Copyright: 1981

Population: Children; ages 3 to 8

Purpose: Assesses the creativity of young children; used as part of a program to develop promising creative talent among young children

Description: Show–tell test assessing the creativity of young children, especially preschoolers. The responses are appropriate to the developmental characteristics of the younger child and are physical in nature, although verbal responses are acceptable. A booklet, manual, and set of equipment are used. Raw scores and standard scores are yielded. Examiner must be certified for assessment.

Format: Individually administered; examiner required; not suitable for group use; timed: 10–30 minutes

Scoring: Examiner evaluated; machine-scored; scoring service available from publisher

Cost: Starter Set $38.55

Publisher: Scholastic Testing Service, Inc.

Thinking Creatively with Sounds and Words (TCSW)
E. Paul Torrance, Joe Khatena, Bert F. Cunnington

Copyright: 1973

Population: Grades 3 and above

Purpose: Measures ability to create images for words and sounds; used to identify gifted and creative individuals and to teach imagery

Description: Two-test battery assessing creativity by measuring the originality of ideas stimulated by abstract sounds and spoken onomatopoetic words. TCSW is a battery of two tests: Sounds and Images and Onomatopoeia and Images. It is available in equivalent forms (A and B) on two levels: Level I (Grades 3–12) and Level II (adult). One cassette provides the stimuli for each level. Raw scares are yielded. A booklet and pencil are used. Examiner must be certified for assessment.

Format: Examiner required; suitable for group use; untimed: 30 minutes per test

Scoring: Examiner evaluated; machine-scored; scoring service available from publisher

Cost: Specimen Set $18.90

Publisher: Scholastic Testing Service, Inc.

Torrance Tests of Creative Thinking (TTCT)
E. Paul Torrance

Copyright: 1962

Population: Grades K and above

Purpose: Assesses the ability to visualize and transform words, meanings, and patterns; used to identify gifted and creative individuals

Description: Paper–pencil criterion-referenced measure of an individual's creativity assessing four mental characteristics: fluency, flexibility, originality, and elaboration. The test is available in two editions: Verbal TTCT (seven word-based exercises) and Figural TTCT (three picture-based exercises). The Verbal TTCT can be administered orally to students in kindergarten through Grade 3 and is easily scored. Individuals with psychometric training should interpret the subtest and total scores. "Streamlined" scoring of the figural forms of the overall test is available. This alternative scoring yields norm-referenced measures for fluency, originality, abstractness of titles, elaboration, and resistance to premature closure. It provides an overall Creativity Index and criterion-referenced national percentiles and standard scores for several creativity indicators. The Verbal and Figural tests are available in two equivalent forms (A and B). A scoring guide is included in the directions manual. A booklet and pencil are used for both forms.

Format: Examiner required; suitable for group use; timed: Figural TTCT—30 minutes, Verbal TTCT—45 minutes

Scoring: Examiner evaluated; machine-scored; scoring service available from publisher

Cost: Specimen Set (specify form) $18.90

Publisher: Scholastic Testing Service, Inc.

Watson-Glaser Critical Thinking Appraisal™ (WGCTA™)
Goodwin Watson, Edward M. Glaser

Copyright: 1980

Population: Grades 9 through 12, college students, and professionals

Purpose: Assesses critical thinking abilities; used for evaluation of gifted and talented individuals; used to select candidates for positions in which analytic reasoning is an important part of the job

Description: Paper–pencil 80-item test measuring five aspects of the ability to think critically: inference, recognition of assumptions, deduction, interpretation, and evaluation of arguments. The subject responds to the exercises, which include problems, statements, arguments, and interpretation of material encountered on a daily basis. Two alternate and equivalent forms, A and B, are available.

Format: Examiner required; suitable for group use; untimed: 50 minutes

Scoring: Hand key; may be machine scored

Cost: Examination kit (Form A test booklet, answer document, manual, and class record) $38.50

Publisher: Harcourt® Brace Educational Measurement

Learning Disabilities

Analytic Learning Disability Assessment (ALDA)
Thomas D. Gnagey, Paticia D. Gnagey

Copyright: 1982

Population: Children, adolescents; ages 8 to 14

Purpose: Measures the skills necessary to read, spell, write, and work with numbers; aids in the neuropsychological evaluation of students with learning disabilities, educable mental retardation, and behavioral disturbance

Description: Multiple-item test assessing a student's strengths and weaknesses in 77 skills underlying basic school subjects. The strengths and weaknesses are matched with the student's most appropriate learning method for each subject: 11 reading methods, 23 spelling methods, 6 math computation methods, and 8 handwriting methods. The results are transferred to the Recommendation Pamphlet to create an individualized teaching plan providing specific procedures and methods for teachers. Materials include a student learning plan, a teacher recommendation pamphlet, also with tear-out sections, four colored scoring pencils, tape, and a straight-edge ruler in a leather carrying case. The test should not be used unless a learning dysfunction is suspected.

Format: Examiner required; not suitable for group use; untimed: 75 minutes

Scoring: Hand key

Cost: Complete kit (test book, manual, scoring straight edge, four colored scoring pencils, tape, chalk, 20 complete testing forms, teaching plan, carrying case) $148.00

Publisher: Slosson Educational Publications, Inc.

Boder Test of Reading–Spelling Patterns
Elena Boder, Sylvia Jarrico

Copyright: 1982

Population: All ages

Purpose: Differentiates specific reading disability (developmental dyslexia) from nonspecific reading disability through reading and spelling performance; used to classify dyslexic readers into one of three subtypes

Description: Paper–pencil 300-item tests of reading and spelling ability. The Reading Test uses 13 graded word lists of 20 words each, half of which are phonetic and half of which are nonphonetic. The words, which are presented flash and untimed, require sight vocabulary and phonic word analysis skills. The Spelling Test uses two individualized spelling lists (10 known words and 10 unknown) based on the student's reading performance. Both the reading and spelling tests tap the central visual and auditory processes required for reading and spelling, making it possible to diagnose developmental dyslexia by the joint analysis of reading and spelling as interdependent functions. The results should be supplemented with testing that uses instructional materials to which the child already has been and will be exposed.

Format: Examiner required; not suitable for group use; timed: 30 minutes

Scoring: Examiner evaluated

Cost: Examination kit $118.00

Publisher: The Psychological Corporation

Career Inventory for the Learning Disabled (CILD)
Carol Weller, Mary Buchanan

Copyright: 1983

Population: Age 6 to adult

Purpose: Assesses the personality, abilities, and interests of students with learning disability to help them make intelligent and realistic career choices

Description: Multiple-item paper–pencil test consisting of three inventories: Attributes, Ability, and Interest. The Attributes Inventory assesses the individual's dominant personality characteristics; the Ability Inventory provides a profile of strengths and weaknesses across the auditory, visual, and motor areas; and the Interest Inventory can be used to determine whether the individual's career goals are realistic. Attributes and Ability Inventories are com-

pleted by the examiner, while the Interest Inventory may be completed by the individual. Job Finder is included in the manual. The instrument is criterion referenced.

Format: Individual or group use; 20 to 30 minutes

Scoring: Examiner administered and interpreted

Cost: Complete kit (manual and protocols in vinyl folder) $50.00

Publisher: Academic Therapy Publications

Cognitive Control Battery
Sebastiano Santostefano

Copyright: 1988

Population: Children, adolescents; ages 4 to 12

Purpose: Predicts the presence of learning disabilities and assesses the role of cognitive dysfunction in school and adjustment problems

Description: Three tests comprise the battery: Fruit Distraction, Scattered Scanning, and Leveling–Sharpening House. The Fruit Distraction is a verbal measure of an individual's ability to selectively attend even when there is interference from competing stimuli. The child responds by naming a series of colors presented with and without distractions or contradictions. The Scattered Scanning Test is a paper–pencil test of an individual's preferred way of scanning information (broad vs. narrow). The child scans a display of geometric shapes randomly scattered over a sheet of paper and marks certain ones. The Leveling–Sharpening House Test consists of 60 drawings of a house in which elements of the drawing are cumulatively omitted on successive cards. The child's task is to tell the examiner when the picture changes. The CCB tests can be individually administered or combined.

Format: Examiner required; not suitable for group use; untimed

Scoring: Examiner interpretation

Cost: Kit (25 record booklets, 25 Form 1 test sheets for the SST, 25 Form 2 test sheets for the SST, 25 motor tempo test forms for the SST, 25 training forms for the SST) $325.00

Publisher: Western Psychological Services

Cognitive Control Battery: The Scattered Scanning Test
Sebastiano Santostefano

Copyright: 1988

Population: Children, adolescents; ages 4 to 12

Purpose: Predicts the presence of learning disabilities and assesses the role of cognitive dysfunction in school and adjustment problems

Description: This test, along with the Leveling–Sharpening House Test and the Fruit Distraction Test, comprise the Cognitive Control Battery. The test is available in two forms: Form 1 (ages 3 to 8) and Form 2 (ages 9 to 12).

Format: Examiner required; not suitable for group use; untimed: typical time not available

Scoring: Examiner evaluated

Cost: Kit (all test materials, 1 manual, 25 record booklets, 25 Form 1 test sheets for the SST, 25 Form 2 test sheets for the SST, 25 motor tempo test forms for the SST, 25 training forms for the SST) $325.00

Publisher: Western Psychological Services

Dyslexia Schedule
John McLeod

Copyright: 1987

Population: Grades K through 1

Purpose: Gathers relevant social data and developmental information from parents or guardians about a child who is suspected of having a reading disability

Description: Paper–pencil 89-item questionnaire completed by the parents or guardians before the child visits a clinic; results provide the clinician with background data to help evaluate characteristics associated with childhood dyslexia before testing begins.

Format: Individual administration; 20–30 minutes

Scoring: Examiner administration and interpretation

Cost: Specimen Set $7.05

Publisher: Educators Publishing Service, Inc.

Learning Disabilities Evaluation Scale (LDES)–Renormed
Stephen B. McCarney

Copyright: 1996

Population: Children, adolescents; ages 4 years 5 months to 18 years

Purpose: Diagnoses learning disabilities

Description: The instrument utilizes performance observations of the classroom teacher or other instructional personnel. The instrument is designed to provide a profile based on the most commonly accepted definition (IDEA) of learning disabilities. This profile classifies whether the student's difficulties are in the areas of Listening, Thinking, Speaking, Reading, Writing, Spelling, or Mathematical Calculations. Appropriate for initial referral and screening procedures.

Format: Individual administration; untimed: 20 minutes

Scoring: Self/computer scored

Cost: Complete kit $133.50

Publisher: Hawthorne Educational Services, Inc.

Learning Disability Rating Procedure (LDRP)
Gerald J. Spadafore, Sharon J. Spadafore

Copyright: 1981

Population: Ages 6 through 18

Purpose: Provides a focus for discussion and facilitates agreement among participants of IEP meetings concerning eligibility

Description: Brief rating procedure that summarizes 10 areas that are important to consider when determining placement. The student is rated on each indicator, ranging from general intelligence and listening comprehension to socially inappropriate behavior and learning motivation. Criteria describe the student as a poor, fair, good, or excellent candidate for LD placement.

Format: Individual rating scale for each meeting participant; 15 minutes

Scoring: Examiner administered and interpreted

Cost: Test kit (manual and rating forms in vinyl folder) $37.00

Publisher: Academic Therapy Publications

Self-Perception Profile for Learning Disabled Students
Susan Harter Renick

Copyright: 1988

Population: Ages 8 to 18

Purpose: Assesses general intellectual ability, reading competence, math competence, writing competence, spelling competence, social acceptance, athletic competence, physical appearance, behavioral conduct, and global self-worth

Description: The manual includes a teacher rating scale, as well as a rating scale to tap children's perceptions of the importance of each domain.

Format: Examiner required; individual administration; time varies

Scoring: Hand key

Cost: $15.00

Publisher: Susan Harter

Slingerland College Level Screening
Carol Murray

Copyright: 1991

Population: Adults

Purpose: Identifies specific language disabilities, shows how a student learns, and screens for dyslexia

Description: Multiple-choice paper–pencil short-answer test comprised of the following subtests: visual to kinesthetic, visual to kinesthetic–motor, visual perception–memory, visual discrimination, visual perception and memory to kinesthetic–motor, auditory to visual–kinesthetic, auditory to visual, comprehension, and auditory to kinesthetic.

Format: Individual administration; suitable for group use; examiner required; timed: approximately 1½ hours

Scoring: Examiner evaluated

Cost: Manual $11.35; tests $15.95/dozen; cards and charts $15.95

Publisher: Educators Publishing Service, Inc.

Slingerland High School Screening
Carol Murray, Patricia Beis

Copyright: 1993

Population: Adolescents, adults; Grades 9 through 12

Purpose: Screens for dyslexia and specific language disabilities; shows how the student learns by identifying strengths and weaknesses

Description: Ten-item multiple-choice paper–pencil short-answer test comprised of the following items: visual to kinesthetic–motor, visual to kinesthetic–motor, visual perception and memory, visual discrimination, visual perception–memory to kinesthetic–motor, auditory to visual–kinesthetic, auditory to visual, comprehension, and auditory to kinesthetic.

Format: Individual administration; suitable for group use; examiner required; timed: 60 minutes

Scoring: Hand key, examiner evaluated

Cost: Manual $11.35; tests $15.95; cards and charts $15.95

Publisher: Educators Publishing Service, Inc.

Slingerland Screening Tests for Identifying Children with Specific Language Disability
Beth H. Slingerland

Copyright: 1984

Population: Grades 1 through 6

Purpose: Screens elementary school children for indications of specific language disabilities in reading, spelling, handwriting, and speaking

Description: Four forms (A, B, C, and D) each contain eight subtests. Five of the subtests evaluate visual–motor coordination and visual memory linked with motor coordination. Three subtests evaluate auditory–visual discrimination or auditory–memory-to-motor ability. Form D contains a ninth subtest that evaluates personal orientation in time and space and the ability to express ideas in writing. All the forms contain separate Echolalia tests and include individual auditory tests. Also available in Spanish.

Format: Group except for Echolalia; 1½ hours

Scoring: Examiner administration and interpretation

Cost: Forms A, B, C, and D $13.65/dozen; manual for Forms A, B, and C $6.85; manual for Form D $5.15

Publisher: Educators Publishing Service, Inc.

Specific Language Disability Tests
Neva Malcomesius

Copyright: 1967

Population: Grades 6 through 8

Purpose: Screens entire classroom groups or individual students and identifies those who show specific language disability

Description: Subtests I–V evaluate perception in visual discrimination, visual memory, and visual–motor coordination. Subtests VI–X evaluate perception in auditory discrimination, auditory–visual coordination, auditory–motor coordination, and comprehension.

Format: Group; 1–1½ hours

Scoring: Examiner administration and interpretation

Cost: Test $14.10; charts and cards $14.10; manual $1.90; Specimen Set $2.10

Publisher: Educators Publishing Service, Inc.

Weller-Strawser Scales of Adaptive Behavior: For the Learning Disabled (WSSAB)
Carol Weller, Sherri Strawser

Copyright: 1981

Population: Ages 6 to 18

Purpose: Assesses the adaptive behavior of elementary and secondary school students with learning disabilities; used to determine severity of disabilities and to identify areas requiring remedial attention

Description: Multiple-item paper–pencil norm-referenced scales covering social coping, relationships, pragmatic language, and production. The scales are completed by a teacher or diagnostician following a period of observation of the student. The total score and subtest scores define behavior problems as mild to moderate or moderate to severe. Using the results and following suggestions in the manual, the examiner may develop compensatory teaching techniques to help the student cope with situations in school, home, social, and job environments.

Format: Individual administration; 15 minutes

Scoring: Examiner evaluated

Cost: Test kit, elementary or secondary (manual, 50 forms, in vinyl folder) $36.00

Publisher: Academic Therapy Publications

Mental Retardation

AAMR Adaptive Behavior Scale–Residential and Community: Second Edition (ABS–RC:2)
Kazuo Nihira, Henry Leland, Nadine Lambert

Copyright: 1993

Population: Ages 18 to 60 and over

Purpose: Identifies individuals who are significantly below their peers in important areas of adaptive behavior and to determine strengths and weaknesses among adaptive domains and factors

Description: This instrument is a revision of the 1969 and 1974 *AAMD Adaptive Behavior Scales*. The items measure the following domains: Independent Functioning, Physical Development, Economic Activity, Language Development, Numbers and Time, Domestic Activity, Prevocational/Vocational Activity, Self-Direction, Responsibility, Socialization, Social Behavior, Conformity, Trustworthiness, Stereotyped/Hyperactive Behavior, Sexual Behavior, Self-Abuse Behavior, Social Engagement, and Disturbing Interpersonal Behavior.

Factor scores of Personal Self-Sufficiency, Community Self-Sufficiency, Personal–Social Responsibility, Social Adjustment, and Personal Adjustment are available from the domain scores.

Format: Individual interview format; 15–30 minutes

Scoring: Examiner scored and interpreted; computer (IBM, Apple II, and Mac) interpretation available

Cost: Complete kit (examiner's manual, protocols, and storage box) $104.00

Publisher: PRO-ED, Inc.

AAMR Adaptive Behavior Scale–School: Second Edition (ABS-S:2)
Nadine Lambert, Kazuo Nihira, Henry Lambert

Copyright: 1993

Population: Ages 3 years to 18 years 11 months

Purpose: Identifies individuals who are significantly below their peers in important areas of adaptive behavior and determines strengths and weaknesses among adaptive domains and factors

Description: This instrument is a revision of the 1969 and 1974 *AAMD Adaptive Behavior Scales*. The items measure the following domains in Part One: Independent Functioning, Physical Development, Economic Activity, Language Development, Numbers and Time, Prevocational/Vocational Activity, Self-Direction, Responsibility, and Socialization. Part Two measures Social Behavior, Conformity, Trustworthiness, Stereotyped/ Hyperactive Behavior, Self-Abusive Behavior, Social Engagement, and Disturbing Interpersonal Behavior. Factor scores of Personal Self-Sufficiency, Community Self-Sufficiency, Personal–Social Responsibility, Social Adjustment, and Personal Adjustment are available from the domain scores.

Format: Individual interview format; 15–30 minutes

Scoring: Examiner scored and interpreted;

computer (IBM, Apple II, and Mac) interpretation available

Cost: Complete kit (examiner's manual, protocols, and storage box) $104.00

Publisher: PRO-ED, Inc.

Adaptive Behavior Inventory (ABI)
Linda Brown, James E. Leigh

Copyright: 1986

Population: Ages 6 years to 18 years 11 months

Purpose: Evaluates the functional, daily living skills of school-aged children; used to identify children with mental retardation and emotional disturbance

Description: Paper–pencil 150-item test assessing functional skills in five scale areas: Self-Care Skills, Communication Skills, Social Skills, Academic Skills, and Occupational Skills. The test yields an Adaptive Behavior Quotient, standard scores, and percentiles. The ABI–Short Form, which contains 50 items and yields the same scores as the complete form, is also available.

Format: Individual interview format; 15–30 minutes

Scoring: Examiner scored and interpreted; computer (IBM and Apple II) interpretation available

Cost: Complete kit (examiner's manual, short form and long form protocols, and storage box) $74.00

Publisher: PRO-ED, Inc.

CASAS STRETCH Competency Tests

Copyright: 1992

Population: Adults, adolescents

Purpose: Assesses life skill competencies for use with learners with developmental disabilities

Description: Set of 15 tests, each targeting one of the following transition domains: domestic self-care, domestic home care, vocational, recreation/leisure, and community resources. The tests consist of informal inventories and are used with the STRETCH Curriculum Guide that coincides with each transition domain.

Format: Checklist

Scoring: Standardized observational scoring rubric provided

Cost: 15 reusable tests $75.00

Publisher: Comprehensive Adult Student Assessment System

CASAS Tests for Special Populations

Copyright: 1991

Population: Adults, adolescents

Purpose: Used with learners with developmental disabilities to assess competencies across a range of life skills and may be used to measure learning progress

Description: Multiple-choice tests. Highest test level provides transition into regular CASAS life skill series. Four levels of tests, AAAAA (most basic) through AA. Training required to implement the program. CASAS scaled scores identify general skill level and enable comparison of performance across CASAS tests.

Format: Examiner required; not suitable for group administration

Scoring: Hand scored

Cost: $11.00 per test

Publisher: Comprehensive Adult Student Assessment System

Developmental Assessment for the Severely Handicapped (DASH)
Mary K. Dykes

Copyright: 1980

Population: Children; developmental ages birth to 8

Purpose: Assesses the development of individuals with severe disabilities; used to establish IEPs

Description: Five multiple-item paper–pencil observational scales assessing development in the following domains: sensorimotor, language,

preacademic, activities of daily living, and social–emotional. The five Pinpoint Scales are sensitive to small changes in skill performance. The skills assessed are identified as either present, emerging, task-resistive, nonrelevant, or unknown.

Format: Examiner required; not suitable for group use; untimed: time varies

Scoring: Examiner evaluated

Cost: Complete kit (manual, 5 each of 5 Pinpoint Scales, 25 daily plan sheets, 1 pad comprehensive program records, and 25 individualized education plans) $119.00

Publisher: PRO-ED, Inc.

Inventory for Client and Agency Planning (ICAP)
Robert H. Bruininks, Bradley K. Hill, Richard F. Weatherman, Richard W. Woodcock

Copyright: 1986

Population: Infants to adults

Purpose: Measures the adaptive and problem behaviors and service needs of individuals with moderate to severe disabilities or mental retardation in residential rehabilitation, education, and human service programs; also used by geriatric service agencies

Description: Multiple-item paper–pencil self-report inventory providing client information in the following areas: diagnostic and health status, adaptive behavior, problem behavior, service history, residential placement, projected service needs, functional limitations, and social–leisure history. The results can be used by administrators and supervisors to determine the client's current status and eligibility for services and to manage programs and facilities by assisting in their accreditation, coordinating and planning project costs and reimbursement, and obtaining funding. Age scores, adaptive behavior indexes, standard scores, and service level index scores are obtained.

Format: Individual administration; examiner required; 20 minutes

Scoring: Examiner evaluated; may be computer scored

Cost: Complete kit (manual, 25 response booklets) $103.00

Publisher: Riverside Publishing Company

Prevocational Assessment and Curriculum Guide (PACG)
Dennis E. Mithaug, Jeffrey E. Stewart, Deanna K. Mar

Copyright: 1993

Population: Children to adults

Purpose: Measures the skills of individuals with severe to profound mental retardation for entrance into a sheltered workshop; used for vocational planning

Description: Multiple-choice 46-item paper–pencil test measuring the following: attendance/endurance, independence, production, learning, behavior, communication, social skills, grooming/eating, and toileting.

Format: Individual administration; examiner required; untimed: 15 minutes

Scoring: Hand key; no scoring service available

Cost: Manual and 10 forms $12.00

Publisher: Exceptional Education

Progress Assessment Chart (PAC)
Herbert C. Gunzburg

Copyright: Not provided

Population: All ages

Purpose: Assesses the ability to cope with everyday situations; intended for use with individuals with disabilities

Description: Paper–pencil criterion-referenced assessment of abilities composed of four subcategories: socialization, occupation, self-help, and communication. Available in German, French, Spanish, Dutch, Norwegian, Polish, Icelandic, and Danish.

Format: Individual administration; examiner required; untimed

Scoring: Examiner evaluated

Cost: Contact publisher

Publisher: SEFA (Publications) Ltd.

Social and Prevocational Information Battery–Revised (SPIB–R)
Andrew Halpern, Paul Raffeld, Larry K. Irvin, Robert Link, Ardan Munkres

Copyright: 1985

Population: Students with mental retardation in junior and senior high school, adults

Purpose: Assesses a student with educable mental retardation for knowledge of skills and competencies important for community adjustment; used by educators as an evaluative device in programs for students with EMR

Description: Orally administered 277-item paper–pencil test consisting of nine subtests (job search skills, job-related behavior, banking, budgeting, purchasing, home management, physical health care, hygiene and grooming, functional signs) measuring a student's attainment of five long-range goals of work-study or work experience programs in secondary schools: employability, economic self-sufficiency, family living, personal habits, and communication. SPIB–T for TMR students is an alternate edition consisting of one form and one level designed for use with students with mild to moderate retardation.

Format: Examiner required; suitable for use by groups not exceeding 20 students; untimed: 15–25 minutes per subtest

Scoring: Hand key; may be computer scored

Cost: Hand-scorable test books (includes manual) $77.75

Publisher: CTB/McGraw-Hill

Street Survival Skills Questionnaire (SSSQ)
Dan Linkenhoker, Lawrence T. McCarron

Copyright: 1993

Population: Ages 9 and older; Grades 2 and above

Purpose: Measures specific aspects of the adaptive behavior of special education students; used as a baseline behavioral measure of the effects of training and to predict one's potential for adapting to community living conditions and vocational placement

Description: Oral-response and point-to 216-item test consisting of nine subtests, each presented in a separate booklet containing 24 picture plates. The examiner orally presents the question, and the examinee responds by pointing to one of the four pictures presented. Fundamental reading skills are required. The large-print and graphic format is designed for use with individuals with visual acuity of 20/200 or better in either eye. A booklet for administering the SSSQ in sign language is available. The SSSQ Report (sold separately) provides narrative interpretations of the examinee's performance in each area as well as more specific area analyses.

Format: Examiner required; not suitable for group use; untimed: 30–45 minutes

Scoring: Hand key; may be computer scored

Cost: Complete $310.00; computer scoring service $225.00

Publisher: McCarron-Dial Systems

T.M.R. School Competency Scales
Samuel Levine, Freeman F. Elzey,
Paul Thormahlen, Leo F. Cain

Copyright: Not provided

Population: Children, adolescents, ages 5 and older

Purpose: Assesses students' adaptive skills in trainable mentally retarded (T.M.R.) classroom settings; used to evaluate strengths and weaknesses and to measure progress

Description: Paper–pencil 91- or 103-item rating scale measuring five school competence skill areas: perceptual–motor, initiative–responsibility, cognition, personal–social, and language. Items are rated on a 4-point scale by the classroom teacher. Materials include separate scales for each of five age groups: 5 to 7, 8 to 10, 11 to 13, 14 to 16, and 17 and older. Scales are published in two forms: one for the two younger age groups (91 items) and one for the three older age groups (103 items).

Format: Examiner required; not suitable for group use; untimed: typical time not available

Scoring: Examiner evaluated

Cost: Preview kit (Rating Scale I, Scale II, Manual) $19.00

Publisher: Consulting Psychologists Press, Inc.

VCWS 17—Pre-Vocational Readiness Battery

Copyright: 1978

Population: Adults

Purpose: Measures an individual's ability to function independently; may be used with individuals with mental retardation to determine whether the individual requires a sheltered environment or can function independently

Description: Assessment and training tool containing five subtests: Development Assessment, Workshop Evaluation, Vocational Interest Screening, Interpersonal/Social Skills, and Independent Living Skills. The developmental assessment subtest contains functional nonmedical measures of physical and mental abilities. The workshop evaluation is a simulated assembly process designed to determine if the examinee is appropriately placed in a work or training setting. The vocational interest screening subtest, presented in an audiovisual format, identifies job interests. The interpersonal/social skills subtest identifies barriers to employment or independent living. The independent living skills subtest measures skill and knowledge in transportation, money handling, grooming, and living environment. The tasks in each subtest vary in difficulty from very simple recognition of rooms to more complex processes relating to work. The test is designed in such a way that a lack of language or reading skills does not present a barrier to evaluation. The test should not be administered to individuals with severe impairment of the upper extremities.

Format: Examiner required; not suitable for group use; timed: time not available

Scoring: Examiner evaluated

Cost: $3,695.00

Publisher: Valpar International Corporation

Vineland Adaptive Behavior Scales

Sara S. Sparrow, David A. Balla,
Dominic V. Cicchetti

Copyright: 1984, 1985

Population: Birth to 18 years 11 months (and low-functioning adults)

Purpose: Assesses individuals with mental retardation or those who have difficulty performing in testing situations

Description: Semistructured interviews and a questionnaire that assess personal and social skills. Available in an Expanded Form, Survey Form, and Classroom Edition. Each has a starter set consisting of the appropriate manual, 10 item or record booklets, and samples of parent reports. Expanded Form also has a sample Program Planning Report. Optional materials in Spanish.

Format: Individual parent/caregiver interviews; individual teacher questionnaires, Interview Edition: Expanded Form 60–90 minutes, Survey Form 20–60 minutes. Classroom Edition: 20 minutes

Scoring: Items are examiner-scored; ASSIST scoring software is available for Apple II and IBM computers for the Interview Edition (Expanded and Survey Forms) and for IBM only for Classroom Edition

Cost: Complete Starter Set (one each of the Starter Sets TG3010, TG3040, and TG3080) $134.95

Publisher: American Guidance Service

Vocational Adaptation Rating Scales (VARS)

Robert G. Malgady, Peter R. Barcher,
John Davis, George Towner

Copyright: Not provided

Population: Adolescents; adults

Purpose: Measures maladaptive behavior in individuals with mental retardation

Description: The rating can be done by any adult who has had sufficient contact with the individual being rated and covers maladaptive behavior in six areas: verbal manners, communication skills, interpersonal skills, respect for property, rules and regulations, attendance and punctuality, grooming and personal hygiene. Ratings are totaled to produce frequency and severity scores for each area and are used to make placement decisions; used to help determine individual vocational activity.

Format: Individually administered; examiner completed; 30 minutes

Scoring: Examiner evaluated

Cost: Kit (25 rating booklets and profile forms, 1 manual) $50.00

Publisher: Western Psychological Services

Vocational Assessment and Curriculum Guide (VACG)

Frank R. Rusch, Richard P. Schutz,
Dennis E. Mithaug, Jeffrey E. Stewart,
Deanna K. Mar

Copyright: 1993

Population: Children to adults

Purpose: Measures skills of individuals with mental retardation essential for competitive employment; used for vocational planning

Description: Multiple-choice 49-item paper–pencil test with the following categories: attendance/endurance, independence, production, learning, behavior, communication, social skills, grooming, eating, reading/writing, math.

Format: Individual administration; examiner required; untimed: 15 minutes

Scoring: Hand key; no scoring service available

Cost: Manual and 10 forms $12.00

Publisher: Exceptional Education

Washer Visual Acuity Screening Technique (WVAST)

Rhonda Wiczer Washer

Copyright: 1984

Population: Age 2 to adult; mentally challenged

Purpose: Measures the visual abilities of severely mentally challenged (mental age 2.6 years to adult), low-functioning, and very young children; used for screening groups of children to identify those with possible visual impairments

Description: Point-to vision test for screening both near- and far-point acuity. The testing procedure omits as many perceptual, motor, and verbal skills as possible. A conditioning process is outlined for familiarizing individuals with the symbols, matching skills, and eye occlusion used in the screening. Examiner must be certified for assessment.

Format: Examiner required; suitable for group use; untimed

Scoring: Examiner evaluated

Cost: Specimen Set $22.00

Publisher: Scholastic Testing Service, Inc.

Visual Impairment

Hill Performance Test of Selected Positioned Concepts
Everett Hill

Copyright: 1981

Population: Children; ages 6 to 10

Purpose: Measures the development of spatial concepts in children with visual impairments; used by teachers and mobility specialists to diagnose visually impairment in children

Description: Task assessment of basic spatial concepts such as front, back, left, and right, with 72 items. The development of these positional concepts is tested through performance on four types of tasks: identifying body relationships, demonstrating positional concepts of body parts to one another, demonstrating positional concepts of body parts to other objects, and forming object-to-object relationships. The test may be used as a criterion-referenced instrument to identify individual strengths and weaknesses in the area of spatial concepts or as a norm-referenced test.

Format: Examiner required; not suitable for

group use; untimed: typical time not available

Scoring: Examiner evaluated

Cost: Complete kit (20 record forms, manual) $33.00

Publisher: Stoelting Company

School Readiness Tests for Blind Children (STBC)

Copyright: 1979

Population: Children with blindness

Purpose: Assesses cognitive abilities of children with blindness; used for determining school readiness

Description: Seven-subtest measure of cognitive skills important to school readiness, including Information Test, Kinesthesis Test, Vocabulary Test, Number Concept Test, Motor Development Test, Memory Test, and Reasoning Test. The examiner may make subjective evaluations of the child's perseverance, readiness to follow instructions, and social adjustment.

Format: Examiner required; not suitable for group use; untimed: 1½ hours

Scoring: Examiner evaluated

Cost: Contact publisher

Publisher: Human Sciences Research Council

South African Individual Scale for the Blind (SAISB)

Copyright: 1979

Population: Children, adolescents; ages 6 to 18

Purpose: Measures general intelligence of children with blindness; used for psychological and educational evaluations

Description: Nine-subtest measure of general intellectual ability. Five subtests are verbal, and four are nonverbal. Materials include Braillon sheets for the Pattern Completion and Dominos subtests, a form board, and wooden blocks. The test was adapted from the New South African Individual Scale (NSAIS).

Format: Examiner required; not suitable for group use; untimed: typical time not available

Scoring: Hand key; examiner evaluated

Cost: Contact publisher

Publisher: Human Sciences Research Council

VCWS 18—Conceptual Understanding Through Blind Evaluation (CUBE)

Copyright: 1980

Population: Adults with blindness

Purpose: Measures the perceptive abilities that help a person compensate for visual disabilities; used with adults who are congenitally and adventitiously blind

Description: Performance-based battery of six tests assessing a person's perceptual skills in meeting the basic needs of judgment, mobility, orientation, discrimination, and balance. The subtests are Tactual Perception, Mobility/Discrimination Skills, Spatial Organization and Memory, Assembly and Packaging, and Audible Perception. Administration of the tests varies according to the factors being assessed: mobility or job skills.

Format: Examiner required; not suitable for group use; timed: time not available

Scoring: Examiner evaluated

Cost: $3,995.00

Publisher: Valpar International Corporation

Social Studies

. . . .

ACT PEP RCE: Arts and Sciences: American Dream (Part I)

Copyright: 1993

Population: Adults; college level

Purpose: Used by adults wanting to earn college credit by examination; assesses interdisciplinary humanities at the upper level

Description: Essay test with three extended-response questions. Two forms are available. A test booklet, answer sheet, and pen are used. A college reading level is required. Examiner must have experience with college-level test administration. Available in large print. May be used for persons with visual, physical, hearing, and mental disabilities.

Format: Suitable for group use; examiner required; timed: 3 hours

Scoring: Examiner evaluated

Cost: $140.00

Publisher: American College Testing

ACT PEP RCE: Arts and Sciences: Ethics: Theory and Practice

Copyright: 1996

Population: Adults; college level

Purpose: Measures knowledge and understanding of ethics; used to grant college credit and/or advanced placement in academic courses

Description: Multiple-choice 120-item test assessing knowledge of material taught in one semester. A test booklet, answer sheet, and pencil are used. Examiner must have experience with test administration at the college level. May be used for persons with visual, physical, hearing, and mental disabilities.

Format: Suitable for group use; examiner required; timed: 3 hours

Scoring: Machine scored

Cost: Contact publisher

Publisher: American College Testing

ACT PEP RCE: Arts and Sciences: History of Nazi Germany

Copyright: 1993

Population: Adults

Purpose: Measures upper-level knowledge of history of Nazi Germany; used to grant college credit and advanced placement in academic courses

Description: Three-item essay test. Two forms are available. A test booklet, answer document, and pen are used. A college reading level is required. Examiner must have experience with test administration at the college level. Available in large print. May be used with individuals with visual, physical, hearing, and mental disabilities.

Format: Suitable for group use; examiner required; timed: 3 hours

Scoring: Examiner evaluated

Cost: $140.00

Publisher: American College Testing

ACT PEP RCE: Arts and Sciences: New Rule of Reason: Philosophy and Security in the Seventeenth Century

Copyright: 1994

Population: Adults; college level

Purpose: Used by adults wanting to earn college credit by examination; assesses knowledge of 17th-century Western European philosophy

Description: Essay test with three extended response questions. Two forms are available. A test booklet, answer document, and pen are used. A college reading level is required. Examiner must have experience as a college test administrator. Available in large print. May be used for persons with visual, physical, hearing, and mental disabilities.

Format: Suitable for group use; examiner required; timed: 3 hours

Scoring: Examiner evaluated

Cost: $140.00

Publisher: American College Testing

Informeter: An International Technique for the Measurement of Political Information
Panos D. Bardis

Copyright: 1972

Population: Adolescents; Grades 10 and above

Purpose: Measures political knowledge and

awareness of local, national, and international affairs; used for research on political information in the general population and discussion in social sciences classes

Description: Paper–pencil 100-item test in which the subject is asked to list important names, dates, events, and issues in response to specific questions about politics, government, and current events. Suitable for use with individuals with physical and hearing disabilities.

Format: Examiner/self-administered; suitable for group use; 15 minutes

Scoring: Examiner evaluated

Cost: Free

Publisher: Panos D. Bardis, Ph.D.

Irenometer
Panos D. Bardis

Copyright: 1985

Population: Adolescents, adults

Purpose: Measures attitudes and beliefs concerning peace; used for discussion purposes

Description: Ten-item paper–pencil inventory in which an individual rates 10 statements about peace and its effects on individuals and society on a 5-point scale ranging from 0 (strongly disagree) to 4 (strongly agree). All statements express positive attitudes toward peace. The score equals the sum of the 10 numerical responses. Suitable for use with individuals with physical and hearing disabilities.

Format: Self-administered; suitable for group use; untimed: varies

Scoring: Self-scored

Cost: Free

Publisher: Panos D. Bardis, Ph.D.

National Proficiency Survey Series (NPSS): Social Studies
Dale P. Scannell

Copyright: 1989

Population: Grades 8 to 12

Purpose: Assesses student proficiency in high school courses

Description: Multiple-item multiple-choice paper–pencil tests used for evaluation of student proficiency in social studies courses. The World History test examines world geography and early civilizations up to the current age. The U.S. History test spans early exploration to the present. The American Government test measures information about state and federal governments, elections, and the Constitution.

Format: Examiner required; suitable for group use; 40 minutes

Scoring: Self-scored; hand key

Cost: Scanning and Scoring System Kit available; contact publisher for current prices

Publisher: Riverside Publishing Company

World Government Scale
Panos D. Bardis

Copyright: 1985

Population: Adolescents, adults

Purpose: Measures attitudes and beliefs concerning world government and the possible effects world government might have on society; used for discussion and educational purposes

Description: Six-item paper–pencil inventory in which individuals rate six statements about world government and its effects on society on a 5-point scale from 0 (strongly disagree) to 4 (strongly agree). All statements express positive attitudes toward world government. The score equals the sum of the six numerical responses. The theoretical range extends from 0 (complete rejection of the concept of world government) to 24 (complete acceptance). Suitable for use with individuals with physical and hearing disabilities.

Format: Self-administered; suitable for group use; untimed: time varies

Scoring: Self-scored

Cost: Free

Publisher: Panos D. Bardis, Ph.D.

Student Opinion

. . . .

Diagnostic Teacher-Rating Scale
Mary Amatora

Copyright: 1983

Population: Adolescents; adults; Grades 7 and above

Purpose: Measures students' perceptions of their teachers; used to analyze and improve student–teacher relations

Description: This is a 56-item inventory consisting of two scales. The Area Scale (7 items) consists of a list of attributes related to effective teaching and good student–teacher relations. Students rate their teacher for each attribute on a 5-point scale from "worst" to "best." The Diagnostic Checklist (49 items) consists of true–false statements assessing seven factors: liking for teacher; ability to explain; kindness; friendliness, and understanding; fairness in grading; discipline; amount of work required; and liking for lessons. The checklist is available

in two similar forms, A and B.

Format: Examiner required; suitable for group use; untimed: typical time not available

Scoring: Hand key; examiner evaluated

Cost: Specimen Set $5.00; complete kit (35 record sheets for scale, checklist, manual) $12.00

Publisher: Educators'/Employers' Tests and Services Associates

Student Instructional Report (SIR)

Copyright: Not provided

Population: Adolescents, adults; college students

Purpose: Measures teacher performance; used for instructional improvement, administrative decisions, and student course selection

Description: Paper–pencil 39-item test assessing six aspects of teacher performance: course organization and planning, faculty–student interaction, communication; course difficulty and workload, textbooks and readings, and tests and exams. The instrument is administered to students during regular class sessions. Available in French (for Canadian universities) and Spanish.

Format: Examiner required; suitable for group use; untimed: 50 minutes

Scoring: Computer scored

Cost: First 20,000 forms $0.18 each; processing of first 5,000 forms $0.35 each

Publisher: Educational Testing Service

Teacher Attitude

Class Activities Questionnaire (CAQ)
Joe M. Steele

Copyright: 1982

Population: Grades 4 to 12

Purpose: Assesses the instructional climate of upper-elementary and high school classrooms; enables teachers to determine whether goals and expectations are clearly defined in the classroom; assesses openness, independence, divergence, and grades

Description: Paper–pencil 30-item questionnaire assessing five dimensions of instructional climate in the classroom: lower thought processes, higher thought processes, classroom focus, classroom climate, and student opinions. Items 1–27 assess cognitive emphasis and classroom conditions by asking students to rate statements about their classroom experiences on a 4-point scale ranging from "strongly agree" to "strongly disagree." Items 28–30 allow the students to describe in their own words what they perceive to be the strengths and weaknesses of their class. Teachers complete the questionnaire twice, once to indicate what they intend to emphasize in the classroom and a second time to indicate what they predict the students as a group will say. Computer scoring compares the teacher's responses to those provided by the students.

Format: Examiner required; suitable for group use; untimed: 20–30 minutes

Scoring: Computer scored

Cost: Test kit (30 student forms, two teacher forms, manual, and computer analysis) $24.95; Specimen Set $8.95

Publisher: Creative Learning Press, Inc.

Instructional Styles Inventory (ISI)
Albert A. Canfield, Judith S. Canfield

Copyright: Not provided

Population: Adults

Purpose: Identifies a teacher's preferred instructional methods; used in conjunction with the Learning Styles Inventory to maximize teaching and learning efficiency

Description: Paper–pencil 25-item forced-rank inventory assessing a teacher's preference concerning learning environments, instructional modalities, and topical interests. The inventory also measures how much responsibility the instructor will assume for student learning (instead of measuring performance expectancy), identifies areas where instructional training would be most beneficial, provides information to help instructors interpret classroom problems and student reactions, and measures the same dimensions as the *Canfield Learning Styles Inventory* to allow for one-to-one comparison between the two inventories. The test booklets are reusable. Separate norms are provided for male and female instructors.

Format: Self-administered; suitable for group use; untimed: 20–30 minutes

Scoring: Self-scored

Cost: Kit (5 inventories, 1 manual) $60.00

Publisher: Western Psychological Services

Opinions Toward Adolescents (OTA Scale)
William T. Martin

Copyright: 1972

Population: Adolescents, adults; Grades 5 through 7

Purpose: Evaluates attitudes and personality factors that may help or inhibit interpersonal relationships between adults and adolescents; used to screen persons who will be working with adolescents and to educate current staff members

Description: Paper–pencil 89-item inventory examining bipolar attitudes on the following subscales: conservative–liberal, permissive–punitive, morally accepting–morally restrictive, democratic–authoritarian, trust–mistrust, acceptance–prejudice, misunderstanding–understanding, and sincerity–skepticism (a validity scale reflecting test-taking attitude). Norms are provided for various adult and college groups. A fifth- to seventh-grade reading level is required.

Format: Self-administered; suitable for group use; untimed: 20 minutes

Scoring: Hand key

Cost: Examiner's set (manual, keys, 25 test books, 25 answer sheets, 25 profile sheets) $40.00; 25 tests $15.00; 25 profile sheets $8.25; 25 answer sheets $6.75; keys $6.75; manual $4.50

Publisher: Psychologists and Educators, Inc.

Scales for Effective Teaching (SET)
Stevan J. Kukic, Susan L. Fister, Donald P. Link, Janet L. Freston

Copyright: 1989

Population: Adults

Purpose: Used in staff development to assess teacher effectiveness

Description: Fifteen scales of behaviorally anchored items that describe five levels of teaching performance in 14 areas of effective teaching. SET is based on a cohesive group of characteristics that identify classrooms that promote high student achievement. Characteristics include high student expectations; active student learning; well-organized classroom environments; congruence among outcomes, methods, and evaluation; frequent monitoring and feedback of student progress; positive rewards for correct student responses; and planned experiences that promote student involvement. SET includes an administration manual and enough evaluation forms for an average elementary school.

Format: Individual administration; examiner required; untimed

Scoring: Examiner evaluated

Cost: $29.00

Publisher: Sopris West, Inc.

Teacher Motivation Diagnostic Questionnaire
Kenneth M. Matthews

Copyright: 1985

Population: Adults

Purpose: Used for improving teacher motivation

Description: Paper–pencil 16-item test using a numerical Likert scale; assesses self-concept, principal expectations, future utility, and attitudes toward principal

Format: Self-administered; suitable for group use; examiner required; untimed: 10 to 20 minutes

Scoring: Hand key; test scoring service available from publisher

Cost: 25 forms $55.00

Publisher: Kenneth M. Matthews, Ed.D.

Teacher Stress Inventory (TSI)
Michael J. Fimian

Copyright: 1988

Population: Adults; teachers

Purpose: Measures the occupational stress of teachers; used by teachers to assess their own stress levels; by teacher groups in workshop and other similar settings; and by researchers interested in school-, system-, or statewide surveys of teacher stress

Description: Paper–pencil rating scale with 58 items (49 stress related and 9 optional demographic) measuring five stress source factors and five stress manifestation factors in teachers. The stress source factors are Time Management, Work-Related Stressors, Professional Distress, Discipline and Motivation, and Professional Investment. The stress manifestation factors are Emotional, Fatigue, Cardiovascular, Gastronomic, and Behavioral. Raw scores may be compared to cutoff scores by using deciles or by comparison to the norm. The manual provides norms for regular and special education teachers by sex and grade level.

Format: Self-administered; not suitable for group use; untimed: 15 minutes

Scoring: Hand key; examiner evaluated

Cost: Complete kit (manual and protocols) $34.00

Publisher: PRO-ED, Inc.

Visual Processing

Basic Visual Motor Association Test
James Battle

Copyright: 1990

Population: Ages 6 to 15; elementary through junior high students

Purpose: Measures visual motor skills; applicable for tutoring and remediation

Description: Multiple-item paper–pencil test of visual integration, symbol integration, visual association, recall of visual symbols, and visual sequencing. Available in two forms, A and B (60 items each). Available in large print and in French.

Format: Individual/group administration; examiner required; timed: 3 minutes

Scoring: Hand key; test scoring service available from publisher

Cost: $20.00 U.S., $32.00 Canadian

Publisher: James Battle and Associates, Ltd.

Benton Visual Retention Test®, Fifth Edition
Abigail Benton Sivan

Copyright: 1991

Population: Ages 8 to adults

Purpose: Measures visual memory, visual perception, and visual attention

Description: Ten-item test of visual perception, visual memory, and visuoconstructive abilities. Items are designs that are shown to the subject one-by-one. The subject studies each design and reproduces it as exactly as possible by drawing it on plain paper. Materials include Design Cards and three alternate and equivalent forms, C, D, and E.

Format: Examiner required; not suitable for group use; untimed: 5 minutes

Scoring: Examiner evaluated

Cost: Complete set (manual, stimulus booklet—all 30 designs, scoring templates, and 25 response booklets–record forms) $114.00

Publisher: The Psychological Corporation

Comprehensive Test of Visual Functioning (CTVF)
Sue Larson, Evelyn Buethe, Gary J. Vitali

Copyright: 1990

Population: Ages 8 to adults

Purpose: Provides a profile of a person's ability in total visual processing

Description: The CTVF was designed to be a brief and meaningful assessment device to accurately detect and discriminate visual processing problems. The CTVF is an excellent complement to traditional assessments of IQ and standardized reading and neuropsychological evaluations. It is appropriate for multiple professions.

No specific training is required. The CTVF may be used with populations manifesting visual–perceptual problems secondary to acute or chronic disorder processes.

Format: Individual administration; examiner required; untimed: 25 minutes

Scoring: Examiner evaluated

Cost: CTVF Complete (CTVF–2 to CTVF–5 and stimulus items) $102.00

Publisher: Slosson Educational Publishing, Inc.

DeGangi-Berk Test of Sensory Integration (TSI)
Georgia A. DeGangi, Ronald A. Berk

Copyright: 1983

Population: Children; ages 3 to 5

Purpose: Measures overall sensory integration in preschool children; screens for young children with delays in sensory, motor, and perceptual skills in order to facilitate intervention programs

Description: Performance test of three subdomains of sensory integration: postural control, bilateral motor integration, and reflex integration. The examiner rates the child's response to each of 36 items on a numerical scale indicating abnormal to normal development.

Format: Examiner required; not suitable for group use; untimed: 30 minutes

Scoring: Examiner required

Cost: Kit (test materials, 25 star design sheets, 25 protocol booklets, manual, and carrying case) $165.00

Publisher: Western Psychological Services

Denver Eye Screening Test (DEST)
William K. Frankenburg, J. Goldstein, A. Barker

Copyright: 1973

Population: Children; ages 6 months to 7 years

Purpose: Helps evaluate eye problems and strabismus in children to determine if a child needs specialized testing

Description: Performance test in which the examiner shows seven picture cards and asks the child to name the picture at 15 feet. For children age 6 months to 2 years 5 months, the examiner uses an "E" card and a spinning toy to attract the child's attention and examines the eyes to see if they track; first one eye is tested, then the other. Materials consist of picture cards, cord, toy, and "E" card. A flashlight is required. The alternate cover test and pupillary light reflex test are used to detect strabismus.

Format: Examiner required; not suitable for group use; untimed: 10 minutes

Scoring: Examiner evaluated

Cost: Complete kit $13.50; manual/workbook $13.00; 25 test forms $4.50

Publisher: Denver Developmental Materials, Inc.

Developmental Test of Visual Perception–Second Edition (DTVP–2)
Donald D. Hammill, Nils A. Pearson, Judith K. Voress

Copyright: 1993

Population: Ages 4 years through 10 years 11 months

Purpose: Distinguishes between visual–perceptual and visual–motor problems

Description: Multiple-item instrument that yields scores for both pure visual perception with no motor response and visual–motor integration ability. These eight subtests are Eye–Hand Coordination, Copying, Spatial Relations, Position in Space, Figure–Ground, Visual Closure, Visual–Motor Speed, and Form Constancy. Standard scores, percentiles, and age equivalents are provided for each subtest as well as the composites of General Visual Perception, Motor-Reduced Perception, and Visual–Motor Integration.

Format: Individual administration; 35 minutes

Scoring: Examiner administration and interpretation; computer scoring on IBM and Mac available

Cost: Complete kit (manual, picture book, protocols, and storage box) $149.00

Publisher: PRO-ED, Inc.

Developmental Test of Visual–Motor Integration–Fourth Edition (VMI)
Keith E. Beery

Copyright: 1997

Population: Ages 3 to 18

Purpose: Measures students' visual–motor skills by duplicating geometric figures

Description: Multiple-item paper–pencil test measuring the integration of visual perception and motor behavior. Test items, arranged in order of increasing difficulty, consist of geometric figures that the children are asked to copy. The Short Test Form (15 figures) is used with children ages 3 to 8. The Long Test Form (24 figures) is used with children ages 3 to 18 and adults with developmental delays. The manual includes directions for administration, scoring criteria, developmental comments, age norms, suggestions for teaching, percentiles, and standard score equivalents.

Format: Examiner required; suitable for group use; untimed: time varies

Scoring: Hand key

Cost: Contact publisher

Publisher: Modern Curriculum Press, Inc.

Dvorine Color Vision Test
Israel Dvorine

Copyright: 1988

Population: All ages

Purpose: Identifies individuals with defective color vision; used for screening for color blindness in schools and industrial settings

Description: Fifteen-item test for determining the type and degree of color vision defect. The subject reads numbers or traces paths consisting of multicolored dots presented against a background of contrasting dots. Materials include 15 plates and 8 auxiliary plates for verification.

Format: Examiner required; not suitable for group use; untimed: 2–3 minutes

Scoring: Examiner evaluated

Cost: Booklet of color plates $284.00; record forms $27.00

Publisher: The Psychological Corporation

Inventory of Perceptual Skills (IPS)
Donald R. O'Dell

Copyright: 1983

Population: Children

Purpose: Assesses visual and auditory perceptual skills and provides the structure for individual remedial programs; aids in instructional planning for students at all age levels and in the development of IEPs

Description: Oral-response and task-performance 79-item test assessing perceptual skills in the following areas: visual discrimination, visual memory, object recognition, visual–motor coordination, auditory discrimination, auditory memory, auditory sequencing, and auditory blending. Once scored and recorded on the student profile (included in the student record booklet), a graphic comparison can be made of all of the subtests. A score below the mean on any subtest indicates a weakness in that area. The test may be administered by teachers, aides, or specialists without special training. The teacher's manual contains many educational activities in visual and auditory perception. Games, exercises, and activities provide the teacher with a variety of approaches and materials to use with the student. The student workbook includes 18 exercises to improve the areas in need of remediation.

Format: Examiner required; not suitable for group use; untimed: time varies

Scoring: Examiner evaluated

Cost: Complete set (manual, student workbook, 10 student record booklets, stimulus cards) $45.00

Publisher: Stoelting Company

J-K Screening Test
Rosalie C. Johnson

Copyright: 1973

Population: Ages 5 to 6

Purpose: Identifies children who may have perceptual–motor problems that would interfere with adequate development in reading

Description: Instrument provides scores in number concepts (counting/recognition and writing numerals), visual–motor coordination, discrimination of form, symbol recognition, spatial relations, position in space, perceiving relationships, auditory discrimination, color recognition, and draw-a-person. A total score is available.

Format: Group; 1½ to 2 hours

Scoring: Examiner administration and interpretation

Cost: Contact publisher

Publisher: J-K Screening

Kent Visual Perceptual Test (KVPT)
Lawrence E. Melamed

Copyright: 1996

Population: Ages 5 to 11

Purpose: Measures visual–perceptual skills through three perceptual processing tasks

Description: Multiple-item paper–pencil test that measures Discrimination, Memory, and Copy. The Copy subtest includes three levels of testing. The use of an integrated set of items allows for ease in comparison of performance level across the different perceptual tasks. Interpretive data include suggestions for use in school, clinical, and neuropsychological evaluation. Research norms are provided for ages 18–22 and 55–74. Separate norms are provided for males and females.

Format: Examiner required; individual administration; 20–30 minutes

Scoring: Examiner evaluated; Copy subtest requires precise measurement

Cost: Complete kit (manual, three tests; scoring, and error analysis) $154.00

Publisher: PRO-ED, Inc.

Learning Efficiency Test II–Revised
Raymond E. Webster

Copyright: 1992

Population: Ages 5 to adults

Purpose: Used in education, rehabilitation, and cognitive assessment to measure information processing in auditory and visual modalities

Description: The LET–II provides a quick and reliable measure of visual and auditory memory characteristics and is useful in determining memory deficits that may be related to learning problems in the classroom. The test yields information about a person's preferred modality for learning and provides valuable insights about the impact of interference on memory storage and retrieval. The revised edition features an updated literature review, new case studies, expanded remediation strategies, and an improved record form and scoring system. The norms have been expanded to include adult values (up to 75+ years of age). Memory is assessed in two modalities (visual and auditory) and in three recall conditions (immediate recall, short-term recall, and long-term recall). The six subtest scores can be collapsed into Modality Scores and into a Global Memory Score; each score can be converted into standard scores and percentiles for comparison with other tests.

Format: Individual administration; examiner required; presentation timed; response untimed

Scoring: Examiner evaluated

Cost: Test kit (manual, stimulus cards, 50 record forms, vinyl folder) $70.00

Publisher: Academic Therapy Publications

McDowell Vision Screening Kit
P. Marlene McDowell, Richard L. McDowell

Copyright: Not provided

Population: Children

Purpose: Used for testing preschool and severely disabled children for vision problems

Description: This test assesses the functional vision of children previously considered untestable. It gives a behavioral assessment of visual performance in five areas: distance visual acuity, near-point visual acuity, ocular alignment and motility, color perception, and ocular function. The kit contains all the toys, objects, and recording forms necessary for a comprehensive screening. The test requires no matching or verbal skills.

Format: Individual administration; examiner required; 10–20 minutes

Scoring: Examiner evaluated

Cost: Kit (includes all test materials, 100 recording forms, 1 manual) $110.00

Publisher: Western Psychological Services

Minnesota Spatial Relations Test–Revised Edition

Copyright: 1979

Population: Ages 16 and above

Purpose: Assesses spatial visualization and three-dimensional object manipulation

Description: Consists of transferring blocks from one board to another and fitting the blocks into similarly shaped cutouts. The test can be purchased as a complete set of two units (Boards A and B and Boards C and D), allowing a variety of uses, or the units may be purchased separately and used as a short form.

Format: Individual administration; 10–20 minutes

Scoring: Examiner interpreted; standard scores

Cost: 4 test boards (A, B, C, D), shape sets, manual, 50 record forms $995.95

Publisher: American Guidance Service

Modified Version of the Bender-Gestalt Test for Preschool and Primary School Children (Modified B-G Test)
Gary G. Brannigan, Nancy A. Brunner

Copyright: Not provided

Population: Ages 4 years 6 months to 8 years 5 months

Purpose: Measures the development of visual–motor integration skill; designed to be used as

an aid in identifying children with learning difficulties

Description: This manual is intended to be used with six of the nine Bender-Gestalt Test designs. Scored by a newly developed qualitative scoring system.

Format: Examiner required; suitable for group setting; untimed: 5 minutes

Scoring: Examiner evaluated

Cost: Complete kit (manual and scoring forms) $34.00

Publisher: PRO-ED, Inc.

Motor-Free Visual Perception Test–Revised (MVPT–R)
Ronald R. Colarusso, Donald D. Hammill

Copyright: 1996

Population: Ages 4 years through 11 years 11 months

Purpose: Assesses visual perception without reliance on a student's motor skills

Description: Multiple-item point-and-tell test in which the individual is shown a line drawing and asked to match the stimulus by pointing to one of a multiple-choice set of other drawings. Norm-referenced scores are provided.

Format: Individual administration; 15 minutes

Scoring: Examiner administered and interpreted

Cost: Test kit (manual, test plates, and protocols in vinyl folder) $75.00

Publisher: Academic Therapy Publications

Ontario Society of Occupational Therapists Perceptual Evaluation Kit (OSOT)
Marian Boys, Pat Fisher, Claire Holzberg

Copyright: Not provided

Population: Adults

Purpose: Assesses perceptual impairment; used for identification and monitoring of perceptual dysfunction

Description: Paper–pencil oral response short-answer show-tell point-to test with 18 subtests:

scanning, spatial neglect, motor planning, copying 2-D designs, copying 3-D designs, body puzzle, draw-a-person, *r/l* discrimination, clock, peg board, draw-a-house, shape recognition, color recognition, size recognition, *f/g* discrimination, proprioception, stereognosis r., and stereognosis l. Examiner must be a qualified occupational therapist.

Format: Individual administration; examiner required; timed and untimed

Scoring: Hand key; no scoring service available

Cost: Kit $650.00

Publisher: Nelson Canada

Perceptual–Motor Assessment for Children (P–MAC)
Jack G. Dial, Lawrence T. McCarron, Garry Amann

Copyright: 1988

Population: Children, adolescents; ages 4 years to 15 years 11 months

Purpose: Screens perceptual–motor skills; used by diagnosticians and classroom teachers to identify needs and provide educational management for students with special needs

Description: Multiple-item oral-response point-to task-performance battery of perceptual–motor skills. The battery consists of selected subtests from the McCarron Assessment of Neuromuscular Development (MAND), Haptic Visual Discrimination Test (HVDT), and Perceptual Memory Task (PMT). The P–MAC Computer Program provides scores for each area assessed. Four types of printed reports are offered: Educational Analysis Report, Classroom Report, Report of Trait Scores, and Comprehensive Evaluation Report. The computer program operates on Apple, IBM PC and compatible, and Macintosh systems.

Format: Examiner required; not suitable for group use; untimed: time varies

Scoring: Examiner evaluated; hand key; may be computer scored

Cost: Complete set (assessment battery in single case, comprehensive manual, scoring forms, 5-volume set of *Guides for Educational Man-*

agement, computer program, and operating manual) $1,995.00

Publisher: McCarron-Dial Systems

Sensory Integration and Praxis Tests (SIPT)
A. Jean Ayres

Copyright: 1987

Population: Children; ages 4 years to 8 years 11 months

Purpose: Measures sensory integration processes that underlie learning problems and emotional disorders; used for analyzing sensory integrative dysfunction and planning treatment disorders

Description: Seventeen tests assessing aspects of sensory processing in the vestibular, proprioceptive, kinesthetic, tactile, and visual systems as well as the behavior and learning disorders (including learning disabilities, emotional disorders, and minimal brain dysfunction) associated with inadequate integration of sensory input from these systems. The subtests are Space Visualization, Figure–Ground Perception, Manual Form Perception, Kinesthesia, Finger Identification, Graphesthesia, Localization of Tactile Stimuli, Praxis on Verbal Command, Design Copying, Constructional Praxis, Postural Praxis, Oral Praxis, Sequencing Praxis, Bilateral Motor Coordination, Standing and Walking Balance, Motor Accuracy, and Postrotary Nystagmus.

Format: Examiner required; not suitable for group use; untimed: time not available

Scoring: Computer scored

Cost: Set (all test materials, 25 copies of all consumable test forms, 10 complete sets of all 17 computer-scored answer sheets, 10 transmittal sheets, 1 manual, carrying case) $150.00

Publisher: Western Psychological Services

Spatial Orientation Memory Test
Joseph M. Wepman, D. Turaids

Copyright: 1985

Population: Children; ages 5 to 9

Purpose: Measures a child's ability to retain and recall the orientation of visually presented forms; used to identify children facing potential learning difficulties

Description: Multiple-item response test. The examiner presents a target page with a nonalphabetic design to the child, asking the child to select the same design from the response page, which contains four or five samples of the same design in different rotational positions. Spatial orientation ability prepares the child for individual letter discrimination recall, sequential ordering of letters in words, and related skills essential for reading. Adequacy scores are indicated for ages 5, 6, 7, 8, and 9. The test is available in two forms for retesting.

Format: Examiner required; not suitable for group use; untimed: 10–15 minutes

Scoring: Hand key

Cost: Complete kit (1 set of reusable stimulus cards, 25 score sheets, 1 manual) $75.00

Publisher: Western Psychological Services

Test of Visual Motor Integration (TVMI)
Donald D. Hammill, Nils A. Pearson, Judith K. Voress

Copyright: 1996

Population: Ages 4 years through 17 years 11 months

Purpose: Measures visual–motor ability

Description: Multiple-item paper–pencil test that consists of 30 items (12 for ages 4 to 8 and 12 for ages 8 to 17) that are copied by students. Each item is rated 0, 1, 2, or 3. This range of points makes it possible for the examiner to distinguish readily among students with severe visual–motor problems and students with exceptional copying skills. Results are reported in standard scores, percentiles, and age equivalents.

Format: Individual or group administration; 20 minutes

Scoring: Examiner administered and interpreted

Cost: Complete kit (manual, protocols, and storage box) $106.00

Publisher: PRO-ED, Inc.

VCWS 204—Fine Finger Dexterity

Copyright: 1989

Population: Adolescents, adults; ages 13 and older

Purpose: Assesses worker qualification profile factors for job/curricula placement and career planning

Description: Criterion-referenced test consisting of demonstrated performance of dominant and nondominant fine finger dexterity. The test yields MTM standard and percentile scores. Materials include wiring box and tweezers. This test is suitable for individuals with hearing, physical, and mental impairments. Signing for hearing impairment necessary.

Format: Examiner required; timed: 10–15 minutes

Scoring: Examiner evaluated

Cost: $695.00

Publisher: Valpar International Corporation

VCWS 204—Independent Perceptual Screening (Special Aptitude)

Copyright: 1989

Population: Adolescents, adults; ages 13 and older

Purpose: Assesses worker qualification profile factors for job/curricula placement and career planning

Description: Criterion-referenced test consisting of demonstrated performance of pin placement, pin assembly, six-part assembly, and three-dimensional assembly. Measures special aptitude, reasoning, general learning ability, form perception, motor coordination, and finger and manual dexterity. The test yields MTM standard and percentile scores. Materials include assembly board, parts bin, and assorted assembly parts. This test is suitable for individuals with hearing, physical, and mental impairments. Signing for hearing impairment necessary.

Format: Examiner required; not suitable for group use; timed: 25–30 minutes

Scoring: Examiner evaluated

Cost: $595.00

Publisher: Valpar International Corporation

Visual Memory Test
Joseph M. Wepman, Anne Morency, Maria Seidl

Copyright: 1983

Population: Children; ages 5 to 8

Purpose: Measures a child's ability to remember nonalphabetical, visual forms; used to identify any perceptual inadequacy that might reduce the ability to learn to read

Description: Sixteen-item test measuring a child's ability to recall unfamiliar forms that cannot readily be named. The examiner shows the child a design on a target page, and the child chooses the design from four designs on a response page. Norms are provided for ages 5, 6, 7, and 8. Adequacy threshold scores indicate the need for additional evaluation.

Format: Examiner required; not suitable for group use; untimed: 10–15 minutes

Scoring: Hand key

Cost: Kit (1 set of reusable stimulus cards, 25 score sheets, 1 manual) $85.00

Publisher: Western Psychological Services

Visual Skills Appraisal (VSA)
Regina G. Richards, Gary S. Oppenheim, G. N. Getman

Copyright: 1984

Population: Ages 5 to 9

Purpose: Assesses visual skills of students in Grades K–4; used by teachers who may not have specialized training in visual skills assessment for identifying visual inefficiencies that affect school performance

Description: Multiple-item task-performance test assessing pursuit, scanning, alignment, and locating movements; eye-hand coordination;

and fixation unity. The test identifies students who should be referred for a comprehensive visual examination. The test is self-contained and does not require the use of other equipment. The manual includes many visual training techniques keyed to each subtest.

Format: Individual administration; 10–15 minutes

Scoring: Examiner administered; hand key

Cost: Test kit (manual, stimulus cards, 25 design completion forms, 25 red/green train forms, 25 score sheets, red/green glasses, in vinyl folder). $60.00

Publisher: Academic Therapy Publications

Visual-Aural Digit Span Test (VADS)
Elizabeth M. Koppitz

Copyright: 1977

Population: Children; ages 5 to 12 years

Purpose: Diagnoses specific problems in reading recognition and spelling for children who can read and write digits; used to develop individual educational programs for learning disabled children

Description: Multiple-item test in which digit sequences on 26 test cards must be reproduced from memory, first orally, then in writing after being presented orally; and, finally, as a separate series, visually. The test measures auditory, visual, visual–auditory, and auditory–visual integration; sequence and recall of digits; and organization of written material. There are 11 scores, which are interpreted individually. Available in Spanish.

Format: Examiner required; suitable for group use; untimed: 10 minutes

Scoring: Examiner evaluated

Cost: Examination kit $38.00

Publisher: The Psychological Corporation

Wepman's Visual Assessment Battery
Joseph M. Wepman, Anne Morency, Maria Seidl, D. Turaids

Copyright: Not provided

Population: Ages 5 to 9

Purpose: Used to measure visual skills essential to reading

Description: Battery of three tests: The Visual Memory Test measures ability to retain immediate memory of visually presented, nonalphabetic forms; the Visual Discrimination Test measures ability to discriminate between similar visually perceived forms; the Spatial Orientation Memory Test measures a child's ability to retain and recall the orientation of visually presented forms.

Format: Individually administered; examiner required

Scoring: Hand key

Cost: Set (includes one kit for each of the three tests) $230.00

Publisher: Western Psychological Services

Wide Range Assessment of Visual Motor Ability (WRAVMA)

Wayne Adams, David Sheslow

Copyright: 1995

Population: Ages 3 to 17; Grades K through 12

Purpose: Intended for school populations, children's hospitals, and occupational therapists to assess visual motor ability

Description: Multiple-choice paper–pencil pegboard test with three subtests: Visual Spatial, Visual Motor, and Fine Motor Subtests. Scale Scores, percentiles, age equivalents, and a Visual Motor Composite Score are yielded. Drawing, matching, and examiner forms are available.

Format: Individual/group administration; examiner required; timed and untimed

Scoring: Hand key; examiner evaluated

Cost: Introductory kit $195.00

Publisher: Wide Range, Inc.

Business Instruments

The tests described in the Business section generally are used for personnel selection, evaluation, development, and promotion. In addition, the reader is encouraged to consult the Psychology and Education sections for other assessment instruments that may be of value in the area of business.

General Aptitude

Adaptability Test
Joseph Tiffin, C. H. Lawshe

Copyright: 1942

Population: Adults

Purpose: Measures mental adaptability and alertness; distinguishes between people who should be placed in jobs requiring more learning ability and those who should be in more simple or routine jobs

Description: Paper–pencil 35-item test consisting primarily of verbal items. The test predicts success in a variety of business and industrial situations. The test is available in two forms, A and B.

Format: Examiner required; suitable for group use; timed: 15 minutes

Scoring: Hand key

Cost: 25 test booklets (specify form) $40; examiner's manual $15

Publisher: McGraw-Hill/London House

....

Adaptive Ability Test–Language
Colin D. Selby

Copyright: 1989

Population: Adolescents, adults; ages 11 and above

Purpose: Used in educational and industrial applications to assess verbal critical reasoning

Description: Multiple-choice 30-item computer-administered test. An 11-year-old reading level is required. A computer version using PC DOS is available.

Format: Individual/self-administered; suitable for group use; examiner required; timed: 15 minutes

Scoring: Computer scored

Cost: Specimen Set $50.00

Publisher: Selby MillSmith Ltd.

....

Adaptive Ability Test–Numeracy
Colin Selby

Copyright: 1989

Population: Adolescents, adults

Purpose: Used in education and employment applications to assess numerical critical reasoning

Description: Multiple-choice 30-item computer-administered test. A computer version using PC DOS computers is available. An 11-year-old reading level is required.

Format: Individual/self-administered; suitable for group use; examiner required; timed: 15 minutes

Scoring: Computer scored

Cost: Specimen Set $50.00

Publisher: Selby MillSmith Ltd.

....

Applied Technology Series (ATS) Diagrammatic Thinking (DTS6)

Copyright: 1988

Population: Adults

Purpose: Looks at the ability to follow a sequence of interdependent symbols arranged in a logical order

Description: This 36-item test is arranged in the form of simple flowcharts and involves keeping track of changes in shape, size, and color of objects. This aptitude to apply checks and follow sequences is likely to be relevant in following process control systems, debugging software, and in systems design.

Format: 20 minutes

Scoring: Hand key; machine scored; scoring service available

Cost: Contact publisher

Publisher: Saville and Holdsworth Ltd.

Applied Technology Series (ATS) Fault Finding (FTS4)

Copyright: 1988

Population: Adults

Purpose: Assesses the ability to identify faults in logical systems

Description: Test with 36 items which requires no specialized knowledge of fault finding but rather the ability to locate what element in an arrangement of color-coded symbols is not working as specified. This ability is appropriate in many applications, including those of electronics fault finding, debugging of software, process control systems, and systems design.

Format: 20 minutes

Scoring: Hand key; machine scored; scoring service available

Cost: Contact publisher

Publisher: Saville and Holdsworth Ltd.

Applied Technology Series (ATS) Spatial Checking (STS5)

Copyright: 1988

Population: Adults

Purpose: Measures the ability to locate differences between complex designs rotated and reversed in two or three dimensions

Description: Forty-item test that measures the ability to locate differences between complex designs rotated and reversed in two or three dimensions. This ability is important in the checking and design of electronic systems and engineering components and in some applications of computer-aided design. Each item in this test involves identifying mismatches between master and copy designs.

Format: 15 minutes

Scoring: Hand key; machine scored; scoring service available

Cost: Contact publisher

Publisher: Saville and Holdsworth Ltd.

Arithmetic Reasoning Test (ART), High Level

Copyright: 1985

Population: Adults

Purpose: Measures arithmetic reasoning ability; used to select applicants to positions requiring "hard" science, engineering, and quantitative technical activities

Description: Paper–pencil or computer-administered 24-item (high level) or 30-item (intermediate level) multiple-choice test. Each item consists of a numerical expression with selected digits and operators replaced by symbols. The examinee must determine the value of the missing digits. Using algebraic operations to solve the problems is difficult; applying reasoning strategies requires less effort. The computer version operates on Plato System. Purchasers of the test must be registered with the South African Medical and Dental Council. Available in Afrikaans.

Format: Examiner required; suitable for group use; timed: intermediate level 35 minutes, high level 39 minutes

Scoring: Hand key

Cost: Contact publisher

Publisher: Human Sciences Research Council

Bennett Mechanical Comprehension Test™ (BMCT™)
G. K. Bennett

Copyright: 1968 (manual 1994)

Population: Adults

Purpose: Measures ability to understand mechanical relationships and physical laws in practical situations; used to screen job applicants for positions requiring practical application

Description: Multiple-item paper–pencil multiple-choice test assessing understanding of mechanical relationships. Materials include two equivalent forms, S and T. Tape recordings of the test questions read aloud are available for applicants with limited reading skills.

Format: Examiner required; suitable for group use; timed: 30 minutes

Scoring: Hand key; may be machine scored

Cost: Examination kit (booklets, answer documents for both forms and manual) $34.00

Publisher: The Psychological Corporation

Blox Test (Perceptual Battery)

Copyright: 1983

Population: Adolescents, adults

Purpose: Measures visual perception; used with subjects with 10 to 12 years of education for purposes of employee selection and placement in a variety of clerical and technical positions

Description: Multiple-item paper–pencil test measuring spatial relations. The subject must analyze given geometric figures and then find them in a series as seen from another angle. The test is restricted to competent persons properly registered with the South African Medical and Dental Council. Afrikaans version available.

Format: Examiner required; suitable for group use; timed: 30 minutes

Scoring: Hand key; examiner evaluated

Cost: Contact publisher

Publisher: National Institute for Personnel Research

Classification Test Battery (CTB)

Copyright: 1972

Population: Adults

Purpose: Evaluates general thinking and adaptability skills of illiterate and semiliterate applicants for unskilled and semiskilled jobs

Description: Four apparatus tests measuring nonverbal reasoning and spatial ability. The battery contains the Pattern Reproduction Test, Circles Test, Forms Series Test (Mines Version), and Colored Peg Board. The battery was devised as a unit and can be used only as described in the manual. Pretest instructions are available in any of nine African languages and English. The test itself is administered at centers established by firms employing the publisher's consultation and training services; use is restricted to competent persons properly registered with the South African Medical and Dental Council.

Format: Examiner required; suitable for group use

Scoring: Examiner evaluated

Cost: Contact publisher

Publisher: Human Sciences Research Council

Closure Flexibility (Concealed Figures)

L. L. Thurstone, T. E. Jeffrey

Copyright: 1984

Population: Adolescents, adults

Purpose: Measures the ability to hold a configuration in mind despite distracting irrelevancies as indicated by identification of a given figure "hidden" or embedded in a larger more complex drawing; used for vocational counseling and selection of personnel

Description: Paper–pencil 49-item test measuring visual and space perception skills. Each item consists of a figure, presented on the left of the page, followed by a row of four more complex drawings. The subject must indicate whether the figure appears or does not appear in each of the drawings.

Format: Examiner required; suitable for group use; timed: 10 minutes

Scoring: Hand key

Cost: 25 test booklets $36; score key $10; examiner's manual $15

Publisher: McGraw-Hill/London House

Comprehensive Ability Battery (CAB)

A. Ralph Hakstian, Raymond B. Cattell

Copyright: 1975

Population: Adolescents, adults; Grades 10 and above

Purpose: Measures a variety of abilities important in industrial settings for individuals of high school age and older; used in career and vocational counseling and employee selection and placement

Description: Twenty paper–pencil subtests, each measuring a single primary ability factor related to performance in industrial settings. The tests in the battery may be used individually or in combination. The subtests are grouped and presented in four test booklets (CAB–1, 2, 3/4, and 5). CAB–1 contains Verbal Ability, Numerical Ability, Spatial Ability, and Perceptual Completion. CAB–2 contains Clerical Speed and Accuracy, Reasoning, Hidden Shapes, Rote Memory, and Mechanical Ability. CAB–3/4 contains Meaningful Memory, Memory Span, Spelling, Auditory Ability, and Esthetic Judgment. CAB–5 contains Organizing Ideas, Production of Ideas, Verbal Fluency, Originality, Tracking, and Drawing.

Format: Examiner required; suitable for group use; timed: 5–7 minutes per subtest

Scoring: Hand key

Cost: Specimen Set (4 test booklets, answer and profile sheets for all tests, manual) $31.25; 10 CAB–1, CAB–2, CAB–3/4 or CAB–5 test booklets $19; 50 answer sheets $13

Publisher: Institute for Personality and Ability Testing, Inc.

Concept Attainment Test

J. M. Schepers

Copyright: 1968

Population: Adolescents, adults

Purpose: Measures conceptual and rational mental abilities of science and technical graduates; used for employee screening and selection

Description: Multiple-item paper–pencil test measuring the ability to attain concepts through the use of rational strategies of thought. The test consists of 10 problems for which solutions can be obtained only if a well-defined and logical strategy is followed consistently. Norms are provided for science graduates. The test is restricted to competent persons properly registered with the South African Dental Council. Afrikaans version available.

Format: Examiner required; suitable for group use; timed: 50 minutes

Scoring: Hand key; examiner evaluated

Cost: Contact publisher

Publisher: Human Sciences Research Council

Creativity Measure— The SRT Scale

William C. Kosinar

Copyright: 1960

Population: Adolescents, adults; Grades 10 and above

Purpose: Assesses level of creativity; used for career guidance with youths and to select research and scientific personnel

Description: Multiple-item forced-choice paper–pencil test of creativity. The manual provides norms on scientific personnel, National Science Talent Search winners, college students, and high school students.

Format: Examiner required; suitable for group use; untimed: 5 minutes

Scoring: Examiner evaluated

Cost: Specimen Set 44.00; 25 tests $4.50

Publisher: Psychometric Affiliates

Cree Questionnaire

Thelma Gwinn Thurstone, J. Mellinger

Copyright: 1995

Population: Adults

Purpose: Evaluates an individual's overall creative potential and the extent to which his or her behavior resembles that of identified creative individuals; used for selection and placement of managerial and professional personnel and career counseling

Description: Paper–pencil 58-item test measuring the 10 factorially determined dimensions of the creative personality: dominance vs. submission, independence vs. conformity, autonomous vs. structured work environment, pressured vs. relaxed situation, high vs. low energy level, fast vs. slow reaction time, high vs. low ideational spontaneity, high vs. low theoretical interests, high vs. low artistic interests, and high vs. low mechanical interests.

Format: Self-administered; suitable for group use; untimed: 15 minutes

Scoring: Hand key

Cost: 25 test booklets $36; 25 score sheets $30; examiner's manual $15

Publisher: McGraw-Hill/London House

Critical Reasoning Test Battery (CRTB) Diagrammatic Series (DC3.1)

Copyright: 1991

Population: Age 16 to adult

Purpose: Measures critical reasoning ability for thinking sequentially

Description: Paper–pencil 40-item test assessing the logical or analytical ability to follow a sequence of diagrams and select the next one in a series from five alternatives. The test is appropriate where logical or analytical reasoning is required, such as technical research or computer programming positions.

Format: 20 minutes

Scoring: Hand key; machine scored; scoring service available

Cost: Contact Publisher

Publisher: Saville and Holdsworth Ltd.

Deductive Reasoning Test

Copyright: 1972

Population: Adolescents, adults

Purpose: Measures logical thinking abilities; used with matriculants and higher for purposes of employee screening and selection for a wide variety of technical positions

Description: Multiple-item paper–pencil test based on formal syllogisms. Each syllogism contains either factual, contrafactual, or nonsense premises. The test provides a measure of the ability to deduce logically correct conclusions from the information contained in the premises. The test is restricted to competent persons properly registered with the South African Medical and Dental Council. Afrikaans version available.

Format: Examiner required; suitable for group use; timed: 40 minutes

Scoring: Hand key; examiner evaluated

Cost: Contact publisher

Publisher: Human Sciences Research Council

Employee Aptitude Survey Test #10—Symbolic Reasoning (EAS#10)

G. Grimsley, F. L. Ruch, N. D. Warren, J. S. Ford

Copyright: 1985

Population: Adults

Purpose: Measures ability to manipulate abstract symbols and use them to make valid decisions; used to evaluate candidates for positions requiring a high level of reasoning ability, such as troubleshooters, computer programmers, accountants, and engineers

Description: Paper–pencil 30-item multiple-choice test consisting of a list of abstract symbols (and their coded meanings) used to establish relationships in the pattern of "A" to "B" to "C." Given the statement, the examinee must decide whether a proposed relationship between "A" and "C" is true, false, or unknown from the given statement. The test is available in two equivalent forms. Available in Spanish and French.

Format: Examiner required; suitable for group use; timed: 5 minutes

Scoring: Hand key; may by computer scored

Cost: 25 tests per package: 1–19 packages $42.50; 20–149 packages $36.25; 200+ packages $28.75

Publisher: Psychological Services, Inc.

Employee Aptitude Survey Test #1—Verbal Comprehension (EAS#1)

G. Grimsley, F. L. Ruch, N. D. Warren, J. S. Ford

Copyright: 1984

Population: Adults

Purpose: Measures ability to use and understand the relationships between words; used for selection and placement of executives, secretaries, professional personnel, and high-level office workers; also used in career counseling

Description: Paper–pencil 30-item multiple-choice test measuring word-relationship recognition, reading speed, and ability to understand instructions. Each item consists of a word followed by a list of four other words from which the examinee must select the one meaning the same or about the same as the first word. The test is available in two equivalent forms.

Format: Examiner required; suitable for group use; timed: 5 minutes

Scoring: Hand key; may be computer scored

Cost: 25 tests per package: 1–19 packages $42.50; 20–149 packages $36.25; 200+ packages $28.75

Publisher: Psychological Services, Inc.

Employee Aptitude Survey Test #2—Numerical Ability (EAS#2)

G. Grimsley, F. L. Ruch, N. D. Warren

Copyright: 1980

Population: Adults

Purpose: Measures basic mathematical skill; used for selection and placement of executives, supervisors, engineers, accountants, salespersons, and clerical workers; also used in career counseling

Description: Paper–pencil 75-item multiple-choice test arranged in three 25-item parts assessing addition, subtraction, multiplication, and division skills. Part I covers whole numbers, Part II decimal fractions, and Part III common fractions. The test is available in two equivalent forms. Available in Spanish. Parts

may be administered and timed separately.

Format: Examiner required; suitable for group use; timed: 10 minutes

Scoring: Hand key; may be computer scored

Cost: 25 tests per package: 1–19 packages $42.50; 20–149 packages $36.25; 200+ packages $28.75

Publisher: Psychological Services, Inc.

Employee Aptitude Survey Test #3—Visual Pursuit (EAS#3)

G. Grimsley, F. L. Ruch, N. D. Warren, J. S. Ford

Copyright: 1985

Population: Adults

Purpose: Measures speed and accuracy in visually tracing lines through complex designs; used for selection and placement of drafters, design engineers, technicians, other technical and production positions; also in career counseling

Description: Paper–pencil 30-item multiple-choice test consisting of a maze of lines that weave their way from their starting points (numbered 1 to 30) on the right-hand side of the page to a column of boxes on the left. The task is to identify for each starting point the box on the left at which the line ends. Examinees are encouraged to trace with their eyes, not their pencils. The test is available in two equivalent forms. Available in Spanish and French.

Format: Examiner required; suitable for group use; timed: 5 minutes

Scoring: Hand key; may be computer scored

Cost: 25 tests per package: 1–19 packages $42.50; 20–149 packages $36.25; 200+ packages $28.75

Publisher: Psychological Services, Inc.

Employee Aptitude Survey Test #4—Visual Speed and Accuracy (EAS#4)

G. Grimsley, F. L. Ruch, N. D. Warren

Copyright: 1980

Population: Adults

Purpose: Measures ability to see details quickly and accurately; used to select bookkeepers, accountants, clerical and administrative personnel, and supervisors; also used in career planning

Description: Paper–pencil 150-item multiple-choice test in which each item consists of two series of numbers and symbols that the subject must compare and determine whether they are "the same" or "different." The test may be administered to applicants for sales, supervisory, and executive positions with the expectation that their scores will be above average. The test is available in two equivalent forms. Available in Spanish.

Format: Examiner required; suitable for group use; timed: 5 minutes

Scoring: Hand key; may be computer scored

Cost: 25 tests per package: 1–19 packages $42.50; 20–149 packages $36.25; 200+ packages $28.75

Publisher: Psychological Services, Inc.

Employee Aptitude Survey Test #5—Space Visualization (EAS#5)

G. Grimsley, F. L. Ruch, N. D. Warren, J. S. Ford

Copyright: 1985

Population: Adults

Purpose: Measures ability to visualize and manipulate objects in three dimensions by viewing a two-dimensional drawing; used to select employees for jobs requiring mechanical aptitude like drafters, engineers, and personnel in technical and production positions

Description: Paper–pencil 50-item multiple-choice test consisting of 10 perspective line drawings of stacks of blocks. The blocks are all the same size and rectangular in shape so that they appear to stack neatly and distinctly. Five of the blocks in each stack are lettered. The subjects must look at each lettered block and determine how many other blocks in the stack the lettered block touches. The test is available in two equivalent forms. Available in Spanish.

Format: Examiner required; suitable for group use; timed: 5 minutes

Scoring: Hand key; may be computer scored

Cost: 25 tests per package: 1–19 packages $42.50; 20–149 packages $36.25; 200+ packages $28.75

Publisher: Psychological Services, Inc.

Employee Aptitude Survey Test #6—Numerical Reasoning (EAS#6)

G. Grimsley, F. L. Ruch, N. D. Warren, J. S. Ford

Copyright: 1985

Population: Adults

Purpose: Measures the ability to analyze logical relationships and discover principles underlying such relationships, an important ingredient of "general intelligence"; used to select employees for professional, managerial, supervisory, and technical jobs

Description: Paper–pencil 20-item multiple-choice test in which each item consists of a series of seven numbers followed by a question mark where the next number of the series should be. Examinees must determine the pattern of each series and select (from five choices) the number that correctly fills the blank. Logic and deduction, rather than computation, are emphasized. The test is available in two equivalent forms. Available in Spanish and French.

Format: Examiner required; suitable for group use; timed: 5 minutes

Scoring: Hand key; may be computer scored

Cost: 25 tests per package: 1–19 packages $42.50; 20–149 packages $36.25; 200+ packages $28.75

Publisher: Psychological Services, Inc.

Employee Aptitude Survey Test #7—Verbal Reasoning (EAS#7)

G. Grimsley, F. L. Ruch, N. D. Warren, J. S. Ford

Copyright: 1985

Population: Adults

Purpose: Measures ability to analyze information and make valid judgments about that information; also measures the ability to decide whether the available facts provide sufficient information to support a definite conclusion; used for employee selection

Description: Paper–pencil 30-item multiple-choice test consisting of six lists of facts (one-sentence statements) with five possible conclusions for each list of facts. The subject reads each list of facts and then looks at each conclusion and decides whether it is definitely true, definitely false, or unknown from the given facts. The test is available in two equivalent forms. Available in Spanish and French.

Format: Examiner required; suitable for group use; timed: 5 minutes

Scoring: Hand key; may be computer scored

Cost: 25 tests per package: 1–19 packages $42.50; 20–149 packages $36.25; 200+ packages $28.75

Publisher: Psychological Services, Inc.

Employee Aptitude Survey Test #8—Word Fluency (EAS#8)
G. Grimsley, F. L. Ruch, N. D. Warren, J. S. Ford

Copyright: 1981
Population: Adults
Purpose: Measures flexibility and ease in verbal communication; used to select sales representatives, journalists, field representatives, technical writers, receptionists, secretaries, and executives; also used in career counseling

Description: Open-ended paper–pencil test measuring word fluency by determining how many words beginning with one specific letter, given at the beginning of the test, a person can produce in a 5-minute test period (75 answer spaces are provided).

Format: Examiner required; suitable for group use; timed: 5 minutes

Scoring: Hand key

Cost: 25 tests per package: 1–19 packages $42.50; 20–149 packages $36.25; 200+ packages $28.75

Publisher: Psychological Services, Inc.

Employee Aptitude Survey Test #9—Manual Speed and Accuracy (EAS#9)
G. Grimsley, F. L. Ruch, N. D. Warren, J. S. Ford

Copyright: 1984
Population: Adults
Purpose: Measures ability to make fine-finger movements rapidly and accurately; used to select clerical workers, office machine operators, electronics and small parts assemblers, and employees for similar precision jobs involving repetitive tasks

Description: Multiple-item paper–pencil test consisting of a straightforward array of evenly spaced lines of 750 small circles. The applicant must place a pencil dot in as many of the circles as possible in five minutes. Available in Spanish.

Format: Examiner required; suitable for group use; timed: 5 minutes

Scoring: Hand key

Cost: 25 tests per package: 1–19 packages $42.50; 20–149 packages $36.25; 200+ packages $28.75

Publisher: Psychological Services, Inc.

English Language Achievement Test

Copyright: Not provided
Population: Adolescents, adults; Grades 12 and above

Purpose: Measures achievement of basic English language skills; suitable for use with matriculants and higher; used in employee selection and placement

Description: Multiple-item paper–pencil test assessing English language abilities in spelling, comprehension, and vocabulary. Norms are based on a group of matriculants. The test is restricted to competent persons properly registered with the South African Medical and Dental Council. Afrikaans version available.

Format: Examiner required; suitable for group use; timed: 19 minutes

Scoring: Hand key; examiner evaluated

Cost: Contact publisher

Publisher: Human Sciences Research Council

ETSA Tests 1-A—General Mental Ability

George A. W. Stouffer, Jr., S. Trevor Hadley

Copyright: 1990

Population: Adolescents, adults; Grades 10 and above

Purpose: Measures general intelligence and learning ability; used for employee selection, placement, and promotion

Description: Paper–pencil 75-item test of general learning ability consisting of both verbal and nonverbal items. The test may be used in conjunction with ETSA 8-A, Personal Adjustment Index, and any ETSA test measuring a specific skill area.

Format: Examiner required; suitable for group use; untimed: 45 minutes

Scoring: Hand key; examiner evaluated; scoring service available

Cost: 10 tests with key $15.00; manual $5.00; handbook $15.00

Publisher: Educators'/Employers' Tests and Services Associates

Figure Classification Test

Copyright: 1983

Population: Adolescents, adults

Purpose: Measures abstract reasoning ability; used with examinees with 7 to 9 years of education for purposes of employee selection and placement

Description: Multiple-item paper–pencil test measuring conceptual reasoning abilities by requiring the examinee to analyze sets of figures and deduce the basic relationships that divide each set into two groups. The relationships are indicated by uniformity, symmetry, inversion, repetition, and series. The test is restricted to competent persons properly registered with the South African Medical and Dental Council. Afrikaans version available.

Format: Examiner required; suitable for group use; timed: 1 hour

Scoring: Hand key; examiner evaluated

Cost: Contact publisher

Publisher: Human Sciences Research Council

Form Series Test A

Copyright: 1975

Population: Adolescents, adults

Purpose: Measures nonverbal reasoning ability; used with groups of individuals with 6 years or less of education for purposes of employee selection and placement

Description: Multiple-item apparatus test measuring nonverbal reasoning ability using a board printed with a series of patterns made up of forms of different sizes, shapes, and colors. Each pattern must be continued by inferring from the given series of shapes, sizes, and colors what the next two must be. The test is restricted to competent persons properly registered with the South African Medical and Dental Council. Afrikaans version available.

Format: Examiner required; suitable for group use; timed: 25 minutes

Scoring: Hand key; examiner evaluated

Cost: Contact publisher

Publisher: Human Sciences Research Council

Industrial Test Battery (ITB)

Copyright: 1988

Population: Adults

Purpose: Measures general reasoning ability in adults with less than 8 years of formal education; used for job selection and placement

Description: Multiple-item paper–pencil multiple-choice battery consisting of three screening tests. The Anomalous Concept Test (ACT) assesses concept formation. The Anomalous Figure Test (AFT) measures spatial relations. The Series Induction Test (SIT) measures the conception of relationships and trends. Examinees use an erasable pen to mark their answers on plastic-covered test pages. After a stencil is used to score answers, the plastic sheets are wiped clean.

Format: Examiner required; suitable for group use; timed: ACT 20 minutes; AFT 25 minutes; SIT 30 minutes

Scoring: Hand key

Cost: Contact publisher

Publisher: Human Sciences Research Council

Information Technology Test Series (ITTS) Spatial Reasoning (SIT7)

Copyright: 1988

Population: Adults

Purpose: Measures ability to visualize and manipulate shapes in three dimensions when given a two-dimensional drawing

Description: Multiple-choice 40-item test consisting of a series of folded-out cubes and perspective drawings of assembled cubes. The respondents must identify the assembled cubes that could be made from the folded-out cube, each face of which has a different pattern. The test discriminates at a high level and would be relevant for engineers, designers, architects, and IT staff.

Format: 20 minutes

Scoring: Hand key; machine scored; scoring service available

Cost: Contact Publisher

Publisher: Saville and Holdsworth Ltd.

IPI Employee Aptitude Series: Blocks

Copyright: 1986

Population: Adults

Purpose: Measures aptitude to visualize objects on the basis of three-dimensional cues; used to screen applicants for mechanical and technical jobs

Description: Paper–pencil 32-item test of spatial relations and quantitative ability. The test does not require the ability to read. Also available in French and Spanish.

Format: Suitable for group use; examiner required; timed: 6 minutes

Scoring: Hand key

Cost: Introductory kit (20 test booklets, scoring key, manual) $30

Publisher: Industrial Psychology International Ltd.

IPI Employee Aptitude Series: Dexterity

Copyright: 1986

Population: Adults

Purpose: Determines ability to rapidly perform routine motor tasks involving eye–hand coordination; used to screen applicants for mechanical and technical jobs

Description: Three 1-minute paper–pencil subtests (maze, checks, dots) assesses one's ability to perform routine motor tasks. The test does not require the ability to read or write. Also available in French and Spanish.

Format: Suitable for group use; examiner required; timed: 3 minutes

Scoring: No key required

Cost: Introductory kit (20 test booklets, scoring key, manual) $30

Publisher: Industrial Psychology International Ltd.

IPI Employee Aptitude Series: Dimension

Copyright: 1986

Population: Adults

Purpose: Evaluates ability to visualize objects drawn in their exact reverse; used to screen applicants for mechanical and technical jobs

Description: Paper–pencil 48-item test measuring spatial relations at a high level. The test does not require the ability to read or write. Also available in French and Spanish.

Format: Suitable for group use; examiner required; timed: 6 minutes

Scoring: Hand key

Cost: Introductory kit (20 test booklets, scoring key, manual) $30

Publisher: Industrial Psychology International Ltd.

IPI Employee Aptitude Series: Fluency

Copyright: 1981

Population: Adults

Purpose: Assesses aptitude to think of words rapidly and easily; used to screen applicants for clerical, sales, and supervisory jobs

Description: Three 2-minute paper–pencil subtests measuring the ability to write or talk without mentally blocking or searching for the right word. Also available in French and Spanish.

Format: Suitable for group use; examiner required; timed: 6 minutes

Scoring: No key required

Cost: Introductory kit (20 test booklets, scoring key, manual) $30

Publisher: Industrial Psychology International Ltd.

IPI Employee Aptitude Series: Judgment

Copyright: 1981

Population: Adults

Purpose: Evaluates an individual's ability to think logically and to deduce solutions to abstract problems; used to screen applicants for clerical, sales, and supervisory positions

Description: Paper–pencil 54-item test measuring aptitude to think logically, plan, and deal with abstract relations. Also available in French and Spanish.

Format: Suitable for group use; examiner required; timed: 6 minutes

Scoring: Hand key

Cost: Introductory kit (20 test booklets, scoring key, manual) $30

Publisher: Industrial Psychology International Ltd.

IPI Employee Aptitude Series: Motor

Copyright: 1986

Population: Adults

Purpose: Measures ability to coordinate eye and hand movements in a specific motor task; used to screen applicants for mechanical and technical jobs

Description: Three 2-minute trials of the same task that demonstrate manual dexterity and eye–hand coordination. The test requires a special motor apparatus for administration. Also available in French and Spanish.

Format: Suitable for group use only if more than one apparatus is available; examiner required; timed: 6 minutes

Scoring: No key required

Cost: Introductory kit (20 test booklets, scoring key, manual) $30; motor board $150

Publisher: Industrial Psychology International Ltd.

IPI Employee Aptitude Series: Numbers

Copyright: 1981

Population: Adults

Purpose: Measures ability to perform numerical computations rapidly and accurately; used to screen applicants for clerical, administrative, mechanical, sales, technical, and supervisory positions

Description: Paper–pencil 54-item test measuring the ability to perform numerical computations and to understand mathematical concepts. Numbers are highly related to record keeping, typing, work planning, computational skills, and coding.

Format: Suitable for group use; examiner required; timed: 6 minutes

Scoring: Hand key

Cost: Introductory kit (20 test booklets, scoring key, manual) $30

Publisher: Industrial Psychology International Ltd.

IPI Job-Field Series: Writer

Copyright: 1960

Population: Adults

Purpose: Assesses skills and personality of applicants for writing positions requiring fluent expression and the ability to write freely; used to screen for advertising, author, copywriter, critic, editor, journalist, and public relations positions

Description: Multiple-item paper–pencil battery of six aptitude and three personality tests. The tests are Fluency, Sales Terms, CPF, MPF, Memory, Judgment, 16PF, Perception, and Parts. For individual test descriptions, see the IPI Employee Aptitude Series. Also available in French and Spanish.

Format: Suitable for group use; examiner required; timed: 82 minutes

Scoring: Hand keys

Cost: Starter kit (test materials for five applicants, scoring keys, manuals) $80; test package $12/applicant

Publisher: Industrial Psychology International Ltd.

Kirton Adaption–Innovation Inventory (KAI)
Michael J. Kirton

Copyright: 1977

Population: Adolescents, adults

Purpose: Measures problem-solving and creativity styles

Description: Paper–pencil 33-item test containing three factor traits: Sufficiency of Originality, Efficiency Style, and Rule/Group Conformity Style. Requires training course before use. Also available in Italian, Dutch, French, and Slovak/Czech.

Format: Suitable for group use; untimed: 10–15 minutes

Scoring: Administrator required; computer scored on NCR form

Cost: $150 for 50

Publisher: Occupational Research Centre

Learning Ability Profile (LAP)
Margarita Henning

Copyright: 1989

Population: Adults

Purpose: Assesses a person's ability to learn; may be used to determine the potential for job success

Description: Paper–pencil 80-item test measuring overall learning ability, flexibility, frustration level, problem-solving ability, and decisiveness. Available in French.

Format: Examiner required; suitable for group use; untimed: 1 hour

Scoring: Hand key; examiner evaluated

Cost: Complete set (1 test booklet, answer sheet, manual) $79.00

Publisher: Walden Personnel Testing and Training, Inc.

Mental Alertness–Advanced and Intermediate

Copyright: Not provided

Population: Adults

Purpose: Measures general intelligence for purposes of employee screening and selection; used with matriculants and higher and individuals with 10 to 12 years of schooling

Description: Two paper–pencil tests measuring general intelligence, mainly verbal, at two levels of education. The High Level Battery is suitable for matriculants and higher. The Intermediate Battery is for candidates with 10 to 12 years of education. Both tests are available in two parallel forms. Norms are provided for each test. The tests are restricted to competent persons properly registered with the South African Medical and Dental Council. Afrikaans version available.

Format: Examiner required; suitable for group use; timed: 35 minutes each

Scoring: Hand key; examiner evaluated

Cost: Contact publisher

Publisher: Human Sciences Research Council

National Firefighter Selection Test (NFST)

Copyright: 1994

Population: Adults

Purpose: Assesses basic cognitive skills; used for pre-employment screening

Description: Multiple-choice 70-item paper–pencil test with three subtests: Reading Comprehension (25 items, 25 minutes), Mathematics (25 items, 30 minutes), and Listening (20 items, 20 minutes). Scores are provided for each subtest. Forms A and B are available.

Format: Examiner required; individual administration; suitable for group use; timed: time varies

Scoring: Machine/self-scored

Cost: Contact publisher

Publisher: Stanard and Associates, Inc.

National Police Officer Selection Test (POST)

Copyright: 1991

Population: Adults

Purpose: Assesses cognitive basic skills; used for pre-employment screening

Description: Multiple-choice 75-item paper–pencil short-answer true–false test with four subtests: Reading Comprehension (20 items, 20 minutes), Mathematics (20 items, 20 minutes), Grammar (25 items, 25 minutes), Writing (10 items, 20 minutes). Forms A, B, and C are available.

Format: Examiner required; individual administration; suitable for group use; timed: time varies

Scoring: Machine/self-scored

Cost: Contact publisher

Publisher: Stanard and Associates, Inc.

Non-Verbal Reasoning

Copyright: Not provided

Population: Adults

Purpose: Assesses nonverbal reasoning (spatial analysis) abilities; used with applicants to technical and engineering positions

Description: Paper–pencil 45-item test of nonverbal reasoning. Each test item consists of 10 figures, the first 4 of which are alike. Applicants select two of the last six figures which are like the first four. A variety of elements are tested, including squareness, angle bisection, differential shading, number relationships, and arrangement relationships. Examinee must be able to read numbers. The test has been used successfully with applicants with low educational levels and with technical and managerial personnel with high educational levels.

Format: Examiner required; suitable for group use; timed: 15 minutes

Scoring: Hand key

Cost: 1–24 packages $55.00; score key $7.50; manual $5.00

Publisher: Richardson, Bellows, Henry, and Company, Inc.

Nonverbal Reasoning
Raymond J. Corsini

Copyright: 1985

Population: Adults

Purpose: Assesses capacity to reason logically as indicated by solutions to pictorial problems; used for job screening and selection and for vocational counseling

Description: Pictorial paper–pencil 44-item test. The subject studies one picture and then selects from among four others the one which best compliments the first picture.

Format: Examiner required; suitable for group use; untimed: 20 minutes

Scoring: Hand key

Cost: 25 test booklets $37; score key $10; examiner's manual $15

Publisher: McGraw-Hill/London House

Normal, Intermediate and High Level Batteries

Copyright: N 1989; I 1989; H 1975

Population: Adults

Purpose: Measures mental abilities and verbal skills related to many clerical and technical positions; suitable for matriculants and higher

Description: Three batteries of paper–pencil tests measuring three levels of mental and verbal abilities. The Normal Battery, used with standards 6 to 10 and job applicants with 8 to 11 years of education, contains five tests: Mental Alertness, Reading Comprehension, Vocabulary, Spelling, and Computation. The Intermediate Battery, used with standards 7 to 10 and job applicants with 9 to 12 years of education, contains seven tests covering mental alertness, arithmetical problems, computation, spotting errors, reading comprehension, vocabulary, and spelling. The High Level Battery, used with a wide range of groups at matrix and higher levels, contains six tests covering reading and vocabulary, mental alertness, and mathematics skills.

Format: Examiner required; suitable for group use; timed: Normal Level 120 minutes, Intermediate Level 165 minutes, High Level 117 minutes

Scoring: Hand key; examiner required

Cost: Contact publisher

Publisher: Human Sciences Research Council

Omnia Profile®, Omniafax® in Europe
J. B. Caswell, H. F. Livingstone

Copyright: 1985

Population: Adults

Purpose: Measures a job applicant's vocational and environmental fit in a specific job and workplace; used for pre-employment screening, career counseling, and as a management tool for existing employees

Description: Part 1: Applicant's/employee's work concept. Part 2: Applicant's/employee's self-concept. Part 3: Applicant's/employee's description of appropriate behavior for the position. Part 4: Applicant's/employee's description of the ideal supervisor/manager or workplace. Scores yielded: For job applicants: 1–10. Applicants who receive scores of 8.0 and higher are recommended. Applicants who receive 7.9–7.3 are conditionally recommended, 7.3–7.0 receive a marginal recommendation. Those who receive a 6.9 or less are not recommended.

Available in Spanish, Japanese, French, German, Dutch, and Italian.

Format: Individual administration; suitable for group use; untimed: 10–12 minutes

Scoring: Computer scored; test scoring service available from publisher

Cost: $90.00

Publisher: Omnia Group, Inc.

Pattern Relations Test

Copyright: 1969

Population: Adults

Purpose: Measures inductive reasoning abilities; used with university-level and graduate job applicants for a variety of science and technical positions

Description: Multiple-item paper–pencil test measuring the ability to recognize associated concepts that fit sets of data and the consequent forming and testing of hypotheses. The test is similar to *Raven's Progressive Matrices.* Norms have been established on scientific research workers with degrees and first-year engineering students. The test is restricted to competent persons properly registered with the South African Medical and Dental Council. Afrikaans version available.

Format: Examiner required; suitable for group use; timed: 50 minutes each

Scoring: Hand key; examiner evaluated

Cost: Contact publisher

Publisher: Human Sciences Research Council

Personnel Tests for Industry (PTI)
A. G. Wesman, J. E. Doppelt

Copyright: 1969

Population: Adults

Purpose: Assesses general ability; used to select workers for skilled positions in industrial settings

Description: Multiple-item paper–pencil multiple-choice tests covering two dimensions of general ability: verbal and numerical competence. Some items involve problem solving.

Two equivalent forms and tapes for administering the test are available.

Format: Examiner required; suitable for group use; timed: Verbal 5 minutes, Numerical 20 minutes

Scoring: Hand key

Cost: Examination kit $32.00

Publisher: The Psychological Corporation

Personnel Tests for Industry–Oral Directions Test (PTI–ODT™)

C. R. Langmuir

Copyright: 1974 (manual 1995)

Population: Adults

Purpose: Assesses general mental ability and the ability to understand oral directions

Description: Recorded-format test measuring general mental ability of individuals with low education levels or who speak English as a second language. Scores reflect minimal proficiency in conversational English and the ability to comprehend oral directions. May be used to determine whether individuals can benefit from basic skills training, vocational training, training in conversational English, or educational remediation programs. Two alternate forms, S and T.

Format: Examiner required; suitable for group use; untimed: approximately 15 minutes

Scoring: Hand key

Cost: Complete set (recording, manual, script, key, 100 answer documents, and directions for administering) $132.75

Publisher: The Psychological Corporation

Professional Employment Test

Copyright: Not provided

Population: Adults

Purpose: Measures three cognitive abilities—verbal comprehension, quantitative problem solving, and reasoning—important for successful performance in many professional occupations; used to select professional, technical, and managerial personnel

Description: Paper–pencil 40-item multiple-choice test measuring the ability to understand and interpret complex information, determine the appropriate mathematical procedures to solve problems, and analyze and evaluate information to arrive at correct conclusions. The test includes four item types: reading comprehension, quantitative problem solving, data interpretation, and reasoning. The test is available in two alternate forms and in a short-form (20 questions).

Format: Examiner required; suitable for group use; timed: regular form 80 minutes, short form 40 minutes

Scoring: Hand key; may be computer scored

Cost: $5.95

Publisher: Psychological Services, Inc.

RBH Test of Learning Ability, Form STR

Copyright: Not provided

Population: Adults

Purpose: Assesses general aptitudes; used for screening, selection, placement, and upgrading of personnel

Description: Paper–pencil 108-item multiple-choice test assessing general aptitude. Examinees must choose the correct answer for each problem from four alternatives. Answers are recorded in the test booklet. This test is a compilation of two shorter forms (S89 and T89) and provides a "floor" low enough to accommodate all but the illiterate and mentally deficient and a "ceiling" high enough for individuals with upper levels of education or ability. The test is organized so that each three consecutive items contain a block-counting, vocabulary, and arithmetic item. Each series of items is more difficult than the preceding series. Reading and understanding directions is not part of the STR administration time.

Format: Examiner required; suitable for group use; timed: 25 minutes

Scoring: Hand key

Cost: 1–24 packages $60.00; score key $10.00; manual $5.00

Publisher: Richardson, Bellows, Henry and Company, Inc.

Revised Beta Examination–Second Edition (BETA–II)
D. E. Kellogg, N. W. Morton

Copyright: 1978

Population: Adults

Purpose: Measures mental ability of nonreading applicants; used for testing applicants in settings with large numbers of unskilled workers

Description: Six separately timed paper–pencil tests of mental ability, including mazes, coding, paper form boards, picture completion, clerical checking, and picture absurdities. Directions are given orally to the applicant. Available in Spanish.

Format: Examiner required; suitable for group use; untimed: 30 minutes

Scoring: Hand key

Cost: Examination kit $34.75

Publisher: The Psychological Corporation

Space Relations (Paper Puzzles)
L. L. Thurstone, T. E. Jeffrey

Copyright: 1984

Population: Adolescents, adults

Purpose: Assesses facility in visual perceptual skills; used in vocational counseling or for selection for positions requiring mechanical ability and experience

Description: Paper–pencil 30-item test of the ability to visually select a combination of flat pieces that, together, will cover a given two-dimensional space.

Format: Examiner required; suitable for group use; timed: 9 minutes

Scoring: Hand key

Cost: 25 test booklets $36; score key $10; examiner's manual $15

Publisher: McGraw-Hill/London House

Space Thinking (Flags)
L. L. Thurstone, T. E. Jeffrey

Copyright: 1984

Population: Adolescents, adults

Purpose: Assesses the ability to visualize a rigid configuration (a stable figure, drawing, or diagram) when it is moved into different positions; used for vocational counseling or selection for positions requiring mechanical ability or experience

Description: Paper–pencil 21-item test in which a solid object (flag) is pictured on the left and pictures of six positions into which the object has been moved are on the right. The examinee must identify whether each position represents the same or the opposite side of the object.

Format: Examiner required; suitable for group use; timed: 5 minutes

Scoring: Hand key

Cost: 25 test booklets $36; score key $10; examiner's manual $15

Publisher: McGraw-Hill/London House

SRA Nonverbal Form
Robert N. McMurry, Joseph E. King

Copyright: 1986

Population: Adults

Purpose: Assesses general learning ability; measures learning potential of individuals who have difficulty reading or understanding the English language; used with adults with a high school education or less and for employee selection and placement

Description: Paper–pencil 60-item test consisting of five drawings, each measuring recognition of differences.

Format: Examiner required; suitable for group use; timed: 10 minutes

Scoring: Hand key

Cost: 25 test booklets $47; examiner's manual $15

Publisher: McGraw-Hill/London House

SRA Pictorial Reasoning Test (PRT)
Robert N. McMurry, Phyllis D. Arnold

Copyright: 1966

Population: Adolescents, adults

Purpose: Measures general reasoning ability of

students, especially older nonreaders; used with individuals with a high school education or less, for predicting job success, and as a basic screening test for entry-level jobs

Description: Paper–pencil 80-item pictorial test measuring aspects of learning ability. The test is culturally unbiased and does not require previously learned reading skills.

Format: Examiner required; suitable for group use; timed: 15 minutes (may also be given untimed)

Scoring: Hand key

Cost: 25 test booklets $43; examiner's manual $15

Publisher: McGraw-Hill/London House

SRA Verbal Form
L. L. Thurstone, Thelma Gwinn Thurstone

Copyright: 1955
Population: Adults
Purpose: Measures an individual's overall adaptability and flexibility in comprehending and following instructions and in adjusting to alternating types of problems on the job; used in both school and industry for selection and placement

Description: Paper–pencil or computerized test of general mental abilities. The test measures both linguistic (vocabulary) and quantitative (arithmetic) factors. Items of both types are interspersed with a time limit. The test is similar to the Thurstone Test of Mental Alertness but has a time limit of 15, rather than 20 minutes. The test is available in two forms, A and B.

Format: Examiner required; suitable for group use; timed: 15 minutes

Scoring: Hand key; computer scored

Cost: 25 test booklets $39; examiner's manual $15

Publisher: McGraw-Hill/London House

Strategic Assessment of Readiness for Training (START)
Claire E. Weinstein, David R. Palmer

Copyright: 1994

Population: Adults

Purpose: Diagnoses learning strengths and weaknesses in a work setting; used to increase a trainee's experience of the training experience; suitable for new employees and employees entering training programs

Description: Eight-scale 56-item multiple-choice computer-administered or paper–pencil test measuring anxiety, attitude, motivation, concentration, identifying important information, knowledge acquisition strategies, monitoring learning, and time management. A chart yielding total scale scores and average item scores is used, as is a self-scored form or a computerized version. A Macintosh version is available.

Format: Individually/self-administered; untimed: 20–30 minutes

Scoring: Computer scored, self-scored

Cost: 1–99 $9.95 each, 100–259 $8.95 each, 251–1,000 $7.95 each

Publisher: H and H Publishing Co., Inc.

Technical Test Battery (TTB) Spatial Recognition (ST8.1)

Copyright: 1988
Population: Adults
Purpose: Measures basic spatial ability
Description: Test with 36 items measures the ability to recognize shapes in two dimensions.
Format: 10 minutes
Scoring: Hand key; machine scored; scoring service available
Cost: Contact publisher
Publisher: Saville and Holdsworth Ltd.

Technical Test Battery (TTB) Visual Estimation (ET3.1)

Copyright: 1992
Population: Adults
Purpose: Measures important elements of spatial perception
Description: Multiple-choice 36-item test involving the estimation of lengths, angles, and

shapes. In each item, the respondent must select the two figures from a set of five which are identical in form, although in many cases they are rotated on the page.

Format: 10 minutes

Scoring: Hand key; machine scored; scoring service available

Cost: Contact publisher

Publisher: Saville and Holdsworth Ltd.

Test of Learning Ability, Forms S-89 and T-89

Copyright: Not provided

Population: Adults

Purpose: Assesses general aptitude; used for screening, selection, placement, and upgrading of personnel

Description: Paper–pencil 54-item multiple-choice test assessing general aptitude. The test is organized into 18 three-item series, each containing a block-counting, vocabulary, and arithmetic part. Each series of items is more difficult than the preceding series. The three types of items can be scored separately. The test is available in two forms: S-89 and T-89. Reading and understanding of the test directions is not included in the administration time of the test. Norms are available for both male and female employees and applicants.

Format: Examiner required; suitable for group use; timed: 12 minutes

Scoring: Hand key

Cost: 1–4 packages $53.00; score key $7.50; manual $25.00

Publisher: Richardson, Bellows, Henry and Company, Inc.

Verbal Reasoning
Raymond J. Corsini, Richard Renck

Copyright: 1958

Population: Adults

Purpose: Assessing individual capacity to reason logically as indicated by solutions to verbal problems; used for job selection and vocational counseling

Description: Paper–pencil 36-item test of mental reasoning consisting of 12 statements with three questions each.

Format: Examiner required; suitable for group use; timed: 15 minutes

Scoring: Hand key

Cost: 25 tests $36.00; score key $10.00; examiner's manual $15.00

Publisher: McGraw-Hill/London House

Wesman Personnel Classification Test (PCT)
A. G. Wesman

Copyright: 1965

Population: Adults

Purpose: Assesses general mental ability; used for selection of employees for sales, supervisory, and managerial positions

Description: Multiple-item paper–pencil test of two major aspects of mental ability: verbal and numerical. The verbal items are analogies. The numerical items test basic math skills and understanding of quantitative relationships. Three forms, A, B, and C, are available. The verbal part of Form C is somewhat more difficult than the verbal parts of Forms A and B.

Format: Examiner required; suitable for group use; timed: Verbal 18 minutes, Numerical 10 minutes

Scoring: Hand key

Cost: Examination kit $26.25

Publisher: The Psychological Corporation

Wonderlic Personnel Test
E. F. Wonderlic

Copyright: 1988

Population: Adults

Purpose: Measures level of mental ability in business and industrial situations; used for selection and placement of business personnel and for vocational guidance

Description: Paper–pencil 50-item or PC test measuring general learning ability in verbal, spatial, and numerical reasoning. The test is used to predict an individual's ability to adjust to complex and rapidly changing job requirements and complete complex job training. Test items include analogies, analysis of geometric figures, arithmetic problems, disarranged sentences, sentence parallelism with proverbs, similarities, logic definitions, judgment, direction following, and others. Available in Spanish, French, Mexican, Cuban, Puerto Rican, Canadian, Chinese, German, Japanese, Korean, Portuguese, Russian, Tagalog, and Vietnamese.

Format: Examiner required; suitable for group use; timed: 12 minutes: may also be administered untimed

Scoring: Hand key and test scoring available from publisher

Cost: Paper–pencil version: 25 tests $75.00, 100 tests $155.00, ADA kit $155.00 (includes large print, audio and scoring key); PC version: 25 tests $75.00, 100 tests $155.00

Publisher: Wonderlic Personnel Test, Inc.

Work Keys Listening Test

Copyright: 1992

Population: Adolescents, adults

Purpose: Used in program evaluation, skills profiling, and selection to assess listening skills

Description: Criterion-referenced 6-point test across five levels. Form 10CC is available. An audiotape, answer folder, administrator's manual and video administrator's manual are used.

Format: Individual administration; suitable for group use; examiner required; timed: 40 minutes

Scoring: Holistic scoring by publisher only

Cost: $13.40 per examinee; Listening and Writing Test $16.00

Publisher: American College Testing

Work Keys Locating Information Test

Copyright: 1993

Population: Adolescents, adults

Purpose: Used in program evaluation, skills profiling, and selection to assess locating information in business graphics and other materials

Description: Multiple-choice 32-item criterion-referenced test across four levels. Form 10DD is available. A test booklet, answer folder, administrator's manual, and videotape administrator's manual are used.

Format: Individual administration; suitable for group use; examiner required; timed: 35 minutes

Scoring: Machine scored; test scoring service available from publisher only

Cost: $4.00 per examinee; 15% discount for K–12 schools

Publisher: American College Testing

General Skills

Adaptive Ability Test—Detailed Checking
Colin D. Selby

Copyright: 1989

Population: Adolescents, adults; ages 11 and above

Purpose: Used in educational and industrial applications to assess accuracy with detailed work under pressure

Description: Multiple-choice 40-item computer-administered test. Three subtests assess speed and accuracy of perception and checking ability. An 11-year-old reading level is required.

Format: Individual/self-administered; suitable for group use; examiner required; timed: 20 minutes

Scoring: Computer scored

Cost: Specimen Set $50.00

Publisher: Selby MillSmith Ltd.

Applied Technology Series (ATS) Following Instructions (VTS1)

Copyright: 1988

Population: Adults

Purpose: Assesses the ability to follow simple technical instructions

Description: Test with 36 items measures the ability to follow written instructions. The topics covered are designed to be relevant in a technical environment and draw on the kind of materials often associated with equipment manuals or operating instructions. No prior knowledge of technical words is assumed.

Format: 20 minutes

Scoring: Hand key; machine scored; scoring service available

Cost: Contact publisher

Publisher: Saville and Holdsworth Ltd.

Applied Technology Series (ATS) Numerical Estimation (NTS2)

Copyright: 1988

Population: Adults

Purpose: Estimates answers to numerical calculations

Description: Forty-item test measures the ability to estimate quickly the answers to numerical calculations. Fractions and percentages are included, as well as basic arithmetic. The task involves selecting an answer of an appropriate order of magnitude from a number of possible answers.

Format: 10 minutes

Scoring: Hand key; machine scored; scoring service available

Cost: Contact publisher

Publisher: Saville and Holdsworth Ltd.

Arithmetic Fundamentals, Forms I and II

Copyright: Not provided

Population: Adults

Purpose: Assesses the ability to perform arithmetic calculations quickly and accurately; used with applicants for hourly and clerical positions

Description: Paper–pencil 42-item test of arithmetic skills. Items are arranged in order of difficulty progressing from simple addition through subtraction, multiplication, and division of whole numbers to handling fractions and decimals. Individuals are provided with printed symbols and verbal instructions indicating which operation to perform on each problem. The test is available in two forms, I and II. The booklet contains space for figuring problems, and answers are recorded in the margins. Norms are available for male clerical and sales applicants, mechanical and operating applicants, and employees. Norms are also available for female applicants for nurses' training, student nurses, and clerical applicants.

Format: Examiner required; suitable for group use; timed: 20 minutes

Scoring: Hand key

Cost: 1-24 packages $45.00; score key $7.50; manual $5.00

Publisher: Richardson, Bellows, Henry and Company, Inc.

Automated Office Battery (AOB) Numerical Estimation (NE1)

Copyright: 1988

Population: Ages 16 to adult

Purpose: Measures the ability to estimate the answers to a variety of numerical calculations

Description: Multiple-choice 50-item test assessing the ability to quickly estimate the answers to calculations. Candidates are presented with calculations requiring addition, subtraction, multiplication, division, and percentages. Candidates are required to estimate the order of magnitude of the solution and choose the correct one from five alternatives. Candidates are discouraged from making precise calculations, and the time constraint encourages estimation.

Format: 10 minutes

Scoring: Hand key; machine scored; scoring service available

Cost: Contact publisher

Publisher: Saville and Holdsworth Ltd.

Biographical Index
Williard A. Kerr

Copyright: 1983

Population: Adults

Purpose: Quantifies background data; used for predicting success in managerial and sales positions and in recruitment programs for general business

Description: Multiple-item paper–pencil measure of personal background information. The instrument yields five scores: stability, drive to excel, human relations, financial status. and personal adjustment. Three middle scores provide an estimate of basic energy level. The instrument predicts the annual salary increment of executives.

Format: Examiner required; suitable for group use; untimed: 30 minutes

Scoring: Hand key

Cost: Specimen Set $5.00; 25 indices $8.75; 25 answer sheets $5.00

Publisher: Psychometric Affiliates

Bruce Vocabulary Inventory
Martin M. Bruce

Copyright: 1974

Population: Adults

Purpose: Determines how a subject's vocabulary compares to the vocabulary of individuals employed in various business occupations

Description: Paper–pencil 100-item multiple-choice test in which the subject matches one of four alternative words with a key vocabulary word. Measures the ability to recognize and comprehend words. The subject's score can be compared to the scores of executives, middle managers, white-collar workers, engineers, blue-collar workers, and the total employed population. Suitable for individuals with physical, hearing, and visual disabilities.

Format: Self-administered; suitable for group use; untimed: 15–20 minutes

Scoring: Hand key

Cost: Reusable tests $51.50; manual $5.50; manual supplement $22.50, fan key $2.75; IBM answer sheets $24.50; Specimen Set IBM Form $36.50; Specimen Set Fan Key Form $32.50

Publisher: Martin M. Bruce, Ph.D.

CareerPak
Samuel J. Wein

Copyright: 1995

Population: Ages 21 to 65

Purpose: Used as career assessment

Description: Combines the *Strong Interest Inventory* with the *Comprehensive Personality Profile* along with the book *Wing Walking*.

Format: Group or individual administration; 2 hours

Scoring: Computer scored

Cost: $99.50

Publisher: Behaviordyne, Inc.

Clark Wilson Group Surveys (CWG)
Clark L. Wilson

Copyright: Updated yearly

Population: Adults

Purpose: Measures skills for five different roles in the organization: Quality, Leadership, Management, Sales, and Teams

Description: There are 13 surveys in the standard battery of CWG surveys. Each survey is constructed around a Task Cycle with five or six phases (skills groups). Each phase has up to four dimensions of more specific behaviors. Surveys comprise between 50 and 145 items, paper–pencil and on-line option. Some surveys include open-ended questions where respondents may write comments. Surveys may be customized to fit company needs. The feedback report presents data from all respondent groups in Task Cycle sequence. A narrative report is optional. Surveys are normed. Validity studies for standard surveys available upon request. Modifications necessary to accommodate individuals with visual, physical, hearing, and mental impairment.

Format: Self-administered; suitable for group use; untimed: 20–45 minutes

Scoring: Self-scored/computer scored; test scoring service available from publisher and from another company

Cost: Contact publisher

Publisher: Clark Wilson Group

Critical Reasoning Test Battery (CRTB) Verbal Evaluation (VC1.1)

Copyright: 1993

Population: Age 16 to adult

Purpose: Measures ability to understand and evaluate the logic of arguments

Description: Sixty-item test measuring the ability to understand and evaluate the logic of various types of arguments. The candidate must decide if a statement is true or untrue, or whether there is insufficient information to judge.

Format: 30 minutes

Scoring: Hand key; machine scored; scoring service available

Cost: Contact publisher

Publisher: Saville and Holdsworth Ltd.

Critical Reasoning Test Battery (CRTB) Interpreting Data (NC2.1)

Copyright: 1993

Population: Age 16 to adult

Purpose: Measures ability to make correct decisions or inferences from numerical data

Description: Forty-item paper–pencil test assessing the ability to interpret statistical and other numerical data presented as tables or diagrams. Candidates must select the correct answer to a question from five alternatives. The test is appropriate for jobs involving analysis or decision making based on numerical facts.

Format: 30 minutes

Scoring: Hand key; machine scored; scoring service available

Cost: Contact publisher

Publisher: Saville and Holdsworth Ltd.

Customer Service Skills Inventory (CSSI)

Juan Sanchez, Scott Frazer

Copyright: 1995

Population: Adults

Purpose: Determines whether an individual has critical customer service skills; used for selection and placement

Description: Multiple-choice 63-item inventory assessment measures skills, behavior, and traits indicative of success in service-oriented positions. The individual responds to situational type questions to determine whether applicants show a desire to help customers, understand and satisfy customer's needs, take responsibility for assisting customers, cooperate with co-workers, put forth extra job efforts, and keep a reasonable balance between customer requests and company interests.

Format: Examiner required; untimed: 30 minutes

Scoring: Hand key; computer

Cost: 10 test booklets $97.50; examiner's manual $15.00

Publisher: McGraw-Hill/London House

Customer Service Skills Test

Copyright: Not provided

Population: Adults

Purpose: Measures clerical, intellectual, and administrative as well as specific skills required in a customer service environment

Description: Provides a five-page report to the client. Measures the following: verbal communication skills, numerical skills, attention to detail, problem solving ability, customer service skills, customer service problem solving, and customer service logic.

Format: 1 hour

Scoring: Scoring service available from publisher

Cost: Basic $319.00; Comprehensive $599.00

Publisher: Walden Personnel Testing and Training, Inc.

Employee Application Resume Rating and Categorizing Scale
Thomas J. Rundquist

Copyright: 1995

Population: Adolescents, adults

Purpose: Allows an employer to rate and categorize employment applications per their resume and/or application in a simple and organized fashion

Description: The computer-administered version is available on 3½″ diskettes for Windows IBM PC–compatible computers. The test may be administered to thousands of applicants' resumes or applicants in short order. This will save untold amounts of time and effort as well as provide the best qualified employee applicants for interviews. Also, the database can be programmed to give the Human Resources Department data for researching their employees both present, past, and future in the company's own criteria. Criteria include Job Categories from a list of 75 selections for three choices—Salary (4 Levels) Requirements, Geographic Preferences, and Work Experience (three most recent)—for four criteria. Industries Categories are divided into 10 major headings.

Format: Untimed: 5 minutes

Scoring: Computer scored

Cost: Unlimited usage at a particular site for $50.00

Publisher: Nova Media, Inc.

Empowerment Inventory (EI)
Kenneth W. Thomas, Walter G. Tymon

Copyright: Present

Population: Adults

Purpose: Used in training and development to assess task empowerment

Description: Likert scale with 24 items. Choice, competence, meaningfulness, and pro-gress are the scores yielded. An eighth-grade reading level is required.

Format: Individual/self-administered; suitable for group use; untimed

Scoring: Self-scored

Cost: $6.75

Publisher: Xicom, Inc.

ESSI In-Depth Interpretations
Terry D. Anderson, Howard L. Shenson

Copyright: 1988

Population: Adults

Purpose: Assesses entrepreneurial style preferences and success indicators

Description: Forced-choice 21-item test. A 10th-grade reading level is required.

Format: Individual administration; suitable for group use; examiner required; untimed

Scoring: Self-scored

Cost: $9.95

Publisher: Consulting Resource Group International, Inc.

Estimation Test, High Level

Copyright: 1985

Population: Adults

Purpose: Assesses numerical ability; used for selection of positions requiring quantitative abilities; also used in vocational guidance

Description: Paper–pencil or computer-administered 26-item multiple-choice test. Each item consists of a complex numerical expression and five possible answers. The correct answer may be determined through rounding strategies. The computer version operates on Plato System. Purchasers of the test must be registered with the South African Medical and Dental Council. Available in Afrikaans.

Format: Examiner required; suitable for group use; timed: 26 minutes

Scoring: Hand key

Cost: Contact publisher

Publisher: Human Sciences Research Council

Flanagan Aptitude Classification Tests (FACT)
John C. Flanagan

Copyright: 1953

Population: Adolescents, adults

Purpose: Assesses skills necessary for the successful completion of particular occupational tasks; used for vocational counseling, curriculum planning, and selection and placement of employees

Description: Battery of 16 multiple-item paper–pencil aptitude tests designed to help the subject understand his or her abilities relative to others in the total population and in specific occupations. Each test is printed as a separate nonreusable booklet and may be administered individually or in combination. The FACT battery differs from the Flanagan Industrial Tests (FIT) battery in that the tests are generally of a lower level and have longer time limits.

Format: Self-administered; suitable for group use; timed: 2 to 40 minutes per test

Scoring: Hand key

Cost: 25 test booklets (specify test) $48; examiner's manual $15

Publisher: McGraw-Hill/London House

Flanagan Industrial Tests (FIT)
John C. Flanagan

Copyright: 1960

Population: Adults

Purpose: Predicts success for given job elements in adults; used for employee screening, hiring, and placement in a wide variety of jobs

Description: Battery of 18 paper–pencil tests designed for use with adults in personnel selection programs. Each test is printed as a separate booklet and may be administered individually or in combination.

Format: Examiner required; suitable for group use; timed: 5–15 minutes per test

Scoring: Hand key

Cost: 25 test booklets $40.00; scoring stencil $11.50; examiner's manual $15.00

Publisher: McGraw-Hill/London House

Gottschaldt Figures Test

Copyright: Not provided

Population: Adults

Purpose: Measures visual perception and analytical ability; used with job applicants with at least 10 years of education for purposes of employee screening and selection

Description: Multiple-item paper–pencil test requiring the applicant to find given embedded figures in more complex diagrams. The test is restricted to competent persons properly registered with the South African Medical and Dental Council. Afrikaans version available.

Format: Examiner required; suitable for group use; timed: 20 minutes

Scoring: Hand key

Cost: Contact publisher

Publisher: Human Sciences Research Council

Hay Aptitude Test Battery: Warm-Up
Edward N. Hay

Copyright: 1984

Population: Adults

Purpose: Introduces job applicants to the testing procedures of the *Hay Aptitude Test Battery*

Description: Unscored 20-item paper–pencil test providing a warm-up for the Hay aptitude tests. The exercise is intended to quiet nervous applicants and to familiarize applicants with the format of the other tests. Available in French and Spanish.

Format: Examiner required; suitable for group use; timed: 1 minute

Scoring: Hand key

Cost: 25 forms $41.25; 100 forms $80.00

Publisher: Wonderlic Personnel Test, Inc.

Individual Service Strategy Portfolio
LaVerne Ludden

Copyright: 1993

Population: Adults

Purpose: Captures essential intake information for participants in JTPA and other employment programs

Description: Documents and evaluates 84 assets or barriers to employment opportunities; used by counselors and intake workers. Meets JTPA data collection requirements.

Format: Administered individually; examiner required; untimed

Scoring: Examiner evaluated

Cost: 25 forms $32.95

Publisher: JIST Works, Inc.

Industrial Reading Test (IRT)

Copyright: 1978

Population: Adolescents, adults; Grades 10 and above

Purpose: Measures reading comprehension; used for selecting job applicants and screening trainees for vocational or technical programs

Description: Paper–pencil 38-item test of reading comprehension covering nine reading passages of graded difficulty. Some passages are sections of technical manuals; others take the form of company memoranda. Materials include two forms, A and B. Sales of Form A are restricted to business and industry. Form B is available to both schools and businesses.

Format: Examiner required; suitable for group use; timed: 40 minutes

Scoring: Hand key; may be machine scored locally

Cost: Examination kit $25.68

Publisher: The Psychological Corporation

Information Technology Test Series (ITTS) Diagramming (DIT5)

Copyright: 1988

Population: Adults

Purpose: Measures logical analysis through the ability to follow complex instructions; appropriate for technical occupations and jobs involving systems design, flow charting, and similar skills

Description: Multiple-choice 50-item test consisting of a series of abstract designs in logical sequences. Respondents must select, from five choices, the design which completes the logical sequence. Candidates must think logically and flexibly.

Format: 20 minutes

Scoring: Hand key; machine scored; scoring service available

Cost: Contact publisher

Publisher: Saville and Holdsworth Ltd.

IPI Employee Aptitude Series: Memory

Copyright: 1984

Population: Adults

Purpose: Determines ability to remember visual, verbal, and numerical information; used to screen applicants for clerical, sales, and supervisory jobs

Description: Three 2-minute paper–pencil subtests demonstrating aptitude to recognize and recall associations with names, faces, words and numbers. Also available in French and Spanish.

Format: Suitable for group use; examiner required; timed: 6 minutes

Scoring: Hand key

Cost: Introductory kit (20 test booklets, scoring key, manual) $44

Publisher: Industrial Psychology International Ltd.

IPI Employee Aptitude Series: Applied Math

Copyright: 1995

Population: Adolescents, adults

Purpose: Measures the ability to solve one- and two-step algebra problems; used for employee selection, promotion, and training

Description: Multiple-choice 18-item paper–pencil test. A fourth-grade reading level is required. Scores predict abstract and numeric estimation skills.

Format: Examiner required; suitable for group use; timed: 12 minutes

Scoring: Hand key

Cost: 20 packages $21.00

Publisher: Industrial Psychology International Ltd.

IPI Employee Aptitude Series: Office Terms

Copyright: 1981

Population: Adults

Purpose: Measures ability to understand special terminology used in business and industry; used to screen applicants for clerical, sales, and supervisory jobs

Description: Paper–pencil 54-item test measuring comprehension of information of an office or business nature. It also indicates over-qualification for routine, repetitive assignments. Also available in French and Spanish combined with sales terms.

Format: Suitable for group use; examiner required; timed: 6 minutes

Scoring: Hand key

Cost: Introductory kit (20 test booklets, scoring key, manual) $30

Publisher: Industrial Psychology International Ltd.

IPI Employee Aptitude Series: Parts

Copyright: 1984

Population: Adults

Purpose: Assesses ability to see the whole in relation to its parts; used to screen applicants for clerical, mechanical, technical, sales, and supervisory positions

Description: Paper–pencil 48-item test measuring aptitude for visualizing size, shape, and spatial relations of objects in two and three dimensions. The test reveals one's sense of layout and organization. Also available in French and Spanish.

Format: Suitable for group use; examiner

required; timed: 6 minutes

Scoring: Hand key

Cost: Introductory kit (20 test booklets, scoring key, manual) $30

Publisher: Industrial Psychology International Ltd.

IPI Employee Aptitude Series: Perception

Copyright: 1981

Population: Adults

Purpose: Measures ability to perceive differences in written words and numbers; used to screen applicants for clerical, sales, and supervisory jobs

Description: Paper–pencil 54-item test measuring the ability to rapidly scan and locate details in words and numbers and to recognize likenesses and differences. Also available in French and Spanish.

Format: Suitable for group use; examiner required; timed: 6 minutes

Scoring: Hand key

Cost: Introductory kit (20 test booklets, scoring key, manual) $30

Publisher: Industrial Psychology International Ltd.

IPI Employee Aptitude Series: Precision

Copyright: 1986

Population: Adults

Purpose: Determines ability to perceive details in objects; used to screen applicants for technical and mechanical jobs requiring visual accuracy, such as inspector-related jobs

Description: Paper–pencil 48-item test using pictures to test the ability to perceive details in objects and rapidly recognize differences and likenesses. The test does not require the ability to read or write. Also available in French and Spanish.

Format: Suitable for group use; examiner required; timed: 6 minutes

Scoring: Hand key

Cost: Introductory kit (20 test booklets, scoring key, manual) $30

Publisher: Industrial Psychology International Ltd.

IS Manager Consultant Skills Evaluation

Copyright: 1990

Population: Adults

Purpose: Measures technical, intellectual, and supervisory skills required for a senior-level IS consultant, manager, or trainer

Description: Available in English and French

Format: Timed: 3 hours 30 minutes

Scoring: Scoring service available from publisher

Cost: $319.00

Publisher: Walden Personnel Testing and Training, Inc.

IS Project Leader Skills Evaluation

Copyright: 1988

Population: Adults

Purpose: Evaluates all essential skills for the project leader position, including procedural and analytical ability and knowledge of project organization, control, scheduling, and planning concepts

Description: Available in English and French

Format: 3 hours

Scoring: Scoring service available from publisher

Cost: Test booklet and detailed report on each candidate, Basic $319.00, Comprehensive $699.00

Publisher: Walden Personnel Testing and Training, Inc.

Job Style Indicator (JSI)
Terry D. Anderson, Everett T. Robinson

Copyright: 1988

Population: Adults

Purpose: Assesses work style behaviors; used in job placement/evaluation

Description: Forced-choice 16-item test. A 10th-grade reading level is required.

Format: Individual administration; suitable for group use; examiner required; untimed

Scoring: Self-scored

Cost: $5.95

Publisher: Consulting Resource Group International, Inc.

La Monica Empathy Profile (LEP)
Elaine L. La Monica

Copyright: Present

Population: Adults

Purpose: Used in training for nurses, educators, and customer service to assess helping styles

Description: Forced-choice 30-item test. Nonverbal behavior, perceiving feelings and listening, responding verbally, respect of self and others, openness, honesty, and flexibility are the scores yielded. An eighth-grade reading level is required.

Format: Individual/self-administered; untimed

Scoring: Self-scored

Cost: $6.25

Publisher: Xicom, Inc.

Lead Profile

Copyright: 1994

Population: Managers, supervisors, leaders, and staff people

Purpose: Charts responses from the *Lead Self* and *Lead Other* tests

Description: Gives average and individual scores of *Lead Self* and *Lead Other* instruments. Measures perceptions of supervisors, associates, and colleagues against perceptions of the examinee. Materials used include a self-administered instrument and scoring form. An eighth-grade reading level is required. Available in Spanish, German, Japanese, and French. Suitable for individuals with physical and hearing disabilities.

Format: Individual/group administration; self-administered; untimed

Scoring: Self/computer scored; test scoring service available from publisher

Cost: Contact publisher

Publisher: Center for Leadership Studies, Inc.

Ligonde Equivalence Test
Paultre Ligonde

Copyright: Not provided

Population: Adults

Purpose: Measures grade-level ability of adults who have been out of school 20–30 years; used when determination of school grade level is relevant to employment qualifications and for placement in adult education programs

Description: Multiple-item paper–pencil test assessing the grade level of adults who have been out of school several years. Scoring is based on what students from a particular grade level should retain in terms of verbal and numerical skills. The test is used to select employees for positions requiring verbal communication or clerical skills, to determine school levels for trade or labor unions, and to issue competency cards. The test was normed on 3,000 French and English Canadians who left school 20–30 years ago. The test is available in two forms, GE and HE. Both include questions on knowledge of the second language.

Format: Examiner required; suitable for group use; timed: 15 minutes

Scoring: Hand key

Cost: Specimen Key $12.00

Publisher: Institute of Psychological Research, Inc.

Listening Styles Profile
Kittie W. Watson, Larry L. Barker, James Weaver

Copyright: 1995

Population: All employees

Purpose: Identifies listening style, teaches participants how to adapt their listening style for different situations and people

Description: Helps people understand how they listen and what type of information they prefer to listen to. Once they learn about their personal "listening style," they can explore other styles and learn how to adapt their behaviors accordingly to maximize communication. By understanding listening style, people will be better able to determine the communication channel that is best for themselves and others; adapt behavior to match a speaker's needs, time constraints, and settings, and understand others' viewpoints. The instrument is complete with a self-scoring answer sheet and an interpretation guide, allowing participants to immediately see results.

Format: 15 minutes

Scoring: Self-scored or examiner scored

Cost: $69.95; Trainer's Package $19.95

Publisher: Pfeiffer and Company International Publishers, Inc.

Mathematical Achievement Test

Copyright: 1968

Population: Adults

Purpose: Measures general skills of algebra, geometry, and mathematics at the secondary school level; used in employee selection for clerical and technical positions

Description: Multiple-item paper–pencil achievement test assessing the extent to which the subject can apply the principles of algebra, geometry, and general mathematics as taught in secondary schools. Norms are based on a group of matriculated boys and girls. The test is restricted to competent persons properly registered with the South African Medical and Dental Council. Afrikaans version available.

Format: Examiner required; suitable for group use; timed: 23 minutes

Scoring: Hand key; examiner evaluated

Cost: Contact publisher

Publisher: Human Sciences Research Council

Mechanical Comprehension Test A3/1

Copyright: 1978

Population: Adolescents

Purpose: Measures mechanical abilities

Description: Multiple-item paper–pencil test assessing the ability to apply the laws and principles of physics and mechanics. The test is based on the secondary school syllabus.

Format: Examiner required; suitable for group use; untimed: 30–35 minutes

Scoring: Hand key

Cost: Contact publisher

Publisher: Human Sciences Research Council

Multimethod Job Design Questionnaire (MJDQ)
Michael A. Campion

Copyright: 1985

Population: Adults

Purpose: Measures new employee's job qualifications; used in career counseling

Description: Paper–pencil 70-item questionnaire containing the following subtests: organized psychology approach, motivation, mechanics, biomechanics, and motor approach.

Format: Group or individual administration; examiner required; untimed

Scoring: Hand key; examiner evaluated

Cost: $18.00

Publisher: Select Press

My Presentation Style
James H. Brewer

Copyright: 1989

Population: Adults

Purpose: Used to assist individuals in making more effective presentations

Description: Used by trainers, conference leaders, and sales consultants to improve their own presentations. The instrument shows how personality type can dictate an individual's presentation style, outlines techniques for more effec-

tive presentations, explores strengths and weaknesses of each style of presentation, and promotes cross-type understanding.

Format: Individual/self-administered; untimed: 15–20 minutes

Scoring: Hand key

Cost: $4.95 each

Publisher: Associated Consultants in Education

My Timestyle
James H. Brewer

Copyright: 1990

Population: Adults

Purpose: Used to develop more productive time usage

Description: Sixteen items yield accurate information about an individual's time awareness. Four time styles are identified by the instrument: Road Runner (high-velocity person who does not waste words or time); Race Horse (time conscious team worker); New Pup (believes people are more important than time); Tom Cat (independent worker with a low awareness of time and people). The instrument determines one's time usage style, describes how each style behaves, explores more positive time use, and promotes a better understanding of others.

Format: Individual/self-administration; untimed: 10–15 minutes

Scoring: Hand key

Cost: $2.95 each

Publisher: Associated Consultants in Education

Numerical Skills Scale

Copyright: 1996

Population: Adults

Purpose: Identifies applicants who possess precise and fast business math skills

Description: Scale with 25 questions used for determining an applicant's potential for errors in customer transactions, cash and inventory counting accuracy, numerical calculations, and cash-handling speed. Applicants who score well on this scale earn high performance ratings for fast, accurate, and complaint-free performance.

Format: 15 minutes

Scoring: I-Fax (automated scoring platform that returns test results via fax), Fax-In, Phone-In, Mail-In or PC software

Cost: Ranges from $8.50 to $18.00

Publisher: Reid Psychological Systems

Personnel Test Battery (PTB) Numerical Computation (NP2.1)

Copyright: 1993

Population: Adults

Purpose: Measures basic numbers skills

Description: Multiple-choice 30-item test measuring the understanding of relationships between numbers and operations, as well as quick and accurate calculations. In each item, one number has been omitted from an equation. The examinee must select (from five choices) the number that will correctly complete the equation. Simple fractions and decimals are used, and some problems are expressed in numbers, but more complex notation or operations are deliberately omitted. The test is suitable for individuals with minimal educational qualifications.

Format: 7 minutes

Scoring: Hand key; machine scored; scoring service available

Cost: Contact publisher

Publisher: Saville and Holdsworth Ltd.

Personnel Test Battery (PTB) Verbal Comprehension (VP5.1)

Copyright: 1993

Population: Adults

Purpose: Assesses an individual's knowledge of the meanings of words and the relationships between them; used where verbal communication skills are important

Description: Multiple-choice 40-item test requiring the candidate to identify the relationship (same or opposite) between one pair of words and to select (from five choices) the word which relates in the same way to a third given word. The vocabulary used is nonspecialist, everyday language. VP5.1 is more difficult than VP1.1 of the same battery.

Format: 18 minutes

Scoring: Hand key; machine scored; scoring service available

Cost: Contact publisher

Publisher: Saville and Holdsworth Ltd.

Personnel Test Battery (PTB) Numerical Reasoning (NP6.1, NP6.2)

Copyright: 1993

Population: Adults

Purpose: Assesses simple numerical reasoning skills

Description: Tests assessing simple reasoning skills with numbers. Both have short written problems which involve using decimals, fractions, or graphs. Test content includes items based on subjects relevant to sales, clerical, and general staff. NP6.2 (24 items) allows aids to calculation to be used, and candidates are supplied with a calculator. NP6.1 (30 items) is completed without a calculator.

Format: 15 minutes

Scoring: Hand key; machine scored; scoring service available

Cost: Contact publisher

Publisher: Saville and Holdsworth Ltd.

Personnel Test Battery (PTB) Verbal Comprehension (VP5.1)

Copyright: 1993

Population: Adults

Purpose: Measures ability to understand written information

Description: Forty-item test measuring the ability to understand written information. The task is to read a variety of office memos, written instructions, etc., and to decide whether given statements are true or false, or whether there is insufficient information to judge. Applicable where verbal communication skills are important.

Format: 18 minutes

Scoring: Hand key; machine scored; scoring service available

Cost: Contact publisher

Publisher: Saville and Holdsworth Ltd.

Position Analysis Questionnaire (PAQ)
Ernest J. McCormick, P. R. Jeanneret, Robert C. Meacham

Copyright: Not provided

Population: Adults

Purpose: Analyzes jobs in terms of job elements that reflect directly or infer the basic human behaviors involved, regardless of their specific technological areas or functions; used with jobs at all levels

Description: Paper–pencil 187-item job analysis rating scale in which the examiner/analyst indicates the degree of involvement of each of the elements listed using appropriate rating scales such as importance, frequency, etc. The job elements are organized so that they provide a logical analysis of the job's structure. Six broad areas are assessed: information input, mental processes, work output, relationships with other persons, job context, and other job characteristics. Examples of specific job elements are the use of written materials, the level of decision making, the use of mechanical devices, working in a hazardous environment, and working at a specified pace. Analysis of the questionnaire is in terms of job dimensions. The results are used as the basis for job aptitude requirements, deriving point values for jobs that in turn can be used to establish compensation rates and classifying jobs into clusters that have similar profiles.

Format: Self-administered by analyst, personnel staff, job supervisors, and in some cases the workers themselves; suitable for group use; untimed: typical time not available

Scoring: Examiner evaluated; computer processing available

Cost: Preview Kit (booklet, answer sheet) $11.00; Job Analysis Manual $55.65; User's Manual $37.40; Technical Manual $21.05

Publisher: Consulting Psychologists Press

Position Classification Inventory (PCI)
Gary Gottfredson, John L. Holland

Copyright: 1991

Population: Adults

Purpose: Used by human resources development and career counselors to classify positions or job classes

Description: Paper–pencil 84-item 3-point scale inventory. An SDS summary code is produced. Materials used include a manual, reusable item booklet, and answer/profile form.

Format: Self-administered; suitable for group use; untimed: 10 minutes

Scoring: Computer scored; test scoring service available from publisher

Cost: Intro Kit $55.00

Publisher: Psychological Assessment Resources, Inc.

Press Test
Melany E. Baehr, Raymond J. Corsini

Copyright: 1985

Population: Adults

Purpose: Assesses adults' ability to work under pressure by comparing objective measures of reaction time under normal and high-pressure conditions; used for selection, career counseling, and placement of high-level personnel, where efficiency must be maintained

Description: Multiple-item paper–pencil test measuring speed of reaction to verbal stimuli, color stimuli, and color stimuli under distraction caused by interfering verbal stimuli. For valid results, stopwatch time limits and strict monitoring must be employed in the administration of the test, which is not designed to be completed in the allotted time. The test has been used to select high-level managers, professionals, and airline pilots.

Format: Examiner required; suitable for group use; timed: 10 to 12 minutes

Scoring: Hand key

Cost: 25 test booklets $51; examiner's manual $15

Publisher: McGraw-Hill/London House

Problem-Solving Skills Questionnaire (PSSQ)
Dennis C. Kinlaw

Copyright: 1989

Population: Adults; managers

Purpose: To be used as a larger package on coaching (see also *Coaching Skills Inventory*)

Description: Self-scoring instrument used to assess participants' understanding and use of specific conversational skills.

Format: Self-administered; 2 hours

Scoring: Self-scored

Cost: $7.95

Publisher: Pfeiffer and Company International Publishers, Inc.

Project Implementation Profile (PIP)
Jeffrey K. Pinto, Dennis P. Slevin

Copyright: Present

Population: Adults

Purpose: Used in project management to assess variables that affect project success

Description: Likert scale 57-item test. Project mission, technical tasks, personnel, troubleshooting, top management support, client acceptance, project schedule, monitoring and feedback, client consultation, and communication. An eighth-grade reading level is required.

Format: Individual/self-administered; untimed

Scoring: Self-scored

Cost: $6.75

Publisher: Xicom, Inc.

Purdue Pegboard Test

Copyright: 1992

Population: Adults

Purpose: Measures hand–finger–arm dexterity required for certain types of manual work; used in the selection of business and industrial personnel

Description: Multiple-operation manual test of gross- and fine-motor movements of hands, fingers, arms, and tips of fingers. The test measures the dexterity needed in assembly work, electronic production work, and similarly related jobs. Materials consist of a test board with two vertical rows of holes and four storage wells holding pegs, washers, and collars. The subject must complete as many assemblies as possible in the allotted time.

Format: Examiner required; suitable for group use; timed: 3 to 9 minutes

Scoring: Hand key

Cost: Complete (board, manual) $237.00; 100 profiles $50.00; complete replacement set (pegs, washers, collars) $39.00; manual $15.00

Publisher: McGraw-Hill/London House

Quality Service Audit for Employees
James H. Brewer

Copyright: 1992

Population: Adults

Purpose: Used to give employees an opportunity to evaluate how they rate in quality customer service

Description: The instrument measures employee's beliefs, knowledge, commitment and performance in quality customer service, promotes more positive attitudes toward quality customer service, uses self-assessment as a tool for change, and shows how each employee is vital to quality customer service.

Format: Individual/self-administered; untimed: 15–20 minutes

Scoring: Hand key

Cost: $5.95 each

Publisher: Associated Consultants in Education

RBH Arithmetic Reasoning Test, Forms I and II

Copyright: Not provided

Population: Adults

Purpose: Assesses an individual's ability to solve problems using basic arithmetical operations; used with technical and professional, sales, clerical, mechanical, and operating personnel

Description: Test with 25 items assessing an individual's ability to solve arithmetic problems covering the following areas: determination of selling price, distribution of costs, discounting, production rates, wage and salary rates, payments, overtime procedures, dividend and profit determinations, percentages, and proportions. Examinees mark their answers directly in the test book in boxes placed next to the problem. Space for figuring the problems is provided. The score is the number of items answered correctly. The test is available in two forms, I and II.

Format: Examiner required; suitable for group use; timed: 15 minutes

Scoring: Hand key

Cost: 1–24 packages $45.00; score key $7.50; manual $15.00

Publisher: Richardson, Bellows, Henry, and Company, Inc.

RCJS Arithmetic Test—Form A
Roland T. Ramsay

Copyright: 1991

Population: Adults

Purpose: Measures the ability of industrial workers to perform basic computations

Description: Paper–pencil 24-item multiple-choice test assessing the ability to perform computations involving addition, subtraction, multiplication, and division of whole numbers and fractions.

Format: Examiner required; suitable for group use; timed: 20 minutes

Scoring: Hand key

Cost: 5 booklets $29.75; manual with scoring key $24.95

Publisher: Ramsay Corporation

RCJS Maintest Form NL–1 and Form B
Roland T. Ramsay

Copyright: 1991

Population: Adults

Purpose: Assesses maintenance ability for trade/craft jobs; used for hiring and promotion

Description: Multiple-choice 153-item paper–pencil test. Use Form NL–1 or alternate Form B. Materials used include paper, pencil, and a separate answer sheet.

Format: Suitable for group use; examiner required; untimed: 2 hours 30 minutes

Scoring: Machine scored by publisher

Cost: 10 booklets, 10 answer sheets, and manual $500.00

Publisher: Ramsay Corporation

RCJS Measurement, Reading, and Arithmetic
Roland T. Ramsay

Copyright: 1990

Population: Adults

Purpose: Measures reading, arithmetic, and measurement skills for pre-employment

Description: Multiple-choice 101-item paper–pencil test with three subtests: Reading (40 items), Measurement (21 items), and Arithmetic (40 items). One composite score and three subscores are yielded. Materials used include a pencil, scrap paper, and separate answer sheet.

Format: Individual administration; suitable for group use; examiner required; timed: 85 minutes

Scoring: Hand key; machine scoring service available from publisher

Cost: (10 booklets, 1 key, 1 manual, 100 answer sheets) $498.00

Publisher: Ramsay Corporation

RCJS Reading Test—Form A
Roland T. Ramsay

Copyright: 1991

Population: Adults

Purpose: Assesses the ability to read, comprehend, and answer written questions

Description: Paper–pencil 40-item multiple-choice test designed to measure an individual's ability to read, comprehend, and answer questions based on a printed passage. The topics of the passages are Plant Safety, Hydraulic Systems, Industrial Machines, Lubrication, and Operating a Computer Terminal.

Format: Examiner required; suitable for group use; timed: 35 minutes

Scoring: Hand key

Cost: 5 booklets $29.75; manual with scoring key $24.95; consumable, self-scoring booklet $10.00

Publisher: Ramsay Corporation

Reading Comprehension

Copyright: Not provided

Population: Adults

Purpose: Measures reading comprehension of applicants to industrial positions

Description: Multiple-item paper–pencil test assessing the ability to comprehend reading material related to business and industry. The test contains six articles taken from training and safety manuals and publicity releases. Each article is followed by several questions that test the examinee's understanding of the article. The test is not intended to measure critical thinking. For males, the test has been used almost exclusively with industrial employees and applicants. With a maximum score of 40, examinees average about 30 with a standard deviation of 7.

Format: Examiner required; suitable for group use; timed: 20 minutes

Scoring: Hand key

Cost: 1–24 packages $60.00; score key $5.00; manual $5.00

Publisher: Richardson, Bellows, Henry and Company, Inc.

Rotate and Flip Test (RAFT)
Terence R. Taylor, Monica R. Ebertsohn

Copyright: 1989

Population: Adolescents, adults

Purpose: Assesses visualization, spatial relations, and orientation

Description: Multiple-choice 24-item paper–pencil test of spatial visualization that yields a total test score. Materials include test booklet, answer sheet, pencil, eraser, and manual. Available in Afrikaans.

Format: Examiner required; suitable for group use; timed: 25 minutes

Scoring: Hand key

Cost: Contact publisher

Publisher: Human Sciences Research Council

Self-Employment Questionnaire (SEQ)
Frank W. D. Thaxton

Copyright: 1995

Population: Adults

Purpose: Used in employment counseling to measure skill and readiness for self-employment

Description: Multiple-choice computer-administered projective test with a narrative text. An 11-year-old reading level is required.

Format: Individual/self-administered; timed: 90 minutes

Scoring: Computer scored

Cost: $47.00

Publisher: Selby MillSmith Ltd.

Selling Skills Series (SSS) Reasoning with Data (NS2)

Copyright: 1988

Population: Adults

Purpose: Assesses ability to use numerical data

Description: Test with 35 items measuring the ability to understand and use numerical data in order to answer questions. The task is to utilize tables provided in order to solve basic numerical problems. These involve addition, subtraction, multiplication, division, and percentages. However, candidates are allowed to use a pocket calculator during the test, so the emphasis is on understanding and reasoning rather than arithmetic and calculation. The data and the questions have been designed to simulate the kind of numerical information which individuals may encounter in sales jobs.

Format: 20 minutes

Scoring: Hand key; machine scored; scoring service available

Cost: Contact publisher

Publisher: Saville and Holdsworth Ltd.

Selling Skills Series (SSS) Using Written Information (VS1)

Copyright: 1988

Population: Adults

Purpose: Assesses written communication skills

Description: Test with 36 items measuring the ability to understand written information in order to arrive at reasoned conclusions. Performance on the test depends on the precise extraction of relevant information from a paragraph of text. The task is to use this information to decide whether given statements are true or untrue, or whether there is insufficient information to judge. This task is relevant to sales jobs where incumbents receive product information in written form as well as written communication from customers and/or colleagues.

Format: 12 minutes

Scoring: Hand key; machine scored; scoring service available

Cost: Contact publisher

Publisher: Saville and Holdsworth Ltd.

Shop Arithmetic Test, Forms I and II

Copyright: Not provided

Population: Adults

Purpose: Assesses arithmetic reasoning abilities; used with applicants for operations and craft positions and engineering aides

Description: Paper–pencil 20-item test of mathematical abilities related to industrial situations. Content includes simple arithmetic operations (fractions and decimal fractions form the upper limit) involved in figuring sums or remainders on problems of weight or length; computing measures of distance, area, or volume; and analyzing operations data from tables. Illustrations and diagrams are provided to define and illustrate some problems. Space is provided in the test booklet for figuring problems, and answers are recorded in the margin. The test is available in two forms.

Format: Examiner required; suitable for group use; timed: 15 minutes

Scoring: Hand key

Cost: 1–24 packages $55.00; score key $7.50; manual $5.00

Publisher: Richardson, Bellows, Henry and Company, Inc.

Skills and Attributes Inventory
Melany E. Baehr

Copyright: 1976

Population: Adults

Purpose: Assesses the relative importance of 13 skill and attribute factors necessary for successful job performance and the degree to which the incumbent possesses the skills and attributes; used for systematic job analysis, test validation, and selection

Description: Paper–pencil 96-item test measuring general functioning, intelligence, visual activity, visual and coordination skills, physical coordination, mechanical skills, graphic and clerical skills, general clerical skills, leadership ability, tolerance in interpersonal relations, organization identification, conscientiousness and reliability, efficiency under stress, and solitary work. Each item is rated on importance to the job, on a 4-point, equal-interval scale ranging from "little or none" to "outstanding." An ability form also may be used to assess the incumbent's strength in the relative skills and attributes.

Format: Examiner required; suitable for group use; untimed: 45 minutes

Scoring: Hand key; may be computer scored

Cost: 25 tests $34; 25 score sheets $12; examiner's manual $15

Publisher: McGraw-Hill/London House

South African Wechsler Adult Individual Intelligence Scale

Copyright: 1983

Population: Adults; ages 18 to 59

Purpose: Assesses intelligence of Afrikaans and English-speaking South Africans

Description: Multiple-item paper–pencil and performance test consisting of five verbal tests covering information, comprehension, arithmetic, digit span, and similarities, and five performance tests covering picture completion, object assembly, block design, digit symbols, and picture arrangement. An IQ score can be obtained by adding the standard scores of the tests.

Format: Examiner required; not suitable for group use; timed: time not available

Scoring: Not available

Cost: Contact publisher

Publisher: Human Sciences Research Council

SRA Reading–Arithmetic Index (RAI–12)

Copyright: 1995

Population: Adults

Purpose: Assesses general reading and computational achievement up to grade level of 12; used for entry-level position and training programs where basic skills of applicants are often too low to be reliably evaluated by typical selection of tests

Description: Two multiple-item tests measuring reading skills (picture–word association, word decoding, phrase comprehension, sentence comprehension, paragraph comprehension I, and paragraph comprehension II) and arithmetic skills (addition and subtraction, multiplication and division, fractions, decimals

and percentages, square roots and powers, and geometry and word problems). The score reflects the highest developmental level passed.

Format: Examiner required; suitable for group use; untimed: 35 minutes

Scoring: Hand key; computer scored

Cost: 25 test booklets $42.00; examiner's manual $15.00

Publisher: McGraw-Hill/London House

TABE™ Work-Related Foundation Skills (TABE–WF)

Copyright: 1994

Population: Adults

Purpose: Assesses adults' foundation skills in reading, mathematics, and language

Description: Multiple item paper–pencil multiple-choice test that evaluates basic reading, math, and language skills. There are three forms, each presenting all questions and situations within the context of a specific workplace environment: Health, Business/Office, and Trade/Technical. In addition, there is a fourth, General Form, that covers a variety of work contexts. The test produces a variety of results including norm-referenced scores useful for growth measurement and student placement for reading, language, mathematics computation, applied mathematics, total mathematics, and total battery. Computer version available.

Format: Examiner required; suitable for group use; untimed: 120 minutes

Scoring: Machine scored; hand key; computer scored

Cost: 25 test books and examiner's manual $59.25

Publisher: CTB/McGraw-Hill

TABE™ Work-Related Problem Solving (TABE–PS)

Copyright: 1994

Population: Adults

Purpose: Measures a wide range of problem-solving competencies in a variety of work-related applications

Description: Multiple-item paper–pencil essay/short-answer and verbal performance assessment that helps employers, educators, and training professionals diagnose how an examinee deals with various aspects of problem solving: defining the problem, examining the problem, suggesting possible solutions, evaluating solutions, and extending the meaning of the solution. Tasks are based on realistic workplace situations and measure problem-solving skills. Computer version available.

Format: Examiner required; suitable for group use; untimed: 60 minutes

Scoring: Machine scored; hand key; computer scored

Cost: 25 test books and examiner's manual/scoring guide $34.75

Publisher: CTB/McGraw-Hill

Technical and Scientific Information Test, Technical Reading Comprehension Test, and General Science Test

Copyright: 1983

Population: Adolescents, adults

Purpose: Measures technical and scientific knowledge and technical reading comprehension; used with matriculated students in standards 7 to 9

Description: The General Science Test consists of two multiple-item paper–pencil subtests: The Technical and Scientific Information Test, which contains informational questions over general science topics, and The Technical Reading Comprehension Test, which contains a number of paragraphs with questions to determine the extent to which articles of a technical nature can be understood. The two tests are administered in separate booklets. The tests are restricted to competent persons properly registered with the South African Medical and Dental Council. Available in Afrikaans.

Format: Examiner required; suitable for group use; timed: time not available

Scoring: Hand key; examiner evaluated

Cost: Contact publisher

Publisher: Human Sciences Research Council

Technical Test Battery (TTB) Numerical Computation (NT2.1)

Copyright: 1995

Population: Adults

Purpose: Measures basic ability to work with numbers in a technical setting

Description: Multiple-choice 36-item test assessing the understanding of mathematical relationships and operations and the ability to calculate quickly and accurately. In each item, one number or operation has been omitted from an equation. The examinee must select the missing element from five possible answers. Fractions, decimals, and percentages are included, but more complex notations or operations are omitted deliberately. The range extends from minimal educational qualifications to high school graduate level.

Format: 10 minutes

Scoring: Hand key; machine scored; scoring service available

Cost: Contact publisher

Publisher: Saville and Holdsworth Ltd.

Test A/8: Arithmetic

Copyright: Not provided

Population: Adolescents, adults

Purpose: Measures general arithmetic ability; used with technical college students and applicants for clerical and trade positions with 8 to 12 years of education for employee selection and placement

Description: Multiple-item paper–pencil test measuring general arithmetic ability. Norms are available for technical college students and matriculated males. The test is restricted to competent persons properly registered with the South African Medical and Dental Council. Available in English and Afrikaans.

Format: Examiner required; suitable for group use; timed: Matriculants 30 minutes; nonmatriculants 40 minutes

Scoring: Hand key; examiner evaluated

Cost: Contact publisher

Publisher: Human Sciences Research Council

Test of English for International Communication (TOEIC)

Copyright: Not provided

Population: Adults nonnative speakers of English

Purpose: Measures English language proficiency required in business; used as a basis for employee selection and placement, for decisions concerning assignment, and to measure achievement in company-sponsored English language programs

Description: Paper–pencil 200-item multiple-choice test of English language skills. Section I contains 100 listening comprehension items administered via audiotape. Section II contains 100 reading items. Total test scale scores range from 10 to 990; scale subscores for Sections I and II range from 5 to 495. The scores are correlated to direct measures of listening, speaking, reading, and writing, as well as to indirect measures. The test is used by multinational corporations, language schools, government agencies, public/private organizations for hiring, assignment to overseas posts, and assignment to/promotion within departments where English is desirable. Application to take the test is made through national/regional offices. A cassette player is required.

Format: Examiner required; suitable for group use; timed: 2 hours 30 minutes

Scoring: Hand key; may be computer scored

Cost: Contact publisher

Publisher: Educational Testing Service

Test of Practical Judgment—Form 62
Alfred J. Cardall

Copyright: Not provided

Population: Adults

Purpose: Determines employee ability to use practical judgment in solving problems; used to screen for management and sales positions

Description: Multiple-item paper–pencil multiple-choice test of judgment factors that may be used in conjunction with intelligence testing. The test also may be used for screening and for selection and placement of individuals whose work involves thinking, planning, or getting along with people. The test examines such factors as empathy, drive, and social maturity. Materials include five tests, a key, and a manual. Also available in French.

Format: Examiner required; suitable for group use; untimed: 30 minutes

Scoring: Hand key

Cost: Contact publisher

Publisher: Institute of Psychological Research, Inc.

Test of Work Competency and Stability
A. Gaston Leblanc

Copyright: Not provided

Population: Adults; ages 21 to 67

Purpose: Measures stress levels in motor coordination and mental concentration; used to evaluate psychological capacity for work performance

Description: Multiple-item paper–pencil interview and manual dexterity test of six factors related to work competency in industry, including work stability, assertiveness, persistence and concentration, psychomotor steadiness, capacity, and stress tolerance. Scores screen workers and provide information for rehabilitation. The materials are provided in a set that includes a manual, interview questionnaire sheets, mirror tracing patterns, tapping patterns, and record blanks. Also available in French.

Format: Examiner required; not suitable for group use; untimed: time varies

Scoring: Hand key

Cost: Contact publisher

Publisher: Institute of Psychological Research, Inc.

Thurstone Test of Mental Alertness

L. L. Thurstone, Thelma Gwinn Thurstone

Copyright: 1959

Population: Adults

Purpose: Measures an individual's capacity to acquire new knowledge and skills and to use what has been learned to solve problems; measures individual differences in ability to learn and perform mental tasks of varying types and complexity

Description: Test with 126 items measuring linguistic (vocabulary) and quantitative (arithmetic) factors. This test is available in two forms, A and B.

Format: Examiner required; suitable for group use; timed: 20 minutes

Scoring: Hand key; computer scored

Cost: 25 test booklets $49.00; examiner's manual $15.00

Publisher: McGraw-Hill/London House

Understanding Communication

Thelma Gwinn Thurstone

Copyright: 1984

Population: Adults

Purpose: Measures comprehension of verbal material in short sentences and phrases; used for industrial screening and selection of clerical, first-line supervisor, or other positions that need to understand written material and communications

Description: Paper–pencil 40-item single-score test measuring verbal comprehension through the ability to identify the one of four words that will complete a given sentence.

Format: Examiner required; suitable for group use; timed: 15 minutes

Scoring: Hand key

Cost: 25 test booklets $36; score key $10; examiner's manual $15

Publisher: McGraw-Hill/London House

VCWS 14—Integrated Peer Performance

Copyright: 1977

Population: Adults

Purpose: Measures an individual's instruction-following ability and color discrimination skills; stimulates interaction among workers

Description: Manual test measuring an individual's ability to follow instructions and discriminate between colors. The test emphasizes the ability to interact effectively with both peers and supervisors and the ability to work as a team member in order to complete a task. Three or four examinees are seated and given colored assembly pieces and an assembly pattern booklet. The examiner places assembly boards on the table and moves them from worker to worker every 20 seconds. Each examinee performs his or her portion of the assembly and then waits for the next assembly board. As each assembly board is completed, the examiner inspects each board and informs the appropriate examinee of any errors made.

Format: Examiner required; suitable for group use; timed: time not available

Scoring: Examiner evaluated

Cost: $2,695.00

Publisher: Valpar International Corporation

VCWS 3—Numerical Sorting

Copyright: 1974

Population: Adults

Purpose: Measures an individual's ability to perform work tasks requiring sequential sorting of a combined numerical/alphabetical problem; provides insight into spatial and form perception, accuracy, and attention to detail in transferring data

Description: Manual test measuring the ability to sort, file, and categorize objects using a numerical code. The individual must transfer 42 of 56 numerically ordered white plastic chips inserted into correspondingly marked slots in Board I to the appropriate slots in Board II. After the chip placements on Board II are scored, the individual transfers the chips back to Board I. Work activities related to the test include examining, grading, and sorting; keeping records and receipts; recording or transmitting verbal or coded information; and posting verbal or numerical data on stock lists. The test should not be used with individuals with severe impairment of the upper extremities.

Format: Examiner required; not suitable for group use; timed: time not available

Scoring: Examiner evaluated

Cost: $1,495.00

Publisher: Valpar International Corporation

VCWS 6—Independent Problem Solving

Copyright: 1974

Population: Adults

Purpose: Measures the ability to perform work tasks requiring visual comparison and proper selection of abstract designs; may be used with individuals with mental retardation and hearing impairment

Description: Manual test measuring a person's ability to perform work tasks requiring a visual comparison of colored shapes. Work activities relating to the test are characterized by emphasis on decision-making and instruction-following abilities. The test should not be used with individuals with severe impairment of the upper extremities or severe visual impairment.

Format: Examiner required; not suitable for group use; timed: time not available

Scoring: Examiner evaluated

Cost: $1,495.00

Publisher: Valpar International Corporation

Wonderlic Basic Skills Test (WBST)
Eliot R. Long, Winifred L. Clonts, Victor S. Artese

Copyright: 1994

Population: Adolescents, adults; ages 15 and above

Purpose: Used in employment and job training to measure job-related math and verbal skills and for vocational guidance

Description: Multiple-choice paper–pencil test with two subtests: Test of Verbal Skills (50 questions, 20 minutes) and Test of Quantitative Skills (45 questions, 20 minutes). JRT scale scores, scores by job requirements, and scores by grade level are yielded. Verbal forms VS1, VS2, and Quantitative forms QS1, QS2 are available. A sixth-grade reading level is required.

Format: Examiner required; timed: 40 minutes

Scoring: Computer scored; test scoring service available from publisher

Cost: Composite of both tests: 25 tests $110.00, 100 tests $245.00; Verbal Skills: 25 tests $80.00, 100 tests $165.00; Quantitative: 25 tests $80.00, 100 tests $165.00

Publisher: Wonderlic Personnel Test, Inc.

Word Fluency

Copyright: 1961

Population: Adults

Purpose: Determines the speed of relevant verbal associations and an individual's ability to produce appropriate words rapidly; used for vocational counseling and personnel selection in fields requiring communication skills, such as supervision, management, and sales

Description: Paper–pencil 80-item test measuring verbal fluency.

Format: Examiner required; suitable for group use; timed: 10 minutes

Scoring: Hand key

Cost: 25 test booklets $34; examiner's manual $15

Publisher: McGraw-Hill/London House

Work Environment Questionnaire for Identification of Original Problems (WEQ)
John R. Turney, Stanley L. Cohen

Copyright: 1977

Population: Adults

Purpose: Measures problem areas, corrections, and job satisfaction of specific army work settings; used in career counseling of soldiers

Description: Multiple-item paper–pencil questionnaire

Format: Group or individual administration; examiner required; untimed

Scoring: Hand key; examiner evaluated

Cost: $24.00

Publisher: Select Press

Work Keys Applied Mathematics Test

Copyright: 1992

Population: Adolescents, adults

Purpose: Assesses mathematical problem solving

Description: 30-item multiple-choice criterion-referenced test across five levels. Form 10BB is available. A test form, formula sheet, answer folder, administrator's manual, and videotaped administrator's manual are used.

Format: Individual administration; suitable for group use; examiner required; timed: 45 minutes

Scoring: Machine scored; test scoring service available from publisher

Cost: $4.00 per examinee; 15% discount for K–12 schools

Publisher: American College Testing

Work Keys Observation Test

Copyright: 1995

Population: Adolescents, adults

Purpose: Assesses observation skills in the workplace

Description: 36-item multiple-choice criterion-referenced test across four levels. A test videotape, answer folder, administrator's manual, and videotaped administrator's manual are used.

Format: Individual administration; suitable for group use; examiner required; timed: 60 minutes

Scoring: Machine scored; test scoring service available from publisher

Cost: $7.00 per examinee; 15% discount for K–12 schools

Publisher: American College Testing

Work Keys Reading for Information Test

Copyright: 1992

Population: Adolescents, adults

Purpose: Used in program evaluation, skills profiling, and selection to assess reading skills

Description: Multiple-choice 30-item criterion-referenced test across five levels. Form 13AA is available. A test booklet, answer folder, administrator's manual, and videotaped administrator's manual are used.

Format: Individual administration; suitable for group use; examiner required; timed: 45 minutes

Scoring: Machine scored; test scoring service available from publisher

Cost: $4.00 per examinee; 15% discount for K–12 schools

Publisher: American College Testing

Work Keys Writing Test

Copyright: 1992

Population: Adolescents, adults

Purpose: Used for program evaluation, skills profiling, and selection to assess business writing skills

Description: Six-prompt essay test across five levels. Form 10CC is available. An audiotape, answer folder, administrator's manual, and videotaped administrator's manual are used.

Format: Individual administration; suitable for group use; examiner required; timed: 40 minutes

Scoring: Holistic scoring by publisher only

Cost: $12.50 per examinee; $16.00 if administered with *Work Keys Writing Test*

Publisher: American College Testing

Work Readiness Profile

Helga A. Rowe

Copyright: 1995

Population: Adolescents, adults; ages 15 and above

Purpose: Used with individuals with impairments or disabilities as a preparation for employment

Description: Multiple-choice 12-factor paper–pencil oral response interview with the following categories: health, hearing, vision, travel, movement, fine motor, gross motor, social skills, communication, literacy, and numeracy. A generic answer booklet is available.

Format: Individual/self-administered; examiner required; untimed

Scoring: Examiner evaluated

Cost: A $70.00

Publisher: The Australian Council for Educational Research Limited

Work Skills Series (WSS) Understanding Instructions (VWP1)

Copyright: 1988

Population: Adults

Purpose: Assesses the ability to follow and understand simple written instructions

Description: Test with 39 items measuring the ability to follow and apply instructions in practical and work-related situations. Candidates read a series of paragraphs outlining particular work procedures and are then tested on their understanding of these. The contents have been designed to look like those typically found in many technical, production, or manufacturing environments.

Format: 12 minutes

Scoring: Hand key; machine scored; scoring service available

Cost: Contact publisher

Publisher: Saville and Holdsworth Ltd.

Work Skills Series (WSS) Visual Checking (CWP3)

Copyright: 1990

Population: Adults

Purpose: Assesses the ability to check that one set of visual indicators corresponds with another

Description: Thirty-item test measuring the ability to check that one set of indicators corresponds to another set of indicators according to a number of simple rules. This skill is important whenever production or control equipment is used by semiskilled operators.

Format: 7 minutes

Scoring: Hand key; machine scored; scoring service available

Cost: Contact publisher

Publisher: Saville and Holdsworth Ltd.

Work Skills Series (WSS) Working with Numbers (NWP2)

Copyright: 1988

Population: Adults

Purpose: Assesses the ability to perform simple numerical computations, such as in stock control

Description: Test with 36 items measuring the ability to apply the basic rules of arithmetic to practical and work-related situations. The test content involves dealing quickly with stock levels and use of various types of mechanical components. This test is relevant to any job in industry or manufacturing where the appropriate application of basic arithmetical skills is important.

Format: 10 minutes

Scoring: Hand key; machine scored; scoring service available

Cost: Contact publisher

Publisher: Saville and Holdsworth Ltd.

Attitudes

Abbreviated Reid Report

Copyright: 1996

Population: Adults

Purpose: Assesses an applicant's attitudes and

experiences related to integrity, social behavior, substance abuse, and personal achievements

Description: Multipurpose 55-question test; used to hire more productive, conscientious employees and reduce turnover, shrinkage, and absenteeism

Format: 15 minutes

Scoring: I-Fax (automated scoring platform that returns test results via fax), Provoice (front-end applicant telephone testing program), Fax-In, Phone-In, Mail-In or PC software

Cost: Ranges from $8.50 to $18.00

Publisher: Reid Psychological Systems

Alienation Index Survey (AI Survey)

Copyright: 1978

Population: Adults

Purpose: Assesses work-related attitudes of job applicants; identifies individuals with alienated attitudes that reduce performance and cause poor morale; used for applicant screening and employee selection

Description: Multiple-item paper–pencil pre-employment survey assessing the attitudes of job applicants toward employers, supervisors, co-workers, work, pay, and benefits. The survey identifies applicants with alienated attitudes in these areas who have a high potential for becoming problem employees. The survey is administered, scored, and interpreted in-house for immediate use by personnel/human relations/security specialists by license to Psychological Systems Corporation. The survey is also available as part of the PASS Booklet (which includes the Trustworthiness Attitude Survey and the Emotional Stability Survey) or PASS-II Booklet (along with Trustworthiness Attitude Survey) for more complete applicant assessment.

Format: Examiner required; suitable for group use; untimed: 8–12 minutes

Scoring: Examiner evaluated

Cost: Contact publisher

Publisher: Predictive Surveys Corporation

Attitude Survey Program for Business and Industry: Organization Survey

Copyright: 1984

Population: Adults

Purpose: Measures attitudes of hourly employees and first-line supervisors and provides an overview of company conditions; used to identify reasons for low morale, productivity, and absenteeism; assess employee acceptance of change; and determine training needs

Description: 93-item paper–pencil survey assessing the priorities and concerns of employees. Items cover the following areas: organization identification, job satisfaction, pay, benefits, supervisory leadership practices, work associates, general administrative practices, supervisory administrative practices, work organization, work efficiency, performance and personal development, communication effectiveness, and reactions to survey. A general comment section is also included; transcription and analysis are optional. Administration occurs on company premises under the supervision of a company official or McGraw-Hill/London House employee. Narrative reports, feedback presentations, and follow-up surveys are also available.

Format: Examiner required; suitable for group use; untimed: 50 minutes or less

Scoring: Computer scored by London House

Cost: Standard surveys $10/each; 100 modified surveys $1,500.00; 100 customized surveys $1,500.00

Publisher: McGraw-Hill/London House

Campbell Organizational Survey (COS)

David P. Campbell

Copyright: 1995

Population: Adults

Purpose: Assesses employee attitudes toward organizations

Description: Paper–pencil 67-item test with 17 scales plus an overall index. A sixth-grade reading level is required. Examiner must have taken psychology courses. Available also in

Spanish and French.

Format: Self-administered; suitable for group use; untimed

Scoring: Computer scored; test scoring service available from publisher

Cost: Varies by volume

Publisher: NCS Assessments

Career Attitudes and Strategies Inventory
John L. Holland, Gary D. Gottfredson

Copyright: 1994

Population: Adults

Purpose: Assesses an employee's current work situation and includes common attitudes as well as strategies for coping with job, family, co-workers, and supervisors; used for career counseling

Description: Multiple-choice 130-item true–false test with nine scales: geographical barriers, job satisfaction, work involvement, skill development, dominant style, career worries, interpersonal abuse, family commitment, and risk-taking style. Materials used include a manual, inventory booklet, hand-scorable answer sheet, and interpretive summary booklet.

Format: Self-administered; suitable for group use; untimed

Scoring: Hand key; self scored

Cost: Introductory kit $60.00

Publisher: Psychological Assessment Resources, Inc.

Career Decision Scale (CDS)
Samuel H. Osipow, Clarke G. Carney, Jane Winer, Barbara Yanico, Maryanne Koschir

Copyright: 1987

Population: Adolescents, adults; Grade 9 through college

Purpose: Identifies barriers preventing an individual from making career decisions; used as a basis for career counseling, to monitor the effectiveness of career counseling programs, and for research on career indecisiveness

Description: Paper–pencil 10-item inventory assessing a limited number of circumstances that cause problems in reaching and implementing educational and career decisions. Items 1 and 2 measure degree of certainty (Certainty scale). Items 3–18 measure career indecision (Indecision scale). Item 19 is open-ended. Individuals rate each item on a 4-point scale from 1 ("not like me") to 4 ("like me") to indicate the extent to which each item describes their personal situations. Scores are reported as percentiles. The manual includes data regarding validity and reliability and norms for various age and grade levels.

Format: Examiner/self-administered; suitable for group use; untimed: 10–15 minutes

Scoring: Hand scorable answer sheet; examiner evaluated

Cost: Kit (manual, 50 test booklets) $34.00

Publisher: Psychological Assessment Resources, Inc.

Career Survival: Strategic Job and Role Planning
Edgar H. Schein

Copyright: 1993

Population: Adults; managers, employees, human resources specialists

Purpose: Identifies the key elements of an individual's job now and in the future and how to set appropriate priorities

Description: Helps managers, employers, and human resources specialists answer such questions as What does the job currently involve? How will the job itself change over the next few years? How will the environment around the job change? Do these changes mean that the job may require a different person? *Career Survival* helps organizations more accurately forecast their needs, and individual employees effectively structure their priorities and future plans.

Format: Self-paced

Scoring: Self-scoring

Cost: $9.95

Publisher: Pfeiffer and Company International Publishers, Inc.

Change Agent Questionnaire (CAS)
Jay Hall, Martha S. Williams

Copyright: 1995

Population: Adults

Purpose: Evaluates attitudes toward change; used in programs on the dynamics of change with teachers, trainers, managers, members of the clergy, politicians, probation officers, counselors, and social workers to bring about positive changes

Description: Multiple-item paper–pencil self-report inventory assessing an individual's philosophies, strategies, and approaches concerning the concept of change. The inventory measures basic assumptions regarding the process and duration of change, particularly that which is brought about through the efforts of change agents (individuals who effect change by actively influencing the thoughts and behaviors of others). The inventory yields five scores, which are profiled according to a grid format based on the work of Herbert Kelman concerning change agents.

Format: Self-administered; suitable for group use; untimed: time varies

Scoring: Self-scored

Cost: $8.95 each

Publisher: Teleometrics International, Inc.

Child/Elder Care Survey

Copyright: 1994, 1996

Population: Adults

Purpose: Assesses employees' concerns regarding their family and work responsibilities

Description: Survey with 76 questions designed to provide a comprehensive analysis of employee care concerns and how they affect work performance. The survey results focus on the entire workforce and deliver information in a group format so that decisions can be made that will benefit the entire organization.

Format: 15 minutes

Scoring: Fax-In, Phone-In, Mail-In or PC software

Cost: Ranges from $8.50 to $18.00

Publisher: Reid Psychological Systems

Conflict Management Survey (CMS)
Jay Hall

Copyright: 1996

Population: Adults

Purpose: Assesses the manner in which individuals interpret the meaning of conflict and, consequently, the manner in which they handle it; used in labor–management sessions and community relations laboratories to identify outcomes of conflict

Description: Multiple-item paper–pencil self-report inventory assessing an individual's reaction to, and consequent handling of, interpersonal, group, and intergroup conflict. Analysis employs a grid format measuring two dimensions: concern for personal goals and concern for relationships. The survey identifies five styles of conflict management: win–lose, yield–lose, lose–leave, compromise, and synergistic. Normative data and conversion tables are provided for transforming raw scores on the five styles into a fivefold conflict management profile. These profiles provide a basis for establishing constructive conflict-handling behavior.

Format: Self-administered; suitable for group use; untimed: time varies

Scoring: Self-scored

Cost: $8.95 each

Publisher: Teleometrics International, Inc.

Creativity Questionnaire
Allan Cameron

Copyright: 1994

Population: All ages

Purpose: Assesses innovation, creativity, and rule-conformity

Description: Multiple-choice 48-item computer-administered paper–pencil test. The categories are originality, rule consciousness, openness to change, assertiveness, and independence. An 11-year-old reading level is required.

Format: Individual/self-administered; suitable for group use; examiner required; untimed: 10 minutes

Scoring: Computer scored; test scoring service available from publisher

Cost: Specimen Set $60.00

Publisher: Selby MillSmith Ltd.

Cross-Cultural Adaptability Inventory™ (CCAI™)
Colleen Kelley, Judith Meyers

Copyright: 1995

Population: Adults

Purpose: A "culture general" test used to assess an individual's ability to adapt to other cultures

Description: Paper–pencil 50-item test that measures an individual's cultural adaptability

Format: Self-administered; not suitable for group use; untimed

Scoring: Self-scored

Cost: $5.00

Publisher: NCS Assessments

Culture Shock Inventory (CSI)
W. J. Reddin

Copyright: 1994

Population: Adults

Purpose: Assesses an individual's susceptibility to culture shock; used to acquaint those who expect to work outside their own culture with potentially difficult areas

Description: Multiple-item paper–pencil test consisting of scales assessing Western ethnocentrism, cross-cultural experience, cognitive flex, behavioral flex, cultural knowledge (specific and general), customs acceptance, and interpersonal sensitivity. The test may be used with managers, spouses, and older children and in colleges.

Format: Self-administered; suitable for group use; untimed: 20–30 minutes

Scoring: Hand key

Cost: Test kit (10 test copies, fact sheet, user's guide) $40.00

Publisher: Organizational Tests Ltd.

Decision Making Inventory
Richard Johnson, William Coscarelli, JaDean Johnson

Copyright: 1983

Population: Adolescents, adults

Purpose: Identifies an individual's preferred decision-making style; used in career counseling, marriage therapy, task groups, and instructional programs

Description: Paper–pencil 20-item one-page instrument assessing an individual's preferred style of making decisions. Individuals rate a series of statements concerning steps in the decision-making process on a 6-point scale ranging from "never" to "always" to indicate the degree to which each item is true for themselves. Scoring and interpretation are based on Johnson's theory that suggests that information can be gathered in a systematic or spontaneous manner and this information is analyzed either externally or internally. The manual describes the theory in detail, as well as the development of the scale, scoring procedures, and examples of its use in counseling and task groups.

Format: Examiner required; suitable for group use; untimed: time varies

Scoring: Examiner evaluated

Cost: Kit (manual, 2 scoring grids, 25 inventories) $35; 50 inventories $28

Publisher: Marathon Consulting and Press

Development and Use of the Adjective Rating Scale (ARS)
Edward F. Kelly, Ernest T. Pascarella, Patrick Terenzini

Copyright: 1978

Population: Adults

Purpose: Assesses students' attitudes toward courses and programs

Description: Paper–pencil 4-point scale questionnaire containing 24 adjectives

Format: Group administered; requires examiner; untimed

Scoring: Examiner evaluated

Cost: $27.84

Publisher: Select Press

Development of a Core Attitude Study Questionnaire for International Use
Geert Hofstede

Copyright: 1977

Population: Adults

Purpose: Measures employee attitudes

Description: Multiple-choice 60-item questionnaire

Format: Examiner required; suitable for group use; untimed

Scoring: Examiner evaluated

Cost: $24.00

Publisher: Select Press

Diagnosing Organizational Culture
Roger Harrison, Herb Stakes

Copyright: 1993

Population: Adults; organizations

Purpose: Designed to help identify the shared values and beliefs that constitute an organization's culture

Description: Organizations can use *Diagnosing Organizational Culture* for team building, organizational development, productivity improvement, and human resources development. It defines four cultures basic to most organizations: Power, Role, Achievement, and Support.

Format: Self-administered; 2–4 hours

Scoring: Self-scored

Cost: $8.95; Trainer's Package $24.95

Publisher: Pfeiffer and Company International Publishers, Inc.

Diversity Awareness Profile (DAP)
K. Stinson

Copyright: 1992

Population: Adults

Purpose: Helps people become more aware of their behaviors, evaluate their own behaviors, and modify behaviors to be empowering and respectful to all people

Description: The DAP is based on the belief that if people discriminate, judge, or isolate others, it is unintentional. These self-scoring instruments are based on information gathered in a series of focus groups and one-on-one interviews. The groups included older workers, women, people with disabilities, African Americans, Native Americans, Hispanics, and other groups that experience discrimination.

Format: Self-administered; 2 hours

Scoring: Self-scored

Cost: $3.95

Publisher: Pfeiffer and Company International Publishers, Inc.

Empathy Test
Williard A. Kerr, B. J. Speroff

Copyright: 1993

Population: Adolescents, adults

Purpose: Measures empathic ability; used to select managerial and supervisory personnel and graduate students

Description: Multiple-item paper–pencil test measuring the ability to put oneself in another person's position, establish rapport, and anticipate another person's reactions, feelings, and behavior. Empathy is measured as a variable unrelated to intelligence and most other attitudes. Three forms—Form A, blue-collar emphasis; Form B, white-collar emphasis; and Form C, Canadian emphasis—are available.

Format: Examiner required; suitable for group use; timed: 15 minutes

Scoring: Examiner evaluated

Cost: Specimen Set $4.00; 25 tests (specify form) $3.50

Publisher: Psychometric Affiliates

Employee Attitude Inventory (EAI)

Copyright: 1989

Population: Adults

Purpose: Identifies employees who might steal or engage in costly counterproductive acts in the workplace; used in investigative and organizational assessment of honesty and as a guide for in-house promotions

Description: Paper–pencil 179-item test measuring theft admissions, attitudes, and suspicions; drug-abuse tendencies; and job dissatisfaction and burnout. A validity scale is included. Although the test is self-administered, it may be given orally to illiterates.

Format: Suitable for group use; untimed: 30 minutes

Scoring: Computer scored; scoring service available from publisher

Cost: $9 to $18 per booklet depending on scoring method and volume ordered

Publisher: McGraw-Hill/London House

Employee Safety Inventory (ESI)

Copyright: 1988

Population: Adults

Purpose: Assesses attitudes toward on-the-job safety; used for screening, placement, and training of job applicants and current employees

Description: Paper–pencil multiple-choice short-answer test yielding scores in four areas (Risk Avoidance, Stress Tolerance, Safety Control, and Validity). Scores on a supplemental scale (Driver Attitudes), and a composite are also available. Materials include ESI test booklet, ESI Interpretation Guide, and ESI Administrator's Guide. Must purchase a minimum of 25 booklets.

Format: Examiner required; suitable for group use; untimed: time varies

Scoring: Computer scored; test scoring service available from publisher

Cost: $6 to $13 per test depending on volume ordered

Publisher: McGraw-Hill/London House

Employment Inventory (EI)
George Paajanen

Copyright: 1986

Population: Adolescents, adults; ages 15 and older

Purpose: Assesses job applicants' probability of productive and counterproductive job behavior

Description: Paper–pencil 97-item multiple-choice and true–false test assessing job applicants' probability of engaging in counterproductive behavior in an hourly job and probability of voluntarily remaining on the job for at least 3 months. Questions are directed toward the applicant's opinions, attitudes, and background. The test yields a Performance score and a Tenure score. The Performance score indicates the likelihood the employee will be reliable, follow rules, have a good attendance record, and be strongly motivated. The Tenure score indicates the likelihood of premature turnover, another aspect of counterproductive job behavior. Scoring is accomplished using a disk-based software operating on PC systems, or by faxing/phoning to the publisher.

Format: Examiner required; suitable for group use; untimed: 15–20 minutes

Scoring: Computer scored

Cost: Based on volume: contact publisher

Publisher: Personnel Decisions International

Employment Values Inventory (EVI)
Adrian Savage

Copyright: 1990

Population: Adolescents, adults

Purpose: Used in education and employment applications to assess work and educational values

Description: Multiple-choice 168-item computer-administered paper–pencil criterion-referenced test with 14 work-related factors. A computer version using DOS is used. An 11-year-old reading level is required.

Format: Individual/self-administered; suitable for group use; examiner required; untimed: 20 minutes

Scoring: Computer scored; test scoring service available from publisher

Cost: Specimen Set $50.00

Publisher: Selby MillSmith Ltd.

Integrity Attitude Scale (Part I)

Copyright: 1988, 1996

Population: Adults

Purpose: Identifies trustworthy, productive employees who are likely to stay on the job; used as the foundation for many organizations' screening programs

Description: Scale with 83 questions allows applicants to reveal their attitudes toward integrity and general counterproductivity. Integrated Attitude scores have been shown to correlate with other measures of psychological balance: work motivation, low job turnover, and overall job performance. Extensive research demonstrates that this test strongly resists faking, is free of adverse impact, and produces little applicant resistance.

Format: 15 minutes

Scoring: Fax-In, Phone-In, Mail-In, or PC software

Cost: Ranges from $8.50 to $18.00

Publisher: Reid Psychological Systems

Interest Questionnaire for Indian South Africans (IQISA)

Copyright: 1969

Population: Adolescents

Purpose: Assesses interests of Indian pupils; used for vocational guidance

Description: Paper–pencil 210-item measure of seven categories of interests: language, art, social service, science, mechanical, business, and office work. The subject responds "like," "indifferent," or "dislike" for each item.

Format: Examiner required; suitable for group use; untimed: 2 hours

Scoring: Hand key; examiner evaluated

Cost: Contact publisher

Publisher: Human Sciences Research Council

Job Descriptive Index–Revised (JDI–REV)
Patricia C. Smith, Lorne M. Kendall, Charles L. Hulin

Copyright: 1985

Population: Ages 17 to 100

Purpose: Assesses an individual's job satisfaction

Description: Paper–pencil 72-item test consisting of five scales: Satisfaction with Work (18 items), Pay (9 items), Promotions (9 items), Supervision (18 items), and Co-Workers (18 items). Items are answered in "yes–no" format. The test yields five scores, one per scale. A scoring service is available by special arrangement with the publisher. A second-grade reading level is required. The *Job in General* (JIG) test may be administered as a follow-up. Suitable for use with individuals with hearing and physical disabilities. Available in French, Spanish, Chinese, etc.

Format: Self-administered; suitable for group use; untimed: 5 minutes

Scoring: Hand key; may be computer/machine scored

Cost: 100 test booklets (includes *Job in General*) $42.00; postage and handling $5.00

Publisher: Bowling Green State University

Job in General (JIG)
Gail H. Ironson, Patricia C. Smith, Michael T. Brannick

Copyright: 1985

Population: Adults

Purpose: Assesses overall job satisfaction

Description: Paper–pencil 18-item yes–no test assessing workers' job satisfaction. The test is to be administered following the *Job Descriptive Index* (JDI), which measures five specific areas of job satisfaction (see separate description). A scoring service is available by special arrangement with the publisher. A second-grade reading level is required. Suitable for use with individuals with hearing and physical disabilities.

Format: Self-administered; suitable for group use; untimed: 1 minute

Scoring: Hand key; may be computer/machine scored

Cost: 100 questionnaires $8; $2 postage and handling if administered separately from *Job Descriptive Index;* JIG is included with the JDI at no charge.

Publisher: Bowling Green State University

Job Search Attitude Inventory
John J. Liptak

Copyright: 1994

Population: Adolescents, adults

Purpose: Identifies positive and negative job search attitudes; used in employment counseling

Description: Paper–pencil 32-question test. A seventh-grade reading level is required.

Format: Individual/self-administered; untimed: 20 minutes

Scoring: Self-scored; no scoring service available

Cost: 25 forms $37.50

Publisher: JIST Works, Inc.

Kilmann-Saxton Culture-Gap Survey (CGS)
Ralph H. Kilmann, Mary J. Saxton

Copyright: 1983

Population: Adults

Purpose: Used in organizational development to assess corporate culture (actual vs. desired)

Description: Forced-choice 56-item test. Task support, task innovation, social relationships, and personal freedom are the scores yielded. Actual norms—28 items, desired norms—28 items. An eighth-grade reading level is required.

Format: Individual/group administered; untimed

Scoring: Self-scored

Cost: $6.75

Publisher: Xicom, Inc.

Kilmanns Organizational Belief Survey (OBS)
Ralph H. Kilmann, Ines Kilmann

Copyright: 1994

Population: Adults

Purpose: Used in organizational development

Description: Thirty-item Likert scale. External control, internal control, and mixed control are the scores yielded. An eighth-grade reading level is required.

Format: Individual/self-administered; suitable for group use; untimed

Scoring: Self-scored

Cost: $6.75

Publisher: Xicom, Inc.

Leadership Practices Inventory—Individual Contributor: Observer
James M. Kouzes, Barry Z. Posner

Copyright: 1993

Population: Informal leaders

Purpose: Helps nonmanagers understand behaviors that characterize exemplary leadership, identify their personal strengths as leaders, identify areas for improvement in their leadership practices, develop action plans, and plan how to share their results

Description: This instrument helps participants gather input from colleagues and/or supervisors. It can be administered to five to ten people, and it provides a helpful comparison of how others view a participant's current behaviors.

Format: 2 to 4 hours

Scoring: Peer scored

Cost: $3.95

Publisher: Pfeiffer and Company International Publishers, Inc.

Leadership Practices Inventory— Individual Contributor: Self
James M. Kouzes, Barry Z. Posner

Copyright: 1993

Population: Informal leaders

Purpose: Helps nonmanagers understand behaviors that characterize exemplary leadership, identify their personal strengths as leaders, identify areas for improvement in their leadership practices, and develop action plans for becoming better leaders

Description: Participants evaluate their own performance and effectiveness as leaders with this 30-item instrument. The accompanying guidebook includes instructions for scoring, interpreting the scores, and comparing scores from the observer instruments, worksheets to help interpret feedback and make improvement plans, and suggested action steps for developing the necessary leadership skills with an action-planning worksheet.

Format: 2 to 4 hours

Scoring: Self-scored

Cost: Contact publisher

Publisher: Pfeiffer and Company International Publishers, Inc.

M-Scale: An Inventory of Attitudes Toward Black/White Relations in the U.S.
James H. Morrison

Copyright: 1969

Population: Adults

Purpose: Assesses attitudes toward black/white relations; used in diversity training and research

Description: Likert-like scale 28-item test measuring race separationist attitudes vs. race integrationist attitudes. A 10th-grade reading level is required.

Format: Individual administration; suitable for group use; examiner required; untimed

Scoring: Examiner evaluated

Cost: $4.00 for 20 inventories with manual

Publisher: James H. Morrison

Management Change Inventory
W. J. Reddin, E. Keith Stewart

Copyright: 1981

Population: Adults

Purpose: Measures knowledge about change relations

Description: True–false 80-item test of knowledge of sound methods of introducing change at a worker and supervisory level. Topics covered include participation, speed, degree of information, training, resistance, and planning. The test emphasizes principles and common sense. Scores are reported in percentiles.

Format: Examiner required; suitable for group use; untimed: 2–5 minutes

Scoring: Self-scored; examiner evaluated

Cost: Kit (10 tests, instructions) $40.00

Publisher: Organizational Tests Ltd.

Management Inventory on Leadership, Motivation, and Decision-Making (MILMD)
Donald L. Kirkpatrick

Copyright: 1993

Population: Adults

Purpose: Assesses attitudes and knowledge; used as a training tool to determine the training needed, to stimulate classroom discussion, and to evaluate training programs

Description: Paper–pencil agree–disagree test

Format: Self-administered; suitable for group use; untimed: 15–20 minutes

Scoring: Self-scored

Cost: 20 tests and answer booklets, instructor's manual $30.00

Publisher: Donald L. Kirkpatrick, Ph.D.

Mentoring Style Appropriateness Scale
William A. Gray, Terry D. Anderson

Copyright: 1990

Population: Adults

Purpose: Assesses how accurately mentoring help is provided

Description: Multiple-choice paper–pencil test comprised of two subtests: one rates mentor's mentoring style appropriateness, and the other rates protégé's mentoring style appropriateness. A 10th-grade reading level is required.

Format: Self-administered; suitable for group use; untimed: 15 to 20 minutes

Scoring: Self-scored

Cost: $4/test

Publisher: Mentoring Institute, Inc.

Mentoring/Coaching Skills Assessment (MCSA)
Linda Phillips-Jones

Copyright: 1995

Population: Adults

Purpose: Assesses mentoring/coaching skills; used in business, industrial psychology, and self-improvement

Description: Likert scale 36-item 4-point test covering Listening, Encouraging, Inspiring/ Instilling Vision, Coaching, Instructing, Managing Risks, Opening Doors, Demonstrating Personal Mastery, and Giving Constructive Feedback. A mentor version and a colleague version are available.

Format: Individual administration; untimed

Scoring: Computer scored; test scoring service available from publisher

Cost: $60.00

Publisher: Mind Garden, Inc.

Miner Sentence Completion Scale: Form H
John B. Miner

Copyright: 1961

Population: Adults

Purpose: Measures an individual's hierarchic (bureaucratic) motivation; used for employee counseling and development and organizational assessment

Description: Multiple-item paper–pencil free-response or multiple-choice sentence completion test measuring an individual's motivation in terms of motivational patterns which fit the hierarchic (bureaucratic) organizational form. Both forms (free-response version or multiple-choice version, offering six alternatives for each stem) measure the following subscales: authority figures, competitive games, competitive situations, assertive role, imposing wishes, standing out from the group, and routine administrative functions. The basic scoring guide (for use with the free-response version) discusses categorizing the responses, the subscales, supervisory jobs, total scores, and the sample scoring sheet.

Format: Examiner required; suitable for group use; untimed: time varies

Scoring: Examiner evaluated

Cost: 50 Scales (specify free-response or multiple-choice version) $30.00; 64-page Basic Scoring Guide (includes supplementary scoring guides) $10.00

Publisher: Organizational Measurement Systems Press

Miner Sentence Completion Scale: Form P
John B. Miner

Copyright: 1981

Population: Adults

Purpose: Measures an individual's professional (specialized) motivation; used for employee counseling and development and organizational assessment

Description: Multiple-item paper–pencil free-response sentence completion test measuring motivation in terms of motivational patterns that fit the professional (specialized) organizational form. The test measures the following subscales: acquiring knowledge, independent action, accepting status, providing help, and professional commitment. Each test item consists of a sentence stem that individuals complete in their own words. The scoring guide discusses categorizing the responses, the subscales, actual scoring, reliability, normative data, use of Form P, and bibliographic notes.

Format: Examiner required; suitable for group use; untimed: time varies

Scoring: Examiner evaluated

Cost: 50 scales $30.00; scoring guide $10.00

Publisher: Organizational Measurement Systems Press

Miner Sentence Completion Scale: Form T
John B. Miner

Copyright: 1984

Population: Adults

Purpose: Measures an individual's task (entrepreneurial) motivation; used for employee counseling and development and organizational assessment

Description: Multiple-item paper–pencil free-response sentence-completion test measuring an individual's motivation in terms of patterns that fit the task (entrepreneurial) organizational form. The test measures the following subscales: self-achievement, avoiding risks, feedback of results, personal innovation, and planning for the future. These subscales are generally parallel to the five aspects of David McClelland's achievement situation. Each test item consists of a sentence stem that individuals complete in their own words. The scoring guide discusses categorizing the responses, the subscales, actual scoring, reliability, normative data, the use of the MSCS–Form T, and bibliographic notes.

Format: Examiner required; suitable for group use; untimed: time varies

Scoring: Examiner evaluated

Cost: 50 scales $30.00; scoring guide $10.00

Publisher: Organizational Measurement Systems Press

Motivation Analysis Test (MAT)
Arthur B. Sweney, Raymond B. Cattell, John L. Horn

Copyright: 1982

Population: Adolescents, adults; Grades 12 and above

Purpose: Measures motivational patterns in high school seniors and adults; used in a variety

of counseling situations in education and business

Description: Paper–pencil 208-item multiple-choice test providing 10 measures of comfort, social, and achievement needs. Five are basic drives: caution, sex, self-assertion, aggressiveness, and self-indulgence. Five are interests that develop and mature through learning experience: career, affection, dependency, responsibility, and self-fulfillment. For each of the 10 interest areas, scores measure drive or need level, satisfaction level, degree of conflict, and total motivational strength. Standard scores are provided for men and women together.

Format: Self-administered; suitable for group use; untimed: 50–60 minutes

Scoring: Hand key; computer scored; scoring service available from publisher

Cost: MAT Introductory Kit $33.75; 25 test booklets $30; 25 machine-scorable answer sheets $12.75; 50 hand-scorable answer sheets $10.50; 50 profile sheets $10.60; 4 scoring keys $16.25; manual $12.95; individual scoring report certificates $4.00–20.00

Publisher: Institute for Personality and Ability Testing, Inc.

MSI Mentoring Style Indicator for Business and Government
William A. Gray, Terry D. Anderson

Copyright: 1987

Population: Adults

Purpose: Selects, matches, and trains mentors and protégés

Description: Six-situation multiple-choice paper–pencil test. A 10th-grade reading level is required.

Format: Self-administered; suitable for group use; untimed: 15 to 20 minutes

Scoring: Self-scored

Cost: $8/test

Publisher: Mentoring Institute, Inc.

Observational Assessments of Temperament

Melany E. Baehr

Copyright: 1979

Population: Adults

Purpose: Provides self-assessment or observational assessments of behavior that can be used in either counseling or assessment center settings

Description: Paper–pencil test assessing three behavior factors that have been shown to be the most effective in predicting significant aspects of performance in higher-level positions: introversive/cautious vs. extroversive/impulsive, emotional/responsive vs. nonemotional/controlled, dependent/group oriented vs. self-reliant/self-oriented. When used in conjunction with the *Temperament Comparator*, the instrument provides a measure of insight through comparison of disguised and undisguised assessments of the same three behavior factors.

Format: Examiner required; suitable for group use; untimed: 10 minutes

Scoring: Hand key

Cost: 25 test booklets and manual $36

Publisher: McGraw-Hill/London House

Occupational Stress Inventory (OSI): Research Version

Samuel H. Osipow, Arnold Spokane

Copyright: 1985

Population: Adults

Purpose: Measures dimensions of occupational adjustment of individuals employed primarily in technical, professional, and managerial positions in school, service, and manufacturing settings

Description: Paper–pencil 140-item test measuring three dimensions of occupational adjustment: occupational stress, psychological strain, and coping resources. The instrument consists of three separate questionnaires. The Occupational Roles Questionnaire (ORQ; 6 scales with 10 items each) analyzes stress due to occupational roles. The Personal Strain Questionnaire (PSQ; 4 scales with 10 items each) measures psychological strain as reflected in behaviors and attitudes. The Personal Resources Questionnaire (PRQ; 4 scales with 10 items each) analyzes effective coping via personal resources. The profile form is used to convert raw scores to T-scores. The questionnaires may be administered together or separately. Can be used on IBM PCs and compatibles.

Format: Self-administered; suitable for group use; untimed: 20–40 minutes

Scoring: Self-scored; scoring/test scoring service available from publisher

Cost: Kit (manual, 25 reusable item booklets, 50 rating sheets, 50 profile forms) $67.00; Computer Version $295.00

Publisher: Psychological Assessment Resources, Inc.

Organizational Assessment Survey

Larry A. Braskamp, Martin L. Maehr

Copyright: 1985

Population: Adults

Purpose: Assesses organizational culture and employee commitment, assesses worker motivation by determining personal values and incentives, and evaluates the opportunities for fulfillment that individuals perceive in their present jobs

Description: Two hundred Likert-scale items measuring four aspects of the worker, job, and organization: accomplishment, recognition, power, and affiliation. Both group and individual reports are available. Individual reports provide employees feedback about their incentives, personal values, and job opportunities. A second type of individual report provides supervisors with insights into their own management style and the impact their styles have on the people they supervise. The group report provides feedback on organizational culture, degree of employee commitment, and areas of job satisfaction.

Format: Examiner/self-administered; suitable for group use; untimed: 1 hour

Scoring: Computer scored through publisher

Cost: Introductory kit (test materials, manual, and processing of 2 reports) $49.50

Publisher: MetriTech, Inc.

Personal Achievements Questionnaire

Copyright: 1996

Population: Adults

Purpose: Provides insight on how applicants assess their prior work performance

Description: Questionnaire with 19 items that can be used in conjunction with other screening tests to bring all of the relevant biographical and work history information together in one place to help verify the accuracy of information supplied by the applicant.

Format: 10 minutes

Scoring: Fax-In, Phone-In, Mail-In, or PC software

Cost: Ranges from $8.50 to $18.00

Publisher: Reid Psychological Systems

Personal Outlook Inventory (POI)

Copyright: 1987

Population: Adults

Purpose: Assesses the likelihood that a potential employee will try to steal cash, merchandise, or other company assets; designed to reduce employee theft

Description: Multiple-choice 37-item test has two scales: V-scale score indicates whether the instrument is valid for the examinee; S-scale score indicates the probability that the examinee will be fired for stealing.

Format: Examiner required; suitable for group use; untimed: 30 minutes

Scoring: Hand key

Cost: 25 test booklets $105.00; examiner's manual $13.00

Publisher: McGraw-Hill/London House

Personal Reaction Index (PRI)
Jay Hall

Copyright: 1980

Population: Adults

Purpose: Measures the degree to which employees feel they are encouraged to participate in the decision-making process; used in programs evaluating job satisfaction at all occupational levels and in management training and development programs

Description: Multiple-item paper–pencil inventory assessing the attitudes of subordinates toward the decision structure which governs their work. Measures the amount of influence subordinates feel they have in making work-related decisions and their consequent satisfaction with and commitment to those decisions. The resulting information provides information concerning the manager's use of/lack of use of the participative ethic with subordinates. Normative data are provided.

Format: Self-administered; suitable for group use; untimed: time varies

Scoring: Self-scored

Cost: $2.95 each

Publisher: Teleometrics International, Inc.

Personnel Reaction Blank (PRB)
Harrison G. Gough

Copyright: Not provided

Population: Adults

Purpose: Measures a dependability–conscientiousness factor among rank-and file workers; used by personnel officers for selecting new employees

Description: Paper–pencil 70-item test assessing interests and attitudes related to dependability and conscientiousness. The test is used with rank-and-file workers and is not recommended for management personnel. A manual explains the meaning of high and low scores. The test is restricted, and scoring keys are sold only to registered users.

Format: Self-administered; suitable for group use; untimed: 10–15 minutes

Scoring: Hand key

Cost: Preview kit (booklet, scoring keys, manual) $39.00

Publisher: Consulting Psychologists Press, Inc.

PSC-Survey A. D. T.
(For Alienation and Trustworthiness/Leniency)
Alan L. Strand, Mark L. Strand

Copyright: 1987

Population: Adolescents, adults; ages 16 and older

Purpose: Assesses predisposing attitudes toward work; assists in pre-employment screening of minimum-wage and high turnover positions

Description: True–false 100-item paper–pencil test with questions concerning alienation/motivation (40 items) and trustworthiness/leniency (60 items). This is one test in the PSC Survey series used in pre-employment screening. A fourth-grade reading level is required. This is a condensed version of the M. A. and L. T. Available in Spanish.

Format: Examiner required; suitable for group use; untimed: 15 minutes

Scoring: Self-scored; examiner evaluated

Cost: $6.00; volume discount

Publisher: Predictive Surveys Corporation

PSC-Survey L. T.
(For Leniency/Trust)
Alan L. Strand, Mark L. Strand

Copyright: 1987

Population: Adolescents, adults; ages 16 and older

Purpose: Assesses predisposing attitudes toward work; used for pre-employment screening

Description: True–false 100-item (2 subfactor) paper–pencil test with questions concerning leniency (20 items) and trustworthiness (80 items) yielding numerical scores. This is a revision of the 1987 T. A. Survey. It can be used for the Non-Management program (in conjunction with the Survey–S. A. and/or the Survey–A. D.). The Non-Management program screens for positions that have an advanced level of responsibility and/or security risk but are not in a supervisory capacity. The Management program screens for beginning and mid-level man-

agement positions. A fourth-grade reading level is required.

Format: Examiner required; suitable for group use; untimed: 15 minutes

Scoring: Self-scored; examiner evaluated

Cost: $6.00; volume discount

Publisher: Predictive Surveys Corporation

PSC-Survey M. A.
(For Motivation/Alienation)
Alan L. Strand, Mark L. Strand

Copyright: 1986

Population: Adolescents, adults

Purpose: Assesses predisposing attitudes toward work; assists in pre-employment screening of nonmanagement positions

Description: True–false 60-item (4 subfactor) paper–pencil test with questions concerning supervisors (18 items), companies (18 items), motivation (14 items), and workers (10 items). It is appropriate for positions that have an advanced level of responsibility and/or security risk but are not in a supervisory capacity. For a more comprehensive screening, use a combination of two or three of the following surveys: Survey–M. A., Survey–LT, Survey–A. D. A fourth-grade reading level is required. This is a revision of the 1986 A. I. Survey.

Format: Examiner required; suitable for group use; untimed: 15 minutes

Scoring: Self-scored; examiner evaluated

Cost: $6.00; volume discount

Publisher: Predictive Surveys Corporation

Quality Potential Assessment
Jay Hall

Copyright: 1995

Population: Adults

Purpose: Analyzes how the policies, practices, and procedures of an organization affect human potential

Description: Paper–pencil 40-question three-capsule answer test.

Format: Self-administered; untimed

Scoring: Computer scored

Cost: $1,500.00 for 1 to 150 persons; $10.00 for each additional person

Publisher: Teleometrics International, Inc.

Retirement Descriptive Index (RDI)
Patricia C. Smith, Lorne M. Kendall, Charles L. Hulin

Copyright: 1975

Population: Adults

Purpose: Assesses satisfaction with activities, finances, people, and health; used with retired persons and other nonworking adults

Description: Paper–pencil 63-item test consisting of four scales measuring satisfaction: Activities (18 items), Income (9 items), Persons (18 items), and Health (18 items). The items follow a "yes–no" format. The test yields scores for each of the four scales. A scoring service is available by special arrangement with the publisher. A second-grade reading level is required.

Format: Self-administered; suitable for group use; untimed: 10 minutes

Scoring: Hand key; may be computer/machine scored

Cost: 100 booklets $34

Publisher: Bowling Green State University

Risk Avoidance Scale

Copyright: 1996

Population: Adults

Purpose: Accurately assesses applicants' attitudes toward substance use

Description: Forty-question scale designed to provide employers with a cost-effective alternative or prescreen to expensive and invasive biochemical testing. This scale predicts the likelihood of substance use on the job, as well as compliance with safety regulations and policies in the workplace.

Format: 15 minutes

Scoring: I-Fax (automated scoring platform that returns test results via fax), Provoice (front-end applicant telephone testing program), Fax-In, Phone-In, Mail-In, or PC software

Cost: Ranges from $8.50 to $18.00

Publisher: Reid Psychological Systems

Safety and Substance Abuse Questionnaire

Copyright: 1996

Population: Adults

Purpose: Provides employers with admissions of recent drug use and information regarding safety attitudes and experiences

Description: Questionnaire with 46 items designed to reduce the number of applicants who have recently used illegal substances. In addition, this questionnaire helps save money by reducing the number of applicants whose previous behaviors might pose extreme risks to the workplace.

Format: 10 minutes

Scoring: Fax-In, Phone-In, Mail-In, or PC software

Cost: Ranges from $8.50 to $18.00

Publisher: Reid Psychological Systems

Self-Actualization Inventory (SAI)
W. J. Reddin

Copyright: 1994

Population: Adults

Purpose: Measures the degree to which an individual's needs are fulfilled; used to compare responses of managers and their subordinates

Description: Paper–pencil test covering the following needs: physical, security, relationships, respect, independence, and self-actualization.

Format: Self-administered; suitable for group use; untimed: 20–30 minutes

Scoring: Hand key

Cost: Test kit (10 test copies, fact sheet, user's guide) $40.00

Publisher: Organizational Tests Ltd.

Social Behavior Questionnaire

Copyright: 1996

Population: Adults

Purpose: Identifies social behavior that might not come out during an interview

Description: Questionnaire with 73 items that uncovers an applicant's experiences at work and elsewhere. These comprehensive questions offer an opportunity to uncover significant information about previous criminal behavior and relevant job experiences.

Format: 10 minutes

Scoring: Fax-In, Phone-In, Mail-In, or PC software

Cost: Ranges from $8.50 to $18.00

Publisher: Reid Psychological Systems

Specific Case Inventory (SCI)

Copyright: 1988

Population: Adolescents, adults

Purpose: Assesses the amount of information a subject has about a theft issue

Description: Paper–pencil 62-item multiple-choice survey that identifies persons with critical information about a specific theft incident. One score, the Information Index, is provided. The score rates the subject's knowledge about the incident from "no or very little information" to "substantial information." Suggested questions can be used by the investigator to conduct an individualized follow-up interview. Objective decisions concerning further action can then be based on the score and the accompanying follow-up data. An eighth-grade reading level is required. Computer version available for IBM and compatibles. Examiner must be trained in security interviewing as it relates to investigations.

Format: Examiner required; suitable for group use; untimed: 20 minutes

Scoring: Computer scored; scoring service available from publisher

Cost: $12 to $18 per test depending on volume ordered

Publisher: McGraw-Hill/London House

Stress Resiliency Profile (SRP)
Kenneth W. Thomas, Walter G. Tymon

Copyright: Present

Population: Adolescents, adults; Grades 9 through 12

Purpose: Assesses effective mental habits for managing stress

Description: Eighteen-item Likert scale. Deficiency focusing, necessitating, and low skill recognition are scores yielded. An eighth-grade reading level is required.

Format: Individual/self-administered; suitable for group use; untimed

Scoring: Self-scored

Cost: $6.75

Publisher: Xicom, Inc.

Supervisory Communication Relations Test (SCOM)
W. J. Reddin

Copyright: 1995

Population: Adults

Purpose: Measures an individual's understanding of sound communication methods; used before or after coaching training

Description: True–false 80-item paper–pencil test covering communication with subordinates, co-workers, and superiors. The test also assesses the ability to give orders and introduce change. The test covers verbal and nonverbal communication. Suitable for either blue- or white-collar supervision.

Format: Self-administered; suitable for group use; untimed: 20–30 minutes

Scoring: Hand key

Cost: Test kit (10 test copies, fact sheet, user's guide) $30.00

Publisher: Organizational Tests Ltd.

Supervisory Human Relations Test (SHR)
W. J. Reddin

Copyright: 1995

Population: Adults

Purpose: Measures an individual's attitude toward others; used before or after instruction in human relations

Description: True–false 80-item paper–pencil test measuring an individual's attitude toward superiors, co-workers, and subordinates. The test is not recommended as a test–retest device to discover the effects of training. Suitable for white- or blue-collar supervision.

Format: Self-administration; suitable for group use; untimed: 20–30 minutes

Scoring: Hand key

Cost: Test kit (10 test copies, fact sheet, user's guide) $30.00

Publisher: Organizational Tests Ltd.

Survey III

Copyright: 1996

Population: Adults

Purpose: Identifies the likelihood of current employees' participation in internal theft, on-the-job drug use, and other forms of counter-productive behavior

Description: Survey with 116 items that ranks employees on their attitudes regarding drug use and theft so that problem employees can be quickly identified. The survey helps answer organization needs for loss prevention, operations, general management, and human resources.

Format: 30 minutes

Scoring: Fax-In, Phone-In, Mail-In, or PC software

Cost: Ranges from $8.50 to $18.00

Publisher: Reid Psychological Systems

Survey of Work Values (SWV)
Steven Wollack, James G. Goodale,
Jan P. Wijting, Patricia C. Smith

Copyright: 1976

Population: Adults

Purpose: Assesses an individual's work values

Description: Paper–pencil 72-item test in which examinees use a 5-point scale (strongly agree to strongly disagree) to rate statements. The test contains six scales consisting of nine items each: Pride in Work, Social Status of Job, Attitude Toward Earnings, Activity Preference, Upward Striving, and Job Involvement. The test can be scored to measure two factors, Intrinsic Values and Extrinsic Values. The test yields scores for each of the scales and factors. A scoring service is available by special arrangement with the publisher. A fifth-grade reading level is required. Available in Arabic. Suitable for use with individuals with hearing and physical disabilities.

Format: Self-administered; suitable for group use; untimed: 10 minutes

Scoring: Hand key: may be computer scored; may be machine scored

Cost: 100 booklets $21.00; 100 answer sheets $5.00; 100 scoring sheets $5.00; postage and handling $5.00

Publisher: Bowling Green State University

Temperament and Values Inventory (TVI)
Charles B. Johansson, Patricia L. Webber

Copyright: 1977

Population: Adolescents, adults; Grades 9 and above

Purpose: Measures an individual's attitudes and work values; used for career development, personnel counseling, and training needs assessment

Description: Paper–pencil 230-item test containing 133 true–false statements and 97 5-point scale items. The test covers seven bipolar temperament scales: Routine–Flexible, Quiet–Active, Attentive–Distractible, Serious–Cheerful, Consistent–Changeable, Reserved–Sociable, and Reticent–Persuasive. The test also contains seven reward value scales: Social Recognition, Managerial Sales Benefits, Leadership, Social Service, Task Specificity, Philosophical Curiosity, and Work Independence. The test may be computer scored via mail-in service or using Arion II Teleprocessing.

Format: Self-administered; suitable for group use; untimed: 20 to 30 minutes

Scoring: Computer scored

Cost: Manual $13.50; Interpretive Report $6.95–$8.50 depending on quantity; Profile Report $4.25–$4.95 depending on quantity

Publisher: NCS Assessments

Time Problems Inventory
Albert A. Canfield

Copyright: 1987

Population: Adults

Purpose: Evaluates an individual's time-use problems; identifies personal and internal causes of time-use problems; used for group discussions and to assess organizational time-use problems

Description: Multiple-item paper–pencil inventory measuring the comparative level of an individual's time-use problems in four areas: priority setting, planning, task clarification, and self-discipline. Questions are largely work related, representing time problems in all aspects of daily living. Interpretation focuses on internal causes of time-use problems and may be used to identify time-use problems common to members of any organization. Scoring provides information for the discussion of internal and external factors related to ineffective time use.

Format: Self-administered; suitable for group use; untimed: 20–25 minutes

Scoring: Self-scored

Cost: Kit (10 inventories, 1 manual) $38.50

Publisher: Western Psychological Services

Time Use Analyzer
Albert A. Canfield

Copyright: 1981

Population: Adults

Purpose: Evaluates a person's time-use habits; provides a basis for discussions of time quality versus time quantity

Description: Multiple-item paper–pencil test assessing how individuals feel about how their time is being spent in eight aspects of life: at work, asleep, on personal hygiene, taking care of personal/family business, in community and church activities, with family or home members, in education and development, and on recreational and hobby activities. Test booklets contain a discussion of the implications of the results and the general findings. The test produces an awareness of common areas in which most people express some level of dissatisfaction with their time use and helps individuals differentiate between time efficiency and time effectiveness and stimulates concerns for improvement in both areas.

Format: Self-administered; suitable for group use; untimed: 20 minutes

Scoring: Self-scored

Cost: Kit (10 inventories, 1 manual) $38.50

Publisher: Western Psychological Services

Values Preference Indicator (VPI)
Everett T. Robinson

Copyright: 1990

Population: Adults

Purpose: Ascertains the most important values

Description: Forced-choice 21-item test.

Format: Individual administration; suitable for group use; examiner required; untimed

Scoring: Self-scored

Cost: $10.95

Publisher: Consulting Resource Group International, Inc.

Whisler Strategy Test
Lawrence Whisler

Copyright: Not provided

Population: 1973

Purpose: Assesses strategy used in approaching problems; used to evaluate applicants for employment

Description: Multiple-item paper–pencil measure of six aspects of strategy: solutions, speed, boldness, caution, hypercaution, and net strategy. The test detects both risk takers and risk avoiders and evaluates the subject with respect to the wisdom of his or her strategy.

Format: Examiner required; suitable for group use; timed: 25 minutes

Scoring: Hand key

Cost: Specimen Set $5.00; 25 tests $5.00, 25 answer sheets $5.00

Publisher: Psychometric Affiliates

Work Aspect Preference Scale (WAPS)
R. Pryor

Copyright: 1983

Population: Adolescents, adults; Grades 10 and above

Purpose: Measures work qualities that individuals consider important; used in career counseling, vocational rehabilitation, the study of personal and work values, and research on career development and worker satisfaction

Description: Paper–pencil or computer-administered 52-item inventory assessing an individual's work values along 13 scales: altruism, co-workers, creativity, detachment, independence, lifestyle, management, money, physical activity, prestige, security, self-development, and surroundings. Computer scoring converts raw scores on each scale to percentiles and ranks the scales in order of raw score and percentile. The computer-administered and -scored version requires an Apple II+, IIe, or IIc computer with 48K, an 80-column printer, and a single or dual disk drive.

Format: Examiner required; suitable for group use; untimed: 10–20 minutes

Scoring: Hand key; may be machine scored; may be computer scored

Cost: Contact publisher

Publisher: The Australian Council for Educational Research Limited

Work Attitudes Questionnaire
M. S. Doty, N. E. Betz

Copyright: 1981

Population: Adults

Purpose: Measures an individual's commitment to work and the degree to which such commitment is psychologically healthy or unhealthy; used for research purposes and to identify "workaholics"

Description: Paper–pencil 45-item questionnaire consisting of two scales: one assessing high versus low commitments to work (23 items) and the second assessing the degree to which work attitudes are psychologically healthy or unhealthy (22 items). Test items consist of statements regarding work or career orientation or the role which work plays in the larger scheme of life. Individuals rate each item on a 5-point scale to indicate the degree to which the statement expresses their personal beliefs. Results differentiate the Type A personality from the highly committed worker who manages to lead a balanced, psychologically healthy life.

Format: Examiner required; suitable for group use; untimed: time varies

Scoring: Examiner evaluated

Cost: Kit (manual, 25 questionnaires) $25; 50 questionnaires $20

Publisher: Marathon Consulting and Press

Work Motivation Inventory
Larry A. Braskamp, Martin L. Maehr

Copyright: 1986

Population: Adults

Purpose: Measures individual work motivation factors; used for employee selection/promotion and career counseling

Description: Paper–pencil or computer-administered 77-item multiple-choice test measuring four basic work motivation factors: accomplishment, recognition, power, and affiliation. The information obtained from the test helps predict job success and aids in understanding burnout and stress. Responses to the paper–pencil version may be entered into a computer for scoring and analysis. The computer version, which operates on IBM PC systems, administers and scores the test and generates reports. This test is an adaptation of the Organizational Assessment Survey.

Format: Examiner/self-administered; suitable for group use; untimed: 15 minutes

Scoring: Computer scored

Cost: Kit (test materials, manual, and processing of 5 reports) $49

Publisher: MetriTech, Inc.

Work Motivation Inventory (WMI)
Jay Hall, Martha S. Williams

Copyright: 1995

Population: Adults

Purpose: Assesses the work-related needs and motivations of both managers and subordinates; used for employee training and development and as a basis for discussion

Description: Multiple-item paper–pencil self-report inventory assessing work-related needs actually experienced by an individual. The inventory yields five scores which provide a personal motivational profile according to the five-need systems established in Maslow's need-hierarchy concept. The inventory may be administered in conjunction with the *Management of Motives Index* (MMI) in two ways. When used as a subordinate instrument and compared to the manager's MMI profile, discrepancies are identified between what an employee feels is important and what the manager offers in the way of motivational support. Normative data are provided.

Format: Self-administered; suitable for group use; untimed: time varies

Scoring: Self-scored

Cost: $7.95 each

Publisher: Teleometrics International, Inc.

Interests

Canadian Occupational Interest Inventory (COII)
G. Booth, Luc Begin

Copyright: 1982

Population: High school students, adults

Purpose: Identifies an individual's interest in occupationally related activities

Description: Paper–pencil 70-item measure of attitudes as they relate occupationally to activities. Interests and activities are measured by the following bipolar factors: things vs. people, business contact vs. scientific, routine vs. creative, social vs. solitary, and prestige vs. production. The test relates to the Canadian computer guidance programs DISCOVER and CHOICES. An IBM microcomputer program, Profile, which accesses 6,000+ occupations, is available for administration and scoring. Available also in French.

Format: Examiner required; suitable for group use; untimed: 40 minutes

Scoring: Hand key; computer scored

Cost: 25 booklets $74.95; manual $37.95; 100 sheets and charts $75.00; key $9.95; profile $750.00

Publisher: Nelson Canada

Curtis Interest Scale
James W. Curtis

Copyright: 1964

Population: Adolescents, adults; Grades 10 and above

Purpose: Assesses individual vocational interest patterns; used for vocational guidance, screening, and selection

Description: Paper–pencil 55-item test of vocational interests in 10 occupational areas: applied arts, business, computation, direct sales, entertainment, farming, interpersonal, mechanics, production, and science. The test yields an estimate of "level of responsibility."

Format: Self-administered; suitable for group use; untimed: 10 minutes

Scoring: Examiner evaluated; scoring service available

Cost: Specimen Set (test, manual, profile sheet) $4.00; 25 scales $7.00; 25 profiles $4.00

Publisher: Psychometric Affiliates

World of Work Inventory
Robert E. Ripley, Karen Hudson, Gregory P. M. Neidert

Copyright: 1995

Population: Adolescents, adults; ages 13 to 65 and over

Purpose: Measures temperaments, interests, and aptitudes related to *Dictionary of Occupational Titles* career families; used for employee selection, career counseling, vocational rehabilitation, and adult/career education classes

Description: Standard Form is a 516-item paper–pencil inventory. The 98 multiple-choice items assess the following achievement–aptitude areas: abstractions, spatial-form, verbal, numerical, mechanical–electrical, and clerical. The 418 rating items (subject responds "like," "dislike," or "neutral") assess 12 job-related temperament factors and career interests in activities related to 17 professional and industrial career areas. Short Form is comprised of 330 items. Results for both forms are provided in profile and narrative summary formats. An audiocassette tape is available for instruction of examiners. Available for IBM PC compatible. Spanish and modified English versions available.

Format: Self-administered; suitable for group use; untimed: Standard Form 2 hours, Short Form 1 hour

Scoring: Machine scored, computer scored, test scoring service available from publisher

Cost: Reusable test booklet $5.00; single answer sheet $11.00; coupon for single narrative summary $10.00; interpretation manual $19.95; service included with cost of answer sheets

Publisher: World of Work, Inc.

Management

Access Management Survey
Jay Hall

Copyright: 1989

Population: Adults

Purpose: Ensures employee access to five critical supports for involvement; used for management development; gives information about how effectively one manages the sociotechnical aspects of work and to provide insights into more productive management

Description: Paper–pencil 25-question test

Format: Self-administered; untimed

Scoring: Self-scored

Cost: $8.95 each

Publisher: Teleometrics International, Inc.

Advanced Managerial Tests (AMT) Numerical Analysis (NMT4)

Copyright: 1995

Population: Adults

Purpose: Assesses numerical skills of managers, professional staff, and work-experienced graduates across a range of functions

Description: Thirty-item test measuring the ability to interpret and utilize complex business-related numerical information. The test consists of a number of charts, tables, and graphs relating to one business organization. Candidates are required to interpret the data and combine the information from different sources in order to answer the questions. Calculators may be used. This test would be used in assessing a manager's ability to identify trends across a wide range of data or combine statistics from different departments to establish new information.

Format: 35 minutes

Scoring: Hand key; machine scored; scoring service available

Cost: Contact publisher

Publisher: Saville and Holdsworth Ltd.

Advanced Managerial Tests (AMT) Numerical Reasoning (NMT2)

Copyright: 1995

Population: Adults

Purpose: Assesses verbal skills of managers, professional staff, and work-experienced graduates across a range of functions

Description: Test with 35 items measuring the ability to understand the relationship between pieces of numerical information and complete the relevant operations needed to solve specific problems. The test consists of a series of short problems set in a range of business contexts. Candidates are required to use the information given and, with the aid of a calculator, reach appropriate solutions. Problem types range from arithmetic to proportions, ratios, and probabilities. The main use of this test would be to establish a manager's competence in handling basic business data.

Format: 20 minutes

Scoring: Hand key; machine scored; scoring service available

Cost: Contact publisher

Publisher: Saville and Holdsworth Ltd.

Advanced Managerial Tests (AMT) Verbal Analysis (VMT3)

Copyright: 1995

Population: Adults

Purpose: Assesses numerical skills of managers, professional staff, and work-experienced graduates across a range of functions

Description: Test with 35 items measuring the ability to interpret high-level written information in a variety of ways. The test consists of a series of passages of complex information. The questions asked address a broad range of verbal analysis skills such as summarizing, drawing appropriate inferences, and logical reasoning. This test would assess a manager's ability to interpret complex reports and documents.

Format: 35 minutes

Scoring: Hand key; machine scored; scoring service available

Cost: Contact publisher

Publisher: Saville and Holdsworth Ltd.

Advanced Managerial Tests (AMT) Verbal Application (VMT1)

Copyright: 1995

Population: Adults

Purpose: Assesses verbal skills of managers, professional staff, and work-experienced graduates across a range of functions

Description: Test with 35 items measuring the ability to understand the meaning of words, logic within sentences, and the use of grammar. The test consists of short sentences from which two or three words have been omitted. Candidates are required to select the correct combination of words to complete the sentences. One use of this test would be to assess a candidate's ability to understand, complete, or correct high-level written text.

Format: 20 minutes

Scoring: Hand key; machine scored; scoring service available

Cost: Contact publisher

Publisher: Saville and Holdsworth Ltd.

ASSET (A Supervisory Selection Tool)

Copyright: 1990

Population: Adults

Purpose: Assesses supervisory skills; used for the selection and development of employees in financial services companies

Description: Multiple-choice paper–pencil tests yielding an overall score for hiring purposes and an individual profile for development. Examiner must be trained by LOMA. Use is restricted to financial service companies.

Format: Individual administration; suitable for group use; examiner required; timed: time varies

Scoring: Hand key, computer scored

Cost: Contact publisher

Publisher: Life Office Management Association

BEST Leaderstyle Match (Computer Software)
James H. Brewer

Copyright: 1989

Population: Adults

Purpose: Used to improve leadership skills

Description: This computer program calculates the leader's personality type, the leadership role characteristics in the leader's current position, and the compatibility between the two. With this information, the leader can modify his or her behavior to match the organization's needs.

Format: Individual/self-administered; untimed: 15–20 minutes

Scoring: Hand key

Cost: $99.95 each

Publisher: Associated Consultants in Education

Coaching Skills Inventory (CSI): Other
Dennis C. Kinlaw

Copyright: 1990

Population: Adults; managers

Purpose: Helps managers develop skills in counseling, mentoring, tutoring, and confronting

Description: Measures participants' coaching skills and helps them create action plans for improvement. They measure the coaching skills used by superior leaders: Contact and Core Skills, Counseling, Mentoring, Tutoring, Confronting, and Challenging.

Format: Self-administered; untimed

Scoring: Peer scored

Cost: $3.95

Publisher: Pfeiffer and Company International Publishers, Inc.

Coaching Skills Inventory (CSI): Self
Dennis C. Kinlaw

Copyright: 1990

Population: Adults; managers

Purpose: Helps managers develop skills in counseling, mentoring, tutoring, and confronting

Description: Measures participants' coaching skills and helps them create action plans for improvement. Measures the coaching skills used by superior leaders: Contact and Core Skills, Counseling, Mentoring, Tutoring, and Confronting and Challenging.

Format: Self-administered; 2 hours

Scoring: Self-scored

Cost: $7.95

Publisher: Pfeiffer and Company International Publishers, Inc.

Communication Knowledge Inventory
W. J. Reddin

Copyright: 1994

Population: Adults

Purpose: Assesses a manager's general knowledge of communication

Description: Paper–pencil 80-item test covering verbal and nonverbal communication fallacies

Format: Self-administered; suitable for group use; untimed: 20–30 minutes

Scoring: Hand key

Cost: Test kit (10 test copies, fact sheet, user's guide) $40.00

Publisher: Organizational Tests Ltd.

Communication Sensitivity Inventory
W. J. Reddin

Copyright: 1981

Population: Adults

Purpose: Determines the characteristic response of a manager to whom others come with problems; used as a pretest in courses in listening, coaching, and communication

Description: Paper–pencil 10-item multiple-choice test measuring a manager's reaction to problems expressed by subordinates. Responses are categorized as feeling, challenge, more information, or recommendation.

Format: Self-administered; suitable for group use; untimed: 20–30 minutes

Scoring: Hand key

Cost: Test kit (10 test copies, fact sheet, user's guide) $40.00

Publisher: Organizational Tests Ltd.

Conflict Management Appraisal
Jay Hall

Copyright: 1995

Population: Adults

Purpose: Provides companion feedback to *Conflict Management Survey*; used in management development

Description: Paper–pencil survey divided into four major categories appropriate to conflict issues: personal orientation, interpersonal relationships, small group relationships, intergroup relationships.

Format: Self-administered; untimed

Scoring: Self-scored

Cost: $7.95 each

Publisher: Teleometrics International, Inc.

Critical Thinking Test (CTT) Numerical Critical Reasoning (NCT1)

Copyright: 1988

Population: Adults

Purpose: Assesses numerical critical reasoning skills in managers

Description: Multiple-choice 40-item test measuring understanding and reasoning of numerical data, rather than pure computation. Candidates are required to make decisions or inferences from numerical data presented in a variety of formats. The use of calculators is permitted. The format has clear relevance to management decision-making based on numerical and statistical data.

Format: 35 minutes

Scoring: Hand key; machine scored; scoring service available

Cost: Contact Publisher

Publisher: Saville and Holdsworth Ltd.

Critical Thinking Test (CTT) Verbal Critical Reasoning (VCT1)

Copyright: 1988

Population: Adults

Purpose: Assesses verbal critical reasoning skills in managers

Description: Multiple-choice 52-item test measuring the ability to evaluate the logic of various kinds of argument within a realistic context. Candidates are given passages of information followed by series of statements. The candidates must decide whether a given statement is true or untrue, or whether there is insufficient information to make the judgment. The test clearly relates to a key element in managerial or senior specialist jobs in which decisions or inferences must be made or evaluated either on paper or in meetings.

Format: 25 minutes

Scoring: Hand key; machine scored; scoring service available

Cost: Contact Publisher

Publisher: Saville and Holdsworth Ltd.

Developing the Leader Within (DLW)
Linda Phillips-Jones

Copyright: 1995

Population: Adults

Purpose: Assesses leadership skills levels; used in psychology and leadership development

Description: Likert scale 45-item test covering Developing Within, Helping Others Excel, Improving Critical Processes, and Showing Commitment to the Team; 360-degree feedback used.

Format: Individual administration; untimed: 15 minutes

Scoring: Computer scored

Cost: Multi-rater $125.00, single version $30.00

Publisher: Mind Garden, Inc.

Diversity Awareness Profile: Manager's Version
K. Stinson

Copyright: 1992

Population: Adults; managers

Purpose: Helps managers to be aware of their actions or inactions that inhibit the success of others; the profile also reveals areas where they could be proactive in eliminating biases

Description: Questions are based on those in the DAP but are stated in ways that are relevant to managers. It will help managers to be aware of their actions or inactions that inhibit the success of others. The profile also reveals areas where they could be proactive in eliminating biases. Trainer's Notes include an overview, discussion questions, and instructions for administering and helping participants create action plans. Use these instruments as stand-alone interventions or as part of a program on improving working relationships.

Format: Self-administered; 2 hours

Scoring: Self-scored

Cost: $3.95

Publisher: Pfeiffer and Company International Publishers, Inc.

Employee Involvement Survey (EIS)
Jay Hall

Copyright: 1988

Population: Adults

Purpose: Assesses the extent to which employees are provided opportunities for personal involvement and influence at work (i.e., opportunities for making suggestions, decision making, influencing how trips are done) by management.

Description: Paper–pencil 50-item criterion-referenced instrument that is a companion to the *Participative Management Survey* (PMS). The test provides feedback to the manager about influence opportunities afforded to employees. Using the same 50 items as the PMS, the EIS gives employees the opportunity to rate their manager's actual practices, as well as how frequently employees would desire such practices.

Format: Self-administered; suitable for group use; untimed: time varies

Scoring: Self-scored

Cost: $7.95 each

Publisher: Teleometrics International, Inc.

Executive Profile Survey (EPS)
Virgil R. Lang

Copyright: 1978

Population: Adults

Purpose: Measures executive potential and identifies individuals likely to succeed; assesses an organization's executive strengths and identifies future needs; used for employee evaluation and placement, screening job applicants, and professional development

Description: Paper–pencil 94-item (61 on a 7-point Likert scale and 33 multiple choice) test measuring self-attitudes, values, and beliefs of individuals in comparison with over 2,000 top-level executives. Based on a 15-year study of the "executive personality," EPS measures the 11 personality-profile dimensions most important in business, management, and executive settings. The profile dimensions include ambitious, assertive, enthusiastic, creative, spontaneous, self-focused, considerate, open-minded, relaxed, practical, and systematic traits of the individual. The survey also provides two validity scales. Norms, reliability, validity, and developmental background are explained in "Perspectives on the Executive Personality."

Format: Self-administered; suitable for group use; untimed: 1 hour

Scoring: Computer scored; scoring service available from publisher

Cost: Introductory kit $36.75

Publisher: Institute for Personality and Ability Testing, Inc.

Experience and Background Inventory (EBI)
Melany E. Baehr, Ernest C. Froemel

Copyright: 1996

Population: Adults

Purpose: Evaluates an individual's past performance and experience on nine factorially determined dimensions of quantified personal background data; used for selection, promotion, and career counseling of higher-level managerial and professional personnel

Description: Paper–pencil 55-item multiple-choice inventory assessing the following background areas: school achievement, choice of a college major, aspiration level, drive/career progress, leadership and group participation, vocational satisfaction, financial responsibility, general responsibility, and relaxation pursuits. Different combinations of factors have been validated for selection and evaluation of potential for successful performance in higher-level managerial and professional positions.

Format: Self-administered; suitable for group use; untimed: 20 minutes

Scoring: Hand key

Cost: 25 test booklets $34; 25 score sheets $12; examiner's manual $15

Publisher: McGraw-Hill/London House

Field Officer Descriptive Questionnaire (FODQ)
Joseph Schneider

Copyright: 1980

Population: Adults

Purpose: Assesses leadership behavior of regional field officers supervising 5–20 people

Description: Paper–pencil 53-item test measuring the following areas: competence, reliability, respect, influence, and role definition.

Format: Group or individual administration; examiner required; untimed

Scoring: Hand key; examiner evaluated

Cost: $18.00

Publisher: Select Press

IPI Job-Field Series: Factory Supervisor

Copyright: 1988

Population: Adults

Purpose: Assesses skills and personality for supervisory positions in a factory setting; used to evaluate the achievement and personality of maintenance and production people, foremen, and superintendents

Description: Multiple-item paper–pencil battery of eight aptitude and three personality tests. The tests are 16 PF, Factory Terms, Parts, NPF, Office Terms, Tools, Numbers, Judgment, CPF, Fluency, and Memory. For individual test descriptions, see the IPI Employee Aptitude Series. Also available in French and Spanish.

Format: Suitable for group use; examiner required; timed 128 minutes

Scoring: Hand keys

Cost: Starter Kit (test materials for five applicants, scoring keys, manuals) $80; test package $12/applicant

Publisher: Industrial Psychology International Ltd.

IPI Job-Field Series: Sales Supervisor

Copyright: 1960

Population: Adults

Purpose: Assesses skills and personality of applicants for supervisory positions in various sales fields; used to screen for advertising, credit, merchandise, service, and store sales supervisor positions

Description: Multiple-item paper–pencil battery of seven aptitude and three personality tests. The tests are 16PF, Fluency, Sales Terms, Memory, Judgment, CPF, Parts, Numbers, NPF, and Perception. For individual test descriptions, see the IPI Employee Aptitude Series. Available in French and Spanish.

Format: Suitable for group use; available in French and Spanish; timed: 82 minutes

Scoring: Hand keys

Cost: Starter kit (test materials for five applicants, scoring keys, manuals) $80; test package $12/applicant

Publisher: Industrial Psychology International Ltd.

Job Analysis Kit (JAK)
Sandra A. McIntire, Mary Ann Bucklan, Deonda R. Scott

Copyright: 1995

Population: Adults

Purpose: Used as a step-by-step method for conducting job analysis by human resources management and industrial psychologists; intended for supervisors

Description: Oral-response short-answer verbal measure of knowledge, skills, abilities, and other characteristics

Format: Individual administration; examiner required; untimed

Scoring: Hand-scorable answer sheet; examiner evaluated

Cost: Kit $97.00

Publisher: Psychological Assessment Resources, Inc.

Lead Other

Copyright: 1993

Population: Managers, supervisors, leaders, and staff people

Purpose: Measures what others perceive about a leader's style

Description: Multiple-choice 12-question paper–pencil test measuring a leadership style profile. An eighth-grade reading level is required. Available in Spanish, German, Japanese, and French. Suitable for individuals with physical and hearing disabilities. Materials include self-administered instrument and scoring form. Computer version available.

Format: Individual/group administration; self-administered; untimed

Scoring: Computer/self scored

Cost: $1.95 each with quantity discounts

Publisher: Center for Leadership Studies, Inc.

Lead Self

Copyright: 1993

Population: Managers, supervisors, leaders, and staff people

Purpose: Measures which leadership behaviors one uses and the extent to which one matches the behavior of others

Description: Multiple-choice 12-question paper–pencil test resulting in a leadership style profile. Available forms include Lead Self perception and Lead Others perception. Materials used are a self-administered instrument and scoring form. Available also in Spanish, German, Japanese, and French. An eighth-grade reading level is required. Suitable for individuals with physical and hearing impairments.

Format: Individual/group administered; self-administered; untimed

Scoring: Self/computer scored; test scoring service available from publisher

Cost: $2.95 each

Publisher: Center for Leadership Studies, Inc.

Leadership Ability Evaluation
Russell N. Cassel, Edward J. Stancik

Copyright: 1982

Population: Adolescents, adults; Grades 9 and above

Purpose: Measures leadership abilities, behavior, and style in adults and high school students; used for counseling and self-analysis

Description: Paper–pencil 50-item multiple-choice test consisting of eight pages of leadership-decision problems, each with four possible solutions. Responses reflect specific decision modes or social climate structures and classify decision-making patterns into one of four types: laissez-faire, democratic–cooperative, autocratic–submissive, or autocratic–aggressive. The test was normed on 2,000 individuals; additional norms are provided for 400 outstanding leaders and 100 U.S. Air Force Officers.

Format: Self-administered; suitable for group use; untimed: 15 minutes

Scoring: Hand key

Cost: Kit (20 tests, manual) $48.50

Publisher: Western Psychological Services

Leadership Appraisal Survey (LAS)
Jay Hall

Copyright: 1986

Population: Adults

Purpose: Evaluates a leader's behavior from the associates' point of view; used for assessment and development purposes with nonmanagement supervisory personnel, campus and community groups, volunteer organizations, and administrative personnel

Description: Multiple-item paper–pencil inventory assessing a leader's impact on and stimulus value for the group from the associates' point of view. The inventory identifies blindspots, pinpoints strengths and weaknesses, and confirms the way leadership practices come across to associates. The inventory yields analyses of overall leadership style, including four components of leadership: philosophy, planning, implementation, and evaluation. The inventory may be administered in conjunction with the *Styles of Leadership Survey* (SLS) to provide a comparison of the associates' ratings with the leaders self-ratings on the SLS. Normative data are provided.

Format: Self-administered; suitable for group use; untimed: time varies

Scoring: Self-scored

Cost: $7.95 each

Publisher: Teleometrics International, Inc.

Leadership Opinion Questionnaire (LOQ)
Edwin A. Fleishman

Copyright: 1989

Population: Adults

Purpose: Measures leadership style; used in a variety of industrial and organizational settings for selection, appraisal, counseling, and training of employees

Description: Paper–pencil or computer 40-item test measuring two aspects of leadership: consideration (how likely it is that an individual's job relationship with subordinates is characterized by mutual trust, respect, and consideration) and structure (how likely an individual is to define and structure personal and subordinates' roles toward goal attainment).

Format: Self-administered; suitable for group use; untimed: 10–15 minutes

Scoring: Hand key; computer scored

Cost: 25 test booklets $37; examiner's manual $15

Publisher: McGraw-Hill/London House

Leadership Practices Inventory (LPI)
James M. Kouzes, Barry Z. Posner

Copyright: 1993

Population: Managers and supervisors

Purpose: Helps managers set goals, create solid action plans, cultivate innovative thinking, improve interpersonal skills, and take other positive steps to develop essential leadership traits

Description: Helps participants understand specific behaviors that characterize exemplary leadership, identify their personal strengths as leaders, identify areas for improvement in their leadership practices, develop action plans for becoming better leaders, and plan how to share their results and what they learned from the feedback session with co-workers and colleagues.

Format: 2 to 4 hours

Scoring: Self-scored

Cost: $9.95

Publisher: Pfeiffer and Company International Publishers, Inc.

Leadership Practices Inventory: Observer
James M. Kouzes, Barry Z. Posner

Copyright: 1992

Population: Adults

Purpose: Provides a balanced picture of leadership traits and allows for constructive discussion of ways to improve

Description: The anonymous perceptions of constituents and colleagues combined with the manager's self-assessment provide a clear picture of how the manager functions as a team leader

Format: 2–4 hours

Scoring: Peer scored

Cost: $3.95

Publisher: Pfeiffer and Company International Publishers, Inc.

Leadership Practices Inventory: Self
James M. Kouzes, Barry Z. Posner

Copyright: 1992

Population: Adults

Purpose: Evaluates managers' performance and effectiveness as leaders

Description: When used in concert with the LPI: Observer, up to 10 observers' scores can be combined with self-assessment scores. Using the results, you can help the manager develop plans for improvement. The accompanying guidebook includes a worksheet to help interpret feedback on and plan improvement in each leadership practice assessed, action planning worksheets for determining specific improvement actions, and sections on how to compare scores with the normative sample and on how to share feedback with constituents.

Format: 2 to 4 hours

Scoring: Peer scored

Cost: $9.95

Publisher: Pfeiffer and Company International Publishers, Inc.

Leadership Skills Inventory: Other's (LSI)
Terry D. Anderson

Copyright: 1992

Population: Adults

Purpose: Assesses others' leadership skills; used in leadership development

Description: Ranking test with 56 items. A 10th-grade reading level is required. Available in Swedish.

Format: Individual administration; suitable for group use; examiner required; untimed

Scoring: Self-scored

Cost: $7.95

Publisher: Consulting Resource Group International, Inc.

Leadership Skills Inventory: Self (LSI)
Terry D. Anderson

Copyright: 1992

Population: Adults

Purpose: Measures leadership skills; used in leadership development

Description: Rating test with 56 items. A 10th-grade reading level is required.

Format: Individual administration; suitable for group use; examiner required; untimed

Scoring: Self-scored

Cost: $12.95

Publisher: Consulting Resource Group International, Inc.

Leatherman Leadership Questionnaire (LLQ)
Richard W. Leatherman

Copyright: 1992

Population: Adults

Purpose: Used in career counseling and training needs assessment to determine the organization's needs and also to provide the individual with specific career development "prescriptions" based on objective information of strengths and areas of needed improvement

Description: Multiple-choice 339-item test with one most correct answer and three distractors, with 27 scales. A summary report, two transparency bar charts, Training Needs Analysis, and individual report are available. A 129-page administrator's manual, 143-page questionnaire (part 1 and part 2), two answer sheets, a 109-page research report, and a 346-page development manual for each test taker are used. A high school reading level is required. Also available in German.

Format: Individual/self-administered; suitable for group use; examiner required; untimed: approximately 270 minutes

Scoring: Machine scored

Cost: Complete testing kit for 10 people $1,500.00; additional testing service $95.00 per person

Publisher: International Training Consultants, Inc.

Management Appraisal Survey (MAS)
Jay Hall, Jerry B. Harvey, Martha S. Williams

Copyright: 1986

Population: Adults

Purpose: Assesses an individual's style of management from the subordinate's point of view; used for management training and development and as a basis for discussion

Description: Multiple-item paper–pencil inventory assessing subordinates' perceptions of their manager's practices. Analysis is based on the Blake-Mouton managerial grid—a model of management behavior that is an extension of Likert's production-morale theory relating production concerns with people concerns. The inventory provides a total score for each of the five management styles described by the model, as well as scores for each style on four components: philosophy, planning, implementation,

and evaluation. The survey may be administered in conjunction with the Styles of Management Inventory to provide a comparison between subordinate ratings and manager self-ratings on the SMI. Normative data are provided.

Format: Self-administered; suitable for group use; untimed: time varies

Scoring: Self-scored

Cost: $7.95 each

Publisher: Teleometrics International, Inc.

Management Burnout Scale
John W. Jones, Donald M. Moretti

Copyright: 1980

Population: Adults

Purpose: Assesses burnout or work stress among managerial-level employees

Description: Multiple-item paper–pencil test assessing burnout or work stress through four types of factors: cognitive reactions, affective reactions, behavioral reactions, and psychophysiological reactions.

Format: Self-administered; suitable for group use; untimed: 10 minutes

Scoring: Hand key

Cost: 25 tests $23; Specimen Set (interpretation manual, validation studies) $10; examiner's manual $10

Publisher: McGraw-Hill/London House

Management Coaching Relations Test (MCR)
W. J. Reddin

Copyright: 1981

Population: Adults

Purpose: Measures a manager's knowledge of sound methods of coaching subordinates who may be supervisors or managers; used before or after a discussion of coaching

Description: True–false 80-item paper–pencil test measuring knowledge of performance appraisal, effectiveness criteria, coaching interview, and training.

Format: Self-administered; suitable for group use; untimed: 20–30 minutes

Scoring: Hand key

Cost: Test kit (10 test copies, fact sheet, user's guide) $40.00

Publisher: Organizational Tests Ltd.

Management Inventory on Managing Change (MIMC)
Donald L. Kirkpatrick

Copyright: 1994

Population: Adults

Purpose: Measures a manager's attitudes and knowledge in regard to managing change within an organization; used in conjunction with training programs aimed at teaching managers how to deal with change; used with all levels of management

Description: Paper–pencil 65-item inventory measuring attitudes, knowledge, and opinions regarding principles and approaches for managing change. Items 1–50 are statements of beliefs or attitudes concerning organizational change and various ways of implementing such change. Individuals indicate whether they agree or disagree with each statement. Items 51–60 are free-response questions asking for a list of reasons why people might accept or resist change. Items 61–65 are multiple-choice items calling for an assessment of a situation involving change within an organization. Item content is intended to help managers understand their role in managing change.

Format: Self-administered; suitable for group use; untimed: 20 minutes

Scoring: Self-scored

Cost: 20 tests and answer booklets, instructor's manual $30.00

Publisher: Donald L. Kirkpatrick, Ph.D.

Management Inventory on Modern Management (MIMM)
Donald L. Kirkpatrick

Copyright: 1992

Population: Adults

Purpose: Measures philosophy, principles, and approaches related to the effective performance of middle- and upper-level managers; used to determine need for training, as a tool for conference discussions, and to evaluate effectiveness of a training program

Description: Paper–pencil 80-item agree–disagree test of eight topics important to managers: leadership styles, selection and training, communicating, motivating, managing change, delegating, decision making, and managing time. Other available materials include an explanatory cassette, a book on communication, and a communication training kit.

Format: Examiner/self-administered; suitable for group use; untimed: 20 minutes

Scoring: Self-scored

Cost: 20 tests and answer booklets, instructor's manual $30.00

Publisher: Donald L. Kirkpatrick, Ph.D.

Management Inventory on Performance Appraisal and Coaching (MIPAC)
Donald L. Kirkpatrick

Copyright: 1992

Population: Adults

Purpose: Measures knowledge and agreement with principles and techniques in performance appraisal and coaching; used in conjunction with management training programs

Description: Paper–pencil 45-item two-choice test measuring the extent to which supervisors understand and accept the principles, facts, and techniques of performance appraisal and coaching. Individuals indicate whether they agree or disagree with each statement about beliefs or behaviors presented in each test item. The answer booklet provides a rationale for each correct answer. Test results identify topics that should be emphasized in training programs and provide information for on-the-job coaching.

Format: Self-administered; suitable for group use; untimed: 15 minutes

Scoring: Self-scored

Cost: 20 tests and answer booklets, instructor's manual $30.00

Publisher: Donald L. Kirkpatrick, Ph.D.

Management Inventory on Time Management (MITM)
Donald L. Kirkpatrick

Copyright: 1994

Population: Adults

Purpose: Measures a manager's knowledge and attitudes regarding effective management of time and delegation; used in conjunction with training programs on time management

Description: Paper–pencil 60-item two-choice test assessing managers' knowledge of the principles and practices concerning the effective management of time. Test items are statements about time use within an organization. Individuals indicate for each item whether they agree or disagree with the statement. The answer booklet includes the rationale for all correct answers. Test results identify topics that should be emphasized in training programs, serve as a tool for conference discussions, measure the effectiveness of training programs, and provide information for on-the-job coaching. A list of books and films for use in time management training programs is included.

Format: Self-administered; suitable for group use; untimed: 15 minutes

Scoring: Self-scored

Cost: 20 tests, answer booklets, and instructor's manual $30

Publisher: Donald L. Kirkpatrick, Ph.D.

Management of Motives Index
Jay Hall

Copyright: 1995

Population: Adults

Purpose: Identifies manager's theories of what stimulates subordinates, their assumptions about why people work, and the approaches to motivation which result from those assumptions

Description: The profile gives managers a basis for comparing their emphasis with what their colleagues and/or direct reports say they need. Reveals the emphasis that managers place on each of Maslow's five need systems to manage others. Ideally, managers complete the *Management of Motives Index* and have their colleagues and direct reports complete the *Work Motivation Inventory.*

Format: Self-administered; suitable for group use; untimed: time varies

Scoring: Self-scored

Cost: $8.95 each

Publisher: Teleometrics International, Inc.

Management Potential Report

Copyright: 1995, 1996

Population: Adults

Purpose: Identifies candidates who are true performers and committed to quality leadership; provides accurate and objective information to make the best possible decisions about management candidates

Description: Highly psychometric 145-question screening test designed to predict a candidate's potential for managerial success. Job performance is measured on five dimensions: productivity, adaptability, problem solving skills, ambitiousness, and social skills.

Format: 30 minutes

Scoring: Fax-In, Phone-In, Mail-In, or PC software

Cost: Ranges from $8.50 to $18.00

Publisher: Reid Psychological Systems

Management Readiness Profile (MRP)

Copyright: 1988

Population: Adults

Purpose: Evaluates job applicants or employees for managerial interests and basic management orientation

Description: Paper–pencil 188-item multiple-choice test with seven subtests: Management Interests, Leadership, Energy and Drive, Practical Thinking, Management Responsibility, Sociability, and Candidates. Subscale scores and a composite Management Readiness Index are generated.

Format: Suitable for group use; untimed: 20 minutes

Scoring: Computer scored

Cost: $8 to $15 based on volume ordered

Publisher: McGraw-Hill/London House

Management Relations Survey (MRS)
Jay Hall

Copyright: 1995

Population: Adults

Purpose: Measures a manager's communications/employee relations skills from the subordinates' point of view; used for employee training and development

Description: Multiple-item paper–pencil inventory assessing management/employee relations from the subordinates' point of view. The inventory provides a manager with feedback from associates and subordinates and allows subordinates to examine their own practices with the manager. The inventory may be administered in conjunction with the *Personnel Relations Survey* for self–other comparisons of management communication skills and effectiveness. Normative data are provided.

Format: Self-administered; suitable for group use; untimed: time varies

Scoring: Self-scored

Cost: $7.95 each

Publisher: Teleometrics International, Inc.

Management Style Diagnosis Test
W. J. Reddin

Copyright: 1977

Population: Adults

Purpose: Measures managers and supervisors against the eight styles of the 3-D Theory of Leadership Effectiveness; used in management and supervisory training seminars

Description: Multiple-item paper–pencil test in which the manager responds "agree" or "disagree" to descriptive statements of a hypothetical manager's actions. Test scores relate to styles such as deserter, missionary, autocrat, compromiser, bureaucrat, developer, benevolent autocrat, task orientation, relationships orientation, and effectiveness.

Format: Self-administered; suitable for group use; untimed: 20–30 minutes

Scoring: Hand key

Cost: Test kit (10 test copies, fact sheet, user's guide) $40.00

Publisher: Organizational Tests Ltd.

Management Styles Inventory
Jay Hall, Jerry B. Harvey, Martha S. Williams

Copyright: 1995

Population: Adults

Purpose: Provides profiles in four components of managerial style: Philosophy, Planning and Goal Setting, Implementation, and Evaluation; used for management development

Description: Paper–pencil inventory; 60 management alternatives presented five at a time under 12 different situations

Format: Self-administered; untimed

Scoring: Self-scored

Cost: $8.95 each

Publisher: Teleometrics International, Inc.

Management Transactions Audit (MTA): Self
Jay Hall, C. Leo Griffith

Copyright: 1973

Population: Adults

Purpose: Designed to provide managers with some information about the effects that their feelings and practices in responding to others' comments have on the quality and subsequent success of their managerial transactions

Description: Paper–pencil criterion-referenced instrument which is a companion to the *Management Transactions Audit: Other.* Eric Berne's model of Transactional Analysis postulates three positions from which individuals can communicate and is widely used to sharpen individual self-awareness. The three-part MTA is based on Berne's model and measures the size of the Parent, Adult, and Child in the manager's transactions with direct reports, colleges, and superiors. Completed by managers, the MTA also taps transaction contamination, crossed and complementary transactions, and constructive and disruptive tension.

Format: Self-administered; suitable for group use

Scoring: Self-scored

Cost: $8.95 each

Publisher: Teleometrics International, Inc.

Management Transactions Audit (MTA): Other
Jay Hall

Copyright: 1989

Population: Adults

Purpose: Assesses how employees view the manager's transactions and interact with the manager

Description: Paper–pencil criterion-referenced instrument which is a companion to the *Management Transactions Audit: Self.* Designed to provide managers with some information about the effects that their feelings and practices in responding to others' comments have on the quality and subsequent success of their managerial transactions.

Format: Self-administered; suitable for group use; untimed: time varies

Scoring: Self-scored

Cost: $7.95 each

Publisher: Teleometrics International, Inc.

Manager Profile Record (MPR)

Copyright: Not provided

Population: Adults

Purpose: Assesses the managerial qualities of employees or applicants; used for predicting managerial success

Description: Multiple-item computer-administered predictive inventory indicating the degree to which an individual resembles successful managerial employees in the areas of background and judgment. The test yields 11 separate scores for individuals with more than 10 full years of full-time work experience and 9 separate scores for those with 10 or less years of full-time work experience. Validity data are extensive across organization type, functional area, race, and sex.

Format: Self-administered; suitable for group use; untimed: time varies

Scoring: Computer scored

Cost: Contact publisher

Publisher: Richardson, Bellows, Henry and Company, Inc.

Manager Styles Appraisal
Jay Hall, Jerry B. Harvey, Martha S. Williams

Copyright: 1995

Population: Adults

Purpose: Provides companion feedback to Management Styles Inventory; used in management development

Description: Paper–pencil appraisal; 60 management alternatives presented five at a time under 12 different situations

Format: Self-administered; untimed

Scoring: Self-scored

Cost: $7.95 each

Publisher: Teleometrics International, Inc.

Manager/Supervisor Staff Selector

Copyright: 1984

Population: Adults

Purpose: Measures intellectual and personality characteristics of candidates for manager and supervisor positions

Description: Multiple-item paper–pencil set of seven subtests assessing logic, problem-solving, planning, and conceptualizing skills; numerical skills and reasoning; verbal fluency and communication skills; business judgment and ability to deal with peers; supervisory practices and practical leadership; emotional stability; and people contact skills. The test is used for selecting first- and second-line supervisors for all positions and as a screening test for middle and senior management candidates. Three subtests are timed. Available in Basic, Screening, or Comprehensive versions depending on depth of assessment required. Available in French.

Format: Examiner required; suitable for group use; timed/untimed: 120 minutes

Scoring: Scoring service provided

Cost: $499.00 each

Publisher: Walden Personnel Testing and Training, Inc.

Managerial and Professional Job Functions Inventory (MP-JFI)
Melany E. Baehr, Wallace G. Lonergan, Bruce A. Hunt

Copyright: 1978

Population: Adults

Purpose: Assesses the relative importance of functions performed in higher-level managerial and professional positions and the incumbent's ability to perform them; used to clarify job positions and organizational structure, and to diagnose training needs

Description: Multiple-item paper–pencil inventory assessing the relative importance of job functions in the following 16 categories: setting organizational objectives, financial planning and review, improving work procedures and practices, interdepartmental coordination, developing and implementing technical ideas, judgment and decision-making, developing teamwork, coping with difficulties and emergencies, promoting safety attitudes and practices, communications, developing employee potential, supervisory practices, self-development and improvement, personnel practices, promoting community–organization relations, and handling outside contacts. Items are rated by incumbent employees for each position. The test may be used for self- or supervisory ratings.

Format: Examiner required; suitable for group use; untimed: 40–60 minutes

Scoring: Hand key

Cost: 25 test booklets $34; 25 score sheets $12; examiner's manual $15

Publisher: McGraw-Hill/London House

Managerial Competence Index–Revised D
Jay Hall

Copyright: 1989

Population: Adults

Purpose: Assesses managerial beliefs, involvement practices, motivation, and interpersonal competence

Description: Paper–pencil 60-item criterion-referenced test consisting of 12 typical management situations. The individual chooses one of five alternative ways of handling each situation. Answers indicate the individual's personal style of managerial decision making.

Format: Self-administered; suitable for group use; untimed: time varies

Scoring: Self-scored

Cost: $8.95 each

Publisher: Teleometrics International, Inc.

Managerial Competence Review–Revised
Jay Hall

Copyright: 1989

Population: Adults

Purpose: Assesses managerial beliefs, involvement practices, motivation, and interpersonal competence as viewed by other workers

Description: Paper–pencil 60-item criterion-referenced test consisting of 12 typical management situations. The individual chooses one of five alternative ways of handling each situation. Answers indicate the manager's personal style of managerial decision making. This is a companion to the Managerial Competence Index.

Format: Self-administered; suitable for group use; untimed: time varies

Scoring: Self-scored

Cost: $7.95 each

Publisher: Teleometrics International, Inc.

Managerial Philosophies Scale (MPS)
Jacob Jacoby, James Terborg

Copyright: 1995

Population: Adults

Purpose: Evaluates managers in terms of Douglas McGregor's Theory X and Theory Y types of managers; differentiates between high-, average-, and low-achieving managers

Description: Multiple-item paper–pencil self-report inventory measuring the degree to which managers adhere to either of two theories concerning the philosophical motivation behind management practices: Theory X and Theory Y. Theory X managers are authoritarian and intent on others' compliance with their commands. Theory Y managers see the potential of satisfaction and self-fulfillment for all who work. The inventory yields scores for both X and Y dimensions. Normative data and interpretive guidelines are provided for purposes of comparison, reflection, and evaluation. The inventory may be used for pre- and posttesting to measure the impact of training intervention programs.

Format: Self-administered; suitable for group use; untimed: time varies

Scoring: Self-scored

Cost: $8.95 each

Publisher: Teleometrics International, Inc.

My Best Leadership Style
James H. Brewer

Copyright: 1994

Population: Adults

Purpose: Used to improve leadership skills

Description: Using My Best Leadership Style, human resource developers can help supervisors, managers, executives, and others understand how to modify their behaviors to deal more effectively with subordinates. The test gives examples of how personality types affect leadership styles, suggests modification techniques for more successful leadership, describes how to lead different personality types, and discusses organization needs vs. personal leadership style.

Format: Individual/self-administered; untimed: 15–30 minutes

Scoring: Hand key

Cost: $4.95 each

Publisher: Associated Consultants in Education

Negotiating Style
James H. Brewer

Copyright: 1991

Population: Adults

Purpose: Used to build productive negotiating strategies

Description: The instrument identifies negotiating style, describes how styles behave in negotiating sessions, suggests ways to improve each style, and promotes more productive negotiating techniques.

Format: Individual/self-administered; untimed: 10–15 minutes

Scoring: Hand key

Cost: $2.95 each

Publisher: Associated Consultants in Education

Organization Health Survey (OHS)
W. J. Reddin

Copyright: 1981

Population: Adults

Purpose: Reveals the attitudes of managers in an organization; used as a training device or as feedback to top management

Description: True–false 80-item paper–pencil test providing a separate score on productivity, leadership, organization structure, communication, conflict management, participation, human resource management, and creativity.

Format: Self-administered; suitable for group use; untimed: 20–30 minutes

Scoring: Hand key

Cost: Test kit (10 test copies, fact sheet, user's guide) $40.00

Publisher: Organizational Tests Ltd.

Participative Management Survey
Jay Hall

Copyright: 1988

Population: Adults

Purpose: Assesses the extent to which managers provide opportunities for employee involvement

Description: Paper–pencil 50-item criterion-referenced instrument generating a Personal Participative Management Profile. The items are expressed in behavioral terms (i.e., as actual practices which may or may not be used). Employees are asked to respond to each item in terms of actual frequency of use (i.e., how often such an influence opportunity is extended to employees being managed). To be used in conjunction with the *Employee Involvement Survey.*

Format: Self-administered; not suitable for group use; untimed: time varies

Scoring: Self-scored

Cost: $8.95 each

Publisher: Teleometrics International, Inc.

Personal Achievement Formula (PAF)
Jay Hall

Copyright: 1976

Population: Adults

Purpose: Assesses managers' overall approach to managing and their organization's most rewarded practices

Description: Two-part paper–pencil instrument measuring managerial strategy and the organization through the use of a value matrix. The Personal Achievement Formula is intended to be used with the film *Search for Achievement.* It personalizes the message of the film and the report on managerial achievement. Matrix items reflect those dimensions found to distinguish among high-, average-, and low-achieving managers.

Format: Self-administered; suitable for group use; untimed: time varies

Scoring: Self-scored

Cost: $8.95 each

Publisher: Teleometrics International, Inc.

Personal Opinion Matrix (POM)
Jay Hall

Copyright: 1983

Population: Adults

Purpose: Assesses the overall approach of both manager and organization

Description: Paper–pencil questionnaire in two parts: Manager's Approach to Management and Job and Workplace. As a companion piece to the *Personal Achievement Formula* (PAF), the Personal Opinion Matrix (POM) provides feedback for the manager. The POM utilizes the same matrix item pool as the PAF and, when the two are used in tandem, the resulting action dynamics enable constructive critique of personal assumptions and practices.

Format: Self-administered; suitable for group use; untimed: time varies

Scoring: Self-scored

Cost: $7.95 each

Publisher: Teleometrics International, Inc.

Personnel Performance Problems Inventory (PPPI)
Albert A. Canfield

Copyright: 1987

Population: Adults

Purpose: Assesses the use of delegation skills at all levels of management; identifies specific elements in the delegation process which are creating problems; used for manager/supervisor training and development

Description: Paper–pencil 30-item test assessing the effectiveness of a supervisor's delegation relationships in the following areas: mutual understanding of job responsibilities, authority, accountability, results expected, and employment conditions. Each test item describes a common performance problem of subordinates. The supervisor or manager must indicate the extent to which each is a problem with a present employee or group of employees. Test booklets contain complete descriptions of areas for improvement. Norms are provided for supervisors/managers to identify key areas for improvement. A bibliography for additional reading also is included.

Format: Self-administered; suitable for group use; untimed: 30 minutes

Scoring: Self-scored

Cost: Kit (10 inventories, 1 manual) $38.50

Publisher: Western Psychological Services

Personnel Relations Survey
Jay Hall, Martha S. Williams

Copyright: 1995

Population: Adults

Purpose: Assesses the communications skills of managers; used for employee training and development

Description: Multiple-item paper–pencil self-report inventory assessing the communications tendencies of managers in three areas: with employees, with colleagues, and with superiors. Normative data provide a basis for comparison with the "average" manager on both the exposure and feedback dimensions. The inventory may be administered in conjunction with the *Management Relations Survey* for a more complete assessment of managers' communication skills.

Format: Self-administered; suitable for group use; untimed: time varies

Scoring: Self-scored

Cost: $8.95 each

Publisher: Teleometrics International, Inc.

Power Base Inventory (PBI)
Kenneth W. Thomas, Gail Fann Thomas

Copyright: 1985

Population: Adults

Purpose: Used in management development to assess leadership and influencing styles

Description: Forced-choice 30-item test.

Information, expertise, goodwill, authority, reward, and discipline are the scores yielded. An eighth-grade reading level is required.

Format: Individual/self-administered; suitable for group use; untimed

Scoring: Self-scored

Cost: $6.25

Publisher: Xicom, Inc.

Power Management Inventory (PMI)
Jay Hall, James Hawker

Copyright: 1995

Population: Adults

Purpose: Evaluates a manager's use of power; used for management training and development and as a basis for discussion

Description: Multiple-item paper–pencil self-report inventory assessing the motivations for power and power styles of managers. The first part of the inventory examines an individual's personal motivations for power, including needs for impact, strength, and influence, that guide behavior. The second part of the inventory analyzes how the individual uses power and assesses two bipolar dimensions of power of style: autocratic–democratic and permissive–authoritarian. The analysis of individual power dynamics includes assessments of both motive and style, focusing on the interaction between the two. Normative data are provided.

Format: Self-administered; suitable for group use; untimed: time varies

Scoring: Self-scored

Cost: $8.95 each

Publisher: Teleometrics International, Inc.

Power Management Profile (PMP)
Jay Hall, James Hawker

Copyright: 1995

Population: Adults

Purpose: Evaluates a manager's use of power from the viewpoint of subordinates or associates; used for management training and development and as a basis for discussion

Description: Multiple-item paper–pencil inventory assessing a manager's power style and related behaviors as seen by the manager's subordinates or co-workers. Elicits feedback for managers concerning how their approaches to power are viewed by those on the receiving end of their behavior. Analysis of responses provides a structure for after-the-fact discussions with subordinates and develops a statement of the general morale that exists in the workplace as a function of the manager's use of power. Normative data are provided. The inventory may be administered in conjunction with the *Power Management Inventory* to provide a comparison of managers' self-ratings with those of their subordinates.

Format: Self-administered; suitable for group use; untimed: time varies

Scoring: Self-scored

Cost: $7.95 each

Publisher: Teleometrics International, Inc.

Productive Practices Survey
Jay Hall

Copyright: 1996

Population: Adults

Purpose: Measures the degree to which managers employ practices which research has shown lead to higher productivity and a healthier work environment

Description: Paper–pencil 72-item criterion-referenced self-assessment instrument that provides profiles on three dimensions and nine components of competence which are tied to productivity. Normative data provide a basis for comparison with the "average" manager on all scales.

Format: Self-administered; suitable for group use; untimed: time varies

Scoring: Self-scored

Cost: $8.95 each

Publisher: Teleometrics International, Inc.

PSC Survey–S.A.
(For Supervisory Attitudes)
Mark L. Strand

Copyright: 1987

Population: Adolescents, adults; ages 16 and older

Purpose: Assesses predisposing attitudes toward work; assists in pre-employment screening of managers and supervisors

Description: True–false paper–pencil 60-item (5 subfactor) test with questions concerning managers (10 items), being a supervisor (10 items), companies and business (10 items), peers and associates (10 items), and subordinates (20 items). This is one test in the PSC Survey series that is appropriate for beginning and mid-level management positions. Can be used for new applicants or for screening current employees being considered for advancement. Used in a combination with two or three of the following surveys: Survey–S. A., Survey–L. T., Survey–A. D.

Format: Untimed: 15 minutes

Scoring: Self-scored; examiner evaluated

Cost: $6.00; volume discount

Publisher: Predictive Surveys Corporation

Quality Improvement Audit for Leaders
James H. Brewer

Copyright: 1990

Population: Adults

Purpose: Assesses the leader's knowledge and behaviors during quality improvement (TQM) implementation as compared with leading Japanese and American firms

Description: Serves as a guide for implementing basic quality improvement behaviors while helping the leader take a personal assessment of his or her quality improvement knowledge and behaviors. The instrument assesses personal leadership factors in quality implementation, compares achievement to accepted Total Quality Management models, and increases leadership skills.

Format: Individual/self-administered; untimed: 20–30 minutes

Scoring: Hand key

Cost: $6.95 each

Publisher: Associated Consultants in Education

Reality Check Survey
Jay Hall

Copyright: 1995

Population: Adults

Purpose: Used as a companion to *Managerial Philosophies Scale;* survey is designed to provide managers with an opportunity for reflection

Description: Paper–pencil test consisting of true–false statements. Part I allows employees to describe the circumstance under which they feel they do or would do their best work and be most productive. Part II, using the same 20 true–false statements, employees are asked to (1) consider one's manager's actions toward others, and (2) on the basis of those actions, to estimate the circumstances which he or she appears to believe are necessary for employees to do their best and be most productive.

Format: Self-administered; untimed

Scoring: Self-scored

Cost: $7.95 each

Publisher: Teleometrics International, Inc.

Retail Management Assessment Inventory (RMAI)

Copyright: 1989

Population: Adults

Purpose: Selects and screens applicants for the position of unit manager in retail or restaurant outlets

Description: Multi-item multiple-choice paper–pen test comprised of 10 subtests: Background and Work Experience, Management and Leadership Interests, Management Responsibility, Understanding Management Procedures and Practices, Customer Service, Applied Management Computations, Energy Level, Job Stability, Business Ethics, and Management Orientation. Scores are provided for each subtest and for an overall Management Potential Index. In addition to scores, the RMAI generates positive indicators, training needs, and follow-up interview questions. Three scoring options are available from McGraw-Hill/London House.

Format: Suitable for group use; examiner required; untimed: 75 minutes

Scoring: Computer scored

Cost: $14 to $27 depending on scoring method and volume

Publisher: McGraw-Hill/London House

Station Manager Applicant Inventory (SMAI)

Copyright: 1987

Population: Adults

Purpose: Screens gas station dealers and managers for operating a gas station; also used for franchise screening for gas stations

Description: Paper–pencil 218-item multiple-choice test used for screening station manager applicants. The test contains eight subtests: Background, Managerial Arithmetic, Honesty, Interpersonal Cooperation, Drug Avoidance, Temperament, Understanding Organizational Policies and Practices, and Distortion. Eight subtest scores and a composite Manager Potential Index are generated.

Format: Examiner required; suitable for group use; untimed: 1 hour 30 minutes

Scoring: Computer scored; scoring service available from publisher

Cost: $11–$25 depending on scoring method and volume ordered

Publisher: McGraw-Hill/London House

Styles of Leadership Survey
Jay Hall, Martha S. Williams, Jerry B. Harvey

Copyright: 1968

Population: Adults

Purpose: Assesses leadership styles in terms of "concern for people" and "concern for purpose." Used with nonmanagement supervisory personnel, campus and community groups, volunteer organizations, and administrative personnel.

Description: Multiple-item paper–pencil self-report inventory assessing leadership behavior in terms of the Blake-Mouton model of management behavior. The Blake-Mouton managerial grid is an extension of Likert's production-morale theory and measures two dimensions of leadership behavior: concerns for people and concerns for purpose. The inventory yields analyses of overall leadership style, including four components of leadership: philosophy, planning, implementation, and evaluation. Normative data are provided. The inventory may be administered in conjunction with the Leadership Appraisal Survey for a more complete assessment of leadership styles and effectiveness.

Format: Self-administered; suitable for group use; untimed: time varies

Scoring: Self-scored

Cost: $8.95 each

Publisher: Teleometrics International, Inc.

Styles of Management Inventory (SMI)
Jay Hall, Jerry B. Harvey, Martha S. Williams

Copyright: 1995

Population: Adults

Purpose: Evaluates an individual's style of management in terms of the assumptions made about the relationship between production concerns and people concerns; used for management training and development and as a basis for discussion

Description: Multiple-item paper–pencil self-report inventory assessing styles of management based on the Blake-Mouton managerial grid, a model of management behavior based on Likert's morale-production theory. The inventory yields a total score for each of the five styles described by the Blake-Mouton model, as well as subscores for each style on four components of management: philosophy, planning, implementation, and evaluation. The inventory provides managers with a way of relating their behavior with their on-the-job practices and discovering areas needing change. Normative data and conversion tables afford personal comparison with both the "average" manager and a theoretical ideal.

Format: Self-administered; suitable for group use; untimed: time varies

Scoring: Self-scored

Cost: $8.95 each

Publisher: Teleometrics International, Inc.

Supervisory Behavior Description (SBD) Questionnaire
Edwin A. Fleishman

Copyright: 1989

Population: Adults

Purpose: Measures leadership style as perceived by supervisors, peers, and subordinates; used in a variety of industrial and organizational settings for selection, appraisal, counseling, and training of employees

Description: Multiple-choice 48-item test measures two aspects of leadership: consideration (how likely it is that an individual's job relationship with subordinates is characterized by mutual trust, respect, and consideration) and structure (how likely an individual is to define and structure personal and subordinates' roles toward goal attainment).

Format: Examiner required; suitable for group use; untimed: 20 minutes

Scoring: Hand key; computer

Cost: 25 test booklets $37.00; examiner's manual $15.00

Publisher: McGraw-Hill/London House

Supervisory Change Relations Test (SCHR)
W. J. Reddin

Copyright: 1981

Population: Adults

Purpose: Measures a supervisor's knowledge of sound methods of introducing change; used before or after training in change techniques

Description: True–false 80-item paper–pencil test measuring a supervisor's understanding of how change can be affected by participation, speed, and degree of information, training, resistance, and planning. Suitable for blue- or white-collar supervision. The test is based on Chapter 13 of W. J. Reddin *Managerial Effectiveness* (McGraw-Hill, 1970).

Format: Self-administered; suitable for group use; untimed: 20–30 minutes

Scoring: Hand key

Cost: Test kit (10 test copies, fact sheet, user's guide) $30.00

Publisher: Organizational Tests Ltd.

Supervisory Coaching Relations Test (SCORE)
W. J. Reddin

Copyright: 1981

Population: Adults

Purpose: Measures a supervisor's knowledge of the methods of coaching subordinates; used before or after coaching training

Description: True–false 80-item paper–pencil test covering performance appraisal, effectiveness criteria, coaching interview, and training. Suitable for white- or blue-collar supervision.

Format: Self-administered; suitable for group use; untimed: 20–30 minutes

Scoring: Hand key

Cost: Test kit (10 test copies, fact sheet, user's guide) $30.00

Publisher: Organizational Tests Ltd.

Supervisory Inventory on Communication (SIC)
Donald L. Kirkpatrick

Copyright: 1995

Population: Adults

Purpose: Measures knowledge of proper supervisory use of communication procedures within an organization; used in conjunction with training programs aimed at improving the communication effectiveness of supervisors

Description: Paper–pencil 80-item two-choice test assessing knowledge and understanding of communication philosophy, principles, and methods for supervisors. Each item describes an action or belief concerned with on-the-job communication. Individuals indicate whether they agree or disagree with each statement. Test results identify topics that should be emphasized in training programs, serve as a tool for

conference discussions, measure the effectiveness of training programs, provide information for on-the-job coaching, and assist in the selection of supervisory personnel. The instructor's manual includes a discussion of the inventory's development, normative data, research data, and interpretive guidelines.

Format: Self-administered; suitable for group use; untimed: 20 minutes

Scoring: Self-scored

Cost: 20 tests and answer booklets, instructor's manual $30.00; *No-Nonsense Communication* (book) $5.50 (discount for multiple orders)

Publisher: Donald L. Kirkpatrick, Ph.D.

Supervisory Inventory on Human Relations (SIHR)
Donald L. Kirkpatrick

Copyright: 1994

Population: Adults

Purpose: Measures knowledge of basic human relations principles involved in effective supervisory job performance; used in conjunction with management training programs aimed at increasing knowledge and improving attitudes in dealing with people

Description: Paper–pencil 80-item two-choice test measuring the extent to which supervisors understand and accept the principles, facts, and techniques of human relations in management. Test items cover human relations issues in the following areas: the supervisor's role in management, understanding and motivating employees, developing positive employee attitudes, problem-solving techniques, and principles of learning and training. Individuals indicate whether they agree or disagree with the statement about beliefs or behaviors presented in each test item. The answer booklet provides a rationale for each correct answer. Test results identify topics that should be emphasized in training programs and provide information for on-the-job coaching.

Format: Self-administered; suitable for group use; untimed: 15 minutes

Scoring: Self-scored

Cost: 20 tests and answer booklets, instructor's manual $30.00

Publisher: Donald L. Kirkpatrick, Ph.D.

Supervisory Job Discipline Test (SJD)
W. J. Reddin

Copyrigt: 1981

Population: Adults

Purpose: Determines an individual's knowledge of accepted disciplinary techniques; used before or after training in disciplinary training techniques

Description: True–false 80-item paper–pencil test covering lateness, horseplay, appropriate punishments, corrective interview techniques, handling errors, long coffee breaks, visiting other departments, and eating lunch at desk. Suitable for either blue- or white-collar supervision.

Format: Self-administered; suitable for group use; untimed: 20–30 minutes

Scoring: Hand key

Cost: Test kit (10 test copies, fact sheet, user's guide) $30.00

Publisher: Organizational Tests Ltd.

Supervisory Job Instruction Test (SJI)
W. J. Reddin

Copyright: 1981

Population: Adults

Purpose: Measures an individual's knowledge of how to instruct others on the job; used before or after job instruction training

Description: True–false 80-item paper–pencil test measuring understanding of learning environment; suitable for either blue- or white-collar supervision

Format: Self-administered; suitable for group use; untimed: 20–30 minutes

Scoring: Hand key

Cost: Test kit (10 test copies, fact sheet, user's guide) $30.00

Publisher: Organizational Tests Ltd.

Supervisory Job Safety Test (SJS)
W. J. Reddin

Copyright: 1981

Population: Adults

Purpose: Measures an individual's attitudes toward an understanding of good safety practices; used before or after safety training

Description: True–false 80-question paper–pencil test covering safety instruction, safety devices, safety responsibilities, safety causes, corrective practices, work methods, types of accidents, hazard analysis, accident investigation, and role of supervisors. Suitable for either blue- or white-collar supervision.

Format: Self-administered; suitable for group use; untimed: 20–30 minutes

Scoring: Hand key

Cost: Test kit (10 test copies, fact sheet, user's guide) $30.00

Publisher: Organizational Tests Ltd.

Supervisory Potential Test (SPT)
W. J. Reddin

Copyright: 1981

Population: Adults

Purpose: Measures an individual's understanding of supervisory methods, principles, and techniques; used as a training tool

Description: True–false 80-item paper–pencil test covering subordinate evaluation techniques, disciplinary principles, promotion criteria, change introduction, superior relations, new supervisor attachment, and subordinate motivation. Suitable for either blue- or white-collar supervision.

Format: Self-administered; suitable for group use; untimed: 20–30 minutes

Scoring: Hand key

Cost: Test kit (10 test copies, fact sheet, user's guide) $30.00

Publisher: Organizational Tests Ltd.

Supervisory Practices Inventory (SPI)

Judith S. Canfield, Albert A. Canfield

Copyright: 1981

Population: Adults

Purpose: Evaluates how an individual prefers to be supervised, how the individual's supervisor actually functions, and the difference between preferred and actual supervisory behaviors

Description: Paper–pencil 20-item inventory assessing a subordinate's view of 10 areas of supervisory behavior: setting objectives, planning, organization, delegation, problem identification, decision making, performance evaluation, subordinate development, team building, and conflict resolution. The test items consist of a list of supervisory behaviors, which the subordinate must rank first in order of personal preference and second to indicate how his or her supervisor actually functions. Questions measure supervisory behavior rather than trait or personality characteristics. Dissonance scores are developed from the difference between preferred and actual rankings. Test booklets include explanations for the scales and possible interpretations.

Format: Self-administered; suitable for group use; untimed: 20–40 minutes

Scoring: Self-scored

Cost: Kit (10 inventories, 1 manual) $38.50

Publisher: Western Psychological Services

Supervisory Practices Test (Revised)

Martin M. Bruce

Copyright: 1976

Population: Adults

Purpose: Evaluates supervisory ability and potential in a business-world setting; used for personnel selection, evaluation, and training

Description: Paper–pencil 50-item multiple-choice test indicating the extent to which the subject is able to choose a desirable course of action (as compared with the perceptions and attitudes of managers and subordinates) when presented with a business decision. Minority group data are available. Suitable for individuals with physical, hearing, or visual disabilities. Available also in French, Spanish, and German.

Format: Self-administered; suitable for group use; untimed: 20 minutes

Scoring: Hand key

Cost: Manual and manual supplement (1984) $38.50; key $2.85; forms $53.50; Specimen Set $42.50

Publisher: Martin M. Bruce, Ph.D.

Supervisory Profile Record (SPR)

Copyright: Not provided

Population: Adults

Purpose: Assesses qualities related to successful first-line supervision

Description: Multiple-item paper–pencil computerized questionnaire system designed for predicting an individual's potential for success as a first-line supervisor. The Supervisory Profile Record Report yields information in the areas of background (present self-concept evaluation and present word-values orientation) and judgment (employee communication–motivation, employee training–evaluation, problem resolution, disciplinary practices, and general style practices). Validity data are extensive across functions, organization types, race, and sex.

Format: Examiner required; suitable for group use; untimed: time varies

Scoring: Computer scored

Cost: Contact publisher

Publisher: Richardson, Bellows, Henry and Company, Inc.

Supervisory Union Relations Test (SUR)

W. J. Reddin

Copyright: 1981

Population: Adults

Purpose: Measures a supervisor's attitudes toward unions; used to evaluate supervisors' and managers' attitudes

Description: True–false 80-item paper–pencil test covering motives of union leadership, the reasons men join unions, effective methods for working with unions, management rights, role of shop steward, foreman–union relationship, labor benefits, and company benefits. Respondents answer on the basis of what they believe is best for their position or company at the present time. Suitable for either blue- or white-collar supervision.

Format: Self-administered; suitable for group use; untimed: 20–30 minutes

Scoring: Hand key

Cost: Test kit (10 test copies, fact sheet, user's guide) $30.00

Publisher: Organizational Tests Ltd.

Survey of Employee Access
Jay Hall

Copyright: 1995

Population: Adults

Purpose: Provides companion feedback to *Access Management Survey.* Designed to give an opportunity to evaluate how effectively managers handle problem-solving processes, information flow, budgets, work design, technical resource allocation and employee morale.

Description: 25-question paper–pencil survey.

Format: Self-administered; untimed

Scoring: Self-scored

Cost: $7.95 each

Publisher: Teleometrics International, Inc.

Survey of Management Practices
Jay Hall

Copyright: 1995

Population: Adults

Purpose: Assesses how productive a manager's practices are

Description: Paper–pencil 72-item criterion-referenced test consisting of items which address some of the specific behaviors that a manager may or may not engage in. Two sets of ratings are used: ACTUAL, employee's assess-ment of current managerial practices, and DESIRED, employee's assessment of how often the employees would like for the manager to use a practice. The test uses a 9-point scale ranging from 1 (never) to 9 (always) for each set of ratings. This is a companion to the *Productive Practices Survey.*

Format: Self-administered; suitable for group use; untimed: time varies

Scoring: Self-scored

Cost: $7.95 each

Publisher: Teleometrics International, Inc.

System for Testing and Evaluation of Potential (STEP)
Melany E. Baehr

Copyright: 1986

Population: Adults

Purpose: Estimates potential for successful performance (PSP) and current skills in present and future positions; used for selection, placement, promotion, succession planning, diagnosis of training needs, and individual or management development

Description: Based on two interlocking paper–pencil measurement systems: The *Managerial and Professional Job Functions Inventory* (MP-JFI), which analyzes the demands of a job, and *The Managerial and Professional Test Battery,* which assesses an individual's abilities, skills, and attributes. Given the administration of the relevant test battery and the job skills questionnaire, a single test administration will provide information about the individual's potential for successful performance and present skill level for all three positions in a selected managerial hierarchy.

Format: Examiner required; suitable for group use; timed: 1½ to 4½ hours depending on version

Scoring: Mail scoring or ITAC (Immediate Telephone Analysis by Computer)

Cost: Contact publisher; $120 to $200 per test depending on volume ordered

Publisher: McGraw-Hill/London House

Thomas-Kilmann Conflict Mode Instrument (TKI)
Ralph H. Kilmann, Kenneth W. Thomas

Copyright: 1974

Population: Adults

Purpose: Used for management development, counseling, and negotiating to assess conflict handling techniques.

Description: Forced-choice 30-item test. Competing, collaborating, compromising, avoiding, and accommodating. Also available in French and Spanish.

Format: Individual/self-administered; suitable for group use; untimed

Scoring: Self-scored

Cost: $6.50

Publisher: Xicom, Inc.

TQManager Inventory (TQMI)
Warren H. Schmidt, Jerome P. Finnigan

Copyright: 1994

Population: Adults

Purpose: Used in management development to assess managerial skills critical to TQM

Description: Likert scale with 25 items. Openness and trust, collaboration and teamwork, managing by fact, recognition and reward, and learning organization are the scores yielded. A 10th-grade reading level is required. Available in Spanish.

Format: Individual/self-administered; untimed

Scoring: Self-scored

Cost: $6.75

Publisher: Xicom, Inc.

Values Inventory (VI)
W. J. Reddin

Copyright: 1981

Population: Adolescents, adults

Purpose: Reveals a manager's value system; used in college and industry

Description: Multiple-item paper–pencil test consisting of quotations among which the manager chooses preferred statements. The values tested are theoretical, power, effectiveness, achievement, human, industry, and profit.

Format: Self-administered; suitable for group use; untimed: 20–30 minutes

Scoring: Hand key

Cost: Test kit (10 test copies, fact sheet, user's guide) $40.00

Publisher: Organizational Tests Ltd.

Wilson Multi-Level Management Surveys
Clark L. Wilson

Copyright: 1978

Population: Adults

Purpose: Measures refinement and replication of MLMS Scales

Description: Multiple-item paper–pencil questionnaire with 15 measures of managerial practices

Format: Group administration; examiner required; untimed

Scoring: Examiner evaluated

Cost: $21.00

Publisher: Select Press

Women as Managers (WAMS)
Lawrence H. Peters, James R. Terborg, Janet Taynor

Copyright: 1974

Population: Adults

Purpose: Measures attitudes toward women in management positions; used in career counseling of male and female college students

Description: Paper–pencil 21-item questionnaire

Format: Group or individual administration; examiner required; untimed

Scoring: Examiner evaluated

Cost: $18.00

Publisher: Select Press

X-Y-Z Inventory
W. J. Reddin

Copyright: 1981

Population: Adults

Purpose: Reveals a manager's basic, underlying, philosophical assumptions about humans; used in business to help understand a manager's frame of reference in assessing employees' performances

Description: Multiple-item inventory reveal-ing some elements of a manager's assumptions that the human is a beast (X), a self-actualizing being (Y), or a rational being (Z). The test is used prior to discussion of X, Y, and Z theories.

Format: Self-administered; suitable for group use; untimed: 20–30 minutes

Scoring: Hand key

Cost: Test kit (10 test copies, fact sheet, user's guide) $40.00

Publisher: Organizational Tests Ltd.

Personality

Adult Personality Inventory
Samuel E. Krug

Copyright: 1982

Population: Adults

Purpose: Assesses personality characteristics, interpersonal style, and career preferences for personnel evaluation, career planning, rehabilitation counseling, and family therapy

Description: Series of computer-administered multiple-item multiple-choice paper–pencil subtests yielding scores in three areas: Personality Characteristics (extroverted, adjusted, tough-minded, independent, disciplined, creative, enterprising), Interpersonal Style (caring, adapting, withdrawn, submissive, hostile, rebellious, sociable, assertive), Career Orientation (practical, scientific, aesthetic, social, competitive, structured). Four validity scales (Good Impression, Bad Impression, Infrequency, Uncertainty) complete the test profile. Reports available through mail-in service or three on-site software programs (MS/PC DOS on IBM systems).

Format: Self-administered; suitable for group use; untimed: 30–60 minutes

Scoring: Computer scored

Cost: Introductory kit available in four different report formats. Kits include test material, manual, and processing of five reports $49 to $59

Publisher: MetriTech, Inc.

Behavioral Profiles: Observer Assessment
Tony Alessandra

Copyright: 1995

Population: Adults/employees

Purpose: Helps people define their own styles; provides a picture of how others perceive an individual's interactions

Description: Used together with the *Self Assessment,* this instrument provides valuable information for personal growth. Participants can recognize differences between the way they think they are and the way they are actually perceived by others. This evaluation provides tangible goals for improving versatility and enhancing relationships.

Format: ½ day or full day

Scoring: Self-scoring

Cost: $3.95

Publisher: Pfeiffer and Company International Publishers, Inc.

Behavioral Profiles: Self Assessment
Tony Alessandra

Copyright: 1995

Population: Adults/employees

Purpose: Helps people define their own styles; determines how a person believes he or she interacts with others

Description: Used together with the *Observer Assessment,* this instrument provides valuable information for personal growth. Participants can recognize differences between the way they think they are and the way they are actually perceived by others. This evaluation provides tangible goals for improving versatility and enhancing relationships.

Format: ½ day or full day

Scoring: Self-scoring

Cost: $3.95

Publisher: Pfeiffer and Company International Publishers, Inc.

Business Judgment Test–Revised
Martin M. Bruce

Copyright: 1984

Population: Adults

Purpose: Evaluates the subject's sense of "social intelligence" in business-related situations; used for employee selection and training

Description: Paper–pencil 25-item multiple-choice test in which the subject selects one of four ways to complete a stem statement, allowing the examiner to gauge the subject's sense of socially accepted and desirable ways to behave in business relationships. The score suggests the degree to which the subject agrees with the general opinion of businesspeople as to the proper way to handle various relationships. Available in French.

Format: Self-administered; suitable for group use; untimed: 10–15 minutes

Scoring: Hand key

Cost: Manual and manual supplement $37.50; key $2.75; forms $53.50; Specimen Set $37.50

Publisher: Martin M. Bruce, Ph.D.

CandRT (Creativity and Risk Taking)
Richard E. Byrd

Copyright: 1986

Population: Adults

Purpose: Assesses an individual's creativity and risk-taking orientations, the implications of these orientations for management styles, what contributions a person with this style is likely to make, and how this person might hinder organizational progress

Description: Participants respond to a series of questions and are able to calculate their own score to see immediate results. The instrument includes a section on the possibility of changing styles, a background of the inventory, a bibliography, and trainer's guidelines.

Format: 2 hours

Scoring: Self-scoring

Cost: $7.95

Publisher: Pfeiffer and Company International Publishers, Inc.

Campbell Leadership Index
David P. Campbell

Copyright: 1991

Population: Adults

Purpose: Measures personality characteristics directly related to the nature and demands of leadership; used for measuring an individual's effectiveness as a leader

Description: Paper–pencil 100-item test with 21 dimensions, plus an overall index. Compares self vs. other. A sixth-grade reading level is required. Examiners must be qualified in psychology.

Format: Individual administration; untimed

Scoring: Computer scored; test scoring service available from publisher

Cost: $165.00

Publisher: NCS Assessments

Career Anchors: Discovering Your Real Values
Edgar H. Schein

Copyright: 1990

Population: Adults

Purpose: Helps people define dominant themes

and patterns in their lives, understand their own approach to work and a career, find reasons for choices they make, and take steps to fulfill their self-image

Description: Helps people uncover their real values and use them to make better career choices. The instrument includes the orientations inventory, the career anchor interview, and conceptual material. The Trainer's Manual provides facilitation instructions for a two-hour workshop and an extended workshop of four hours or more. A short lecture on the concept of career anchors is included.

Format: Suitable for group use; 2 hours or 4 hours

Scoring: Self-scoring

Cost: Career Anchors Package $24.95; instrument $9.95

Publisher: Pfeiffer and Company International Publishers, Inc.

Career Suitability Profile
Christopher P. Harding

Copyright: 1991

Population: Adults

Purpose: Measures fundamental personality characteristics which control career interests, abilities, and the capacity to perform; used for recruiting, screening candidates, organization design, succession planning, training and assistance, and reassignment

Description: Multiple-choice 70-item paper–pencil or computer-administered test based on 12 personality factors defined by Christopher Harding to characterize an individual's personality structure. The test determines which factors most control an individual's performance potential in his or her work and personal life, one's suitability for various career fields, the outlook for achievement and fulfillment in one's most appropriate career area(s), and the type of business in which he or she will function most effectively. An individual's results are classified into one of several hundred possible profile patterns. The Career Suitability Profile Report provides a personalized 30-page description of the profile and what each element means.

Format: Self-administered; suitable for group use; untimed: 10 minutes

Scoring: Computer scored

Cost: Test and report $250.00 per person

Publisher: Management Strategies, Inc.

Career/Personality Compatibility Inventory (C/PCI)
James H. Brewer

Copyright: 1989

Population: Adults

Purpose: Used in career planning, placement, training and development to improve career selection

Description: The instrument determines personality type, explores the individual's career preferences, charts the compatibility between personality type and career, suggests job selection criteria, and suggests careers based on personality type. Contains a Personality Inventory and score sheet, a Career Characteristic Inventory and score sheet, and a compatibility graph.

Format: Individual/self-administered; untimed: 20–30 minutes

Scoring: Hand key

Cost: $6.95 each

Publisher: Associated Consultants in Education

Comprehensive Personality Profile
Larry L. Craft

Copyright: 1980

Population: Adults; ages 18 and above

Purpose: Used in pre-employment selection to measure personality and assess job compatibility

Description: Paper–pencil 88-item test with seven primary scales, 10 secondary scales, and sales training reports. A ninth-grade reading level is required. Available in Spanish and French.

Format: Individual/self-administered; suitable for group use; untimed

Scoring: Computer scored; test scoring service available from publisher

Cost: 5 tests $25.00; 25 tests $500.00

Publisher: Wonderlic Personnel Test, Inc.

Comprehensive Personnel System (CPS)
Terry D. Anderson, Brian Zeiner

Copyright: 1989

Population: Adults

Purpose: Screens for selection and development of exceptional employees; used for employee selection

Description: Projective test with 14 items. A 10th-grade reading level is required.

Format: Individual administration; suitable for group use; examiner required; untimed

Scoring: Self-scored

Cost: $19.95

Publisher: Consulting Resource Group International, Inc.

Education Position Analysis (EPA)
William J. Reddin

Copyright: Not provided

Population: Adults

Purpose: Used for diagnosis

Description: Multiple-choice paper–pencil test with eight styles, 20 elements/relative effectiveness, 20 elements/dominance, and task relationships orientation.

Format: Individual/self-administered; suitable for group use; untimed: 60 minutes

Scoring: Self-scored

Cost: Set of 10 tests $150.00

Publisher: Organizational Tests Ltd.

Emo Questionnaire
George O. Baehr, Melany E. Baehr

Copyright: 1995

Population: Adults

Purpose: Determines an individual's personal–emotional adjustment; used to evaluate

the potential of sales, managerial, and professional personnel and to screen applicants for jobs requiring efficient performance under pressure

Description: Paper–pencil 140-item examination measuring 10 traditional psychodiagnostic categories (rationalization, inferiority feelings, hostility, depression, fear and anxiety, organic reaction, projection, unreality, sex problems, withdrawal) and three composite adjustment factors (internal, external, somatic). The results reflect both the individual's internal psychodynamics and his or her relationship with the external environment. In combination with other instruments, the test has been validated for selection of salespersons, police and security guards, and transit operators. In hospital settings, it is useful as a diagnosis of emotional health and to chart the course of psychotherapy. Basic reading skills required.

Format: Examiner required; suitable for group use; untimed: 20 minutes

Scoring: Hand key

Cost: 25 test booklets $36; 25 score sheets $10; examiner's manual $20

Publisher: McGraw-Hill/London House

Emotional Stability Survey (ES Survey)

Copyright: 1973

Population: Adults

Purpose: Measures the emotional stability of applicants for sensitive positions; used for applicant screening and employee selection

Description: Multiple-item paper–pencil pre-employment survey measuring emotional stability and control. The survey is highly job related for police and security positions. The self-report questionnaire format requires no interpretive analysis. In addition to the standard scoring template, a critical factor score template also is provided to identify false positive scores indicating attempts to bias answers. The survey was developed according to guidelines established by the EEOC and reviewed by FEPC and EEOC examiners. It may be administered, scored, and interpreted in-house by personnel/human resource/security specialists by license to Psychological Systems Corporation. The survey is also available as part of the PASS Booklet.

Format: Examiner required; suitable for group use; untimed: 5–10 minutes

Scoring: Hand key

Cost: Contact publisher

Publisher: Predictive Surveys Corporation

Employee Reliability Inventory (ERI)®

Gerald L. Borofsky

Copyright: 1986

Population: Adults; job applicants

Purpose: Assesses seven dimensions of behavior; used to help screen job applicants

Description: Paper–pencil 81-item true–false test designed to screen job applicants for unreliable and unproductive behavior. The seven areas of behavior assessed are Freedom from Disruptive Alcohol and Substance Abuse, Courteous Job Performance, Emotional Maturity, Conscientiousness, Trustworthiness, Long Term Job Commitment, and Safe Job Performance. Available in Chinese, Hindi, Spanish, French. Suitable for those with visual, physical, and hearing disabilities. A sixth-grade reading level is required. Available in large print, on audiocassette, and in Braille.

Format: Individual/self-administered; untimed

Scoring: Hand key, computer (IBM) scored; test scoring service available from publisher

Cost: $6–$12 per test; minimum order of 10 tests

Publisher: Bay State Psychological Associates, Inc.

Employment Productivity Index (EPI)

Copyright: Not provided

Population: Job applicants

Purpose: Assesses personality trait combinations that lead to productive and responsible work behavior. Used to identify applicants who will remain on the job, have low absentee rates, and obey company rules, particularly those prohibiting alcohol and drugs

Description: Multiple-item paper–pencil survey consisting of four scales measuring personality traits that lead to productive employment: Dependability, Interpersonal Cooperation, Drug Avoidance, and Validity. Standard scores, percentile scores, and a Composite Productivity Index are provided. In addition, a test analysis report includes a Significant Behavioral Indicators section highlighting specific responses that may be useful in making decisions about borderline candidates. The EPI–3S version includes a safety scale measuring safety consciousness and identifying applicants at risk for on-the-job accidents.

Format: Self-administered; suitable for group use; untimed: 30 minutes

Scoring: Operator-assisted telephone; computer scored

Cost: Kit (administration materials, operator-assisted telephone scoring, and reports) $9–$13 depending on quantity and scoring method; EPI–3S $14

Publisher: McGraw-Hill/London House

Employment Productivity Index (EPI–3 and EPI–3S)

Copyright: 1989

Population: Job applicants

Purpose: Assesses personality trait combinations that lead to productive and responsible work behavior; used to identify applicants who will remain on the job, have low absentee rates, obey company rules, and cooperate with supervisors, customers, and co-workers.

Description: Multiple-item paper–pencil survey consisting of four scales measuring personality traits that lead to productive employment: Dependability, Interpersonal Cooperation, Drug Avoidance, and Validity. Standard scores, percentile scores, and a Composite Productivity Index are provided. In addition, a test analysis report includes Significant Behavioral Indicators highlighting specific responses that may be useful in making decisions about borderline candidates. The EPI–3S version includes a safety scale measuring safety consciousness and identifying applicants at risk for on-the-job accidents.

Format: Self-administered; suitable for group use; untimed: 30 minutes

Scoring: Operator-assisted telephone; computer scored; scoring service available from publisher

Cost: $5–$15 depending upon quantity and scoring method

Publisher: McGraw-Hill/London House

Entrepreneurial Quotient (EQ)
Edward J. Fasiska

Copyright: 1984

Population: Adults

Purpose: Assesses adaptability, management, and personality traits to measure entrepreneurial potential

Description: Multiple-choice 100-item paper–pencil test. The following reports are yielded: four summary scales—adaptability, managerial traits, personality traits, and EQ index.

Format: Individual/self-administered; suitable for group use; untimed

Scoring: Computer scored

Cost: 5 tests $125.00; 25 tests $500.00

Publisher: Wonderlic Personnel Test, Inc.

ETSA Tests 8-A—Personal Adjustment Index
George A. W. Stouffer, Jr., S. Trevor Hadley

Copyright: 1990

Population: Adolescents, adults; Grades 10 and above

Purpose: Measures personality traits for all types of jobs; used for employee selection, placement, and promotion

Description: Paper–pencil 105-item test measuring seven components of personal adjustment: community spirit, attitude toward cooperation with employer, attitude toward health, attitude toward authority, lack of nervous tendencies, leadership, and job stability. The test may be used in conjunction with ETSA 1-A, General Mental Ability, and any ETSA test measuring a specific skill area.

Format: Examiner required; suitable for group use; untimed: 1 hour

Scoring: Hand key; examiner evaluated; scoring service available

Cost: 10 tests with key $15.50; manual $5.00; handbook $15.00

Publisher: Educators'/Employers' Tests and Services Associates

Famous Sayings (FS)
Bernard M. Bass

Copyright: 1958

Population: Adolescents, adults; Grades 10 and above

Purpose: Assesses personality; used for industrial and professional screening and for research in social psychology

Description: Paper–pencil 131-item test of four vocationally important aspects of personality, including hostility, fear of failure, social acquiescence, and acceptance of conventional mores. Items are general statements consisting mainly of famous sayings, proverbs, and adages. Instructions are read aloud by the examiner while the subjects read along silently. The subjects indicate whether they agree or disagree with the statements or are uncertain.

Format: Examiner required; suitable for group use; untimed: 15–30 minutes

Scoring: Hand key; examiner evaluated

Cost: Kit $13.00

Publisher: Psychological Test Specialists

Gordon Personal Profile–Inventory (GPP–I™)
Leonard V. Gordon

Copyright: 1978 (Manual 1993)

Population: Adults

Purpose: Provides measurement of factors in the personality domain

Description: Eight factors provide coverage of five personality traits (extroversion, agreeableness, conscientiousness, emotional stability, and openness). Respondents select one item in each group of four as being most like themselves and one as being least like themselves.

Format: Examiner required; suitable for group use; untimed: 20–30 minutes

Scoring: Hand key or machine scorable

Cost: Examination kit (booklets, answer document, and manual) $48.00

Publisher: The Psychological Corporation

GuidePak
Doris J. Pick

Copyright: 1991

Population: Ages 18 and older

Purpose: Identifies an individual's interests and personality characteristics; used for career guidance and selection

Description: Paper–pencil 805-item multiple-choice and true–false instrument that combines the California Psychological Inventory and the Strong-Campbell Interest Inventory to measure aspects of an individual's personality and interests that are related to vocational choice. A narrative report, personal interest profile, and workbook are provided.

Format: Group or individual administration, 2 hours

Scoring: Computer scored

Cost: $89.50

Publisher: Behaviordyne, Inc.

Hilson Management Survey (HMS)
Robin E. Inwald

Copyright: 1995

Population: Adults; ages 18 and above

Purpose: Assesses work-related behavioral characteristics

Description: Paper–pencil 103-item true–false test with a profile graph within a computer-generated report. A test book and scannable answer sheets are used. A fifth-grade reading level is required. A computer version is available using software for IBM and compatible computers.

Format: Suitable for group use; examiner required; untimed: 15 minutes

Scoring: Computer scored; test scoring service available from publisher

Cost: Contact publisher

Publisher: Hilson Research, Inc.

Hilson Personnel Profile/Success Quotient (HPP/SQ)
Robin E. Inwald

Copyright: 1988

Population: Adolescents, adults; ages 15 and older; Grades 7 and above

Purpose: Assesses behavioral patterns and characteristics related to success in the working world; measures individual strengths and positive features; used for pre-employment screening and in-house staff training programs

Description: Behaviorally oriented 15-item paper–pencil true–false instrument consisting of one validity measure and five scales: Candor, Achievement History, Social Ability, "Winner's" Image, Initiative, and Family Achievement Expectations. Content areas for the SA scale include Extroversion, Popularity, and Sensitivity. Areas covered by the WI scale include Competitive Drive and Self-Worth. For the IN scale, four content areas are included: Drive, Preparation Style, Goal Orientation, and Anxiety about Organization. A narrative report and two profile graphs of six scales and nine scale content areas are provided with raw scores and t-scores. Local/specific job category norms are also available. A fifth-grade reading level is required.

Format: Self-administered; suitable for group use; untimed: 20 minutes

Scoring: Computer scored

Cost: Reusable test booklets $1.50; processing fees $6.00–$20.00; Contact publisher for additional information

Publisher: Hilson Research, Inc.

Hogan Personality Inventory (HPI)
Robert Hogan, Joyce Hogan

Copyright: 1992

Population: Adults

Purpose: Assesses the major components of normal personality in organizationally appropriate terms for career counseling, individualized assessment, employee selection, placement, promotion, and succession planning.

Description: Test consists of 206 true–false items that are generated into reports to help determine whether persons are suited for a particular occupation. There are six occupational scales that predict organizational effectiveness. Three measure characteristics that are important for all jobs (service orientation, reliability, and stress tolerance). Three additional scales forecast performance in clerical, sales, and managerial jobs (clerical potential, sales potential, and managerial potential). Also included are seven primary scales measuring characteristics that influence a variety of organizational behaviors.

Format: Examiner required; suitable for group use; times: 15–20 minutes

Scoring: Computer scored

Cost: Examination kit (technical manual, test booklet, and answer sheet) $38.75

Publisher: The Psychological Corporation

INQ—Your Thinking Profile
Allen Harrison, Robert Bramson, Susan Bramson, Nicholas Parlette

Copyright: 1994

Population: Adults

Purpose: Identifies one's preferred mode of thinking; used in training, team-building, and sales

Description: Multiple-choice 18-item test yielding scores in five categories: Analyst, Synthesist, Pragmatist, Idealist, and Realist. Also available in Spanish and French.

Format: Suitable for group use; untimed: 15–20 minutes

Scoring: Self-scored

Cost: 10 Tests $59.95

Publisher: INQ Educational Materials

Inwald Survey 2 (IS2)
Robin E. Inwald

Copyright: 1994

Population: Adults; ages 18 and above

Purpose: Assesses violence-related behavior characteristics; used for pre-employment and promotional screening for job applicants

Description: Paper–pencil 110-item true–false test with a profile graph and computer-generated report. A test book and scannable answer sheets are used. Scales include denial of shortcomings—validity scale, risk-taking tendencies, lack of temper control, reckless driving/safety patterns, firearms interest, work difficulties, lack of social sensitivity, lack of leadership interest; attitudes—antisocial behaviors, and behavior patterns—integrity concerns. A fifth-grade reading level is required. A computer version is available using software for IBM compatibles. Also available in Spanish.

Format: Suitable for group use; examiner required; untimed: 15 minutes

Scoring: Computer scored; test scoring service available from publisher

Cost: Contact publisher

Publisher: Hilson Research, Inc.

Inwald Survey 5 (IS5)
Robin E. Inwald

Copyright: 1991

Population: Adults

Purpose: Assesses behavioral characteristics; used for pre-employment screening for job candidates

Description: Paper–pencil 162-item true–false test with three overall scales. A profile graph is contained in a computer-generated report. A computer version using software for IBM compatibles is available. A fifth-grade reading level is required.

Format: Suitable for group use; examiner required; untimed: 20 minutes

Scoring: Computer scored; test scoring service available from publisher

Cost: Contact publisher

Publisher: Hilson Research, Inc.

IPI Employee Aptitude Series CPF
Raymond B. Cattell, J. E. King, A. K. Schuettler

Copyright: 1992

Population: Adults

Purpose: Measures extroversion vs. introversion; used for screening, placement, and promotion of employees

Description: Paper–pencil 40-item personality test determines contact vs. noncontact factor in personalities. Also available in French and Spanish.

Format: Suitable for group use; examiner required; untimed: 5–10 minutes

Scoring: Hand key

Cost: Introductory kit (20 test booklets, scoring key, manual) $30

Publisher: Industrial Psychology International Ltd.

IPI Employee Aptitude Series NPF
Raymond B. Cattell, J. E. King, A. K. Schuettler

Copyright: 1992

Population: Adults

Purpose: Measures emotional balance, stability, and stress tolerance; used to screen applicants for a variety of positions and to place and promote employees

Description: Paper–pencil 40-item test measuring an individual's general stability and emotional balance. Also available in French and Spanish.

Format: Suitable for group use; examiner required; untimed: 5–10 minutes

Scoring: Hand key

Cost: Introductory kit (20 test booklets, scoring key, manual) $30

Publisher: Industrial Psychology International Ltd.

Leadership/Personality Compatibility Inventory (L/PCI)
James H. Brewer

Copyright: 1994

Population: Adults

Purpose: Used to promote more productive leadership in organizations

Description: Helps respondents determine and understand three major factors affecting their leadership: basic personality style, present leadership role, and the compatibility between the two. The instrument consists of two inventories: a personality inventory and a leadership role inventory. The respondents first learn about their dominant personality using the Brewer framework: Bold, Expressive, Sympathetic, or Technical. Their leadership role characteristics are determined by their organizational environment: Active/Competitive; Persuasive/Interactive; Precise/Systematic; and Willing/Steady. A full interpretation is included.

Format: Individual/self-administered; untimed: 15–30 minutes

Scoring: Hand key

Cost: $6.95 each

Publisher: Associated Consultants in Education

Management Position Analysis (MPA)

Copyright: 1991

Population: Adults

Purpose: Used for diagnosis

Description: Multiple-choice paper–pencil test with eight styles, 20 elements on relative effectiveness, 20 elements on dominance and task–relationship orientation.

Format: Individual/self-administration; suitable for group use; untimed: 60 minutes

Scoring: Self-scored

Cost: Set of 10 tests $150.00

Publisher: Organizational Tests Ltd.

Meyer-Kendall Assessment Survey (MKAS)

Henry D. Meyer, Edward L. Kendall

Copyright: 1997

Population: Adults

Purpose: Surveys work-related personality and interpersonal functioning for use in personnel assessment

Description: Paper–pencil 105 dichotomous-item test of 10 aspects of personal functioning relevant to performance at work. The scales are dominance, attention to detail, psychosomatic tendencies, independence, extroversion, anxiety, determination, people concern, stability, and achievement motivation. Scores are also obtained for two broad-band scales: Assertive Drive and Self-Assurance. An optional feature of the MKAS is the Pre-Assessment Worksheet, which determines the profile of an "ideal" applicant for a position. Computer scoring is achieved using the WPS Test Report mail-in service.

Format: Examiner/self-administered; suitable for group use; untimed: 15 minutes

Scoring: Computer scored

Cost: Kit (2 WPS Test Report assessment sheets, 2 WPS Test Report pre-assessment sheets, 1 manual) $95.00

Publisher: Western Psychological Services

My BEST Profile (Computer Software)

James H. Brewer

Copyright: 1989

Population: Adults

Purpose: Used to improve self-understanding and interpersonal relations

Description: Determines personality types, fosters positive interpersonal relations, creates self-awareness, and promotes greater productivity

Format: Individual/self-administered; untimed: 15–20 minutes

Scoring: Hand key

Cost: $99.95 each

Publisher: Associated Consultants in Education

Occupational Personality Questionnaire (OPQ)

Copyright: 1987

Population: Adults

Purpose: Assesses 30 work-relevant personality traits used in personnel selection, placement, counseling, and development

Description: Multiple-choice 248-item paper–pencil or computer-administered questionnaire measuring 30 work-related personality traits covering relationships with people (persuasive, outgoing, democratic), thinking style (practical, conceptual, conscientious), and feelings and emotions (worrying, critical, competitive) along with others. Application expanded by using in conjunction with Hurmis EXPERT Software to produce 25-page interpretive report.

Format: Approximately 35 minutes

Scoring: Hand key; machine scored; scoring service available

Cost: Contact Publisher

Publisher: Saville and Holdsworth Ltd.

Occupational Relationships Profile (ORP)

Colin D. Selby

Copyright: 1991

Population: Adolescents, adults

Purpose: Used in employment counseling to assess social behavior at work

Description: Multiple-choice 102-item computer-administered paper–pencil criterion-referenced projective test. The categories are sociability, power, teamwork, and warmth. Narrative reports are available. A computer version using DOS is available. An 11-year-old reading level is required. Available in French.

Format: Individual/self-administered; suitable for group use; examiner required; untimed: 20 minutes

Scoring: Computer scored; test scoring service available from publisher

Cost: Specimen Set $60.00

Publisher: Selby MillSmith Ltd.

Occupational Type Profile (OTP)
Colin D. Selby

Copyright: 1991

Population: Adolescents, adults

Purpose: Used in employment counseling to assess Jungian type in the workplace

Description: Multiple-choice 88-item computer-administered paper–pencil criterion-referenced projective test. Psychological type profile norms, an uncertainty index, and narrative reports are available. A computer version using PC DOS computers is available. Available in French.

Format: Individual/self-administered; suitable for group use; examiner required; untimed: 20 minutes

Scoring: Computer scored; test scoring service available from publisher

Cost: Specimen Set $60.00

Publisher: Selby MillSmith Ltd.

PEP/Pre-Evaluation Profile
James H. Brewer

Copyright: 1989

Population: Adults

Purpose: Prepares supervisors for performance evaluation of employees without personality type bias

Description: Provides a profile of the supervisor and the employee being evaluated, leads supervisor to understand how personality may affect employee evaluation, explores methods of fair employee evaluations, and describes how to interpret personality factors in the evaluation process. The taker must know the other person well enough to make valid observations.

Format: Individual/self-administered; untimed: 15–30 minutes

Scoring: Hand key

Cost: $4.95 each

Publisher: Associated Consultants in Education

Personal Audit
Clifford R. Edams, William M. Lepley

Copyright: Not provided

Population: Adolescents, adults; Grades 7 and above

Purpose: Assesses an individual's personality as a factor of how well that person will perform in school or industry; also used for clinical diagnosis of maladjustment

Description: Paper–pencil 450-item personality test. Nine scales of 50 items each measure relatively independent components of personality: seriousness–impulsiveness, firmness–indecision, tranquillity–irritability, frankness–evasion, stability–instability, tolerance–intolerance, steadiness–emotionality, persistence–fluctuation, and contentment–worry. The test acquaints teachers with personality characteristics of students, is an aid to vocational and educational counseling, and provides an index of employees' job satisfaction and success in terms of their personal adjustment. Two forms are available.

Format: Self-administered; suitable for group use; untimed: Form LL 40–50 minutes; Form SS 30–40 minutes

Scoring: Hand key

Cost: 25 test booklets Form LL $50.00; 25 test booklets Form SS $43.00; examiner's manual $10.00

Publisher: McGraw-Hill/London House

Personal Style Indicator (PSI)
Terry D. Anderson, Everett T. Robinson

Copyright: 1988

Population: Adults

Purpose: Assesses personal style preferences; used for marital counseling, conflict resolutions, leadership and personal development, and team building

Description: Forced-choice 16-item test. An 11th-grade reading level is required. Available in Japanese, French, and Dutch. Individuals with special needs will need assistance.

Format: Self-administered; suitable for group use; examiner required; untimed

Scoring: Examiner evaluated; self or computer scored

Cost: $12.95

Publisher: Consulting Resource Group International, Inc.

Personnel Selection Inventory (PSI)

Copyright: 1988

Population: Job applicants

Purpose: Assesses personality trait combinations that lead to honest, productive, and service-oriented employees; designed to reduce absenteeism, shrinkage, turnover, on-the-job accidents, and substance abuse; meets both human resources and loss-prevention needs

Description: Multiple-item paper–pencil test survey. Eight versions of the PSI are available to meet various companies' screening needs. The forms range from PSI–1, which assesses honesty only, to PSI–7ST, which assesses a wide range of attributes. The various forms contain combinations of the following scales: Honesty, Supervision Attitudes, Employee/Customer Relations, Drug Avoidance, Work Values, Safety, Emotional Stability, Nonviolence, and Tenure. A distortion and an accuracy scale are included. Some versions contain a detailed personal and behavioral history section that aids in making decisions about borderline candidates. Industry specific norms are available for some PSI versions. A seventh-grade reading level is required.

Format: Self-administered; suitable for group use; untimed: 30–40 minutes

Scoring: Computer scored

Cost: Complete $8.00 to $17.00 depending on scoring method and volume ordered

Publisher: McGraw-Hill/London House

Picture Situation Test

Copyright: 1971

Population: Adult males

Purpose: Measures an individual's response to aggression-provoking stimuli within an every-day context; used for personnel screening and placement and clinical research on aggression

Description: Paper–pencil 20-item test measuring the type of aggression an individual displays and the effect it is likely to have on the interpersonal situation in which aggression appears. The test items consist of partially structured pictures depicting aggression-provoking situations. The individual must complete the situation by giving personal responses. Responses are scored for type of aggression (direct, denial) and effect of response (constructive, destructive). A method for standardized scoring is provided. The test is restricted to competent persons properly registered with the South African Medical and Dental Council. Afrikaans version available.

Format: Examiner required; suitable for group use

Scoring: Hand key; examiner evaluated

Cost: Contact publisher

Publisher: Human Sciences Research Council

Power Management
James H. Brewer

Copyright: 1987

Population: Adults

Purpose: Provides a systematic approach to improving leadership through an understanding of the forces of power

Description: The three-in-one package can be used as a text, a workbook, or for the fullest comprehension—a "worktext" complete with personality profiles. It provides complete flexibility for group training or independent study. A video supplement and computer software are also available.

Format: Individual/self-administered

Scoring: Self-scored

Cost: Complete package (worktext, video and computer program) $149.95

Publisher: Associated Consultants in Education

Power Selling
James H. Brewer

Copyright: 1995

Population: Adults

Purpose: Enables one to understand how to behave in each new selling situation and how to communicate with prospects of different personality types

Description: The model identifies critical elements of your personality that will help or hurt your selling, analyze your prospects' personality types so that you can "speak their language," and plan the best sales approach based on your prospect's personality and situation.

Format: Individual/self-administered

Scoring: Self-scored

Cost: Power Selling (test only) $19.95; My BEST Presentation Style $4.95; Sales Style $2.95; Complete Set $22.95

Publisher: Associated Consultants in Education

Projective Personality Test (Analogous to the TAT)

Copyright: 1972

Population: Adults

Purpose: Evaluates basic personality characteristics; intended for use exclusively with black African subjects

Description: The test's 16–18 picture cards provide the stimuli for a projective personality assessment analogous to the TAT. Each picture presents some degree of ambiguity to facilitate a variety of interpretations. Where humans are depicted, black characters are used except where the situation, according to the test publisher, "requires a Caucasian." There is one set of cards for each of the following groups: urban men, urban women, rural men, and rural women. Use is restricted to competent persons properly registered with the South African Medical and Dental Council.

Format: Examiner required; not suitable for group use; untimed: open ended

Scoring: Examiner evaluated

Cost: Contact publisher

Publisher: Human Sciences Research Council

PSI In-Depth Interpretations
Terry D. Anderson, Everett T. Robinson

Copyright: 1988

Population: Adults

Purpose: Assesses personal style preferences; used for personal development

Description: Test with 21 items. Available in Japanese, French, and Dutch. A 10th-grade reading level is required.

Format: Individual administration; suitable for group use; examiner required

Scoring: Self-scored

Cost: $9.95

Publisher: Consulting Resource Group International, Inc.

Rahim Organizational Conflict Inventories (ROCI)
Afzalur Rahim

Copyright: Not provided

Population: Adults

Purpose: Measures conflict experienced within an organization and assesses varying styles of handling the conflict

Description: Paper–pencil 105-item self-report inventory in two parts assessing the types of conflict and the various styles of handling conflict found within an organization. ROCI I contains 21 items assessing three dimensions or types of organizational conflict: intrapersonal, intergroup, and intragroup. ROCI II consists of three 28-item forms assessing conflict with one's boss (Form A), with one's subordinates (Form B), and with one's peers (Form C). Five styles of handling interpersonal conflict are identified: integrating, obliging, dominating, avoiding, and compromising. Both parts use a 5-point Likert scale. Limited norms are provided for college students and managerial groups.

Format: Examiner required; suitable for group use; untimed: 10–12 minutes

Scoring: Examiner evaluated

Cost: Preview kit (Inventories I and II, answer sheets, manual) $29.00

Publisher: Consulting Psychologists Press, Inc.

Reaction to Everyday Situations Test
Sheena M. A. Waterhouse

Copyright: 1972

Population: Adolescents, adults; ages 16 and older

Purpose: Measures general anxiety shown by individuals in their day-to-day lives; used for employee selection and screening and clinical research

Description: Paper–pencil 50-item questionnaire measuring the general anxiety shown by examinees in everyday situations. Each test item relates to a particular situation in which anxiety might be displayed. The test is restricted to competent persons properly registered with the South African Medical and Dental Council. Afrikaans version available.

Format: Examiner required; suitable for group use; untimed: no time limit

Scoring: Hand key

Cost: Contact publisher

Publisher: Human Sciences Research Council

Sales Position Analysis (SPA)
William J. Reddin

Copyright: 1988

Population: Adults

Purpose: Used for diagnosis

Description: Multiple-choice, paper–pencil test with eight styles, 20 elements/relative effectiveness, 20 elements/dominance, and task–relationships orientation.

Format: Individual/self-administered; suitable for group use; untimed: 60 minutes

Scoring: Self-scored

Cost: Set of 10 tests $150.00

Publisher: Organizational Tests Ltd.

Sales Productivity Scale

Copyright: 1996

Population: Adults

Purpose: Identifies applicants who rely upon their influential, competitive, and sociable personalities to produce significant sales results

Description: Scale with 45 questions designed to increase profits and reduce training costs and turnover by placing only those applicants or employees with strong sales and service skills in positions requiring motivated selling and sensitivity to customer needs.

Format: 10 minutes

Scoring: I-Fax (automated scoring platform that returns test results via fax), Provoice (front end applicant telephone testing program), Fax-In, Phone-In, Mail-In, or PC software

Cost: Ranges from $8.50 to $18.00

Publisher: Reid Psychological Systems

Self Worth Inventory (SWI)
Everett T. Robinson

Copyright: 1990

Population: Adults

Purpose: Identifies self-worth

Description: Forced-choice 40-item test. A 10th-grade reading level is required.

Format: Individual administration; suitable for group use; examiner required; untimed

Scoring: Self-scored

Cost: $10.95

Publisher: Consulting Resource Group International, Inc.

Self-Description Inventory
Charles B. Johansson

Copyright: 1977

Population: Adolescents, adults; Grades 9 to adult

Purpose: Evaluates an individual's personality strengths relevant to world of work; used for career counseling, training, and development

Description: Inventory with 200 items covering 11 basic personality scales and six vocational scales. Items are self-descriptive adjectives. The bipolar personal scales are Cautious/Adventurous, Nonscientific/ Analytical, Tense/Relaxed, Insecure/Confident, Conventional/Imaginative, Impatient/Patient, Unconcerned/Altruistic, Reserved/Outgoing, Soft-Spoken/Forceful, Lackadaisical/Industrious, and Unorganized/Orderly. The vocational scales cover the following RIASEC factors: Realistic, Investigative, Artistic, Social, Enterprising, and Conventional.

Format: Self-administered; suitable for group use; untimed: 15–20 minutes

Scoring: Computer scored

Cost: Manual $12.50; answer sheets (includes test items) $4.25–$5.00 depending on quantity

Publisher: NCS Assessments

South African Personality Questionnaire

Copyright: 1974

Population: Adolescents, adults; Grades 10 and above

Purpose: Measures general personality traits in the context of South African society; used for employee screening and selection; suitable for matriculants and higher

Description: Paper–pencil 150-item test consisting of bipolar forced-choice items measuring the following personality traits: social responsiveness, dominance, hostility, flexibility, and anxiety. Use is restricted to competent persons properly registered with the South African Medical and Dental Council.

Format: Examiner required; suitable for group use; untimed: open ended

Scoring: Hand key; examiner evaluated

Cost: Contact publisher

Publisher: Human Sciences Research Council

SRA Sales Aptitude Test

Copyright: 1993

Population: Adults

Purpose: Measures behavioral and personality characteristics indicative of success in sales positions; used for sales selection programs

Description: Multiple-choice 86-item test measures eight traits important to sales success:

ego strength, persuasiveness, sociability, entrepreneurship, achievement motivation, energy, self-confidence, and empathy.

Format: Examiner required; suitable for group use; untimed: 30 minutes

Scoring: Hand key, computer scored

Cost: 25 test booklets $77.00; examiner's manual $15.00

Publisher: McGraw-Hill/London House

Stress Indicator and Health Planner (SHIP)
Gwen Faulkner, Terry D. Anderson

Copyright: 1990

Population: Adults

Purpose: Assesses personal distress, interpersonal stress, wellness, time stress, and occupational stress

Description: Five-item forced-choice test. A 10th-grade reading level is required.

Format: Individual administration; suitable for group use; examiner required; untimed

Scoring: Self-scored

Cost: $12.95

Publisher: Consulting Resource Group International, Inc.

Sup'r Star Profiles
James H. Brewer

Copyright: 1994

Population: Adults

Purpose: Used for a more advanced and in-depth study of personality types

Description: Updates personality assessment by using color and integrating additional research findings for a more complete study of personality types. The four types of personality now become Self-Reliant, Upbeat, Patient, and Reasoning.

Format: Individual/self-administration; untimed: 20–25 minutes

Scoring: Hand key

Cost: $5.95 each

Publisher: Associated Consultants in Education

Survey of Personal Values
Leonard V. Gordon

Copyright: 1965

Population: Adolescents, adults; Grades 10 and above

Purpose: Measures the critical values that help an individual determine coping ability with everyday problems; used for employee screening and placement, vocational guidance, and counseling

Description: Paper–pencil 30-item inventory assessing personal values. Each item consists of a triad of value statements. For each triad, examinees must indicate most and least important values. Six values are measured: practical mindedness, achievement, variety, decisiveness, orderliness, and goal orientation.

Format: Self-administered; suitable for group use; untimed: 15 minutes

Scoring: Hand key

Cost: 25 test booklets $44; scoring stencil $10; examiner's manual $15

Publisher: McGraw-Hill/London House

Temperament Comparator
Melany E. Baehr

Copyright: 1985

Population: Adults

Purpose: Determines the strength of relatively permanent temperament traits characteristic of an individual's behavior; used to evaluate the potential of sales and of higher-level managerial and professional personnel and for job screening and vocational counseling

Description: Paper–pencil 66-item test consisting of trait pairs derived from the application of a paired comparison technique to 12 individual traits. Emphasis is on individual variations in significant dimensions within the "normal" range of behavior. The factors measured are the 12 individual traits and three factorially determined behavior factors: extroversive/impulsive vs. introversive/cautious, emotional/responsive vs. nonemotional/controlled, self-reliant/self-oriented vs. dependent/group oriented. The test provides a measure of internal consistency of response.

Format: Examiner required; suitable for group use; untimed: 15 minutes

Scoring: Hand key

Cost: 25 test booklets $36; score sheet $10; examiner's manual $15

Publisher: McGraw-Hill/London House

Thurstone Temperament Schedule
L. L. Thurstone, Thelma Gwinn Thurstone

Copyright: 1991

Population: Adults

Purpose: Evaluates permanent aspects of personality and how normal, well-adjusted people differ from one another; used by managers to determine employee suitability for particular jobs

Description: Paper–pencil or computerized 120-item inventory assessing seven areas of temperament: active, vigorous, impulsive, dominant, stable, sociable, and reflective. The inventory is limited to use by individuals with advanced training in personality instruments.

Format: Self-administered; suitable for group use; untimed: 15–20 minutes

Scoring: Hand key; computer scored

Cost: 25 booklets $40.00; examiner's manual $15.00

Publisher: McGraw-Hill/London House

Time Perception Inventory
Albert A. Canfield

Copyright: 1987

Population: Adults

Purpose: Measures the difference between physical and mental presence; helps employees understand how much of their time is wasted due to mental preoccupation; identifies an individual's particular preoccupation and evaluates causes and debilitating nature

Description: Multiple-item paper–pencil inventory measuring an individual's tendencies to focus attention on the past, future, or present. Percentile comparison on perceived time effectiveness (typically related to an individual's motivation to improve) is provided. All scales provide opportunities to consider positive and negative aspects of thinking in a particular time reference. Group patterns can be identified through a simple show of hands. The test booklet provides interpretations of scales and implications of scores on scales. Recommendations for additional reading are included. Normative data are available.

Format: Self-administered; suitable for group use; untimed: 10 minutes

Scoring: Self-scored

Cost: Kit (10 inventories, 1 manual) $38.50

Publisher: Western Psychological Services

Trait Evaluation Index
Alan R. Nelson

Copyright: 1967

Population: Adults

Purpose: Assesses adult personality traits; used for job placement and career counseling

Description: Paper–pencil 125-item two-choice test measuring 24 personality dimensions, including social orientation, elation, self-control, sincerity, compliance, ambition, dynamism, caution, propriety, and intellectual orientation. Materials consist of a test manual, keys, answer sheets, and academic and industrial-business profile sheets. Available also in German.

Format: Self-administered; suitable for group use; untimed: 30–40 minutes

Scoring: Hand key

Cost: 20 reusable tests $55.00; manual and manual supplement (1984) $42.50; 24 IBM scoring stencils $43.50; 20 profile sheets $25.50; Specimen Set $63.00; Specimen Set without scoring stencils $29.50

Publisher: Martin M. Bruce, Ph.D.

Trustworthiness Attitude Survey (T. A. Survey)
Alan L. Strand, R. W. Cormack

Copyright: 1976

Population: Adults

Purpose: Measures attitudes and personality characteristics related to trustworthiness; used to screen applicants for jobs involving security, money, and product handling

Description: Paper–pencil 118-item multiple-choice and short-answer test measuring attitudes and beliefs. The test must be administered by a qualified, licensed company or government agency examiner.

Format: Examiner required; suitable for group use; untimed: 20–30 minutes

Scoring: Hand key

Cost: Specimen Set: free, 25 tests $6.00; scoring templates leased yearly $60.00

Publisher: Predictive Surveys Corporation

Values Scale–Second Edition
Donald E. Super, Dorothy D. Nevill

Copyright: Not provided

Population: Adults

Purpose: Measures intrinsic and extrinsic life-career values

Description: Paper–pencil 106-item inventory measuring intrinsic and extrinsic life-career values and many cultural perspectives of adults. Items are rated on a 4-point scale ranging from "little or no importance" to "very important." The 21 scales are Ability, Utilization, Achievement, Advancement, Aesthetics, Altruism, Authority, Autonomy, Creativity, Economic Rewards, Lifestyle, Personal Development, Physical Activity, Prestige, Risk, Social Interaction, Social Relations, Variety, Working Conditions, Cultural Identity, Physical Prowess, and Economic Security. The scale was developed as part of the international Work Importance Study and has international norms. The profile available through the computer scoring service plots 21 subscales and provides local percentiles and group summary data for answer sheets scored stimultaneously.

Format: Examiner required; suitable for group use; untimed: 30–45 minutes

Scoring: Hand scored; computer scoring service available

Cost: Preview kit (booklet, answer sheet, manual) $39.00

Publisher: Consulting Psychologists Press

Working With My Boss

Copyright: 1989

Population: Adults

Purpose: Used to improve the productive relationship between an employee and supervisor

Description: Uses BEST personality dimensions to help people understand the personality of their bosses and what they need to do to work successfully with them. Assesses both employee and employer personality types, explores consequences of similarities and differences, and suggests how to develop a more productive relationship, identifies more productive approaches to boss.

Format: Individual/self-administered; untimed: 15–30 minutes

Scoring: Hand key

Cost: $4.95 each

Publisher: Associated Consultants in Education

Team Skills

. . . .

Assessing Your Team: 7 Measures of Team Success
Dick Richards, Susan Smyth

Copyright: 1995

Population: Intact work group or new team

Purpose: Helps secure high-quality team performance, enhances productivity, increases involvement, and clarifies roles and procedures

Description: This instrument focuses on team interaction and creates a group profile based on each member's perceptions of overall group functioning. It can be administered by the team leader or an outside facilitator and scored in-house. The Team Leader's Manual provides guidance to follow up actions.

Format: ½ day

Scoring: Scored by team leader/facilitator

Cost: Team Leader's Package $24.95; Team Member's Manual $9.95

Publisher: Pfeiffer and Company International Publishers, Inc.

Campbell-Hallam Team Development Survey (TDS)
David P. Campbell, Glenn Hallam

Copyright: 1994

Population: Adults

Purpose: Assesses perceptions of team effectiveness; used for identifying team strengths and weaknesses

Description: Paper–pencil 72-item test with 18 dimensions, plus an overall index. A sixth-grade reading level is required. Examiner must have taken psychology coursework.

Format: Self-administered; suitable for group use; untimed

Scoring: Computer scored; test scoring service available from publisher

Cost: $15.00 per member

Publisher: NCS Assessments

Herrmann Brain Dominance Instrument (HBDI)
William E. Herrmann

Copyright: 1995

Population: Adults

Purpose: Assesses thinking style preferences; used with teams, communication, personal development, and learning

Description: Paper–pencil 120-item test. Examiner must be HBDI certified. Available in French, Spanish, German, Turkish, and Portuguese.

Format: Self-administered; untimed

Scoring: Computer scored

Cost: $49.00

Publisher: The Ned Herrmann Group

I-Speak Your Language®
Paul Mok

Copyright: Updated yearly

Population: Adults

Purpose: Assesses communications style of all levels of employees as it relates to teambuilding, interviewing, and influencing

Description: Paper–pencil 18-question multiple-choice test consisting of nine questions under normal conditions and nine questions under stressful conditions that evaluates communications style. Yields primary and secondary communications styles under normal and stressful conditions. Paper form and computerized version (I-SPEAK 2000™) available. Materials include manual, strategies book, videos (2 current), and overheads. Available in English, Spanish, French, Italian, and Japanese.

Format: Self-administered; suitable for group use; untimed

Scoring: Self scored; computer scored; examiner evaluated

Cost: 10 tests $45.00

Publisher: DBM Publishing

Lake St. Clair Incident
Albert A. Canfield

Copyright: 1988

Population: Adults

Purpose: Examines individual and group decision-making processes; used to improve decision-making, communication skills, and teamwork

Description: Multiple-item paper–pencil test requiring a team of three to seven individuals to work together to solve a hypothetical problem situation involving cold weather and cold water survival. Participants are provided with considerable information on the subject, maps, charts, drawings, and a list of 15 items available for them to use in their struggle for survival. The team must reach a decision on what action to take and the relative importance of the 15 items. Three different decision-making processes are required: independent, consultative, and participative/consensual. Scoring procedure uses Coast Guard officer decisions and rankings as "expert" opinions. Scores are provided for three types of decision-making processes.

Format: Self-administered (teams must cooperate to get team performance scores). Suitable for group use. Untimed: 1½ to 2 hours

Scoring: Self-scored

Cost: Kit (10 booklets, 1 manual) $37.50

Publisher: Western Psychological Services

NASA Moon Survival
Jay Hall

Copyright: 1989

Population: Adults

Purpose: Results of this decision-by-consensus tool prove the potential of group decision making. Presents a problem for participants to solve, consensus rules to use in the solving, and an exercise to analyze member contributions to the team's consensus task.

Description: Paper–pencil consensus decision-making exercise. Fifteen survival items to be ranked. It lays to rest the "individual vs. group" controversy regarding decision quality and generates group diagnostic data. The Manned Spacecraft Center's solution to problem affords immediate assessment and feedback of individual and group performance.

Format: Self-administered; suitable for group use; untimed

Scoring: Self-scored

Cost: $8.95 each

Publisher: Teleometrics International, Inc.

Our BEST Team
James H. Brewer

Copyright: 1989

Population: Adults

Purpose: Used to build more productive teaming

Description: The instrument identifies team members' personality types, determines the mix of types in a team, explores decisions made by different types of personality mixes, helps teams overcome poor decision making caused by personality conflicts, suggests kinds of tasks each team member should be assigned based on personality.

Format: Individual/self-administered; untimed: 20–30 minutes

Scoring: Hand key

Cost: $6.95 each

Publisher: Associated Consultants in Education

Parker Team Player Survey (PTPS)
Glenn M. Parker

Copyright: 1990

Population: Adults

Purpose: Used in team building to assess team player styles

Description: Eighteen-item rating scale. Contributor, collaborator, communicator, and challenger are the scores yielded. An eighth-grade reading level is required. Available in Spanish and French.

Format: Individual/self-administered; suitable for group use; untimed

Scoring: Self-scored

Cost: $6.50

Publisher: Xicom, Inc.

Personal Style Inventory (PSI)
William Taggart, Barbara Taggart-Hausladen

Copyright: 1993

Population: Adults

Purpose: Used by personnel development to increase personal flexibility and team productivity

Description: Multiple-choice paper–pencil inventory with the following profiles: Rational Modes (planning, analysis, control), and Intuitive Modes (vision, insight, sharing). Materials used include a trainer's manual, overhead transparencies, survey booklets, strategy profile, personal development booklets, and PDP booklets.

Format: Individual administration; suitable for group use; examiner required

Scoring: Self-scored

Cost: Kit $95.00

Publisher: Psychological Assessment Resources, Inc.

Styles of Teamwork Inventory
Jay Hall

Copyright: 1995

Population: Adults

Purpose: Assesses team members' understanding of their own styles and the impact a particular style is apt to have on the team

Description: Paper–pencil 80-item instrument which addresses how one functions as a member of various work teams—the behaviors a team member has and the feelings the individual has interacting with others in a team setting. The inventory results in an overall preferred style and provides specific scores on individual attitude, the handling of conflict, leadership preference, and intergroup relations. Normative sample is 1,000.

Format: Self-administered; suitable for group use; untimed: time varies

Scoring: Self-scored

Cost: $8.95 each

Publisher: Teleometrics International, Inc.

Team Effectiveness Survey (TES)
Jay Hall

Copyright: 1985

Population: Adults

Purpose: Assesses team functioning and identifies individuals who are primarily responsible for the team's style of functioning; used for employee training and development and discussion purposes

Description: Multiple-item paper–pencil inventory assessing team functioning on the exposure and feedback dimensions inherent in the Johari Window model of interpersonal relations. Each team member rates self and others on items related to both dimensions. The resulting individual and team profiles serve as immediate feedback to confirm or deny self-ratings and furnish an overview of team functioning. Defensive versus supportive climate scores also are obtained.

Format: Self-administered group exercise; untimed: time varies

Scoring: Self-scored

Cost: $8.95 each

Publisher: Teleometrics International, Inc.

Team Process Diagnostic
Jay Hall

Copyright: 1989

Population: Adults

Purpose: Assesses member contributions to team functioning

Description: 32-item paper–pencil criterion-referenced instrument utilizing a matrix format and scoring wheel. The matrix indices yield behavioral assessments of the dynamics underlying individuals' behavior and of the impact of their behavior on the group. In addition, the instrument provides diagnostic information about the group's climate resulting from the problem-solving, "flight or fight" behaviors of its members.

Format: Self-administered; suitable for group use; untimed: time varies

Scoring: Self-scored

Cost: $8.95 each

Publisher: Teleometrics International, Inc.

Teamness Index
Jay Hall

Copyright: 1995

Population: Adults

Purpose: Assesses whether or not team members meet the minimal conditions for teamness

Description: Paper–pencil 24-item criterion-referenced test using a 9-point scale that reflects how characteristic each statement is for an individual. Each item is presented in two parts; the first part is the condition of interest being sur-

veyed, and the second part serves as a reference of the opposite condition. Answers indicate how each team member characterizes particular work relationships.

Format: Self-administered; suitable for group use; untimed: time varies

Scoring: Self-scored

Cost: $8.95 each

Publisher: Teleometrics International, Inc.

Teamwork Appraisal Survey
Jay Hall

Copyright: 1987

Population: Adults

Purpose: Assesses how personal practices impact others when working in teams or groups

Description: Paper–pencil 80-item criterion-referenced survey which focuses on how associates function as members of various work teams. It is a companion instrument to the *Styles of Teamwork Inventory* (STI) and is filled out by other team members to provide a person using the STI with comparative assessments of that person's team behavior. The TAS is arranged to permit direct, question-by-question comparisons between it and the STI. It is these comparisons and the discussions surrounding them that enable an individual to come to know and think about the impact of his or her behavioral practices.

Format: Self-administered; suitable for group use; untimed: time varies

Scoring: Self-scored

Cost: $7.95 each

Publisher: Teleometrics International, Inc.

Teamwork–KSA Test
Michael J. Stevens, Michael A. Campion

Copyright: 1995

Population: Adults

Purpose: Assesses individuals who work well in a team-oriented work environment

Description: Multiple-choice 35-item test measures the essential knowledge, skills, and abilities that individuals must have to work effectively in teams. Three interpersonal skills areas (conflict resolution skills, collaborative problem-solving skills, and interpersonal communicative skills) and two self-management areas (team goal setting and performance management, team planning and task coordination) are measured.

Format: Examiner required; suitable for group use; untimed: 30–40 minutes

Scoring: Hand key; computer scored

Cost: 10 test booklets $97.50; examiner's manual $15.00

Publisher: McGraw-Hill/London House

The Team Leadership Practices Inventory
James M. Kouzes, Barry Z. Posner

Copyright: 1992

Population: All types of work teams

Purpose: Helps identify leadership practices currently used within the team, helps identify areas for enhancing and improving leadership practices within the team, and creates action plans for becoming a more effective team through enhanced leadership

Description: Thirty-item questionnaire designed to be used by every team member. The accompanying guidebook includes instructions for scoring, comparing scores from each team member, and interpreting scores; and worksheets for creating team action plans and keeping commitments.

Format: 2–4 hours

Scoring: Facilitator scored

Cost: $5.95

Publisher: Pfeiffer and Company International Publishers, Inc.

The Team-Review Survey
Dave Francis, Don Young

Copyright: 1992

Population: Adults; team members

Purpose: Helps team members assess team strengths and weaknesses, identify blockages to high performance, determine whether the group has the desire and the energy to begin a team-building program, and understand the characteristics of effective teamwork

Description: Contains 18 statements that relate to team effectiveness. Team members who complete the survey give an accurate picture of what works and what doesn't in the day-to-day functioning of the team. That information is then used to create action plans for improvement. The entire exercise takes about 2 hours to complete.

Format: 2 hours

Scoring: Self-scored

Cost: $7.95

Publisher: Pfeiffer and Company International Publishers, Inc.

Work Keys Teamwork Test

Copyright: 1993

Population: Adolescents, adults

Purpose: Assesses teamwork skills

Description: Multiple-choice 36-item criterion-referenced test across four levels. Form 10EE is available. A videotape, answer folder, administrator's manual, and videotape administrator's manual are used.

Format: Individual administration; suitable for group use; examiner required; timed: two 40-minute parts

Scoring: Machine scored; test scoring service available from publisher

Cost: $7.00 per examinee; 15% discount for K–12 schools

Publisher: American College Testing

Work Environment

. . . .

Learning Organization Practices Profile
Michael J. O'Brien

Copyright: 1994

Population: All employees

Purpose: Used to diagnose an organization's ability to learn and change and to create action plans to help an organization learn and change

Description: Results of the instrument reveal how your organization measures up in 12 key areas: Vision and Strategy, Executive Practices, Managerial Practices, Climate, Organizational and Job Structure, Information Flow, Individual and Team Practices, Work Processes, Performance Goals and Feedback, Training and Education, Rewards and Recognition, and Individual and Team Development.

Format: Approximately 30 minutes

Scoring: Self-scored

Cost: $6.95; Professional Set $24.95

Publisher: Pfeiffer and Company International Publishers, Inc.

Oliver Organization Description Questionnaire (OODQ)
John E. Oliver

Copyright: 1981

Population: Adults

Purpose: Evaluates the organizational form of a particular organization

Description: Multiple-item paper–pencil questionnaire measuring the extent to which four organizational forms exist within a particular organization. The forms are hierarchic (bureaucratic), professional (specialized), task (entrepreneurial), and group (sociotechnical). The scoring guide discusses the form of the instrument, the four domains, scoring, potential uses of the scores, development of the instrument, interpretation of individual scores, and interpretation of organization scores.

Format: Examiner required; suitable for group use; untimed: time varies

Scoring: Examiner evaluated

Cost: 50 questionnaires $30.00; scoring guide $5.00

Publisher: Organizational Measurement Systems Press

Productivity Environmental Preference Survey (PEPS)
Rita Dunn, Kenneth Dunn, Gary E. Price

Copyright: 1995

Population: Adults

Purpose: Assesses the manner in which adults prefer to function, learn, concentrate, and perform in their occupational or educational activities; used for employee placement, counseling, office design, and layout

Description: Paper–pencil or computer-administered 100-item Likert scale inventory measuring the following environmental factors related to educational or occupational activities: immediate environment (sound, temperature, light, and design), emotionality (motivation, responsibility, persistence, and structure), sociological needs (self-oriented, peer-oriented, authority-oriented, and combined ways), and physical needs (perceptual preferences, time of day, intake, and mobility). Test items consist of statements about the ways people like to work or study. Respondents are asked to indicate whether they agree or disagree with each statement.

Format: Self-administered; suitable for group use; untimed: 20–30 minutes

Scoring: Computer scored

Cost: Specimen Set (manual, answer sheet) $11.00; Diskette (100 administrations per licensing agreement) $295.00; each 100 additional administrations $60.00; NCS scanner program $395.00; 100 answer sheets for NCS scanner program $60.00

Publisher: Price Systems, Inc.

Work Environment Scale (WES)

Paul Insel, Rudolf H. Moos

Copyright: Not provided

Population: Adults

Purpose: Evaluates the social climate of work units; used to assess correlates of productivity, worker satisfaction, quality assurance programs, work stressors, individual adaptation, and supervisory methods

Description: Paper–pencil 90-item measure of 10 dimensions of work social environments: involvement, peer cohesion, supervisor support, autonomy, task orientation, work pressure, clarity, control, innovation, and physical comfort. These dimensions are grouped into three sets: relationships, personal growth, and system maintenance and change. Three forms are available: the Real Form (Form R), which measures perceptions of existing work environments; the Ideal Form (Form I), which measures conceptions of ideal work environments; and the Expectations Form (Form E), which measures expectations about work settings. Forms I and E are not published although items and instructions will be provided upon request.

Format: Examiner required; suitable for group use; untimed: 20 minutes

Scoring: Hand key; computer scoring service available

Cost: Preview kit (booklet, narrative answer sheet) $13.00; self-scorable preview kit (booklet, answer sheet, interpretive report) $10.00

Publisher: Consulting Psychologists Press, Inc.

Aptitudes and Skills

Banking

Assessment of Service Readiness (ASR)

Copyright: 1993

Population: Adults

Purpose: Assesses entry-level customer service skills; used for selection and development of employees in insurance/financial services

Description: Multiple-choice 182-item paper–pencil test yielding a predicted performance score and development information. A videotape, TV, VCR, and computer are used. Use is restricted to insurance/financial services.

Format: Individually administered; examiner required; suitable for group use; timed: 90 minutes

Scoring: Computer scored

Cost: Contact publisher

Publisher: Life Office Management Association

Basic Bank Skills Battery

Copyright: 1987

Population: Adults; ages 16 and older

Purpose: Measures potential for successful performance as a bank teller and customer service representative; used for employee selection and promotion

Description: Multiple-choice 317-item paper–pencil battery measuring potential in several key areas related to an applicant's ability to perform as a teller or customer service representative. Scores are provided for 13 scales: Drive, School Achievement, Arithmetic Computation, Interpersonal Relations, Cognitive Skills, Error Recognition, Motor Ability, Math Ability, Name Comparison, Self-Discipline, Leadership, Number Comparison, and Perceptual Skills. The battery yields a single score, the Potential Estimate, for the bank teller and customer service positions. Form A combines the timed and untimed tests. A Short Form is comprised of the timed tests only.

Format: Examiner required; suitable for group use; timed: time varies

Scoring: Computer scored

Cost: Contact publisher

Publisher: McGraw-Hill/London House

Personnel Selection Inventory for Banking (PSI–B)

Copyright: 1987

Population: Job applicants

Purpose: Identifies banking job applicants who might engage in theft or counterproductive behavior in the workplace; designed to help banks select quality employees and reduce losses

Description: Multiple-item paper–pencil survey designed to enable employers to screen job applicants. Four versions of the inventory, PSI–B1, PSI–B3, PSI–B7, and PSI–B77 are available. The PSI versions contain one or more of the following scales: Honesty, Drug-Avoidance, Non-Violence, Customer/Employee Relations, Work Values, Supervision Attitudes, Tenure, and Employability. Significant Behavioral Indicators and follow-up interview questions are available for the PSI–B7 and PSI–B77. Banking industry norms are available for all three versions. All versions contain a distortion and an accuracy scale. Scoring options include operator-assisted scoring. Touch-Test telephone, microcomputer, and mail-in service.

Format: Self-administered; suitable for group use; untimed: 30–45 minutes

Scoring: Computer scored; scoring service available from publisher

Cost: $3–$17 depending on scoring method and volume ordered

Publisher: McGraw-Hill/London House

Clerical

ACER Short Clerical Test (Forms C, D, and E)

Copyright: 1984

Population: Adolescents, adults; ages 15 and older

Purpose: Measures speed and accuracy in checking names and numbers and in basic arithmetic; used as a test of clerical aptitude in selecting employees for routine clerical jobs

Description: Multiple-item paper–pencil test measuring an individual's ability to perceive, remember, and check written or printed material (both verbal and numerical), and to perform arithmetic operations. The test is available in 3 forms: Forms C and D are used for personnel selection and Form E for guidance and counseling in business training colleges. Australian norms are provided. British norms are available for Form C in British Supplement of Norms for Tests Used in Clerical Selection, available from NFER-Nelson.

Format: Examiner required; suitable for group use; timed: 5 minutes per part

Scoring: Hand key

Cost: Contact publisher

Publisher: The Australian Council for Educational Research Limited

ACER Speed and Accuracy Test–Form A

Copyright: 1963

Population: Adolescents, adults; ages 13 years 6 months and older

Purpose: Measures the checking skills of individuals ages 13 and older; useful in the selection of clerical personnel

Description: Multiple-item paper–pencil test measuring the ability to perceive, retain, and check relatively familiar material in the form of printed numbers and names while working in a limited amount of time. The test contains two sections: name checking and number checking. Australian norms are available for school, university, adult, and some occupational groups. British normative data are available in British Supplement of Norms for Tests Used in Clerical Selection, available from NFER-Nelson.

Format: Examiner required; suitable for group use; timed: 6 minutes per part

Scoring: Hand key

Cost: Contact publisher

Publisher: The Australian Council for Educational Research Limited

Automated Skills Assessment Program (ASAP)
Wallace Judd

Copyright: 1992

Population: Adolescents, adults; ages 18 and above

Purpose: Measures clerical skills; used in pre-employment selection

Description: Computer-administered test with five subtests: typing, 10 key, data entry, spelling, and filing.

Format: Individual/self-administeredl; timed/untimed

Scoring: Computer scored

Cost: 25 forms $65.00; 100 forms $135.00

Publisher: Wonderlic Personnel Test, Inc.

Candidate Profile Record

Copyright: Not provided

Population: Adults

Purpose: Assesses background characteristics related to success in office positions

Description: Multiple-item paper–pencil questionnaire designed to predict an individual's potential for success in teller and customer service positions, processing and verifying positions, and secretarial and clerical positions. The autobiographical questionnaire covers an individual's early development influences, academic history and accomplishments, self-esteem and description, work history, and work-related values and attitudes. Normative, reliability, and validity data are contained in the manual.

Format: Self-administered; suitable for group use; untimed: time varies

Scoring: Self-scored; computer scored

Cost: Contact publisher

Publisher: Richardson, Bellows, Henry and Company, Inc.

Clerical Abilities Battery (CAB)

Copyright: 1987

Population: Adults

Purpose: Assesses clerical skills

Description: Instrument contains seven subtests that measure clerical tasks of filing, copying information, comparing information, using tables, proofreading, addition and subtraction, and reasoning with numbers.

Format: Examiner required; suitable for group use; timed: 5–20 minutes

Scoring: Hand key

Cost: Examination kit (one booklet for each test and manual) $41.00

Publisher: The Psychological Corporation

Clerical Aptitude Tests
Andrew Kobal, J. Wayne Wrightstone, Andrew J. MacElroy

Copyright: 1961

Population: Adolescents, adults; Grades 7 and above

Purpose: Assesses aptitude for clerical work; used for screening job applicants

Description: Three-part paper–pencil test measuring clerical aptitudes, including business practice; number checking; and date, name, and address checking. Scores correlate with job success.

Format: Examiner required; suitable for group use; timed: 40 minutes

Scoring: Hand key

Cost: Specimen Set $4.00; 25 tests $8.75

Publisher: Psychometric Affiliates

Clerical Skills Series–Revised
Martin M. Bruce

Copyright: 1990

Population: Adults

Purpose: Assesses the language, physical coordination, and mathematical abilities necessary for various clerical jobs; used for screening prospective employees, measuring student skills, and evaluating current employees

Description: Ten-category paper–pencil test series covering alphabetizing, filing, arithmetic, clerical speed and accuracy, coding, eye–hand accuracy, grammar and punctuation, spelling, vocabulary, and word fluency. The series consists of 10 short tests, six of which are timed. Suitable for individuals with physical, hearing, or visual disabilities.

Format: Separate or unit administration; examiner required for timed items; suitable for group use; timed: 2–8 minutes per section

Scoring: Hand key

Cost: Specimen Set $52.50; manual $13.50; manual supplement $22.50 (1984); profile sheets $24.50; key $2.85 per test; forms $41.50 and $40.50

Publisher: Martin M. Bruce, Ph.D., Publishers

Clerical Skills Test

Copyright: Not provided

Population: Adults

Purpose: Assesses the clerical skills required to perform a variety of occupational tasks; used for job placement

Description: Six paper–pencil and performance subtests measuring the subject's ability to type from plain copy, take dictation, spell, type statistics, and spell medical and legal terms. Only those subtests that relate to significant job skill needs should be administered. A skilled worker will score higher than an unskilled worker. Norm tables are used to convert raw scores to deciles based on representative samples of experienced workers. Materials required include a typewriter, typing paper, and pencils.

Format: Examiner required; suitable for group use; timed: time varies

Scoring: Hand key

Cost: Contact publisher

Publisher: Walden Personnel Testing and Training, Inc.

Clerical Skills Test Series

Copyright: 1990

Population: Adults

Purpose: Used for measuring clerical skills

Description: Series of tests that measure attention to detail, problem solving, numerical skills, spelling, alphabetizing and filing, grammar and punctuation, vocabulary, reading comprehension, receptionist skills, keyboard skills, 10- key calculator, bookkeeping, PC graphics, coding, manual dexterity, electronics knowledge, mechanical comprehension, and spatial perception.

Format: Examiner required; suitable for group use; timed: time varies

Scoring: Hand key

Cost: 20 tests $219.00

Publisher: Walden Personnel Testing and Training, Inc.

Clerical Staff Selector

Copyright: 1984

Population: Adults

Purpose: Evaluates candidates of all levels of experience for clerical positions

Description: Multiple-item tests measuring skills required for various clerical positions, including accounting, inventory, secretarial, and factory. Skills measured are problem-solving, coding, attention to detail, manual dexterity, alphabetizing and filing, spelling, grammar and punctuation, and numerical facility. Also available in French.

Format: Examiner required; suitable for group use; timed: 30 minutes; untimed: 30 minutes

Scoring: Hand key; scoring service provided

Cost: $45.00 per person

Publisher: Walden Personnel Testing and Training, Inc.

CRT Skills Test

Copyright: 1995

Population: Adults

Purpose: Measures individual's ability to enter alpha and numeric data and retrieve and interpret files; used to measure skills for selection and placement decisions for data-entry operators and customer service representatives

Description: Computerized test consists of

three parts. The first part assesses speed and accuracy in entering both alpha and numeric data. The second part assesses speed and accuracy in entering numeric data only. The third part assesses the ability to retrieve customer files and identify the correct answers to assorted customer questions.

Format: Examiner required; timed: 5–10 minutes; practice sections are untimed

Scoring: Computer scored

Cost: 5 reusable test booklets $40.00; 25 administrations on diskette $100.00; audiocassette $25.00; examiner's manual $15.00

Publisher: McGraw-Hill/London House

Curtis Verbal–Clerical Skills Tests
James W. Curtis

Copyright: 1964

Population: Adolescents, adults; ages 16 and older

Purpose: Assesses clerical and verbal abilities; used to evaluate job applicants

Description: Four multiple-item paper–pencil tests of clerical abilities. The tests are Computation, measuring practical arithmetic; Checking, measuring perceptual speed and accuracy; Comprehension; measuring reading vocabulary; and Capacity, measuring logical reasoning ability.

Format: Examiner required; suitable for group use; timed: 2 minutes per test

Scoring: Hand key

Cost: Specimen Set $5.00; 25 tests (specify form) $4.00

Publisher: Psychometric Affiliates

Data Entry, Data Checking Tests (DEDC)

Copyright: 1989

Population: Adults

Purpose: Assesses data entry and checking skills for data entry employees

Description: The four tests are Verbal Data Entry, Numerical Data Entry, Verbal Data Checking, and Numerical Data Checking and are administered on any IBM-compatible PC. The candidate sits at the computer keyboard and is given on-screen instructions, then proceeds through the four tests. Data must be entered from a booklet into the computer system. Scores are given for speed, accuracy, learning speed, and not having to make corrections. The data-checking tasks involve checking and correcting pre-entered data against a paper copy. This product is available only as a customized piece of software.

Format: Approximately 10 minutes per test

Scoring: Computer scored

Cost: Contact publisher

Publisher: Saville and Holdsworth Ltd

Dictation Test

Copyright: Not provided

Population: Adults

Purpose: Provides a quick screening of an individual's dictation abilities

Description: Manual test assessing an individual's dictation speed and accuracy in which the examiner dictates a business letter to the examinee. The examiner adjusts his dictation speed to the examinee's pace. The examiner dictates only words; the examinee must supply appropriate punctuation, capitalization, and spelling. After the letter is dictated, the examiner notes the amount of time that elapsed from the beginning to the end of the dictation. The examinee then reads the notes back to the examiner, who marks errors of interpretation and estimates the examinee's dictation speed. The test yields an estimate of dictation speed accurate to within five words per minute.

Format: Examiner required; not suitable for group use; untimed: 5 minutes

Scoring: Hand key

Cost: 1–24 packages $45.00

Publisher: Richardson, Bellows, Henry and Company, Inc.

ETSA Tests 2-A—Office Arithmetic Test
George A. W. Stouffer, Jr., S. Trevor Hadley

Copyright: 1990

Population: Adolescents, adults; Grades 10 and above

Purpose: Measures ability to use office arithmetic; used for employee selection, placement, and promotion

Description: Paper–pencil 50-item test assessing arithmetic skills used in office work. The areas tested include whole number computation, mixed number computation, written problems, reading tables, reading graphs, and advanced office computation. The test is one in a series of ETSA tests.

Format: Examiner required; suitable for group use; timed: 40 minutes

Scoring: Hand key; examiner evaluated; scoring service available

Cost: 10 tests with key $15.00; manual $5.00; handbook $15.00

Publisher: Educators'/Employers' Tests and Services Associates

ETSA Tests 3-A—General Clerical Ability Test

George A. W. Stouffer, Jr., S. Trevor Hadley

Copyright: 1990

Population: Adolescents, adults; Grades 10 and above

Purpose: Measures general skills required of clerks in routine office work; used for employee selection, placement, and promotion

Description: Paper–pencil 131-item test assessing general clerical skills. The items include alphabetizing, checking lists of numbers and names, spelling, office vocabulary, and basic information. Speed and accuracy are emphasized. The test is one in a series of ETSA tests.

Format: Examiner required; suitable for group use; timed: 20 minutes

Scoring: Hand key; examiner evaluated; scoring service available

Cost: 10 tests with key $15.00; manual $5.00; handbook $15.00

Publisher: Educators'/Employers' Tests and Services Associates

ETSA Tests 4-A—Stenographic Skills Test

George A. W. Stouffer, Jr., S. Trevor Hadley

Copyright: 1990

Population: Adolescents, adults

Purpose: Measures typing, shorthand, and general skills required of secretaries and stenographers; used for employee selection, placement, and promotion

Description: Paper–pencil 120-item test measuring four basic office skills: spelling, filing, grammar, and general office information. Materials include supplemental performance evaluations of typing and shorthand, either or both of which may be used with the basic scale. The test is one in a series of ETSA tests. Examiner required. Suitable for group use.

Format: Examiner required; suitable for group use; untimed: 45 minutes; Typing Test Supplement 5 minutes; Shorthand Test 18 minutes

Scoring: Hand key; examiner evaluated; scoring service available

Cost: 10 tests with key $15.00; manual $5.00; handbook $15.00

Publisher: Educators'/Employers' Tests and Services Associates

General Clerical Test (GCT)

Copyright: 1988

Population: Adults

Purpose: Assesses clerical aptitude; used for selecting applicants and evaluating clerical employees for promotion

Description: Multiple-item paper–pencil test of three types of abilities needed for clerical jobs: clerical speed and accuracy, numerical ability, and verbal ability. The clerical subtest involves finding errors by comparing copy with the original and using an alphabetical file. The numerical subtest requires the applicant to solve arithmetic problems, find numerical errors, and solve numerical word problems.

The verbal subtest involves correcting spelling errors, answering questions about reading passages, understanding word meanings, and correcting grammatical errors. Separate booklets for the clerical and numerical subtests combined and the verbal subtest only are available for use where one or the other of the abilities is of consideration.

Format: Complete test 46 minutes

Scoring: Hand key

Cost: Examination kit $34.00

Publisher: The Psychological Corporation

Hay Aptitude Test Battery
Edward N. Hay

Copyright: 1984

Population: Adults

Purpose: Identifies job applicants with the greatest aptitude for handling alphabetical and numerical clerical detail; used to select personnel for office and clerical positions, and trainee positions requiring innate perceptual skills

Description: Four paper–pencil tests assessing clerical and numerical aptitude: Warm-Up, Number Perception Test, Name Finding Test, and Number Series Completion Test (NS). The Warm-Up Test, which is not scored, is designed to prepare the examinee for testing. The Number Perception Test (4 minutes) assesses numerical accuracy. Applicants must identify exact pairs of numbers from groups of similar pairs. Results do not necessarily indicate general mental ability. The Name Finding Test (4 minutes) screens the applicant's short-term memory and word accuracy. The examinee must read words and retain them long enough to verify them. Available in Spanish and French.

Format: Examiner required; suitable for group use; timed: 13 minutes total

Scoring: Hand key

Cost: 25 of each form $130.00; 100 sets $300.00

Publisher: Wonderlic Personnel Test, Inc.

Hay Aptitude Test Battery: Name Finding
Edward N. Hay

Copyright: 1984

Population: Adults

Purpose: Measures ability to check and verify names quickly and accurately; used to select office and clerical personnel

Description: Paper–pencil 32-item multiple-choice test assessing the ability to read names and hold them in memory long enough to accurately identify them from four similarly spelled names on the back of the same sheet. The task is similar to many clerical tasks, including making bookkeeping entries or typing invoices or checks. Available in French and Spanish.

Format: Examiner required; suitable for group use; timed: 4 minutes

Scoring: Hand key

Cost: 25 forms $52.50; 100 forms $105.00

Publisher: Wonderlic Personnel Test, Inc.

Hay Aptitude Test Battery: Number Perception
Edward N. Hay

Copyright: 1984

Population: Adults

Purpose: Measures ability to check pairs of numbers and identify those which are the same; used to select office and clerical personnel

Description: Paper–pencil 200-item test measuring speed and accuracy of numerical checking. Each test item consists of a pair of numbers that the applicant decides are the same or different. Items are designed to include the most common clerical errors.

Format: Examiner required; suitable for group use; timed: 4 minutes

Scoring: Hand key

Cost: 25 forms $52.50; 100 forms $105.00

Publisher: Wonderlic Personnel Test, Inc.

Hay Aptitude Test Battery: Number Series Completion

Edward N. Hay

Copyright: 1984

Population: Adults

Purpose: Measures the ability to deduce the pattern in a series of six numbers and provide the seventh and eighth numbers in the series; used to select office and clerical personnel

Description: Paper–pencil 30-item test assessing numerical reasoning abilities. Each item presents a series of six numbers (1–3 digits) related by an unknown pattern. Applicants must provide the next two numbers in the series. Good clerks can find the additional numbers more readily than poor ones. Available in French and Spanish.

Format: Examiner required; suitable for group use

Scoring: Hand key

Cost: 25 forms $52.50; 100 forms $105.00

Publisher: Wonderlic Personnel Test, Inc.

IPI Job-Field Series: General Clerk

Copyright: 1981

Population: Adults

Purpose: Assesses skills of applicants for general clerical positions; used to evaluate typing, filing, billing, transcribing, sorting, writing, and phone answering skills

Description: Multiple-item paper–pencil battery of seven aptitude tests. The tests are Perception, Judgment, Numbers, Office Terms, Memory, Parts, and Fluency. For individual test descriptions, see the IPI Employee Aptitude Series. Also available in French and Spanish.

Format: Suitable for group use; also available in French and Spanish; timed: 42 minutes

Scoring: Hand key

Cost: Starter kit (test materials for five applicants, scoring keys, manuals) $80; test package $12/applicant

Publisher: Industrial Psychology International Ltd.

IPI Job-Field Series: Numbers Clerk

Copyright: 1989

Population: Adults

Purpose: Assesses skills and personality of applicants seeking clerical positions that are mathematical in nature; used to screen for accounting, billing, insurance, inventory, payroll, and statistical positions

Description: Multiple-item paper–pencil battery of four aptitude and personality tests. The tests are Numbers, Judgment, Perception, Office Terms, and NPF. For individual test descriptions, see the IPI Employee Aptitude Series. Also available in French and Spanish.

Format: Suitable for group use; examiner required; timed: 34 minutes

Scoring: Hand key

Cost: Starter kit (test materials for five applicants, scoring keys, manuals) $80; test package $12/applicant

Publisher: Industrial Psychology International Ltd.

IPI Job-Field Series: Office Machine Operator

Copyright: 1989

Population: Adults

Purpose: Assesses skills and personality of applicants for positions utilizing office machines; used to screen for accounting, billing, keypunch, and typist positions

Description: Multiple-item paper–pencil battery of four aptitude tests and two personality tests. The tests are Perception, Dexterity, Parts, Office Terms, CPF, and NPF. For individual test descriptions, see the IPI Employee Aptitude Series. Also available in French.

Format: Suitable for group use; examiner required; timed: 41 minutes

Scoring: Hand key

Cost: Starter kit (test materials for five applicants, scoring keys, manuals) $80; test package $12/applicant

Publisher: Industrial Psychology International Ltd.

IPI Job-Field Series: Office Supervisor

Copyright: 1960

Population: Adults

Purpose: Assesses skills and personality of applicants for supervisory positions in an office setting; used to screen for the positions of administrator, controller, department head, and vice-president

Description: Multiple-item paper–pencil battery of seven aptitude and three personality tests. The tests are 16 PF, Judgment, Parts, Fluency, Office Terms, Numbers, NPF, CPF, Perception, and Memory. For individual test descriptions, see the IPI Employee Aptitude Series. Also available in French and Spanish.

Format: Suitable for group use; examiner required; timed: 82 minutes

Scoring: Hand key

Cost: Starter kit (test materials for five applicants, scoring keys, manuals) $80; test package $12/applicant

Publisher: Industrial Psychology International Ltd.

IPI Job-Field Series: Office Technical

Copyright: 1960

Population: Adults

Purpose: Assesses skills and personality of applicants for various office technical positions; used to evaluate the achievement and personality of accountants, estimators, methods clerks, statisticians, and time-study experts

Description: Multiple-item paper–pencil battery of six aptitude and three personality tests. The tests are Office Terms, Perception, CPF, NPF, Judgment, Numbers, 16PF, Parts, and Memory. For individual test descriptions, see the IPI Employee Aptitude Series. Also available in French and Spanish.

Format: Suitable for group use; also available in French and Spanish; timed: 76 minutes

Scoring: Hand key

Cost: Starter kit (test materials for five applicants, scoring keys, manuals) $80; test package $12/applicant

Publisher: Industrial Psychology International Ltd.

IPI Job-Field Series: Secretary

Copyright: 1981

Population: Adults

Purpose: Assesses skills of applicants for secretarial positions; used to screen for stenographers and executive, legal, private, and social secretaries

Description: Multiple-item paper–pencil battery of six aptitude tests. The tests are Perception, Office Terms, Judgment, Memory, and Parts. For individual test descriptions, see the IPI Employee Aptitude Series. Also available in French or Spanish.

Format: Suitable for group use; examiner required; timed: 30 minutes

Scoring: Hand key

Cost: Starter kit (test materials for five applicants, scoring keys, manuals) $80; test package $12/applicant

Publisher: Industrial Psychology International Ltd.

IPI Job-Field Series: Senior Clerk

Copyright: 1981

Population: Adults

Purpose: Assesses skills of applicants for high-level clerical or administrative positions; used to screen for administrative, bookkeeping, correspondence, cost, and production positions

Description: Multiple-item paper–pencil battery of six aptitude tests. The tests are Office Terms, Judgment, Perception, Parts, Numbers, and Memory. For individual test descriptions, see the IPI Employee Aptitude Series. Also available in French and Spanish.

Format: Suitable for group use; examiner required; timed: 36 minutes

Scoring: Hand key

Cost: Starter kit (test materials for five applicants, scoring keys, manuals) $80; test package $12/applicant

Publisher: Industrial Psychology International Ltd.

Language Skills, Form G

Copyright: Not provided

Population: Adults

Purpose: Measures word meaning, spelling, hyphenation, and punctuation skills; used with applicants to clerical positions

Description: Paper–pencil 84-item test assessing the ability of clerical personnel to handle job-related tasks. A portion of the test is multiple-choice. Another portion consists of brief paragraphs containing no punctuation within the sentences. Key words in the sentences are underlined at points where punctuation may be needed. The examinee chooses from among two to four punctuation marks. All answers are marked in the test booklet.

Format: Examiner required; suitable for group use; timed: 25 minutes

Scoring: Hand key

Cost: 1–24 packages $55.00; score key $5.00; manual $5.00

Publisher: Richardson, Bellows, Henry and Company, Inc.

Minnesota Clerical Test (MCT)
D. M. Andrew, D. G. Peterson,
H. P. Longstaff

Copyright: 1979

Population: Adults

Purpose: Measures ability to see differences or errors in pairs of names and pairs of numbers; used to select clerical applicants

Description: Multiple-item paper–pencil test of speed and accuracy of visual perception. Items are pairs of names and numbers. The applicant checks each pair that is identical. The test predicts performance in numerous jobs, including adding-machine operators, clerical employees, key machine operators, and filing

and cataloging personnel. Materials include optional tapes for test administration.

Format: Examiner required; suitable for group use; timed: 15 minutes

Scoring: Hand key

Cost: Examination kit $26.25

Publisher: The Psychological Corporation

Office Skills Achievement Test
Paul L. Mellenbruch

Copyright: 1970

Population: Adolescents, adults; Grades 10 and above

Purpose: Assesses clerical skills; used for educational and vocational guidance and for screening applicant for employment

Description: Multiple-item paper–pencil test measuring several important office and clerical skills, including business letter writing, English usage, checking, filing, simple arithmetic, and following written instructions. The test was developed in office work situations, using clerical employees.

Format: Examiner required; suitable for group use; timed: 20 minutes

Scoring: Hand key

Cost: Specimen Set (test, manual, key) $5.00; 25 tests $8.75

Publisher: Psychometric Affiliates

Office Skills Tests

Copyright: 1977

Population: Adults

Purpose: Assesses clerical ability of job applicants; used for employee selection and placement

Description: Twelve tests suitable for screening clerks, accounting clerks, typists, secretary/stenographers, library assistants, and other office personnel. The tests are Checking, Coding, Filing, Forms Completion, Grammar, Numerical Skills, Oral Directions, Punctuation, Reading Comprehension, Spelling, Typing, and Vocabulary. Each test is available in two forms (A and B). Norms are provided for timed and untimed administration.

Format: Examiner required; suitable for group use; untimed: 3–10 minutes per test

Scoring: Hand key; computer scored

Cost: 25 booklets (specify test) $34; scoring stencils $10 each; oral directions cassette $30; examiner's manual $15

Publisher: McGraw-Hill/London House

Perceptual Speed (Identical Forms)
L. L. Thurstone, T. E. Jeffrey

Copyright: 1984

Population: Adults

Purpose: Measures ability to identify rapidly the similarities and differences in visual configurations; used to select clerical personnel or workers in occupations that require rapid perception of inaccuracies in written materials and diagrams

Description: Paper–pencil 140-item test of perceptual skill. The subject selects the figure among five choices that appears to be most similar to the illustration.

Format: Examiner required; suitable for group use; timed: 5 minutes

Scoring: Hand key

Cost: Specimen Set $8; 25 test booklets $20

Publisher: McGraw-Hill/London House

Personnel Test Battery (PTB) Audio Checking (CP8.1)

Copyright: 1991

Population: Adults

Purpose: Assesses an individual's ability to receive and check information that is presented orally; used to select clerical staff who must process information presented orally as in telesales or airline/hotel bookings

Description: Multiple-choice 60-item test in which the task is to listen to a string of numbers or letters presented on an audiotape and select the identical string from the five choices presented in the question booklet. There are three subtests covering letters, numbers, and letters

and numbers mixed. The test is suitable for individuals with minimal educational qualifications.

Format: 10 minutes

Scoring: Hand key; machine scored; scoring service available

Cost: Contact publisher

Publisher: Saville and Holdsworth Ltd.

Personnel Test Battery (PTB) Basic Checking (CP7.1)

Copyright: 1991

Population: Adults

Purpose: Measures speed and accuracy in checking a variety of materials at a very basic level; used for selection of clerical and general staff concerned with simple routine checking

Description: Multiple-choice 40-item test consisting of two subtests. One involves checking a list of numbers and the other involves checking a list of letters. In each list, a series of strings of numbers or letters is presented. These are compared with another page from which the identical string must be selected (from five choices). The test is suitable for individuals with minimal educational qualifications.

Format: 5 minutes

Scoring: Hand key; machine scored; scoring service available

Cost: Contact Publisher

Publisher: Saville and Holdsworth Ltd

Personnel Test Battery (PTB) Classification (CP4.1)

Copyright: 1993

Population: Adults

Purpose: Measures the ability to perceive and classify material in accordance with a set of instructions; appropriate when data handling, filing, or the following of instructions are important skills

Description: Sixty-item test representing a clerical task in which a number of sales order forms must be filed. The candidate classifies each order and then records the order in coded form. Some orders ("account sales") must be filed alphabetically, and others ("cash sales") must be classified under seven categories of goods purchased.

Format: 7 minutes

Scoring: Hand key; machine scored; scoring service available

Cost: Contact Publisher

Publisher: Saville and Holdsworth Ltd

Personnel Test Battery (PTB) Clerical Checking (CP3.1)

Copyright: 1993

Population: Adults

Purpose: Measures ability to perceive and check a variety of material quickly and accurately

Description: Forty-item proofreading test in which two lists of information about hotels are presented; one list is handwritten and the other is printed. The material contained in the lists includes names, numbers, and symbols. The candidates must compare the two lists and note any errors in accordance with a given code (designed to represent an actual clerical task).

Format: 7 minutes

Scoring: Hand key; machine scored; scoring service available

Cost: Contact publisher

Publisher: Saville and Holdsworth Ltd

Personnel Test Battery (PTB) Verbal Usage (VP1.1)

Copyright: 1993

Population: Adults

Purpose: Assesses verbal usage skills essential in business correspondence

Description: Thirty-item test which measures vocabulary, spelling, and grammatical skills necessary for drafting and processing of business correspondence. Candidates must select the correct words to complete sentences drawn from common commercial contexts.

Format: 10 minutes

Scoring: Hand key; machine scored; scoring service available

Cost: Contact publisher

Publisher: Saville and Holdsworth Ltd.

Personnel Test Battery (PTB) Text Checking (CP9.1)

Copyright: 1993

Population: Adults

Purpose: Measures proofreading speed and accuracy

Description: Fifty-item test which assesses speed and accuracy in proofreading, an important skill in the production of all kinds of documents. The test requires detailed proofreading from one set of texts to another, with candidates required to specify the exact nature of errors identified.

Format: 10 minutes

Scoring: Hand key; machine scored; scoring service available

Cost: Contact publisher

Publisher: Saville and Holdsworth Ltd.

PSI Basic Skills Tests for Business, Industry, and Government: Classifying (BST #11)
W. W. Ruch, A. N. Shub, S. M. Moinat, D. A. Dye

Copyright: 1981

Population: Adults

Purpose: Measures ability to place information into appropriate categories; used to select clerical and administrative personnel

Description: Multiple-choice 48-item test presenting four sets of data. Each set contains 12 items that must be properly categorized. The test is available in two equivalent paper–pencil forms and in computerized form. Transported validity study is available.

Format: Examiner required for paper–pencil forms; suitable for group use; timed: 5 minutes

Scoring: Hand key; may be computer scored

Cost: Paper–pencil: 25 tests per package: 1–19 packages $53.25; 20–199 packages $44.25;

200+ packages $36.25; Computerized form: 150–499 tests $2.50 each; 500–4,999 tests $2.25 each; 5,000–49,999 tests $2.00 each; 50,000+ tests $1.75 each

Publisher: Psychological Services, Inc.

PSI Basic Skills Tests for Business, Industry, and Government: Coding (BST #12)
W. W. Ruch, A. N. Shub, S. M. Moinat, D. A. Dye

Copyright: 1981

Population: Adults

Purpose: Measures ability to code information according to a prescribed system; used to select clerical and administrative personnel

Description: Multiple-choice 72-item test in which the subjects are given systems for coding information (each system codes four categories of related information). For each test item, the subject must code the given information into categories. The test is available in two equivalent paper–pencil forms and in computerized form. Transported validity study is available.

Format: Examiner required for paper–pencil forms; suitable for group use; timed: 5 minutes

Scoring: Hand key; may be computer scored

Cost: Paper–pencil: 25 tests per package: 1–19 packages $53.25; 20–199 packages $44.25; 200+ packages $36.25; Computerized form: 150–499 tests $2.50 each; 500–4,999 tests $2.25 each; 5,000–49,999 tests $2.00 each; 50,000+ tests $1.75 each

Publisher: Psychological Services, Inc.

PSI Basic Skills Tests for Business, Industry, and Government: Computation (BST #4)
W. W. Ruch, A. N. Shub, S. M. Moinat, D. A. Dye

Copyright: 1981

Population: Adults

Purpose: Measures ability to solve arithmetic problems; used to select clerical and administrative personnel

Description: Multiple-choice 40-item test measuring the ability to add, subtract, multiply, and divide, using whole numbers, fractions, and decimals. The test is available in two equivalent paper–pencil forms and in computerized form. Transported validity study is available.

Format: Examiner required for paper–pencil forms; suitable for group use; timed: 5 minutes

Scoring: Hand key; may be computer scored

Cost: Paper–pencil: 25 tests per package: 1–19 packages $53.25; 20–199 packages $44.25; 200+ packages $36.25; Computerized form: 150–499 tests $2.50 each; 500–4,999 tests $2.25 each; 5,000–49,999 tests $2.00 each; 50,000+ tests $1.75 each

Publisher: Psychological Services, Inc.

PSI Basic Skills Tests for Business, Industry, and Government: Decision Making (BST #6)
W. W. Ruch, A. N. Shub, S. M. Moinat, D. A. Dye

Copyright: 1981

Population: Adults

Purpose: Measures ability to read a set of procedures and apply them to new situations by determining the appropriate action; used to select clerical and administrative personnel

Description: Paper–pencil 20-item multiple-choice test in which sets of procedures (related to clerical or office duties) are described along with a set of action codes for implementing the procedures. The examinee is presented with a number of problems in which he or she must decide the course of action for each item and mark the appropriate action code. The test is available in two equivalent paper–pencil forms. Transported validity study is available.

Format: Examiner required; suitable for group use; timed: 5 minutes

Scoring: Hand key; may be computer scored

Cost: 25 tests per package: 1–19 packages $53.25; 20–199 packages $44.25; 200+ packages $36.25

Publisher: Psychological Services, Inc.

PSI Basic Skills Tests for Business, Industry, and Government: Filing Names (BST #13)

W. W. Ruch, A. N. Shub, S. M. Moinat, D. A. Dye

Copyright: 1981

Population: Adults

Purpose: Measures ability to file simple entries alphabetically; used to select clerical and administrative personnel

Description: Multiple-choice 50-item test in which the subject is presented with a name, followed by a list of four other names (arranged alphabetically). The subject "files" the given name at the beginning, between two of the names, or at the end of the list. The test is available in two equivalent paper–pencil forms and in computerized form. Transported validity study is available.

Format: Examiner required for paper–pencil forms; suitable for group use; timed: 1½ minutes

Scoring: Hand key; may be computer scored

Cost: Paper–pencil: 25 tests per package: 1–19 packages $53.25; 20–199 packages $44.25; 200+ packages $36.25; Computerized form: 150–499 tests $2.50 each; 500–4,999 tests $2.25 each; 5,000–49,999 tests $2.00 each; 50,000+ tests $1.75 each

Publisher: Psychological Services, Inc.

PSI Basic Skills Tests for Business, Industry, and Government: Filing Numbers (BST #14)

W. W. Ruch, A. N. Shub, S. M. Moinat, D. A. Dye

Copyright: 1981

Population: Adults

Purpose: Measures ability to file numbers in numerical order; used to select clerical and administrative personnel

Description: Multiple-choice 75-item test in which each test item consists of a six-digit number to be filed numerically in a list of four other six-digit numbers (already arranged in numeri-

cal order). The test is available in two equivalent paper–pencil forms and in computerized form. Transported validity study is available.

Format: Examiner required for paper–pencil forms; suitable for group use; timed: 2 minutes

Scoring: Hand key; may be computer scored

Cost: Paper–pencil: 25 tests per package: 1–19 packages $53.25; 20–199 packages $44.25; 200+ packages $36.25; Computerized form: 150–499 tests $2.50 each; 500–4,999 tests $2.25 each; 5,000–49,999 tests $2.00 each; 50,000+ tests $1.75 each

Publisher: Psychological Services, Inc.

PSI Basic Skills Tests for Business, Industry, and Government: Following Oral Directions (BST #7)

W. W. Ruch, A. N. Shub, S. M. Moinat, D. A. Dye

Copyright: 1981

Population: Adults

Purpose: Measures ability to listen to information and instructions presented orally and answer questions about what is heard; used to select clerical and administrative personnel

Description: Paper–pencil 24-item multiple-choice test in which the subjects listen to a 6½ minute prerecorded audiotape and then answer questions about the content of the tape. The tape is played only once (no rewinding or stopping of the tape is allowed), and subjects are encouraged to take written notes during the playing of the tape. The tape is a recording of conversations that take place in an employment setting.

Format: Examiner required; suitable for group use; timed: 5 minutes

Scoring: Hand key; may be computer scored

Cost: 25 tests per package: 1–19 packages $53.25; 20–199 packages $44.25; 200+ packages $36.25

Publisher: Psychological Services, Inc.

PSI Basic Skills Tests for Business, Industry, and Government: Following Written Directions (BST #8)
W. W. Ruch, A. N. Shub, S. M. Moinat, D. A. Dye

Copyright: 1981

Population: Adults

Purpose: Measures ability to read, understand, and apply sets of written instructions; used to select clerical and administrative personnel

Description: Multiple-choice 36-item test requiring examinees to read sets of rules and apply them to a number of case examples. The test is available in two equivalent paper–pencil forms and in computerized form. Transported validity study is available.

Format: Examiner required for paper–pencil forms; suitable for group use; timed: 5 minutes

Scoring: Hand key; may be computer scored

Cost: 25 tests per package: 1–19 packages $42.50; 20–199 packages $35.50; 200+ packages $29.00

Publisher: Psychological Services, Inc.

PSI Basic Skills Tests for Business, Industry, and Government: Forms Checking (BST #9)
W. W. Ruch, A. N. Shub, S. M. Moinat, D. A. Dye

Copyright: 1981

Population: Adults

Purpose: Measures ability to verify the accuracy of completed forms; used to select clerical and administrative personnel

Description: True–false 42-item test in which the examinee verifies the accuracy of information in clerical forms filled out using information in written paragraphs. The examinee must check a number of the entries on each form against the information in the paragraphs to determine whether the entries are correct or incorrect. The test is available in two equivalent paper–pencil forms and in computerized form. Transported validity study is available.

Format: Examiner required for paper–pencil forms; suitable for group use; timed: 5 minutes

Scoring: Hand key; may be computer scored

Cost: Paper–pencil: 25 tests per package: 1–19 packages $53.25; 20–199 packages $44.25; 200+ packages $36.25; Computerized form: 150–499 tests $2.50 each; 500–4,999 tests $2.25 each; 5,000–49,999 tests $2.00 each; 50,000+ tests $1.75 each

Publisher: Psychological Services, Inc.

PSI Basic Skills Tests for Business, Industry, and Government: Language Skills (BST #1)
W. W. Ruch, A. N. Shub, S. M. Moinat, D. A. Dye

Copyright: 1981

Population: Adults

Purpose: Measures language skills used in proofing written material

Description: Multiple-choice 25-item test in which examinee reads a sentence, part of which is underlined, and determines whether the underlined portion contains errors in spelling, punctuation, capitalization, grammar, or usage. The test is available in two equivalent paper–pencil forms and in computerized form. Transported validity study is available.

Format: Examiner required for paper–pencil forms; suitable for group use; timed: 10 minutes

Scoring: Hand key; may be computer scored

Cost: Paper–pencil: 25 tests per package: 1–19 packages $53.25; 20–199 packages $44.25; 200+ packages $36.25; Computerized form: 150–499 tests $2.50 each; 500–4,999 tests $2.25 each; 5,000–49,999 tests $2.00 each; 50,000+ tests $1.75 each

Publisher: Psychological Services, Inc.

PSI Basic Skills Tests for Business, Industry, and Government: Problem Solving (BST #5)
W. W. Ruch, A. N. Shub, S. M. Moinat, D. A. Dye

Copyright: 1981

Population: Adults

Purpose: Measures ability to solve written math problems

Description: Multiple-choice 25-item test in which examinee reads a word problem and applies the appropriate arithmetic operations to solve the problem. The test is available in two equivalent paper–pencil forms and in computerized form. Transported validity study is available.

Format: Examiner required for paper–pencil forms; suitable for group use; timed: 5 minutes

Scoring: Hand key; may be computer scored

Cost: Paper–pencil: 25 tests per package: 1–19 packages $53.25; 20–199 packages $44.25; 200+ packages $36.25; Computerized form: 150–499 tests $2.50 each; 500–4,999 tests $2.25 each; 5,000–49,999 tests $2.00 each; 50,000+ tests $1.75 each

Publisher: Psychological Services, Inc.

PSI Basic Skills Tests for Business, Industry, and Government: Reading Comprehension (BST #2)
W. W. Ruch, A. N. Shub, S. M. Moinat, D. A. Dye

Copyright: 1981

Population: Adults

Purpose: Measures basic reading comprehension; used to select clerical and administrative personnel

Description: Paper–pencil 23-item multiple-choice test measuring the ability to read short passages and answer literal and inferential questions about them.

Format: Examiner required; suitable for group use; timed: 10 minutes

Scoring: Hand key; may be computer scored

Cost: Paper–pencil: 25 tests per package: 1–19 packages $53.25; 20–199 packages $44.25; 200+ packages $36.25; Computerized form: 150–499 tests $2.50 each; 500–4,999 tests $2.25 each; 5,000–49,999 tests $2.00 each; 50,000+ tests $1.75 each

Publisher: Psychological Services, Inc.

PSI Basic Skills Tests for Business, Industry, and Government: Reasoning (BST #10)
W. W. Ruch, A. N. Shub, S. M. Moinat, D. A. Dye

Copyright: 1981

Population: Adults

Purpose: Measures ability to analyze a list of facts and draw valid and logical conclusions from that information; used to select clerical and administrative personnel

Description: Multiple-choice 30-item test consisting of six lists of facts (one-sentence statements), with five possible conclusions for each list of facts. The examinee must read each list of facts and decide whether each conclusion is definitely true, definitely false, or unknown based on the given facts. The test is available in two equivalent paper–pencil forms and in computerized form. Transported validity study is available.

Format: Examiner required for paper–pencil forms; suitable for group use; timed: 5 minutes

Scoring: Hand key; may be computer scored

Cost: Paper–pencil: 25 tests per package: 1–19 packages $53.25; 20–199 packages $44.25; 200+ packages $36.25; Computerized form: 150–499 tests $2.50 each; 500–4,999 tests $2.25 each; 5,000–49,999 tests $2.00 each; 50,000+ tests $1.75 each

Publisher: Psychological Services, Inc.

PSI Basic Skills Tests for Business, Industry, and Government: Visual Speed and Accuracy (BST #15)
W. W. Ruch, A. N. Shub, S. M. Moinat, D. A. Dye

Copyright: 1981

Population: Adults

Purpose: Measures ability to see details quickly and accurately; used to select clerical and administrative personnel

Description: Multiple-choice 150-item test in which each test item consists of two series of numbers and symbols. The examinee compares the numbers or symbols and determines whether they are the same or different. The test is available in two equivalent paper–pencil forms and in computerized form. Transported validity study is available.

Format: Examiner required for paper–pencil forms; suitable for group use; timed: 5 minutes

Scoring: Hand key; may be computer scored

Cost: Paper–pencil: 25 tests per package: 1–19 packages $53.25; 20–199 packages $44.25; 200+ packages $36.25; Computerized form: 150–499 tests $2.50 each; 500–4,999 tests $2.25 each; 5,000–49,999 tests $2.00 each; 50,000+ tests $1.75 each

Publisher: Psychological Services, Inc.

PSI Basic Skills Tests for Business, Industry, and Government: Vocabulary (BST #3)
W. W. Ruch, A. N. Shub, S. M. Moinat, D. A. Dye

Copyright: 1981

Population: Adults

Purpose: Measures the ability to identify the correct synonym for the word underlined in each sentence; used to select clerical and office workers

Description: Multiple-choice 45-item test in which each item consists of a sentence with one word underlined, followed by four words. The examinee must select the word meaning the same or about the same as the word that is underlined in the sentence. The test is available in two equivalent paper–pencil forms and in computerized form. Transported validity study is available.

Format: Examiner required for paper–pencil forms; suitable for group use; timed: 5 minutes

Scoring: Hand key; may be computer scored

Cost: Paper–pencil: 25 tests per package: 1–19 packages $53.25; 20–199 packages $44.25; 200+ packages $36.25; Computerized form: 150–499 tests $2.50 each; 500–4,999 tests $2.25 each; 5,000–49,999 tests $2.00 each; 50,000+ tests $1.75 each

Publisher: Psychological Services, Inc.

RCJS Office Arithmetic Test– Form CA
Roland T. Ramsay

Copyright: 1990

Population: Adults

Purpose: Assesses math skills necessary for the position of office clerk; used for hiring

Description: Multiple-choice 40-item paper–pencil test assessing addition and subtraction of 1-, 2-, and 3-digit whole numbers and decimals; multiplication and division of 1- and 2-digit whole numbers and decimals; and reading simple charts and tables. Materials include reusable booklet, answer sheet, and manual with key.

Format: Examiner required; suitable for group use; timed: 30 minutes

Scoring: Hand key; machine scoring service available from publisher

Cost: Kit (10 test booklets, 100 answer sheets, scoring key, 1 test manual) $200.00

Publisher: Ramsay Corporation

RCJS Office Reading Test–Form G
Roland T. Ramsay

Copyright: 1990

Population: Adults

Purpose: Assesses reading skills necessary for office workers; used for hiring

Description: Multiple-choice 40-item paper–pencil test based on five written passages: Operating the Copier, Travel Arrangements, Operating a Computer, The Business Letter, and Telephone Procedures. Materials include reusable booklet, answer sheet, and manual with key.

Format: Examiner required; suitable for group use; timed: 30 minutes

Scoring: Hand key; machine scoring service available from publisher

Cost: Kit (10 test booklets, 100 answer sheets, scoring key, test manual) $200.00

Publisher: Ramsay Corporation

Secretarial Staff Selector

Copyright: 1984

Population: Adults

Purpose: Evaluates candidates of all levels of experience for secretarial positions

Description: Multiple-item paper–pencil set of seven timed subtests and two optional subtests available in three formats for assessing attention to detail, alphabetizing and filing skills, grammar and punctuation, spelling and vocabulary, manual dexterity, logical and problem-solving abilities, numerical skills, desire for people contact (optional), and emotional stability (optional). The tests are used for selecting senior clerks, secretaries, and administrative assistants. Available in French.

Format: Examiner required; suitable for group use; timed: 75 minutes

Scoring: Scoring service available from publisher

Cost: $299.00 each

Publisher: Walden Personnel Testing and Training, Inc.

Short Employment Tests® (SET®)
G. K. Bennett, Marjorie Gelink

Copyright: 1951 (Manual 1993)

Population: Adults

Purpose: Measures verbal, numerical, and clerical skills; used to select qualified individuals for a variety of administrative and entry-level positions

Description: Three 5-minute subtests: verbal, numerical, and clerical aptitude. May be used as a complete battery to produce a total score or as individual tests. Available in four forms.

Format: Examiner required; suitable for group use; timed: 5 minutes per subtest

Scoring: Hand key

Cost: Examination kit (booklet for each of three tests and manual) Form 1 $35.75; Forms 2, 3, and 4 $40.00

Publisher: The Psychological Corporation

Short Tests of Clerical Ability (STCA)

Copyright: 1959

Population: Adults

Purpose: Assesses aptitudes and abilities important to the successful completion of typical office tasks; used for selection and placement in office personnel

Description: Multiple-item paper–pencil battery consisting of seven tests; the battery includes arithmetic skills, business vocabulary, checking accuracy, coding, oral and written directions, filing, and language (grammar and mechanics).

Format: Examiner required; suitable for group use; untimed: 3–6 minutes per subtest

Scoring: Hand key

Cost: 25 test booklets (specify test) $32.00; scoring stencils (specify test) $10.00; examiner's manual $15.00

Publisher: McGraw-Hill/London House

SRA Clerical Aptitudes

Copyright: 1947

Population: Adults

Purpose: Assesses general aptitudes necessary for clerical work; used in employee screening and placing

Description: Three-part paper–pencil test measuring office vocabulary, office arithmetic, and office checking. The tests indicate the ability to learn tasks usually performed in various clerical jobs. The office vocabulary test (48 items) measures command of basic vocabulary and verbal relations. The arithmetic test (24 items) requires application of basic math processes to the solution of practical problems. The checking test (144 items) measures the ability to perceive details easily and rapidly.

Format: Examiner required; suitable for group use; timed: 25 minutes

Scoring: Hand key

Cost: 25 reusable test booklets $90; 25 answer sheets $24; 100 profile sheets $24; examiner's manual $15

Publisher: McGraw-Hill/London House

SRA Typing 5

Copyright: 1975

Population: Adults

Purpose: Measures a person's ability to type a particular kind of assignment; used with a variety of typing positions requiring different skills

Description: Task assessment consisting of three forms measuring typing speed and accuracy. Typing Speed, Form A, consists of a letter with approximately 215 words measuring key stroking speed and accuracy. Business Letter, Form B, for the more experienced typist, measures the ability to set up a business letter and type it quickly and accurately. Numerical, Form C, containing approximately 115 words and 40 numbers, measures speed and accuracy in typing complex material containing words, symbols, and numbers in columns with headings.

Format: Examiner required; suitable for group use; timed: 5 minutes per test (after practice time)

Scoring: Hand key

Cost: 25 test booklets (specify test) $35; 25 practice sheets $10; examiner's manual $15

Publisher: McGraw-Hill/London House

Typing Test for Business (TTB)

J. E. Doppelt, A. D. Hartman,
F. B. Krawchick

Copyright: 1984 (Manual 1991)

Population: Adults

Purpose: Assesses typing skills; used to test applicants for typist, keypunch operator, secretarial, and other positions in which typing skill is necessary

Description: Test of five kinds of typing used in business: straight copy, letters, revised manuscript, numbers, and tables. The warm-up practice copy is administered first. The straight copy test may be given as a quick screening test. Two alternate forms, AR and BR, are available. The test is sold only to personnel departments of business and industrial firms for the testing of applicants and employees. It is not sold to schools or employment agencies.

Format: Examiner required; suitable for group use; timed: time varies

Scoring: Hand key

Cost: Examination kit $46.00

Publisher: The Psychological Corporation

Typing Test I and II

Copyright: Not provided

Population: Adults

Purpose: Provides a quick screening of an individual's typing ability; used to estimate the typing skills of applicants for general clerical or clerk–typist positions

Description: Manual test measuring an individual's typing speed and accuracy in which the examinee is presented with a double-spaced letter to type. After reading the test directions, adjusting the machine settings, and typing the practice copy, the examinee types the test letter exactly as it appears. If the examinee completes the letter before the allotted time expires, he or she begins retyping the letter. The test yields a words-per-minute score and an accuracy score. A more comprehensive test should be used for promoting present personnel or hiring secretarial or stenographic applicants. The following materials are required: one test folder and one typewriter for each examinee and a timing device for the examiner.

Format: Examiner required; suitable for group use; timed: 5 minutes

Scoring: Hand key

Cost: 1–24 packages $45.00

Publisher: Richardson, Bellows, Henry and Company, Inc.

VCWS 5—Clerical Comprehension and Aptitude

Copyright: 1974

Population: Adults

Purpose: Measures basic clerical aptitude and the ability to perform a variety of answering, mail sorting, alphabetical filing, bookkeeping, and typing tasks and to communicate effectively both verbally and in writing; used as a screening device for entry-level jobs

Description: Manual test featuring three separate work samples measuring an individual's ability to perform a variety of clerical tasks and to learn the tasks. The test begins with mail sorting and simultaneous phone answering. A tape plays a series of phone conversations at prerecorded intervals, requiring the individual to stop the mail sorting in order to take the phone message. The individual also must complete an alphabetical filing task. In the second section of the test, the individual must use a 10-key adding machine to perform three exercises emphasizing accurate recording of numerical data and basic math skills. In the typing section, the typewriter has been modified to measure a person's typing coordination skills.

Format: Examiner required; not suitable for group use; timed: time not available

Scoring: Examiner evaluated

Cost: $2,495.00

Publisher: Valpar International Corporation

Computer

Aptitude Assessment Battery: Programming (AABP)

Jack M. Wolfe

Copyright: 1967

Population: Adults

Purpose: Determines a person's aptitude for computer programming; may be used to select job candidates, as a guide for training programs, and for revealing work habits and task preference

Description: Five-problem paper–pencil tests measuring ability to draw deductions, understand complicated instructions, interpret intricate specifications, reason, desk-check, debug, and document and annotate work. Available in French, Spanish, and Braille.

Format: Examiner required; suitable for group use; untimed: 3 hours

Scoring: Scoring service provided

Cost: Complete (test, evaluation, report) $245.00

Publisher: Rose Wolfe

Automated Office Battery (AOB) Coded Instructions (CI3)

Copyright: 1988

Population: Ages 16 to adult

Purpose: Measures the ability to understand and follow instruction coded into machine-oriented language

Description: Forty-item test assessing the ability to understand and follow coded instructions. Candidates are presented with instructions on how to enter and retrieve information from a machine. They must understand the instruction in the text and decide on the appropriate course of action for each question. The content is office-based and related to new technology within the office environment, particularly to the kinds of instructions that an individual must follow when operating computer systems and word processors.

Format: 18 minutes

Scoring: Hand key; machine scored; scoring service available

Cost: Contact Publisher

Publisher: Saville and Holdsworth Ltd.

Automated Office Battery (AOB) Computer Checking (CC2)

Copyright: 1988

Population: Ages 16 to adult

Purpose: Measures the abilities of scanning, reasoning, and checking documentation against computer-screen and printer output by comparing input

Description: Forty-item test assessing the ability to check computerized information against typewritten copy. The candidate must identify quickly and accurately whether the information has been correctly transferred to a facing representation of a computer screen or a page of computer printout. The information may have been reordered and added to other information during input to the computer. To complete the checking task, the candidate must find the relevant data, understand its new representation, and then make the final check on its correct transfer.

Format: 12 minutes

Scoring: Hand key; machine scored; scoring service available

Cost: Contact Publisher

Publisher: Saville and Holdsworth Ltd.

Business Analyst Skills Evaluation (BUSAN)

Copyright: 1984

Population: Adults

Purpose: Evaluates aptitude and potential for positions in business systems analysis, procedures analysis, and user department/EDP department interface; used with candidates with prior business experience; no previous data processing knowledge is required

Description: Multiple-item paper–pencil test in two groups of subtests used for evaluating candidates for positions such as business analyst, procedures analyst, business systems analyst, and user/EDP department interface. Section 1 subtests measure analytical ability, flow charting, deductive reasoning, procedures and systems analysis, and development of departmental user reports and subsystems. Section 2 subtests measure horizontal interpersonal relationship abilities, people contact desired, emotional stability, stress tolerance, group participation skills, consistency, dominance, adventurousness, maturity, enthusiasm, tough-mindedness, practicality, sophistication, self-sufficiency, and leadership potential.

Format: Examiner required; suitable for group use; timed: 1 hour 45 minutes

Scoring: Scoring service provided

Cost: $319.00–$699.00 depending on depth of assessment required

Publisher: Walden Personnel Testing and Training, Inc.

Computer Operator Aptitude Battery (COAB)

Copyright: 1973

Population: Adults

Purpose: Helps predict job performance of computer operators; used by data processing managers and personnel directors to select applicants for computer operator positions

Description: Paper–pencil test predicting success as a computer operator; the test consists of three separately timed subtests: Sequence Recognition, Format Checking, and Logical Thinking.

Format: Examiner required; suitable for group use; timed: 45 minutes

Scoring: Hand key

Cost: 5 reusable test booklets $90; 25 answer sheets $59; examiner's manual $15

Publisher: McGraw-Hill/London House

Computer Programmer Aptitude Battery (CPAB)

Copyright: 1964

Population: Adults

Purpose: Measures potential for success in the computer programming field; used by data processing managers and personnel directors to identify people with the aptitude for computer programming

Descripton: Five separately timed paper–pencil subtests measuring verbal meaning, reasoning, letter series, number ability, and diagramming (problem analysis and logical solution). The test is available in a short version which includes reasoning and diagramming.

Format: Examiner required; suitable for group use; timed: 1 hour 19 minutes

Scoring: Hand key

Cost: 5 reusable test booklets $90; 25 answer sheets $59; examiner's manual $15

Publisher: McGraw-Hill/London House

Database Analyst Staff Selector

Copyright: Not provided

Population: Adults

Purpose: Measures analytical reasoning and detail skills necessary for the position of database analyst or database programmer

Description: Multiple-item tests measuring skills

Format: 85 minutes

Scoring: Scoring service

Cost: $319.00

Publisher: Walden Personnel Testing and Training, Inc.

IPI Job-Field Series: Computer Programmer

Copyright: 1984

Population: Adults

Purpose: Assesses skills and aptitudes of applicants for entry-level computer programmer positions; used for employee selection and placement

Description: Multiple-item paper–pencil battery of five aptitude tests measuring skills that predict success as an entry-level computer programmer. The tests include Office Terms, Numbers, Judgment, Parts, and Perception. For individual test descriptions, see the IPI Employee Aptitude Series. Also available in French and Spanish.

Format: Suitable for group use; examiner required; timed: 30 minutes

Scoring: Hand keys

Cost: Starter kit (test materials for five applicants, scoring keys, manuals) $80; test package $12/applicant

Publisher: Industrial Psychology International Ltd.

Microcomputer User Aptitude Test
   Richard Label

Copyright: 1986

Population: Adults

Purpose: Measures aptitude and potential for work with a microcomputer

Description: Multiple-item test measuring the following abilities necessary for working with a microcomputer: logical ability; ability to work with spreadsheets, databases, and operating sys-

tems; and vendor manual interpretation. The test consists of five problems that simulate the use of the most commonly used microapplications. Skills are assessed independent of any specific hardware or software.

Format: Examiner required; timed: 1 hour

Scoring: Scoring service provided

Cost: $139.00

Publisher: Walden Personnel Testing and Training, Inc.

Network Analyst Staff Selector

Copyright: Not provided

Population: Adults

Purpose: Measures basic knowledge of data communication systems components and evaluates the candidate's problem-solving ability relevant to common network problems

Description: Multiple-item test measuring the abilities necessary for working with a microcomputer

Format: 1 hour and 45 minutes

Scoring: Scoring service provided

Cost: Test booklet and detailed report on each candidate $319.00

Publisher: Walden Personnel Testing and Training, Inc.

Network Technician Staff Selector

Copyright: Not provided

Population: Adults

Purpose: Measures basic knowledge of data communication systems components and evaluates the candidate's problem-solving ability relevant to common network problems

Description: Multiple-item test measuring the abilities necessary for working with a microcomputer

Format: 1 hour and 45 minutes

Scoring: Scoring service provided

Cost: Test booklet and detailed report on each candidate $319.00

Publisher: Walden Personnel Testing and Training, Inc.

Object-Oriented Programmer Analyst Staff Selector

Copyright: Not provided

Population: Adults

Purpose: Measures object-oriented programming ability and specific knowledge of C++

Description: Multiple-item test measuring the abilities necessary for working with a microcomputer

Format: 2 hours

Scoring: Scoring service provided

Cost: Test booklet and detailed report on each candidate $319.00

Publisher: Walden Personnel Testing and Training, Inc.

Programmer Analyst Aptitude Test (PAAT)

Copyright: 1984

Population: Adults

Purpose: Evaluates aptitude and potential for computer programming and business analysis positions; used for prescreening entry-level candidates with no prior experience, computer trainees, computer science graduates, and experienced applicants

Description: Six-item paper–pencil test assessing logical ability, skill in interpreting business specifications, potential for translating business problems into symbolic logic, and ability to follow complex business procedures and analyze them to supply specific requirements. Available with interpersonal measures.

Format: Examiner required; suitable for group use; timed: 2 hours

Scoring: Scoring service provided

Cost: $269.00–$699.00 depending on depth of assessment

Publisher: Walden Personnel Testing and Training, Inc.

Programmer Aptitude Battery (PAB)

Terence R. Taylor

Copyright: 1988

Population: Adolescents, adults

Purpose: Assesses aptitude for computer programming

Description: Multiple-choice 102-item paper–pencil test with three subtests: Procedures Test–logical reasoning, number ability, perseverance, short–medium-term memory, reading comprehension, precise methodological approach to problems (36 items, 60 minutes); Matrices Test I—speed and accuracy (36 items, 10 minutes); Matrices Test II—forming and checking hypotheses (30 items, 30 minutes). Materials include test booklet, answer sheets, rough paper, and manual. Available in Afrikaans.

Format: Examiner required; suitable for group use; timed: 100 minutes

Scoring: Hand key and computer scored

Cost: Contact publisher

Publisher: Human Sciences Research Council

Software Knowledge Series

Copyright: 1994

Population: Adults

Purpose: Measures knowledge of software for microcomputers

Description: Additions to the five-minute knowledge test series: Mac, OS/2, WordPerfect, Novell Netware, Excel, dBASE, Harvard Graphics, Windows, Windows 95, DOS, Word for Windows, UNIX, Lotus, Sybase, and C.

Format: Examiner required; suitable for group use; timed: 75 minutes

Scoring: Scoring service available from publisher

Cost: 20 tests $219.00

Publisher: Walden Personnel Testing and Training, Inc.

Systems Analyst Aptitude Test (SAAT)

Jack M. Wolfe

Copyright: 1971

Population: Adults

Purpose: Measures a person's aptitude for business systems design; used for hiring, training, and promotion of systems analysts

Description: Single-item (case study) test evaluating interpretation of specifications, ability to plan a logical procedure, recognition of alternative solutions, clarity of explanation, quality of organization, attention to detail, and effectiveness and efficiency of design. Available in French.

Format: Examiner required; suitable for group use; untimed: 3 hours

Scoring: Scoring service provided

Cost: Complete (test, evaluation, and report) $419.00

Publisher: Rose Wolfe

Systems Programming Aptitude Test (SPAT)
Jack M. Wolfe

Copyright: 1979

Population: Adults

Purpose: Measures a person's aptitude for systems and software programming; may be used for hiring, training, and promotion decisions at all levels of skill

Description: Five-part paper–pencil test measuring accuracy, reasoning, and ability to deal with complex relationships and skills in deductive, interpretive, and analytic reasoning.

Format: Examiner required; suitable for group use; untimed: 3 hours

Scoring: Scoring service provided

Cost: Complete (test, evaluation, and report) $419.00

Publisher: Rose Wolfe

Technical Support Staff Selector

Copyright: Not provided

Population: Adults

Purpose: Evaluates knowledge and ability to work in Client/Server and Help Desk environments; the candidate generally provides technical user support for those who must interface with IS departments

Description: Multiple-item tests measuring skills

Format: 1 hour 45 minutes

Scoring: Scoring service available from publisher

Cost: Test booklet and detailed report on each candidate $319.00

Publisher: Walden Personnel Testing and Training, Inc.

W-Apt Programming Aptitude Test
Jack M. Wolfe

Copyright: 1983

Population: Adults

Purpose: Measures aptitude and potential for applications programming; used for screening entry-level candidates, computer trainers, and computer science graduates and for prescreening experienced applicants

Description: Five-item paper–pencil or computer-administered test assessing logical ability, interpretation of intricate specifications, ability to follow instructions precisely, attention to detail, accuracy, and problem solving using reasoning with symbols. A microcomputer version is available. Available in French.

Format: Examiner required; suitable for group use; untimed: 1 hour

Scoring: Hand key; scoring service provided

Cost: $109.00 per person

Publisher: Rose Wolfe

Wolfe Computer Operator Aptitude Test (WCOAT)
Jack M. Wolfe

Copyright: 1985

Population: Adults

Purpose: Evaluates the aptitude for computer operations at all experience levels

Description: Generalized aptitude test measuring manual dexterity and the ability to solve problems logically, follow procedural logic, and precisely follow all instructions and rules. Available in French.

Format: Examiner required; suitable for group use; timed: 1 hour

Scoring: Scoring service provided

Cost: Complete (test, computer report) $129.00 per person

Publisher: Rose Wolfe

Wolfe Programming Aptitude Test–Form W
Jack M. Wolfe

Copyright: 1978

Population: Adults

Purpose: Measures a person's aptitude for computer programming; used by schools and placement agencies

Description: Three-part paper–pencil test measuring attention to detail, ability to solve problems, and ability to interpret specifications. Available in French.

Format: Examiner required; suitable for group use; timed: 45 minutes

Scoring: Scored by publisher

Cost: Booklets $89.00 each

Publisher: Rose Wolfe

Wolfe Programming Language Test: COBOL (WCOBOL)
Jack M. Wolfe

Copyright: 1977

Population: Adults

Purpose: Assesses a person's knowledge of COBOL. Used for screening experienced programmers.

Description: Paper–pencil 47-item test measuring speed of work and evaluating coding skills, documentation, and knowledge of COBOL. Suitable for junior and intermediate programmers with detailed knowledge of the COBOL manual.

Format: Examiner required; suitable for group use; timed: 3 hours

Scoring: Scoring service provided

Cost: Complete (test, evaluation, and report) $109.00

Publisher: Rose Wolfe

Wolfe-Spence Programming Aptitude Test (WSPAT)
Jack M. Wolfe, R. J. Spence

Copyright: 1979

Population: Adults

Purpose: Screens entry-level candidates for computer programming work; may be used for hiring or selecting candidates for training classes

Description: Eight-item paper–pencil test measuring a person's logical capabilities and ability to interpret intricate specifications. Candidates passing the test should be given the AABP test prior to making hiring decisions.

Format: Examiner required; suitable for group use; timed: 2 hours

Scoring: Scoring service provided

Cost: Complete (test, evaluation, and report) $149.00 per person

Publisher: Rose Wolfe

Wolfe-Winrow CICS/VS Command Level Proficiency Test (WWCICS)
B. W. Winrow

Copyright: 1982

Population: Adults

Purpose: Measures a person's knowledge of IBM CICS/VS Command Level; used for hiring, training, and promoting applications programmers and software specialists

Description: Five-part paper–pencil test measuring general knowledge of CICS/VS concepts, facilities, and commands, and the ability to code CICS/VS commands from specifications and debug and test in a CICS/VS environment. The test also includes an optional measure of specific knowledge of Basic Mapping Support and related commands.

Format: Examiner required; suitable for group use; timed: 30 minutes

Scoring: Scoring service provided

Cost: Complete (detailed report) $109.00

Publisher: Walden Personnel Testing and Training, Inc.

Wolfe-Winrow DOS/VS JCL Proficiency Test
B. W. Winrow

Copyright: 1982

Population: Adults

Purpose: Measures a person's knowledge of DOS, DOS/VS, or DOS/VSE JSL language; may be used for hiring, training, and promoting purposes

Description: Five-part paper–pencil test measuring the ability to identify common JCL errors, code, overwrite catalogued procedures, and specific knowledge of JCL parameters. Suitable for examining computer operators, DOS JCL analysts, and applications programmers at all experience levels.

Format: Examiner required; suitable for group use; timed: 30 minutes

Scoring: Scoring service provided

Cost: Complete (test, computer report) $109.00 per person

Publisher: Walden Personnel Testing and Training, Inc.

Wolfe-Winrow OS JCL Proficiency Test
B. W. Winrow

Copyright: 1982

Population: Adults

Purpose: Measures a person's knowledge of IBM OS/JCL language; used for hiring, promoting, and training computer operators, analysts, and programmers

Description: Five-part paper–pencil test measuring general knowledge of JCL statements and parameters and understanding of JCL parameters, catalogued procedures, symbolic parameters, GDGs, and overriding JCL. The test also assesses the ability to identify OS/JCL errors and code OS/JCL.

Format: Examiner required; suitable for group use; timed: 30 minutes

Scoring: Scoring service provided

Cost: Complete (test, computer report) $109.00 per person

Publisher: Walden Personnel Testing and Training, Inc.

Wolfe-Winrow Structured COBOL
B. W. Winrow

Copyright: 1982

Population: Adults

Purpose: Assesses a person's knowledge of structured COBOL; used for hiring, evaluating existing staff, evaluating training needs and effectiveness, and promotion

Description: Five-question paper–pencil test measuring the ability to identify structured programming tools for COBOL, use concepts such as table look-up and debugging aids, define storage attributes and code PICTURE clauses for COBOL, code from specifications, and understand arithmetic operations and programming efficiencies.

Format: Examiner required; suitable for group use; timed: 30 minutes

Scoring: Scoring service provided

Cost: Complete (includes report) $109.00 per person

Publisher: Walden Personnel Testing and Training, Inc.

Wolfe-Winrow TSO/SPF Proficiency Test (WWTSO)
B. W. Winrow

Copyright: 1982

Population: Adults

Purpose: Assesses a person's knowledge of IBM TSO/SPF. Used for hiring, training, and promoting programmers and software specialists.

Description: Five-part paper–pencil test evaluating an applicant's knowledge of TSO/SPF features and commands.

Format: Examiner required; suitable for group use; timed: 30 minutes

Scoring: Scoring service provided

Cost: Complete (test, detailed report) $109.00

Publisher: Walden Personnel Testing and Training, Inc.

Work Keys Applied Technology Test

Copyright: 1993

Population: Adolescents, adults

Purpose: Used for program evaluation, skills profile, and selection to assess technological problem solving

Description: Multiple-choice 32-item criterion-referenced test across four levels. Form 10FF is available. A test booklet and answer folder, administrator's manual, and video administrator's manual are used.

Format: Individual administration; suitable for group use; examiner required; timed: 45 minutes

Scoring: Machine scored; test scoring service available from publisher

Cost: $4.00 per examinee; 15% discount for K–12 schools

Publisher: American College Testing

Education

Inventory of Activities of an Academic Psychologist
Joel W. Smith

Copyright: 1973

Population: Adults

Purpose: Measures activities of academic psychologists during a workday; used for job justification

Description: Inventory with 107 items

Format: Individual/self-administered; untimed

Scoring: Examiner evaluated

Cost: $15.00

Publisher: Select Press

IPI Job-Field Series: Instructor

Copyright: 1960

Population: Adults

Purpose: Assesses skills and personality of applicants for various teaching positions; used to screen for counselors, instructors, safety directors, teachers, and training directors

Description: Multiple-item paper–pencil battery of six aptitude and three personality tests. The tests are Fluency, 16PF, Sales Terms, Parts, Memory, Judgment, CPF, NPF, and Perception. For individual test descriptions, see the IPI Employee Aptitude Series. Also available in French and Spanish.

Format: Suitable for group use; examiner required; timed: 76 minutes

Scoring: Hand keys

Cost: Starter kit (test materials for five applicants, scoring keys, manuals) $80; test package $12/applicant

Publisher: Industrial Psychology International Ltd.

Electrical

RCJS Elec Test–Form A
Roland T. Ramsay

Copyright: 1994

Population: Adults

Purpose: Assesses the ability to answer electrical/electronics questions; used for hiring and promotion for trade/craft jobs

Description: Multiple-choice 60-item paper–pencil test. The categories are Power Distribution, Tools, Motors, Digital and Analog Electronics, Schematics, Print Reading, AC/DC Theory and Electrical Maintenance, Computers/PLC, and Power Supplies. Materials used include paper, pencil, and a separate answer sheet.

Format: Suitable for group use; examiner required; untimed: approximately 60 minutes

Scoring: Hand key; scoring service available from publisher

Cost: (10 reusable test booklets, 100 answer sheets, manual, key) $498.00

Publisher: Ramsay Corporation

RCJS Electronics Test–Form G2
Roland T. Ramsay

Copyright: 1990

Population: Adults

Purpose: Measures knowledge and skill in the area of electronics

Description: Paper–pencil 125-item multiple-choice test assessing AC/DC theory (15 items), digital electronics (16 items), analog electronics (12 items), print reading (7 items), power supplies (11 items), regulators (9 items), test instruments (11 items), motors (5 items), electronic equipment (7 items), radio theory (7 items), power distribution (4 items), computers and PLC (17 items), and mechanical (4 items).

Format: Examiner required; suitable for group use; untimed: 2 hours

Scoring: Hand key

Cost: 10 reusable test booklets, 100 answer sheets, manual, and key $498.00

Publisher: Ramsay Corporation

RCJS Technician Electrical Test–Form A2 and Form B
Roland T. Ramsay

Copyright: 1989

Population: Adults

Purpose: Measures knowledge and skills in various electrical areas

Description: Paper–pencil 132-item multiple-choice test covering motors (17 items), digital electronics (8 items), analog electronics (12 items), print reading (11 items), control circuits (13 items), power supplies (10 items), basic AC and DC theory (11 items), power distribution (6 items), test instruments (8 items), mechanical (11 items), computers and PLC (5 items), hand and power tools (6 items), electrical maintenance (8 items), and construction and installation (6 items).

Format: Examiner required; suitable for group use; untimed: 2 hours

Scoring: Hand key; machine scoring service available from publisher

Cost: 10 reusable test booklets, 100 answer sheets, manual, and key $498.00

Publisher: Ramsay Corporation

VCWS 12—Soldering and Inspection (Electronic)

Copyright: 1975

Population: Adults

Purpose: Measures an individual's ability to acquire and apply basic soldering techniques to tasks requiring varying degrees of precision; provides insight into the ability to follow sequential instructions and acquire new tool use skills

Description: Manual test measuring an individual's ability to acquire and apply basic skills necessary to perform soldering tasks. The examinee uses wire cutters, wire strippers, needle-nose pliers, a soldering iron, and a solder to perform exercises involving the use of the tools in precision solder tasks. Exercises include work with both wires and circuit board assemblies. Performance indicates the individual's degree of ability to become a successful worker in jobs related to electronic assembly and soldering. Work activities related to the test include fabricating, processing, or repairing materials and examining and measuring for the purpose of grading and sorting.

Format: Examiner required; not suitable for group use; timed: not available

Scoring: Examiner evaluated

Cost: $1,695.00

Publisher: Valpar International Corporation

Factory

IPI Employee Aptitude Series: Factory Terms

Copyright: 1985

Population: Adults

Purpose: Determines ability to understand the words and information used in factory and mechanical settings; used to screen applicants for mechanical and technical jobs

Description: Paper–pencil 54-item test measuring comprehension of high-level mechanical, engineering, and factory information

Format: Suitable for group use; examiner required; timed: 10 minutes

Scoring: Hand key

Cost: Introductory kit (20 test booklets, scoring key, manual) $30

Publisher: Industrial Psychology International Ltd.

IPI Job-Field Series: Inspector

Copyright: 1989

Population: Adults

Purpose: Assesses skills of applicants for inspector-oriented positions; used to evaluate checking, classifying, examining, grading, pairing, scaling, and sorting skills

Description: Multiple-item paper–pencil battery of four aptitude tests. The tests are Dimension, Numbers, Tools, and Blocks. For individual test descriptions, see the IPI Employee Aptitude Series. Also available in French and Spanish.

Format: Suitable for group use; examiner required; timed: 24 minutes

Scoring: Hand keys

Cost: Starter kit (test materials for five applicants, scoring keys, manuals) $80; test package $12/applicant

Publisher: Industrial Psychology International Ltd.

IPI Job-Field Series: Vehicle Operator

Copyright: 1989

Population: Adults

Purpose: Assesses skills of applicants for positions involving operation of moving vehicles;

used to screen for crane, elevator, motorman, taxi, teamster, tractor, and truck-driving positions

Description: Multiple-item paper–pencil battery of five aptitude tests. The tests are Numbers, Dexterity, Precision, Blocks, and Tools. For individual test descriptions, see the IPI Employee Aptitude Series. Also available in French and Spanish.

Format: Suitable for group use; examiner required; timed: 27 minutes

Scoring: Hand keys

Cost: Starter kit (test materials for five applicants, scoring keys, manuals) $80; test package $12/applicant

Publisher: Industrial Psychology International Ltd.

VCWS 10—Tri-Level Measurement

Copyright: 1974

Population: Adults

Purpose: Measures an individual's ability to perform inspecting and measuring tasks ranging from the very simple to the very precise; measures ability to use independent judgment in following sequences of operations, and selecting proper instruments

Description: Manual test measuring a person's ability to perform very simple to very precise inspection and measurement tasks. The individual must sort 61 incorrectly or correctly machined parts into nine inspection bins. The seven inspection tasks involved are visual and size discrimination, comparison (using jigs), and measurement with a ruler, micrometer, and vernier caliper. Performance indicates the ability to succeed in jobs requiring varying degrees of measurement and inspection skills and decision-making abilities. The test should not be administered to individuals with severe impairment of the upper extremities.

Format: Examiner required; not suitable for group use; untimed: not available

Scoring: Examiner evaluated

Cost: $1,995.00

Publisher: Valpar International Corporation

VCWS 8—Simulated Assembly

Copyright: 1974

Population: Adults

Purpose: Measures an individual's ability to work at an assembly task requiring repetitive physical manipulation and evaluates bilateral use of the upper extremities; determines standing and sitting tolerance

Description: Manual test measuring an individual's ability to work at conveyor-assembly jobs. The individual stands or sits in front of two parts bins, one containing metal pins and the other containing a black washer and white cap. The individual must place the pin, then the washer, and then the cap on the assembly board, which rotates automatically at a constant speed. Correct assemblies are counted automatically, and all assemblies are recycled to the parts bins automatically. Work activities relating to the test, including placing materials in or on automatic machines, following simple instructions, and starting, stopping, and observing the functions of machines and equipment, are included.

Format: Examiner required; suitable for group use; timed: time not available

Scoring: Examiner evaluated

Cost: $2,595.00

Publisher: Valpar International Corporation

Health Services

Attitude Survey Program for Health Care: Nursing Staff Survey

Copyright: 1985

Population: Adults

Purpose: Assesses the concerns of the nursing staff in hospitals, HMOs, clinics, and nursing care facilities; used by health care administrators to assess employee acceptance of organizational and procedural changes and to determine training needs

Description: Paper–pencil 93-item survey assessing the priorities and concerns of nursing

staff members. Items cover the following areas: organization identification, job satisfaction, material rewards: pay, benefits, supervisory leadership practices, work associates, general administrative effectiveness, supervisory administrative practices, work organization, work efficiency, performance and personal development, communication effectiveness, relationship with physicians, nursing office practices, professional nursing role, and reactions to survey. London House psychologists help administrators plan and conduct a survey. Administration occurs on organization premises under the supervision of an organization official or London House employee.

Format: Examiner required; suitable for group use; untimed: 60 minutes or less

Scoring: Computer scored by London House

Cost: 100 Standard Surveys $950.00; 100 Modified Surveys $1,150.00; 100 Customized Surveys $1,500.00 (specify survey title); Customized Transcriptions $2.00 per unit

Publisher: McGraw-Hill/London House

Attitude Survey Program for Health Care: Paraprofessionals Survey

Copyright: 1985

Population: Adults

Purpose: Assesses the concerns of licensed practical nurses, nurses' aides, and orderlies in hospitals, HMOs, clinics, and nursing care facilities; used by health care administrators to assess employee acceptance of organizational and procedural changes

Description: Paper–pencil 93-item survey assessing the priorities and concerns of paraprofessionals. Items cover the following areas: organization identification, job satisfaction, material rewards (pay, benefits), supervisory leadership practices, work associates, general administrative effectiveness, supervisory administrative practices, work organization, work efficiency, performance and personal development, communication effectiveness, paraprofessional role, and reactions to survey. A general comments section is also available;

transcription and analysis are optional. London House psychologists help administrators plan and conduct a survey. Administration occurs on organization premises under the supervision of an organization official/London House employee.

Format: Examiner required; suitable for group use; untimed: 50 minutes or less

Scoring: Computer scored by London House

Cost: 100 Standard Surveys $950.00; 100 Modified Surveys $1,150.00; 100 Customized Surveys $1,500.00 (specify survey title); Comment Transcription $2.00 per unit

Publisher: McGraw-Hill/London House

Attitude Survey Program for Health Care: Physicians Survey

Copyright: 1985

Population: Adults

Purpose: Assesses the concerns of physicians in hospitals, HMOs, clinics, and nursing care facilities; used by health care administrators to assess employee acceptance of organizational and procedural changes and to determine training needs

Description: Paper–pencil 93-item survey assessing the priorities and concerns of physicians. Items cover the following areas: organization identification, job satisfaction, work associates, general administrative effectiveness, work organization, work efficiency, relationship with administration, medical staff organization, medical staff relations, relationship with nursing, diagnostic and therapeutic services, patient services, and reactions to survey. London House psychologists help administrators plan and conduct a survey. Administration occurs on organization premises under the supervision of an organization official or London House employee.

Format: Examiner required; suitable for group use; untimed: 50 minutes or less

Scoring: Computer scored by London House

Cost: 100 Standard Surveys $950.00; 100 Modified Surveys $1,150.00; 100 Customized Surveys $1,500.00 (specify survey title); Comment Transcriptions $2.00 per unit

Publisher: McGraw-Hill/London House

IPI Job-Field Series: Dental Office Assistant

Copyright: 1981

Population: Adults

Purpose: Assesses skills of applicants for dental office assistants; used to screen assistants who will work chairside, perform light secretarial duties, and work with patients and the dentist

Description: Multiple-item paper–pencil battery of four aptitude and two personality tests. The tests are Numbers, Perception, CPF, Office Terms, NPF, and Judgment. For individual test descriptions, see the IPI Employee Aptitude Test Series. Also available in French and Spanish.

Format: Suitable for group use; timed: 44 minutes

Scoring: Hand key

Cost: Starter kit (test materials for five applicants, scoring keys, manuals) $80; test package $12/applicant

Publisher: Industrial Psychology International Ltd.

IPI Job-Field Series: Dental Technician

Copyright: 1989

Population: Adults

Purpose: Assesses skills and personality of applicants for dental laboratory technician positions requiring good manual dexterity and visualization skills

Description: Multiple-item paper–pencil battery of three aptitude and two personality tests. The tests are CPF, NPF, Dexterity, Dimension, and Blocks. For individual test descriptions, see the IPI Employee Aptitude Test Series. Also available in French and Spanish.

Format: Suitable for group use; examiner required; timed: 35 minutes

Scoring: Hand key

Cost: Starter kit (test materials for five applicants, scoring keys, manuals) $80; test package $12/applicant

Publisher: Industrial Psychology International Ltd.

IPI Job-Field Series: Optometric Assistant

Copyright: 1967

Population: Adults

Purpose: Assesses skills and personality of applicants for optometric assistant positions; used to screen individuals who will act as support people for optometrists, work with the practitioner and patients, and perform reception and secretarial duties

Description: Multiple-item paper–pencil battery of five aptitude and two personality tests. The tests are Numbers, NPF, CPF, Office Terms, Judgment, Perception, and Fluency. For individual test descriptions, see the IPI Employee Aptitude Series. Also available in French and Spanish.

Format: Examiner required; suitable for group use; timed: 50 minutes

Scoring: Hand keys

Cost: Starter kit (test materials for five applicants, scoring keys, manuals) $80; test package $12/applicant

Publisher: Industrial Psychology International Ltd.

NCLEX–RN Success Test (1989)

Copyright: 1989

Population: Graduate nurses

Purpose: Assesses nursing ability, skill, and knowledge at the RN entry level

Description: Multiple-choice 200-item paper–pencil test measuring nursing ability, skill, and knowledge at the RN entry level. Percent correct and percentile scores are provided for total score and two subscales. Materials include test and answer sheet included in the book *American Nursing Review for NCLEX–RN*.

Format: Self-administered; not suitable for group use; untimed: time varies

Scoring: Computer scored; test scoring service available from publisher

Cost: $23.00 per answer sheet scored

Publisher: National League for Nursing

NLN Employee Assessment Series: Basic Proficiency in Medication Administration

Copyright: 1988

Population: Nurses (RN and LPN/LVN)

Purpose: Identifies nursing staff needs for instruction in pharmacology; used to assess need for in-service education

Description: Paper–pencil 60-item multiple-choice test covering dosage calculations (15 items), principles of drug administration (about 20 items), and effects of commonly used drugs (about 25 items). Subscores can be obtained for each of the three areas assessed. Two forms of the test are available. Available only to nursing practice agencies.

Format: Examiner required; suitable for group or individual use; untimed: 1 hour

Scoring: Hand key

Cost: Package (25 test booklets, manual, scoring key) $75.00

Publisher: National League for Nursing

NLN Employee Assessment Series: Caring for Persons with AIDS

Copyright: 1988

Population: Registered nurses

Purpose: Measures the nurse's knowledge and ability to apply basic principles necessary to provide safe care to persons with AIDS; used to assess need for inservice education

Description: Paper–pencil 60-item multiple-choice test including etiology and epidemiology; prevention and education for community and family; infection control; clinical nursing management; and ethical–legal issues for persons with AIDS and for health care workers. Two subscores are available: Knowledge (21 items) and Application (39 items). This test was designed to conform to the Centers for Disease Control MMWR publication "Recommendations for Prevention of HIV Transmission in Health-Care Settings," August 21, 1987, Vol. 36, No. 2S. Available only to nursing practice agencies.

Format: Examiner required; suitable for group use; untimed: 1 hour

Scoring: Hand key

Cost: Package (25 test booklets, manual, scoring key) $75.00

Publisher: National League for Nursing

NLN Employee Assessment Series: Home Health Aide Skills Assessment

Copyright: 1988

Population: Adults; home health aides

Purpose: Measures the ability to apply the basic principles needed for safe patient care

Description: Paper–pencil 60-item multiple-choice test covering the home health aide's role and function (15 items), the basic care needs of patients (25 items), and caring for patients with special needs (20 items). Subscores are yielded for each of the three areas assessed.

Format: Group administration; 1 hour

Scoring: Examiner administration and interpretation

Cost: 10 test booklets, manual, scoring key $50.00

Publisher: National League for Nursing

NLN Employee Assessment Series: Long-Term Care Nursing Assistant Test

Copyright: 1988

Population: Nursing assistants

Purpose: Measures knowledge and ability to apply the basic principles necessary to provide safe care to residents in long-term care facilities; used to assess need for inservice education

Description: Multiple-choice 60-item paper–pencil test of content on normal aging; psychological needs of residents; basic personal care for residents; care for residents who are disabled, ill, or dying; resident safety; observing and report-

ing signs and symptoms; and the nursing assistant's role and function. Two subscores are provided: Knowledge (23 items) and Application (37 items). Available only to nursing practice agencies.

Format: Suitable for group or individual administration; examiner required; untimed: 1 hour

Scoring: Hand key

Cost: Package (10 test booklets, manual scoring key) $50.00

Publisher: National League for Nursing

NLN Employee Assessment Series: Medications for Coronary Care

Copyright: 1988

Population: Registered nurses

Purpose: Measures nurse's knowledge and skills related to drugs used in the care of patients with coronary problems; used to assess need for inservice education

Description: Paper–pencil 60-item multiple-choice test covering the major groups of coronary care medications and asks for interpretation of selected EKG rhythm strips. Subscores are available for calculations (11 items), therapeutic effects and actions (29 items), and side and untoward effects (20 items). Available only to nursing practice agencies.

Format: Suitable for group or individual use; examiner required; untimed: 1 hour

Scoring: Hand key

Cost: Package (10 test booklets, manual, scoring key) $50.00

Publisher: National League for Nursing

NLN Employee Assessment Series: Psychotropic Drug Administration

Copyright: 1988

Population: Registered nurses

Purpose: Measures registered nurse's knowledge of drugs used in the treatment of patients with psychiatric disorders; used to assess need for inservice education

Description: Paper–pencil 60-item multiple-choice test covering the major groups of psychotropic medications in terms of actions, untoward effects, interactions, and implications for nursing interventions. A small number of items deal with some commonly abused substances. Subscores are available for actions (13 items), untoward effects and interactions (24 items), and nursing implications (23 items). Available only to nursing practice agencies.

Format: Individual administration; suitable for group use; examiner required

Scoring: Hand key

Cost: Package (0 test booklets, manual, scoring key) $50.00

Publisher: National League for Nursing

Staff Burnout Scale for Health Professionals

John W. Jones

Copyright: 1980

Population: Adults

Purpose: Assesses burnout or work stress among health care professionals

Description: Multiple-item paper–pencil test assessing burnout or work stress through four types of factors: cognitive reactions, affective reactions, behavioral reactions, and psychophysiological reactions.

Format: Self-administered; suitable for group use; untimed: 10 minutes

Scoring: Hand key

Cost: 25 tests $23; Specimen Set (interpretation manual, validation studies) $10; examiner's manual $10

Publisher: McGraw-Hill/London House

Insurance

Insurance Selection Inventory (ISI)

Copyright: 1986

Population: Adults; ages 16 and older

Purpose: Evaluates potential for success as a claims examiner, customer service representative, and correspondence representative; used for employee selection and promotion

Description: Multiple-choice 275-item paper–pencil test measuring 11 basic functions necessary to succeed in key insurance positions: Number Comparison, Verbal Reasoning, Applied Arithmetic, Arithmetic Computation, Error Recognition, Drive, Interpersonal Skills, Cognitive Skills, Self-Discipline, Writing Skills, and Work Preference. Potential estimate scores for the positions of claims examiner, customer service representative, and correspondence representative are yielded. Standard scores for each of the 11 measures are also profiled.

Format: Examiner required; suitable for group use; timed: time varies

Scoring: Computer scored

Cost: Contact publisher

Publisher: McGraw-Hill/London House

Job Effectiveness Prediction System: Coding and Converting (JEPS: Test Code K)

Copyright: Not provided

Population: Adults

Purpose: Measures the ability to quickly and accurately use conversion tables and coding guides; used for selection and placement of entry-level clerical and technical/professional employees in life and property/casualty insurance companies

Description: Paper–pencil or computerized multiple-choice 85-item test in three sections measuring the ability to use conversion tables and coding guides. In the first section, the examinee uses a table that converts monthly premiums to annual premiums in order to indicate the correct annual premium for 20 monthly premiums. In the second section, the examinee uses a table of letter codes for annual premiums to indicate the correct letter code for 25 annual premiums. In the third section, the examinee uses both tables to indicate the correct code for 40 monthly premiums. Use is restricted to insurance companies.

Format: Examiner required; suitable for group use; timed: 8 minutes

Scoring: Hand key; computer scored

Cost: Contact publisher

Publisher: Life Office Management Association

Job Effectiveness Prediction System: Comparing and Checking (JEPS: Test Code L)

Copyright: Not provided

Population: Adults

Purpose: Measures ability to compare numbers and words and detect the differences; used for selection and placement of entry-level clerical and technical/professional employees in life and property/casualty insurance companies

Description: Paper–pencil or computerized 40-item multiple-choice test measuring the ability to compare words and numbers and detect differences. The examinees are presented with correct lists of words and numbers (names, addresses, dollar amounts, etc.) and lists to be checked. The subjects are asked to count the number of errors per line. Use is restricted to insurance companies.

Format: Examiner required; suitable for group use; timed: 7 minutes

Scoring: Hand key; computer scored

Cost: Contact publisher

Publisher: Life Office Management Association

Job Effectiveness Prediction System: Filing (JEPS: Test Code J)

Copyright: Not provided

Population: Adults

Purpose: Measures general filing skills; used for selection and placement of entry-level clerical and technical/professional employees in life and property/casualty insurance companies

Description: Paper–pencil or computerized 60-item multiple-choice test measuring the ability to file materials according to given instructions. The examinee is presented with existing files with numbered slots between en-

tries and lists of entries to be filed. The examinee indicates the number of the slot into which each of the entries should be filed. Use is restricted to insurance companies.

Format: Examiner required; suitable for group use; timed: 5 minutes

Scoring: Hand key; computer scored

Cost: Contact publisher

Publisher: Life Office Management Association

Job Effectiveness Prediction System: Language Usage (JEPS: Test Code E)

Copyright: Not provided

Population: Adults

Purpose: Measures proper usage of the English language; used for selection and placement of entry-level clerical and technical/professional employees in life and property/casualty insurance companies

Description: Paper–pencil or computerized 94-item test measuring knowledge of grammar, punctuation, capitalization, and formation of plurals. The subject indicates whether there are any errors in a reading selection that is divided into two parts; use is restricted to insurance companies

Format: Examiner required; suitable for group use; timed: 12 minutes

Scoring: Hand key; computer scored

Cost: Contact publisher

Publisher: Life Office Management Association

Job Effectiveness Prediction System: Mathematical Skill (JEPS: Test Code C)

Copyright: Not provided

Population: Adults

Purpose: Measures the ability to work with mathematical relationships and formulas; used for selection and placement of entry-level clerical and technical/professional employees in life and property/casualty insurance companies

Description: Paper–pencil or computerized

23-item multiple-choice test measuring skill in solving and manipulating mathematical relationships and formulas. One section involves solving formulas, and the other requires selecting the appropriate formula to use for problem solving. Use is restricted to insurance companies.

Format: Examiner required; suitable for group use; timed: 20 minutes

Scoring: Hand key; computer scored

Cost: Contact publisher

Publisher: Life Office Management Association

Job Effectiveness Prediction System: Numerical Ability–1 (JEPS: Test Code A)

Copyright: Not provided

Population: Adults

Purpose: Measures the ability to add, subtract, multiply, and divide; used for selection and placement of entry-level clerical and technical/professional employees in life and property/casualty insurance companies

Description: Paper–pencil or computerized 50-item multiple-choice test measuring the ability to perform basic arithmetic operations, including the addition, subtraction, multiplication, and division of whole numbers, fractions, decimals, and percentages. Use is restricted to insurance companies.

Format: Examiner required; suitable for group use; timed: 8 minutes

Scoring: Hand key; computer scored

Cost: Contact publisher

Publisher: Life Office Management Association

Job Effectiveness Prediction System: Numerical Ability–2 (JEPS: Test Code B)

Copyright: Not provided

Population: Adults

Purpose: Measures the ability to perform operations with decimals and percentages; used for selection and placement of entry-level clerical

and technical/professional employees in life and property/casualty insurance companies.

Description: Paper–pencil or computerized 50-item test with multiple-choice and true–false sections measuring numerical ability. Problems require the subject to perform operations with percentages, round off decimal numbers, and approximate correct answers. Use is restricted to insurance companies.

Format: Examiner required; suitable for group use; timed: 15 minutes

Scoring: Hand key; computer scored

Cost: Contact publisher

Publisher: Life Office Management Association

Job Effectiveness Prediction System: Reading Comprehension–1 (JEPS: Test Code F)

Copyright: Not provided

Population: Adults

Purpose: Measures the ability to understand written instructions; used for selection and placement of entry-level clerical and technical/professional employees in life and property/casualty insurance companies

Description: Paper–pencil or computerized 30-item multiple-choice test measuring the ability to understand written directions, definitions, and procedures. The subject reads several passages and answers questions about each passage. Use is restricted to insurance companies.

Format: Examiner required; suitable for group use; timed: 30 minutes

Scoring: Hand key; computer scored

Cost: Contact publisher

Publisher: Life Office Management Association

Job Effectiveness Prediction System: Reading Comprehension–2 (JEPS: Test Code G)

Copyright: Not provided

Population: Adults

Purpose: Measures level of general reading comprehension; used for selection and placement of entry-level clerical and technical/professional employees in life and property/casualty insurance companies

Description: Paper–pencil or computerized 35-item multiple-choice test measuring reading comprehension at approximately a Grades 11–13 reading level. The subject reads several reading passages and answers questions about each passage. Use is restricted to insurance companies.

Format: Examiner required; suitable for group use; timed: 30 minutes

Scoring: Hand key; computer scored

Cost: Contact publisher

Publisher: Life Office Management Association

Job Effectiveness Prediction System: Spelling (JEPS: Test Code D)

Copyright: Not provided

Population: Adults

Purpose: Measures the ability to recognize whether words are correctly spelled; used for selection and placement of entry-level clerical and technical/professional employees in life and property/casualty insurance companies

Description: Paper–pencil or computerized 85-item test consisting of a list of words. The examinee indicates whether each word is spelled correctly. Use is restricted to insurance companies.

Format: Examiner required; suitable for group use; timed: 7 minutes

Scoring: Hand key; computer scored

Cost: Contact publisher

Publisher: Life Office Management Association

Job Effectiveness Prediction System: Verbal Comprehension (JEPS: Test Code H)

Copyright: Not provided

Population: Adults

Purpose: Measures general word knowledge; used for selection and placement of entry-level clerical and technical/professional employees in life and property/casualty insurance companies

Description: Paper–pencil or computerized 35-item multiple-choice test measuring vocabulary and word knowledge. The words tested are general vocabulary words rather than words from specialized or esoteric vocabularies. Use is restricted to insurance companies.

Format: Examiner required; suitable for group use; timed: 6 minutes

Scoring: Hand key; computer scored

Cost: Contact publisher

Publisher: Life Office Management Association

LIMRA Career Profile System

Copyright: 1992

Population: Adults

Purpose: Evaluates the career experience and expectations of individuals considering an insurance sales career; used for employee screening and selection

Description: Multiple-choice 162-item paper–pencil questionnaire assessing career information related to future success as an insurance salesperson. The Initial Career Profile is used with applicants who have no prior insurance sales experience. The Advanced Career Profile is used with experienced applicants. The Student Career Profile is used with current or recent students. The questionnaire is available to insurance company home offices only. Both forms may be administered in Canada and are available in French.

Format: Examiner required; suitable for group use; untimed: varies

Scoring: Computer scored

Cost: Test booklet (specify profile) $7; administrative manual $7; Cost includes scoring answer sheets $15.50

Publisher: LIMRA International

Mechanical

ACER Mechanical Comprehension Test

Copyright: 1989

Population: Adolescents, adults; ages 13 years 6 months and older

Purpose: Measures mechanical aptitude; used for employee selection and placement for positions requiring some degree of mechanical aptitude

Description: Paper–pencil 45-item multiple-choice test consisting of problems in the form of diagrams that illustrate various mechanical principles and mechanisms. Australian norms are provided for various age groups, university and technical college groups, and national service trainees and applicants for apprenticeships. Materials include a reusable booklet, separate answer sheet, scoring key, manual, and specimen set.

Format: Examiner required; suitable for group use; timed: 30 minutes

Scoring: Hand key; may be computer scored

Cost: Contact publisher

Publisher: The Australian Council for Educational Research Limited

ACER Mechanical Reasoning Test–Revised Edition

Copyright: 1989

Population: Adolescents, adults; ages 15 and older

Purpose: Measures basic mechanical reasoning abilities; used for employee selection and placement for positions requiring some degree of mechanical aptitude

Description: Multiple-item paper–pencil multiple-choice test consisting of problems in the form of diagrams that illustrate various mechanical principles and mechanisms. This test is a shortened version of the ACER Mechanical Comprehension Test and contains some different items and less verbal content. Australian norms are provided for apprenticeship appli-cants for a variety of trades and for apprentices beginning training. Materials include a reusable booklet, answer sheet, score key, manual, and specimen set.

Format: Examiner required; suitable for group use; timed: 20 minutes

Scoring: Hand key; may be machine scored

Cost: Contact publisher

Publisher: The Australian Council for Educational Research Limited

Applied Technology Series (ATS) Mechanical Comprehension (MTS3)

Copyright: 1988

Population: Adults

Purpose: Assesses the understanding of basic mechanical principles

Description: Test with 36 items assesses the understanding of basic mechanical principles and their application to such devices as pulleys, gears, and simple structures. The task involves selecting the answer to a short written question from a number of alternatives, which is supported by a realistic technical drawing.

Format: 15 minutes

Scoring: Hand key; machine scored; scoring service available

Cost: Contact publisher

Publisher: Saville and Holdsworth Ltd.

Closure Speed (Gestalt Completion)
L. L. Thurstone, T. E. Jeffrey

Copyright: 1984

Population: Adolescents, adults

Purpose: Measures the ability to hold a configuration in mind despite distracting irrelevancies as indicated by identification of a given figure "hidden" or embedded in a larger, more complex drawing; used for vocational counseling and selection of personnel

Description: Paper–pencil 24-item test in which each item consists of an incomplete picture drawn in black on a white background. The subject must identify and briefly describe the subject of the picture.

Format: Examiner required; suitable for group use; timed: 3 minutes

Scoring: Hand key

Cost: 25 test booklets $36; score key $10; examiner's manual $15

Publisher: McGraw-Hill/London House

Crawford Small Parts Dexterity Test (CPSDT)

John Crawford

Copyright: 1981

Population: Adolescents, adults

Purpose: Measures fine-motor dexterity and eye–hand coordination; used for selecting applicants for such jobs as engravers, watch repairers, and telephone installers

Description: Two-part performance measure of dexterity. Part 1 measures dexterity in using tweezers to assemble pins and collars. Part 2 measures dexterity in screwing small screws with a screwdriver after placing them in threaded holes. The test may be administered in two ways. In the work-limit method, the subject completes the task and the total time is the score. Using the time-limit procedure, the score is the amount of work completed during a specified time. Materials include an assembly plate, pins, collars, and screws.

Format: Examiner required; suitable for group use; timed: 10–15 minutes

Scoring: Examiner evaluated

Cost: Complete set (manual and spare parts) $385.00

Publisher: The Psychological Corporation

Curtis Spatial Tests: Object Completion Test and Space–Form Test

James W. Curtis

Copyright: 1961

Population: Adults

Purpose: Assesses perceptual efficiency; used for screening applicants for jobs requiring manual skills

Description: Two paper–pencil tests of perceptual efficiency. One test is two-dimensional and one is three-dimensional. The tests may be used in conjunction with Holmes' One Minute Per-Flu-Dex Tests for screening of factory aptitudes.

Format: Examiner required; suitable for group use; timed: 1 minute per test

Scoring: Hand key

Cost: Specimen Set $4.00; 25 tests (specify form) $3.50

Publisher: Psychometric Affiliates

ETSA Tests 5-A—Mechanical Familiarity

George A. W. Stouffer, Jr., S. Trevor Hadley

Copyright: 1990

Population: Adolescents, adults; Grades 10 and above

Purpose: Measures ability to recognize common tools and instruments; used for employee selection, placement, and promotion

Description: Paper–pencil 50-item nonverbal test of background in mechanical activities. The items are commonly used tools, which the applicant identifies. The test is one in a series of ETSA tests.

Format: Examiner required; suitable for group use; untimed: 1 hour

Scoring: Hand key; examiner evaluated; scoring service available

Cost: 10 tests with key $15.00; manual $5.00; handbook $15.00

Publisher: Educators'/Employers' Tests and Services Associates

ETSA Tests 6-A—Mechanical Knowledge

George A. W. Stouffer, Jr., S. Trevor Hadley

Copyright: 1990

Population: Adolescents, adults; Grades 10 and above

Purpose: Measures mechanical insight and understanding; used for employee selection, placement, and promotion

Description: Paper–pencil 121-item test assessing six areas of mechanical knowledge. The test discriminates between novices, journeymen, and experts. The test is one in a series of ETSA tests.

Format: Examiner required; suitable for group use; untimed: 1 hour 30 minutes

Scoring: Hand key; examiner evaluated; scoring service available

Cost: 10 tests with key $15.00; manual $5.00; handbook $15.00

Publisher: Educators'/Employers' Tests and Services Associates

---

Hand-Tool Dexterity Test
G. K. Bennett

Copyright: 1981

Population: Adults

Purpose: Measures manipulative skill in using ordinary mechanic's tools, wrenches, and screwdrivers; used in selecting applicants for mechanical and industrial jobs

Description: Task test of mechanical skill in which the subject takes apart 12 assemblies of nuts, bolts, and washers from a wooden frame according to a prescribed sequence and then reassembles them. The score is the time required to perform the tasks. Materials include a wooden frame, nuts, bolts, washers, and tools.

Format: Examiner required; not suitable for group use; timed: 7 minutes

Scoring: Score obtained by timing

Cost: Complete set $298.00

Publisher: The Psychological Corporation

Intuitive Mechanics
(Weights and Pulleys)
L. L. Thurstone, T. E. Jeffrey

Copyright: 1984

Population: Adolescents, adults

Purpose: Measures ability to understand mechanical relationships and to visualize internal movement in a mechanical system; used for vocational counseling or for selection in positions requiring mechanical interest and experience

Description: Paper–pencil 32-item test in which each item is a drawing that represents a system of weights and pulleys. For each system, the examinee must determine whether the system is stable (will not produce movement) or unstable (will produce movement).

Format: Examiner required; suitable for group use; timed: 3 minutes

Scoring: Hand key

Cost: 25 test booklets $36.00; score key $10.00; examiner's manual $15.00

Publisher: McGraw-Hill/London House

IPI Employee Aptitude Series: Tools

Copyright: 1986

Population: Adults

Purpose: Measures ability to recognize simple tools and mechanical equipment; used to screen applicants for mechanical and technical jobs

Description: Paper–pencil 48-item test measuring the ability to recognize pictures of common tools, equipment, and machines used in factory and mechanical areas. The test does not require the ability to read or write. Also available in French and Spanish.

Format: Suitable for group use; examiner required; timed: 6 minutes

Scoring: Hand key

Cost: Introductory kit (20 test booklets, scoring key, manual) $30

Publisher: Industrial Psychology International Ltd.

IPI Job-Field Series: Factory Machine Operator

Copyright: 1989

Population: Adults

Purpose: Assesses skills of applicants for various factory machine-oriented positions requiring equipment operation; used to screen for cutter, screw machine, lathe, press, sewing, and welder jobs

Description: Multiple-item paper–pencil battery of five aptitude tests. The tests are Numbers, Dexterity, Precision, Blocks, and Tools. For individual test Descriptions, see the IPI Employee Aptitude Series. Also available in French and Spanish.

Format: Suitable for group use; examiner required; timed: 27 minutes

Scoring: Hand keys

Cost: Starter kit (test materials for five applicants, scoring keys, manuals) $80; test package $12/applicant

Publisher: Industrial Psychology International Ltd.

IPI Job-Field Series: Semi-Skilled Worker

Copyright: 1989

Population: Adults

Purpose: Assesses skills of applicants for middle-level mechanical positions; used to screen for assembler, construction, helper, and production positions

Description: Multiple-item paper–pencil battery of four aptitude tests. The tests are Motor, Precision, Tools, and Blocks. For individual test descriptions, see the IPI Employee Aptitude Series. Also available in French and Spanish.

Format: Suitable for group use; examiner required; timed: 24 minutes

Scoring: Hand keys

Cost: Starter kit (test materials for five applicants, scoring keys, manuals) $80; test package $12/applicant

Publisher: Industrial Psychology International Ltd.

IPI Job-Field Series: Skilled Worker

Copyright: 1989

Population: Adults

Purpose: Assesses skills of applicants for mechanically complex and difficult positions; used to screen for linemen, machinists, maintenance workers, mechanics, and tool makers

Description: Multiple-item paper–pencil battery of six aptitude tests. The tests are Dimension, Dexterity, Parts, Blocks, Motor, and Precision. For individual test descriptions, see the IPI Employee Aptitude Series. Also available in French and Spanish.

Format: Suitable for group use; examiner required; timed: 33 minutes

Scoring: Hand keys

Cost: Starter kit (test materials for five applicants, scoring keys, manuals) $80; test package $12/applicant

Publisher: Industrial Psychology International Ltd.

IPI Job-Field Series: Unskilled Worker

Copyright: 1988

Population: Adults

Purpose: Assesses skills of applicants for lower-level mechanical jobs; used to screen janitors, laborers, loaders, material handlers, packers, and truckers

Description: Multiple-item paper–pencil battery of four aptitude tests. The tests are Motor, Precision, Tools, and Blocks. For individual test descriptions, see the IPI Employee Aptitude Series. Also available in French and Spanish.

Format: Suitable for group use; examiner required; timed: 24 minutes

Scoring: Hand keys

Cost: Starter kit (test materials for five applicants, scoring keys, manuals) $80; test package $12/applicant

Publisher: Industrial Psychology International Ltd.

Mechanical Movements
L. L. Thurstone, T. E. Jeffrey

Copyright: 1984

Population: Adolescents, adults

Purpose: Determines degree of mechanical interest and experience; used for vocational counseling and to select persons for mechanical occupations in industry

Description: Paper–pencil 37-item multiple-choice measure of mechanical comprehension indicating the ability to visualize a mechanical system in which there is internal movement or displacement of the parts.

Format: Examiner required; suitable for group use; timed: 14 minutes

Scoring: Hand key

Cost: 25 test booklets $36; score key $10; examiner's manual $15

Publisher: McGraw-Hill/London House

Minnesota Rate of Manipulation Tests

Copyright: 1969

Population: Adults

Purpose: Measures finger–hand–arm dexterity; used for employee selection for jobs requiring manual dexterity and in vocational and rehabilitation training programs

Description: Five-test battery measuring manual dexterity. The five tests are The Placing Test, The Turning Test, The Displacing Test, The One Hand Turning and Placing Test, and The Two-Hand Turning and Placing Test. Materials consist of two test boards with holes and blocks. Each block is painted orange on the upper half and yellow on the lower half. The blocks are manipulated in prescribed ways. Specific tests assess movements with the preferred hand and with both hands. The five tests may be administered separately. All tests are repeated for four complete trials. The Displacing and Turning tests are suitable for use with the blind.

Format: Individual administration; 10 minutes for each test

Scoring: Examiner interpreted

Cost: Complete kit (manual, protocols, test boards, blocks, carrying case) $353.95

Publisher: American Guidance Service

Pennsylvania Bi-Manual Worksample
John R. Roberts

Copyright: 1969

Population: Adolescents, adults; ages 16 and older

Purpose: Measures manual dexterity and eye–hand coordination; used for employee placement

Description: Multiple-operation manual dexterity test utilizing an 8″×24″ board containing 100 holes arranged in 10 rows and a set of nuts and bolts to test finger dexterity of both hands, whole movement of both arms, eye–hand coordination, and bimanual coordination. The employee grasps a nut between the thumb and index finger of the other hand, turns the bolt into the nut, and places both in a hole in the board. Twenty practice motions are allowed, and 80 motions are timed. Disassembly reverses the process and involves timing 100 motions. A special supplement contains directions for administration to blind employees.

Format: Individual and small (4) group; 12 minutes

Scoring: Examiner interpreted

Cost: Complete kit (manual, protocols, board, bolts, nuts, carrying case) $199.95

Publisher: American Guidance Service

RCJS Machinist Test–Form A
Roland T. Ramsay

Copyright: 1989

Population: Adults

Purpose: Assesses the ability to perform machinist job requirements; used in hiring and promotion for trade/craft jobs

Description: Multiple-choice 120-item paper–pencil test; materials used include paper, pencil, and a separate answer sheet

Format: Suitable for group use; examiner required; untimed: approximately 120 minutes

Scoring: Hand key, machine scored; test scoring service available from publisher

Cost: (10 reusable test booklets, 100 answer sheets, manual, key) $498.00

Publisher: Ramsay Corporation

RCJS Measurement Test–Form A
Roland T. Ramsay

Copyright: 1982

Population: Adults

Purpose: Assesses an individual's ability to measure accurately with a ruler; used to predict job performance in areas such as maintenance, machine operation, and quality control

Description: Paper–pencil 20-item multiple-choice test designed to assess an individual's ability to measure accurately with a scale in rule dimensions of wholes, halves, quarters, eighths, and sixteenths. The test is available in two forms, A and B.

Format: Examiner required; suitable for group use; timed: 15 minutes

Scoring: Hand key

Cost: 5 consumable booklets $29.75; manual with scoring key $24.95

Publisher: Ramsay Corporation

RCJS Mec Test–Form AU
Roland T. Ramsay

Copyright: 1993

Population: Adults

Purpose: Assesses mechanical ability for trade/craft jobs; used for hiring and promotion

Description: Multiple-choice 60-item paper–pencil test. Materials used include paper, pencil, and a separate answer sheet.

Format: Suitable for group use; examiner required; untimed: approximately 60 minutes

Scoring: Consumable, self-scoring booklet

Cost: Booklet $10.00

Publisher: Ramsay Corporation

RCJS Reading Prints and Drawings—Form A
Roland T. Ramsay

Copyright: 1990

Population: Adults

Purpose: Assesses ability to read mechanical prints and drawings; used for hiring and promotion

Description: Multiple-choice 33-item paper–pencil test assessing ability to read mechanical prints and drawings. Materials include reusable booklet, answer sheet, and manual with key.

Format: Examiner required; suitable for group use; timed: 30 minutes

Scoring: Hand key; machine scoring service available from publisher

Cost: Kit (10 test booklets, 100 answer sheets, 1 scoring key, and 1 test manual) $498.00

Publisher: Ramsay Corporation

RCJS Technician Mechanical Test–Form A2 and Form B
Roland T. Ramsay

Copyright: 1990

Population: Adults

Purpose: Measures knowledge and skills in mechanical areas such as hydraulics, pneumatics, print reading, pumps, and welding

Description: Paper–pencil 124-item multiple-choice test covering hydraulics (15 items), pneumatics (7 items), print reading (7 items), welding (17 items), power transmission (16 items), lubrication (5 items), pumps (12 items), piping (12 items), rigging (7 items) mechanical maintenance (11 items), and shop machines, tools, and equipment (15 items).

Format: Examiner required; suitable for group use; untimed: 2 hours

Scoring: Hand key; machine scoring service available from publisher

Cost: 10 reusable test booklets, 100 answer sheets, manual, and key $498.00

Publisher: Ramsay Corporation

RCJS Tool Knowledge and Use Test–Form JLR
Roland T. Ramsay

Copyright: 1994

Population: Adults

Purpose: Assesses knowledge of tools and their uses; used for hiring for trade/craft jobs

Description: Multiple-choice 70-item paper–pencil test. Materials used include paper, pencil, and a separate answer sheet.

Format: Suitable for group use; examiner required; untimed: approximately 60 minutes

Scoring: Hand key, machine scored; test scoring service available from publisher

Cost: (10 reusable tests, 100 answer sheets, manual, and key) $498.00

Publisher: Ramsay Corporation

RCJS Welding Test–Form A
Roland T. Ramsay

Copyright: 1987
Population: Adults
Purpose: Assesses welding ability for trade/craft jobs; used for hiring and promotion

Description: Multiple-choice 100-item paper–pencil test. Materials used include paper, pencil, and a separate answer sheet.

Format: Suitable for group use; examiner required; untimed: approximately 120 minutes

Scoring: Hand key; machine scoring service available from publisher

Cost: 10 reusable test booklets, 100 answer sheets, manual, and key $498.00

Publisher: Ramsay Corporation

Revised Minnesota Paper Form Board Test™ (RMPFBT™)
Rensis Likert, W. H. Quasha

Copyright: 1941 (Manual 1995)
Population: Adolescents, adults
Purpose: Measures ability to visualize and manipulate objects in space; used to select applicants for jobs requiring mechanical–spatial ability

Description: Multiple-item paper–pencil test of spatial perception. The applicant is required to visualize the assembly of two-dimensional geometric shapes into a whole design. The test is related to both mechanical and artistic ability.

Two equivalent forms, AA and BB (hand scoring) and MA and MB (machine scoring), are available. Available in French-Canadian.

Format: Examiner required; suitable for group use; timed: 20 minutes

Scoring: Hand key; may be machine scored locally

Cost: Examination kit $39.75

Publisher: The Psychological Corporation

SRA Mechanical Aptitudes

Copyright: 1947
Population: Adolescents, adults: Grades 10 and above

Purpose: Evaluates an individual's mechanical aptitude; used for employee selection and placement

Description: Three-part paper–pencil aptitude test measuring mechanical knowledge, space relations, and shop arithmetic. The Mechanical Knowledge subtest consists of 46 pictures of common tools and measures general mechanical background. The Space Relations subtests (40 items) measures the ability to visualize and mentally manipulate objects in space. The Shop Arithmetic subtest (24 problems) measures application of quantitative reasoning and fundamental math operations.

Format: Examiner required; suitable for group use; timed: 35 minutes

Scoring: Hand key

Cost: 25 reusable test booklets $90; 25 answer sheets $24; 100 profile sheets $24; examiner's manual $15

Publisher: McGraw-Hill/London House

SRA Test of Mechanical Concepts

Copyright: 1975
Population: Adults
Purpose: Measures an individual's ability to visualize and understand basic mechanical and spatial interrelationships; used for employee selection and screening for such jobs as assembler, maintenance mechanic, machinist, and factory production worker

Description: Paper–pencil 78-item test consisting of three subtests measuring separate skills or abilities necessary for jobs requiring mechanical ability. The Mechanical Interrelationships subtest consists of 24 drawings depicting mechanical movements and interrelationships. The Mechanical Tools and Devices subtest consists of 30 items measuring knowledge of common mechanical tools and devices. The Spatial Relations subtest consists of 24 items measuring the ability to visualize and manipulate objects in space. The test is available in two forms, A and B.

Format: Examiner required; suitable for group use; untimed: 35–45 minutes

Scoring: Hand key

Cost: 25 test booklets (specify form) $69; examiner's manual $15

Publisher: McGraw-Hill/London House

Stromberg Dexterity Test (SDT)
E. L. Stromberg

Copyright: 1981

Population: Adults

Purpose: Measures manipulative skill in sorting by color and sequence; used to select applicants for jobs requiring manual speed and accuracy; also used for assessing manual dexterity of individuals with disabilities in vocational training programs

Description: Two-trial performance test of manual dexterity in which the applicant is asked to discriminate and sort biscuit-sized discs and to move and place them as quickly as possible. The score is the number of seconds required to complete the two trials. Materials include assembly board and discs.

Format: Examiner required; not suitable for group use; timed: 5–10 minutes

Scoring: Score obtained by timing

Cost: Complete set $530.00

Publisher: The Psychological Corporation

Technical Test Battery (TTB) Mechanical Comprehension (MT4.1)

Copyright: 1992

Population: Adults

Purpose: Measures understanding of basic mechanical principles

Description: Multiple-choice 36-item test measuring knowledge of the classic mechanical elements, such as gears, pulleys, and levers, and a wide range of domestic and leisure applications of physics and mechanics, from electric ovens to billiard balls. Each item consists of a three-choice question about a technical drawing. The drawings are presented in technical workshop style without demanding any specific preknowledge to interpret them.

Format: 18 minutes

Scoring: Hand key; machine scored; scoring service available

Cost: Contact publisher

Publisher: Saville and Holdsworth Ltd.

VCWS 11—Eye–Hand–Foot Coordination

Copyright: 1974

Population: Adults

Purpose: Measures eye, hand, and foot coordination; provides insight into individual concentration, learning, planning, spatial discrimination, and reaction to immediate positive and negative feedback

Description: Manual test measuring an individual's ability to use his or her eyes, hands, and feet simultaneously and in a coordinated manner. The examinee sits in front of the work sample and maneuvers nine steel balls, one at a time, through a maze containing 13 holes into which the steel balls may drop, thus ending the examinee's attempt to make it to the end of the maze with that particular ball. In order to move the ball, the examinee tilts the maze left and right with the hands, forward and backward with the feet, and traces the track of the ball with the eyes. Work activities related to the test include starting, stopping, and observing the function of machines; perceiving relationships between moving objects, fixtures, and surfaces; and planning the order of operation

Format: Examiner required; not suitable for group use; timed: time not available

Scoring: Examiner evaluated

Cost: $1,695.00

Publisher: Valpar International Corporation

VCWS 4—Upper Extremity Range of Motion

Copyright: 1974

Population: Adults

Purpose: Measures an individual's upper extremity range of motion, including the shoulders, upper arms, forearms, elbows, wrists, and hands; provides insight into factors such as neck and back fatigue, finger dexterity, and finger tactile sense

Description: Manual test measuring the range of motion and work tolerances of an individual in relation to his or her upper torso. The individual works through an opening in front of the work sample, the inside of which is half red and half blue. Using opposite hands for each color, the individual fastens two sizes of nuts to bolts on each of five panels. The design of the work sample allows the examiner to view muscle action in the individual's wrist and fingers. Performance indicates coordination, spatial and perceptual skills, susceptibility to fatigue, and the ability to succeed in jobs requiring reaching, handling, fingering, feeling, and seeing. The test should not be used with individuals with severe impairment of the upper extremities.

Format: Examiner required; not suitable for group use; timed: time not available

Scoring: Examiner evaluated

Cost: $1,595.00

Publisher: Valpar International Corporation

VCWS 7—Multi-Level Sorting

Copyright: 1974

Population: Adults

Purpose: Measures an individual's decision-making ability while performing tasks requiring physical manipulation and visual discrimination of colors, color–numbers, color–letters, and combinations of the three

Description: Manual test measuring an indi-vidual's ability to make decisions while performing work tasks requiring physical manipulation and visual discrimination. The individual sorts 168 coded chips into 48 sorting slots showing on a board. Each chip is coded in one of the following ways: color; color and letter; color and number; or color, letter, and number. The test allows the examiner to observe the individual's orientation, approach, and organization in regard to the task, color, and letter; number discrimination skills; simple decision making; and physical manipulation. A time/error score relating directly to the level of supervision the individual will need while performing a particular job is derived.

Format: Examiner required; not suitable for group use; timed: time not available

Scoring: Examiner evaluated

Cost: $1,695.00

Publisher: Valpar International Corporation

VCWS 9—Whole Body Range of Motion

Copyright: 1974

Population: Adults

Purpose: Assesses the ability to perform successfully gross- and fine-finger dexterity tasks while in kneeling, crouching, stooping, bending, and stretching positions; may be used with individuals with hearing and visual disabilities

Description: Nonmedical measurement of gross body movements of the trunk, hands, arms, legs, and fingers as they relate to an individual's functional ability to perform job tasks. The individual stands in front of the work sample, with the frame adjusted to six inches above the head. The individual takes three colored shapes, one at a time, and transfers them from shoulder height to overhead. The individual then transfers the shapes to waist level, which requires bending forward at the waist; to knee level, which requires crouching or kneeling; and then back to shoulder height. In each transfer, the individual must remove a total of 22 nuts and then replace them, using one hand, onto each of the three colored shapes.

Format: Examiner required; not suitable for group use; timed: time not available

Scoring: Examiner evaluated

Cost: $2,095.00

Publisher: Valpar International Corporation

VCWS 1—Small Tools (Mechanical)

Copyright: 1974

Population: Adults

Purpose: Measures an individual's understanding of small tools and ability to work with them; may be used with individuals with institutional retardation, visual disabilities, and hearing disabilities

Description: Manual test measuring understanding of small tools and the ability to work with them. The design of the test challenges the individual to demonstrate skill in working in small, confined spaces while using the fingers and hands to manipulate tools to perform the assigned task. The individual works through a small hole in the work sample in order to simulate working conditions in which an individual is unable to view the work she or he is doing. The individual completes five panels. In each panel, the individual uses a different set of tools to insert fasteners such as screws, bolts, and hitch pin clips. Performance indicates the ability to complete successfully jobs requiring various degrees of ability in using small tools.

Format: Examiner required; not suitable for group use; timed: 1½ hours

Scoring: Examiner evaluated

Cost: $1,695.00

Publisher: Valpar International Corporation

VCWS 2—Size Discrimination

Copyright: 1974

Population: Adults

Purpose: Measures an individual's ability to perform tasks requiring visual size discrimination; provides insight into problem-solving abilities, work organization, ability to follow directions, and psychomotor coordination

Description: Manual test measuring an individual's ability to visually discriminate sizes. The individual must use her or his dominant hand to screw 49 hex nuts onto 32 bolt threads of various sizes. Both hands may be used to remove the nuts during disassembly. Performance indicates the ability to work successfully in occupations requiring visual size discrimination, eye–hand coordination, and bilateral dexterity. Work activities related to the test include examining and measuring for purposes of grading and sorting; tools; and working within prescribed tolerances or standards. The test should not be used with individuals with severe impairment of the upper extremities.

Format: Examiner required; not suitable for group use; timed: time not available

Scoring: Examiner evaluated

Cost: $1,395.00

Publisher: Valpar International Corporation

Work Skills Series (WSS) Findex

Copyright: 1991

Population: Adults

Purpose: Measures the ability to manipulate small objects requiring fine finger dexterity

Description: The candidate is required to insert thin steel rods into small holes and secure them with the aid of a screwdriver. The working area is restricted and both hands need to be used to complete the task.

Format: 7 minutes

Scoring: Hand score

Cost: Contact publisher

Publisher: Saville and Holdsworth Ltd.

Work Skills Series (WSS) Mandex

Copyright: 1991

Population: Adults

Purpose: Measures ability to manipulate and construct components using medium finger–hand dexterity

Description: The candidate is presented with a pre-assembled structure (mounted on one end of a wood base) consisting of six steel plates joined together by an assortment of nuts, bolts, washers, and spacers. Using this as a model, the task is to build an identical structure on the other end of the base using a set of plates and related materials provided. No tools are necessary. Scoring is achieved by awarding points for the correct selection and positioning of plates. The number of nuts, bolts, washers, and spacers used is also taken into account.

Format: 15 minutes

Scoring: Hand score

Cost: Contact publisher

Publisher: Saville and Holdsworth Ltd.

Municipal Services

Correctional Officers' Interest Blank (COIB)
Harrison G. Gough

Copyright: Not provided

Population: Adults

Purpose: Measures an individual's potential for correctional work; used for screening and placement

Description: Paper–pencil 40-item interest and attitude scale identifying applicants and officers of both sexes who possess the temperament and personal qualities required for work in correctional agencies and institutions. Sale is restricted to state and federal correctional agencies and penal institutions.

Format: Examiner required; suitable for group use; untimed: 10 minutes

Scoring: Hand scored

Cost: Preview Kit (booklet, key, manual) $47.00

Publisher: Consulting Psychologists Press, Inc.

Firefighter Selection Test

Copyright: 1987

Population: Adults

Purpose: Measures three abilities important for learning and performing the job of firefighter:

mechanical comprehension, reading comprehension, and report interpretation; used to select applicants for entry-level firefighter positions or training programs

Description: Paper–pencil 100-item multiple-choice test measuring the understanding of mechanical principles relevant to the fire fighting job (39 items), the ability to read and interpret a passage (51 items), and the ability to read and interpret charts and reports (10 items). The items consist of drawings and passages based on firefighter training materials and sample charts and reports presenting fire department data.

Format: Examiner required; suitable for group use; timed: 2 hours 30 minutes

Scoring: Hand key; may be computer scored; scoring service available from publisher

Cost: Test package (10 reusable tests, 10 answer sheets, scoring key, administrator's guide, and technical manual) $155.00; 2–9 additional packages $62.00 each; 50–99 additional packages $46.50 each; 100+ additional packages $44.00 each

Publisher: Psychological Services, Inc.

Inwald Personality Inventory (IPI)
Robin E. Inwald

Copyright: 1980

Population: Adults

Purpose: Assesses behavior patterns and characteristics of police, security, firefighter, and correction officer candidates; used for pre-employment screening

Description: Paper–pencil 310-item true–false instrument consisting of a validity measure and 25 scales assessing specific external behavior, attitudes and temperament, internalized conflict measures, and interpersonal conflict measures: Guardedness, Alcohol, Drugs, Driving Violations, Job Difficulties, Trouble with the Law and Society, Absence Abuse, Substance Abuse, Antisocial Attitudes, Hyperactivity, Rigid Type, Type "A," Illness Concerns, Treatment Programs, Anxiety, Phobic Personality, Obsessive Personality, Depression, Loner Type, Unusual Experience/Thoughts, Lack of

Assertiveness, Interpersonal Difficulties, Undue Suspiciousness, Family Conflicts, Sexual Concerns, and Spouse/Mate Conflicts. The test yields raw scores and *t*-scores.

Format: Self-administered; suitable for group use; available in Spanish; untimed: 30–45 minutes

Scoring: Computer scored

Cost: Starter kit (technical manual, test booklet, answer sheets for 3 computer-scored reports) $45.00; reusable test booklets $2; processing fees range from $10 to $23

Publisher: Hilson Research, Inc.

Law Enforcement Candidate Record (LECR)

Copyright: 1988

Population: Adults

Purpose: Used for police, corrections, and sheriff's officers

Description: Multiple-choice test with three subtests: 70 verbal, 100 recall, and 185 biodata

Format: Examiner required; suitable for group use

Scoring: Computer scored, test scoring service available from publisher

Cost: $7.00–$10.00 per candidate

Publisher: Richardson, Bellows, Henry, and Company, Inc.

Police Selection Test

Copyright: 1989

Population: Adults

Purpose: Measures five abilities important in learning and performing the job of police officer: reading comprehension, quantitative problem solving, data interpretation, writing skills, and reasoning; used to select applicants for entry-level police positions

Description: Paper–pencil 100-item multiple-choice test measuring the ability to read and interpret a passage (19 items), the ability to analyze logical numerical relationships (20 items), the ability to interpret data and other informa-

tion (23 items), the ability to express information in writing (15 items), and the ability to analyze information and make valid judgments based on available facts (23 items). The test consists of passages, tables, forms, and maps based on police officer training material. Scoring service available. Study guide available.

Format: Examiner required; suitable for group use; timed: 2 hours

Scoring: Hand key; may be computer scored

Cost: Paper–pencil: 25 tests per package: 1–19 packages $53.25; 20–199 packages $44.25; 200+ packages $36.25; Computerized form: 150–499 tests $2.50 each; 500–4,999 tests $2.25 each; 5,000–49,999 tests $2.00 each; 50,000+ tests $1.75 each

Publisher: Psychological Services, Inc.

Staff Burnout Scale for Police and Security Personnel
John W. Jones

Copyright: 1991

Population: Adults

Purpose: Assesses burnout or work stress among police and security personnel

Description: Multiple-item paper–pencil test assessing burnout or work stress through four types of factors: cognitive reactions, affective reactions, behavioral reactions, and psychophysiological reactions.

Format: Self-administered; suitable for group use; untimed: 10 minutes

Scoring: Hand key

Cost: 25 tests $23; examiner's manual $10

Publisher: McGraw-Hill/London House

Sales

Aptitudes Associates Test of Sales Aptitude–Revised
Martin M. Bruce

Copyright: 1983

Population: Adults

Purpose: Evaluates an individual's aptitude for selling; used as an aid in vocational guidance and in the selection and training of sales personnel

Description: Paper–pencil 50-item test measuring the subject's knowledge and understanding of the principles of selling a wide variety of goods ranging from heavy industrial capital items to door-to-door housewares. Norms are available to compare the subject's score with salespeople, men, women, and selected "special sales groups." The subject reads the directions and completes the test. Suitable for individuals with physical, hearing, or visual disabilities.

Format: Self-administered; suitable for group use; untimed: 20–30 minutes

Scoring: Hand key

Cost: Manual $9.00; key $2.85; forms $52.50; Specimen Set $41.50

Publisher: Martin M. Bruce, Ph.D.

Assessment Inventory for Management (AIM)

Copyright: 1991

Population: Adults

Purpose: Assesses sales management potential

Description: Multiple-choice paper–pencil test divided into four subtests: biodata, cognitive ability, personality, and situational judgment. Available also in French Canadian.

Format: Individual/self-administered; untimed

Scoring: Computer scored; test scoring service available from publisher

Cost: Contact publisher

Publisher: LIMRA International

Customer Reaction Survey

Jay Hall, C. Leo Griffith

Copyright: 1995

Population: Adults

Purpose: Assesses customer reaction to a salesperson's interpersonal style and customer preferences regarding salesperson behavior; used for employee training and development and as a basis for discussion

Description: Multiple-item paper–pencil inventory assessing an individual's success as a salesperson from the customer's point of view. In the first part of the inventory, the customer rates the salesperson's use of exposure and feedback. In the second part, the customer states preferred salesperson behavior. The resulting profiles may be combined with self-ratings from the Sales Relations Survey to make sales training relevant to the realities of the field. Normative data are provided.

Format: Suitable for group use; untimed: time varies

Scoring: Self-scored

Cost: $7.95 each

Publisher: Teleometrics International, Inc.

Diplomacy Test of Empathy

Willard A. Kerr

Copyright: 1984

Population: Adults

Purpose: Measures empathic ability; used for selecting applicants for sales positions

Description: Multiple-item paper–pencil test measuring the ability to sell and be persuasive, tactful, and diplomatic. Items correlate with the mean salary increases of executives but have little or no relationship with intelligence. Norms are available for general adults, management, sales, and sales management.

Format: Examiner required; suitable for group use; untimed: 20 minutes

Scoring: Hand key

Cost: Specimen Set $5.00; 25 tests $5.00; 25 answer sheets $5.00

Publisher: Psychometric Affiliates

Drug Store Applicant Inventory (DSAI)

Copyright: 1989

Population: Adults

Purpose: Assesses potential for successful employment; used in selection and screening of drugstore cashier/clerk applicants

Description: Paper–pencil 144-item multiple-choice test with eight diagnostic scales yielding scores in Background and Work Experience, Applied Arithmetic, Customer Service, Job Stability, Honesty, Interpersonal Cooperation, Drug Avoidance, and Risk Avoidance. Two validity scales, Distortion and Accuracy, are also included. A composite Employability Index based on the eight diagnostics is provided for decision-making purposes. In addition to scores, the DSAI generates behavioral indicators and training needs based on examinee responses to individual items.

Format: Examiner required; suitable for group use; untimed: 45 minutes

Scoring: Computer scored; test scoring service available form publisher

Cost: $18.00; minimum order of 25

Publisher: McGraw-Hill/London House

ETSA Tests 7-A—Sales Aptitude

George A. W. Stouffer, Jr., S. Trevor Hadley

Copyright: 1990

Population: Adolescents, adults; Grades 10 and above

Purpose: Measures abilities and skills required for effective selling; used for employee selection, placement, and promotion

Description: Paper–pencil 100-item test assessing seven aspects of sales aptitude: sales judgment, interest in selling, personality factors, identification of self with selling occupation, level of aspiration, insight into human nature, and awareness of sales approach. The test is one in a series of ETSA tests.

Format: Examiner required; suitable for group use; untimed: 1 hour

Scoring: Hand key; examiner evaluated; scoring service available

Cost: 10 tests with key $15.00; manual $5.00; handbook $15.00

Publisher: Educators'/Employers' Tests and Services Associates

Field Sales Skills Test

Copyright: 1990

Population: Adults

Purpose: Measures aptitude for work as a field sales representative, including general sales knowledge and understanding of sales principles

Description: Provides a five-page report to the client. Measures the following: verbal communication skills, numerical skills, attention to detail, problem solving ability, customer service skills, customer service problem solving, and customer service logic.

Format: 51 minutes

Scoring: Scoring service available from publisher

Cost: $319.00

Publisher: Walden Personnel Testing and Training, Inc.

Incentives Management Index (IMI)

Jay Hall, Norman J. Seim

Copyright: 1995

Population: Adults

Purpose: Assesses the incentives used by a sales manager to motivate the sales force; used for training and development of sales managers and as a basis for discussion

Description: Multiple-item paper–pencil self-report inventory identifying which incentives a sales manager emphasizes and assessing the sales manager's personal theories about what motivates the sales force. The inventory yields a managerial profile that may be used as feedback for the sales force. The inventory may be administered in conjunction with the Sales Motivation Survey (SMS) in two ways: to indicate areas in which the sales manager's own needs influence the incentives that are emphasized with the sales force and to assess the sales manager's own motivational theory in light of the needs of the sales force. Normative data are provided.

Format: Self-administered; suitable for group use; untimed: time varies

Scoring: Self-scored

Cost: $7.95 each

Publisher: Teleometrics International, Inc.

IPI Employee Aptitude Series: Sales Terms

Copyright: 1984

Population: Adults

Purpose: Measures ability to understand information of a sales or contract nature; used to assist employers in the selection, placement, promotion and training of different levels of sales personnel

Description: Paper–pencil 54-item test measuring comprehension of sales-related information. The test also indicates whether a person is overqualified for routine or repetitive assignments. French and Spanish versions are a combination of Sales Terms and Office Terms.

Format: Suitable for group use; examiner required; timed: 5 minutes

Scoring: Hand key

Cost: Introductory kit (20 test booklets, scoring key, manual) $30

Publisher: Industrial Psychology International Ltd.

IPI Job-Field Series: Contact Clerk

Copyright: 1981

Population: Adults

Purpose: Assesses skills of applicants for public relations positions; used to screen for complaint, information, receptionist, and customer service positions

Description: Multiple-item paper–pencil battery of five aptitude tests. The tests are Fluency, Perception, Memory, Judgment, and Numbers. For individual test descriptions, see the IPI Employee Aptitude Test Series. Also available in French and Spanish.

Format: Suitable for group use; examiner required; timed: 30 minutes

Scoring: Hand keys

Cost: Starter kit (test materials for five applicants, scoring keys, manuals) $80; test package $12/applicant

Publisher: Industrial Psychology International Ltd.

IPI Job-Field Series: Customer Service Representative

Copyright: 1989

Population: Adults

Purpose: Assesses skills and personality of applicants for customer service representative positions involving customer account maintenance and selling

Description: Multiple-item paper–pencil battery of five aptitude tests and one personality test. The tests are CPF, Memory, Fluency, Perception, Office Terms, Judgment, and Numbers. For individual test descriptions, see the IPI Employee Aptitude Series. Also available in French and Spanish.

Format: Suitable for group use; examiner required; timed: 46 minutes

Scoring: Hand keys

Cost: Starter kit (test materials for five applicants, scoring keys, manuals) $80; test package $12/applicant

Publisher: Industrial Psychology International Ltd.

IPI Job-Field Series: Sales Clerk

Copyright: 1960

Population: Adults

Purpose: Assesses skills and personality of applicants for lower-level sales positions; used to screen for department store, post office, teller, ticketer, and waitress positions

Description: Multiple-item paper–pencil battery of one personality and five aptitude tests. The tests are CPF, Numbers, Perception, Memory, Sales Terms, and Fluency. For individual test descriptions, see the IPI Employee Aptitude Series. Also available in French and Spanish.

Format: Examiner required; suitable for group use; timed: 40 minutes

Scoring: Hand key

Cost: Starter kit (test materials for five applicants, scoring keys, manuals) $80; test package $12/applicant

Publisher: Industrial Psychology International Ltd.

IPI Job-Field Series: Sales Engineer

Copyright: 1960

Population: Adults

Purpose: Assesses skills and personality of applicants for technically oriented sales positions; used to screen for claims work, adjusting, purchasing, technical sales, and underwriting

Description: Paper–pencil battery of six aptitude and three personality tests. The tests are Sales Terms, 16PF, Parts, Judgment, Numbers, Fluency, Memory, CPF, and NPF. For individual test descriptions, see the IPI Employee Aptitude Series. Also available in French and Spanish.

Format: Examiner required; suitable for group use; timed: 75 minutes

Scoring: Hand keys

Cost: Starter kit (test materials for five applicants, scoring keys, manuals) $80; test package $12/applicant

Publisher: Industrial Psychology International Ltd.

IPI Job-Field Series: Salesperson

Copyright: 1960

Population: Adults

Purpose: Assesses skills of applicants for higher-level sales positions; used to screen for agent, demonstrator, insurance, retail, wholesale, and route sales positions

Description: Multiple-item paper–pencil battery of five aptitude and two personality tests; the tests are 16PF, Numbers, Sales Terms, Fluency, Memory, CPF, and Perception. For individual test descriptions, see the IPI Employee Aptitude Series. Also available in French and Spanish.

Format: Examiner required; suitable for group

use; timed: 60 minutes

Scoring: Hand keys

Cost: Starter kit (test materials for five applicants, scoring keys, manuals) $80; test package $12/applicant

Publisher: Industrial Psychology International Ltd.

IS Sales Assessment Battery

Copyright: 1988

Population: Adults

Purpose: Measures logic and reasoning ability, as well as understanding of sales and problem solving in a sales environment

Description: Available in English and French.

Format: 1 hour 40 minutes

Scoring: Scoring service available from publisher

Cost: Test booklet and detailed report on each candidate $319.00

Publisher: Walden Personnel Testing and Training, Inc.

PDI Customer Service Inventory (CSI)

Copyright: 1991

Population: Adults

Purpose: Assesses customer service orientation; used for employee selection

Description: Multiple-choice 64-item paper–pencil true–false test. A PC version is available. A sixth-grade reading level is required. Available also in Spanish and French.

Format: Individual administration; suitable for group use; examiner required; untimed: 10–15 minutes

Scoring: Computer scored; test scoring service available from publisher

Cost: Based on volume; contact publisher

Publisher: Personnel Decisions International

Retail Sales Skills Test

Copyright: Not provided

Population: Adults

Purpose: Tests for retail sales knowledge, problem solving ability in a retail environment, and sales logic

Description: Multiple-item tests measuring skills

Format: 45 minutes

Scoring: Scoring service provided

Cost: Test booklet and detailed report on each candidate: Basic $199.00

Publisher: Walden Personnel Testing and Training, Inc.

Sales Attitude Checklist
Erwin K. Taylor

Copyright: 1992

Population: Adults

Purpose: Measures attitudes and behaviors involved in sales and selling; used for sales selection programs

Description: Paper–pencil 31-item test assessing basic attitudes toward selling and habits in the selling situation.

Format: Examiner required; suitable for group use; untimed: 10–minutes

Scoring: Hand key

Cost: 25 test booklets $59; examiner's manual $15

Publisher: McGraw-Hill/London House

Sales Motivation Inventory–Revised
Martin M. Bruce

Copyright: 1985

Population: Adults

Purpose: Assesses interest in and motivation for sales work, both commission and whole-sale/retail

Description: Paper–pencil 75-item test measuring sales motivation and drive. Consists of multiple-choice triads. Available also in French. Suitable for individuals with physical, hearing, and visual disabilities.

Format: Self-administered; suitable for group use; untimed: 20–30 minutes

Scoring: Hand key

Cost: Manual and manual supplement $39.50 (1984); key $2.85; profile sheets $25.50; forms $53.50; Specimen Set $42.50

Publisher: Martin M. Bruce, Ph.D.

Sales Motivation Survey
Jay Hall, Norman J. Seim

Copyright: 1995

Population: Adults

Purpose: Assesses the needs and motivations of salespersons; used for employer training and development and as a basis for discussion

Description: Multiple-item paper–pencil self-report inventory measuring the personal needs and goals of salespersons. The inventory provides a profile of personal motivations. The results may serve as a basis for reordering personal priorities and better understanding of personal performance. Normative data are provided. The inventory may be administered in conjunction with the Incentive Management Index for assessment of sales managers.

Format: Self-administered; suitable for group use; untimed: time varies

Scoring: Self-scored

Cost: $8.95 each

Publisher: Teleometrics International, Inc.

Sales Professional Assessment Inventory (SPAI)

Copyright: 1989

Population: Adults

Purpose: Assesses potential for success in sales positions; used for selection and screening of candidates for direct sales to business and retail sales of consumer durable goods or special services

Description: Paper–pencil 210-item multiple-choice test with 12 diagnostic scales yielding scores in Sales and Work Experience, Sales Interest, Sales Responsibility, Sales Orientation, Energy Level, Self Development, Sales Skills,

Sales Understanding, Customer Service, Business Ethics, and Job Stability. Two validity scales, Candidness and Accuracy, are provided. A sales Potential Index that is a composite of the 12 diagnostic scales is provided for decision-making purposes. In addition to scores, the SPAI generates positive indicators, training needs, and follow-up interview questions, based on examinee responses to individual items.

Format: Examiner required; suitable for group use; untimed: 60 minutes

Scoring: Computer scored; test scoring service available from publisher

Cost: $23.00–$36.00 depending on quantity and method of scoring; minimum order of 25

Publisher: McGraw-Hill/London House

Sales Relations Survey (SRS)
Jay Hall

Copyright: 1995
Population: Adults
Purpose: Assesses an individual's interpersonal sales style; used for employee training and development and as a basis for discussion

Description: Multiple-item paper–pencil self-report inventory assessing the quality of a salesperson's relationships with customers along exposure and feedback dimensions. The inventory is used to introduce and assess concepts such as blindspots, facades, and hidden potentials. Scores may be used to plot Johari Window profiles for an entire sales force. Normative data are provided. The inventory may be administered in conjunction with the Customer Reaction Survey for a more complete assessment of an individual's interpersonal sales style.

Format: Self-administered; suitable for group use; untimed: time varies

Scoring: Self-scored
Cost: $8.95 each
Publisher: Teleometrics International, Inc.

Sales Sentence Completion Blank–Revised
Martin M. Bruce

Copyright: 1982

Population: Adults
Purpose: Aids in evaluating and selecting sales personnel by providing insight into how the applicant thinks and his or her social attitudes and general personality

Description: Paper–pencil 40-item test consisting of sentence fragments to be completed by the subject. The examiner assesses the responses by scoring them on a 7-point scale. Responses are a "projection" of the subject's attitudes about life, self, and others. Suitable for individuals with physical, hearing, or visual disabilities.

Format: Self-administered; suitable for group use; untimed: 20–35 minutes

Scoring: Hand key
Cost: Manual $18.50; forms $52.50; Specimen Set $24.50
Publisher: Martin M. Bruce, Ph.D.

Sales Style
James H. Brewer

Copyright: 1990
Population: Adults
Purpose: Used to sharpen sales skills

Description: Identifies four general patterns: the "Quick-Sell" type; the "Talkative-Sell"; the "Persistent-Sell," and the "Precise-Sell." The instrument relates personality type to sales style, identifies strengths and weaknesses of each personality type, helps sales people develop new approaches, and explores other styles.

Format: Individual/self-administered; untimed: 10–15 minutes

Scoring: Hand key
Cost: $2.95 each
Publisher: Associated Consultants in Education

Sales Style Diagnosis Test
W. J. Reddin, David Forman

Copyright: 1977
Population: Adults
Purpose: Measures a salesperson's selling style and effectiveness; used to screen, coach, and train salespersons

Description: Multiple-item paper–pencil test designed to provide scores on the following selling styles: deserter, missionary, autocrat, compromiser, bureaucrat, developer, benevolent autocrat, and executive. Task orientation, relationships orientation, and effectiveness are assessed as well. The individual responds to actions of a hypothetical salesperson and receives a score indicative of selling style.

Format: Self-administered; suitable for group use; untimed: 20–30 minutes

Scoring: Hand key

Cost: Test kit (10 test copies, fact sheet, user's guide) $40.00

Publisher: Organizational Tests Ltd.

Sales Style Indicator (SSI)
Terry D. Anderson, Bruce R. Wares

Copyright: 1991

Population: Adults

Purpose: Assesses sales style preferences; used in sales training

Description: Forced-choice 16-item test. A 10th-grade reading level is required.

Format: Individual administration; suitable for group use; examiner required; untimed

Scoring: Self-scored

Cost: $14.95

Publisher: Consulting Resource Group International, Inc.

Sales Transaction Audit (STA)
Jay Hall, C. Leo Griffith

Copyright: 1980

Population: Adults

Purpose: Assesses the interpersonal transactions of salespeople with their customers in terms of Eric Berne's model of transactional analysis; used for employee training and development and as a basis for discussion

Description: Multiple-item paper–pencil self-report inventory measuring the size of the parent, adult, and child—the three positions from which individuals can communicate according to the model of transactional analysis—in a salesperson's transactions with customers. The inventory also provides scores for transaction contamination, crossed and complementary transactions, and constructive and disruptive tension in the sales relationship. Normative data are provided.

Format: Self-administered; suitable for group use; untimed: time varies

Scoring: Self-scored

Cost: $8.95 each

Publisher: Teleometrics International, Inc.

Selling Judgment Test
Martin M. Bruce

Copyright: 1959

Population: Adolescents, adults

Purpose: Measures sales comprehension; used by sales trainers to develop discussion topics

Description: Five-item paper–pencil multiple-choice test assessing sales competence in the retail and wholesale fields. The items in this test are taken from the *Sales Comprehension Test* and were chosen by the Associated Merchandising Corporation as particularly pertinent to the department retail store field. The test is used primarily for training and discussion purposes. The *Sales Comprehension Test* is more appropriate for assessment purposes. Suitable for individuals with physical, hearing, or visual disabilities.

Format: Self-administered; suitable for group use; untimed: 3 minutes

Scoring: Examiner evaluated

Cost: 20 forms $17.50

Publisher: Martin M. Bruce, Ph.D., Publishers

Service Relations Scale

Copyright: 1989, 1996

Population: Adults

Purpose: Identifies applicants who are most likely to be successful in positions requiring excellent customer service skills

Description: Fifty-question scale designed to reduce turnover and increase employee service by placing only those applicants or employees with strong communication skills in positions requiring sensitivity to customer and co-worker needs.

Format: 10 minutes

Scoring: I-Fax (automated scoring platform that returns test results via fax), Provoice (front-end applicant telephone testing program), Fax-In, Phone-In, Mail-In, or PC software

Cost: Ranges from $8.50 to $18.00

Publisher: Reid Psychological Systems

SSI In-Depth Interpretation
Terry D. Anderson, Bruce R. Wares

Copyright: 1991

Population: Adults

Purpose: Assesses sales style preferences; used in sales training

Description: Test with 21 items. A 10th-grade reading level is required.

Format: Individual administration; suitable for group use; untimed

Scoring: Self-scored

Cost: $9.95

Publisher: Consulting Resource Group International, Inc.

Station Employee Applicant Inventory (SEAI)

Copyright: 1986

Population: Adults

Purpose: Assesses the on-the-job attitudes and behaviors of gas station and convenience store cashier applicants; used to predict which applicants will have low rates of tardiness and absenteeism, safeguard funds, and handle cash and charge transactions accurately

Description: Multiple-choice 144-item paper–pencil test assessing the attitudes and behavior of gas station and convenience store cashier applicants. The test evaluates characteristics in five major areas measured by the following scales: Honesty, Interpersonal Cooperation, Drug Avoidance, Arithmetic Skills, and Job-Specific Skills and Abilities. An Applicant Employee Index and a validity scale are included also. Optional scales include safety attitudes and a tenure scale that predicts turnover. Standard and percentile scores are available in each of the five major areas. Three scoring options are available from London House: operator-assisted telephone, Touch-Test, and PC based. Results are available immediately, and written confirmation is mailed the next day.

Format: Examiner required; suitable for group use; untimed: 45 minutes

Scoring: Operator-assisted telephone; computer scored

Cost: $6.00–$16.00 based on scoring method and volume ordered

Publisher: McGraw-Hill/London House

Test of Retail Sales Insight (TRSI)
Russell N. Cassel

Copyright: 1971

Population: Adults

Purpose: Assesses degree of knowledge of retail selling; used for foreign-service education of retail sales clerks and assessing progress in distributive education courses

Description: Paper–pencil 60-item multiple-choice test measuring five areas of retail sales: general sales knowledge, customer motivation and need, merchandise procurement and adaptation, sales promotion procedures, and sales closure. Five alternatives are provided for each item. A fifth-grade reading level is required.

Format: Examiner required; suitable for group use; untimed: 30 minutes

Scoring: Hand key

Cost: Specimen Set $9.00; 25 tests $27.50; 25 answer sheets $6.75; 25 profile sheets $8.25; keys $6.75; manual $6.75

Publisher: Psychologists and Educators, Inc.

Technical

Chemical Comprehension, Forms S and T

Copyright: Not provided

Population: Adults

Purpose: Assesses understanding of concepts related to chemistry; used with applicants for operation, craft, and lab technician positions

Description: Paper–pencil 50-item multiple-choice test measuring general knowledge of chemistry. Content could be learned in school, but persons without formal training in chemistry can achieve high scores. Answers are marked in the test booklet. The test is helpful to applicants choosing between process or mechanical positions in industry. Norms are available for male process and laboratory applicants, process workers, and mechanical workers. Norms are also available for female student nurses and nurses' training applicants. The test is available in two forms, S and T.

Format: Examiner required; suitable for group use; timed: 30 minutes

Scoring: Hand key

Cost: 1–24 packages $45.00; score key $10.00; manual $15.00

Publisher: Richardson, Bellows, Henry and Company, Inc.

Development and Application of Absolute Scales of Electronic Job Performance
Arthur I. Siegel, Douglas G. Schultz, Richard S. Lanterman

Copyright: 1976

Population: Adults

Purpose: Evaluates performance of naval avionics technicians

Description: Paper–pencil test measuring fleet objectives. Adaptation of the *Guttman Scale.*

Format: Examiner required; not suitable for group use; untimed

Scoring: Examiner evaluated

Cost: $24.00

Publisher: Select Press

Development of a Psychophysical Photo Quality Measure
R. I. Welch, F. R. Clarke, T. E. Jeffrey

Copyright: 1975

Population: Adults

Purpose: Measures aerial reconnaissance

Description: Criterion-referenced paper–pencil questionnaire measuring image interpretation.

Format: Individually administered; examiner required; untimed

Scoring: Examiner evaluated; hand key

Cost: $24.00

Publisher: Select Press

Performance Evaluative Measures
Arthur I. Siegel, Philip J. Pederson

Copyright: 1976

Population: Adults

Purpose: Measures navy fleet posttraining performance/evaluation systems

Description: Eight-factor paper–pencil test. Two instruments available.

Format: Group or individual administration; examiner required; untimed

Scoring: Hand key; examiner evaluated

Cost: $24.00

Publisher: Select Press

VCWS 16—Drafting

Copyright: 1977

Population: Adults

Purpose: Measures an individual's potential to compete in an entry-level position requiring basic drafting and print reading skills; provides insight into the ability to visualize abstract problems and to acquire new tool use skills

Description: Manual test measuring the potential to compete in an entry-level position requiring basic drafting skills. The examinee performs a series of exercises measuring ability to measure objects accurately in inches and centimeters; learn the use of drafting tools such as a T square, compass, circle template, and triangles; and read blueprints. The examinee must produce three view drawings of three wooden blocks. Each subtest screens the examinee in terms of ability to cope successfully with the next subtest. The test is designed to accommodate a range of needs within the drafting industry from minimal expertise to sophisticated high-level performance.

Format: Examiner required; not suitable for group use; timed: time not available

Scoring: Examiner evaluated

Cost: $1,595.00

Publisher: Valpar International Corporation

Indexes

Index of Test Titles

653

Index of Tests Not in the Fourth Edition

Index of Publishers Not in the Fourth Edition

....

Administrative Research Associates, Incorporated; forwarding order expired

Alemany Press; forwarding order expired

Allen House; no forwarding order

Allington Corporation; no reply

American Automobile Association; not a test publisher

American Chemical Society; no reply

American Council on Education; no reply

American Foundation for the Blind; no reply

American Orthopsychiatric Association, Incorporated, 330 Seventh Avenue, 18th Floor, New York, NY 10001, 212-564-5390, FAX 212-564-6180

American Printing House for the Blind; no tests in catalog

American Testronics; instruments with American College Testing

Appenfeldt, Linda, PhD; no contact since 1988

Applied Innovations, Incorporated; no contact since 1987

ARBOR, Inc; Academic Therapy now publishes

Associated Services for the Blind; no longer publishes tests

Association of American Medical Colleges; forwarding order expired; no reply

Aurora Publishing; no contact since 1987

Australian Government Publishing Service, GPO Box 84, Canberra ACT 2601 AUSTRALIA, 00800049, 06954861, FAX 06954888

Ballard and Tighe, Incorporated; no reply

Barber Center, Incorporated; no reply

Beckham, E. Edward, 408 French Park Drive Suite B, Edmond, OK 73034, 405-59-0029, FAX 405-59-0095

Behar, PhD, Lenore; no reply

Behavior Arts Center; no reply

Behavior Science Press, 3710 Resource Dr., Tuscaloosa, AL 35401, 205-758-2823, FAX 205-758-3222

Behavior Science Systems, Incorporated, PO Box 580274, Minneapolis, MN 55458, 612-929-6220

Behavioral Science Research Press, Incorporated; no contact since 1987

Bilingual Media Productions, Incorporated; no contact since 1987

Bingham Button Test; no contact since 1987

Biobehavioral Associates; no reply

Bitter, James A.; no reply

BJK Associates; no reply

Bloom, Philip; no contact since 1987

Bond Publishing Company; no reply

Book-Lab; no reply

Brador Publications, Incorporated; no contact since 1987

Brain Train, Incorporated; forwarding order expired; no reply

Branden Publishing Company, Incorporated; no reply

Brook Educational Publishing Limited; box closed

Brown University Family Research Program; no contact since 1988

Brown, Company Publishers, W.C.; no reply

Bureau of Business and Economic Research; no contact since 1987

Callier Center for Communication Disorders; no reply

Cambridge University Press; forwarding order expired; no reply

Carlson, Bernadine P.; no reply

Carney, Weedman and Associates; no reply

Carroll Publications; no contact since 1987

Cedars Press; no contact since 1987

Center for Advanced Study in Theoretical Psychology; no contact since 1987

Center for Cognitive Therapy; no longer publishing

Center for Educational assessment; no reply

Center for Faculty Evaluation and Development; requested delete from listing

Frost, PhD, Barry P.; no contact since 1987

Functional Assessments and Training Consultants; no reply

Gallaudet University Press; no longer publishing tests

Gibson Publisher, Robert; no contact since 1987

Gordon Systems, Incorporated, PO Box 746, DeWitt, NY 13214, 315-446-4849, FAX 315-446-2012

Goyer, PhD, Robert S.; no contact since 1987

Guglielmino and Associates, Incorporated, 734 Marble Way, Boca Raton, FL 33432, 407-392-0379, FAX 407-392-0379

Guidance Centre; no contact since 1987

Guidance Testing Associates; no contact since 1988

Halgren Tests; no contact since 1988

Hanson, Silver, Strong, and Associates, Incorporated, 34 Washington Road, Princeton Junction, NJ 08550, 609-799-6300, FAX 609-799-6301

Harding Tests; not a publisher of tests

Harvard University Press, 75 Garden St., Cambridge, MA 018, 617-495-4608, 617-495-2600, FAX 617-495-5898

Haverly Systems, Incorporated; no contact since 1988

Heath, PhD, S. Roy; no contact since 1988

Heinemann Publishers Australia Pty Limited; no reply

Hill, William Faucett; no reply

Hodder and Stoughton; no reply

Hodges, PhD, Kay; no contact since 1988

Hoeflin, Ronald K.; box closed

Howarth, PhD, Edgar; no contact since 1988

Hughes, PhD, Jeanne E.; no contact since 1988

Human Synergistics, 9819 Plymouth Road #C-8020, Plymouth, MI 48170, 313-459-100, FAX 313-459-5557

Illinois Critical Thinking Project; no reply

Independent Assessment and Research Centre; no contact since 1988

Institute for Behavioral Research in Creativity; no reply

Institute for Character Development; no reply

Institute for Child Behavior Research; no reply

Institute for Psycho-Imagination Therapy; no reply

Institute for the Development of Human Resources; no contact since 1987

Institute of Athletic Motivation; no reply

Instructional Materials and Equipment Distributors (IMED); no contact since 1987

Instructional Materials Laboratory; forwarding order expired

Integrated Professional systems, Incorporated; no contact since 1987

Interdatum; no longer publishing

International Association for the Study of Pain; no reply

Intrex Interpersonal Institute, Incorporated; no reply

IPS Publishing; forwarding order expired

Ishmael and Associates, R. B.; forwarding order expired; no reply

ISU Research Foundation; no reply

Jansky, Jeannette J.; no reply

Johnson, Suzanne Bennett; no contact since 1988

Joint Council on Economic Education; no reply

Kahn, PhD, Marvin W.; no contact since 1988

Katz, PhD, Martin M.; no reply

Keegan, Warren, Associates Press; no reply

Keeler Instruments, Incorporated; no reply

Keeler Limited; no reply

Keller, MD, Martin B.; unable to contact

Kew, Clifton E.; unable to contact

Keystone View; no reply

Khavari, Khalil A.; no reply

Kovacs, PhD, Maria; no reply

Krieger Publishing Company, Incorporated, Robert E.; no contact since 1988

Kundu, Ramanath; no reply

Lafayette Instrument Company; no reply

LaForge, Rolfe; no reply

Laidlaw Brothers/Doubleday; no contact since 1988

Lake Publishers, David S.; no contact since 1987

Larlin Corporation; unable to contact

Law School Admission Council; no contact since 1988

Lea and Febiger; no reply

Learning Publications, Incorporated; no reply

Learning Time Products; no reply

Lefkowitz, PhD, Monroe M.; no contact since 1988

Leonard Publishing Corporation, Hal; no reply

Leonardo Press, PO Box 1326, Camden, ME 04843, 207-236-8649

Lewis and Company Limited, H. K.; mail returned with no explanation

Libraries Unlimited, PO Box 6633, Englewood, CO 80155-6633, 800-237-6124, 303-220-8843

Lingua Press; no contact since 1988

Linguametrics Group; no contact since 1988

Lippincott/Harper Publisher, Incorporated; do not publish tests

M and M Systems; no reply

M.A.A. Committee on High School Contests; no reply

MacKeith Press; no forwarding order

Macmillan Education Limited; no reply

Mafex Associates, Incorporated; no contact since 1987

Manasayan, Agarwal Complex, S-524 School Block, Shakarpur, Delhi 110092, INDIA, 222-919, FAX 327-1584

Marriage Council of Philadelphia, Incorporated; no contact since 1988

Matisak, Rick; not a test publisher

McCann Associates, Incorporated; no reply

McCartney, William A.; no contact since 1987

McCormick and Associates, R. R.; requested removal from listing

McGraw-Hill Ryerson; unable to contact

Meeting Street School; no contact since 1987

Merrill Publishing, Charles E.; no contact since 1987

Miami University Alumni Association; no reply

Midwest Music Tests; no reply

Miller, Incorporated, G. E.; no contact since 1988

Mings and Associates, Jerry; unable to contact

Ministry Inventories; unable to contact

Mississippi State University Rehabilitation Research and Training Center on Blindness and Low Vision; instruments out of print

MKM, Incorporated, 401 3rd Street, Suite 1, Rapid City, SD 57701, 605-342-7284

Modern Curriculum Press, Incorporated; no reply

Monitor; no reply

Morgan, Robert F., Morgan Foundation Publishers: International Published Innovations, #7 Wild Oak Drive, Billings, MT 59102, 406-652-8123

Morrisby Organisation, 83 High Street, Hemel Hempstead, Hertfordshire HP1 3AH, UK, 01442-68645, FAX 01442-240531

Morstain, Barry R.; no reply

Multimodal Publications, Incorporated; no reply

Munksgaard; no reply

Munsell Color; unable to contact

National Business Education Association; no reply

National Computer Systems, Incorporated, 510 North Dodge Street, PO Box 30, Iowa City, IA 52240, 319-339-6463, FAX 319-339-6477

National Institute for Automotive Service Excellence; no reply

National Institute for Personnel Research; no reply

National Institute on Mental Retardation (NIMR); no contact since 1987

National Occupational Comprehensive Testing Instruments, NOCTI, National Occupational Competency Testing Institute, 500 N. Bronson, Big Rapids, MI 4907, 800-334-6283, 616-796-4695, FAX 616-796-4699

National Study of School Evaluation; no contact since 1988

Neimeyer, Robert A.; no reply

Nevins Printing Company, C. H.; no reply

New Zealand Council for Educational Research; no reply

Newbury House Publishers, Incorporated; no contact since 1987

NFER-NELSON Publishing Company Limited; no reply

Nisonger Center; no contact since 1987

Northwestern University Press; no contact since 1987

NSW Department of Industrial Relations; no contact since 1988

NTS Research Corporation; no reply

Nursing Research Associates; no contact since 1988

Ontario Institute for Studies in Education, Guidance Centre, 712 Gordon Baker Road, Toronto, Ontario M2H 3R7 CANADA, 800-668-6247, 416-502-1262, FAX 416-502-1101

Ottowa Civic Hospital; no reply

Oxford University Press; no reply

Oy Integro Finland Ab; no reply

Pacific Psychological; unable to contact

Paulist Press; no reply

Pediatric Psychology Press; no longer publishing tests

Perceptual Learning Systems; unable to contact

Perfection Form Company; no reply

Person-O-Metrics, Incorporated, 20504 Williamsburg Road, Dearborn Heights, MI 48127, 313-271-4631

Personality Research Services, Limited; no reply

Personnel Assessment Centers, Incorporated; forwarding order expired

Phoenix Institute of California; no contact since 1988

Phonovisual Products, Incorporated, 18761 N. Fredrick Road #BB, PO Box 1410, Germantown, MD 20875, 800-283-4888, 301-869-6190

Pikunas, Justin, PhD; unable to contact

Pilowsky, MD, I.; no reply

Planet Press; unable to contact

Planetree Medical Systems, Incorporated; no reply

Polymath Systems; no reply

Precision People; no contact since 1987

Prentice Hall/Cambridge; no reply

Prep, A Division of Educational Technologies, Incorporated; no reply

Priority Innovations, Incorporated; no reply

Professional Resource Exchange; no longer publishing test

Programs for Education, Incorporated; no reply

Psychodiagnostic Test Company; no reply

Psychodynamic Instruments; unable to contact

Psychological & Educational Publications, Incorporated, 1477 Rollins Road, Burlingame, CA 94010, 800-523-5755, FAX 800-447-0907

Psychological Assessment and Services, Incorporated; no reply

Psychological Measurement Systems; forwarding order expired

Psychological Surveys Corporation; unable to contact

Psychologistics, Incorporated, 68 N. Babcock Street #B-1, Melbourne, FL 32935, 407-259-7811, FAX 407-259-7811

Psytec, Incorporated; forwarding order expired

Purdue Research Foundation, Division of Sponsored Programs, 328 ENAD, West Lafayette, IN 47907, 317-494-2610, FAX 317-496-1277

Quay, PhD, Herbert C.; retired

Ray Publishing, Steven; no contact since 1988

Reason House; forwarding order expired

Reddin and Associates, W. J.; unable to contact

Reitan Neuropsychology Laboratory; no forwarding order, no reply

Renovex; no reply

Research and Training Center Press; no reply

Research Concepts; no contact since 1987

Research Press; no longer publishing tests

Revrac Publications, Incorporated, 207 W. 116th Street, Kansas City, MO 64114

Richmond Products; no reply

Roll, PhD, Samuel; no contact since 1987

Rucker Gable Associates; no contact since 1987

SAFE, Incorporated; Stoelting now publishes

Saleh, Shoukry; no reply

Sauls, PhD, Charles; no contact since 1987

Sbordone, PhD, Robert J.; forwarding order expired, no reply

SCANTRON Corporation; forwarding order expired, no reply

Schubert, Herman; does not wish to participate

Scrima, Lawrence, PhD; no reply

Sensonics, Incorporated; unable to contact

Sewall Rehabilitation Center; no contact since 1987

Sheridan Psychological Services, Incorporated; Consulting Psychology Press now publishes

Skillcorp Software, Incorporated; unable to contact

Smith, Sandman and McCreery; no reply

SOARES Associates, Management Specialists, 111 Teeter Rock Road, Trumbull, CT 06611, 203-375-5353

Social and Behavioral Sciences Documents; Psychological Assessment Resources now publishes

SOI Systems; no forwarding order

Spivack, George Institute for Graduate Clinical Psychology, Widner University, Chester, PA 19013, 610-499-1209, FAX 610-499-4625

Springer Publishing Company; no contact since 1987

SRA; no longer publishing tests

Stanton Corporation; no reply

Statistical Publishing Society; no contact since 1987

Stein, Morris I.; no contact since 1987

Stevens, Thurow, and Associates, 100 W. Monroe St. #2200, Chicago, IL 60603, 312-332-6277

Stratton-Christian Press, Incorporated; no reply

Swensen, Clifford H.; no reply

Swift, Marshall, 319 South Ivy Lane, Glen Mills, PA 19342, 610-358-1289

T.E.D. Associates; no contact since 1987

T.O.T.A.L. Child, Incorporated; no reply

Tabin, Johanna Krout; no reply

TAV Selection System, 12807 Arminta Street, North Hollywood, CA 91605, 818-765-1884

Teachers College Press, Teachers College, Columbia University, 1234 Amsterdam Avenue, New York, NY 10027, 212-678-3919, FAX 212-678-4149

Teaching and Testing Resources; no contact since 1987

Telemarketing Design, Incorporated; no reply

Templer, Donald I.; no reply

Test Agency Limited, Cray House, Woodlands Road, Henley, Oxon RG9 4AE United Kingdom, 01491-413413, FAX 01491-572249

Test Systems International; no contact since 1987

Thelen, Mark H.; no longer publishing

Thomas, Charles C., Publisher; instruments out of print

Titmus Optical, Incorporated; no reply

Twitchell-Allen, Doris; unable to contact

U.S. Department of Labor; no contact since 1988

United Educational Services, Incorporated; no longer publishing

University Associates, Incorporated; no reply

University of Illinois Press, 1325 S. Oak Street, Champaign, IL 61820, 217-333-0950, FAX 217-244-8082

University of Minnesota Press, 111 Third Avenue South Suite 290, Minneapolis, MN 55401-2520, 612-627-1963, 612-627-1980

University of New England, Publications Office, Armidale, NSW 2351 AUSTRALIA, 067 73 3448, FAX 067 72 5272

University Press of America; no contact since 1988

Village Publishing; no reply

Vocational and Rehabilitation Research Institute; no reply

Vocational Psychology Research, University of Minnesota, N620 Elliot Hall, Minneapolis, MN 55455-0344, 612-625-1367, FAX 613-626-2079

VORT Corporation; no reply

Walker Educational Book Corporation; no longer publishing

Washington Pre-College Program; no contact since 1988

Index of Tests Available in Foreign Languages

. . . .

Spanish

3-R's® Test

16PF Questionnaire Fourth Edition

Ability Explorer

ACDI-Corrections Version II

Adaptive Behavior Evaluation Scale (ABES)–Revised

Adaptive Behavior Inventory for Children (ABIC)

Adolescent Chemical Dependency Inventory (ACDI)

Adult Basic Learning Examination–Second Edition (ABLE)

Adult Neuropsychological Questionnaire

American Drug and Alcohol Survey™

Anxiety Scales for Children and Adults (ASCA)

AP Examination: Advanced Placement Program

APTICOM

Aptitude Assessment Battery: Programming (AABP)

Aptitude Based Career Decision

Association Adjustment Inventory (AAI)

Attention Deficit Disorders Evaluation Scale (ADDES)–Revised

Basic Inventory of Natural Language (BINL)

Behavior Dimensions Scale (BDS)

Behavior Disorders Identification Scale (BDIS)

Ber-Sil Spanish Tests: Elementary Test 1987 Revision

Ber-Sil Spanish Tests: Secondary Test

Bi/Polar® Inventories of Core Strengths

Bilingual Syntax Measure I and II (BSM)

Boehm Test of Basic Concepts–Revised (BOEHM-R)

Brigance® Diagnostic Assessment of Basic Skills— Spanish Edition

California Critical Thinking Disposition Inventory (CCTDI)

California Critical Thinking Skills Test (CCTST)

California Program for Learning Assessment

Campbell Organizational Survey (COS)

Career Assessment Inventory—Vocational Version

Career Exploration Inventory (CEI)

Carlson Psychological Survey (CPS)

CASAS Basic Citizenship Skills Examination

Child Neuropsychological Questionnaire

Children of Alcoholics Screening Test (CAST)

Children's Apperception Test (CAT-A)

Children's Apperception Test—Human Figures (CAT-H)

Children's Apperception Test—Supplement (CAT-S)

Children's Personality Questionnaire (CPQ)

Chronic Pain Battery™ (CPB)

Columbia Mental Maturity Scale (CMMS)

Composition Profile

Comprehensive Identification Process (CIP), Second Edition

Comprehensive Personality Profile

Compton Speech and Language Screening Evaluation

Copsystem Interest Inventory (COPS)

Culture Fair Intelligence Tests

Denver II

Derogatis Interview for Sexual Functioning (DISF/DISF-SR)

Developing Skills Checklist (DSC)

Domestic Violence Inventory

Driver Risk Inventory (DRI)

Early School Personality Questionnaire (ESPQ)

Employee Aptitude Survey Test #10—Symbolic Reasoning (EAS#10)

Employee Aptitude Survey Test #2—Numerical Ability (EAS#2)

Employee Aptitude Survey Test #3—Visual Pursuit (EAS#3)

Junior Eysenck Personality Inventory (JEPI)

Kent Infant Development Scale (KID Scale)
Kirton Adaption-Innovation Inventory (KAI)

Language Assessment Scales-Oral (LAS-O)
Language Proficiency Test (LPT)
LAS® Reading/Writing (LAS R/W)
Lead Other
Lead Profile
Lead Self
Learning Style Inventory (LSI)
Lindamood Auditory Conceptualization Test
   (LAC)
Lista de Destrezas en Desarrollo (La Lista)
Lollipop Test: A Diagnostic Screening Test of
   School Readiness

Myers-Briggs Type Indicator (MBTI)

National Spanish Examinations
Non-Verbal Scale of Suffering (N-V SOS)
North American Depression Inventories (NADI)

Oars Multidimensional Functional Assessment
   Questionnaire
Omnia Profile®, Omniafax® in Europe
Oral English or Spanish Proficiency Placement
   Test

Parent as a Teacher Inventory (PAAT)
Parental Acceptance-Rejection Questionnaire
   (PARQ)
Parker Team Player Survey (PTPS)
PDI Customer Service Inventory (CSI)
Performance Assessment in Spanish (PAIS)
Personal Styles Inventory PSI-120
Personality Assessment Inventory (PAI)
Personality Research Form (PRF)
Phelps Kindergarten Readiness Scale
Physical Punishment Questionnaire (PPQ)
Pre-LAS
Preschool Evaluation Scale (PES)
Preschool Language Scale-3 (PLS-3)
Prescreening Developmental Questionnaire
   (PDQ)

Prison Inmate Inventory
Progress Assessment Chart (PAC)
PSC-Survey A. D. T. (For Alienation and
   Trustworthiness/Leniency)
Psychological Screening Inventory (PSI)
Purpose in Life (PIL)

Reading Style Inventory (RSI)
Revised Beta Examination–Second Edition
   (BETA-II)
Riley Preschool Developmental Screening
   Inventory

SAQ-Adult Probation II
SAT II: Subject Tests
Self Concept As A Learner (SCAL)
Self Directed Search® Form E (SDS® Form E)
Self-Directed Learning Readiness Scale (SDLRS)
Senior Apperception Technique (SAT)
Sequenced Inventory of Communication
   Development, Revised Edition
Shoplifting Inventory
Skills Assessment Module (S.A.M.)
Slingerland Screening Tests for Identifying
   Children with Specific Language Disability
Spanish & English Reading Comprehension Test
Spanish Assessment of Basic Education, Second
   Edition (SABE®/2)
Spanish Computerized Adaptive Placement Exam
   (S-CAPE)
Spanish Proficiency Test (SPT)
Spanish Reading Comprehension Test (Evaluacion
   de Comprension de la Lectura)
Spanish Speaking Test (SST)
Spiritual Well-Being Scale
Standardized Bible Content Tests
Standardized Bible Content Tests-E, F
Strong Interest Inventory
Structured Photographic Expressive Language
   Test-Preschool (SPELT-P)
Student Instructional Report (SIR)
Substance Abuse Questionnaire (SAQ)
Supervisory Practices Test (Revised)
Survey of Study Habits and Attitudes (SSHA)
System of Multicultural Pluralistic Assessment
   (SOMPA)

Temperament Inventory Tests

TerraNova (CTB5-5)

Test de Vocabulario en Imagenes Peabody (TVIP)

Tests of Adult Basic Education (TABE), Forms 7 and 8

Thomas-Kilmann Conflict Mode Instrument (TKI)

TMJ Scale™

TQManager Inventory (TQMI)

Vineland Adaptive Behavior Scales

Visual-Aural Digit Span Test (VADS)

Vocational Research Interest Inventory (VRII)

Wechsler Scales: Wechsler Adult Intelligence Scale–Revised (WAIS-R)

Wonderlic Personnel Test

Woodcock Language Proficiency Battery–Revised (WLPB-R) English Form

Woodcock Language Proficiency Battery–Revised (WLPB-R) Spanish Form

Woodcock-Muñoz Language Survey, English Form, Spanish Form

World of Work Inventory

French

Anxiety Scales for Children and Adults (ASCA)

AP Examination: Advanced Placement Program

Aptitude Assessment Battery: Programming (AABP)

Assessment Inventory for Management (AIM)

Basic Visual Motor Association Test

Business Judgment Test, Revised

California Critical Thinking Disposition Inventory (CCTDI)

Campbell Organizational Survey (COS)

Canadian Occupational Interest Inventory (COII)

Canadian Test of Basic Skills: Mathematics French Edition (CTBS), Levels 9-14, Form 7

Canadian Tests of Basic Skills: Multilevel, (CTBS), Levels 5-18 Form 7/8

Career Assessment Inventory—Vocational Version

Career Beliefs Inventory (CBI)

Carlson Psychological Survey (CPS)

Children of Alcoholics Screening Test (CAST)

Children's Apperception Test (CAT-A)

Children's Apperception Test—Supplement (CAT-S)

CLEP Subject Examination: Foreign Languages: College French Levels 1 and 2

Clerical Staff Selector

Composition Profile

Comprehensive Personality Profile

Defense Mechanisms Inventory

Derogatis Interview for Sexual Functioning (DISF/DISF-SR)

Employee Aptitude Survey Test #10—Symbolic Reasoning (EAS#10)

Employee Aptitude Survey Test #3—Visual Pursuit (EAS#3)

Employee Aptitude Survey Test #6—Numerical Reasoning (EAS#6)

Employee Aptitude Survey Test #7—Verbal Reasoning (EAS#7)

Employee Reliability Inventory (ERI)®

French Computerized Adaptive Placement Exam (F-CAPE)

French Speaking Test (FST)

Frenchay Dysarthria Assessment

Graduate Record Examinations (GRE)

Hay Aptitude Test Battery

Hay Aptitude Test Battery: Name Finding

Hay Aptitude Test Battery: Number Series Completion

Hay Aptitude Test Battery: Warm-Up

Henmon-Nelson Test of Mental Ability (Canadian Edition)

Henmon-Nelson Tests of Mental Ability

Herrmann Brain Dominance Instrument (HBDI)

I-Speak Your Language®

INQ- Your Thinking Profile

Sales Motivation Inventory, Revised

SAT II: Subject Tests

Secretarial Staff Selector

Self-Directed Learning Readiness Scale (SDLRS)

Spiritual Well-Being Scale

Strong Interest Inventory

Structured Addictions Assessment Interview for Selecting Treatment (ASIST)

Student Instructional Report (SIR)

Supervisory Practices Test (Revised)

Systems Analyst Aptitude Test (SAAT)

Temperament Inventory Tests

Test of Attitude Toward School (TAS)

Test of Practical Judgment—Form 62

Test of Work Competency and Stability

Thomas-Kilmann Conflict Mode Instrument (TKI)

Vocational Preference Inventory

W-Apt Programming Aptitude Test

Wolfe Computer Operator Aptitude Test (WCOAT)

Wolfe Programming Aptitude Test—Form W

Wonderlic Personnel Test

Various Languages

19 Field Interest Inventory (19FII)

Academic Aptitude Test, Standard 10 (AAT)

Academic Aptitude Test, University (AAT)

Academic-Technical Aptitude Tests for Coloured Pupils in Standards 6, 7, and 8 (ATA)

Academic-Technical Aptitude Tests—ATA and SATA

ACTFL Oral Proficiency Interview

Adult Basic Learning Examination–Second Edition (ABLE)

Adult Language Assessment Scales (Adult LAS®)

Anxiety Scales for Children and Adults (ASCA)

Aptitude Assessment Battery: Programming (AABP)

Aptitude for and Sensitivity to Music—Junior Form (ASM J)

Aptitude for and Sensitivity to Music—Senior Form (AGM S)

Aptitude Test Battery for Pupils in Standards 6 and 7 (ATB)

Aptitude Test for Adults (AA)

Aptitude Tests for Indian South Africans— JATISA and SATISA

Aptitude Tests for School Beginners (ASB)

Arithmetic Test A/8

Assessment Inventory for Management (AIM)

Association Adjustment Inventory (AAI)

Bar-Ilan Picture Test for Children

Ber-Sil Spanish Tests: Elementary Test 1987 Revision

Ber-Sil Spanish Tests: Secondary Test

Bi/Polar® Inventories of Core Strengths

Blue Pearl

Business Judgment Test, Revised

Canadian Test of Basic Skills: Mathematics French Edition (CTBS), Levels 9-14, Form 7

Canadian Tests of Basic Skills: High School Battery, (CTBS), Levels 15-18, Form 7

Canadian Tests of Basic Skills: Multilevel, (CTBS) Levels 5-18 Form 7/8

Canadian Tests of Basic Skills: Primary Battery, (CTBS) Levels 5-8, Form 7

Career Assessment Inventory—Vocational Version

Children's Apperception Test (CAT-A)

Children's Apperception Test—Human Figures (CAT-H)

Children's Apperception Test—Supplement (CAT-S)

CHIPS–Children's Problem Solving

Comprehensive Personality Profile

Denver II

Derogatis Interview for Sexual Functioning (DISF/DISF-SR)

Derogatis Sexual Functioning Inventory (DSFI)

Diagnostic Math Tests

Eating Disorder Inventory-2 (EDI-2)

Employee Reliability Inventory (ERI)®

English First and Second Language Tests

Index of Computer-Scored Tests

Index of Authors

Index of Publishers

Camelot Unlimited; 6 North Michigan Avenue; Suite 1502; Chicago, IL 60602-4809; 312-251-8484; FAX 312-251-8486

Carousel House; 212 Aguello Boulevard; San Francisco, CA 94118; 800-526-4824; 415-777-2334; FAX 415-777-9832

Centec Learning; 310 Airport Road; Jackson, MS 39208; 800-626-8235; FAX 601-939-7969

Center for Applied Linguistics; 1118 22nd Street NW; Washington, DC 20037; 202-429-9292; FAX 202-429-9292

Center for Leadership Studies, Inc.; 230 West Third Avenue; Escondido, CA 92025; 619-741-6595; FAX 619-747-9384

Center for Talented Youth; 2701 North State Street; Baltimore, MD; 301-405-2801

Center for the Study of Aging and Human Development; Duke University Medical Center; PO Box 3003; Durham, NC 27710; 919-660-7500; FAX 919-684-8569

Center for the Study of Ethical Development; 206 A Burton Hall; 178 Pillsbury Drive SE; Minneapolis, MN 55455; 612-624-0876; FAX 612-624-8241

Center for the Study of Parental Acceptance and Rejection; University of Connecticut; U-158, Department of Anthropology; Storrs, CT 06269-2158; 203-486-0073; FAX 203-486-4865

CHECpoint Systems, Inc.; 1520 N. Waterman Avenue; San Bernadino, CA 92404; 909-888-3296; FAX 909-384-0519

CHES; 6031 Saint Andrews; Dallas, TX 75205; 214-559-7525

Chronicle Guidance Publications, Inc.; 66 Aurora Street; PO Box 1190; Moravia, NY 13118-1190; 800-622-7284; 315-497-0330; FAX 315-497-3359

Clark Wilson Group; 1320 Fenwick Lane; Suite 708; Silver Spring, MD 20910; 800-537-7249; 301-587-2591; FAX 301-495-5842

Clinical Psychometric Research, Inc.; PO Box 619; 100 W. Pennsylvania Avenue; Suite 302; Riderwood, MD 21139; 800-245-0277; 410-321-6165; FAX 410-321-6341

College Board, The; 45 Columbus Avenue; New York, NY 10023-6992; 212-713-8060; FAX 212-713-8063

Communication Skill Builders; Division of Psychological Corporation; 555 Academic Court; San Antonio, TX 78204-2498; 800-228-0752; FAX 800-232-1223

Comprehensive Adult Student Assessment System (CASAS); 8910 Clairemont Mesa Boulevard; San Diego, CA 92123; 800-255-1036; 619-292-2900; FAX 619-292-2910

Consulting Psychologists Press, Inc.; PO Box 10096; 3803 E. Bayshore Road; Palo Alto, CA 94303; 800-624-1765; 415-969-8901; FAX 415-969-8608

Consulting Resource Group International, Inc.; 200 West Third Street #386; Sumas, WA 98295-8000; 604-852-0566; FAX 604-850-3003

Creative Learning Press, Inc.; PO Box 320; Mansfield Center, CT 06250; 203-429-8118; FAX 203-429-7783

Critical Thinking Press & Software; PO Box 448; Pacific Grove, CA 93950; 800-458-4849; 408-393-3288; FAX 408-393-3277

CTB/McGraw-Hill; 20 Ryan Ranch Road; Monterey, CA 93940; 800-538-9547; 408-393-0700; FAX 800-282-0266

Curriculum Associates, Inc.; PO Box 2001; North Billerica, MA 01862-0901; 800-225-0248; 508-667-8000; FAX 508-663-0521

Dansk psykologisk Forlag; Hans Knudsens Plads 1A; DK-2100 Copenhagen 0 Denmark; 45 3118 2757; FAX 45 3118 5758

DBM Publishing; 100 Park Avenue; New York, NY 10017; 212-692-2100; FAX 212-972-2120

Defense Manpower Data Center; DOD Center—Monterey Bay; 400 Gigling Road; Seaside, CA 93955-6771; 408-583-2400; FAX 408-583-2339

Denver Developmental Materials, Inc.; PO Box 6919; Denver, CO 80206-0919; 303-355-4729; FAX 303-355-5622

Developmental Reading Distributors; 5879 Wyldewood Lakes Court; Ft. Myers, FL 33919; 813-481-2318

Devereux Foundation; ICTR; 19 South Waterloo Road; Box 400; Devon, PA 19333; 610-964-3000; 610-964-3090; FAX 610-964-3092

Dragon Press; 127 Sycamore Avenue; Mill Valley, CA 94941; 415-383-3736; FAX 415-383-3736

Ed & Psy Associates, Inc.; 2071 South Atherton Street; Suite 900; State College, PA 16801; 814-235-9115

EdITS/Educational and Industrial Testing Service; PO Box 7234; San Diego, CA 92107; 619-222-1666; FAX 619-226-1666

Education Associates, Inc.; PO Box Y; 8 Crab Orchard Road; Frankfort, KY 40602; 502-227-4783; FAX 502-227-8608

Educational & Psychological Consultants, Inc.; 601 East Broadway; Suite 301; Columbia, MO 65201; 314-875-6640; FAX 314-875-6640

Educational Activities, Inc.; 1937 Grand Avenue; Baldwin, NY 11520; 800-645-3739; FAX 516-623-928

Educational Assessment Service, Inc.; W6050 Apple Road; Watertown, WI 53098; 414-261-1118; FAX 414-261-6622

Educational Evaluation Enterprises; Awre; Newnham, Gloucestershire GL14 1ET, England; 01594-510503; FAX 01594-510503

Educational Records Bureau, Inc.; 140 West 65th Street; New York, NY 10023; 212-873-9108; FAX 212-873-0020

Educational Testing Service—TOEFL; PO Box 6155; Rosedale Road; Princeton, NJ 08541; 609-951-1691; FAX 609-520-1093

Educators Publishing Service, Inc.; 31 Smith Place; Cambridge, MA 02138-1000; 800-225-5750; 617-547-6706; FAX 617-547-0412

Educators'/Employers' Tests & Services Associates; 341 Garfield Street; Chambersburg, PA 17201; 717-264-9509

Elbern Publications; PO Box 09497; Columbus, OH 43209; 614-235-2643; FAX 614-237-2637

English Language Institute Test Publications; University of Michigan; 3021 North University Building; Ann Arbor, MI 48109-1057; 313-763-3452; FAX 313-763-0369

Exceptional Education; 18518 Kenlake Pl. N.E.; PO Box 15308; Seattle, WA 98155; 206-486-4510

Faculty of Education, Memorial University of Newfoundland; G. A. Hickman Building; Street John's, Newfoundland A1B 3X8, Canada; 709-737-8625; FAX 709-737-2429

Family Social Science; 290 McNeal Hall; University of Minnesota; 1985 Buford Avenue; Street Paul, MN 55108; 612-625-7250; FAX 612-625-4227

Four Oaks Institute; PO Box 279; Dover, MA 02030; 508-785-2527; FAX 508-785-2526

GIA Publications, Inc.; 7404 S. Mason Avenue; Chicago, IL 60638; 708-496-3800; FAX 708-496-3828

Gough, Harrison G.; PO Box 909; Pebble Beach, CA 93953; 408-642-6000; FAX 408-624-4579

H & H Publishing Company; 1231 Kapp Drive; Clearwater, FL 34625; 813-442-7760; FAX 813-442-2195

Harter, Susan; Department of Psychology; University of Denver; 2155 South Race Street; Denver, CO 80208-0204; 303-871-3789

Harcourt® Brace Educational Measurement, 555 Academic Court, San Antonio, TX 78204, 800-228-0752, 210-299-1061, FAX 800-232-1222

Hawthorne Educational Services, Inc.; 800 Gray Oak Drive; Columbia, MO 65201; 800-542-1673; 314-874-1710; FAX 800-442-9509

Heinemann; 361 Hanover Street; Portsmouth, NH 03801-3912; 800-541-2086; FAX 800-847-0938

Hilson Research, Inc.; PO Box 150239; 82-28 Abingdon Road; Kew Gardens, NY 11415-0239; 718-805-0063; FAX 718-849-6238

Hirsch, Joseph A.; 55 Perry Street #4D; New York, NY 10014-3278; 212-807-6530

Hogan Assessment Systems, Inc.; PO Box 521176; 2622 E. 21st Street; Suite 14; Tulsa, OK 74152; 918-749-0632; 800-756-0632; FAX 918-749-0635

Hogrefe & Huber Publishers; PO Box 2487; Kirkland, WA 98083; 206-820-1500; 800-228-3749; FAX 206-823-8324

Human Sciences Center; PO Box 270169; San Deigo, CA 92198-2169; 619-487-5532

Human Sciences Research Council; 134 Pretorius Street; Private Bag X41; Pretoria, South Africa 0001; 012-202-2224; FAX 012-202-2553

Mentoring Institute, Inc.; 675 Inglewood Avenue; West Vancouver, BC V7T 1X4, Canada; 604-925-2295; 604-925-1124; FAX 604-925-1162

MetriTech, Inc.; 4106 Fieldstone Road; Champaign, IL 61821; 217-398-4868; FAX 217-398-5798

Mind Garden, Inc.; PO Box 60669; Palo Alto, CA 94306; 415-424-8493; FAX 415-424-0475

Modern Curriculum Press, Inc., A Division of Paramount, Customer Service Center, 4350 Equity Dr., Columbus, OH 43216, 800-321-3106, 201-739-8000, FAX 614-771-7360

Moreno Educational Company; PO Box 19329; San Diego, CA 92159; 619-461-0565; FAX 619-469-1073

Morrison, James H.; 10932 Rosehill; Overland Park, KS 66210; 913-339-6670

Multi-Health Systems, Inc.; 908 Niagara Falls Boulevard; North Tonawanda, NY 14120-2060; 800-456-3003; FAX 416-424-1736

National League for Nursing; 350 Hudson Street; New York, NY 10014; 800-669-9656; FAX 212-675-2878

National Reading Styles Institute, Inc.; PO Box 737; 179 Lafayette Drive; Syosset, NY 11791; 800-331-3117; 516-921-5500 FAX 516-921-5591

National Spanish Exam; 2051 Mt. Zion Drive; Golden, CO 80401-1737; 303-278-1021; FAX 303-278-6400

NCS Assessments; 5605 Green Circle Drive; Minnetonka, MN 55343; 612-939-5000; FAX 612-939-5099

Ned Herrmann Group, The; 2075 Buffalo Creek Road; Lake Lure, NC 28746; 704-625-9153; FAX 704-625-1402

Nelson Canada; 1120 Birchmount Road; Scarborough, Ontario, M1K 5G4, Canada; 416-752-9100; FAX 416-752-9365

New Standards, Inc.; 1080 Montreal Avenue; Suite 300; Street Paul, MN 55116-2325; 800-755-6299; 616-690-1002; FAX 612-690-1303

Nichols and Molinder Assessments; 437 Bowes Drive; Tacoma, WA 98466-7047; 206-565-4539; FAX 206-565-0164

Northwest Publications; 710 Watson Drive; Natchitoches, LA 71457; 318-352-5313; FAX 318-352-8345

Nova Media, Inc.; 1724 N. State; Big Rapids, MI 49307; 616-796-7539; FAX 616-796-0486

Occupational Research Centre; Highlands, Gravel Path; Berkhamsted, Hertfordshire, HP4 2PQ, United Kingdom; 442-871200; FAX 442-871200

OMNIA Group Incorporated; 601 S. Boulevard 4th Floor; Tampa, FL 33606; 813-254-9449; FAX 813-254-8558

Optometry Admission Testing Program; 211 East Chicago Avenue; Suite 1846; Chicago, IL 60611-2678; 312-440-2693; FAX 312-440-2915

Organizational Measurement Systems Press; PO Box 70586; 34199 Country View Drive; Eugene, OR 97401; 503-484-2715; FAX 503-465-1602

Organizational Tests Limited; PO Box 324; Fredericton, N. B. E3B 4Y9 Canada; 5 06-452-7194; FAX 506-452-2931

Owens M.Ed., Inc., Ned.; 629 W. Centerville; Garland, TX 75041; 214-278-1387; FAX 214-278-1387

Pain Resource Center; PO Box 2836; 1314 Broad Street; Durham, NC 27715; 800-542-7246; 919-286-9180 FAX 919-286-4506

Personnel Decisions, Inc.; 2000 Plaza VII Tower; 45 South Seventh Street; Minneapolis, MN 55402-1608; 612-339-0927; FAX 612-339-8292

PESCO International; 21 Paulding Street; Pleasantville, NY 10570; 800-431-2016; FAX 914-769-2970

Pfeiffer & Company International Publishers; 2780 Circleport Drive; Erlanger, KY 41018; 800-274-4434; 606-647-3030; FAX 800-569-0443

Phylmar Associates; 191 Iroquois Avenue; London, Ontario M6C 2K9, Canada; 519-433-2052.

Piney Mountain Press, Inc.; PO Box 333; Cleveland, GA 30528; 800-255-3127; FAX 800-905-3127

Predictive Surveys Corporation; 5802 Howard Avenue; LaGrange, IL 60525; 708-246-2985; FAX 708-969-8349

Preventive Measures, Inc.; 1115 W. Campus Road; Lawrence, KS 66044; 913-842-5078; FAX 913-842-5078

Price Systems, Inc.; 1714 E. 700 Road; Lawrence, KS 66049; 913-843-7892; FAX 913-843-0101

PRO-ED, Inc.; 8700 Shoal Creek Boulevard; Austin, TX 78757; 512-451-3246; FAX 800-397-7633

Psychological Assessment Resources, Inc.; PO Box 998; Odessa, FL 33556; 800-331-8378; FAX 800-727-9329

Psychological Corporation, The; A Subsidiary of Harcourt, Brace, Jovanovich, Inc.; 555 Academic Court; San Antonio, TX 78204; 800-228-0752; 210-299-1061; FAX 800-232-1223

Psychological Publications, Inc.; 290 Conejo Ridge Avenue #100; Thousand Oaks, CA 91361; 805-373-7360; FAX 805-373-1753

Psychological Services Bureau, Inc.; PO Box 327; 8918 Fort McCord Road; Street Thomas, PA 17252; 717-369-4222; FAX 717-369-2344

Psychological Services, Inc.; Test Publication Division; 100 W. Broadway; Suite 1100; Glendale, CA 91210; 818-244-0033; FAX 818-247-7223

Psychological Test Specialists; PO Box 9229; Missoula, MT 59807; 406-728-1702

Psychologists and Educators, Inc.; PO Box 513; Chesterfield, MO 63006; 314-536-2366; 314-576-9127; FAX 314-878-3090

Psychology Press, Inc.; PO Box 328; 39 Pearl Street; Brandon, VT 05733-0328; 802-247-8312; 800-639-4122; FAX 802-247-8312

Psychometric Affiliates; PO Box 807; 1805 Lexington Trace; Murfreesboro, TN 37133-0807; 615-898-2565; FAX 615-890-6296

Psychometric Software, Inc.; PO Box 1677; 2210 S. Front Street; Suite 208; Melbourne, FL 32901; 800-882-9811; 407-729-6390; FAX 407-951-9508

Pumroy, Donald K.; 4006 Oliver Street; Hyattsville, MD 20782; 301-864-8935

Ramsay Corporation; Boyce Station Offices; 1050 Boyce Road; Pittsburgh, PA 15241-3907; 412-257-0732; FAX 412-257-9929

Reid Psychological Systems; 200 S. Michigan Avenue; Suite 900; Chicago, IL 60604; 800-922-7343; 312-938-9200; FAX 312-294-0140

Richardson, Bellows, Henry and Company, Inc.; 1140 Connecticut Avenue, NW; Suite 610; Washington, DC 20036; 202-659-3755; FAX 202-659-9360

Risk & Needs Assessment, Inc.; PO Box 32818; Phoenix, AZ 85064-2818; 800-231-2401; 602-234-2888; FAX 602-266-8227

Riverside Publishing Company, The; 8420 Bryn Mawr Boulevard; Chicago, IL 60631-3476; 800-767-8378; 312-714-6194; FAX 312-693-2248

Rocky Mountain Behavioral Science Institute, Inc.; 419 Canyon Avenue; Suite 316; Fort Collins, CO 80521; 800-447-6354; 970-221-0602

SASSI Institute; PO Box 5069; 1928 Arlington Road; Bloomington, IN 47403; 812-333-6434; FAX 800-546-7995

Saville & Holdsworth Ltd.; 575 Boylston Street; Boston, MA 02116-3607; 617-236-1550; FAX 617-236-2092

Schmeck, Ph.D., Ronald R.; Department of Psychology; Southern Illinois University at Carbondale; Carbondale, IL 62901; 618-453-3535

Schneider, Ph.D., Nina G.; Nicotine Research Unit; VA Medical Center, Brentwood T350; Mail Code: 691/B151D; Los Angeles, CA 90073; 310-312-0564; FAX 310-478-6349

Scholastic Testing Service, Inc.; 480 Meyer Road; PO Box 1056; Bensenville, IL 60106-1617; 800-642-6787; 708-766-7150; FAX 708-766-8054

Search Institute; 700 S. 3rd Street; Suite 210; Minneapolis, MN 55415; 612-376-8955; 800-888-7828; FAX 612-376-8956

SEFA (Publications) Ltd.; "The Globe"; 4 Great William Street; Stratford-Upon-Avon CV37 6RY United Kingdom; FAX 49-8136-8157

Selby MillSmith Ltd.; 30 Circus Mews; Bath, Avon BA1 2PW, United Kingdom; 1225-446655; FAX 1225-446643

Select Press; PO Box 37; 45 San Clemente Drive; Suite D130; Corte Madera, CA 94976-0037; 415-924-1612; FAX 415-924-7179

Sigma Assessment Systems, Inc.; PO Box 610984; 1110 Military Street; Port Huron, MI 48061-0984; 800-265-1285; FAX 800-361-9411

Slosson Educational Publications, Inc.; PO Box 280; East Aurora, NY 14052; 800-828-4800; 716-652-0930; FAX 716-655-3840

Sopris West, Inc.; 1140 Boston Avenue; PO Box 1809; Longmont, CO 80501; 800-547-6747; 303-651-2829; FAX 303-776-5934

Stanard & Associates, Inc.; 309 West Washington Street; Suite 1000; Chicago, IL 60606; 800-367-6919; FAX 312-573-0218

Steck-Vaughn/Berrent Publishing Company; 1025 Northern Boulevard; Roslyn, NY 11576; 516-365-4040; FAX 516-365-4013

Stoelting Company; 620 Wheat Lane; Wood Dale, IL 60191; 708-860-9700; FAX 708-860-9775

Student Development Associates, Inc.; 110 Crestwood Drive; Athens, GA 30605; 706-549-4122; FAX 706-542-4130

Swets Test Services; PO Box 820; Heereweg 347b; 2160 SZ Lisse, The Netherlands; 2521-35375; FAX 2521-15888

Teleometrics International; 1755 Woodstead Court; The Woodlands, TX 77380; 713-367-0060; FAX 713-292-1324

Test Analysis and Development Corporation; 2400 Park Lake Drive; Boulder, CO 80301; 303-666-8651

Timao Foundation for Research & Development; 1815 N. Broadway #29; Escondido, CA 92026-2065; 619-480-0260

Touchstone Applied Science Association, Inc.; PO Box 382; Fields Lane; Brewster, NY 10509; 914-277-8100; FAX 914-277-3548

TRT Associates; 65 Eagle Ridge Dirve; Highlands, NC 28741; 704-526-9561

Twenty-first Century Assessment; PO Box 608; 1909 Oxley Street; South Pasadena, CA 91031-0608; 818-441-0614; 800-374-2100; FAX 818-441-0614

University of Iowa; Publications Order Department; Oakdale, IA 52242-5000; 800-235-2665; FAX 319-335-4039

University of Maryland; 3404 Benjamin; College Park, MD 20742; 301-405-2801

University of Vermont Department of Psychiatry; One South Prospect Street; Burlington, VT 05401-3456; 802-656-8313; FAX 802-656-2602

University of Washington Press; PO Box 50096; Seattle, WA 98145-5096; 800-441-4115; FAX 800-669-7993

Valpar International Corporation; PO Box 5767; 2450 W. Ruthrauff Road; Suite 180; Tucson, AZ 85705; 800-528-7070; 520-293-1510; FAX 520-292-9755

Variety Pre-Schooler's Workshop; 47 Humphrey Drive; Syosset, NY 11791; 516-921-7171; FAX 516-921-8130

Vine Publishing Ltd.; 10 Elgin Road; Bournsmouth, Dorset BH4 9NL United Kingdom; 01202-761766; FAX 01202-761766

Vocational Research Institute; 1528 Walnut Street; Suite 1502; Philadelphia, PA 19102; 215-875-7387; FAX 215-875-0198

Waetjen, Walter B.; 4790 Sailors Retreat Road; Oxford, MD 21654; 410-822-9172; FAX 410-822-9172

Walden Personnel Testing & Training, Inc.; 750 Lauren Room B-60; Montreal, Quebec H4M 2M4, Canada; 514-748-7448; FAX 514-748-1013

Weider, Arthur; 552 LaGuardia Place; New York, NY 10012; 212-777-7303

Western Psychological Services; 12031 Wilshire Boulevard; Los Angeles, CA 90025-1251; 310-478-2061; FAX 310-478-7838

Wide Range, Inc.; 15 Ashley Place; Suite 1A; PO Box 3410; Wilmington, DE 19804-0250; 800-221-9728; 302-658-4990; FAX 302-652-1644

Williams & Wilkins; Rose Tree Corporate Center, Building II; 1400 North Providence Road; Suite 5025; Media, PA 19063-2043; 800-638-0672

Wintergreen/Orchard House, Inc.; PO Box 15899; 629 Cherokee Street; New Orleans, LA 70175-5899; 504-866-8658; 800-321-9479; FAX 504-866-8710

Wolfe, Rose; 750 Lauren Room B-60; Montreal, Quebec H4M 2M4, Canada; 514-748-7448; FAX 514-748-1013

Index of Cross-References

Psychology Instruments

Attention Deficit

Adult Attention Deficit Disorder Behavior Rating Scale, 1

Attention Deficit Disorder Behavior Rating Scales (ADDBRS), 1

Attention Deficit Disorders Evaluation Scale (ADDES)–Revised, 2

Attention-Deficit Hyperactivity Disorder, 2

Attention-Deficit/Hyperactivity Disorder Test (ADHDT), 2

Brown Attention-Deficit Disorder Scales, 2–3

Children's Attention and Adjustment Survey (CAAS), 3

Conners' Continuous Performance Test (CPT) Version 3.1, 3

Conners' Parent and Teacher Rating Scales, 3

Disruptive Behavior Rating Scale (DBRS), 4

Early Childhood Attention Deficit Disorders Evaluation Scale (ECADDES), 4

Tachistoscopic Reading (FASTREAD), 80

Visual Search and Attention Test (VSAT), 4

Drug Knowledge

Information Test on Drugs and Drug Abuse, 5

Smoking and Health, 5

Family

Ackerman-Schoendorf Scales for Parent Evaluation of Custody (ASPECT), 5

American Home Scale, 5–6

Borromean Family Index: For Married Persons, 6

Borromean Family Index: For Single Persons, 6

Children of Alcoholics Screening Test (CAST), 28

Children's Version of the Family Environment Scale, 6–7

Dyadic Parent-Child Coding System (DPICS II), 7

Faces II, 7

Eidectic Parents Test, 56–57

Familism Scale, 7

Familism Scale: Extended Family Integration, 7–8

Familism Scale: Nuclear Family Integration, 8

Family Adjustment Test (Elias Family Opinion Survey), 8

Family Apperception Test, 8–9

Family Assessment Measure (FAM III), 9

Family Environment Scale, 9

Family Relationship Inventory (FRI), 9–10

Family Story Pictures, 10

Family Violence Scale, 10

Grandparent Strengths and Needs Inventory (GSNI), 10

Home Screening Questionnaire (HSQ), 10–11

Interview Questionnaire on Attitudes Toward Family Planning in Black Community, 11

Inventory of Anger Communication, 11

Life Interpersonal History Enquiry (LIPHE), 11

Marriage and Family Attitude Survey, 53–54

Marital Attitudes Evaluation (MATE), 58

Marital Communication Inventory, 11

Maryland Parent Attitude Survey (MPAS), 11–12

Michigan Screening Profile of Parenting (MSSP), 12

Parent as a Teacher Inventory (PAAT), 12

Parent Behavior Form, 12–13

Parent–Adolescent Communication Inventory, 13

Parent–Child Relationship Inventory (PCRI), 13

Parental Acceptance-Rejection Questionnaire (PAPQ), 13

Parental Acceptance-Rejection Questionnaire (PARQ), 13–14

Parenthood Motivation Questionnaire, 14

Parenting Stress Index (PSI), 14

Perceptions of Parental Role Scales, 14–15

Religion Scale, 15

Rossetti Pediatric Case History and Family Needs Profile, 15

Staffan Roijeus Family Game (SRF), 15

Tasks and Rating Scales for Lab Assessment of Infant Temperament, 16

Intelligence

Marital

Premarital

Relations

Neuropsychology

Multiage

Academic Aptitude

Auditory

Behavior and Counseling

Attitudes

Study Skills

Business Education

Development and Readiness

Driver's Education

English As a Second Language and Bilingual Education

Fine Arts

Foreign Language

Guidance

General

Health Education

Industrial Arts

Library Skills

Math

Basic

Religious

Speech and Language

Comprehensive Language

Speech and Language

Articulation and Phonology

Aphasia, Apraxia, Dysarthria, and Dysphagia

School and Institutional Environments

Business Instruments
General Aptitude

General Skills

Attitudes

Personality

Team Skills

Work Environment

Aptitude and Skills

Banking

About the Editor

Taddy Maddox joined PRO-ED as associate director of research in 1994 after completing her doctorate in special education at the University of Texas at Austin. Previously she had worked as an educational diagnostician in Texas public schools for 15 years. Prior to that, Maddox was a special education teacher in self-contained and resource settings. In addition, she has been active in the Texas Educational Diagnosticians' Association and the Texas Council for Exceptional Children.